The Russian Officer Corps in the Revolutionary and Napoleonic Wars

1792-1815

Also by Alexander Mikaberidze

Lion of the Russian Army:
Life and Career of General Peter Bagration

Alexander Mikaberidze

The Russian Officer Corps in the Revolutionary and Napoleonic Wars

1792-1815

SPELLMOUNT

Staplehurst

British Library Cataloguing in Publication Data:
A catalogue record for this book is available
from the British Library

Copyright © Alexander Mikaberidze 2005

ISBN 1-86227-269-7

Published in the UK in 2005 by

Spellmount Limited
The Village Centre
Staplehurst
Kent TN12 0BJ

Tel: 01580 893730
Fax: 01580 893731
E-mail: enquiries@spellmount.com
Website: www.spellmount.com

1 3 5 7 9 8 6 4 2

Also published in the United States of America by

Savas Beatie LLC
521 Fifth Avenue, Suite 3400
New York, NY 10175

All rights reserved. No part of this publication may be
reproduced, stored in a retrieval system or transmitted in
any form or by any means, electronic, mechanical,
photocopying, recording or otherwise,
without prior permission in writing from
Spellmount Limited, Publishers.

Printed in the United States of America

To my parents,
Levan and Marina Mikaberidze,
who gave up so much for their children
and instilled in them a passion for learning.

Russian officers: Karl Fedorovich Baggovut (top left); Joseph Kornilovich O'Rourke (top right); Peter Ivanovich Bagration (center); Pavel Vasilievich Golenischev-Kutuzov (bottom left); Aleksey Petrovich Ermolov (bottom right).

Contents

Introduction

ix

Foreword

xiii

Author's Note

xv

The History of the
Russian Officer Corps: An Overview

xvii

The Biographies

1-468

Bibliography

469

Introduction

The sun burned brightly on 11 September 1815. Anyone traveling to Vertus, 100 miles from Paris, beheld an awe-inspiring sight: more than 150,000 men dressed in parade uniforms deployed on a vast field near the town. Around noon, the soldiers marched past Emperor Alexander I of Russia and his entourage, thundering shouts of "hurrah" and playing music. The scene was breathtaking indeed, a triumphant conclusion to the titanic struggle between two opposing worlds and a showcase of Russian military might and success.

Only three years earlier, Europeans watched in suspense as Emperor Napoleon led more than 500,000 men into Russia. However, within a year, the once-mighty Grand Army was destroyed and tens of thousands of its soldiers killed, captured, or frozen to death in the vastness of Russia. After the Russian army emerged victorious from the depths of the East, it marched across the continent into the heart of France. Despite many defeats along the way, on 11 September 1815, few questioned whether the final victory over Napoleon would have been possible without the Russian army and its officers.

When discussing the Russian army during the Age of Napoleon, people often forget that, unlike other European powers, Russia was at war for virtually all of the late 18th and early 19th centuries. The Russian army participated in the seven campaigns against France (1799, 1805, 1806-1807, 1812-1814); three Russo-Turkish Wars (1769-1774, 1787-1791, 1806-1812); the annexation of the Crimea (1783-1784); the Russo-Persian War (1804-1813); two Russo-Swedish Wars (1789-1791, 1808-1809); two partitions of Poland (1792-1794); and annexations of the principalities in Georgia and Northern Caucasus. Therefore, in this study the term "Revolutionary and Napoleonic Wars" includes all of these military operations.

Many Russian officers rose to prominence during this period. The names of Generals Mikhail Kutuzov, Mikhail Barclay de Tolly, Peter Bagration, Peter Wittgenstein, and many others evoke memories of Russian triumphs, glorious days gone by, numerous battles fought, and victories celebrated. For decades, their names were venerated in Russia. These officers spent the best years of their lives serving in the Russian armies. Some were talented commanders and administrators; others were less gifted leaders and arrogant courtiers. They came from all over the world—Alexander Langeron, Antoine Jomini, and Emmanuel St. Priest from France; Peter Bagration, Ivan Djavakhishvili (Zhevakhov), and Levan Panchulidze from Georgia; Joseph O'Rourke from Ireland; Mikhail Barclay de Tolly from Scotland; Levin Bennigsen, Peter Wittgenstein, Karl Clausewitz, and others from various German states. Russia embraced them all and, in return, they defended their adopted Motherland. Many paid the ultimate price for the well-being of Russia.

* * *

The idea for this volume originated during work on my dissertation at the Institute on Napoleon and the French Revolution at Florida State University. When researching numerous archival materials, I found myself wishing there were dictionaries describing Russian officers similar to the classical studies on the French officer corps by Georges Six and C. Mullié, and on the British officers by John A. Hall.[1] Left on my own, I began gathering biographical details on the Russian senior officers. In late 2002, I contacted Robert Burnham, the editor of the fine Napoleon Series (www.napoleon-series.org), one of the best on-line collections related to the Age of Napoleon. I proposed creating an online dictionary of the Russian officer corps. Robert supported me in this undertaking and, encouraged by the response, I decided to expand the number of biographical sketches and combine them into a single volume. The result you now hold in your hands.

The Russian Officer Corps in the Revolutionary and Napoleonic Wars is divided into two parts. The first section contains information on the development of the Russian officer corps and analytical tables on enlistment, education, social status, and experience of the Russian officers.[2] I did not include any material on officer uniforms because Alexander Viskovatov's superb work on this topic is much better than anything I could produce.[3] The second section of this book contains more than 800 biographies of these officers, arranged in alphabetical order. I included biographies of both junior and senior officers. Although some of them, particularly those of lieutenants and captains, at first blush appear unimportant based on their contributions to the war effort, they illustrate the technicalities of the Russian officer corps and in my opinion, help flesh out this study.

* * *

This book could not have been completed without the assistance of individuals too numerous to mention. I cannot possibly list everyone, so if you are not named, you know who you are and know that I am in your debt. I will be forever grateful to Dr. Donald D. Horward, who changed my life when he invited me from the faraway Republic of Georgia to study the Age of Napoleon under his direction. It was indeed a dream come true! I am thankful to Darrin McMahon and Samuel "Skip" Vichness, whose support made it possible for me to complete the manuscript.

This book would not have been made without tremendous help from my publisher, Theodore P. Savas, of Savas Beatie LLC. Ted saw its potential and took a real risk to publish it.

Matt De La Matter and Dana Lombardy helped with editing the manuscript and offered many helpful comments and suggestions that greatly improved its value. Lee Merideth did a superb job formatting and preparing numerous files and images for print, and Sarah Stephan of Savas Beatie LLC assisting with the final proofing.

Thanks also to the Strozier Library Special Collections and Documents Department staff at Florida State University: Dr. Lucia Patrick, Deborah Rouse, and Patricia Brinkely were courteous and helpful. The Interlibrary Loan Section (ILS) of the Strozier Library was remarkable and indispensable. The staff helped locate materials, and provided me with hundreds of volumes from libraries throughout the United States. Without their quick and effective help, my work would have continued for many more years.

My contact with scholars and enthusiasts at the Napoleon Series Discussion Forum was beneficial. To name just a few: Steven Smith, Robert Goetz, Robert Burnham, George Nafziger, Digby Smith, Robert Mosher, Howie Muir, Robert Ouvrard, Tom Holmberg, Tony Broughton, Alain Chappet, Kevin Kiley, and Rory Muir all helped me with numerous details of the Napoleonic campaigns. I am indebted to Jack Sigler, Kenny Johnson, Josh Moon, Jason Musteen, and Rick Black for their wonderful discussions at the Napoleon seminars. My Russian friends Alexander Zhmodikov and Boris Megorsky greatly assisted me in acquiring Russian sources. I am especially grateful to my Georgian friends Shalva Lazariashvili, Paata Buchukuri, George Zabakhidze, and Dmitri Khocholava, each of whom cheered me on despite our distance apart. I will forever cherish their friendship.

Finally, I would like to thank my family, whose blessings and support have kept me moving forward against all hardships. Last but not least, I am indebted to my dear Anna for her constant encouragement and ceaseless aid in all my undertakings. Without you, nothing would have been accomplished.

End Notes

1. Georges Six, *Dictionnaire biographique des généraux & amiraux Français de la révolution et de l'empire, 1792-1814*, 2 vols. (Paris: G. Saffroy, 1934), 2 volumes; C. Mullié, *Biographie des célébrités militaires des armées de terre et de mer de 1789 à 1850*, 2 vols. (Paris: Poignavant, 18??).

2. Tables are based on various works consulted during the research. I also used data from my personal researches to verify and compliment these studies. Most useful works in this respect were Liubomir Besrovny's two classical studies on the Russian army in the 18th and 19th centuries, and Dmitry Tselorungo's excellent book *Ofitsery Russkoi Armii–uchastniki Borodinskogo Srazhenia* [Officers of the Russian Army: Participants of the Battle of Borodino].

3. A. V. Viskovatov, *Istorciheskoe opisanie odezhdy i vooruzheniia Rossiiskikh voisk* [*Historical Description of the Clothing and Arms of the Russian Army*], Vols. 1-30 (St. Petersburg, 1841-62), 2nd ed., Vols. 1-34 (St. Petersburg-Novosibirsk- Leningrad, 1899-1948). This work is based on remarkable archival documents and contains some 4,000 colored illustrations.

Foreword

The Hermitage Palace in St. Petersburg has a grand hall dedicated to the Russian army generals who served in the wars waged during the Napoleonic period. When Westerners pass through the hall and see the portraits of more than 330 generals, they recognize very few by name or appearance with the exception of the most prominent, such as Mikhail Barclay de Tolly, Mikhail Kutusov, Peter Bagration, Dmitry Dokhturov, and Matvei Platov. Nevertheless, the hall is a pantheon of Russian heroes who fought and often died in the struggle against Napoleon's armies and allies.

The Revolutionary period was one of great activity for the Russian army. Although officially neutral during the War of the First Coalition, Emperor Paul made a major commitment against Republican France in 1799 and sent three armies west. The main Russian army, under the command of the legendary Field Marshal Alexander Suvorov, employed many young inexperienced officers in Italy and Switzerland. Despite the ultimate withdrawal of these armies following General André Masséna's victories during the Zurich campaign, the Russian officers gained valuable experience and exposure to the tactical and strategic changes in warfare spawned by Napoleon and the armies of Republic.

In 1805, the Russian armies faced the Grand Army and Napoleon for the first time. The leadership in the Russian armies proved to be formidable at Amstetten, Durenstein, and Schöngraben, but suffered humiliation at Austerlitz. Nevertheless, the Russian officers continued to improve in leadership and their understanding of Napoleonic tactics. Fourteen months later, they demonstrated these qualities in the battle at Eylau, denying Napoleon the decisive victory he sought. Although successful in repulsing the Grand Army at Heilsburg, four days later the Russian army was lured across the Alle River and crushed at Friedland. After Tilsit, they served as Napoleon's ally in the War of the Fifth Coalition against Austria; meanwhile, other army units were deployed against the Ottoman Empire and the Swedes.

By 1812, after a decade of almost constant warfare, the leadership in the Russian army had improved markedly. Many officers had served in various European theaters and compiled impressive records of success on the battlefield. They faced their greatest challenge and achieved their greatest success in 1812 when Napoleon invaded Russia, only to be driven out six months later. The defeat of Napoleon in the east was the Russian army's crowning achievement for the next 130 years. Now, for the first time, Western readers will have an opportunity to familiarize themselves with the Russian army officers who made these victories possible.

Hundreds of books, including memoirs, journals, and correspondence, have been published in English, French, and German on the Napoleonic period. The names of very few Russian officers appear on their pages. Their names and titles stand out in Russian publications, but are lost to most Western readers. With the completion of this volume by Alexander Mikaberidze, readers interested in the Russian army during the Napoleonic period now have a valuable research tool available. Having just completed a doctoral dissertation on General Prince Peter Bagration, who served in almost every Russian campaign during the period, Dr. Mikaberidze has had the opportunity to delve into the careers of hundreds of Russian officers, as well as the administration of the Russian army.

After tracing the evolution of the Russian army in the 18th century and the Napoleonic period, Dr. Mikaberidze examines the system of enlistments and promotion; the military schools and educational programs; the social composition and status in Russian society; the system of recognition and awards; and the strengths and weaknesses of the Russian army. Biographical sketches are provided for each general, many of the colonels, and some of the lieutenants. There are extensive details on each officer's origin, education, military service, and military awards. In the tradition of the distinguished French historian George Six and his *Dictionnaire bibliographique des Généraux & Amiraux français de la Révolution et de l'empire (1792-1814)*, Dr. Mikaberidze has produced a book that will be invaluable to anyone interested in the Russian army and the campaigns of the Napoleonic period.

Professor Donald D. Horward
Institute on Napoleon and the French Revolution
Florida State University

Author's Note

A few names in the book have Roman numerals attached to them. The rule of "numbering" officers in the Russian army originated because there were often several officers with the same last names, i.e., four Tuchkovs, 12 Ilovaiskys, and 18 Grekovs. Therefore, numbers were attached to their last names to distinguish them: Tuchkov I, Ilovaisky IX, and Grekov XVIII. Dates in original Russian documents are tied to the Julian calendar, which was used in Russia until the October Revolution of 1917. To convert a date to the modern calendar, I added 11 days to dates prior to 1 March 1800, and 12 days to dates after 1 March 1800.

Tables are based on works consulted during research and illustrate different aspects of the officer corps. The most important of them are Liubomir Besrovny's two classical studies on the Russian army in the 18th and 19th centuries, and Dmitry Tselorungo's excellent work *Ofitsery Russkoi Armii—uchastniki Borodinskogo Srazhenia*. I also used data from my research to verify and complement these studies. The analytical tables are primarily based upon data collected on 2,074 officers who served with the 1st and 2nd Western Armies in 1812.

The History of the Russian Officer Corps: An Overview

Origins, Enlistment and Promotions

The beginning of the Russian officer corps is closely tied to Peter the Great's military reforms. Peter realized the importance of having well-trained and professional officers leading his army.[1] Modernizing the state was especially crucial in light of the Great Northern War between Russia and Sweden (1700-1721). When the Swedish army, under the maverick King Charles XII, defeated the Russians from 1700 to 1704, Peter began inviting foreign officers to train and lead his troops.[2] He hired 700 foreign officers in 1698, though the majority of them were fired within a couple of years.[3] In most cases, these men were adventurers, renegades, or inexperienced officers with military experience but no prospects in their native countries. General A. Golovin complained, "They had no experience or knowledge of military affairs and had to be themselves trained first. . . . [I]t is better to conscript [Russian nobles], educate and train them."[4]

Peter shifted his attention to recruiting Russian nobility and creating the professional officer corps.[5] To increase the number of nobles available for service, he established obligatory military service. He also prohibited noblemen younger than 60 from joining the monastery. Those who avoided service faced persecution and confiscation of property. Noblemen were eligible for conscription at 13, serving first as soldiers and then as officers. Peter prohibited granting officer's rank to any noble who did not serve as a soldier in the Guard units. He hoped this arrangement would enable noblemen to gain experience while serving in the lower ranks of regiments. In 1700, 1,091 Russian nobles were conscripted into the army. Within two years, another 2,913 were reviewed and 940 started service in the army.[6] In 1700 there were 264 officer vacancies in eight infantry regiments; 33 of the 78 positions were filled by foreigners.[7] By 1701, a third of the 1,137 infantry officers were foreigners. In contrast to the infantry regiments, virtually every cavalry officer was of Russian origin.[8]

Although army commanders could nominate nobles for officer's rank, two special institutions, Voennii Prikaz (Military Agency) and Inozemnii Prikaz (Foreign Agency), supervised and confirmed these promotions. The nobles exploited a loophole in this system by enlisting their children in the Guard at birth or during infancy. When the children were grown, they already had officer's rank without any experience or training. Peter tried to prohibit this procedure by requiring all officers in the regiment to vote on granting new officer rank, with the emperor having the final say. In 1764, new regulations prohibited enlisting any youth before age 15. The only exception was children of soldiers, who could be assigned to units as clerks or musicians before age 15.[9] Emperor Alexander forbade accepting noblemen in the Quartermaster Section of the Imperial Retinue and the artillery before age.[10]

Still, this process continued for decades through nepotism and rampant army corruption. While many young noblemen began their service as rank and file soldiers, others from prominent families with connections were enrolled in regiments as infants and granted leaves until they completed their "studies" at home. For example, future Field Marshal Rumyantsev enlisted in the Imperial Guard at age five, future Minister of Police Alexander Balashov joined the Guard at age six, and Senator Bibikov's son enlisted at age two and conferred officer's rank by age nine. Peter Volkonsky (1776-1852) was enlisted in the Life Guard Preobrazhensk Regiment on the day of his baptism. He began active service at 16 and received the rank of ensign within a matter of weeks. Two years later, Volkonsky was already an adjutant in his own regiment. Similarly, Prince Peter Dolgoruky was enlisted in the Life Guard Izmailovsk Regiment on 15 March 1778 at two and a half months old. He became a captain at 15, major at 16, colonel at 20, and major general at 21. These Guard officers took advantage of their status and transferred to the Regular Army, receiving a two-rank promotion.(14) [11]

Patronage was important for finding any position or vacancy because of the abundance of young noblemen ready for service. Sergey Glinka noted that new appointments usually took place on the first day of each new year in the Guard regiments. This way, at the end of December, the secretary would be pestered with questions such as, "Will my son get in?" or "Has my nephew been put on the list?"[12] Another contemporary described the significance of becoming an officer by stating, "Everyone who has obtained his first officer rank and a sword knows that there is scarcely any pleasure on earth to compare with this reward."[13]

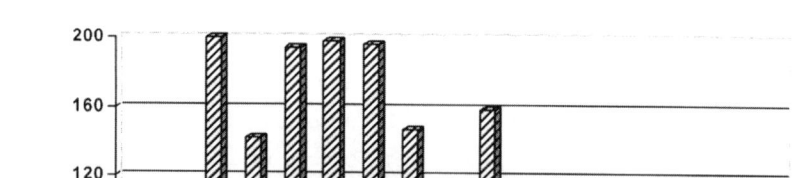

Age at Enlistment of the Officers Serving in 1812 Campaign [14]

Age	2 to 5	6 to 12	13 to 15	16	17	18	19	20	21	22	23	24	25	26	27	28	29-36
Officers	13	89	222	142	194	198	196	147	102	159	29	24	17	15	7	2	7

Initially, the length of service for nobles was undetermined, and they often served for life. In 1736, new regulations allowed nobles to keep one son at home to take care of the family property; other male children could study until the age of 20 when they had to enlist in the army for 25 years. They were usually registered at age seven and called to St. Petersburg at 16, where they would undergo a knowledge examination. Well-educated nobles could choose civil careers while others continued their studies until the age of 20, when they were called to the Heraldry (geroldia) to begin military service. Nobles who did not receive education by 16 were enlisted in the navy and unable to receive an officer's rank.

Age of Officers at the Start of Service [15]

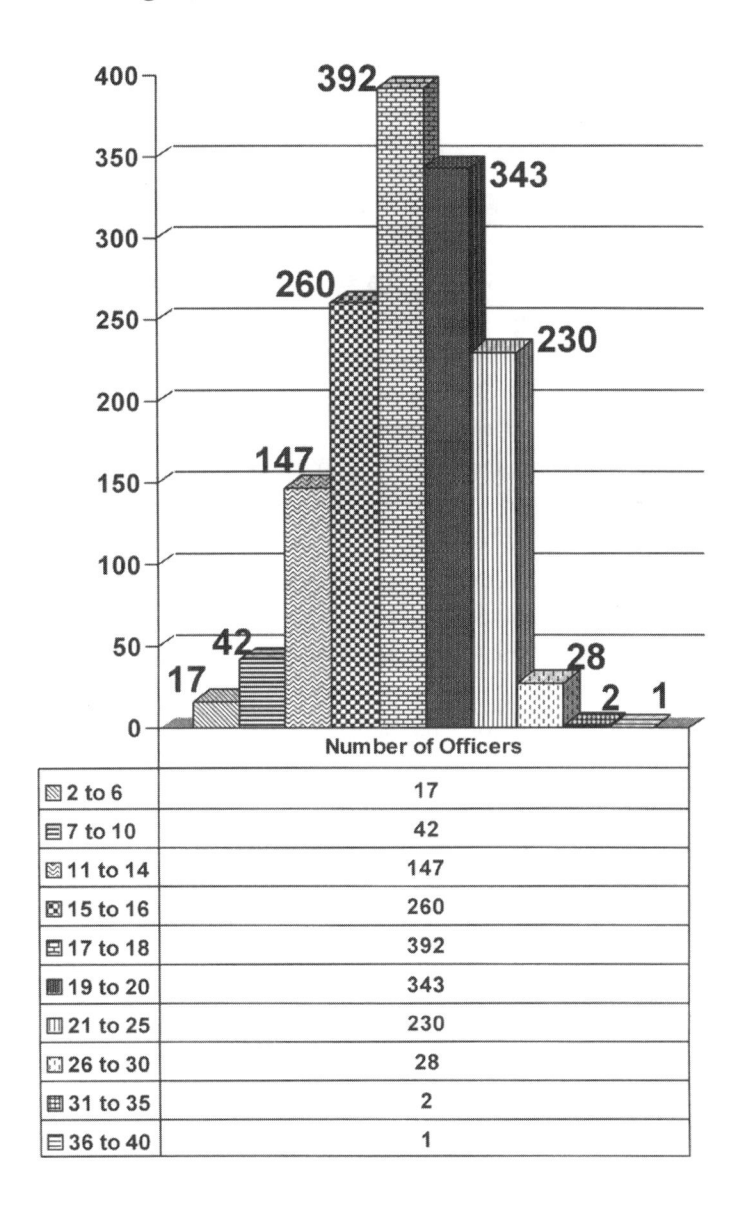

Age	Number of Officers
2 to 6	17
7 to 10	42
11 to 14	147
15 to 16	260
17 to 18	392
19 to 20	343
21 to 25	230
26 to 30	28
31 to 35	2
36 to 40	1

Although Emperor Peter III promulgated the Charter of Liberties in 1762[16] that abolished mandatory military service for nobles, the number of noblemen enlisting in the army kept increasing. The army was the only honorable career for young noblemen and the Russian monarchy created a hallowed tradition of service. By 1782, 108,000 male nobles in Russia had flooded the army.[17] New vacancies of supernumeraries (sverkhkomplektnye) were created because the regimental ranks were full. Eventually, the excess of supernumeraries, particularly of Guard officers, turned into a major problem. By 1792 there were 6,134 non-commissioned officers in the Life Guard Preobrazhensk Regiment and 3,502 privates. Although the Guard officially had vacancies for only 400 non-commissioned officers, the actual number of officers exceeded 11,500.[18] Therefore, large groups of officers were frequently appointed to regular units; 250 in 1782 and 400 in 1796.[19] The size of the Officer Corps varied during the Napoleonic Wars. In 1797 there were 399 generals, 297 colonels, 466 lieutenant colonels, and 1,654 majors; 12 years later there were 495 colonels, 442 lieutenant colonels, and 1,176 majors. The total size of the Officer Corps was 12,000 men in 1803, more than 14,000 from 1805 to 1807, and between 15,000 and 17,000 by 1812.[20]

Enlisted noblemen were usually conferred the rank of non-commissioned officer, but had to serve as a soldier for three months before actually receiving the rank. Patronage and nepotism played an important role in advancement. Many senior officers arranged for sons or relatives to serve in their units and receive promotions in a timely or expedited fashion. On average, noblemen served two months to three years to earn an officer's rank. In 1812, 16.5% of officers in the First and Second Western Armies served two years as NCOs before earning an officer's rank, 12.6% received the rank in a year, and 7.5% within several months of enlistment.[21] Civilians who transferred to the military service usually had their officer epaulettes within one to three years, depending on their previous civil rank and position. The timeline was considerably longer for non-nobles, who waited five to seven years before becoming an officer. NCOs from the soldier ranks were in the worst position, and usually served a decade or more before receiving an officer's rank. In 1812, 64 out of these 92 officers had to serve between 10 and 25 years, while three of them remained in the NCO ranks for an incredible 24 to 27 years.[22]

Russian rulers established various regulations in attempts to improve the promotion process. Prior to 1742, candidates were selected by the vote (balotirovanie) of their fellow officers. Peter the Great established this process to ensure that promotions were based on merit. However, in 1726, Empress Catherine I abolished it because corruption and nepotism prevented objective voting. Instead, candidates were promoted based on merit and experience. Empress Anna Ioanovna revived the voting procedure with certain limitations in February 1731. Under new regulations, the Russian sovereign had to confirm officer transfers between regiments as well as any promotions to colonel. Five years later, Empress Anna made further changes to the system. She kept the voting process for junior and staff officer ranks, but senior officer ranks were awarded only on merit. Finally, in March 1742, Empress Elisabeth declared that promotions be made based on seniority and merit.

Junior officers and NCOs had their subsequent career chosen for them by their supervising colonel with evaluations in attestats (certificates of service). These documents were supposed to be signed by the candidate's comrades before being sent to their superiors.

However, some men signed whatever their commander showed them for fear of receiving a bad evaluation.[23] Thus, a commanding officer could determine the composition of his unit and indirectly influence the social composition of the officer corps by delaying promotions to non-nobles. Candidates had to pass military examinations to qualify for officer's rank. In 1808, General Aleksey Arakcheyev established the Committee on Artillery to supervise artillery examinations and to ensure the quality of artillery officers. Similar exams also existed for other branches, but they were rarely enforced because of rampant favoritism.[24]

Differences also existed between ober (junior rank) and staff officer to senior rank promotions. Generals to captains could promote candidates to ober officer ranks. Only army commanders, field marshals, and the president of the War College could promote candidates to major and lieutenant colonel. The number of vacancies in each regiment limited these promotions. Staff officers could be transferred from their regiment to a vacancy in another unit. When a vacancy appeared, the most senior officer was promoted.[25] Therefore, dating seniority in ranks became extremely important, and often led to squabbles between officers of the same rank but different seniority. To accelerate their promotions, many officers transferred to units where they could receive a higher rank. Such transfers were particularly widespread in the artillery, where 80% of the officers changed regiments at least twice during their careers. Once they achieved senior rank, officers remained in their units for extended periods of time.

Number of Transfers During Military Service[26]

Number of Transfers	Guard #	Guard %	Infantry #	Infantry %	Cavalry #	Cavalry %	Artillery #	Artillery %	Total #	Total %
0	188	58,6	682	55,4	208	54,9	28	19,7	1,106	53,3
1	93	28,9	321	26,1	102	26,9	39	27,5	555	26,8
2	27	8,4	138	11,2	53	14	31	21,8	249	12
3	7	2,2	52	4,2	9	2,4	13	9,2	81	3,9
4	6	1,9	21	1,7	4	1,1	14	9,9	45	2,2
5	-	-	11	0,9	1	0,3	7	4,9	19	0,9
6	-	-	5	0,4	1	0,3	3	2,1	9	0,4
7	-	-	1	0,1	-	-	2	1,4	3	0,1
8	-	-	1	0,1	1	0,3	1	0,7	3	0,1
9	-	-	-	-	-	-	1	0,7	1	0,05
10	-	-	-	-	-	-	3	2,1	3	0,1

Protocol for promotions in the Russian army commonly caused confusion and upset. Promotions could be delayed for a number of reasons, such as lack of a vacancy, an influx of new officers from privileged families, and the transfer of Guard officers to the Regular Army. Officers resuming active duty after retirement also caused a problem. Upon retirement, an officer who had served for at least one year in his current rank (five years in the case of colonels) was promoted by one grade.[27] Seniority gained while in the civil service was often taken into account when a man returned to the army.[28]

During wartime there were many chances to distinguish oneself in battle and receive a higher rank. En masse promotions, designed to mark victories, led to many complaints because they were often accompanied by uncontrolled favoritism. This was especially true during the Russo-Turkish Wars in the 1770s and 1780s, where some regiments had up to 60 majors.[29] "I was always against promotions for distinction [in battle]," complained Colonel Marin in a letter in January 1813. "It causes so much wickedness! [*skolko tut zla!*] For every good officer promoted, there are five dreadful [*dryannoi*]."[30] In another case, General Alexander Kutaysov, who was credited for bringing artillery companies to hold the Russian left flank at Eylau on 8 February 1807, was awarded the Order of St. George (third class) and praised by Emperor Alexander himself. Many contemporaries decried this award and asserted that Generals Osterman and Ermolov should receive credit for these decisive actions. They stated that Ermolov, acting on Osterman's orders, was the first to arrive with 36 guns, Kutaysov only followed him with an additional 12 guns. Rumor had it that Kutaysov received an award because he was a cousin to the commander of the Russian artillery. Aleksey Ermolov received a lesser award, the Order of St. Vladimir (third class). According to Denis Davidov, Prince Peter Bagration was extremely upset by this favoritism and appealed to Commander-in-Chief Levin Bennigsen to award Ermolov a higher decoration. However, Prince Peter did not press the matter because Kutaysov's mother helped him at his wedding in 1800. Instead, Peter made sure that Ermolov received the Order of St. George (third class) for his actions in June 1807.[31]

Disagreements with senior officers or men in powerful positions could also delay promotions. General Dmitry Rezvyi, who commanded the Russian artillery in the 1806-1807 campaigns, offers a good example. In early 1812, Rezvyi unwisely made fun of the powerful minister Arakcheyev in a private conversation. Arakcheyev learned about this joke and persecuted Rezvyi for the rest of his life. He refused to let Rezvyi command the Russian artillery in late 1812. Two years later, Arakcheyev denied Rezvyi's promotion to lieutenant general, although he served as major general for more than 15 years. When Rezvyi tried to meet Arakcheyev and solve this predicament, Arakcheyev refused to meet him and had Rezvyi discharged from the army on 29 December 1815.

The Russian government also changed the process of accepting foreign officers. Those entering Russian service were initially accepted with their previous rank. However, the Russian government realized the importance of regulating the process as foreign officers continued to fill the Russian army. Under Empress Elisabeth, foreign officers were reduced by one rank and only the Russian sovereign could make an exception to this rule. In some cases, foreigners were refused service because of their criminal past or other activities. While French émigrés were encouraged to enter Russian service (Prince Condé had an entire such corps in Russian service), Russian authorities were suspicious of French deserters and often refused to accept them into the army.

Civil officials also served as officers in the Russian army, though with certain restrictions. Noble civil officials were allowed to begin military service with the rank of junker. Non-noble officials could only join the military with the Imperial consent as NCOs. This restriction was implemented to prevent an influx of non-noble civilians from receiving an officer's rank, which carried the status of nobility. Retired military officers or those in civil service were accepted back into the army with a military rank corresponding to their civil rank. Seniority was determined by the date of their retirement. To be considered, military retirees had to appeal to the Emperor and submit required documents. Upon acceptance, they had to pledge an oath to the Emperor. Beginning in 1808, those who failed to join their units within four months of acceptance were discharged from the army without a right to enlist; however, they could submit documents explaining their absence. Depending on the severity of their crimes, court-martialed officers could return to the military. Those discharged for intoxication or insubordination could rejoin the army as privates or, in a few cases, as NCOs. In some cases, a discharged or court-martialed officer could serve in opolchenye (militia) forces without officially returning to military service. During the 1812 Campaign in Russia, hundreds of former officers volunteered for the army and many of them had to serve in opolchenye forces without formal acceptance into the military. They were usually restored in rank after a year of service.

Education

Despite the perennial problem of incompetent army officers, the Russian military education system was surprisingly multifaceted. The system was created during the reign of Peter the Great. As early as 1698, Peter established the Artillery School of the Life Guard Preobrazhensk Regiment, whose graduates began service as non-commissioned officers in the army. The following year, he founded the Naval School to train crews of the Baltic and Azov Fleets. In 1701, Peter drafted curriculum for the School of Mathematical and Navigation Sciences.[32] This school proved to be of greater importance. Under Peter's decree, 500 children of noble descent from ages 15 to 17 were enrolled to study Russian grammar, geometry, trigonometry, navigation, artillery, and fencing. The graduates usually served in the artillery, navy, and the corps of engineers. Some were also dispatched to provinces to educate the local population. Non-nobles were only accepted in the school to study grammar and graduate as clerks.[33] In 1715, the Naval Academy was established and virtually replaced the School of Mathematical and Navigation Sciences. By 1718, the Academy had 865 students who studied mathematics, navigation, artillery, fortifications, geography, drawing, and astronomy. Peter the Great also founded the Artillery School in 1701,[34] the Engineer School in 1712,[35] and another two artillery schools in 1712 and 1721.[36] To satisfy the increased demand for non-commissioned officers, he established 50 Garrison Schools and 13 Admiralty Schools in major towns across the country.

The education system rapidly developed under Peter's successors. The Shliakhetsky Kadetskii Korpus (Noble Cadet Corps) was founded in 1731 to train noble children before active service.[37] Students were divided into three companies of 100 to study mathematics, fortifications, artillery, painting, fencing, history, geography, dancing, and music.[38] From 1731 to 1761, the corps produced 1,557 graduates and 1,200 of them received officer's rank.[39] However, low wages and lack of funding resulted in poor training. In 1737, a report to the Imperial Senate stated that a quarter of graduates had "no knowledge in any sciences."[40]

Despite these findings, the corps became one of the best institutions in the empire during the reign of Catherine the Great (1762 to 1796). Renamed the Sukhoputnii Korpus (Infantry Cadet Corps), it was directed by the excellent administrator I. Betskoy, who reorganized the school and introduced new regulations.[41]

Under the Statute of 1766, the corps organized its students in companies: three musketeer, one grenadier, and one horse. The curriculum included five classes of three years each. Students were enrolled in the first class from age five to nine and tended by nurses. Male officers supervised the other classes.[42] Curriculum included mathematics, logic, physics, chemistry, eloquence, history, geography, astronomy, foreign languages, state law, political economy, military art, fortifications, and artillery. There were nine art classes, three special classes, and nineteen general subject classes. Students in junior classes had examinations every four months while seniors were only examined once a year.[43] The corps lacked experienced and able instructors, so the quality of education remained poor. In 1784, Catherine made major changes to the curriculum. Female nurses were excluded and better instructors were hired. On 22 March 1800, the institution was renamed Pervii Kadetskii Korpus (First Cadet Corps). Between 1762 and 1800, more than 2,180 students studied in the Corps; 985 of them graduated and 820 received regimental assignments.[44] In 1812, the Corps produced 180 officers for the army. The graduates were some of the best officers in the Russian army, including General Field Marshals Peter Rumyantsev, Alexander Prozorovsky, and Mikhail Kamensky, Generals Mikhail Volkonsky, Karl Toll, Peter Repnin, Ivan Weilmarn, Peter Melissino, and Mikhail Kakhovsky, and Admiral Ivan Kutuzov.

Empress Elisabeth also worked to advance the Russian education system. She set up the Morskoi Korpus (Naval Cadet Corps) in 1752. The new institution combined existing naval schools and trained the naval officers for three years. More than 360 students[45] were organized into one guard marine and two cadet classes.[46] The first class studied mathematics (arithmetic, geometry, and trigonometry) and foreign languages, the second class concentrated on navigation and other naval sciences, and the third class covered practical training. This corps produced many skilled Russian officers, including Admirals Fedor Ushakov, Dmitry Senyavin, and Mikhail Lazarev.

From 1730 to 1735, three new engineering schools were created in St. Petersburg and Moscow: Arifmeticheskaia Shkola (Arithmetic School, later renamed the Artillery Arithmetic School), Inzhinernaia Shkola (Engineer School), and Chertezhnaia Artilleriiskaia Shkola (Drawing Artillery School). Empress Elisabeth also increased the number of garrison schools training non-commissioned officers. By the 1740s, these schools were established in every garrison throughout the empire, training more than 6,000 men.[47] On 3 September 1758, the engineering and artillery schools joined to form the Soedinennaya Artilleriskaya i Inzhinernaya Shkola (Combined Artillery and Engineer School).[48]

Another center for military education was established in 1758, the Artilleriiskii i Inzhinernii Shliakhetsky Kadetskii Korpus (Artillery and Engineer Noble Cadet Corps). This institution was directed by prominent Russian military officer General Feldzugmeister Prince Peter Shuvalov. It consisted of two schools, Soedinennaia soldatskaia shkola (Combined School for Soldiers) and Artilleriiskaya i inzhenernaya dvoryanskaya shkola (Artillery and Engineer Noble School). With a curriculum devised by famous Russian scientist Mikhail

Lomonosov, its 150 students[49] learned tactics, history, geography, mathematics, mechanics, hydraulics, physics, chemistry, architecture, artillery, fortification, foreign languages, fencing, and dancing.[50] Directed by General Peter Melissino after 1783, the Corps became one of the best military institutions in the empire. Melissino reorganized the school into three companies based on age. The first two groups received theoretical training while the third existed for special training. Between 1765 and 1800, the corps trained more than 1,500 cadets. In 1800, the corps was renamed *Vtoroi Kadetskii Korpus* (Second Cadet Corps). In the first quarter of the 19th century, it supplied 793 officers, 184 of whom graduated in 1812. The corps produced such distinguished officers as Field Marshal Mikhail Kutuzov and Generals Fedor Buxhöwden, Aleksey Arakcheyev, Peter Müller-Zakomelsky, Aleksey Korsakov, Alexander Zasyadko, Vladimir Iashvili, and Alexander Seslavin.

Graduates of the Artillery and Engineer Cadet Corp / 2nd Cadet Corps in 1762-1855[51]

	Artillery	Engineer	Guard	Army	Cavalry	Other	Expelled
Catherine II	703	210	35	336	-	76	48
Paul I	248	50	1	66	2	17	14
Alexander I	781	140	11	536	-	35	90
Nicholas I	495	83	112	782	101	286	444

As Russian monarchs expanded their influence to the Balkans, they invited families of pro-Russian factions to send their children to Russia for studies. During the Russo-Turkish War from 1769 to 1774, the Russian navy squadron recruited 50 Greek boys. These students were sent to St. Petersburg, where *Grecheskii Kadetskii Korpus* (Greek Cadet Corps) was established in 1774. In April 1775, the school was organized into a cadet corps and its name changed to *Korpus Chuzhesterannikh Edinovertsev* (Corps of Foreign Fellow Believers) to reflect the addition of students from other Balkan nations.[52] The curriculum provided general courses for junior students, such as French, German, Greek, Italian, Russian, Turkish, arithmetic, geometry, geography, drafting, and dance. Students who completed these courses continued training for their branch of service. The corps existed until 1796 and prepared 200 officers, including 100 naval officers.[53] This school was an effective training ground for offspring of petty Greek nobility, who entered the Russian service and achieved high positions in society.

In 1778, General Sergey Zorich established *Shklovskoe blagorodnoe uchilishe* (Schklov Noble Boarding School), which was intended for noble orphans and petty nobility. The military college provided eight years of training and was initially organized into two cavalry squads and two infantry companies. Students advanced through five classes: first, second, and third classes (one year each) taught foreign languages, mathematics, history, geography, theology, and drawing; fourth class (two years) and fifth class (three years) provided advanced courses in mathematics, artillery, tactics, military architecture, horse riding, fencing, drilling, dancing, and music.[54] The school was reorganized into *Shkovskii kadetskii Korpus* (Shklov Cadet Corps) in 1799. Later that same year, the school burned down and the corps was transferred first to

Grodno (Grodno Cadet Corps) and then to Smolensk (Smolensk Cadet Corps) in 1807.[55] Between 1778 and 1800, it produced 665 graduates, including 470 army and artillery officers.[56]

While the corps supplied the army with officers, garrison schools trained non-commissioned officers and clerks. Set up as garrison regiments, these institutions were reorganized into garrison battalions in 1764, and 112 of them were established throughout the empire. Each school divided its 50 students into groups and trained them for 15 years.[57] Ten students were taught artillery and engineering, 20 others music and singing for regimental bands, and 10 were instructed in weapon repairs. The final 10 learned grammar and writing to become non-commissioned officers and clerks. Students were assigned to units at age 18, but musicians could be sent to regiments as young as 15. The total number of students enrolled in these schools varied. During the Russo-Turkish Wars in the late 18th century, there were more than 10,000 men training at the garrisons. In 1798, Emperor Paul established the Imperial Military Orphan Home (*Imperatorskii Voenno-Sirotskii Dom*).[58] Beginning in 1805, military orphanages were established throughout the empire and supervised by the Permanent Council for Military Schools. Children enrolled in these orphanages were referred to as cantonists. In 1810, they started annually providing trained soldiers to sapper and pioneer companies. The number of graduates grew steadily, with 12,000 in 1797, 16,000 in 1801, and 19,000 in 1812.[59]

Emperor Alexander also founded several important educational institutions. The Page Corps (*Pazheskii Ego imperatorskogo Velichestva korpus*) was established for upper nobility in 1802. By 1810, 66 students were attending. The corps was organized into three page (50 men) and one kamer page (116 men) classes, providing general and military education. The seven-year program consisted of five years of general education and two years of specialized instruction. The curriculum included mathematics, history, foreign languages, geography, diplomacy, political economy, physics, statistics, mechanics, fortifications, artillery, and mining. Between 1800 and 1825, the corps produced 624 officers, among them General Field Marshal Ivan Paskevich, Alexander Tormasov, Dmitry Dokhturov, and Alexander Chernishev.

Following the Franco-Russian campaigns in Poland from 1806 to 1807, Emperor Alexander set up the Volunteer Cadet Corps to supply junior infantry officers. With a two-year curriculum, the corps was able to train 500 officers a year.[60] In 1808, it was converted to *Dvorianskii Polk* (Noble Regiment, or Regiment of the Nobility) and attached to the Second Cadet Corps. Directed by General Kleinmichel, the regiment was organized into two battalions led by Majors Holdgoyer and Engelhardt. This effective military institution produced 2,665 ensigns in the first five years.[61] Simultaneously, the 110-men Cavalry Squadron of the Nobility was formed to provide junior officers for the Russian cavalry.

The final addition to the education system, *Tsarsko Selskii litsei* (Tsarskoe Selo Lycée), was founded in 1811 to train personnel for civil and military service. It quickly became a privileged institution for the offspring of wealthy and prominent noble families. In 1822, it became purely a military institution under jurisdiction of the Council of the Military Educational Institutions. On the eve of the French invasion in 1812, Emperor Alexander also established the Finnish Topographic Academy on the Gaapanemi peninsula in the Kuopio province. Located at the former Swedish military school, its four-year program trained 60 professional topographers for the Russian army.[62]

Despite the increasing number of cadet corps and other institutions, the quality of the graduates remained poor. The curriculum emphasized general subjects that broadened students' intellectual horizons and made them fit for civil service. The ratio of students per instructor remained low: 4.7 students per instructor at the Page Corps, 8.4 students per instructor at the Second Cadet Corps, and 10.8 students per instructor at the First Cadet Corps. The two-year program at the Noble Regiment was an exception to the low ratio, with 44.7 students per instructor.[63]

The quality of the instructors was also low. Many officers could barely read and write when they entered the army. Military subjects were taught briefly and erratically. Sergey Tuchkov's memoir provides insight into the education of Russian officers. Tuchkov's training began at age three with two tutors, "a deacon and soldier," who took care of him, although "[neither] ...had any abilities to convey their meager knowledge to [a child]." Later, Tuchkov's father hired a Danish tutor, who "also taught without any methodology, forcing [Tuchkov] to write citations from the Holy Scripture and learn by heart excerpts from his own works. [His] Russian language instructor had no understanding of the grammar or spelling and barely taught [him] to read and write." Tuchkov was greatly influenced by his father, who "believed that physics, chemistry and mechanics were the most useful subjects to the future officers; yet, he could not tutor us in them. Father thought that literature, eloquence and music were worthless and did not want us to study any Latin, which, he believed, was necessary only for priests and physicians. He considered theology and philosophy inappropriate to the future officer."[64]

Service records demonstrate interesting data on the education of military institution graduates. In 1812, the majority of Russian officers (1,061 out of 2,074 men) could only read and write. At the same time, many were fluent in several languages, with 30.4% (630 men) able to speak French and 25.2% (522 men) fluent in German. English and Italian were less popular languages, with 17 and 10 men speaking them, respectively. Only 61 officers (2.9%) studied military sciences and seven (0.3%) were taught tactics. Many officers, especially those in the artillery, were familiar with mathematics. Twenty-three percent showed competence in arithmetic, 10.6% in geometry, 6.5% in algebra, and 3.5% in trigonometry.

Even if a young nobleman completed the cadet corps, he still faced the problem of adapting to army life. According to Sergey Glinka, a Russian officer and cadet corps graduate, "after completing a classical education, [his fellow cadets] collapsed under the weight of their learning when they encountered ordinary officers [in the army]; in despair, they took to Bacchus' cup and so were prematurely lost to the service." Some of them perished imitating the feats of classical heroes on the battlefield.[65]

Knowledge of Subjects by the Russian Officers in 1812-1813[66]

Subject	Officers familiar with subject	Subject	Officers familiar with subject
French	630	Military Drawing	11
German	522	Logic	11
Arithmetic	482	Italian	10
Geography	320	Tactics	7
History	265	Philosophy	7
Basic Mathematic	238	Ancient Greek	6
Geometry	220	Natural history	6
Artillery Science	184	Fortress defense	5
Fortification	182	Engineering	5
Drawing	143	Topography	5
Algebra	134	Hydraulics	5
Physics	96	Swedish	4
Trigonometry	72	Technical drawing	3
Military sciences	61	Politics	3
Military operations	46	Diplomacy	3
Theology	46	Rhyming (Poetry)	3
Latin	43	Parade Execution	3
Architecture	42	Geodesy	2
Grammar	40	Mountain Engineering	2
Advanced Geometry	36	Astronomy	2
Mechanics	36	Jurisprudence	2

Subject	Officers familiar with subject	Subject	Officers familiar with subject
Russian	35	Literature	2
Horse Riding	29	Music	2
Polish	24	Finnish	1
Dancing	23	Military regulations	1
Chemistry	22	Naval science	1
Fencing	21	Political economy	1
Statistics	20	Catechizes	1
Military laboratory	18	Calligraphy	1
English	17	Only read/write	1061
Advanced Mathematic	45	Illiterate	2
Rhetoric	13	No information	6

During the 1812 Campaign, General V. Vyazemsky complained to Emperor Alexander, "There are many schools [in Russia], but only a few of them are first-rate."[67] In 1809, Commander-in-Chief Peter Bagration, Army of Danube, criticized the inexperienced officers arriving from St. Petersburg. The newly arrived officers were mostly foreigners who did not speak Russian and were "arrogant and disrespectful."[68] Prince Peter wrote, "I need Russians, not foreigners; they are not accustomed to serve one [monarch] and switch sides [when it suits them]." Bagration explained his position more fully to Aleksey Arakcheyev:

> [These officers] neither know nor understand anything. They should be still studying in [military] schools. I need experienced officers! The war with Turks is very different from the campaign against European states. Here, the officers had to accompany the Cossacks on reconnaissance, locate the enemy positions and determine the distance for the maneuvers. The Asiatic [sic] attack often continues along hundred square *versts* [66 miles]. Yet, despite these factors, I keep receiving young and inexperienced officers.[69]

By 1811, 34% of Noble Regiment graduates could only read and write. Another 23% were described as "able to read and write, understands arithmetic." Twenty-five percent of graduates were acquainted with two or three subjects, 11% with four or five, and 7% with six to ten.[70] As this data indicates, the level of illiteracy in officers graduating from the highest military institutions was simply appalling.

During the Napoleonic Wars, the artillery received the most qualified and educated officers. By 1812, 67.6% of the artillery's officers were graduates of the cadet corps. In contrast, only 10.5% of officers in the guard cavalry and 10% in the regular cavalry were cadet corps graduates. On a better note, 21.6% of the regular infantry received a cadet corps education. Similarly, 21.2% of the guard infantry officers studied in the highest military institutions, albeit the majority of them were from the Noble Regiment. Only 21.8% of the officers in the Quartermaster Section of the Imperial Retinue were educated at the best military institutions and another 10% graduated from civil schools.[71]

In the upper levels of the officer corps, 500 generals participated in the 1812 to 1815 campaigns. Forty-five graduated from the Artillery and Engineer Corps (Second Cadet Corps), 35 from the Infantry Cadet Corps (First Cadet Corps), 22 from the Page Corps, seven from the Corps of Fellow Believers, four from the Schklov Cadet Corps, and 11 from the Naval Cadet Corps.[72] Some prominent commanders, such as Peter Bagration, did not receive any formal military education.

This information reveals interesting correlations between educated officers who served during the 1812 to 1815 campaigns. The Noble Regiment was a principal source of junior and middle rank officers. Its graduates constituted 25% of educated officers in the guard infantry, 58.3% in the grenadiers, 60.2% in the regular infantry, 62% in the jager units, and 35% in the cavalry. In the artillery, 52.1% of the literate officers came from the Second Cadet Corps, where curriculum focused on technical subjects. It is noteworthy that the majority of officers in the Imperial Retinue graduated from the First Cadet Corps.

Officers of the 1st and 2nd Western Army and their Graduate Institutions, 1812

	1st Cadet Corps	2nd Cadet Corps	Military Orphan Homes	Smolensk (Grodno) Cadet Corps	Noble Regiment	Page Corps	Foreign Fellow Believers Corps	Naval Corps	Institution Unknown
Guard Infantry	10	5	1	-	13	19	-	2	2
Guard Cavalry	2	1	-	1	1	3	-	-	-
Grenadiers	4	2	2	-	14	2	-	-	-
Regular Infantry	18	13	10	13	103	1	-	3	10
Jagers	10	7	2	2	44	-	-	-	6
Cuirassiers	6	2	1	-	6	1	1	-	-
Dragoons	-	-	1	-	1	-	-	-	-
Hussars	4	4	-	1	4	-	-	-	2
Uhlans	-	2	-	-	3	1	-	-	-
Artillery	9	50	8	7	19	-	-	-	3
Imperial Retinue	16	2	1	6	-	4	-	-	9

Officer Literacy by Ranks, 1812[73]

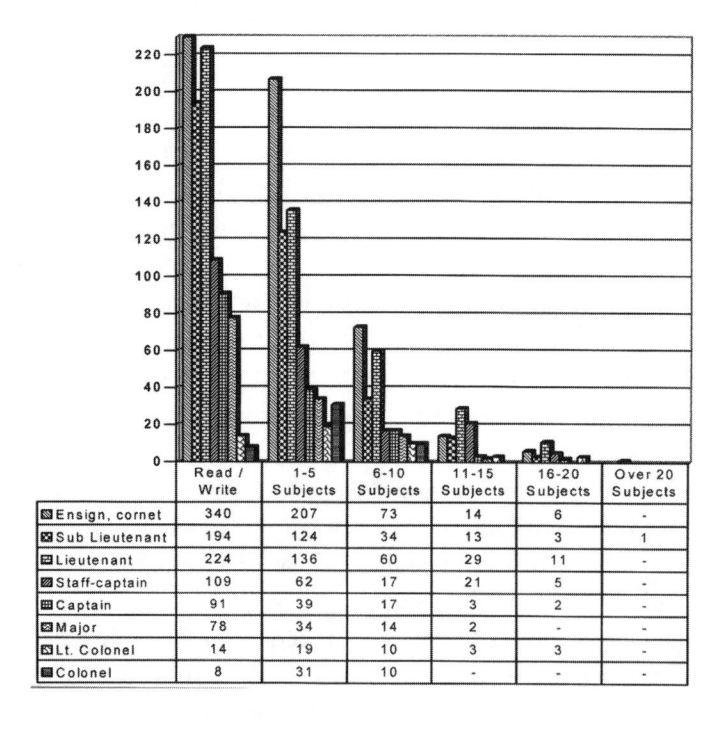

	Read / Write	1-5 Subjects	6-10 Subjects	11-15 Subjects	16-20 Subjects	Over 20 Subjects
Ensign, cornet	340	207	73	14	6	-
Sub Lieutenant	194	124	34	13	3	1
Lieutenant	224	136	60	29	11	-
Staff-captain	109	62	17	21	5	-
Captain	91	39	17	3	2	-
Major	78	34	14	2	-	-
Lt. Colonel	14	19	10	3	3	-
Colonel	8	31	10	-	-	-

Officer Literacy by Army Branches

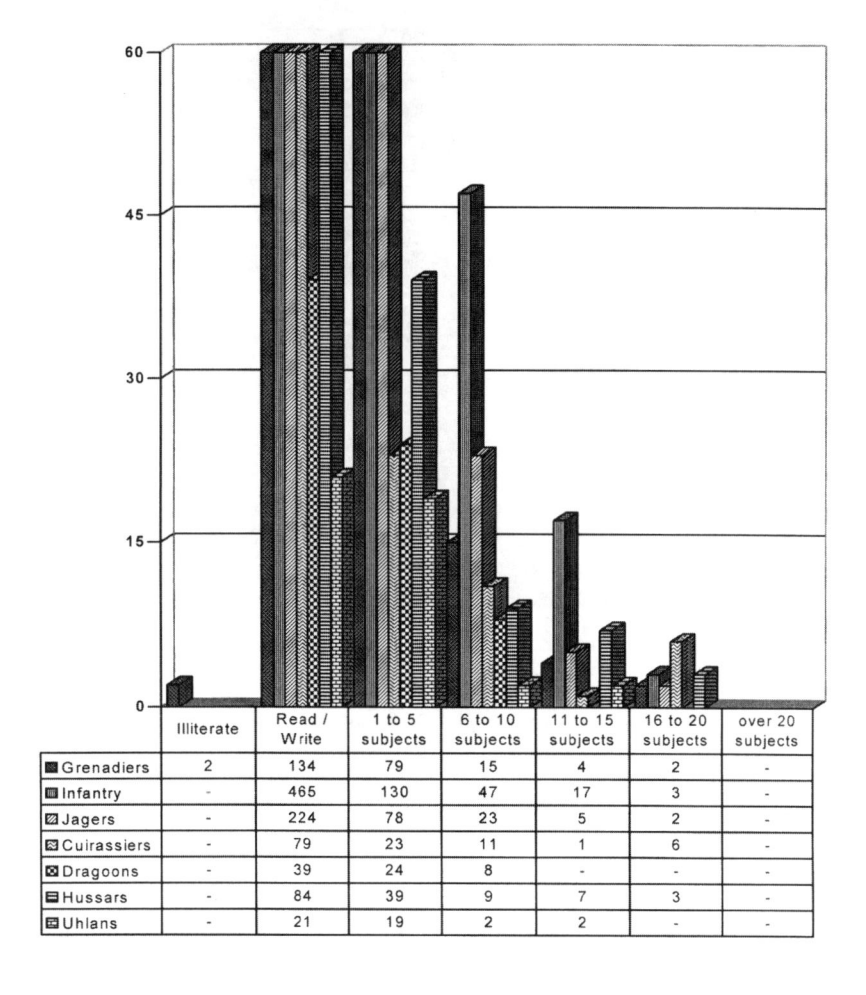

	Illiterate	Read / Write	1 to 5 subjects	6 to 10 subjects	11 to 15 subjects	16 to 20 subjects	over 20 subjects
Grenadiers	2	134	79	15	4	2	-
Infantry	-	465	130	47	17	3	-
Jagers	-	224	78	23	5	2	-
Cuirassiers	-	79	23	11	1	6	-
Dragoons	-	39	24	8	-	-	-
Hussars	-	84	39	9	7	3	-
Uhlans	-	21	19	2	2	-	-

Social Composition and Status

Throughout the 18th and 19th centuries, officers held a distinguished social status in Russian society. One of Peter the Great's priorities was to increase the social stature of his newly-created officer corps. In January 1712, he decreed that officers would enjoy a higher standing than any other noble "notwithstanding his family ancestry."[74] The officer corps was also opened to every estate to enhance its prestige in lower social strata. Peter's successors underlined the importance of serving in the army and granted many privileges to the officer corps. Thus, in 1775, nobles who did not have an officer's rank lost their voting rights in the provincial assemblies. The monarchy also perpetuated the notion of honorably serving to defend the motherland. The military was the only respected professional career for nobles.

Officer Literacy in Artillery and the Guard

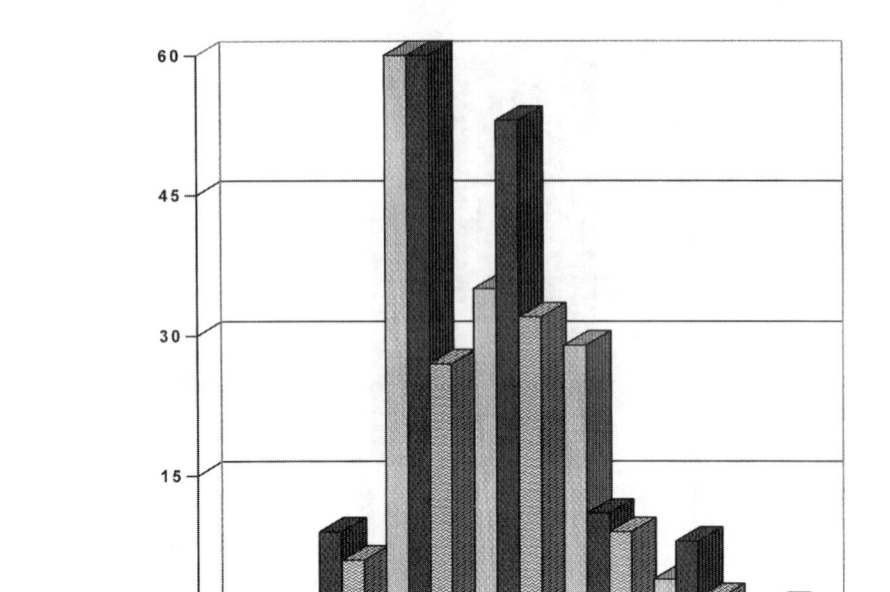

	Illiterate	Read / Write	1 to 5 subjects	6 to 10 subjects	11 to 15 subjects	16 to 20 subjects	over 20 subjects
Artillery	-	-	74	35	29	4	-
Guard Infantry	-	9	161	53	11	8	1
Guard Cavalry	-	6	27	32	9	2	-

Historian Christopher Duffy described the stereotype of a Russian officer: "For most of us, terms like 'the Russian officer' have connotations of dissolute young wastrels, who were freed of care and responsibility by the labor of thousands of serfs, who spent their evenings throwing vodka glasses against the wall, and who finally subsided into unconsciousness among a wreckage of a gilded furniture."[75] The reality was considerably different from this impression. Many Russian officers lived in poverty, without property or serfs. These officers were obligated to maintain clothing, equipment, and horses with meager salaries that barely covered living costs. The average pay during the Napoleonic Wars was as follows: ensigns received 125 rubles a year; sub-lieutenants, 142 rubles; lieutenants, 166 rubles; staff captains, 192 rubles; captains, 200 rubles; majors, 217 rubles; lieutenant colonels, 250 rubles; colonels, 334 rubles; major generals, 655; lieutenant generals, 794 rubles; and generals, 1,302 rubles. The artillery and cavalry officers received 10% higher salaries and the Guard officers earned 20% to 50% more than their regular infantry counterparts.[76] A complete officer uniform cost approximately 200 rubles, while dinner at a nice restaurant was about five rubles.

Young officers from petty noble families often owned nothing but a bundle of clothes when they joined the regiment. Officer quarters held only objects essential for existence. According to Colonel Ilya Radozhitsky, "Beside his hand baggage, pipe with scanty tobacco and stacks of cards spread around on the floor, [the average] Russian officer had virtually nothing in his quarters."[77] Cossack Major General Adrian Denisov stated in his memoirs that his inadequate salary made him "short even of necessities." Many times officers could not accumulate enough savings for equipment and food. General Arsenii A. Zakrevsky recalled that when he was stationed in Lithuania, he could afford nothing but eggs.[78] In some cases, officers followed the example of the rank and file and organized cartels (corporations) to help each other survive the campaign. There were also commanding officers who took care of their subordinates. Lieutenant General F. M. Numsen, who served as the Cavalry Inspector in Livonia, held weekly dinners for his officers to help them survive on their salaries.[79]

The records of service show that 77% of Russian officers in 1812 did not own property or serfs. The remaining 16% had serfs owned by their fathers, who supported them, and less than four percent had property owned by other members of their families. Almost all foreign officers in the Russian army held no assets in Russia and depended on their salaries to survive. The same condition applied to 88.6% of the Polish officers and 83.1% of officers from the Baltic provinces. Virtually no junior officers, including non-commissioned officers, owned estates or serfs.[80]

The data on army branches also shows the difference in financial and property status between the officers. Naturally, the Guard units had the most affluent officers: 38% of them owned serfs and property. The cavalry officers were the least affluent (21.95%) followed by infantry's 20.3% and artillery's 15.4%. Despite its imposing name, the officers in the Quartermaster Section of the Imperial Retinue were the most deprived; only 9.8% of them owned any property or serfs.

Serfs Owned by the Russian Officers in 1812[81]

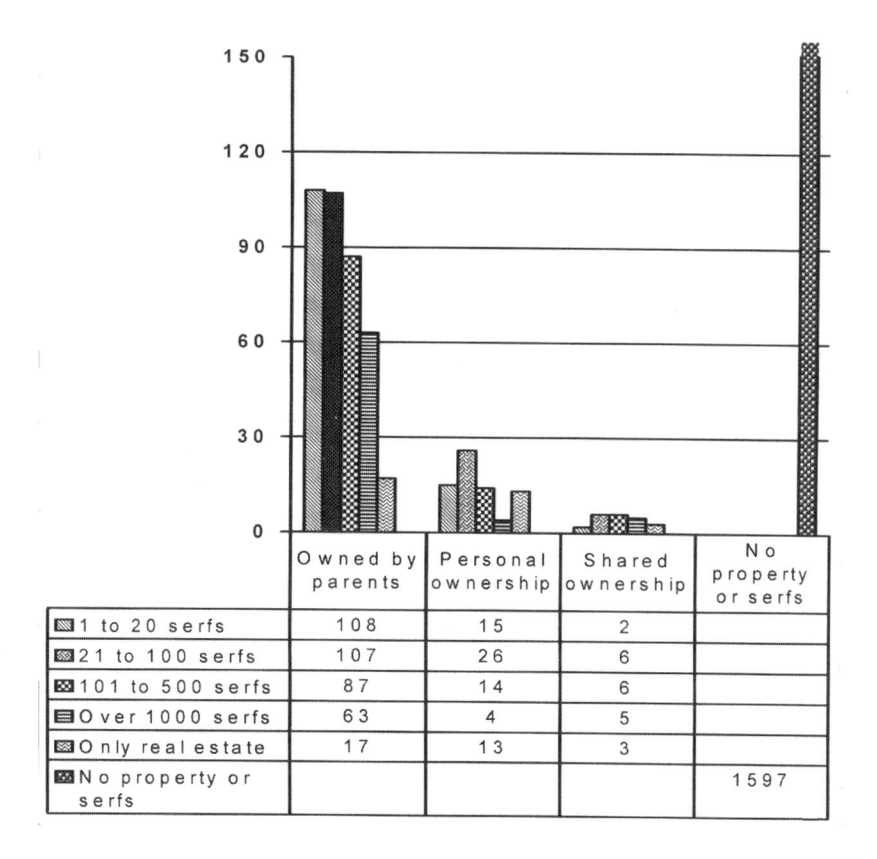

	Owned by parents	Personal ownership	Shared ownership	No property or serfs
1 to 20 serfs	108	15	2	
21 to 100 serfs	107	26	6	
101 to 500 serfs	87	14	6	
Over 1000 serfs	63	4	5	
Only real estate	17	13	3	
No property or serfs				1597

Guard

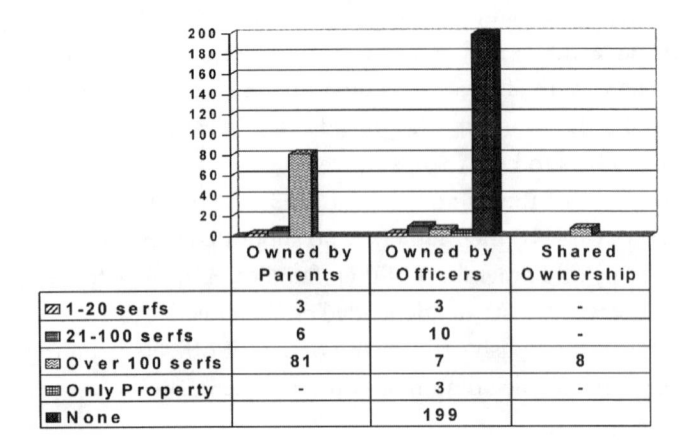

	Owned by Parents	Owned by Officers	Shared Ownership
1-20 serfs	3	3	-
21-100 serfs	6	10	-
Over 100 serfs	81	7	8
Only Property	-	3	-
None		199	

Cavalry

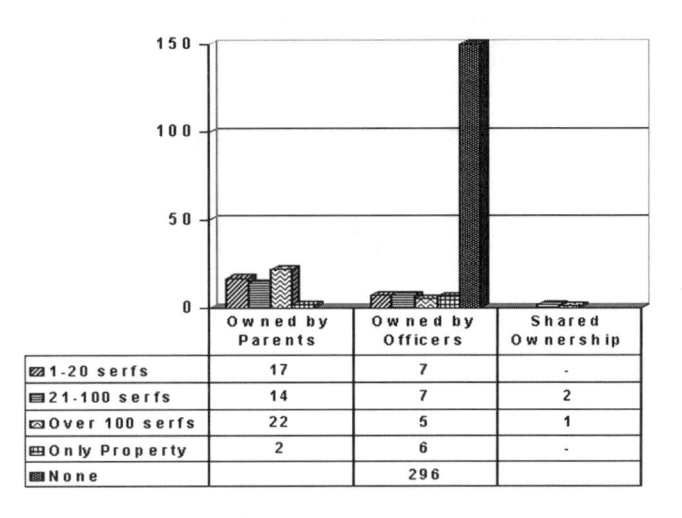

	Owned by Parents	Owned by Officers	Shared Ownership
1-20 serfs	17	7	-
21-100 serfs	14	7	2
Over 100 serfs	22	5	1
Only Property	2	6	-
None		296	

Infantry

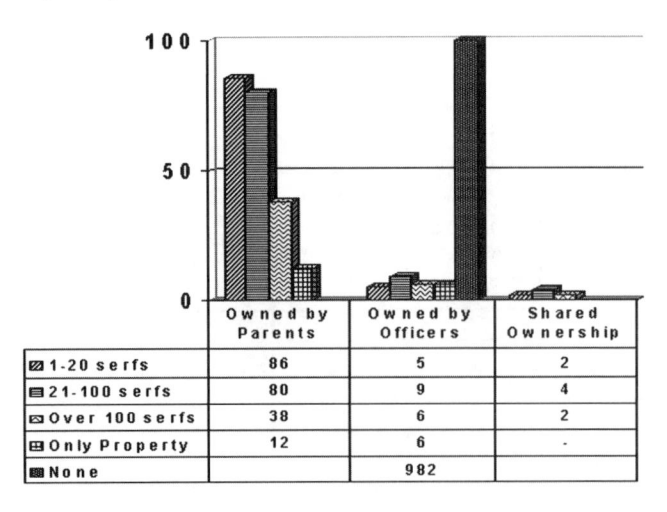

	Owned by Parents	Owned by Officers	Shared Ownership
1-20 serfs	86	5	2
21-100 serfs	80	9	4
Over 100 serfs	38	6	2
Only Property	12	6	-
None		982	

Artillery

Looking at the data on senior officers (major generals, lieutenant generals, and generals), it is surprising to find that 13 (4.4%) owned less than 20 serfs, 34 (11.5%) owned between 20 and 100 serfs, and 79 (26.8%) owned more than 100 serfs. Only 2.7% of generals possessed estates. The majority of senior officers (54.2%) had neither serfs nor property.[82]

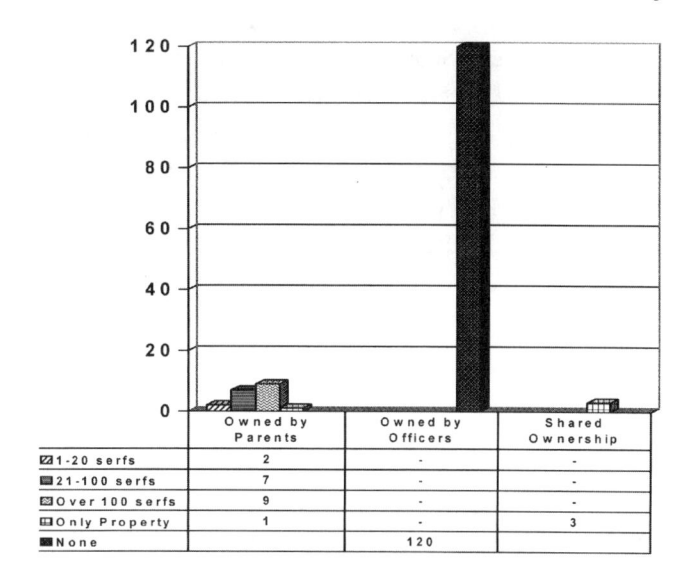

	Owned by Parents	Owned by Officers	Shared Ownership
1-20 serfs	2	-	-
21-100 serfs	7	-	-
Over 100 serfs	9	-	-
Only Property	1	-	3
None		120	

An officer's marital status was closely connected to his finances and property. A Russian serving in the military did not need his parents' consent to marry, but only the permission of his commanding officer. However, insufficient military salaries prevented them from marrying until retirement. As a result, an overwhelming majority of Russian officers (91.3%) were single. They usually married in their late 30s and had one or two children.

Marital Status

Age	Single	Married	Widower
14	1	-	-
15-16	18	-	-
17-18	88	-	-
19-20	275	1	-
21-25	774	7	1
26-30	376	43	2
31-35	208	47	1
36-40	88	30	-
41-45	38	24	-
46-50	5	9	-
51-60	2	5	-

Children

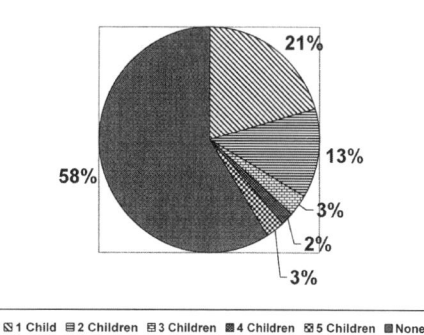

- 1 Child: 21%
- 2 Children: 13%
- 3 Children: 3%
- 4 Children: 2%
- 5 Children: 3%
- None: 58%

At the same time, many officers and prominent commanders had huge debts. In 1813, General Mikhail Vorontsov owed more than 65,000 rubles to General Dokhturov and another 62,000 to General Sabaneyev. Some officers ran up enormous debts from gambling, which was part of the accepted lifestyle.[83] Upon receiving their salaries, many officers spent their nights gaming and gambling on their pledged word or making over their houses, serfs, and other possessions. Gambling was not limited to the lower ranks. In 1809, Prince Peter Bagration criticized General Mikhail Miloradovich for excessive gambling after the latter lost 35,000 rubles in Bucharest. According to Alexander Langeron, several months later, "Miloradovich gambled [another] 250,000 rubles... and was soon 600,000 rubles in debt."[84]

Prince Bagration was another important Russian commander in debt. Bagration's annual income was an impressive 2,200 rubles, but his debts slowly accumulated because he had to keep up with social etiquette in the capital of the Russian Empire.[85] Bagration mortgaged his personal estates and, in early 1802, the Imperial treasurer informed Emperor Alexander that Bagration had to sell his estate back to the treasury. "[Bagration] did not determine any price on it, but informed me that he was 28,000 rubles in debt to the treasury, in addition to another 52,000 rubles in debt, for a total 80,000 rubles." In February 1802, Alexander gave consent for the treasury to buy Bagration's estate for 70,650 rubles. As often happens with bureaucracy though, Bagration did not receive the money for six months. On 1 July, he wrote to the state treasurer asking for an advance on the estate he sold.[86] Meanwhile, Bagration continued borrowing. In March 1804, merchant Bartholomew de Farge loaned him 3,381 rubles, which Bagration promised to repay in two months. When he could only pay back 500 rubles, the merchant sued him in court. Fortunately for Prince Peter, he was sent to fight the French in 1805 and under existing legislation, officers could not be prosecuted for debts during wartime. Returning to Russia, Bagration covered his debt to de Farge in 1806. Three years later, Bagration again approached the Imperial Treasurer to advance him two years rent from his estates.[87] In December 1810, Bagration sold his two houses near Constantine Palace in Pavlovsk, one of which was bought by Empress Maria Feodorovna.[88] However, debts quickly mounted when Bagration found himself unemployed in 1811. Etiquette required that Bagration frequently attend and serve dinners, which forced him to borrow even more money.[89] Fortunately, Minister of War Mikhail Barclay de Tolly helped him obtain a furlough with 9,000 rubles from the Imperial Treasury in 1811.

Besides gambling, there was also excessive indulgence in alcohol. When the Russians launched an offensive move near Smolensk in 1812, the Second Grenadier Division did not make the movement and in turn delayed other divisions stacked up behind it. Aleksey Ermolov recalled, "This division was commanded by Lieutenant General Prince Karl von Mecklenburg. Having spent the previous night feasting with friends, he was drunk, unable to command and woke up very late the next day; only then, he was able to order his troops to march."[90]

Nobles in the Officer Corps

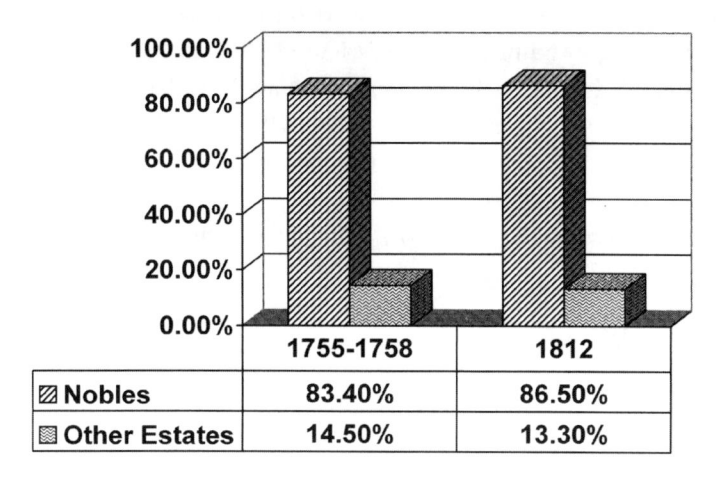

	1755-1758	1812
Nobles	83.40%	86.50%
Other Estates	14.50%	13.30%

The Russian officer corps overwhelmingly consisted of noblemen. These nobles enjoyed advantages in both the enlistment process and subsequent promotions. The class-conscious noble officers erected barriers that made it difficult for non-nobles to get advance into their ranks. Non-nobles had to serve as non-commissioned officers for extended periods of time and could only hope for promotion after four, eight, or twelve years of service. If non-nobles persevered to receive an officer's rank, they obtained the title of personal nobility. They could not receive hereditary nobility, however, which would have transferred to their offspring.

After 1796, Emperors Paul and Alexander considerably restricted this procedure by insisting officers be of noble origins. Commoners promoted to officer rank were only allowed to serve in administrative capacities, such as auditors or commissariat officials. When Paul assumed the throne, he ordered the War College give preference to nobles over non-nobles, and reprimanded regimental commanders who recommended non-nobles for officer ranks. Paul also decreed that promotions into the officer corps must be signed by the emperor. Emperor Alexander continued his father's policies. He required that non-nobles serve as NCO's for at least 12 years before qualifying for promotion to officers.[91] Soldiers' children had some advantage in this process. They were considered to be in military service upon birth and in actual service at 15 years of age. After 15 years in the army, they were eligible for discharge. The recruits, however, had to serve for 25 years before qualifying for advancement.

The demand for officers during the Napoleonic Wars rapidly increased, which in turn led to changes in regulations. Non-noble NCOs were allowed to receive an officer's rank in the army and the Guard, while ober officers were promoted without vacancies. After the 1805 Campaign, university students also enjoyed benefits. Despite their social background, they only had to serve as privates for three months and sub-ensigns for another three months before receiving an officer's rank without vacancy.

While Russian noble officers often held non-noble NCOs in contempt, they were more concerned about the increasing number of foreign noblemen joining the officer corps. Ever since Peter the Great employed large numbers of foreigners, the friction between Russian and "foreign" officers preoccupied the Russian military. In 1722, 13 out of 49 generals (26.5%) were of non-Russian origin.[92] The percentage increased during the reign of Empress Anna Ioanovna, who surrounded herself with foreigners, most of them of German stock. Empress Elizabeth, who promoted herself as a true Russian sovereign, made efforts to reduce the number of foreigners in the Russian army. The Seven Year War led to increasing anti-German sentiments in Russia and facilitated this process. The brief reign of Peter III intensified antagonism against the "Germans" when the Russian Emperor tried to impose Prussian-style and manners upon Russia. Peter III openly admired Prussia's King Frederick the Great and recruited the elite guard from his native Holstein. By the time Catherine II took power in the coup d'état of 28 June 1762, more than 34% of majors and 41% of 402 senior officers were non-Russians. The proportion was even higher among lieutenant generals (63.7%).[93]

Nobles and Social Composition in the Officer Corps

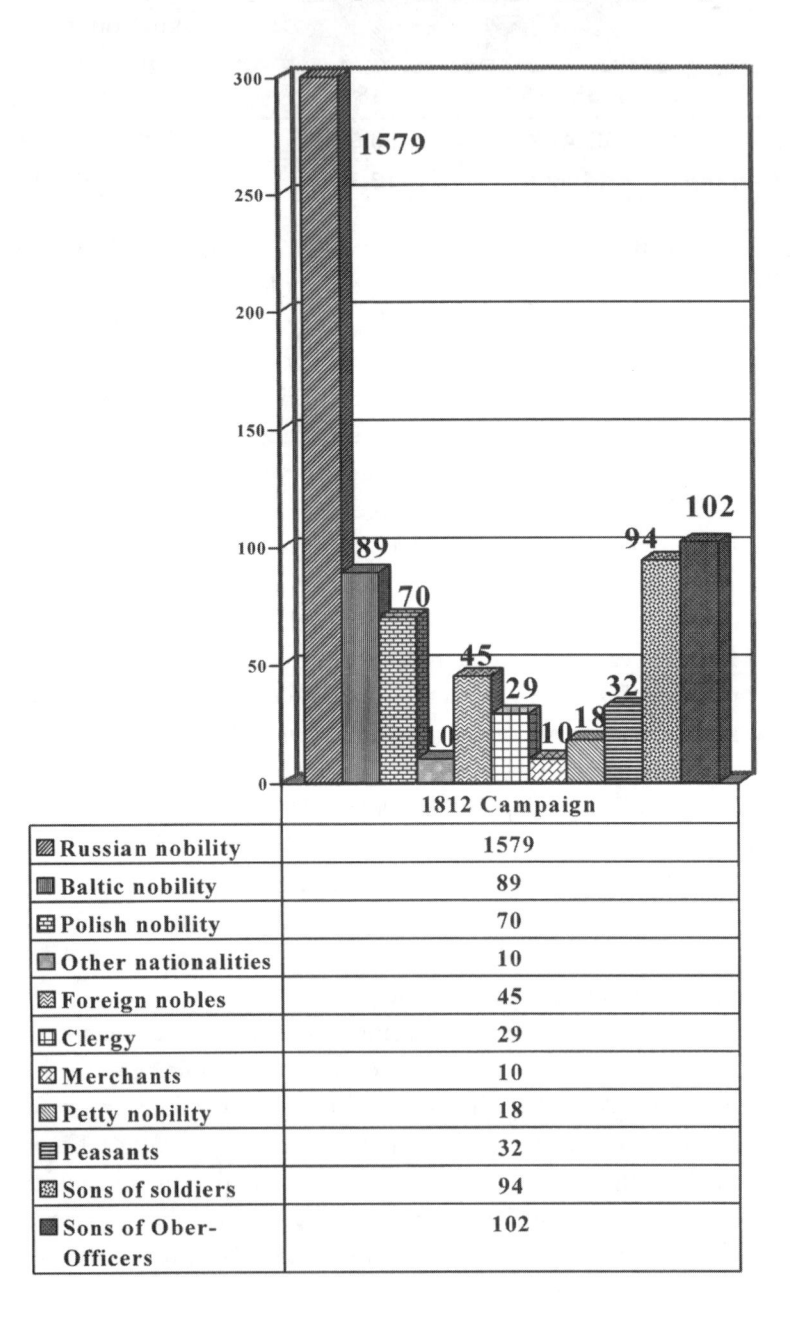

	1812 Campaign
Russian nobility	1579
Baltic nobility	89
Polish nobility	70
Other nationalities	10
Foreign nobles	45
Clergy	29
Merchants	10
Petty nobility	18
Peasants	32
Sons of soldiers	94
Sons of Ober-Officers	102

The antagonism against foreigners remained strong in the Russian army during the Napoleonic Wars. From 1806 to 1807, the "Russian" officers opposed the appointment of Levin Bennigsen to command the Russian army, noting that there were genuine Russian commanders available for this post. During the campaign, bickering between Generals Bennigsen and Buxhöwden led to the latter's dismissal (Buxhöwden later challenged Bennigsen to a duel). In June 1807, Bennigsen launched an offensive around Guttstadt, hoping to destroy Marshal Michel Ney's corps. However, General Fabian Osten-Sacken's column failed to support Prince Bagration's attack, allowing the French to safely retreat. Some claimed General Sacken, who had strained relations with Bennigsen, intentionally delayed the advance to undermine the entire operation and have Bennigsen removed from the army.[94] In a letter to Alexander, Bennigsen accused Sacken of insubordination and held him responsible for the failure of the maneuver at Guttstadt.[95] Sacken, who was eventually court-martialed, tried to justify his actions by referring to Bennigsen's confusing orders.[96]

A more important conflict took place during the 1812 Campaign, which could have led to disastrous consequences for Russia. This disagreement illustrates the complexities and intrigues swirling through the Russian officer corps. When Napoleon invaded Russia in June 1812, the Russian armies quickly retreated eastward. Mikhail Barclay de Tolly's First Western Army moved toward the entrenched camp at Drissa, seeking a junction with the Second Western Army of General Peter Bagration. After marching through Drissa and Vitebsk, the First Western Army finally arrived at Smolensk on 1 August. Meanwhile, Bagration's Second Western Army out-marched Marshal Davout's entrapment at Moghilev and proceeded to Smolensk. Bagration himself arrived there on 2 August to discuss war plans with Barclay de Tolly.[97]

This meeting influenced the fate of the Russian army. The continuous retreat was generating discontent and demoralizing the soldiers. Most senior officers, including Bagration, opposed Barclay de Tolly's Fabian (passive) defensive strategy. Though Bagration agreed with Barclay on the necessity of the retreat, he also insisted on "active defensive warfare," which meant combining the retreat with counterattacks.[98] The discord that developed between Barclay and Bagration was neither a simple quarrel between two generals nor a mere disagreement on strategy. This conflict stemmed from a political friction between the "foreigners" and old Russian aristocracy. The "real" Russian preferred a straightforward, stand-up fight to maneuvering, and bitterly resented the surrender of every inch of Russian soil, blaming the foreigners for all their misfortunes.[99]

The main reason for this tension was the different views on strategy among the senior officers and army commanders, who represented opposing factions within the officer corps. Barclay de Tolly[100] was surrounded by the so-called "German party," which consisted mainly of the émigré officers, some of whom settled in Russia generations earlier. These non-Russians did not form a homogeneous or isolated group in the army or in noble society generally. Many of them assimilated into the Russian society and learned the Russian language. However, in 1812, many of these non-Russians, led by Barclay de Tolly, supported a defensive doctrine. Opposing them was the "Russian party" of old Russian families who were proponents of offensive warfare. Led by Prince Peter Bagration (a Georgian), they reflected the majority opinion of the Russian army which believed in defeating Napoleon with vigorous counterattacks and offensive action.[101]

Prince Bagration and most Russian generals resented foreign officers in the army, claiming they brought the spirit and influence of the Prussian military into the Russian army. In a letter to Aleksey Arakcheyev, Chief of Imperial Chancellery, Bagration complained, "the whole headquarters is so full of Germans that a Russian cannot breathe."[102] Bagration described Barclay's headquarters in a letter to Prince Paul Stroganov, specifying that "people around the minister [Barclay de Tolly] wish to become field marshals without reading any military journals or [other writings]. . . . Today the rogues and impudent upstarts are in favor."[103] Denis Davidov, who later became a famous guerrilla leader, recalled that "inspired with ardent love of our mother land, Prince [Bagration], with unrestrained ardor characteristic of all Asians, felt anger against Barclay; this feeling, based only on antipathy to the German party, increased considerably due to constant retreat of our troops."[104]

Personal relations between Bagration and Barclay de Tolly were complex. The generals were cordial when they fought in the Polish campaigns (1806-1807) and the Swedish War in Finland (1808-1809). According to a contemporary, "after the battles at Pultusk and Eylau, Prince Bagration respected Barclay de Tolly and often praised him."[105] In 1812, however, their relationship rapidly deteriorated.

Barclay de Tolly had to perform under a significant moral stress. Most of the army opposed him, believing that the deep retreat into Russia was proof of his betrayal. Even his own staff members, led by General Alexander Ermolov, intrigued against him.[106] Officers taught the rank and file to call Barclay de Tolly by the nickname "Boltai da i tolko" (All talk and nothing else).[107] Barclay de Tolly's position was a precarious one from the outset of the campaign. Confidence in him was undermined, and every new stage of the retreat intensified the malicious rumors against him. It was hard for him to parry Bagration's thrusts. Barclay had neither a heroic career nor a brilliant reputation as a disciple of Suvorov. He lacked everything Bagration had in abundance. A diligent administrator and reformer, Barclay gained Alexander's confidence by his executive ability and firmness.

In contrast, Prince Bagration was respected throughout the army for his military talents. He retained an extraordinary presence of mind in the most desperate situations, and was known to endanger his life in circumstances where the odds were significantly against him. The rank and file knew this trait well; he had a charismatic personality that could fire his men to attempt the impossible. Unfortunately, Bagration had an uncontrollable temper. Although he was often calm, taciturn, and even restrained, his anger knew no bounds when he found an object worthy of his wrath. This contempt was often out of proportion to the situation. Bagration regarded Barclay's tactics as ineffective and so he proposed the army go over to the offensive. Barclay, however, ignored his proposals, and Bagration's rage continued increased.

Bagration is often portrayed as a reckless general, whose only strategy was to blindly attack and confront the enemy. Known for his violent temper, some claimed he had limited strategic sense and moderate tactical skills.[108] This is incorrect. Bagration proved in a series of earlier campaigns that he was an equally effective offensive and defensive commander. However, in 1812, he was not informed of the overall strategy.[109] "I was neither provided with the essential information, nor acquainted with our policy," he complained to Tsar Alexander.[110] Bagration appealed directly to Barclay for adequate information, but his requests were ignored. He wrote to Alexander Ermolov, Barclay's Chief of Staff:

> I have written to you twice, but there is no answer. I asked the minister [Barclay de Tolly] where is he leading the army? I wrote to him, but there is no answer. I do not understand. What does it mean?! What is happening with you? Why do you neglect me? It is no time for jokes. If I write, it is necessary [for you] to answer.[111]

Lacking sufficient intelligence on the French invasion, Bagration believed it was possible to defeat Napoleon on the battlefield. However, he withdrew on his own initiative when faced with the advancing Grand Army. This proved vitally important to the Russians, for it provided the army with a three- to four-day advantage over the French before Bagrations' route of retreat could be cut by the coordinated forces of King Jérôme and Marshal Davout. After successful actions at Mir and Moghilev, Bagration was convinced the Russian army could launch its own offensive. He appealed for an attack and criticized Barclay's strategy in a series of letters to his Russian compatriots. For example, he wrote to Arakcheyev:

> You will get no one in the army, or in Russia, to believe that we have not been betrayed. I cannot defend all Russia alone.... One feels ashamed.... If I cannot be supported, better have me released from the yoke and send someone else to command. But why torment the soldiers without purpose and satisfaction?[112]

Unaware of the actual situation facing Barclay, Bagration complained to Ermolov, "One feels ashamed to wear the [Russian] uniform. I feel sick.... What a fool.... The minister [Barclay de Tolly] himself is running away, yet he orders me to defend all of Russia."[113] Commanders exchanged bitter letters,[114] with Bagration, who focused his frustration on Tsar Alexander, as well. Bagration also knew his own chief of staff, Colonel Emmanuel Saint Priest, was in secret correspondence with the Tsar, informing him of the condition of the Second Western Army.[115]

Accompanied by an imposing escort of generals and aide-de-camps, Bagration reached Smolensk on 2 August, exhausted and ready to see an insult in every trifle. However, Barclay displayed unusual tact.[116] To show his respect for Bagration, Barclay de Tolly met him wearing a parade uniform complete with medals, sash, sword, and plumed bicorne in hand. This unanticipated action had a tremendous effect on Bagration.[117] Both commanders apologized for any injustice he might have caused the other. Bagration praised Barclay's withdrawal from Vitebsk, and Barclay complimented Bagration on the skillful manner in which he eluded Napoleon's trap. Bagration seemed surprised by Barclay's tact and his readiness to cooperate. He was pleased with this conversation and, though senior in rank, gallantly agreed to subordinate himself to Barclay de Tolly.[118] Furthermore, Bagration wrote to the Tsar suggesting that he appoint Barclay de Tolly Commander-in-Chief of all the armies, advising him that "a single overall command is necessary to save the fatherland."[119]

After the failure of the counter-offensive at Smolensk on 8-12 August, and the subsequent surrender of the city on 19 August, relations between the two commanders deteriorated. Bagration was particularly enraged that Barclay de Tolly had broken his pledge not to surrender Smolensk. He complained to the Tsar that Barclay did not consider his suggestions and tried to mislead him.[120] Bagration wrote to Moscow Governor Feodor Rostopchin, "I do not rely on Barclay anymore and . . . can assure you that he will bring the enemy to [Moscow]."[121] Two days after the battle of Smolensk, Bagration complained to Arakcheyev, "Your minister [Barclay de Tolly] may be good at ministerial affairs, but as a general he is not only bad, but simply worthless. I am truly going out of my mind from grief."[122]

Anti-Barclay sentiments were also strong among senior officers who still intrigued for the appointment of Bagration to supreme command. The demands for Barclay's dismissal showed signs of a mutiny.[123] General Alexander Ermolov, who provided Bagration with information from the First Western Army headquarters, appealed to the Tsar requesting that Bagration replace Barclay de Tolly—unbeknownst to Bagration.[124] Senior officers detested Barclay de Tolly, his associates, and the current strategy.[125] Bagration's consent to obey Barclay de Tolly irritated them. A contemporary recalled, "The reconciliation between two commanders infuriated all our generals and officers, who unanimously detested Barclay."[126] These misguided officers tried to persuade Bagration to oppose Barclay de Tolly publicly. The Quartermaster General of the Second Western Army, Mikhail Vistitskii, stated that Bagration "was encouraged by the senior officers to replace Barclay by force."[127]

Fortunately, Bagration rejected these treasonous suggestions and refused to openly engage Barclay de Tolly. But Bagration's true feelings and passionate temper often came out in private letters to Arakcheyev and Rostopchin. "I have no power over the minister even though I am senior [in rank]," he complained. "When the Tsar departed [the army], he did not leave any instructions as to who should be in command in case the two armies united, and hence Barclay, as a Minister of War, would be superior."[128]

Bagration also complained in a letter to Admiral Paul Tchichagov: "I am senior in rank, but His Majesty does not want to give overall command to one person; meanwhile he [Barclay] is allowed to do everything. . . . I call for the offensive, he for the retreat."[129] Alexander Ermolov urged Bagration to write directly to the Tsar and boldly suggest that he be named supreme commander of the Russian armies. "Please write to His Majesty [and appeal for the command]. You must fulfill your duty. . . . I will write to the Tsar and describe your deeds and impediments you have overcome. Take overall command of the armies. . . . "[130]

Although Bagration's secret ambition was undoubtedly to command the Russian armies, he hesitated to reach that high. The proud scion of the Bagration Kings of Georgia was a man of dignity. Too high and noble to commit willful insubordination, he rejected all appeals to write to the Tsar. Instead he wrote to Ermolov: "I will not write the Tsar asking for the command, because this would be attributed to my ambition and vanity, not my merit and abilities."[131] Perhaps Bagration realized Alexander would never give him supreme command of the Russian army. He knew Alexander's feelings toward him, especially in light of their conflict during the 1809 campaign in the Danube Valley, current disagreements on strategy, and his liaison with Alexander's sister, Catherine.[132]

The loss of Smolensk made Barclay's position even more tenuous. According to Sir Robert Wilson, British commissioner to the Russian army, "The spirit of the army was affected by a sense of mortification and all ranks loudly and boldly complained; discontent was general and discipline relaxing. The removal [of Barclay de Tolly] . . . had become a universal demand."[133] The retreat through Lithuania and Byelorussia was reluctantly accepted due to the enemy's numerical superiority. However, the main theater of fighting was now on ancient Russian soil and the Holy City of Smolensk was in ruins. Thoughts of further retreat became unbearable, especially when after the successful actions (Mir, Klyastitsy, Romanovo, Moghilev, Polotsk, and Kobrin) that had taken place during the early stages of the retreat.[134] These alleged successes fueled a determination to attack the French. Bagration wrote to Ermolov, "The retreat is intolerable and dangerous. . . . The army was in excellent condition, but now it is exhausted. . . . Ten days it marched on sandy terrain, in hot weather . . . surrounded by the enemy. Nevertheless, we defeated the adversary every time we opposed him! I do not understand these witty maneuvers. My maneuver is to seek and attack!"[135]

Most Russian generals and officers opposed the surrender of Smolensk. Barclay's favorite young general, Count Alexander Kutaysov, spoke with him on behalf of the senior officers and requested to continue the battle. Barclay de Tolly listened attentively and then replied, "Lets everyone mind his own business and I shall mind mine."[136] In Dorogobuzh, the corps commander complained to the Grand Duke Constantine about Barclay's leadership. According to a contemporary, "soldiers were disappointed, downcast. . . . Everybody was concerned with the future of the army."[137] To their own dishonor, many officers publicly slandered Barclay de Tolly. Grand Duke Constantine was even more disgraceful in his attempts to discredit the Commander-in-Chief, telling the rank and file, "we can do nothing [for] there is not a single drop of Russian blood in our commander's veins."[138] In Dorogobuzh, Constantine brutally insulted Barclay in the presence of aide-de-camps and staff members, "You are *German*, a traitor, vermin, and you are betraying Russia!"[139] Motivated by bigotry, jealousy, and self-interest, many Russian generals opposed Barclay de Tolly no matter what he did. Despite Barclay de Tolly's loyalty and commitment to Russia, he was increasingly unpopular among the superstitious soldiers, who saw "irrefutable" evidence of his betrayal. In their eyes, Barclay de Tolly was "German" and therefore a traitor.[140]

Considering the events prior to and during operations around Smolensk, Barclay de Tolly's generalship saved the army and allowed it to pass to his successor intact and battle-worthy. At the beginning of the campaign, the ratio of forces was against the Russians. Luckily for Russia, Bagration and his supporters were not given high command, for a battle at that time may well have led to the destruction of both Russian armies, which in turn would have exposed all of Russia to Napoleon's armies. Instead, Barclay opposed most of the army (and especially the Russian nobility) and continued his retreat deep into the heart of Russia. To his credit, Barclay stoically endured disgrace. Despite humiliation and insult, he assured Alexander he was devoted to the motherland and eager "to serve the country at any post or assignment."[141] To justify his actions, Barclay wrote, "Had I been motivated by blind and reckless ambition, Your Majesty would probably have received a number of reports of battles fought, and nevertheless the enemy would still be at gates of Moscow without retaining sufficient forces to resist him."[142]

The retreat toward Moscow during the summer of 1812 demonstrates well the competition and jealousy seething within the Russian army. On many occasions, senior Russian officers showed little judgment and behaved childishly. They accused Barclay of betraying Russia based on his alleged "German" origins. Ermolov recalled that the two Commanders-in-Chief had a passionate argument near Smolensk: Bagration yelled at Barclay, "You are German! That is why you do not care about Russia," to which Barclay defiantly replied, "You are fool and do not even understand why you call yourself Russian."[143] Georgian Bagration acted as an out-and-out Russian nationalist against Barclay, whose own origins were Scottish.[144] If Bagration and his supporters had gained control of the army, it could have had disastrous repercussions for the future of Russia and its leadership.

Military Ranks

The Russian rank structure was determined by a decree levied by Peter the Great on 4 February 1722. This order provided the army branches and civilian service with rank equivalencies. When Peter launched reforms in the early 1700s, a new promotion system was required to organize the army and society. This was particularly important for noblemen, who were obligated to serve in the army under his decree. Peter the Great had two goals while forming his army along the European lines: to simplify the transfer from one branch of service to another, and to determine the precedence of officials in civilian service and court.

The Table of Ranks[145] was comprised of 14 chins, classes of ranks, and 262 service titles. It was organized by the military branches (infantry, cavalry, guard, artillery, and navy), civilian, and court positions. A system of properly addressing the ranks was also set up. The Guards, as a privileged corps, were given higher classes of rank than an equivalent rank in other military branches. Non-nobles particularly benefited from the Table of Ranks because it allowed sons of secretaries and scribes to be promoted through the ranks. The seventh class awarded men of non-noble descent the status of nobility (*dvorianskoe zvanie*). The Table was divided into three parts: classes XIV to IX were given ober officer (junior officer) ranks, classes VIII to V staff officer ranks, and classes IV to I general ranks. The rank of *Generalissimus* was an exceptional distinction not included in the Table. During the 18th century, it was only awarded to three generals: Menshikov, Suvorov, and Prince Anton Ulrich von Braunschweig.

The Table used specialized terminology. The official title literally translates to "Table of Rangs," where the word *rang* (rank) referred to a person's status determined by his *chin* (rank) and *klass* (class). In addition, the Table established a relative correspondence between the rank (chin) and position (*dolzhnost*). A person would not be considered for a position unless he held a rank of appropriate class. In some cases, a promotion to a higher class also meant a promotion in position. Most classes had more than two ranks; each originally intended to describe a distinct position. The Table was modified several times throughout the two centuries it was used. In the late 19th century, the table contained 12 ranks and many titles of civilian positions were simplified. The Bolshevik government abolished the Table of Ranks in the 23 November and 29 December 1917 decrees.

Officer Ranks under the original "Table of Ranks" of 1722

Class	Infantry/Cavalry	Guard	Engineers	Artillery	Navy
I	General Field Marshal	-	-	-	General Admiral
II	General of Infantry, General of Cavalry	-	-	General[146] Feldzeugmeister	Admiral
III	Lieutenant General; General Kriegscommissar[147]	-	-	Lieutenant General	Vice Admiral, General Kriegscommissar
IV	Major General	Colonel	Major General of Fortifications	Major General	Rear Admiral; Sautbenacht; Ober-zeugmeister
V	Brigadier, Ober-ster-Kriegscommissar, General Proviantmeister	Lieutenant Colonel		Colonel	Captain Commander, Captain of Kronsdat Port, Intendant, Zeugmeister, Ober-ster-Kriegscommissar
VI	Colonel, Treasurer, General-[148] Proviantmaster, Ober-Commissar, General Adjutant, Prosecutor, General-Quartermaster-Lieutenant[149]	Major	Colonel	Lieutenant Colonel, Ober-Commissar	Captain (1st class), Captain of other ports, Ship Surveyor, Prosecutor, Intendant of St. Petersburg Warf, Treasurer, Ober-Proviantmeister, Ober-Commissar
VII	Lieutenant Colonel, General Auditor,[150] Ober-proviantmeister, General-Wagonmeister, General-Gelwadiger,[151] General Adjutant to General Fieldmarshal, Controller	Captain	Lieutenant Colonel	Major, Ober-Controller	Captain (2nd class), Controller
VIII	Major, General Adjutant to General, Ober Auditor, General-Staff-Quartermaster, Ober-Zalmeister	Lieutenant Captain	Major	Captain, Ober-Zeichwarter, Controller	Captain (3rd class)

Officer Ranks under the original "Table of Ranks" of 1722 (continued)

IX	Captain, Flügel Adjutant to General Fieldmarshal or full General, Adjutant to Lieutenant General, Ober-Proviantmeister, General-Staff-Quartermaster, Ober-Auditor, Field Postmeister, General Provost	Lieutenant	Captain	Lieutenant Captain, Ober-Auditor, Quartermaster, Commissar to gunpowder factory	Lieutenant Captain, Gallery Master
X	Lieutenant Captain	Unter Lieutenant	Lieutenant Captain	Lieutenant	Lieutenant
XI	-	-	-	-	Ship Secretary
XII	Lieutenant	Fendrik	Lieutenant	Unter-Lieutenant, Wagonmeister	Unter Lieutenant, Skipper (1st class)
XIII	Unter Lieutenant, Flügel Adjutant to Lieutenant General	-	Unter-Lieutenant	Shtyk junker[152]	-
XIV	Fendrik, Flügel Adjutant to Major General or Brigadier, Staff furrier	-	Fendrik[153]	-	Ship Commissar, Skipper (2nd class)

To illustrate changes introduced to the Table of Ranks throughout the 18th and early 19th centuries, the following tables (beginning on the facing pages) listed only major ranks between 1765 and 1815:

1765-1798

Class	Infantry	Cavalry	Guard	Engineer/Artillery
I	General Field Marshal	-	-	-
II	Gènèral-en-Chef	General of Cavalry	-	General, General Feldzugmeister
III	Lieutenant General	Lieutenant General	-	Lieutenant General
IV	Major General	Major General	Colonel	Major General
V	Brigadier	Brigadier	Lieutenant Colonel	Colonel
VI	Colonel	Colonel	Premier/Second Major	Lieutenant Colonel
VII	Lieutenant Colonel	Lieutenant Colonel	Captain, Rotmistr	Major
VIII	Premier/Second Major	Premier/Second Major	-	Captain
IX	Captain	Rotmistr	Lieutenant	Lieutenant Captain
X	-	-	Sub-Lieutenant	Lieutenant
XI	Lieutenant	Lieutenant	-	Sub-Lieutenant
XII	Sub-Lieutenant	-	Ensign, Cornet	-
XIII	-	-	Feldfebel	Ensign
XIV	Ensign	Cornet	Sergeant	-

1765-1798 (continued)

	Unter Officers (Non-Commissioned Officers)			
	Senior Sergeant	Senior Sergeant	Sub-Ensign	Feldfebel
	Junior Sergeant	Junior Sergeant	Kaptenarmus[154]	Sergeant
	Sub Ensign	Sub Ensign	Fourrier	Sub-Ensign
	Kaptenarmus	Kaptenarmus	Corporal	Kaptenarmus
	Fourrier	Fourrier	-	Fourrier
	Corporal	Corporal	-	Corporal
	-	-	-	Gunner, Sapper, Pioneer, Miner

As Russia expanded its influence to Ukraine, the Hetman (Cossack) state developed its own rank system. The Cossack state was dominated by the Cossack *starshynas*, a general title applied to people of authority in the Ukrainian Cossack Regiments and the administration of the Hetman state (1648-1781). In order to preserve its autonomy from Russia, the Cossack *starshynas* wanted Moscow to recognize Cossack titles and offices. In 1756, Hetman Kiril Razumovsky established a Ukrainian table of ranks consisting of 12 classes, excluding the two highest positions: the hetman and acting hetman. This system operated until 1784, when all Ukrainian titles were officially prohibited and Ukrainian nobles were encouraged to enter Russian service. When the Russian judicial system was introduced in 1796, the Ukrainian administrative positions were redefined according to the Table of Ranks (and are reproduced on the facing page).[155]

1798-1800

Emperor Paul made considerable changes to the Table of Ranks, hoping to simplify the promotion system and purge the military of its excessive number of officers. The Guard ranks remained two classes higher than an equivalent rank in other branches of the military, but the artillery and engineering ranks matched the infantry classes. Paul I also made an important change in the regimental structure, introducing the chef (*shef*, colonel proprietor) of the regiment. Chef became a senior officer in the regiment and was responsible for maintenance and service of the unit. The dual command of regiments occurred with chefs and regimental commanders having similar authority. The regimental commander gradually became the second senior officer in the unit. He was to comply with the chef's orders and only assumed full command in the chef's absence.

Hetman K. Razumovsky's Table of Ranks, 1756-1784

1st Rank	General Quartermaster
2nd Rank	General judge; General treasurer
3rd Rank	General chancellor, general flag-bearer, general esaul, general standard-bearer
4th Rank	Colonel
5th Rank	Fellow of the standard; esaul of the general artillery, colonel of mercenary cavalry regiment, secretary of the general military court, senior chancellor of the general military chancellery
6th Rank	General artillery flag-bearer, regimental judge, quartermaster of mercenary cavalry regiment
7th Rank	Regimental secretary, esaul, and flag bearer, translator of the general military chancellery
8th Rank	Captain, chancellor of the general military chancellery, ataman of the general artillery, esaul, flag bearer and secretary of the mercenary cavalry regiment
9th Rank	Fellow of the banner, regimental court secretary, captain of the hetman's personal guard, ataman of company city, captain of mercenary cavalry
10th Rank	Ataman of the hetman's personal guard, company esaul, flag bearer, secretary, regimental chancellor, regimental artillery flag-bearer and ataman, mercenary company officer
11th Rank	Kurin ataman, mayor (*gorodnychyi*) of company city, village ataman
12th Rank	Cossack, guard, member of the hetman's guard (*zholdak*) mercenary cavalryman (*kompaniiets*), artilleryman (*pushkar*)

In 1796, Paul abolished the rank of brigadier and combined the ranks of premier and second majors. He removed the rank of *shtyk-Junker* (artillery) and allowed non-nobles to receive the rank of *vakhmistr* (sergeants).[156] Paul made efforts to curb the policy of enlisting noble infants in regiments. Under the new system, a nobleman could receive an officer's rank after serving three years as a private and another three years as an *estandart junker* (*fanen junker* in dragoons and *portupey junker* in light cavalry). On 12 November 1796, Paul abolished the rank of sub-lieutenant in the hussar regiments and ensigns were renamed to cornets. The following year, on 7 November 1797, he turned lieutenant captain into staff captain and the second *rotmistr* into staff *rotmistr*. In the Cossack forces, the ranks were titled *Polkovnik* (colonel), *Voiskovoi starshina* (major), *Esaul* (captain), *Sotnik* (lieutenant), and *Khorunzhii* (cornet). In 1798, he introduced special ranks for non-commissioned officers: *estandart-junker* in heavy cavalry regiments, *fanen-junker* in dragoon regiments, *portupey-junker* in light cavalry and artillery, and *portupey-praporshchik* (*portupey* ensign) in the infantry.[157]

Ranks in the Russian Officer Corps under Emperor Paul

Class	Infantry	Cavalry	Guard	Engineer/Artillery[158]
I	General Field Marshal	-	-	-
II	Gènèral-en-Chef	General of Cavalry	-	General, General Feldzugmeister
III	Lieutenant General	Lieutenant General	-	Lieutenant General
IV	Major General	Major General	Colonel	Major General
V	-	-	Lieutenant Colonel	-
VI	Colonel	Colonel	Major	Colonel
VII	Lieutenant Colonel	Lieutenant Colonel	Captain, Rotmistr	Lieutenant Colonel
VIII	Major	Major	Staff Captain, Staff Rotmistr	Major
IX	Captain	Rotmistr	-	Captain
X	Staff Captain	Staff Rotmistr	Lieutenant	Staff Captain
XI	-	-	Sub-Lieutenant	-
XII	Lieutenant	Lieutenant	Ensign, Cornet	Lieutenant
XIII	Sub-Lieutenant	-		Sub-Lieutenant
XIV	Ensign	Cornet	Feldfebel, Vakhmistr	-

Ranks in the Russian Officer Corps under Emperor Paul (continued)

	Unter Officers (Non-Commissioned Officers)			
	Feldfebel	Vakhmistr	Portupey-Ensign, Estandart Junker	Feldfebel
	Portupey-Ensign	*Estandart Junker* in heavy cavalry regiments, *Fanen-Junker* in dragoon regiments, Portupey-*Junker* in the light cavalry	Sub-Ensign	Portupey-junker
	Sub Ensign	Sub Ensign	Junior Unter Officer	Sub-Ensign
	Junior Unter Officer	Junior Unter Officer	Private of higher pay	Fireworker [159]
	Private of higher pay [160]	Private of higher pay	Private of minor pay	Private of higher pay
	Private of minor pay [161]	Private of minor pay	-	Private of minor pay

The Table of Ranks also regulated promotions within the Imperial Retinue (Imperial Suite). In 1711, Peter the Great established the positions (*dolzhnost*) *flügel* adjutant and general adjutant. These positions enabled officers attached to the Commanders-in-Chief and the Emperor to carry out specific missions. From 1722 to 1731, the position of *flügel* adjutant to the general field marshal was assigned to the XI class and was equivalent to the rank of army captain; general adjutant to general field marshal was assigned to the VII class and was equivalent to the rank of lieutenant colonel; general adjutant was assigned to the VI class and was equivalent to army colonel. Because of the prestige associated with these positions, Empress Catherine declared that general adjutants were only appointed to the sovereign and matched the rank of army lieutenant general. Emperor Paul regulated appointments to these positions. Under the new system, officers of classes VIII to VI (major, lieutenant colonel, and colonel) were eligible to become *flügel* adjutant, while officers of classes III to I (lieutenant general, general, and general field marshal) were eligible to become general adjutant. If a *flügel* adjutant was promoted to lieutenant general, he surrendered his position as *flügel* adjutant.

Ranks in the Russian Officer Corps, 1800-1826

Class	Infantry	Cavalry[162]	Guard	Engineer /Artillery[163]
I	General Field Marshal	-	-	-
II	General	General of Cavalry	-	General, General Feldzugmeister
III	Lieutenant General	Lieutenant General	-	Lieutenant General
IV	Major General	Major General	Colonel	Major General
V	-	-	Lieutenant Colonel	-
VI	Colonel	Colonel	Major	Colonel
VII	Lieutenant Colonel	Lieutenant Colonel	Captain, Rotmistr	Lieutenant Colonel
VIII	Major	Major	Staff Captain	Major
IX	Captain	Rotmistr	-	Captain
X	Staff Captain	Staff Rotmistr	Lieutenant	Staff Captain
XI	-	-	Sub-Lieutenant	-
XII	Lieutenant	Lieutenant	Ensign, Cornet	Lieutenant
XIII	Sub-Lieutenant	-	-	Sub-Lieutenant
XIV	Ensign	Cornet	Feldfebel, Vakhmistr	-

	Unter Officers (Non-Commissioned Officers)			
	Feldfebel	Vakhmistr	Portupey-Ensign, Estandart Junker	Feldfebel
	Portupey Ensign	Estandart Junker	Sub-Ensign	Portupey Junker
	Sub Ensign	Sub Ensign	Junior Unter Officer	Sub Ensign
	Junior Unter Officer	Junior Unter Officer	Private of higher pay	Fireworker
	Private	Private	Private of minor pay	Private

Addressing the Ranks

Classes of Ranks	Addressing Form
I - II	Your High Excellency (*Vashe vysokoprevoskhoditelstvo*)
III - IV	Your Excellency (*Vashe prevoskhoditelstvo*)
V	Your Highly Born (*Vashe vysokorodie*)
VI, VII, VIII	Your Right Highly Born (*Vashe vysokoblagorodie*)
XI, X, XI, XII, XIII, XIV	Your Wellborn (*Vashe blagorodie*)

Major Russian Military Orders[164]

Unlike European orders with their century-old traditions, Russian Imperial decorations were established in the early 18th century. Peter the Great adopted European style awards and ceremonies during his reforms. Over the next century, his successors established more orders. Emperor Paul I then organized them into a hierarchy of orders in a unified chapter (*kapitul*).

Order of St. Andrew the First-Called (*Orden Sv. Andreia Pervosvannogo*) was established by Peter the Great in 1698. Named after Apostle Andrew, it became the highest order of the Russian Empire. To be considered, candidates had to be either a prince or count, hold the position of senator, minister, or ambassador, and have the military rank of general or admiral. In some cases, governor generals of the provinces were eligible for the order after 10 years of service. The order could not be awarded to disabled persons or noblemen younger than 25. Peter the Great awarded 40 of these orders during his reign. Another 231 men were honored between 1725 and 1796. In April 1797, Emperor Paul specified the cloth color and type and how the nominee must wear the order. He also allowed male members of the Imperial family to receive the Order of St. Andrew the First-Called upon birth. The rank of Commander of the Order was conferred to 12 recipients based on when they received the award. Three senior Commanders received 1,000 serfs each, four received 800 each, and the final five received 700 each. Upon the Commander's death, these serfs were transferred to the next recipient. During the Napoleonic Wars, Emperor Alexander bestowed this order on Emperor Napoleon, King Jerome of Westphalia, Prince Charles Talleyrand, and Marshals Alexander Berthier and Joachim Murat at Tilsit in 1807. Eight years later, Arthur Wellesley, Duke of Wellington, was also honored with the Order of St. Andrew the First-Called.

Motto: "For Faith and Fidelity" (*Za veru i vernost*)
Color of the Ribbon: Blue

Order of St. Andrew with
the Grand Cross on Parade Uniform

Order of St. Andew
on Common Uniform

Order of St. Vladimir (*Orden Sv. Vladimira*) was established by Catherine the Great in 1782 on the twentieth anniversary of her reign. Named after prominent Prince Vladimir of Ancient Kiev, it became the second highest order in the Russian empire. The order had four classes and was awarded for distinguished military and civil service. During the Napoleonic Wars, 12 first class and 95 second class orders were awarded. Third and fourth classes were awarded frequently.

Motto: "Advantage, Honor and Glory" (*Polza, chest i slava*)
Color of Ribbon: Red with Black edges

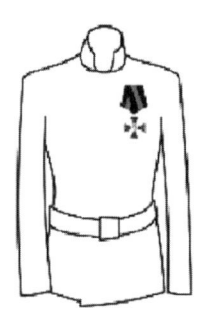

Order of St. Vladimir
4th Class

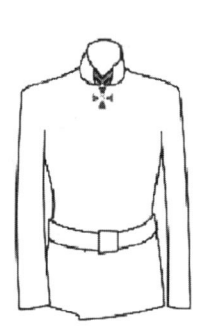

Order of St. Vladimir
3rd Class

Order of St. Vladimir
2nd Class

Order of St. Vladimir
1st Class

Order of St. Alexander of Neva (*Orden Sv. Aleksandra Nevskago*) was set up by Empress Catherine I in 1725. It was named after Prince Alexander of Novgorod, who crushed the Swedes and Teutonic Crusaders (1240-1241). The order became the third highest award in the Russian Empire. Although it did not have classes, there were additions to this award that enhanced its prestige. After receiving the original award, the recipient could earn swords, diamond signs, and diamond swords to add to the Order. From 1800 to 1825, Emperor Alexander conferred more than 250 Orders of St. Alexander of Neva, including 48 during the Napoleonic Wars from 1812 to 1814.

Motto: "For Labor and Motherland" (*za trudy i otechestvo*)
Color of Ribbon: Red

Order of St. Alexander of Neva

Order of St. George (*Orden Sv. Georgia*) was founded by Catherine the Great in 1769. Named after Saint George, it became one of the most popular and widespread Russian awards. With four classes, the Order of St. George was awarded for excellence in military service and courage in military operations. The fourth class order was also awarded for 25 years of army service or 18 naval campaigns. However, special circumstances could substantially reduce the "twenty-five years of service" requirement. Officers who participated in celebrated battles (Ochakov, Ismail, Praga, Eylau, and Bazardjik) were eligible to receive this distinction in 22 years. Earning the Order of St. Vladimir (fourth class) reduced this requirement by three years; a golden sword for courage by two years; the Order of St. Anna (third class) by two years; and the Order of St. Anna (fourth class) by another year. Officers who received Imperial letters of gratitude (*visochaishee blagovelenie*) could subtract another full year. Although the fourth class was awarded frequently, the higher classes were some of the most difficult decorations to garner. Between 1769 and 1869, 2,239 men received the fourth class order, 512 men earned the third class, and 100 men were decorated with the second class. Only 20 received the first class Order of St. George.

In 1807, Alexander I also established the Medal of Distinction for the Order of St. George (*Znak otlichia Voennogo Ordena*). Meant for soldiers and non-commissioned officers, it was often referred to as "St. George Cross for Soldiers" (*Soldatskii georgievskii kross*). Its recipients received higher pay and could not be sentenced to corporal punishment. Between 1807 and 1812, 12,871 men were awarded this medal. The awards were not initially numbered, but in 1809, Alexander ordered all crosses be registered. NCO Yegor Mityukhin of the Chevalier Guard Regiment received the first cross for his actions at Friedland and Cavalry maiden Natalya Durova, aka Alexander Sokolov, received cross number 5,723. In 1812, 6,783 men were decorated with the medal. Another 21,939 crosses were distributed from 1813 to 1815. In total, Emperor Alexander granted 46,527 "St. George Crosses" during his reign.

Motto: "For Service and Courage" (*Za sluzhbu i khrabrost*)
Color of Ribbon: Orange with Black Edges

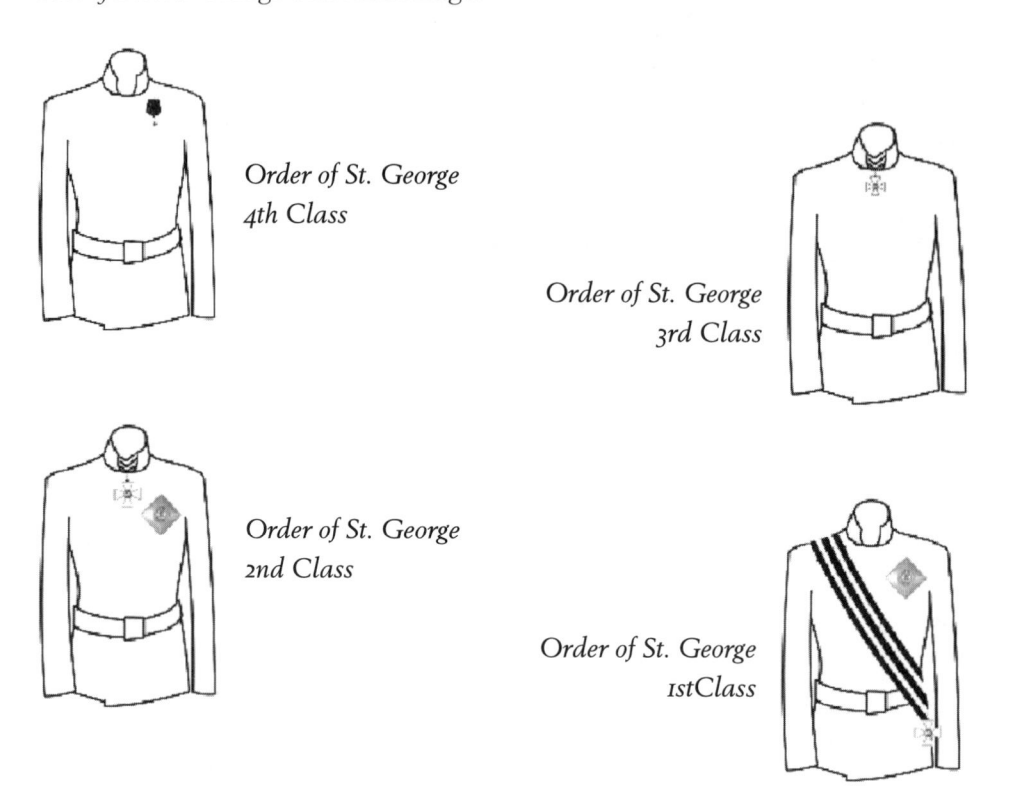

Order of St. George 4th Class

Order of St. George 3rd Class

Order of St. George 2nd Class

Order of St. George 1stClass

Order of St. Anna (*Orden Sv. Anny*) was established by Prince Karl Friedrich of Holstein in 1735 to honor his wife, Anna Petrovna (daughter of Peter the Great). When his son Prince Karl Peter Ulrich became Emperor Peter III of Russia, the Order was officially proclaimed one of the highest Russian awards. While the first and second class Orders were variations of the cross, the third (fourth after 1815) class Order was a small badge fastened to an officer's sword or saber. The first class Order was reserved primarily for generals and second and third classes for senior officers. During the Napoleonic Wars, many officers received the third class Order, including 664 men in 1812, 751 in 1813, and more than 1,090 in 1814. In some cases, soldiers and non-commissioned officers were decorated with the Medal of Distinction of the Order of St. Anna (*znak otlichia ordena sv. Anny*) when they participated in celebrated campaigns or engagements. Soldiers who earned the medal received higher pay and could not be sentenced to corporal punishment. Three hundred men in Prince Peter Bagration's troops received this medal after the famous rearguard action at Schöngrabern in November 1805. In 1807, Emperor Alexander included awarding of this medal to soldiers and non-commissioned officers who served 20 years.

Motto: "*Amantibus Justitiam, Pietateret Fidem*" (Truth, Honor, and Fidelity to the Beloved)
Color of Ribbon: Red with Yellow hems

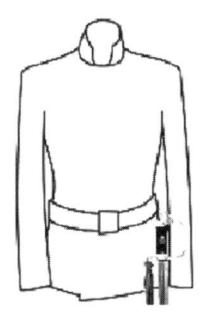

Order of St. Anna 4th (3rd) Class. A Small badge fastened to an officer's sword

Order of St. Anna 3rd Class

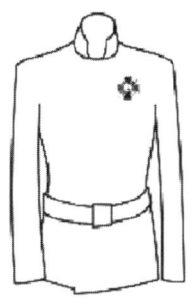

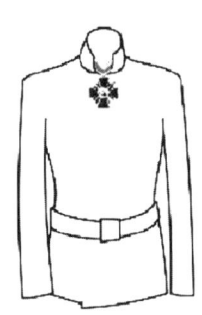

Order of St. Anna 2nd Class

Order of St. Anna 1st Class

Order of St. John of Jerusalem was created by Emperor Paul in 1798 after he became the protector of the Order of Malta in 1797, and the Grand Master of the Order in 1798. Paul established two types of the award: Commanders of the Cross of St. John of Jerusalem for Catholic and Orthodox Christians, and Honorary Commanders and Chevaliers of Order. In 1800, he also created a special medal (*donat*) of the Order for lower officer ranks. The Order lost its function after Paul's death in 1801.

Color of Ribbon: Black (no image)

Correlation Between the Orders and the Rank Classes[165]

Orders	Class	Classes of Rank											
		I	II	III	IV	V	VI	VII	VIII	IX	X	XI	XII
Order of St. Andrew the First Called		*	*	*									
Order of St. Alexander of Neva		*	*	*									
Order of St. George	I	*	*										
	II	*	*	*									
	III	*	*	*	*	*	*						
	IV	*	*	*	*	*	*	*	*	*	*	*	
Order of St. Vladimir	I	*	*										
	II	*	*	*									
	III	*	*	*	*	*							
	IV				*	*	*	*	*	*	*		
Order of St. Anna	I	*	*	*	*								
	II					*	*	*	*				
	III								*	*	*		
	IV									*	*	*	
Order of the White Eagle		*	*	*	*								
Order of St. Stanislaus	I	*	*	*	*	*	*						
	II								*	*	*		
	III									*	*	*	*

End Notes

1. Peter the Great dispatched about 150 men to study in Europe in 1697. *Istoria Severnoi voini, 1700-1721* [History of the Northern War, 1700-1721] (Moscow, 1987), 31-32.

2. For the new conscription laws, see *Polnoe sobranie zakonov rossiiskoi imperii* [Complete Compilation of Laws of the Russian Empire, hereafter cited as *PSZ*], 46 vols. (St. Petersburg, 1830-1839), vol. IV.

3. S. Volkov, *Russkii ofitserskii korpus,* [Russian Officer Corps], (Moscow, 1993), 69.

4. M. Bogoslovsky, *Peter I*, (Moscow, 1948), IV, 183. Also see, *Istoria Severnoi voini 1700-1721*, 34.

5. Military expenditures increased seven-fold during Peter's reign:

Year	Revenue	Expenditures
1680	1,500,000 rubles	Ca. 750,000 rubles
1701	2,500,000 rubles	1,839,600 rubles
1710	3,133,879 rubles	2,566,324 rubles (army) 433,966 rubles (navy)
1724	8,546,000 rubles	4,003,348 rubles (army) 1,400,000 (navy)

During the reign of Alexander I, the military expenditures varied between 60% and 90% of normal revenues. For details, see *Ministerstvo Finansov, 1802-1902* [Ministry of Finances, 1802-1902] (St. Petersburg, 1902), 616-21; Christopher Duffy, *Russia's Military Way to the West: Origins and Nature of Russian Military Power, 1700-1800* (London, 1981), 36.

6. Liubomir Beskrovny, *Russkaia armia i flot v XVIII veke* [Russian Army and Fleet in XVIII Century] (Moscow, 1958), 167-168, 170.

7. Volkov, *Russian Officer Corps*, 69.

8. According to Avtokratov, in 1695 there were 178 foreigners and 1,129 officers in the Russian army. "*Voennii prikaz, k istorii komplektovania i formirovania voisk v Rossii v nachale XVIII v.*" in *Poltava K 250-letiu Poltavskogo srazhenia* (Moscow, 1959), 238-40.

9. *PSZ*, V, No. 2,775, 3,265.

10. Ibid., XXX, No, 23,641.

11. A. Romanovich-Slavatinsky, *Dvorianstvo v Rossii ot nachala XVIII veka do otmeny krepostnogo pravas* [Nobility in Russia from early XVIII century to Abolishment of Serfdom] (St. Petersburg, 1870), 128-30, N. Pavlov-Silvansky, *Gosudarevy sluzhilie ludi: proiskhozhdenie russkogo dvorianstvo* (St. Petersburg, 1898), 272-73. Zapiski Vinskago, in *Russkii Arkhiv*, 1877, 98-99, 162-63.

12. S. Glinka, *Zapiski* [Recollections] (St. Petersburg, 1895), 136.

13. Martos, A. N., *Zapiski inzhenernogo ofitsera Martosa o turetskoi voine v tsartsvovanii Aleksandra Pavlovicha* [Recollections of Engineer Officer Martos on the Turkish Campaign during the Reign of Alexander Pavlovich], in *Russkaya Starina*, 77/2 (1893), 306.

14. Based on the records of service of 2,074 officers involved in the Battle of Borodino. Tselorungo, *Officers of the Russian Army*, 152

15. Based on the records of service of 1,462 officers, serving in 1812, who had not graduated from the military institutions.

16. The original title was "Decree Concerning the Granting of Privileges and Freedom to All the Russian Nobility." Catherine the Great confirmed this ruling by issuing another "Charter of Rights, Privileges and Preferences of the Esteemed Russian Nobility."

17. Keep, *The Soldiers of the Tsar*, 232.

18. Volkov, *Russian Officer Corps*, 55.

19. "*Chinoproizvodstvo po voennomu vedomstvu*" in *Stoletie Voennogo ministerstva, 1802-1902* [Centennial Anniversary of the Ministry of War, 1802-1902] (St. Petersburg, 1912), IV, part 3, 5-6.

20. Volkov, *Russian Officer Corps*, 87.

21. Tselorungo, *Officers of the Russian Army*, 139.

22. Ibid., 140-141.

23. Rzhevsky, S. M. "*O Russkoi armii vo vtoroi polovine Ekateriniskogo tsarstvovsnia,*" in *Russkii Arkhiv*, 3 (1879), 361; Semen Vorontsov, "*Zapiska, o russkom voiske, predstavlennaia imperatoru Aleksandru Pavlovichu* v *1802*," in *Arkhiv Kniazia Vorontsova*, X (1876), 487.

24. N. Durnovo, *Dnevnik 1812 g.,* in *1812 god. Voennie dnevniki* (Moscow, 1991), 50-51;

25. *PSZ*, Nos. 2,795, 3,120, 3,997, 7,022, 7,487, 8,724.

26. Based on the records of service of 2,074 officers involved in the Battle of Borodino. Tselorungo, *Officers of the Russian Army*, 152

27. *PSZ*, XXVII, 3 July 1802, No. 20,358.

28. Kharkevich V. *1812 god v dnevnikakh, zapiskakh i vospominaniyakh sovremennikov* [1812 Campaign in Diaries, Notes and Memoirs of Contemporaries] (Vilno, 1900-1904), II, 151.

29. For details see, John LeDonne, "*Outlines of Russian Military Administration 1762-1796: The High Command*," in *Jahrbücher für Geschichte Osteuropas*, 33 /2 (1985), 192.

30. Marin to Vorontsov, 2 January 1813, *K chesti Rossii: Iz chastnoi perepiski 1812 goda* [To Russia Honor: From Private Correspondence of 1812] (Moscow, 1988), 192-93.

31. Aleksey Ermolov, *Zapiski A.P. Ermolova* [Memoirs of A.P. Ermolov], (Moscow, 1991), 94; Davidov, <u>Sochinenia</u>, (St. Petersburg, 1893), I, 142, 206-208, 221-22; G. Ratch, "*Publichnie lektsii, chitannie gospodam ofitseram gvardeiskoi artillerii*" [Public Lectures Presented to the Officers of the Guard Artillery], in *Artilleriiskii Zhurnal*, 11(1861), 842; P. Pototsky, "*Sto ler Russkoi konnoi artillerii*," [Hundred Years of the Russian Horse Artillery], in *Artilleriiskii Zhurnal*, 3 (1894) 41-42; Alexander Mikhailovsky-Danilevsky, *Opisanie vtoroi voini Imperatora Aleksandra s Napoleonom v 1806-1807 godakh* [Description of the Second War of the Emperor Alexander against Napoleon in 1806-1807, hereafter cited as Campaigns of 1806-1807], (St. Petersburg. 1846), 202-203.

32. *PSZ*, V, No. 2,798,

33. M. Lalaev, *Istoricheskii ocherk voennikh zavedenii, podvedomstvennikh Glavnomu ikh upravleniu* [Historical Survey of Military Institutions] (St. Petersburg, 1880), 6-8.

34. V. Krylov, *Kadetskie korpusa i Rossiiskie kadeti* [Cadet Corps and the Russian Cadets] (St. Petersburg, 1998), 15-16. The school curriculum was divided into sections. The 1st Section included mathematics, fortifications, and artillery, and each graduate received an officer's rank. In the 2nd Section, students studied the Russian language and mathematics, graduating as regimental clerks.

35. *PSZ*, IV, No., 2,467; V, Nos. 2,739, 2,798. Peter the Great also set up the Engineer Company directed by the French Colonel Coulon. V. Stroev, N. Zherve, *Istoricheskii ocherk 2-go Kadetskogo korpusa, 1712-1912* [Historical Survey on 2nd Cadet Corps, 1712-1912], (St. Petersburg, 1912), I, 2-9.

36. The first school was established at the Artillery Regiment in March 1712. Directed by the German Major General Gunter, it trained the soldiers of Life Guard Preobrazhensk and Semeyonovsk Regiments in mathematics (arithmetic, geometry, and trigonometry), fortifications, and artillery. The graduates received the rank of bombardier, and in some cases even became officers. The second school was founded in St. Petersburg in March 1721.

37. *PSZ*, VIII, No. 5,811.

38. *PSZ*, VIII, No. 6,050.

39. Beskrovny, *Russian Army and Fleet in XVIII Century*, 179.

40. Krylov, *Cadet Corps*, 21

41. *PSZ*, XVII, Nos. 12,670, 12,741.

42. The 1st class (ages five to nine) was divided into ten sections of twelve students each. The 2nd class (ages nine to twelve) was comprised of eight sections of 15 men each, and the 3rd class (ages twelve to fifteen) had six sections of twenty students each. The 4th and 5th classes were organized into

civil and military groups. The military group comprised two companies commanded by captains, while a special instructor directed the civil group.

43. The best students received special silver and golden medals as a reward for their excellence.

44. Beskrovny, *Russian Army and Fleet in XVIII Century*, 448-50. According to Krylov, some 3,300 students graduated between 1731 and 1801. Krylov, *Cadet Corps*, 25.

45. The corps was expanded to 600 students in 1783 and to 700 in 1817.

46. Guard marine derived from French *garde-marine*. Peter the Great established this rank for the graduates of the Naval Academy in 1716. Beginning in 1752, the rank was conferred to graduates of the Naval Cadet Corps.

47. Krylov, *Cadet Corps*, 17-18

48. N. Loman, *Istoricheskoe obozrenie 2-go kadetskogo korpusa* [Historical Survey on the 2nd Cadet Corps], (St. Petersburg, 1862), 71-98; Lalaev, *Istoricheskii ocherk*, 35-37.

49. The corps was later expanded to 274 students and then to 400 in 1784.

50. Krylov, *Cadet Corps*, 28-30

51. Ibid., 123.

52. *PSZ*, XX, Nos. 14,299, 14,300. For details see, N. Korguev, "*Korpus Chuzhesterannikh Edinovertsev,*" in *Morskoi sbornik*, 7 (1897), 155-59. Prince Gregory Potemkin wanted to transfer this Cadet Corps to Kherson in the Crimea, but decided to keep it in St. Petersburg, establishing instead a smaller Greek school in the Crimea in 1785. *PSZ*, XXI, No. 15,658; Korguev, *Korpus Chuzhesterannikh Edinovertsev*, 161.

53. Beskrovny, *Russian Army and Fleet in XVIII Century*, 452; Krylov, *Cadet Corps*, 32-33. For details on Paul's decision to abolish the corps, see *PSZ*, XLIII, No. 17,746; Korguev, *Korpus Chuzhesterannikh Edinovertsev*, 163-64.

54. Beskrovny, *Russian Army and Fleet in XVIII Century*, 452.

55. During the 1812 Campaign, the Smolensk Cadet Corps was evacuated to Tver and then to Kostroma, where it remained for the next twelve years. In August 1824, it was moved to Moscow and renamed to the Moscow Cadet Corps.

56. Krylov, *Cadet Corps*, 35.

57. In 1785, four schools for 100 men each were opened at the fortresses of Omsk, St. Peter, Yamishev and Biisk. There were also Special Military Schools at Mozdok, Kizlyar, and Ekaterinograd in the Caucasus to train the local nobility.

58. Imperial Military Orphan Home was divided into two sections. The first section trained some 200 children who graduated with the ranks of junker and portupei-ensign. The second section trained some 800 orphans, who received the rank of non-commissioned officer upon graduation. The best fifty students from both sections were selected to continue education in the higher Cadet Corps.

59. Liubomir Beskrovny, *The Russian Army and Fleet in the Nineteenth Century*, ed. by David R. Jones (Academic International Press, 1996), 80-81.

60. Krylov, *Cadet Corps*, 33.

61. For details see, M. Holmdorf, *Materialy dlia istorii bivshego Dvorianskogo polka, 1807-1859* [Materials for History of the Former Noble Regiment, 1807-1859], (St. Petersburg 1882).

62. Dmitry Tselorungo, *Ofitsery Russkoi armii–uchastniki Borodinskogo Srazhenia* [Officers of the Russia Army – Participants of the Battle of Borodino] (Moscow, 2002), 115; Beskrovny, *The Russian Army and Fleet in the Nineteenth Century*, 80-81.

63. Krylov, *Cadet Corps*, 132.

64. Sergey Tuchkov, *Zapiski, 1766-1808* [Recollections, 1766-1808], (St. Petersburg, 1908), 2.

65. Glinka, *Zapiski*, 100.

66. Based on the records of service of 2,074 officers involved in the Battle of Borodino. Tselorungo, *Officers of the Russian Army*, 129.

67. V. Vyazemsky, *Zhurnal: 1812 g.* in *1812 god: Voennie dnevniki* (Moscow, 1990), 211-12.

68. Bagration did not specify who these officers were, although three years later, he often referred to the Prussian and officers from other German states as "the foreigners."

69. Bagration to Arakcheyev, 7 October 1809, *Voennii sbornik*, 10 (1864): 63.

70. Tselorungo, *Officers of the Russian Army*, 118.

71. Ibid., 119-20.

72. Based on author's research for the present volume.

73. Based on the records of service of 2,074 officers of 1st and 2nd Western Armies. Tselorungo, *Officers of the Russian Army*, 125

74. S. Troitsky, *Russkii absolutism i dvorianstvo v XVIII veke* [Russian Absolutism and Nobility in XVIII Century], (Moscow, 1974), 41-42.

75. Duffy, *Russia's Military Way to the West*, 136

76. Volkov, *Russian Officer Corps*, 344.

77. Ilya Radozhitsky, *Pokhodnmie zapiski artillerista s 1812 po 1816 gg.* (Moscow, 1833), II, 43

78. D. Drutsky-Sokolinsky, "*Biograficheskaia zametka o zhizni grafa Arsenia Andreevicha Zakrevskogo*," in *SIRIO*, 78 (1890) I-xvi.

79. Waldemar Hermann Löwernstein, *Memoires du general-major russe baron de Löwernstein 1776-1858*, (Paris, 1903), I, 25.

80. Tselorungo, *Officers of the Russian Army*, 104.

81. Based on the records of service of 2,074 officers involved in the Battle of Borodino.

82. Tselorungo, *Officers of the Russian Army*, 107. Tselorungo considered 295 generals serving in the 1st and 2nd Western Armies in 1812. I also verified that in 1812, there were 327 generals of the guard and army, and 14 Cossack generals.

83. Lowernstern, *Memoirs*, I, 155-162; Glinka, *Zapiski*, 13, 137.

84. Bagration to Arakcheyev, 10 January 1810, *Letters of Prominent Statesmen ... in 1807-1829*, 120. Langeron, *Recollections*, in *Russkaia starina*, 135 (1908): 175, 664.

85. V. Gribanov, *Bagration v Peterburge* [Bagration in St. Petersburg], (Leningrad 1979), 82. Despite his hardships, Bagration spent his own meager fortune on his soldiers and their families and, in 1803, was caring for forty-seven children fathered by his soldiers.

86. Bagration to Vasiliev, 1 July 1802, in Gribanov, *Bagration in St. Petersburg*, 73.

87. Ibid., 157.

88. Ibid., 161.

89. In 1811, Bagration borrowed 5,000 rubles from Prince David of Georgia, 7,500 rubles from Major General Bulatov, and another 9,000 rubles from Engelhardt.

90. Ermolov, *Memoirs*, I, 163.

91. *PSZ*, Nos. 17,534, 18,486, 20,542.

92. Emperor Peter I to the Senate, 11 January 1722, in SIRIO 11(1873): 440-442.

93. A. Lebedev, *Russkaia armia v nachale tsarstvovania imperatritsy Ekaterini II: materiali dlia russkoi voennoi istorii* [Russian Army at the Beginning of Empress Catherine II's Reign: Materials for the Russian Military History], (Moscow, 1898), 4-69; Duffy, *Russia's Military Way*, 147.

94. Emperor Peter I to the Senate, 11 January 1722, in SIRIO 11(1873): 440-442.

95. A. Lebedev, *Russian Army at the Beginning of Empress Catherine II's Reign*, 4-69; Duffy, *Russia's Military Way*, 147

96. The hearings on Sacken's case continued for more than three years. The court found him guilty but did not impose any punishment because of Sacken's distinguished career.

Mikhailovsky-Danilevsky, *Campaigns of 1806-1807*, 298-300; Höpfner, *Der Krieg von 1806 und 1807 [i.e. achtzehnhundertsechs und achtzehnhundertsieben]: ein Beitrag zur Geschichte der Preussischen Armee nach den Quellen des Kriegs-Archivs bearbeitet*, (Berlin 1850), III, 583.

97. *General Bagration: Sbornik dokumentov i materialov* [General Bagration: Compilation of Documents and Materials, hereafter cited as Correspondence of Bagration], (Moscow, 1945), 213; V. M. Vorontsov, *Otechestvennaya voina 1812 g. v predelakh Smolenskoi gubernii* [The Patriotic War of 1812 in the Smolensk Gubernya], (St. Petersburg, 1912), 75-76; A. Tartarovsky, *Nerazgadannyi Barklai: legendy i byl' 1812 goda* [Unknown Barclay: Legends and Tales of 1812], (Moscow, 1996), 63-65; Michael Josselson, *The Commander: Life of Barclay de Tolly*, (Oxford, 1980), 113-14.

98. See footnote 99.

99. Tartarovsky, *Unknown Barclay*, 63-65; Nikolay Troitsky, *1812: Velikii god Rossii* [1812: The Glorious Year of Russia], (Moscow, 1988), 121; Josselson, *Barclay de Tolly*, 113-14

100. Barclay de Tolly was third-generation Russian from Livonia, where his Scottish ancestors settled in the 17th century. Josselson, *Barclay de Tolly*, vii, 1-5; Tartarovsky, *Unknown Barclay*, 5-15.

101. These fraction members included Grand Duke Constantine and Generals Peter Bagration, Alexander Ermolov, Nikolay Rayevsky, Dimitry Dokhturov, Matvei Platov, Illarion Vasyl'chykov, Nikolay Tuchkov, Paul Tuchkov and Alexander Tuchkov, Peter Konovnitsyn, Paul Shuvalov and many others.

102. Bagration to Arakcheyev, 10 August 1812, *Correspondence of Bagration*, 226.

103. Bagration to Stroganov, circa July 1812, *Pisma kniazya P.I. Bagrationa grafu P.A. Stroganovu* [Correspondence of Prince P. I. Bagration with Count P.A. Stroganov], in *Istoricheskoe issledovanie epokhi imperatora Alexandra I* (St. Petersburg, 1903), III, 259.

104. Tartarovsky, *Unknown Barclay*, 65.

105. *Vospominania F. Bulgarina*, [Memoirs of F. Bulgarin] (St. Petersburg, 1848) IV, 172.

106. Tartarovsky, *Unknown Barclay*, 84; Fabry, *Campaign de Russie*, (Paris, 1900), IV, 320.

107. Nikolay Muravyev, *Zapiski* [Recollections], in *Russkii arkhiv*, 9(1885): 49; Josselson, *Barclay de Tolly*, 118; Eugene Tarle, *Napoleon's Invasion of Russia, 1812*, (New York: 1942), 163-65; Tartarovsky, *Barclay de Tolly*, 64-66; Alan Palmer, *Napoleon in Russia* (London, 1967), 57; Troitsky, *1812: The Glorious Year of Russia*, 121.

108. John Elting, *A Military History and Atlas of the Napoleonic Wars* (London, 2000), biographical sketches, entry on Bagration.

109. Tsar Alexander and his headquarters come in for some legitimate criticism. Alexander trusted foreign generals more than the Russians commanders, although he had little regard for either of them. In February 1812, he is quoted as saying there are good soldiers in Russia, but only incompetent generals. The crushing defeat at Austerlitz in 1805 revealed Alexander's military incompetence, and by 1812, the Tsar was no longer the self-confident commander who had led the army seven years earlier. He was so distrustful of his own generals that he considered calling General Jean Victor Moreau from the United States and offering him command of the Russian armies in 1811. The following year, Alexander toyed with the idea of offering command to generals Arthur Wellington and Jean Baptist Bernadotte. In 1813, he wanted to offer joint command to generals Jean Moreau and Antoine-Henri Jomini. For more information see, *Russkaya Starina*, 6 (1892): 190-191; *Rossia i Shvetsia: dokumenti i materiali 1809-1818* [Russia and Sweden: Documents and Materials 1809-1818] (Moscow, 1985), 100; V. Pugachev, *Podgotovka Rossii k voine s Napoleonom v 1810-1811* [Preparations of Russia in 1810-1811 to the War against Napoleon], University of Gorky Press, 1964, No.72, 97.

110. Bagration to Alexander, 19 August 1812, *Correspondence of Bagration*, 234.

111. Bagration to Ermolov, 29 July 1812, Ermolov, *Memoirs*, I, 178.

112. Bagration to Arakcheyev, 8 July 1812, *Otechestvennaia voina 1812 g.: Materiali Voenno-Uchebnogo arkhiva Glavnogo Shtaba* [Patriotic War of 1812: Materials of Military-Academic Archive of the General Staff, hereafter cited as *General Staff Archives*], XVI, 215-16.

113. Bagration to Ermolov, 27 June 1812, Tarle, *Napoleon's Invasion of Russia*, 91.

114. Bagration to Barclay de Tolly, 1 August 1812, *General Staff Archives*, XVI, 214.

115. Bagration to Ermolov, circa July 1812, Gribanov, *Bagration in St. Petersburg*, 186.

119. Troitsky, *1812: The Glorious Year of Russia*, 105; Josselson, *Barclay de Tolly*, 113; Joseph Baye, *Smolensk; les origines, l'épopée de Smolensk en 1812,* (Paris, 1912), 100.

116. Löwernstein, *Memoires*, I, 218-19.

117. Tartarovsky, *Unknown Barclay*, 87-89; Vorontsov, *The Patriotic War of 1812 in Smolensk Gubernya*, 80; Baye, *L'épopée de Smolensk en 1812*, 100.

118. Bagration to Alexander, 4 August 1812, *General Staff Archives*, XVI, 219; Fabry, *Campaign de Russie*, IV, 320.

119. Bagration to Alexander, 19 August 1812, *Correspondence of Bagration*, 235.

120. Bagration to Rostopchin, 26 August 1812, in Dubrovin, *The Patriotic War in Correspondence of the Contemporaries*, 96.

121. Bagration to Arakcheyev, 19 August 1812, *Otechestvennaya voina 1812 goda: sbornik dokumentov i materialov* [The Patriotic War of 1812: a Compilation of Materials and Documents], (Moscow, 1941), 54.

123. Russian historian Tartarovsky described this dissatisfaction as "the Mutiny of Generals." *Unknown Barclay*, 79. See also Michael Glover, *A Very Slippery Fellow: The Life of Sir Robert Wilson, 1777-1849,* (Oxford, 1978), 104.

124. *General Staff Archives*, XIV, 259-61.

125. Cossack Ataman Matvey Platov said to Barclay, "You see, Sir, I wear only a cloak. I will no longer put on the Russian uniform. I consider it a disgrace." General Dokhturov considered Barclay a "stupid and loathsome person." Sir Robert Wilson, *Narrative of Events During the Invasions of Russia by Napoleon Bonaparte and the Retreat of the French Army in 1812* (London, 1860), 114-15; Dokhturov to his wife, circa August 1812, Russkii Arkhiv, 1874, N1, 1101, 1118.

126. Muravyev, *Writings and Letters*, 102.

127. *Iz zapisok Vistitskogo* [From Vistitskii's Recollections, hereafter cited as Vistitskii's Memoirs], in V. Kharkevich, *1812 god v dnevnikakh, zapiskakh i vospominaniakh sovremennikov* [1812 Campaign in Diaries, Memoirs and Correspondence of the Contemporaries], (Vilna, 1900), 184.

128. Bagration to Rostopchin, July 1812, (undated), in Dubrovin, *Patriotic War in Letters of Contemporaries*, 72-73.

129. Bagration to Tchichagov, 15 August 1812, A. Afanasiev, *1812-814: Sekretnaya perepiska General P. I. Bagrationa, iz sobrania Gosudarstvennogo Istoricheskogo Muzea* [1812-1814: Secret Correspondence of General P. I. Bagration, from the collection of the State Historical Museum, hereafter cited as Secret Correspondence], (Moscow, 1992), 168.

130. Ermolov to Bagration, 1 August 1812, *Secret Correspondence*, 178; Ermolov to Bagration, 31 July 1812, Ibid., 177; Fabry, *Campaign de Russie*, IV, 320, 356.

131. Bagration to Ermolov, July 1812, Ermolov, *Memoirs*, I, 176; Fabry, *Campaign de Russie*, IV, 358-59.

132. Grand Duke Nikolay Mikhailovich, *Correspondence de l'Empereur Alexandre Ier avec sa souer la Grande Duchesse Catherine* (St. Petersburg, 1912), 85; Tartarovsky, *Unknown Barclay*, 59-60; Gribanov, *Bagration in St. Petersburg*, 147-48, 206-207.

133. Wilson, *Narrative of Events*, 130. Wilson also wrote in his diary, "I cannot express the indignation that prevailed. The sacrifice of so many brave man; the destruction of an important town ... the sight of the holy city in flames, and etc, etc, worked strongly on the feelings of the Russians." *Private*

Diary of Travels, Personal Services and Public Events During Mission and Employment in 1812, 1813 and 1814 Campaigns, ed. By H. Randolph, (London, 1861), i, 149

134. Carl von Clausewitz, *The Campaign of 1812* (London, 1970), 113.

135. Bagration to Ermolov, 7 July 1812, in M. Boitsov, *K chesti Rossii: iz chastnoi perepiski 1812 goda* [To Russia's Honor: From the Private Correspondence of 1812], (Moscow, 1988), 50.

136. Paul Grabbe, *Iz pamiatnikh zapisok* [From the Memorable Notes], (Moscow, 1873), II, 57.

137. Radozhitsky, *Poxodnie zapiski,* I, 125, 129.

138. Ivan Zhirkevich, *Zapiski* [Recollections], in *Russkaya Starina*, 8(1874): 648.

139. A. Muraviyev, *Avtographiobicheskie zapiski* [Autobiographical notes], in Dekabristi: Novie materialy, (Moscow, 1955), 187.

140. Barclay de Tolly was third-generation Russian from Livonia, where his Scottish ancestors settled in the 17th century. Josselson, *Barclay de Tolly*, vii, 1-5; Tartarovsky, *Unknown Barclay*, 5-15.

141. Barclay de Tolly to Alexander, 28 August 1812, in Kharkevich, *Barclay de Tolly v otechestvennoi voine: posle soedinenia armii pod Smolenskon* [Barclay de Tolly During the Patriotic War: After the Junction of Armies at Smolensk], (St. Petersburg, 1904), 23-24.

142. Barclay de Tolly to Alexander, 28 August 1812, Ibid., 24.

143. Zhirkevich, *Recollections,* in *Russkaya Starina*, 8(1874): 650.

144. In nineteenth century Russia, the term "German" was used for anyone coming from Livonia, the various German states, and Prussia. Thus Barclay de Tolly, himself of Scottish origin and born in Livonia, was usually referred as "German."

145. The official title of the system was "Tabel o rangakh vsekh chinov voinskikh, statskikh i pridvornikh, kotorie v kakom klasse chini obretautsia [Table of Ranks of Military, Civil and Court Ranks and the Classes They are Conferred in]. For information on the Table, see Table of Ranks, 24 January (4 February) 1722, No. 3,890, *PSZ*, VI, 284; V. Zwegintsov, *Russkaya armiia. 1700-1855* (Paris, 1967-1979) 5 vols.; James Hassel, "Implementation of the Russian Table of Ranks During the Eighteenth Century," in *Slavic Review,* 29 (1970): 283-95; Helju Aulik Bennett, "Chiny, Ordena, and Officialdom," in *Russian Officialdom: The Bureaucratization of Russian Society from the Seventeenth to the Twentieth Century*, ed. by Walter McKenzie Pinter and Don Karl Rowney (Chapel Hill, 1980); Helju Aulik Bennet, "Evolution of the Meaning of Chin: An Introduction to the Russian Institution of Rank Ordering and Niche Assignment from the Time of Peter the Great's Table of Ranks to the Bolshevik Revolution," in *California Slavic Studies*, 10 (1977): 1-43; L. Shepelev, *Chinovnii mir rossii XVIII – nachalo XX v.* [Russia's Officialdom in XVIII – early XX centuries] (St. Petersburg, 1999).

146. General *Feldzeugmeister*, derived from German *Feldzeugmeister*, was head of the artillery. Peter the Great established it as a permanent position in 1699, conferring first rank to Georgian Prince Alexander Imeretinsky (Bagration).

147. General *Kriegscommissar* derived from German *Kriegskomissar*. An officer with the latter rank supervised the financial and supply aspects of the armies. In 1812, a new position of Field General *Kriegscommissar* was established to direct the field commissariats.

148. There were several types of adjutants in the Russian army: 1. General adjutant, who attended the emperor with a rank of colonel, general field marshal with a rank of lieutenant colonel and full general with a rank of major; 2. Flügel adjutant served field marshals and full generals with a rank of captain. 3. "Generals adjutant" was a senior adjutant in the unit.

149. Quartermasters were attached to divisions, ober quartermasters were attached to corps, and quartermaster generals to armies.

150. A General Auditor headed the General Audit—the Russian military police. Established in 1797, it was attached to the War College and, initially, was considered Emperor's chancellery on military court-martials. General Audit was reorganized in 1805, becoming an independent institution

under direct control of the Senate and Emperor. It comprised of six members: 2 generals, 2 admirals and 2 civil counselors. In 1812, General Audit was reorganized again and incorporated as a department in the Minister of War. General Auditor accompanied the armies on the campaign and directed the field audits through his divisional auditors; they ensured proper enforcement of the regulations and presided over court-martials.

151. *Gelwadiger* (Hevaldiger) meant a military police officer, derived from German *Gewaldiger*. A General Gewaldiger was responsible for the discipline and order in the army and, in urgent situations, had authority to enforce sentences, including the death penalty. He usually directed corps and divisional gewaldigers. During the battles, these officers supervised assembling and transportation of the wounded.

152. *Shtyk junker* literally means "bayonet junker." Junker itself referred to an officer candidate.

153. Fendrik was similar to cornet, derived from the German *Fähnric*.

154. *Kaptenarmus* originated from French *capitaine d'armes*. It was a non-commissioned officer rank established in 1716. During action, *kaptenarmus* had to be with the ammunition wagons and provide munitions to the troops. On the bivouacs, *kaptenarmus* were often in charge of provisions within the unit.

155. For details, see Z. E. Kohut, *Russian Centralism and Ukrainian Autonomy: Imperial Absorption of the Hetmanate, 1760s-1830s* (Cambridge, 1988) D. Miller, *Ocherki iz istorii i iuridicheskogo byta staroi Malorossii: Prevrashenie kozatskoi starshiny v dvorianstvo, Kievskaia Starina*, 1892, No. 1-4.

156. *Vakhmistr* derived from German *Wachtmeister*, a non-commissioned officer in the cavalry and horse artillery.

157. *Portupey* junker meant an officer candidate who received an officer's pouch strap (*portupeya*).

158. In the corps of engineers, the non-commissioned officers were also called conductors [*konduktora*].

159. "Feyerveiker" literally means "fireworker," i.e. an artillery specialist, derived from German *Feuerwerker*.

160. In Russian, "Ryadovoi starshego oklada."

161. In Russian, "Ryadovoi mladshego oklada."

162. To match ranks in the heavy and light cavalry, the rank of sub-lieutenant was abolished and a major (VIII Class) was instituted.

163. In 1811, the rank of major was abolished in the artillery and the corps of engineers. The rank of ensign was introduced for XIII class for these branches of service.

164. This list excludes the Polish Orders of the White Eagle, Stanislaus, and *Virtuti Militari* because they were included into the Russian hierarchy of orders after the Napoleonic Wars. For details see, N. Panov, *Istoricheskii ocherk rossiiskikh ordenov I sbornik osnovnykh ordenskikh statutov* (St. Petersburg, 1892); P. von Vinkler, *Ocherki istorii ordenov I znakov otlichia Rossii* (St. Petersburg, 1899); V. Durov, *Ordena Rossii* (Moscow, 1993); L. Shepelev, *Tituli, mundiry, ordena v Rossiiskoi imperii* (St. Petersburg, 1991).

The Biographies

ABAKUMOV, Andrey Ivanovich (b. 1772 — d. 1841) was born to a merchant family and began service as a clerk in the Life Guard Preobrazhensk Regiment in 1787, rising to an ensign in 1802. During the 1812 Campaign, he served in the Moscow Supply Depot and was later appointed the ober-proviantmeister of the 4th Corps. In 1813, he served as ober-proviantmeister of Russian advance guards and, in 1816, became the head of the Supply Department of the Ministry of War. He was instrumental in reorganizing the supply system in the Russian army in 1817-1825. Abakumov was promoted to privy counsellor and appointed to the Senate on 3 September 1826. During the Russo-Turkish War in 1828-1829, he headed the Commissariat of the main Russian army and, in 1831, served as the General Intendant of the Russian army in Poland. He retired because of a major disagreement with Commander-in-Chief General Diebitch over requisitioning supplies from local populations in Poland. Abakumov served for ten years in the Senate.

ADADUROV, Vasily Vasilievich (b. 1765 – d. 10 May 1845, St. Petersburg) was born to a noble family in the St. Petersburg *gubernia* (province). He enlisted as a sergeant in the Life Guard Preobrazhensk Regiment in 1781 and was promoted to ensign on 12 January 1783. He fought against the Swedes in 1788-1790, rising to colonel of the Life Guard Izmailovsk Regiment. On 17 April 1798, he was promoted to major general and appointed chef of the Tiflis Musketeer Regiment. Adadurov's subsequent service is not clear. Some authors claim him serving as chef of the Novobadensk Musketeer Regiment, but this regiment was not established yet. He probably continued his service in the Tiflis Musketeer Regiment, but was discharged on 16 October 1798 for being absent from his regiment. In March 1801, he rejoined the army and was eventually appointed chef of the Tobolsk Musketeer Regiment on 20 November 1804. Yet, he retired again in February 1805 only to return to service on 19 September 1805, when he became chef of the Penza Musketeer Regiment. He retired for a third time on 16 February 1808.

During the 1812 Campaign, Adadurov commanded the 2nd Company (*druzhina*) in the St. Petersburg *opolchenye*, fighting at Polotsk and Chashniki. In 1813, he participated in the siege of Danzig, commanding the 1st Company (*druzhina*) of the same *opolchenye*. In May 1813, Adadurov assumed command of the entire Saint Petersburg *opolchenye*. He distinguished himself in repulsing the French sortie on 16 August 1813 and was awarded a golden sword with diamonds. On 24 June 1815, he retired for a final time and settled in St. Petersburg, where he died on 10 May 1845 and was buried at the Lazarev Cemetery of St. Alexander of Neva Monastery.

AGALIN, Afanasy Kornilovich (b. 18 February 1764 – d. 28 April 1846) was born to a noble family in the Yaroslavl *gubernia*. He enlisted in the Gatchina Troops at Pavlovsk on 15 November 1789. In 1790, he participated in the campaign against Sweden and received the rank of sub-lieutenant on 16 August 1793. Three years later, Agalin joined the Life Guard Semeyonovsk Regiment, becoming a colonel on 5 February 1800. In 1806, he was appointed chef of the Kursk Musketeer Regiment and remained at this position until September 1814. He served with the 10th Division during the 1806-1807 Campaigns in Poland, receiving promotion to major general on 12 December 1807.

In 1810-1812, Agalin fought the Turks in the Danubian Principalities and distinguished himself at the siege of Silistra for which he was awarded the Order of St. Vladimir (3rd class). In 1812, Agalin's Kursk Infantry Regiment was attached to the 2nd Brigade of the 10th Division of the 3rd Corps in the Army of Danube. In 1813, he served in the Duchy of Warsaw and then commanded a brigade during the military operations in Saxony. He was named a brigade commander of 10th Division, but could not assume his duties because of his poor health. Instead, he served as an assistant to the commander of the 26th Infantry Division. On 19 March 1816, Agalin took command of the 1st Brigade of the 18th Division; later, he transferred to the 26th Division. He retired on 6 January 1820 and died on 28 April 1846.

AGTE (Akhte), Yegor Andreyevich (b. 23 August 1777, Arensburg, Lifland *gubernia* – d. 7 September 1826, Kremechug, Poltava *gubernia*) was born to a noble family of Estland origins. Enlisted as a corporal in the Life Guard Horse Regiment on 16 June 1792, he transferred as a lieutenant to the Malorossiisk (Little Russia) Grenadier Regiment on 12 January 1796. He served in the 1805 Campaign, distinguishing himself at Austerlitz. In 1806-1811, Agte took part in campaigns against the Turks in the Danubian Principalities. On 31 November 1809, he became the commander of the Malorossiisk Grenadier Regiment. In 1810, he distinguished himself at Ruse (Ruschuk, lightly wounded) and Batin, for which he received the Order of St. George (4th class) on 22 March 1812.

During the 1812 Campaign, Agte served with the 3rd Brigade of 2nd Grenadier Regiment of the 8th Infantry Corps and took part in Prince Bagration's successful retreat to Smolensk. At Borodino, he was wounded in the right hand. On 9 September 1812, he took command of the St. Petersburg Grenadier Regiment in the 1st Western Army and later participated in the battle at Krasnyi, where he got wounded for the second time. For his bravery, he was promoted to colonel on 2 December 1812. The following year, Agte became chef of the St. Petersburg Grenadier Regiment (9 February) and took part in the 1813-1814 Campaigns, receiving the Order of the Red Eagle (3rd class). He rose to major general on 1 August 1814. As his health deteriorated, he retired with a full pension on 27 April 1816 and died ten years later on 7 September 1826.

AKHLESTYSHEV, Mikhail Fedorovich (date of birth unclear, 1778 or 1782 – d. 12 January 1829) was born to a noble family in the Tula *gubernia*. He enlisted in the Life Guard Preobrazhensk Regiment on 26 April 1791, transferred to the Chevalier Guard Squadron on 2 February 1797 and then returned to the Preobrazhensk Regiment as an ensign on 18 October 1797. He participated in the 1805 Campaign and was wounded in the right arm at Austerlitz. During the 1807 Campaign in Poland, he fought at Heilsberg and Friedland. In January 1810, he was promoted to colonel and transferred to the Narva Musketeer Regiment (25 June 1810) that was deployed in the Danube Valley against the Turks.

Akhlestyshev took part in the failed assault on Ruse in 1810 and was wounded in the left foot. In September 1810, he distinguished himself at the battle of Batin, for which he garnered a golden sword for bravery. He also took part in the capture of Sistov and Nikopol. On 18 November 1810, he was appointed commander of the 41st Jager Regiment. In 1811, he took part in Kutuzov's entrapment of the Turkish army near Ruse and was appointed chef of the 39th Jager Regiment on 28 August 1811.

During the 1812 Campaign, Akhlestyshev served with the 3rd Brigade of the 10th Infantry Division of the 3rd Corps of the Army of Danube. He fought the French at Kovel, Lubomle, Golovnya, Gornostayevchi and Volkovysk. In 1813, he fought near Helm, Lublin and Czenstochowa and was awarded the Order of St. George (4th class, 13 April 1813). He then fought at Bautzen, where he was wounded in the the chest, and Katzbach. He was seriously wounded in the the left hip and right foot at Leipzig. For his bravery, he was promoted to major general on 1 January 1814 (confirmed on 22 November). In early 1814, he returned to the army and participated in the siege of Metz, where he was wounded in the the right hip during a French sortie. After recuperating, he was given command of a jager brigade of the 10th Infantry Division (11 October 1814). In July 1817, he was appointed commander of the 2nd Brigade of the 9th Division and was then transferred to the 6th Division. On 23 May 1824, he was appointed commander of the 1st Brigade of the 13th Division and later served as commander of the 1st Brigade of the Combined Division of the 5th Corps. On 28 September 1826, he was appointed commander of the 6th Infantry Division. He died on 31 January 1829 in Moscow and was buried at the cemetery of the Spaso-Andronevsky Monastery.

AKHSHARUMOV, Dmitri Ivanovich (b. 1792 – d. 25 January 1837) graduated from the 1st Cadet Corps and began service as an ensign in the Chernigov Infantry Regiment in 1803. He participated in the 1806-1807 Campaign in Poland and 1809-1811 Campaigns in the Danubian Principalities. He was awarded the Order of St. Vladimir (4th class) for his actions at Bazardjik. In 1812, he served in the Life Guard Jager Regiment and fought at Smolensk, Borodino, Tarutino and Maloyaroslavets (received the Order of St. George, 4th class). In 1813, he distinguished himself at Lutzen, receiving promotion to colonel. After the war, he served at the headquarters of the Russian Occupation Corps in France. He was promoted to major general in March 1820 and later commanded the 2nd Brigade of the 17th Division. However, Akhsharumov transferred to civil service in 1821 and served in the Commissariat. In 1826-1837, he compiled the first Russian code of military regulations published in 1838. In 1819, he wrote "*Opisanie voini 1812 g.* [Description of the War of 1812]," which was based upon primary documents and was the first Russian military history of the campaign with relatively objective interpretation of events.

AKHVERDOV, Fedor Isaevich (b. 1773 – d. 1820) was born to a Georgian noble family. He began military service in the Artillery and Engineer Cadet Corps in 1788 and was promoted to shtyk-junker in 1791. He transferred to the 1st Cannonier Regiment in 1793 and served as a flügel adjutant to Prince V. Zubov. During the Persian Campaign of 1796, he participated in the actions at Shemakha and Gandja. In 1797, he joined the 5th Artillery Regiment and was promoted to lieutenant colonel in 1798 and to colonel in 1799. In 1800, Akhverdov commanded pontoon companies and took part in the suppression of an uprising in Kabarda (received the Order of St. John of Jerusalem). In 1803, he served in the 9th Artillery Battalion and fought at Gandja in 1804. Two years later, he took command of the 9th Artillery Brigade and participated in the operations against the Turks in southern Georgia. For his actions, he was promoted to major general and awarded the Order of St. George (4th class) in 1808. He took command of the 19th Division in 1812 and participated in peace negotiations with Turkey. Beginning in 1816, he commanded the Independent Georgian Corps.

AKLECHEYEV, Ivan Matveyevich (b. 30 October 1758 – d. 15 January 1824) was born to a noble family in the Vologda *gubernia*. He enlisted in the Life Guard Horse Regiment in 1771 and, three years later, he transferred to the Life Guard Izmailovsk Regiment. Over the next eight years, Aklecheyev was promoted to corporal and transferred to the army with the rank of sub-lieutenant on 12 January 1780. He joined the Neva Infantry Regiment on 10 March 1780. During the Russo-Turkish War of 1787-1791, he distinguished himself at Ochakov, where he was injured to the right arm. For his bravery, he was promoted to second major and awarded a golden cross. In 1794, he fought the Poles at Maciejowice, earning promotion to lieutenant colonel on 27 October 1794. The same year, he transferred to the Military Order Of Holy Martyr and Victorious Saint George

Regiment, also known as the Military Order Regiment.

On 14 March 1797, Aklecheyev joined the Kharkov Cuirassier Regiment. He participated in the Persian Campaign of 1796-1797 and received a golden sword for courage during the assault on the fortress of Derbent. Promoted to colonel on 22 February 1798, he was dismissed from service during Emperor Paul's purges on 1 July 1798. He returned to the service with a rank of major general on 31 December 1799. Aklecheyev then served as a counsellor in the Forest Department of the State Admiralty Board. Despite some claims, Aklecheyev did not serve in the 1805 Campaign but remained at his department. After the department was abolished in December 1811, he transferred to the Heraldry Board.

In 1812, Aklecheyev commanded the 17th Company (*druzhina*) of the St. Petersburg *opolchenye* and fought at Polotsk and Chashniki. In 1813, he served under Count Wittgenstein and took part in the battles of Lutzen, Bautzen, Dresden and Leipzig. In 1814, he fought at Bars sur Aube, Arcis and was wounded in the left foot at Paris. For his actions in these campaigns, he was awarded the Orders of St. Anna (1st class), of St. George (4th class), of St. Vladimir (4th class) and the Prussian Order of the Red Eagle (2nd class), He retired in October 1814 and served in the Ministry of Finance for the remaining years. He passed away in Petersburg on 15 January 1824 and was buried at the Tikhvinsk Cemetery of St. Alexander of Neva Monastery.

ALALYKIN, Alexander Alexandrovich (b. 1769 - d. 1818) was born to a noble family in the Kostroma *gubernia*. He enlisted as a non-commissioned officer in the Life Guard Preobrazhensk Regiment on 24 February 1781, rising to an ensign twelve years later. He took part in the 1807 Campaign in Poland, fighting at Heilsberg and Friedland. Alalykin was promoted to captain on 23 December 1807 and to colonel on 26 April 1809; however, on 14 October 1809, he transferred to the Intendant Service as a college counsellor (*kolezhsky sovetnik*). In 1812, he took command of the 10th *Opolchenye* Company (*druzhina*) and then led the 4th Brigade of the St. Petersburg *opolchenye*. He fought at Polotsk and served as the Commandant at Keydan in late 1812. In 1813-1814, he took part in the siege of Danzig, where he earned the rank of major general. He returned to civil service after the war.

ALBRECHT, Aleksandr Ivanovich (b. 14 November 1788, St. Petersburg – d. 27 August 1828, Warsaw) was born to a Prussian noble family in the St. Petersburg *gubernia*. His grandfather settled in Russia under Peter the Great and his father served as a colonel in the Life Guard Semeyonovsk Regiment. Albrecht initially enlisted in the Quartermaster Service and then joined as a cadet the Chevalier Guard Regiment on 24 March, 1803. He was promoted to cornet in October 1804. At Austerlitz, he commanded the 1st Company of the Leib Squadron (Leib-Eskadron), that was decimated in the action. Albrect was one of two men surviving from his entire company, but he was twice wounded in the head, once to the right hand and suffered a blank shot that burned his face. He lost consciousness and remained on the battle field until the night, when the French looters tried to undress him and stabbed him in the thigh. However, after realizing he was alive, they also took him to hospital, where Albrecht remained for a couple of weeks before being released. After returning to Russia, Albrecht was awarded a golden sword for courage and promoted to lieutenant in December 1806. During the 1807 Campaign in Poland, he fought at Heilsberg and Friedland. In December 1809, Albrecht transferred to the Life Guard Dragoon Regiment, receiving promotions to captain on 15 January 1810 and to colonel on 23 October 1811.

During the 1812 Campaign, Albrecht served in the 1st Corps and commanded the Combined Guard Cavalry Regiment comprised of the reserve squadrons of the Life Guard Dragoon, Life Guard Uhlan and Life Guard Hussar Regiments. He took part in the actions at Volyntsy, Golovchitsy, Kokhanovichy, Belyi, Druya and Belmon, garnering the Order of Vladimir (4th class) and the Order of St. Anna (2nd class). During the battle of Polotsk, Albrecht captured twelve guns while also being wounded in the right hand and was later decorated with the Order of St. George (4th class) on 4 January 1813. Albrecht also distinguished himself in the combat at the village of Kublichi in late November, where his regiment captured 107 men, several Bavarian flags and over 40 wagons with loot. For this action, he was awarded the Order of St. Vladimir (3rd class). During the French retreat, Albrecht took part in the actions at Smolnya and Borisov, earning the diamond signs of the Order of St. Anna (2nd class) and the second golden sword for courage.

In 1813, Albrecht commanded a squadron of the Life Guard Dragoon Regiment and fought at Lutzen, Bautzen (wounded), Kulm, Leipzig, Eckartsberg and Buttelstadt. During the invasion of France in 1814, he served at Brienne, Arcis sur Aube, Sezanne, Montmirail, Rheims and Le Fère Champenoise (promoted to major general on 22 May 1814 and awarded the Prussian Pour le Merite and the Bavarian Order of Maximilian Joseph). Albrecht then took part in the capture of Paris, for which he received a special medal commemorating this event. In 1815, he briefly travelled to Russia to recuperate and then returned to Poland. On 21 April 1816, he was appointed to command the 1st Brigade of the 3rd Cuirassier Division, and, on 19 December 1817, he became commander of the Life Guard Uhlan Regiment.

On 12 April 1818, Albrecht was awarded the Order of St. Anna (1st class) for exemplary discipline in his regiment. His further service in Poland was highlighted by additional rewards: the Order of St. Stanislaus (1st class) on 17 October 1819, a golden snuffbox with Alexander I's anagram on 18 October 1820 and the Order of St. Vladimir (2nd class) on 14 June 1825. On 7 October 1823, Albrecht assumed command of the Guard Cavalry Division of the Independent Lithuanian Corps in Poland. He rose to lieutenant general during the coronation of Nicholas I on 3 September 1826. Albrecht died on 27 August 1828 in Warsaw and was buried at the Kotelskoye estate near Yamburg in the St. Petersburg *gubernia*.

ALEDINSKY, Alexander Pavlovich (b. 1775 – date of death unclear, c. 1850) was born to a noble family in the Pskov *gubernia*. He graduated from the Infantry Cadet Corps and enlisted as a lieutenant in the Moscow Grenadier Regiment in 1790. He took part in the campaigns in Poland in 1792-1794 and fought at Vilna and Warsaw. In 1799, he served in Italy and Switzerland, participating in the actions at Lecco, on the Adda River, at Bassignana, on the Tidone, Trebbia and Nure Rivers (received the Order of St. Anna, 4th class), at Tortona and Novi (received the Order of St. Anna, 2nd class). He distinguished himself during Field Marshal Suvorov's ill-fated campaign in the Alps, fighting at the Devil's Bridge and in the Muothatal Valley, for which he received the Order of St. John of Jerusalem and a rise to captain. After brief retirement in 1803, he was promoted to major in 1804 and appointed to tutor Grand Dukes Nicholas and Mikhail. He became a lieutenant colonel of the Life Guard Preobrazhensk Regiment in 1810 and a major general in 1816. He accompanied both Grand Dukes during the trips to Europe in 1814-1823 and served as hofmeister at the court of Grand Duke Mikhail Pavlovich in 1828-1841.

ALEKSAPOL, Fedor Panteleymonovich (b. 23 December 1758 – date of death unknown) was born to a Greek family resettled to Russia. He was enrolled in the Cadet Corps on 13 December 1775 and transferred as an ensign to the Riga Infantry Regiment on 27 June 1781. He fought the Turks in 1787-1791 and participated in the assaults on Ochakov (1788) and Izmail (1791). On 9 May 1799, he was appointed commander of the 15th Jager Regiment and served at this position until 20 March 1800, when his regiment was transformed into the 14th Jagers (he commanded it until 29 December 1802). Aleksapol rose to colonel on 20 June 1800, received the Order of St. John of Jerusalem and served in the Caucasus from 1800-1802. On 29 December 1802, he became chef of the 18th Jager Regiment. Five years later, Aleksapol was promoted to major general on 24 December 1807 and, the next year, he became a brigade commander of the 23rd Division.

During the 1812 Campaign, Aleksapol commanded the 2nd Brigade (the Koporsk Infantry Regiment and the 18th Jagers) of the 23th Division of the 4th Corps and fought at Smolensk and Borodino, where his jagers recaptured the Great Redoubt. Aleksapol was wounded in the left thigh in this action and, for his bravery, he garnered the Order of St. Vladimir (3rd class). In 1813, he served with the reserves in the Duchy of Warsaw and supervized the arrival of reinforcements. In 1814, he commanded the 4th and 21st Divisions of the Army of Reserve. In 1815, he led the 3rd Brigade of the 6th Division. On 26 March 1816, he retired because of poor health and was given a full pension.

ALEKSEYEV, Ilya Ivanovich (b. 29 July 1772 – d. 15 October 1830, Moscow) was born to a petty noble family in the Moscow *gubernia*. He was enlisted in the Life Guard Preobrazhensk Regiment in 1782 and was promoted to sergeant in 1789. He participated in the Russo-Swedish war in 1789, serving on the galley flotilla under Prince Nassau-Zigen and in Brigadier Baikov's detachment. He was twice injured in the actions and was later transferred as a vakhmistr to the Life Guard Horse Regiment. He volunteered for service against the Turks and participated in the assault on Ismail. In 1791-1794, he served as an adjutant to General Count Ivan Saltykov, who patronized him for the next several years. In 1795, Alekseyev transferred as a captain to the Sumsk Light Horse Regiment (later Sumsk Hussars) and served in Poland. In 1796, on Saltykov's recommendation, he was promoted to major and remained an adjutant to Saltykov, then the Military Governor of Moscow. Promoted to colonel on 20 August 1799, Alekseyev was dismissed from service in February 1800, but re-enlisted in September 1800 and, with the help of the notorious Count Aleksey Arakcheyev, he was appointed the head of the Moscow police.

Alekseyev became chef of the Mitau Dragoon Regiment on 5 July 1806 and participated in the 1807 Campaign in Poland, rising to major general on 5 June 1807. He distinguished himself at Eylau (received the Orders of St. Anna, 2nd class and of St. Vladimir, 3rd class), Heilsberg (received a golden sword for courage) and Friedland. During the Russo-Swedish War in 1808, he successfully commanded the advance guards in the Savolax region and was awarded the Order of St. Anna (1st class) with diamonds. In early 1809, he led the advance guard of Shuvalov's Corps, making flanking march around the Gulf of Bothnia. He undertook a daring crossing of the Gulf of Bothnia at Skellefteå on 2 May, where his detachment marched for twenty-six miles up to their knees in the melting ice to surprise the Swedish garrison and capture the town. For this conduct, Alekseyev was awarded the Order of St. George (3rd class). During the actions in the summer of 1809, Alekseyev distinguished himself at Umeo, Herenfors and Sevar, where he led a counterattack and was wounded in the left foot. For this action, he was decorated with the diamond signs of the Order of St. Anna (1st class). In 1809-1811, Alekseyev remained on a garrisson duty in Finland.

In 1812, Alekseyev commanded a brigade of the Mitau and Finland Dragoon Regiments in Wittgenstein's 1st Corps. He fought at Polotsk, Chashniki, Stolbtsy, Smolyani and Studyanka, garnering the Order of St. Vladimir (2nd class). In 1813, he took part in the battle of Lutzen, where he was seriously wounded in his left foot. After recovering, he commanded the 3rd Dragoon Division in August 1814 and took part in the siege of Metz in 1815. He was promoted to lieutenant general on 11 September 1815 and remained with the Allied occupational forces in France until 1818. He returned to Russia in early 1819 and briefly commanded the 1st Dragoon Division before retiring the same year. He died in poverty and poor health on 15 October 1830 and was burried at the Simonov Cemetery in Moscow.

ANDREEVSKY, Stepan Stepanovich (b. 9 July 1782 - d. 1 November 1842) was born to a noble family in the Tver *gubernia*. He enlisted as a junker in the Life Guard Horse Regiment on 12 July 1799 and was promoted to cornet in March 1801. He took part in the 1805 Campaign and fought at Austerlitz on 2 December. He was promoted to colonel on 9 December 1809. In 1812, his regiment was attached to the Guard Cuirassier Brigade of the 1st Cuirassier Division of the 5th Reserve Corps and Andreevsky fought at Smolensk and Borodino; his participation in the battles at Vitebsk, Maloyaroslavets and Krasnyi could not be verified. In 1813, he was promoted to major general on 27 April 1813 and fought at Bautzen, Drezden, Kulm (received the Prussian Iron Cross) and Leipzig. In 1814, he participated in the combats at Le Fère Champenoise and Paris, receiving a golden sword with diamonds.

For his actions in 1813-1814, Andreevsky was also decorated with the Order of St. Anna (1st class) with diamonds, the Order of St. George (4th class), the Austrian Order of Leopold (2nd class), the Prussian Order of Red Eagle and the Bavarian Order of Maximilian Joseph. He retired on 12 September 1814, but returned to the service on 11 March 1819, serving in the Life Guard Uhlan Regiment. Andreevsky took command of the 2nd Brigade of the 1st Uhlan Division in October 1819 of the Life Guard Uhland Regiment on 30 April 1821 and of the 2nd Brigade of the Guard Light Cavalry Division on 13 January 1827. He retired on 14 July 1828 and died on 1 November 1842. He was buried in the village of Zhdanovo in the Simbirsk *gubernia*.

ANHALDT, Victor Amadeus, Prince of Anhalt Bernburg Schaumburg Hoym (May 1744 – 29 April 1790) was born to the family of Prince Victor Amadeus Adolf of Anhalt Bernburg Schaumburg Hoym. He entered the Russian service in 1772, rising to a major general in 1775 and to a lieutenant general in 1782. During the Russo-Turkish War in 1787-1791, he distinguished himself at Ochakov (received the Order of St. George, 2nd class), Kaushani (commanded the advance guard, received the Order of St. Alexander of Neva) and Bender (received the Order of St. Andrew the First Called). Anhaldt then participated in the Russo-Swedish War in 1790 and was mortally wounded, when a cannonball cut off his right leg during the battle near Kernikoski on 29 April 1790. On his deathbed, he presented his sword to Mikhail Barclay de Tolly, whom he praised for the military skills.

ANREP, (Kameke von der Hey-Henant-Wolfenschild Anrep-Elmpt), Roman Karlovich (date of birth unknown – d. 25 January 1807) descended from an ancient German noble family. He joined the Russian service and participated in the naval expedition to the Ionian Islands in 1801. Four years later, he took part in the operations in the Naples. In 1806, he took command of the 14th Division in Buxhöwden's corps and participated in the opening moves of the 1807 Campaign. He was killed during the battle at Mohrungen, where he brought cavalry to reinforce Major General Markov's advance guard against French General Charles Bernadotte.

ANSIO (Anzio), Alexander Yegorovich (b. 1776 – d. 19 July 1830, Vyborg) was born to a petty noble family. He graduated from the Artillery and Engineer Cadet Corps (2nd Cadet Corps since March 1800) with specializaion in the artillery in 1794. Promoted to a sub-lieutenant in 1796, he fought at Austerlitz in 1805, where he was wounded in the leg and captured. Released in 1806, he again served against the French during the 1807 Campaign in Poland, fighting at Eylau, Heilsberg and Friedland. For his actions, he was promoted to colonel and given command of the 12th Artillery Brigade on 2 January 1808. In 1809-1812, Ansio served against the Turks in the Danubian Principalities and distinguished himself at Bazardjik and Ruse (Ruschuk). For his courage, he was promoted to major general on 4 July 1810 and received the Orders of St. George of the 4th class (8 July 1810) and of 3rd class (1 March 1812).

In 1812, Ansio served as a duty officer in the headquarters of the Army of the Danube, fighting on the Berezina and at Vilna, and later commanded the light artillery in the Army of Reserve. On 17 June 1816, he took command of the artillery of the 7th Corps and then led the artillery parks of the 2nd Army. On 28 April 1817, he was discharged for financial embezzelement and was ordered to reimburse over 25,000 rubles in compensations. He was allowed to return to military service in December 1824 and became commander of artillery garrisons in the Old Finland District on 8 April 1825. He died on 19 July 1830 at Vyborg.

APRAKSIN, Stepan Stepanovich (b. 24 June 1757, Riga – d. 20 February 1827, Moscow) was born to a prominent Russian family, the son of Field Marshal Stepan Fedorovich Apraksin. He was enlisted as ensign in the Life Guard Semeyonovsk Regiment upon his birth in 1757 and was promoted to captain in 1772. Apraksin later transferred as a colonel to the Kiev Infantry Regiment and was appointed a flügel adjutant in 1777. He took command of the Kiev Infantry Regiment in 1782 and participated in the operations against the Turks in the Crimea. In 1783, he became a brigadier and served with the Astrakhan Carabineer Regiment in the Caucasus and Kuban Valley, receiving the Order of St. Vladimir (3rd class). He was promoted to major general and appointed chef of the Astrakhan Carabineer Regiment on 23 February 1786.

Apraksin took part in the Russo-Turkish War in 1787-1791, distinguishing himself at Ochakov. In 1793, he became a lieutenant general and served in Poland in 1794. He rose to a lieutenant general on 13 September 1794, to general of cavalry on 23 March 1798 and took command of the Astrakhan Dragoon Regiment on 14 December 1796. Apraksin retired because of poor health in December 1798 but returned to the army in 1801, serving as the head of the Moscow and Smolensk Inspections. In 1803, he

ARAKCHEEV, Aleksey Andreyevich (b. 4 October 1769, Bezhetsk district of Tver *gubernia* – d. 3 June 1834, Gruzino estate, Novgorod *gubernia*.) was born to a petty noble family in the Tver *gubernia*. He graduated from the Artillery and Engineer Cadet Corps with the rank of sub-lieutenant on 8 October 1787 and remained at the Corps as an instructor and librarian. In 1790-92, he served as a senior adjutant to the director of the Artillery and Engineering Cadet Corps. In 1792, he was appointed commander of the Gatchina Artillery with the rank of captain. He became very close with Grand Duke Paul and, over the next three years, he was promoted to major and colonel and became infantry inspector at Gatchina. After Paul became an emperor in November 1796, Arakcheyev rose to major general and received command of a battalion of the Life Guard Preobrazhensk Regiment, quickly followed by appointment as the Commandant of St. Petersburg. On 16 April 1797, Arakcheyev was conferred the title of baron of the Russian Empire and, on 30 April of the same year, he became the Quartermaster General of the Russian army. He became the Military Governor of Smolensk. Four years later, he organized the 16th Division and commanded it against the Turks in the Danubian Principalities in 1807-1808. He retired again in 1809 and settled in Moscow, where he died on 20 February 1827.

However, Arakcheyev was dismissed with the rank of lieutenant general on 29 March 1798. Emperor Paul soon forgave him and returned him to service in January 1799, making him commander of the Life Guard Artillery Battalion and the Inspector of All Russian Artillery. On 16 May 1799, Arakcheyev was given the title of count of the Russian Empire with the motto "Devoted without Flattery" composed by Paul himself. However, Arakcheyev's aloofness and gloomy personality, straight forward and rough character made him disliked by many. In the fall of 1799, he was dismissed for concealing his brother's financial machinations. He remained at his estate in Gruzino for the next four years, except for a brief trip to St. Petersburg on the eve of Paul's assassination.

Arakcheyev was reinstated to his position of Inspector of All Artillery in 1803 and was instrumental in launching artillery reforms in the Russian army. On 9 July 1807, he was promoted to general of artillery. In 1808, Emperor Alexander appointed him the Minister of War and General Inspector of the Infantry and Artillery. In September 1808, the Rostov Musketeer Regiment was renamed to Count Arakcheyev's Musketeer (later Grenadier) Regiment.

In 1809, Arakcheyev briefly ventured to Finland where he participated in Prince Peter Bagration's crossing of the Gulf of Bothnia. In 1810, he presided over the Department of War within the State Council. In early 1812, Arakcheyev remained with the Imperial headquarters at the 1st Western Army and then travelled to St. Petersburg. He returned to the army in December 1812 and served as the head of the Imperial Field Chancellery in 1813-1814. In April 1814, Alexander I promoted him to field marshal, but Arakcheyev asked him to annul this order because he did not command any troops. Instead, Arakcheyev received the Emperor's portrait with diamonds.

Arakcheyev's power increased beginning in 1815, when Alexander was preoccupied with foreign affairs and depended on Arakcheyev for domestic administration. Arakcheyev served as the Inspector of all infantry and artillery and supervised the State Council and the Cabinet of

Ministers during Alexander's absence. He was in charge of the infamous system of military colonies and created a network of settlements with some 400,000 men. This period is often referred to as *Arakcheyevschina* (Era of Arakcheyev). Arrogant and ruthless, Arakcheyev virtually governed the empire during the time and made numerous enemies through his callous and brusque decisions. By the end of Alexander's reign, he was one of the most despised, yet feared, men in the empire. Immediately after Alexander's death, Emperor Nicholas I removed him from all positions of power. Arakcheyev retired to his estate at Gruzino where he died on 4 June 1834 and was buried in the local Church of St. Andrew.

ARBUZOV, Yevgeny Fedorovich (b. 1771 – d. 1834) was born to a noble family in the Smolensk *gubernia*. He began his service as a sergeant at the Life Guard Preobrazhensk Regiment in 1786, becoming an ensign in 1788. He fought against the Swedes in 1788-1790. In 1794, he transferred as a premier major to the Byelorussia Jager Corps and fought the Polish insurgents. Promoted to colonel in 1797, he participated in the expedition to Holland in 1799 and distinguished himself at the Helder Island. For his actions, he was promoted to major general on 21 September 1799.

In 1801, Arbuzov retired because of poor health and returned to service in 1806. He served as a supply inspector in the Russian army during the 1807 Campaign in Poland. In 1808, he was in charge of the supply depots for the Army of Finland. Two years later, he served in the Department of Commissariat of the Ministry of War. In 1812, he joined the St. Petersburg *opolchenye* and the next year, he served as a supply inspector for the Army of Reserve. In 1814, he took part in the siege of Hamburg. After the war, he returned to the Ministry of War. In 1831, he supervised main supply depot in the western *gubernias*. He retired in 1834 because of poor health.

ARGAMAKOV (Argamakov II), Ivan Andreyevich (b. 26 December 1775, Osokino, Kostroma *gubernia* – d. 21 March 1820) was born to a noble family from the Kostroma *gubernia*. After studying in the Infantry Cadet Corps in 1782-1793, he began service as a lieutenant in the Ingermanland Carabinier Regiment on 6 July 1793. He served in Poland in 1794 and, for his actions at Vilna, he was promoted to rotmistr and took command of a squadron of the Ingermanland Carabiniers. In February 1798, Argamakov rose to a major and, in September of the same year, he transferred to the newly formed Tver Dragoon Regiment. For his role in forming this regiment, Argamakov received the Commandor Cross of the Order of St. John of Jerusalem and a 1,000 rubles annual pension. In June 1800, he was promoted to lieutenant colonel.

In 1805, Argamakov served in the Tver Dragoon Regiment and fought under Prince Bagration at Wischau, Possoritz and Austerlitz. The next year, he took command of the Tver Dragoon Regiment on 11 July 1806 and transferred to the Danubian Principalities, where he fought the Turks for the next six years. He distinguished himself in the actions at Buzeo and Braila and was promoted to colonel on 24 December 1807. On 15 April 1810, he became chef of the Zhitomir Dragoon Regiment. In late 1811, he transferred to the Army of Volhynia (later Army of Podolsk, 2nd Western Army), and then joined the 3rd Reserve Army of Observation, serving in the 16th Brigade of the 5th Cavalry Division of General Lambert's Cavalry Corps.

In June-October 1812, during Napoleon's invasion of Russia, Argamakov participated in the minor raids on the Austrian and French forces in Volhynia. On 15 November, he distinguished himself at Kaidanov, capturing some 3,000 men, two guns and two flags, for which he was later awarded the Order of St. George (4th class). He also participated in the capture of Minsk and Borisov, and in the operations on the Berezina. In 1813, he took part in the siege of Danzig and fought at Koenigswarta, Bautzen, Hanau (received the Orders of St. Anna, 2nd class, and of St. Vladimir, 3rd class) and Leipzig (received the

Order of St. Anna, 1st class). For his courage, he was promoted to major general on 27 September 1813.

In 1814, he participated in the siege of Hamburg. In 1815, he commanded 2nd Brigade of the 3rd Uhlan Division and attended the grand military parade at Vertus. After the war, Argamakov was deployed with his regiments in the Kharkov *gubernia*. In 1818, he took command of the 1st Brigade of the 3rd Uhlan Division in the Sloboda *gubernia* and, in February 1820, he became commander of the 1st Brigade of the 3rd Dragoon Division. He died on 21 March 1820.

ARGAMAKOV (Argamakov I), Ivan Vasilyevich (b. 1763 – d. 1834) was born to a noble family in the Ryazan *gubernia*. He began service in the Life Guard Izmailovsk Regiment in 1775 and then transferred to the Life Guard Horse Regiment in 1783. In 1789, he joined the Kazan Cuirassier Regiment and fought the Swedes. In 1794, he transferred to the Sofia Cuirassier Regiment and took part in the campaigns against the Polish insurgents, distinguishing himself at Praga. In 1805, he served in the Tver Dragoon Regiment and fought at Austerlitz, receiving the Order of St. Vladimir (4th class). Promoted to colonel on 5 May 1806, he commanded the Yamburg Dragoon Regiment in 1807.

In 1808, he took part in the campaign against the Swedes in Finland. The next year, he was appointed commander of the Vladimir Dragoon Regiment on 23 November. In 1810-1811, he served with his regiment in the Caucasus and the Crimea. In 1812, Argamakov served with the 24th Brigade of the 8th Cavalry Division of General Lambert's Corps and participated in the operations in Volhynia. In 1813-1814, he fought at Dresden, Leipzig and Hamburg. He was promoted to major general on 28 May 1815 and appointed commander of the 1st Brigade of the 2nd Horse Jager Division. Argamakov retired because of poor health on 26 January 1816 and lived in his estate of Ivanovo in the Tver *gubernia* until his death in 1834.

ARMFELT, Gustav Maurice Maksimovich (b. 12 April 1757, Abo – d. 31 March 1814, Tsarskoe selo) descended from an ancient Swedish noble family. He was a favorite of the Swedish King Gustavus III and served as a general in the Swedish army during the Russo-Swedish War of 1788-1790. Armfelt represented Sweden at the peace negotiations in 1790, and was awarded the Orders of St. Andrew and of St. Alexander of Neva on 19 September 1790. After the assassination of King Gustavus III in 1792, he served as the Swedish envoy to Naples but was involved in a plot against King Gustavus IV and fled to Russia, where he lived in Kaluga until 1797. He then moved to Germany and, in 1799, Gustavus IV granted him amnesty. Armfelt returned to Sweden in 1801 and was appointed the Swedish ambassador to Vienna in 1802-1804 and then Governor General of Finland in 1805-1807. He commanded forces against the Danes in Norway in 1807.

During the Russo-Swedish War in 1808, Armfelt was nominated to become commander-in-chief of the Swedish army, but was replaced by General Klingspor. In 1809, he served as the president of the Military College of Sweden and a member of the State Council. After a coup d'etat of 13 March 1809 removed King Gustavus IV from the throne, Armfelt left Sweden to enter Russian service. He became general of infantry on 22 March 1812, the title of count (September 1812), and appointed to the State Council. He influenced Alexander I in granting Finland an autonomous status within the empire.

In 1812, Armfelt served at the headquarters of the 1st Western Army and took part in the war council at Drissa. He accompanied Emperor Alexander to St. Petersburg and negotiated a treaty with Sweden. In July 1813, he served in the headquarters of the Army of North led by Swedish Crown Prince Karl Bernadotte, and took part in the battles of Gross-Beeren, Dennewitz, and Leipzig. He died on 31 March 1814 at Tsarskoe selo and was buried at his estate near Abo in South Finland.

ARNOLDI, Ivan Karlovich (b. 1783 – d. 23 October 1860) was born to a noble family in the Courland *gubernia*. After graduating from the Cadet Corps, he enlisted as a sub-lieutenant in the field artillery battalion in St. Petersburg on 19 December 1799. He participated in 1806-1807 Campaigns in Poland, serving as an adjutant to Major General Alexander Kutaisov, and distinguished himself at Eylau, Lomitten (awarded the Order of St. Anna, 4th class), Heilsberg and Friedland (earned a golden sword for courage). In 1809, he took part in the campaign against Austria, and two years later, he received another award for excellent service: under the Imperial order, he was allowed to wear a golden badge on the collar. In 1812, Arnoldi commanded the 13th Horse Artillery Company in Admiral Paul Chichagov's army and fought on the Berezina in November 1812, garnering the Order of St. Vladimir (4th class). For his actions in 1812, he was promoted to lieutenant colonel.

In February 1813, Arnoldi commanded an artillery company in Count Vorontsov's advance guard and fought at Rogozhnyi and Obernik. During a six-week truce in the summer of 1813, he was at Magdeburg, and then fought at Dennewitz, where he led his gunners in counterattack and captured two French cannon. In September 1813, Arnoldi fought at Torgau, for which he received the Order of St. George (4th class) and the Prussian Pour le Merite. He then joined Swedish Crown Prince Bernadottes's troops at Leipzig, where he was first wounded in the left leg, but remained with the ranks until moments later a French projectile cut off this leg; notwithstanding his wound, Arnoldi continued commanding his battery lying on the ground near one of his guns. For his courage, Alexander sent his personal physician to treat him and promoted him to colonel on the battlefield; Prince Bernadotte awarded him the Swedish Order of the Sword. Despite his serious injury, Arnoldi commanded his artillery company during the Russian army's march to France in 1815.

After the war, Arnoldi took command of the artillery of the 5th Reserve Cavalry Corps in 1817 and of the Life Guard Horse Artillery in 1820. He rose to a major general in 1821 and served on Count Aleksey Arakcheyev's staff. In 1822, he commanded artillery in the military colonies in Kherson and Ekaterinoslavl *gubernia*s and, four years later, he became adjutant to Grand Duke Mikhail Pavlovich.

During the Russo-Turkish War of 1828-1829, Arnoldi led the Russian artillery at Silistra and Kulevchi, and received the Order of St. Anna (1st class). He followed the army across the Balkans and fought at Slivno and Adrianople. After the war, he continued as an adjutant to Grand Duke Mikhail. In 1834, Arnoldi became a lieutenant general and commander of the reserve horse artillery. In 1841, he was appointed inspector of the reserve artillery. In 1849, he received the Order of St. Alexander of Neva for fifty years of distinguished service; two years later he was promoted to general of artillery. In 1853, he was appointed to the Senate. He had two brothers, Peter and Otto, who served with him in the 13th Horse Artillery Brigade during the 1812-1814 Campaigns.

ARSENYEV (Arsenyev I), Mikhail Andreyevich (b. 1779 – d. 18 November 1838) was born to a noble family in the Tula *gubernia*. He enlisted in Life Guard Horse Regiment in 1791, but did not start active service until 1796 when he transferred to the Chevalier Guard Corps. However, the corps was disbanded after Empress Catherine II's death and Arsenyev transferred back to the Life Guard Horse Regiment in November 1797. Serving in this unit, he rose to a cornet on 21 July 1799, to lieutenant in 1801, to captain in 1804 and to colonel on 24 August 1807. In 1812, he served as a commanding officer of the Life Guard Horse Regiment attached to the 1st Cuirassier Division of the 5th Corps of the 1st Western Army. He fought at Vitebsk, Smolensk, Borodino (wounded in the left hand, awarded the Order of St. George, 4rd class, 2 December 1812, promoted to major general on 7 January 1813), Tarutino, Maloyaroslavets and Krasnyi.

In 1813, Arsenyev participated in the battles at Lutzen, Bautzen, Dresden, Kulm (received the Order of St. Vladimir, 3rd class) and Leipzig, taking commmand of the 1st Brigade of 1st Cuirassier Division in late 1813. The next year, he took part in the invasion of France and fought at Brienne, Le Fère Champenoise and Paris, receiving Order of St. Anna (1st class), the Austrian Order of Leopold (2nd class), the Prussian Order of the Red Eagle (2nd class) and the Bavarian Order of Maximilian Joseph. On 28 January 1819, Arsenyev assumed command of the 1st Dragoon Division but then resigned because of poor health in November 1819. He served on various military committees until December 1833, when he retired with a full pension. He passed away from pneumonia on 18 November 1838 at his estate in the Tula *gubernia*.

ARSENYEV, Nikolay Dmitrievich (date of birth unclear, c. 1739 – d. 1796) enlisted in the Life Guard Preobrazhensk Regiment in 1760 and participated in the Russo-Turkish War of 1769-1774, fighting at Kafa and Obashtu. He was promoted to colonel in 1780, to brigadier in 1787 and to major general on 16 February 1790. He participated in the Russo-Turkish War of 1787-1791 and fought at Tulcea and Ismail (awarded the Order of St. George, 3rd class, 5 April 1791). In 1792-1794, he served in Poland and fought at Nesvizh, Slutsk and Brest Litovsk, receiving Order of St. Vladimir (2nd class). He was captured by the Poles in Vilna on 20 April 1794 and remained in captivity the Russian occupied the town in late 1794.

ARSENYEV (Arsenyev II), Nikolay Mikhaylovich (b. 1764 – d. 1830) was born to a noble family in the Tula *gubernia*. He graduated from the Cadet Corps and joined army as a lieutenant on 1 March 1785. However, he transferred to civil service and served as a prosecutor in Irkutsk. He returned to the military in 1791 and received the rank of major. He participated in the 1794 Campaign in Poland, where he was wounded in both feet and promoted to lieutenant colonel. Promoted to colonel on 14 February 1798, he took command of the Old Badensky (later Kozlovsky) Musketeer Regiment. The following year, he was promoted to major general on 9 February and appointed chef of the Voronezh Musketeer Regiment. On 27 November 1804, he was court martialed for failing to properly maintain his regiment, but was restored the next year. On 5 August 1805, Arsenyev became chef of the Navaginsk Musketeer Regiment.

During the 1806-1807 Campaigns in Poland, Arsenyev served with the 4th Division and fought at Pultusk, Eylau (wounded in the leg), Danzig and Koenigsberg. He distinguished himself at Heilsberg, garnering the Order of St. George (4th class, 1 June 1808). Arsenyev then participated in the Russo-Swedish War in 1808 before retiring because of health complications on 2 February 1809. During the 1812 Campaign, he organized the 7th Infantry Regiment of the Moscow *opolchenye* and commanded this *opolchenye* at Borodino, Tarutino, Maloyaroslavets and Krasnyi. Beginning in December 1812, he supervised the Russian wounded and disabled soldiers at Orsha. In October 1816, he officially re-enlisted in the regular military service and was appointed to the 4th, and later to the 7th District of the Independent Corps of the Internal Guard [*otdelnii korpus Vnutrennei strazhi*]. He retired with a full pension on 18 January 1825 and died five years later.

B

BAGGOVUT, Karl Fedorovich (Karl Gustav) (b. 27 September 1761, Pergel, Eastland – d. 18 October 1812, Tarutino) was born to an ancient Norwegian noble family, settled in the Eastland *gubernia*. He joined the Russian army on 4 April 1779 and served as lieutenant in the Tobolsk Infantry Regiment. On 12 September 1779, he transferred to the 2nd Battalion of the Finland Jager Corps. In January 1781, he joined the Dnieper Regiment in the south of Russia and fought against the Crimean Tartars. He was soon promoted to captain and transferred to the Siberia Grenadier Regiment. Baggovut took part in the Russo-Turkish War in 1787 and fought at Salchi and Bender in late 1789. On 21 February 1791, he retired because of poor health with the rank of premier major.

However, Baggovut returned to the army the next year and served in Poland as a volunteer. He distinguished himself in several engagements, including those on the River Bug and at Dubenka, and he was reinstated in his rank to the Siberia Grenadier Regiment on 25 December 1792. He fought the Poles near Warsaw in the spring of 1794 and then commanded a detachment in the actions at Kotomo (1 May), Belyi (26 May), Lishanov (1 August) and Galkovo (9 August). He took part in the battle at Maciejowice on 10 October, where General Ivan Ferzen defeated Thaddeus Kosciusko, and earned promotion to lieutenant colonel. Baggovut then served under Suvorov during the rest of campaign and fought at Praga and Warsaw. In May 1795 he became commander of the 1st Battalion of the Byelorussia Jager Regiment and within two years, he rose to commander of the 14th Jager Regiment. In February 1798, he was promoted to colonel and, within a year, in January 1799, he became chef of the 14th Jagers. On 9 February 1799, he became a major general. In August 1800, Baggovut retired again only to return to service in August 1801 becoming chef of the 4th Jager Regiment on 17 November.

Baggovut joined Bennigsen's troops in 1806 and fought at Pultusk on 26 December. For this battle, he was awarded the Order of St. George (3rd class) and the Prussian Order of Red Eagle. In February 1807, Baggovut was wounded in the chest at Eylau and was decorated with the Order of St. Anna (1st class). He fought at Guttstadt, on the Passarga River and at Heilsberg. He was seriously wounded at Friedland on 14 June 1807. For his actions during the 1807 campaign, Baggovut was promoted to lieutenant general on 24 December 1807. After his convalescence, he joined the Russian troops in Finland in the spring of 1808 and took command of the 5th Division. He fought at Iverismo (near Abo), in June 1808 and then at Helsing on 27 September 1808.

In 1812, Baggovut commanded 2nd Corps of the 1st Western Army and fought at Valutino near Smolensk in August 1812. At Borodino, Baggovut's corps was on the Russian right flank and his troops performed a critical march to reinforce Bagration's battered troops on the left, where his timely arrival helped the Russians hold. Baggovut was awarded the Order of Alexander of Neva for this battle. However, he was mortally wounded at Tarutino in October 1812, when he was leading the flanking maneuver. He was buried at the Lavrentiev Monastery in Kaluga.

BAGRATION, Constantine Davidovich (b. 1793 – date of death unclear) was born to the Imeretian branch of the Bagration royal house of Georgia. In 1812, Prince Constantine began service as a rotmistr in the Life Guard Cossack Regiment and distinguished himself on the Dvina River, at Vitebsk, Porechye, Smolensk (commanded Life Guard Black Sea Company, *leib-gvardii Chernomorskaia sotnya*) and Borodino (earned the Order of St. Vladimir, 4th class). After October 1812, he served as a flügel adjutant to Emperor Alexander. In 1813, he fought at Lutzen, Bautzen (earned promotion to colonel in June 1813) and Leipzig, and, in 1814, he took part in the battle for Paris in March. After the war, he rose to major general in December 1817.

BAGRATION, Peter Ivanovich (b. July 1765, Georgia – d. 24 September 1812, Simy) descended from the Bagration royal dynasty that ruled Georgia for over nine hundred years. His father immigrated to Russia in 1766 and served at a garrison of Kizlyar. Despite some claims that Bagration was born in Kizlyar, Prince Peter's was born in Georgia (probably in Tbilisi) in the summer of 1765 and traveled with his parents to Kizlyar in 1766. Brought up in Daghestan, Bagration received basic education at a garrison school. He enlisted as a supernumerary [*sverkh-komplekta*] in the Astrakhan Infantry Regiment on 12 May 1783 and became a private on 4 September 1783. During the Russo-Turkish War of 1787-1791, Bagration served under Alexander Suvorov in the Crimea, distinguishing himself at Ochakov in 1788, for which he was promoted to captain skipping the rank of sub-lieutenant, perhaps due to Potemkin's patronage. Thus, Bagration rose to an ensign on 9 July 1787, to captain on 18 December 1788 and nominally given rank of sub lieutenant on 9 July 1789.

In 1789-1790, Bagration served in Gregory Potemkin's staff and participated in the negotiations with representatives of Ali Mahmud Khan of Persia. He also served as an adjutant to various generals, including Count Ivan Saltykov and Johann Herman, who commanded the Russian troops in the Caucasus. In 1790, he participated in the campaign against the Chechens and was seriously wounded in an action near village of Alda on the Sunzha River. By early 1792, Bagration had transferred to the Kiev Horse Jager Regiment, becoming a second major on 9 July 1792 and a premier major on 8 December 1793.

On 15 May 1794, Bagration transferred to the Sofia Carabineer Regiment, and in Poland in late 1794, he participated in the actions at Brest-Litovsk, Sedlitsy, Deryachin, Tatarovka and Sokolnya. In October, he led his squadron in a surprise attack against a 1,000-men strong Polish detachment and captured 250 men and a gun, for which Bagration was promoted to a lieutenant colonel on 27 October 1794. In November of the same year, he followed the main army to Praga, a suburb of Warsaw, but he did not participate in the subsequent assault. After the war in Poland, Bagration returned to Russia and, in June 1795, he took command of the 1st Battalion of the Lifland Jagers at Volkovisk in the Grodno *gubernia*. After the military reorganization in 1796, Bagration became commander of the 7th Independent Jager Battalion on 28 May 1797 and his unit was soon converted to the 7th Jager Regiment. On 24 February 1798, Bagration took promotion to colonel and, on 28 January 1799, he became chef of the 7th Jager Regiment, now renamed as Prince Bagration's Jager Regiment.

During Alexander Suvorov's campaigns in Italy and Switzerland in 1799, Bagration led both the advance and rearguards of the Russian army and distinguished himself in the battles at Brescia, Lecco, Tortona, Alexandria, Marengo, Turin, on the Tidone and Trebbia Rivers and at Novi in Italy. In Suvorov's ill-fated campaign in Switzerland, Bagration served during the crossing of the St. Gottard Pass, the storming of the Devil's Bridge, the actions in Muothatal Valley, at Nafels, Netstal, Glarus and he was pivotal during the harrowing escape through the Panixer Pass. For his actions, Bagration garnered the Orders of St. Anna (1st class), of St. Alexander of Neva, of St. John of Jerusalem, the Sardinian Order of Saints Maurice and Lazarus and the Austrian Order of Maria Theresa. On 10 April 1800, his regiment was transformed into the 6th Jagers and Bagration became chef of the Life Guard Jager Battalion on 21 June. In 1801, he became the commandant of the Imperial residence at Pavlovsk.

In 1805, Bagration commanded the rearguard of the Austro-Russian army and fought with determination at Lambach and Amstetten. At Schöngraben (Hollabrunn) on 16 November 1805, he commanded 7,000 men against 30,000 French under Marshals Joachim Murat and Jean Lannes. Loosing two thirds of his troops, Bagration halted the French for over eighteen hours and let the main Allied forces escape to safety. For his actions, he was promoted to a lieutenant general and decorated with the Order of St. George (2nd class) on 20 November 1805.

During the Allied offensive, he fought at Wischau and Raussnitz and commanded the right wing of the Allied army at Austerlitz on 2 December 1805. After the battle, he covered the retreat of the Russian army to Hungary. He was again appointed commander of the Russian advance guard in early January 1807 and he assumed this position on 25 January. Bagration then distinguished himself at Wolfsdorf, Eylau, Altkirch, Guttstadt, Quest, Deppen, Heilsberg, Friedland and Tilsit; in consequence he garnered the Order of St. Vladimir (2nd class) and Prussian Orders of the Red and Black Eagles.

During the Russo-Swedish War, he commanded the 21st Division and successfully occupied southwestern Finland and occupied Abo, where he later defeated the Swedish landing force in September 1808. On 15 March 1809, he led the famous march across the frozen Gulf of Bothnia to occupy the Aland Islands and his advance guard reached the Swedish shores in the vicinity of the Swedish capital, precipitating the *coup d'etat* in Stockholm. For his actions against the Swedes, Bagration was promoted to a general of infantry on 21 March 1809 and appointed an assistant to the Commander-in-Chief General Prozorovsky of the Army of Moldavia on 13 July 1809. After Prozorovsky's death on 21 August 1809, he took command of the army and immediately launched an offensive southward against the Turks, capturing the fortresses of Macin, Constanta (Kustendji) and Girsov on his way to Cavarna and Bazardjik. On 16 September 1809, Bagration defeated the Turks at Rassevat and, on September 22, he invested Silistra, forcing the Grand Vizier Yussuf to cancel his invasion of Serbia and Wallachia.

Bagration halted the superior Turkish army at Tataritsa on October 22, but had to lift the siege of Silistra because of lack of supplies and ammunition. He succeeded in taking Ismail and Braila in late 1809. In March 1810, he resigned after a disagreement with Emperor Alexander on the overall strategy being pursued in the Danubian Principalities. He briefly traveled to Vienna in late 1810 and became involved in a diplomatic scandal between France and Russia after he unsuccessfully tried to obtain secret documents on Franco-Persian relations. After returning to Russia, Bagration was appointed to command the Army of Podolsk on 25 August 1811; this army had been later reorganized into the 2nd Western Army in March 1812.

During the 1812 Campaign, Bagration successfully eluded Napoleon's enveloping maneuvers and achieved victories at Mir and Romanovo. He outmaneuvered Marshal Nicholas Davout at Moghilev and joined Barclay de Tolly's 1st Western Army at Smolensk on 3 August. The aggressive Bagration was the chief proponent of the Smolensk offensive, but he was ultimately able to perceive Napoleon's designs to outflank the Russians. Falling back from the French envelopment in time, he successfully defended Smolensk on 15-16 August. His bitter opposition to Barclay de Tolly's policy of scorched earth and retreat led to Barclay's replacement by Mikhail Kutuzov. On 7 September, Bagration commanded the Russian left flank at Borodino and fiercely defended the flèches against the main French attacks. However, he was seriously wounded by a shell splinter in his left leg and died of wound complications on 24 September at the village Simy in the Vladimir *gubernia*. He was buried at a local church but his remains were transferred to the Great Redoubt at the Borodino Battlefield in August 1839. His grave was destroyed by the communists in 1932, but restored in 1987. He was unhappily married to Countess Ekaterina Skavronsky, who left him within a year of marriage and had an illegitimate child with Austrian Diplomat Clemence von Metternich in 1801. Princess Bagration later played important role in the Congress of Vienna in 1815.

Prince Peter Bagration was one of the best tactical commanders in Europe during the Napoleonic Wars. His rearguard actions in Moravia in 1805 and Poland in 1807 were truly remarkable. However, he also demonstrated poor strategic abilities in 1812. He was a man of an uncontrolled, ambitious and violent temper, who expressed his feelings in a passionate manner. He was one of the most beloved generals in the Russian army and was often called "the Glory of the Russian army" (S. Volkonsky) and "Bog-rati-on"—"the God of the Army" (G. Derzhavin).

BAGRATION, Roman (Revaz) Ivanovich (b. 1778, Kizlyar, — d. 14 March 1834, Tbilisi; excluded from rosters on 28 April 1834) descended from the Georgian royal family; Roman was the younger brother of Peter Bagration. He enlisted in the Life Guard Horse Regiment on 27 April 1790 and served as an adjutant to Count V. Zubov until April 1796. On 21 May 1796, he transferred as an ensign to the Kuban Jager Corps. He took part in minor operations in the North Caucasus in 1797-1800 before being transferred to the Life Guard Hussar Regiment in May 1802. Bagration participated in the 1805 and 1807 Campaigns against Napoleon, and then fought against the Turks in 1809-1810. He was promoted to colonel on 8 December 1810.

During the 1812 Campaign, Bagration served in the Alexandria Hussar Regiment in the 3rd Reserve Army of Observation (later 3rd Western Army) and fought at Kobryn, Brest and Gorodechnya. In 1813, he distinguished himself at Bautzen and became a major general on 2 June 1813. Bagration then served with the Austrian troops at Dresden (earned the Order of St. Anna, 1st class) before joining Major General Bulatov's detachment and participating in the rear guard actions around Dresden in October 1813. In early 1814, Bagration commanded advance guard of Bulatov's detachment and later served at Hamburg, garnering the Order of St. George (3rd class). He participated in 1828-1829 Campaign against the Turks and was promoted to lieutenant general on 7 July 1829. Three years later, he returned to Georgia and served in Abkhazia, where he contracted a fever and died on 14 March 1834. He is buried in the Church of St. David in Tbilisi. In addition to the mentioned awards, he received the Order of St. John of Jerusalem and Prussian Pour le Merite. He had a son Peter Romanovich Bagration, who became lieutenant general and governor general of the Lifland, Courland and Estland *gubernia*s.

BAKHMETYEV (Bakhmetyev III), Aleksey Nikolayevich (b. 1774, Penza *gubernia* – d. 27 September 1841, Podolsk *gubernia*) descended from a Tatar noble family living in the

Penza *gubernia*. He enlisted in the Life Guard Preobrazhensk Regiment on 21 September 1777 and transferred as an ensign to the Life Guard Izmailovsk Regiment on 13 January 1790. He participated in the Russo-Swedish War of 1788-1790. He was promoted to colonel in December 1798 and to major general on 12 April 1800 and received appointment as chef of the Siberia Grenadier Regiment. In 1805, he took part in the expedition to Naples, and in 1806-1811, he served in the Danube Valley against the Turks. He distinguished himself at Giurgiu, Obilesti and Braila in 1807, at Girsov, Rassevat, Tataritsa (was seriously wounded and received the Order of St. George (3rd class, 6 August 1810), Silistra and Shumla in 1809-1810. He was seriously wounded during the assault on Ruse in 1810, where he commanded General Uvarov's reserves and spent the rest of campaign recuperating. On 29 January 1811, he was appointed commander of the 26th Division, and, on 12 April, he took command of the 23rd Division.

In 1812, Bakhmetyev's division was attached to the 4th Corps of the 1st Western Army. He fought at Ostrovno, Smolensk and Zabolotye. At Borodino, he was seriously wounded when a cannonball tore off his right leg. For his courage, he was promoted to lieutenant general on 12 November 1812 with a seniority starting on 5 September 1812. After recuperating from the wound, he became governor of Kamenets-Podolsk on 8 April 1814.

Two years later he served as the Governor of Bessarabia. He was promoted to general of infantry on 24 December 1823. In 1828 he was appointed the Governor of Nizhegorod, Kazan, Simbirsk and Penza *gubernias* and became a member of the State Council. In addition to the previously mentioned decorations, Bakhmetyev also had the Order of Alexander of Neva, a medal "For XLV years of Distinguished Service" and a golden sword with diamonds for courage.

BAKHMETYEV (Bakhmetyev I), Nikolay Nikolayevich (b. 1772 – d. 1831) was born to a noble family in the Kursk *gubernia*, brother of Aleksey Bakhmetyev. He began service as a sergeant in the Life Guard Preobrazhensk Regiment in 1789, and then participated in the campaign against the Swedes in 1789-1790. He was promoted to colonel in 1797; the next year, he became a major general and chef of the Rylsk Musketeer Regiment on 10 June 1798. In October of the same year, he took over the governorship of Orenburg, where he remained until 26 July 1803. He retired in December 1804, but returned to the service in June 1811 and received another appointment as governor, this time of Smolensk in September 1811. On 4 April 1812, Bakhmetyev was given command of the Combined Grenadier Division of the 1st Western Army. However, on 4 May, he took command of the 11th Division of the 4th Corps. During the 1812 Campaign, he fought at Ostrovno, Smolensk and Borodino, where he was seriously wounded. Bakhmetyev spent the rest of the campaign recuperating and was discharged on 6 May 1813. During his career, he was honored with the Orders of St. Anna with diamonds (1st class), of St. Vladimir (3rd class), of St. John of Jerusalem as well as a golden sword with diamonds for courage.

BAKLANOVSKY, Mikhail Alekseyevich (b. 11 November 1760, Tver *gubernia* — d. 5 August 1823, Tver *gubernia*) was born to a noble family in the Tver *gubernia*. He enlisted as a private in the Life Guard Izmailovsk Regiment in 1772 and was promoted to ensign on 1 January 1778. The following January, he transferred as a captain to the Nasheburg Infantry Regiment, where he served for eight years. On 21 December 1787, he transferred to the Tobolsk Musketeer Regiment. Baklanovsky took part in the campaigns in Poland (1779-1781, 1794), Crimea (1783) and Sweden (1789-1790). On 12 July 1798, he took command of the Tobolsk Musketeer Regiment and later received promotion to colonel on 7 November 1798. He participated in the expedition to Holland in 1799. On 7 February 1800, he became a major general as well as chef of the Ukraine Musketeer Regiment, where he served until 28 August 1804. Baklanovsky retired on 18 November 1806 and commanded militia in the Kashinsk district of the Tver *gubernia*.

In 1807, Baklanovsky led a militia brigade of the Tver province and was deployed at Vilno to guard the frontiers. He was elected head of the nobility assembly [*zemstvo*] of the Tver *gubernia* in January 1809. In 1812, he commanded the 1st Dismounted Cossack Regiment of the Tver Militia comprised of the detachments of Kashinsk, Kalyazinsk, Kimrsk and Bezhetsk districts. He participated in minor actions during the retreat of the Grand Army. In 1813, he participated in the siege of Modlin. After the Tver militia was disbanded in February 1814, Baklanovsky retired to his estate in the Tver *gubernia*, where he died on 5 August 1823 and was buried at the Troitsky Monastery in Kalyazin. During his service, Baklanovsky was awarded a golden cross for Praga, the Orders of St. George (4th class), of St. Anna (2nd class) with diamonds, of St. Vladimir (4th class) and of St. John of Jerusalem.

BALABIN, Peter Ivanovich (b. 2 May 1776 — d. 21 October 1856) enlisted in the service at an early age, but his active service began as an army captain in the Black Sea Navy on 12 January 1794. Conferred the rank of navy lieutenant on 13 June 1785, he participated in the expeditions of Black Sea Fleet in the Mediterranean Sea throughout 1794-1798. In 1797-1798, Balabin served as adjutant to Admiral Fedor Ushakov. In 1798, he took part in the expedition to the Ionian Archipelago and, the next year, he was in the landing force at Naples that marched on Rome. In 1801, he transferred to the Baltic Galley Fleet. In 1802, he transferred as a lieutenant to the Chevalier Guard Regiment and served as adjutant to General Fedor Uvarov.

Balabin participated in the 1805 Campaign and fought at Austerlitz on 2 December. In 1807, he distinguished himself at Heilsberg and Friedland. In 1808, he fought against the Swedes in Finland; on 26 August 1808, he was dispatched with Alexander's letters to Napoleon in Paris. On his return, he was promoted to flügel adjutant to Emperor Alexander I on 13 October 1808. During the 1812 Campaign, he served under Governor of Riga Ivan Essen and fought at Eckau, Memel and Mitau. In 1813, he participated in the battles at Bautzen, Dresden, Kulm and Glogau. For his actions, he was promoted to major general on 27 September 1813 and awarded the Prussian Pour le Merite and Order of Red Eagle (2nd class). Balabin participated in the 1814 Campaign in France and returned with the Russian army in 1815. He retired because of poor health on 19 January 1818, but returned to service 28 November 1826. Over the next six years, he served as the head of the 1st Region of the Independent Gendarmerie Corps. He was discharged on 22 February 1832 with promotion to a lieutenant general. Balabin died on 21 October 1856 and was buried at the Lazarev Cemetery of Alexandra Neva Monastery in St. Petersburg.

BALABIN (Balabin II), Stepan Fedorovich (b. 1763- date of death unknown; removed from rosters on 31 May 1818) was born to a priest family at the Don Cossack *stanitsa* Razdorskoe. His military service began on 21 March 1778 and, eleven years later, he was promoted to sotnik (15 September 1789). He participated in various campaigns in the North Caucasus region from 1778-1785 and then served in Russo-Turkish War of 1787-1791; he injured his arm at the battle of Large in 1788 and took a wound to the foot during the assault on Ismail in 1790. In 1792, Balabin transferred to Poland in order to fight the Polish insurgents. From 1796-1797, he participated in the Persian Campaign and took part in the capture of the fortress of Derbent in Daghestan. In 1806, he was given command of the elite Ataman Cossack Regiment.

Balabin participated in the 1807 Campaign in Poland and distinguished himself at Hanau for which he was honored with the Order of St. George (4th class, 17 August 1807). In 1809, he transferred to the Danube Valley and distinguished himself at the battle of Rassevat, receiving colonelcy on 5 February 1810. In 1812, Balabin served in Ataman Platov's Cossack Corps attached to the 2nd Western Army. He covered the retreat of the 2nd Western Army and fought at Mir and Romanovo. After the junction of the two Russian armies, Balabin fought at Borodino and Tarutino. During the French retreat, he harassed the French forces and nearly captured Napoleon at Maloyaroslavets. He became ill in December 1812 and remained at Kovno, commanding a Cossack brigade. On 31 October 1813, he took command of the regiment later designated as the Balabin's Cossack Regiment. He participated in the 1814 Campaign and fought at Soissons earning the Order of St. George (3rd class, 14 February 1814) and promotion to major general on 15 January 1815 with seniority dating from 1 December 1813.

BALASHOV, Alexander Dmitryevich (b. 24 July 1770, Moscow – d. 20 May 1837, Kronshdadt) was born to a noble family in the Tula *gubernia*. He enlisted in the Life Guard Preobrazhensk Regiment on 15 October 1775. On 12 September 1781, he was accepted as a page to the Imperial court. Ten years later, he was conferred the rank of lieutenant and received command of a company in the Life Guard Izmailovsk Regiment. In September 1798, Balashov was appointed commander of the Kazan Garrison Regiment and the following year he was promoted to major general and appointed the commandant of the Omsk Fortress and chef of the Omsk Garrison Regiment.

Balashov retired in February 1800 but returned on 31 November of the same year to become the Military Governor of Revel (8 December) and chef of the Combined Garrison Regiment comprised of the battalions of the Revel and Pernovsk Garrison Regiments. In July 1801, this unit was disbanded and Balashov was appointed chef of the Revel Garrison Regiment. Balashov served as the Military Governor of Revel until 29 December 1802. In September 1804, he was appointed chef of the Troitsk Musketeer Regiment, but was then discharged in October of the same year. He returned to the service within a few weeks and was appointed head of the Moscow Police on 10 January 1805. While serving at this position, he was also briefly appointed general kriegscommissar in 1807. In April 1808, Balashov was appointed head of the St. Petersburg Police. For his exemplary service at these positions, he was promoted to general adjutant on 14 February 1809 and was appointed the Military Governor of St. Petersburg. Furthermore, on 9 April 1809, he took promotion to lieutenant general and, the next year, he became a member of the State Council (13 January) and the Minister of Police (July 1810).

In June 1812, Balashov was dispatched on a diplomatic mission to Napoleon and later executed various diplomatic assignments as well, including negotiations with Murat in Naples in 1814. In 1819, the Ministry of Police was abolished and Balashov was appointed the Governor General of the Orel, Tula, Ryazan, Tambov and Voronezh *gubernia*s. He was promoted to general of infantry on 24 December 1823. In June 1832, he became member of the Council of War of the Ministry of War. However, he retired two years later on 5 October 1834. Balashov died on 20 May 1837 and was buried at the village of Pokrovskoe in the Petersburg *gubernia*.

BALATUKOV, Cyril Matveyevich (Kaya Bey) (b. 1774, Crimea — date of death unknown; excluded from rosters on 10 September 1827) descended from a Tatar noble family. On 12 October 1786, he enrolled into the Corps of Foreign Fellow Believers and was assigned as a lieutenant to the Sebastopol Infantry Regiment on 15 July 1793. From 1798-1800, he took part in naval operations in the Mediterranean, including the capture of Corfu. He retired with a rank of major in January 1802 and served as the leader of the Simferopol nobility. He returned to military service in 1806 and participated in the campaign in Poland. On 1 July 1807, he received command of the Simferopol Horse Tatar Regiment. In 1812, he served in Ataman Platov's Cossack Corps and fought at Mir, Romanovo, Borodino and Tarutino (received the Order of St. George 4th class, 12 January 1813). In 1813, he served in the siege of Danzig and earned promotion to colonel on 30 May, and to major general on 19 December 1813.

BALK, Mikhail Dmitryevich (b. 1764, Kursk *gubernia* — d. 19 December 1818, Moghilev) descended from an Austrian noble family. He began military service in the Kursk Infantry Regiment on 12 January 1776 and was promoted to ensign on 5 January 1783. He became a sub-lieutenant in 1786 and a lieutenant on 3 July 1787. He participated in the campaigns against the Turks in 1788 and the Swedes in 1790, although his regiment was kept in reserve and Balk did not take part in any battles. He was promoted to captain in 1791 and transferred to the St. Petersburg Dragoon Regiment. Three years later, Balk was sent to Poland to suppress the Polish uprising and fought at Borun (17 June), Novoselok (18 June), Lyda (5 July), Vilna (19 July) and Pogulyanka (11 August). For his actions, he was promoted to second major. Two year later, he was promoted to premier major, but was then discharged on 15 February 1797.

Balk returned to service in April 1802 as a lieutenant colonel of the St. Petersburg Dragoon Regiment. In May 1805, he was promoted to colonel and participated in the campaign against the French in 1805, fighting at Wischau and Austerlitz, where he was wounded in the neck. In 1806-1807, Balk served in the advance and rear guards and took part in numerous rear-guard actions as well as the battles at Eylau, Guttstadt and Heilsberg. At Friedland, he was seriously wounded when a cannonball splinter fractured his skull. He was fortunate to survive this horrible wound and wore a silver plate in his skull for the rest of life. For his actions, he was promoted to major general (24 December 1807), given a substantial allowance, awarded the Order of St. George (4th class) and appointed chef of the Riga Dragoons Regiment (23 January 1808.) During the Russo-Swedish War, Balk was dispatched to Friedrixhamn but did not participate in the military operations. In 1809, he was attached to the Russian army operating against Austria, but did not fight once again. The same year, he was appointed commander of cavalry brigade comprised of Riga and St. Petersburg Dragoon regiments.

In 1812, Balk commanded the 3rd Brigade of the 1st Cavalry Division of Wittgenstein's Corps. He provided crucial intelligence on French movements prior to the battle of Klyastitsy, where Balk commanded ten infantry battalions and his cavalry. For his actions, he received the Order of St. Anna (1st class). He then commanded Wittgenstein's right wing advance guard and fought at Polotsk on 17 August, earning the Order of St. George (3rd class) for his actions at this combat. During the French retreat, Balk led Wittgenstein's advance guard and engaged the French at Yurievich (16 October) but was wounded in the head in the fighting near village of Gromy on 18 October. He was decorated with the Order of St. Vladimir (2nd class) for his actions.

Balk recuperated for the rest of campaign and returned to service in late 1813. He participated in the Invasion of France in 1814 and fought at Laon and St. Dizier. For his conduct, he received the diamond signs of the Order of St. Anna and was promoted to lieutenant general on 13 June 1815. In September 1815, he was appointed commander of the 1st Horse Jager Division. He was discharged with full pension on 29 January 1816, but returned to service in the next May and continued commanding this division until his death on 19 December 1818.

BALLA, Adam Ivanovich (b. 1764 — d. 17 August 1812) was born to a Greek family from Morea. He was taken to Russia at the age of ten and enrolled in the Artillery and Engineer Corps College for Foreigners on 11 August 1778. After graduation in 1782, he began service as a lieutenant in the Aleksopol Infantry Regiment on 13 July 1782 and went on to fight the Turks in the Crimea. On 1 August 1786, he transferred to the 4th Battalion of the Lifland Jager Regiment and promoted to captain. He participated in Potemkin's campaigns against the Turks and distinguished himself at Ochakov (promoted to second major) on 17 December 1788 and Ismail (promoted to premier major) on 22 December 1790; he also received golden crosses for both these combats.

Balla next served under Suvorov in Poland in 1792-1793 and commanded the 4th battalion of Lifland Jagers. In November 1797, he was appointed commander of the 12th Jager Regiment. In 1798, he was promoted to colonel. Between 18 January and 19 May 1799, he also served as chef of the 12th Jager Regiment and, in March 1800, he was appointed commander of the 11th Jager Regiment. On 13 March 1799, he received the rank of major general. In 1806–1811, Balla served in the Army of Moldavia, participating in numerous battles against the Turks and earning the Order of St. Anna (1st class). In 1812, Balla commanded the 3rd Brigade of the 7th Division of General Dorokhov's 6th Corps and took part in the battle of Smolensk on 16 August 1812, where he was mortally wounded. He died the following day and was buried at Smolensk. In his career, Balla also received the Order of St. Vladimir (3rd class) and a golden sword for courage.

Two other Ballas fought in the Napoleonic Wars. **Alexander Ivanovich Balla,** was promoted to a colonel on 12 December 1803 and commanded the Olonetsk Musketeer Regiment in 16 November 1799- 9 July 1807; **Alexander Fedorovich Balla** commanded the Kherson Grenadier Regiment from 16 August 1803 – 5 September 1806 and served as chef of the Neyshlodt Musketeer Regiment from 5 September 1806 – 4 July 1815.

BALMAIN, Antoine Bogdanovich (b. 1741 — d. 15 October 1790) descended from the Scotch family Ramsay of Balmain, which had left Scotland in the 17th century and immigrated to Russia. He enlisted as a sergeant in the Life Guard Izmailovsk Regiment in 1751 and rose to ensign in 1758. In 1761, he transferred as a lieutenant colonel to the army and served as adjutant to Field Marshal Razumovsky. He became colonel on 10 January 1769 and commanded the Rostov Carabinier Regiment in 1770. During the Russo-Turkish War in 1770-1772, he fought at Bender and Kafa. He was promoted to major general on 28 March 1774 and transferred to the Ukraine. In 1776, he served in the Crimea and, for his outstanding conduct, Balmain received both the Orders of St. Anna (1st class, 9 July 1777) and of St. Alexander of Neva (7 July 1783) and promotion to lieutenant general in 1780. He directed the Infantry Cadet Corps in 1784 and served as the Governor General of the Kursk and Orlov *gubernia*s in 1786. During the second Russo-Turkish War in 1789-1790, he commanded a corps in the Caucasus but became seriously ill and died at Georgievsk on 12 October 1790.

His one son, **Alexander Antonovich Balmain**, began service in the Life Guard Horse Regiment, but he was reduced in ranks for beating a police officer in March 1801. After Alexander's accession to the throne, he joined the diplomatic corps and served on missions to Sardinia in 1801, Naples in 1803 and Vienna in 1810. In late 1812, he was appointed to the Russian embassy in London before returning to military service with a rank of lieutenant colonel in April 1813. Balmain took part in the battles at Gross-Beeren, Dennewitz (received the Order of St. Vladimir, 4th class), Kassel (received the Order of St. Anna, 2nd class), Hanau and other lesser actions. In September 1815, he was appointed the Russian representative to St. Helena during Napoleon's exile to this island. He remained on the island for four years but had to leave it because of deteriorating health in 1820. Returning to Russia, he was appointed to the Russian embassy in London in 1822-1826. During the Russo-Turkish War in 1828-1829, he served in the headquarters, was promoted to major general and awarded the Order of St. Anna (2nd class). He participated in the suppression of the Polish uprising in 1831 and retired in 1837. He died on 29 April 1848 in St. Petersburg. He left interesting memoir on Napoleon's life on St. Helena, "The Reports of Count Balmain, Russian Commissioner on the Island of St. Helena, 1816-1820." Balmain's second son, **Major General Karl Antonovich Balmain**, was appointed chef of the 49th Jager Regiment on 29 January 1811 and chef of the Sofia Infantry Regiment on 24 March 1811. He died on 9 May 1812.

BARATINSKY, Ilia Andreyevich (b. 1776 – d. 1837) was educated in the Naval Cadet Corps and served as a guard marine in the Baltic Fleet during the Russo-Swedish War of 1788-1790, fighting at Gogland, Eland and Vyborg. After the war, he served in Arkhangelsk and Kronshtadt from 1792-1793, sailed in the Baltic and North Seas in 1793-1794 and joined the British fleet in 1795, participating in the naval battle at St. Vincent. He was promoted to captain lieutenant in 1797, and returning to Russia, was appointed flügel adjutant in 1798 and commanded the ships-of-the-line "*Parmen*" and "*Yaroslavl*." In 1799-1800, he sailed in the North Sea and evacuated Russian troops from Netherlands. Baratinsky was awarded the Order of St. John of Jerusalem and rose to captain (1st class) in March 1801. In 1802-1805, he commanded a galley flotilla in the Gulf of Finland. In 1806-1807, he commanded the ship-of-the-line "*St. Peter*" in Admiral Senyavin's squadron in the Adriatic Sea, blockaded Raguse and Dalmatia and took part in naval actions at Tenedos, Dardanelle and Mt. Athons. After Tilsit, he opposed the surrender of the territories in the Adriatic Sea to the French and was recalled in 1808. He was promoted to rear admiral in 1811 but retired in December 1813. His older brother, Lieutenant General **Peter Andreyevich Baratinsky** served in the Naval Cadet Corps in 1791-1813, taking part in the naval actions against the Swedes in the Baltic Sea in 1808-1809 before receiving appointment to the Senate.

BARCLAY de TOLLY, Mikhail Bogdanovich (Michael Andreas) (b. 24 December 1757, Lithuania — d. 26 May 1818, Insterburg, Prussia) descended from an ancient Scottish family resettled to Lifland in the 17th century. He enlisted in the Pskov Carabineer Regiment on 13 May 1767 and rose to the rank of cornet by May 1778. In 1783-1790, Barclay served as an adjutant to various senior officers. He became a second lieutenant in 1783, lieutenant in 1786, captain in 1788, major in 1788 and lieutenant colonel in 1794. In 1794, he was appointed commander of a battalion of the Estland Jager Corps. On 29 May 1797, Barclay became commander of the 4th Jager Regiment, and on 29 January 1799, he became chef of the same unit. After the military re-organization in 1800, he served as chef of the 3rd Jager Regiment. Barclay de Tolly participated in the Russo-Turkish War of 1787-1791, Russo-Swedish War of 1788-1790, and the Polish Campaign of 1794. For his actions against the Poles, he received the Order of St. George (4th class). He was promoted to colonel on 18 March 1798 and to major general on 13 March 1799.

Barclay de Tolly highly distinguished himself in the 1806-1807 Campaigns in Poland, while commanding the rearguard under Prince Peter Bagration. He fought at Pultusk (earned the Order of St. George, 3rd class), Hoff and Eylau, where he was seriously wounded in the right hand. For his heroic actions at Eylau, he received promotion to lieutenant general on 21 April 1807 and took command of the 6th Division. He returned to active service in late 1807 and participated in the Russo-Swedish War of 1808-1809. In 1808, he occupied the Savolax Region and Kuopio and, in 1809, he distinguished himself during the crossing of the frozen Gulf of Bothnia near Kvarken and in the subsequent capture of the town of Umeo in Sweden. For his actions, Barclay was promoted to general of infantry on 1 April 1809 and appointed commander-in-chief of the Russian forces in Finland.

On 30 January 1810, Barclay de Tolly became the Minister of War and launched a series of important military reforms in the Russian army while also planning for Napoleon's invasion of Russia. On 31 March 1812, he was appointed the commander-in-chief of the 1st Western Army. De Tolly led this force in the during the retreat before Napoleon's invasion of Russia that summer, fighting at Ostrovno, Vitebsk, and Smolensk. He was responsible for conceiving and carrying out the policy of retreat during the initial stages of the campaign, despite the bitter opposition of the majority of the Russian officers (Bagration being a prominent example) and the public at large. Under intense public pressure, Emperor Alexander finally replaced him with General Mikhail Kutuzov in August 1812. Barclay distinguished himself at Borodino, where five horses were shot under him and nine of his twelve adjutants were wounded around him. For these actions, he received the Order of St. George (2nd class).

Barclay retired because of poor health and public pressure in October 1812, but returned to the army in 1813 to command the 3rd Western Army (14 February 1813) before becoming the commander-in-chief of the Russo-Prussian armies on 29 May 1813. Late that year, he fought at Koenigswarta, Kulm (awarded the Order of

St. George, 1st class, 31 March 1814) and Leipzig (received title of count, 28 October 1813). Barclay de Tolly then commanded the Russian forces during the invasion of France. After the capture of Paris, he was promoted to field marshal (31 March 1814) and was conferred a title of prince of the Russian Empire (11 September 1815). In 1815-1816, he commanded the 1st Army but retired because of poor health in April 1818. He died at Insterburg on 26 May 1818 and was buried at his estate in Estland.

Barclay was awarded almost every Russian military decoration, including the Orders of St. Andrew, of St Vladimir (1st class), of St. Alexander of Neva with diamonds, of St. Anna (1st class) and of St. Catherine. He also received the Prussian Orders of Black and Red Eagles (1st class), the Swedish Order of the Sword (1st class), the Austrian Order of Maria Theresa and the French Order of St. Louis and Legion of Honor, the British Order of Bath (1st class), the Dutch Order of Wilhelm (1st class) and the Saxon Order of St. Henry (1st class).

Barclay de Tolly was one of the best Russian commanders of the Napoleonic Wars. He excelled on the tactical level commanding units in Poland and Finland, and demonstrated excellent strategic abilities during the 1812-1814 Campaigns. Unfortunately, his abilities were ignored because of his alleged German origins and unpopular policy of retreat in 1812. For almost two hundred years, Russian and Soviet historians have ignored his contributions and concentrated primarily on Field Marshal Mikhail Kutuzov who, in many respects, simply continued de Tolly's strategy against Napoleon in 1812. However, interest in Barclay de Tolly has revived recently, and several volumes have been published on his involvement in the Napoleonic campaigns.

BARDAKOV, Peter Grigorievich (b. 1756 — d. 16 January 1821, Moscow) was born to a noble family in the Kostroma *gubernia*. He began service as a corporal the Life Guard Izmailovsk Regiment on 2 June 1767 and rose to sergeant on 13 January 1771, to ensign on 13 January 1778 and to lieutenant on 13 January 1779. Three years later, he transferred as a lieutenant colonel to the Moscow Infantry Regiment. On 20 March 1787, he was assigned to form a battalion of the Ekaterinoslavl Jager Corps. He participated in the Russo-Turkish War of 1787-1791 and fought at Focsani and Macin. For his actions, he was awarded the Order of St. George (4th class) on 25 April 1789 and a few weeks later received promotion to colonel on 2 May 1789. The same month, he was assigned to form the Tula Infantry Regiment. In April 1793, he transferred to the Ingermanland Carabineer Regiment and participated in the campaign in Poland. For his actions against the Poles, he was awarded the Order of St. George (3rd class) on 26 September 1794.

In the spring of 1797, Bardakov was appointed chef of the Kazan Cuirassier Regiment and rose to major general on 1 May. The following year, he was conferred the rank of lieutenant general (29 October), but was discharged on 18 February 1799. He returned to service only in May 1801 and served as the Commandant of Vilna. He was dismissed from this position in October 1801 and discharged from service in January 1804. Bardakov returned to the military only in 1812, when he organized the Kostroma *opolchenye*. In 1813, he led this force in the sieges of Breslavl and Glogau. The following October, the Kostroma *opolchenye* was disbanded and Bardakov returned to his estate, where he remained for the rest of his life.

BARTOLOMEY, Aleksey Ivanovich (Baltazar Ludwig Alexis) (b. 28 June 1784 – d. 6 January 1839) was born to a Lifland noble family. He enlisted in the Arensburg Garrison Battalion on 30 April 1798 and soon rose to an ensign. In January 1803, he transferred to the 3rd Jager Regiment and became adjutant to Barclay de Tolly. He participated in the 1805 Campaign in Moravia and 1806-1807 Campaigns in Poland, distinguishing himself at Pultusk, Eylau (received cross), Heilsberg and Friedland. In February 1808, Bartolomey transferred as a captain to the Life Guard Jager Regiment and took part in Russo-Swedish War of 1808, fighting at Joris and Kuopio. In October 1808, he became adjutant to the Prince of Holstein-Oldenburg who served as the governor of Revel.

In 1812, Bartolomey served as an adjutant to both Barclay de Tolly and Kutuzov at the battles of Vitebsk, Smolensk, Borodino, Tarutino, and Maloyaroslavets. On 15 September 1813, he was promoted to flügel adjutant to Emperor Alexander. He took part in the battle of Leipzig and was promoted to major general on 20 October 1813. Bartolomey then participated in the Invasion of France and fought at Soissons, Laon and Paris. In September 1814, he became commander of a brigade of the 14th Division, but retired the next year because of poor health. He soon returned to service and was given command of the 4th Division. In February 1826, he was appointed commander of the 9th Division and promoted to lieutenant general on 3 September 1826.

Bartolomey participated in the Russo-Turkish War of 1828-1829 and fought at Shumla, where he was wounded in the head. Commanding the 10th Division beginning on 16 October 1829, he took part in the campaign against the Polish insurgents in 1830-1831. On 14 April 1833, Bartolomey was appointed commander of the 8th Division but he retired because of poor health on 27 October 1834. He died on 6 January 1840. Bartolomey is buried at Volkovo Lutheran Cemetery in St. Petersburg. During his military service, he was awarded the Orders of St. Anna (1st class) with a crown, of St. Vladimir (2nd class), of St. George (3rd class), Medal of Military Merit (*Voennoe Dostointsvo*) (2nd class), two golden swords for courage, the Prussian Order of Red Eagle (2nd class) and Pour le Merite, the Austrian Order of Leopold (2nd class) and the Bavarian Order of Maximilian Joseph (3rd class).

BASHILOV, Alexander Alexandrovich (b. 11 September 1777, Glukhovo – d. 12 January 1848, Moscow) was born to a wealthy Russian noble family; his father Alexander Bashilov was a prominent official under Catherine II. Bashilov began his career as a page to Catherine II and kamer-page to Paul I. In February 1798, he enlisted as a lieutenant in the Life Guard Preobrazhensk Regiment and, the following year, he was promoted to colonel (2 November) and became flügel adjutant to Paul (5 November). He served on various diplomatic missions to Austria, France and Italy. However, Bashilov was reduced in ranks for imprudent behavior on 21 February 1802 and transferred to the Navaginsk Musketeer Regiment. He retired on 12 December 1803, but returned to service to take command of the Tambov Musketeer Regiment on 15 December 1806.

Bashilov took part in the 1807 Campaign in Poland and in the 1809 Campaign against Austria. He then transferred to the Danube Valley against the Turks and commanded a brigade of the 18th Division. He distinguished himself during the assault on Bazardjik and was promoted to major general on 26 June 1810. For his actions at Shumla, he received the Order of St. Anna (1st class). In 1812, Bashilov served as the chef of the Tambov Infantry Regiment attached to the 1st Brigade of the 18th Division of the 3rd Reserve Army of Observation. He participated in battle at Gorodechna but then retired on 27 May 1813. Bashilov returned to service in 1825 and was appointed to the staff of the military governor of Moscow. He participated in the Russo-Turkish War of 1828-1829, serving as head of the mobile supply train of the 2nd Army. He was later appointed to the Senate and promoted to privy counselor (equivalent of the rank of lieutenant general in military service) in January 1830. In 1831-1832, Bashilov directed the Commission on Construction in Moscow.

BASHUTSKY, Paul Jakovlevich (b. 28 August 1771 — d. 23 January 1836, St. Petersburg) descended from a Polish family of Bakhovsky, who immigrated to Russia in 1709. He enlisted in the 3rd Marine Battalion on 24 June 1786 and took part in the Russo-Swedish War of 1788-1790, fighting at Seskar and Vyborg. In June 1796, he transferred as a lieutenant to the Gatchina Troops and, on 20 November of the same year, was again transferred to the Life Guard Izmailovsk Regiment. Bashutsky was promoted to colonel on 9 September 1799 and to major general on 8 September 1803. In December 1803, he was appointed commandant of St. Petersburg.

During the 1807 Campaign, Bashutsky commanded a brigade consisting of the Life Guard Semeyonovsk and Izmailovsk Regiments and he led them at Heilsberg and Friedland, earning the Order of St. George (3rd class, 2 June 1808). In February 1808, he became commander of the Life Guard Izmailovsk Regiment. Bashutsky retained this position for the next three years before taking command of the 25th Division on 10 November 1811. During Napoleon's invasion, he was recruiting and training reserve battalions. In 1813, he commanded the 1st Reserve Infantry Corps and took part in the siege of Modlin and Danzig. In March 1814, General Veliaminov replaced him and Bashutsky returned to his previous position of the Commandant of St. Petersburg. He was promoted to lieutenant general on 11 September 1816. Bashutsky took part in suppression of the Decembrist Uprising in December 1825 and was promoted to general adjutant. Three years later, he became general of infantry on 7 July 1828. After 1832, he served in the Ministry of War. During his service, Bashutsky was awarded the Orders of St. Anna with diamonds (1st class), of St. Alexander of Neva with diamonds, of St. Vladimir (1st class), of St. John of Jerusalem, of St. George (3rd class) and a medal "For XLV Years of Distinguished Service."

BAUMGARTEN, Ivan Evstafievich (Hans Nils Gustav) (b. 19 May 1782, Kerro, Estland — d. 2 May 1846, Moscow) descended from a Swedish family living in the Estland *gubernia*. He enlisted in the Revel Garrison Regiment on 11 November 1791 and was promoted to ensign in March 1797. In October 1793, he transferred as a captain to the Servsk Musketeer Regiment. On 15 May 1806, he rose to major and transferred to the Permsk Musketeer Regiment. He then participated in the 1806-1807 Campaigns in Poland and was wounded in the right foot at Eylau. After recuperating, he took part in the 1808-1809 Campaigns in Finland and distinguished himself at Oravais, for which he received the Order of St. George (4th class) on 1 June 1808, and Karstule, where he was seriously wounded. After he spent the next year recuperating, Baumgarten was appointed commander of the Permsk Musketeer Regiment on 22 May 1810.

In 1812, Baumgarten's regiment was attached to the 5th Division of Wittgenstein's Corps. He took part in actions at Wilkomir, Jakubovo, Klyastitsy and at Polotsk, where he was again seriously wounded. He returned in time to take part in the capture of Polotsk in October and took another wound in the left foot. However, Baumgarten remained with his regiment and fought at Chashniky and on the Berezina River. For his actions, he was promoted to a lieutenant colonel on 30 October 1812 and to a colonel on 23 February 1813. In the Saxon Campaign, he took part in the occupation of Warsaw and Berlin and fought at Lutzen, where he continued commanding his regiment despite being wounded in his right foot. Hit again in the right hand while defending the crossing on the Elbe River, the rather unlucky Baumgarten spent the rest of the campaign at the hospital. He returned to service in late 1813 and took part in the capture of Cologne. In 1814, he fought at Strasburg, Nojan, Troyes, Bars-sur-Aube, Labrussel (received a golden sword for courage), Ligny, Arcis sur Aube, Le Fère Champenoise and Paris (promoted to major general on 13 June 1815, seniority from 30 March 1814).

After the war, Baumgarten returned with his regiment to Russia but was recalled to France in 1815, where he commanded the 2nd Brigade of the 6th Division. He retired with a full pension because of poor health on 21 January 1821, but returned to service on 20 October 1834 and served as the Commandant of Nikolaev. He was discharged with a pension in September 1836. During his career, Baumgarten received the Orders of St. Stanislaus (1st class), of St. Anna (3rd class) with diamonds, of St. George (4th class), of St. Vladimir (3rd class), the Prussian "Pour le Merite" and a golden sword for courage. Another **Baumgarten, Karl Ivanovich** led the Muromsk Musketeer Regiment from 31 August 1804 - 9 July 1807; Karl rose to major general on 19 August 1810 and served as chef of the Crimea Musketeer Regiment in 9 July 1807 – 22 January 1812.

BEDRIAGA (Bedriaga I), Mikhail Grigorievich (b. 1780 – date of death unknown) was born to a noble family from Voronezh *gubernia* and enlisted as a cadet in the Akhtyrsk Hussar Regiment in 1793. In 1794, he was promoted to cornet and served in Poland, fighting at Skalmerzh, Roslovitse, Mstetz, Maciejowice, Kobylka and Praga. In 1806-1807, he commanded 1st Squadron of the Akhtyrsk Hussar Regiment and distinguished himself at Pultusk (received the Order of St. Anna, (3rd class) and a golden saber). In 1809, he took part in the campaign in Galicia and was promoted to a rotmistr.

During the Russian Campaign, his regiment was attached to the 2nd Western Army and Bedriaga took part in actions at Mir, Romanovo and Saltanovka. At Borodino, he was seriously wounded in the head and in recognition for his service Bedriaga received promotion to major and was decorated with the Order of St. Vladimir (4th class). Recuperating from his wound, Bedriaga transferred to the Life Guard Horse Jager Regiment in 1814 but had to retire because of poor health in 1824. His father **Gregory Vasilievich Bedriaga** commanded the Akhtyrsk Hussar Regiment between 26 July 1799 and 27 April 1804. He served as chef of the Chuguev Cossack Regiment in 4 April 1805 – 18 January 1808 and was promoted to major general on 5 June 1807. His two brothers **Nicholas and Sergey Bedriaga** served in the regiment during the Napoleonic Wars as well.

BEGICHEV, Ivan Matveyevich (b. 25 February 1766 – d. 4 January 1816) was born to a noble family in the Ryazan *gubernia*. He enlisted in the artillery in February 1772. Three years later, after promotion to sergeant, he transferred to the Bombardier Artillery Regiment in 1778. Three years later, he was appointed shtyk junker to his father Matvei Begichev, who was a lieutenant general of artillery. In 1786, Begichev received promotion to lieutenant and transferred to the 2nd Fusilier Regiment, and, in 1787, he became a captain and served as adjutant to his father. In 1788-1791, he took part in the Russo-Turkish War and fought at Akkerman, Bender and Macin. He then served in the Polish Campaign of

1794 and took part in the assault on Praga (received a cross). For his courage, he was promoted to major and appointed to the Kiev Artillery Garrison. In 1796, he transferred to General Brevern's Artillery Battalion. He was promoted to colonel on 29 March 1798. The next year, he was promoted to major general (10 October) and appointed chef of the 1st Siege Artillery Battalion. In March-October 1800, he also served as chef of the 1st Artillery Regiment.

Begichev retired on 19 October 1800 after a disagreement with General Aleksey Arakcheyev, but he returned to service on 29 May 1801 and worked at the Kazan Gunpowder Factory. In 1806, he was sent to the Army of Moldavia and participated in the landing operation at Trapezund on the southern Black Sea Coast. He then participated in the siege of Izmail, where he was wounded. He retired again only to return in 1812 to command the 2nd Company of the St. Petersburg *opolchenye*. He fought at Polotsk, Chashniki and Berezina receiving the Order of St. George (15 January 1813). In 1813, he served in the siege of Modlin and Danzig and then retired for the final time.

BEKHLY, Fedor Matveevich (b. 1759 — date of death unknown) descended from a Bohemian noble family. He began service in the Austrian army, but then joined the Russian service on 12 April 1779 and initially served as a second-class guide (*kolonovozhatii*) with the main headquarters. On 12 August of the same year, he enrolled in the Artillery and Engineer Cadet Corps, and after its graduation, he was appointed as a first-class column guide (*kolonovozhatii*). Bekhly next advanced to lieutenant on 5 January 1783 and took part in the Russo-Swedish War of 1788-1790, fighting at Neschlodt, Mikkeli and Parasalmi. He distinguished himself during the capture of the Swedish positions on the western bank of the Saimaa Lake, for which he received a promotion to second major.

In 1794, Bekhly fought against the Polish insurgents at Brest and Vilna. Three years later, he joined the Engineer Corps and took part in repair works on the fortifications along the Baltic Sea. Promoted to colonel on 16 January 1799, Bekhly received the Order of St. John of Jerusalem and continued his service in the Engineer Corps for the next nine years. During the Russo-Swedish War of 1808, he took part in the sieges of Sveaborg and Svartholm; during the following year, he supervised construction of fortifications at Revel and was awarded the Order of St. George (4th class, 8 December 1809). In 1810, he was sent to the Army of Moldavia and fought at Shumla and Ruse, where he was wounded in right foot. On 1812, he served in the headquarters of the Army of Danube and fought at Borisov and on the Berezina. In early 1813, Bekhly took part in minor operations and was promoted to major general on 10 April 1813. He then took part in the sieges of Modlin and Glogau. In 1814, he was appointed commander of the Caucasian Engineer District and served in the Caucasus for two years. Recalled on 31 January 1818, Bekhly returned to the Engineer Department of the Ministry of War. He retired on 6 June 1821 with a full pension.

BELLI, Genrikh (Henry) Genrikhovich (date of birth unknown — d. 14 June 1826) descended from a British noble family and joined the Russian navy in 1783. He served on the Black Sea Fleet in 1787-1798 and fought the Turks at Fidonisi (14 July 1788), Kerch Straits (19 July 1790), Hadjibey (8-9 September 1790) and Kaliakria (11 August 1791, received the Order of St. Vladimir, 4th class). In 1798, he served under Admiral Fedor Ushakov in the Mediterranean Sea and took part in actions at Corfu and the Ionian Islands (received the Order of St. Anna, 2nd class).

Belli became a lieutenant captain in 1799, commanded frigate "*Schastlivii*" and took part in operations against the French in southern Italy, including capture of Foggia (awarded the Order of St. John of Jerusalem), Naples (received the Order of St. Anna, 1st class, and the Neapolitan Order of St. Ferdinand), Castel de Nuovo and Capua. He remained in Naples for two years and, returning to Sebastopol in 1803, Belli was promoted to captain (1st class). In 1805-1807, he served under Admiral Senyavin in the Adriatic Sea and occupied Cattaro and other local islands. Sailing back to Russia, Senyavin's fleet was blockaded in Lisbon and detained by the British.

Returning to St. Petersburg, Belli was disgraced because of his British origins and exiled to Saratov in 1808-1812. During the Russian Campaign, he commanded the ship-of-the-line "*Asia*" in the Black Sea Fleet. Ultimately, Belli rose to the rank of rear admiral in 1816 and commanded the 3rd Fleet Division (*flotskaia divizia*).

BELLEGARDE, Alexander Alexandrovich (b. 1774 – date of death unknown; excluded from rosters as deceased on 22 June 1816) descended from a French noble family. He served in the French royal artillery but then fled France during the Revolution and entered Russian service on 25 December 1793. After becoming a captain in the 2nd Bombardier Regiment, Bellegarde took part in the campaign against the Poles in 1794, earning a cross for assault on Praga. In the spring of 1799, he was promoted to colonel (3 April) and then participated in Suvorov's campaign in Italy; although his participation in this war is still unclear. In 1805, he took part in the expedition to Hanover. His participation in 1806-1807 Campaigns is often cited, but could not be verified.

During the Russo-Swedish War, Bellegarde commanded the 21st Artillery Brigade and took part in the capture of Sveaborg, for which he was promoted to major general (28 March 1808) and received the Order of St. George (4th class) on 22 April 1808. Bellegarde then served as the commandant of Sveaborg between 29 September 1808 and 9 June 1810. In the fall of 1810, he was appointed artillery commander of the Finish Corps. In 1812, he fought at Riga and Polotsk and participated in minor actions during the French retreat. In 1813, he became seriously ill and was hospitalized at Koenigsberg. After recuperating, he commanded the light artillery reserves in the Army of Reserve. During his career, Bellegarde was also decorated with the Order of St. Anna with diamonds (2nd class) and Order of St. Vladimir (3rd class).

BELOGRADSKY, Gregory Grigorievich (b. 1773, Poltava — d. 21 February 1857, Konevetz) was born to a noble family in the Poltava *gubernia*. He graduated from the Cadet Corps on 16 January 1790 and joined the Ekaterinoslavl Cuirassier Regiment with the rank of sub-lieutenant. He served against the Turks in 1787-1791 and the Poles in 1794. In 1805, Belogradsky was appointed to the Duben Supply Depot and, three years later, he joined General Buxhöwden's staff during the Russo-Swedish War of 1808-1809. In 1810, he served under General Barclay de Tolly in the Ministry of War. The following year, he was appointed to the Life Guard Preobrazhensk Regiment (27 September) and promoted to colonel (7 November).

During the 1812 Campaign, Belogradsky supervised the hospitals and in 1813-1814, he served as the hospital inspector in Germany and France. He was promoted to major general on 17 April 1814. After the Napoleonic Wars, Belogradsky served on various minor positions in the army before being appointed chair of the Field Audit [*polevoi auditoriat*] of the 1st Army on 15 November 1828. The next year, he attained the rank of lieutenant general on 26 April. He became member of the General Audit of the Ministry of War on 12 July 1835. He became general of infantry on 29 March 1845; however, in February 1849, he was discharged for inappropriate behavior and banished to the Konevets Monastery on Ladoga Lake. He died two years later and was buried at Konevetz. During his military career, Belogradsky received the Orders of St. Anna with crown (1st class), of

St. George (4th class), of St. Vladimir (2nd class), a medal "L Years of Distinguished service" as well as several foreign decorations that included the Polish Order of the White Eagle, the Prussian Pour le Merite and the French Legion of Honor and Order of Lily.

BENARDOS, Panteleimon Egorovich (date of birth unclear, c. 1761-1763, Moreya, Greece – d. 1839) descended from a Greek noble family. He enrolled in the Greek Gymnasium of the Artillery and Engineer Cadet Corps in September 1775, and after graduation, was promoted to ensign in the Schlüsseburg Infantry Regiment on 27 June 1781. Five years later, he transferred as a lieutenant to the 1st Battalion of the Ekaterinoslavl Jager Corps. He took part in the Russo-Turkish War in 1787-1791 and fought at Ochakov (received a golden cross), Kaushani, Akkerman, Bender and Ismail (promoted to second major). In 1792-1794, he participated in the suppression of the Polish uprising. In 1802, Benardos was appointed commander of the Nizhegorod Musketeer Regiment (11 October) and later became chef of the Vladimir Musketeer Regiment on 17 March 1806.

Benardos participated in the 1806-1807 Campaigns in Poland and distinguished himself at Golymin (received a golden sword), Eylau (received the Order of St. Anna, 2nd class), Lomitten (received the Order of St. Vladimir, 3rd class), Heilsberg and Friedland (wounded in the left leg, received the diamond signs of Order of St. Anna, 2nd class). For his actions, he was promoted to major general on 24 December 1807. In 1812, Benardos commanded the 1st Brigade of the 18th Division in the 3rd Reserve Army of Observation. He fought at Kobryn, Gorodechnya (received the Order of St. Anna, 1st class), Stakhov and other minor actions. In 1813, Benardos took part in the actions at Thorn, Koenigswartha, Bautzen, Katzbach and received the Order of St. George (3rd class). In 1814, he fought at Brienne and was wounded at La Rothière. He retired because of wounds on 28 March 1816 and spent the rest of his life at his estate.

BENCKENDORFF, Alexander Khristoforovich (Constantine Alexander Karl Wilhelm), (b. 4 July 1781, St. Petersburg – 23 September 1844, aboard the ship "*Hercules*" near Island of Dago) descended from a noble family from Brandenburg that settled in Lifland in late 16th century. His father served in the Russian army, becoming general of infantry and military governor of Riga; his mother, Baroness Anna Schilling von Kanschtadt was close friend of Empress Maria Fedorovna, consort of Paul I. Benckendorff was educated in a Jesuit boarding school and began service in the Life Guard Semeyonovsk Regiment in 1798; he became flügel adjutant to Emperor Paul on 11 January 1799. He participated in operations in the

Caucasus in 1803-1804 and briefly served on the Island of Corfu in 1804.

In 1806-1807, Benckendorff served as a duty officer to General P.A. Tolstoy and received promotion to colonel on 25 February 1807. He distinguished himself at Eylau and took part in negotiations at Tilsit. In 1807-1809, he served in the Russian embassy in Paris. In 1809, he volunteered for service in the Danubian Principalities and commanded cavalry detachments against the Turks. Benckendorff fought at Braila, Silistra and distinguished himself at Ruse in 1811, receiving the Order of St. George (4th class, 7 June 1812). During the 1812 Campaign, he commanded the advance guard in the corps of Generals Winzegorode and Paul Golenischev-Kutuzov. He fought at Velizh, Zvenigorod, Spassk and other minor actions. He was promoted to major general on 28 September 1812 with seniority dating from 8 August 1812. Benckendorff briefly served as commandant of Moscow in October 1812.

During the 1813 Campaign, Benckendorff commanded cavalry detachments and fought at Tempelburg (received the Order of St. George, 3rd class), Furstenwald, Leipzig and Luttich, receiving a golden sword for courage from the Prince-Regent of Britain. In 1814, he distinguished himself at Craonne, Laon and St. Dizier. He was appointed commander of the 2nd Brigade of the 1st Uhlan Division on 10 September 1814; two years later, he became commander of the 2nd Dragoon Division (21 April 1816). He was appointed head of the Independent Guard Corps on 30 March 1819 and promoted to adjutant-general on 3 August 1819.

Benckendorff became very close to Emperors Alexander and Nicholas, who in turn showered him with promotions and awards. In 1821, he was promoted to lieutenant general (2 October) and took command of the 1st Cuirassier Division. On 6 August 1826, he was appointed head of the Gendarmerie Corps and the 3rd Section of His Imperial Majesty's Personal Chancellery; also the same year, he became a senator in addition to his other duties. Benckendorff was one of the closest associates of Nicholas I. He participated in the Russo-Turkish War of 1828-1829 and was promoted to general of cavalry on 3 May 1829. Two years later, he became a member of the State Council and the Cabinet. In 1832, he was conferred the title of the count of the Russian Empire. He died aboard the ship *"Hercules"* returning from Amsterdam to Revel on 23 September 1844.

Benckendorff was one of the most decorated officers in the Russian army. He received almost every Russian awards, including the Orders of St. Andrew with diamonds, of St. Vladimir (1st class), of St. Alexander of Neva with diamonds, of St. Anna with diamonds, of St. George (3rd class), of St. Stanislaus and of Catherine as well as a medal "For 35 Years of Distinguished Service." He was also awarded nine foreign orders – the Prussian Orders of Black and Red Eagles with diamonds and Pour le Merite, the Swedish Orders of the North Star and of the Sword, the Austrian Order of St. Stephan, the Bavarian Order of Humbert, the Saxon Order of White Hawk, the Polish Order of the White Eagle.

BENCKENDORFF, Constantine Khristoforovich (Constantine Friedrich), (b. 11 February 1783, St. Petersburg — d. 18 August 1828, Pravoda) was born to a German noble family in the St. Petersburg; he was the brother of Alexander Benckendorff. Unlike his brother, Constantine chose a diplomatic career and began service in the College on Foreign Affairs in August 1797. In May 1803, he was conferred the rank of kamer-junker and served in various diplomatic missions in the German states. In March 1810, he was appointed secretary to the Russian Embassy in Naples. The next year, he became Russian *chargé d'affaires* in Naples and was promoted to kamerger on 11 September 1812.

During the 1812 Campaign, Benckendorff enlisted in the army on 31 October 1812 and served as a major under General Winzegorode. He took part in the actions at Vyazma, Smolensk and Vilna. In 1813, he fought at Belzig and Leipzig and was promoted to colonel with appointment as flügel adjutant to the Emperor on 29 October 1813. In 1814, he took part in the battles at Soissons, Craonne, Brienne and Paris and was promoted to major general on 9 November 1814. For his actions at Soissons and Craonne, he received the Order of St. George (3rd class) on 22 September 1815. After 1815, he commanded the 2nd Brigade of the 4th Dragoon Division.

In 1820-1826, Benckendorff served as ambassador to Württemberg and Baden. He was promoted to adjutant-general on 26 October 1826 and commanded cavalry detachment during the Russo-Persian War of 1826-1828. He fought at Akzibuk, Bezobdal, Echmiadzin, Djevan-Bulak and along the Araks and Abiran Rivers. For his actions, he was promoted to lieutenant general on 29 May 1827. The next year, Benckendorff joined the Russian army in the Danubian Principalities and commanded a cavalry detachment against the Turks. However, he contracted a serious illness on campaign and died at Pravoda on 18 August 1828. During his career, Benckendorff also received the Orders of St. Anna with diamonds (1st class), of St. Vladimir (2nd class), a golden sword for courage, the Prussian Order of Red Eagle (2nd class), the Swedish Order of the Sword, the Bavarian Order of Maximilian Joseph and the Austrian Order of Leopold.

BENNIGSEN, Leontii Leontievich (Levin August Theophile) (b. 10 February 1745, Brunswick – d. 3 October 1826, Hannover) was born to a Hanoverian noble family in the Brunswick, where his father was a colonel in the guards. His family also owned estates at Banteln in Hanover. Due to his father's connections at the Hanoverian court, Bennigsen began his service at the age of ten as a page. Four years later he was commissioned as ensign in the guard and, in 1763, as a captain, he participated in the final campaign of the Seven Years War. A year later, after the death of his father and his own marriage to the Baroness Steimberg, he retired to his estates at Banteln, disillusioned with military service and widely regarded as an unpromising officer. Bennigsen apparently squandered his inheritance and, after his wife's untimely death, he briefly reentered Hanoverian service before deciding to seek a career in Russia. He was accepted into the Russian service with a rank of premier major and assigned to the Vyatka Musketeer Regiment in 1773.

During the Russo-Turkish War, Bennigsen served in the Narva Musketeer Regiment and was noticed by Rumyantsev and Saltykov. In January 1779, he became a lieutenant colonel in the Kiev Light Cavalry Regiment. In 1787, he was appointed commander of the Izumsk Light Cavalry Regiment and fought at Ochakov and Bender, receiving promotion to brigadier in 1788. In 1792-1794, Bennigsen took part in the operations against the Polish insurgents, was promoted to major general on 9 July 1794 and awarded the Order of St. George (3rd class) on 26 September 1794. In 1795, he commanded a brigade at Vasilkov. After returning to St. Petersburg, he formed a close association with Valerian Zubov, the brother of the Empress' last favorite. In 1796, he took part in the Persian Campaign along the Caspian Sea and fought at Derbent. After Paul's accession to the throne, Bennigsen was named chef of the Rostov Dragoons Regiment (14 December 1796) and was promoted to lieutenant general (25 February 1798). However, he was dismissed from service on 11 October 1798 during Paul's military purge of high-ranking officers. He participated in the conspiracy to overthrow Paul and according to the memoirs of the participants, was chosen to lead the *coup d'état* because of his reputation for audacity and courage. Despite his role in the conspiracy, Bennigsen's career did not suffer under Alexander. He was appointed the Military Governor of Vilna and inspector of the Lithuanian Inspection on 23 July 1801. Bennigsen was then promoted to general of cavalry on 23 June 1802 with seniority dating from 4 December 1799.

During the 1805 Campaign, Bennigsen commanded a reserve corps of some 48,000 men arranged between Taurrogen and Grodno. In 1806, he was directed to take up quarters in Silesia and assist the Prussians against the French. After the Prussian defeat, Bennigsen withdrew to Poland, where he fought the French army at Golymin and Pultusk He claimed these battles as decisive Russian victories, received the Order of St. George (2nd class) on 8 January 1807 and was appointed commander-in-chief of the Russian army on 13 January 1807. He launched an offensive in January 1807 and fought the French army at Eylau (received the Order of St. Andrew the First Called), Guttstadt, Heilsberg and Friedland, where his poor tactics resulted in the Russian defeats with heavy losses. Displeased with his actions, Emperor Alexander discharged Bennigsen on 9 July 1807. Bennigsen remained in exile until 1812, when he was ordered to join the Imperial Retinue (8 May 1812). He was considered for the post of commander-in-chief in August 1812, but was rejected in favor of Mikhail Kutuzov. Instead, he was appointed the chief of staff of the united Russian armies and bickered with Kutuzov for command throughout the campaign. After Borodino, he advised against abandoning Moscow to the French. He distinguished himself at Tarutino, where he was wounded in the leg. However, in late 1812, Bennigsen was finally dismissed because of his ongoing disagreements with Kutuzov.

Bennigsen returned to the army in early 1813 and received command of the Army of Poland. He later fought at Lutzen, Bautzen and Leipzig and besieged Torgau and Magdeburg; for his actions, he was conferred the title of count of the Russian Empire on 10 January 1814. He then commanded the Russian troops besieging Hamburg and was decorated with the Order of St. George (1st class) on 3 August 1814 for his conduct. He commanded the 2nd Army in 1815-1817 but was criticized for poor administration and forced to retire on 15 May 1818. He spent next eight years at Hanover. He was awarded almost all the highest Russian awards, including the Orders of St. Andrew with diamonds, of St. Vladimir (1st class), of St. Alexander of Neva, of St. Anna (1st class), of St. George (1st class) and a golden sword with diamonds for courage. In addition, he had six foreign decorations, the Prussian Order of Black Eagle, the Hanoverian Order of Guelf, the Dutch Order of the Elephant, the French Legion of Honor, the Swedish Order of the Sword and the Austrian Order of Maria Theresa.

Bennigsen is an over rated general. Brave officer, he showed no tactical or strategic abilities in 1806-1807 and 1813 Campaigns. Despite his claims to victories, the battles of Pultusk and Eylau were draws at best. At Heilsberg, he lost consciousness and other senior Russian commanders conducted the battle. At Friedland, he chose disadvantageous positions that led to heavy Russian casualties. Bennigsen was very ambitious officer and able courtier, who easily navigated in the court politics. His three-volume *Mémoires du général Bennigsen*, published in Paris in 1907-1908, contain fascinating details on the Russian operations in 1806-1813 but often embellish facts.

BERDYAEV, Alexander Nikolaevich (b. 1778 — d. 1824) began service as a *reitar* in the Life Guard Horse Regiment on 7 July 1784. He served at this regiment for ten years and, after briefly retiring to civil service (January-February

1794), he was appointed rotmistr (captain) of the 3rd Chuguev Regular Cossack Regiment. In 1798, he transferred to the Tver Cuirassier Regiment and rose to colonel on 19 December 1800. He participated in the 1805 Campaign and distinguished himself at Posoritz on 20 November, where he was surrounded and captured. However, he was exchanged on 27 November and was awarded the Order of St. George (4th class, 24 January 1806). He fought at Austerlitz where a canister shot seriously damaged his left arm. After recuperating, Berdyaev was appointed chef of the Tversky (Tver) Dragoon Regiment on 19 February 1806 and dispatched to the Danube Valley against the Turks. He remained there for the next six years, distinguishing himself at Ruse and earning promotion to major general on 16 July 1811.

During the 1812 Campaign, Berdyaev served in the 3rd Reserve Army of Observation commanding the 15th Brigade of the 5th Cavalry Division of General Lambert's Cavalry Corps. He fought at Slonim, Kobryn and on the Berezina, ultimately receiving the Order of St. Anna (1st class). In 1813, he fought at Thorn, Koenigswart, Bautzen, Dresden and Leipzig, where he remained during the 1814 Campaign. He retired on 21 September 1821 because of poor health. He spent the rest of his life at his estate at Letichev in the Podolsk *gubernia*, where he died in 1824. During his service, Berdyaev was also awarded the Order of St. Vladimir (3rd class) and two golden swords (one of them with diamonds) for courage.

BERG, Burhardt Maximovic (Bernhardt Magnus), (b.19 May 1764, Derpt — d. 31 July 1838, Vyborg) was born to a German noble family in the Derpt in the Lifland *gubernia*. At the age of ten, he was enlisted by his family as a sergeant in the Voronezh Infantry Regiment on 20 January 1774. The following year, he was promoted to ensign (20 December) and served as adjutant to General Ingelstrom. He participated in the Russo-Turkish War of 1787-1791 and was awarded a golden cross for the capture of Ismail. In 1799, he took part in expedition to Holland. After his return to Russia, he was promoted to colonel (1 September 1801) and appointed to the Imperial Retinue. In 1805, he was dispatched on a diplomatic mission to Sweden to facilitate the Russian landings in Swedish Pomerania.

Berg participated in the 1806-1807 Campaigns and distinguished himself at Pultusk and Eylau (was wounded in the right arm); for his actions, he was awarded the Order of St. George (4th class) on 10 February 1807 and promoted to major general on 24 August 1807. Berg then fought against the Swedes in Finland from 1808-1809. In 1812, he served as a quartermaster general of the Army of Danube and took part in operations on the Berezina and around Vilna. In 1813, Berg fought at Thorn, Lutzen and Bautzen, receiving the Order of St. George (3rd class, 6 May 1813). On 19 July, he was appointed a quartermaster general of the Army of Poland and fought at Leipzig in October. In 1814, he took part in the sieges of Magdeburg and Hamburg. Through 1816-1818, Berg served as chief of staff of the 2nd Corps and, in July 1819, was appointed commandant of Vyborg. He was promoted to lieutenant general on 3 August 1826. During his career, he received the Orders of St. Anna with diamonds, of St. Vladimir (3rd class), of St. John of Jerusalem, the Prussian Pour le Merite, a golden sword for courage and a medal "For L Years of Distinguished Service."

BERG, Grigory Maximovich (27 August 1765, Lunya estate, Lifland – 7 April 1833, Revel) was born to a German noble family in the Lifland *gubernia*. His father Magnus Berg rose to the rank of general-en-chef in the Russian army under Catherine the Great. Berg enlisted as a sergeant in the Siberia Infantry Regiment in 1778. He was promoted to lieutenant on 13 January 1782 and served as ober-auditor of the Lifland Division. During the Russo-Swedish War of 1787-1790, Berg served as a second major in the Neva Infantry Regiment and distinguished himself at Mikkeli, Pomarsund and Pardakoski, where he was wounded in the left foot. In 1792-1794, he was sent against the Polish insurgents. Berg was promoted to colonel on 19 October 1797. In 1798, he became commander of the Tambov Musketeer Regiment (27 August 1798) but, four days later, he was promoted to major general and appointed chef of the Ukraine Musketeer Regiment.

Berg remained at this regiment until 19 February 1800 when he was discharged for alleged embezzlement of regimental funds. Berg was acquitted and returned to service nine months later as chef of the Malorossiisky (Little Russia) Grenadier Regiment on 1 December 1800. The following year, Alexander I made Prince Karl of Baden chef of this regiment and Berg was appointed its commander on 28 July 1801. He commanded this regiment during the 1805 Campaign and distinguished himself at Amstetten, where he was wounded in the head, and Austerlitz, where he was bruised twice to the left foot and captured. Berg remained in captivity for a couple of weeks and returned to Russia in January 1806. He became commandant of Revel on 23 October 1806 and remained at this position for next six years. He became commander of the 5th Division on 4 April 1812 but kept his previous position as well. During the 1812 Campaign, Berg's division was attached to Wittgenstein's corps and fought at Jakubovo and Klyastitsy. Berg particularly distinguished himself at Nischy and Golovchyn attaining the rank of lieutenant general (promotion granted on 30 October 1812, with seniority dating from 30 July 1812) After fighting on the Svolnya River on 11 August 1812, he was wounded at Polotsk but remained in the ranks commanding his troops (received the Order of St. Anna, 1st class).

After recuperating, Berg took part in the second battle of Polotsk in October 1812 and earned the Order of St. Vladimir (2nd class). He personally led a counterattack against the French cavalry at Smolnya on 14 November 1812. In 1813, Berg fought at Danzig, participated in the retaking of Berlin and the battles at Mockern (received the Prussian Order of Red Eagle) and Lutzen, where he covered the retreat of the Allied forces and received the Order of St. George (3rd class, 14 June 1813). He then distinguished himself at Bautzen and Reichenbach where he was seriously wounded in the left foot. Berg had to leave army and returned to his duty of commandant at Revel. He served at this position for the next ten years. On 24 December

1823, Berg was promoted to general of infantry, and five years later, he became the Military Governor of the Revel *gubernia* (6 April 1828). He retired on 21 February 1832 and died on 7 April 1833 at Revel.

BEZOBRAZOV, Nikolay Alekseyevich (b. 1770 – d. 1831) was born to a noble family. He enlisted to the Life Guard Semeyonovsky Regiment in 1777 and fought against the Swedes in 1789-1790 receiving the rank of ensign (13 January 1789) and the Order of St. George (4th class, 7 December 1789). In 1796, he transferred as a lieutenant colonel to the army and participated in the Persian Campaign. Two years later, he was promoted to colonel (7 July) and then served as commander of Astrakhan Dragoon Regiment (18 January 1799 – 21 March 1800). Promoted to major general on 15 May 1800, Bezobrazov served as chef of the Moscow Dragoon Regiment.

Bezobrazov participated in the 1805 Campaign and then retired in July 1807. He returned to service in December 1812 and served under General Kologrivov with the cavalry reserves. In 1813, he fought in Poland and Germany, where he commanded the Penza Cossack Regiment and distinguished himself at Leipzig, receiving the Order of St. Vladimir, 3rd class). In 1814, Bezobrazov remained in Saxony securing the communication and supply lines. Two years later, he was given command of the 1st Brigade of the 2nd Horse Jager Division (13 March) and then appointed commander of the 1st Hussar Division on 4 November 1819. He was promoted to lieutenant general on 24 December 1824. During his service, he also received the Order of St. Anna (1st class) and a golden sword for courage.

BEZRODNY, Vasily Kirilovich (b. 13 January 1768, Novgorod — d. 16 September 1847, St. Petersburg) was born to a noble family in the Novgorod *gubernia*. In October 1780, he began service as a clerk (*podkantselarist*) at the Novorosiisk *gubernia* chancellery and was promoted to the college registrar in March 1786. He then served in Ekaterinoslavl administration where Gregory Potemkin noticed his abilities and helped procure his appointment as the *gubernia* secretary (*gubernsky sekreta*r) with the rank of sub-lieutenant in the army on 26 June 1794. Bezrodny served under Alexander Suvorov in Poland in 1794 and was appointed to the Supply Commissariat of the War College on 21 August 1795. The following year, he was promoted to captain on 29 November 1796.

In 1799, Bezrodny became a military counselor of the 6th class (24 October 1799) and headed the Statistics Section (*schetnoe otdelenie*) of the Commissariat. In 1801, he was promoted to military counselor of the 5th class and served as a head of the Kiev Supply Commissariat. He received the rank of major general with appointment to the Ministry of War on 3 November 1803. He served at this position for the next nine years until appointed head of the 1st Division of the Supply Department of the Ministry of War in 1812. After the 1812 Campaign, Bezrodny worked in the supply commissariat of the main Russian army and took part in the campaigns in Germany and France. On 15 January 1816, he was appointed head of the chancellery of the commander-in-chief of the 1st Army. He served at this position until 6 August 1825, when he transferred as a privy counselor to the Senate.

In January 1828, Bezrodny became a member of the Commission for Appeals, and in April 1829, was appointed lieutenant general–proviantmeister (head of the commissariat) of the Army of the Danube. Two years later, he returned to St. Petersburg and was appointed as a senator in February 1831. After ten years at this position, he became an actual privy counselor on 28 April 1841.

Bezrodny died six years later on 16 September and was buried at the Smolensk cemetery in St. Petersburg. During his career, he was awarded the Orders of St. John of Jerusalem, of the White Eagle, of St. Anna with diamonds (1st class), of St. Alexander of Neva, of St. Vladimir (2nd class) and the Prussian Order of Red Eagle (2nd class).

BIBIKOV, Alexander Alexandrovich (b. 18 January 1765 — d. 20 July 1822, Dresden) was born to a prominent noble family of Tatar origins; his grandfather Ilya Bibikov was a powerful official under Elizabeth and Catherine II, while his father General-en-Chef Alexander Bibikov was instrumental in suppressing Pugachev's Rebellion in the 1770s. Bibikov enlisted in the Life Guard Izmailovsk Regiment in 1767 at age of two; after his father's death, Catherine II promoted the nine-year-old Bibikov to ensign of the Life Guard Izmailovsk Regiment in 1774. Bibikov rose to captain of the Life Guard Preobrazhensk Regiment on 12 January 1787 and accompanied Catherine II in her famous travel to the Crimea. He participated in the Russo-Swedish War in 1788-1790, fighting at Wilmanstrand, Parosalmi and Rotensalmi; he was awarded a golden sword for courage and the Order of St. George (4th class, 20 June 1789).

In August 1789, Bibikov took command of a battalion of Life Guard Preobrazhensk Regiment and served in the galley fleet of Prince Nassau-Zigen. In 1790-1795, Bibikov continued his service in the Guard before transferring to the civil service with a rank of kamer-junker. In June 1796, he was promoted to actual kamerger and joined the diplomatic corps. In October 1798, he became privy counselor and was appointed ambassador to Portugal (2 January 1799) and Saxony (12 January 1799). He was appointed the senator in January 1800 but was then dismissed by Emperor Paul.

Bibikov briefly returned to military service only six years later, when he was elected commander of the Oranienbaum District Militia in the St. Petersburg *gubernia* on 28 December 1806. However, in February 1808, Alexander appointed him Ambassador to Naples, where he remained for the next three years and received the Order of St. Anna (1st class). Recalled in March 1810, Bibikov returned to work in the 3rd Department of the Senate. In 1812, he was elected commander of the St. Petersburg and Novgorod *opolchenyes* and was attached to Wittgenstein's corps. During the operations in August-September, Bibikov commanded the 1st *Opolchenye* Brigade comprised of Voronezh Infantry Regiment, 1st and 3rd *Opolchenye* Companies (*druzhini*), later reinforced by the Grodno Hussars and Polish Uhlans. In October, he took part in the second battle at Polotsk and was awarded the Order of St. George (3rd class, awarded 15 January 1813) for courage. He was also given command of the 5th Infantry Division and fought at Smolnya, where he took a wound in the leg. Unable to ride, he commanded his troops from a carriage and fought at Borisov and on Berezina. For his courage, he was awarded a golden sword with inscription "For Faith and the Tsar."

In 1813, Bibikov participated in the siege of Danzig but had to leave the army because of poor health. He retired in July 1813 with permission to wear a general's uniform. In 1829, Bibikov traveled to Dresden to recuperate from his wounds but died there on 2 July 1829. His body was returned and buried at Alexander of Neva Lavra in St. Petersburg. Several other Bibikovs served in the Russian army during Napoleonic Wars. Two of them, whose first names are unknown, became colonels: one served as chef of the Belev Musketeer Regiment from 26 January 1809 to 13 January 1810, the second Bibikov commanded the Vyatka Musketeer Regiment from 31 August 1804 to 17 October 1806. In addition, Colonel **Stepan Matveevich Bibikov** commanded the Grodno Hussar Regiment in 17 October 1806–7 November 1809. Major General **Alexander Bibikov** served as chef of the Kursk Musketeer Regiment from 1796-1797 and of the Poltava Musketeer Regiment from 1802-1803.

BISTROM, Adam Ivanovich (b. 3 November 1774, Estland *gubernia* – d. 29 October 1828, Dresden) was born to a noble family in the Estland *gubernia*; brother of Karl Bistrom. Adam Bistrom was enrolled as a private in Life Guard Preobrazhensk Regiment in January 1782 and the next year he transferred to the Life Guard Semeyonovsk Regiment, where he served for the next eight years. In 1791, he became a sergeant and two years later he transferred as a captain to the Finland Jager Corps in January 1793; he fought in the Polish Campaign of 1794. In 1797, after Emperor Paul's military reorganization, Bistrom served in the 2nd Marine Regiment and then at Bolotnikov's Garrison Regiment (later known as the Kronstadt Regiment). In 1802, he was appointed to the Lithuania Musketeer Regiment and, two years later, was promoted to lieutenant colonel.

In 1806-1807, Bistrom fought the French in Poland and distinguished himself at Pultusk and Eylau, where he was seriously wounded in the head and earned the Order of St. Vladimir (4th Class). He took part in the battles at Guttstadt and Heilsberg; at Friedland, Bistrom was wounded in the chest. For his actions, Bistrom was promoted to colonel (24 December 1807) and, on 18 March 1808, was appointed to command the Lithuania Musketeer Regiment. He participated with this regiment in the Russo-Swedish War of 1808-1809, and distinguished himself in battle near Oravais on 14 September. He was awarded a gold sword for courage. In 1810, the Lithuania Musketeer Regiment was converted to the 33rd Jagers Regiment (31 October 1810), and Bistrom became chef of the regiment on 8 December 1810. The next year, he took command of 3rd Brigade (1st and 33rd Jagers Regiments) of the 11th Division.

During 1812 Campaign, Bistrom served in the 1st Western Army and fought at Ostrovno, Vitebsk, Smolensk, Borodino (awarded the Order of St. Vladimir 3rd class), Mozhaisk, Tarutino, and Maloyaroslavets. For his actions at Maloyaroslavets, Kutuzov recommended him for promotion; Bistrom was promoted on 10 May 1813 with seniority dating from 24 October 1812. He received the Order of St. George (4th class, 23 July 1813) for his action at Vyazma. During 1813-1814 Campaigns, he took part in battles at Labau, Ottendorf, Leipzig (received the Swedish Order of the Sword), Coblenz, Rheims (was wounded in left shoulder) and Laon (awarded the Order of St. Anne, 1st Class, with diamond signs). For his actions at Paris, Bistrom was given Order of St. George (3rd Class, 30 March 1814). After the Treaty of Paris, Bistrom began the long march home to Russia, but was recalled in 1815 when Napoleon escaped from Elba; Bistrom took part in the siege of the fortress of Pfalzburg. On 28 December 1815, he was appointed commander of the Life Guard Pavlovsk Regiment, where he remained for the next ten years. He also briefly commanded the 2nd Brigade of the 2nd Guard Infantry Division. In March 1825, he was appointed to the Imperial Retinue and, on 13 January 1826, he was promoted to lieutenant general. However, he soon resigned because of poor health and traveled to Dresden to recuperate. He died there on 27 October 1828 (excluded from the rosters on 21 November 1828).

BISTROM, Karl Ivanovich (b. 13 May 1770, Estland *gubernia* — d. 28 June 1838, Kissingen, Bavaria) was born to a noble family in the Estland *gubernia*; he was the brother of Adam Bistrom. Karl Bistrom enlisted as a corporal in the Life Guard Izmailovsk Regiment on 19 June 1784, where he passed through the ranks, rising to sergeant in 1787. He participated in the Russo-Swedish War in 1788-1789 and transferred as a captain to the Neva Musketeer Regiment on 12 January 1790. Bistrom became commander of the 1st Jager Regiment on 29 May 1797 and rose to lieutenant colonel on 29 January 1799. He was also awarded the Commander Order of the St. John of Jerusalem. He was given command of the 20th Jagers on 19 March 1805 and promoted to colonel on 22 July 1805.

During the 1806-1807 Campaigns in Poland, Bistrom fought at Czarnowo (received the Order of St. George, 4th class, 10 February 1807), Pultusk (wounded in the left foot, awarded the Prussian Pour le Merite), and Eylau (wounded in the left shoulder, awarded a golden sword for courage). In June 1807, he participated in the minor actions at Zecher, Peterswald, Altkirchen, and along the Passarga River, and was awarded the Order of St. Vladimir (3rd Class.) He distinguished himself at Guttstadt on 9-10 June, where his regiment covered the retreat of the Russian forces for almost fourteen hours. He was seriously wounded in his right cheek by a musket ball that damaged his jaw. As a result, Bistrom had difficulty speaking for the rest of his life. For his courage, Emperor Alexander personally awarded him with the Order of St. Anne (2nd class) with diamond signs.

After Tilsit, Bistrom was named a battalion commander in the Life Guard Jager Battalion, and, on 31 December 1809, he received command of the entire regiment, serving in this capacity throughout the 1812-1814 Campaigns. In 1812, his unit was attached to the 3rd Brigade of the Guard Infantry Division of the 5th Reserve (Guard) Corps of the 1st Western Army. Bistrom fought at Smolensk in August 1812 and then at Borodino in September. For his bravery at Borodino, he was promoted to major general on 2 December 1812 with seniority dating from 7 September 1812. He the participated in the actions at Tarutino, Maloyaroslavets, and Klementino, and distinguished himself in the fighting at Dobraya, near Krasnyi, where Bistrom's troops captured Marshal Davout's correspondence and baton. For his actions, Bistrom received the Order of St. George (3rd Class, received on 15 June 1813). In 1813, Bistrom fought at Lutzen, Bautzen, Kulm and Leipzig, and in 1814 – at Brienne, Arsi-sur-Aube, Le Fère Champenoise and Paris.

After the conclusion of war, Bistrom returned to St. Petersburg. In June 1821, he received command of the 2nd Guard Infantry Division and was promoted to lieutenant general on 24 December 1824. In March 1825, he was given command of the infantry of the Separate Guards Corps; he was promoted to general-adjutant for suppressing the Decembrist Uprising in St. Petersburg in December 1825. During the Russo-Turkish War of 1828-29, Bistrom commanded the Guard Corps and invested the fortress of Varna in August. On 16-18 September he fought a major battle there against a coordinated assault of the Turkish forces. He captured Varna on 29 September and was awarded the Order of Alexander of Neva. In 1830, Bistrom took leave because of poor health, however he returned to the army during the Polish Uprising. He commanded the advance guard during the campaign and fought at Ostrolenko, where he received a serious contusion by a cannonball to his right thigh. For his actions, Bistrom received the Order of St. George (2nd Class, 11 June 1831). Bistrom took part in the assault on Warsaw and, after his promotion to general of infantry on 3 September 1831, he commanded the Russian forces in the Polish capital after Field Marshal Paskevich departed.

Bistrom returned to Russia in 1832 and took extended leave to recuperate. In December 1835, he was awarded the Order of St. Vladimir (1st Class) and, in July 1837, he was appointed deputy commander of the Separate Guard Corps, commanded by Grand Duke Michael Pavlovich. However, his health rapidly deteriorated and Bistrom traveled to Kissingen in Bavaria to recuperate but died there on 28 June 1838. Bistrom was buried at his estate at Yamburg in Russia. In addition to abovementioned awards, Bistrom also had the Prussian Pour le Merite and Order of Red Eagle (2nd class), medals "For Military Merit" (1st class) and "Twenty Four Years of Distinguish Service." Another Bistrom, **BISTROM, Gustav Fedorovich** became colonel on 11 January 1801 and commanded the Novgorod Musketeer Regiment in May 1800 to July 1802 and from July 1803 to March 1805.

BODISKO, Nikolay Andreyevich (date of birth unclear — d. 13 January 1815) studied in the Navy Cadet Corps and began his service in the Baltic Fleet, rising to a midshipman in 1777. In 1780-1784, he took part in the expeditions to Italy and, in 1786, he commanded the yacht '*Schastie*.' During the Russo-Swedish War of 1788-1790, he commanded a transport vessel at Gogland, where he briefly commanded the captured Swedish ship-of-the-line '*Prince Gustav*' in 1788. The following year, he took command of the frigate '*Nadezhda Blagopoluchia*,' fighting at Gangut. In 1790, he served under Admiral Chichagov in the battles at Eland, Revel and Vyborg, where he captured six enemy vessels and received the Order of St. George (4th class).

In 1793, Bodisko commanded the frigate '*Venus*,' taking part in the cruises to the British shores in 1795-1797. He rose to a captain (1st class) on 28 November 1798 but then took a discharge. He returned to the service in the summer of 1801, commanding various vessels in Revel. He became a captain commander in 1804 and a rear admiral in 1808. During the Russo-Swedish War, he captured the Island of Gotland; however, he then hastily withdrew the Russian landing forces that allowed the Swedes to recapture the island. Bodisko was initially awarded the Order of St. Anna (1st class) for the capture of the Gotland; but, as the news of the Swedish success reached St. Petersburg, Bodisko was courtmartialed and, on 7 June 1809, he was discharged from the service, deprived of the Order of St. Anna and exiled to Vologda. He was pardoned two years later and restored in the service on 16 October 1811. On 19 November 1812, he became the commander of the port of Sveaborg and received the Order of St. Anna (1st class) on 5 August 1814.

BOGDANOV (Bogdanov II), Nikolay Ivanovich (b. 1752 — date of detath unclear) rose to a major general in October 1798 and served as chef of the 8th Artillery Regiment in March 1800 - September 1801. He commanded the Russian artillery at Austerlitz in 1805. Later, he served as the Civil Governor of Tula in 1811-1814 and organized the Tula *opolchenye* in 1812. Several other Bogdanovs served in the Russian army during the Napoleonic era. **Colonel Bogdanov** (first name unclear) commanded the Riga Musketeer regiment between 21 January 1805 and 28 March 1807; Lieutenant General **Bogdanov (Bogdanov III)** served as chef of the garrison regiments at Birsk and Selengisnk in 1797-1802.

BOGDANOVICH, Ivan Fedorovich (b. 1783 — date of death unclear) was born to an officer's family. Graduating from the 2nd Cadet Corps, he began service as sub lieutenant in the 6th Artillery Battalion in 1803. He participated in the 1805 Campaign and, in 1806-1807, he fought at Pultusk, Heislberg (received the Order of St. Anna, 3rd class) and Friedland. He transferred to the 1st Artillery Brigade on 26 February 1811 and became staff captain on 3 March 1812. During the 1812 Campaign, he fought at Vitebsk, Smolensk and Borodino (received the Order of St. Vladimir, 4th class). In 1813, he took part in actions at Kalisch, Lutzen, Bautzen, Dresden, Leipzig and Strasburg. He rose to lieutenant colonel on 5 February 1814.

BOGDANOVICH, Ivan Fedorovich (b. 1784, Poltava — date of death unknown; excluded from rosters on 1 September 1840) began his career as a guide (*kolonovozhatii*) in the quartermaster service of the Imperial entourage in 1802. He was dispatched to Bukhara in late 1802 and next year served in Kurgizia, where he distinguished himself fighting the local tribes. On 21-22 September 1803, his detachment of some 30 Cossacks held out in a fortified camp against a much superior tribal army (official record of service showed 3,000 Kirgiz-kaisaks) before fighting its way back to the Russian frontiers. After returning to St. Petersburg in March 1804, Bogdanovich was promoted to sub-lieutenant on 31 December 1804 and awarded 2,000 rubles. In 1805, he took part in a diplomatic mission to China and, having returned to St. Petersburg in January 1807, he received a diamond ring with 450 rubles.

In August 1808 – November 1809, Bogdanovich served in Bukhara and was promoted to lieutenant on 25 October 1809. In 1810-1811, he took part in topographical project to create a detailed map of Russia. In 1812, he served in Platov's Cossack Corps and took part in the retreat of the 2nd Western Army. He fought at Mir and Romanovo and was promoted to staff-captain (4 December 1812). He later took part in battles at Borodino, Tarutino and various minor actions during the French retreat.

For his actions, Bogdanovich received the Orders of St. Vladimir (4th class) and of St. Anna (2nd class). He was promoted to captain in March 1813 and appointed to Adjutant-General Chernyshev's detachment. He fought at Luneburg (received the Imperial letter of gratitude and the Prussian Pour le Merite), Halberstadt and Tuas (promoted to lieutenant colonel on 13 July and awarded a golden sword for courage), Dennewitz (received the Swedish Order of the Sword), Beltzen (received the Order of St. Anna with diamonds) and Kassel. For his actions, he was promoted to colonel on 30 September 1813. During 1814 Campaign, he fought at Soisson (received the Order of St. Vladimir, 3rd class) and Laon (received the Imperial letter of gratitude).

After the war, Bogdanovich became chief of staff of the 7th Corps on 17 December 1814 (served until March 1818). A year later, he was dispatched on a topographical survey mission to the Danube Valley. In January 1817, he was appointed to the Russian embassy in Istanbul to negotiate the state borders on the Danube River. After he returned to St. Petersburg in September 1817, Bogadnovich was again sent to the Danube to delimit state borders. He was then dispatched to Novocherkask and served in the Committee to Establish Don Cossack Army with instructions to survey the Don Cossack territories. Bogdanovich was soon generously awarded for his services. He was promoted to major general on 31 March 1820 and awarded a state-paid rent for 12 years (17 January 1822). The next year, he received the Order of St. Anna (1st class) on 7 June 1823 and the Order of St. George (4th class) for 25 years of distinguished service on 8 December 1826. In 1829, he received the Order of St. Anna (1st class) with an imperial crown and a diamond ring (21 March 1833) for the topographical map of the Don Cossack territories. He was promoted to lieutenant general on 13 January 1835 and appointed to the Senate. Date of his death is unknown but he was removed from military rosters on 1 September 1840.

BOGDANOVSKY, Andrey Vasilievich (b. 1780 — d. 1864) was born to a noble family in the Little Russia. He graduated from the Cadet Corps with a rank of sub-lieutenant in the 12th Jager Regiment on 16 June 1798. He took part in the Russo-Turkish War of 1806-1812 and fought at Bender, Ismail, Bazardjik (received a cross)

and Ruse. He became commander of the Odessa Musketeer Regiment on 16 October 1810; this regiment was converted to the 40th Jager Regiment on 31 October 1810. On 2 February 1811, he took command of the Narva Musketeer Regiment, which in turn was renamed into an infantry regiment a month later.

During the 1812 Campaign, Bogdanovsky commanded the Narva Infantry Regiment attached to the 1st Brigade of the 12th Division of the 7th Corp of the 2nd Western Army. He participated in Bagration's successful retreat and fought at Smolensk and Borodino, where he was wounded in the foot. Promoted to colonel on 28 March 1813, he took part in the siege of Modlin and the battle of Leipzig. In 1814, he fought at Craonne and was promoted to major general on 13 December 1814 with seniority dating from 7 March 1814. He assumed command of the 1st Brigade of the 12th Division on 13 June 1815. He continued commanding this unit for the next five years and was discharged in January 1820 with full pension. He became an actual civil counsellor and served as the Governor of Kerch in October 1823. He was promoted to privy counsellor on 30 August 1828 and to actual privy counsellor on 15 April 1849. He retired on 21 March 1856. During his career, Bogdanovsky received the Orders of St. Vladimir (2nd class), of St. Anna with crown (1st class), of the White Eagle, the Prussian Pour le Merite, the Swedish Order of the Sword and the French Legion of Honor.

BOGUSLAVSKY, Alexander Andreyevich (b. 1771 — d. 16 June 1831, Perm) was born to a noble family in the Poltava *gubernia*. He graduated from the Artillery and Engineer Cadet Corps in 1789 and began service as a shtyk-junker in the Bombardier Regiment on 8 January 1789. He participated in the Russo-Turkish War in 1790-1791 and fought at Macin, recieving the rank of lieutenant for courage. He then fought against the Polish insurgents in 1792-1794. Throughout the 1805 Campaign, Boguslavsky served in the 4th Artillery Regiment and distinguished himself at Austerlitz, where he was wounded in the foot. The following year, he transferred to the Danube Valley and spent his next four years fighting the Turks. He took part in the siege of Ruse in 1810 and earned the Order of St. George (4th class, 18 March 1811).

In 1811, Boguslavsky became a colonel on 23 May and took command of the 11th Artillery Brigade. His unit was later renamed to the 2nd Field Artillery Brigade and was attached to the 2nd Grenadier Division of the 8th Division of the 2nd Western Army. He fought at Smolensk and Borodino receiving a golden sword for courage. In October-November 1812, he fought at Tarutino, Maloyaroslavets and Krasnyi. During the 1813 Campaign, he commanded artillery at the siege of Zamostye and served as the commandant of this fortress in 1814. Boguslavsky was dispatched with his unit to France during the Hundred Days in 1815. He was promoted to major general on 1 December 1815 and given command of the artillery of the 5th Corps. Beginning on 1 June 1826, Boguslavsky supervised the artillery garrisons in the Danube District, and on 3 May 1827, he became head of the defense factories in the Urals. Promoted to lieutenant general on 26 April 1829, he died only two years later at Perm. During his military service, Boguslavsky was awarded the Orders of St. George (3rd class), of St. Anna with diamonds (1st class), of St. Vladimir (2nd class) and of St. John of Jerusalem.

BOLOGOVSKY, Dmitry Nikolaevich (b. 1780 — d. 6 September 1852) was born to a Russian noble family. He was enlisted in the Life Guard Izmailovsk Regiment at an early age and began active service as an ensign in 1797. He took a discharge with a rank of captain in 1802 and returned to the army only ten years later, when he was appointed to the Moscow Infantry Regiment in July 1812. Bologovsky fought at Borodino and replaced Major General Monakhtin as the Chief of Staff of the 6th Corps.

In 1812-1814, he distinguished himself at Maloyaroslavets, Krasnyi, Leipzig (wounded, received the Order of St. George, 4th class), Magdeburg and Hamburg. After the Napoleonic Wars, he rose to a major general on 2 March 1820 and commanded the 2nd Brigade of the 22nd Division and the 1st Brigade of the 16th Division. He took a discharge on 12 February 1834 but returned to the army in March 1836 serving as a *chargé d'affaires* for the military governor of the Vologda *gubernia*. He was appointed to the Senate in 1841.

BOMBEL, Alexander was promoted to colonel on 5 May 1806 and commanded the Vladimir Dragoon Regiment from 28 February 1805 to 16 December 1807.

BOROZDIN, Andrey Mikhaylovich (b. 1765 — d. 21 December 1838) was born to a Russian noble family in the Pskov *gubernia*; his grandfather General-en-Chef Kornilii Borozdin was instrumental in establishing the horse artillery in Russian service during the Seven Years War. Andrey Borozdin was the brother of Generals Mikhail and Alexander Borozdin. He enlisted as a kaptenarmus in the Life Guard Semeyonovsk Regiment in 1773 and rose to an ensign in 1784. He participated in the Russo-Swedish War of 1788-1790 and took part in subsequent operations in Poland from 1792-1794.

Rising to a major general in 1798, Borozdin became chef of the Troitsk Musketeer Regiment on 16 March 1798. Two years later, he was promoted to lieutenant general on 17 February 1800, but he retired in November 1804. In 1806, he served in the Kiev militia and was appointed the Civil Governor of Tavrida on 14 November 1807, earning the Order of St. Anna (1st class) on 24 March 1809. He remained at this position for the next nine years, becoming a senator in March 1812. During 1812 Campaign, he commanded the troops in the Crimea and was instrumental in suppressing the cholera epidemic in this region. He was relieved of command on 1 August 1816 and worked in the Senate for the next twelve years.

BOROZDIN (Borozdin I), Mikhail Mikhailovich (b. 19 July 1767, Pskov *gubernia* — d. 26 October 1837, Simferopol) was born to a Russian noble family in the Pskov *gubernia*; the brother of Andrey and Alexander Borozdin. He was enrolled in the Artillery and Engineer Cadet Corps in 1773, and on 30 September of the same year, he enlisted as a corporal in the Life Guard Semeyoenovsk Regiment at the age of six. He began actual military service as a sergeant in this regiment on 18 June 1780 and was promoted to ensign on 12 January 1784. On 16 March 1790, he transferred to the 1st Marine Battalion with a rank of lieutenant colonel (he was captain in the guard regiment). He fought the Swedes in 1790 and the Turks in 1791, distinguishing himself at the battle of Macin. After serving against the Polish insurgents in 1792-1794, Borozdin was promoted to colonel on 12 January 1795. On 13 November 1797, he took command of the Yeletsk Musketeer Regiment, but was appointed chef of the Astrakhan Grenadier Regiment on 10 December 1797.

In March 1799, Prince von Mecklenburg replaced Borozdin as chef of the Astrakhan Grenadier Regiment and Borozdin then served as the commander of this regiment until 24 May 1799. He took part in the expeditions of the Russian Black Sea Fleet in the Mediterranean Sea in 1799 and fought the French on the Ionian Islands. He was promoted to lieutenant general on 16 November 1799. He served as the Commandant of Vilna between 19 November 1799 and 23 March 1800 and became the Military Governor of Kiev and inspector of the Ukraine Inspection on 22 September 1800. In 1800-1802, he commanded the Neapolitan Guard and marines in Naples and Palermo. At the same time, he served as chef of Tenginsk Musketeer Regiment between 23 March and 15 May 1800, and as chef of Smolensk Musketeer Regiment between 22 September and 18 October 1800.

Borozdin retired on 9 January 1804 and remained at his estate until 4 May 1812 when he was appointed commander of the 8th Infantry Corps of the 2nd Western Army. He participated in Bagration's retreat and fought at Smolensk, Shevardino and Borodino, receiving the Order of St. George (3rd class, 1 November 1812). In October-November 1812, he fought at Tarutino, Maloyaroslavets and Krasnyi. In 1813, he participated in the siege of Danzig and, after its capture, he commanded the Russian garrison of the town. On 22 December 1814, he became commander of the 27th Division, but retired on 9 January 1817 because of poor health. During his career, Borozdin was decorated with the

Orders of St. Anna with diamonds (1st class), of St. Vladimir (2nd class), of St. John of Jerusalem and of St. George (3rd class) as well as a golden sword for courage.

BOROZDIN (Borozdin II), Nikolay Mikhailovich (b. 13 November 1777, Pskov *gubernia* – d. 26 November 1830, St. Petersburg) was born to a Russian noble family in the Pskov *gubernia*; the brother of Mikhail and Andrey Borozdin. Borozdin enlisted as a private in the Life Guard Preobrazhensk Regiment in 1782 at the age of five and was promoted to sergeant on 21 January 1784. The same year, he transferred as a vakhmistr to the Life Guard Horse Regiment (22 March) and rose to a cornet on 12 January 1794. He transferred to the His Majesty's Life Guard Cuirassier Regiment on 10 December 1796, but the next year he returned to his previous regiment (Life Guard Horse Regiment) on 16 April 1797. In fairly rapid succession, Borozdin rose to a lieutenant on 28 September 1798, to staff-rotmistr on 29 August 1798 and to rotmistr (captain) on 18 June 1799. He joined the Chevalier Guard Regiment on 15 October 1799. He was promoted to a colonel on 23 January 1800. In 1803, Alexander I made him a flügel adjutant. Between 29 August 1806 and 24 October 1811, Borozdin served as chef of the Finland Dragoon Regiment and, then between 24 October 1811 and 13 September 1814, as chef of the Astrakhan Cuirassier Regiment.

Borozdin participated in the 1807 Campaign in Poland and distinguished himself at Myschenitz (awarded the Order of St. Anna, 2nd class) and Guttstadt (received the Order of St. Vladimir, 3rd class, and a golden sword for courage). He was promoted to major general on 5 June 1807. Borozdin also took part in the Russo-Swedish War in 1808-1809 and served with his regiment (the Finland Dragoons) in the 14th Division. He took part in a series of minor actions, including those at Aborfors and Borgo, receiving the Order of St. Anna (1st class) for his conduct. In late spring of 1808, Borozdin took part in the siege of Sveaborg and then was given a coast guard duty along the southern shores of Finland. He repulsed the Swedish landing force on 19-20 June near Lemo, and served under Bagration during the battle at Helsinge on 26 September 1808. In early 1809, he was left on the garrison duty in Abo.

In 1810, Borozdin took command of the 1st Brigade of the 1st Cuirassier Division, comprised of His and Her Majesty Life Guard Cuirassier Regiments. In the fall of 1811, he became chef of the Astrakhan Cuirassier Regiment (24 October). During the 1812 Campaign, Borozdin commanded the 1st Cuirassier Brigade of the 1st Cuirassier Division in the 5th Reserve (Guard) Corps of the 1st Western Army. He fought at Ostrovno and Borodino, where he defended the village of Semeyonosvkoe and received the Order of St. George (3rd class, 1 November 1812) for his gallant actions. In October-November, Borozdin's brigade was kept in reserves during the battles of Tarutino, Maloyaroslavets and Vyazma. On 16 November, Kutuzov appointed him to command General Orlov-Denisov's cavalry detachment and Borozdin distinguished himself during the pursuit of the French army, fighting at Krasnyi, Lyadi, Dubrovna, Orsha, on Berezina River and at Vilna.

In mid-December 1812, Borozdin took a furlough because of poor health and returned to the army in June 1813; he was initially given command of the 1st Dragoon Division but later commanded the 8th Corps of the Army of Silesia. He fought in several minor actions (Schmideberg, Greifenberg, Lauban and others) as well as in the major battles at Bautzen and Katzbach (earned the diamond signs of the Order of St. Anna, 1st class). After his promotion to lieutenant general on 27 September 1813, Borozdin fought at Leipzig and took part in the pursuit of the retreating French. During the 1814 Campaign, he took part in the siege of Metz in January and then fought at Craonne, Laon and Le Fère Champenoise, where Alexander witnessed his actions and awarded him the Order of St. Vladimir (2nd class). On 30 March, Borozdin took part in the battle for Paris, reinforcing General Emmanuel's troops.

After the war, Borozdin commanded the 1st Dragoon Division in the 2nd Infantry Corps. He returned to Russia in late 1814, but had to march back to France during the Hundred Days in 1815. He reached Bavaria when Napoleon was defeated at Waterloo. In January 1817, he took command of the 4th Reserve Cavalry Corps (confirmed on 24 March 1823) and rose to an adjutant general on 9 August 1820. He became general of cavalry on 3 September 1826. Two years later, Borozdin led his 4th Corps to the Danube Valley to fight the Turks. However, his health deteriorated and he could not personally participate in the actions and had to leave army. He died on 26 November 1830 in St. Petersburg and was buried at his estate in Kostyzhetsy in the Pskov *gubernia*.

BOUR, Karl Fedorovich was appointed chef of the Pavlograd Hussar Regiment on 10 December 1796 and rose to a major general on 7 February 1797 and to a lieutenant general on 17 September 1797. He participated in the 1805 Campaign and distinguished himself at Austerlitz on 2 December 1805. Bour was relieved of command on 10 April 1806.

BRANITSKY, Vladislav Grigorievich (b. 1782, St. Petersburg — d. 27 August 1843, Warsaw) was born to a Polish noble family; his father served in the Russian army as a general-en-chef. Just after his birth, Branitsky enlisted as an ensign in the Life Guard Preobrazhensk Regiment on 24 February 1782; he was promoted to sub lieutenant on 12 January 1791. However, he was soon dismissed for failure to appear in the regiment. Branitsky was restored in the regiment on 12 January 1797 but four years later he transferred as kamer-junker to the civilian service. Branitsky returned to military service in January 1809 and was given the rank of staff captain.

Branitsky participated in the Russo-Turkish War and was promoted to flügel adjutant on 13 August 1809. In 1812, he rose to the rank of colonel (29 April) and served in Emperor Alexander's entourage and at the headquarters of the 1st Western Army. He took part in the battles at Smolensk, Borodino, Tarutino and Krasnyi. In 1813, he fought at Kulm (earned the Prussian Iron Cross) and Leipzig, while in 1814 he participated in the combats at La Rothière, Arcis sur Aube and Paris. He was promoted to major general on 8 April 1814 with seniority dating from 30 March 1814. Branitsky served in the Imperial Retinue for the next twelve years and was appointed a jagermeister in September 1826. Five years later, he became a senator (20 May) and rose to an actual privy counsellor in 1838.

During his career, Branitsky received the Orders of the White Eagle, of St. Anna (1st class), of St. Vladimir (3rd class), of St. John of Jerusalem, of St. George (4th class), the Prussian Orders of Red Eagle and Pour le Merite, the Austrian Order of Leopold, the Bavarian Order of Maximilian Joseph and the Württemberg Order of Military Merit.

BREZHINSKY, Semen Petrovich (b. 1780 – d. 11 October 1817, Kursk) was born to a Polish noble family. He studied in the Cadet Corps and joined the Pskov garrison Battalion with a rank of ensign on 30 December 1797. After promotion to lieutenant in 1798 and to staff captain on 23 December 1799, he transferred to the Belozersk Musketeer Regiment on 8 April 1802. During the 1805 Campaign, he took part in the expedition to Hanover. In 1806, he fought at Pultusk and was wounded in the right arm. In 1807, he participated in the actions at Guttstadt, Heilsberg and Friedland, receiving a golden sword for courage.

In 1808-1809, Brezhinsky fought in Finland and, after 31 August 1809, served as commander of the Kholmsk Recruit Depot. On 19 July 1811, he became adjutant to Prince Peter Bagration and was promoted to lieutenant colonel on 17 May 1812. He participated in the retreat of the 2nd Western Army and fought at Romanovo, Mir, Saltanovka, Smolensk, Dorogobouzh and Vyazma. For his actions at Shevardino and Borodino, he was awarded the Order of St. Anna (2nd class).

In 1813, Brezhinsky became a colonel on 28 March 1813 and fought at Lutzen, Bautzen and Kulm (received the Order of St. Anna with diamonds, 2nd class). At Leipzig, he was wounded in the right shoulder and afterwards awarded the Prussian Pour le Merite. In 1814, he took part in the action at Labrussel, Troyes and Paris and was awarded the Order of St. George (4th class). He was promoted to major general on 13 June 1815 with seniority dating from 30 March 1814. Between 14 April 1814 and 13 June 1815, Brezhinsky served as chef of the 23rd Jager Regiment. After 13 June 1815, he served as an assistant to the commanders of the 27th and the 28th Infantry Division. He died on 11 October 1817 at Kursk.

BRIZEMAN VON NETTING, Ivan Ivanovich, (Johann Ludwig) (b. 1762 — d. 1 March 1814, Riga) descended from a Prussian family living in the Lifland *gubernia*. He enlisted in the Smolensk Infantry Regiment on 12 January 1771 and rose to ensign on 20 February 1778 while serving as adjutant to the regiment commander. On 21 June 1790, he transferred to the Fanagoria Grenadier Regiment and took part in the Russo-Swedish War. In 1792-1794, he fought against the Polish insurgents and received a golden sword for his actions at Vilna. He rose to colonel on 14 March 1798. and soon after became a major general. In March 1799, he was appointed chef of the Kazan Musketeer Regiment, and on 13 March 1799, he became the Commandant of Kizlyar and chef of the Kizlyar Garrison Regiment. On 16 March 1800, Brizeman, during the reorganization of garrison regiments, found himself discharged with a rank of lieutenant general.

Brizeman von Netting was restored to service on 1 December 1800 and appointed the Commandant of the fortress of Dünamund on 6 December 1800. The following year, he became chef of the Dneprovsk Musketeer Regiment on 25 September. He served at this position for the next five years until retiring on 27 January 1807. He returned to service on 29 September 1812, serving as the commandant of Dünamund and a duty officer to General Ivan Essen.

Brizeman took part in the minor actions against the retreating French forces at Riga (received the Order of St. Anna of 1st class), Mittau, Koenigsberg and Elbing, where he was seriously wounded. He spent the next two years recuperating from his wound, but died from complications on 1 March 1814. His son **Fedor Ivanovich Brizeman von Netting** served in the Lithuanian Infantry Regiment and fought at Polotsk, Chasniky and on the Berezina River before being killed at Leipzig. His brother, **Anton Ivanovich Brizeman von Netting** served in the Belostock Infantry Regiment and fought at Borisov. Another brother, **Wilhelm Ivanovich Brizeman von Netting,** commanded the Revel Musketeer Regiment between 18 July 1800 and 5 July 1806.

BUCHOLTZ, Otto Ivanovich (b. 1770 — date of death unknown) was born to a German noble family settled in the Estland *gubernia*. He enlisted in the Nasheburg Infantry Regiment on 21 November 1784 and transferred as a lieutenant to the 2nd Cannonier Regiment in July 1788. He participated in the campaigns against the Turks in 1787-1791, distinguishing himself at Ochakov (received a cross) and against the Poles in 1792-1794. In 1797, he transferred to the 10th Artillery Battalion and rose to colonel on 15 November 1799. In 1804-1808, he participated in Admiral Dmitry Senyavin's naval expedition in the Mediterranean Sea.

Bucholtz was promoted to major general on 28 March 1808 and took command of the 13th Artillery Brigade. On 12 April 1808, he became commander of the Kiev Artillery Garrison and Polotsk Reserve Artillery Park. He later commanded the artillery of the 7th Infantry Corps. During the 1812 Campaign, Bucholtz commanded artillery in the 1st Western Army and fought at Smolensk (wounded twice), Tarutino and Krasnyi. In 1813, he commanded the reserve artillery in Warsaw. In 1814, he took command of the artillery in the 6th Infantry Corps, and later commanded the artillery of the 2nd Army. He was discharged because of poor health in January 1818. During his military career, Bucholtz received the Orders of St. Anna (1st class), of St. Vladimir (3rd class), of St. George (4th class) as well as a golden sword with diamonds for courage.

BUDBERG, Karl Vasilievich (Karl Ludwig), (b. 9 July 1775 — d. 8 September 1829) was born to a German noble family in the Lifland *gubernia*. He enlisted in the Life Guard Semeyonovsk Regiment on 14 June 1785 and rose to sergeant in February 1792. On 12 July 1795, he became senior adjutant to Lieutenant General B. Lassi. In 1797, he transferred as a rotmistr to the Riga Cuirassier Regiment. He participated as a major in the expedition to Holland in 1799. Budberg also took part in the 1806-1807 Campaigns in Poland fighting at Golymin, Eylau (wounded in the left arm), Lomitten, Guttstadt, Heilsberg and Friedland. He was promoted to colonel on 24 December 1808 and took part in the 1809 Campaign against Austria. In 1811, he took command of His Majesty's Life Guard Cuirassier Regiment on 12 February and later that year he became chef of this unit on 15 November.

During the 1812 Campaign, Budberg's regiment was attached to the 1st Cuirassier Brigade of the 1st Cuirassier Division of the 5th Reserve (Guard) Corps of the 1st Western Army. Budberg fought at Vitebsk, Smolensk and Vyazma. At Borodino, he was wounded in the right foot, but continued commanding his regiment. In October-November 1812, he took part in the battles at Krasnyi, Orscha and Borisov. For its distinguished service, his regiment was awarded the St. George flags and assigned to the guard on 25 April 1813. During the War of Liberation in Saxony, Budberg was promoted to major general on 11 September with seniority dating from 30 August 1813. He fought at Lutzen, Bautzen, Koenigstein, Kulm (received the Prussian Iron Cross) and Leipzig. In 1814, he participated in the actions at Brienne, Arcis sur Aube, Le Fère Champenoise and Paris.

In 1816, he was appointed commander of the 2nd Brigade of the 1st Cuirassier Division. On 5 November 1824, he took command of the 2nd Hussar Division and two years later was promoted to lieutenant general on 3 September. Budberg participated in the Russo-Turkish War of 1828-1829, but died on 8 September 1829. During his career, he was awarded the Orders of St. Anna with diamonds (1st class), of St. George (4th class), of St. Vladimir (2nd class), the Prussian Order of Red Eagle (2nd class), the Austrian Order of Leopold (3rd class) and the Bavarian Order of Maximilian Joseph (3rd class).

BULATOV, Mikhail Leontievich (b. 1760 — d. 14 May 1825, Omsk) was born to a noble family in the Ryazan *gubernia*. He enlisted as a private in the Life Guard Izmailovsk Regiment in March 1776 and transferred as a lieutenant to the Vladimir Infantry Regiment on 3 February 1781. Two years later, he joined the Ladoga Infantry Regiment with a rank of captain. He served in the Caucasus in 1783-1787. In 1788, Bulatov was appointed ober-quartermaster in the headquarters of the Army of Ekaterinoslavl and, in 1790-1791, he served in the Danube Valley, distinguishing himself at Bender, Akkerman and Ismail (received the Order of St. Vladimir, 4th class). In 1792-1794, he participated in the suppression of the Polish uprising. In 1794-1796, he served as a quartermaster general in the Russian army. Promoted to colonel on 1 January 1798 and to major general on 30 May 1799, Bulatov served in the depot at St. Petersburg, receiving the Order of St. John of Jerusalem in 1801 and the Order of St. George (4th class) in 1803.

During the 1807 Campaign in Poland, Bulatov served as a quartermaster in Bennigsen's army and later commanded a brigade in Tuchkov's corps. He was appointed chef of the Moghilev Musketeer Regiment on 24 December 1807. The following year, he fought the Swedes in Finland, distinguishing himself at Kuopio. On 27 April 1808, Bulatov was seriously wounded at Revolax, receiving three musket ball wounds to the chest. He was captured and treated in Sweden. When offered to return to Russia on the condition of not fighting against Sweden, Bulatov declined it and remained in captivity until the Swedish King Gustavus Adolf released him in early 1809. Returning to Russia, Bulatov was under investigation for the defeat at revolax, but the court had acquited him. On 21 July 1809, he was dispatched to the Danubian Principalities, where he fought the Turks at Isaccea, Tulcea, Constanta, Rassevat, Silistra, Sumla (received the diamond signs of the Order of St. Anna), Ruse (received the Order of St. George, 3rd class, 3 December 1810) and Nikopol. He distinguished himself during the operations at Ruse that resulted in surrender of the entire Turkish army in early 1812.

During the 1812 Campaign, Bulatov commanded a corps in the Army of Danube and fought at Gornostaev, Volkovysk and Pinsk. In 1813-1814, he participated in the actions at Czenstochow, Krakow, Dresden and Hamburg, where he was wounded twice. After the war, Bulatov commanded detachments deployed on the Dniestr and Prut Rivers before becoming commander-in-chief of the Russian forces in Bessarabia in 1820. He was promoted to lieutenant general on 8 December 1823 and took command of the 27th Division. In 1824, he became the Governor General of Siberia, but died at Omsk on 14 May 1825.

BURSAK, Fedor Jakovlevich (date of birth unknown — died after 1816) was born to a prominent Cossack family and participated in the Russo-Turkish War in 1787-1791, distinguishing himself at Ismail. By 1799, he had risen to lieutenant colonel and ataman of the Cossack forces in the Kuban Valley. He reorgazied the Cossack forces in 1803 and launched a series of campaigns against the mountaineers in the North Caucasus region from 1800-1811. He defeated the Circassians in the Kuban Valley in May 1802 and was promoted to colonel. In 1804, he secured the Kuban Valley and was awarded the Order of St. Anna (2nd class) with diamonds.

BUTURLIN, Dmitry Petrovich (d. 1790 – d. 21 October 1849) was born to a prominent Russian noble family and began his service as a sub-lieutenant in the Imperial Retinue. He distinguished himself during the 1812 Campaign, garnering the Orders of St. Anna (4th class), of St. Vladimir (4th class) and a golden sword for courage. In 1813, he fought at Leipzig and received the Order of St. Anna (2nd class). After the war, he became flügel adjutant in 1817 and received his promotion to colonel in 1819. He served as a military adviser in the French Army during the French invasion of Spain in 1823 and was awarded the Order of St. Vladimir for his actions at Trocadero (31 August 1823).

In 1824-1829, Buturlin served as a quartermaster general of the 1st Army and during the Russo-Turkish War in 1829, he was appointed quartermaster general of the 2nd Army. He distinguished himself at Kulevchi and Silistra, receiving the Order of St. Vladimir (2nd class). He then transferred to civil service with a rank of privy counsellor and was appointed to the Senate in 1835. Buturlin became a member of the State Council in 1840, the director of the Imperial Library in 1842 and head of the Censorship Committee in 1848. Buturlin was a prolific writer and historian. His most important works include *Relation historique et critique de la guerre Austro-Russe en Italie en 1799* (St. Petersburg, 1812), *Précis des événements militaires de la derniére guerre des Espagnols contre les Francais* (St. Petersburg, 1819), *Tableau de la campagne d'automne de 1813 en Allemagne etc., par un officier russe, reviv le baron de Jomini"* (Paris, 1817-1818), *Histoire militaire de la campagne de Russie en 1812* (Paris, 1824), *"Kutuzov v 1812 g."* (*Russkaya Starina*, 1894) and *Kartina voin Rossii s Turtsiei* (St. Petersburg, 1829).

BUXHÖWDEN, Fedor Fedorovich (Friedrich Wilhelm), (b. 13 September 1750, estate Magnustal on Island of Ezel – 4 September 1811, Lode) descended from a noble family in the Lifland *gubernia*. He enrolled in the Artillery and Engineer Cadet Corps in 1764. Six years later, he went with the Russian army to fight the Turks and distinguished himself at Bender, receiving promotion to engineer ensign in 1770. He was seriously wounded during the assault on Braila in 1771 and earned the Order of St. George (4th class) for his valor. In 1772, he became adjutant to General Felzugmeister Prince Orlov and accompanied him in his travels in Germany and Italy. Under Orlov's patronage, Buxhöwden was quickly promoted through the ranks. In 1783, he became a colonel; four years later, he was appointed a flügel adjutant to Catherine II and took command of the Keksholm (Kexholm) Infantry Regiment. He participated in the Russo-Swedish War in 1788-1790 serving as a brigadier in the galley fleet of Vice Admiral Prince Nassau-Zigen. In 1789, he distinguished himself in the action at Rochensalmi for which he was promoted to major general and awarded the Order of St. George (3rd class). For his actions in the 1790 Campaign, he received the Order of St. Anna (1st class).

Buxhöwden then commanded a division in the campaign against the Polish insurgents in 1793-1794, fought at Praga and was appointed the Commandant of Warsaw. He was generously rewarded for his services receiving the Order of St. Vladimir (2nd class), a medal from the citizens of Warsaw and a golden sword with diamonds for courage. In December 1795, he was conferred the title of count by the King of Prussia and awarded the Orders of the White Eagle, of St. Stanislaus (1st class) and of St. John of Jerusalem. Serving under Emperor Paul I, Buxhöwden became the Military Governor of St. Petersburg and was decorated with the Order of St. Alexander of Neva. Between 23 November 1796 and 1 September 1798 he served as chef of Keksholm Musketeer Regiment. On 16 April 1797, he was conferred the title of count of the Russian Empire. However, in September of the same year, he was discharged from military service. After travelling in Germany, Buxhöwden returned to Russia in early 1802 and was restored in the army in 1803 with a rank of general of infantry. The same year, he became head of the Lifland Inspection.

In 1805, Buxhöwden brought reinforcements to Olmutz and, at Austerlitz, he commanded one of the Russian columns on the Allied left flank and suffered appalling losses. After the battle, he had only two battalions intact out of the forty-four he led into action. Despite this catastrophe, he was awarded the Order of St. Vladimir (2nd class). In 1806-1807 Campaign, Buxhöwden commanded one of the Russian corps but had strained relations with Levin Bennigsen. The two commanders detested each other and refused to cooperate. After Bennigsen became the commander-in-chief of the Russian army, Buxhöwden left army for Riga and complained to Alexander about his rival. When his appeals were ignored, Buxhöwden challenged Bennigsen to a duel but the two never fought each other. In 1807, he served as the Military Governor of Riga and was awarded the Order of St. Andrew the First Called for mobilizing the local militia.

In 1808, Buxhöwden took command of the Russian army to invade Finland and successfully drove the Swedish army out of Finland. For his success, he was awarded the diamond signs of the Order of St. Andrew the First Called and the Order of St. George (2nd class). On 29 September 1808, the Swedes offered a cease-fire, which Buxhöwden welcomed because his army suffered from the lack of supplies, ammunition and reinforcements. However, Emperor Alexander, as he traveled to meet Napoleon at Erfurt, disapproved the armistice and ordered Buxhöwden to resume the offensive. The armistice ended on 27 October and, by 13 December, all of Finland was finally under the Russian control. Yet, Buxhöwden opposed to Alexander's aggressive policy in Finland. The Russian emperor, anxious to expand his territory in the north, dismissed Buxhöwden in early December and appointed a new commander-in-chief, General von Knorring. Buxhöwden retired to his estate in Estland, where he died on 4 September 1811.

BUXHÖWDEN, Ivan Filipovich served as chef of the Voronezh Musketeer Regiment (7 October 1807 – 21 November 1807) and led his unit in the 7th Division during the 1806-1807 Campaigns in Poland, fighting at Eylau, Heilsberg and Friedland. He commanded the Astrakhan Grenadier Regiment between 21 November 1807 and 7 September 1812. During the 1812 Campaign, he served at Smolensk but was mortally wounded at the battle of Borodino on 7 September 1812.

BUXHÖWDEN, Peter Fedorovich (b. 1790 – d. 1863) was born to General Fedor Buxhöwden and was educated at home before being enlisted in the Polish army by his family. In 1805, he transferred to the Tavrida Grenadier Regiment with a rank of ensign, where he served as adjutant to his father and participated in the campaign against Napoleon. In 1806, he entered the Life Guard Preobrazhensk Regiment and became flügel adjutant to the Emperor on 24 March 1808. He participated in the Russo-Swedish War of 1808-1809 and received the Order of St. Vladimir (4th class) for his actions.

Buxhöwden retired in 1811 but returned to service during the Russian Campaign of 1812. He served in the Alexandria Hussar Regiment in the 3rd Reserve Army of Observation and fought at Kobryn, Pruzhany and other minor actions earning the Order of St. George (4th class). In late 1812, Buxhöwden transferred to the Life Guard Hussar Regiment and fought at Lutzen and Bautsen in May 1813. He then served in the cavalry detachment and fought at Bunzlau, Katzbach and Leipzig, where he was wounded in the left foot and garnered a golden sword for courage. However, he took a long furlough because of poor health and retired in 1816. Four years later, he returned to service and was appointed lieutenant colonel in the Elizavetgrad Hussar Regiment. In 1824, he became a colonel and transferred to the Life Guard Hussar Regiment.

During the Russo-Turkish War in 1828, Buxhöwden served in the St. Petersburg Uhlan Regiment attached to the 6th Corps. He commanded a cavalry detachment at the siege of Silistra amd distinguished himself in the actions of 22 July. Buxhöwden retired again in late 1829 and served as an actual civil counsellor in the Ministry of Internal Affairs. He was instrumental in battling a cholera epidemic in St. Petersburg in 1831 and was awarded the Order of St. Vladimir (3rd class) for his efforts. In 1833-1840, he was elected leader (marshal) of the St. Petersburg *uezd* nobility. In 1840, he was promoted to major general and two years later he was appointed head of the 4th Gendarmerie District. Buxhöwden became a lieutenant general in April 1850 and served in the 3rd Department of the Senate. He was awarded the Order of St. Alexander of Neva in 1861.

CARBONIER (Karbonier), Leo Lvovich (Louis Barthelemy) (b. 3 December 1779, St. Petersburg — d. 9 May 1836) descended from the French noble family Carbonier de Grogniac that settled in Russia in the early 18th century. He enlisted as a sergeant in the Life Guard Preobrazhensk Regiment in 1786 and made an ensign in 1788. The next year, he transferred as a captain to the St. Petersburg Grenadier Regiment and participated in the Russo-Swedish War in 1789-1790. In 1791, he was sent to the Danube Valley and fought the Turks at Braila, Babadag and Macin. In 1794-1795, he served in the Black Sea Grenadier Corps in Odessa. Carbonier transferred to the quartermaster service in 1801 and trained cadets in the 2nd Cadet Corps in 1802-1807, receiving the rank of lieutenant colonel. In 1808, he transferred as a captain (2nd class) to the Ministry of Navy and supervised the construction of fortifications at Revel.

After becoming colonel in 1809, Carbonier served in the fortress of Kronshtadt. He rose to a major general on 19 October 1810 and served in the Engineer Corps for the next two years, becoming inspector general of the corps in 1811. He participated in the 1813-1814 Campaigns and fought at Dresden, Kulm, Leipzig and Hamburg, earning the Order of St. Anna (1st class) with diamonds, the Prussian Order of Red Eagle and the Austrian Order of Leopold.

From 1815 - 1816, he was in charge of the engineer schools and worked on improving navigation on the Volga, Gzhat and Moscow Rivers. In 1818, Carbonier supervised the military colonies and later served on the Council of Transportation. After retirement from 20 December 1824 to 1826, Carbonier was appointed to the Engineer Corps in February 1826 and rose to lieutenant general on 3 September 1826. He also served as the head of the main censorship committee. He became director of the Marine Section of the Department of Constructions on 19 March 1827 and was promoted to general of the Engineer Corps on 4 May 1834. Carbonier died on 9 May 1836 and was buried at the Smolensk Lutheran Cemetery in St. Petersburg.

CASTELLI, Stepan Nikolaevich (b. 1753 — d. 1806) descended from an Italian noble family. He began service as a sergeant in the Kozlovsk Musketeer Regiment in 1771 and took part in the Russo-Turkish War in 1771-1774 and in the operations in the Crimea in 1778. He transferred to the Elisavetgrad Garrison in 1779 and later commanded the Black Sea Grenadier Battalion. In 1792, he joined the Arkhangelogorod Musketeer Regiment and was promoted to colonel on 29 October 1798. Castelli took command of the Arkhangelogorod Musketeer Regiment on 20 October 1798 and participated in the 1799 Campaign in Italy, fighting at Serravalle and Novi. On 31 January 1800, he became a major general and chef of the Velikii Lutsk Musketeer Regiment. He was appointed chef of the Kazan Garrison Regiment on 14 December 1802 and served there until his death on 28 January 1806.

CASTRO-LAZERDA, Jacob Antonovich (b. 1733 — d. 1800) descended from a Spanish noble family. He served in the Spanish and Prussian armies before entering the Russian service as a captain in the Revel Dragoon Regiment in 1761. He was later transferred to the Polotsk Infantry Regiment and took part in the Russo-Turkish War of 1787-1791, fighting at Ochakov in 1788. Castro-Lazerda was appointed chef of the Old Ingermanland Musketeer Regiment on 14 December 1796, and then became chef of the Revel Garrison Regiment on 18 October 1798. Castro-Lazerda rose to general of infantry on 3 October 1798 and commanded the Revel Garrison Regiment until his death in the spring of 1800 (excluded from rosters on 3 June 1800).

CHALIKOV (Shalikashvili), Anton Stepanovich (b. 21 July 1754 — d. 9 April 1821) was born to a Georgian noble family and began service as a private in the Life Guard Preobrazhensk Regiment on 12 March 1774. He transferred as a rotmistr to the regular army in January 1788 and took part in the Russo-Turkish War of 1789-1791. He served in Poland in 1792-1794 and participated in the campaign in Switzerland under General Rimsky-Korsakov in 1799. Promoted to colonel on 7 April 1800, Chalikov commanded the Sumsk Hussar Regiment between 21 February and 1 June 1802. In 1805, he distinguished himself at Austerlitz, where he was wounded in the left leg. In 1807, he served in Poland, fighting at Heilsberg and Friedland (received the Order of St. George, 4th class, 1 June 1808).

Chalikov took command of the His Majesty Grand Duke Constantine's Uhlan Regiment (later Life Guard Uhlan Regiment) on 10 December 1807 and was promoted to major general on 24 December 1807. In 1812, he commanded the Guard Light Cavalry Brigade and fought at Vitebsk, Smolensk, Borodino and Tarutino. In 1813, Chalikov participated in the battles at Lutzen, Bautzen, Kulm (received the Prussian Iron Cross) and Leipzig. In 1814, he took part in the actions at Brienne, Montmirail, Le Fère Champenoise (received the Order of St. George, 3rd class, 25 March 1814) and Paris. For his actions in 1813-1814, Chalikov was also awarded the Prussian Orders of Red Eagle (2nd class) and the Pour le Merite, the Austrian Order of Leopold, the Bavarian Order of Maximilian Joseph and the French Legion of Honor. After the war, he commanded the 2nd Brigade of the Guard Light Cavalry Division and the Guard Light Cavalry Division (29 July 1818).

CHAPLITS, Yefim Ignatievich (b. 1768 — d. December 1825) was born to a Polish noble family. He began service in the Polish army but entered the Russian service with a rank of second major on 26 October 1783. During the Russo-Turkish War in 1788-1791, he served in Prince Gregory Potemkin's staff and distinguished himself at Ochakov, Bender, Akkerman and Ismail. For his actions against the Turks, Chaplits received the Order of St. Vladimir (4th class) and promotion to premier major. In 1792, he became a lieutenant colonel and transferred to the Smolensk Dragoon Regiment. In 1792-1794, he served against the Polish insurgents and was wounded and captured at Warsaw in 1794. Chaplitz was soon released and participated in the Persian Campaign in 1796, commanding the Grebensk and Semeiny Cossack Regiments. He became a colonel on 30 July 1796, was discharged from the army in March 1798, and returned to service with the rank of major general on 27 March 1801. Chaplitz was appointed to the Imperial Retinue on 23 October 1803.

During the 1805 Campaign, Chaplits served under Prince Peter Bagration and participated in the actions at Lambach, Amstetten (received the Order of St. George, 3rd class, 24 January 1806), Schöngrabern (Hollabrunn) and Austerlitz. He became chef of the Pavlograd Hussar Regiment on 4 August 1806 and commander of the cavalry brigade on 4 November 1806. Chaplitz distinguished himself at Golymin, Allenstein, and briefly served as the Commandant of Koenigsberg. In 1809-1810, he commanded the 7th Division and, in November 1810, he took command of the Reserve Cavalry Corps.

Chaplitz briefly led the 4th and 8th Cavalry Divisions in early 1811 before taking command of the 3rd Reserve Cavalry Corps of the 3rd Reserve Army of Observation on 19 April 1812. During the 1812 Campaign, he fought at Kobryn and Slonim for which he was later promoted to lieutenant general on 12 November 1812. In September 1812, Chaplitz was appointed commander of the infantry corps and led the advance guard of Admiral Paul Chichagov's army to the Berezina River. Chaplitz fought the French at Borisov on 26 November 1812, where he was lightly wounded in the head. Two days later, he captured Vilna.

In 1813, Chaplitz served at Thorn before taking command of cavalry of the Army of Poland; he fought at Leipzig in October of the same year. In 1814, he participated in the siege of Hamburg and assumed command of the 3rd Corps of the Army of Poland on 18 April 1814. In 1817, Chaplitz became commander of the 3rd Hussar Division and was relieved of command on 27 February 1823. During his career, he also received the Prussian Order of Red Eagle, the French Legion of Honor, the Russian Orders of St. Alexander of Neva, of St. Anna (1st class) with diamonds, of St. Vladimir (2nd class) and a golden sword with diamonds.

CHARNYSH (Chernysh), Ivan Ivanovich (b. 1767 — date of death unclear, c. 1831) was born to a Cossack noble family in the Poltava *gubernia*. He enlisted in the Mirgorod Regiment of the Little Russia (Malorossiisky) Cossack Host and was promoted to esaul on 16 April 1784. He began service in the regular Russian army as a second major of the Poltava Light Horse (*legkokonnii*) Regiment on 30 December 1792. Charnysh served in Poland in 1792 and distinguished himself at Praga. Promoted to colonel on 24 May 1799, he took command of the Seversk Dragoon Regiment on 28 September 1799.

Charnysh became a major general on 31 January 1805 with seniority since November 1803; he was also appointed chef of the Kazan Dragoon Regiment on 31 January 1805. Charnysh participated in the campaign in Poland in 1807, serving with the 5th Division at Eylau (received the Order of St. George, 4th class) and Guttstadt. During the 1812 Campaign, Charnysh commanded the 4th Brigade of the 1st Cavalry Division of the 1st Reserve Cavalry Corps and took part in several rear guard actions, including the combats at Zvenigorod and Moscow. In 1813, he served at Danzig and, in 1814, he remained in the Duchy of Warsaw. He was relieved of command in 1815 and was discharged from the army in March 1831.

CHECHENSKY (Chichensky) Alexander was born to a Chechen noble family. In 1812, he commanded the 1st Bug Cossack Regiment and distinguished himself at Borodino, garnering the Order of St. George (4th class). He then served in Denis Davydov's detachment, fighting in the Vyazma region, and distinguished himself during the French retreat, capturing hundreds of French stragglers. Chechensky took part in the 1813-1814 Campaigns as well and later rose to major general before dying in 1834.

CHEREMISINOV, Yakov (Jacob) Yakovlevich (b. 1784, Gurova — date of death unclear) was born to an officer's family in the Kursk *gubernia*. He graduated from the 2nd Cadet Corps and began service as a sub lieutenant in the 3rd Artillery Regiment in 1804. During the 1805 Campaign, he fought at Austerlitz and received the Order of St. Anna (3rd class). In 1807, he took part in the battles at Eylau, Heilsberg and Friedland (earned the Order of St. Vladimir, 4th class). Cheremisinov served in Finland in 1808-1809 and transferred to the Danubian Principalities in late 1809. In 1810-1811, he fought at Turtukai (garnered a golden sword), Ruse (wounded in the head, received an Imperial letter of gratitude) and Lovchea. He took command of the 14th Light Artillery Company on 25 April 1811 and was promoted to lieutenant colonel on 30 July 1811. During the 1812 Campaign, he took part in the actions on the Narva River and at Mukhovets (received the Order of St. Anna (2nd class) with diamonds). In 1813-1814, he served at Glogau, Lutzen, Bautzen, Leipzig (severely wounded by canister to both hands, decorated with the Order of St. George, 4th class) and Paris.

CHERNOZUBOV (Chernozubov IV), Ilya Fedorovich (b. 1765 — d. 1821) was born to a Don Cossack staff officer's family. He began service on 21 June 1777 and rose to sotnik on 13 July 1783. He served in the Kuban Valley in 1778-1783 and participated in the Russo-Turkish War of 1787-1791, distinguishing himself at Ismail. In 1794, he took part in the operations in Poland. Under Emperor Paul, Chernozubov was appointed to the Cossack Expeditionary Corp assigned to invade India that marched only as far as Orenburg. He participated in the 1807 Campaign in Poland under Ataman Platov. During the 1812 Campaign, Chernozubov commanded a Don Cossack *opolchenye* and distinguished himself at Krasnyi, receiving promotion to major general on 30 July 1813 with seniority dating from 16 November 1812. In 1813-1814, he served in the Duchy of Warsaw before retiring in January 1820.

CHERNISHEV (Chernyshev), Alexander Ivanovich (b. 10 January 1786, Moscow — d. 20 June 1857, Castellamare di Stabia, Italy) was born to a prominent Russian noble family. He was home educated by Jesuit Priest Perron and began service as a kamer page in 1801. He transferred as a cornet to the Chevalier Guard on 2 October 1802 and served as an adjutant to General Fedor Uvarov. Chernishev participated in the 1805-1807 Campaigns and distinguished himself at Austerlitz and Friedland (received the Order of St. George, 4th class, 1 June 1808). He was dispatched on several diplomatic missions to France in 1808, where he became close to Napoleon. Chernishev served as the Russian observer to the French army during Napoleon's campaign against Austria in 1809, witnessed the battles of Aspern-Essling and Wagram and was appointed a flügel adjutant to Alexander I on 18 June 1809.

In 1810-1812, Chernishev served on numerous diplomatic and secret missions to Napoleon as well as worked as a Russian spymaster in Paris. Chernishev successfully infiltrated the French Ministry of War and obtained many secret documents on Napoleon's preparations against Russia. He was promoted to colonel on 18 November 1810 and left France in 1811, after his undecorver operations were discovered by the French secret police. During the 1812 Campaign, he accompanied Emperor Alexander, then served on Kutuzov's and

Chichagov's staffs. In November-December 1812, he commanded a cavalry detachment and participated in the pursuit of the French army. He became a major general and adjutant general on 4 December 1812. In 1813, Chernishev distinguished himself at Marienwerder, Berlin (earned the Order of St. George, 3rd class, 1 March 1813), Luneburg, Kassel and commanded a cavalry detachment during his famous raid into Westphalia. In 1814, he fought at Soissons and was promoted to lieutenant general on 4 March 1814. The following year, Chernishev again commanded a cavalry detachment during the Hundred Days and captured Chalons.

After the war, Chernishev served on the committee to reorganize the Don Cossack Host in 1819-1821. He took command of the Guard Light Cavalry Division on 30 April 1821, served on the investigation commission on the Decembrists in 1826 and was conferred the title of count of the Russian Empire on 3 September 1826. He was appointed to the Senate in 1827 and rose to general of cavalry on 14 October 1827 and chargè d'affaires of Minister of War on 7 September 1827. Chernishev became the Deputy Chief of General Staff on 15 February 1827 and a member of the State Council in 1828. He served as the Minister of War between 13 May 1832 and 7 September 1852. He was appointed chef of the St. Petersburg Uhlan Regiment on 14 April 1833, received the title of prince of the Russian Empire on 28 April 1841 and became chef of the Kabarda Jager Regiment on 23 April 1843. For his service, the St. Petersburg Uhlans and the Kabarda Jagers were renamed to Chernishev Uhlan and Jagers Regiments on 6 April 1844.

In 1848, Chernishev became the head of the State Council (15 November), the chairman of the Committee of Ministers and the president of the Caucasian and Siberian Committies. He was conferred the title of his highness prince (*svetleishii kniaz*) on 3 September 1849. Chernishev was relieved of all positions because of poor health on 17 April 1856. He travelled to Italy to recuperate, but died at Castellamare di Stabia on 20 June 1857. Chernishev was one of the most decorated Russian officers. During his career, he received the Russian Orders of St. Andrew the First Called with diamonds, of St. Vladimir (1st class), of St. Alexander of Neva with diamonds, of St. Anna (1st class) with diamonds, a medal "For L Years of Distinguished Service," the Polish Order of the White Eagle, the Prussian Orders of Red and Black Eagles and the Pour le Merite, the Austrian Orders of St. Stephan and Maria Theresa (3rd class), the Swedish Orders of the Sword and of the Seraphim, the Bavarian Order of Maximilian Joseph (2nd class), the Dutch Order of Wilhelm (2nd class), the French Legion of Honor and Order of St. Louis, the Hessian Orders of the Lion and of the Military Merit, the Sardinian Order of St. Maurice and Lazarus and the Portugese Military Order of St. Benedict of Avis (1st class).

CHICHAGOV, Pavel Vasilievich (b. 8 July 1767, St. Petersburg — d. 1 September 1849, Paris) was the son of Admiral Vasily Chichagov. He studied in the Naval Corps and began service as a sergeant in the Life Guard Preobrazhensk Regiment in 1779. In January 1782, he transferred to the 1st Marine Battalion and, in 1782-1784, he took part in the campaign in the Mediterranean Sea as an aide-de-camp to his father. Chichagov became a naval lieutenant on 17 September 1783 and captain lieutenant on 25 April 1787 before serving on the ship-of-the-line "*Iezekil*" under Rear Admiral Kozlyaninov in the Danish waters in 1788. During the Russian-Swedish War of 1789-1790, he distinguished himself serving on the ship-of-the-line "*Rostislav*" in the naval engagements at Eland, Vyborg and Revel. For his actions, Chichagov was promoted to captain 2nd class and awarded the Order of St. George (4th class, 29 May 1790) and a golden sword. He had the honor of delivering news of the victory at Vyborg to the Empress Catherine II for which he was promoted to captain (1st class) on 8 July 1790.

After the war, Chichagov studied in Great Britain from 1792-1793. He took command of the captured Swedish ship-of-the-line "*Sophia-Magdalena*" on 19 July 1793 and, in 1794-1796, he commanded the ship-of-the-line "*Retvizan*" in the Baltic Sea. Chichagov rose to captain brigadier on 24 November 1796 and took part in the naval maneuvers at Krasnyi Gorky in June 1797, receiving the Order of St. Anna (2nd class). However, Chichagov was discharged because of a disagreement with Emperor Paul in October 1797. Paul pardoned him two years later and promoted him to rear admiral on 20 May 1799. Yet, Chichagov was soon falsely accused of treason and imprisoned in the Petropavlosvk Fortress on 2 July 1799. After investigating the case, Paul acquitted him and restored his rank on 13 July 1799. Late that year, Chichagov participated in the expedition to Holland and fought at Helder and Texel. For his actions, he received the Order of St. Anna (1st class) and a golden sword with diamonds (gift from the British sovereign).

Returning to Russia, Chichagov became an adjutant general to Alexander on 24 May 1801, a member of the Committee on Navy Reorganization on 5 September 1802, vice admiral on 25 November 1802 and the Deputy Minister of Navy on 12 December 1802. Over the next five years, Chichagov introduced a series of reforms to modernize the Russian navy. He was appointed the Minister of Navy with the rank of admiral on 1 August 1807. He became a member of the State Council on 25 November 1811. However, Chichagov resigned because of poor health on 10 December 1811 and served as an adjutant general to Emperor Alexander. The following year, Alexander appointed him the Commander-in-Chief of the Army of Danube and of the Black Sea Fleet and the Governor General of Moldavia and Wallachia on 16 July 1812. However, the Treaty of Bucharest was concluded before Chichagov arrived to the army so he did not participate in the military operations against the Turks.

Late in 1812, the Army of Danube merged with the 3rd Reserve Army of Observation (30 September) and Chichagov took command of the newly created 3rd Western Army. He drove the Austrian troops to the Bug and advanced to Kamenetz and Visoko-Litovsk. Chichagov attempted to cut Napoleon's line of retreat on the Berezina on 25-26 November 1812 but failed and was largely blamed for this fiasco, although Kutuzov and Wittgenstein should have shared the responsibility as well. He captured Smorgon on 7 December and pursued the French into Poland in January 1813. In 1813, he was relieved of command because of "poor health," but, in reality, he was harshly criticized and blamed in the Russian society for mishandling the operation on the Berezina.

Chichagov was offended by such criticism and requested an indefinite furlough in March 1814 settling in France. He was relieved of all positions but remained a member of the State Council for the next twenty years. In 1834, he disregarded Emperor Nicholas' decree limiting staying abroad to five years and was discharged from the Russian service on 29 October 1834; he was also dismissed from the State Council and his property was requisitioned. Chichagov died on 1 September 1849 in Paris. He interesting memoirs were published in Paris after his death.

CHICHERIN, Alexander Vasilievich (b. 1793 — d. 29 August 1813, Kulm) was born to a prominent Russian family; the son of Lieutenant General Vasily Chicherin (see below). After studying in the Page Corps, he began service as a page at the Imperial Court in 1806, becoming a kamer page two years later. Chicherin then enlisted in the Life Guard Semeyonovsk Regiment and rose to a lieutenant in 1811.

During the 1812-1813 Campaigns, Chicherin served with the 3rd Battalion of this regiment at Borodino, Vilna, Lutzen and Bautzen before being mortally wounded at Kulm on 29 August 1813. He was buried in Prague later that year. Checherin wrote one of the most insightful Russian memoirs on the 1812-1813 Campaigns, published as *Dnevnik Aleksandra Checherina* [Diary of Alexander Chicherin] in Moscow in 1966. The manuscript was lost in the piles of materials in the Russian archives for some hundred thirty years before it was accidentally found and printed. It contains detailed information on the daily life in the Russian army and introduces reader to the fascinating world of the Russian officer of the Napoleonic Wars.

CHICHERIN (Chicherin I), Nikolay Alexandrovich (b. 1807 — date of death unclear) was born to a Russian noble family. He began service as a sergeant in the Life Guard Preobrazhensk Regiment on 25 January 1782, and transferred as a vakhmistr to the Life Guard Horse regiment on 18 February 1787. He was rapidly promoted during the next eleven years, becoming cornet on 12 January 1792, a sub-lieutenant on 14 January 1797, a lieutenant on 20 August 1797, and a staff rotmistr on 29 August 1798. However, he was discharged from the army during Emperor Paul's purges in November 1798. Chicherin returned to the service four years later, becoming a lieutenant colonel and adjutant to the Grand Duke in February 1802. Six months later, Chicherin transferred to the Life Guard Horse Regiment on 9 August, and rose to colonel on 16 September. He participated in the 1805 Campaign and distinguished himself at Austerlitz, earning a golden sword for courage. In 1807, he served under Grand Duke Constantine and participated in the operations on the Passarge River and at Heilsberg and Friedland, earning the Orders of St. George (4th class), of St. Vladimir (3rd class) and the Prussian Pour le Merite. Chicherin took a discharge with a rank of major general on 27 November 1807 but returned to the army five years later, when he became adjutant to Grand Duke Constantine on 22 August 1812. Chicherin served under Grand Duke for the rest of the war and participated in operations in Germany and France in 1813-1814. On 23 October 1815, Chicherin was transferred to the 27th Infantry Division and took command of the 1st Brigade of this division on 6 January 1816. However, he retired because of poor health on 22 January 1815. The date of his death has not been established.

CHICHERIN (Chicherin II), Peter Alexandrovich (b. 21 February 1778 — d. 8 January 1849, St. Petersburg) was born to a noble family from the Tula *gubernia*. He enlisted as a sergeant in the Life Guard Preobrazhensk Regiment on 19 April 1785 and transferred as a vakhmistr to the Life Guard Horse Regiment on 12 May 1789. He rose to colonel on 16 December 1803. During the 1805 Campaign, Chicherin participated in the battle of Austerlitz on 2 December. In 1807, he took part in the battles of Guttstadt, Heilsberg and Friedland, earning the Order of St. George (4th class, 1 June 1808). He took command of the Life Guard Dragoon Regiment on 24 December 1809. During the 1812 Campaign, Chicherin served in the 1st Western Army and took part in the battles at Wilkomir, Vitebsk, Smolensk and Borodino. Late in 1812, he was attached to Dorokhov's detachment and distinguished himself at Krasnyi for which he was decorated with the Order of St. George (3rd class, 15 June 1813). He rose to major general on 18 December 1812.

In 1813, Chicherin served at Lutzen, Bautzen, Kulm (received the Prussian Iron Cross) and Leipzig (wounded) and, in 1814, he fought at Le Fère Champenoise and Paris. After 1815, he commanded the 1st Brigade of the Guard Light Cavalry Division, was appointed adjutant general on 27 December 1825 and promoted to lieutenant general on 13 January 1826. He became commander of the 1st Guard Light Cavalry Division on 18 December 1826. In 1828-1829, Chicherin participated in the Russo-Turkish War and, in 1830-1831, he served against the Poles, commanding the Combined Guard Corps. He was appointed to the Imperial Retinue on 30 December 1833 and received promotion to general of cavalry on 4 May 1834. During his service, Chicherin received the Orders of St. Alexander of Neva with diamonds, of St. Anna (1st class) with diamonds, of St. Vladimir (2nd class), a golden sword with diamonds, a medal "For XL Years of Distinguished Service," the Prussian Orders of Red Eagle and the Pour le Merite and the Bavarian Order of Maximilian Joseph.

CHICHERIN, Vasily Nikolayevich (b. 1754 – d. 17 April 1825) was born to a noble family in the Tambov *gubernia*. He enlisted as a corporal in the Life Guard Izmailovsk Regiment on 28 February 1761 and transferred as a lieutenant to the His Majesty's Cuirassier Regiment on 12 January 1769. He served in Poland in 1771-1773 and commanded the 2nd Marine Battalion during the Russo-Swedish War of 1788-1790. He fought at Gogland in 1788, where he was wounded in the right shoulder and later received promotion to second major. The next year, Chicherin became a lieutenant colonel and commander of the 4th Battalion of the Estland Jager Corps (1 June) and distinguished himself at Bjorkezund, Krasnyi Gorky (received a golden sword), Vyborg and Swenkzund (wounded in the chest). In 1792-1794, he served in Poland, receiving promotion to colonel on 16 January 1793 and the Order of St. George (4th class, for exemplary service) on 7 December 1794. Chicherin distinguished himself during the assault on Praga, the suburb of Warsaw, for which he earned promotion to brigadier and the Order of St. George (3rd class) on 12 January 1795.

Promoted to major general on 24 January 1798, Chicherin took command of the Pskov Dragoon Regiment on 24 January 1798 before becoming chef of this unit on 21 February of the same year. He was discharged from the army in October 1798. Under Alexander I, he returned to the army and was appointed to the Imperial Retinue on 27 March 1801. Chicherin retired with the rank of lieutenant general on 1 January 1810. During the 1812 Campaign, he organized and briefly commanded the Moscow *opolchenye*, taking part in the battles at Borodino, Maloyaroslabets, Vyazma and Krasnyi. In 1813, he served at Modlin for which he was decorated with the Order of St. Vladimir (2nd class). Chicherin retired after the war and settled in Moscow, where he died in April 1825.

CHOGLOKOV, Pavel (Paul) Nikolayevich (b. 29 January 1772, St. Petersburg *gubernia* — d. 15 April 1832, St. Petersburg) was born to a prominent noble family of Prussian origins that settled in Russia in the 13th century. He studied in the Cadet Corps and began service as a lieutenant in the Pskov Infantry Regiment on 19 June 1790. He served on the galley fleet against the Swedes in 1790, but did not participate in any major military actions. Choglokov was promoted to adjutant with the rank of captain in 1792 and transferred as a ober-provianmeister (with the rank of major) to the Comissariat in 1793.

Choglokov volunteered for service in Poland in 1794 and was appointed to General Derfelden's detachment, fighting at Slonim,

Brestovtsy, Grodno, Skolky, Ostrolenka and Kobylka. He distinguished himself during the assault on Praga for which he was transferred as a major to the Neva Infantry Regiment and awarded the Order of St. George (4th class) on 12 January 1795. Two years later, Choglokov transferred to the Keksholm (Kexholm) Musketeer Regiment and rose to lieutenant colonel on 22 October 1798. He was discharged on 11 July 1799 but returned to service on 16 November 1800, receiving promotion to colonel on 19 November 1800. Three years later, he was appointed commander of Keksholm Musketeer Regiment on 24 October 1803.

During the 1805 Campaign, Choglokov's regiment was attached to General Tolstoy's corps operating near Hanover. Choglokov served in the blockade of Hameln and his regiment was reviewed by the Prussian King in late 1805. He became chef of the Pernov Musketeer Regiment on 5 September 1806. During the 1807 Campaign, Choglokov's unit was attached to the 1st Division and participated in the actions at Guttstadt, Heilsberg and Friedland. His regiment captured two French eagles at Heilsberg and Friedland and was awarded the St. George flags, while Choglokov was decorated with the Order of St. Vladimir (3rd class) for Heilsberg and a golden sword for Friedland. During the Russo-Swedish War of 1808-1809, Choglokov served in the siege of Sveaborg and repulsed the Swedish landing force near Abo in June 1808. For his actions, he earned promotion to major general on 6 July 1808. In 1809, he served under Prince Bagration during the crossing of the Gulf of Bothnia and the capture of the Aland Islands. In 1811, Choglokov took command of the 1st Brigade of the 11th Division.

During the 1812 Campaign, Choglokov took part in the actions at Ostrovno, Smolensk and Borodino (received the Order of St. Anna, 1st class). After General Bakhmetyev was wounded at Borodino, Choglokov became commander of the 11th Division and fought at Chirikov and Vyazma (earned the Order of St. George, 3rd class, 15 June 1813); he remained in reserves at Krasnyi in November 1812. In early 1813, Choglokov served with the 4th Corps in the Duchy of Warsaw and took part in the siege of Glogau. He became the Commandant of Dresden on 26 April 1813 and took command of the 1st Grenadier Division. Choglokov participated in the battles of Bautzen, Reichenbach and Leipzig, where he earned the rank of lieutenant general on 20 October 1813. During the 1814 Campaign, Choglokov was kept in reserve at Brienne, but fought at Arcis sur Aube and Paris, where he was decorated with the Order of St. Vladimir (2nd class). After the war, he continued commanding the 1st Grenadier Division until 18 October 1817 when he was relieved of command. He retired on 5 October 1818 and spent the next fourteen years at St. Petersburg, where he died on 15 April 1832.

DAMAS, Maxim Ivanovich (Ange-Hyacinthe-Maxence) (b. 1785 — d. 6 May 1862, Paris) was born to a prominent French noble family that fled to Russia during the French Revolution. Damas studied in the Artillery and Engineer Cadet Corps and began service with a rank of sub-lieutenant in the Pioneer Regiment on 30 October 1800. He soon joined the Life Guard Semeyonovsk Regiment and participated in the battle of Austerlitz in 1805. Beginning in 1806, he trained recruits in Russia and received the rank of colonel on 12 May 1811. In 1812, he commanded a battalion of the Life Guard Semeyonovsk Regiment and was wounded in the hand at Borodino, for which he earned the Order of St. Anna (2nd class).

Damas took command of the Astrakhan Grenadier Regiment on 5 January 1813 and, during the 1813 Campaign, led a grenadier brigade at Lutzen, Bautzen, and Leipzig, for which he was decorated with the Order of St. Vladimir (3rd class). He rose to a major general on 27 September 1813. During the 1814 Campaign, Damas fought at Brienne, La Rothière (received a golden sword), Arcis sur Aube, and Paris, where he garnered the Order of St. George (3rd class) on 17 May 1814. After the war, he left the Russian service on 22 May 1814 and returned to France, where he enjoyed a brilliant career serving as the Minister of War in 1823-1824 and Minister of Foreign Affairs in 1824-1828.

DANILOV, Pavel Fedorovich (b. 1776 — date of death unclear; removed from rosters on 26 January 1833) was born to a Russian noble family. He studied in the Artillery and Engineer Cadet Corps and began service as a shtyk junker in the Artillery Battalion of the Baltic Galley Fleet [*artilleriiskii batalion Baltiiskogo grebnogo flota*] on 17 July 1796. During the Russo-Swedish War of 1808-1809, he served at Sveaborg. He then transferred as a major to the 1st Pioneer Regiment and rose to lieutenant colonel on 25 May 1811. On 1 March 1813, he took command of the Sapper Regiment, serving at the siege of Danzig. After the war, he became a colonel and commanded a battalion of the 2nd Sapper Regiment in 1816. Rising to major general in 1820, he took command of the 1st Combined Pioneer Brigade. In 1824, he commanded the 1st Pioneer Brigade in the 2nd Division. In 1831, he became the Military Governor of Dünaburg.

DANZAS, Karl Ivanovich (b. 1762 — d. 27 May 1831) was born to a noble family from the Estland *gubernia*. He enlisted as a sergeant in the Noteburg Infantry Regiment on 12 January 1786 and, the same year, he transferred to the staff of Général-en-Chef Elmpt. He rose to major in 1796 and transferred as a lieutenant colonel to the St. Petersburg Grenadier Regiment in 1798. Danzas became a colonel and took command of the St. Petersburg Grenadier Regiment on 10 June 1799. Promoted to major general on 26 September 1800, he became chef of the Taurida Grenadier Regiment on the same day. Danzas served as the commander of this unit between 18 April 1801 and 16 March 1807, when he took a discharge because of poor health.

DAVYDOV (Davidov), Alexander Lvovich (b. 1773 – d. 1833) was born to a prominent Russian noble family; the brother of General Nikolay Rayevsky. He enlisted as a sergeant in the Life Guard Preobrazhensk Regiment in 1785 and soon transferred to the Life Guard Horse Regiment, becoming a cornet in 1799 and a colonel on 7 June 1804. In 1805, he fought at Austerlitz and, in 1807-1809, he served with the Grodno Hussar Regiment in Poland and Finland. He took a discharge because of poor health on 23 January 1810.

During the 1812 Campaign, Davydov returned to the army, serving in Miloradovich's advance guard at Tarutino, Maloyaroslavets, Vyazma and Krasnyi, where he garnered the Order of St. Vladimir (3rd class). In 1813, he distinguished himself at Lutzen, Bautzen, Dresden (received the Order of St. George, 4th class) and Kulm. The following year, Davydov served at Bar sur Aube, Troyes, Arcis sur Aube, Le Fère Champenoise and Paris. He was promoted to a major general on 16 June 1815 with seniority dating from 29 January 1814.

DAVYDOV, Artemii Ivanovich commanded the Vladimir Dragoon Regiment between 1 July 1801 and 2 June 1803 and served as chef of the Vladimir Dragoon Regiment from 4 November 1806 to 1 January 1807 and chef of the Serpukhov Dragoon Regiment from 1 January 1807 to 18 June 1809.

DAVYDOV (Davidov), Denis Vasilievich (b. 27 July 1784, Moscow – d. 4 May 1839, Verkhnaya Maza, Simbirsk *gubernia*) was born to a prominent Russian noble family; the son of Brigadier Vasily Denisov, who commanded the Poltava Light Horse Regiment under Alexander Suvorov. He enlisted as an estandart junker in the Chevalier Guard Regiment on 10 October 1801, rising to cornet on 21 September 1802 and a lieutenant on 14 November 1803.

For writing satires about his superiors, Davydov was transferred to the Byelorussia Hussar Regiment on 25 September 1804 and, then on 16 July 1806, he joined the Leib Hussar (Life Guard Hussar) Regiment with a rank of lieutenant. On 15 January 1807, he was appointed an adjutant to Prince Peter Bagration and rose to staff rotmistr on 26 January 1807. During the campaign in Poland, he served in Bagration's detachment, participating in numerous rearguard actions as well as in the major battles of Eylau (garnered a golden cross), Guttstadt, Heilsberg and Friedland. For his actions, Davydov was decorated with the Order of St. Anna (2nd class) and the Prussian Pour le Merite.

In February-April 1808, Davydov again served under Bagration in Finland and then joined Kulnev's advance guard, fighting at Sikaioki, Karloe, Lappo, Perho, Kuhalambi, Kuortain, Salmi, Oravais and Gamle-Kamlebi. In April 1809, he took part in Bagration's expedition to the Åland Islands. In July 1809, he followed Prince Bagration to the Danubian Principalities, where Davydov fought at Macin, Girsov, Rassevat, Silistra, Tataritsa and Shumla (received the Order of St. Anna, 2nd class). Promoted to rotmistr of the Leib Hussar Regiment on 16 March 1810, he transferred as a lieutenant colonel to the Akhtyrsk Hussar Regiment on 20 April 1812.

During the 1812 Campaign, Davydov served in the 14th Brigade of the 4th Cavalry Division in the 7th Corps of the 2nd Western Army and participated in the battles at Romanovo, Saltanovka (Moghilev) and Smolensk. Following the battle at Smolensk, Davydov organized, with Bagration's consent, a guerrilla detachment to harrass the French communication and supply lines. He distinguished himself at Lyakhov, where his troops captured an entire French brigade of General Augereau. He then fought at Vyazma, Krasnyi, Kopys (received the Order of St. George, 4th class), Shklov, Starosel and Grodno; for his actions in 1812, Davydov was promoted to a colonel and awarded the Order of St. Vladimir (3rd class).

In 1813, Davydov commanded a detachment in Winzegorode's forces at Kalisch and later made a daring raid on Dresden, capturing Heustadt in March. However, Davydov acted without orders during this operation, for which he was relieved of command and transferred to Major General Lanskoy's detachment. He then took part in the actions at Predel, Ezdorf, Uebigau, Dresden, Bautzen, Reichenbach, Zeitz, Altenburg, Chemnitz, Naumburg, Leipzig as well as in the pursuit of the French army to the Rhine River. For his actions in 1813, he received an Imperial letter of gratitude. The following year, Davydov commanded the Akhtyrsk Hussar Regiment in France, distinguishing himself at Brienne, La Rothière (promoted to a major general on 2 January 1816 with seniority dating from 1 February 1814), Montmirail, Chateau Thierry, Laon, Le Fère Champenoise, Craonne and Paris.

Returning to Russia, Davydov served as an assistant to the commander of the 1st Dragoon Division (2 January 1815) and then in the same capacity in the 2nd Horse Jager Division (26 March 1816) and the 2nd Hussar Division (3 June 1816). On 19 November 1817, he took command of the 1st Brigade of the 2nd Hussar Division. On 3 March 1818, he became the Chief of Staff for the 7th Infantry Corps and, on 6 March 1819, for the 3rd Infantry Corps.

He was relieved of command on 29 March 1820 and retired because of illness on 26 November 1823 but returned to the army on 4 April 1826. Davydov participated in the Russo-Persian War in 1826, fighting at Amymly and Alagez, and constructed the fortress of Djelal-Oghlu. However, his health quickly deteriorated and Davydov had to take an extended furlough to recuperate in 1827. Four years later, he returned to the army during the Polish Uprising, taking command of a cavalry detachment of three cossack and one dragoon regiments. He captured the town of Vladimir (Volhynia) on 18 April 1831. He then commanded the advance guard in General Ridiger's corps, earning his promotion to lieutenant general on 18 October 1831 and the Orders of St. Anna (1st class) and of St. Vladimir (2nd class).

After the campaign, Davydov returned to his estate of Verkhnaya Maza in the Simbirsk *gubernia*, where he died on 4 May 1839. Before his death, he organized the transfer of Prince Bagration's remains from the village of Simy for reinternment on the Borodino Battlefield. Davydov left a diverse literary legacy. In addition to his numerous poems and lyrics, Davydov's articles and memoirs remain important sources for the study of the Napoleonic Wars. His most important works include: "*Opyt teorii partizanskogo dvizhenia* [Practice of Theory of the Guerrilla Movement]" (1821), "*Vstrecha s velikim Suvorovym* [Meeting the Great Suvorov]" (1835), "*Moroz li istrebil frantsuzskuiu armmiu v 1812* [Was it the Frost that Destroyed the French Army in 1812]" (1835), "*Dnevnik partizanskikh deistvii* [Diary of the Guerrilla Operations]" (1860). Davydov's memoirs were translated by Greg Troubetskoy and published under title of "*In the Service of the Tsar Against Napoleon: the Memoirs of Denis Davidov, 1806-1814*" in 1999. They contain vivid and insightful accounts of the military actions and interesting characterizations of the prominent Russians. Davydov served as a model for Vasily Denisov in Tolstoy's *War and Peace*.

DAVYDOV, Evgraf Vladimirovich (b. 1775 — date of death unclear; removed from rosters on 1 January 1824) was born to a noble family in the Tula *gubernia*. He enlisted as a vakhmistr in the Life Guard Horse Regiment on 9 September 1791 and transferred as a cornet to the Leib Hussar (Life Guard Hussar) Regiment in 1798. Made a colonel on 12 April 1803, he took part in the battles at Austerlitz in 1805 and at Guttstadt, Heilsberg and Friedland in 1807. During the 1812 Campaign, Davydov served in the 2nd Brigade of the Guard Cavalry Division of the 1st Reserve Cavalry Corps in the 1st Western Army and was seriously wounded in the left hand at Ostrovno. After recuperating, he distinguished himself at Kulm in August 1813, for which he was promoted to major general on 5 September 1813 with seniority dating from 30 August 1813; he was also appointed chef of the Lubensk Hussar Regiment on 5 September 1813. On 18 October 1813, he took part in the Battle of Leipzig, where he lost his right arm and left leg and was decorated with the Order of St. George (3rd class) on 22 February 1814. He was relieved of command on 20 January 1814 but remained in the military service until his death in 1823.

DAVYDOV, Nikolay Fedorovich (b. 1773 — date of death unknown) was born to a noble family from the Tula *gubernia*. He enlisted in the Life Guard Izmailovsk Regiment in 1779 and rose to sergeant in 1784 before transferring as a vakhmistr to the Life Guard Horse Regiment in 1785. Cornet on 12 January 1791, Davydov received promotion to the rank of colonel on 3 October 1801 and was wounded at Austerlitz on 2 December 1805. In 1807, he served at Eylau (received a golden cross), Heilsberg and Friedland (wounded); he was appointed chef of the Moscow Dragoon Regiment on 9 July 1807. In 1812, Davydov commanded the 6th Brigade of the 2nd Cavalry Division of the 2nd Reserve Cavalry Corps in the 1st Western Army, distinguishing himself at Borodino and Krasnyi. In 1813, after earning the rank of major general on 30 July 1813, he distinguished himself at Leipzig, where he was wounded. After fighting in France in 1814, Davydov retired on 6 January 1816.

DAVYDOV, Peter Lvovich (b.1782 — d. 1842) was born to a prominent Russian noble family; the brother of Alexander Davydov and Nikolay Rayevsky. He enlisted in the Life Guard Horse Regiment in 1797 and took a discharge with the rank of lieutenant in 1799. Over the next thirteen years, he served on various positions at the Imperial Court. He returned to the army with the rank of major in early 1812 and served under Miloradovich throughout the 1812 Campaign, rising to a lieutenant colonel. During the following year, he again served under Miloradovich in Saxony, distinguishing himself at Leipzig, for which he was promoted to a colonel with seniority dating from 14 October 1813. In 1814, he served in France, receiving promotion to major general on 17 April 1814.

After the war, he transferred to the civil service in February 1818 and eventually rose to a privy counsellor.

DAVYDOVSKY (Davydovsky I), Yakov Yakovlevich (b. 1758 — d. 12 January 1807) was born to a petty noble family in the Kiev *gubernia*. He enlisted as a private in the Moscow Carabinier Regiment in 1771 and rose to ensign in the Kiev Light Horse Regiment in 1778. In 1783-1784, he served in the Crimea and joined the Pereyaslavl Carabinier Regiment in 1785. Rising to a lieutenant in 1786, he transferred to the 1st Battalion of the Byelorussia Jager Corps in 1788. During the Russo-Turkish War of 1787-1791, Davydovsky distinguished himself at Rimnic (promoted to a captain) and Ismail (wounded). Promoted to second major in 1790, he served in Poland from 1792-1794. He rose to a lieutenant colonel in 1799 and colonel in the following year. He commanded the 10th Jager Regiment between 8 September 1800 and 24 November 1802. Davydovsky became chef of the 1st Jager Regiment on 24 November 1802. In 1805, he served in Finland and, in 1806, he joined the 9th Division in Poland. He distinguished himself in the battle of Pultusk, where he was twice wounded in the head and left shoulder. He died of his wounds on 12 January 1807.

DEBU, Osip (Joseph) Lvovich (b. 30 December 1774, Livorno, Italy — d. 22 April 1842, Moscow) was born to a prominent French noble family living in Italy. He studied in the Artillery and Engineer Cadet Corps and began service in the Life Guard Semeyonovsk Regiment in 1793. In 1800, he joined the Lithuanian Musketeer Regiment. He rose to colonel and commander of the Kaluga Musketeer Regiment on 4 April 1806. In 1806-1807, he served with the 5th Division in Poland. He became chef of the Kazan Musketeer Regiment on 28 November 1809 and fought the mountaineers in the North Caucasus region for the next six years. He commanded the Kazan Infantry Regiment between 4 July 1815 and 11 September 1816. Rising to a major general in 1816, he commanded the 1st Brigade of the 22nd Division. In 1826, he left the army for the civil service, becoming the Civil Governor of Orenburg in 1827. Rising to a privy counselor in 1832, he later served in the Senate in St. Petersburg. Among Debu's literary works is *Zapiski o Kavkazskoi linii i prisoedinennikh k onoi Chernomorskikh voiskakh* [Recollections on the Caucasian Line and the Black Sea Troops Deployed There], published in Moscow in 1829.

DEDULIN, Jacob Ivanovich (b. 29 October 1772, Ratmirovo – d. 6 May 1836) was born to a noble family from the Yaroslavl *gubernia*. He enlisted as a sub-ensign in the Life Guard Preobrazhensk Regiment on 13 February 1787. During the Russo-Swedish War of 1788-1790, he served in Prince Nissau-Zigen's galley fleet. Promoted to an ensign in 1792, he rose to a colonel on 29 September 1802. Dedulin was wounded at Austerlitz on 2 December 1805 and, two years later, he served at Guttstadt and Heilsberg before being wounded at Friedland. Dedulin took a discharge with a rank of major general on 1 May 1810. During the 1812 Campaign, he organized the Yaroslavl *opolchenye* and returned to the service on 31 December 1812. In 1813, he led the Yaroslavl *opolchenye* at Modlin and Glogau, where he was again wounded. After the war, he returned to his estate of Ratmirovo in the Yaroslavl *gubernia*.

DEKHTEREV, Nikolay Vasilievich (b.1775 — d.17 September 1831) was born to a noble family from the Voronezh *gubernia*. He enlisted as a furier in the Life Guard Preobrazhensk Regiment on 20 January 1784 and transferred as a captain to the Pskov Dragoon Regiment on 12 January 1792. He took part in the operations in Poland in 1792-1794, earning the rank of major. In 1799, he served under General Rimsky-Korsakov in Switzerland and was promoted to colonel on 7 December 1800. The following year, he took command of the St. Petersburg Dragoon Regiment on 19 March 1801. Dekhterev distinguished himself during the 1805 Campaign in Moravia, fighting at Austerlitz.

In 1806-1807, he served with the 8th Division in Poland, receiving the Order of St. George (3rd class, 8 May 1807) for Eylau. On 30 October 1808, he became chef of the Oliviopol Hussar Regiment and served with the Army of Moldavia in the Danubian Principalities. He distinguished himself again at Bazardjik in 1810, receiving a golden cross and promotion to a major general on 26 June 1810. However, he was seriously wounded in the chest at Shumla in June 1810. In early 1812, Dekhterev served with the 23rd Brigade of the 7th Cavalry Division of the Army of Danube and, during the 1812 Campaign, he commanded a cavalry detachment in the Volhynia and the Duchy of Warsaw. In 1813-1814, he performed well at Leipzig, Brienne, Bar sur Aube and Paris. He retired because of poor health on 28 January 1816.

DELAGARDE, August Osipovich (Augusten Marie Balthazar Charles Peletie) (b. 1780 — d. 1834) was born to a French noble family that fled to Russia during the French Revolution. He entered the Russian quartermaster service on 3 October 1801 and was later appointed an adjutant to General Dotichamp, Cavalry Inspector of the Dniestr Inspection in 1802-1806. In 1805, he served in the quartermaster service of Kutuzov's army in Moravia and fought at Austerlitz. He transferred to the Life Guard Jager Regiment in late 1806, participating in the 1807 Campaign in Poland. In 1808-1809, Delagarde fought the Swedes in Finland, receiving the Order of St. George (4th class) for his actions at Idensalmi. Promoted to colonel in 1811, he served with the 3rd Brigade of the Guard Infantry Division of the 1st Western Army in 1812 and was wounded in the left side at Borodino. The following year, he distinguished himself at Lutzen, Bautzen, Kulm (received the Prussian Iron Cross) and Leipzig. In 1814, he took part in the actions at La Rothière, Le Fère Champenoise and Paris, for which he was promoted to a major general on 27 May 1814. On 26 August 1814, he became chef of the 48th Jager Regiment and later commanded a jager brigade of the 17th Division. However, he left the Russian service in early 1815 and returned to France.

DELYANOV (Delakyan), David Artemyevich (b. 4 August 1763, Moscow — d. 19 July 1837) was born to an Armenian noble family. He enlisted as a vakhmistr in the Narva Carabinier Regiment on 2 September 1773 and transferred as a sub-lieutenant to the Voronezh Infantry Regiment on 19 January 1786. He served in Poland in 1792-1794 and joined the Sumsk Hussar Regiment on 8 February 1801. During the 1806-1807 Campaigns in Poland, he served with the 3rd Division at Eylau, Heilsberg and Friedland, for which he was promoted to a colonel on 24 December 1807. In 1812, he served with the 3rd Brigade of the 3rd Cavalry

Division in the 1st Western Army, participating in numerous rearguard actions as well as in the battles of Smolensk, Borodino and Krasnyi. In 1813, he fought at Lutzen, Dresden, Kulm and Leipzig, rising to a major general on 27 September 1813. In 1814, he participated in the actions at Bar sur Aube, Arcis sur Aube and Paris. After the war, he commanded the 2nd Brigade of the 2nd Dragoon Division (6 January 1816) and the 2nd Brigade of the 2nd Hussar Division (20 February 1823). He was relieved of command on 16 July 1827 and retired on 11 January 1833.

DEMIDOV, Nikolay Ivanovich (b. 1773 — d. 1833) was born to a Russian noble family and enlisted in the Life Guard Preobrazhensk Regiment immediately upon his birth, rising to sergeant three years later. Promoted to an ensign in January 1790, he rose to a captain in 1798 and colonel in 1799. Four years later, he became a major general in the Life Guard Izmailovsk Regiment and chef of the Petrov Infantry Regiment on 28 May 1803. In 1807, his unit was deployed on the frontier with Poland but did not participate in military operations against the French; during this campaign, Demidov organized the Libau Infantry Regiment.

In 1808, Demidov commanded a detachment defending Vaasa in Finland. Misinformed by his reconnaissance on the direction of the Swedish attack, Demidov marched his entire detachment out of Vaasa while the Swedes landed their forces from the sea and captured the town. Nevertheless, at the price of heavy casualties, Demidov recaptured the town, earning the Order of St. George (3rd class). He then fought at Kuortain and Oravais, for which he earned the Order of St. Vladimir (3rd class). In 1809, he was garrisoned on the Aland Islands and, on 24 December of the same year, Demidov took command of the 21st Division in Finland, remaining here for the next five years. Promoted to a lieutenant general in 1816, he became commander of the 1st Grenadier Division in late 1817. He resigned from the command because of poor health in 1824. The next year, he became adjutant general on 27 December 1825 and was appointed to the Senate. In 1826, he became the Director of the Page and Cadet Corps and was promoted to a general of infantry in 1828.

DENISIEV, Luc Alekseyevich (b. 1762 — d. 1846) was born to a Russian noble family and enlisted as a sub-ensign in the Life Guard Preobrazhensk Regiment on 12 January 1773. He transferred as a captain to the regular army in 1787 and participated in the Russo-Swedish War in 1788-1790. After serving in Poland in 1792-1794, Denisiev took command of the Chernigov Cuirassier Regiment on 18 August 1799 and rose to colonel on 30 June 1800. Between 31 March and 2 June 1803, he commanded the Chernigov Dragoon Regiment before taking command of the Novorossiisk Dragoon Regiment on 24 November 1803. He became chef of the Seversk Dragoon Regiment on 10 October 1806 and participated in the Russo-Turkish War of 1806-1812, fighting at Ismail, Macin and Silistra. Denisiev rose to a major general on 24 December 1807. During the 1812 Campaign, he served in the 2nd Corps of the Army of Danube, taking part in the battles at Brest-Litovsk, Borisov and on the Berezina. His regiment was converted to the Seversk Horse Jagers on 29 December 1812. Denisiev then participated in the actions at Thorn, Bautzen, Leipzig in 1813 and the invasion of France in 1814. He retired on 29 January 1816.

DENISIEV, Peter Vasilievich (b. 1766 — date of death unknown) was born to a noble family from the Kursk *gubernia*. He enlisted as a vakhmistr in the Life Guard Horse Regiment on 25 April 1785 and transferred as a captain to the Malorossiissk Grenadier Regiment on 12 January 1794. After fighting the Poles in 1794, Denisiev returned to Poland in 1806-1807, distinguishing himself at Eylau and Friedland. He rose to colonel on 25 December 1807 and took command of the Uglitsk Musketeer Regiment on 10 December 1808. Two years later, he became chef of the Butyrsk Musketeer Regiment on 31 October 1810. During the 1812 Campaign, Denisiev commanded the 2nd Brigade of the 24th Division of the 6th Corps in the 1st Western Army, fighting at Smolensk, Borodino, Tarutino, Maloyaroslavets and Krasnyi. In 1813, he distinguished himself at Leipzig, earning his promotion to major general on 23 January 1814 with seniority dating from 18 October 1813. In 1814, he took part in the actions at Craonne, Laon and Paris. His sibling, **DENISIEV, Stepan Vasilievich** rose to the rank of colonel on 29 September 1800 and commanded the Malorossiisk Grenadier Regiment between 31 May 1800 and 28 July 1801. He served as a chef of the 25th Jager Regiment from 3 August 1808 to 11 August 1812.

DENISOV (Denisov VI), Adrian Karpovich (b. 1763 — d. 1841) was born to a Don Cossack noble family. After styding in the Neva Monastery and at Masson's private boarding school in St. Petersburg, he enlisted in the Cossack troops on 12 August 1776 and rose to esaul on 23 August 1777 and then to lieutenant in 13 May 1780. In 1783, Denisov served with his uncle Major Timofei Denisov's Cossack Regiment in the Crimea. On 11 January 1785, he was promoted to a Cossack sergeant [*voiskovoi starshina*] and returned to the Don Host. In 1787-1788, he served with Matvei Platov's Cossack Regiment in the Crimea, fighting at Hadjibey (Odessa) and Ochakov. In 1789, he transferred to Prince Repnin's corps, distinguishing himself at Ismail, where he was wounded but led the charge to capture the Turkish battery; for his valor, he garnered the Order of St. George (4th class). In 1791, he again distinguished himself at Macin and was awarded a golden medal. In 1792, Denisov commanded a Cossack regiment in Poland, fighting at Murozh, Shpinchintza, Gorodnitze (received the Order of St. Vladimir, 4th class), Ostrog, Verkhovoi, Dubna, Dubenka For his excellent service, Denisov received promotion to a lieutenant colonel on 9 July 1794. Late that year, he again fought the Polish insurgents at Maciejowice, Slonim (wounded in the neck and hand), Lipovo Pole (received the Prussian Pour le Merite), Warsaw and Praga (earned a golden sabre).

Returning to the Don Host in early 1795, Denisov took part in the Persian Campaign along the Caspian Sea in 1796. In 1797-1798, he served in the Cossack Chancellery. Promoted to colonel on 3 February 1798, he became a campaign ataman [*pokhodnoi ataman*] of the Cossack troops deployed for the campaign in Italy. Arriving to Verona, Suvorov appointed him to Prince Bagration's detachment. However, Denisov resented being subordinated to Bagration, whom he considered junior in rank. The relations between two commanders became strained; when Bagration criticized him for an ineffective reconnaissance, Denisov challenged him to a duel and offered to choose any weapon, except for a sword because he could not fence. Fortunately, Bagration had a presence of mind not to aggravate situation and simply ignored the Cossack's behavior. Later, Denisov was disciplined for his insubordination at Novi.

During the campaign in Italy, Denisov distinguished himself capturing Bergamo on 24 April 1799 and fighting at Lecco, on the Adda River, Milan, Marengo (received the Order of St. John of Jerusalem), Turin and Novi (received the Order of St. Anna, 2nd class). He was promoted to a major general on 1 July 1799. Denisov then distinguished himself during the crossing of the Alps, garnering the Order of St. Anna (1st class).

Returning to Russia, Denisov raised eleven Cossack regiments for the expedition to India in 1800 and marched as far as the Volga River when he was recalled. Between 20 October 1805 and 7 April 1806, he served as *chargè d'affaires* of the campaign ataman Matvei Platov and as the governing ataman [*nakaznoi ataman*] of Don Host from 1 January to 11 February 1807. He joined the Russian army in the spring of 1807 and, in June of the same year, Denisov led three Cossack regiments at Guttstadt, Deppen (received the Order of St. Vladimir, 3rd class), Zomerfield, Arensdorf and Heilsberg. After the battle of Friedland, he covered, along with Prince Bagration, the Russian retreat to Tilsit. For his actions in 1807, Denisov was decorated with the Prussian Orders of Red Eagle and the Pour le Merite. In 1808, he was dispatched to the Danubian Principalities, where he commanded Cossacks at Rassevat, Silistra and Shumla, garnering the Order of St. Anna (1st class) for his skirmishes with the Turkish raiding parties. However, following his argument with Commander-in-Chief Kamensky, Denisov was removed from command in 1810 and returned to St. Petersburg.

In 1812, Denisov again became the governing ataman of the Don Cossack Host and raised several Cossack regiments for the 1812-1813 Campaigns, for which he received the Order of St. Vladimir (2nd class) and promotion to lieutenant general on 2 June 1813. After Platov's death in 1818, Denisov became the Ataman of the Don Cossack Host. His attempts at reforming the Cossack administration led to discontent among the Cossack nobility, who accused him of embezzlement and abuse of power. Denisov was discharged from the army on 12 February 1821. During his retirement, Denisov wrote very interesting but biased memoirs about his service in the Napoleonic Wars. Entitled *"Zapiski Donskogo Atamana Denisova* [Recollections of the Don Cossack Ataman Denisov]," the manuscript was published in parts in the *Russkaya Starina* in 1875 and as a separate volume in 2000.

Denisov descended from a prominent Cossack family and many of his relatives served in the Russian army:

1. His father, **DENISOV (Denisov II) Karp Petrovich** (b. ca. 1732 – date of death unclear) participated in the Seven years War and the Russo-Turkish War of 1769-1774, rising to a major general in 1795.

2. His uncle, **DENISOV, Fedor Petrovich** (b. 1735/1738 – d. 1801) began service in 1756 and distinguished himself during the Russo-Turkish Wars of 1769-1774. He rose to a Don Cossack colonel in 1770 and became a major of regular army in 1773, a lieutenant colonel in 1774, a colonel in 1777, a brigadier in 1784, a major general in 1787 and a lieutenant general in 1798. Promoted to general of cavalry on 18 April 1798, Denisov became the first commander of the Leib Cossack (Life Guard Cossack) Regiment on 4 February 1798 and was conferred the title of count of the Russian Empire on 16 April 1799. He served as chef of the Leib Cossack Regiment between 21 November 1800 and 16 January 1801.

3. His another uncle, **DENISOV (Denisov V), Timofei Petrovich** served as the campaign ataman of Cossack forces in the Crimea during the Russo-Turkish War of 1787-1791.

4. His brother **Login Karpovich (Denisov IV)** and two cousins, **Vasily Denisov** (see below) and **Peter Timofeyevich (Denisov (VIII)** rose to major generals and commanded Cossack detachments throughout the Napoleonic campaigns.

DENISOV (Denisov VII), Vasily Timofeyevich (b. 1777 — d. 1822) was born to a prominent Don Cossack noble family (see previous entry). He began service as a Cossack at an early age and rose to esaul on 26 March 1788. He participated in the Russo-Swedish War of 1789-1790, rising to a lieutenant in the Leib Cossack Escort Company [*leib kazachia konvoinaia* *komanda*] in July 1789, to captain on 12 September 1790 and to a second major on 25 November 1791. In 1792-1794, Denisov commanded a Cossack Regiment in Poland, distinguishing himself at Maciejowice (received a golden sabre) and Praga, for which he garnered the Order of St. George (4th class, 12 January 1795).

Promoted to major on 10 December 1794, Denisov quickly advanced through the ranks becoming lieutenant colonel on 9 July 1795, Cossack campaign ataman on 22 February 1798, colonel on 18 March 1798 and major general on 10 January 1799. He served in the Novorossiisk *gubernia* in 1798-1801 before joining Platov's Cossack forces during the 1806-1807 Campaigns in Poland. In 1812, Denisov commanded a Cossack brigade in Platov's Cossack Corps, fighting at Molodechno, Rudnya, Inkovo, Krasnyi, Borisov, Vilna and Kovno. In 1813-1814, he distinguished himself in the operations in Saxony and, in France, at Soissons, Rheims, Craonne, Laon, St. Dizier and Paris. After the war, Denisov returned to the Don Cossack Host, where he died in 1822.

DEPRERADOVICH, Nikolay Ivanovich (b. 24 October 1767 — d. 28 December 1843, St. Petersburg) descended from a Serbian noble family that immigrated to Russia in 1752. He enlisted as a cadet in the Volozh Hussar Regiment on 12 December 1777 and transferred as a cornet to the Ukraine Hussar Regiment in 1778, rising to a sub-lieutenant in 1782. He took part in the Russo-Turkish War of 1787-1791, fighting at Kaushani, Akkerman and Bender. From 1792-1794, he served in Poland, first with the Elisavetgrad Light Horse Regiment and then in the Smolensk Dragoon Regiment. In 1798, he was appointed a colonel in the Leib Hussar (Life Guard Hussar) Regiment and, five years later, became a major general and commander of the Chevalier Guard Regiment on 28 May 1803. He distinguished himself commanding this regiment at Austerlitz on 2 December 1805, receiving the Order of St. George (3rd class) on 8 March 1806. In June 1807, Depreradovich led his unit at Guttstadt, Heilsberg and Friedland.

In 1810, Depreradovich took command of the 1st Cuirassier Division, keeping the command of the Chevalier Guard Regiment. During the 1812 Campaign, he commanded this division at Vitebsk, Smolensk, Borodino, Tarutino, Vyazma and Krasnyi. In 1813, he fought at Lutzen, Bautzen, Dresden and Leipzig; he distinguished himself at Kulm, earning the Prussian Iron Cross and promotion to lieutenant general on 11 September 1813 with seniority dating from 29 August 1813.

In 1814, Depreradovich received a golden sword with diamonds for his conduct at Le Fère Champenoise. For his service in 1814, he was also decorated with the Austrian Order of Maria Theresa, the Prussian Order of Red Eagle and the Bavarian Order of Maximilian Joseph. After the war, Depreradovich became an adjutant general on 3 August 1819. Two years later, he was relieved of command of the Chevalier Guard Regiment and appointed commander of the 1st Reserve Cavalry Corps. He rose to a general of cavalry on 3 September 1826 and commanded the Guard Reserve Cavalry Corps between 14 April 1833 and 12 March 1835. He then served on the Committee on Wounded until his death on 28 December 1843.

His brother, **DEPRERADOVICH, Leontii Ivanovich** (b. 1766 – d. 19 February 1844) commanded the Astrakhan Grenadier Regiment between 16 July 1798 and 24 August 1799. Promoted to a major general on 24 August 1799, he commanded the Life Guard Semeyonovsk Regiment between 26 August 1799 and 9 July 1807. He took part in the battle of Austerlitz, garnering the Order of St. George (3rd class). He participated in the 1807 Campaign in Poland, serving at Guttstadt, Heilsberg and Friedland.

DERFELDEN, Otto Wilhelm Khristoforovich (b. 1735 – d. 1819) was born to a noble family in the Estland *gubernia*. He enlisted as a *reitar* in the Life Guard Horse Regiment in 1754, rising to a cornet in 1761 and rotmistr in 1768. Two years later, he transferred as a colonel to the Tver Carabinier Regiment. He participated in the Russo-Turkish War in 1770-1774 and became a brigadier in 1775, major general in 1777 and lieutenant general in 1784. In 1783-1784, Derfelden served in Poland. During the Russo-Turkish War in 1787-1791, he commanded the 4th Division at Byrlad, Maksimeni, Galati.(received the Order of St. George, 2nd class), Focsani and Rimnic. He left the army because of illness in early 1791 and commanded the Russian corps in Lithuania in 1792. During the 1792 Campaign in Poland, he captured Kamenetz-Podolsk. Two years later, he repulsed initial attack of the Polish insurgents, for which he garnered the Order of St. Alexander of Neva.

In the fall of 1794, Derfelden served under General Alexander Suvorov in Poland, distinguishing himself at Pankova and Praga; for his service in this campaign, Derfelden received promotion to général-en-chef on 12 January 1795. He later served as a cavalry inspector in the St. Petersburg and Finland Inspections. During Paul's coronation on 16 April 1797, Derfelden was decorated with the Order of St. Andrew the First Called.

After a brief retirement, Derfelden was ordered to accompany Grand Duke Constantine to the Russian army in Italy, with instructions to replace Alexander Suvorov if necessary. He commanded a division under Suvorov during the operations in Italy, distinguishing himself at Novi, St. Gothard, Devil's Bridge and Muothatal Valley. For his actions, Derfelden garnered the Order of St. John of Jerusalem. Returning to Russia, he took a discharge on 9 November 1799 and lived in St. Petersburg until his death in 1819.

DEVOLAN, Franz Pavlovich (date of birth unclear – d. 12 December 1818) descended from a Dutch noble family. He entered Russian service as a major in the corps of engineers in 1787. He participated in the Russo-Swedish War in 1788, fighting at Gotland. In 1789-1791, Devolan served in the Danubian Principalities, where as a chief engineer he fought the Turks at Kaushani, Palanka, Akkerman, Bender, Killia, Ismail, Babadag, Braila and Macin. In 1793, he became chief engineer in General Suvorov's army and served in Poland in 1794, earning promotion to colonel. Beginning in 1795, Devolan directed renovation works at the fortresses of Fanagoria, Akhtyar, Kinburn, Tiraspol, Ovidiapol, Grigoriopol, Voznesensk and other lesser sites; for his service, Catherine II presented him with 10,000 rubles in December 1795. He also designed and directed the construction of the fortress and harbor of Hadjibey (Odessa) in 1795-1796. Under Emperor Paul, Devolan rose to a major general and worked on the fortifications in the western and southern provinces of Russia. He took a discharge with a rank of general of the corps of engineers in late 1797. After two years of travelling in Europe, he returned to service as a member of the Department of Marine Communications in 1799. Over the next nineteen years, he designed and constructed numerous harbors, canals and inland waterways throughout Russia, including the Tikhvinsk and Mariinsk water system and the port of Taganrog.

DIEBITCH, Ivan Ivanovich (Johann Karl Friedrich Anton) (b. 13 May 1785, Gross-Leipe, Silesia — d. 10 June 1831) was born to a German noble family, the son of retired Prussian Lieutenant Colonel Baron Hans Ehrenfried Diebitch. He studied in the Berlin Cadet Corps, which he entered at the age of twelve in 1797. The following year, his father entered Russian service, becoming a major general in 1800 and Diebitch followed his father's footsteps by enlisting as an ensign in the Life Guard Semeyonovsk Regiment in 1801. During the 1805 Campaign in Moravia, he distinguished himself at Austerlitz, where he was wounded in the right hand but remained with the ranks and led the attack of his unit; for his valor, he was awarded a golden sword. In 1806-1807, Diebitch took part in the battles at Eylau, Guttstadt, Heilsberg and Friedland, garnering the Orders of S. George (4th class), of St. Vladimir (4th class) and the Prussian Pour le Merite.

In 1810, he transferred to the Quartermaster Section of the Imperial Retinue and served as a duty officer in Wittgenstein's corps. Promoted to colonel on 27 September 1811, he served as ober-quartermaster of the 1st Corps in 1812, fighting at Jakubovo, Klyastitsy, Golovchin (received the Order of St. George, 3rd class, 5 September 1812), Chashniki, Smolnya, Borisov, Studyanka and etc. For his actions in the two battles of Polotsk, Diebitch garnered the Orders of St. Vladimir (3rd class) and of St. Anna (1st class) as well as promotion to major general on 30 October 1812 with seniority dating from 18 August 1812.

In late 1812, Diebitch helped negotiate the Tauroggen Convention for which he received 10,000 rubles. In 1813, he became general quartermaster of the Allied armies, fighting at Lutzen, Bautzen, Dresden, Kulm (received the Order of St. Vladimir, 2nd class and the Prussian Iron Cross) and Leipzig, where he earned the Austrian Order of Maria Theresa and the rank of lieutenant general on 20 October 1813 with seniority dating from 16 October 1813. In 1814, Diebitch participated in the battles of La Rothière, Arcis sur Aube and Paris, for which he was decorated with the Order of St. Alexander of Neva. In 1815, Diebitch served as the Chief of Staff for the 1st Army and, at the grand military review at Vertus, he was awarded the diamonds signs of the Order of St. Alexander of Neva. He rose to adjutant general on 20 June 1818 and became a member of the State Council on 11 September 1823, *chargé d'affaires* of Chief of Staff of the Imperial General Staff on 12 May 1823 and Chief of Staff of the Imperial General Staff on 18 April 1824.

Diebitch accompanied Emperor Alexander to the Congress of Lambach, where he was decorated with the Austrian Order of Leopold and the Russian Order of St. Vladimir (1st class). He was promoted to general of infantry on 3 September 1826. Diebitch briefly served in Georgia in 1827 and was conferred the title of count of the Russian Empire on 7 July 1827. During the Russo-Turkish War of 1828-1829, he replaced General Wittgenstein as Commander-in-Chief of the 2nd Army on 21 February 1829 and was promoted to general field marshal on 4 October 1829. He received the Order of St. George (2nd class) for the battle of Kulevchi and the Order of St. George (1st class) for the capture of Silistra. For his successful operations in the Balkan Mountains, he was conferred the name of Zabalkansky [Transbalkan] in 1829. Diebitch then took command of the Russian army to suppress the Polish Uprising on 12 December 1830 but died from the cholera epidemic during the campaign.

DMITRYEV-MAMONOV, Matvei Alexandrovich (b. 25 September 1790 — d. 23 June 1863) was born to an ancient Russian family from the Smolensk *gubernia*; the son of Adjutant General Alexander Dmitryev-Mamonov, one of Empress Catherine II's favorites. He began his career at the Imperial Court, becoming a kamer junker in 1808 and ober-prosecutor in the Senate in 1810. During the 1812 Campaign, Dmitryev-Mamonov joined the Moscow *opolchenye*, fighting at Borodino, Tarutino and Maloyaroslavets. In late 1812, he personally organized a cavalry regiment, later named the Dmitryev-Mamonov's Moscow Cossack Regiment, and served as a major general and chef of this unit beginning on 24 March 1813.

However, Dmitryev-Mamonov did not participate in the major operations in Saxony and briefly served with his regiment in France. The unit was disbanded on 8 September 1814 and Dmitryev-Mamonov served as an assistant to the commander of the 2nd Horse Jager Division until 26 March 1816. Retiring in 1819, he lived in Moscow and was considered one of the richest men in Russia. He refused to pledge allegiance to Emperor Nicholas in early 1826 and lived secluded at his estate of Vasilievskoe. He suffered from madness late in his life before dying on 23 June 1863.

DOKHTUROV, Dmitry Sergeyevich (b. 12 September 1759, Krutoe, Tula *gubernia* — d. 26 November 1816, Moscow) was born to a Russian noble family from the Tula *gubernia*. He began service at the Imperial Court, becoming a page in 1771 and a kamer page in 1775. Dokhturov enlisted as a lieutenant in the Life Guard Preobrazhensk Regiment on 17 April 1781, becoming lieutenant captain in 1784 and captain in 1788. He participated in the Russo-Swedish War of 1788-1790, fighting at Rochensalmi (wounded in the right shoulder), near the estuary of the Kumen River, at Hervanland (received a golden sword) and Vyborg (wounded). Dokhturov became a colonel and commander of the Yeletsk Infantry

Regiment on 12 January 1795. Two years later, he rose to a major general and chef of the Sofia Musketeer Regiment on 13 November 1797. Between 11 November 1798 and 3 August 1800, this unit was named Dokhturov's Musketeer Regiment. Dokhturov received promotion to lieutenant general on 5 November 1799.

After brief retirement in July-November 1800, Dokhturov became chef of the Olonetsk Musketeer Regiment on 11 August 1801 and chef of the Moscow Musketeer Regiment and infantry inspector of the Kiev Inspection on 7 February 1803. During the 1805 Campaign, he commanded one of the columns in the Russian army, distinguishing himself at Krems (Dürrenstein, received the Order of St. George, 3rd class, 24 January 1806) and Austerlitz (received the Order of St. Vladimir, 2nd class). In 1806-1807, he led the 7th Division in Poland, fighting at Golymin (received the Order of St. Anna, 1st class), Eylau (wounded in the right leg, earned a golden sword with diamonds), Lomitten (received the Prussian Order of Red Eagle, 1st class), Heilsberg (received the Order of St. Alexander of Neva) and Friedland. In 1809, he took part in the operations against the Austrian army in Galicia, for which he received the Order of St. Catherine. Promoted to general of infantry on 1 May 1810, he took command of the 4th Corps on 7 November 1810 and of 6th Corps of the 1st Western Army in early 1812.

During the 1812 Campaign, Dokhturov defended Smolensk, for which he later received 25,000 rubles, and distinguished himself at Borodino, where he took command of the 2nd Western Army after Prince Bagration was injured. For his actions in this battle, Dokhturov was decorated with the diamond signs of the Order of St. Alexander of Neva. At the council of war at Fily, he recommended the army engage Napoleon in the vicinity of Moscow, and in October-November led his command at the battles of Aristovo, Maloyaroslavets (garnered the Order of St. George, 2nd class), and Krasnyi.

In 1813, Dokhturov commanded the right flank of the Army of Poland, fighting at Berggieshubel, Dohna, Dresden, Leipzig (received the Order of St. Vladimir, 1st class), Magdeburg and Hamburg, where he remained until the end of the war. In late 1814, Dokhturov took a furlough to recuperate and nominally commanded the 3rd Corps. During the Hundred Days, Dokhturov returned to the army, commanding the right flank of the Russian army. Returning to Russia, he took a discharge because of poor health on 13 January 1816 and died on 26 November 1816 in Moscow.

DOLGORUKOV, Aleksey Alekseyevich (b. 25 May 1767 — d. 23 August 1834) was born to a prominent Russian noble family. He was enlisted in the artillery in January 1776 before transferring to the Guard. In 1791, he began actual service as an ensign in 1791 and rose to premier major in 1795. Under Emperor Paul, Dolgorukov enjoyed rapid promotions, becoming lieutenant colonel in 1798 and colonel in October 1799 as well as garnering the Order of St. John of Jerusalem. He commanded the Keksholm (Kexholm) Musketeer Regiment from 3 January 1800 to 18 July 1803. In July 1803, he transferred to civil service with a rank of actual state counselor and later served in the Heraldry before becoming the Civil Governor of Simbirsk gubernia in 1808.

In 1810, Dolgorukov was decorated with the Order of St. Anna (1st class) for his effective government of the Simbirsk province. In 1812, he organized and commanded the Simbirsk opolchenye. On 29 May 1815, he was appointed the Civil Governor of Moscow and, the following year, he was promoted to privy counselor. In 1817, Dolgorukov became a member of the Senate. In 1818-1826, he traveled throughout Russian provinces to review local conditions and, for his efforts, he received the Order of St. Vladimir (2nd class) in 1823, the diamond signs of the Order of St. Anna (1st class) and the Order of St. Alexander of Neva (1827). In October 1827, he was appointed Minister of Justice. Two years later, he was relieved of this position and appointed a member of the State Council.

DOLGORUKOV, Mikhail Petrovich (b. 1780 — d. 27 October 1808) was born to a prominent Russian noble family, the son of General Peter Petrovich Dolghorukov and brother of Peter Petrovich Dolgorukov (see below). He was enlisted in the Life Guard Preobrazhensk Regiment at the age of four in 1784 and transferred as a rotmistr to the Pavlograd Light Horse Regiment on 12 January 1795. In 1796, he participated in the Persian Campaign along the Caspian Sea and fought at Gandja.

After serving in Georgia for a year, Dolgorukov transferred as a captain to the Arkharov Garrison Regiment in Moscow in 1797, rose to major on 26 June 1798 and then joined the Chevalier Guard Corps in February 1799. A year later, he returned for service in the Life Guard Preobrazhensk Regiment, rising to lieutenant colonel on 18 October 1799 and colonel in June 1800.

After Napoleon offered to return Russian prisoners of war, Dolgorukov was sent on a mission to Paris, where he was introduced to the First Consul and his entourage. Dolgorukov returned to Russia after Emperor Paul's death and became flügel adjutant to Emperor Alexander on 26 April 1801. However, he took an extended furlough to study abroad and spent the next four years traveling throughout Europe. He returned to Russia in late 1805 and attended Emperor Alexander during the opening moves of the 1805 Campaign. After completing a diplomatic mission to Berlin, he joined the Russian army and took part in the Allied advance from Olmutz and the battle of Austerlitz, where he was wounded in the chest; for his actions he was awarded a golden sword for courage and the Order of St. George (4th class).

In early 1806, Dolgorukov was dispatched to Vienna to arrange exchange of prisoners of war. In late 1806, he took part in the operations against the French and distinguished himself at Pultusk (garnered the Order of St. Vladimir, 3rd class), Mohrungen (commanded the Courland Dragoon Regiment), Passenheim, Wolfsdorf and Eylau (earned the Order of St. George, 3rd class). For his actions, Dolgorukov was promoted to major general on 21 April 1807 and appointed general adjutant and chef of the Courland Dragoon Regiment (served between 21 April 1807 and 9 May 1808). In June 1807, he participated in the battles at Guttstadt, Heilsberg (earned the Order of St. Anna, 1st class) and Friedland (garnered the Prussian Order of the Red Eagle).

After Tilsit, Dolgorukov had the honor to deliver the news of peace to St. Petersburg. He remained in the capital for over a year. In the summer of 1808, Dolgorukov took command of the Serdobol Detachment in Lieutenant General Nikolay Tuchkov's division in Finland. In August 1808, Dolgorukov operated against the Swedes in the Kuopio region, but had an argument with Tuchkov over the strategy and temporarily resigned from command. He returned to command in September 1808 and, after an armistice in October, he commanded advance guard of Tuchkov's division during the Russian advance to Gamlerkarlebu. On 27

October 1808, Dolgorukov approached Himango, where he attacked the Swedish positions with inferior troops and was killed by a cannonball while rallying troops in action. His body was transported to St. Petersburg and buried at the Alexander of Neva Monastery.

DOLGORUKOV (Dolgorukov III), Peter Petrovich (b. 30 December 1777 — d. 20 December 1806) was born to a prominent noble family, the second son of General Peter Dolgorukov, Governor of St. Petersburg under Catherine the Great. Dolgorukov was enlisted in the Life Guard Izmailovsk Regiment at the age of three months on 15 March 1778. In January 1792, he was promoted to captain and transferred to the Moscow Grenadier Regiment. In June 1793, he rose to a premier major and served as an adjutant to his uncle General Prince Dolgorukov. In November 1795, he joined the Lieutenant General Arkharov II's Garrison Regiment in Moscow, earning promotion to colonel on 13 May 1797 at the age of twenty. Bored by garrison duty, he appealed to Emperor Paul to transfer him to army service but was repeatedly declined. Finally, he approached Crown Prince Alexander, who procured for him an appointment as the Governor of Smolensk and chef of the Smolensk Garrison Regiment on 22 September 1798; the same day, Dolgorukov became a major general at the age of twenty-one. For his service in Smolensk, he was appointed adjutant general to Paul I in January 1799.

While in St. Petersburg, Dolgorukov befriended Alexander and, arguably, was among the conspirators against Paul I. Under the new emperor, Dolgorukov enjoyed a brilliant career. He served on secret diplomatic missions to Prussia and Sweden in 1802. In late 1804, Alexander dispatched him on another diplomatic mission to Prussia to negotiate the Prussian involvement in coalition. Dolgorukov accompanied Emperor Alexander during his visit to King Frederick William of Prussia, and then to the main Russian army. Dolgorukov then played a crucial role in the events leading to Austerlitz. Following the successful action at Wischau (25 November 1805), he led a group of young arrogant officers, who urged Alexander to attack Napoleon. He personally met Napoleon, who was annoyed by young prince's arrogance and used him to provoke the Allies on offensive. Misled by Napoleon, Dolgorukov persuaded Alexander to attack the French army at Austerlitz. During the battle, he fought under Prince Bagration and was later awarded the Order of St. George (3rd class, February 1806) and a golden sword (March 1806) for his valor.

After the battle, Alexander sent Dolgorukov on a diplomatic mission to Prussia. Dolgorukov returned to St. Petersburg in February 1806, and late that year, he was appointed to General Michelson's army to fight the Turks. However, he was soon recalled to join the Russian army in Poland. Traveling in bad weather, Dolgorukov became seriously ill and died upon his arrival at St. Petersburg on 20 December 1806, at the age of twenty nine.

DOLGORUKOV (Dolgorukov II), Sergey Nikolayevich (b. 1769 — d. 27 June 1829, Paris) was born to a prominent Russian noble family. He was enlisted as a sergeant in the Life Guard Semeyonovsk Regiment on 27 February 1773 and rose to ensign in 1785. He participated in the Russo-Swedish War in 1788-1790 and transferred with a rank of lieutenant colonel to the regular army. Dolgorukov became a colonel in 1796 and led the Keksholm (Kexholm) Musketeer Regiment between 20 December 1796 and 10 January 1798. Promoted to major general on 11 January

1798, he served in the War College and received promotion to lieutenant general on 29 December 1799. He became the Commandant of the fortress of St. Petersburg and chef of the St. Petersburg Garrison Regiment on 11 May 1799.

In 1805, Dolgorukov served as the Russian envoy to Vienna and, in 1808, he became the Russian ambassador to Holland. Three years later, he became the Russian envoy to the Naples. He returned to Russia in 1812 and joined the Russian army at the Tarutino Camp. In October-December 1812, he commanded the 2nd and, later, the 8th Corps. In early 1813, he took command of the 3rd Corps but was dispatched on a diplomatic mission to Copenhagen in May. He retired because of poor health in 1816 and later lived in France. Dolgorukov wrote interesting work on the Russian army, entitled *Khronika Rossiiskoi Imperatorskoi Armii* [Chronicles of the Russian Imperial Army] published in 1799.

DOLGORUKOV (Dolgorukov V), Vasily Yurievich, (b. 1776 — date of death unclear; removed from rosters on 7 October 1810) enlisted in the Life Guard Preobrazhensk Regiment in 1789. In 1798, he was promoted to colonel, but he retired the next year. In 1801, Dolgorukov returned to active service and rose to major general in the Astrakhan Grenadier Regiment. From 5 July 1802 to 14 October 1809, he served as chef of the Chernigov Musketeer Regiment.

During the 1806-1807 Campaigns, Dolgorukov distinguished himself at Pultusk, Eylau and Friedland, becoming adjutant general in July 1807. In 1809, he took part in the campaign against Austria but did not participate in any actions. Between 14 October 1809 and 7 October 1810, he was chef of the Tambov Musketeer Regiment. In 1810, Dolgorukov took part in the Russo-Turkish war, commanding the 18th Division and fought at Bazardjik, Shumla, Varna, Shumla and other actions before dying of illness in September 1810.

DOLGORUKOV (Dolgorukov IV), Vladimir Petrovich (b. 1773 — d. 1817) was enlisted in the Guard immediately after his birth and rose to a sergeant by 1781. Two years later, he was promoted to a junior adjutant to Lieutenant General Nashokin. On 9 December 1784, Dolgorukov received the rank of flügel adjutant and, in 1789, he was promoted to adjutant general to Prince Yuri Dolgorukov. On 4 November 1789, he became a lieutenant colonel in the Aleksandria Light Horse Regiment and, in 1790, he transferred to the Smolensk Dragoon Regiment. Dolgorukov took part in the Russo-Swedish War in 1790-1791 and served in Poland in 1794. In 1795, he rose to a colonel and took command of the Pavlograd Light Horse Regiment. In 1796, he participated in the Persian Campaign along the Caspian Sea. However, Emperor Paul had him arrested for alleged treason in 1797. Dolgorukov was soon acquitted and promoted to major general on 5 December 1798, receiving the Order of St. John of Jerusalem. On 3 April 1799, Dolgorukov became chef of the Chevalier Guard Regiment and served in Switzerland in 1799.

Returning to Russia, Dolgorukov served on several military committees before taking a discharge on 19 March 1800. On 20 November 1800, he returned to the army, taking command of the Tatar Lithuanian Regiment but retired again on 1 February 1801. After the accession of Alexander I, he became chef of the Kinburn Dragoon Regiment on 24 July 1801. He successfully petitioned the Russian emperor to send him to Kutuzov's army and arrived there on the eve of the battle of Austerlitz. In 1807, Dolgorukov transferred to the Moldavian Army and captured an enemy supply magazine at Galati. His deteriorating health forced him to retire on 23 February 1808. He spent the rest of his life in Speshnev estate in the Tula *gubernia* before dying on 24 November 1817.

Other Dolgorukovs serving in the Russian army included: **DOLGORUKOV, Aleksey Alekseyevich,** who commanded the Keksholm (Kexholm) Musketeer Regiment from 3 January 1800 to 18 July 1803; **DOLGORUKOV (Dolgorukov III), Mikhail Petrovich**, who served as chef of the Courland Dragoon Regiment in 21 April 1807 – 9 May 1808; **DOLGORUKOV, Pavel Vasilievich**, who served as chef of the Siberia Grenadier Regiment in November-December 1796 and chef of the Uglitsk Musketeer Regiment between 31 December 1796 and 24 March 1798; **DOLGORUKOV Yuri Vladimirovich**, chef of the Astrakhan Grenadier Regiment from 13 December 1796 to 10 December 1797.

DOLON (d'Olon), Osip Frantsevich (Gabriel Joseph) (b. 14 April 1774, Nancy – d. 25 May 1821) was born to a French noble family and began service in Prince Conde's émigré corps. He entered Russian service as a captain in the Siberia Dragoon Regiment in 1798.

During the Russo-Turkish War of 1806-1812, Dolon commanded the 1st Horse Volunteer Regiment [*konnii volonternii polk*] before taking command of the Izumsk Hussar Regiment on 5 July 1811. During the 1812 Campaign, he served in the 8th Brigade of the 2nd Cavalry Division of the 4th Corps, fighting at Smolensk, Lubino (promoted to a colonel, 12 November 1812), Borodino (wounded), Maloyaroslavets and Krasnyi. In 1813, he served at Danzig and Torgau before joining Chernyshev's flying detachment. Dolon distinguished himself at Lüneburg (received the Order of St. George, 4th class, 4 January 1814), Dennewitz and Leipzig.

The following year, he served at Craonne, Rheims, St. Dizier and Paris, rising to a major general on 13 June 1815 with seniority dating from 26 March 1814. He briefly served as the Commandant of Nancy in 1815. After the war, Dolon commanded the 2nd Brigade of the Bug Uhlan Division between 28 November 1817 and 18 May 1818, and the 1st Brigade of the same division from 18 May 1818 to 7 November 1819 when he took a discharge because of poor health.

DOROKHOV, Ivan Semenovich (b. 4 October 1762 — d. 7 May 1815, Tula) was born to a Russian noble family. He graduated from the Artillery and Engineer Cadet Corps and began service as a lieutenant in the Smolensk Infantry Regiment in 1787. He distinguished himself in the campaign against the Turks in 1788-1789, fighting at Maksimeni on the Siret River, Focsani, Rimnic and Macin and served as a duty officer to General Alexander Suvorov. In 1794, Dorokhov took part in the campaign against the Poles. In April, he defended Warsaw for thirty-six hours against the superior Polish troops and was wounded twice. In late 1794, he fought at Maciejowice and Praga, garnering a golden cross. In 1798, Dorokhov was promoted to colonel and retired from the military only to return to the service in March 1802. From 1 June 1802 to 16 August 1803, he commanded the Sumsk Hussar Regiment. He became a major general and chef of the Izumsk Hussar Regiment on 16 August 1803.

During the 1806-1807 Campaign in Poland, Dorokhov fought at Pultusk (received the Order of St. George, 3rd class, 2 February 1807), Hof (wounded in the left leg), Eylau and Friedland. In 1808-1809, Dorokhov commanded the coastal defense on the Baltic Sea. In 1812, he led the advance guard of the 4th Corps. In late June, while retreating to Drissa camp, Dorokhov was cut off from the 1st Western Army and fought several rearguard actions against the French at Olshani and Bolshie Solechniki before joining the 2nd Western Army. He followed Bagration's army to Smolensk, where he took part in battles at Molevo Boloto and Lubino (wounded in the left hand).

At the Battle of Borodino, Dorokhov was attached to the 2nd Cavalry Corps and distinguished himself at Bagration's fleches, for which he was promoted to lieutenant general on 12 November 1812. After Borodino, Dorokhov covered the retreat of the main army and fought at Znamensky on 19 September. He then harassed the French supply lines between Smolensk and Moscow. In October, Dorokhov was dispatched by Kutuzov to take Vereya, which he captured with its entire French garrison on 11 October; for this success, he garnered a golden sword with diamonds inscribed "For Liberating Vereya." Dorokhov then fought at Maloyaroslavets, where he was seriously wounded in the left leg. He died of the wound complications on 7 May 1815 and was buried at Vereya.

DOTICHAMP, Jean Frank Louis was born to a French marquis. Fleeing the French Revolution, he entered Russian service taking command of the Chevalier Guard Regiment on 20 June 1797. He became chef of the Yamburg Cuirassier Regiment on 5 August 1798. Promoted to general of cavalry on 31 March 1799, he served as chef of the Rostov Dragoon Regiment between 24 November 1799 and 11 January 1800. He served as cavalry inspector of the Dniestr Inspection in 1802-1806.

DOVRE (D'Auvray), Fedor Filippovich (Friderich Anton Philipp August) (b. 12 September 1764 — d. 6 September 1846, St. Petersburg) descended from a French noble family living in Saxony. He studied in the Dresden Engineer Academy and began service in the Polish army as an adjutant to General Feldzugmeister Brule in Warsaw. During the Polish Uprising of 1794, he was imprisoned for refusing to join the insurgents. Liberated in late 1794, he entered Russian service as a captain in the corps of engineers on 4 March 1795. He then taught fortifications and military art at the Artillery and Engineer Cadet Corps, rising to major in January 1797, to lieutenant colonel on 16 August 1798 and to colonel on 19 October 1799. On 31 August 1801, he was appointed to the Quartermaster Section of the Imperial Retinue and served in the embassy to China in 1805.

Returning to Russia, Dovre joined the 1st Guard Division during the campaign in Poland in 1807, fighting at Guttstadt, Heilsberg and Friedland and earning the Orders of St. Vladimir (3rd class) of St. Anna (2nd class) and the Prussian Pour le Merite. In 1809-1810, he worked on a detailed map of the western Russia and prepared various plans for the defense of the western provinces; for his service, Dovre received the rank of major general on 27 September 1811. Two months later, he became quartermaster general of the 1st Corps and a duty officer to General Wittgenstein. During the 1812 Campaign, he served as the Chief of Staff for Wittgenstein's corps, fighting at Jakubovo, Klyastitsy, Golovchin, on Svolnya River (garnered the Order of St. George, 3rd class, 1 October 1812), two battles of Polotsk, for which he received the Orders of St. Anna (1st class) and of St. Vladimir (2nd class), at Chashniki, Smolnya, Borisov and on the Berezina River (earned the diamond signs of the Order of St. Anna, 1st class). He helped negotiate the Tauroggen Convention in late December 1812.

In the spring of 1813, Dovre served as the Chief of General Staff of the Russian army and took part in the actions at Pillau, Berlin, Wittenberg, Spandau (received the Prussian Order of Red Eagle, 1st class), Torgau, Lutzen (promoted to a lieutenant general on 27 September 1813 with seniority dating from 2 May) and Bautzen. In August-December 1813, Dovre was the Chief of Staff of Wittgenstein's corps and participated in the battles at Dresden and Leipzig, for which he received a golden sword with diamonds. In 1814, he took part in the battles at Mormant, Bar sur Aube, Labrusselle, Troyes, Arcis sur Aube, Le Fère Champenoise and Paris. For the first four battles, Dovre was awarded a twelve-year rent; for his conduct at Paris, he was decorated with the Order of St. Alexander of Neva and the Austrian Order of Maria Theresa. In addition to previous decorations, he also received the Bavarian Order of Maximilian Joseph for his service in 1814. After the war, Dovre took part in demarcation of the state borders between Austria, Prussia and Russia in 1815-1818 for which he garnered the diamond signs of the Order of St. Alexander of Neva and a diamond encrusted golden snuffbox with the portrait of the King of Prussia.

Between 17 July 1819 and 1 March 1827, Dovre commanded the Independent Lithuanian Corps, earning two diamond encrusted golden snuffboxes with the portraits of the Russian Emperor and the King of Prussia. He rose to general of infantry on 3 September 1826 and garnered the Order of the White Eagle on 17 May 1827. On 16 June 1827, he became *chargè d'affaires* of the Quartermaster General of the Imperial General Staff. During the Russo-Turkish War of 1828-1829, he commanded the troops in the siege of Silistra, for which he received the Order of St. Vladimir (1st class, 14 September 1829) and a twelve-year rent. In 1830, Dovre was decorated with the Austrian Order of Leopold (1st class) and became the Chief of Staff of the Army of Reserve on 21 April 1831. After participating in the suppression of the Polish Uprising in 1831, Dovre returned to St. Petersburg, where he headed the Committee on Determining the Strategic Sites on the Borders of the Russian Empire. He died on 6 September 1846 in St. Petersburg.

DREVICH, Fedor Ivanovich (b. 1767 — d. 1816) was born to a noble family from the Vitebsk *gubernia*. He enlisted in the Life Guard Horse Regiment in 1776 and transferred as a captain to the Dnieper Infantry Regiment in 1786. He participated in the Russo-Turkish War of 1787-1791 and served in Poland in 1792-1794, retiring with a rank of major in 1795. During the 1806 Campaign in Poland, Drevich enlisted in the Vitebsk *opolchenye* and later served as an adjutant to Buxhöwden, following him to Finland in 1808. He took command of the Finland Dragoon Regiment on 2 January 1811. The same year, he rose to colonel and became chef of the Finland Dragoons on 10 November.

During the 1812 Campaign, Drevich served in the Finland Corps and participated in the operations in the Baltic provinces and in the battles at Riga, Polotsk and on the Berezina River. In 1813, he joined Chernyshev's cavalry detachment, distinguishing himself at Lüneburg and Halberstadt, where he was wounded and earned promotion to major general on 13 July 1813. However, due to his poor health, Drevich left his unit without leave in late 1813 and was court martialed for his absence and poor maintenance of the regiment. He died in 1816 before the final sentence was announced.

DRIZEN (Drizen II), Fedor Vasilievich (Friedrich Wilhelm) (b. 21 August 1781 — d. 12 October 1851) was born to a Prussian noble family that settled in Russia in the mid-18th century. He enlisted as an ensign in the Life Guard Preobrazhensk Regiment on 28 August 1797. Promoted to staff captain, he took part in the battles of Austerlitz (received the Order of St. Anna, 4th class), Heilsberg and Friedland in 1805-1807. For his actions, he was promoted to colonel on 23 February 1808 and appointed commander of the Vilna Musketeer Regiment on 24 April 1808. Two years later, he became chef of the Muromsk Musketeer Regiment on 31 October 1810.

During the 1812 Campaign, Drizen served with the 1st Brigade of the 3rd Division of the 3rd Corps, fighting at Sventsyani, Vitebsk, Smolensk (received the Order of St. Vladimir, 4th class), Zabludye (bruised in the left leg by a cannoball) and Borodino, where he lost his left leg. For his courage, Drizen was decorated with the Order of St. George (4th class, 4 January 1813) and earned promotion to major general on 27 September 1813 with seniority dating from 7 September 1812. Because of his injury, Drizen could not participate in the campaigns of 1813-1814. After the war, he served in the Supply Department of the Ministry of War before becoming an adjutant to the Minister of War in 1817. Promoted to a lieutenant general on 13 January 1826, Drizen was appointed the Commandant of Riga on 10 November 1828 and received the Order of St. Vladimir (2nd class) in 1832 and the rank of general of infantry on 29 March 1845. His brother, **DRIZEN, Yegor Vasilievich** commanded the Life Guard Preobrazhensk Regiment between 26 September 1810 and 25 September 1812, taking part in the Battle of Borodino in September 1812.

DRUTSKOY-SOKOLINSKY, Eliferii Vasilievich commanded the Oliviopol Hussar Regiment between 10 December 1804 and 24 December 1807 and participated in the 1806-1807 Campaigns in Poland. Promoted to a major general on 24 December 1807, he served as chef of the Kharkov Dragoon Regiment from 22 March 1808 to 1 July 1810.

DUKA, Ilya Mikhailovich (b. 1768 — d. 28 February 1830, Ivnya, Kursk *gubernia*) descended from a Serbian family. He enlisted as a furier in the Nasheburg Infantry Regiment on 27 May 1776 and transferred as a vakhmistr to the Ukraine Light Horse Regiment in 1780 before joining the Smolensk Dragoon Regiment with the rank of cadet in 1782. In 1783, he fought the Poles and, in June 1787, Duka became a senior adjutant with lieutenant's rank in General

Shevich's staff. During the Russo-Turkish War of 1787-1791, he served with the Kuban Corps in the Kuban Valley, distinguishing himself at Anapa. In June 1789, Duka transferred to the Ostrogozh Light Horse Regiment and fought at Kinburn, Bender and Killia. During the 1794 Campaign in Poland, he fought at Krupchitze, Brest-Litovsk, Kobylka and Praga (received a golden cross). He distinguished himself at Radozhitze, where he captured Polish General Warwzhewsky and his entire staff. He had honor of delivering the news of the Russian victories in Poland to Empress Catherine II. For his conduct, Duka was promoted to rotmistr in January 1795 and to second major on 6 July of the same year. Three months later, on 20 October 1795, he transferred to the Aleksandria Light Horse Regiment receiving the rank of major in late 1796.

Duka became a colonel on 1 May 1799 and joined the Life Guard Hussar Regiment. In 1805, he participated in the battle of Austerlitz, garnering the Order of St. Vladimir (4th class). On 23 October 1806, Duka was appointed chef of the Malorossiisk (Little Russia) Cuirassier Regiment. He took part in the 1806-1807 Campaigns, distinguishing himself at Golymin (received a golden sword), Lockau, Allenstein, Jankovo, Landsberg and Eylau (garnered the Order of St. George, 3rd class). Promoted to major general on 16 May 1807, he fought at Heilsberg on 10 June 1807, where he was seriously wounded and earned a golden sword with diamonds. In 1808-1811, he was deployed with his regiment in the Kiev *gubernia*. In July-August 1812, Duka served with the 2nd Cuirassier Division of the 2nd Western Army, fighting at Smolensk on 15-16 August. On 22 August 1812, he took command of the 2nd Cuirassier Division and distinguished himself at Shevardino, Borodino (earned the Order of St. Anna, 1st class), Tarutino, Maloyaroslavets and Krasnyi (received the Order of St. Vladimir, 2nd class).

In early 1813, Duka took command of the 3rd Cuirassier Division and fought at Dresden, Peterswalde and Leipzig, where he was wounded in the head. He received promotion to lieutenant general on 27 September and, for his actions at Leipzig in October 1813, he earned a golden sword with diamonds. In 1814, he distinguished himself at Brienne, Arcis sur Aube and Paris, garnering the Prussian Order of Red Eagle and the Austrian Order of Leopold. During the Hundred Days, Duka commanded the 3rd Cuirassier Division of the 3rd Reserve Cavalry Corps and took part in the military parade at Vertus in September 1815. Upon his return to Russia, Duka commanded the 3rd Cuirassier Division before taking command of the 2nd Reserve Cavalry Corps on 20 September 1823. On 3 September 1826, he was promoted to general of cavalry and then retired because of poor health on 17 February 1827. He died at his estate at Ivnya in the Kursk *gubernia* on 28 February 1830.

DURNOVO, Ivan Nikolayevich (b. 1784 — d. 1850, St. Petersburg) was born to a prominent Russian noble family. He was enlisted in the Life Guard Semeyonovsk Regiment in June 1786 and rose to ensign in January 1793. Durnovo began active service as a sub-lieutenant in 1799 and rose to a lieutenant in 1802 and staff captain in 1806. In 1807, he took part in the campaign in Poland, fighting at Guttstadt and Friedland, where he was seriously wounded in the left leg and earned the Order of St. Vladimir (4th class). Promoted to captain in 1808 and colonel on 26 April 1809, Durnovo took command of the reserve battalions of the 9th Division. He served in the Danubian

Principalities in 1810-1811, distinguishing himself at Ruse, where he took a serious wound to the left hand. He took command of the 18th Jager Regiment on 17 February 1811 and became chef of the 29th Jager Regiment on 31 March 1812.

During the 1812 Campaign, Durnovo served with the 3rd Brigade of the 22nd Division in the Army of Danube, fighting at Lubomle, Terebun, Vysoko-Litovsk and Volkovysk, where he earned the Order of St. George (4th class, 13 September 1813). In 1813, Durnovo served at Warsaw, Krakow, Prausnitz, Katzbach (wounded in the chest), Lobau, Hochkirch, Neustadt, Stolpen (received the Order of St. Anna, 2nd class and the Prussian Pour le Merite), Düben, Leipzig and Mainz. In 1814, he took part in the actions at Soissons (received a golden sword) and Paris. For his excellent service in 1813-1814, Durnovo was promoted to major general on 13 June 1815 with seniority dating from 18 October 1813, while his regiment was renamed to the 29th Grenadier Jager Regiment on 15 April 1814. The following year, this unit was converted to the 6th Carabinier Regiment on 11 September 1815. Durnovo commanded the 3rd Brigade of the 15th Division in 1815 and, after a brief retirement in 1816, he took command of the 1st Brigade of the 15th Division in 1817 and of the 2nd Brigade of the 1st Division in 1820. Durnovo finally retired on 6 December 1821 and lived in Moscow and St. Petersburg before dying in 1850.

DUROVA, Nadezhda Andreyevna (b. 1783 – d. 4 April 1866) was born to a minor official's family in the Vyatka *gubernia*. In 1801, she married Vasily Chernov, a local official in Sarapul, and had a daughter in 1802. However, the marriage soon ended as Durova met a Cossack esaul and decided to enlist in the army. She disguised herself as a nobleman Aleksandr Andreyevich Aleksandrov and joined the Polish Horse Uhlan Regiment. She took part in the 1807 Campaign in Poland, fighting at Guttstadt, Heilsberg and Friedland, where she was promoted to ensign in the Mariupol Hussar Regiment. However, she was wounded in one of the skirmishes and her deception was revealed. Nevertheless, Emperor Alexander commended her for her valor and allowed her to remain in the army.

In 1812, Durova served with the Luthuanian Uhlan Regiment, fighting at Smolensk, Kolotsk and Borodino, where she was bruised in the leg. In September-December 1812, she served on Kutuzov's staff and, the following year, she participated in the sieges of Modlin and Hamburg. After the war, she retired with a rank of staff rotmistr in 1816 and returned to her family in Sarapul. Durova is the only known female officer of the Russian army during the Napoleonic Wars. She wrote very interesting and vivid military recollections entitled "*Kavalerist*

Devitsa [Cavalry Maiden]." The work was published in English under titles "*The Cavalry Maiden: Journals of a Female Russian Officer in the Napoleonic Wars*" (London, 1988) and "*The Cavalry Maid: the Memoirs of a Woman Soldier of 1812*" (Ann Arbor, 1988).

DYACHKIN, Grigoriy Andreevich (b. 1756 — d. 15 January 1819) was born to a Don Cossack staff officer's family in Cherkassk. He enlisted as a private in the Don Cossack Host in 1773 and rose to esaul in 1774. Serving in the Caucasus, he took command of a Cossack regiment in 1783 and received promotion to Cossack colonel (major of the regular army) on 26 July 1788. The same year, Dyachkin organized a new Cossack regiment that he commanded during the Russo-Swedish War in 1789-1790. In 1794, he served in Poland, garnering the Order of St. Vladimir (4th class). He then returned to the Don Cossack Host, participating in the operations in the North Caucasus region. He became colonel of the Russian regular army on 27 July 1798.

During the 1812 Campaign, Dyachkin commanded a Cossack regiment in the 3rd Reserve Army of Observation and fought at Kobryn, Slonim and on the Berezina. He was promoted to a major general on 26 November 1812 (officially conferred on 28 June 1813) but took a discharge because of poor health in January 1813.

DYATKOV, Stepan Vasilievich (b. 1759 — date of death unknown) was born to a noble family from the Tambov *gubernia*. He enlisted as a private in the Life Guard Semeyonovsk Regiment on 12 March 1771, and transferred as a lieutenant to the Chevalier Guard Corps in 1776. Twelve years later, he joined the Pereyaslavl Horse Jager Regiment and took part in the Russo-Turkish War in 1788-1791, distinguishing himself at Ismail and Bender. Promoted to colonel on 10 November 1799, Dyatkov became commander of the Malorossiisk (Little Russia) Cuirassier Regiment on 13 January 1804, and chef of this unit on 6 October 1806.

During the 1806-1807 Campaigns in Poland, Dyatkov served with the 3rd Division at Eylau (wounded in the stomach), Guttstadt, Heilsberg and Friedland. He became chef of the Orenburg Dragoon Regiment on 11 September 1807, and received promotion to major general on 24 December 1807. During the 1812 Campaign, Dyatkov served with the 9th Brigade of the 3rd Cavalry Division of the 3rd Reserve Cavalry Corps, distinguishing himself at Smolensk (wounded) and Borodino, where he was seriously wounded in the right arm. After recuperating, Dyatkov fought at Dresden, Leipzig and Hamburg in 1813-1814. He retired because of poor health on 11 January 1819.

EFIMOVICH, Andrey Alexandrovich (b. 1773 — date of death unclear; removed from rosters on 5 September 1823) was born to a petty noble family in the Kiev *gubernia*. He began service in the Life Guard Preobrazhensk Regiment and served against the Turks in 1787-1790. He transferred as a lieutenant to the Prince Potemkin's Cuirassier Regiment (later Ekaterinoslavl Cuirassiers) in 1792. During the 1806-1807 Campaigns in Poland, he served in the 6th Division and fought at Heilsberg and Friedland (received the Order of St. George, 4th class). He was promoted to colonel on 24 December 1808 and became commander of the Alexandria Hussar Regiment on 24 May 1809. He served in the Danubian Principalities in 1810-1811.

During the Russian Campaign of 1812, Efimovich served in the 17th Brigade of the 5th Cavalry Division in the 3rd Reserve Army of Observation and fought at Kobryn, Gorodechnya, Minsk and Borisov. In 1813, he took part in the actions at Kalisch, Lutzen (wounded in the head), Bautzen and Katzbach. In 1814, Efimovich distinguished himself at Brienne (promoted to major general on 11 September 1814 with seniority dating from 29 January 1814), La Rothière, Craonn, Le Fère Champenoise and Meaux. After the war, he was given command of the 1st Brigade of the 2nd Dragoon Division on 1 January 1819.

EFREMOV, Ivan Grigorievich (b. 1773 — date of death unclear) was born to a noble family and studied in the Artillery and Engineer Cadet Corps. He began service as a shtyk-junker in the 3rd Bombardier Regiment in 1790 and participated in the Russo-Swedish War serving on the galley fleet. He took part in the 1806-1807 Campaigns in Poland and fought at Pultusk, Eylau (wounded in the left leg and hand; received a golden sword), Heilsberg and Friedland (earned the Order of St. Vladimir, 4th class).

Efremov was promoted to lieutenant colonel on 21 February 1811 and was appointed commander of the 24th Artillery Brigade on 29 September 1811. During the 1812 Campaign, he fought at Smolensk and Borodino (received the Order of St. Anna, 2nd class), where he was seriously wounded in the left leg. After recuperating, he served in the Duchy of Warsaw in 1813-1814.

EISMANDT, Aleksey Matveyevich (b. 1789 — date of death unclear) was born to a noble family in the Grodno *gubernia*. He studied in the Grodno Cadet Corps and began service as a sub-lieutenant in the 4th Artillery Brigade in 1806. He participated in the campaign in Poland in 1806-1807 and fought at Pultusk and Eylau. He was promoted to lieutenant on 21 February 1811 and transferred to the Life Guard Artillery Brigade on 6 February 1812. During the 1812 Campaign, Eismandt fought at Borodino and Krasnyi. In 1813-1814, he participated in the battles at Lutzen, Bautzen, Dresden, Kulm, Leipzig and Paris.

EMELYANOV, Nikolay Filippovich (b. 1768 — d. 1829) was born to a Russian noble family. He enlisted as a sergeant in the Chernigov

Infantry Regiment on 20 June 1779. He fought in the Russo-Swedish War of 1788-1790 and was promoted to ensign. In 1799, he distinguished himself in the Italian and Swiss Campaigns of Field Marshal Alexander Suvorov. Six years later, he participated in the campaign against Napoleon and fought at Austerlitz. He was then transferred to the Danube Valley to fight the Turks. Emelyanov took command of the Vyborg Musketeer Regiment on 3 August 1809 and distinguished himself at Braila, Ruse and Lovchea. For his actions, he was promoted to colonel on 25 April 1811 and appointed chef of the Kabarda Infantry Regiment on 5 September 1811. However, three months later, he became chef of the Keksholm (Kexholm) Infantry Regiment on 22 November 1811.

During the 1812 Campaign, Emelyanov's regiment was attached to the 1st Brigade of the 11th Division of the 4th Corps of the 1st Western Army. He fought at Ostrovno, Borodino, Tarutino, Maloyaroslavets, Vyazma and Krasnyi. In 1813, Emelyanov fought at Modlin, Bautzen, Dresden, Kulm (rose to major general on 27 September 1813) and Leipzig. The following year, he took part in the battle of Paris and took command of the 2nd Brigade of the 1st Grenadier Division on 20 December 1814. He was appointed head of the 2nd District of Internal Guard in 1821 and retired on 19 December 1829 with a full pension. During his career, Emelyanov received the Russian Orders of St. Anna (1st class), of St. Vladimir (3rd class), of St. George (4th class) and of St. John of Jerusalem, the Prussian Order of the Red Eagle (2nd class) and a golden sword with diamonds for courage.

EMMANUEL (Manuilovich), George (Yegor) Arsenyevich (b. 13 April 1775 — d. 26 January 1837, Elizavetgrad) was born to a petty noble family in Serbia. From an early age, he participated in actions against the Turks. In 1791, he joined the Austrian service to fight the Porte. At the battle of Landau in 1792, Emmanuel was seriously wounded receiving a bayonet wound into stomach and a cannonball splinter to his right hand. The same year, he was hit with canister in the right leg. For his courage, he was awarded a gold medal with the inscription "Der Tapferkeit" and was appointed to the Hungarian Guard with the rank of sub-lieutenant in 1794. However, Emmanuel soon resigned because of the Austrian reluctance to support the Serbian independence. He traveled to Moscow in April 1797 and met Emperor Paul I, who liked him and praised his Hungarian uniform. The same day (20 April), Emmanuel was enlisted in the Life Guard Hussar Regiment with the rank of lieutenant. The next year, he became staff-rotmistr and, in 1799, he rose to rotmistr. He was promoted to colonel on 7 October 1800.

With accession of Emperor Alexander, Emmanuel's promotions slowed down. In 1802, he transferred to the Kiev Dragoon Regiment and then participated in the 1806-1807 Campaigns against Napoleon. At Pultusk, he commanded two squadrons and was seriously wounded, but remained with the ranks and later received a golden sword for courage. After recuperating, he served in General Essen I's corps in April-May 1807. In June 1807, he fought at Guttstadt, where he led a cavalry charge and garnered the Order of St. Vladimir (4th class). Emmanuel then distinguished himself at Heilsberg and received the Order of St. Anna (2nd class). At Friedland, he served with the Kiev Dragoon Regiment, covering the retreat of the main forces and destroying the bridges over the Nieman River. On 24 May 1808, he was appointed commander of the Kiev Dragoon Regiment and, on 23 December 1808, he became chef of the Courland Dragoon Regiment. Two months later, on 2 February 1808, he became chef of the Kiev Dragoon Regiment.

During the 1809 Campaign against Austria, Emmanuel's regiment was assigned to Sergey Golitsyn's corps to fight the Austrians, but Emmanuel appealed to Alexander for permission to avoid this service because he served in the Austrian army before. His petition was satisfied and he did not participate in the actions of that year. In 1812, Emmanuel commanded the 13th Brigade of the 4th Cavalry Division of the 4th Reserve Cavalry Corps in the 2nd Western Army. He distinguished himself at Mir on 9 July (received the Order of St. Vladimir, 3rd class) and took part in the actions at Novoselk and Saltanovka and in the battles of Smolensk and Shevardino. He led several charges against the French at Shevardino, but was wounded in the chest and later received the Order of St. George (4th class, 4 January 1813).

Emmanuel spent several weeks recuperating and joined the army in late September at Tarutino. In October he was assigned to the advance guard and fought at Maloyaroslavets, Vyazma and several other minor actions. For his conduct, he was promoted to major general on 7 January 1813. During the campaign in Saxony, Emmanuel took part in the sieges of Modlin, Glogau and then commanded a detachment around Zwenkau. He was one of the first Allied commanders to cross the Elbe River and participated in minor actions prior to the battle of Bautzen, where he distinguished himself fighting Marshal Macdonald. During the armistice in the summer of 1813, he served on the Bohemian borders. For his actions in the spring of 1813, he was awarded the Order of St. Anna (1st class) and the Prussian Order of the Red Eagle (2nd class). As the hostilities resumed, Emmanuel commanded the cavalry of the advance guard of Langeron's corps. On 19 August, he fought the French near Ziben-Eichen on the Bobr River and then had several minor actions before the battle of Katzbach, where, according to the official rosters, he captured over 1,100 men and 7 guns. He then engaged the French at Löwenberg (awarded the Order of St. George. 3rd class, 29 August 1813) as well as in the minor actions at Stolpen, Rotmeritz, Bischofswerda, Elster, Duben, Rodefeld and Badefeld.

Emmanuel took part in the Battle of Leipzig on 16-18 October and distinguished himself by capturing 2 generals, including General Loriston, 17 officers and 400 soldiers. Emmanuel, however, was not awarded for his actions because of his argument with Field Marshal Gebhard Blücher. He was soon transferred to St. Priest's corps and fought at Rheims, where he covered the retreat of the Russian troops. He took part in the capture of Paris on 30 March 1814 and was promoted to lieutenant general on 8 April 1814 with seniority dating from 30 March 1814. He also received the Prussian Order of the Red Eagle (1st class) and the Swedish Order of the Sword (2nd class). In 1815, Emmanuel took command of the 4th Dragoon Division and remained at this position for the next ten years. On 7 July 1826, he assumed command of the Russian forces in the Caucasus. For his actions against Caucasian mountaineers, he received the Order of St. Alexander of Neva.

During the Russo-Turkish War of 1828-1829, Emmanuel occupied and annexed several major regions in the North Caucasus, including Karachaevo, and suppressed uprisings in the Kuban Valley. For his actions, he was promoted to general of cavalry on 7 July 1828. Emmanuel led an expedition to Mountain Elbrus, the highest peak in the Caucasus, in 1829 and was awarded a lifetime pension and an estate in 1830. Emmanuel retired in 1831 and lived at Elizavetgrad until dying on 26 January 1837.

EMME, Ivan Fedorovich (b. 5 August 1763 — d. 24 September 1839, Moscow) was born to a noble family in the Lifland *gubernia*. He studied at the Infantry Cadet Corps and began service as a lieutenant in the Tobolsk Infantry Regiment on 25 March 1782. He participated in the Russo-Swedish War in 1789-1790 and distinguished himself on the Kummen River (received the Order of St. Vladimir, 4th class) and at Kernikoski (promoted to lieutenant colonel). He became colonel and commander of the Ryazan Musketeer Regiment on 21 January 1797, commander of the Sofia Musketeer Regiment on 28 July 1798 as well as major general and chef of the Pavlovsk Grenadier Regiment on 6 September 1798.

Emme participated in the expedition to Holland in 1799 and fought at Bergen (wounded in the right leg) and Alkmar (wounded in the left hand). Returning to Russia, he was discharged on 20 April 1800 but he returned to service on 26 November 1800 receiving appointment to the Life Guard Preobrazhensk Regiment. He was discharged for the second time for improper reporting on 17 March 1801 but returned to the army on 26 March 1801. Emme became the Commandant of Riga on 21 January 1802, chef of the Riga Garrison Regiment on 10 October 1803 and served in Riga for the next nine years. In 1812-1813, he organized the defense of Riga (promoted to lieutenant general on 7 January 1813) and fought at Mittau, Memel, Elbing and Danzig. In late 1813-1814, he commanded the 26th Division during the siege of Hamburg and was awarded the Order of St. George (3rd class) on 10 February 1814. After the war, Emme commanded the 26th Division for five years. He became commander of the 17th Division on 27 February 1820 and later commanded the 5th Division. He was relieved of command on 5 November 1824 and retired on 1 January 1834.

EMME (Emme I), Aleksey Fedorovich (b. 1775 — d. 8 October 1849) was born to a noble family in the Lifland *gubernia*. He enlisted in the Life Guard Izmailovsk Regiment on 12 January 1793 and transferred to the Tobolsk Infantry Regiment in March 1794. The same year, he participated in the campaign against the Poles. In 1799, he took part in the expedition to Holland and was wounded in the action at Bergen. He was promoted to staff-captain in May 1800 and to captain in December 1804. During the Polish Campaigns of 1806-1807, Emme fought at Pultusk, Eylau, Danzig and Memel. In 1812, he served as a duty officer under Lieutenant General Löwis and fought at Eckau, Beberbeck, Kalideni, Wolhont, Dalen-Kirck and Memel. The following year, he took part in the siege of Danzig, for which he received promotion to colonel as well as the Order of St. Anna (2nd class), the Prussian Pour le Merite and a golden sword for courage.

In March 1814, Emme transferred to the Tavrida Grenadier Regiment and three years later he became commander of the Moscow Grenadier Regiment. He was promoted to major general in August 1823. Emme was named commander of the 2nd Brigade of the 2nd Grenadier Division in January 1825 and served as the Commandant of Bender beginning in March 1831. However, while remaining at the military settlement of the 2nd Grenadier Division, he was attacked by mutinious soldiers, thrown out of the second floor window and severely beaten with spikes, having his thigh and head broken in several places. He barely survived these wounds and later assumed his position as the Commandant of Bender in October 1831. He was promoted to lieutenant general in 1846.

EMME (Emme II), Alexander Ivanovich (b. 1794 — date of death unknown) descended from a noble family in the Lifland *gubernia*. He began service as a page on 8 January 1810 and was appointed a cornet in the Sumsk Hussar Regiment in 1812. During the Russian Campaign of 1812, he served under Count Wittgenstein and fought at Chashniky and Smolyani, rising to lieutenant. In 1813, he served under Major General Dörenberg and took part in the battles at Dresden (received the Order of St. Anna, 4th class), Heilsdorf, Kulm, Wachau and Leipzig (earned the Order of St. Vladimir, 4th class) and

Betelstedt. In 1814, Emme fought at Bar sur Aube, Labrusselle, Troyes, Arcis sur Aube, Le Fère Champenoise and Paris. For his actions in these battles, he was promoted to rotmistr and awarded the Prussian Pour le Merite and the Baden Order of Military Merit.

In January 1815, Emme was promoted to staff-rotmistr and transferred as a captain to the Life Guard Horse Jager Regiment on 7 April 1815. Two years later, he was appointed as major to the Akhtyrsk Hussar Regiment, receiving promotion to lieutenant colonel in 1826. During the Russo-Turkish War of 1828-1829, Emme served under General Ridiger and fought at Constanta, Shumla, Esk-Istambul and in other minor actions. In 1829, he was promoted to colonel and, in 1830, he transferred to the Kargopol Dragoon Regiment. The following year, he became commander of the Kargopol Dragoons and took part in the suppression of the Polish uprising for which he garnered the Order of St. Anna (2nd class). In 1834, he briefly commanded the Courland Dragoon Regiment before taking extended furlough becase of poor health. He retired with the rank of major general in January 1837.

ENGELHARDT, Anton Evstafievich (b. 1795 — d. 8 September 1872, St. Petersburg) was born to a noble family in the Lifland *gubernia*. He enlisted as a junker in the Grodno Hussar Regiment on 13 August 1812 and participated in minor actions at Kirka, Eklau, Stishani, Gorden, and Yanishek and other places. He was promoted to cornet on 4 November 1812 and appointed adjutant to Major General Ridiger. During the 1813 Campaign, Engelhardt took part in the combats on the Vistula River, at Koenigsberg, Berlin, Magdeburg, (promoted to lieutenant on 2 May 1813), Bautzen, Dresden, Leipzig (received the Order of St. Anna, 3rd class and the Prussian Pour le Merite) and Strasbourg. For his courage in these battles, he was also awarded the Order of. St. Vladimir (4th class). In 1814, Engelhardt fought at Brienne, Bar sur Aube, Arcis sur Aube, Le Fère Champenoise and Paris, earning the Order of St. Anna (2nd class) and a golden sword for courage.

In 1815-1820, Engelhardt served as an adjutant to General Ridiger, becoming a rotmistr on 19 May 1820 and transferring as a captain to the Life Guard Horse Jager Regiment in August 1820. He was promoted to lieutenant colonel in 1823 and served in the Wittgenstein's Hussar Regiment. He participated in the Russo-Turkish War of 1828-1829, fighting in numerous battles including the actions at Constanta and Shumla. Engelhardt was appointed commander of the Kinburn Dragoon Regiment on 11 October 1829 and rose to colonel on 13 August 1830. The next year, he served in Poland, taking part in the capture of Warsaw for which he was decorated with the Orders of St. George (4th class) and of St. Vladimir (3rd class). He took command of the 1st Brigade of the 2nd Dragoon Division in December 1837, rose to major general in 1838 and earned the Order of St. Stanislaus (1st class) in 1839.

In April 1843, Engelhardt became commander of the Life Guard Hussar Regiment and, a year later, he assumed command of the 2nd Brigade of the 1st Life Guard Cavalry Division (7 April 1844). He was awarded the Order of St. Anna (1st class) with an Imperial crown in 1846 and promoted to lieutenant general on 23 April 1848. In November 1848, Engelhardt was appointed commander of the 1st Guard Light Cavalry Division, and later took command of the 2nd Guard Light Cavalry Division in February 1849. He commanded this unit for the next seven years receiving the Order of St. Vladimir (2nd class) in December 1849 and the Order of the White Eagle four years later. In January 1856, he was appointed commander of the Combined Guard Cavalry Corps and later commanded the Reserve Guard Cavalry. Engelhardt became general of cavalry in 1858 but retired later that year and settled in St. Petersburg. He died there on 8 September 1872.

ENGELHARDT, Fedor Antonovich (b. 1763 — d. 1831) was born to a noble family in Riga and enlisted as a corporal in the Life Guard Preobrazhensk Regiment on 14 March 1781. He was appointed adjutant to Gregory Potemkin's staff and promoted to lieutenant in the Novotroitsk Cuirassier Regiment on 13 January

1783. He transferred as a second major to the Smolensk Dragoon Regiment on 7 July 1785. In 1787, he was sent to the Caucasus and participated in the campaigns against the local mountaineers. In 1789-1790, he took part in the Russo-Turkish War and fought at Kaushani, Akkerman, Bender, Ismail (wounded in the head, awarded the Order of St. George, 4th class) and Macin. For his actions, he was promoted to colonel on 5 April 1791. Engelhardt served in Lithuania and Poland in 1792-1794 and fought at Belostock, Shekochin, Maciejowice and Praga (wounded in the right leg, awarded the Order of St. Vladimir, 3rd class). He retired with the rank of brigader on 31 January 1795. During the 1806 Campaign in Poland, he participated in the formation of the Lifland *zemstvo* militia. During the 1812 Campaign, he took part in the defense of Riga. He died in Riga during the cholera epidemic in 1831.

ENGELHARDT, (Engelhardt I), Grigory Grigorievich (b. 1759 — d. 5 March 1834) was born to a noble family in the Courland *gubernia*. He enlisted as a kaptenarmus in the Life Guard Izmailovsk Regiment on 17 May 1776. Three years later, he transferred as a lieutenant to the Neva Infantry Regiment (14 December 1779) and then as a captain to the Ryazan Infantry Regiment in 1785. He served in the Russo-Swedish War from 1789-1790, taking two wounds at Friedriksh and receiving promotion to premier major. He took part in the Polish Campaign of 1794 and rose to lieutenant colonel and commander of the Ryazan Musketeer Regiment on 12 July 1798. Engelhardt was promoted to colonel on 6 November 1798, to major general on 17 February 1800 and appointed chef of the Old Ingermanland Musketeer Regiment on 27 March 1800.

Engelhardt participated in the 1805 Campaign and served under Prince Bagration at Austerlitz. In 1807, he took part in the battles at Eylau (wounded in the right leg, received a golden cross), Lomitten, Heilsberg amd Friedland (wounded in the left thigh, stomach and left hand; garnered the Order of St. George, 3rd class, 1 June 1808). In 1808, he transferred to the Danubian Principalities and commanded a detachment in Little Wallachia in 1809-1810. In the summer of 1811, he commanded a brigade during the battle at Ruse. During the 1812 Campaign, Engelhardt served in the 2nd Brigade of the 8th Division in the Army of Danube and fought at Gornostay, Volkovysk and Kamenets-Zhuravky. The following year, he participated in the actions at Belostock, Warsaw, Lutzen and Bautzen, where he was seriously wounded in the left thigh. He left the army to recuperate and did not participate in the invasion of France.

In 1815, Engelhardt commanded the 1st Brigade of the 8th Division besieging Metz and Saarlouis. Returning to Russia, he briefly commanded the 3rd brigade of the 23rd Division and retired because of poor health on 11 March 1816. During his career, he was awarded two Orders of St. Vladimir (2nd and 3rd classes), the Order of St. Anna (1st class) with diamonds, the Prussian Order of the Red Eagle (2nd class) and a golden sword with diamonds.

ENGELHARDT, Leo Nikolaevich (b. 21 February 1765 — d. 16 November 1836, Moscow) was born to a noble family in the Smolensk *gubernia*. He enlisted in the Life Guard Preobrazhensk Regiment in January 1779 and studied in Count Zorich's Cadet Corps in 1779-1783. He began active service as a sergeant in the Life Guard Preobrazhensk Regiment in September 1783 and was promoted to ensign on 12 January 1784. Two years later he transferred as a second major to the Smolensk Dragoon

Regiment on 18 June 1786. Engelhardt participated in the Russo-Turkish War in 1787-1790 and fought at Ochakov (received a golden cross and promotion to premier major, 25 April 1789), Focsani, Rimnic (awarded the Order of St. Vladimir, 4th class, promoted to lieutenant colonel) and Macin (promoted to colonel, 9 July 1791). He served in Poland in 1792, commanding the Kozlov Infantry Regiment at Dubenka and Gorodische.

During the 1794 Campaign in Poland, Engelhardt distinguished himself at Shekochin, Kobylka and Praga (received a golden cross). Three years later, he transferred to the Caucasus region and was appointed commander of the Ufa Musketeer Regiment on 24 September 1798. He participated in numerous clashes with Caucasian mountaneers and was promoted to major general and appointed chef of the Ufa Musketeer Regiment on 15 February 1799. However, he retired on 29 October 1799 and spent the next seven years at his estate in the Kazan *gubernia*. During the 1806 Campaign in Poland, he organized and commanded the Kazan *zemstvo* militia and was awarded the Order of St. Anna (2nd class) with diamonds. During the Russian Campaign of 1812, he helped to organize the Kazan *opolchenye* but, according to his memoirs, he did not participate in actions.

ENGELHARDT, Paul Mikhailovich (b. 1766 – date of death unclear) was born to a noble family in the Smolensk *gubernia*. After graduating from the Infantry Cadet Corps, he began service as a lieutenant in the Her Majesty's Cuirassier Regiment on 26 November 1787. He participated in the Russo-Turkish War in 1788-1790 and fought at Gangar, Kaushani, Bender, Killia, Tulcea and Ismail (wounded in the neck and right hand; received a golden cross and promotion to second major). He served in Poland in 1792-1794 and fought at Shekochin, Maciejowice (received the Order of St. Vladimir, 4th class, and a golden sword) and Praga (earned a golden cross and promotion to premier major). He was promoted to lieutenant colonel and appointed commander of the Her Majesty's Cuirassier Regiment in 1798.

In 1799, Engelhardt rose to colonel (31 March) and served under Rimsky-Korsakov in Switzerland, where he distinguished himself at Zurich. For his actions, he was promoted to major general and appointed chef of the St. Petersburg Dragoon Regiment on 8 November 1800. He became commander of the St. Petersburg Dragoons on 25 November 1803 but was discharged on 6 April 1804. Engelhardt returned to military service eight years later, when, during the Russian Campaign, he joined the Smolensk *opolchenye* and commanded the Poretsk and Rudnya companies (*druzhina*) at Gedeonovo, Valutina Gora (wounded in the left hand) and Borodino. In October-November 1812, he fought at Maloyaroslavets, Vyazma and Krasnyi; at the latter, he took a severe wound in the right leg and left the army. He retired on 1 April 1814.

ERMOLOV (Yermolov), Aleksey Petrovich (b. 4 June 1772, Moscow – 23 April 1861, Moscow) was born a Russian noble family from the Orlov *gubernia*. He graduated from the boarding school of the Moscow University and enlisted in the Life Guard Preobrazhensk Regiment on 16 January 1787. Four years later, he was promoted to lieutenant and transferred to the Nizhegorod Dragoon Regiment with the rank of captain. He briefly taught at the Artillery and Enginrer Cadet Corps in 1793 before being sent to fight the Polish insurgents in 1794. He participared in the assault on Praga and received the Order of St. George (4th class) on 12 January 1795. The next year, Ermolov took part in the Persian Campaign along the Caspian Sea. However, he was arrested on 7 January 1799 for alleged participation in conspiracy against the Tsar and Ermolovspent two years in exile. He was restored under Alexander I and appointed to the 8th Artillery Regiment on 13 May 1801; he then transferred to the horse artillery company on 21 June 1801.

During the 1805 Campaign, Ermolov served in the rear and advance guards and distinguished himself at Amstetten and Austerlitz. For his actions, he was promoted to colonel on 16 July 1806. The following year, he participated in the campaign in Poland, where he served in Prince Bagration's advance guard. Ermolov distinguished himself commanding an artillery company in numerous rearguard actions during the retreat to Landsberg as well as in the Battle of Eylau. In June 1807, Ermolov commanded horse artillery company in the actions at Guttstadt, Deppen, Heilsberg and Friedland, garnering the Order of St. George (3rd class, 7 September 1807). He was promoted to major general on 28 March 1808 and was appointed inspector of horse artillery companies. In early 1809, he inspected artillery companies of the Army of Danube. Although his division took part in the 1809 Campaign against Austria, Ermolov commanded the reserves in Volhynia and Podolsk *gubernia*s where he remained for the next two years. In 1811, he took command of the guard artillery company and in 1812, became the Chief of Staff of the 1st Western Army.

During the 1812 Campaign, Ermolov took part in the retreat to Smolensk and played an important role in the quarrel between Generals Barclay de Tolly and Bagration. He opposed Barclay's strategy and appealed to Emperor Alexander to replace him with Bagration. After the Russian armies united on 2 August, Ermolov fought at Smolensk and Lubino (Valutina Gora) for which he was promoted to lieutenant general on 12 November 1812 with seniority dating from 16 August 1812. He distinguished himself at Borodino, where he was lightly wounded leading a counterattack that recaptured the Great Redoubt. For his courage, Ermolov received the Order of St. Anna (1st class). During the rest of campaign, he served as a duty officer in the headquarters of the main Russian army and fought at Maloyaroslavets.

In October-November 1812, Ermolov served in the advance guard under Miloradovich and fought at Vyazma and Krasnyi. In late November, he commanded one of the detachments in the advance guard under General Rosen taking part in the combats on the Berezina. On 3 December 1812, he was recalled to the main headquarters where he became the Chief of Staff of the Russian army. Three weeks later, he was appointed commander of the artillery of the Russian armies.

In 1813, Ermolov fought at Lutzen, where he was accused of insubordination and transferred to command the 2nd Guard Division. He then fought at Bautzen, commanding the Russian rearguard during the retreat, and at Kulm where he was decorated with the Prussian Iron Cross. In 1814, he distinguished himself in the battle around Paris and was awarded the Order of St. George on 7 April 1814. Two years later, Ermolov was appointed as commander-in-chief of the Russian forces in Georgia and commander of the Independent Georgian Corps on 21 April 1816. He proved himself an able administrator and successfully negotiated with Persia in 1818, receiving promotion to general of infantry on 4 March 1818 (Ermolov was in retirement in 1827-1831 so his seniority was changed to 1 February 1822).

Ermolov served in Georgia for nine years but was dismissed on 9 April 1827 because of his argument with General Ivan Paskevich, who was patronized by Emperor Nicholas I; Ermolov was discharged on 7 December 1827 with a full pension. However, four years later, Emperor Nicholas restored him in the rank (6 November 1831) and appointed him to the State Council; Ermolov's rank of general of infantry was confirmed in 1833. During the Crimean War, Ermolov was elected the head of the Moscow *opolchenye* on 10 March 1855. He died on 23 April 1861 in Moscow and was buried at the Trinity Church in Orel. In addition to the already mentioned decorations, Ermolov was also decorated with the Russian Orders of St. Andrew the First Called, of St. Vladimir (1st class), of Alexander of Neva, of the White Eagle, and of St. Anna (1st class); foreign orders received included the Prussian Orders of Red Eagle (1st class) and the Pour le Merite, the Austrian Order of Maria Theresa (3rd class), the Baden Order of Karl Friedrich, the Persian Order of the Lion and the Sun, and two golden swords for courage (including one with diamonds).

Ermolov was one of the best artillery officers in the Russian army. He proved his abilities throughout the Napoleonic Wars and later in the Caucasus. However, he was also shrewd and cunning courtier, who often intrigued against his superiors. Because of his enigmatic character, Ermolov was often described as the "Modern Sphinx." He proved himself a ruthless ruler in the Caucasus and distinguished himself brutally suppressing Chechen uprisings. Ermolov left very interesting and valuable memoirs on his service in 1796-1816. His "Zapiski" are divided into three parts covering his early career, the Napoleonic wars and his service in the Caucasus.

ERSHOV, Ivan Zakharovich (b. 7 January 1778, Moscow — d. 30 January 1852, Aleshna, Orlov *gubernia*) was born to a noble family from the Orlov *gubernia*. Orphaned at an early age, he was brought up by his uncle and studied at a private boarding school in Moscow. He enlisted as a corporal in the Life Guard Horse Regiment in 1786 and transferred as a cornet to the Sumsk Hussar Regiment (then known as the Shevich's Hussar Regiment) on 2 February 1797. He transferred to the Chorba's Hussar Regiment on 3 September 1798 and returned to the Sumsk Hussar Regiment on 3 October 1798. In 1799, he served under Lieutenant General Rimsky-Korsakov in Switzerland and fought at Zurich.

Returning to Russia, Ershov transferred to the Chevalier Guard Regiment on 5 April 1801 and was promoted to lieutenant on 29 September 1802, to staff rotmistr on 30 June 1803 and to rotmistr on 10 April 1806. During the 1807 Campaign, he served as a squadron commander in the Chevalier Guard Regiment and distinguished himself at Guttstadt, on the Passarge River, at Heilsberg and Friedland. He was promoted to colonel on 6 July 1809. During the Russian Campaign of 1812, he commanded a reserve squadron of the Chevalier Guard Regiment in the Combined Cuirassier Regiment in Wittgenstein's Corps. He took part in the both battles at Polotsk (received the Order of St. George, 4th class, and the Order of St. Anna, 2nd class) and in the actions at Svolnya, Chashniki, Smolnya (received the diamond signs of the Order of St. Anna, 2nd class, 13 April 1813, confirmed in 1821), Batura, Borisov and Studenka (earned the Order of St. Vladimir, 3rd class, for last three battles, 23 July 1813).

In 1813-1814, Ershov participated in the actions at Lutzen, Bautzen, Kulm (garnered the Prussian Iron Cross and the Pour le Merite), Magdeburg and Hamburg. For his actions, he was promoted to major general on 27 September with seniority dating from 29 August 1813. He became assistant to commander of the 4th Dragoon Division on 10 September 1814, commander of the 2nd Brigade of the 4th Dragoon Division on 6 January 1816, commander of the 2nd Brigade of the 2nd Cuirassier Division on 2 September 1821 and commander of the 2nd Cuirassier Division on 10 April 1825. He was promoted to lieutenant general on 3 September 1826. Ershov was relieved of command on 31 December 1827 and discharged from the army on 28 December 1833.

ERTEL, Fedor (Friedrich) Fedorovich (b. 23 January 1767, Labau — d. 20 April 1825, Moghilev) was born to a Prussian noble family. He studied at the Smolensk Cadet Corps and began service as a junker in the Tsastrov's Infantry Regiment in 1778. Six years later, he was promoted to ensign and appointed to the Gatchina Troops, where he served as an ensign in the 1st Marine Battalion (11 April 1785). He became a sub-lieutenant on 12 May 1786 and lieutenant on 12 January 1788. Ertel participated in the Russo-Swedish War in 1788-1790, commanding a gunboat, and distinguished himself in the naval actions near Friedrichsham and Rochensalmi in August 1789. On 1 September, he commanded a landing force on the southern shores of Finland and captured two Swedish batteries. For his actions, he was promoted to second major. However, in a naval combat on 3 September, Ertel was seriously wounded in the the head and lost his right eye. Before retiring on 14 October 1789, he was awarded 400 rubles in pension and promoted to premier major.

Ertel returned to service in 1791 after a fire destroyed his estate, and served as the head of the Yamburg *uezd* court. In 1793, he was instructed to form a grenadier battalion and was appointed major in the 1st Marine Battalion. Three years later, Ertel had to retire again because of poor health (10 February) and served as a prosecutor in Vyborg. He returned to military service eight months later when he was appointed as a major in the Life Guard Grenadier Regiment (23 November 1796) to train and maintain this unit. The regiment was soon reviewed by Emperor Paul, who awarded Ertel with the Order of St. Anna (3rd class) for successful training. Ertel then briefly served in the Siberia Inspection and rose to lieutenant colonel in March 1797 and to colonel in 1798. On 16 March 1798, he was instructed to form a battalion of the Life Guard Preobrazhensk Regiment, for which he later received the Order of St. Anna (2nd class) and an estate in Podolsk *gubernia*.

Ertel was promoted to major general on 21 December 1798 and served as the head of the Moscow Police until 1800. On 29 January 1802, he was appointed chef of the Butyrsk Musketeer Regiment. Eight month later, on 19 September 1802, he became the head of the St. Petersburg Police and remained at this position for the next six years. During this period, he garnered the Orders of St. Anna (1st class), St. Vladimir (3rd class), a diamond ring and an allowance of 6,000 rubles. He became the Commandant of St. Petersburg on 25 February 1807 and transferred from this position to the Imperial Retinue on 10 April 1808.

Two years later, Ertel was appointed quartermaster general to the Army of Danube. He participated in the actions at Silistra and Ruse, for which he was awarded the Order of St. Vladimir (2nd class) and promoted to lieutenant general on 1 March 1811. In April-May 1811, Ertel was instructed to investigate the peasant uprisings in the Western *gubernia*s and was awarded 25,000 rubles for accomplishing this mission. On 24 October 1811, he became the head of the recruit depots of the 2nd Defense Line, and, on 4 December, he was appointed commander of the 2nd Reserve Corps.

During the 1812 Campaign, Ertel remained with his troops around Mozyr but was instrumental in securing communications between the Russian armies and pacifying local uprisings. In late September, his troops were attached to the Army of Danube and Ertel made several raids against the French at Glusk, Pinsk and Gorbachevichy. For this actions, he was awarded the Order of St. George (3rd class). In

October, Admiral Paul Chichagov replaced Ertel with General Tuchkov II and court-martialed him for disobeying his orders to move his corps to join the Army of Danube. However, Emperor Alexander intervened in the hearing and appointed Ertel the Military Prosecutor (general policemeister) of the Russian armies in January 1813. Ertel served at this position for the next two years and participated in the campaigns of 1814-1815. He took a furlough in late 1815 because of poor health and travelled to various resorts to recuperate in 1816-1818.

He served as the General Policemeister of the 1st Army in 1818-1821. Ertel was discharged on 2 November 1821 but two years later he was restored to the position of the General Policemeister of the 1st Army, appointed to the Imperial Retinue and promoted to general of infantry on 24 December 1823. The following year, Ertel was dispatched on a mission to Kiev, where he got ill with fever and died on 20 April 1825 at Moghilev.

ESHIN, Vasily Vasilievich (b. 1771 — d. 10 June 1825) was born to a petty noble family and began his career in the civil service. Hearing about the start of Russo-Turkish War, he volunteered to fight the Turks and was appointed as a corporal in the Ekaterinoslavl Cuirassier Regiment in 1787. He participated in the assault on Ochakov in December 1788, rose to vakhmistr in the Voronezh Hussar Regiment in 1789 and fought at Ismail and Macin in 1790-1791. Eshin served in Poland in 1792-1794 and distinguished himself at Maciejowice (where he was wounded in the leg) and Praga. He transferred to the Alexandria Hussar Regiment in 1797 and rose to lieutenant in 1798, to staff rotmistr in 1800 and to rotmistr in 1803. In 1805, Eshin volunteered to fight the French and distinguished himself at Austerlitz. For his actions, he transferred as a rotmistr to the Life Guard Hussar Regiment in early 1806.

In June 1807, Eshin participated in the battles at Guttstadt, Heilsberg (received the Order of St. Vladimir, 4th class) and Friedland (earned a golden sword and Prussian Pour le Merite). He transferred as a lieutenant colonel to the Tatar Uhlan Regiment in 1808 and participated in the campaign against Austria in 1809. He was promoted to colonel on 22 August 1811 and was appointed commander of the Tatar Uhlan Regiment on 10 June 1812. During the Russian campaign of 1812, he served in the 17th Brigade of the 5th Cavalry Division in the 3rd Reserve Army of Observation and fought at Brest-Litovsk, Kobryn, Gorodechnya (received the Order of St. Vladimir, 3rd class) and Kaidanov (received the Order of St. Anna, 2nd class). In March-May 1813, Eshin served in Winzegorode's detachment and fought at Kalisch, Lutzen and Bautzen earning the diamond signs of the Order of St. Anna (2nd class) and the Prussian Red Eagle (2nd class).

In July 1813, Eshin's unit was attached to Osterman-Tolstoy's detachment and he took part in the battle at Kulm as well as rearguard actions at Hellendorf and Peterswalde among others. He was promoted to major general on 27 September 1813. In late 1813, Eshin took part in the Battle of Leipzig and in the sieges of Torgau and Magdeburg. In August 1814, he transferred to the 2nd Uhlan Division and, in 1815, commanded the 1st Brigade of this division during the march to France. In September 1815, he became commander of the 2nd Brigade of the same division. After returning to Russia, he was appointed commander of the 1st Brigade of the 1st Horse Jager Division on 26 April 1818 and commander of the 2nd Brigade of the 2nd Cuirassier Division on 26 February 1820. He was relieved of command on 2 September 1821, but became commander of the 2nd Uhlan Regiment on 11 September 1821. Eshin died on 10 June 1825.

ESSEN (Essen I), Ivan Nikolayevich (Magnus Gustav) (b. 30 September 1758, Peddes — d. 20 July 1813, Baldone) was born to a noble family in the Estland *gubernia*. He enlisted as a private in the Life Guard Izmailovsk Regiment on 20 February 1772 and transferred as a lieutenant to the Nasheburg Infantry Regiment on 12 January 1775. He served in Poland in 1783-1785, was seriously wounded at Byala and retired because of wounds with the rank of premier major on 25 June 1786. After recuperating, he was appointed to the Narva Infantry Regiment in early 1788 and was soon transferred to the 3rd Battalion of the Estland Jager Corps. Essen took part in the Russo-Swedish War in 1788-1790 and fought at Abber-Fors, Wolkolabi and Tranzund. In 1792-1794, he served in Poland and fought at Selvi, Vilna, Kobylka (promoted to colonel, awarded the Order of St. George, 4th class, 26 September 1794) and Maciejowice. He transferred to the St. Petersburg Grenadier Regiment on 26 September 1794 and commanded this regiment from 1796-1797. He became a major general and chef of the Chernigov Musketeer Regiment on 12 October 1797. In 1799, he participated in the expedition to Holland, where Essen assumed command of the Russian corps after the French captured General Hermann and launched an offensive seizing Alkmar and Bergen. For his actions, he was promoted to lieutenant general on 19 September 1799 and awarded the Order of St. Anna (1st class).

Returning to Russia, he was discharged on 10 November 1799 after the intervention of the Russian ambassador to London, Semen Vorontsov, who was concerned about Essen's crticism of the British actions in Holland. However, Essen was soon restored in his rank and returned to his regiment on 14 November 1800. He became the Military Governor of Smolensk and infantry inspector of the Smolensk Inspection on 5 July 1802. He was appointed the Military Governor of Kamenets-Podolsk and infantry inspector of the Dnestr Inspection on 23 October 1803. During the 1805 Campaign, he commanded a corps but did not participate in any actions. In 1806, he was sent to the Army of Moldavia and participated in the Russo-Turkish War, capturing Khotin (received the Order of St. Vladimir, 2nd class). He was then directed to reinforce the Russian army in Poland, where Essen fought the French at Ostrolenka.

In April 1807, Essen became seriously ill and was appointed duty officer to the main headquarters of the Russian army. He was severely bruised by a cannonball at Friedland and left the army to recuperate. In 1809, he took command of a reserve corps in the Army of Moldavia. He became the Military Governor of Riga and the Governor General of Lifland on 14 June 1812. During the Russian Campaign of 1812, he organized the defense of the Lifland *gubernia*. Concerned by the French success at Eckau and possible siege of Riga, he ordered the demolition of three suburbs (Moscow, St. Petersburg and Zadvin) of Riga to improve the defense of the city; however, these drastic measures antagonized the city inhabitants. Essen was criticised for his actions and eventually replaced by Lieutenant General Paulucci in late 1812. After taking a furlough on 24 January 1813, Essen retired to his estate and drowned (allegedly committed suicide) while recuperating at the water resort in Baldona on 20 July 1813.

ESSEN (Essen III), Peter Kirillovich (b. 22 August 1772 — d. 5 October 1844, St. Petersburg) was born to a prominent noble family in the Lifland *gubernia*; his father served in the Russian army during the Seven Years War. Essen was enlisted as a vakhmistr in the Life Guard Cuirassier Regiment on 24 May 1777 and transferred as a sub-ensign to the Grand Duke Constantine's Battalion in the Gatchina Troops on 12 March 1790. He was promoted to sub-lieutenant on 12 January 1791, to lieutenant on 2 April 1793, to captain on 26 September 1793 and to second major on 14 September 1795.

After Paul's accession to the throne, Essen enjoyed a series of rapid promotion, becoming lieutenant colonel of the Life Guard Izmailovsk Regiment on 20 November 1796 and colonel on 8 January 1797. He was appointed major general and chef of the Vyborg Musketeer Regiment on 25 February 1798. In late Spring 1798, Paul praised his regiment at the military parade at Moscow and awarded Essen Order of St. Anna (2nd class). In 1799, Essen served under Rimsky-Korsakov in Switzerland and fought at Walishof (received the Order of St. Anna, 1st class), Zurich and Dizenhof. Returning to Russia, he was promoted to lieutenant general on 7 February 1800 and appointed the Military Governor of Vyborg, chef of the Vyborg Garrison Regiment and infantry inspector of the Finland Inspection on 30 August 1800. Two years later, Essen was appointed chef of the Vyborg Musketeer Regiment (for second time) on 16 February 1802, and chef of the Schlüsseburg Musketeer Regiment on 17 March 1802.

During the 1805 Campaign, Essen served under Essen I and did not participate in any actions. In 1806, he took command of the 8th Division and participated in the campaign in Poland in 1807. He reinforced Prince Bagration at Eylau on 7 February and distinguished himself on the second day of the battle. For his actions, he was awarded the Order of St. George (3rd class, 20 April 1807) and the Prussian Red Eagle (1st class). In June 1807, he fought at Lomitten (received the Order of St. Vladimir, 2nd class), Guttstadt, Heilsberg and Friedland. Essen was appointed to the Army of Moldavia in 1808 and, in 1809-1811, he took part in the actions at Frasin (earned a golden sword with diamonds), Braila (garnered the Order of St. Alexander of Neva), Ruse (received the diamond signs of the Order of St. Alexander of Neva) and Slobodzea (received the Order of St. Vladimir, 1st class).

During the 1812 Campaign, Essen commanded the 2nd Corps of the Army of Danube and took part in the actions at Brest, Drogochin, Byala, Ustilug, Gornostaevichi, Volkovysk and Brest. For his conduct, he was awarded a golden sword with diamonds. In late 1812, Essen was ordered to form 48 new battalions at Bobruisk and Chernigov and was awarded 15,000 rubles for accomplishing this mission in short time. In early 1813, he assumed command of the 4th Division in the Army of Reserve and remained in the Duchy of Warsaw in 1814. During the Hundred Days in 1815, he served in the sieges of Metz and Charlois and temporarily commanded Count Langeron's Corps on the return to Russia.

Essen became commander of the 27th Division on 29 December 1815 and of the 4th Division on 21 April 1816. He was relieved of command on 9 December 1816 and then appointed commander of the Independent Orenburg Corps and the Military Governor of Orenburg on 31 January 1817. Essen rose to general of infantry on 13 January 1819 and received the Prussian Order of the Black Eagle in June 1829. He became the Military Governor of

St. Petersburg on 19 February 1830, a member of the State Council in March 1830 and greatly contributed to suppressing the cholera epidemic in 1831. For his service in St. Petersburg, Essen received a golden snuffbox with the portrait of Nicholas I (1831), a diamond ring with Nicholas' portrait (1832), the title of count of the Russian Empire (13 July 1833), the Orders of St. Andrew the First Called and of the White Eagle (24 April 1834) and the diamond signs of the Order of St. Andrew the First Called (28 April 1841). Essen was relieved of position on 14 December 1842, but remained a member of the State Council until his death on 5 October 1844. During his career, Essen was also awarded the Order of St. John of Jerusalem, two golden swords with diamonds and a medal "For XLV Years of Distinguished Service."

EYCHEN (Eychen I), Yakov (Jacob) Yakovlevich (b. 1770 – date of death unclear) was born to an ober-officer's family. He studied in the Mountain Engineer Corps (*gornii korpuss*) and was assigned to the Department of Geography of this Corps in 1790. He entered military service as a lieutenant on the General Staff in 1793. In 1794, he served under Général-en-chef Repnin in Riga and took part in operations in Poland. In 1796-1797, he participated in the demarcation of the Russian and Prussian state frontiers along the Narev and Bug Rivers.

In 1805, Eychen served in General Bennigsen's corps in Silesia. In 1806, he served with the 6th Division in Poland and fought at Naselsk and Pultusk. In the spring of 1807, he supervised construction of the military camp at Heilsberg and served at the headquarters of the Russian army. In 1810-1812, Eychen served on various missions in the Volhynia and Podolsk *gubernia*s. After the war, he was promoted to major general in 1819 and appointed the Commandant of the Petergof Palace in 1826, earning promotion to lieutenant general in 1831. He was removed from this position in 1841 and discharged from service in 1843.

His brother **EYCHEN (Eychen II), Fedor Yakovlevich** (date of birth unclear — d. 25 February 1847) also studied in the Mountain Engineer Corps. He entered military service as a lieutenant in the General Staff on 27 December 1793 and took part in operations in Poland in 1794. In 1795-1798, Eychen II served on topographic missions in the Baltic provinces. In 1799, he participated in the campaign in Holland. Returning to Russia, he served as an adjutant to Grand Duke Constantine in 1801-1805. In 1806, he served under Lieutenant General Essen I and was dispatched to the main army, taking part in the battle at Eylau. In May-June 1807, he took part in the actions at Guttstadt, on the Passarge River, at Heilsberg and Friedland. In 1808-1811, Eychen served on topographic missions along the southern coastline of the Gulf of Finland. He participated in the 1812-1813 Campaigns in Russia and Germany and retired in 1814. Eychen returned to service as a colonel in the quartemaster service in 1822 and was promoted to major general in 1826. In 1839, he rose to lieutenant general and served in the General Audit.

EYLER, Alexander Khristoforovich (b. 28 February 1773 — d. 27 March 1849, St. Petersburg) was born to a prominent Lutheran family, the grandson of well known scientiest Leonard Eyler. After studying in Weidemeir's private boarding school in St. Petersburg, Eyler enlisted as a sergeant in the Bombardier Regiment on 16 June 1790 and participated in the Russia-Swedish War, serving on the galley fleet in the Baltic Sea. He was promoted to ensign on 12

November 1790, transferred to the 2nd Horse Artillery Regiment on 18 December 1794, briefly served in the 1st Battalion of the Baltic Fleet (26 May 1796) and was appointed lieutenant in the Life Guard Artillery Battalion on 7 December 1796. Eyler was awarded the Order of St. John of Jerusalem in 1800.

Eyler participated in the 1805 Campaign and distinguished himself at Austerlitz (earned promotion to captain and the Order of St. Anna, 3rd class). He then took part in the campaign in Poland in 1807 and served at Heilsberg and Friedland (wounded in the right hand, received the Order of St. Vladimir, 4th class, and the rank of colonel, 12 August 1807). During the Russian Campaign of 1812, he commanded a company of the Life Guard Artillery Brigade and, at Borodino, he commanded the artillery reserve of the 1st Western Army (received the Order of St. Vladimir, 3rd class). For his actions at Krasnyi, Eyler was promoted to major general on 7 January 1813. During the campaign in Germany, Eyler participated in the battles at Lutzen, Bautzen, Dresden and Leipzig (received the Order of St. Anna, 2nd class, with diamonds). In 1814, he distinguished himself at La Rothière, Soissons and Paris.

After the war, Eyler was appointed artillery commander of the Grenadier Corps on 7 August 1814 and commander of the horse and field artillery companies in the Novgorod and Pskov *gubernia*s on 4 January 1815. In 1815, he was sent to the Bryansk Armory to work on new types of artillery and later assumed command of the artillery companies in Orel and Karachev. He became commander of the Novgorod Military Battalion, comprised of the artillery and engineer companies on 27 March 1819. Eyler received the Order of St. Vladimir (2nd class) in 1823, the Order of St. Anna (1st class) with diamonds on 28 July 1825 and the Order of the White Eagle on 4 May 1834. He was promoted to lieutenant general on 9 February 1826 and was appointed a member of the Council of War of the Ministry of War on 17 October 1826.

Eyler was appointed the deputy director of the Artillery Department of the Ministry of War on 14 April 1833. He became general of artillery and director of the Artillery Department of the Ministry of War on 18 December 1834. He received the Order of St. Alexander of Neva on 10 April 1836. Eyler was relieved of his position because of poor health on 18 December 1840 and died on 27 March 1849. During his service, Eyler also garnered a medal "For L Years of Distinguished Service."

EYLER (Eyler II) Pavel (Paul) Khristoforovich (b. 1787 — date of death unclear) was born to a noble family in the Lifland *gubernia*; the brother of Alexander Eyler. He graduated from the 1st Cadet Corps and began service as an ensign in the Ryazan Musketeer Regiment. He participated in the 1805 Campaign in Pomerania and the 1806-1807 Campaigns in Poland. In 1808, he took part in the Russo-Swedish War and served at Sveaborg. In 1809, he participated in Prince Bagration's daring march to the Aland Islands across the frozen Gulf of Bothnia. During the Russian Campaign of 1812, he took part in the battles at Borodino, Tarutino, Maloyaroslavets, Vyazma and Krasnyi. In 1813, Eyler fought at Kalisch, Lutzen, Kulm and Leipzig. In 1814, he distinguished himself at Bar sur Aube.

In 1815, Eyler returned with the Russian army during the Hundreds Days and attended the military parade at Vertus. He was appointed duty officer in the headquarters of the 4th Corps in early 1816 and took command of the Yeletsk Infantry Regiment on 11 May 1823. He retired because of poor health in 1827 but returned to military service three years later and was appointed lieutenant colonel in the Gendarmerie Corps. In September 1830, Eyler became staff officer in the 1st District (*okrug*) Gendarmerie Corps in the Courland *gubernia* and was later transferred to the 3rd District in the Volhynia *gubernia*. In 1831, he became the head of the Secret Chancellery in Zhitomir and served in the commission investigating the Polish uprising in the Volhynia and Podolsk *gubernia*s. He served as the Governor of Lifland *gubernia* from 1833-1834 and was promoted to major general in 1839 before dying on 23 November 1840. During his service, Eyler received the Orders of St. Anna (2nd and 3rd classes), of St. Vladimir (3rd and 4th classes), of St. George (4th class) and a medal for 25 years of service.

FALK, Karl Evstafievich commanded the Kargopol Dragoon Regiment between 28 April 1807 and 14 December 1810. He rose to colonel on 24 December 1807 and served as chef of the Yamburg Dragoon (later Uhlan) Regiment between 14 December 1810 and July 1815.

FEDOROV, Alexander Ilyich commanded the 4th Jager Regiment from 28 November 1809 to 16 October 1813. He was promoted to colonel on 30 March 1810 and was killed at Leipzig on 16 October 1813.

FENSHAW (Fensh), Andrey Semenovich (b. 1757 — date of death unknown; removed from rosters in March 1828) was born to an English noble family. He entered Russian service in 1784 and served as a sub-lieutenant in the 1st Battalion of Ekaterinoslavl Jager Corps.

In 1788, he transferred as a captain to the Yeletsk Infantry Regiment, served on Prince Nissau-Zigen's flotilla during the Russo-Turkish War and fought at Ochakov in 1788 (received the Order of St. George, 4th class, 25 July 1788, promoted to second major). He was transferred to the Baltic fleet in early 1789 and took part in the naval battles at Bjorkzund, Vyborg and Rochensalmi. For his actions, Fenshaw was promoted to lieutenant colonel in 1790.

Fenshaw served in Poland and Lithuania in 1792-1794 and was promoted to brigadier in October 1794. He participated in the Persian Campaign in 1796, distinguished himself at Derbent and earned promotion to major general on 9 July 1796. He became chef of the Moscow Musketeer Regiment on 21 January 1797. Fenshaw was promoted to lieutenant general on 23 March 1798 and to general of infantry on 25 February 1800. He was appointed infantry inspector of the Ukraine Inspection and the Military Governor of Kiev on 6 October 1800 and became the Military Governor of Feodosia in the Crimea on 10 April 1803. He retired because of poor health in 1800 and returned to service on 7 August 1812. Because of retirement, his rank seniority was changed to 6 August 1804. During the Russian Campaign of 1812, Fenshaw organized *opolchenyes* in the Kherson and Tavrida *gubernia*s and operated in Volhynia. He took part in the siege of Danzig in 1813, became a senator in 1815 and left military service in 1817.

His son, **Gregory Andreyevich Fenshaw** (b. 1789 — d. 1869) entered Russian service as a sub-lieutenant in the Quartermaster Section of the Imperial Retinue in 1807. He served in the Danubian Principalities in 1807-1808 and, after retirement from 1809-1810, he transferred to the Life Guard Semeyonovsk Regiment in 1811. He served with this regiment throughout the 1812-1814 Campaigns, garnering a golden sword and the Order of St. Vladimir (4th class) for Borodino and the Prussian Iron Cross and the Order of St. Anna (2nd class) with diamonds for Kulm.

FERZEN, Ivan Evstafievich (b. 1739 — d. 28 July 1800) was born to a prominent noble family from the Lifland *gubernia*. He began service as a sergeant in the artillery in 1760 and rose to sub-lieutenant in 1762. After transferring as a captain to the Elisavetgrad Pikinier Regiment in 1769, he took part in the

Russo-Turkish War in 1770-1774, fighting at Khotin, on the Prut River and at Silistra. For his conduct, he was quickly promoted to second major on 12 January 1770, to premier major on 18 July 1770 and to lieutenant colonel in 1771; he later received the Order of St. George (3rd class) in 1775. Ferzen became a brigadier in 1782 and rose to major general in 1784. He participated in the Russo-Swedish War from 1787-1790 and distinguished himself in the battle at Vyborg, for which he garnered a golden sword with diamonds and 5,000 rubles.

Promoted to lieutenant general in 1791, Ferzen commanded a corps in Lithuania and suppressed the Polish uprising in 1792, for which he was decorated with the Order of St. Alexander of Neva. Ferzen then participated in the 1794 Campaign in Poland, defeating Thaddeus Kosciusko at Maciejowice, taking part in the assault on Praga and capturing the Polish troops at Radochin. For his success, he was awarded the Order of St. George (2nd class) and large estates in the Lifland province; he was also conferred the title of count of the Russian Empire in 1795. After brief retirement in September 1797, Ferzen became the Director of the Cadet Corps on 4 January 1798 and received promotion to general of infantry on 15 January 1798 before retiring in December of the same year. He settled at Dubno where he died on 28 July 1800. There was also another Ferzen serving in the Russian army: **FERZEN, Ermolai Yegorovich** served as chef of the Kiev Grenadier Regiment from 14 December 1796 – 28 September 1797. He became a lieutenant general on 30 July 1797 and general of infantry on 9 April 1799. He served as chef of the Tobolsk Musketeer Regiment between 12 October 1798 and 25 January 1801.

FIGNER, Alexander Samoilovich (d. 1787 — d. 13 October 1813) was born to a court official's family and, after graduating from the 2nd Cadet Corps, he began service as a sub-lieutenant in the 6th Artillery Regiment in 1805. He participated in the expedition to Corfu and Naples in 1805-1806. Figner rose to lieutenant on 29 January 1807 and took command of the 3rd Light Artillery Company of the 13th Artillery Brigade on 28 March 1807. In 1808-1811, he served in the Danubian Principalities, distinguishing himself at Turtukai and Ruse, for which he garnered the Order of St. George (4th class). In 1812, he fought at Borodino and, in October 1812, he took command of a partisan detachment.

Fluent in French and Italian languages, he often disguised himself as an enemy officer and gathered intelligence on the French deployment. He even attempted to assassinate Napoleon in the Kremlin, but barely escaped after the Old Guard sentry suspected his intentions. Figner demonstrated fanatical hatred against the French and, on some occasions, brutally executed prisoners of war. Yet, his daring raids on the French supply and communication lines caused great distress to Napoleon, who called him 'A True Tartar.' Figner distinguished himself at Lyakhov on 9 November 1812, where his troops helped Denis Davydov to capture an entire French brigade. For his excellent service, Figner quickly advanced through the ranks, becoming captain, lieutenant colonel and colonel within couple of months in 1812. In 1813, he formed a special detachment from Italian and German deserters and harassed the French troops throughout Saxony. He was finally surrounded by the French near Dessau on 13 October 1813 and drowned while attempting to swim across the river.

FILIPSTALSKY (Philippsthal), Ernst Constantine (b. 8 August 1771, Philippstal — d. 25 December 1849, Meiningen) was born to a prominent Prussian family of princes, the son of Landgrave Wilhelm of Hesse-Philippsthal-Barchfeld. He began service in Hesse-Cassel army and entered Russian service with the rank of lieutenant colonel in the 6th Jager Regiment on 10 June 1808. He was appointed adjutant to Prince Prozorovsky and participated in the Russo-Turkish War from 1809-1811. He was wounded in the left leg at Braila in May 1809 and was seriously bruised to the chest during an assault on Ruse in 1810. He retired because of wounds in 1811 and, after recuperating, returned to military service in early 1812, when he was promoted to colonel and appointed ober-quartemaster in Platov's Corps on 23 June 1812.

Filipstalsky participated in Bagration's retreat from Volkovysk and fought at Mir and Saltanovka. He was severely wounded at Borodino when a cannonbal cut off his right leg. He spent the rest of campaign recovering and returned to the army in early 1813. He served at the main headquarters and took part in the battles at Lutzen, Bautzen and Reichenbach. For his conduct, he was promoted to major general on 27 July 1813 and became commander of a Cossack detachment in General Winzegorode's corps. In late 1813, he fought at Gross-Beeren, Dennewitz and Leipzig and, in 1814, Filipstalsky remained at the siege of Hamburg. After the war, he served as an assistant to the commander of the Light Guard Cavalry Division and was promoted to lieutenant general on 3 September 1826. Filipstalsky retired with the rank of general of cavalry on 21 September 1836 and returned to Hesse-Philippstal.

FILISOV, Pavel Andreyevich (b. 1769 — d. 12 February 1821) was born to a noble family in the Jaroslavl *gubernia*. He enlisted as private in the Life Guard Semeyonovsk Regiment on 12 January 1785 and transferred as a lieutenant to the Belozersk Infantry Regiment in 1789. He participated in the Russo-Swedish War in 1789-1790 and distinguished himself at Kaipias. He transferred as a captain to the Moscow Grenadier Regiment in 1790 and served in Poland from 1792-1794, where he was promoted to second major for his actions at Vilna. In 1799, he commanded a battalion of the Moscow Grenadier Regiment and served under Suvorov in Italy and Switzerland. Filisov distinguished himself at Trebbia (received the Order of St. Anna, 2nd class), Novi (received the Order of St. John of Jerusalem), St. Gothard and in the Muothatal Valley.

Returning to Russia, Filisov became commander of the Moscow Grenadier Regiment on 7 November 1800 and rose to colonel on 26 September 1803. In 1806, his regiment was attached to the 8th Division of General Essen III and, in 1807, he fought at Eylau (received the Order of St. George, 4th class). He became chef of the Polotsk Musketeer Regiment on 2 May 1807 and took part in operations around Danzig, where he was seriously wounded. After recuperating, Filisov returned to his regiment, now attached to the Russian army in Finland and participated in Barclay de Tolly's daring crossing of the Gulf of Bothnia in 1809. He was promoted to major general on 9 April 1809. In 1812, Filisov commanded the 2nd Brigade of the 11th Division of the 4th Corps in the 1st Western Army, fought at Ostrovno, Smolensk and was severely wounded at Kolodnya. He left the army to recuperate and did not participate in 1813-1814 Campaigns. In 1815-1821, he commanded the 10th Division.

FOCH, Alexander Borisovich (b. 13 May 1763, Oranienbaum — d. 15 April 1825, Oranienbaum) was born to a Dutch noble family from Holstein; his father, Bernhardt Foch, was chief gardener of Catherine II. He began service in the College on Foreign Affairs and enlisted as a sergeant in the Bombardier Regiment in August 1780. He became a lieutenant on 21 September 1787 and participated in the Russo-Swedish War in 1788-1790. He distinguished himself at Pardakoski, where he was wounded in the leg and received the Order of St. George (4th class, 7 December 1791). In 1794, Foch served in Poland and distinguished himself at Vilna, where he was wounded in the stomach. In 1795-1798, he organized horse artillery units and was promoted to major general before taking command of the Rochensalmi Artillery Garrison on 21 September 1799.

Foch was discharged from the army in February 1800 but returned to service in April 1801 and was appointed chef of the 2nd Artillery Battalion on 8 September 1801. He retired two years later and returned to the army on 22 January 1807, when he was appointed a duty officer to the Russian army in Poland. He took part in the battle of Eylau (received the Order of St. George, 3rd class, 20 April 1807) and was seriously wounded in the chest and right hand at Heilsberg (received the Order of St. Vladimir, 2nd class). After recuperaing, Foch was appointed a duty general to Minister of War Mikhail Barclay de Tolly on 1 May 1810. He became commander of the 18th Division on 24 September 1811 and the Chief of Staff of the Finland Corps on 21 April 1812. During the Russian Campaign, he took part in the actions at Eckau, Zemalen, Polotsk and Chashniky. He was promoted to lieutenant general on 15 January 1813 with seniority dating from 19 October 1812. Foch took a discharge because of poor health in early 1813 and settled in estate at Oranienbaum, where he died on 15 April 1825.

FOCH, Boris Borisovich (b. 1760 — date of death unknown) was born to a Dutch noble family from Holstein; the brother of Alexander Foch. He began service as a sergeant in the Bombardier Regiment on 19 June 1775 and became flügel adjutant (with the rank of ensign)

to Lieutenant General Müller in 1780. He was promoted to sub-lieutenant on 21 January 1785 and to captain in 1788. Foch participated in the Russo-Turkish War in 1788 and Russo-Swedish War in 1790. In 1792-1794, he served in Poland and transferred from artillery to infantry as a lieutenant colonel in the Estland Jager Corps. He was appointed commander of the 6th Jager Regiment on 28 May 1797, rose to colonel on 17 April 1798 and became chef of the 6th Jager Regiment on 28 January 1799 and major general on 3 May 1799.

Foch was discharged on 14 January 1800 and returned to service in March 1807. He was appointed chef of the 24th Jager Regiment on 21 April and commander of the Astrakhan Grenadier Regiment (attached to the 9th Division of Essen I's corps) on 2 May 1807. He retired with the rank of lieutenant general on 4 November 1807. He returned to service four years later with the rank of major general and was appointed chef of the St. Petersburg Grenadier Regiment on 10 March 1812. During the Russian Campaign, he led the 3rd Brigade of the 1st Grenadier Division of the 3rd Corps at Vitebsk, Smolensk, Borodino (received the Order of St. George, 3rd class) and the 24th Division at Tarutino and Maloyaroslavets. He retired because of poor health on 10 January 1813.

FÖRSTER (Foerster), Egor Khristianovich (b. 1756 — d. 16 November 1826, Bender) was born to a Prussian noble family. He served in the Prussian army before entering Russian service as a sub-lieutenant in the Life Guard Preobrazhensk Regiment in 1786. After retirement from 1787-1788, he was appointed Captain in the 1st Marine Battalion and participated in the Russo-Swedish War, earning a golden sword for his actions at Savonlinna. He was appointed second major to the Engineer Corps in May 1790 and served in the Crimea, where he supervised construction of fortresses. He was promoted to major and became the Commandant of Ovidiopol fortress in 1796. Promoted to lieutenant colonel in April 1797, Förster was discharged from the army in January 1799. He returned to service on 19 June 1801 and supervised depots in Odessa. He was promoted to colonel on 27 September 1802 with seniority dating from 21 February 1799.

After another retirement in 1799-1801, Förster headed the engineer troops at Odessa. He took part in the Russo-Turkish War in 1806-1812, briefly serving as the Commandant of Akkerman. He then captured Killia in March 1807. Serving in the corps of engineers, Förster was seriously wounded at Ismail in June 1807. After recuperating, he led a detachment during the expedition to Anapa in June 1809 and was promoted to major general on 21 October 1809. Förster became chief engineer of the 2nd Western Army on 31 March 1812. During the 1812 Campaign, he was instrumental in organizing Bagration's retreat and took part in the battles at Saltanovka, Smolensk, Borodino (received the Order of St. Anna, 1st class), Maloyaroslavets, Vyazma and Krasnyi (earned a golden sword).

In early 1813, Förster served at Thorn and Glogau before becoming chief engineer of the Army of Poland. He served at Hamburg in 1813-1814, garnering the Order of St. Vladimir (2nd class), the Swedish Order of the Sword and the French Legion of Honor. After the war, he inspected the fortresses of Akkerman, Ismail, Khotin and Bender in the Danube Valley before becoming the head of the Danube Engineer District on 17 November 1817. Two years later, he was appointed chief engineer of the 2nd Army and was promoted to lieutenant general on 2 October 1821. Förster died on 16 November 1826 and was buried at a local cemetery at Bender. Another **Förster, Ivan Ivanovich** rose to major general and served as chef of the Tambov Musketeer Regiment between 15 June 1797 and February 1803. Promoted to lieutenant general on 2 February 1799, he became chef of the Archangelsk Garrison Regiment on 5 February 1803, and led this unit until his death on 9 July 1807.

FULL, Karl Ludwig, *see* **Phull, Karl Ludwig**

GAGARIN, Gregory Ivanovich (b. 28 March 1782 — d. 24 February 1837) was born to a prominent Russian noble family. He studied in the Boarding School of the Moscow University, upon where he graduated with honors and a golden medal. He began service in the College of Foreign Affairs on 20 June 1797 and transferred to the Moscow Archive of Foreign Affairs on 12 October 1798. He was awarded the Order of St. John of Jerusalem on 31 October 1800 and appointed to the Russian embassy in Vienna in 25 May 1802. In May 1805, he transferred to the Russian embassy in Istanbul.

During the 1806-1807 Campaign, Gagarin served as adjutant to General Levin Bennigsen and took part in negotiations at Tilsit. In October 1807, he joined the Russian embassy in Paris, serving as a charge d'affairs in late 1808, and received a rank of actual kamerger in April 1809. In late 1809, he returned to the College of Foreign Affairs and then served in the Ministry of Finances in 1810. He became a state counsellor in January 1811 and the State Secretary of the State Council in October 1811. He took a discharge with a rank of actual state counsellor in 1816, but returned six years later to serve in the Russian mission in Rome. He took part in the Congress at Verona in 1822. Under Nicholas I, he became the Russian Envoy to Rome in 1827 and to Munich in 1832.

GAGARIN, Ivan Alekseyevich (b. 27 September 1771 — d. 24 October 1832) was born to a prominent Russian noble family. He was enlisted in the Life Guard Preobrazhensk Regiment at the age of two on 21 January 1773, transferred to the Life Guard Izmailovsk Regiment in 1776 at age fifteen and rose to ensign on 12 January 1790. During the Russo-Turkish War in 1788-1791, he distinguished himself at Ismail, for which he received the Order of St. George (4th class) on 5 April 1791. He rose to the rank of lieutenant on 12 January 1792, lieutenant captain on 12 January 1796, kamerger (5th class) on 12 February 1796, actual kamerger (4th class) on 14 January 1797, stalmeister to Grand Duches Helen Pavlona on 24 June 1799 and stalmeister to Grand Duchess Catherine Pavlovna on 24 October 1799. Eleven years later, he administered the court of Grand Duchess Catherine Pavlovna in Tver. In 1816, he became a stalmeister in the Imperial Court and, three years later, was appointed to the Senate with a rank of privy counsellor. He was murdered by one of his servants during an altercation on 6 August 1842.

GAGARIN, Pavel Gavrilovich (b. 19 January 1777— d. 14 January 1850) was born to a prominent Russian noble family. He was enlisted as a sergeant in the Life Guard Preobrazhensk Regiment at the age of three in 1780 and transferred as a vakhmistr on 3 May 1788. He became flügel adjutant to Général-en-Chef N. Repnin on 9 July 1793 and served in Lithuania and Poland in 1794. The following year, he attended the Polish King Stanisnilas Auguste and rose to the rank of second major on 29 December 1795. The following year, he joined the Moscow Grenadier Regiment on 16 May 1796. He participated in the 1799 Campaign in Italy, serving as an adjutant to Suvorov (26 July

1799). On 30 July 1799, he was promoted to a colonel of the Life Guard Preobrazhensk Regiment. After delivering news of the Russian victories in Italy to Emperor Paul, he was appointed flügel adjutant on 6 December 1799 and adjutant general on 7 December 1799. Gagarin's rapid promotions were facilitated by the fact that he was engaged to Princess Anna Lopukhina, one of Emperor Paul's favorites.

In 1801-1802, Gagarin served as a Russian envoy to Sardinia and, in 1808-1809, he accompanied Emperor Alexander to Erfurt and Finland. In May 1809, he delivered Alexander's letter to Napoleon concerning the Russian operations in Galicia. He took charge of the Inspection Department on 21 August 1812 but left on 25 December 1814. He spent the rest of his life secluded in his house in St. Petersburg and died on 14 January 1850. His literary legacy includes numerous lyrics and a memoir on travels to Finland, "*Les treize journées ou la Finlande*," published in Moscow in 1809.

GALATTE DI JEPOLA, Joseph Nikolaevich (b. 1760 — date of death unclear) descended from a Piedmontese noble family. He entered the Russian service with a rank of captain on 23 July 1799 and served with Suvorov in the closing stages of the 1799 Campaign in Italy and Switzerland. He participated in the 1805 Campaign in Moravia, for which he received promotion to a lieutenant colonel on 11 February 1806 and was appointed to the Quartermaster Section of the Imperial Retinue. Galatte served under Vice Admiral Senyavin in the Mediterranean Sea in 1806-1807, where he garnered the Order of St. George (4th class, 21 September 1807) for a heroism in the naval engagement of 1 July 1807.

Returning to Russia, Galatte was appointed a platz major in Sveaborg on 18 September 1810 and rose to colonel on 2 December 1810. In 1812, he served in the Finland Corps in operations along the Baltic coastline. In 1813-1814, he fought at Dennewitz (received the Order of St. Vladimir, 3rd class), Leipzig (received a golden sabre with diamonds and promotion to major general on 27 December 1813), St. Dizier (received the Order of St. Anna, 2nd class) and Paris. He took a discharge on 17 April 1816 and returned back to Piedmont, where he continued service in the Piedmontese army.

GAMEN, Aleksey Yurievich (b. 29 May 1773, Gzhatsk — d. 23 June 1829, St. Petersburg) was born to a noble family from the Smolensk *gubernia*; his father was a physician in Catherine II's court. He studied in the Infantry Cadet Corps, which he graduated with a rank of lieutenant on 12 June 1789. He participated in the Russo-Swedish War in 1789-1790, serving on the galley flotilla, and, on 24 November 1789, received a promotion to captain for his actions in a naval engagement near the Kumen River. In 1791, he joined the 2nd Admiralty Battalion in Finland, and two years later, transferred to Major

Brimmer's Battalion in the Black Sea Fleet. He became a second major on 17 May 1796 and major on 10 December 1796.

In 1799-1800, Gamen served on the Russian squadron in the Adriatic Sea, where he distinguished himself during the capture of the Island of Vido and actions at Corfu and in Naples (received the Order of St. Anna, 2nd class). Returning to Russia, he became a lieutenant colonel and commander of the 6th Marine *Ekipash* [flotskii ekipazh] on 3 March 1802, a colonel on 26 September 1803 and took command of the 3rd Marine Regiment on 2 January 1804. During the 1805 Campaign, he served under Count Tolstoy in Pomerania. He became chef of the 3rd Marine Regiment on 21 November 1807 and defended the Baltic coast against the Swedes and the British, earning the diamond sign of the Order of St. Anna (2nd class) on 21 January 1809 and the Order of St. Vladimir (4th class) in May 1811. He rose to a major general on 13 November 1811.

During the 1812 Campaign, Gamen served in Wittgenstein's corps. On 17-18 August 1812, he commanded the Russian center in the battle at Polotsk, receiving four light wounds and afterwards the Order of St. Anna (1st class). In second battle of Polotsk on 19 October, Gamen took a serious wound in the stomach and was decorated with the Order of St. George (3rd class) on 15 January 1813. Gamen spent the rest of the campaign recuperating and did not participate in the battles of 1813-1814. He took command of troops in St. Petersburg on 27 October 1813 and organized a guard and a regular infantry division. After the war, Gamen commanded a brigade of the 23rd Division (September 1814) and the 2nd Reserve Division (14 May 1815) before resigning on 22 April 1816. After travelling in Europe to recuperate, he became the Second Commandant of the Kronshtadt Fortress on 9 March 1820, rose to lieutenant general and the Commandant of the Kronshtadt Fortress in St. Petersburg on 13 January 1826. He died on 23 June 1829 in St. Petersburg, after forty years of service in the Russian army.

GAMPER, Yermolai Yermolayevich, *see* **Hamper, Yermolay Yermolayevich**

GANGEBLOV (Gangeblishvili), Semen Georgievich (b. 4 June 1757, Moscow — d. 1 March 1837) was born to a Georgian noble family that resettled to Russia in 1724. He enlisted as a corporal in the Black Hussar Regiment on 12 January 1771. After his unit was disbanded, he transferred as a cadet to the Moldavia Hussar (later Kherson Light Horse) Regiment in 1777. He became an ensign in 1778, a lieutenant in 1783, and transferred to the Orel Infantry Regiment in 1788. During the Russo-Turkish War in 1788-1791, Gangeblov distinguished himself at Ochakov in 1788, where he was wounded in the left leg and received a promotion to captain as well as a golden cross. In late 1789, he participated in the capture of Hadjibei (Odessa) and joined Rear Admiral Ushakov's squadron in the Black Sea in 1790. In 1792, he served in Poland and was promoted to second major on 12 January 1793.

During the Polish uprising in Warsaw in 1794, he was saved by a Polish family and later commanded a battalion of the Ekaterinoslavl Jager Corps. Gangeblov distinguished himself at Maciejowice, for which he was promoted to premier major on 10 October 1794. During the assault on Praga, he captured the Polish battery and the bridge to Warsaw, for which Suvorov personally promoted him to a lieutenant colonel on 9 July 1795; Gangeblov also garnered a golden cross for Praga. He transferred to the 1st Jager Battalion on 25 November 1795, became a colonel on 11 May 1798, commander of the 9th Jager Regiment on 18 May 1799 and a major general and chef of the 13th Jager Regiment (known as Gangeblov's Jager Regiment) on 9 October 1799. Although his unit fought in Italy and Switzerland in 1799, Gangeblov joined it in early 1800.

In 1803-1804, Gangeblov served in the Kuban Valley and the Crimea. During the Russo-Turkish War in 1806-1812, he served in the Caucasus, participating in operations at Anapa (received the Order of St. Vladimir, 3rd class), in the Kuban Valley (received the Order of St. Anna, 1st class) and Trapezund in 1810. He was discharged from the service for defeat at Trebizond on 8 December 1810 but returned to the army as a chef of the 12th Jager Regiment on 1 June 1811. In 1812, he served in the 3rd Brigade of the 13th Division in the Crimea. During the 1812 Campaign, he joined the Army of Danube and took part in actions on the Berezina. In 1813, Gangeblov served at Thorn, Koeniswartha and took a serious wound in the right side at Bautzen, for which he received the Order of St. George (4th class) on 1 November 1813. He left the army to recuperate and did not participate in the subsequent operations. After the war, he briefly commanded the 13th Division, but had to resign because of poor health. He took a discharge on 1 April 1818 and spent the rest of his life at the estate of Bogodarovka in the Ekaterinoslabvl *gubernia*. His son Alexander Gangeblov left interesting memoirs describing in details his father's career, published as "Vospominania A.S. Gangeblova" in the *Russkii Arkhiv* in 1886.

GANSKAU, Yakov Fedorovich (b. 1787 — d. 10 April 1841) was born to a noble family from the Liflan *gubernia*. He studied in the 1st Cadet Corps and began service as a ensign in the Nizov Infantry Regiment on 21 February 1805. He rose to the rank of sub-lieutenant on 12 August 1805 and transferred to the Vilna Infantry Regiment (later the 34th Jager Regiment) on 18 December 1805. He participated in the 1806-1807 Campaigns in Poland, fighting at Pultusk, Guttstadt and Friedland. He was promoted to a lieutenant on 21 November 1807 and staff captain on 4 January 1810. On 11 July 1811, he became adjutant to Lieutenant General Baggovut and rose to a captain on 1 May 1811.

During the 1812 Campaign, Ganskau fought at Smolensk, Gedeonovo, Borodino (received the Order of St. Vladimir, 4th class) and Tarutino (received the Order of St. Anna, 4th class). After Baggovut was killed at Tarutino, Ganskau became adjutant to Prince Dolgorukov II and participated in actions at Maloyaroslavets and Vyazma. In May 1813, he served as an adjutant to Eugene of Wuttemberg, fighting at Lutzen and Bautzen. On 28 July 1813, he transferred to the 4th Jager Regiment and was appointed senior adjutant in the 2nd Corps. In August-October 1813, he distinguished himself at Kulm (earned the Prussian Pour le Merite) and Leipzig, for which he transferred with the same rank to the Life Guard Jager Regiment.

In 1814, Ganskau served at Vassy, Nogent, Bar sur Aube, Troyes (received a golden sword), Le Fère Champenoise and Paris, for which he was decorated with the Order of St. Anna (2nd class) with diamonds. In 1815, he took part in the march to France during the Hundred Days. He became colonel in the Chernigov Infantry Regiment on 29 March 1817 and, after taking a discharge from the army, joined the civil service with a rank of actual state counsellor on 15 March 1823. In 1827-1841, he served in succession as governor of Arkhangelsk, Kursk and Kherson (9 May 1830). He died on 10 April 1841 and was buried in St. Petersburg.

GARNAULT (Harnault), Ivan Ivanovich (b. 1758 — date of death unknown; removed from rosters on 15 February 1822) was born to a French noble family settled in Russia in the early 18th century. He enlisted as a private in the Keksholm Infantry Regiment on 12 January 1768 and rose to a regimental adjutant in 1771. He served in Poland in 1772-1774, becoming lieutenant by the end of the campaign. He participated in the Russo-Swedish War in 1787-1790, earning a rank of second major for his actions. He took command of the Neva Musketeer Regiment on 30 September 1799 and received his colonelcy on 23 March 1800. He became chef of the Perm Musketeer Regiment on 17 March 1806.

During the 1806-1807 Campaigns in Poland, Garnault served with 5th Division at Eylau (received the Order of St. Anna, 2nd class), Guttstadt, Heilsberg (received the Order of St. Vladimir, 3rd class) and Friedland. He became a major general on 24 December 1807. During the Russo-Swedish War in 1808-1809, he served with the 5th Division in the Savolax region in northern Finland. In the battle of Revolaks in April 1808, his troops left their positions on the left flank leading to a Russian defeat. After investigating this incident, the military court court martialed Garnault and relieved him of command on 3 August 1808. He remained unemployed for three years and appealed to be restored in the army during the 1812 Campaign. Alexander allowed him to serve only as a staff officer. Garnault joined the army as it pursued the French in late 1812. The following year, he served at Thorn and distinguihsed himself on the Bobr Regiver on 19 August 1813. After the war, Garnault was pardoned because of the recommendations of Generals Barcla de Tolly and Langeron.

GARPE, Vasily Ivanovich, *see* **Harpe, Vasily Ivanovich**

GARTING, Martyn Nikolayevich, *see* **Harting, Martyn Nikolayevich**

GECKEL, Yegor Fedorovich (b. 1764— d. 6 February 1832) descended from a Saxon noble family. He began service in the Polish army but then entered the Russian service with a rank of captain in 1795. He worked in the Engineer Corps for three years but then he joined the Prussian army, where he served for six years. He returned to Russia in late 1804 and received his colonelcy on 19 August 1805. In 1805-1807, he served as an engineer with the Russian headquarters in Moravia and Poland. During the 1808-1809 war in Finland, Geckel directed siege works at Sveaborg and, after its capture, worked on reinforcements of the fortress.

In 1810-1811, Geckel directed construction of a new fortress at Dunaburg, which was not completed by 1812. He was promoted to a major general on 11 September 1811. During the 1812 Campaign, Geckel repulsed the initial French attack on Dunaburg and then served at Rezhitz, Polotsk before returning to Dunaburg to complete the fortress. In 1814, he joined the Quartermaster Section of the Imperial Retinue and marched with the Russian army to France during the Hundred Days in 1815. After the war, he became commandant of Odessa on 11 June 1819 and of Kamenetz-Podolsk on 18 July 1822. He rose to a lieutenant general on 3 September 1826.

GEDEONOV, Alexander Mikhailovich (b. 1791— d.) was born to a noble family from the Smolensk *gubernia*. He began service as a junker in the Moscow Archive of the Foreign Affairs and transferred as a column guide [*kolonovozhatii*] to the Quartermaster Section of the Imperial Retinue on 11 April 1805. Promoted to sub-lieutenant on 20 November 1808, he transferred to the Chevalier Guard Regiment on 20 January 1810 and was appointed adjutant to N. Depreradovich in April 1810. A lieutenant in September 1810, he transferred as a captain to the Yamburg Dragoon regiment in June 1811. In 1812, he served in Wittgenstein's Corps, fighting at Klyastitsy and Polotsk. Gedeonov joined the Kazan Dragoon Regiment in March 1813 and participated in the siege of Danzig, where he garnered the Orders of St. Anna (4th class), of St. Vladimir (4th class) and the Prussian Pour le Merite. In late 1813, he served as an adjutant to Alexander of Wuttemberg, negotiated the surrender of Danzig and delivered the news to Emperor Alexander in France.

In 1814, Gedeonov attended Alexander at the battles of Bar sur Aube, Le Fère Champenoise and Paris. He returned to his duties of adjutant to Alexander of Württemberg in August 1814 and took a discharge with a rank of major in March 1816. He entered the civil service in 1817 and, over the next fifty years, made considerable contributions to the development of the Russian theater. During his career, he was bestowed with numerous awards, including the Orders of St. Anna (1st and 2nd classes) with crow, of St. Vladimir (2nd and 3rd classes) and of the White Eagle; he was promoted to actual privy counsellor on 11 July 1846. Gedeonov died in April 1867 in Paris and was buried at the cemetery of Père Lachaise.

GEIDEN, Login Petrovich, *see* **Heiden, Login Petrovich**

GEISMAR, Fedor Klementievich *see* **Heismar, Fedor Klementievich**

GELFREICH, Bogdan Borisovich, *see* **Helfreich, Bogdan Borisovich**

GELFREICH, Yegor Ivanovich, *see* **Helfreich, Yegor Ivanovich**

GERMAN, Ivan Ivanovich, *see* **Hermann, Ivan Ivanovich**

GERMES, Bogdan Andreyevich, *see* **Hermes, Bogdan Andreyevich**

GERNGROSS, Rodion Fedorovich (Renatus Samuel Auguste) (b. 4 July 1775, Wittkop – d. 22 June 1860, St. Petersburg) was born to a Lifland noble family. He enlisted in the Life Guard Horse Regiment in 1777, began active service in 1787 and transferred to the regular army with a rank of a captain in 1794. He served in Poland in 1794, and five years later, was under General Rimsky-Korsakov in Switzerland. He took command of the Mittau Dragoon Regiment on 4 November 1807 and became a colonel on 24 December 1807. Gerngross served in the Caucasus in 1807 and in Finland from 1809-1811. In 1812, he commanded a detachment in the Finland Corps and fought at Riga, Chashniki and Smolyani, for which he was promoted to major general on 8 June 1813 with seniority dating from 31 October 1812. In 1813-1814, he commanded a flying detachment, earning the Order of St. George (3rd class) on 37 September 1813. After the war, he briefly commanded the 1st Dragoon Division before taking his discharge on 19 November 1816.

GERTSDORF, Karl Maksimovich, *see* **Herzdorf Karl Maksimovich**

GERUA (Gueroi), Alexander Klavdievich (b. 1784 — d. 24 February 1852) was born to a French noble family that settled in Russia in the middle of the 18th century; his father served as an architect under Catherine II. Gerua studied in the 2nd Cadet Corps and began service as a sub-lieutenant in the Pioneer Regiment on 8 November 1800. In 1803-1811, he served in the 2nd Pioneer Regiment, and, in 1812, he transferred as a captain to the 1st Pioneer Regiment. During the 1812 Campaign, he served with the 1st Corps at Jakubovo, Klyastitsy, Golovchyn (received the order of St. Vladimir, 4th class) and both battles of Polotsk. In 1813, Gerua took command of a company in the Sapper Regiment, fighting at Lutzen, Bautzen (received a rank of lieutenant colonel), and Leipzig for which he garnered the Order of St. Anna (2nd class). In 1814, he took part in actions at Nogent, Troyes and Paris, earning the Prussian Pour le Merite. Returning to France during the Hundred Days in 1815, he took command of the 3rd Pioneer Battalion (later 5th Pioneer Battalion) in 1816. He transferred to the Life Guard Sapper Battalion in April 1819 and was appointed adjutant to Grand Duke Nicholas on 21 August 1819. The following year, he took command of the Life Guard Sapper Battalion. For his dedicated service, Gerua received the Order of St. Vladimir (3rd class) in 1821 and became a flügel adjutant on 11 September 1825.

During the Decembrist Uprising in December 1825, Gerua defended the Winter Palace and was promoted to a major general on 13 January 1826 and, in March of the same, he became the Chief of Staff of the Moscow Detachment of the Guard Corps [*Moskovskii otriad gvardeiskogo korpusa*]. He rose to adjutant general on 3 September 1826 and served as chief of staff for the General Inspector of the Corps of Engineers in October 1826. During the Russo-Turkish War of 1828-1829, he served with the 2nd Army in the Danubian Principalities, garnering the Order of St. Anna (1st class). After the war, Gerua served on the Committee for the Wounded in 1833 and, three years later, he supervised the engineer schools. In December 1837, he became director of the Engineer Department of the Ministry of War. For his service, he earned the Orders of St. Vladimir (2nd class) in 1835, of the White Eagle in 1840, of St. Alexander of Neva in 1842 and the diamond signs of St. Alexander of Neva in 1846. On 30 September 1849, he became a member of the Council of War and died on 24 February 1852.

GESSE, Ivan Krestyanovich, *see* **Hesse, Ivan Krestyanovich**

GESSE, Karl Fedorovich, *see* **Hesse, Karl Fedorovich**

GESSE, Vladimir Antonovich, *see* **Hesse Vladimir Antonovich**

GEYDENREYKH, Ivan Grigorevich, *see* **Heidenreich, Ivan Grigorevich**

GICK (Gicka), Ivan Karlovich (b. 1765 — date of death unknown) was born to a Greek noble family. After studying in the Greek Gimnasium, he began service as a sub-lieutenant in the Kozlov Musketeer Regiment on 12 January 1781 and rose to a lieutenant on 5 December 1781 and to captain on 12 January 1786. Two years later, he transferred as a second major to the Ekaterinoslavl Grenadier Regiment. During the Russo-Turkish War in 1787-1791, he distinguished himself at Ochakov (wounded) and Killia, for which he was promoted to a premier major on 18 November 1791. In 1792-1794, he served in Poland, transfering as a lieutenant captain to the Life Guard Preobrazhensk Regiment on 9 June 1792. Gick became a captain on 12 January 1795, colonel on 26 November 1796, major general on 12 February 1798 and lieutenant general on 17 January 1800. He took command of the grenadier battalion of the Life Guard Preobrazhensk Regiment on 12 February 1798. On 28 April 1800, he became commandant of Smolensk and chef of the Smolenck Garrison Regiment. In June of the same year, Gick became the military governor of Smolensk and the infantry inspector for the Smolensk Inspectorate. He was removed from these positions on 5 July 1802 and took a discharge because of poor health on 1 January 1803.

GINTZEL, Yegor Karlovich (b. 1790 — date of death unclear) was born to a noble family from the Riga *gubernia*. He studied in the 2nd Cadet Corps and began service as a sub-lieutenant in the 7th Artillery Regiment in 1806. He participated in the Russo-Turkish War of 1806-1812, fighting at Braila, Silistra, Shumla and Ruse. He rose to a lieutenant on 9 March 1810 and transferred to the 14th Artillery Brigade on 18 June 1811. During the 1812 Campaign, he served with the 1st Corps at Klyastitsy (received a golden sword), at the two battles of Polotsk (received the Order of St. Vladimir, 4th class) and at Chashniki (promoted to staff captain). In 1813, Gintzel took part in actions at Magdeburg, Lutzen (received the Order of St. Anna, 2nd class, and the Prussian Pour le Merite), Kulm (promoted to captain) and Leipzig (received the diamond signs of Order of St. Anna, 2nd class), while the following year, he distinguished himself at Bar sur Aube (promoted to a lieutenant colonel) and Paris.

GIRSCH, Karl Krestyanovich (b. 1779 – d. 7 September 1812, Borodino) descended from a Saxon noble family. He studied in the Artillery and Engineer Cadet Corps and began service as a sub-lieutenant in Lieutenant General Eyler's Battalion in 1798. He participated in the 1799 Campaign in Switzerland and the 1805 Campaign. During the Russo-Turkish War of 1806-1812, he took command of the 22nd Light Artillery Company of the 12th Artillery Brigade and fought at Bender, Ismail, Braila, Bazardjik, Shumla and Nikopol. He rose to a lieutenant colonel on 21 February 1811. During the 1812 Campaign, he was mortally wounded at Borodino.

GIZHITSKY, Bartholomey Kaetanovich (b. 1775 — d. 7 May 1826) was born to a prominent Polish noble family. He studied in the boarding school in Warsaw, mastering several European languages. He took part in the Polish uprising in 1792, becoming a colonel. After the Polish defeat, he entered the Russian service, joining the Horse Grenadier [*konnogrenaderskii*] Regiment. He rose to the rank of colonel on 2 December 1797 and took command of the Pavlograd Hussar Regiment on 27 August 1798. He served in the Caucasus in 1797-1798, becoming a major general on 20 September 1798. In 1799, he briefly commanded a cavalry brigade but was disgraced by Paul I and discharged from the army in November 1799. He returned to service on 20 December 1800 and became chef of the Kharkov Dragoon Regiment on 30 November 1804. During the 1805 Campaign, he commanded a cavalry brigade in Uvarov's division and was wounded at Austerlitz, for which he was decorated with the order of St. Vladimir (3rd class).

In early 1806, Gizhitsky commanded a brigade consisting of the Kharkov Dragoons, Chernigov Dragoons and the Akhtyrsk Hussar Regiments. In January-February 1807, he commanded the advance guard of Essen I's corps, distinguishing himself at Shumov. In late 1807, he was dispatched to the Army of Moldavia, where he temporarily commanded the Kinburn Dragoon Regiment before taking a discharge on 1 March 1808. Living at his estate for next six years, Gizhitsky was elected leader of the Volhynia *gubernia* nobility on 30 January 1814 and returned to the military service on 11 September 1814. However, he was discharged from the army again in 1815 for supporting the Polish nobles in Volhynia. He became civil governor of the Volhynia *gubernia* on 26 March 1816 and turned against the Polish nobility. Gizhitsky was removed from the position for abusing his authority on 27 March 1825 and died on 7 May 1826.

GIZHITSKY, Ignatius Ivanovich (b. 1752 — date of death unclear) was born to a Polish noble family. He began service as a kamerger at the Polish royal court in 1770 and entered the Russian civil service in 1780. After serving two years in the Moghilev *gubernia* court, he transferred to the army as a lieutenant colonel in the Life Cuirassier Regiment in 1782; three years later, he joined the Riga Cuirassier Regiment and, in 1790, served with the Aleksandria Light Horse Regiment. Gizhitsky participated in the Russo-Turkish War in 1790-1791, where he distinguished himself at Killia (received a rank of colonel) and Macin, for which he garnered a golden sabre. In 1792-1794, he served in Poland, where he distinguished himself at Gorodische (received the Order of St. Vladimir, 4th class), Krupchitse, Brest (wounded in the right leg, received the Order of St. Vladimir, 3rd class), Kobylka (received the Order of St. George, 4th class) and Warsaw.

Gizhitsky rose to a brigadier on 3 October 1795 and to a major general on 27 July 1797. Gizhitsky became chef of the Aleksandria Hussar Regiment on 20 October 1797 but took a discharge on 6 November 1798. In 1812, he commanded the Zhitomir *opolchenye* and organized reinforcements in Ukraine. In 1812-1813, he took part in actions at Kovel, Lubomle and Zamostye. After briefly serving as a commandant of Zamostye, he became civil governor of Volhynia on 26 March 1816 with a rank of actual state counsellor. His one son, **Peter Ignatiyevich Gizhitsky** (b. 1791) studied in the 2nd Cadet corps and began service as a sub-lieutenant in the Life Guard Horse Artillery Regiment. In 1812, he took part in battles at Smolensk, Borodino (received the Order of St. Anna (3rd class), Tarutino, Maloyaroslavets (received the order of St. Vladimir, 4th class), Vyazma (promoted to a lieutenant), Krasnyi, Borisov and Vitebsk. In 1813-1814, he distinguished himself at Lutzen, Bautzen, Kulm and Paris. Another son, **Alexander Ignatievich Gizhitsky** (b. 1791) studied in the 2nd Cadet Corps and began service as an ensign in the 15th Artillery Brigade in 1811. During the 1812 Campaign, he served with the 3rd Reserve Army of Observation and took part in actions at Borisov, Kobryn and Gorodechna. In 1813-1814, he fought at Thorn, Bautzen, Leipzig, Brienne and La Rothière (received the Order of St. Anna, 2nd class).

GLADKOV, Ivan Vasilievich (b. 7 February 1766 — d. 19 August 1832) was born to a Russian noble family from the Penza *gubernia*. He enlisted as a furier (fourrier) in the Cadet Company of the Life Guard Izmailovsk Regiment on 12 January 1774 and rose to sergeant on 12 January 1780. Eight years later, he transferred as a captain to the Belozersk Infantry Regiment on 12 September 1788. During the Russo-Swedish War in 1788-1790, he commanded a detachment of horse jagers and Cossacks and earned a rank of second major. He transferred to the Ukraine Light Horse Regiment in 1791. In 1792-1794, he served in Poland, commanding cavalry detachments; in one of the skirmishes in 1792, he took a serious wound to the right hand that partially paralyzed his arm. He became a premier major on 13 June 1795 and served as an assistant to the Governor General of Byelorussia in 1795-1796, earning the Order of St. Vladimir (4th class) in July 1796. On 12 December 1796, Gladkov transferred to the Lindener's Hussar Regiment and received a rank of lieutenant colonel on 31 August 1798. He rose to a colonel of Life Guard Hussar Regiment on 25 September 1798.

In 1799-1800, Gladkov took part in the expedition to Holland, receiving the Order of St. Anna (2nd class) on 4 November 1799. Returning to Russia, he became chef of the Chuguev Cossack Regiment on 9 October 1800, a cavalry inspector of the Kharkov Inspectorate on 18 October 1800 and a major general on 17 November 1800.

During the 1805 Campaign, Gladkov commanded a cavalry brigade and distinguished himself at Austerlitz, where he was wounded in the right hand and garnered the Order of St. Vladimir (3rd class) on 8 March 1806. He served as the ober-policemeister of Moscow in 1807-1809 and was appointed head of the 2nd District of the Internal Garrisons (later Internal Guard) on 19 January 1811. During the 1812 Campaign, he supervised training of the new regiments in Tver and Rostov. In 1813, Gladkov commanded the 2nd Reserve Corps at Modlin, and the following year, he organized twenty guard companies in the Duchy of Warsaw. After the war, he again became head of the 2nd District of the Internal Guard and became ober-policemeister of St. Petersburg on 3 September 1821. He was promoted to a lieutenant general on 2 October 1821 and was relieved of command on 15 August 1825.

GLAZENAP, Gregory Ivanovich (date of birth unclear, ca. 1750/1751 — d. 22 March 1819, Omsk) was born to a noble family from the Lifland *gubernia*. He began service in the 3rd Grenadier Regiment on 25 July 1764 and rose to sub ensign on 29 September 1764 and to sergeant on 29 September 1765. He transferred as an ensign to the Simbirsk Musketeer regiment on 12 January 1770. During the Russo-Turkish War in 1769-1774, he fought at Rybaya Mogila, Larga, Kagul, Giurgiu, Bucharest and Silistra. He took promotion to sub-lieutenant on 12 January 1771 and, less than a month later, he became a lieutenant in the Staroskol Musketeer Regiment on 4 February 1771. Two years later, he transferred to the Life Guard Cuirassier Regiment, becoming a rotmistr on 5 October 1776 and a second major on 9 September 1784. During the Russo-Turkish War of 1787-1791, Glazenap commanded a cavalry detachment, fighting at Tsyganka, Sang, Ismail, Karnatokh-Krasne and other minor skirmishes, for which he was promoted to a lieutenant colonel in the Military Order [*Ordenskii*] Cuirassier Regiment on 20 October 1792. Three years later, he joined the Nezhinsk Carabinier Regiment on 26 March 1795 and received the Order of St. George (4th class) on 7 December 1795 for twenty five years of service.

On 1 April 1797, Glazenap transferred to the Yamburg Cuirassier Regiment and rose to a colonel on 26 July 1798, to a major general 29 October 1798 and chef of a dragoon regiment (Glazenap's Dragoon Regiment) on 20 January 1799. He took a discharge with a rank of lieutenant general on 16 March 1800 but returned to the service on 29 March 1801, becoming chef for the Nizhegorod Dragoon Regiment on 11 April 1801. On 25 November 1803, he was appointed cavalry inspector of the Caucasus Inspectorate, and the following year, he took command of the Russian troops in the North Caucasus on 10 April 1804. He pacified

Kabarda in 1804, for which he was decorated with the Order of St. Vladimir (2nd class) on 4 September 1804. In October 1804 – January 1805, he cleared the passes to secure communications with Georgia across the Caucasian mountains, and pacified the tribes along the Kuban Valley, for which he earned the Order of St. Anna (1st class) with diamonds on 13 March 1805.

After Commander-in-Chief General Paul Tsitsianov's murder at Baku in early 1806, Glazenap took command of the Russian troops. In June 1806, he captured Derbent and repulsed the Persian raids into Georgia. He was appointed inspector of the Siberia Inspectorate and commander of the Russian troops in Siberia on 16 February 1807. After the abolition of the inspections, Glazenap took command of the Independent Siberia Corps on 6 January 1816. He died three years later, on 22 March 1819 in Omsk.

GLAZENAP, Vladimir (Otto Waldemar) Grigorievich (b. 14 February 1784 — d. 28 December 1862) was son of Lieutenant General Gregory Glazenap. He studied in the 1st Cadet Corps and began service as a cornet in the Pavlograd Hussar Regiment. In 1805, he fought at Amstetten, Schöngrabern, Wischau and Austerlitz (received the Order of St. Anna, 3rd class). He transferred to the Grand Duke Constantine's Uhlan Regiment on 29 August 1806 and took part in battles at Guttstadt, Heilsberg and Friedland, for which he earned a golden sabre. Glazenap rose to a lieutenant on 19 December 1807 and to a staff rotmistr on 24 December 1810. In 1812, he served with 1st Corps at Polotsk (received the Order of St. Vladimir, 4th class), Belyi, Chashniki and Borisov and he was promoted to rotmistr on 12 November 1812. The following year, he fought at Lutzen, Bautzen, Dresden, Kulm (received the Order of St. Anna, 2nd class and the Prussian Iron Cross) and Leipzig.

During the 1814 Campaign, Glazenap distinguished himself at Brienne, Montmirail, Sompuis (received the diamond signs of the Order of St. Anna, 2nd class and the Bavarian Order of Maximilian Joseph), Le Fère Champenoise (wounded in the right side) and Paris. Promoted to colonel on 3 November 1816 and major general on 30 April 1826, he took command of the Life Guard Dragoon Regiment on 18 December 1826. He distinguished himself during the Russo-Turkish War of 1828-1829, fighting at Hadji-Hassan (received the Order of St. Vladimir, 3rd class), Varna (wounded) and Silistra. He took command of the 2nd Brigade of the 1st Guard Light Cavalry Division on 26 March 1829 and participated in the suppression of the Polish Uprising in 1830; he garnered the Order of St. Anna (1st class) for advance guard actions, the Order of St. Vladimir (2nd class) for the battle of Ostrolenka and the order of St. George (3rd class) for actions at Warsaw. He commanded the 1st Brigade of the 1st Guard Light Cavalry Division (1 February 1832), the 2nd Uhlan Division (September 1832), the 5th Light Cavalry Division (16 February 1836) and the 2nd Uhlan Division (August 1842). He rose to a lieutenant general on 18 December 1833. Glazenap died on 28 December 1862 in St. Petersburg.

GLAZOV, Pavel Mikhailovich (b. 1747 — d. 28 May 1814) was born to a Russian noble family. He began service as a reitar in the Life Guard Horse Regiment in May 1763, rose to kaptenarmus in 1768 and then to lieutenant in 1769. During the Russo-Turkish War of 1769-1774, he fought at Bucharest and Silistra, for which he received a rank of captain. He became a second major on 19 May 1777, commander of a squadron of the Life Guard Hussar Regiment on 10 February 1780 and a premier major on 19 June 1781. He attended Prince Gregory Potemkin in 1783-1788, communicating letters to and from Empress Catherine II, for which he received a promotion to a lieutenant colonel on 27 May 1784 and to a colonel on 25 July 1788 quickly followed by a transfer to the Ekaternislavl Cuirassier Regiment on 22 August 1788.

During the Russo-Turkish War of 1787-1791, Glazov distinguished himself at Ochakov, earning the Order of St. George (4th class) on 25 April 1789. After the war, he became charge d'affairs of ober-policemeister of

Moscow on 30 May 1790, then a brigadier and ober-policemeister of Moscow on 27 May 1793 and lastly ober-policemeister of St. Petersburg on 13 September 1793. Promoted to a major general on 9 July 1796, he was discharged from the army by Paul I in July 1797. Glazov died in retirement on 28 May 1814.

GLEBOV, Andrey Saviichevich (b. 1770, Berezna — d. 24 September 1854) was born to a Russian noble family from the Chernigov *gubernia*. He began service as a private in the 3rd Battalion of the Lifland Jager Corps in January 1791. He served in Poland in 1792-1794. He transferred to the 7th (later 6th Jager) Regiment on 30 July 1797. During the campaigns in in Italy and Switzerland in 1799, he distinguished himself at Brescia, Lecco (wounded in the left leg, received the Order of St. Anna, 4th class), Marengo, on the Tidone and Trebbia (wounded in the right leg, promoted to portupei-junker), Novi (wounded in the head, promoted to a sub-lieutenant on 25 August 1799), St. Gothard (wounded in the left hand) and Schwanden, where he was wounded in the head and captured by the French. Glebov remained in the French captivity for two years.

Returning to Russia, Glebov joined the 6th Jager Regiment, becoming a lieutenant on 8 August 1802, staff captain on 29 October 1804 and captain on 31 January 1805. In 1805, he served under Prince Bagration and participated in the rear guard actions at Lambach, Amstetten, Krems, Schöngrabern, Wischau as well as in the battle of Austerlitz, where he was wounded in the right side and later received the Order of St. George (4th class) on 24 April 1806. From 1806-1811, he served with the 6th Jager Regiment in the Danubian Principalities, fighting at Bucharest, Chediroghlu (wounded in the left hand), Giurgiu (received a golden sword), Obilesti (promoted to a major on 23 February 1808), Kladovo (wounded in the right leg and left hand), Bartokert (promoted to a lieutenant colonel on 11 October 1809) Rassevat, Dudu (wounded in the left leg), Vidrovitz (took command of the 6th Jager Regiment on 17 May 1810, promoted to a colonel on 24 July 1810), Praiova (received the Orders of St. Vladimir, 4th class and of St. Anna, 2nd class) and Bregov.

In 1812, Glebov served in the 3rd Brigade of the 12th Division of 7th Corps in the 2nd Western Army. He participated in Prince Bagration's retreat from Volkovisk and fought at Saltanovka (Moghilev), Smolensk, Shevardino and Boorodino, where he was wounded in the head. For his actions in the last two battles, he was promoted to a major general on 3 December 1812. After recuperating, Glebov took part in battles at Maloyaroslavets and Krasnyi, for which he earned the Order of St. Vladimir (3rd class). In 1813, he fought at Lutzen, Bautzen, Modlin, Dresden, Leipzig (received the Order of St. George, 3rd class) and Hamburg. The following year, he distinguished himself at Soissons, Craonne and Laon. He became chef of the 6th Jager Regiment on 12 May 1814 and, in 1814-1815, served as an assistant to the commander of the 6th Division. He took command of the 1st Brigade of the 12th Division on 20 March 1816 but took a discharge on 23 September 1816.

GLINKA, Fedor Nikolaevich (b. 19 June 1786, Sutoki, Smolensk *gubernia* — d. 23 February 1880) was born to a Russian noble family from the Smolensk *gubernia*; brother of Sergey Glinka. He studied in the 1st Cadet Corps and began service as an ensign in the Apsheron Infantry Regiment in 1802. During the 1805 Campaign, he served as an adjutant to Major General Miloradovich, participating in the rear guard actions during the retreat from Braunau and in the battle of Austerlitz. He took a discharge because of poor health on 23 September 1806 but, the next year, he briefly joined the Smolenck *opolchenye* in February 1807.

While in retirement, Glinka began writing his recollections of the 1805 Campaign, *"Pismarusskago ofitsera o Polshe, Avstriiskikh vladeniakh i Vengrii s podrobnim opisaniem pokhoda Rossian protiv frantsuzov v 1805 i 1806 godakh* [Letters of the Russian Officer on Poland, Austrian Territories and Hungary With Detailed Description of the Russian Campaign Against the French in 1805 and 1806]" published in Moscow in 1808. In 1812, he returned to the Apsheron Infantry Regiment and served as an adjutant to Miloradovich throughout the 1812-1814 Campaigns, earning the Orders of St. Vladimir (4th class) of St. Anna (2nd class), the Prussian Pour le Merite and a golden sword. He was appointed to the Life Guard Izmailovsk Regiment in 1816 and served in the Guard General Staff. Promoted to a colonel in 1819, he served as an adjutant to Miloradovich, then Military Governor General of St. Petersburg. He transferred from the guard to the regular army in 1822.

Glinka was implicated in the Decembrist Uprising and transferred to the civil service in 1826. In 1826-1852, he served in administrations of Petrozavodsk and Tver. Over the years, he wrote numerous poems and novels as well as historical works. His main publications include: five volumes of *"Pisma Russkago ofitsera* [Letters of the Russian Officer]" (Moscow, 1870), *"Podvigi grafa Mikhaila Andreyevicha Miloradovicha v Otechestvennuiu voinu 1812 goda, s prisovokupleniem nekotorikh pisem ot raznikh osob* [Exploits of Count Mikhail Andreyevich Miloradovich During the Patriotic War of 1812, Annexed With Some Additional Letters from Various Persons]" (Moscow, 1814), *"Cherti iz zhizni Tadeusha Kostiushki, plenennago rossiiskim generalom Ferzenom* [Features From the Life of Thaddeus Kosciusko, Captured by the Russian General Ferzen]" (St. Petersburg, 1815), *"Kratkoe obozrenie voennoi zhizni i podvigov grafa Miloradovicha* [Brief Description of the Military Career and Exploits of Count Miloradovich]" (St. Petersburg, 1818) and *"Lettres d'un officier russe sur quelques évenements militaires de l'année 1812"* (Moscow, 1821).

GLINKA, Sergey Nikolaevich (b. 16 July 1775, Sutoky – d. 17 April 1847, St. Petersburg) was born to a noble family from the Smolensk *gubernia*; brother of Fedor Glinka. He studied in the Infantry Cadet Corps in 1782-1795, graduating with a rank of lieutenant in January 1795. He briefly served as an adjutant to Prince Yuri Dolgorukov in Moscow and then transferred to a regiment in Lithuania. In 1799, he volunteered for service in Italy but the campaign ended before he reached Suvorov's army. Promoted to captain in late 1799, he soon retired with a rank of major in 1800. During retirement, Glinka proved himself prolific writer and completed several theatrical plays. During the 1806 Campaign, he enlisted in the militia, serving with a rank of brigade major in one of the companies. He continued working on theatrical productions and published numerous historical plays and articles.

After Emperor Alexander signed Peace of Tilsit, Glinka became very patriotic and anti-French, publishing a journal *Russkii Vestnik*, where he expressed his ideas. In July-August 1812, as Napoleon invaded Russia, Glinka became one of most active and influential public orators in Moscow calling for people to rise against the French. Emperor Alexander realised the potential benefit of Glinka's actions, awarding his the Order of St. Vladimir (4th class) and 300,000 rubles to continue shaping the public opinion. Throughout the 1812 Campaign, Glinka's *Russkii Vestnik* turned into an influential periodical that promoted official propaganda. However, with the end of the Napoleonic Wars, the popularity of this publication fell and Glinka found himself in poverty. He published six-part 'History of Russia' (1816) and became a member of the Moscow Censorship Committee in 1827. However, Glinka often refused to censor manuscripts and gave his consent to some publications directed against autocracy. He was removed from his position in December 1830.

Over the next five years, Glinka travelled to Moscow, Smolensk and St. Petersburg, publishing various articles and historical works, including '*Zapiski o Moskve I o zagranichnikh proisshestviakh ot iskhoda 1812 goda do polovini 1815 g.*' [Recollections on Moscow and Foreign Affairs from late 1812 to the Summer of 1815] (St. Petersburg, 1837). He died on 17 April 1847 in St. Petersburg. His recollections '*Zapiski*' were later published in 1895.

GLINKA, Vladimir Andreyevich (b. 15 December 1790 — d. 31 January 1862, St. Petersburg) was born to a Russian noble family in the Smolensk *gubernia*. He studied in the 1st Cadet Corps and began service as a sub-lieutenant in the Life Guard Artillery Battalion on 8 November 1806. In 1807, he participated in the battles of Guttstadt, Heilsberg and Friedland, for which he was decorated with the Order of St. Anna (3rd class) on 24 April 1808. In 1808-1809, he served in Finland, defending the southern coastline. He transferred as a staff captain to the horse company of the 10th Artillery Brigade in 1810 and served in the Danubian Principalities, fighting at Nikopol. In 1811, he rose to a captain in the reserve artillery brigade, which he commanded throughout the 1812-1814 Campaigns. Glinka became a lieutenant colonel in 1813 and took command of the horse artillery brigade of the 4th Dragoon Division in 1818.

Promoted to a colonel in 1820, Glinka took command of the artillery of the 4th Reserve Cavalry Corps and of the horse artillery brigade of the 1st Dragoon Division in 1824. Although he was involved in the secret societies in 1818-1824, Glinka did not participate in the Decembrist Uprising. During the Russo-Turkish War of 1828-1829, he commanded the reserve artillery of the 2nd Army in 1828, earning a golden sword and the order of St. Vladimir (3rd class). He became a major general on 18 December 1828 and took command of the artillery of the 4th Reserve Cavalry Corps. After the war, he commanded artillery of the Russian troops in Moldavia and was appointed to attend Emperor Nicholas in January 1831. One month later, he served as an assistant to General Diebitch against the Polish insurgents and, during the campaign in Poland, he briefly served in the capacity of artillery chief of staff and commander of the reserve artillery. He distinguished himself at Grochow, where he was wounded in the left arm and stomach and earned the Order of St. Anna (1st class).

In 1832, Glinka served on the committee reforming the field and horse artillery and, the next year, he became artillery chief of staff of the 1st Army. In 1836, he joined the Artillery Department and, in 1837, was appointed director of the factories in the Ural mountains. He was promoted to a lieutenant general on 30 April 1837 and to a general of artillery on 8 December 1852. He became a senator on 8 November 1856 and a member of the Council of War on 12 February 1857. He was discharged on 13 February 1860 and died on 31 January 1862. During his career, he was decorated with the Orders of St. George (4th class) in 1830, of St. Anna (1st class) with a crown in 1834, of the White Eagle in 1841, of St. Alexander of Neva in 1851, the diamond signs of St. Alexander of Neva in 1854 and the Order of St. Vladimir (1st class) with swords in 1856 for fifty years of service.

GLUKHOV, Vasily Alekseyevich (b. 1762 — date of death unclear) was born to a Russian noble family and studied in the Artillery and Engineer Cadet Corps, graduating as a shtyk junker in the Fusilier Regiment in 1781. He served in the Caucasus in 1784 and participated in the Russo-Turkish War in 1787-1791, distinguishing himself at Killia and Ismail (received the Order of St. George, 4th class). In 1792, he served in Poland. He took command of the 6th Artillery Brigade on 4 September 1806. During the 1806-1807 Campaigns in Poland, he fought at Pultusk (promoted to a colonel on 29 January 1807), Jankovo, Eylau and Heilsberg. During the 1812 Campaign, he distinguished himself at Tarutino on 18 October 1812.

GOGEL, Fedor Grigorevich (b. 12 March 1775, Saratov — d. 29 April 1827, Belaya Tserkov, Kiev *gubernia*) was born to a noble family in Saratov; brother of Ivan Gogel. He enlisted in the Life Guard Horse Regiment on 12 January 1785 and rose to captain on 12 January 1792. In 1794, he transferred to Arkharov's

Moscow Garrison Regiment and received a rank of a lieutenant in 1799. He became a colonel on 6 December 1800 and took command of the Moscow Garrison Regiment on 14 October 1800. Gogel was appointed commander of the 20th Jager Regiment on 13 February 1804, commander of the 5th Jager Regiment on 7 May 1804 and chef of the 5th Jager Regiment on 18 December 1804. In 1805, he served in Buxhöwden's corps and fought at Austerlitz on 2 December 1805. In 1806-1807, his unit was attached to the 7th Division and fought at Liebstadt, Mohrungen (received the Order of St. Anna, 2nd class), Wolfsdorf, Eylau, Guttstadt, Heilsberg and Friedland, for which he received the Order of St. George (4th class, 8 January 1808) and the Prussian Pour le Merite.

In 1812, Gogel commanded the 3rd Brigade of the 26th Division in the 7th Corps. He participated in actions at Saltanovka, Smolensk, Shevardino, Borodino, Vyazma and Krasnyi. For his actions at Shevardino, he was promoted to a major general on 3 December 1812 with seniority dating from 5 September 1812. In 1813-1814, Gogel served at Modlin and Hamburg, for which he garnered the Order of St. George (3rd class) on 9 February 1814. After the war, he commanded the 26th Division (21 April 1816), the 28th Division (3 August 1817) and the 25th Division. He became a lieutenant general on 24 December 1824. Another **GOGEL, Alexander Grigorevich** (b. 1787) graduated from the Page Corps in 1805 and began service as a lieutenant in the Life Guard Artillery Battalion. In 1807, he served at Guttstadt, Heilsberg and Friedland, earning the Order of St. Anna (3rd class). He rose to a staff captain on 12 february 1810 and commanded the 2nd Light Artillery Company in 1812. During the 1812 Campaign, he distinguished himself at Borodino, where he was wounded and received the Order of St. George (4th class).

GOGEL, Ivan Grigorevich (b. 22 November 1773 – d. 4 December 1834) was born to a noble family; brother of Fedor Gogel. He studied in the Infantry Cadet Corps and began service as a captain in the army in ealy 1793 and transferred to the 1st Fusilier Regiment in 1794. Two years later, he joined the Black Sea Fleet Bombardier Battalion and rose to a major in 1797. He became a lieutenant colonel in the Akhtiarsk Artillery Company in early 1798, quickly followed by a promotion to colonel in April of the same year. In 1801-1805, Gogel served in several regiments, starting with the 6th Artillery Regiment in February 1801, the 12th Artillery Battalion in August 1801, the 8th Artillery Regiment in July 1803 and the 1st Artillery Regiment in May 1805.

During the 1805 Campaign, Gogel served in Tolstoy's corps at Hannover. He was appointed the director of the Page Corps on 1 November 1806 and rose to a major general on 29 March 1808. In 1809, he attended the Prussian King during his visit to Russia and was decorated with the Prussian Red Eagle (1st class). Gogel became inspector of the Sestroretsk weapon factory in November 1810, a member of the Artillery Expedition in June 1811 and the Deputy Director of the Artillery Department in early 1812. In December 1812, he organized the Russo-German Legion for which he received the Order of St. Vladimir (2nd class) on 12 August 1813. During the 1813-1814 Campaigns, he served on the Committee on German Affairs. After the war, he headed the Inspection Department in 1815 and directed the Military Educational Committee in 1819. He was promoted to lieutenant general on 24 December 1824. He was removed from position of Deputy Director of the Artillery Department in April

1826 and of the Director of the Page Corps in April 1830. He rose to general of artillery on 4 May 1834.

During his career, Gogel was also actively involved in historical research. He published materials in the "*Artilleriiskii Zhurnal*" and "*Voennii Zhurnal*," translated numerous artillery manuals and treatises and wrote a few original works on the Russian artillery. His main studies include "*Nuzhneishie poznania inzheneru i artilleristu v pole, obrabotannie dlia poniatia i polzi drugikh ofitserov, dalnikh svedenii v matematike ne imeiushikh* [Important Information For Engineer and Artillerist on the Battle Field, Written for Understanding and Use of Other Officers Less Familiar with Mathematics" (1803), "*Kratkoe nastavlenie o soldatskom ruzhie* [Brief Manual on Soldier's Musket]" (1809), "*Pravila maloi voini i upotreblenia legkikh voisk, obiasnennie primerami iz frantsuzskoi voini maiorom Valentini* [Rules of Minor Tactics and Use of Light Troops, with Examples from the French Wars by Major Valentini] (1811) and "*Osnovania artillerii i pontonnoi nauki* [Basics of the Artillery and Pontoon Science]" (1812).

GOLENISCHEV-KUTUZOV, Mikhail Illarionovich, *see* **Kutuzov, Mikhail Illarionovich**

GOLENISCHEV-KUTUZOV, Pavel Vasilievich (b. 23 June 1772 — d. 13 November 1843, St. Petersburg) was born to an ancient Russian noble family from the Novgorod *gubernia*. He began service as a page at the Imperial Court and enlisted as a vakhmistr in the Life Guard Horse Regiment in 1782 and rose to a cornet in 1784. Under Emperor Paul, he became a flügel adjutant on 14 December 1796 and colonel on 28 April 1798. Two years later, on 4 January 1801, he transferred as a major general to the Life Guard Hussar Regiment and took command of the Chevalier Guard Regiment on 28 March 1801. He formed the Byelorussia Hussar Regiment in 1802-1803 and became chef of this unit on 28 May 1803.

Golenischev-Kutuzov participated in the Russo-Turkish War in 1806-1807, fighting at Bucharest, Turbat and Ismail for which he garnered the Order of St. George (3rd class) on 17 August 1807. Golenischev-Kutuzov took a discharge because of poor health on 21 December 1807 but returned to military service on 14 February 1809, when he was appointed to the Imperial retinue; he was restored to the rank of major general but the seniority was changed to 28 February 1802. In 1810-1811, he served as a ober-policemeister of St. Petersburg and became adjutant general on 11 September 1810. In 1812, he attended Emperor Alexander in the 1st Western Army and was wounded at Ostrovno. After recuperating, he formed the Yamsk Horse Regiment and commanded Winzegorode's mobile detachment, harrassing the French communication and supply lines. Golenischev-Kutuzov distinguished himself during the pursuit of the French in November 1812–January 1813, for which he received the Order of St. Vladimir (2nd class).

In 1813, Golenischev-Kutuzov participated in battles at Lutzen, Bautzen, Dresden, Kulm (promoted to a lieutenant general on 27 September 1813) and Leipzig, for which he received a golden sword with diamonds. He had the honor of delivering the news of the victory at Leipzig to the Empress Maria Feodorovna in St. Petersburg, for which he earned a diamond ring. For his actions in 1813, he also received the Austrian Order of Leopold, the Prussian Red Eagle, the Bavarian Order of Maximilian Joseph, and the Swedish Order of the Sword. During the 1814 Campaign, Golenischev-Kutuzov attended Emperor Alexander at Brienne, Arcis sur Aube,

Le Fère Champenoise and Paris. He delivered new of the Allied capture of Paris to the Empress Maria Feodorovna. After the war, Golenischev-Kutuzov served on the committee concerning the wounded and disabled soldiers and accompanied Emperor Alexander to the Congress of Vienna. In 1816-1817, he accompanied Grand Duke Nicholas travelling in Europe and received numerous awards, including honorary citizenship from Edinburg and Liverpool, a honorary doctoral degree from Oxford and the Order of St. Alexander of Neva.

Returning to Russia, Golenischev-Kutuzov commanded troops in St. Petersburg in 1821-1822 and became director of the Page and other cadet Corps, including Tsarskoe Selo Lyée, on 4 February 1823. After the Decembrist Uprising, he was appointed the Military Governor of St. Petersburg and served on the committee investigating the uprising. He became general of cavalry on 3 September 1826. Due to health problems, he resigned from the position of the Military Governor of St. Petersburg on 19 February 1830, became a member of the State Council in 1832 and chaired the Council of Military Educational Institutions in May-October 1836. For his dedicated service, Golenischev-Kutuzov received the diamond signs of the Order of St. Alexander of Neva in December 1828, the Order of St. Andrew the First Called on 17 April 1830, a title of count of the Russian Empire on 20 November 1832, and the Order of St. Vladimir (1st class) in April 1841. He died on 13 November 1843 in St. Petersburg and was buried in the village of Shubino of the Tver *gubernia*.

GOLITSYN, Alexander Borisovich (b. 10 October 1792, Moscow — d. 1 February 1865, St. Petersburg) was born to Prince Boris Andreyevich Golitsyn and Princess Anna Alexandrovna Gruzinskaya, aunt of Prince Peter Bagration. He enlisted as junker to the College for Foreign Affairs on 12 October 1803 and then transferred as portupei-junker to the Life Guard Jager Regiment on 18 December 1807. The following year, he again transferred, this time as an estandart-junker, to the Life Guard Horse Regiment (March 1808) and took promotion to cornet on 20 June.

During the 1812 Campaign, Golitsyn fought at Vitebsk, Smolensk and Borodino, serving as Kutuzov's courier for the rest of war. For his actions, he was awarded the Orders of St. Anna (2nd class) and of St. Vladimir (4th class). He was promoted to lieutenant on 3 March 1813 and fought at Lutzen, Bautzen, Dresden and Kulm, receiving diamond signs of Order of St. Anna (2nd class). In 1814, he took part in battles at Brienne, Le Fère Champenoise (awarded a golden sword for courage) and Paris. On 14 October 1814, Golitsyn was appointed adjutant to Grand Duke Constantine and put on fast track promotion to staff-rotmistr (28 November 1815), rotmistr (4 November 1816) and to colonel (16 October 1819). He retired on 16 October 1820, and was appointed Governor of Saratov on 29 November 1826. He served at this position for next four years before retiring for the final time. Golitsyn was elected as the leader of nobility of the Vladimir *gubernia* in 1839-1842, was promoted to actual state counsellor and awarded the Order of St. Anna (1st class). He died on 1 February 1865 in St. Petersburg. His recollections on the 1812 Campaign were published in *Voennii Zhurnal* (1859) and "*Otechestvennaya voina v zapiskakh sovremennikov*" by K. Voensky (St. Petersburg, 1911).

GOLITSYN, Alexander Sergeyevich (b. 3 December 1789, Zubrilovka, Saratov *gubernia* — d. 24 September 1858, Kalisch) was born to Général-en-Chef Prince Sergey Fedorovich Golitsyn (1749-1810) and Barbara Vasilievna Engelhardt, the niece of Potemkin. He was educated at Abbot Nichola's boarding school and enlisted in the guard at an early age. His actual service began as portupei-ensign at the Life Guard Semeyeonovsky Regiment on 5 October 1806 and was promoted to ensign on 16 February 1807. Golitsyn took part in the campaign in Poland and fought at Guttstadt, Heilsberg and Friedland, where he was wounded in the leg and received a golden sword for courage. He became a sub-lieutenant on 4 February 1808 and to lieutenant on 29 August 1810.

During the 1812-1813 Campaigns, Golitsyn served as an adjutant to Bennigsen and fought at Borodino (received the Order of St. Vladimir, 4th class), Tarutino (received the Order of St. Anna, 2nd class) and Dohna on 8 September 1813 (received diamond signs of Order of St. Anna, 2nd class). He was promoted to staff-captain on 5 October and to captain on 19 October 1813. He retired in January 1816, but returned to the army ten months later and was appointed a lieutenant colonel in Life Guard Uhlan Regiment on 21 August 1817. The same year, he transferred to the Grand Duke Constantine's Life Guard Uhlan Regiment. He was promoted to colonel on 22 March 1818 and retired on 25 February 1819. He returned to military service for the second time over twenty years later. In 1843-1844, he served as the military governor of the Lublyan *gubernia* and the Kalisch *okrug*. He was promoted to major general on 29 May 1845 and was discharged from service on 25 June 1858. He died on 24 September 1858 at Kalisch. During his service, Golitsyn was awarded the Orders of St. Vladimir (3rd class, 1842), St. Stanislaus (1st class, 1846), St. Anna (1st class, 1849) and St. George (4th class, 1854).

GOLITSYN, Andrey Borisovich (b. 1791, St. Petersburg — d. 23 April 1861) was son of Prince Boris Andreyevich Golitsyn. He enlisted as a junker in the College for Foreign Affairs on 1 October 1805. Two years later, he transferred as a portupei-junker to the Life Guard Jager Regiment on 18 December 1807, and then as an estandart-junker to the the Life Guard Horse Regiment in March 1808 and became a cornet on 18 June 1808. During the 1812 Campaign, he fought at Vitebsk, Smolensk and Borodino (received the Order of St. Anna, 4th class). Later, he served as an adjutant to Miloradovich and participated in actions at Chirikov, Gremyachev (received the Order of St. Vladimir, 4th class), Chernigov, Vyazma, Dorogobouzh and Krasnyi (received a golden sword for courage). Golitsyn was promoted to lieutenant in March 1813 and fought at Lutzen, Bautzen, Dresden and Kulm, where he was wounded in the leg and awarded the Order of St. Anna (2nd class).

In 1814, Golitsyn took part in the battles at Brienne, Le Fère Champenoise and Paris. After the war, he was promoted to staff-rotmistr on 28 January 1816, appointed flügel-adjutant (24 December 1817), promored to rotmistr (10 March 1819) and to colonel on 10 December 1819. Over the next seven years, he served at various civilian positions and was awarded the diamond signs of the Order of St. Anna (2nd class, 18 December 1826). He participated in the Russo-Turkish War in 1828 and was promoted to major general on 8 July of the same year. In 1829, he was appointed to the Caucasus Corps and commanded an infantry brigade consisting of the Kabarda and Sebastopol regiments. He was appointed as adjutant to the commander-in-chief in July and, in September, he was given command of a cavalry brigade. For his actions, Golitsyn was awarded the Order of St. Vladimir (3rd class) and a golden sword. In 1831, he was charged with false accusations and sent to the Kekholm Fortress, where he remained for a couple of months before being discharged on 16 December 1831. However, he continued to make allegations on various personalities and was exiled to his estate in the Vladimir *gubernia* and placed under police supervision. In 1841, he was given permission to leave his estate, but he was prohibitted to enter St. Petersburg and Moscow. He was finally pardonned in 1844, although ordered to live in Moscow only. He died on 23 April 1861 and was buried at Svyatogorsk.

GOLITSYN (Golitsyn I), Boris Andreevich (b. 26 May 1766, Simy, Vladimir *gubernia* — d. 11 April 1822) was born to the Vladimir branch of the prominent Russian noble family of Golitsyn's. He enlisted as a furier (fourrier) in the Life Guard Preobrazhensk Regiment in 1779 and rose to ensign in 1783. After serving in the Russo-Swedish War in 1790, he transferred as a colonel to the Sofia Carabinier Regiment in 1792.

Golitsyn served in Poland in 1794, earning the Order of St. George (4th class) for his actions at Praga. In 1794-1796, he served as hofmarshal in Grand Duke Constantine's court and rose to major general on 9 December 1796 and chef of the Sofia Cuirassier Regiment on 14 December 1796. Golitsyn became a lieutenant general on 29 March 1798 and transferred to the Life Guard Horse Regiment on 8 December 1798. He took a discharge on 17 January 1800 and spent the next twelve years in his estate in the Vladimir *gubernia*. In 1812-1813, he commanded the Vladimir *opolchenye* and participated in the siege of Danzig.

GOLITSYN (Golitsyn II), Boris Vladimirovich (b. 17 January 1769, Moscow — d. 18 January 1813, Vilna) was born to the Moscow branch of the Golitsyn family. He enlisted as a sergeant in the Life Guard Semeyonovsk regiment in 1781 but spent the next ten years studying at the University of Strasburg and Æcole Militaire in Paris. Returning to Russia, he took part in final phase of the Russo-Swedish War in 1790. He served in Poland in 1794 and rose to colonel in 1796. He became a major general and chef of the St. Petersburg Grenadier Regiment on 21 January 1798. Two years later, he was promoted to a lieutenant general on 12 January 1800, but was discharged from the army on 5 April 1800.

Golitsyn returned to the military service under Alexander I in 1801 and became chef of the Pavlovsk Grenadier Regiment on 1 June 1802 and infantry inspector of the Smolensk Inspectorate on 23 October 1803. He participated in the 1805 Campaign and was seriously wounded at Austerlitz. He took another discharge on 19 September 1806. In 1812, he returned to the military service and served at Smolensk, Gedeonovo and Borodino, where he was seriously wounded. After recuperating, he returned the the main headquarters of the Russian armies, participated in the French pursuit and died at Vilna on 18 January 1813.

GOLITSYN (Golitsyn V), Dmitry Vladimirovich (b. 9 November 1771, Yaropoltsy, Moscow *gubernia* — d. 8 April 1844, Paris) was born to the Moscow branch of the Golitsyn family; brother of Boris Vladimirovich Golitsyn. He enlisted in the Life Guard Preobrazhensk Regiment in 1774 and rose to sergeant in 1777. He studied in the University of

Strasburg and travelled extensively in Germany, Britain and France in 1786. In 1786-1789, he studied in the École Militaire in Paris. Simultaneously, Golitsyn was promoted to vakhmistr and transferred to the Life Guard Horse Regiment on 22 December 1785.

While he studied abroad for six years, Golitsyn was promoted to cornet (12 January 1786), sub-lieutenant (12 January 1788), lieutenant (12 January 1789) and second rotmistr (12 January 1791). In 1794, he became rotmistr and fought the Polish confederates, distinguishing himself in combat at Praga, for which he received the Order of St. George (4th class) on 12 January 1795. He was promoted to colonel on 12 May 1797, received the Order of St. Anna (4th class, 1797), rose to major general on 16 August 1798 and lieutenant general on 2 September 1800. He also was awarded the Order of St. John of Jerusalem in 1800 and served as chef of a cuirassier regiment that was named the Prince Golitsyn 5th Cuirassier Regiment (later renamed to the Military Order Cuirassier Regiment) between 3 May 1800 and 20 April 1809.

In 1805, Golitsyn served in Bennigsen's corps and did not participate in major operations. In 1806, he was given command of the 4th Division and participated in the campaign against the French in Poland. He fought at Golymin (received the Order of St. George, 3rd class, 2 February 1807) in December 1806. In January 1807, Golitsyn commanded the cavalry of the left wing and, at Eylau, he led a series of cavalry charges for which he garnered the Order of St. Vladimir (2nd class) and the Prussian Red Eagle on 30 May 1807. He then distinguished himself at Wolfsdorf (received a golden sword for courage), Heilsberg and Friedland (received the Prussian Order of Black Eagle, 7 July 1807). In late 1807, Golitsyn remained at Vilna and, in 1808, he was dispatched to Finland, where he commanded a corps at Vaasa. In 1809, he made preparations to cross the Gulf of Bothnia, but was replaced by Barclay de Tolly. Upset by this replacement, Golitsyn retired on 20 April 1809 and travelled in Germany before returning to Moscow.

In 1812, Golitsyn returned to the army and commanded the 1st and then the 2nd Cuirassier Divisions in the 2nd Western Army. He fought at the battles of Shevardino, Borodino, Tarutino, Maloyaroslavets, Vyazma, and Krasnyi (received the Order of Alexander of Neva). In 1813, he remained with his cuirassier divisions in reserve at Lutzen and Bautzen but fought at Dresden, Kulm (earne the Order of St. Vladimir, 1st class) and Leipzig (received the Austrian Order of Maria Theresa, 3rd class). In 1814, Golitsyn participated in the battles at Brienne, Malmaison, La Ferte, Arcis sur Aube, Le Fère Champenoise and Paris. He was promoted to general of cavalry on 14 April 1814. Four months later, he became commander of the 1st Reserve Cavalry Corps on 21 August. He was also given command of the 1st and 2nd Guard Divisions on 14 September 1814 and of the Guard Light Cavalry Division on 14 March 1815. On 24 July 1818, he became commander of the 2nd Infantry Corps, where he served for two years.

Golitsyn was appointed Military Governor of Moscow on 18 January 1820. He was instrumental in rebuilding Moscow devastated by the great fire of 1812. While serving in this position, Golitsyn became a member of the State Council on 12 November 1821 and was awarded the Order of St. Andrew (6 January 1826), the diamonds signs of the Order of St. Andrew the First Called (31 March 1830) and was allowed to wear a monogram of Emperor Nicholas I on his epaulettes (20 November 1831). He became chef of the Military Order Cuirassier Regiment on 2 November 1834. However, Golitsyn became seriously ill in late 1830 and travelled extensively in Europe for treatment. He resigned from his governorship on 20 January 1841 but remained a member of the State Council. He died on 8 April 1844 in Paris, where he had gone to recuperate from his illness. His body was transported to Moscow where he was buried with great honors on 31 May. Golitsyn's literary legacy includes "*Manuel du volontaire en campagne*" (1794) and "*Opyt nastevlenii, kasaushikhsia do ekzertsitsii i manevrov kavaleriiskogo polka* [Manual Concerning the Tactics and Maneuvers of Cavalry Regiment" (1804).

GOLITSYN, Mikhail Mikhailovich (b. 16 February 1793 — d. 1 June 1856) was born to a prominent Russian noble family. He was educated at Abbot Nichola's boarding school before entering engineering school in Vienna and the École Polytechnique in Paris. He returned to Russia in 1811 and served as a column guide (*kolonovozhatii*) under N.N. Muravyev. He was promoted to ensign on 8 February 1812 and served in the 4th Corps. During the 1812 Campaign, he fought at Ostrovno, Smolensk and Borodino, where he was seriously wounded. For his actions, he was awarded the Order of St. Anna (4th class) and of St. Vladimir (4th class). Golitsyn was able to rejoin the army (8th Corps) in early 1813 and fought at Lebau, Puzkau, Wartemburg and Leipzig (promoted to sub-lieutenant). He then took part in the capture of Koblentz, Mainz and Rheims. For his actions in 1813, he received the Prussian "Pour le Merite" and a golden sword for courage. Golitsyn was then appointed to the Guard Headquarters on 13 August 1814 and served as adjutant to Chief of Staff Prince Volkonsky between 17 April and 13 December 1815.

Golitsyn accompanied the Russian army to Paris in 1815 and was promoted to lieutenant on 19 March 1816. He served in the Guard Corps in 1818, was promoted to captain on 20 April 1821 and transferred to the Chancellery of the Chief of Staff, where he served from 14 January 1822 to 27 March 1823. He returned to the Guard General Staff in 1823 and attained the rank of colonel on 20 February 1824. The next year, he was appointed ober-quartermaster for the 1st Reserve Cavalry Corps on 13 March 1825. He was discharged from military service and transferred to civilian service with a title of kamerger and rank of actual state counsellor on 26 March 1829. He served under the Governor General of Novorosiisk from 16 March 1833 before retiring on 6 December 1837. He was restored to military service in June 1839 and served at the General Staff. He became a member of the Military Censorship Committee (8 February 1841) and was promoted to major general (28 April 1841). He served as ober-quartermaster for the Orenburg Corps and the Internal Guard in 1841-1852. He was then appointed to the main headquarters, where he served for the rest of his life. He was awarded the Order of St. George (4th class) for 25 years of distinguished service on 13 January 1847 and Order of St. Vladimir (2nd class, 1851). He died on 1 June 1856 and was buried at the Lazarev Cemetery of the Alexander of Neva Lavra. He was married to Maria Arkadyevna Suvorov (granddaughter of Field Marshal Suvorov) and had three daughters.

GOLITSYN, Mikhail Nikolayevich (b. 18 October 1796, village Arkhangelskoe near Moscow — d. 6 November 1863, Moscow) began service as a junker at the Collegium for Foreign Affairs. He became a column guide (*kolonovozhatii*) in the Imperial Retinue on 29 March 1810, but transferred as a junker-ensign to the Life Guard Preobrazhensk Regiment on 27 May 1811. He was promoted to ensign on 27 April 1812, and fought at age 16 at the battle of Borodino on 7 September 1812. In the 1813 Campaign, he took part in the battles at Lutzen, Bautzen, Pirna, Kulm, and Leipzig. For his actions at Pirna and Kulm, he was awarded the Order of St. Anna of 4th class and the Prussian Iron Cross. He was promoted to sub-lieutenant on 5 October 1813.

In 1814, Golitsyn followed the main army to France and took part in the battle of Paris. After the war, he was appointed adjutant to Lieutenant General Baron Rosen and promoted to lieutenant (13 October 1816), staff captain (13 February 1820) and captain (25 March 1821). In 1822-1823, he served as adjutant to Chief of Staff Prince Volkonsky and transferred to civilian service with a rank of college counsellor and title of kamerger on 4 May 1823. For next twenty years, he worked at various position in the Senate; he was promoted to state counsellor on 6 May 1836, to actual state counsellor on 15 December 1839 and to privy counsellor on 13 July 1854. Since 1852, he directed military hospital in Moscow. He died on 6 November 1863 in Moscow and was buried in a church at the village of Nikosk-Urupin in Zvenigorod *uezd*. In addition to previously mentioned decorations, Golitsyn was also awarded the Orders of St. Vladimir (3rd class, 1834), St. Stanislaus (1st class, 1842), St. Anna (1st class, 1856) and of the White Eagle (1856).

GOLITSYN, Nikolay Borisovich (b. 20 December 1794, Moscow — d. November 1866, Svyatogorsk) was born to the Vladimir branch of the Golitsyn family. He enlisted as portupei-junker to the Life Guard Horse Artillery on 14 September 1810 and was promoted to sub-lieutenant on 21 December of the same year. He was discharged on 18 December 1812 for misbehavior but restored in military service in early 1812. He served as courier under Prince Bagration and fought at Shevardino, where he was wounded in the head. He was promoted to ensign on 10 September, and fought at Krasnaya Pakhra, Chirikov, Tarutino, Vyazma, Dorogobouzh, and Kobychev. Golitsyn served as adjutant to Generals Sievers and Osterman-Tolstoy in 1813, fighting at Bautzen (received the Order of St. Anna of 4th class) and Marn (received the Order of St. Vladimir 4th class).

Golitsyn was promoted to lieutenant in August 1813 and took part in the invasion of France in 1814, fighting at Rheims (promoted to staff-captain) and Paris (received a golden sword for courage). He was promoted to captain on 12 May 1817 and transferred to the Life Guard Pavlovsk Regiment in August 1822. He was discharged with a rank of lieutenant colonel in December 1821, but returned to his regiment two years later and was promoted to colonel on 9 February 1826. In 1830, he briefly commanded a garrison battalion during the riots in Tambov and later headed the gendarmerie company in the same town in 1831. He was discharged from military service and transferred with a rank of college counsellor to the Ministry of Finances in April 1832. He was well-known in music circles for organizing over three hundreds concerts and ordering numerous musical works, including several by Beethoven. He died in November 1866 and was buried at Svyatogorsk.

GOLITSYN, Nikolay Yakovlevich (b. 16 September 1788, Moscow — d. 30 January 1850, Moscow) was born to Prince Yakov (Jacob) Alexandrovich Golitsyn and Countess Natalya Golovina. He enlisted as a junker in the Life Guard Horse Regiment on 3 April 1805 and promoted to estandart-junker on 24 August of the same year. He participated in 1805 Campaign and fought at Austerlitz. He was promoted to cornet in May 1807 and was dispatched with reinforcements to join Bennigsen's army. He fought at Heilsberg and Friedland, where he was wounded and later awarded a golden sword for courage and the Order of St. Anna (4th class). Golitsyn was promoted to lieutenant on 24 July 1808 and served in his regiment for the next four years. In 1812, he fought at Vitebsk, Smolensk, Borodino (received the Order of St. Vladimir, 4th class), Tarutino, Maloyaroslavets and Krasnyi.

In 1813, Golitsyn became staff-rotmistr on 20 January and rotmistr on 5 October, fighting at Lutzen, Bautzen and Leipzig. The following year, he participated in the invasion of France, distinguishing himself at Brienne. He became a colonel on 11 December 1817 and major general on 27 December 1825. He was given command of the 2nd Brigade of the 1st Cuirassier Division on 3 May 1828; two years later, he commanded the 1st Brigade of the same division (18 December 1830) and then led the 1st Cuirassier Division (17 January 1831). He fought against the Poles in 1831 and took part in the capture of Warsaw. He was discharged with a rank of lieutenant general on 6 February 1836. He died on 30 January 1850 in Moscow and was buried in the Don Monastery.

GOLITSYN, Peter Aleksandrovich commanded the Elizavetgrad Hussar Regiment in July-August 1802, became a major general on 19 May 1803 and served as a chef of the Lithuanian Horse (Uhlan) Regiment between 19 Mayn 1803 and 7 August 1809.

GOLITSYN, Sergey Fedorovich (b. 16 November 1749 – d. 1 February 1810, Tarnopol) descended from one of the most prominent family of Russian princes. He enlisted as a corporal in the artillery in 1 January 1757 and rose to sergeant in 1757 and then to shtyk junker on 12 March 1761. Graduating from the University of Moscow and the Infantry Cadet Corps, he received a rank of lieutenant and became an adjutant to a general-en-chef (probably, Général-en-Chef Bruce) on 14 May 1764 and a captain on 3 February 1766. During the Russo-Turkish War in 1768-1774, he fought at Rachev Cape, Kagul (received the Order of St. George, 4th class) and Silistra; his actions earned him quick promotions as Golitsyn received the rank of second major on 30 December 1769 and premier major on 1 August 1770. Golitsyn became a lieutenant colonel of the Smolensk Dragoon Regiment on 5 December 1771. On 3 October 1775, he became a flügel adjutant and colonel of the Smolensk Dragoon Regiment. Three years later, on 3 October 1798, he transferred as a brigadier to the Life Guard Preobrazhensk Regiment and, on 16 May 1779, he was promoted to a major general. The same year, he married Varvara Vasilievna Engelhardt, niece of Prince Gregory Potemkin. In 1782, he served in the Crimea; he was decorated with the Polish Orders of the White Eagle and of St. Stanislaus in 1787 and received the rank of lieutenant general on 25 July 1788.

During the Russo-Turkish War of 1787-1791, Golitsyn fought at Ochakov (commanded reserve of the left flank, received a golden sword with diamonds), on the Prut River (commanded a reserve corps) Macin and Braila. For his actions in the last two battles, he garnered the Orders of St. George (2nd class) and of St. Alexander of Neva. In 1794, he commanded a corps in General N. Repnin's army in Poland, for which he earned the Order of St. Vladimir (1st class) on 6 November 1794. In 1796-1797, he served as a battalion commander of the Life Guard Preobrazhensk Regiment and briefly commanded this entire unit as well. He was promoted to general of infantry on 21 April 1797. The following year, he had an argument with Emperor Paul due to intrigues of Count Kutaysov, whom Golitsyn detested for his low origins. Golitsyn was discharged from the army on 12 September 1798 and retired to his estate in the Kiev *gubernia*. While preparing for the campaigns against France in late 1798, Paul I recalled Golitsyn on 29 December 1798 and gave him command of a corps. However, as the corps marched to Italy, Golitsyn was relieved of command on 18 January 1799 because of his criticism of Paul I.

Golitsyn remained at his estate of Zubrilovka in the Saratov *gubernia* until the assassination of Paul I in March 1801, when the new Emperor Alexander I recalled him and appointed him the Governor General of Riga and infantry inspector for the Lifland *gubernia* on 17 July 1801. On 27 September 1801, Golitsyn received the diamond signs of the Order of St. Alexander of Neva and, on 8 June 1802, the Order of St. Andrew the First Called. Golitsyn retired for the third time in September 1804. During the 1806-1807 Campaigns, he became the commander-in-chief over the militia (zemskoe voisko) of the 3rd Region and received the diamond signs of the Order of St. Andrew the First Called in 1807. He returned to the military service on 8 April 1809 and took command of a corps in Galicia against the Austrians. However, he adamantly opposed to the war against Austria and avoided actions with the Austrians. After the campaign, he was appointed a member of the State Council on 13 January 1810, but he died of a stroke on 1 February 1810 at Tarnopol. He had ten sons: Gregory (1779-1848), Fedor (1781-1826), **Sergey** (1783-1838, see below), Mikhail (1784-1807, mortally wounded at Pultusk), Zakhar (1785-1792), Nikolay (1787-1807), Pavel (1788-1837), Alexander (1789-1858), Vasily (1792-1856) and **Vladimir** (1794-1861, see below).

GOLITSYN, Sergey Sergeyevich (b. 28 February 1783 — d. 26 March 1833, St. Petersburg) was born to a prominent Russian princely family, third son of Général-en-Chef Sergey Golitsyn. He enlisted in the guard in 1797 and served at Austerlitz and Friedland in 1805-1807. He became a flügel adjutant on 15 May 1806 and served as a kamer junker at the Imperial court in February – July 1808 before receiving his colonelcy on 15 July 1808. In 1812, Golitsyn attended General Levin Bennigsen and, during the 1813-1814 Campaigns, he took part in the battles at Lutzen, Bautzen (promoted to major general on 27 September 1813), Leipzig and Paris. For his actions in these campaign, he garnered the Prussian Orders of the Red Eagle and the Pour le Merite. He retired in 1815 and spent the rest of his life at his estate.

GOLITSYN, Vladimir Sergeyevich (b. 28 March 1794, Moscow – d. 31 January 1861, Moscow) was the youngest son of Général-en-Chef Prince Sergey Fedorovich Golitsyn (1749-1810) and Barbara Vasilievna Engelhardt, niece of Potemkin. He was home-educated by I.A. Krylov and began his career as a junker at the Ministry of Commerce. He became a kamer-junker on 4 June 1810. Two years later, during the 1812 Campaign, he enlisted as cornet in the 3rd Ukraine Cossack Regiment on 22 August and participated in minor skirmishes during the French retreat. He distinguished himself at Kalisch and was awarded the Order of St. Anna (4th class).

In 1813, Golitsyn commanded the advance guard of General Madatov and took part in the actions at Weissenfels, Lutzen (where he covered the Allied retreat and received the Orders of St. Anna, 4th class) and Vladimir. He also fought at Bautzen, Reichenbach, Dresden (wounded in the left thigh), Katzbach (received a sabre cut to the right hand), Bunzlau (wounded in the right leg), Leipzig and Mainz, where he was first to reach the French artillery batteries.

In 1814, Golitsyn participated in the battles at Brienne and La Rothière (received the Order of St. Anna, 2nd class), Montmirail, Chateau Thierry, Laon, St. Dizier, Bar-sur-Aube and Paris (wounded in the leg). For his actions, he was promoted to staff-rotmistr in the Life Guard Horse Jager Regiment on 7 May 1814. Two years later, he became adjutant to General Barclay de Tolly on 17 January 1816, and, the following year, he was promoted to flügel-adjutant (11 October 1817). He was promoted to captain on 27 March 1818 and to major in the Tiraspol Horse Jager Regiment (other sources referred to the Pereyaslavl Horse Jagers) on 1 February 1819. He became a lieutenant colonel on 22 August 1820 and a colonel on 24 December 1823. Two years after, he took command of the Tiraspol Horse Jagers, but had an altercation with his corps commander and was discharged after being reduced in ranks. He was restored in ranks (flügel-adjutant) on 5 October 1826 and served at Nizhegorod Dragoon Regiment. He briefly commanded this regiment between 8 December 1826 and 15 January 1827 and took part in the Russo-Persian War.

In March 1827, Golitsyn was appointed duty officer to General Madatov and fought at Sardar-Abat and Yerivan, where he was wounded in the shoulder and subsequently awarded the Order of St. Anna (2nd class) with diamonds. However, his problems with his superiors continued; on 15 November 1827, he was excluded from the court and appointed to the Independent Caucasus Corps (1 January 1828). The next January, he was discharged for gambling with fellow officers (14 January 1829) and transferred to the Ministry of Internal Affairs (28 January). He was promoted to actual state counsellor on 6 April 1829. He was discharged again in March 1835, but was restored in military service four years later. He was given the rank of colonel in the Independent Caucasus Corps in March 1838, and commanded cavalry in the campaigns against the North Caucasian Mountaineers in 1840-1841. He was promoted to major general in 1842 or 1843, and was awarded the Order of Staniuslaus (1845) and St. Anna (1st class) and Prussian "Pour le Merite" in 1847. He retired with a title of privy counsellor in 1849 after an argument with General Vorontsov. He settled in Moscow and wrote several plays and poems. In 1855, he organized and commanded a company of Moscow *opolchenye* during the Crimean War. He died in Moscow on 31 January 1861 and was buried at Miusky Cemetery.

GOLOVIN, Yevgeny Alexandrovich (b. 1782 — date of death unclear; removed from roster on 7 August 1858) was born to a noble family from the Smolensk *gubernia*. He studied in the University of Moscow and began military service as a sub ensign in the Life Guard Preobrazhensk Regiment in April 1797. On 25 December 1797, he transferred as an ensign to the Moghilev Garrison Battalion and, in 1801, joined the Fanagoria Grenadier Regiment. In 1805, he served in Buxhöwden's corps and fought at Austerlitz, where he was wounded in the left leg. In 1807-1810, he was in retirement. In 1810, he joined his regiment in the Danubian Principalities and distinguished himself at Shumla (promoted to a lieutenant colonel), Batin (received the Order of St. George, 4th class, 26 January 1812) and Bazardjik. Golovin took command of the Fanagoria Grenadier Regiment on 12 February 1811.

In 1812, Golovin served in the 1st Western Army and was seriously wounded at Borodino. He rose to colonel on 3 December 1813. In the 1813 Campaign, Golovin participated in actions at Lutzen, Bautzen and Leipzig, where he was wounded in the left hand and later received promotion to a major general on 1 August 1814 with seniority dating from 16 October 1813. The following year, he took part in the invasion of

France and fought at Paris. After the war, he commanded a brigade of the 3rd Grenadier Division and became commander of the Life Guard Jager Regiment on 22 August 1821 and commander of the 4th Brigade of the 2nd Grenadier Division on 26 March 1825.

Golovin opposed the Decembrist Uprising in December 1825, for which he received promotion to adjutant general on 27 December 1825 and lieutenant general on 3 September 1826. He participated in the Russo-Turkish War in 1828-1829, taking command of the 19th Division on 5 October 1828 and serving as commandant of Varna. After the war, he became the Military Governor of Orenburg and the commander of the Orenburg Corps on 19 February 1830. Golovin retired on 30 April 1830 but returned to the army the following year, taking command of the 26th Division on 29 February 1831. He participated in the suppression of the Polish Uprising in 1831, for which he garnered the Order of St. George (3rd class) on 25 September 1831. Golovin took command of the 2nd Division on 13 November 1831 and served on the various committes in the Kingdom of Poland. From December 1837 to November 1842, he commanded the Caucasian Corps, and served as civil governor in the Transcaucasia. He became general of infantry on 13 July 1839. In 1845-1848, he served as a governor general for the Lifland, Estland and Courland *gubernia*s. He was appointed a member of the State Council in 1848. During the Crimean War, he was elected the commander of the Smolensk *opolchenye* on 25 March 1855.

GORBUNTSOV, Yegor Sergeyevich (b. 1768 — d. 4 June 1813, Danzig) was born to an ober-officer's family. He began service as a sergeant in the Life Grenadier Regiment in 1783. During the Russo-Swedish War in 1789-1790, he earned the Order of St. George (4th class) and rose to ensign. Under Paul I, he enjoyed quick promotions becoming a lieutenant in 1797, a captain of the Life Guard Preobrazhensk Regiment in 1798 and colonel in 1799. He served as a platz-major in St. Petersburg in 1799 and a commandant of Revel in 1800. Gorbuntsov rose to a major general on 26 September 1800, but after Paul's assassination, was discharged from the army on 20 January 1802. He returned to the service six years later and took command of the Pskov Garrison Battalion on 24 May 1808; however, his rank was reduced to colonel. The following year, he became a major general and chef of the Aland Garrison Regiment on 28 November 1809. Gorbuntsov was appointed chef of the Bryansk Infantry Regiment on 29 January 1811. In 1812, he commanded the 1st Brigade of the 6th Division in the Finland Corps and took part in operations in the Baltic *gubernia*s. In 1813, he participated in the siege of Danzig, where he died on 4 June 1813.

GORCHAKOV (Gorchakov I), Aleksey Ivanovich (b. 31 May 1769, Moscow — d. 24 December 1817, St. Petersburg) was born to a prominent Russian noble family; cousin of Field Marshal Alexander Suvorov and brother of Andrey Gorchakov. He enlisted as a corporal in the Life Guard Preobrazhensk Regiment in 1774 and began service in 1781. He transferred as a captain to the regular army in 1786 and served as an adjutant to Alexander Suvorov in 1788. During the Russo-Turkish War, he distinguished himself at Ochakov (received the Order of St. George, 4th class, promoted to lieutenant colonel, adjutant to Prince Potemkin), Kaumany, Bender and Akkerman. Gorchakov rose to a colonel and commander of the Azov Infantry Regiment in 1791. In 1792, he served in Poland and garnered the Order of St. Vladimir (4th class). Two years later, he returned to Poland, fighting at Kobryn, Krupchitse, Brest and Warsaw, for which he earned a golden sword and the rank of brigadier on 17 September 1794. Gorchakov became chef of the Riga Musketeer Regiment on 15 December 1796 and rose to major general on 8 February 1797. The following year, he became chef of the Ekaterinoslavl Musketeer Regiment on 16 March and chef of the Shirvan Musketeer Regiment on 30 March 1798, remaining at this position for eight months. He was promoted to a lieutenant colonel on 20 September 1798.

In 1799, Gorchakov served with General Rimsky-Korsakov in Switzerland and covered the Russian retreat after the defeat at Zurich.

Returning to Russia, he became chef of the Neva Musketeer Regiment on 7 February 1800 and served as the Military Governor of Vyborg and chef of the Vyborg Garrison Regiment in March-August 1800. He was accused of embezzeling the regimental funds and was discharged from the army on 30 August 1800. Under Alexander I, he returned to the army on 20 April 1801 and served as an inspector in the Ukraine and Brest Inspectorates in 1801-1803. He was appointed to the Senate in March 1804 and chef of the Belozersk Musketeer Regiment on 2 May 1807. In February 1812, he became a member of the Council of War and, from August 1812 to December 1815, he served as a head of the Ministry of War, receiving the rank of general of infantry on 11 September 1814. He was again accused of embezzelement in December 1815 and removed from command. He took a discharge in September 1817 and died three months later in St. Petersburg.

GORCHAKOV (Gorchakov II), Andrey Ivanovich (b. 1779, Moscow – d. 23 February 1855, Moscow) was born to a prominent Russian noble family; cousin of Field Marshal Alexander Suvorov and brother of Aleksey Gorchakov. He was enlisted in the guard at the age two in 1781 and began service as an ensign on 12 January 1793. Four years later, he rose to lieutenant colonel and flügel adjutant. He became colonel in early 1798 and major general of the Life Guard Preobrazhensk Regiment on 5 April 1798. He was discharged on 12 November 1798 but returned to the service in the War College on 20 January 1799.

Gorchakov volunteered to serve on Alexander Suvorov's staff during the campaigns in Italy and Switzerland in 1799. He distinguished himself on the Trebbia River, at Novi and during the crossing of the Alps, for which he received promotion to lieutenant general on 23 February 1800. Gorchakov became chef of the Neva Musketeer Regiment on 20 March 1800, chef of the Tamborv Musketeer Regiment on 1 March 1803 and garrison inspector of the Moscow Inspectorate on 29 August 1805. In 1806, he formed the 18th Division, which he commanded in the 1807 Campaign in Poland; he distinguished himself at Heilsberg and Friedland in June 1807. Two years later, he commanded division in Sergey Golitsyn's corps, but was opposed to any military operations against the Austrians. He corresponded with the Austrian generals and, in one of his letters to Archduke Ferdinand, he stated that the Austrian and the Russian armies should unite against Napoleon. The French intercepted this letter and demanded the dismissal of Gorchakov. Alexander had him court martialed and discharged from the army on 11 October 1809. Three years later, Gorchakov was restored in the army on 13 July 1812 and appointed to the headquarters of the 2nd Western Army. He participated in actions at Saltanovka, Smolensk and distinguished himself at Shevardino and Borodino, where he was seriously wounded. For his actions in the last two battles, he was decorated with the Order of St. George (3rd class) on 1 November 1812.

After recuperating, Gorchakov joined the army in the summer of 1813 and fought at Leipzig, for which he garnered the Order of St. Vladimir (1st class) and the Prussian Red Eagle (1st class). In 1814, he took part in battles at Brienne, La Rothière, Bar sur Aube and Paris, for which he received the Order of St. George (2nd class) on 31 March 1814. After the war, he became a member of the State Council in 1817, general of infantry on 13 January 1819, commander of the 3rd Corps on 26 January 1819 and commander of the 2nd Corps on 29 February 1820. He retired in 1847.

GOVE (Howe), Alexander Petrovich (b. 1765 — date of death unknown) descended from a French noble family. He enlisted as a sergeant in the 2nd Fusilier Regiment on 19 January 1770 and took a discharge with a rank of sub-lieutenant in May 1782. Two years later, he returned to the army as a cornet in the Sofia Carabinier Regiment. He fought the Turks in 1787-1791 and the Poles in 1794, earning a golden cross for Praga. He transferred as a major to the Commissariat in 1795, where he remained for the rest of his career. He served as a supply commissar in the Russian headquarters in 1805-1807 campaigns in Moravia and Poland. During the 1812 Campaign, Gove served as a general proviantmeister of the 1st Western Army. He became a state counsellor on 12 March 1812, and received a military rank of major general on 21 March 1813. In 1813-1814, he served in the main headquarters of the Russian army. After the war, Gove served as a deputy director of the Supply Department of the Ministry of War before retiring in 1834.

GREIG, Aleksey Samuilovich (b. 17 September 1775, Kronstadt — d. 30 January 1845, St. Petersburg) was born to a prominent Scottish noble family, the son of Admiral Samuil Greig, he was baptized by Empress Catherine II. He was enlisted as a midshipman on 23 October 1775 and, ten years later, studied navigation in Britain and traveled to India. He served in the British Royal Navy against the French and Spanish fleets in 1789-1792. Returning to Russia, he rose to a captain 1st class on 12 January 1799 and participated in the expedition to Holland. Greig was promoted to captain commander on 21 January 1803. In 1804-1806, he commanded a Russian squadron in the Adriatic Sea, where he distinguished himself during the operations in Dalmatia and Naples, for which he earned a rank of rear admiral on 8 January 1806. In 1807, he served under Vice Admiral Senyavin against the Turks, fighting in the battles of the Dardanelles, Tenedos and Mt. Athos.

In 1809, Greig was appointed to the Black Sea Fleet and commanded a squadron against the Turks. In 1812, he served as one of the Russian representatives during the negotiations with the Porte. In 1813, he commanded a Russian flotilla during the blockade of Danzig (received the Order of St. Vladimir, 2nd class) and was promoted to a vice admiral on 6 November 1813. In 1815, Greig was given command of the Black Sea Fleet and become the Military Governor of Sebastopol. During the Russo-Turkish War of 1828-1829, he participated in the captures of Varna (received the Order of St. George, 2nd class, 11 October 1828) and Anapa, for which he received promotion to admiral on 1 August 1828. On 26 August 1830, he became chair of the Committee to Reform the Russian Fleet and, three years later, was appointed a member of the State Council on 15 August 1833.

GRABBE, Paul (Pavel) Khristoforovich (b. 14 December 1789, Keksholm — d. 27 July 1875) was born to a noble family from the Lifland *gubernia*. He studied in the Infantry Cadet Corps and graduated as a sub-lieutenant in the 2nd Artillery Regiment in 1805. He marched with Essen's column to Moravia but was ordered back after the battle of Austerlitz. Grabbe participated in the 1806-1807 Campaign in Poland, fighting at Golymin (received the Order of St. Anna, 3rd class), Eylau (received a golden cross), Guttstadt, Heilsberg and Friedland. In 1808, he served as an adjutant to General Yermolov in Poland. Two years later, he became a military agent in the Russian embassy in Munich.

In 1812, Grabbe became adjutant to Minister of War Barclay de Tolly. In June 1812, on the eve of the French invasion, he was dispatched to negotiate with the French and had a secret mission to determine the enemy deployment. Serving as adjutant to Generals Yermolov and Miloradovich, he then took part in battles of Vitebsk, Smolensk (received the Order of St. George, 4th class), Borodino, Tarutino, Maloyaroslavets, Vyazma and Krasnyi; for his actions, he was decorated with the Orders of St. Vladimir (4th class) and of St. Anne (2nd class) and was promoted to staff captain. In 1813, Grabbe served in the mobile detachment of Count Wallmoden and distinguished himself in numerous raids on the French communication and supply lines. After the war, in 1816, Grabbe was promoted to a colonel and, the following year, he took command of the Lubensk Hussar Regiment. He became involved with the secret societies but did not participate in the Decembrist movement. On 4 March 1822, he was removed from command for ignoring the service regulations but was soon appointed in the Seversk Horse Jager Regiment in 1823. Four years later, he transferred to the Novorossiisk Dragoon Regiment and participated in the Russo-Turkish War in 1828-1829, fighting at Calafat, Golentsy, Boelesti (received a golden sabre), Rakhov, on the Isker River and other actions; for military distinction, he received the Order of St. Vladimir (3rd class) and promotion to a major general.

In 1831, Grabbe served as a chief of staff of the 1st Corps and fought the Polish insurgents at Minsk, Kaluszin (wounded in the thigh), Ostrolenko (received the Order of St. George, 3rd class) and Warsaw (decorated with the Order of St. Anna, 1st class). After the campaign, he took command of the 2nd Dragoon Division in 1832. Five years later, he was promoted to a lieutenant general on 30 April 1837 and, then, received command of troops in the Caucasus and on the Black Sea coast 30 April 1838. Faced with the Chechen uprising led by Imam Shamil, Grabbe led several expeditions into the mountains, fighting bloody engagements at the villages [*auls*] of Tarengul, Arguan (promoted to adjutant general) and Akhulgo (received the Order of St Alexander of Neva) in 1839. He believed Chechnya was pacified and withdrew troops from occupied territories. However, he soon faced the rallied forces of the Chechens and spent the next two years fighting Shamil in Chechnya and Daghestan.

Following his unsuccessful expedition into Chechnya in the summer of 1842, Grabbe was relieved of command and spent several years at his estate. With the outbreak of the Hungarian revolt in 1849, he took command of the forces defending Galicia. For his part in the actions at Rozenberg, Sen-Marton, Sen-Miklosh and Komorn, Grabbe received a golden sabre with diamonds and inscribed "For the Campaign in Hungary in 1849." In 1852, he became a member of the Committee on Invalids. However, the following year, he and other members of this committee were court-martialed for failing to carry out their duties that resulted in embezzlement of funds by the committee's executive clerk. Grabbe was later pardoned and took command of the Kronstadt Garrison on 1 April 1854. Two years later, he rose to general of cavalry and commanded the troops in Estland. On 1 October 1862, he was named governing ataman [*nakaznoi ataman*] of the Don Cossack Host and was awarded the Order of St. Andrew the First-Called in 1863. On 28 October 1866, Grabbe received the title of count and became a member of the State Council. He died on 27 July 1875. Grabbe left insightful memoirs on his participation in the Napoleonic campaigns, "*Iz Zapisok P. Kh. Grabbe*," published in the *Russkii Arkhiv* in 1873-1889 as well as in a separate volume in Moscow in 1873.

GREKOV (Grekov IX), Aleksey Yevdokimovich (b. 1760 — date of death unknown) was born to a Cossack officer's family, son of Colonel Evdokim Grekov. He began service as a private in the Don Cossack Host on 12 May 1773 and rose to sauryad-esaul in 1775 and esaul in 1780. In 1780-1784, he served in Life Cossack Escort. He participated in the

Russo-Turkisgh War in 1787-1791. In 1796, Grekov took command of the Life Cossack Escort and became a colonel on 8 November 1799. In 1806-1807, he commanded a Cossack Regiment in the 4th Division and fought at Golymin and Eylau. In 1812, he served in Ertel's corps and took part in minor engagements with the French. In 1813-1814, he served at Kalisch, Wittenberg, Magdeburg, Torgau, Leipzig and Paris, for which he was promoted to a major general on 16 June 1815 with seniority dating from 26 March 1814.

GREKOV (Grekov III), Boris Alekseyevich (b. 1752 — date of death unclear) was born to a Don Cossack family. He began service as a private in the Don Cossack Host on 15 September 1770 and rose to sotnik on 16 May 1772. From 1777-1782, he served in the Life Cossack Escort in St. Petersburg, becoming a lieutenant in January 1780. In 1784-1789, he served in the Kuban Valley. He became a starshina and commander of a Cossack regiment in 1786. In 1794, he served in Poland, where he garnered the Order of St. Vladimir (4th class) for his actions at Praga. In 1795-1798, Grekov served in the western Russian *gubernia*s and was promoted to colonel on 16 March 1798. He soon retired with a rank of major general and spent almost a decade in Donetsk. In 1812, he organized the *opolchenye* regiments in the Donetsk Regione and led five Cossack regiments to the Tarutino Camp. In November-December 1812, he fought at Vyazma and Krasnyi, receiving the Order of St. Vladimir (3rd class). No details were available on his subsequent career.

GREKOV (Grekov I), Dmitry Yevdokimovich (b. 1748 — d. 1820) was born to a Cossack officer's family, son of Colonel Evdokim Grekov. He began service in the Don Cossack Host on 26 April 1761 and served in Daghestan in 1764-1766. He rose to esaul on 17 March 1766. During the Russo-Turkish War in 1769-1774, he distinguished himself at Akkerman (received a golden medal), Perekop and Feodosia. On 31 January 1771, Grekov became a Cossack colonel. In 1783-1786, he served in the Caucasus and participated in the operations in the Kuban Valley, where he was captured by the mountaineers in 1786. After paying a ransom, Grekov returned to his unit and became a lieutenant colonel of the Russian army on 12 July 1787. He took part in the Russo-Turkish War in 1787-1791, fighting at Ochakov (received a golden cross), in the Crimea and in Caucasus (Djeme-Tasi, Anapa), garnering the Order of St. George (4th class). In 1794, he served in Poland, where he distinguished himself at Praga and received a promotion to colonel on 2 December 1794. Four years later, he rose to a major general on 18 September 1798. Grekov was discharged on 10 June 1800 and returned to Daghestan, where he served at Derbent. In 1812, he formed the Don Cossack *opolchenye* and brought a brigade of three cossack regiments to the Tarutino Camp. He then participated in the battles at Tarutino, Kolotsk Monastery, Solvyeovo, Dukhovshina, Smolensk, Krasnyi and on the Berezina.

GREKOV (Grekov VIII), Peter Matveyevich (date of birth unclear, ca. 1762/1764 — d. 15 February 1817, Dyachkina) was born to a Don Cossack noble family. He began service as a private in the Don Cossack Host on 12 May 1784 and, for his actions in the battle at Malka against the Turks, he was promoted to *khorunjii* on 30 June 1785. He participated in the Russo-Turkish War in 1788-1791, fighting at Bender, Kaushani, Akkerman, Macin and Ismail (received a golden cross); during the war, he was promoted to lieutenant and captain. In 1792-1794, Grekov served in Poland and, for his actions at Maciejowice, he received the Order of St. George (4th class) and a rank of premier major. He became a colonel on 20 February 1799 and participated in the 1799 Campaign in Italy and Switzerland, fighting at Bergamov, Lecco, Turin, Tortona, Trebbia and Novi. In 1801, he took part in the expedition to India, although the Cossack Corps got only as far as Orenburg. In 1802-1807, he served in the civil administration of the Don Cossack Host.

In 1808-1811, Grekov was dispatched to the Danubian Principalities, where he commanded three Cossack regiments and distinguished himself at Ruse (received the Order of St. George, 3rd class) and Turtukai, for which he was promoted to a major general on 30 January 1812. During the 1812 Campaign, he commanded ten Cossack regiments in the Army of Danube and fought at Lubolme, Brest, Kaidanov, Borisov and was seriously wounded at Khataevichi on 1 December 1812; for his actions, he was decorated with the Order of St. Anna (1st class). After recuperating, he commanded Cossack detachments throughout the 1813-1814 Campaigns, distinguishing himself at Bautzen, Colberg, Levenberg, Leipzig, Nemours, Le Fère Champenoise and Paris. He died while visiting General Karpov at the village of Dyachkina in the Donetsk district on 15 February 1817.

GREKOV (Grekov V), Stepan Yevdokimovich (b. 1768, Cherkassk — d. 1833) was born to a Cossack officer's family, son of Colonel Evdokim Grekov. He began service as a private in the Don Cossack Host on 12 May 1786 and rose to an esaul on 24 February 1788. He participated in the Russo-Turkish War in 1787-1791, fighting at Focsani, Rimnic, Ismail (wounded in the right leg, received a golden cross) and Macin (received a medal); he quickly advanced through the ranks, becoming captain, second major and premier major by the end of war. On 11 November 1798, Grekov rose to a colonel. For the next decade, he served in Don Cossack Host. In 1812, he organized the Don Cossack *opolchenye* and took two Cossack regiments to join the main Russian army at the Tarutino Camp. He distinguished himself in operations against the Italians on the Vop' River, for which he earned the Order of St. George (4th class, 7 April 1813). He continued commanding Cossack detachments throughout the 1813-1814 Campaign, becoming a major general on 30 May 1813. After the war, he served in the Don Cossack Chancellery.

GREKOV (Grekov XVIII), Timofey Dmitryevich (b. 1770 — d. 1 September 1831) was born to a prominent Cossack family; son of Major General Dmitry Grekov. He began service as a private in the Don Cossack Host on 26 March 1788 and was promoted to esaul late that year. He participated in the Russo-Turkish War in 1788-1791, fighting in the Crimea and the Kuban Valley. In 1794, he served in Poland, receiving a golden cross for Praga. He took command of a Cossack regiment (designated Grekov XVIII's Cossack Regiment) in 1800. Grekov took part in the campaign in Poland in 1806-1807, serving with the 4th Division. In 1812, he participated in 2nd Western Army's retreat from Volkovisk, fighting at the battles of Mir, Romanovo, Molevo Boloto, Tarutino, Maloyaroslavets (received the Order of St. Vladimir, 3rd class), Vyazma, and on the Berezina. For his actions, he was promoted to a colonel on 28 December 1812. In 1813, Grekov took command of the Ataman Cossack regiment and distinguished himself at Leipzig, for which he received a rank of major general. In 1814, he made a daring raid on Nemours and fought at Le Fère Champenoise and Arcis sur Aube. After the war, Grekov commanded the Ataman Cossack Regiment until 1819 before retiring on 18 April 1822.

GRESSER, Alexander Ivanovich (b. 1772 — d. 1822) was born to a noble family in the Liflan *gubernia*. He enlisted as a corporal in the Life Guard Preobrazhensk Regiment on 23 January 1778 and rose to lieutenant in 1783. He took part in the Russo-Turkish War in 1787-1791, distinguishing himself at Kinburn and Ochakov. In 1794, he fought in Poland, receiving a golden cross for Praga. In 1801, he joined the Quartermaster Section of the Imperial Retinue and became a colonel on 31 December 1801. Grekov was appointed chef of the 2nd Pioneer Regiment on 8 August 1803. During the 1805 Campaign, he was captured at Austerlitz on 2 December 1805 and released in February 1806. In 1812, he served in the 2nd Western Army and supervised the construction of the fortifications at Bobruisk and Borisov.

During the 1812 Campaign, Grekov commanded two reserve battalions of the 1st and 33rd Jager regiment and a sapper company at Borisov. As the French forces approached Borisov, Gresser abandoned the town and withdrew to Moghilev, where he had a minor skirmish with Marshal Davout's forces before joining Prince Bagration's 2nd Western Army. He fought at Salatanovka, Smolensk, Borodino, for which he received the Order of St. Anna (2nd class) and the rank of major general on 6 January 1813. During the 1813-1814 Campaigns, he supervised construction of the fortifications at Borisov. In March 1816, Grekov joined the Engineer Corps; he became the Chief of Staff of the 6th Corps on 21 April 1816 and of the Independent Lithuanian Corps on 14 December 1817. His brother Colonel Maksim Ivanovich Gresser commanded the 10th Jager Regiment from June 1799 – March 1800, and the 9th Jager Regiment from March 1800 – January 1802.

GUDOVICH, Andrey Ivanovich (b. 1782 — d. 1 June 1867, Moscow) was born to a prominent Russian noble family, the son of General Field Marshal Ivan Gudovich. He enlisted as a sergeant in the Life Guard Izmailovsk Regiment on 12 December 1783 and transferred as a vakhmistr to the Life Guard Horse Regiment in January 1784. After becoming a sub-lieutenant in 1797 and a colonel on 17 October 1801, he joined the Grand Duke Constantine's Uhlan Regiment on 2 December 1803 and fought at Austerlitz in 1805. In 1808-1809, Gudovich served in Finland, fighting the Swedes at Kuopio and Uleaborg. He became chef of the Military Order [Ordenskii] Cuirassier Regiment on 20 April 1809. In 1812, he served with the 2nd Cuirassier Brigade of the 2nd Cuirassier Division of the 8th Corps in the 2nd Western Army and distinguished himself at Shevardino, where he was seriously wounded; for his actions, he earned promotion to major general on 28 December 1812 with seniority dating from 5 September 1812, and the Order of St. George (4th class) on 4 January 1813.

After recuperating, Gudovich returned to his unit, participating in the major battles of the 1813-1814 Campaigns. He took command of the 1st Brigade of the 3rd Cuirassier Division on 10 September 1814 and retired because of poor health on 14 April 1816. He served as leader of the Moscow nobility in 1832-1841. In 1844, he became jagermeister of the Imperial court with a rank of privy counsellor and, in September 1856, he rose to ober-jagermeister. Gudovich died in Moscow on 1 June 1867.

GUDOVICH, Ivan Vasilievich (b. 1741 — d. January 1820) was born to a prominent Russian noble family. He went to the universities in Königsburg and Leipzig and began service as an ensign in the corps of engineers in 1759. He then became an adjutant to the Count P.I. Shuvalov, and, in 1761, was assigned as an adjutant to the Prince of Holstein with the rank of lieutenant colonel. As brother of Andrey Vasilievich Gudovich, Emperor Peter III's favorite, Gudovich was imprisoned for three weeks upon the ascension to the throne of Catherine II in 1762. The following year, he took command of the Astrakhan Infantry Regiment and served in Poland in 1764. He participated in the Russo-Turkish War in 1769-1774, fighting at Khotin, Rachevskii Forest (promoted to a brigadier), Larga (received the Order of St. George, 3rd class), Kagul, Braila, Bucharest (promoted to major general), Giurgiu (wounded in the leg) and Podaluny. After the war, he commanded a division in Little Russia and rose to a lieutenant general in 1777. Seven years later, he was appointed the Governor General of the Ryazan and Tambov *gubernia*s.

During the Russo-Turkish War of 1788-1791, Gudovich commanded a separate corps at Hadjibei (Odessa) and Killia. Promoted to general-en-chef, Gudovich took command of the troops in the Caucasus and the Kuban Valley. He captured the fortress of Anapa on 22 June 1791, garnering the Order of St. George (2nd class) and a golden sword with diamonds. Over the next five years, he began construction of a series of fortification along the Caucasus and was awarded the Order of St. Andrew the First Called in 1793.

Disappointed with Valerian Zubov's appointment to command troops against Persia, he resigned from his position in early 1796. However, following Paul's accession to the throne, Gudovich was appointed to replace Zubov in the Caucasus. In 1798, Gudovich became the Governor General of Kiev and the Podolia *gubernia*. However, following a disagreement with the emperor, he was discharged from the army in June 1800. After six years in retirement, he was called back to service in 1806 and took command of the Russian troops in the Transcaucasia. During the Russo-Turkish War of 1806-1811, he fought at Arpachay, Akhaltsikhe, Akhalkalaki and Gumri. In 1808, Gudovich became seriously ill (lost one of his eyes) and resigned from his positions. After recuperating, he became the Governor of Moscow on 7 August 1809 but was removed from this position due to poor health in February 1812. Gudovich spent the last years of his life at his estate at Olgopol in the Podolia *gubernia*, where he died in January 1820.

GUINE (Hoiningen-Guine), Jacob Yegorovich (b. 1769 — d. 18 October 1813, Leipzig) was born to a noble family from the Lifland *gubernia*. He studied in the Infantry Cadet Corps and began service as a sub-lieutenant in the Bombardier Regiment on 27 November 1787. During the Russo-Turkish War in 1787-1791, he distinguished himself at Ochakov, Kaushany, Bender and Ismail, for which he received a golden cross and rank of lieutenant on 22 December 1790. In 1794, Guine served in Poland, fighting at Krupchitse, Brest (received the Order of St. Vladimir, 4th class) and Warsaw. He rose to staff captain in the 8th Artillery Battalion on 22 January 1797, a captain on 15 December 1797, a major on 20 December 1799 and transferred to the 5th Artillery Regiment on 5 July 1803. In 1805, he commanded artillery in Dokhturov's column, fighting at Krems (Durrenstein) and Austerlitz, for which he garnered a golden sword.

In 1806, he joined the 9th Artillery Brigade (4 September) and served with Essen's corps in the opening moves of the Russo-Turkish War. After fighting at Khotin, he marched to Poland, where he took part in operations against the French, including actions at Stanislavov and on the Narew River. Guine became a lieutenant colonel on 3 March 1807 and a colonel and commander of the 2nd Artillery Brigade on 2 January 1808. On 8 December 1810, he receivedthe Order of St. george (4th class) for twenty five years of service. In 1812, he took command of the 21st Artillery Brigade in the Finland Corps. During the 1812 Campaign, he distinguished himself at Chashniki, for which he was promoted to major general on 8 June 1813 with seniority dating from 15 January 1813. In 1813, he served at Lutzen, Bautzen (posthumously awarded the order of St. George, 3rd class) and was mortally wounded at Leipzig on 18 October 1813.

GULEVICH, Lavr Lvovich (b. 1782 — date of death unclear) was born to a noble family from the Chernigov *gubernia*. He studied in the Artillery and Engineer Cadet Corps and began service in the 8th Artillery Battalion in 1797. In 1805, he participated in the battle of Austerlitz, for which garnered the Order of St. Anna (3rd class). During the Russo-Turkish War of 1806-1812, he fought at Bucharest, Giurgiu and Braila, where he was wounded and received a golden sword in 1809. He took command of the 23rd Battery Company of the 23rd Artillery Brigade on 7 February 1811, and rose to lieutenant colonel on 21 February 1811. During the 1812 Campaign, Gulevich participated in the battles at Borodino (received the Order of St. George, 4th class), Vyazma, Gremyachii (received the Order of St. Anna, 2nd class, with diamonds), and in minor actions during the pursuit of the French.

GURIEV, Alexander Dmitryevich (b. 2 July 1786 — d. 28 December 1865) was born to a prominent Russian noble family. He began service as a junker in the College of Foreign Affairs in 1798 and served in the embassies in

China and France, rising to actual state counsellor. In 1812, he joined the the 3rd District *Gubernial* Opolchenya and commanded an *opolchenye* brigade of the 1st Kazxan and 3rd Nizhegorod *Opolchenye* Regiment. In November-December 1812, he served in the advance guard of the main Russian army, fighting in minor skirmishes with the French. The following year, he distinguished himself in the battle of Dresden, receiving the Order of St. George (4th class) on 30 December 1813 and becoming commandant of Dresden. For his actions, Guriev was officially transferred to the military service with a rank of major general on 11 September 1814. After the war, he commanded a brigade of the 12th Division and remained with the occupational forces in France until 1818.

Returning to Russia, Guriev served in the 1st Grenadier Division (18 April 1819) and took command of the 2nd Brigade of the 3rd Grenadier Division on 8 September 1821. On 23 July 1822, he became the Governor of Odessa and, three years later, he transferred to the Ministry of War as an assistant to the minister on 3 May 1825. He was promoted to the rank of lieutenant general on 29 May 1827 and then appointed to the Senate in 1828. In June 1832, he became a member of the Council of War and military governor for the Poltava and Chernigov *gubernia*s. He was appointed the Military Governor of Kiev and the Governor General of the Podolsk and Volhynia *gubernia*s on 21 June 1835. Guriev transferred to the civil service with a rank of actual privy counsellor on 27 November 1837 and served in the State Council until his death on 28 December 1865.

GURIEV, Aleksey Ivanovich (b. 1767 — date of death unknown; removed from rosters on 18 July 1819) was born to a noble family in the Kaluga *gubernia*. He enlisted as a kaptenarmus in the Moscow Carabinier Regiment on 12 May 1784 and transferred to the Life Guard Izmailovsk Regiment on 12 June 1784. After participating in the Russo-Swedish War in 1788-1790, he transferred as a captain to the regular army and served in Poland in 1794. A colonel on 24 December 1808, he took command of the Polish Uhlan Regiment on 11 June 1811. During the 1812 Campaign, Guriev served with the 5th Brigade of the 1st Cavalry Division of the 2nd Reserve Cavalry Corps; he fought at Vitebsk, Smolensk, Borodino, Maloyaroslavets, Vyazma and Krasnyi. In 1813, he served at Glogau and Leipzig (promoted to a major general on 12 December 1813), and, the following year, took part in the invasion of France, garnering the Prussian Red Eagle and the Swedish Order of the Sword. After the war, he took command of the 1st Brigade of the 3rd Hussar Division on 26 March 1818, but died early the following year.

GURIELOV (Gurieli), Ivan Stepanovich (b. 1770 — date of death unknown; removed from rosters on 1 July 1819) was born to a prominent Georgian noble family. He entered the Russian service in 1780 and rose to an ensign in 1786. He took part in the Russo-Turkish war in 1787-1791 and the Polish Campaign in 1794. Promoted to colonel on 6 July 1799 and major general on 28 May 1803, he became chef of the Volhynia Musketeer Regiment on 28 May 1803, the Commandant of Vilna on 28 March 1808 and chef of the Ekaterinburg Infantry Regiment on 24 June 1812. During the 1812 Campaign, Gurielov commanded the 1st Brigade of the 23rd Division opf the 4th Corps in the 1st Western Army and fought at Ostrovno, Smolensk, Borodino, Tarutino and Vyazma. In 1813, he distinguishe dhimself at Bautzen and Lutzen, and the following year, he took part in the invasion of France. After the war, he commanded the 27th Division before dying in early 1818.

GYLLENSCHMIDT, Yakov Yakovlevich (b. 1782 – d. 5 April 1852) was born to a Danish noble family from the Lifland *gubernia*. After studying in a private boarding school, he began service as a kaptenarmus in the 2nd Cannonier Regiment on 7 September 1795. He transferred to the 3rd Bombardier Regiment in early 1797 and later, joined the Vyborg Artillery Garrison. In 1799, he was appointed to Major General Wilde's 2nd Artillery Battalion and rose to a sub-lieutenant on 7 January 1800. In March 1800, he transferred to the 1st Artillery Regiment, then, in August, to the 2nd Artillery

Battalion. Two years later, Gyllenschmidt served in the 9th Artillery Regiment, became a lieutenant in July 1805 and transferred to the 10th Artillery Regiment in September 1805. The following year, he served in the 16th Artillery Brigade. On 18 November 1806, he was promoted to a staff captain in the Kiev Reserve Artillery Brigade.

Made a captain on 13 November 1807, Gyllenschmidt served in the Danubian Principalities in 1809-1810, fighting at Braila (received the Order of St. Vladimir, 4th class, 8 August 1809), Silistra (received the Orders of St. Anna, 3rd and 2nd class, 19 August/1 October 1810.), Ruse, Giurgiu and Shumla. He became a major on 20 January 1810, a lieutenant colonel on 21 February 1811 and a colonel on 13 July 1819. He took command of the 20th Artillery Brigade on 18 July 1821 and, on 21 June 1825, he received the Order of St. George (4th class) for twenty five years of service. He was appointed to the Life Guard 1st Artillery Brigade on 13 March 1827 and participated in the Russo-Persian War in 1827, fighting at Alagez, Sardar-Abbat, Yerivan and Tabriz (received the Order of St. Vladimir, 3rd class, 18 April 1828). Promoted to major general on 27 March 1828, he took command of the artillery of the Caucasian Corps.

During the Russo-Turkish War of 1828-1829, Gyllenschmidt fought at Kars (received a golden sword with diamonds, 12 May 1829), Akhalkalaki (received the Order of St. Anna, 1st class, 3 May 1830), Akhaltsikhe (wounded in the left hand, receicved the Order of St. Vladimir, 2nd class, 3 May 1829), on the Gunker-Su and Kainly River, at Melides, Erzerum (received the Order of St. George, 3rd class, 31 January 1830) and Baiburt (received the Order of St. Anna, 1st class, with a crown, 3 May 1830). In 1830, he participated in the operations against the North Caucasian mountaineers and received a promotion to lieutenant general on 30 October 1831. He participated in the suppression of the Polish Uprising in 1831, becoming a charge d'affairs of the commander of the artillery of the Russian army (30 October 1831); he took command of the artillery on 13 September 1834, and rose to a general of artillery on 13 September 1843. In 1849, he took part in the campaign against the Hungarian insurgents, garnering the Order of St. Vladimir (1st class). He was appointed chief inspector of artillery on 24 September 1849, and chef of the 2nd Battery of the Life Guard 1st Artillery Brigade on 7 January 1850.

Gyllenschmidt fell ill and died on 5 April 1852 in St. Petersburg.

HAMPER, Yermolay Yermolayevich (b. 1750 — date of death unknown; removed from rosters on 25 December 1814) was born to a noble family in the Courland *gubernia*. He enlisted in the Kazan Cuirassier Regiment on 14 February 1766, became a corporal on 18 April 1766 and vakhmistr on 12 January 1768. During the Russo-Turkish war of 1768-1774, he took part in the battles of Larga, Kagul, Bucharest, Giurgiu and Focsani. He rose to cornet in the Riga Carabineer Regiment on 1 August 1770, and to lieutenant on 5 December 1771. In 1773-1774, he participated in actions in Bulgaria, earning promotion to captain on 3 October 1773, before transferring to the Smolensk Dragoon Regiment in November 1773. Hamper was stationed in the Kuban Valley from 1777-1778 and then in Poland in 1779-1782. In 1783, he served in the Crimea and was promoted to second major on 11 January 1786.

In 1792-1794, Hamper served in Poland, fighting at Shekochin, Maciejowice (promoted to major), Kobylka, Praga (awarded a golden cross) and Radozhitzy. On 4 October 1795, he became a lieutenant colonel and, on 1 December of the same year, he received the Order of St. George (4th class) for twenty-five years of service. He rose to a colonel on 10 June 1798, and took command of the Smolensk Dragoon Regiment on 8 August 1798. He became a major general and chef of the Military Order Cuirassier Regiment on 6 March 1800, but was discharged on 2 August 1800. Hamper returned to service on 26 March 1801 and was appointed commander of the Smolensk Dragoon Regiment on 24 April 1801. Two years later, he became chef of the Smolensk Dragoon Regiment on 5 February 1803.

In 1806, Hamper was decorated with the Order of St. Vladimir (4th class) for thirty-five years of service. The following year, he transferred to the Danubian Principalities, fighting at Ismail, Silistra (received the Orders of St. Anna, 1st class, and of St. Vladimir, 2nd class), Shumla, Derekoy (received a golden sword), on the Yantra River, at Batin (received the Order of St. Anna, 1st class, with diamonds) and Turtukai. In 1812, he served in the Army of Danube and took part in operations in Volhynia and on the Berezina. On 10 December 1813, Hamper became head of the Field General Audit [*polevoi general-auditorial*] and died in December 1814.

HARPE, Vasily Ivanovich (Otto Wilhelm) (b. 1765 — d. 3 March 1814, Luneburg) was born to a German noble family in Revel. He enlisted as a *furier* (fourrier) in the Life Guard Preobrazhensk Regiment on 5 July 1781 and transferred as an ensign to the Keksholm (Kexholm) Infantry Regiment in 1783. During the Russo-Swedish Wars of 1789-1790, he served on the galley flotilla of Prince Nassau Zigen, distinguishing himself at Rochensalmi, for which he received the rank of captain. In May 1791, he joined the Narva Infantry Regiment and took part in operations against the Polish insurgents in 1792-1794; he was seriously wounded during the assault on Vilna, when a musket ball shattered his left cheek and jaw. Harpe spent almost two years recuperating before rising to major in 1797 and to lieutenant colonel in 1800.

During the 1805 Campaign, Harpe commanded a battalion of the Narva Infantry Regiment in Prince Bagration's detachment, distinguishing himself at Schöngrabern (received the Order of St. Vladimir, 4th class) and Austerlitz, where he took another serious wound in the right side. In 1806, his regiment was attached to the 12th Division in the Army of Moldavia and Harpe participated in the siege of Ismail on the initial stage of the Russo-Turkish War of 1806-1812. He took command of the Narva Musketeer Regiment on 11 September 1808 and, the following year, he became chef of the Navaginsk Musketeer Regiment in Finland on 2 February 1809. He took part in the Russian offensive along the coast of the Gulf of Bothnia in 1809, fighting at Umea, Sevar and Ratan. After the war, his regiment was renamed to the Navaginsk Infantry Regiment on 6 March 1811 and attached to Wittgenstein's corps in the Baltic provinces.

In 1812, Harpe took command of the 1st Brigade of the 14th Division of Wittgenstein's 1st Corps and participated in the battles of Klyastitsy, both battles of Polotsk (received a rank of major general on 30 October 1812 for the first battle and the Order of St. George, 3rd class, on 15 January 1813 for the second battle), Chashniki, Bocheikovo, Vitebsk (received the Order of St. Vladimir, 3rd class), Borisov (wounded, received the Order of St. Anna, 1st class) and on the Berezina. In 1813, he served under General Shepelev at Labiau, Koenigsberg and Braunsberg and under Major General Sievers at Pillau; Harpe then commanded a detachment of three thousand men in Bülow's corps at Magdeburg, Wittenberg and Luckau, where he was wounded and garnered the Prussian Red Eagle (2nd class).

During the summer of 1813, Harpe transferred to General Vorontsov's corps in the Army of North and took part in the battles at Gros Beeren (remained in reserve) and Dennewitz, where he was wounded again. He distinguished himself commanding troops in Vorontsov's corps during the battle of Leipzig, where he received several wounds and earned a golden sword with diamonds. Although he accompanied his unit to Holstein, Harpe soon had to leave the army because of poor health and died on 3 March 1814 at Luneburg.

HARTING, Martyn Nikolayevich (b. 1785, Netherlands — d. 25 August 1824, Moghilev) was born to a noble family in the Netherlands. He began service in the Dutch army and, with the help of Peter Sukhtelen, he entered Russian service with a rank of sub-lieutenant in the Corps of Engineers in 1803. During the 1805 Campaign, he served in Count Tolstoy's corps in Hanover. He then served in Finland in 1808-1809 and joined the Quartermaster Section of the Imperial Retinue on 22 December 1808. In 1812, he served as a quartermaster of the 17th Division and later as a ober-quartermaster of the 3rd Corps. He took part in the battles at Vitebsk, Smolensk, Borodino (wounded in leg, but remained with ranks), Maloyaroslavets (promoted to colonel) and Krasnyi, for which he garnered a golden sword.

In January 1813, Harting transferred to the main headquarters of the 1st Army, fighting at Lutzen, Bautzen, Dresden and Kulm, where he was severely bruised by canister in the chest and received the Russian Order of St. Vladimir (3rd class), the Prussian Pour le Merite and the Order of the Red Eagle and the Austrian Order of Leopold (3rd class). After recuperating, he fought at Leipzig on 16-18 October 1813, where he received another wound in his left hand but remained on the battlefield; for his conduct, he garnered the Order of St. George (4th class). During the 1814 Campaign, he distinguished himself at Brienne, La Rothière, Arcis sur Aube and Paris.

After the war, Harting became an ober-quartermaster in the newly established General Staff and served as a quartermaster general of the Russian army during the 1815 Campaign. On 11 September 1815, he attended the grand military parade at Vertus and was promoted to a major general for his actions in 1814-1815. In 1816-1823, he served as Quartermaster General of the 1st Army, completing numerous detailed topographic maps of Russia's western provinces and north-eastern France. On 21 July 1824, he became served as the quartermaster general for the Imperial General Staff but died on 25 August of that year.

HEIDENREICH, Ivan Grigorevich (b. 1769 — d. 1839) descended from a German noble family. He enlisted as a corporal in the Life Guard Horse Regiment on 14 April 1789, and transferred as a captain to the St. Petersburg Garrison Battalion in January 1796. On 29 December 1796, he joined the Tenginsk Infantry Regiment, rising to major on 2 December 1799 and to lieutenant colonel on 5 May 1806. During the 1806-1807 Campaigns in Poland, Heidenreich fought at Pultusk (received a golden sword), Eylau (wounded in the left hand, received the Order of St. Vladimir, 4th class), Altkirchen, Guttstadt, Heilsberg and Friedland. He took command of the Kostroma Musketeer Regiment on 24 May 1808 and served against the Austrians in Galicia in 1809.

In 1810-1812, Heidenreich fought the Turks in the Danubian Principalities, distinguishing himself at Shumla and Ruse, where he was wounded in the left shoulder and back in August 1811. For his actions, he was promoted to colonel on 11 September 1811. During the 1812 Campaign, he served with the 2nd Brigade of the 18th Division of the 3rd Reserve Army of Observation at Kobryn, Gorodechnya (received the Order of St. George, 4th class), Ratno, Vyzhva, Stakhov, Brily (received the Order of St. Anna, 2nd class) and on the Berezina. In 1813, he distinguished himself at Thorn, Koenigswartha (promoted to major general on 27 September 1813 with seniority dating from 19 May 1813), Bautzen (wounded in the right thigh) and Goldberg.

The following year, Heidenreich fought at Brienne (received the Order of St. Vladimir, 3rd class), La Rothière, Montmirail and Chateau Thierry, where he was captured by the French. Released on 3 May 1814, he temporarily commanded the 18th Division in June-September 1814 and then served as an assistant to the commander of this division in 1815-1816. He took command of the 3rd Brigade of the 15th Division on 20 March 1816. Suffering from poor health, Heidenreich transferred to the Internal Guard on 10 March 1820 and became a district general for the 4th District (later 1st) of the Independent Corps of the Internal Guard on 15 March 1821. He took a discharge due to illness in March 1834.

HEIDEN, Login Petrovich (Ludwig Sigizmund Jacob) (b. 5 September 1772, Hague — d. 17 October 1850, Revel) was born to a Dutch noble family in Hague; the son of Baron Sigizmund Peter Alexander van Heiden. He began service in the Dutch army and was detained by the French authorities in early 1795. Released three months later, he entered Russian service as a lieutenant captain in the Black Sea Fleet in 1795. In 1799-1800, he commanded the brigantine *Aleksey* in Captain (1st class)

Pustoshkin's squadron, delivering reinforcements to Admiral Fedor Ushakov in the Mediterranean Sea. In late 1800, he took command of the frigate *Ioan Zlatoust* at Ochakov and was dispatched on a diplomatic mission to the Porte in 1802. Promoted to captain (2nd class), Heiden transferred to the Baltic Fleet in 1803 and served in the Navy Cadet Corps and Admiralty in 1804-1808.

During the Russo-Swedish War of 1808-1809, Heiden commanded a galley flotilla in the Gulf of Finland and fought near the Island of Kimito (bruised, received the Order of St. Vladimir, 3rd class), garnering a rank of captain (1st class) on 7 June 1808. Heiden earned the Order of St. Anna (2nd class) for the victory at the Island of Palva in late 1808. In 1809-1811, he was stationed at Abo, defending the coastline of southern Finland. In 1810, after Napoleon annexed Holland, Heiden accepted citizenship of the Russian Empire. In 1812, he transported the Finland Corps to the Baltic provinces and defended the coastline. The following year, Heiden command a galley flotilla at Danzig and repulsed several French attempts to break through the blockade, for which he garnered a golden sword and a rank of captain commander on 16 September 1813. In 1814, he served in the combined British, Russian and Swedish squadron along the German coastline.

After the war, Heiden continued commanding ships in the Baltic Fleet, became military governor of Sveaborg on 1 June 1816, and rose to rear admiral in 1817. He was relieved of command for the alleged abuse of power in 1823, but was acquited and transferred to the Admiralty in 1826. The same year, he commanded the 3rd Division of the Baltic Fleet during the cruise to Scotland. The following year, he led a squadron in the Allied fleet in the Mediterranean Sea, participating in the Battle of Navarino on 20 October 1827, for which he was promoted to vice admiral and received the Order of St. George (3rd class), the French Order of St. Louis (1st class) and the British Order of Bath on 21 November 1827.

During the Russo-Turkish War of 1828-1829, Heiden served as a commander-in-chief of the Russian fleet in the Mediterranean Sea and blockaded the Dardanelles. Returning to Russia, he commanded the 1st Division of the Baltic Fleet, rose to admiral on 18 December 1833 and became the Military Governor of Revel in 1834 and commandant of the Revel harbor in 1838. During his long career, Heiden garnered the Orders of St. Alexander of Neva with diamonds (1839), St. Vladimir (2nd class), St. Anna (1st class) and of the White Eagle (1836) as well as a medal "For XX Years of Distinguished service," the Dutch Orders of Wilhelm (2nd class, 1832) and of the Lion (1st class, 1850), the Greek Order of the Savior (1834) and the Swedish Order of the Sword (1st class, 1843).

HEISMAR, Fedor Klementievich (Friedrich Kaspar) (b. 23 May 1783, Severinghausen, Westphalia — d. 7 May 1848, St. Petersburg) was born to an ancient family of German barons. He studied in a boarding school in Münster and began service in the Austrian army in 1798. The following year, he served in Italy, fighting at Mantua and Novi. In 1800, he took part in the Battle of Marengo, where he was captured but released afterwards. In 1804, he left the Austrian army for the British service in India. However, while travelling, he met Russian General Anrepa on the Island of Corfu, who persuaded him enter the Russian service. So, Heismar began service as an ensign in the Siberia Grenadier Regiment in January 1805. Over the next two years, he fought the French in Naples and the Adriatic Sea. In 1807, he transferred to the Danubian Principalities, where he distinguished himself fighting the Turks at Turbat and Obilesti.

In 1808, Heismar served on several diplomatic missions to the Porte, negotiating the armistice. After the cease fire ended the following year, Heismar garnered the Order of St. George (4th class) for his courage during the assault on Slobodzea in March 1809. Serving as an adjutant to Miloradovich, he negotiated the surrender of Razgrad in June 1810 and later fought at Shimla and Giurgiu. He took a discharge with the rank of lieutenant in 1811 and settled in Romania. He returned to the army in early 1812, becoming adjutant to General Bakhmetyev. Heismar was severely wounded in the left leg at Ostrovno, and, after recuperating, he served as an adjutant to Miloradovich. In 1813, Heismar commanded a flying detachment in Saxony, fighting at Rochlitz (wounded in the right shoulder), Kulm, Altenberg, Zeitz, Leipzig and Weimar, for which he garnered a golden sabre with inscription "Citizens of Weimar to their savior—22 October 1813." He then took part in actions at Hanau and Frankfurt. For his service in the 1813 Campaign, Heismar was promoted to a staff rotmistr in the Life Guard Uhlan Regiment and, for his courage at Hanau, he received the rank of colonel.

In 1814, Heismar commanded a cavalry detachment in Belgium, capturing several small towns. After the war, he took command of the Chuguev Uhlan Regiment in 1814 and the Moscow Dragoon Regiment in 1815. Promoted to major general in 1818, he commanded a cuirassier brigade in the 1820s before taking command of the 1st Horse Jager Division in 1827. During the Russo-Turkish War of 1828-1829, he led the advance guard of the 6th Corps, capturing Bucharest in May 1828. He then fought at Giurgiu, Kalafat, Choroy, Boylesti, Turno, Rakhov, Vratz and Arnaut-Kale, for which he received the Order of St. Vladimir (2nd class). After the war, he commanded the 2nd Dragoon Division before becoming commander of the 2nd Horse Jager Division in 1831.

During the Polish Uprising of 1831, Heismar was defeated at Stoczek but was more successful commanding the advance guard of the 6th Corps at Kalushin, Janov and Grochow. In April 1831, he fought resolute rear guard actions at Milosne, Dembe-Velke and Igane. Despite his success, Heismar was briefly removed from command, returning to the army in July 1831. He distinguished himself during the assault on Warsaw, garnering the Order of St. Alexander of Neva. In 1832, he took command of the 5th Reserve Cavalry Corps and, three years later, of the 1st Infantry Corps. He rose to a general of cavalry in 1841. The following year, he took a discharge from the army and settled in the Podolsk *gubernia*. During the Hungarian Revolt in 1848-1849, he volunteered for service but died of a stroke on 7 May 1848.

HELFREICH, Bogdan Borisovich (Gothard Auguste) (b. 7 February 1776, Purgel — d. 6 December 1843, Revel) was born to a German noble family in the Estland *gubernia*. He enlisted as a private in the Life Guard Preobrazhensk Regiment on 3 March 1790 and transferred as a captain to the Narva Musketeer Regiment in 1793. He became a major in the Kizlyar Garrison in March 1799 and later served at the fortress of St. Dmitry (March 1800), in the Tiflis Musketeer Regiment (June 1803) and the Fanagoria Grenadier Regiment (July 1803). He rose to lieutenant colonel on 18 December 1804 and took command of the battalion of the Fanagoria Grenadier Regiment. During the 1805 Campaign, Helfreich distinguished himself at Austerlitz, where he led several charges and was wounded in the right side; for his actions, he garnered the Order of St. Vladimir (4th class) and took command of the Fanagoria Grenadier regiment on 13 January 1806. The same year, he joined the Army of Moldavia and took part in the opening moves of the Russo-Turkish War of 1806-1812, fighting at Adal-Viziralu, Dudeshti and Ismail, for which he earned the Order of St. George (4th class) on 9 April 1807.

In 1807, Helfreich took part in the battle at Braila, for which he received the Order of St. Anna (2nd class) and rank of colonel on 24 December 1807. Two years later, during the assault on Braila, he was wounded in the right hand while his unit was decimated by Turkish fire. In 1809-1810, he led his unit at Isaccea,

Tulcea, Constanta, Silistra (received a golden sword), Bazardjik (received a golden cross, promoted to a major general on 26 June 1810), Varna, Shumla (received the Order of St. Vladimir, 3rd class), Batin (received the order of St. Anna, 1st class) and Nikopol. Helfreich became chef of the Estland Infantry Regiment on 29 January 1811 and, in early 1812, he took command of the 2nd Brigade of the 14th Division in the 1st Corps.

During the 1812 Campaign, Helfreich fought at Klyastitsy, where he took command of the advance guard after the death of Jacob Kulnev and garnered a golden sword. He then served on the Svolnya River (received the diamond signs of the order of St. Anna), in both battles of Polotsk (received the Order of St. George, 3rd class, 16 September 1812 and the Order of St. Vladimir, 2nd class); he also saw action at Glubokoe (awarded a rent), Lubomle, Chashniki and Smolnya; near the close of the campaign, he took command of the 14th Division during the pursuit of the French army. In 1813, he led his division at Danzig, Kustrin, Spandau, Lutzen, Bautzen (received a golden sword with diamonds and the Prussian Red Eagle, 2nd class), Kulm and Leipzig, where he took a wound in the left leg and received the Austrian Order of Leopold (2nd class); for his actions at Leipzig, he was promoted to a lieutenant general on 1 August 1814 with seniority dating from 18 October 1813.

In 1814, Helfreich served at Morman, Bar sur Aube, Arcis sur Aube, Le Fère Champenoise and Paris, where he was wounded in the head and earned an Imperial letter of gratitude. He took a discharge because of his wound in early 1815 but, during the Hundred Days, he again led the 14th Division during the march to France. After the war, he commanded the 3rd Division for four years before taking command of the 1st Division on 28 February 1819. Helfreich retired because of poor health on 31 December 1823.

HELFREICH, Yegor Ivanovich (b. 4 May 1788 — d. 11 January 1866, Simferopol) was born to a German noble family in the Estland *gubernia*. He studied in the Revel Noble School and began service as a junker in the corps of engineers in 1805. The following year, he served in Essen I's corps in Poland, fighting at Ostrov. Late in 1806, he transferred to the 2nd Horse Pioneer Regiment and served in the Danubian principalities, where he took part in the sieges of Braila, Silistra, Shumla, and Ruse. For his actions, he garnered the Order of St. Anna (3rd class). Rising to staff rotmistr by 1812, he commanded a squadron of the Aleksandria Hussar Regiment in the 3rd Reserve Army of Observation and fought at Kobryn, Pruzhany, Gorodechnya, Kaidany and Borisov, where he took two serious wounds in the head and chest while leading a cavalry charge. For his conduct in these actions, Helfreich garnered the Order of St. Vladimir (4th class).

After recuperating, Helfreich became an adjutant to General Barclay de Tolly and, in 1813, he served at Lutzen (promoted to rotmistr), Freyberg, Grossenheim, Koenigswartha, Bautzen, Dresden, Kulm (received the Order of St. Anna, 2nd class) and Leipzig, where he earned a golden sabre and the Prussian Pour le Merite. He attended Barclay de Tolly throughout the 1814 Campaign, receiving the French Legion of Honor as well as an appointment to the Life Guard Hussar Regiment. However, Helfreich soon requested transfer back to the Aleksandria Hussar Regiment, receiving the rank of lieutenant colonel. During the Hundred Days, he took part in the blockade of Metz.

After the war, Helfreich rose to colonel and commander of the Narva Dragoon Regiment in 1820 and to a major general and commander of the 2nd Brigade of the 4th Cavalry Division in 1829. He participated in the suppression of the Polish Uprising in 1831, fighting at Vileyko, Veprzh, Bechy, Wilkomir, Erogal, and Lukshin. After the campaign, he became commander of the 1st (later 2nd) Brigade of the 7th Cavalry Division and received the Order of St. Stanislaus (2nd class). In 1836, Helfreich took command of the 6th Light Cavalry Division and was decorated with the Order of St. Stanislaus (1st class). The following year, he rose to a lieutenant general and, during the next two years, he earned the Orders of St. Anna (1st class) and St. Vladimir (2nd class).

In 1849, Helfreich took command of the 1st Reserve Cavalry Corps, receiving the Order of the White Eagle in 1850 and the rank of general of cavalry in 1852. During the Crimean War, he led the Cuirassier Corps defending the western provinces from possible Austrian intervention. In 1855, he commanded troops in the engagements at Kurulu-Kipnak and Chebotar. On 13 January 1856, he assumed command of the 4th Corps and was later decorated with the Order of St. Alexander of Neva. On 6 May 1857, he received the Order of St. Alexander of Neva with diamonds for fifty years of distinguished service and, two weeks later, took a discharge from the army. In retirement, Helfreich published several military treatises on cavalry tactics. He died on 11 January 1866 in Simferopol.

HERMAN (Herman von Ferzen), Ivan Ivanovich (date of birth unclear — d. 21 June 1801) descended from a Saxon noble family. He received an excellent education in German universities and entered Russian service on 29 January 1770 as a conductor 2nd class [*konduktor 2-go klassa*] in the engineers; some sources claim he entered as an ensign in 1769. He soon transferred as a divisional quartermaster of lieutenant's rank to the main headquarters on 24 November 1770. During the Russo-Turkish War of 1769-1774, Herman participated in the battles at the Larga and Kagul Rivers and was wounded during a reconnaissance on the Danube; he also completed a detailed map of Moldavia and Wallachia. In 1772, he became a senior quartermaster in Count Elmpt's corps in Poland. The following year, he served in the Corps of Observation on the Swedish border and, after completing a map of Finland, he served as a senior quartermaster to Général-en-Chef Bibikov in Orenburg.

In 1774, Herman took part in the suppression of Emelyan Pugachev's peasant revolt and led the advance guard of Prince Golitsyn's detachment in the actions at Tatishchev, Sakmarsk and other skirmishes, for which he was promoted to ober-quartermaster with a major's rank on 18 May 1774. In 1775, Catherine II ordered Herman to draw up a plan of the Tsaritsyn suburban palace near Moscow. Having completed it, he was dispatched on a secret mission to Astrakhan and Kizlyar to observe the Persian border provinces and to make a detailed map of the area between the Terek, Kuban, Don, and Volga Rivers. In 1776-1777, he served on a similar mission in the lands of Don Cossack Host and was promoted to lieutenant colonel on 24 May 1777. In 1778, he joined the Kabarda Infantry Regiment and served in the Caucasus, where he founded several forts that comprised the basis for the Caucasian Line.

For his service in Caucasus, Herman rose to a colonel on 12 January 1782 and was decorated with the Order of St. Vladimir (4th class) in 1783. The same year, he took command of the Vladimir Infantry Regiment and participated in expeditions against the mountaineers. He also supervised the construction of two major fortresses, Pregradnyi Stan [the Barrier Wall] and Prochnyi Okop [Strong Trench], in the Kuban Valley. In 1787, he took part in the organization of the Caucasus Corps and became a quartermaster general for this unit.

During the Russo-Turkish War of 1787-1791, Herman produced a map of the Caucasus and took part in military actions against mountaineers and Turks at the Laba River, Black Mountain, Mamy River and Anapa. Promoted to brigadier on 2 May 1789, Herman rose to a major general on 16 February 1790, and commanded a brigade comprised of the Kabarda, Vladimir, and Kazan Infantry Regiments. On 11 October 1790, he repulsed major Turkish invasion in the Kuban Valley, for which he received the Order of St. George (2nd class, 1 February 1791).

In 1791, Herman transferred to the Baltic galley fleet and directed the construction of the fortress of Rochensalmi. He was appointed a quartermaster general in the army of Général-en-Chef Krechetnikov in Lithuania in 1792 and produced maps of Lithuania and eastern Poland. In 1793, he commanded a corps on the right wing of Krechetnikov's army, garnering the Order of St. Anna. During the 1794 Campaign in Poland, he commanded a special corps in Prince Repnin's army, earning the Order of St. Vladimir (2nd class). In 1795, he became a quartermaster general in Prince Repnin's headquarters before taking a discharge from the army. He returned to the service one year later, becoming chef of the Schlüsselburg Musketeer Regiment on 14 December 1796 and a major general on 7 January 1798. Late in 1798, he was appointed a quartermaster general of the entire Russian army and was decorated with the Orders of St. Alexander of Neva and of St. John of Jerusalem.

One the eve of the 1799 Campaign in Italy, Emperor Paul I initially wanted Herman to advise the Russian commanders, including Field Marshal Alexander Suvorov, but later gave him command of a corps designated for joint operations with the British in Holland. Arriving in the theater of operations, Herman put up a resolute fight at Bergen before being defeated and captured by the French. However, before the news of his defeat reached St. Petersburg, Herman was promoted to general of infantry on 5 October 1799. Yet, three days later, Emperor Paul learned about the Russian defeat and had Herman discharged from the service. Although the French offered to exchange Herman for French officers captured in Italy, Paul rejected the offer and Herman remained in captivity until 1800. Returning to Russia, he was pardoned and restored in the service on 18 November 1800. Herman died on 21 June 1801 in St. Petersburg. Herman's *"Zhurnal kampanii na Kavkazskoi linii 1790"* [Journal of the Campaign on the Caucasian Line in 1790] was published in the *Otechestvennye Zapiski* in 1825.

HERMES, Bogdan Andreyevich (date of birth unclear, ca. 1758/1759 — d. 14 May 1839) was born to a Prussian noble family in Vilna. He studied in the Artillery and Engineer Cadet Corps and began service as a shtyk junker in the artillery in 1774, rising to a sub-lieutenant in 1779. He served in the Crimea in 1782 and joined the Bombardier Regiment as a lieutenant in 1786. During the Russo-Turkish War of 1787-1791, Hermes distinguished himself at Ochakov, for which he garnered a golden cross. In 1789, he became an adjutant to Général-en-Chef Müller-Zakomelsky and took part in the Russo-Swedish War in 1790, earning a holden sword.

Hermes rose to lieutenant colonel in 1794, to colonel in 1796 and to major general in 1798. In 1798-1799, he trained the artillery battalions in the Ukraine and the Crimea. In February 1800, he took a discharge from the army and transferred to the civil service, receiving the rank of actual state counsellor and becoming Deputy Governor of Novorossiisk on 27 October 1800. The following year, he became the Governor of Tobolsk and, in 1806, the Governor of Perm. Promoted to privy counsellor in 1811, Hermes was appointed in the Senate in 1817 and rose to an actual privy counsellor on 21 April 1832.

HERZDORF, Karl Maksimovich (b. 1761 – date of death unknown; removed from rosters on 4 October 1813) descended from a Danish noble family. He entered Russian service as a captain in the Astrakhan Grenadier Regiment on 16 June 1788. During the Russo-Turkish War of 1788-1791, he distinguished himself at Ochakov (received a golden cross) and Ismail, where he garnered the Order of St. George (4th class) on 11 April 1792. Promoted to colonel on 13 November 1798, Herzdorf served took command of the Sevsk Musketeer Regiment on 16 July 1798.

Herzdorf fought under General Rimsky-Korsakov at Zurich in Switzerland in 1799 and rose to major general and chef of the Uglitsk Musketeer Regiment on 3 April 1800. In 1806-1807, he served with the 14th Division, fighting at Mohrungen, Eylau, Heilsberg and

Friedland. His unit was transformed into the Uglitsk Infantry Regiment in 6 March 1811. The following year, he became head of the military court for the 1st Western Army on 24 June 1812. Late that year, he took part in the organization of the Russo-German Legion.

HESSE, Ivan Krestyanovich (b. 1757 — d. 21 May 1816, Moscow) was born to a Saxon noble family. He began service in the Saxon army and entered Russian service as a sergeant in the Gatchina Artillery on 20 March 1788. He became first instructor of the Gatchina Artillery Company and enjoyed a series of quick promotions, becoming a sub-lieutenant on 24 September 1792, a lieutenant on 6 July 1793, a lieutenant captain in 1795 and a captain on 6 November 1796.

Hesse commanded a company in the Gatchina Artillery Regiment in early 1796 before joining the Life Guard Artillery Battalion on 20 November 1796. A week later, he became a *platz* major of Moscow and then the Commandant of Moscow on 26 May 1797. Over the next two years, Hesse quickly rose through the ranks becoming a major general on 25 August 1799. Under Alexander, his career was not as illustrious since Hesse received promotion to lieutenant general only ten years later on 24 December 1809. He died on 21 May 1816 in Moscow.

HESSE (Hesse II), Karl Fedorovich (b. 1788 — d. 16 December 1842) was born to a noble family in the Lifland *gubernia*; the son of Colonel Fedor Ivanovich Hesse, Commandant of Vyborg until 1800. He was enlisted as a sub-ensign in the Vyborg Garrison in 1793 and rose to portupei-ensign in 1803. The following year, he transferred to the Ryazan Infantry Regiment, where he received promotion to ensign on 19 July 1803. During the 1805 Campaign, he served in Tolstoy's corps in Pomerania. Two years later, he served with the 14th Division in Poland, fighting at Eylau (received a golden cross), Guttstadt, Heilsberg (received the Order of St. Vladimir, 4th class) and Friedland, for which he garnered the Order of St. Anna (4th class). On 24 December 1807, Hesse became a lieutenant.

In 1808-1809, Hesse served as an adjutant to Prince Gorchakov and Count Kamensky in Finland, where he earned the rank of staff captain on 24 December 1808, and a golden sword in 1809. Hesse followed Kamensky to the Danubian Principalities, where he distinguished himself at Silistra, Shumla (received the Order of St. Anna, 2nd class), Ruse, Batin, and Nikopol, earning a promotion to captain on 14 December 1810. The next year, he joined the Schlüsselburg Infantry Regiment on 9 August 1811. During the 1812 Campaign, he served with the Army of Danube on the Berezina and during the pursuit of the French troops; he garnered the rank of major on 16 December 1812. Hesse did not participate in the military operations of 1813 because he remained with the reserves in the Duchy of Warsaw. He transferred to the Arkhangelogorod Infantry Regiment in late 1814 and served in the blockade of Metz during the Hundred Days in 1815.

Returning to Russia, Hesse was promoted to lieutenant colonel in the Life Guard Pavlovsk Regiment on 8 January 1816 and took command of a battalion of this unit on 9 April 1816. Made colonel on 6 January 1818, Hesse took command of the 38th Jager Regiment on 15 March 1820 and received the Order of St. George (4th class) on 24 December 1824 for twenty-five years of service. He rose to a major general on 18 December 1826 and served in the 19th Division before taking command of the 3rd Brigade of the 22nd Division on 15 April 1827. The same year, he became the Civil Governor of the western Georgian provinces of Imereti, Guria, and Mingrelia, garnering the Order of St. Vladimir (3rd class, 20 February 1829) for his effective service.

During the Russo-Turkish War of 1828-1829, Hesse fought at Poti (received the Order of St. Anna, 1st class), Liman, Mukha- Estat, Kintrima and Tsikhis Dziri. For his actions, he received a golden sword with diamonds and took command of the Caucasian Reserve Grenadier Brigade. In 1830, he took part in the suppression of an uprising in Abkhazia. Hesse became a lieutenant general on 18 December 1835 and was relieved of command in October 1837. He took a discharge on 19 December 1838 and died on 16 December 1842.

HESSE, Vladimir Antonovich (b. 1764 — d. 26 April 1828) was born to a noble family from the Lifland *gubernia*. He enlisted as a corporal in the Pskov Carabinier Regiment in 1776, rising to a cornet in 1786. He took part in the Russo-Swedish War of 1789-1790 and the operations against the Poles in 1792. He later transferred to the Kiev Grenadier Regiment and participated in the opening moves of the Russo-Turkish War in 1806-1807, becoming a colonel on 24 December 1807. Three years later, he became chef of the Little Russia (*Malorossiiskii*) Grenadier Regiment on 31 October 1810.

In 1812, Hesse commanded the 3rd Brigade of the 2nd Grenadier Division in the 8th Corps of the 2nd Western Army at Smolensk, Dorogobouzh, Tarutino, Maloyaroslavets (received the Order of St. Anna, 2nd class) and Krasnyi. The following year, he served at Lutzen, Koenigswartha, Bautzen and Leipzig, rising to a major general on 27 September 1813. After serving in France in 1814, he took command of the 1st Brigade of the 10th Division on 10 November 1814. Three years later, he was relieved of command on 23 November 1817 for illegally marrying a Frenchwoman in 1815 despite his previous marriage in Russia. After a clerical court annuled his marriage, Hesse was court martialed for disgracing officer's code and discharged from the army on 8 January 1822. However, later that year, Hesse was restored in the rank and later commanded a brigade of the 27th Division before retiring on 24 November 1824.

HITROVO (Khitrovo), Mikhail Yeliseyevich (b. 1765 — d. 30 July 1848) was born to a noble family and was enlisted as a sergeant in the Life Guard Izmailovsk Regiment in 1775. He transferred to the Bombardier Company of the Life Guard Preobrazhensk Regiment on 22 December 1776. Eleven years later, Hitrovo returned with the rank of captain in 1787 but soon returned to the army becoming a rotmistr in the Kazan Cuirasser Regiment; he later joined the St. Petersburg Dragoon Regiment. On 29 October 1788, he rose to premier major and participated in the Russo-Turkish War of 1787-1791, distinguishing himself at Ochakov (earned the Order of St. Vladimir, 4th class), Kaushani, Akkerman and Bender. Promoted to second major on 20 February 1790, he transferred to the Byelorussia Jager Corps later that year. In 1796, he joined the Nizov Infantry Regiment; two years later, he became commander of this unit on 29 July 1798 and earned promoted to colonel on 13 August 1798.

Hitrovo participated in the 1799 Campaigns in Italy and Switzerland and served in Prince Peter Bagration's detachment, distinguishing himself at Lecco, Marengo (garnered the Order of St. Anna, 2nd class), Alessandria, Serravalle, Novi (awarded the Order of St. John of Jerusalem), St. Gothard, Devil's Bridge and the Panixer Pass. Hitrovo became a major general and chef of the Nizhegorod Infantry Regiment on 13 October 1799 and led this unit until 7 May 1811.

Hitrovo fought at Ismail, Braila (wounded in the neck), Turtukai, and Ruse during the Russo-Turkish War of 1806-1812. He was discharged because of poor health on 5 September 1811, and spent the next six years at his estate. He returned to service on 23 May 1816, becoming commander of the 2nd Brigade of the 27th Division. Three months later, Hitrovo took command of the 1st Brigade of the same division on 26 September. He was relieved of command in 1817 and appointed head of the 9th District of the Internal Guard in 1819. After twelve years of service, Hitrovo retired on 20 December 1833, and died on 30 July 1848.

HITROVO, Nikolay Zakharovich (b. 1779 — d. 1826) was born to a noble family. He was enlisted as a sergeant in the Life Guard Izmailovsk Regiment in 1786 but later transferred as a cornet to the Life Guard Horse Regiment. In 1801, Hitrovo became a flügel adjutant to Emperor Paul. Three years later, he became colonel and commander of the Pskov Dragoon Regiment on 21 February 1804. In 1806-1807, he served with the 4th Division in Poland, fighting at Proschino, Ostrolenka, Pultusk and on the Narew River. Hitrovo was then dispatched to the Danubian Principalities, where he was seriously wounded during the assault on Braila in 1809.

After recuperating, Hitrovo was disgraced (for reasons that still remain unclear) by Emperor Alexander, who exiled him to Vyatka for a year and then lived under house arrest in Kaluga. Hitrovo was pardoned after his father-in-law, Field Marshal Mikhai Kutuzov, appealed to Alexander I. Before his death in 1826, Hitrovo served as a member of the Moscow Historical Society. Another **Hitrovo, Nikolay Fedorovich**, commanded the Sumsk Hussar Regiment between September 1799 and January 1800.

HOLSTEIN-OLDENBURG, Paul Friedrich August (b. 1783 — d. 1853) descended from the ruling house of the Holstein-Oldenburg principality. He arrived to Russia in late 1810 and entered Russian service with the rank of lieutenant general on 3 August 1811; he was also appointed the Military Governor of Revel and chef of the 1st Jager Regiment. During the 1812 Campaign, he served in the headquarters of the 1st Western Army, distinguishing himself at Borodino and Krasnyi, where he was wounded. After the war, he served in the Estland *gubernia*, rising to a general of infantry on 24 December 1823 before returning to Oldenburg in 1836.

I

command and ordered him to return to his estate. Iashvili spent the next three years at Muromtsevo in the Kaluga *gubernia*, where he died on 1 August 1815.

IASHVILI (Yashvil), Vladimir Mikhailovich (b. 26 July 1764 — d. 1 August 1815, Muromtsevo) was born to a prominent Georgian noble family. He graduated from the Artillery and Engineer Cadet Corps in 1786 and served in the Bombardier Regiment and Life Guard Artillery Battallion. He participated in the Russo-Turkish War in 1788-1791 and distinguished himself at Bender, Kinburn and Ismail (received a golden cross). In 1792-1794, he served in Poland and received a golden cross for Praga. He became commander of the 6th Artillery Regiment on 2 May 1800 and was promoted to major general on 15 November 1800. He actively participated in the conspiracy against Emperor Paul in March 1801.

Under Alexander I, Iashvili transferred to the Life Guard Artillery Battalion on 28 March 1801 and became chef of the 10th Artillery Battalion on 8 September 1801. However, Alexander soon disgraced him for his involvement in the conspiracy against Emperor Paul, had discharged him on 25 October 1801 and exiled to the Kaluga *gubernia* in 1803, prohibiting him from entering St. Petersburg and Moscow. Iashvili remained at his estate for the next nine years. During the 1812 Campaign, he volunteered for the *opolchenye* service and was granted permission by General F. Shepelev. Iashvili distinguished himself in the battle at Yelna, but Emperor Alexander, upon hearing about his enlistment, had him removed from the

IASHVILI (Yashvil), Leo Mikhailovich (b. 1768 — d. 1 May 1836, Kiev) was born to a prominent Georgian noble family, the brother of Vladimir Iashvili. He studied in the Artillery and Engineer Cadet Corps and was appointed as shtyk-junker in the Bombardier Regiment on 23 May 1786. He participated in the Russo-Turkish War from 1788-1791, fighting at Akkerman, Bender and Ismail. In 1794, he served in Poland, distinguished himself at Warsaw and Praga and was awarded the Order of St. George (4th class) on 12 January 1795. He transferred to the Life Guard Artillery Battalion in 1799 and was promoted to colonel on 17 May 1800. Iashvili participated in the 1805 Campaign, and distinguished himself in rear guard actions and battles at Wischau and Austerlitz. In 1806-1807, Iashvili served in Poland and took part in the battles at Pultusk, Eylau, Guttstadt, Friedland. For his actions, he was promoted to major general on 28 March 1808 and awarded the Order of St. George (3rd class) on 3 May 1808.

In 1812, Iashvili commanded the 1st Reserve Artillery Brigade of Wittgenstein's corps, fighting at Jakubovo, Klyastitsy, Golovchin, Smolyani and Borisov. For his actions, he was promoted to lieutenant general on 30 October 1812 with seniority dating from 30 July 1812 and he was decorated with the Orders of St. Vladimir (2nd class) and of St. Anna (1st class) with diamonds. In 1813-1814, he served as an artillery commander of the main Russian army and participated in most of the major battles in Germany and France. After the war, he was promoted to general of artillery on 13 January 1819 and served as artillery commander of the 1st Army from 1816-1833. He became a member of the Council of War of the Ministry of War on 23 June 1832. During his career, Iashvili also received the Orders of St. Andrew the First Called, of St. Vladimir (1st class), of St. Alexander of Neva with diamonds, of St. Anna (1st class) with diamonds, the Prussian Pour le Merite and Red Eagle (1st class), two golden swords with diamonds for courage and a career medal "For XXXV Years of Distinguished Service."

IGELSTROM, Alexander Yevstafievich (b. 2 July 1770, Kerrafen — d. 14 May 1855, Revel) was born to a noble family in the Estland *gubernia*. He began service as a page in the Imperial Court on 31 March 1781 and rose to a kamer-page on 18 September 1788. Three years later, he enlisted as a lieutenant in the Life Guard Preobrazhensk Regiment on 22 January 1791. In December of the same year, he transferred as a second major to the Kiev Horse Jager Regiment. He served in Poland in 1792-1794, distinguishing himself at Plotsk (received the Prussian Pour le Merite), Maciejowice (received the Order of St. Vladimir, 4th class) and Praga, for which he was promoted to lieutenant colonel. Made full colonel on 4 January 1798, he took command of the Starodoub Cuirassier Regiment on 22 September 1798. The following year, he rose to a major general and chef of the Sofia Cuirassier Regiment on 5 May 1799 but, on 20 July, he was discharged from the army for his tardy submission of reports.

Igelstrom returned to the military service twelve years later (29 September 1812) and commanded a cavalry reserve in the 1st Corps at Polotsk, Chashniki, Smolyani, on the Berezina, Koenigsberg and Elbing; for his actions, he garnered the Orders of St. Vladimir (3rd class) and of St. Anna (2nd class). In March – May 1813, he served as a duty general in the main headquarters of the Russian army and participated in the battles at Magdeburg, Lutzen (received the Order of St. Anna, 1st class, and the Prussian Red Eagle, 2nd class), Bautzen, Reichenbach and Gorlitz. He became seriously ill in June 1813 and left the army to recuperate. After the war, he supervised cavalry depots of the 1st Army before taking a discharge on 14 January 1836.

IGNATIEV, Dmitry Lvovich (b. 24 April 1771 — d. 27 July 1833, Bogoroditskoe, Tula *gubernia*) was born to a noble family from the Tula *gubernia*. He enlisted as a sub ensign in the Life Guard Preobrazhensk Regiment on 4 November 1795, transferring to the Life Guard Semeyonovsk Regiment in 1804 and to the Leib Hussar (Life Guard Hussar) Regiment in 1807. During the 1807 Campaign in Poland, he fought at Guttstadt, Heilsberg and Friedland. Two years later, he participated in the crossing of the Gulf of Bothnia to capture the Aland Islands.

In 1812, Ignatiev served in the coastal defense of the Lifland and Courland *gubernia*s before joining the 1st Corps. He participated in the actions at Wilkomir, Jakubovo, Klyastitsy, Golovchin, both battles of Polotsk (received the Order of St. George, 4th class, for the first battle; promoted to a colonel for the second), Chashniki, Smolyani, Borisov and on the Berezina. In 1813, he fought at Wittenberg, Lutzen, Bautzen, Pirna, Peterswalde, Dresden, Hollendorf, Kulm and Leipzig, rising to major general on 1 August 1814 with seniority dating from 18 October 1813. After the war, he commanded the 1st Brigade of the 1st Hussar Division before transfering to the 2nd Hussar Division on 24 December 1817 and becoming a duty general in the 2nd Army on 29 July 1818. However, he took a discharge because of poor health on 21 March 1822 and spent the last ten years of his life at his estate in the Tula *gubernia*.

IGNATIEV, Gabriel Alexandrovich (b. 1768 — d. 5 April 1852) was born to a noble family from the St. Petersburg *gubernia*. He studied in the Artillery and Engineer Cadet Corps and began service as an ensign in the Corps of Engineers on 14 September 1785. During the Russo-Turkish War of 1787-1791, he distinguished himself at Ismail, earning a golden cross and rank of lieutenant. In 1793, he served in the Russian embassy in Istambul. Returning to Russia, he participated in Alexander Suvorov's campaigns in Italy and Switzerland in 1799, becoming a colonel on 22 October 1799. In March 1800–July 1801, he commanded the 8th Artillery Regiment.

During the 1805 Campaign, Ignatiev fought at Amstetten, Krems and Austerlitz. Two years later, he served with Essen's corps at Ostrolenka. He rose to major general on 28 March 1808. In 1810, he directed reconstruction of the fortress of Bobruisk. During the 1812 Campaign, he organized the defense of Bobruisk, for which he received the Order of St. Vladimir (2nd class). During the 1813-1814 Campaigns, he remained in the Minsk *gubernia*, organizing supplies and reinforcements. After the war, he commanded artillery in the 6th and 2nd Corps, rising to a lieutenant general on 2 October 1821. He became director of the Artillery Department of the Ministry of War on 20 April 1826 and received a promotion to general of artillery on 3 May 1829. Four years later, he was appointed a member of the General Audit on 5 August 1833.

ILOVAYSKY, Aleksey Ivanovich (date of birth unclear, ca. 1735/1736 — d. 1797) was born to a Cossack noble family. He distinguished himself during the Russo-Turkish War of 1769-1774, and then took part in the suppression of Pugachev's uprising in 1774. He rose to colonel and ataman of the Don Cossack Host in 1795, serving at this position for twenty two years. In late 1796, he was promoted to a general of cavalry but died in Moscow in early 1797. His brother, **Dmitry Ivanovich Ilovaysky** served as a *nakaznoi ataman* [governing ataman] during his term and had six sons, who distinguished themselves commanding Cossack regiments during the Napoleonic Wars.

ILOVAYSKY (Ilovaysky III), Aleksey Vasilievich (b. 1767 — d. 9 February 1842) was born to a Don Cossack noble family. He began service as a esaul in 1776 and served on the Tsarytsino Line in 1776-1778, on the Bug River in 1781-1782 and on the Caucasian Line in 1784-1786. During the Russo-Turkish War of 1787-1791, he distinguished himself at Focsani, Rimnic (promoted to a premier major), Ismail (wounded, promoted to a lieutenant colonel) and Macin. Promoted to a colonel on 25 October

1794, he rose to a major general on 19 November 1798 but was discharged on 21 December 1798. He returned to the Don Cossack Host, where he remained for the next fourteen years, briefly serving in the Cossack Field Chancellery.

In 1812, Ilovaysky served as a campaign ataman [*pokhodnoi ataman*] of the Don Cossack Host, bringing Cossack reinforcements to the Tarutino Camp. In October-December 1812, Ilovaysky led Cossack detachments at Tarutino, Maloyaroslavets, Kolotsk, Gzhatsk, Vyazma, Dorogobouzh, Dukhovshina, and other minor actions during the French pursuit, for which he garnered the Order of St. George (3rd class, 6 April 1813).

During the 1813 Campaign, Ilovaysky participated in the actions at Elbing, Marienburg, Danzig, Stettin, Torgau, Magdeburg, Dennewitz, and others. After the war, he served on the committee to reorganize the Don Cossack Host in 1820. He officially returned to military service on 12 February 1821, serving as a governing ataman [*nakaznoi ataman*] of the Don Cossack Host. Promoted to lieutenant general on 1 October 1821, he became a military ataman [*voiskovoi ataman*] of the Don Cossack Host on 4 May 1822. He was relieved of command for criticism of the government policies in the region on 19 June 1827 and retired on 24 September 1831.

ILOVAYSKY (Ilovaysky IX), Gregory Dmitryevich (b. 4 October 1778 — d. 29 July 1847) was born to a prominent Don Cossack family; the son of General of Cavalry Ataman Dmitry Ilovaysky. He enlisted as a Cossack on 16 January 1787 and rose to a sotnik on 27 May 1788. During the Russo-Turkish War of 1787-1791, he served at Ochakov, Kaushani, Bender, Killia and Ismail (received a golden cross). In 1801, he took part in the expedition to India, but the Cossack corps advanced only as far as Orenburg. He served with his brothers in Poland in 1806-1807, fighting at Eylau (wounded in the right side), Allenstein, Guttstadt, Heilsberg and Friedland, receiving the Order of St. George (4th class) on 17 August 1807.

Made colonel on 23 January 1810, Ilovaysky served in the Don Host in early 1812. During the 1812 Campaign, he brought reinforcements to the Tarutino Camp and later fought at Medyn, Lyakhov, Krasnyi, Orsha and Vilna. In 1813, he served in the siege of Danzig and rose to a major general on 30 July 1813 with seniority dating from 3 November 1812. After the war, he returned to the Don Host, serving in the Don Cossack Field Chancellery, and retired in 1827.

His family included six brothers, all serving in the Napoleonic Wars: **Ivan ILOVAYSKY (Ilovaysky IV)** (see below), **Vasily ILOVAYSKY (Ilovaysky XII)** (see below). **ILOVAYSKY (Ilovaysky II), Pavel (Paul) Dmitryevich** (b. 1764 – d. 1810) commanded a Cossack regiment during the Russo-Turkish War of 1806-1812, distinguishing himself at Ruse in

1810; **ILOVAYSKY (Ilovaysky VIII), Stepan Dmitryevich** (b. 1778 — d. 11 February 1816) participated in General Alexander Suvorov's campaign in Italy and Switzerland in 1799 and commanded a Cossack regiment during the 1806-1807 Campaigns in Poland. **ILOVAYSKY (Ilovaysky XI), Timofei Dmitryevich** (b. 1786 – d. 9 December 1812) commanded a Cossack regiment during the 1812 Campaign and was mortally wounded at Vilna on 9 December 1812.

ILOVAYSKY (Ilovaysky IV), Ivan Dmitryevich (b. 1766 – date of death unclear) was born to a Don Cossack noble family; the son of General of Cavalry Ataman Dmitry Ilovaysky. He began service as a Cossack on 1 June 1772 and rose to a sotnik on 28 March 1775. He served on the Caucasian Line in 1782-1786 and, during the Russo-Turkish War of 1787-1791, he fought at Kinburn, Ochakov (wounded in the leg, earned a golden cross), Kaushani, Bender and Ismail (received a golden cross). He took command of a Cossack regiment in 1789 and became a colonel on 24 December 1797 and a major general on 17 May 1799. He took a discharge on 6 April 1804 but returned to service on 22 May 1806.

During the 1807 Campaign in Poland, Ilovaysky participated in actions at Guttstadt, Heilsberg and Friedland. In 1812, his regiment was attached to Platov's Cossack corps and Ilovaysky took part in the battles at Romanovo, Velizh and Ruza. He was one of the first to enter Moscow after the French abandoned the Russian capital and briefly served as city commandant. Later, Ilovaysky received the Order of St. George (3rd class, 6 October 1813) for his actions during the French retreat. In 1813-1814, he distinguished himself at Lutzen, Bautzen, Leipzig, Craonne, Laon, Rheims and Paris. After the war, he returned to the Don Host and retired on 16 December 1827.

ILOVAYSKY (Ilovaysky V), Nikolay Vasilievich (b. 1772 – d. 26 July 1838) was born to a Don Cossack noble family. He began service as a Cossack on 20 May 1779 and rose to esaul on 7 July 1783. He served in the Caucasian Line in 1784-1787 and, during the Russo-Turkish War of 1787-1791, he distinguished himself at Hajibey (Odessa), Bender, Ismail and Macin. He served in Poland from 1792-1794, and in the Persian expedition along the Caspian Sea in 1796. Made colonel on 3 February 1798, he rose to a major general on 1 July 1799. However, he was discharged from the army on 16 October 1799 and returned to the army on 19 July 1801, serving as a campaign ataman [pokhodnoi ataman] in 1802-1805.

During the 1807 Campaign in Poland, Ilovaysky distinguished himself at Guttstadt, Heilsberg and Friedland, for which he garnered the Order of St. George (3rd class) on 17 August 1807. He was then dispatched to the Danubian Principalities, where he fought the Turks at Braila, Rassevat, Silistra and Shumla in

1809-1810. In 1812, he served in Ataman Platov's Cossack corps, fighting at Mir, Romanovo (wounded in the leg), Molevo Boloto (Inkovo), Smolensk, Borodino, Vyazma, Semlevo, Dukhovshina, Krasnyi, Borisov and Vilna. He rose to lieutenant general on 27 February 1813 and participated in the battles of Lutzen and Bautzen. However, Ilovaysky became seriously ill in June 1813 and took a furlough to recuperate. He returned to the Don Host, where he carried out the duties of governing ataman [*nakaznoi ataman*] between April 1815 and January 1817. He retired on 27 July 1818.

ILOVAYSKY (Ilovaysky X), Osip Vasilievich (b. 1775 – d. 21 February 1839) was born to a Don Cossack noble family. He began service as a Cossack on 26 March 1790 and rose to an esaul on 9 July 1791. He participated in the Russo-Turkish War of 1787-1791, distinguishing himself at Ochakov (received a golden cross) and Macin. He then took part in the operations in Poland from 1792-1794, garnering a golden cross for Praga. In 1796, he took part in the Persian expedition along the Caspian Sea. On 13 March 1800, he took command of a Cossack regiment, distinguishing himself during the 1806-1807 Campaigns in Poland, for which he garnered the Order of St. George (4th class, 17 August 1807) and a golden sword.

Ilovaysky served in the Danubian Principalities in 1809-1810, fighting at Braila, Silistra, Tataritsa and Shumla; for his actions, he was promoted to lieutenant colonel on 10 June 1809 and to colonel on 18 September 1810. In 1812, he served in the 2nd Western Army and took part in the actions at Saltanovka (Moghilev), Smolensk, Borodino, Maloyaroslavets and Vilna. The following year, he fought at Danzig, Lutzen (promoted to a major general on 27 September 1813 with seniority dating from 2 May 1813), Bautzen and Leipzig. In 1814, he served at Le Fère Champenoise, Arcis sur Aube and Sezan. After the war, he returned to the Don Host, where he served as a leader of Cossack nobility in 1821-1824.

ILOVAYSKY (Ilovaysky XII), Vasily Dmitryevich (b. 10 February 1788 — d. 15 November 1860) was the son of General of Cavalry Ataman Dmitry Ilovaysky. He enlisted as a Cossack in the Ataman Cossack Regiment in 1792 and rose to esaul in 1795. Ilovaysky then studied in the Artillery and Engineer Cadet Corps in 1798-1801 and served in the Ataman Cossack Regiment in 1801 before joining Ilovaysky II's Cossack Regiment in October 1802. In 1806-1807, Ilovaysky and his six brothers served in Poland. He commanded Cossack detachments at Pultusk, Jankovo, Eylau (received a golden cross), Guttstadt, Heilsberg and Friedland. For his service in 1807, he was decorated with the Order of St. Anna (4th class) and a golden sabre.

In 1808-1810, Ilovaysky served with Ilovaysky II's Cossack Regiment in the Army of Moldavia, fighting at Braila (received the Order of St. Vladimir, 4th class), Macin, Babadag, Girsov, two combats at Rassevat (received the Orders of St. George, 4th class, and of St. Anna, 2nd class), Silistra (commanded a Cossack regiment), Tataritsa, Bazardjik (promoted to a lieutenant colonel), Shumla, Batin (promoted to a colonel, 7 December 1810) and Nikopol. In 1811, he distinguished himself at Ruse, where General Kutuzov surrounded the entire Turkish army; for his actions, Ilovaysky was decorated with the Order of St. Vladimir (3rd class).

During the 1812 Campaign, Ilovaysky initially commanded a Cossack regiment in the 2nd Western Army, serving at Romanovo and Smolensk. In August–September 1812, Ilovaysky led Cossack detachments at Velizh, Porechye, Surazh, Khimki (promoted to a major general on 28 September 1812). He was one of the first to enter Moscow after the French abandoned the Russian capital. During the French retreat, Ilovaysky distinguished himself at Dukhovshina, Orsha and Kovno, for which he garnered the diamond signs of the Order of St. Anna (2nd class). In the spring of 1813, Ilovaysky led Cossack detachments in Winzegorode's corps, fighting at Nordhausen, Naumburg, Weissenfels, Lutzen, Koenigswartha, Bautzen, and Gorlitz. In June 1813, he took command of all reserve Cossack regiments in the main Russian army. He distinguished himself at Kulm, garnering the Order of St. Anna (2nd class). In October, he served at Pegau, Leipzig, and Hanau, for which he earned the Order of St. George (3rd class, 22 December 1813). In addition, for his service in 1813, Ilovaysky was decorated with the Prussian Red Eagle (2nd class) and a golden saber with diamonds.

During the 1814 Campaign, Ilovaysky took part in the actions at Vassy (received the Order of St. Vladimir, 2nd class), Nogent, Bar sur Aube, Labrusselle, Troyes (received the diamond signs of the Order of St. Anna, 1st class and the Austrian Order of Leopold, 1st class, for the last four actions), Arcis sur Aube, Le Fère Champenoise and Paris, for which he again garnered the diamond signs of the Order of St. Anna (1st class). Returning to Russia, Ilovaysky was appointed ataman of the Don Cossack regiments in the Caucasus in 1823 and rose to a lieutenant general on 7 September 1826. During the Russo-Persian War in 1827, he commanded Cossack detachments in General Paskevich's corps, fighting at Shulaveri, Abbas-Abad, Djavan-Bulah (received a golden snuffbox with diamonds), Echmiadzin and Sardar-Abad, where he became seriously ill and returned to the Don Host. Ilovaysky spent another thirteen years in the service until retiring on 6 April 1840.

INZOV, Ivan Nikitich (b. 1768, St. Petersburg — d. 8 June 1845) was born to a Russian noble family. He enlisted as a cornet in the Sumsk Light Horse Regiment on 17 January 1785. Four months later, he became an auditor with lieutenant's rank and transferred to the Tula Infantry Regiment on 18 May 1785. On 13 February 1787, he received a rank of lieutenant in the Narva Infantry Regiment and then joined the Moscow Grenadier Regiment on 14 May 1789. During the Russo-Turkish War of 1787-1791, Inzov took part in actions on the Salchea River, Ismail, Bender, and Macin, for which he received a promotion to lieutenant and appointment as flügel adjutant to Prince N. Repnin. He served in Poland in 1794 and had honor of delivering the news of the Battle of Maciejowice to Empress Catherine II, for which he was promoted to a premier major. In 1795, he rose to a general adjutant to Prince Repnin and, in 1796, he became an inspector adjutant to Emperor Paul. Two years later, he accomplished a diplomatic mission to Berlin and was promoted to lieutenant colonel.

During the 1799 Campaign in Italy and Switzerland, Inzov replaced the wounded commander of the Apsheron Musketeer Regiment and led this unit at Cassano, Verderio, on the Tidone and Trebbia Rivers, at Novi and across the Alps. For his actions, he was decorated with the Orders of St. Anna (2nd class) with diamonds and of St. John of Jerusalem and was promoted to colonel on 7 January 1800. He officially took command of the Apsheron Musketeer Regiment on 24 August 1800. Four years later, he became a major general and commander of the Kiev Grenadier Regiment on 30 November 1804. During the 1805 Campaign, he served as a duty general to Mikhail Kutuzov, receiving the Order of St. Vladimir (3rd class). In 1806, he took command of a brigade in the 10th Division and participated in the opening moves of the Russo-Turkish War, fighting at Khotin. He then marched with Essen's corps to Poland, where he distinguished himself at Ostrolenka, for which he earned the Order of St. George (4th class).

In 1809, Inzov served in Golitsyn's corps in Galicia and was dispatched to the Danubian Principalities, where hedistinguished himself at Silistra, Shumla (earned a golden sword with diamonds), Ruse, Giurgiu, and Nikopol. In 1812, he was appointed chief of staff of the 3rd Reserve Army of Observation, serving at Kobryn and Gorodechna (earned the Order of St. Vladimir, 2nd class). After the creation of the Army of Danube, Inzov took command of the 9th Division and fought at Borisov, on the Berezina, at Stakhov, Brily, and other minor engagements. In the spring of 1813, he served at Thorn (Order of St. George, 3rd class, 14 May 1813), Koenigswartha, and Bautzen (received the diamond signs of the Order of St. Anna, 1st class). He was appointed chef of the Kiev Grenadier Regiment on 10 May 1813, and a duty general in the Army of Poland on 15 July 1813.

From August 1813—March 1814, Inzov took part in the battles at Dresden and Leipzig, and in the sieges of Magdeburg and Hamburg. For his actions at Hamburg, he was promoted to lieutenant general on 26 August 1814 and received the French Legion of Honor in 1815. After the war, he became chief of staff of the 2nd Army on 2 January 1816 and took command of the 18th Division on 21 April 1816. Two years later, he became Chief Curator and Chair of the Committee of the Colonists of the Souther Regions of Russia on 22 January 1818. He was appointed the Viceroy of Bessarabia on 27 June 1820 and the Governor General of the Novorossiisk *gubernia*s, retaining the position of Viceroy of Bessarabia on 29 July 1822. He was replaced by Count Mikhail Vorontsov on 19 May 1823; Inzov received the Order of St. Alexander of Neva for his service. Promoted to a general of infantry on 7 July 1828, Inzov served in the Committee of the Colonists of the Souther Regions of Russia until 1844, when he retired and settled in Odessa.

IVANOV, Ivan Dmitrievich (b. 1764 — d. 22 August 1828) was born to a petty noble family in the Tver *Gubernia*. He enlisted as a sub ensign in the Novgorod Infantry Regiment on 12 January 1779 and rose to sergeant in 1780 before transferring to the Tula Infantry Regiment in 1785, where he received a rank of ensign on 7 October 1786. During the Russo-Turkish War of 1787-1791, he transferred as a sub-lieutenant to the St. Petersburg Grenadier Regiment and fought on the Salcea River, at Ismail and Bender in 1789. The next year, he joined the Byelorussia Jager Corps, distinguishing himself at Ismail for which he garnered a promotion to lieutenant. In 1792-1794, he served in Poland, fighting at Warsaw, Maciejowice and Praga, for which he earned a rank of captain. Under Emperor Paul I, Ivanov joined the newly established 9th Jager Regiment, later redesignated as the 8th Jager Regiment.

During the 1805 Campaign, Ivanov commanded a battalion of the 8th Jagers at Krems and Austerlitz; for these actions, he was decorated with the Order of St. Anna (3rd class) and the order of St. Vladimir (4th class).

Promoted to colonel on 5 May 1806, he took command of the 8th Jager Regiment on 22 January 1807. He served in Essen's corps in Poland, fighting at Goncharovo, Dronze, Olshevo and Ostrolenka. For his service, Ivanov received the Order of St. Anna (2nd class) and was appointed chef of the 10th Jager Regiment on 24 August 1807. Two years later, he served with Golitsyn's corps in Galicia and, in 1810, joined the Army of Moldavia in the Danubian Principalities. During the next two years, he took part in actions at Plevno, Lovchea (received the Order of St. Vladimir, 3rd class, 1811), Selvi and Ruse (received the diamond signs of St. Anna, 2nd class).

In 1812, Ivanov served with the 3rd Brigade of the 9th Division in the 3rd Reserve Army of Observation at Kobryn, Pruzhany, Gorodechna, on the Styr River (received a golden sword), Turisk, Gorodnya, Lobomle, Mukhavtsy, and Stakhov, where he was seriously wounded in the right side; for his courage at Stakhov, Ivanov was promoted to a major general on 28 July 1813, with seniority dating from 28 November 1812. After recuperating, he returned to his regiment in August 1813, and took command of the 3rd Brigade of the 9th Division in the Army of Silesia. In August-October 1813, he fought at Dohna, Dresden, and Pirna. From December 1813 to May 1814, he participated in the siege of Hamburg, for which he earned the Order of St. George (3rd class).

After the war, Ivanov continued commanding the 3rd brigade of the 9th Division and served in the blockade of Metz during the Hundred Days in 1815. He then served in Vorontsov's corps in France, receiving the French Legion of Honor (2nd class) and the Baden Order of the Lion. Returning to Russia, he became commander of the 16th Division on 30 April 1823, and rose to lieutenant general on 18 January 1826. He took command of the 19th Division on 13 January 1827, and received the Order of St. Anna (1st class) for excellent service on 6 January 1828. During the Russo-Turkish War of 1828-1829, Ivanov commanded the 19th Division of the 7th corps, fighting at Braila (received the Order of St. Vladimir, 2nd class) and Shumla. He was mortally wounded in the left shoulder at Katesh on 22 August 1828, and died that day.

IVANOV, Pavel Andreevich (b. 9 November 1766 — d. 7 June 1839) was born to a noble family in St. Petersburg. He enlisted as a sergeant in the Life Guard Izmailovsk Regiment on 12 January 1781. Two years later, he became a lieutenant in January 1783, but transferred to civil service in the Yaroslavl *guberrnia*. By 1800, he rose to court counsellor [*nadvornii sovetnik*] in the Moscow supply depot and later worked in the Voronezh supply depot. Promoted to military counsellor on 24 July 1801, he directed the Ekaterinoslavl supply depot in 1804-1806 before serving in the same capacity in the Kazan supply depot.

In April 1812, Ivanov became head of the Main Commissariat at Jassy. During the 1812 Campaign, he was appointed general kriegscomissar of the Army of Danube on 25 August 1812 and participated in the military operations in Volhynia. The following year, he rose to general kriegs-commissar of the entire Russian army on 24 June 1813 and was promoted to major general on 18 July 1813. After the war, he directed the supply depots at Kiev (24 April 1815), and Moscow (19 April 1817). On 24 March 1820, he became chief intendant of the military hospitals in St. Petersburg.

IVASHEV, Peter Nikiforovich (b. 18 April 1766 — d. 3 December 1838) was born to a oble family from the Kazan *gubernia*. He was enlisted as a furier (fourrier) in the Life Guard Preobrazhensk Regiment in 1775 and began active service as a sergeant in December 1785, rising to an ensign on 12 January 1787. He transferred as a rotmistr to the Poltava Light Horse Regiment on 13 March 1787. During the Russo-Turkish War of 1787-1791, he distinguished himself at Ochakov (received a golden cross) and Ismail (received a golden cross and a rank of premier major in the Fanagoria Grenadier Regiment). He became close to General Alexander Suvorov and served as a quartermaster in his staff in 1789-1795. In 1794, he fought the Poles and, for his actions at Praga, he earned the Order of St. George (4th class) on 6 November 1794. He became colonel and commander of the Tavrida Horse Jager Regiment on 12 January 1795.

Ivashev rose to a major general and chef of the Taganrog Dragoon Regiment on 18 March 1798. However, Ivashev took a discharge due to illness on 11 December 1798. During the 1806-1807 Campaigns in Poland, he organized militia forces in the Vyatka *gubernia* in january 1807. Four years later, he returned to the military service as a head of the 7th District of the Central Office of Communications on 16 June 1811. During the 1812 Campaign, he was in charge of military communications in the headquarters of the 1st Western Army, serving at Vitebsk, Smolensk, Lubino, Borodino, Tarutino, Maloyaroslavets, Krasnyi and on the Berezina. In 1813-1814, Ivashev took part in operations on the Vistula and Oder Rivers, at Lutzen, Bautzen, Dresden, Magdeburg and Hamburg. After the war, he worked in the Corps of Engineers before retiring in March 1817.

IVELICH (Ivelich IV), Peter Ivanovich (b. 1772, Venice — date of death unknown) descended from a Serbian noble family settled in Venice. He began service in the Venetian forces and entered Russian service as a lieutenant in the Nasheburg Infantry Regiment on 16 June 1788. Rising to captain in October 1788, he joined the 1st Battalion of the Finland Jager Corps and then served in the Shirvan Infantry Regiment. After serving in the Russo-Turkish War of 1787-1791, Ivelich became a major and commander of the Shirvan Musketeer Regiment on 28 January 1799; he rose to lieutenant colonel on 3 May 1799 and to colonel on 22 August 1800. He participated in the 1805-1807 Campaigns in Moravia and was appointed chef of the Brest Musketeer Regiment on 5 September 1806.

During the Russo-Swedish War of 1808-1809, Ivelich served with the 17th Division, earning a rank of major general on 30 October 1808 and the Order of St. George (4th class, 1 March 1809). In 1812, Ivelich served in the 2nd Brigade of the 17th Division in the 2nd Corps of the 1st Western Army and fought at Vitebsk, Smolensk, and was seriously wounded in the right side and shoulder at Borodino, for which he was decorated with the Order of St. Vladimir (3rd class). After recuperating, he participated in the battle of Krasnyi and minor engagements in the Duchy of Warsaw and Saxony in the spring of 1813. He took a furlough because of poor health in May 1813, and returned to the army two years later, when he took command of a brigade of the 17th Division. However, his health soon rapidly deteriorated and Ivelich took a discharge on 17 December 1816.

Other Ivelichs serving in the Russian army were: **IVELICH (Ivelich I), Mark Konstantinovich,** who commanded the Shirvan Musketeer Regiment from 1793 to 20 September 1797, before he rose to major general and chef of the Tomsk Musketeer Regiment. On 25 December 1798, he became chef of the Navaginsk Musketeer Regiment and, on 7 May 1799, was promoted to a lieutenant general; **IVELICH (Ivelich III), Ivan Konstantinovich**, who commanded the 19th Jager Regiment from 12 December 1799 – 20 March 1800, the 18th Jager Regiment from 20 March 1800–21 June 1800, rose to a major general on 3 August 1800 and served as chef of the 6th Jager Regiment between 21 June 1800 and 2 July 1804 and then as chef of the Vladikavkaz Garrison Regiment between 16 January 1805 and 28 February 1810.

IZMAILOV, Lev Dmitrievich (b. 1764 — d. 1834) was born to a noble family in the Ryazan *gubernia*. He enlisted as a sergeant in the Life Guard Semeyonovsk Regiment in 1780, rising to an ensign in 1783. He participated in the Russo-Swedish War in 1788-1790 and in Poland in 1794, becoming a colonel in the Sumsk Hussar Regiment in 1795. He was discharged in 1798 but returned to the army on 31 March 1801 with a rank of major general. However, he was discharged again on 26 October 1801. Living at his estate in the Ryazan *gubernia*, Izmailov organized local militia in 1807. He commanded the Ryazan *opolchenye* during the 1812-1813 Campaigns and was promoted to a lieutenant general on 14 October 1814.

JAVAKHISHVILI, Ivan Semenovich, *see* Zhevakhov, Ivan Semenovich

JAVAKHISHVILI, Philip Semenovich, *see* Zhevakhov, Philip Semenovich

JAVAKHISHVILI, Spiridon Eristovich, *see* Zhevakhov, Spiridon Eristovich

J

JOMINI, Antoine-Henri (b. 6 March 1779, Payerne, Switzerland — d. 22 March 1869, Passy, France) was born to a prominent Swiss banker family. He followed his family tradition by becoming a banker's apprentice in Basel and then began service as a lieutenant in the Swiss troops in March 1798, serving as an adjutant to the Swiss Minister of War. He rose to a captain on 17 June 1799 and chef of battalion on 26 April 1800. Taking a discharge in 1802, Jomini returned to business and wrote his *Traité des grandes opérations militaires*. In 1804, he rejoined the French army as an aide-de-camp of Marshal Michel Ney. He served with the 6th Corps during the 1805 Campaign, fighting at Elchingen and Michelsberg. His service was noted and Jomini received quick promotions to adjutant-commandant on 27 December 1805, and first aide-de-camp of Marshal Ney on 3 September 1806. Jomini served in the General Staff of the Grande Armèe in 1806 before becoming the chief of staff for the 6th Corps on 11 November 1807.

Jomini served in Spain in 1808-1809, where he received the title of baron on 27 July 1808. However, disillusioned in the French service, he considered entering Russian service in 1810. He rose to a general of brigade on 7 December 1810 and director of the historical section of the General Staff on 29 January 1812. During the 1812 Campaign, he served as the Governor of Vilna (11 August 1812) and Smolensk. In 1813, he joined the General Staff of the Grande Armèe on 21 March 1813 and became the chief of staff for the 3rd Corps on 4 May 1813. Jomini fought at Bautzen on 21 May 1813, and was nominated for promotion to general of division. However, Napoleon's Chief of Staff Alexander Berthier, with whom Jomini had strained relations, rejected the promotion. A furious Jomini defected to the Allies on 15 August 1813, and entered Russian service with a rank of lieutenant general.

Jomini advised Emperor Alexander on military matters throughout the campaigns of 1813-1814 and, after the war, accompanied the Emperor to the Congresses at Vienna, Aix la Chapelle, and Verona, held throughout the period of 1815-1822. In 1822-1825, Jomini tutored Grand Duke Nicholas and became his adjutant with a rank of général-en-chef in 1826. He served in the headquarters of the Russian army during the Russo-Turkish War of 1828-1829, and was instrumental in organizing the Russian military academy. Although he soon took a discharge, Jomini was appointed military tutor to Crown Prince Alexander (1837), for whom he wrote *Précis de l'art de la guerre* (1838), which most historians believe is his greatest work.

During the Crimean War (1854-1856), Jomini advised Emperor Nicholas I on a wide variety of military affairs. After the war, Jomini returned to France, where he served as a military adviser to Emperor Napoleon III during the campaigns in Italy in 1859.

During his long and distinguished career, Jomini established himself as one of the most influential military theorists. His works are still studied closely today around the world. Jomini's other works include *Principes de la stratégie*, *Histoire critique et militaire des campagnes de la Révolution, de 1792 à 1801*, and *Vie politique et militaire de Napoléon*.

KABLUKOV, Platon Ivanovich (b. 1779, Ilyinskoe — d. 28 May 1835) was born to a noble family from the Kostroma *gubernia*. He enlisted in the Life Guard Preobrazhensk Regiment on 3 February 1791, and was promoted to ensign in 1798. In 1805, he served in the Chevalier Guard Regiment, was wounded and captured by the French at Austerlitz. Released in early 1806, he received a golden sword for courage. Kablukov participated in the 1807 Campaign and fought at Heilsberg and Friedland. He was promoted to colonel on 16 February 1810, and appointed to the Russian embassy in Paris. Kablukov returned in early 1812, and served in the Chevalier Guard Regiment, attached to the Guard Cuirassier Brigade of the 1st Cuirassier Division of the 5th Reserve (Guard) Corps. He was wounded in the hand at Borodino for which he received the Order of St. Vladimir (4th class).

In 1813, Kablukov took part in the actions at Lutzen, Bautzen, Dresden and Kulm (receiving the Iron Cross) and was promoted to major general on 27 September 1813, with seniority dated 29 August 1813. In 1814, he served at sieges of Magdeburg and Hamburg and was appointed chef of the Courland Dragoon Regiment on 22 May 1814. In 1815-1822, he commanded in succession the 2nd Brigade of the 3rd Dragoon Division and the 1st Brigade of the 3rd Cuirassier Division. He took command of the 3rd Cuirassier Division on 8 December 1823, and was promoted to lieutenant general on 3 September 1826. Kablukov participated in the suppression of the Polish Uprising in 1831, where he took a wound at Grochow, and garnered the Orders of St. George (3rd class, 21 April 1831), and of St. Alexander of Neva for his actions. In April 1832, he became head of the military colonies in the Kherson and Ekaterinoslavl *gubernia*s and received command of the 2nd Reserve Cavalry Corps on 27 October 1833. He died on 28 May 1835 and was buried at the village of Petrikovka, near Elsavetgrad. Kablukov was awarded the Orders of St. Alexander of Neva with diamonds, of St. Vladimir (2nd class), of St. Anna (1st class) with diamonds, the French Legion of Honor and the medal "For Military Honor."

KABLUKOV, Vladimir Ivanovich (b. 15 October 1781 — d. 3 March 1848) was born to a noble family from the Kostroma *gubernia*; brother of Platon Kablukov. He enlisted in the Life Guard Preobrazhensk Regiment on 3 December 1791, and earned a promotion to ensign on 22 December 1798. Four years later, he transferred to the Chevalier Guard Regiment (17 November 1802) and participated in the 1805 Campaign. He distinguished himself at Austerlitz, where he received three sabre cuts to the head and two bayonet wounds to the abdomen. After recuperating, he took part in the 1807 Campaign and fought at Heilsberg and Friedland. He was promoted to colonel on 18 September 1810.

During the 1812 Campaign, Kablukov's regiment was attached to the Guard Cuirassier Brigade of the 1st Cuirassier Division of the 5th Reserve (Guard) Corps and Kablukov fought at Borodino and Krasnyi. In 1813, he took part in the battles at Lutzen, Bautzen, Dresden, Kulm (received the Order of St. George, 4th class, 27 September 1813) and Leipzig. The next year, he distinguished himself at Le Fère Champenoise and was promoted to major general on 22 May 1814 with seniority dated from 25 March 1814. After the war, he remained in the Chevalier Guard Regiment and was given command of the Her Majesty's Cuirassier Regiment on 29 July 1821. He was promoted to lieutenant general on 3 September 1826 and became commander of the 4th Hussar Division on 15 February 1828. He participated in the suppression of the Polish Uprising in 1831 and received command of the 4th Light Cavalry Division on 14 April 1833. He became senator in 1834 and, in October 1843, he transferred to the civil service with a rank of actual privy counselor.

KADYSHEV, Nikolay Gerasimovich, lieutenant colonel, was appointed commander of the Nizhegorod Infantry Regiment on 29 February 1812. During the 1812 Campaign, he was killed at Borodino on 7 September 1812.

KAFTYREV, Jacob Vasilievich (b. 1769 — d. 4 June 1831, Gridinskoe, Jaroslavl *gubernia*) was born to a noble family from the Jaroslavl *gubernia*. He enlisted as a sergeant in the Sevsk Infantry Regiment in 1785 and was promoted to ensign in 1786. He participated in Russo-Turkish War in 1788-1791 and fought the Poles in 1792-1794. In 1799, he served under General Rimsky-Korsakov and fought at Zurich. He participated in the campaigns of 1805-1807 against Napoleon and distinguished himself during the Russo-Swedish war of 1808-1809. For his actions at Kuortaine and Oravais, Kaftyrev was promoted to lieutenant colonel and awarded the Order of St. George (4th class, 8 December 1809). Kaftyrev was appointed commander of the Brest Musketeer Regiment on 14 February 1810 and then, four days later, became commander of the Sevsk Musketeer Regiment. During the 1812 Campaign, Kaftyrev served in the 5th Division of General Wittgenstein's corps and fought at Klyastitsy, Polotsk, and Chashniky. In 1813-1814, he took part in the battles at Bautzen, Dresden, Leipzig (was promoted to colonel), Mainz, and Hamburg, where he was wounded. For his actions at Hamburg, he was promoted to major general on 13 June 1815 with seniority dated from 11 September 1814. After the war, Kaftyrev commanded the 2nd Brigade of the 5th Division, but he retired because of wounds in late 1816.

KAISAROV, Paisii Sergeyevich (b. 1783 — d. 27 February 1844, St. Petersburg) was born to a noble family of Mongol origins. He enlisted as a sergeant in the Life Guard Preobrazhensk Regiment on 2 May 1791, and transferred as a ensign to the Yaroslavl Musketeer Regiment on 2 February 1797. In early 1805, he briefly retired from military service and worked at the Ministry of Commerce. He became staff rotmistr of the Izumsk Hussar Regiment on 26 August 1805, and served as the adjutant to Kutuzov during the

1805 campaign against Napoleon. He transferred as a lieutenant to the Life Guard Semeyonovsky Regiment on 11 February 1806. Same year, Kaisarov was sent to the Danubian Principalities to fight the Turks and served at the main headquarters of the army. Kaisarov was promoted to colonel on 17 October 1811.

During the Russan Campaign, Kaisarov served as chef of the Sebastopol Infantry Regiment between 19 June and 20 August, and became the duty officer to Mikhail Kutuzov. In October-November 1812, he commanded an advance guard of the Cossack Corps. During 1813-1814 Campaigns, he commanded cavalry detachments and fought at Hanau and Arcis sur Aube. Kaisarov was awarded the Orders of St. George (3rd class) and of St. Anna (1st class) with diamonds and was promoted to major general on 14 March 1813 with seniority dating from 7 September 1812.

After the war, Kaisarov became commander of the 2nd Brigade of the 23rd Division on 10 August 1817. Two years later, he was appointed chief of staff of the 1st Infantry Corps on 18 August 1819. Kaisarov received command of the 14th Division on 2 October 1821, and was promoted to lieutenant general on 13 January 1826. He became chief of staff of the 1st Army in March 1829. He participated in the suppression of the Polish uprising in 1830-1831. In 1831, he became commander of the 3rd Infantry Corps (25 March) that was later reorganized into the 5th Infantry Corps (18 October 1831). Promoted to general of infantry on 18 December 1833, Kaisarov commanded the 4th Infantry Corps in 1835. He retired because of poor health on 5 November 1842, and served for the next two years in the Senate.

KAKHOVSKY, Peter Demyanovich (b. 1769, Velizh — d. 1831, Velizh) was born to a noble family from the Smolensk *gubernia*. He enlisted in the Life Guard Horse Regiment on 12 January 1781, was promoted to vakhmistr on 12 January 1787, and became a cornet in 1788. In 1790, he transferred as a rotmistr to the Malorossiisky (Little Russia) Cossack Regular Regiment. He took part in the Russo-Turkish War. He fought at both Ismail and Macin, earning a cross for his actions in the former battle. In 1792-1794, Kakhovsky served against the Polish insurrection. He was promoted to colonel and appointed commander of the Izumsk Hussar Regiment on 2 April 1800. Three years later, Kakhovsky became major general and chef of the Polish Cavalry (Uhlan) Regiment on 18 July 1803.

Kakhovsky participated in the 1805 and 1807 Campaigns against Napoleon and received the Order of St. George (3rd class) on 20 April 1807, for his service at Eylau. He assumed command of the 1st Cavalry Division on 13 February 1811. During the 1812 Campaign, Kakhovsky commanded the cavalry of General Wittgenstein's Corps, and fought at Klyastitsy, Polotsk, and Chashniky. In 1813, he took part in the actions at Lutzen, Bautzen, and Danzig.

Kakhovsky was promoted to lieutenant general on 3 September 1826, and retired in 1829. During his career, Kakhovsky also received the Orders of St. Vladimir (2nd class), of St. Anna (1st class), the Prussian Red Eagle, a golden sabre (with diamonds) and a golden sword for courage.

KAKHOVSKY (Kokhovsky), Mikhail Vasilievich (b. 1734 — d. 1800) was born to a noble family from the Smolensk *gubernia*. He studied in the Infantry Cadet Corps (19 May 1752), was assigned as a sub lieutenant in the 1st Regiment of Shuvalov's Corps of Observation in 1757 and then transferred to the 1st Fusilier Regiment. He participated in the Seven Years War and fought at Zornsdorf, Paltzig, and Kunersdorf in 1758-1759. In 1760, he was promoted to lieutenant, and later the same year was assigned to the Austrian General Laudon, with whom he served at Breslau and Liegnitz. Kakhovsky transferred to Count Chernyshev's corps and took part in the capture of Berlin. In June 1761, he was promoted to captain of the St. Petersburg Infantry Regiment and, in September 1761, was named ober-quartermaster of Chernyshev's corps. In October 1761, Kakhovsky returned to Laudon's Austrian troops and fought at Schweidnitz. In April 1762, he became general quartermaster-lieutenant [*general-kvartermistr-leitenant*] in Chernyshev's corps, and took part in the battle of Burkersdorf. In 1764, he served in Prince M. Volkonsky's Corps. Kakhovsky was promoted to brigadier in 1766 and to quartermaster general in 1768.

Kakhovsky participated in the Russo-Turkish War in 1769-1771, fighting at Khotin, Bender, and in the Crimea (actions on the Perekop Line and at Kaffa). In 1772, he was promoted to major general and commanded troops on the Polish frontiers; later, he became the Governor of the Moghilev *gubernia*. He was promoted lieutenant general in 1773 and became a member of the Military College in 1779. In 1783, he commanded troops in the Crimea and was promoted to général-en-chef on 5 December 1784. In 1787, he was given command of the 2nd Division in the Army of Ekaterinoslavl in the Crimea. In 1791, Kakhovsky took part in expedition against Anapa. After Prince Gregory Potemkin's death, he assumed command of the army in the Crimea despite the opposition of General Mikhail Kamenski.

In 1792, Kakhovsky assumed command of the Army of Ukraine and engaged Prince Joseph Poniatowski's troops in Podolia and Volhynia during the Second Polish Partition. After defeating the Polish troops in a series of actions, he captured Warsaw on 16 August 1792 for which he received the Order of St. Andrew the First Called. In 1793, he was appointed the Governor General of Penza and Nizhegorod and, in 1794, he assumed command of the troops in the Crimea. Under Emperor Paul I, he became general of infantry and the commander of the Tavrida Division in late 1796. However, he was discharged from the army because of poor health on 25 February 1800.

KAMENEV, Sergey Andreevich (b. 1760 — date of death unknown) was born to a noble family from the Kursk *gubernia*. He enlisted in the Sevsk Infantry Regiment on 12 January 1774 and rose to adjutant with the rank of ensign on 13 March 1777. In 1783-1784, he served in Poland and was promoted to lieutenant. He participated in the Russo-Turkish War of 1787-1791 and distinguished himself at Ismail, receiving the rank of premier major. In 1792-1794, Kamenev served in Poland and fought at Praga (Warsaw suburb). Kamenev became colonel on 3 March 1798. The following year, he rose to the rank of major general and was appointed chef of the Kamenev's Cuirassier Regiment on 19 September 1799. Between 14 March 1800 and 21 June 1801, he took retirement and, after brief service in the army in 1802, Kamenev was discharged again on 13 January 1803. He returned to active service only in 1812 (officially accepted on 17 January 1813), and commanded a Cossack brigade in Ataman Platov's advance guard. In 1813, he served in the advance guard of Wittgenstein's corps. In 1814, Kamenev distinguished himself at Brienne, Bar sur Aube, Arcis sur Aube, Le Fère Champenoise, and Paris. He retired because of poor health on 12 April 1816.

KAMENSHIKOV (Kamenshikov I), Ivan Ivanovich, major, became commander of the Tomsk Musketeer Regiment on 9 July 1807. After military reorganization in early 1811, he commanded the Butyrsk Infantry Regiment between 11 June 1811 and 13 June 1815.

KAMENSKI (Kamensky), Mikhail Fedotovich (b. 19 May 1738 — d. 24 August 1809) was born to a prominent noble family of Polish origins that settled in Russian in 17th century. His father, Fedot Mikhailovich Kamenski, served under Peter the Great. He graduated with a rank of lieutenant from the Cadet Corps in 1756, and briefly served in the Chancellery of Constructions. In 1757, he began military service as unter-zeilmeister in the Russian artillery but, in 1758-1759, he served in the French Army and was promoted to captain. After his return to Russia, Kamenski was appointed to the artillery company in Moscow. On 25 February 1761, he transferred to the army with a rank of premier major and later the same year, he rose to colonel and received the appointment as quartermaster-general for Count Peter Rumyantsev's corps. Kamenski took part in the concluding phase of the Seven Years War and then commanded the 1st Moscow Infantry Regiment. In 1765, he was sent on mission to study the Prussian military system and met Frederick the Great. Upon his return, he presented a report, *"Opisanie prusskago lageria"* [Description of the Prussian Camp] in which he praised the Prussian army and its regulations. Kamenski was promoted to brigadier in 1766 and to major general in 1769.

During the Russo-Turkish war in 1769-1771, Kamenski commanded the 4th Brigade and fought at Khotin and Janchintsy, for which he received the Order of St. Anna in 1769. The following year, he commanded the 1st Brigade of the 1st Division and was awarded the Order of St. George for his role in the fight at Bender. After briefly commanding troops in Poland in 1772, he returned to the Danube Valley and participated in operations against the Turks between Craiova and Banat. For his actions, he was awarded the Order of St. George (3rd class) and promoted to lieutenant general in 1773. In 1774, he was given command of the left wing of the Russian army and participated in actions at Bazardjik, Kozludji, Yeni Bazaar, and Shumla. For his actions, he was awarded the Orders of St. George (2nd class) and of St. Alexander of Neva; however, he intrigued against Suvorov, who promptly had him recalled from the army.

In 1775-1785, Kamenski served on various positions, including military adviser to the Prussian army in 1779 and the Governor General of Ryazan and Tombov *gubernia*s in 1783-1785. During the Russo-Turkish War of 1787-1790, he was given command of the 2nd Corps but was compromised after yet another intrigue, this time against Field Marshal Peter Rumyantsev was revealed. He transferred to the 4th Division (Reserve Corps) and took part in operations around Khotin and Bender. He distinguished himself at Gankur in December 1788 and received the Order of St. Vladimir (1st class). He briefly commanded the Army of Ukraine but was involved in conflict with Gregory Potemkin. After Potemkin's death, he claimed the command of the army and refused to transfer the authority to his successor General M. Kakhovsky. He resigned only after the other corps commanders refused to comply with his orders and supported Kakhovsky.

Disgraced by Catherine II, Kamenski retired to his estate and spent next five years there. He returned to active service in 1796, when Emperor Paul I gave him command of the Finland Division and an appointment as chef of the Ryazan Musketeer Regiment; Kamenski was promoted to general of infantry on 14 December 1796. The next year, 1797, he was awarded the Order of St. Andrew the First Called (15 March) and conferred a title of count as well as further promotion to general field marshal on 16 April. However, he soon fell out of favor and was discharged from army on 4 January 1798. Under the new Emperor Alexander I, Kamenski became the Military Governor of St. Petersburg in 1802, but was dismissed for incompetence late in the same year. He spent four years in his estate at Saburovo.

In 1806, faced with a conflict between commanding generals Buxhöwden and Bennigsen, Alexander conceeded to public pressure to appoint Kamenski as the commander-in-chief of the Russian army (22 November). However, Kamenski was in poor health; by the time he reached the army, Kamenski was effectively blind and largely immobilized. However, this did not stop him from ordering an offensive against Napoleon. However, Kamenski demonstrated poor judgment and rank incompetence throughout these operations. He concentrated his forces at Pultusk and planned to fight a major battle there; however, before that took place, he abandoned his command claiming poor health. Kamenski spent the next three years on his estate in Saburovo, where he became notorious for his severe treatment of peasants. Kamenski was murdered by one of his mistreated peasants on 24 August 1809, and was buried in the local church in Saburovo.

KAMENSKI, Nikolay Mikhailovich (b. 7 January 1777 — d. 16 May 1811, Odessa) was born to a prominent Russian family; son of Field Marshal Mikhail Kamenski. He was educated in the Cadet Corps and enlisted as a cornet in the Novotroitsky Cuirassier Regiment on 13 June 1779. His active duty began as adjutant to Lieutenant General Hantwig in April 1785. Two years later, he became adjutant to his father (15 July). In 1795, he transferred as a lieutenant colonel to the Simbirsk Grenadier Regiment, then to the 10th Jager Regiment (9 May 1796) and to the Ryazan Musketeer Regiment on 27 February 1797. Kamenski was promoted to colonel on 27 April 1797 and became major general and chef of the Arkhangelogord Musketeer Regiment on 9 July 1799. He served under Alexander Suvorov in Italy and Switzerland, fighting at St. Gothard, Devil's Bridge, Altdorf, Muothatal (Muttental), Netstal, Nafels and retreat across the Panixer Pass. For his actions, he was awarded the Order of St. Anna (1st class). However, after return to Russia, he misappropriated regimental funds and was discharged between 21 December 1801 and 27 March 1802, when he was restored in his position in the Arkhangelogord Musketeer Regiment.

In 1805, Kamenski served in Buxhöwden's corps and participated in actions at Wischau and Raussnitz. He distinguished himself at Austerlitz, but his regiment suffered horrendous losses; Kamenski barely escaped when a cannonball killed a horse under him; for his actions, he was awarded the Order of St. Vladimir (3rd class). Kamenski then took part in the 1807 Campaign in Poland; he fought at Bergfried and commanded the 14th Division at Eylau, receiving the Order of St. George (3rd class). Through May and June 1807, he fought at Launau, Danzig and Heilsberg. He was promoted to lieutenant general on 24 December 1807.

In January 1808, Kamenski was given command of the 17th Division and participated in the invasion of Finland. In the spring of 1808, he took part in the siege of Sveaborg and protected the southern coast of Finland. In July 1808, he assumed command of General Rayevsky's corps and fought at Alavo, Kuortale, Salmi, Oravais, where he received the Order of St. George (2nd class) and in a series of lesser actions. In 1809, he commanded a corps at Uleaborg and launched offensive around Umea, fighting at Savar and Ratan. For his actions, he was garnered the Order of St. Alexander of Neva with diamonds. On 16 February 1810, he replaced Prince Peter Bagration as commander-in-chief of the Army of Moldavia. During the opening phases of the campaign against the Turks, Kamenski captured the fortresses of Silistra, Razgrad, and Bazardjik, for which he was awarded the Order of St. Vladimir (1st class). He fought the main Turkish army at Shumla, launched an unsuccessful assault on Ruse (losing almost 9,000 men in the process), and annihilated the Turkish army at Batin on 7 September. In August 1810–February 1811, he captured Ruse, Turnu, Plevna, Lovech, and Selvi.

Kamenski became seriously ill in March 1811, and left the army to recuperate in Odessa. He died there on 16 May 1811, and was buried in village of Saburovo in the Orel *gubernia*.

KAMENSKI, Sergey Mikhailovich, (b. 17 November 1771 — d. 20 December 1834, Orel) was born to a prominent Russian family, the son of Field Marshal Mikhail Kamenski and the brother of Nikolay Kamenski. He studied at Cadet Corps and enlisted as a cornet in the Nizhegorod Carabineer Regiment on 17 February 1774. In 1777, he transferred as an ensign to the Life Guard Preobrazhensk Regiment (19 April) and, on 16 May 1789, he became a lieutenant colonel of the Ekaterinoslavl Grenadier Regiment. He participated in the Russo-Turkish War in 1789-1790 and fought at Maximeni and Galati.

In 1792-1794, Kamenski served against the Polish confederates and fought at Shekochin, Pesochna, and Maciejowice and took a minor wound to the stomach at Praga. On 19 May 1794, he was given command of the 3rd Battalion of the Ekaterinoslavl Jager Corps and was awarded the Order of St. Vladimir (4th class) and a golden cross for his participation in the assault on Praga. On 12 January 1797, Kamenski was promoted to colonel and, on 25 March 1798 he was advanced to major general and appointed chef of the Polotsk Musketeers Regiment. Yet, Emperor Paul I soon disgraced him and had him discharged from army on 14 June 1798.

After Paul I's assassination, Kamenski returned to service in April 1801 and became chef of the Phanagoria Grenadier Regiment on 31 August 1801. He participated in the 1805 Campaign and fought in Langeron's column at Austerlitz, for which he was awarded the Order of St. Anna (1st class). Promoted to lieutenant general on 27 June 1806, Kamenski took command of the 12th Division and participated in the 1807-1809 Campaigns against the Turks. He distinguished himself at Braila (awarded the Order of St. Anna, 1st class, with diamonds) and took part in the actions at Constanta, Babadag, and Varna. In late 1809, he commanded a corps at Girsov. In 1810, Kamenski served under his younger brother, General Nikolay Kamenski, and distinguished himself in the battle at Bazardjik, for which he was promoted to general of infantry (26 June 1810). He failed to coordinate his actions with his brother's at Shumla in July, but still managed to defeat the Turkish army there on 4 August 1810, for which he was awarded the Order of St. George (2nd class) on 3 December 1810. He commanded the Russian left wing in the battle of Batin on 7 September 1810. In 1812, Kamenski led the 3rd Corps of the 3rd Reserve Army of Observation of General Alexander Tormasov and took part in the battles of Kobryn and Gorodechna. However, he had a conflict with Tormasov and took a prolonged furlough in late 1812. Kamenski was discharged from army on 18 March 1822, and spent the rest of his life at Orel.

KANCHIALOV, Nikolay Aleksandrovich, colonel, commanded the Sumsk Hussar Regiment between 28 April 1810 and 12 November 1812.

KANKRIN (Cancrin), Yegor Frantsevich (Georg Ludwig) (b. 7 December 1774, Hanau — d. 21 September, Pavlovsk) was born to a German noble family from the Hanau. His father, Franz Ludwig von Cancrin was a well-known German minining engineer and entered Russian service in 1783. Kankrin graduated from the universities at Giessen and Marburg and was accepted into the Russian civil cervice with a rank of court counsellor in 1798. In 1811, Kankrin was appointed to the Ministry of War and drafted new military regulations. In 1812, he became intendant general of the 1st Western Army and was promoted to major general on 13 December 1812. The next year, he served as intendant general of all Russian armies and was promoted to lieutenant general on 11 September 1815.

In 1816-1820, Kankrin served as intendant general of the 1st Army and was appointed to the Council of War of the Ministry of War in 1820. In 1823, he became Minister of Finances and was promoted to general of infantry on 7 July 1826. In 1829, he was conferred the title of count of the Russian Empire. Kankrin supported the Corps of Mining Engineers and the Practical Technological Institute.

During his career, Kankrin received the Russian Orders of St. Andrew the First Called with diamonds, of St. Vladimir (1st class), of Alexander of Neva with diamonds, of St. Anna (1st class), the Polish Order of the White Eagle, the Austrian Order of Leopold, the Prussian Order of the Red Eagle, and two Saxon and Bavarian civil orders. He was highly influential in determining Russia's economic policy under Nicholas I. Kankrin wrote extensively on the logistics and finances. His major works were *Weltreichthum, Nationalreichtum und Staatswirtschaft* was (1821) and *Die Oekonomie der Menschlichen Gesellschaften* (1845).

KANTAKUZEN, Nikolay Egorovich (b. 1773 — d. 1841) was born to a Greek noble family. He briefly served in the Russian army in 1782 before returning to Greece, where he commanded arnaut detachments. In 1790, Potemkin invited him back to Russia, where Kantakuzen received the rank of lieutenant colonel and served in the Bug Cossacks forces. He participated in the Russo-Turkish War in 1790-1791, fighting at Ismail (Order of St. Vladimir) and establishing an arnaut detachment in 1791. Kantakuzen was discharged from the army in 1797, but returned to service four years later with the rank of colonel. In 1806, he became governing ataman of the Bug Cossack Host and took part in another Russo-Turkish War. He distinguished himself at Palanka, Akkerman, and Ismail in 1807 In 1809-1814, he served on the western Russian provinces. On 18 May 1818, he earned promotion to major general and served as a duty officer to General Witte, Commander of the Bug Uhlan Division before retiring in 1833.

Another **Kantakuzen, Gregory Matveyevich**, commanded the 1st Combined Grenadier Brigade of the 5th Corps in the 1st Western Army, and was mortally wounded at Borodino on 7 September 1812.

KAPTSEVICH (Kaptzewitz), Peter Mikhailovich (b. 1772 — d. 15 July 1840, Orenburg) was born to a Byelorussian noble family. He graduated from the Cadet Corps and enlisted in the Gatchina Troops on 18 December 1792. He served in the Life Guard Artillery Battalion and was promoted to colonel on 5 February 1797. He served as commandant of Vilna and became a major general on 1 January 1798. Kaptsevich participated in the expedition to Holland in 1799, rose to lieutenant general on 15 December 1799 and, on 19 March 1800, took appointment as chef of the 3rd Artillery Regiment. From 27 November 1804 to October 1806, he served as chef of the 7th Artillery Regiment and, later, as a duty officer in the Ministry of War (5 February 1808).

During the 1812 Campaign, Kaptsevich commanded the 7th Division of the 6th Corps of the 1st Western Army. He fought at Borodino and was awarded the Order of St. George (3rd class) and a golden sword on 1 November 1812. In 1813, he commanded the 10th Infantry Corps, fought at Kustrin, Goldberg and distinguished himself at Leipzig (wounded, received the Order of St. George, 2nd class, 18 October 1813). He commanded the 10th Corps during the 1814 Campaign. From June 1819 through July 1827, he commanded the Independent Siberia Corps and served as the Governor of Tobolsk and Tomsk. Promoted to general of infantry on 24 December 1823, Kaptsevich took command of the Independent Corps of Internal Guard in October 1828. In 1835, he was conferred rank of general of artillery.

During his career, Kaptsevich was also awarded the Order of St. Alexander of Neva with diamonds, of St. George (2nd), of St. Vladimir (2nd class), of St. Anna (1st class) with diamonds, the Prussian Red Eagle, and the Swedish Order of Sword, a golden sword for courage and medal for "XLV Years of Distinguished Service."

KAPUSTIN, Ivan Fedorovich, (b. 1759 — date of death unknown) was born to a petty noble family from the Ryazan *gubernia*. He enlisted in the Ryazan Infantry Regiment in 1776. During the Russo-Turkish War, he distinguished himself at Ochakov in 1788 receiving the rank of sergeant and a medal for courage. He fought at Akkerman and Bender in 1789 (was promoted to ensign) and at Ismail in 1790 (promoted to sub lieutenant). In 1792-1794, he served in Poland, was wounded at Praga and promoted to captain. In 1799, Kapustin took part in the expedition to Holland, where he was wounded and captured at Bergen. He returned to Russia in the summer of 1800 and became a major. In 1805, he participated in the expedition to Hannover. During the 1806 Campaign in Poland, he fought at Pultusk and, in February 1807, distinguished himself at Eylau, where he took a wound to the left thigh and subsequently received a golden cross. He was promoted to lieutenant colonel on 5 May 1807. Kapustin took part in operations at Guttstadt and Heilsberg and received a golden sword for courage for actions at Friedland. On 11 September 1807, Kapustin was given command of the 20th Jager Regiment.

During the 1812 Campaign, Kapustin served with the 3rd Brigade of the 3rd Division of the 3rd Corps in the 1st Western Army. He fought at Vitebsk and, at Smolensk, he was seriously wounded in the head and received the Order of St. Vladimir (4th class) for his actions.

He spent the rest of the campaign recuperating and returned to the army in late 1812. In the 1813 Campaign, after promotion to colonel on 1 February, he was wounded in the right hand at Kalisch. He then fought at Kustrin, Katzbach and was seriously wounded in the head at Leipzig. Despite the wound, he participated in the 1814 Campaign and distinguished himself ar La Rothière, Arcis sur Aube and Paris. For these actions, he received the Orders of St. Vladimir (3rd and 4th classes) and of St. Anna (2nd class) with diamonds and was promoted to major general on 11 September 1814 with seniority dated from 3 February 1814. After the war, he commanded the 1st Brigade of the 11th Division (23 January 1815) and retired due to his wounds in 1816.

KARATAEV, Vasily Ivanovich took command of the Ekaterinoslavl Cuirassier Regiment on 27 November 1807 and became a colonel on 24 December 1807. He took over the Astrakhan Cuirassier Regiment on 24 October 1811 and rose to major general on 28 March 1813. He died on 19 February 1814.

KARIAGIN, Pavel Mikhailovich, colonel, commanded the 17th Jager Regiment in 1 September 1800 — 5 February 1803. After briefly serving as chef of the 15th Jager Regiment in February–May 1803, he became chef of the 17th Jager Regiment on 25 May 1803 in which he served until his death on 12 August 1807.

KARPENKO, Moisei (Moses) Ivanovich (b. 8 September 1775, Kaluga *gubernia* — d. 16 August 1854, Burinovo, Kaluga *gubernia*) was born to a noble family in the Kaluga *gubernia*. He enlisted as a sub ensign in the Tavrida Grenadier Regiment in 1790 and served in Poland in 1792-1794, receiving the rank of ensign on 3 October 1794. Promoted to lieutenant in 1798, he went on to serve in Georgia in 1803 and took part in operations against Persia in 1804-1805. In 1807, Karpenko served in Poland and, during the Russo-Swedish War of 1808-1809, he fought at Pigaioki, Sigaioki, Skeleftea, and Hernefors. After promotion to colonel on 11 September 1809, he became commander of the 26th Jager

KARPOV (Karpov II), Akim (Yekim) Akimovich (Yekimovich) (date of birth varies between 1762 and 1767, Cherkassk — d. 6 April 1837) was born to a Cossack staff officer's family and enlisted in the Cossack troops on 12 May 1778. He served in Matvei Platov's regiment in 1782-1785 and participated in operations against the North Caucasian mountaineers. He was promoted to esaul on 15 January 1783 and to lieutenant in 1787. In 1796, he served as head of police (*sysk*) in Medveditsk and, the following year, he organized two Don Cossack artillery companies. Karpov was promoted to colonel on 13 November 1799 and took part in the expedition to Orenburg in 1801.

In 1806-1809, Karpov served in the Danube Valley where he distinguished himself at Giurgiu and in other minor actions in Little Wallachia in 1807, receiving the Order of St. George (4th class). In 1808-1809, he fought at Braila, Girsov, Rassevat, and Tataritsa. For his actions, he was promoted to major general on 10 January 1810. He participated in battles at Silistra, Ruse, Shumla, and Batin in 1810. During the 1812 Campaign, he commanded a Cossack detachment in the 2nd Western Army and fought at Mir and Romanovo. He distinguished himself at Tarutino (awarded the Order of St. Anna, 1st class, with diamonds) and in many minor actions during the French retreat, for which he received the Order of St. George (3rd class, 15 June 1813).

Regiment (24 April 1810) and chef of the 1st Jager Regiment on 31 October 1810. After Prince Alexander of Holstein-Oldenburg became the chef of the 1st Jagers, Karpenko served as the commander of the regiment.

During the 1812 Campaign, Karpenko served with the 3rd Brigade of the 11th Division of the 4th Corps in the 1st Western Army. He took part in the retreat to Smolensk and was wounded at Borodino. For his actions, he was promoted to major general on 3 December 1812 with seniority dating from 7 September 1812. In October, he fought at Tarutino and Solovyevo. In 1813, he was wounded at Bautzen and received the Order of St. George (3rd class) on 10 November 1813. In 1815-1816, he led the 3rd Brigade of the 1st Grenadier Division and was given command of the 3rd Brigade of the 5th Division on 18 January 1816.

Karpenko retired on 17 December 1816, but returned to active service on 11 September 1839, although his seniority was changed to 2 June 1835. He was promoted to lieutenant general and became commander of the 2nd Division on 18 December 1840. Four years later, Karpenko became commandant of the Zamostye fortress and a member of the General Audit (April 1849). Karpenko retired because of poor health in 1851, and spent the last three years of his life at estate at Burinovo. His recollections were published in the *Voennii Sbornik* [Military Digest] in 1872.

In 1813, Karpov took part in the actions at Glogau, Bautzen, Dresden, Katzbach and Leipzig. In 1814, he distinguished himself at St. Dizier, Brienne, La Rothière, Montmirail, Craonne, Laon, Le Fère Champenoise, and Paris. For his actions, Karpov was promoted to lieutenant general on 11 September 1814 with seniority dated from 29 January 1814. After the war, he briefly commanded the Don Cossack artillery, served in the committee on establishing the Don Cossack Host, and served as leader of the Don Cossack Nobility (predvoditel donskogo dvoriantsva) in 1817-1821.

Karpov retired on 23 March 1836 and died on 6 April 1837. During his career, he also received the Orders of St. Alexander of Neva, of St. Vladimir, the Prussian Red Eagle (2nd class) and two golden swords for courage.

KARPOV, Jacob Ivanovich (b. 1753 — d. 23 November 1812, Wilkomir) was born to a noble family from the Tver *gubernia*. He was enrolled in the Naval Corps in 1762 and was promoted to guard marine in 1766, serving on the yacht *Paradise* in the Baltic Sea. He became mitchman in 1768 and served in Admiral G. Spiridov's squadrons in the Mediterranean Sea in 1769. During the Russo-Turkish War, Karpov took part in naval battles at Chesma, Negroponto, and Mettelino, and was promoted to lieutenant. In 1775, he was given command of the gunboat *Jupiter* and, in 1778, was promoted to lieutenant captain. In 1786-1789, Karpov served on the flotilla in the Caspian Sea and distinguished himself in actions at the estuary of the Terek River. He became captain (1st class) on 12 January 1795 and took part in the expedition to Holland in 1798-1799. He fought at Helder, Alkmar, and Texcel.

In late 1799, Karpov briefly served under Admiral Fedor Ushakov in the Mediterranean Sea. He became a major general on 4 December 1799 and was appointed to the Admiralty. He retired because of poor health in 1803, but returned to active service in 1806, when he organized the St. Petersburg militia. During the 1812 Campaign, he commanded the 8th Company (druzhina) of the St. Petersburg *opolchenye* and fought at Polotsk, Lepel, and Chaushniky. For his service, Karpov garnered a golden sword for courage and Order of St. Vladimir (3rd class).

His health rapidly deteriorated in late 1812, and Karpov died on 23 November 1812 at Wilkomir. He also earned the Order of St. John of Jerusalem during his career.

KARTSEV, Ivan Petrovich (b. 1770 — d. 16 May 1836) was born to a noble family from the Pskov *gubernia*. He graduated from the Naval Cadet Corps in November 1787 and served as guard marine on the frigate *Hector* in the Baltic Sea. On 26 May 1788, he was promoted to mitchman and served on the ship-of-the-line *Pamiat Evstafia*. He participated in the Russo-Swedish War and fought at Gogland and Eland. Wounded in the right shoulder in naval action at Vyborg, Kartsev was captured in battle at Svenkzund in early 1790 and released in September 1790. Promoted to lieutenant and given command of the schooner *Skoraya* on 12 January 1792, Kartsev earned command of the frigate *St. Paul* within a year. In 1798, he served on the frigate *Alexander* and took part in the expedition to Holland. Kartsev became a lieutenant captain on 23 March 1800, and served on the ship-of-the-line *St. Michael*. In 1804, he became commander of the frigate *Malyi*. In 1808-1810, he commanded the galley *Pallade* on the Neva River. Promoted to captain (2nd class) on 13 March 1810, Kartsev in 1811 organized and commanded the Guard *Ekipazh*.

During the 1812 Campaign, Kartsev fought at Ostrovno, Smolensk, Borodino, Maloyaroslavets, and on the Berezina. In 1813-1814, he was instrumental in constructing the crossings over the major rivers (Vistula, Oder, Elba, Rhine and Seine) and distinguished himself at Bautzen, Kustrin (promoted to captain, 1st class), Koenigstein, Leipzig, Nogent, and Paris. He became a captain-commander on 30 August 1814, and, four years later rose to rear admiral and commander of the Black Sea galley flotilla on 11 September 1818. During the Russo-Turkish War of 1828-1829, Kartsev commanded a flotilla on the Danube and took part in the sieges of Braila, Silistra, Ruse, and Varna. Kartsev was promoted to vice admiral on 3 September 1828, and retired just over two years later on 29 December 1830.

KAZACHKOVSKY, Cyril Fedorovich (b. 1760 – d. 6 July 1829, Tsaritsino) enlisted as a sergeant in the Yeletsk Infantry Regiment on 12 January 1774, and later became ensign on 5 December 1781. He served in Poland in 1783-1784, was promoted to sub lieutenant in 1786 and to lieutenant of the Ekaterinoslavl Jager Corps in 1787. He participated in the Russo-Turkish war in 1787-1791, and distinguished himself at Ochakov in 1788. For his actions there, he received a golden cross and promotion to captain.

In 1790, Kazachkovsky transferred to the Ekaterinburg Field Battalion and became a major in 1791. Appointed commander of the Tomsk Musketeer Regiment on 18 December 1798, Kazachkovsky became lieutenant colonel in 1799 and colonel on 27 June 1800. Kazachkovsky was appointed chef of the 2nd Marine Regiment on 10 April 1806, and later the same year, on 4 November, became chef of the Kaluga Musketeer Regiment. He participated with the 5th Division in the 1807 Campaign in Poland, and fought at Braunsberg, Ditriechdorf, and Heilsberg. His good conduct in these actions earned him a promotion to major general on 24 December 1807, along with the Order of St. Vladimir (3rd class) and the Prussian Pour le Merite.

During the Russo-Swedish War in 1808-1809, Kazachkovsky remained with the 5th Division and fought at Kuopio, Lappo, Kuortane, and Oravais. In 1809, he served in Shuvalov's corps and fought at Torneo, Skelleftea, Hernefors, and Ratan. For his actions in Sweden, he was awarded the Order of St. Anna (1st class) and a golden sword with diamonds. In 1812, he commanded the 1st Brigade of the 5th Division of General Wittgenstein's 1st Independent Corps. He fought at Klyastitsy (received the Order of St. George, 3rd class, 5 September 1812), Svolna (received the Order of St. Anna, 1st class, with diamonds), the two battles at Polotsk (wounded on 18 August, awarded the Order of St. Vladimir, 2nd class) and on the Berezina River. In 1813, he took over command of the 5th Division and fought at Wittenberg (received the Prussian Red Eagle) and was seriously wounded by canister shot in the abdomen at Lutzen. Alexander I witnessed his exploit and promoted him to lieutenant general on 27 September 1813, with seniority dated from 2 May 1813.

After the war, Kazachkovsky became commander of the 16th Division on 26 November 1817. Three years later, he was relieved of duty because of poor health in June 1820. He died nine years later at Tsaritsino.

KAZANTSEV, Ivan Alekseyevich (b. 1770 — d. 4 August 1818, Vyborg) was born to a noble family from the Vologda *gubernia*. He graduated from the Naval Cadet Corps in 1787 and served as a guard marine on the ship-of-the-line *"Rostislav"* in the Gulf of Finland. During the Russo-Swedish War, he took part in the actions at Gogland and Eland and was promoted to mitchman on 22 August 1789. In late 1789, Kazantsev took command of a gunboat in the flotilla on the Danube River and participated in actions at Isaccea, Tulcea, Braila, and Ismail, for which he earned the rank of lieutenant. In 1798, after promotion to lieutenant captain, he received command of the frigate *Constantine* in the Baltic Sea. He participated in the 1799 expedition to Holland and fought at Texcel and Zeidersee. From 1801 to 1807, he commanded gunboats in the Gulf of Finland.

During the Russo-Swedish War, Kazantsev commanded the sloop *Piram* and distinguished himself at Abo, earning the rank of captain (2nd class). In 1809, he supervised the ship wharfs in Arkhangelsk; he was promoted to captain (1st class) and given command of the ship-of-the-line *Emgeiten* on 13 March 1810. During the 1812 Campaign, he commanded a flotilla of forty gunboats and protected the coastline at Riga. In 1813-1814, Kazantsev took part in the actions at Danzig, Wexelmund, and Lubeck, and was promoted to captain commander on 11 September 1814. In 1815, he commanded chip-of-the-line *Prince Gustav* and participated in the blockade of the French coastline during the Hundred Days. In 1818, he became commander of the port of Vyborg.

KERN, Ermolay Fedorovich (b. 1765, Petrovsk, Saratov *gubernia* — d. 20 January 1841, St. Petersburg) descended from a English noble family that settled in Russia in late 17th century. He enlisted as a vakhmistr in the Smolensk Dragoon Regiment on 21 April 1777, and rose to the rank of cadet in 1781. He transferred to the Astrakhan Grenadier Regiment in 1789, and then became sergeant in the Kherson Grenadier Regiment in 1790. Kern participated in the Russo-Turkish War and fought at Ochakov (recived a cross), Bender, Ismail (received a cross and promotion to ensign) and Macin (promotion to sub-lieutenant). In 1792-1794, he served in Poland fighting at Krupchitse, Brest, Kobylka, and Praga (awarded a golden cross) and became a captain.

In 1795-1806, Kern served with the Kherson Grenadier Regiment in the Crimea and Caucasus and was promoted to major in 1800. He participated in operations against the Chechens in 1806, where he was severely wounded in the abdomen. During the 1807 Campaign in Poland, Kern served in the Pernov Musketeer Regiment, but became ill and did not participate in the battles of Heilsberg and Friedland. He became a lieutenant colonel and commander of the Pernov Musketeer Regiment on 16 December 1807. During the Russo-Swedish War in 1808, he marched with his regiment to Sveaborg but fell ill yet again and had to return to St. Petersburg, where he retired because of poor health on 16 December 1808. Kern returned to the army in early 1811 and became commander of the 48th Jager Regiment on 11 April of that year. He transferred to command the Belozersk Infantry Regiment on 28 April 1812, and served in the 1st Brigade of the 17th Division of the 2nd Corps.

During the 1812 Campaign, Kern took part in the defense of Smolensk (wounded), actions at Gedeonovo (bruised in the neck) and Lubino, where he received the Order of St. Anna (2nd class). Kern took command of the 2nd Brigade of the 17th Division and distinguished himself at Borodino (wounded in the left leg,), Tarutino, Vyazma (promoted to major general, 30 July 1813, with seniority dating from 3 November 1812), Krasnyi, and other minor actions. For his service, he accepted his colonelcy on 3 December 1812, as well as two Orders of St. Vladimir (4th and 3rd classes). In early 1813, Kern became commandant of Meissen and later fought at Bautzen (received the Order of St. Anna, 2nd class, with diamonds), Grofenberg, Lobau, the crossing of the Elbe River (received the Prussian Pour le Merite) and at Leipzig (received the Swedish Order of the Sword and the Order of St. Anna, 1st class). He briefly served as the Military Governor of Kassel in late 1813. During the 1814 Campaign, Kern crossed the Rhine River at Kobenz and served in the 22nd Division at Soisson and Paris (awarded the Order of St. George, 4th class).

After the war, Kern commanded in succession the 3rd Brigade of the 17th Division (14 August 1815), the 15th Division (17 May 1816), 2nd Brigade of the 25th Division (22 March 1818) and the 11th Division (6 August 1820). He served as commandant of Riga between 8 October 1823 and 1 August 1827. He became commandant of Smolensk on 12 March 1828 and was promoted to lieutenant general on 26 April 1829. He retired on 29 November 1837, and took part in the grand celebration at Borodino in 1839.

Kern died on 20 January 1841, in St. Petersburg and was buried at the Smolensk Cemetery. During his military service, Kern also received a medal "For XXXV Years of Distinguished Service."

Another **KERN (first name unknown)**, colonel (date of birth unknown — d. 9 July 1807), became commander of the Pernov Musketeer Regiment on 8 December 1806, and was appointed chef of the Dnieper Musketeer Regiment on 27 January 1807. In 1807, he served with the 3rd Division in Poland.

KHANYKOV, Vasily Vasilievich (b. 1759 — d. 24 April 1829) was born to a noble family from the Kaluga *gubernia*. He enlisted in the Life Guard Preobrazhensk Regiment on 27 February 1773, and transferred as a sub lieutenant to the Life Guard Ismailovsk regiment on 8 April 1785. In 1786-1787, he engaged in various diplomatic missions to Berlin and Vienna. During the Russo-Swedish War, he served on the galley flotilla and received the Order of St. George (4th class) for his actions at Rochesalmi. In 1791, he volunteered to fight the Turks and distinguished himself at Babadag and Macin. In 1792, after a diplomatic mission to Istanbul, he received promotion to captain of the Life Guard Ismailovsk Regiment. Khanykov transferred as a colonel to the Rostov Carabineer Regiment on 13 May 1794 and served in Poland fighting at Vilna, Grodno, Brest and Slonim (received a golden sword for courage). Swift promotion followed, to brigadier on 12 March 1795, to major general on 17 April 1797, and finally to lieutenant general on 11 October 1798.

In 1798-1800, Khanykov accomplished several diplomatic missions to Italy and served as the Russian envoy to Dresden from 1802 to 1812. He was arrested by the French in Dresden in the beginning of the 1812 Campaign not gaining release until November 1812. He was appointed to the main headquarters of the Russian army in April 1813 and carried out various diplomatic missions to Vienna. Instrumental during negotiations with King August Wilhelm of Saxony, he received the Order of St. Alexander of Neva for his conduct. He also took part in negotiation of the Treaty of Paris and served again as the Russian envoy to Dresden in late 1814. In May 1815, he became ambassador to Hannover, Saxen-Weimar, Hesse, Oldenburg, and Mecklenburg. Four years later, he became the Russian ambassador to Saxony and transferred to the civil service with a rank of actual privy counsellor (13 January 1819).

KHILKOV, Stepan Alexandrovich (b. 1785, Moscow — d. 1854) was born to an ancient Russian noble family from the Tula *gubernia*. Educated in the private boarding schools in St. Petersburg, he graduated from the Cadet Corp and enlisted as a sub-ensign in the Life Guard Preobrazhensk Regiment on 6 January 1800. In January 1802, he transferred as a junker to the Life Guard Horse Regiment and rose through ranks to standart-junker on 6 February, and cornet on 16 September 1802. Khilkov became lieutenant on 22 August 1805, and participated in the 1805 Campaign, distinguishing himself at Austerlitz, where he led the cavalry charge that captured the eagle of the 1st Battalion of the 4th Line. For his actions, he was awarded the Order of St. Anna (3rd class). In 1807, he fought at Guttstadt, Heilsberg, and was wounded at Friedland, for which he received the Order of St. George (4th class). His promotion to staff rotmistr on 19 November 1807, was followed quickly by his rise to rotmistr on 2 February 1809. In 1810, Khilkov volunteered for service in the Danubian Principalities and fought at Silistra and Shumla. He took command of a squadron of the Life Guard Dragoon Regiment and became a colonel on 25 October 1811.

During the 1812 Campaign, Khilkov's regiment was attached to the 1st Brigade of the Guard Cavalry Division of the 1st Reserve Cavalry Corps of the 1st Western Army. He took part in the actions at Wilkomir, Vitebsk, Smolensk, Borodino, Mozhaisk, and was seriously wounded in the abdomen at Burtsovo, near Mozhaisk. For his service, he was awarded the Orders of St. Vladimir (3rd class) and the diamond signs of Order of St. Anna (2nd class). He returned to the army in November 1812, and commanded the 1st Division of the Life Guard Dragoon Regiment the following year. Khilkov fought at Lutzen, Bautzen, Dresden, Kulm (wounded in the right hand, received a golden sword and the Prussian Iron Cross), and Leipzig. In 1814, he commanded a detachment of the light cavalry and fought at Sézanne, Montmirail, Brienne and Arcis sur Aube. In the battle at Le Fère Champenoise, he was wounded in the right arm; soon thereafter, he became a major general on 25 March 1814. More awards followed for his service, including the Prussian Pour le Merite and the Bavarian Order of Maximilian Joseph.

After recuperating, Khilkov took command of the 2nd Brigade of the 1st Uhlan Division on 21 April 1816. Later, he received the Order of St. Anna (1st class) on 24 October 1821, and rose to command the Life Guard Hussar Regiment on 4 June 1822. He was appointed commander of the 2nd Brigade of the Guard Light Cavalry Division on 8 October 1823, and then took command of the 1st Uhlan Division on 29 May 1824. Khilkov became a lieutenant general on 3 September 1826 and received the Order of St. Vladimir (2nd class, 17 June 1827) and the Order of St. Anna (1st class, with crown) on 18 December 1830. He participated in the suppression of the Polish Uprising in 1830 and, during the following year, led in succession the 4th Reserve Cavalry Corps (18 October 1831), 3rd Reserve Cavalry Corps (22 April 1832), 2nd Reserve Cavalry Corps (14-27 April 1833), 4th Infantry Corps (18 December 1833), and 6th Infantry Corps (24 May – 21 July 1835). He was awarded the Order of St. Alexander of Neva with diamond signs on 27 September 1834. He retired with a full pension on 11 January 1837.

Khilkov briefly returned to active service in 1848. During his long career, he also received the Order of St. John of Jerusalem and medals "For Military Merit" and "For XXX Years of Distinguished Service."

KHOMYAKOV, Aleksey Afanasievich (b. 1765 — d. 1846) was born to a noble family from the Moscow *gubernia*. He graduated from the Cadet Corps in 1785 and enlisted as a lieutenant in the Yamburg Carabineer Regiment. He participated in actions against the Swedes in 1788-1790 and served with the Kazan Cuirassier Regiment in Poland in 1792-1794. He transferred as a major to the Commissariat in March 1797, and then joined Orenburg Dragoon Regiment on 15 April 1800. Five years later, Khomyakov transferred to the Lifland Dragoon Regiment (11 October 1805) and served in the 8th Division during campaign in Poland in 1807. He distinguished himself at Eylau, for which he received a golden cross. He became a colonel and chef of the Lifland Dragoon Regiment on 24 December 1807.

In 1808-1811, Khomyakov served in the Danubian Principalities and distinguished himself at Bazardjik (received a cross) and Shumla in 1810 (received the Order of St. George, 4th class, 23 April 1811). During the 1812 Campaign, he commanded a cavalry detachment and fought at Kovel, Pinsk and was captured by the Austrians at Slonim. He was released in May 1813 and joined the Lifland Horse Jager Regiment, fighting at Jauer, Holdberg and Leipzig. For his service, he received the Order of St. Anna (2nd class) with diamonds and the Prussian Pour le Merite. In 1814, he took part in the battles at Bar sur Aube, Soissons, Arcis sur Aube, Le Fère Champenoise (wounded in the right leg and hand) and Paris (wounded in the head). Khomyakov was promoted to major general in 1815 with seniority dating from 25 March 1814. He took command of the 1st Brigade of the 1st Horse Jager Division on 8 July 1814 and became assistant to the commander of the 2nd Horse Jager Division on 3 June 1816. He received command of the 1st Brigade of the 4th Dragoon Division on 22 January 1817. Khomyakov retired because of poor health on 15 March 1821.

KHOVANSKY, Nikolay Nikolayevich (b. 1777 — d. 2 December 1837, St. Petersburg) descended from a Polish noble family. He enlisted in the Life Guard Preobrazhensk Regiment in December 1791. In January 1793, he became the flügel adjutant to Général-en-Chef Prince Yuri Dolgoruky. He was promoted to second major in the 8th Moscow Field Battalion in February 1796. Under Paul I, he transferred as a major to Revel Musketeer Regiment on 29 November 1796 and promoted to lieutenant colonel on 2 January 1800. In 1803, he transferred to the Tavrida Grenadier Regiment (21 November). Khovansky took part in the 1805 Campaign as an adjutant to General Buxhöwden and distinguished himself at Austerlitz (received the Order of St. Vladimir 4th class). He was promoted to colonel on 5 May 1806, and commanded a battalion of the Tavrida Grenadier Regiment in 1806-1807. He fought at Golymin and, at Eylau, he took command of the Tavrida Grenadier Regiment when its commander, Zhemchuzhnikov, was wounded. For his service, Khovansky received the Order of St. George (4th class) on 7 May 1807. In February 1807, he transferred to the Pernov Musketeer Regiment and fought at Guttstadt, Heilsberg (receuved Order of St. Anna, 2nd class) and was wounded in the left hand at Friedland. For his actions, he was appointed chef of the Dneprovsk Musketeer Regiment on 9 July 1807 and awarded an allowance of 1,000 rubles for 12 years.

In 1809, Khovansky briefly served under Prince Sergey Golitsyn against the Austrians and was sent to the Army of Moldavia in the Danubian Principalities to fight the Turks, where his regiment was attached to the 18th Division of Prince Sherbatov. Khovansky distinguished himself during the assault on Bazardjik (received a golden cross) and became a major general on 26 June 1810. That same year, he fought at Varna, Shumla, and Batin (wounded, received the Order of St. George, 3rd class). During the 1812 Campaign, he commanded the 2nd Brigade of the 18th Division of the 3rd Reserve Army of Observation and participated in minor actions at Divin, Pruzhany, Kobrin, Slonim and Borisov in late 1812.

In 1813-1814, Khovansky commanded the 12th Division and distinguished himself at Leipzig and occupied Hanover. In 1814, he fought at Craonne and Clacy and received the Order of St. Vladimir (2nd class) and promotion to lieutenant general on 11 September of that year. After the war, he commanded the 23rd Division and was appointed to the Senate in 1821. He became the Governor General of the Vitebsk, Moghilev and Smolensk *gubernia*s in 1823, received the Order of St. Alexander of Neva on 3 September 1826 and rose to general of infantry on 6 September 1828. He received the diamond signs of the Order of St. Alexander of Neva on 24 April 1830 and the Order of St. Vladimir (1st class) in 1832. In 1836, he became member of the State Council. During his career, he also received two golden swords with diamonds.

KHOVEN, Grigorii Fedorovich (b. 1772 — date of death unclear) was born to a noble family from the Lifland *gubernia*. He graduated from the Artillery and Engineer Cadet Corps in 1790 and began service as a shtyk junker in the 1st Fusilier Regiment. He served in Poland in 1792-1794, where he engaged in battles at Duchenka, Shekochin, Pesochnoe (received the Order of St. Vladimir, 4th class), Warsaw, Kochenizy, Maciejowice and Praga (received a golden sword and a golden cross). In 1807, Khoven took part in the actions at Eylau, Guttstadt, Heilsberg, and Friedland (received the Order of St. Anna, 2nd class). In 1810-1811, he served in the Danubian Principalities, fighting at Silistra, Shumla (received the Order of St. Anna, 2nd class, with diamonds), Batin and Ruse. In addition, for his service against the Turks, he received a diamond ring on 29 May 1811, and two Imperial letters of gratitudes on 25 June 1811, and 25 August 1812. Khoven rose to a lieutenant colonel on 8 December 1810, and took comand of the 22nd Horse Artillery Company of the 4th Reserve Artillery Brigade on 7 April 1811. During the 1812 Campaign, Khoven distinguished himself at Borodino and received a promotion to colonel on 3 December 1812. In 1813-1814, he served at Dresden and Hamburg, for which he was decorated with the Order of St. Vladimir (3rd class) and the Prussian Pour le Merite.

KHRAPOVITSKY, Matvei Yevgrafovich (b. 20 August 1784, Dobrom — d. 12 April 1847, St. Petersburg) was born to a noble family from the Smolensk *gubernia*. He graduated from the Cadet Corps in 1797, and served as adjutant to Grand Duke Constantine during the 1799 Campaign in Italy and Switzerland. He distinguished himself at Trebbia (promoted to lieutenant of the Life Guard Izmailovsk Regiment, 1 August 1799), and during the campaign in the Alps (received the Order of St. Anna, 3rd class).

Returning to Russia, Khrapovitsky became a colonel and commander of the 1st Battalion of the Life Guard Izmailovsk Regiment. During the 1805 Campaign, he distinguished himself at Austerlitz and received the Order of St. George (4th class) on 8 March 1806. In 1807, he joined the main army in April and took part in battle of Friedland on 14 June. He was appointed commander of the Life Guard Izmailovsk Regiment on 9 November 1811.

During the 1812 Campaign, Khrapovitsky commanded the 2nd Brigade of the Guard Infantry Division of the 5th Reserve (Guard) Corps of the 1st Western Army. He distinguished himself at Borodino, where he was wounded in the left leg and his regiment suffered heavy casualties defending Semeyonovskoe. For his actions, Khrapovitsky was promoted to major general on 2 December 1812, with seniority dating from 7 September 1812. Khrapovitsky's regiment was later awarded flags of St. George on 5 January 1814. During the 1813 Campaign, Khrapovitsky was seriously wounded at Kulm (received the Prussian Iron Cross) and spent a year recuperating. After the war, Khrapovitsky was promoted to adjutant general on 11 September 1816 and commanded the 3rd Grenadier Division between 11 September 1818, and 1 February 1830. He became lieutenant general on 24 December 1824, and general of infantry on 3 September 1831. For his service, Emperor Nicholas I gave Khrapovitsky permission to wear uniform of the

Life Guard Izmailovsk Regiment for the rest of his life. In 1846, he became the Military Governor of St. Petersburg on 19 April, member of the State Council on 29 April and member of the Cabinet on 30 October. During his career, Khrapovitsky also received the Orders of St. Alexander of Neva with diamonds, of St. Vladimir (1st class), of St. Anna (1st class), the Prussian Red Eagle and Pour le Merite and the Swedish Order of the Sword.

KHRUSHCHOV, Ivan Alekseyevich (b. 18 August 1774 — d. 8 December 1824) enlisted in the Life Guard Izmailovsk Regiment on 12 January 1778, and was promoted to ensign in 1793. He transferred as a major to the Elisavetgrad Horse Jager Regiment and served against the Polish insurgents in 1794. In 1796, he took part in the Persian Campaign along the Caspian Sea and, in 1799, he served under Rimsky-Korsakov in Switzerland. He became a colonel on 3 September 1799, commander of the Moscow Dragoon Regiment on 16 July 1805, and chef of the Arzamas Dragoon Regiment on 10 October 1806.

Khrushchov was promoted to major general on 5 June 1807 and served in the Danubian Principalities in 1810. During the 1812 Campaign, he commanded the 16th Brigade of the 5th Cavalry Division in the 3rd Reserve Army of Observation. He fought at Novysverzhen, Borisov and many minor actions during the French retreat. In 1813, he served at the siege of Thorn and, in 1814, Khrushchov fought at Laon, Le Fère Champenoise (received the Order of St. George, 4th class, 25 March 1814), and Paris. After the war, he commanded the 1st Brigade of the 1st Horse Jager Division in 1814-1815, and the 1st Horse Jager Division in December 1816 - May 1817. Khrushchov retired because of poor health on 1 April 1818.

KIKIN, Peter (Varfolomey) Andreevich (b. 1775, Alatyr — d. 30 May 1834) was born to a noble family from the Simbirk *gubernia*. He enlisted in the guard in 1777 and studied in the University of Moscow. Starting active service as sergeant in 1796, Kikin became a flügel adjutant on 10 October 1802. In 1802-1806, he served as adjutant to Generals Michelson, Meyendorff and Prozorovsky and became a colonel in 1806. In 1811, he served in the comission to draft military regulations.

During the 1812 Campaign, Kikin served as duty officer at the headquarters of the 1st Western Army and fought at Ostrovno, Lubino (wounded in the head), Borodino (wounded) and Krasnyi. He was promoted to major general on 12 November 1812 and awarded the Order of St. George (3rd class) on 17 February 1813. In 1813-1814, he commanded the 2nd Brigade of the 6th Division and retired on 29 June 1815.

KINSONA, Viktor Osipovich commanded the Ingermanland Dragoon Regiment between 7 August 1800 and 2 June 1803, the Pereyaslavl Dragoon Regiment from 8 January 1807 to September 1807, and served as chef of the Yamburg Dragoon Regiment between 12 September 1807 and 14 December 1810. He was promoted to major general on 24 December 1807.

KLEINMICHEL, Andrey Andreevich (b. 1757 — d. 17 September 1815, Knischin) was born to a German family in Riga; his father was a minister at local church. He enlisted as a corporal in the Kiev Infantry Regiment on 14 November 1775 and was promoted to ensign in 1779. Kleinmichel participated in the operations against the Crimean Tatars in 1783, and rose to lieutenant of artillery in the Cadet Corps in 1784. In March 1789, he transferred to the headquarters of General P. Melissino and returned to the Cadet Corps in late 1789. He became colonel on 1 January 1798, and major general on 8 February 1799. He was appointed director of the Cadet Corps on 12 October 1799, and the corps was renamed to the 2nd Cadet Corps on 22 March 1800. Kleinmichel was promoted to lieutenant general on 11 September 1811.

During the 1812 Campaign, Kleinmichel organized reserve regiments in Jaroslavl *gubernia*. In 1813, he commanded reserve battalions at the siege of Modlin, and took command the 2nd Corps of the Army of Reserve. In 1814, he was appointed director of the Department of Inspection in the Ministry of War on 25 December. He became chief of staff of the 2nd Army on 7 July 1815, but fell seriously ill and died on 17 September 1815, at Knischin.

During his career, Kleinmichel received the Orders of st. Alexander of Neva, of St. Anna (1st class) with diamonds, of St. Vladimir (2nd class, of St. George (4th class), of St. John of Jerusalem and the Prussian Red Eagle.

KLODT VON URGENSBURG, Karl Fedorovich (Karl Gustav) (b. 5 August 1765, Revel — d. 4 August 1822, Omsk) descended from a German family settled in Estland. Educated at Dohm-Schule at Revel, he enlisted as a sergeant in the Bombardier Regiment on 15 February 1780. From 1783 to 1784, he served in Poland and took promotion to shtyk-junker on 23 May 1786. Klodt transferred as a lieutenant to the main headquarters on 18 December 1787. In 1789-1790, he served against the Turks in Kuban Valley and the Caucasus, and earned his captaincy in 1792. In 1797, he returned to the main headquarters, now renamed as the Quartermaster Section of His Majesty's Retinue, and was promoted to major on 28 November 1797, and then to lieutenant colonel on 20 April 1800. In 1802-1805, Klodt served on several cartographic missions to map the western *gubernia*s. Appointed to General Meyendorf's

Corps in 1806, and promoted to colonel on 20 August 1806, he took part in the actions at Bender and Ismail (received the Order of St. George, 4th class) in 1807.

In 1809, Klodt served in General Zass' corps and fought at Isaccea, Tulcea and Ismail and was awarded another Order of St. George (4th class) for twenty five years of distinguished service. In 1810, he participated in actions at Turtukai, Ruse, Rakovitse, Bregovo (received order of St. Anna, 2nd class, and a golden sword). In 1806-1811, he also made first topographic maps of Moldavia, Wallachia, Serbia and Bessarabia and was awarded a diamond ring. During the 1812 Campaign, he served as ober-quartermaster of the 7th Corps of the 2nd Western Army and participated in the retreat to Smolensk. He fought at Moghilev, Smolensk, Borodino (received diamond signs of Order of St. Anna, 2nd class), Tarutino and Maloyaroslavets.

In early 1813, Klodt served in the Prussian Corps of Bulow and fought at Spandau and Luckau. In June 1813, he transferred as a ober-quartermaster to General Winzegorode's Corps and fought at Gross-Beeren, Dennewitz, and Leipzig. For his actions, he was awarded the Order of St. Vladimir, 3rd class, and a promotion to major general on 23 January 1814, with seniority dating from 18 October 1813. He served as commandant of Bremen in 1814 and was appointed chief of staff of the 3rd Corps in March 1815. Klodt took part in the march of the Russian army to France during the Hundred Days, serving as chief of staff of the 2nd Corps. After returning to Russia, he became chief of staff of the Independent Siberia Corps on 28 March 1817. Klodt became seriously ill and died of fever at Omsk on 4 August 1822.

KNIPER, Fedor Yevstafevich (date of birth unclear, 1767/1768 — d. 14 April 1850) was born to a noble family from the St. Petersburg *gubernia*. He enlisted in the Bombardier Regiment on 25 July 1782 and transferred as a corporal to the Life Guard Horse Regiment in 1784. Four years later, he transferred as a sub lieutenant to the 2nd Admiralty Battalion, later renamed to the 2nd Marine Battalion. He served on the galley flotilla during the Russo-Swedish War and fought at Friedrichshamn and Rochensalme. In 1791, Kniper transferred to the 1st Marine Regiment and then served in sucession in the 2nd Battalion of the Estland Jager Corps (13 May 1793), 2nd Battalion of the Tavrida Jager Corps (11 April 1794), the 15th Jager Battalion in 1797, and the 14th Jager Regiment 1799-1804. He became commander of the 14th Jager Regiment on 2 July 1804, and was promoted to colonel on 22 July 1805. Kniper participated in the expedition to Italy in 1805-1807, and served in the Danubian Principalities. He became chef of the 2nd Jager regiment on 10 February 1810, and fought at Braila and Silistra. During the 1812 Campaign, Kniper commanded the 3rd brigade of the 21st Division of the Finland Corps. He was seriously wounded at Polotsk in October 1812, and returned to the army early the following year. He rose to major general on 27 September 1813, and took his discharge six years later. He returned to the army two years later and was appointed commandant of Vitebsk on 12 May 1821. He retired for the second time on 26 January 1834, and died on 14 April 1850.

Two other Knipers served in the Russian army: **KNIPER (Kniper I) Ivan Karlovich**, colonel, was given command of the Odessa Musketeer Regiment on 28 January 1806, and died on 2 February 1807; **KNIPER (Kniper II), Pavel Karlovich**, briefly commanded the 11th Jager Regiment between April-May 1803, before becoming chef of the 2nd Jager Regiment on 19 May 1803. He was promoted to major general on 24 December 1807, and died on 5 December 1809.

KNORRING, Bogdan Fedorovich (b. 21 November 1746 — d. 29 December 1825) was born to a German noble family from the Liflan *gubernia*. He studied in the Infantry Cadet Corps in 1758-1764 and began service as a lieutenant in the Nizhegorod Infantry Regiment. Over the next four years, he participated in the construction of fortifications in the Baltic provinces. He took part in the Russo-Turkish War in 1769-1774, distinguishing himself at Khotin, Large, Kagul (earned promotion to major and the Order of St. George, 4th class), Bender, Giurgiu, and Silistra. Promoted to major general in 1788, Knorring fought in the Russo-Swedish War in 1789-1790 as a quartermaster general. From 1792-1794, Knorring served in Poland, distinguishing himself at Vilna in 1794, for which he was promoted to lieutenant general and awarded the Order of St. George (2nd class). He took a discharge during the officer purges of Emperor Paul I in 1797.

Knorring returned to the army almost a decade later in 1806, when Emperor Alexander promoted him to general of infantry and dispatched him to the Russian army in Poland to mediate between Generals Bennigsen and Buxhöwden. However, Knorring quarreled with Bennigsen and was recalled from the army in 1807. In November 1808, Knorring replaced General Buxhöwden as the commander-in-chief of the Russian army in Finland. Alexander demanded he launch an offensive across the frozen Gulf of Bothnia. Knorring hesitated, but was finally forced to act by General Aleksey Arakcheyev, who traveled to Finland to enforce Alexander's instructions.

In March 1809, Knorring accompanied Prince Bagration's corps during the crossing of the gulf and capture of the Aland Islands. The Russian advance led to the *coup d'etat* in Stockholm, where King Gustavus IV was overthrown. Knorring immediately began negotiations with new Swedish regent and withdrew Bagration's exposed troops. Exasperated with Knorring's actions, Emperor Alexander removed him from command. Knorring retired to Derpt, where he died on 29 December 1825.

KNORRING, Karl Bogdanovich (b. 23 August 1774, Rasthof, Lifland *gubernia* — d. 29 March 1817, Moscow) was born to a German noble family from the Liflan *gubernia*. He began service as vakhmistr in the Life Guard Horse Regiment in January 1787 and transferred as a captain to the army in 1796. He became adjutant to General Ivan Michelson on 16 September 1805, and took part in the 1805 Campaign against Napoleon. In 1806, Knorring became commander of the Tatar Horse (Uhlan) Regiment on 24 June and fought at Pultusk (promotion to colonel, 24 December 1807). In 1811, he took command of the 17th Cavalry Brigade (16 March) and became chef of the Tatar Uhlan Regiment on 9 June 1812. During the 1812 Campaign, he commanded the 17th Cavalry Brigade of the 5th Cavalry Corps of the 3rd Reserve Army of Observation. Knorring was promoted to a major general on 14 December 1812 with seniority dating from 12 August 1812. In 1813, he took part in the actions at Kalisch and Kulm, where he earned the Orders of St. Anna (1st class) and of St. George (3rd class). During his career, Knorring also received the Order of St. John of Jerusalem, Prussian Orders of Red Eagle and Pour le Merite and Austrian Order of Maria Theresa.

KNORRING, Otto Fedorovich (Otto Wilhelm) (b. 18 November 1759, Ervita, Estland *gubernia* — d. 18 August 1812, Dorogobouzh) was born to a German noble family from the Estland *gubernia*. He enlisted in the Astrakhan Carabineer Regiment on 6 January 1770, and took part in Russo-Turkish War in 1771-1791, fighting in Wallachia, at Bender, and Ismail. In 1792-1794, he served in Poland and distinguished himself at Praga, receiving a rank of lieutenant colonel and Order of St. George on 4-7 November 1794.

After his promotion to colonel on 7 March 1798, Knorring took command of the Kazan Cuirassier Regiment on 9 November 1798. The following year, he rose to major general and chef of the Kazan Cuirassier Regiment on 30 December 1799. However, he was discharged with a rank of lieutenant general on 16 March 1800.

Knorring returned to the army six years later and was restored in rank of major general on 27 March 1806. He participated in campaign in Poland and fought at Heilsberg and Friedland in 1807. He became chef of His Majesty's Life Guard Cuirassier Regiment on 9 July 1807, and served under Bagration during the expedition to the Aland Islands in 1809. In 1811, Knorring became chef of the Novgorod Cuirassier Regiment (24 October), and in 1812, commanded the 2nd Cuirassier Division of the 2nd Western Army. Knorring died during the Russian retreat on 18 August 1812 at Dorogobouzh.

Two other Knorrings served in the Russian army at this time: **Knorring, Vladimir Karlovich** (b. 1784 — d. 1864) was born to a German noble family. He began service in the Life Guard Horse Regiment and rose to a cornet in 1804. Knorring participated in every campaign against France in 1805-1815, fighting at Austerlitz, Heilsberg, Friedland, Berezina, Lutzen, Bautzen, Dresden, Kulm, Leipzig, and Paris. Promoted to major general, he took command of the Life Guard Cuirassier Regiment in 1817. Knorring rose to a lieutenant general in 1829, and took part in the operations against the Poles in 1831. He became commander of the Guard Reserve Cavalry Corps in 1835, becoming general adjutant on 18 December 1838 and general of cavalry in 1841; **Knorring, Karl Fedorovich** served in Transcaucasia, rising to lieutenant general in 1799. He actively participated in the Russian annexation of the east Georgian kingdoms in 1800, and became the governor general of newly acquired territories in May 1802. Three years later, he was dismissed for abuse of authority and replaced by Prince Pavel Tsitsianov.

KNYAZHNIN (Knyazhnin I), Alexander Yakovlevich (b. 9 April 1771, St. Petersburg — d. 8 April 1829, St. Petersburg) was born to a noble family from the St. Petersburg, son of prominent writer Jacob Knyazhnin. He enlisted in the Life Guard Preobrazhensk Regiment in 1784, and transferred on 29 March 1785, to the cadet company of the Life Guard Izmailovsk Regiment. He became a captain in the 1st Marine Regiment on 16 January 1795, and later transferred to the Tenginsk Musketeer Regiment in 1797. Although promoted to major on 2 December 1799, Knyazhnin left army for civil service on 14 October 1802, but later returned to military service as a major of Keksholmn Musketeer Regiment in November 1803.

In 1805, Knyazhnin served in Count Tolstoy's Corps in Pomerania and fought at Hameln. In 1807, he served in the 1st Division of Grand Duke Constantine and fought at Guttstadt, Heilsberg (received the Order of St. George, 4th class, 1 June 1808) and Friedland (wounded).

Knyazhnin became commander of the Keksholmn Musketeer Regiment on 25 January 1808, and received promotion to colonel of the Life Guard Preobrazhensk Regiment on 30 March 1810. However, in December 1810, he was court martialed for embezzlement and abuse and relieved of command. Knyazhnin was pardoned in 1811, and received command of the 1st Brigade of the 27th Division of the 2nd Western Army. He took part in the actions at Krasnyi, Smolensk (received the Order of St. Vladimir, 3rd class) and was severely wounded in the abdomen at Shevardino, just two days before Borodino. Knyazhnin left the army to recuperate and did not take part in the critical battles of 1813-1814, although officially he continued to command the 1st Brigade of the 27th Division. Knyazhnin rose to a major general on 3 December 1812, with seniority dating from 5 September 1812.

After the war, he served as deputy director of the Department of Inspection of the Main Headquarters between February 1816 and September 1823. For his dedicated service, he was awarded the Order of St. Anna (1st class) on 13 January 1819, the diamond signs of this order on 12 January 1820, and Order of St. Vladimir (2nd class) on 24 February 1823. Promoted to lieutenant general on 13 January 1826, he soon took his discharge because of poor health later that year.

Knyazhnin was a skilled writer and his literary legacy includes numerous plays and poems. Knyazhnin had three brothers: **Boris** (see below); **Constantine**, who served in the Vladimir Musketeer Regiment and was killed at Eylau; and **Vladimir**, who served in the Keksholmn Musketeer Regiment, lost leg at Heilsberg, and spent the next thirty years in retirement before dying in 1837.

KNYAZHNIN (Knyazhnin II), Boris Yakovlevich (b. 1 September 1777, St. Petersburg — d. 10 April 1854) was born to a noble family from the St. Petersburg, son of prominent writer Jacob Knyazhnin and brother of Alexander Knyazhnin. He enlisted in the Life Guard Izmailovsk Regiment on 12 October 1786, and began active service in 1793. He transferred as a captain to the St. Petersburg Grenadier Regiment on 12 January 1796. He participated in the 1807 Campaign in Poland and fought at Heilsberg and Friedland (received the Order of St. George, 4th class, 1 June 1808). In 1809, as a lieutenant colonel, Knyazhnin became commander of Count Arakcheyev's Musketeer Regiment (24 December), renamed as Count Arakcheyev's Grenadier Regiment on 8 February 1811.

Promoted to colonel on 19 November 1811, Knyazhnin served in the 1st Brigade of the 1st Grenadier Division of the 3rd Corps of the 1st Western Army during the 1812 Campaign. He fought at Smolensk, Lubino, Borodino, Tarutino, Maloyaroslavets, and Krasnyi. In 1813, he was wounded at Lutzen, but recovered to fight at Dresden, Kulm, and Leipzig, receiving the Prussian Pour le Merite and the Red Eagle. Knyazhnin was promoted to major general on 27 September 1813. In 1814, he fought at Brienne, Arcis sur Aube, Le Fère Champenoise, and Paris.

After the war, Knyazhnin was involved in organizing military colonies in Novgorod *gubernia*. He became chief of police in St. Petersburg on 11 February 1826, and was promoted to lieutenant general on 3 September 1826. Appointed to the Senate on 6 April 1828, he later served as Military Governor of Kiev between November 1829 and February 1832. In June 1832, Knyazhnin became a member of the General Audit and was promoted to general of infantry on 22 October 1843.

KOBLE (Cobley), Foma (Thomas) Alexandrovich (b. 1761 — date of death unknown) descended from an English noble family of Cobley; his father served as a consul in Livorno. He served in the Polish court before entering the Russian service with a rank of captain on 6 July 1788 and then transferred as a second major to the Nikolaev Grenadier Regiment on 20 November 1788. He participated in the Russo-Turkish War and fought at Ochakov, Bender, Akkerman, Ismail (wounded), and Macin. Koble was promoted to premier major in the Smolensk Dragoon Regiment in 1793 and to lieutenant colonel on 9 February 1794. Subsequently, he transferred to the Sumsk Light Horse Regiment in 1795 and then to the Tavrida Horse Jager Regiment in April 1796. Koble became a colonel on 21 January 1798, and a year late rose to major general and chef of the Taritsino Garrison Regiment on 19 January 1799.

Koble retired on 19 June 1799, but returned to service in early 1802. He served as commandant of Odessa and chef of the Ladoga Musketeer Regiment in 8 January 1802 — 6 March 1811. During the 1812 Campaign, Koble took effective measures to contain the cholera epidemic in the Khershon *gubernia* and was awarded the Order of St. Anna (1st class). He retired on 20 February 1819.

KOILENSKY, Ivan Stepanovich (b. 1778 — d. 25 November 1814) was born to a petty noble family. He began service as a corporal in the Bombardier Battalion of the Black Sea Galley Fleet on 12 June 1795. Promoted to lieutenant on 26 March 1798, he served in the Ministry of War until becoming a colonel and duty officer to the Minister of War in December 1811. He attended General Mikhail Barclay de Tolly throughout the opening phase of the 1812 Campaign, taking part in the actions at Vitebsk, Smolensk, Lubino, and Borodino, where he commanded artillery of the 4th Corps. Koilensky continued serving as duty officer to Barclay de Tolly during the 1813-1814 Campaigns and received a promotion to major general on 19 December 1813. Returning from Paris, Koilensky died in the Kursk *gubernia* on 25 November 1814.

KOLOGRIVOV, Aleksey Semenovich (b. 1776 — d. 1818) was born to a noble family from the Orlov *gubernia*. He began service as a rent-page in January 1792 and became a page in January 1797. In 1802, he transferred to the military service and became a sub-lieutenant in the Life Guard Jager regiment on 26 November 1802. He served under Prince Peter Bagration in

1805-1807, and participated in numerous actions in Moravia and Poland. He was promoted to colonel on 12 April 1810 and received command of the 49th Jager Regiment on 10 November 1810. Two years later, on 8 May 1812, Kologrivov became chef of the 49th Jager regiment and was attached to the 3rd Brigade of the 27th Division of the 2nd Western Army. He participated in Bagration's retreat from Volkovisk, and fought at Krasnyi, Smolensk, Borodino, and Maloyaroslavets. In 1813, Kologrivov fought at Luzten, Bauzten, and Leipzig, and received promotion to major general on 27 September 1813.

After the war, Kologrivov became commander of the 3rd Brigade of the 27th Division on 12 September 1815, but retired because of poor health on 23 December 1816. His brother, Colonel **KOLOGRIVOV Ivan Semenovich**, commanded the Ingermanland Dragoon Regiment between 8 August 1804 and 19 May 1807.

KOLOMARA, Dmitry Konstantinovich, commanded 8th Jager Regiment in 11 January 1801–16 September 1809, was promoted to colonel on 13 January 1801 and served as chef of the 22nd Jager Regiment between 16 September 1806 and 15 December 1809.

KOLOTINSKY, Mikhail Mikhailovich (b. 1774 — date of death unclear) was born to a Russian noble family. He graduated from the Infantry Cadet Corps and began service as a sub lieutenant in the horse artillery in 1794. He served under Field Marshal Alexander Suvorov in Italy and Switzerland in 1799, distinguishing himself at Mantua and Novi.

In 1807, Kolotinsky participated in actions at Eylau (received the Order of St. Vladimir, 4th class), Guttstadt, on the Passarge (received a golden sword), Heilsberg, and Friedland (received the Order of St. Anna, 2nd class). In 1809-1810, he served in the Danubian Principalities and fought at Braila, Silistra (received a golden sword), Shumla, and Kalafat (received the Order of St. George, 4th class). Kolotinsky became commander of the 22nd Artillery Brigade on 3 October 1810, and colonel on 25 June 1811. During the 1812 Campaign, he served in the 3rd Western Army and took part in operations in Volhynia. In 1813, Kolotinsky distinguished himself at Leipzig (received the Order of St. Anna, 2nd class, with diamonds) and Hamburg.

KOLYUBAKIN, Peter Mikhailovich (b. 1763 — date of death unknown] was born to a noble family from the Kaluga *gubernia*. He enlisted as a sergeant in the Life Guard Preobrazhensk Regiment on 5 June 1775 and rose to ensign on 12 January 1792. He participated in the Russo-Swedish War in 1788-1790 and served in Poland in 1782-1794. Promotion came rapidly as he became a colonel on 21 December 1798, and major general on 28

April 1800. Kolyubakin was discharged on 22 November 1800, but returned to army on 29 March and was appointed chef of the Smolensk Musketeer Regiment on 19 April 1801. He took part in the 1805 Campaign and was wounded at Austerlitz. In 1806-1811, Kolyubakin served in the Army of Moldavia in the Danubian Principalities. He became commander of the 1st Brigade of the 12th Division on 23 August 1810, and assumed command of the 12th Division on 9 March 1811 (confirmed at this position on 3 September 1814). During the 1812 Campaign, Kolyubakin's division was attached to the 7th Corps of Prince Bagration's 2nd Western Army. After being seriously wounded at Saltanovka (Moghilev), Kolyubakin returned to the army in late 1812. In 1813, he commanded his division during the siege of Danzig and received the Prussian Order of Red Eagle. Kolyubakin retired on 13 December 1814.

KOMAROVSKY, Evgraf Fedotovich (b. 29 November 1769, St. Petersburg — d. 25 October 1843, Gorodische, Orlov *gubernia*) was born to a noble family from the St. Petersburg. He was studied at a private boarding school before enlisting as a sergeant in the Life Guard Preoberazhensk Regiment, and then swiftly transferred to the Life Guard Izmailovsk Regiment. He participated in Empress Catherine II's travels to the Crimea in 1787, and served on missions to London, Paris, and Vienna in 1788-1791. Promoted to ensign on 24 August 1792, and to regimental adjutant in 1794, Komarovsky had been appointed adjutant to Grand Duke Constantine and promoted to captain-lieutenant (kapitan-poruchik) in late 1796. He became a captain on 22 August 1797, and a colonel in 1798.

Komarovsky participated in the 1799 Campaigns in Italy and Switzerland, fighting at Bassignano, Tidone, Trebbia, Nure, and in various actions in the Alps. He was awarded the Order of St. Anna with diamonds, the Order of St. John of Jeruslaem, the Sardinian Order of St. Maurice and Lazarus, and was promoted to major general on 15 November 1799. In 1801, he became adjutant general and appointed assistant to the military governor of St. Petersburg in 1802. In 1803, he attended Archduke Joseph in St. Petersburg and was conferred title of count of the Holy Roman Empire.

Komarovsky became an inspector for the Internal Guard on 19 July 1811 and in 1812-1814, served in southwestern *gubernia*s supervising the recruitment of troops and requisition of horses. After 1816, he commanded a corps of the Internal Guard. He was promoted to general of infantry and appointed to the Senate on 25 October 1828.

Komarovsky's literary legacy includes *Zapiski Grafa E. F. Komarovskogo*, his detailed memoir on the court of Catherine the Great and Paul I, as well as Field Marshal Suvorov's campaign in Italy in 1799, and Komarosvky's travels to Austria and France in 1807-1809.

KONOVNITSYN, Peter Petrovich (date of birth unclear, 19 September/9 October 1764, Kharkov *gubernia* — d. 9 September 1822, Peterhof) was born to a prominent Russian noble family. His father, Peter Konovsnitsyn, was the Governor General of St. Petersburg under Catherine II.

Konovsnitsyn graduated from the Cadet Corps in 1774, enlisted in the Life Guard Semeyonovsky Regiment, and became an ensign on 12 January 1785. He participated in the Russo-Swedish War in 1788-1790, and was promoted to sub-lieutenant. He transferred as a premier major to the Regular Army and became an adjutant to Prince Gregory Potemkin on 3 July 1791; he was promoted to lieutenant colonel in September 1791. Rising to colonel on 23 February 1792, Konovsnitsyn commanded the Staroskol Infantry Regiment in Poland in 1793-1794. He fought at Bar, Khelm, and Slonim and was awarded the Order of St. George (4th class) on 27 September 1794. He was promoted to major general and appointed chef of the Kiev Grenadier Regiment on 29 September 1797. Konovsnitsyn became chef of the Uglitsk Musketeer Regiment on 24 March 1798, but was discharged from the army on 14 November 1798, and settled at his estate at Kiarovo.

Konovsnitsyn returned to military service eight years later. He organized and was elected head of St. Petersburg *opolchenye* in 1806. Alexander I awarded him the Order of St. Anna (1st class) and appointed him to the Quartermaster Section of His Majesty's Retinue on 7 December 1806. During the Russo-Swedish War, he served as duty officer at the main headquarters and took part in the actions at Sveaborg, Svartholm (received a golden snuffbox), Abo, Runsalo, and Sando (received the Order of St. George, 3rd class, 1 March 1809). He was promoted to lieutenant general on 24 April 1808, and became chef of the Chernigov Musketeer Regiment on 14 October 1809. In 1810-1811, he protected the Baltic Sea coastline.

During the 1812 Campaign, Konovsnitsyn commanded the 3rd Division of the 3rd Corps of the 1st Western Army. He fought at Ostrovno, Smolensk, and Lubino, and received the Order of St. Vladimir (2nd class). Between 28 August and 5 September, he commanded the Russian rearguard. Konovsnitsyn led the 3rd Division of Tuchkov's corps at Borodino and was moved to reinforce Bagration. He temporarily commanded the 2nd Western Army after Prince Bagration was mortally injured, but Konovsnitsyn was himself wounded in the hand and back (for which he later received a golden sword for courage). After the battle, he commanded the 3rd Corps and took part in the council of war at Fily. In October-December 1812, he served as a duty officer to Kutuzov and fought at Tarutino, Maloyaroslavets, Vyazma, and Krasnyi (received the Order of St. Alexander of Neva). For his actions, he was promoted to adjutant general on 1 January 1813, and was awarded the Order of St. George (2nd class) on 27 February 1813. In the 1813 Campaign, he led the Grenadier Corps and was wounded in the leg at Lutzen. He was awarded 25,000 rubles and recuperated in Baden. He returned to the army in late September 1813, and fought at Leipzig, for which he earned the Order of St. Vladimir (1st class).

In 1814, Konovsnitsyn accompanied Grand Dukes Nicholas and Mikhail from Mainz to Paris. For his actions in 1813, he was also awarded the Prussian Order of Red Eagle, the Austrian Order of Leopold, the Bavarian Order of Maximilian Joseph and the French Order of St. Louis. He was appointed Minister of War on 24 December 1815, and garnered diamond signs of the Order of St. Alexander of Neva. Konovsnitsyn was promoted to general of infantry on 24 December 1817. On 7 December 1819, he was appointed director of the Page Corps, the 1st and 2nd Cadet Corps, the Smolensk Cadet Corps, the Military Orphanage, the Noble Regiment (*dvorianskii polk*), the Noble Cavalry Squadron (*dvorianskii kavaleriiski eskadron*) and the Lycee of Tsarkoe Selo.

Konovsnitsyn died on 9 September 1822, at Peterhof and was buried at the village of Kiarovo in the St. Petersburg *gubernia*.

KOPIEV, Peter Matveevich (b. 1769 — d. 7 September 1812) was born to an officer's family in Vladimir *gubernia*. He graduated from the Artillery and Engineer Cadet corps and began service as a shtyk junker in the Artillery Battalion in 1791. In 1807, he distinguished himself at Heilsberg (received a golden sword) and Friedland (received the Order of St. Anna, 3rd class). In 1808-1809, Kopiev served in Finland. He became lieutenant colonel on 25 February 1811, and commander of the 2nd Light Artillery Company of the 1st Artillery Brigade on the following day.

Kopiev was mortally wounded at Borodino on 7 September 1812, during the 1812 Campaign against Napoleon.

KORATEYEV (Karataev), Vasily Ivanovich (b. 1762, Bakhmach — date of death unknown; excluded from rosters on 14 February 1814) was born to a petty noble family from the Chernigov *gubernia*. He enlisted in the Novotroitsk Cuirassier Regiment in 1774 and rose to cornet in 1779. He took part in the Russo-Turkish war of 1787-1791 and received a golden cross for Ochakov. In 1792-1794, he served in Poland and received a golden cross for Praga. Korateyev distinguished himself at Heilsberg in 1807, earned appointment as the commander of the Ekaterinoslavl Cuirassier Regiment on 27 November 1807, and rose to colonel less than a month later (24 December 1807). In 1809, Korateyev took part in the campaign against Austria. He became commander of the Astrakhan Cuirassier Regiment on 24 October 1811. During the 1812 Campaign, Korateyev served in the 1st Brigade of the 1st Cuirassier Division of the 5th Reserve (Guard) Corps of the 1st Western army. He distinguished himself at Borodino and was promoted to major general on 26 March 1813. In 1813, Korateyev fought at Kulm (received Iron Cross) and was mortally wounded at Leipzig on 16 October 1813.

KORF, Fedor Karlovich (Friedrich Nicholas Georg) (b. 16 April 1773, Virginalen, Courland — d. 11 September 1823, Orel) was born to a Westphalian noble family settled in the Courland *gubernia* in the 16th century. His ancestors served in the Russian army and achieved prominent positions at the Russian court under Elisabeth and Catherine II. Korf enlisted as a vice vakhmistr in the Life Guard Horse Regiment on 1 May 1787, and was promoted to vakhmistr in July 1787. Korf transferred as a captain to the Horse Grenadier Military Order Regiment in January 1794 and served in Poland, fighting at Brest-Litovsk, Vykhod, Brestovits, Brok, and Praga for which he received the Order of St. George (4th class) on 28 April 1795. Later that year, he transferred as a lieutenant to the Life Guard Horse Regiment, where he earned promotions to staff rotmistr in early 1797, and then to rotmistr on 31 March 1798, before transferring as a colonel to the Khastatov's Dragoon Regiment on 20 October 1798. After his promotion to major general, Korf took command of the Prince Eugene of Wuttemberg's Dragoon Regiment (later the Pskov Dragoon Regiment) on 25 October 1800. On 18 April 1801, he became chef of the Pskov Dragoon Regiment and served at this position until 13 September 1814.

Korf commanded a cavalry brigade of the 4th Division during the 1806-1807 Campaigns in Poland and fought at Golymin (received the Order of St. Vladimir, 3rd class) in December 1806 and in rearguard actions during the retreat from Jankovo in 1807. He was wounded in the left hand at Eylau and later received the Order of St. George (3rd class) on 20 April 1807. After recuperating, he fought at Guttstadt (received the Order of St. Anna, 1st class), Heilsberg, and Friedland, for which he garnered a golden sword with diamonds and the Prussian Order of Red Eagle (1st class). In 1809, Korf ommanded a combined cavalry division in General Sergey Golitsyn's Corps and took part in operations against Austria. After the war, he took part in delimitation of the state frontiers in the Tarnopol region. Korf was promoted to adjutant general on 26 September 1810 and commanded 2nd Cavalry Division in 1811.

In April 1812, Korf was appointed commander of the 2nd Reserve Cavalry Corps in the 1st Western Army. He fought at Sventsyani in June 1812, and covered the retreat of the 1st Western Army to Smolensk, where he defended the St. Petersburg district on 18 August (received the diamond signs of Order of St. Anna, 1st class). Between 25 August and 5 September, he commanded the cavalry of the Russian rearguard. At Borodino, Korf led the 2nd and 3rd Cavalry Corps and led numerous cavalry charges against the French cavalry around the Great Redoubt. For his actions, he was promoted to lieutenant general on 12 November 1812, with seniority dating from 5 September 1812. He commanded the cavalry of the rearguard during the Russian retreat to Moscow and fought at Chirikov, Spas-Kupla, and Chernishna. It was Korf who organized the pursuit of the French after the battle of Tarutino. In October-November 1812, he fought at Maloyaroslavets, Vyazma, and Krasnyi, where, after routing the French cuirassiers, he ordered his troopers to collect the French cuirassies as trophies. For his actions, he was awarded the Order of St. Vladimir (2nd class).

In May 1813, Korf fought at Predel, Rochlitz, Waldheim, Dresden, Bischofswerde, Plov, Bautzen, Reichenbach, and Gorlitz. In August, he commanded the 1st Cavalry Corps in the Army of Silesia, and fought at Zopten, Zibeneihen, Goldberg, Katzbach, Löwenberg (Plagwitz), and Ebersdorf; Korf's corps was kept in reserve at Leipzig. From December 1813-January 1814, he took part in siege of Mainz. During the Invasion of France, Korf fought at Vitry and was given command of the 2nd Dragoon Division of the 5th Corps in 1815. After the war, he became commander of the 2nd Reserve Cavalry Corps on 21 April 1816, and was awarded the Order of St. Alexander of Neva on 14 August 1820. He died on 11 September 1823 at Orel.

KORNILOV, Peter Yakovlevich (b. 1770, Podbornoe, Pskov *gubernia* — d. 22 July 1828) was born to a noble family from the Pskov *gubernia*. He enlisted as a corporal in the Life Guard Izmailovsk Regiment on 21 February 1779 and began active service in 1787. He participated in the Russo-Swedish War in 1789-1790 and served in the Life Guard Horse Regiment. He transferred as a captain to the Tenginsk Infantry Regiment on 12 January 1790. Kornilov served in Poland in 1792-1794 and in Italy in 1799. He took part in actions on the Adda and Trebbia Rivers, at Novi, St. Gothard and Devil's Bridge. He became lieutenant colonel on 27 October 1800 and to colonel on 6 August 1806. Appointed commander of 28th Jager Regiment on 7 October 1807, he became chef of the same regiment on 8 February 1808. In 1809-1810, Kornilov served in the Army of Moldavia and distinguished himself at Shumla (awarded the Order of St. George, 4th class, 10 October 1810) and was wounded at Ruse. He rose to major general on 15 August 1810.

In 1812, Kornilov served with the 3rd Brigade of the 18th Division of the 3rd Reserve Army of Observation and fought at Kobryn, Gorodechna, Dubno, and on the Berezine River. In 1813, Kornilov took part in the battles at Koenigswarte, Bautzen, Katzbach, and Leipzig. In 1814, he commanded the 15th Division and fought at Brienne (received the Order of St. George, 3rd class), Laon, and Paris.

Kornilov continued commanding the 15th Division after the war, and became a lieutenant general on 5 May 1818, and eventually command of the 17th Division in January 1827. He participated in the Russo-Turkish War and took part in the siege of Giurgiu, where he died on 22 July 1828. He was buried in Bucharest.

KOSHELEV, Pavel Ivanovich (b. 1764 — date of death unknown) was born to a noble family from the Orlov *gubernia*. He enlisted in the Life Guard Preobrazhensk Regiment on 12 March 1774, but began his active service as vakhmistr in the Life Guard Horse Regiment on 16 June 1789. Koshelev transferred as a rotmistr to the Yamburg Carabineer Regiment on 12 January 1790, and served in the Russo-Turkish War in 1790-1791. Promoted to second major for his actions at Ismail, he later transferred to the Bug Jager Corps. Rising to colonel on 11 November 1798, he took command of the Moscow Garrison Regiment on 23 April 1800. Between 27 September 1800 and 29 April 1801, he served as commandant of Akhtiarsk (Sebastopol).

After briefly serving in the Belevsk Musketeer Regiment, Koshelev was promoted to major general and appointed chef of the Nizhnekamchatsk Garrison Battalion on 30 January 1802. Two years later, he became the Governor of the Kamchatsk region. However, he was court martialed for abuse of authority in April 1806, and was relieved on 11 September 1808. Koshelev returned to service in 1812 when he enlisted in the St. Petersburg *opolchenye* on 12 August. He commanded the 4th Company (druzhina) and fought at Polotsk, Chashniky, Smolyani, and Berezina. For his actions, he received a pardon and was restored in rank on 14 July 1813. In 1813-1814, he served the Army of Reserve and took part in the siege of Modlin (received the Prussian Order of Red Eagle). Koshelev was appointed head of the 3rd District of the Internal Guard in 1821 and was discharged in January 1828.

KOSTENETSKY, Vasily Grigorevich (b. 1769 — d. 18 July 1831, St. Petersburg) was born to a noble family from the Chernigov *gubernia*. He enrolled in the Cadet Corps on 22 September 1779, and was assigned as shtyk-junker to the 2nd Cannonier Regiment on 23 May 1786. He participated in the Russo-Turkish War and fought at Ochakov (promoted to sub lieutenant), Hajibey, and Bender. After promotion to lieutenant in 1794, he became commander of the Black Sea Artillery Battalion in 1795. Kostenetsky took command of the newly organized horse artillery company in St. Petersburg in 1796. In 1797, he rose to captain and was appointed to the 1st Siege Artillery Battalion. In 1799, he took promotion to colonel and command of a company in the Life Guard Artillery Battalion.

In 1805, Kostenetsky commanded a guard artillery company at Austerlitz and was awarded the Order of St. George (4th class) on 8 March 1806. He participated in the 1807 Campaign in Poland and fought at Heilsberg and Friedland. For his actions, he earned a bump up to major general on 28 March 1808, and was decorated with the Order of St. Vladimir (3rd class). In 1809-1810, Kostenetsky took part in efforts to protect the Baltic coastline and rescued several Russian vessels during a storm at Krasnyi Gorky. In 1811, he became commander of the 2nd and 4th Reserve Artillery Brigades of the 2nd Corps and in early 1812, became commander of artillery of the 6th Corps.

During the 1812 Campaign, as the 6th Corps withdrew to Drissa, Kostenetsky was appointed chief of artillery of the 1st line at Drissa Camp. He took part in the defense of Smolensk for which he receievd Order of St. Anna. He distinguished himself at Borodino when he was attacked by the Polish Uhlans, where Kostenetsky boldly counterattacked with his gunners. Later that day, after the death of General Kutaisov, Kostenetsky assumed command of all the Russian artillery and later received the Order of St. George (3rd class, 1 November 1812) for his actions. After Borodino, he commanded artillery in the Russian rearguard. In October-November, he participated in battles at Tarutino (golden sword), Maloyaroslavets,

Vyazma, and Vilna. In early 1813, he became commander of General Winzegorode's corps and fought at Kalisch (received a golden sword with diamonds).

Kostenetsky commanded artillery of the 6th and 7th Corps between 13 April and 9 May 1813, and became commander of the artillery of the Guard Corps on 9 May 1813. He fought at Lutzen, Bautzen (received third golden sword), Dresden, Kulm, and Leipzig. For his actions, he received the Orders of St. Anna (1st class) and of St. Vladimir (2nd class). In December 1813-January 1814, he served in the siege of Kehl and Strasbourg. In 1814 Campaign, he fought at Barcis sur Aube, Arcis sur Aube, Le Fère Champenoise, and Paris. After the war, he commanded artillery in various infantry corps and was promoted to lieutenant general on 9 February 1826.

Kostenetsky died on 18 July 1831, in St. Petersburg during the cholera epidemic. During his career, Kostenetsky was also awarded the Order of St. John of Jerusalem, the Prussian Orders of Red Eagle and Pour le Merite and the Austrian Order of Leopold.

KOSTROMITINOV, Ivan Fedoseevich commanded the Moscow Infantry Regiment in 2 October 1813 — 13 June 1815 and was promoted to colonel on 28 April 1814.

KOTLYAROV, Aleksandr Fedorovich (b. 1773 — d. 25 July 1812) was born to a staff-officer's family. He graduated from the Infantry Cadet Corps and began service as a sub-lieutenant in the 1st Bombardier Regiment in 1794. He participated in the 1805 Campaign in Pomerania and, in 1806-1807, distinguished himself at Pultusk and Eylau, where he was wounded in his hand. He was decorated with a golden cross. Kotlyarov became commander of the 11th Artillery Brigade on 10 February 1811, and lieutenant colonel eleven days later. During the 1812 Campaign, Kotlyarov served with the 1st Western Army and was mortally wounded at Ostrovno on 25 July 1812.

KOTLYAROVSKY, Peter Stepanovich (b. 1782 — d. 2 November 1852) was the son of an Orthodox priest and graduated from the Kharkov Seminary. In winter of 1792, he met Lieutenant Colonel Lazarev who took notice of the intelligent child and convinced his father to let him into military service. Kotlyarovsky joined Lazarev's regiment, earned promotion to a sergeant in 1793, and participated in a series of campaigns in the Caucasus. In 1799, Kotlyarovsky rose to lieutenant and aide-de-camp to Lazarev, who entrusted him with several secret diplomatic missions. In 1800, he distinguished himself in the actions against the Persians on the Iori River, was awarded the Order of St. John of Jerusalem, and promoted to captain. Kotlyarovsky then served under Prince Paul Tsitsianov and fought the Persians in the khanates of Gandja, Sheki, Shirvan, and Baku. Wounded on 14 December 1803, Kotlyarovsky remained in line and fought at Gandja on 15 January 1804. For his part in the capture of this fortress, he was awarded the Order of St. Anna (3rd class) and promoted to major.

Kotlyarovsky's name became famous after he and his 600 men of the 17th Jagers and two guns halted the advance of Prince Abbas Mirza's army of several thousand men in 1804. Though he lost 1/3 of the detachment, Kotlyarovsky stopped the Persians for two days, retreated to the fortress of Shah-Bulah, and defended it for 13 days until rescued by Tsitsianov. Kotlyarovsky was wounded three times during the fighting. For his actions, Kotlyarovsky was awarded the Order of St. Vladimir (4th class). In August 1804, he suppressed the uprising in Karabakh and fought at Baku. In June 1806, he commanded troops in the battle at Khonashin, where 1,644 Russians defeated 20,000 Persians under Prince Abbas Mirza; Kotlyarovsky was promoted to colonel for this feat. However, he was soon disgraced by Commander-in-Chief Gudovich for petitioning on behalf of Colonel Lisanevich, who was unjustly court-martialed. Kotlyarovsky was discharged from the army and spent the next year and half in Tbilisi.

Kotlyarovsky returned to the service in early 1808 and defeated Prince Abbas Mirza again, this time at Kara-Baba. In 1809, Tormasov dispatched him to protect Karabakh, where Kotlyarovsky successfully fought the Persians over next two years. He became commander of the 17th Jager Regiment on 2 February 1809, and chef of the Caucasus Grenadier Regiment on 26 June 1810. He defeated Abbas Mirza yet again at Migri and a fourth time on the Araks River in July 1810. In October 1810, Kotlyarovsky returned to Tbilisi to recuperate from several wounds. For his victories, Kotlyarovsky was appointed chef of the Georgia Grenadier Regiment (15 February 1811) and awarded the Order of St. George (2nd class) with a golden sword for courage. Late in 1811, he captured Akhalkalaki and defeated the Persians on the Araks and in Karabakh. He became a major general on 30 January 1812, and received the Order of St. Anna (1st class).

In October 1812, Kotlyarovsky, with only 2,000 men and 6 guns, crushed some 30,000 Persians under the hapless Abbas Mirza near Aslanduz on the Araks River, earning a promotion to lieutenant general on 15 December 1812, and the award of the Order of St. George (3rd class). Seriously wounded in the head and leg during the assault on Lenkoran in January 1813, he had to retire from the service and was honored with the Order of St. George (2nd class).

Kotlyarovsky never fully recovered from his wounds, and suffered because of them for the rest of his long life, which he spent secluded on his estate. On 3 September 1826, Nicholas I promoted him to general of infantry.

KOZEN, Peter Andreevich (b. 7 September 1776, Narva — d. 19 December 1853) was born to a noble family from the Lifland *gubernia*. He graduated from the Artillery and Engineer Cadet Corps and was assigned to the horse artillery in 1796. He participated in 1805 Campaign and fought at Austerlitz. In 1807, he took part in battle at Heilsberg (bruised) and Friedland and was promoted to colonel on 2 October 1808. He took command of guard horse artillery brigade in April 1811.

During the 1812 Campaign, Kozen commanded the horse artillery in the 5th Reserve (Guard) Corps of the 1st Western Army and fought at Borodino, Maloyaroslavets (received the Order of St. George, 4th class, 23 July 1813), Vyazma, Krasnyi, Borisov, and Vitebsk. In 1813, he took part in the battles at Lutzen, Bautzen (received the Order of St. George, 3rd class, 10 November 1813), Kulm and Leipzig.

Kozen commanded the guard horse artillery in 1814-1819, and served as adjutant to Grand Duke Mikhail Pavlovich. After a brief retirement, he became lieutenant general on 3 September 1826, and head of the St. Petersburg Arsenal and Okhtenck gunpowder factory in February 1827. During the next year, he became inspector of the arsenals and began developing rockets. Kozen became general of artillery on 29 March 1845.

KOZHIN, Sergey Alekseevich, major general, commanded Life Guard Horse Regiment in October-December 1800 and served as chef of the His Majesty's Cuirassier Regiment between 20 December 1800 and 10 June 1807. He participated in the 1807 Campaign, fighting at Guttstadt and was mortally wounded at Heilsberg.

KOZLOVSKY (Kozlovsky II), Platon Timofeyevich (b. 1779 – date of death unknown) was born to a noble family from the Minsk *gubernia*. He studied in the Cadet Corps and enlisted as a sub ensign in the Life Guard Preobrazhensk Regiment on 15 June 1796. After a brief retirement in October 1800, he was promoted to colonel on 11 September 1802 and appointed commander of the Caucasus Grenadier Regiment on 4 May 1803. Kozlovsky took part in operations against Persians in Armenia and fought at Echmiadzin (received the Order of St. George, 4th class, 4 September 1804) and Erivan (wounded). He became commander of the Moghilev Musketeer Regiment on 26 February 1806, and took part in campaigns in Poland. He fought at Golymin, Jankovo, Landsberg, Eylau (wounded in the right leg; received a golden cross), Danzig. On 2 June 1807, he became chef of Staroskol Musketeer Regiment and, on 2 August 1808, chef of the Oliviopol Hussar Regiment.

In 1809, Kozlovsky was sent to the Danubian Principalities and fought at Macin, Constanta, Pravoda, Silistra (received a golden sword), Bazardjik (received a golden cross), Shumla, and Ruse. He distinguished himself at Batin, capturing twenty Turkish guns, and was promoted to major general on 7 December 1810. The following year, he took a serious wound at Vidin. During the 1812 Campaign, Kozlovsky served with the 23rd Brigade of the 7th Cavalry Division of the Army of Danube. He took part in actions in Volhynia and battles at Kovel, Borisov, and Kovno. In 1813, he participated in occupation of Warsaw and was wounded in the right shoulder at Danzig. Kozlovsky received a furlough to recuperate on 1 June 1813, and retired on 15 October 1814. His brother, **KOZLOVSKY (Kozlovsky I) Mikhail Timofeyevich** commanded the Life Guard Preobrazhensk Regiment from 17 November 1807 - 26 September 1810, and was promoted to major general on 24 December 1807.

KOZLYANINOV, Ivan Timofeyevich (b. 12 August 1781 — d. 24 April 1834) was born to a noble family from the Novgorod *gubernia*. He enlisted in the Life Guard Izmailovsk Regiment on 16 June 1786, and rose to sub ensign on 19 September 1787. He fought at Austerlitz in 1805. In 1807, he took part in the actions at Guttstadt, Heilsberg, and was wounded in the left hand at Friedland (received the Order of St. Vladimir (4th class). For his actions, he earned his colonelcy on 23 December 1807.

During the 1812 Campaign, Kozlyaninov commanded a battalion of the Life Guard Izmailovsk Regiment attached to the 2nd Brigade of the Guard Infantry Division of the 5th Reserve (Guard) Corps. At Borodino, Kozlyaninov temporarily commanded the Life Guard Izmailovsk Regiment, where he was seriously wounded. After recuperating, he returned to the army in early 1813, and fought at Lutzen, Bautzen, Kulm (received the Iron Cross) and Leipzig. For his actions, he was promoted to major general on 27 September 1813, with seniority dating from 28 August 1813. In 1814, he continued his service in the Life Guard Izmailovsk Regiment and became commander of the 1st Brigade of the 13th Division on 30 November 1816. He retired because of poor health on 17 February 1823.

KRASNOV (Krasnov I), Ivan Kozmich (b. 1752, Bukanovskoe — d. 6 September 1812,

Kolotsk) was born to a Don Cossack family and enlisted as a private in the Don Cossack Host in 1773. He became regimental clerk (*pisar*) in 1774, sotnik in 1781 and lieutenant in 1785. He participated in the Russo-Turkish War in 1787-1791, and distinguished himself at Kinburn (wounded in the right foot, promoted to captain), Ochakov, Bender (wounded in the left foot, promoted to second major), Ismail (captured three guns and promoted to premier major), and Macin (captured two flags and received a golden medal). Krasnov served in Poland in 1792-1794, where he was awarded the Order of St. George (4th class) and promoted to lieutenant colonel.

Krasnov became colonel in 1796 and major general on 19 March 1799. He took a discharge from the army in late 1799, but returned to service in September 1803. He served as ataman of the Bug Cossacks beginning in 1803, but was accused of abuse of authority in 1806 and relieved of command in April 1808. Krasnov returned to service in April 1812, and was appointed to Platov's Cossack Corps. During the 1812 Campaign, he followed Bagration's 2nd Western Army to Smolensk and commanded a Cossack detachment in rearguard actions between Smolensk and Borodino. Krasnov was mortally wounded when a cannonball shattered his right leg at the Kolotsk Monastery on 5 September. Despite immediate surgery, he died on 6 August 1812. He is buried at the Don Monastery in Moscow on 8 September.

KRASOVSKY, Afanasii Ivanovich (b. 28 January 1781 — d. 30 May 1843) was born to a noble family from the Slobodsk-Ukraine *gubernia*. He enlisted in the Bug Jager Corps on 4 July 1795, and became a sub lieutenant on 15 January 1800. In 1804, he took part in the expedition of the Russian Black Sea Fleet to Corfu. In 1805, he fought in Naples and served on the Russian fleet in the Adriatic Sea in 1806. Transferred to the Army of Moldavia in 1807, Krasovsky participated in actions at Braila, Macin, Girsov, Constanta, Silistra, Ruse, and Giurgiu. In 1811, he distinguished himself at Vidin, Kalafat and Lom Palanka. Krasovsky was given command of the 14th Jager Regiment on 13 January 1812, and was promoted to colonel on 30 January 1812. During the 1812 Campaign, Krasovsky served in the 3rd Brigade of the 15th Division of the 3rd Reserve Army of Observation. He took part in the actions at Kobryn, Borisov, Berezina and Molodechna (wounded in the abdomen). In 1813, he became chef of the 14th Jager Regiment (25 January) and fought at Kustrin, Magdeburg, Dennewitz and Leipzig.

Krasovsky was promoted to major general on 23 January 1814 with seniority dating from 18 October 1813. During the 1814 Campaign, he fought at Craonne and Rheims and later commanded the 3rd Brigade of the 3rd Grenadier Division. He was relieved of duty because of poor health on 6 November 1819, and returned to service in 1823. He became chief of staff of the 4th Corps on 15 May 1823, and was promoted to lieutenant general on 3 September 1826. Between 1826 and 1829, he commanded in succession the 20th Division (31 October 1826-17 June 1828), the 7th Division (10 October 1828) and 3rd Corps (4 October 1829). Krasovsky took part in Russo-Persian War in 1826-1827 and distinguished himself at Utagan and Erevan.

In 1828-1829, Krasovsky participated in the Russo-Turkish War and fought at Shumla, Silistra and Varna. In 1830-1831, he led troops to suppress the Polish uprising. For his actions, Krasovsky received the Order of St. Alexander of Neva with diamonds and an appointment as chief of staff of the 1st Army on 11 September

1831. Later that year, he was promoted to adjutant general on 2 December 1831. He became member of the Council of War on 15 April 1834, rose to general of infantry on 28 April 1841, and took command of the 1st Corps on 6 November 1842.

During his career, Krasovsky was awarded the Orders of St. Alexander of Neva with diamonds, St. Anna (1st class) with diamonds, St. Vladimir (1st class), Prussian Order of Red Eagle, medals "For Military Honor" and "XXX Years of Distinguished Service," and two golden swords.

KRETOV, Nikolay Vasilievich (b. 23 July 1773, Moscow — d. 23 January 1839, Grafovka, Kursk *gubernia*) was born to a noble family from Moscow. He enlisted as a sergeant in the Life Guard Preobrazhensk Regiment on 6 October 1785 and transferred as a vakhmistr to the Life Guard Horse Jager Regiment on 9 April 1789. He participated in the Russo-Swedish War in 1789-1790. He transferred as a captain in the regular infantry on 12 January 1793, and was appointed krig-zalmeister in the commissariat on 6 March 1793. Kretov served in Poland in 1794 and briefly served in the British Navy in 1795-1796. He was appointed major of the Moscow Dragoon Regiment on 14 June 1797, promoted to lieutenant colonel on 17 October 1798, and appointed flügel adjutant on 3 November 1798. He took part in Field Marshal Suvorov's campaigns in Italy and Switzerland in 1799, rising to colonel on 31 December 1799, and receiving the Order of St John of Jeruslaem and the Sardinian Order of St. Maurice and Lazarus. He retired from the army with a rank of major general on 12 January 1802, and lived London in 1803-1804.

Kretov returned to service in August 1806 and was appointed to the Imperial Retinue. In 1806-1807, he served at the Russian headquarters. He was awarded the Order of St. Vladimir (3rd class) for his actions at Pultusk, and appointed chef of the Ekaterinoslavl Cuirassier Regiment on 6 February 1807. Kretov distinguished himself at Eylau and received the Order of St. George (4th class). In June 1807, he served in Gorchakov's Corps and fought at Guttstadt (golden sword with diamonds), on the Passarge River and at Heilsberg (received the Order of St. Anna and the Prussian Order of Red Eagle). In 1809, he served in Prince Golitsyn's Corps against the Austrians.

During the 1812 Campaign, Kretov commanded the 2nd Cuirassier Brigade of the 2nd Cuirassier Division of the 8th Corps in the 2nd Western Army. He took part in the battles at Smolensk, Borodino (received the Order of St. George, 3rd class, 1 November 1812) and Krasnyi (received the Order of St. Anna, 1st class). In 1813, he took command of the 2nd Cuirassier Division and fought at Lutzen, Bautzen, Dresden, Kulm (received the Order of St. Vladimir, 2nd class), and Leipzig. He was promoted to lieutenant general on 27 September 1813. During the 1814 Campaign, Kretov crossed the Rhine at Basel and took part in the actions at La Rothière, Bar sur Aube, Labruessel, Troyes Arcis sur Aube, Le Fère Champenoise, and Paris (received Bavarian Order of Maximilian Joseph).

Newly returned to Russia, Kretov led the 2nd Cuirassier Division back to France during The Hundred Days. He arrived to Paris after Waterloo and took part in the grand parade of the Russian army at Vertus in August 1815. After the war, he commanded the 2nd Cuirassier Division for eight years, was appointed to the Senate in December 1823 and took indefinite furlough to recuperate in January 1824. He was discharged from the army on 28 January 1831, and died on 23 January 1839, in the Kursk *gubernia*.

KREITZ, Cyprian Antonovich (b. 21 July 1777, Rechitse, Minsk *gubernia* — d. 25 July 1850, Bukhof, Courland *gubernia*) was born to a German noble family. He began service in the Polish army and served as an adjutant to King Stanislaus of Poland. He entered the Russian service on 7 February 1801, and became colonel of Count Zubov's Hussar Regiment (later the Sumsk Hussars). Kreitz took part in the 1805 Campaign and fought at Austerlitz. In 1807, he distinguished himself at Mohrungen, where he was wounded thirteen times and captured by the French. Released in late 1807 after Tilsit, he became commander of the Sumsk Hussar Regiment on 29 February 1808. He became chef of the Siberia Dragoon Regiment on 20 March 1810.

During the 1812 Campaign, Kreitz served in the 10th Brigade of the 3rd Cavalry Division of the 3rd Reserve Cavalry Corps in the 1st Western Army. He fought at Vitebsk, Smolensk, Borodino (wounded four times), Tarutino, Maloyaroslavets, and Vyazma. He was promoted to major general on 28 December 1812, with seniority dating from 27 July 1812. In 1813, he served at Modlin, Magdeburg, Lutzen, Hamburg, and Leipzig. In 1814, he was appointed govenor general of Duchy of Sleiswig. Returning to Russia, he commanded cavalry brigades in 1815-1821, and became commander of the 3rd Dragoon Division on 11 April 1822. He was promoted to lieutenant general on 24 December 1824, and took part in the Russo-Turkish War of 1828-1829. Kreitz was appointed commander of the 2nd Hussar Division on 9 October 1829, then became commander of the 5th Reserve Cavalry Corps on 1 October 1830, and took part in the suppression of the Polish uprising. He was promoted to general of cavalry on 27 April 1831, and was given command of the 2nd Infantry Corps on 18 October 1831.

In 1839, Kreitz was conferred the title of count of the Russian Empire. He was appointed chef of the Siberia Uhlan Regiment on 26 May 1845, but was relieved of other positions on 29 May 1845. He died on 25 July 1850, at his estate at Bukhof in Courland *gubernia*.

During his career, Kreytz was awarded the Orders of St. Alexander of Neva with diamonds, of St. George (2nd class), of St. Anna (1st class) with diamonds, of St. Vladimir (1st class), the Polish Order of St. Stanislaus and the Prussian Order of the Red Eagle, medals "For Military Honor" and "XXXV Years of Distinguished Service," and two golden swords for courage.

KRIDENER, Karl Antonovich, colonel, commander of the Life Guard Semeyonovsk Regiment from 31 December 1809 to 28 December 1812. During the 1812 Campaign, he fought at Borodino and Krasnyi.

KRISHTAFOVICH, Egor Constantinovich (b. 1769, Dergash, Smolensk *gubernia* — d. 15 December 1829) was born to a noble family from the Smolensk *gubernia*. He enlisted as a sergeant in the Smolensk Infantry Regiment on 2 March 1776, and transferred as a corporal to the Life Guard Izmailovsk Regiment on 26 March 1782. He moved as a sub lieutenant to the Malorossiiskii (Little Russia) Grenadier Regiment on 12 October 1787, and took part in the Russo-Turkish War in 1788-1791. He served in Poland in 1794, and transferred as a major to Podolsk Musketeer Regiment in 1803. Two years later, he participated in the campaign against Napoleon and fought at Austerlitz, where he was wounded and received the Order of St. George (4th class) on 24 January 1806.

Krishtafovich participated in the 1807 Campaign in Poland, was appointed commander of Malorossiiskii (Little Russia) Grenadier Regiment on 1 September 1807, and promoted to lieutenant colonel on 24 December 1807. He retired, because of poor health, with a rank of colonel on 6 May 1809. The following year, Krishtafovich returned to military service with a rank of lieutenant colonel and took command of the 1st Marine Regiment on 3 May 1810. On 12 February 1811, he transferred to the Life Guard Jager Regiment and was promoted to colonel on 5 July 1811. Three months later, on 17 October 1811, Krishtafovich became commander of the Ekaterinoslavl Grenadier Regiment.

During the 1812 Campaign, Krishtafovich served in the 2nd Brigade of the 1st Grenadier Division of the 3rd Corps in the 1st Western Army and was wounded at Borodino leading his regiment's attack (received the Order of St. Vladimir, 4th class). Krishtafovich took part in the 1813 Campaign and was promoted to major general on 27 September 1813. In 1815-1816, he served as assistant to commanders of the 1st and 2nd Grenadier Division. He became commander of the 2nd Brigade of the 2nd Grenadier Division on 23 September 1816, briefly commanded brigades in 10th and 12th Divisions, and received command of the 2nd Division on 23 May 1824. He was promoted to lieutenant general on 3 September 1826, and appointed commandant of Dünaburg on 11 April 1829.

KRYZHANOVSKY, Maxim Constantinovich (b. 20 August 1777 — d. 18 May 1839, St. Petersburg) was born to a noble family from the Poltava *gubernia*. He as enlisted in the 3rd Marine Battalion on 7 July 1792 and rose to sub lieutenant on 23 April 1797. In 1807, he was given command of the battalion of Imperial Militia and, the following year, his unit was transformed into the Life Guard Finland Battalion. Kryzhanovsky was promoted to colonel on 7 July 1809, and reorganized his battalion into Life Guard Finland Regiment on 31 October 1811. During the 1812 Campaign, he served in the 3rd Brigade of the Guard Infantry Division of the 5th Reserve (Guard) Corps and distinguished himself at Borodino (received the Order of St. George, 4th class, 2 December 1812), and Krasnyi.

In 1813, Kryzhanovsky took part in the battles at Lutzen, Bautzen, and Kulm. He was promoted to major general on 27 September 1813, with seniority dating from 2 May 1813. He was severaly wounded four times in the leg, hand, and chest at Leipzig, and was forced to leave the army in order to recuperate.

Kryzhanovsky was relieved of duty as the commander of the Life Guard Finland Regiment on 23 January 1816, and became treasurer of the Capitul of the Imperial Orders in July 1817. He rose to lieutenant general on 3 September 1826, and took appointment in the General Audit on 23 June 1832. In 1837, he became commandant of the St. Petersburg fortress and member of the Council of War.

KUDASHEV, Nikolay Danilovich (b. 1784 — d. 9 November 1813, Leipzig) began service as a non-commissioned officer in the Life Guard Horse Regiment on 11 February 1801. He took part in the 1805 Campaign, fought at Ausetrlitz, and was promoted to lieutenant on 13 February 1806. In 1807, he fought at Guttstadt, Heilsberg, and Friedland. He participated in the Russo-Swedish War in 1808-1809, received the Order of St. George (4th class) on 27 February 1809, and became adjutant to Grand Duke Constantine.

Promoted to colonel on 25 October 1811, Kudashev commanded a guerilla detachment in

1812 and was promoted to major general on 7 January 1813. During the 1813 Campaign, he commanded the advance guard of Platov's Corps and was mortally wounded at Leipzig.

KULNEV, Ivan Petrovich (b. 1765 — d. 1840) was born to a noble family from the Kaluga *gubernia*, brother of Jacob Kulnev (below). He graduated from the Cadet Corps and was assigned as a lieutenant to the Chernigov Infantry Regiment on 1 March 1785. He became colonel and took command of the St. Petersburg Grenadier Regiment on 16 July 1798. He was promoted to major general and chef of the Belozersk Musketeer Regiment on 11 May 1799.

The same year, Kulnev became commander of the Astrakhan Grenadier Regiment on 25 May, but was discharged from the army on 3 August. He returned to the military service two years later and was appointed commander of the St. Petersburg Grenadier regiment on 16 June 1801. He became chef of the Revel Garrison Regiment on 31 December 1802. He served in the Army of Moldavia in 1809-1810.

After appointment as chef of the Vologda Infantry Regiment on 29 January 1811, Kulnev soon took a discharge from the army on 9 November 1811. He returned in September 1812, and led a brigade in Wittgenstein's corps. During the 1812 Campaign, Kulnev took part in the actions at Polotsk and on the Berezina River. In 1813-1814, he served in the sieges of Danzig and Hamburg, receiving the Prussian Order of Red Eagle and the French Legion of Honor. Kulnev was relieved of command in 1816 and discharged in January 1834.

KULNEV, Jacob Petrovich (b. 6 August 1763, Lutzin, Vitebsk *gubernia* — d. 1 August 1812, Sivoshino, Vitebsk *gubernia*) was born to a noble family from the Vitebsk *gubernia*. He studied in the Cadet Corps and took assignment as a lieutenant to the Chernigov Infantry Regiment on 1 March 1785. Late that year he joined the St. Petersburg Dragoon Regiment and participated in the Russo-Turkish War in 1787-1792. Kulnev was assigned to the Perejaslavl Horse Jager Regiment on 15 November 1789 and fought in Poland in 1792-1794, distinguishing himself in the actions at Oshmyani, Lida, Kobryn, Brest-Litovsk (promoted to rotmistr) and Praga (promoted to major). In 1797-1798 and 1801-1806, Kulnev served in the Sumsk Hussar Regiment and did not participate in any military operations. He transferred to the Grodno Hussar Regiment as a lieutenant colonel in late 1806.

Kulnev participated in the 1807 Campaign in Poland, fighting at Guttstadt, on the Passarge River (received the Order of St. Vladimir, 4th class) Heilsberg, and Friedland. For his actions, he was promoted to colonel and awarded the Order of St. Anna (2nd class). In 1808, he served under Prince Bagration in Finland and distinguished himself commanding the advance guard. He took part in the actions at Kalaioki, Pihaioki, Sikaioki, Lappo, Kuortane, Salmi, and Oravais (received the Order of St. George, 3rd class, and 5,000 rubles). Decorated with the Order of St. George (3rd class), Kulnev became major general on 24 December 1808. The next year, he led his troops to the Aland Islands and was among the first to reach Sweden across the frozen Gulf of Bothnia. For his actions, Kulnev was awarded the Order of St. Anna (1st class) and appointed chef of the Byelorussia Hussar Regiment on 27 April 1809.

After the war, Kulnev briefly remained in Finland as an assistant to General Demidov, who garrisoned the Aland Islands. In 1810, Kulnev accompanied General Kamenski to the Danubian Principalities and assumed command of the Russian advance guard. He fought at Ruse, Silistra, Shumla, and Batin (received a golden sword). However, he had an argument with Kamenski during the battle at Batin and left the army. Kulnev became chef of the Grodno Hussar Regiment on 29 January 1811. During the 1812 Campaign, he commanded the advance guard of General Wittgenstein's corps and fought in rearguard actions at Wilkomir and Druya. He defeated the French at Klyastitsy on 31 July, but recklessly attacked the French forces on 1 August, and was mortally wounded when a French projectile reaped both his legs. Kulnev was initially buried on the battlefield, but his remains were transferred to Ilsenberg in Vitebsk *gubernia* in 1831. Kulnev's had two brothers, **Ivan** (see above) and **Nicholas**, who commanded the Riga Dragoon Regiment between 13 June 1815 and 11 May 1816.

KURUTA, Dmitry Dmitryevich (b. 1769 — d. 25 March 1833) descended from a Greek family. He enrolled in the Corps of Foreign Fellow Co-Believers in 1787, and transferred as a sub-lieutenant to the St. Petersburg Grenadier Regiment. He tutored Grand Duke Constantine in the Greek and joined the navy in 1788. Five years later, he was appointed to the Imperial Retinue and took part in the 1805 Campaign. He distinguished himself at Austerlitz and was awarded the Order of St. George (4th class). Promoted to colonel on 1 February 1808, he became adjutant to Grand Duke Constantine on 31 July 1810.

During the Russian Campaign, Kuruta served as ober-quartermaster in the 5th Reserve (Guard) Corps and fought at Borodino and Krasnyi. He was promoted to major general on 6 January 1813. During the campaign in Saxony, he fought at Bautzen, Dresden, Kulm (received the Prussian Iron Cross), and Leipzig. He took part in the 1814 Campaign and distinguished himself at Le Fère Champenoise, receiving the Prussian Order of the Red Eagle, the Austrian Order of Leopold and the Bavarian Order of Maximilian Joseph.

In 1815, Kuruta served as Grand Duke Constantine's chief of staff in Warsaw and was appointed director of the 2nd Cadet Corps and chef of the Noble Regiment (*dvorianskii polk*) on

18 November 1815. A line of promotions followed: lieutenant general on 6 October 1816, general of infantry on 7 July 1828; title of count of the Russian empire was conferred on 3 September 1826. Kuruta participated in operations in Poland in 1830-1831, and was awarded the Order of St. George on 19 August 1831. The following year, he became a member of the Council of War (23 June).

KUTAISOV (Kutaysov), Alexander Ivanovich (b. 10 September 1784, St. Petersburg — d. 7 September 1812, Borodino) was born to a prominent noble family. His father was a Turk captured by the Russians at Bender in September 1770, baptized Ivan Pavlovich, and presented to Paul. When Paul became the Emperor, the former captive initially served as the Emperor's barber, but carved out a brilliant career at the court. He became jagermeister on 18 December 1798, and ober-stalmeister on 13 January 1800. He was conferred the title of baron on 5 March, and of count on 17 May 1799, receiving the Orders of St. Anna (1st class), of St. Andrew the First Called and of St. John of Jerusalem.

His son, Alexander (the core subject of this biography), enlisted as a vice vakhmistr in the Life Guard Horse Regiment on 18 January 1793, and rose to vakhmistr in December 1793. On 13 January 1796, Kutaisov transferred as a sergeant to the Life Guard Preobrazhensk Regiment and, on same day, was appointed as captain to the Veliki Lutsk Infantry Regiment. On 13 November 1796, he became ober-provianmeister in the headquarters of Lieutenant General Mikhail Kutuzov's Corps on the Finnish border.

On 18 September 1798, 14-year-old Alexander became general proviantmeister–lieutenant with a rank of lieutenant colonel. His actual service began at 15, when he was promoted to colonel and appointed to the Life Guard Artillery Battalion on 6 February 1799. He studied extensively the artillery science over the next five years and served as adjutant to artillery inspector General A. Korsakov in October 1799 through May 1803. He was transferred to the 2nd Artillery Regiment on 5 July 1803. Two years later, he was dispatched with reinforcements to the main Russian army, but arrived after the battle of Austerlitz. Promoted to major general on 23 September 1806, Kutaisov served in General Fedor Buxhöwden's Corps and took part in battle at Golimyn in December 1806. Kutaisov distinguished himself at Eylau, when, commanding the Russian artillery of the right flank, he diverted his companies to the left flank and halted Marshal Davout's advance. For his actions, he was awarded the Order of St. George (3rd class) on 20 April 1807.

From May to June 1807, Kutaisov commanded artillery at Lomitten (received the Order of St. Vladimir, 3rd class), Heilsberg and Friedland (received a golden sword). Kutaisov commanded the artillery of Golitsyn's Corps during the campaign against Austria in 1809. However, he did not participate in actions and took a prolonged furlough in 1810. Over the next two years, he traveled in Europe, learned six languages (French, German, English, Italian, Turkish and Arabic), and studied artillery and fortifications in France and Austria. Returning to Russia in summer of 1811, he served on the Commission on Military Regulations and contributed articles on the artillery to the *Uchrezhdenie dlia upravlenia bolshoi deistvuiushei armii* [Establishment for the Administration of the Large Active Army]. In addition, he wrote a treatise "General Rules for Artillery Operations on the Battlefield." Kutaisov briefly served as commander of the entire Russian artillery from January to February 1812, and was appointed commander of the artillery in the 1st Western Army on 3 March 1812.

During the 1812 Campaign, Kutaisov commanded the Russian rearguard during the initial retreat of the 1st Western Army and was wounded at Kakuviachina, near Vitebsk in August. He commanded the Russian artillery at Smolensk on 16 August, defending the Malakhov Gates and the Rachenka Suburb, and then took part in the actions at Lubino and Soloveyovo on 19-20 August.

At Borodino, Kutaisov commanded the Russian artillery but was killed while leading the infantry charge against the French at the Great Redoubt. His body was never found, and is probably buried in a common grave at Borodino.

KUTEINIKOV (Kuteinikov II), Dmitry Yefimovich (b. 1766 — d. 1844) was born to a Cossack staff officer's family. His father, Efim Kuteinikov, was campaign ataman (pokhodnoi ataman) and judge (*voiskovoi sudia*). Kuteinikov began service as a private Cossack on 13 January 1778, and took part in operations on the northern Caucasus in 1779-1787. He was promoted to esaul on 31 July 1780, and took part in the Russo-Turkish War in 1787-1790. In 1787, Kuteinikov distinguished himself at Kinburn and was promoted to a Cossack colonel and awarded a golden medal. He served in Poland in 1792-1794 and was promoted to colonel (of regular army) on 8 November 1799. In 1800-1801, he took part in expedition to Orenburg. He participated in the 1807 Campaign in Poland and was awarded the Order of St. George (4th class) on 3 June 1807.

In 1808-1810, Kuteinikov served in the Danubian Principalities and distinguished himself at Braila, Girsov, Rassevat (received the Order of St. George, 3rd class, 3 January 1810) and Tataritsa. He was promoted to major general on 14 June 1809, and commanded the Cossack brigade in Volhynia in 1810-1811.

During the 1812 Campaign, Kuteinikov commanded a brigade in Platov's Corps and fought at Mir, Romanov (wounded in the left hand), Smolensk, Borodino, Maloyaroslavets, Dorogobouzh, Smolensk, and Kovno. He was discharged because of poor health on 4 April 1813. After recuperating, he returned to service and, in 1820, was appointed to the committee to establish the Don Cossack Army. Kuteinikov was elected Don Cossack Ataman on 19 June 1827, promoted to lieutenant general on 18 December 1827, and to general of cavalry on 3 May 1834. He retired on 22 February 1836. During his career, he received the Orders of St. Alexander of Neva with diamonds, of St. Vladimir (2nd class), the Prussian Pour le Merite, medal "For XXX Years of Distinguished Service" and a golden sword with diamonds.

KUTUZOV, Alexander Petrovich (b. 1777, Stavropol — d. 27 September 1817, Tbilisi) was born to a noble family from the Novgorodo *gubernia*. He enlisted in the Life Guard Izmailovsk Regiment in 1788 and was promoted to ensign on 19 September 1798. He took wound to the left hand at Austerlitz in 1805 and to the right shoulder at Friedland in 1807. For his actions, he was awarded the Order of St. George (4th class) on 1 June 1808 and a promotion to colonel on 30 July 1808.

During the 1812 Campaign, Kutuzov served in the Life Guard Izmailovsk Regiment and took part in the battles at Borodino, Tarutino, Maloyaroslavets and Krasnyi. In 1813, he was wounded in the thigh at Lutzen and was promoted to major genetral on 27 September 1813.

In 1815-1816, he led brigades in the 2nd Grenadier Division and took command of the Reserve Brigade of the Independent Georgian Corps on 28 August 1816. Kutuzov became commander of the 20th Division on 16 January 1817, but died on 27 September 1817 in Tiflis (Tbilisi).

KUTUZOV, Ivan Stepanovich (b. 1770 — d. 18 October 1813, Leipzig) was born to a noble family from the Tver Gubernia. He enlisted as a sub ensign in a construction battalion in Pavlovsk, rose to ensign on 28 April 1793, and transferred as a lieutenant to the 6th Marine Battalion on 17 February 1794. Kutuzov served in Poland in 1794, and participated in expedition to Holland in 1799, where he was captured at Alkmar. He returned to Russia in summer of 1800, and after a brief retirement, was appointed lieutenant colonel of the Sofia Musketeer Regiment on 13 January 1802. He participated in the 1807 Campaign in Poland and fought at Eylau (wounded in the abdomen), Guttstadt, Heilsberg (wounded in the right foot), Friedland (wounded in the head) and Tilsit (wounded in the right leg). For his actions, he received his colonelcy on 24 December 1807, and took command of the Sofia Musketeer Regiment on 9 October 1808.

From 1808 to 1811, Kutuzov served in the Army of Danube and fought at Braila (wounded in the chest), Nikopol, Lovchea (received the Order of St. George 4th class, 20 June 1812), Ruse, Silistra and Slobodzea. Kutuzov became commander of the Belostock Musketeer Regiment on 5 July 1810, and chef of the Vyborg Infantry Regiment on 31 October 1810.

During the 1812 Campaign, he served in the 2nd Brigade of the 2nd Division in the Army of Danube and fought at Brest and Volkovisk. In 1813, Kutuzov served in the 3rd Western Army and fought at Thorn, Bautzen (wounded in the left hand), Dresden and was mortally wounded in the chest at Leipzig.

KUTUZOV (Golenischev-Kutusov), Mikhail Illarionovich, (b. 16 September 1747, St. Petersburg — d. 28 April 1813, Bunzlau) was born to an ancient Russian noble family; his father Illarion Golenischev-Kutuzov was a lieutenant general of the Russian Army and the Senator. Mikhail Kutuzov studied in the

Combined Artillery and Engineer School and was promoted to ensign on 12 January 1761. In 1762, he transferred as a captain to the Astrakhan Infantry Regiment commanded by General Alexander Suvorov and fought in Poland in 1764–69. In 1770-1774, he fought the Turks at Ryabaia Mogila, Larga, Kaluga (promoted to a premier major), and Poneshta (promoted to a lieutenant colonel). At Shumy in 1774, Kutuzov took a serious wound to the head and lost his right eye in action. For his courage, he was decorated with the Order of St. George (4th class) on 7 December 1775. In 1776-1777, he traveled to Europe to recuperate. Returning to Russia, he was promoted to colonel on 8 July 1777, and took command of the Lugansk Pikineer Regiment.

Kutuzov served in the Crimea in 1778-1783, commanding the Mariupol Light Cavalry Regiment. He became a major general and chef of the Bug Jager Corps on 5 December 1784. Kutuzov participated in Russo-Turkish War of 1787-1791 and took another serious wound to the head at Ochakov in 1787. From 1789 to 1790, he fought at Kauschanan, Akkerman, Bender, and commanded the Russian left flank column at Ismail. For his actions, he was promoted to a lieutenant general and awarded the Order of St. George (3rd class) on 5 April 1791. He distinguished himself at Babadag and Macin in 1791, and received the Order of St. George (2nd class) on 29 March 1792. After briefly serving Poland in 1792, Kutuzov became ambassador to Turkey in 1793. Returning to Russia, he served as the Governor General of the Kazan and Vyatka *gubernia*s in 1794 before becoming director of the Cadet Corps on 27 September 1794.

From December 1797 to January 1798, Kutuzov served on a diplomatic mission to Prussia and persuaded King Friedrich Wilhelm III to sign a treaty with Russia. For this success, he became chef of the Ryazan Musketeer Regiment on 5 January 1798, was appointed head of the Finland inspectorate and promoted to general of infantry on 15 January 1798. In October 1799, he took command the expeditionary corps in Holland but when he reached Hamburg he learned of the end of hostilities. He served as the Military Governor of Lithuania (6 November 1799–23 July 1801) and chef of the Pskov Musketeer Regiment (6 November 1799). In the summer of 1800, Kutuzov received command of newly organized Army of Volhynia, took part in grand maneuvers at Gatchina and was awarded the Order of St. Andrew the First Called on 20 September 1800. He became very close to Paul I and dined with him the evening the emperor was assassinated. Emperor Alexander appointed Kutuzov as the Military Governor of St. Petersburg on 30 June 1801, but he was relieved of position on 1 September 1802. He retired to his estate Goroshki in Volhynia for the next two years.

In 1805, Kutuzov commanded the Army of Podolsk but, before his force could link up with the Austrians, Napoleon defeated the latter at the battle of Ulm. Kutuzov accomplished a fighting retreat from Branau to Olmutz, defeating the French at Krems (Dürrenstein). In November 1805, he proposed to withdraw to the Russian frontiers and wait for reinforcements, but was ignored by Alexander and his entourage. Lightly wounded at Austerlitz, he was largely blamed for the defeat. After the war, he was appointed the Military Governor of Kiev on 17 October 1806. In 1808, Kutuzov became an assistant to the commander-in-chief of the Army of Moldavia, Field Marshal Prozorosvky, but disagreed with him over strategy. As a result, Kutuzov was recalled from the army and appointed the Military Governor of Vilna on 15 July 1809. Alexander made him commander-in-chief of the Army of Danube on March 1811. The same year, Kutuzov decisively defeated the Turkish army at Ruse and Silistra and was conferred title of count on 10 November 1811. He negotiated and concluded a peace treaty at Bucharest on 28 May 1812. He was appointed member of the State Council on 17 April 1812.

During the 1812 Campaign, Kutuzov was elected a commander of the Moscow and St. Petersburg *opolchenye* on 28-29 July and was conferred title of prince on 10 August. On 20 August, Alexander I appointed him the commander-in-chief of all the Russian forces. Kutuzov's strategy was to wear down the French by incessant minor engagements while retreating and preserving his army. Under public pressure and against his better judgment, he offered a major battle at Borodino on 7 September and, after a council of war at Fily, ordered the surrender of Moscow. He was promoted to general field marshal on 11 September 1812. In October-November, he reorganized his army at the Tarutino Camp and fought the French at Tarutino, Maloyaroslavets, Vyazma, and Krasnyi. For his actions, he was conferred a title of prince of Smolensk. In November-December 1812, he did not pursue the French vigorously, preferring not to engage them and let the severe weather and lack of supplies destroy the enemy. For his service, he was decorated with the Order of St. George (1st class), on 24 December 1812. In January 1813, he opposed Alexander's decision to continue the war in Germany and wanted to return the troops to Russia. As the Russian army advanced through Poland, Kutuzov became seriously ill and died at Bunzlau (now Boleslawiec), on 28 April 1813. His body was transferred to Russia and buried in the Kazan Cathedral in St. Petersburg.

Kutuzov remains one of the most popular and celebrated Russian commanders. He was indeed a gifted general, diplomat, and statesman. During his negotiations with the Turks, he proved himself a tough and shrewd diplomat, successfully achieving his goals both in 1794 and 1812. However, Kutuzov's military career was largely based on the victories against the armies of the decadent Ottoman Empire. Kutuzov never proved himself as a military theorist and, except for his correspondence, left no literary legacy. At the same time, he was an adroit courtier who always endeavoured to win favor from the sovereign. He skillfully played people against each other and highly valued power, honors, and luster. As so often happens with national heroes, Kutuzov gradually became larger than life, a messianic character who led the Holy Russia against the evils of the Revolution and anarchy. Later, the Soviet leaders exploited his personality for more grandiose schemes, forcing many Soviet historians to distort historical facts to create a mythical figure of the Field Marshal.

KUZNETSOV Andrey Andreevich commanded the Perma Musketeer Regiment in January-December 1806 and was promoted to colonel on 24 December 1808. He commanded the Mingrelia Musketeer Regiment in April 1809-May 1811 and served as chef of the Kherson Grenadier Regiment between 27 May 1811 and 6 September 1813.

LACY, Boris Petrovich (b. 1737 — d. 30 January 1820) began service in the Austrian army and entered Russian service as a captain in the Azov Infantry Regiment in 1762. He served in Lithuania and Poland in 1763-1764, and in the Crimea in 1776. During the Russo-Turkish War of 1787-1791, Lacy distinguished himself at Ismail, garnering the Order of St. George (3rd class). He later served in Poland in 1794-1795, where he earned a promotion to lieutenant general. Four years later, he led Russian troops in the Baltic provinces. In 1805, Lacy took command of the Russian expeditionary forces in Naples. He returned to Russia the following year and retired from the army.

LADYZHENSKY, Nikolay Fedorovich (b. 1774 — d. 7 May 1861) was born to a noble family in the Moscow *gubernia*. He enlisted in the Life Guard Preobrazhensk Regiment on 8 February 1790, and rose to ensign on 26 June 1798. Ladyzhensky participated in the 1805 Campaign and was wounded at Austerlitz. Promoted to colonel on 6 October 1806, he was given command of the Keksholm (Kexholm) Musketeer Regiment (served until 21 Decembver 1807). In June 1807, he fought the French at Guttstadt, Heilsberg, and Fiedland, where he was wounded and received the Order of St. George (4th class).

In 1809, Ladyzhensky was appointed commander of the Vyatka Musketeer Regiment (28 November) and served in the Army of Moldavia. He took part in the actions at Turtukai and Ruse in 1810, and was wounded in the left hand during the assault on Ruse in 1811. The same year, he was appointed chef of Nizhegorod Infantry Regiment on 27 May 1811. In 1812, his regiment was attached to the 2nd Brigade of the 26th Division of the 7th Corps of the 2nd Western Army. Ladyzhensky took part in Bagration's retreat from Volkovysk to Moghilev, where he took part in the battle of Satlanovka. Ladyzhensky was seriously wounded when a canister shot hit him in the chest. He spent the rest of campaign recuperating at Ryazan and returned to the army in the summer of 1813.

After a promotion to major general on 27 June 1813, Ladyzhensky led a brigade in the 15th Division. He joined the main army in November 1813, and participated in the invasion of France in 1814, fighting at Brienne, La Rothière, Bar sur Aube, Laon, and Paris (Order of St. Vladimir, 3rd class). After his return to Russia, Ladyzhensky marched with the Russian army to engage Napoleon during The Hundred Days in 1815. After the war, he served in the 15th Division and was discharged with a full pension on 18 March 1817.

In 1819, Ladyzhensky returned to military service and, with his seniority changed to 29 July 1816, served as a duty officer in the 7th and 13th Divisions. In 1820, he commanded the 2nd Brigade of the 10th Division, but was dismissed on 16 September 1823. He retired again on 18 January 1834, but soon returned to service as the Military Governor of Sedletsk. He rose to lieutenant general on 29 March 1845, and directed the 10th District Corps of the Internal Guard. He retired for good with a full pension on 23 February 1850.

During his career, Ladyzhensky received the Orders of St. George (4th class), of St. Vladimir (3rd class), of St. Anna (2nd class) and of St. Stanislaus (1st class), medal "For 35 Years of Distinguished Service" and a golden sword for courage.

LAMBERT, Karl Osipovih (b. 1772 — d. 10 June 1843, Poltava *gubernia*) descended from a prominent French noble family; his father was General Marquis de Saint Bris of the Royal army. Karl Lambert began service in the French Royal Guard but fled France during the Revolution. He joined the Russian service as a second major in the Kinburn Dragoon Regiment on 14 February 1793. In 1794, he took part in operations in Poland, fighting at Khelm, Maciejowice, and

Praga (received the Order of St. George, 4th class, 12 January 1795). In 1796-1797, he participated in the Persian Campaign along the Caspian Sea, where he commanded a Cossack regiment. Lambert was promoted to colonel in March 1798, and became commander of the Starodoub Cuirassier Regiment on 12 August 1799. He served under General Rimsky Korsakov in Switzerland in late 1799, and was wounded in the left leg at Zurich. Lambert was promoted to major general and appointed chef of the Ryazan Cuirassier Regiment on 29 December 1799. However, he was discharged on 20 March 1800, during Paul's military purges.

Lambert returned to service in March 1801, and was appointed commander of the Elizavetgrad Hussar Regiment on 3 August 1802. The next year, he became chef of the Aleksandria Hussar Regiment on 3 March 1803. He participated in the 1806 Campaign and fought at Blon and Czarnowo, where he was wounded but continued in command. For his courage, he received the Order of St. George (3rd class) on 12 February 1807. Lambert distinguished himself at Pultusk, Eylau, and Friedland (Orders of St. Vladimir, 3rd class, St. Anna, 1st class, and the Prussian Red Eagle.

Lambert was promoted to adjutant general on 11 September 1811, and was given command of the 5th Cavalry Division. In 1812, he commanded the 8th Cavalry Division, also known as "Lambert's Cavalry Corps," in the 3rd Reserve Army of Observation. He distinguished himself at Kobryn and Gorodechnya and was promoted to lieutenant general on 2 November 1812, with seniority dating from 12 August 1812. Lambert also fought at Brest, Charukov, Minsk and Borisov, where he was seriously wounded in the leg.

After recuperating from his injuries, Lambert returned to the army in March 1814, and took command of the 2nd Hussar Division in the battles near Paris. In 1816-1825, he commanded the 5th Reserve Cavalry Corps, was promoted to general of cavalry on 24 December 1823, and appointed senator on 26 November 1826. Lambert was conferred the title of count of the Russian Empire in May 1836. During his career, he was also awarded the Order of St. Alexander of Neva with diamonds, the Prussian Order of Red Eagle (1st class), the French Order of St. Louis (2nd class), the Austrian Order of Leopold and the Bavarian order of Maximilian Joseph.

LANGERON, Louis Alexander Andrault (b. 24 January 1763, Paris — d. 16 July, 1831, Odessa) was born to a French noble family; his full name was Louis Alexander Andrault chevalier comte de Langéron, marquis de la Coss, baron de Cougny, de la Ferté Langéron et de Sassy. At an age of 15, he was "*sous-lieutenant des gardes françaises.*" He later served at Caracas and Saint-Domingue in 1782-1783. In 1786, he was promoted to assistant-colonel to the regiment of Médoc, and then colonel to the Armagnac Regiment in 1788. Langeron accompanied the Prince of Nassau to Russia in 1789, and the next year entered Russian service as a colonel in the Siberia Grenadier Regiment (7 May 1790). He distinguished himself in the campaigns against the Swedes, earning the Order of St. George (4th class, 19 September 1790) for actions at Bjork, and commanding the Russian left wing in the battle at Rochensalmi. In 1790-1791, he fought the Turks at Ismail (wounded, awarded a golden sword) and Macin.

With Catherine II's permission, Langeron served in the Prince of Saxony-Teschen's army against the French in Netherlands, and on his return to Russia, was sent as a military observer to the Austrian army in Northern France and Netherlands (1793-1794). In August 1795, Langeron transferred to the Malorossiisk [Little Russia] Grenadiers Regiment and rose to brigadier on 9 July 1796. He became major general and chef of the Ufa (Ufimsky) Musketeer Regiment on 2 June 1797. He was awarded the Order of St. Anna (2nd class) for effective maintenance of his regiment. Under Paul, Langeron also received the Commander Cross of Order of St. John of Jerusalem, and was conferred the title of count of the Russian Empire. He was given the rank of lieutenant general on 5 November 1798, and appointed chef of the Riga (Ryazhsky) Musketeer Regiment 24 May 1799. Langeron became the head of the Brest Inspection on 24 August 1800. Langeron took part in the 1805 Campaign against Napoleon and commanded Russian troops on the Allied left flank at Austerlitz. He was one of the two generals disgraced after the war and was sent to Odessa.

In 1806-1811, Langeron served in the Army of Moldavia against the Ottomans. He fought at Giurgiu, Silistra, Frasin (Order of St. Vladimir, 2nd class), Derekoy (Order of St. George, 3rd class, 1 October 1810), and Ruse (Order of St. Alexander of Neva). Langeron took command of the 22nd Division on 19 August 1810, and temporarily led the Army of Moldavia after General Kamensky died. He participated in the decisive battle at Ruse in 1811, for which he was promoted to general of infantry on 3 September 1811, and awarded the Order of St. Vladimir (1st class). In 1812, Langeron commanded the 1st Corps of the Army of Danube and took part in the actions at Brest-Litovsk and on the Berezina.

In 1813, Langeron was in charge of the blockade of Thorn, for which he received the Order of St. George (2nd class, 23 March 1813), as well as both the Prussian Orders of Black and Red Eagles. Commanding a Russian corps, Langeron participated in the battles of Koenigswarte, Bautzen, Zibeneichen, Lowenberg, Holdberg, Katzbach, Hartau, Bischofsward, and Leipzig (received the diamond signs of Order of St. Alexander of Neva and the Swedish Order of the Sword). In 1814, he led his corps at Soissons, Craonne, Laon, Rheims, Le Fère Champenoise, and Paris for which he garnered the Russian Order of St. Andrew the First Called, the French Orders of St. Louis and Lily, and the Austrian Order of Maria Theresa. In late 1814, Langeron commanded the 4th and 6th Corps in Volhynia, and marched back to France during the Hundred Days. He reached the Rhine when Napoleon was defeated at Waterloo, and turned back to Russia.

After the war, Langeron was appointed the Military Governor of Kherson and Odessa, the Commander-in-Chief of the Bug and Black Sea Cossack Hosts, and the Governor of the Ekaterinoslavl, Kherson, and Tavrida *gubernias* on 28 November 1815. He contributed significantly to the development of the city of Odessa in 1816-1823. Langeron was relieved of his duties because of poor health on 26 May 1823, and traveled to France in 1824-1825.

Langeron was appointed a member of the sentencing panel after the Decembrist Uprising in 1826, and was awarded the diamond signs of the Order of St. Andrew the First Called. During the Russo-Turkish War of 1828-1829, he fought at Satunovo, Shumla, Giurgiu, Turno, and Silistra. Langeron became chef of the Riga Infantry Regiment on 23 February 1829, and left the Turkish front after the appointment of General Diebitsch. He spent the next two years in Odessa and traveled to St. Petersburg in early 1831, where he died during the cholera epidemic on 16 July 1831. Langeron was buried in the Catholic Church in Odessa in 1831.

Langeron was a prolific writer and his memoirs are valuable sources on the period. His literary legacy includes *Mémoires sur les guerres de la première coalition, 1792-1793, Mémoires de Langéron, générale d'infanterie dans l'armée russe. Campagnes de 1812, 1813 et 1814, Journal inedit de la campagne de 1805,* and *Zapiski Grafa Langerona. Voina s Turtsiei v 1806-1812 gg.* [Recollections of Count Langeron. War Against Turkey in 1806-1812].

LANSKOY, Pavel Petrovich (b. 1791 — d. 5 February 1873) was educated at the Page Corps and enlisted as a junker in the Life Guard Horse Regiment in 1809. He was promoted to estandard-junker in 1810, and to cornet in 1811. During the Russian Campain, he fought at Vitebsk, Smolensk, Borodino, Maloyaroslavets, and Krasnyi. In 1813, he took part in the actions at Lutzen, Bautzen, Dresden, Kulm, and Leipzig. For these actions, Lanskoy was promoted to rotmistr and awarded the Orders of St. Vladimir (4th class), and the Prussian Iron Cross. In 1814, Lanskoy fought at Le Fère Champenoise and Paris. He was promoted to colonel in 1820, and after taking part in suppression of the Decembrist Uprising in 1825, was appointed flügel adjutant to Emperor Nicholas I.

Promoted to major general in 1828, Lanskoy served as assistant to the commander of the 1st Cuirassier Division. In 1831, he commanded the Reserve Guard cavalry squadrons. He became a lieutenant general and commander of the 1st Guard Cavalry Division in 1837. He assumed command of the Reserve Guard Cavalry Corps on 5 November 1848. He retired in early 1849, but returned to service to take part in the suppression of the revolt in Hungary. After the war, he served on the committee to reorganize the Russian cavalry, and in 1854, took command of the Reserve Guard cavalry squadrons and the Reserve Brigade of the 1st Cavalry Division. He rose to general of cavalry and took command of the Reserve Guard Cavalry Corps in 1855. Lanskoy served as cavalry inspector in 1862 and accompanied Emperor Nicholas to Prussia, Holland, and Britain in 1863-1865. He died in Naples on 5 February 1873, and was buried at St. Petersburg in March 1873.

LANSKOY, Pavel Sergeyevich (b. 1757 — d. 18 January 1832, St. Petersburg) was born to a noble family in the Novgorod *gubernia*. He enlisted as a private in the Life Guard Semeyonovsk Regiment on 10 September 1768, and transferred as a sergeant to the Life Guard Preobrazhensk Regiment in 1777. He was promoted to ensign in October 1779, and transferred as a captain to the Engineer Section (*ekspeditsia*) of the War College in 1783. Lanskoy participated in the Russo-Swedish War in 1789-1790, the Russo-Turkish War in 1790-1791, and the operations against the Poles in 1792-1794. Despite promotion to colonel on 1 December 1796, Lanskoy transferred to the civil service with a rank of state counsellor on 7 February 1798. He returned to military service in 1801, and was promoted to major general on 17 April.

Over the next seven years, Lanskoy served in the War College, negotiated the exchange of prisoners in 1807, and supervised the Russian field hospitals in 1808-1813. He became a member of the Council of War in 1814, and was awarded the Order of St. Anna (1st class) on 11 September 1814. Seven year later, he was appointed to the Senate and conferred the rank of privy counsellor. He retired in 1830 and settled in St. Petersburg, where he died two years later.

LANSKOY, Sergey Nikolaevich (b. 1774 — d. 7 March 1814, Craonne) was born to a noble family in the Kostroma *gubernia*. He enlisted in the Life Guard Izmailovsk Regiment on 4 December 1783 and rose to ensign on 27 April 1797. He became a lieutenant on 19 September 1798, and three years later, transferred as a staff rotmistr to the Life Guard Horse Regiment. Lanskoy served as an adjutant to Grand Duke Constantine in 1799-1800, and was promoted to rotmistr on 17 October 1801. In 1802, he served in the College on Foreign Affairs earning the civil rank of court counsellor. On 15 July 1802, he was appointed to the Russian embassy in Paris. Three years later, he joined the Russian army serving as a colonel in the Mariupol Hussar Regiment. He participated in the 1805 Campaign against Napoleon and fought at Austerlitz.

During the campaigns in Poland in 1806-1807, Lanskoy commanded the Polish Horse (Uhlan) Regiment between 18 May 1807, and 4 April 1808. In 1809, Lanskoy served against the Turks in the Danube Valley and distinguished himself at Batin in September 1807. He became a flügel adjutant on 4 April 1810, and major general on 15 August 1810, before garnering the Order of St. George on 3 December 1810. The following year, he was appointed chef of the Byelorussia Hussar Regiment on 29 January 1811.

During the 1812 Campaign, Lanskoy served in the 20th Brigade of the 6th Cavalry Division of the Army of Danube and fought on the Berezina. In 1813, Lanskoy fought at Kalisch (Order of St. Vladimir, 2nd class), Halbertstadt, Weisenfeld, Lutzen, Katzbach (promoted to lieutenant general on 27 September 1813), and Leipzig. During the invasion of France, he commanded the advance guard of Mikhail Vorontsov's Corps and was mortally wounded at Craonne on 7 March 1814.

LANSKOY, Vasily Sergeyevich (b. 1754 — d. 1831) was born to a prominent Russian noble family and enlisted in the Life Guard Preobrazhensk Regiment on 22 January 1767. He was promoted to ensign in 1777, to lieutenant colonel of the Life Guard Grenadier Regiment on 12 January 1781, and to general-krieg-commissar on 14 April 1783. Lanskoy served in Poland in 1792-1794, earning his rank of major general. In 1795, he transferred to the civil service with a rank of actual state counsellor and became the Governor of Saratov. In 1796-1803, Lanskoy also served as the Governor of the Tambov and Saratov *gubernia*s. In 1803, he was promoted to privy counsellor and appointed the Governor of Grodno.

Lanskoy became a senator in 1809, and three years later was promoted to the rank of actual privy counsellor and directed the intendant services. In 1813-1814, he governed several *gubernia*s in the Duchy of Warsaw, and after the Congress of Vienna, served as Viceroy of the Kingdom of Poland and as a member of the State Council of the Russian Empire. He was appointed the Minister of Internal Affairs on 1

December 1825, and retired in 1828. A different Lanskoy, **Sergey Stepanovich**, served as the Russian Minister of Internal Affairs in 1855-1861.

LAPTEV, Vasily Danilovich (b. 1758 — d. 14 April 1825) was enlisted in the Life Guard Preobrazhensk Regiment in January 1776, and transferred as a captain to the Tambov Infantry Regiment on 12 January 1789. He participated in the Russo-Turkish War in 1789-1791, and fought at Killia and Ismail, where he was wounded in the chest and earned a golden cross. On 12 March 1790, Laptev transferred to the Astrakhan Grenadier Regiment and thereafter became a major in the 1st Battalion of the Bug Jager Corps on 12 April 1791. In 1792-1794, he participated in the campaign in Poland. In 1797, Laptev was appointed to the 12th Jager Regiment, although the following year he became commander of the Ryazhsky Musketeer Regiment on 23 July 1798.

Promoted to colonel on 22 October 1799, Laptev served as chef of the 8th Jager Regiment from 22 January 1802 to March 1804. He participated in the 1805 Campaign and fought at Lambach, Amstetten (Order of St. George, 4th class, 24 January 1806), and Austerlitz. He rose to major general and chef of the 21st Jager Regiment on 30 January 1806. Laptev also participated in the 1807 Campaign in Poland, where he served with the 3rd Division at Guttstadt, Heilsberg, and Friedland. The next year, he became the Governor of the Island of Esel on 11 September 1808, before taking discharge on 6 February 1809.

In 1812, Laptev supervised the organization of the Moscow *opolchenye* and became commander of the 8th Dismounted Cossack Regiment of the Moscow *opolchenye* on 20 August 1812. As he joined the main Russian army, Laptev took command of the 2nd Brigade of the 11th Division on 6 September 1812. He distinguished himself at Borodino, for which he earned the Order of St. George (3rd class, 1 November 1812). In October, he took command of the 23rd Division, and two month later was instructed to organize the supply system at Nizhni Novgorod. In 1813, Laptev commanded the 21st and 24th Divisions of the Army of North and participated in the Battle of Leipzig, for which he received promotion to lieutenant general on 20 October 1813. In 1814, he was seriously wounded at Craonne on 7 March and retired with a full pension in January 1816.

Laptev returned to the army two years later and was appointed commander of the 25th Division on 29 January 1818. In 1820, his unit was converted to the 1st Infantry Division but he retired for second time on 31 October 1821. During his career, Laptev also earned the Orders of St. John of Jerusalem, of St. Anna (1st class) with diamonds, of St. Vladimir (2nd class) and the Prussian Order of Red Eagle.

LASHKAREV, Pavel Sergeyevich (b. 17 November 1776 — 25 January 1857, St. Petersburg) was born to a prominent Georgian noble family of Lashkarashvili-Bibiluri. His father Sergey Lashkarev was a well-known diplomat under Empress Catherine II. Lashkarev enlisted in the Life Guard Preobrazhensk Regiment on 2 May 1781, and was promoted to sergeant in 1790. In January 1794, he transferred as a lieutenant to the Staroskol Infantry Regiment and participated in operations against the Poles in late 1794, receiving a golden cross for Praga. In 1799, he served in Rimsky-Korsakov's Corps in Switzerland and was wounded at Zurich. Six years later, Lashkarev participated in the 1805 Campaign against the French, distinguishing himself at Austerlitz. He took command of the

Volhynia Musketeer Regiment on 22 November 1806. Five years later, he rose to colonel on 11 September 1811, and became commander of the Simbirk Infantry Regiment on 10 November of the same year. He eventually became chef of this regiment on 9 May 1812.

During the Russian Campaign of 1812, Lashkarev served in the 2nd Brigade of the 27th Division of the 2nd Western Army and participated in Bagration's retreat to Smolensk. Lashkarev distinguished himself in the actions at Krasnyi, Smolensk, and Shevardino. At Borodino, he was seriously wounded in the head and lost some of his vision. After he spent the next two years recuperating, Lashkarev was promoted to major general on 11 September 1814, with seniority dating from 3 February 1814.

Lashkarev took command of the 3rd Brigade of the 28th Division on 13 June 1815, and later served in the Ministry of War. He retired in 1831, and settled in St. Petersburg, where he died in 1857. During his service, he also earned the Orders of St. Anna (2nd class) with diamonds, of St. George (4th class), of St. Vladimir (4th Class), the Prussian Order of Red Eagle and a golden sword for courage.

LASKIN, Aleksey Andreyevich (b.1769 — d. 26 March 1848, St. Petersburg), was born to a noble family in the Kostroma *gubernia*. He enlisted as a private in the Life Guard Preobrazhensk Regiment in 1790, and transferred as a vakhmistr to the Life Guard Horse Regiment on 14 December 1792. After briefly serving in the Austrian army against the French, Laskin was appointed as a captain in the Horse Grenadier Military Order Regiment and fought in Poland in 1794, receiving a golden cross for Praga. In 1796-1798, Laskin served in the Caucasus and participated in the Persian Campaign. He was promoted to colonel on 13 October 1799, and became commander of the Mariupol Hussar Regiment on 26 March 1804.

Laskin participated in the 1805 Campaign and distinguished himself at Austerlitz. In 1806, he was sent to the Danube Valley, where he assumed command of the Her Majesty Cuirassier Regiment on 17 March 1806, and received promotion to major general on 5 June 1807. In 1809, he participated in the campaign against Austria. However, he became seriously ill and was relieved of command on 23 August 1810. Laskin returned to service in March 1812, and was given command of the 11th Cavalry Division, comprised of the reserve squadrons, of the Army of Danube on 27 March 1812. Laskin participated in the actions at Borisov, Smorgon, and Vilna.

In 1813, Laskin fought at Kalisch, Thorn, and was wounded as Koenigswarta. After recuperating, he commanded a cavalry depot of the 1st Army, but was discharged from the army on 7 February 1820, for the cruel treatment of subordinates . He spent the rest of his life in St. Petersburg, where he died on 26 March 1848.

Laskin was also awarded the Orders of St. Anna (1st class), of St. Vladimir (3rd class), a golden sword for courage and the Prussian Orders of Red Eagle and the Pour le Merite.

LAVROV, Nikolay Ivanovich (b. 1761 — d. 22 September 1813, Kholodovo, Orlov *gubernia*) was born to a noble family in the Kaluga *gubernia* and enlisted in the Life Guard Preobrazhensk Regiment on 12 January 1777. He was promoted to ensign on 7 October 1783, and six years later transferred as a second major to the 1st Battalion of the Bug Jager Corps on 26 May 1789. Lavrov participated in the Russo-Turkish War in 1789-1791, and fought at Akkerman, Bender, Killia, Babadag, and Macin (Order of St. George, 4th class). Lavrov distinguished himself during the assault on Ismail, where he was wounded in the left hand and right leg and earned a golden cross and promotion to premier major. In 1792-1794, he served in Poland garnering a golden cross for Praga. Lavrov was promoted to lieutenant colonel on 1 May 1797, and to colonel on 22 September 1798. The following year, he participated in Field Marshal Suvorov's campaign in Italy and Switzerland as his duty staff officer. Lavrov fought at Brescia, Turin, Tidone, Trebbia, Novi, St. Gothard, and Glarus. For his actions, he was promoted to major general on 13 November 1799, and appointed chef of the Tomsk Musketeer regiment.

In 1800, Lavrov became chef of the Shirvan Musketeer Regiment on 27 October 1800, and served at this position until 8 February 1808. He was also appointed the head of the Siberia Inspection, a position he retained for the next six years. In 1806, Lavrov became commander of the 8th Infantry Division (4 September) and fought the French in Poland. He distinguished himself at Pultusk and was seriously wounded at Eylau. In 1808, he transferred to the 11th Infantry Division and rose to lieutenant general in 1811.

Lavrov became the Chief of Staff of the 1st Western Army on 4 May 1812, but was replaced by Aleksey Ermolov (Yermolov) in June 1812. After the battle at Smolensk in August of the same year, he took command of the 5th Infantry (Guard) Corps and distinguished himself at Borodino, earning the Order of St. George (3rd class, 1 November 1812). Lavrov then took part in the battles at Maloyaroslavets, Vyazma and Krasnyi. However, he became seriously ill in early 1813 and died on 22 September 1813. During his career, Lavrov also received the Orders of St. Anna (1st class) with diamonds, St. Vladimir (2nd class), and St. John of Jerusalem, as well as a golden sword for courage.

LEBEDEV, Nikolay Petrovich (b. 1750 — d. 6 January 1813, Kaluga) was born to a noble family in the Smolensk *gubernia*. He enlisted in the Roslavl Dragoon Squadron on 28 August 1756. Two years later, he was promoted to sergeant on 12 December, and transferred to the St. Petersburg Infantry Regiment. He became an ensign on 12 October 1763, and participated in the campaign in Poland in 1766-1768, where he was wounded at Slonim. In 1770-1774, Lebedev fought the Turks in Moldavia, and was appointed second major in the Vyborg Infantry Regiment on 5 December 1774. He transferred to the Apsheron Infantry Regiment in June 1777, and then became a premier major in the Kazan Infantry Regiment on 27 December 1783. In 1783-1785, he served against the local tribes in the Northern Caucasus and transferred to the Caucasian Infantry Regiment in January 1787. Lebedev participated in the Russo-Turkish War of 1787-1790, and for his actions at Anapa, received the Order of St.

George (4th class) and promotion to lieutenant colonel.

In 1796-1797, Lebedev took part in the Persian Campaign along the Caspian Sea, commanding the Selengin Musketeer Regiment (10 December 1796). He was promoted to colonel on 12 October 1796; the next year, on 23 December 1797, he became a major general and the Commandant of Orenburg and chef of the Orenburg Garrison Regiment. In 1798-1799, he engaged the local nomad tribes and was promoted to lieutenant general on 4 December 1799. In 1802, he was made the Governor of the Irkutsk *gubernia* and chef of the Irkutsk Garrisson Regiment on 7 March.

Lebedev retired because of poor health on 1 September 1807, and settled on his estate in the Smolensk *gubernia*. In 1812, he supervised the organization and training of the Smolensk *opolchenye* and fought at Smolensk in August 1812. He was awarded the diamond signs of the Order of St. Anna (1st class). He commanded the Smolensk *opolchenye* at Borodino and Maloyaroslavets, but became seriously ill and left army in December 1812. He failed to rally and died at a hospital in Kaluga on 6 January 1813.

LEONTYEV, Ivan Sergeyevich (b. 1782 — d. 22 August 1824) began his career as a page at the Imperial Court. In 1799, he rose to kamer-page and joined the Life Guard Preobrazhensk Regiment with a rank of lieutenant on 21 February. He participated in the 1805 Campaign and was wounded at Austelitz on 2 December, earning a golden sword for courage. Leontyev then took part in the 1807 Campaign in Poland and distinguished himself at Frieldand, earning promotion to colonel. Two years later, he transferred to the Life Guard Horse Regiment.

During the 1812 Campaign, Leontyev served in the Guard Cuirassier Brigade of the 1st Cuirassier Division of the 5th Reserve (Guard) Corps of the 1st Westren Army. He fought at Borodino and was awarded the Order of St. George (4th class) on 3 December 1812. In 1813, he took part in battles at Lutzen, Bautzen, Dresden and Kulm, where he was wounded in the right leg and garnered the Prussian Iron Cross. After recuperating, he fought at Brienne, Bar sur Aube, Arcis sur Aube, Le Fère Champenoise and Paris in 1814. After the war, Leontyev became commander of the 2nd Brigade of the 3rd Cuirassier Division on 18 October 1817. Two years later, he temporarily commanded the 2nd Hussar Division before being officially confirmed on this position on 27 February 1823. However, he died on 22 August 1824. During his career, Leontyev was also awarded the Orders of St. Anna (1st class) with diamonds, of St. Vladimir (3rd class), of St. George (4th class), the Prussian Order of Red Eagle, the Bavarian Order of Maximilian Joseph and two golden swords for courage.

LESLIE, Dmitry Yegorovich (b. 1758, Smolensk *gubernia* — date of death unknown) descended from an English noble family that settled in Russia during the 17th century. He enlisted as a hefreit-corporal in the Rostov Carabineer Regiment in May 1761, and began active duty as a vakhmitsr in the Smolensk Horse Land Militia (*Konnii Landmilitskii*) Regiment. Leslie participated in the operations in Poland in 1766-1767, and the bloody suppression of Pugachev's peasant uprising in the Orenburg *gubernia* in 1774-1775. Leslie was wounded in the the right leg in the battle at Tatishevo. In 1776, he participated in the suppression of an uprising in Bashkiria and was promoted to cornet on 17 January 1775, and to lieutenant in 1776.

However, he became seriously ill and retired with a rank of captain in November 1779.

Leslie returned to active service nine years later, and was appointed esaul in the Ekaterinoslavl Cossack Corps on 27 June 1788. He participated in the Russo-Turkish War and distinguished himself in a number of actions. In 1788, he took part in the assault at Ochakov, for which he earned promotion to sergeant (voiskovoi starshina) and the Order of St. Vladimir (4th class). The following year, he participated in the operations on the Salcha River and at Hadjibey (Odessa). He was promoted to second major and transferred to the Ukraine Light Horse Regiment in late 1789. After fighting at Killia and Ismail, he was awarded the Order of St. George (4th class) on 5 April 1791, and rose to premier major. Leslie also took part in the battles at Babadag, and was wounded in the right thigh at Macin. For his actions, he was promoted to lieutenant colonel in late 1791, and appointed commander of the 2nd Chuguev Cossack Regiment on 11 March 1792. Later in 1792, he went to fight the Polish insurgents, received a cross for Praga, and he remained in Poland for two years.

After a promotion to colonel, Leslie became chef of the 1st Chuguev Cossack Regiment on 21 May 1797, and later that year was promoted to major general on 28 July. However, he was soon arrested for arriving late to his regiment and was discharged from the army on 22 November 1798. After Paul's death, Leslie was restored in rank on 30 July 1801.

He spent the next eleven years at his estate in the Smolensk *gubernia*. During the 1812 Campaign, he organized a cavalry detachment and took part in the actions at Krasnyi, Smolensk, Lubino, Borodino (received the Order of St. Anna, 2nd class, with diamonds), Tarutino, Maloyaroslavets, Vyazma, and Krasnyi. In 1813, he served at Modlin and Danzig before retiring in August 1814.

LEVASHOV, Constantine Vasilievich (b. 1785 — d. 27 May 1813) was born to a prominent Russian noble family; and was the brother of Vasily Levashov. He began service in 1804 as a junker in Byelorussia Hussar Regiment, and was promoted to cornet in 1806. He took part in the Russo-Turkish War of 1806-1812, and fought at Urzhenits, Turbat (received the Order of St. Anna, 4th class), Giurgiu, Ismail, Obilesti (received the Order of St. Vladimir, 4th class), and Silistra. Levashov transferred to the Life Guard Horse Regiment in 1810, and fought at Borodino, earning a golden sword for courage. He was seriously wounded at Maloyaroslavets (24-25 October). He died on 27 May 1813.

LEVASHOV, Vasily Vasilievich (b. 21 October 1783 — d. 5 October 1848, St. Petersburg) was the son of Vasily Levashov, Actual Privy Counsellor and Ober-Jagermeister, and brother of Constantine Levashov. Vasily Levashov started his career in civil service as a gubernial registrar in 1799, before being appointed a major in the Life Guard Cuirassier Regiment on 25 March 1801. The next year, he transferred as a staff rotmistr to the Chevalier Guard Regiment (25 December) and participated in the campaigns of 1805-1807. Levashov took part in the battles at Austerlitz, Pultusk, Jankovo, Landsberg, Eylau, and Guttstadt. For his actions, he was awarded the Orders of St. Anna (3rd class), of St. Vladimir (4th class), and earned promotion to colonel on 17 November 1808.

In 1812, Levashov served in the 1st Cuirassier Division of the 5th Corps of the 1st Western Army, and fought at Vitebsk, Smolensk, Borodino (Order of St. George, 4th class, 3 December 1812), Tarutino, Maloyaroslavets, and Krasnyi. Promoted to major general on 7 January

1813, Levashov went on to fight at Lutzen, Bautzen, and Dresden in the spring of 1813. He became chef of the Novgorod Cuirassier Regiment on 27 July 1813. During the Battle of Leipzig, he was shot in the chest and his hand was sliced open by a sabre. His actions led to the receipt of the Order of St. Vladimir (3rd class) and the Prussian Order of Red Eagle. In 1814, Levashov fought at Brienne, Troyes, Arcis sur Aube, Le Fère Champenoise, and Paris (awarded the Order of St. Anna, 1st class).

After the war, Levashov commanded the Life Guard Hussar Regiment from April 1815 to June 1822, before becoming flügel adjutant in March 1817. He also commanded the 2nd Brigade of the Guard Light Cavalry Division from 1818-1826. Levashov participated in the court martial of soldiers of the Life Guard Semeyonovsk Regiment in 1821, and in the suppression of the Decembrist Uprising in December 1825. Promoted to lieutenant general on 13 January 1826, he took command of the 1st Cuirassier Division in July of the same year. Six years later, Levashov became the Military Governor of Kiev and the Governor General of Podlosk and Volhynia in March 1832. He was conferred the title of count of the Russian Empire on 13 June 1833, and served as the Governor General of Chernigov, Poltava, and Kharkov *gubernia*s between December 1835 and December 1836. He became a member of the State Council in January 1838, served on the horse production committee in 1841, and supervised construction of the railroad between Moscow and St. Petersburg in 1842. He died on 5 October 1848 in St. Petersburg.

LEVENWOLDE, Karl Karlovich (b. 26 June 1779, Rappin — d. 7 September 1812, Borodino) was born to a noble family in the Lifland *gubernia*. His brother was Kazimir Levenwolde. Karl began service in the Life Guard Horse Regiment in 1790, and was promoted to vakhmistr in 1795. He transferred to the Riga Cuirassier Regiment in 1797, and to Nepluev's Cuirassier Regiment with a rank of lieutenant the following year. Levenwolde served in the Starodoub Cuirassier Regiment in 1800, and in the Life Guard Horse Regiment in 1802. He was promoted to rotmistr in 1804, and took part in the battle of Austerlitz in 1805. After briefly retiring in 1806, he returned with the rank of colonel and took command of the 3rd Squadron of the Life Guard Horse Regiment. During the 1812 Campaign, he was mortally wounded during a cavalry charge at Borodino, and died that same day.

LEVENWOLDE, Kazimir Karlovich (b. 7 August 1780, Rappin — d. 3 December 1805) was born to a noble family in the Lifland *gubernia*; brother of Karl Levenwolde. He began service as a quartermaster for the Life Guard Horse Regiment in 1790, and was promoted to vakhmistr in 1795. He joined the Riga Cuirassier Regiment as a cornet in 1797 and transferred as a lieutenant to Nepluev's Cuirassier Regiment in 1798. Two years later, he was appointed to the Starodoub Cuirassier Regiment, and in 1801, served in the Life Guard Horse Regiment. He was promoted to rotmistr in 1805 and was mortally wounded at Austerlitz on 2 December 1805, and died the following day.

LEVIN, Dmitry Andreyevich (b. 12 January 1777 — d. 12 December 1839, Zakrutoe, Kaluga *gubernia*) was born to a noble family in the Orel *gubernia*. He began service in June 1778, and was promoted to ensign on 1 October 1798. Levin participated in the 1805-1807 Campaigns and fought at Austerlitz, Guttstadt, Heilsberg, and Friedland. Promoted to colonel on 8 January 1808, he became chef of the Siberia Grenadier Regiment on 6 October 1811. During the Russian Campaign of 1812, he served in the 3rd Brigade of the 2nd Grenadier Division of the 8th Corps of the 2nd Western Army. He took part in Prince Bagration's retreat from Volkovysk to Smolensk, and fought at Borodino (received the Order of St. George, 4th class), Tarutino, Maloyaroslavets, Vyazma, and Krasnyi. In 1813, he was wounded in the right hand at Lutzen, rose to the rank of major general on 27 September, and suffered another wound, this time to the right knee, at Leipzig. Levin took part in the 1814 Campaign and fought at Paris. After the war, he commanded a brigade in the 3rd Grenadier Division in 1815-1819, and retired because of poor health on 14 January 1820.

LEVITSKY, Mikhail Ivanovich (b. 1761 — date of death unknown) was born to a noble family in the Moghilev *gubernia*. He enlisted in the Polotsk Infantry Regiment in December 1781, and was promoted to ensign on 8 August 1784. Levitsky participated in operations against the Poles in 1784-1785, and fought the Turks in 1787-1791. He distinguished himself at Ochakov, Kauschany, Akkerman, Bender, Killia, Ismail (wounded), and Macin. In 1792-1794, he again served against the Poles.

Levitsky took command of the Kiev Grenadier Regiment on 23 August 1798, and was as promoted to colonel on 19 June 1799 . On 28 May 1803, he was promoted to major general and chef of the Podolsk Musketeer Regiment. Levitsky participated in the 1805 Campaign and was seriously wounded at Austerlitz on 2 December. In 1806-1807, he served with the 8th Division against the French in Poland and earned the Order of St. George (4th class) for actions at Eylau. In late 1810, his musketeer regiment was transformed into the 36th Jager Regiment. On 31 October 1810, he took command of the 3rd Brigade of the 7th Division of the 6th Corps of the 1st Western Army, but was replaced by Major General Balla in March 1812.

During the 1812 Campaign, Levitsky served as the Commandant of Mozhaisk during the battle of Borodino and covered the retreat of the Russian army through Moscow. In October-November of that year, he fought at Vyazma, Maloyaroslavets, and Krasnyi. In 1813, Levitsky served at the headquarters of the Army of Reserves and became the Commandant of Warsaw on 18 January 1814. He was promoted to lieutenant general on 2 October 1821, and to general of infantry on 3 May 1829.

LIBHARDT, (Liphardt) Anton Ivanovich (Otto Johann Friedrich), (b. 1771 — date of death unknown) was born to a noble family in the Lifland *gubernia*. He began service in the Life Guard Horse Regiment in January 1783, and transferred as a captain to the Nasheburg Musketeer Regiment in January 1790. In 1792-1794, Libhardt served in Poland and was twice wounded in actions there. He demonstrated great bravery in the face of the enemy and was promoted to second major in 1794. Six years later, he took command of the Nasheburg Musketeer Regiment on 27 July 1800, and shortly thereafter was promoted to colonel on 26 September 1803.

In 1806, Libhardt was sent to fight the Turks in the Danube Valley and became chef of the Poltava Musketeer Regiment on 13 March 1807. In early 1812, he was assigned to the 2nd Western Army and commanded the 1st Brigade of the 26th Division of the 7th Corps. He took part in Prince Bagration's retreat and fought at Saltanovka (Moghilev), where he was seriously wounded in the right hand. He retired because of this wound on 28 December 1812 with the rank of major general and full pension. Libhardt returned to active service in October 1814, and became the Commandant of Kherson, where he served until 1830.

LIDERS, Nikolay Ivanovich (b. 1762 — date of death unknown; removed from rosters on 25 August 1823) descended from a Prussian noble family that settled in Russia in the early 18th century. He enlisted as a sergeant in the artillery in January 1767 and transferred as a sergeant to the Life Guard Preobrazhensk Regiment on 12 March 1778. Six years later, on 19 January 1784, Liders was assigned as a vakhmistr to the Life Guard Horse Regiment.

He was promoted to lieutenant in the Tavrida Horse Jager Regiment in January 1786, and then transferred to the Smolensk Light Horse Regiment on 12 April 1787. He participated in the Russo-Turkish War of 1787-1791 and fought at Ochakov. In 1791, he transferred to the Pskov Infantry Regiment and served in Poland in 1792-1794. Liders was promoted to colonel on 17 April 1799, and appointed commander of the Pskov Musketeer Regiment 3 March 1800. He became a major general and chef of the Bryansk Infantry Regiment on 6 October 1800.

Liders participated in the 1805 Campaign and distinguished himself at Austerlitz on 2 December. He was appointed chef of the Okhotsk Musketeer Regiment on 5 September 1806, and from 1806-1811 fought the Ottoman forces in the Danubian Principalities. He was seriously wounded during an assault on Braila in 1809. The following year, he became the Commandant of Khotin on 19 October, and took command of the Khotin Garrison Regiment on 6 November 1810. In August 1812, Admiral Paul Chichagov sent him with a special detachment to harass the French troops in Volhynia and Byelorussia. He took part in the actions at Nesvizh, Borisov, Bryli, and Vilna. In January 1813, Liders returned to his duties as the commandant of Khotin. He retired because of poor health in 1820.

LIEVEN (Lieven III), Ivan Andreyevich (Johann George) (b. 4 June 1775, Kiev — d. 26 February 1848, Mittau) was born to prominent noble family in the Lifland *gubernia*. He began service as a kaptenarmus in the artillery in 1779, and transferred to the Life Guard Semeyonovsk Regiment on 16 December 1790. Lieven became an aide-de-camp to Grand Duke Alexander in 1796. Over the next three years, he was awarded the Order of St. John of Jerusalem, conferred the title of count of the Russian Empire (March 1799), and promoted to colonel (20 April 1799). Lieven became a major general and chef of the Lieven's Combined Grenadier Regiment on 13 October 1800. He was relieved of his duties and ordered to remain with the army on 1 May 1801.

Lieven took part in the 1806-1807 Campaigns in Poland and distinguished himself at Eylau, where he earned the Order of St. George (3rd class) on 20 April 1807. In 1809-1811, he served in the Danubian Principalities and fought at Nikopol, Vidin, and Ruse. During the 1812 Campaign, he led the 10th Division of the 3rd Reserve Army of Observation and fought at Ustilug, Lubomle, and Brest-Litovsk. Lieven served in General Osten-Sacken's detachment in 1813 and fought at Pulawa, Czenstonchov, Breslau, Katzbach, and Leipzig (Order of St. Alexander of Neva). A promotion to lieutenant general followed on 27 September 1813. During the invasion of France, Lieven fought at Brienne and La Rothière, where he was seriously wounded.

After the war, he commanded the 10th Division before retiring on 25 December 1815. Lieven was conferred the title of prince of the Russian Empire in 1826. During his career, he was also decorated with the Orders of St. Anna (1st class) with diamonds, of St. Vladimir (2nd class), the Prussian Order of Red Eagle, the Swedish Order of the Sword and a golden sword for courage.

LIKHACHEV, Yakov (Jacob) Ivanovich (b. 1766 — d. 1821) was born to a noble family from the Jaroslavl *gubernia*. He enlisted as a sub ensign in the Life Guard Semeyonovsk Regiment in 1785, and was promoted to sergeant in January 1788. He participated in the Russo-Swedish War in 1789-1790, fought at Vyborg and Svenkzund, and rose to ensign. In 1792-1794, Likhachev served in the Sofia

Carabineer Regiment in Poland and took part in the actions at Byaloi (promoted to sub-lieutenant) and Gorodische (awarded a golden sword). More promotions followed: colonel on 18 April 1799, major general and chef of the Suzdal Musketeer Regiment on 8 June 1800. In 1801-1804, Likhachev served as a battalion commander in the Life Guard Semeyonovsk Regiment.

On 23 May 1804, Likhachev was appointed chef of the Tobolsk Musketeer Regiment, but he took a discharge from the army on 16 November 1804. Returning to the service, he assumed command of the militia in the Jaroslavl *gubernia* and served in Byelorussia (received the Order of St. Anna, 2nd class, with diamonds). In 1812, he led the Jaroslavl *opolchenye* and operated between Smolensk and Vilna. In 1813, he took part in the sieges of Modlin and Breslau before retiring in November 1814.

LIKHACHEV, Peter Gavrilovich (b. 1758, Tyagushi — d. 6 May 1813, Porkhovo) was born to a Russian noble family in the Pskov *gubernia*. He began military service in the 2nd Fusilier Regiment in 1772, and participated in the Russo-Turkish War in the Crimea in 1783. Likhachev was promoted to lieutenant in 1784, and fought the Swedes in 1788-1790. In 1793-1808, he served in the Caucasus against the local tribes. He was appointed commander of the 17th Jager Regiment on 2 June 1797, and earned promotions to colonel on 25 November 1797, and to major general on 11 November 1798. In 1799, he became chef of the 17th Jager Regiment (later renamed Likhachev's Jager Regiment) on 29 January 1799. In April 1801, Likhachev's regiment was redesignated the 16th Jagers Regiment, and Likhachev served as its chef until 1808. He distinguished himself at Khan-Kale in Chechnya and garnered the Order of St. George (3rd class, 15 February 1808) for his service there. Likhachev retired on 25 January 1808, but returned to service on 24 April 1809, becoming chef of the Tomsk Musketeer Regiment. In 1811, he took command of the 24th Division of the 6th Corps.

During the 1812 Campaign, Likhachev fought at Smolensk and distinguished himself defending the Great Redoubt at Borodino on 7 September. He was captured there by the French and introduced to Napoleon, who returned his sword. Likhachev remained in French captivity for the rest of campaign and was liberated in Koenigsberg in late December 1812. By this time, however, he was seriously ill and died at the village of Porkhovo on 6 May 1813.

LINDFORS, Fedor Andreyevich (Axcel Friedrich) (b. 6 April 1760, Revel — d. 20 October 1813, Leipzig) was born to a Swedish noble family in the Lifland *gubernia*. He enlisted as a private in the Life Guard Semeyonovsk Regiment on 20 April 1777, and transferred as a sub-lieutenant to the Nasheburg Infantry Regiment on 1 February 1781. Lindfors participated in the Russo-Turkish War in 1787-1791, distinguished himself at Ochakov in 1788, and was promoted to second major. In 1789, he transferred to the St. Petersburg Grenadier Regiment on 30 October and served with that unit in Poland from 1792-1794. He was promoted to colonel on 12 February 1800, and took command of the St. Petersburg Grenadier Regiment on 5 February 1803. Two years later, Lindfors became chef of the Tobolsk Musketeer Regiment on 21 February, and rose to major general seven months later.

Lindfors was appointed chef of the Yakutsk Musketeer Regiment on 5 September 1806. During the 1807 Campaign in Poland, his regiment was deployed at Belostock. On 16

March 1810, he was courtmartialed for negligence during the fires at Brest, but was absolved of the charges and restored to his previous position on 24 December 1810. Lindfors was appointed chef of the Galicia Infantry Regiment on 29 January 1811. He led the 1st Brigade of 13th Division in the Crimea during the Russian Campaign of 1812, and participated in the actions on the Berezina in December 1812. In early 1813, he took part in the siege of Modlin. In October 1813, Lindfors was fighting at Leipzig when a cannon ball tore off his right leg. He lingered for two days before dying.

LISANEVICH, Grigory Ivanovich (b. 17 January 1756 — d. 25 February 1832) was born to a noble family in the Polotsk *gubernia*. He joined the Elizavetgrad Pikemen (*Pikinernii*) Regiment in 1771, and fought the Turks at Silistra and Küçük Kaynarca. In 1775, he became an adjutant with a rank of sub-lieutenant and participated in the campaigns against the Crimean Tatars in 1777-1778, and 1782. In 1787, Lisanevich transferred to the Elizavetgrad Horse Jager Regiment and fought at Ochakov (1788) and Akkerman (1789). From 1792-1794, Lisanevich served as a staff officer to General Ferzen in Poland and distinguished himself in the battle at Maciejowice. He rose to lieutenant colonel in 1798, and colonel on 13 September 1799. In 1802, Lisanevich took command of a battalion of the Elizavetgrad Hussar Regiment.

Between 22 July 1803 and 24 December 1807, Lisanevich commanded the Elizavetgrad Hussar Regiment and participated in the 1805 Campaign, distinguishing himself in the fighing at Austerlitz on 2 December 1805. In 1806-1807, he served with the 5th Division in Poland and fought at Eylau, on the Passarga River, at Heilsberg, and Friedland. For his actions, he was promoted to major general on 24 December 1807, and appointed chef of the Chuguev Cossack (Uhlan) Regiment on 18 January 1808. In 1809, Lisanevich commanded this regiment against the Turks in the Danubian Principalities, where he participated in the actions at Braila, Babadag, Girsov, Constanta (Kustendji), and Rassevat. During the siege of Silistra, Lisanevich commanded the Russian rear guard and covered the withdrawal of the Russian army across the Danube in late 1809. In 1810, he fought at Bazardjik, Shumla, Giurgiu, and Ruse. In 1811, he took command of the 2nd Cavalry Brigade of the 7th Cavalry Division and fought the Turks in Little Wallachia.

Lisanevich served in the 23rd Brigade of the 7th Cavalry Division of the 4th Corps of the Army of Danube in 1812. He fought the French and Austrian troops at Volkovysk and throughout the Belostock region. In 1813, he served in the left wing of the Russian army under Miloradovich, and took part in the combats at Glogau, Lutzen, and Bautzen. Lisanevich transferred into the main reserve and was later dispatched to cover Prague. He returned to the main Russian forces after the battle of Kulm and fought at Pirna (8 September), Freyburg (21 October), and Wachau.

At Leipzig, Lisanevich was attached to Count Pahlen's division and distinguished himself on the left flank. In 1814, he led the advance guard of Count Pahlen and fought in a series of actions in France, including Brienne (29 January), Nogent (10 February), Troyes (23-24 February), Bar-sur-Aube (26-27 February), Labrussel (3-4 March), and Le Fère Champenoise (25 March). Once at Paris, Lisanevich joined the 2nd Independent Corps of Count O'Rourke and took command of the 3rd

Uhlan Division, receiving therafter the rank of lieutenant general on 11 September 1814. In 1815, he marched with his division to France during the Hundred Days but was recalled to Russia after Napoleon's defeat at Waterloo.

After the war, Lisanevich worked with General Aleksey Arakcheyev on the organization of the military colonies. He retired on 5 February 1820, and spent the last years of his life on his estate. He attended the coronation of Emperor Nicholas I in September 1826, and died on 25 February 1832.

LOPUKHIN, Peter Andreyevich (b. 1767 — date of death unknown) was born to a prominent Russian noble family; his father Andrey Lopukhin, served as the Governor of Tula under Catherine II. Peter Lopukhin, age five, was enlisted as a corporal in the Life Guard Preobrazhensk Regiment on 12 January 1772, and began active service as a sergeant on 12 January 1782. Promoted to ensign in October 1785, he took part in the Russo-Swedish War in 1788-1790. Lopukhin served on the galley flotilla of Prince Nassau-Zigen and fought at Vyborg and Rochensalmi, receiving a golden sword and the Order of St. Vladimir (3rd class). In 1792-1794, he served as a captain-lieutenant in the Pskov Carabineer Regiment in Poland and fought at Dubeka, Gorodische, and Vladimir (Volhynia), where he was wounded. He rose to colonel on 16 April 1797, and to major general on 16 April 1799.

Lopukhin retired in October 1801 and returned to service in late 1806. In 1807, he commanded militia in the Moscow *gubernia*. During the 1812 Campaign, he organized the Moscow *opolchenye* and served as chef of the 6th Infantry *Opolchenye* Regiment. He took part in the battles at Borodino, Tarutino, Maloyaroslavets, Vyazma, and Krasnyi (received the Order of St. Vladimir, 3rd class). In 1813, he was seriously wounded in the chest at Modlin on 19 March, and spent the rest of the war recuperating. He briefly served at the headquarters of the Army of Reserves in early 1814 before retiring on 20 August 1814.

LÖWENSTERN, Karl Fedorovich, (b. 9 April 1770 — d. 24 June 1840) was born to a Württemberg noble family. He was brought to Russia as a child, and after studying at the Artillery and Engineer Cadet Corps, began service as a guard marine in 1778. He participated in the Russo-Swedish War in 1789-1790, serving on the frigate *Podrazhislav*. In 1789, Löwenstern transferred to the Narva Infantry Regiment with the rank of lieutenant. He rose to colonel in March 1799, and held command of the 2nd Artillery Regiment between 6 April 1800 and 8 September 1801. In 1805, Löwenstern became chef of the 1st Artillery Regiment on 13 June, and served at this position until October 1806. On 23 September 1806, he was promoted to major general and took part in the campaign against the French. At Eylau, he led the center the Russian artillery, and in June 1807, fought at Heilsberg and Friedland.

In 1808-1811, Löwenstern supervised the Baltic coastal batteries. In 1812, he commanded artillery in Bagration's 2nd Western Army and fought at Saltanovka (Moghilev) and Smolensk. After General Kutaysov was killed at Borodino, Löwenstern assumed command of the Russian artillery and distinguished himself, earning in return the Order of St. George (3rd class, 1 November 1812). In October, he was placed in charge of the artillery of the main Russian army, and in December took command of the guard and reserve artilleries. In 1813-1814, Löwenstern fought at Dresden, Pirna, Hollendorf, Kulm,

Leipzig, Thorn, Bar sur Aube, Le Fère Champenoise, and Paris.

In 1815, Löwenstern led the artillery of the 7th Corps before becoming the chief of the artillery of the 2nd Army on 17 June 1816. He was promoted to lieutenant general on 13 May 1818. In 1828, he took part in the campaign against the Turks and fought at Braila, Silistra, and Shumla. He was promoted to general on 3 May 1829. After the conclusion of the war, Löwenstern served as the Chief of Staff of the 2nd Army at Tulcea. In 1832, he became a member of the Council of War. He died in 1840 and was buried at the Volkovo Lutheran Cemetery in St. Petersburg.

LÖWENSTERN, Vladimir Ivanovich (b. 1777, Razik, Estland — d. 2 February 1858) born to an ancient noble family in the Estland *gubernia*. He graduated from the Revel Academy for Nobles and was enlisted as a sergeant in Life Guard Semeyonovsk Regiment in 1793, serving as an adjutant to General Count Saltykov. In December 1794, he transferred to the Horse Guard and, the next year, he served in Ukraine Light Cavalry Regiment (later Starodoub Cuirassiers). From 1798-1799, Löwenstern took part in the campaign against the French on the Rhine, and in 1800 participated in Count Pahlen's expedition along the Baltic Sea. In 1802, he retired because of poor health and returned to active service in 1812, serving as a senior adjutant to General Barclay de Tolly. He participated in the battles of Smolensk, Bodorino, Maloyaroslavets, and Krasnyi. Löwenstern was promoted to lieutenant colonel in 1813 and served as an adjutant to Lieutenant General Vorontsov, taking part in the operations in Saxony and France. In 1815, he became a colonel in the Akhtyrsk Hussar Regiment.

After the war, Löwenstern served in Vorontsov's corps in France in 1815-1819. Arriving to Russia, he transferred to civil service on 12 May 1823, but soon returned to military service becoming the Military Governor of Revel on 26 September 1826. He rose to major general on 18 December 1826, and served in the 3rd Dragoon Division. In April 1828, he took command of the 2nd Brigade of the 3rd Uhlan Division. Löwenstern retired in January 1838, and spent the next twenty years in St. Petersburg, where he died on 2 February 1858. He wrote several recollections concerning his service during the Napoleonic Wars. His *Zapiski* were published in several parts in the *Russkaya Starina*, and his *Denkwurdigkeiten eines Livlanders aus den Jahren 1790-1815* was printed in Leipzig in 1858.

LÖWIS VON MENAR, Fedor (Friedrich) Fedorovich (17 September 1767, Hapsale, Estland — 28 April 1824, Zelen, Wolmar uezd) was born in Estland and descended from a Scottish family that resettled to Russia under Peter the Great. In December 1772, he was enlisted in Moscow Carabineer

Regiment, and then transferred as a vakhmistr to the Kazan Cuirassier Regiment on 10 November 1773. His active duty started in 1782, when Löwis joined the Keksholm (Kexholm) Infantry Regiment as a lieutenant. He took part in the war against Sweden in 1788-1789, and earned his rank of premier major. After the war, Löwis was moved to Polotsk and commanded a grenadier battalion. In 1792-1794, he fought the Poles and was awarded the Order of St. George (4th class) and a golden sword for courage.

In 1795, Löwis joined the Riga Carabineer Regiment; four years later, he was promoted to colonel and commander of this regiment. Late in 1799, he was conferred the rank of major general and became chef of the Kazan Cuirassier Regiment (which was renamed Löwis' Cuirassier Regiment). After brief retirement in August 1800, Löwis returned to service as the commander of His Majesty's Cuirassier Regiment on 19 December 1800. Two years later he was injured while riding his horse and had to retire again on 15 November 1802.

Löwis returned to the army in September 1805, and became chef of the Yaroslavl Musketeer Regiment on 27 November. He served in Buxhöwden's corps during the Russian march to Ulm, and fought at Austerlitz on 2 December, receiving the Order of St. Vladimir (3rd class). In 1806-1807, he served in Essen's corps covering the western frontier of Russia. Löwis was promoted to lieutenant general on 24 December 1807, and appointed commander of the 10th Division. He participated in the 1809 Campaign against Austria in Galicia. In February 1810, he joined the Army of Moldavia and fought the Turks at Silistra and Shumla. However, he became ill with fever and retired on 11 June 1811.

In 1812, Löwis petitioned Emperor Alexander to re-enlist him and was sent to Essen's corps at Riga on 13 July 1812. He fought at Eckau and Bausck against the Prussian General York and was decorated with the Orders of St. Vladimir (2nd class) and of St. George (3rd class). Löwis besieged Danzig in early 1813, an action that garnered the Order of St. Anna (1st class), a golden sword with diamonds, and the Order of St. Alexander of Neva. After the capture of Danzig, Löwis commanded the 25th Infantry Division in the Duchy of Warsaw before retiring because of poor health on 14 October 1814. He lived in the Lifland *gubernia* for the next ten years, served on various civil positions in the province, and accompanied Emperor Alexander and Prussian King Friedrich Wilhelm III during their visit to the region. Löwis died at his estate at Zelen on 28 April 1824.

LUKOV, Fedor Alekseyevich (b. 1761 — d. 26 August 1813, Dresden) was born to a soldier's family in Moscow and enlisted as a private in the Sevsk Infantry Regiment on 16 September 1775. He served in Poland from 1783-1784 and again from 1792-1794, and was promoted to lieutenant on 4 May 1793. In 1799, he served under General Rimsky-Korsakov in Switzerland. Lukov took part in the 1806-1807 Campaigns in Poland, fighting at Jankovo, Eylau, Deppen, and Heilsberg (wounded). From 1808-1809, he served in Tuchkov's corps in Finland and fought at Kuopio, Salmi, Oravais, Torneo, and Umeo. He took command of the Sevsk Infantry Regiment on 16 February 1810, and rose to colonel on 11 September 1811.

During the Russian Campaign of 1812, Lukov served in the 1st Brigade of the 5th Division of Wittgenstein's corps and was seriously wounded at Boyarshina at the opening of the campaign. After recuperating, he took part in the actions at Smolyani and Chashniky in October-November 1812. In 1813, he fought at Lutzen and Bautzen, earning promotion to major general on 8 June 1813, and the Order of St. George (3rd class) on 12 August 1813. Lukov was mortally wounded at the battle of Dresden on 26 August 1813, and died the same day.

LUKOVKIN, Gavriil (Gabriel) Amvrosiyevich (11 March 1772 — 1849) was born to a prominent Cossack family (his father was Avrosii Lukovkin, a major general in the Don Cossack Host). Gavriil Lukovkin began service with the Cossacks in January 1780, and was appointed regimental esaul on 12 August 1783. He rose to sergeant in 1787, and took part in operations in the Kuban Valley in 1790-1792, and in Poland from 1792-1794. Lukovkin was promoted to colonel on 9 February 1799, but retired later that year. He returned to service nine years later, serving as a Cossack brigade commander in Army of Moldavia in 1809-1810, earning the Order of St. George (4th class, 13 March 1811) for his actions at Shumla in 1810.

During the 1812 Campaign, Lukovkin commanded a Cossack brigade and harassed the French lines of communication in Volhynia. In 1813, he served in Chernyshev's cavalry detachment, took part in the operations in the Duchy of Warsaw, and fought at Igumen, Vilna, and Kovno. In early 1813, he served in the corps of Vorontsov and Osten-Sacken and was promoted to major general on 28 June 1813. Lukovkin distinguished himself during the pursuit of the French forces after the battle of Leipzig, for which he received the Order of St. George (3rd class) on 19 October 1813. In 1814, he fought at Brienne, La Rothière, Montmirail, Chateau Thierry, Sezanne, Craonne (wounded in the left hand), Laon, and Le Fère Champenoise. After the war, he served in the Don Cossack Host in 1815-1835, and retired on 23 march 1836.

LVOV, Andrey Lavrentievich (b. 10 December 1751 — d. 29 March 1823, Moscow) was born to a noble family in the Kaluga *gubernia*. He graduated from the Infantry Cadet Corps and enlisted as a sub-lieutenant in the Life Guard Izmailovsk Regiment on 9 March 1770. He served in Poland in 1770-1772, earning promotion to lieutenant. In 1773, Lvov transferred as a second major to the Bakhmutsk Hussar Regiment and took part in the operations in the Crimea in 1774-1775. In 1784, he joined the Ukraine Light Cavalry Regiment with the rank of lieutenant colonel.

Lvov served in the Russo-Turkish War in 1787-1791 and received the Order of St. George (4th class, 25 April 1789) for his actions at Ochakov in 1788. He spent 1789-1791 fighting at Akkerman, Bender, Ismail (wounded in the head and left hand), Babadag, and Macin, where he earned a golden sword for courage. For his conduct throughout the war, Lvov earned promotions to colonel on 13 December 1789, and to brigadier on 14 March 1791. In 1792, he accompanied the Russian mission to Istanbul. He returned to Poland in 1793-1794, fighting at Kobylka, where he was wounded in the right thigh (the Order of St. Vladimir, 3rd class).

Lvov retired on 11 October 1798, and served at the Imperial Court for the next six years. In 1804, he was appointed to the Moscow commissariat and was promoted to privy counsellor in early 1805. He organized the Moscow militia in late 1806, and served in the Moscow Department of the Senate in 1807-1811. During the Russian Campaign of 1812, he led a company (druzhina) of the Kaluga *opolchenye* and took part in the operations at

Maloyaroslavets, Vyazma, and Smolensk. He was wounded at Moghilev late that year and was awarded the Order of St. Vladimir (2nd class). He retired in May 1813. and served in the Senate for the next ten years.

LVOV, Dmitry Semenovich (b. 17 July 1765 — d. 1834) was born to a family of Russian princes. He enlisted as a private in the Life Guard Preobrazhensk Regiment in 1773, and was promoted to ensign on 12 January 1782. Lvov participated in the Russo-Swedish War in 1788-1790, earning the rank of captain and the Order of St. Vladimir (4th class). In 1794, he was appointed to the Imperial Armory in Moscow and was promoted to brigadier in early 1795. He retired in 1796, but returned to service ten years later, organizing the Kaluga Militia in December 1806. During the 1812 Campaign, he led the 1st Infantry Regiment of the Kaluga *Opolchenye* and took part in the complex operations around Maloyaroslavets, Smolensk, and Moghilev. In 1813, Lvov commanded the Kaluga *Opolchenye* and served at the sieges of Modlin and Danzig (received the Orders of St. Anna, 2nd class, with diamonds, and of St. Vladimir, 3rd class). He retired in 1815.

LVOV, Mikhail Lavrentievich (1757 — 9 July 1825) was born to a noble family in the Kaluga *gubernia*. He graduated from the Naval Cadet Corps and began service as a guard marine in the Baltic Fleet on 13 May 1775. Lvov served in Britain in 1778, and was promoted to lieutenant on 2 May 1780. During the Russo-Swedish War, he rose to captain lieutenant and commanded the frigate *St. Marc* at Gogland in 1788. The next year, he transferred to the Black Sea Fleet and served as an adjutant to Prince Gregory Potemkin. He commanded the frigate *St. Nicholas* at Akkerman (Order of St. Vladimir, 4th class), Kerch Straits, Tendra Cape (Order of St. George, 4th class, 19 September 1790), and Kaliakria (wounded, received a golden sword).

Promoted to captain (2nd class) on 27 December 1793, Lvov became captain (1st class) and commander of the ship-of-the-line *Tri Ierarkha* on 12 January 1796. He was promoted to captain commander on 16 April 1797, but retired in March 1798. He joined the civil service in 1803, and served in the Moscow Controller Expedition. He returned to the army and was promoted to major general on 21 December 1803, but retired a second time in 1806. He returned to military service the following year and helped organize militia in the Kaluga *gubernia*. During the 1812 Campaign, Lvov commanded the 3rd Infantry Regiment of the Kaluga *Opolchenye* and participated in the operations in the Kaluga and Smolensk *gubernia*s. He was wounded at Moghilev, for which he received the Order of St. Vladimir (3rd class). Lvov finally retired in the summer of 1813, and lived in Moscow for the next twelve years.

LYALIN, Dmitry Vasilievich (b. 31 october 1772 — d. 9 January 1848) was born to a noble family from the St. Petersburg *gubernia*. He enlisted in the 1st Marine Battalion on 26 May 1786, and later transferred to the Navy Cadet Corps. During the Russo-Swedish War, he was promoted to sub-lieutenant and fought at Gogland, Eland, Krasnyi Gorky, and Vyborg. In 1791-1807, he served in the Moscow inspection and trained marine battalions. He was appointed commander of the Navaginsk Musketeer Regiment on 24 May 1799, and rose to colonel on 8 October 1800. Lyalin participated in the Russo-Swedish War in 1808-1809, and became chef of the Odessa Musketeer Regiment on 28

October 1809. He was appointed chef of the Tenginsk Musketeer Regiment on 9 March 1810. The following year, his regiment was converted to the Tenginsk Infantry Regiment on 6 March.

During the 1812 Campaign, Lyalin served in the 14th Division of Wittgenstein's corps and fought at Wilkomir, Sivosin, Svolnya, Polotsk (promoted to major general on 15 January 1813 with seniority dating from 18 October 1812), Chashniky, Smolyani, Borisov, and Labiau (Order of St. George, 4th class, 10 November 1813). In 1813, Lyalin served at Danzig, Kustrin, Spandau, Lutzen (wounded in the left hand), Koenigswarta, Peterswald, Kulm (wounded in the head), Kolon, and Strasburg. In 1814, he fought at Falzburg, Troyes, Arcis sur Aube, Le Fère Champenoise, and Paris, where he earned the Order of St. George (4th class) on 30 March 1814. He retired because of poor health in January 1817. During his career, he was also awarded the Order of St. Anna (1st class), the Prussian Order of Red Eagle, and a golden sword.

LYAPUNOV, Dmitry Petrovich (b. 1775 — d. 17 March 1821) was born to a noble family from the Ryazan *gubernia*. He enlisted as a sergeant in the Life Guard Semeyonovsk Regiment on 12 January 1784, rose to ensign in January 1792, and to colonel on 28 October 1800. Lyapunov took part in the 1805 Campaign and was awarded the Order of St. George (4th class, 10 March 1806) for his actions at Austerlitz. In 1807, he participated in the battles at Guttstadt, Heilsberg, and Friedland, and became commander of the Pskov Musketeer Regiment on 25 January 1808.

During the 1812 Campaign, Lyapunov served in the 1st Brigade of the 7th Division of the 6th Corps in the 1st Western Army and fought at Smolensk, Borodino, Maloyaroslavets (Order of St. George, 3rd class, 27 February 1813), and Krasnyi. For his actions at Borodino, he was promoted to major general on 2 December 1812, with seniority dating from 7 September 1812. In 1813, he served as a brigade commander in the 7th Division and was later appointed the Commandant of Plotsk. In 1816-1818, Lyapunov served in the Internal Guard Corps before retiring on 30 January 1818.

MADATOV (Mekhrabents), Valerian Grigorievich (b. 1782, Karabagh — d. 14 September 1829) was born to an Armenian noble family from the Karabagh region. At the age of fifteen, he accompanied a delegation to St. Petersburg to appeal for military aid against the Turks. During his stay in Petersburg, young Madatov was fascinated by the Russian guard units and decided to petition Emperor Paul to accept him in the Russian service. Paul I appointed him a portupei-ensign in the Life Guard Preobrazhensk on 25 June 1797, and later transferred him as a sub-lieutenant to the Pavlovsk Grenadier Regiment on 17 May 1802.

The next few years of his career remain unclear. According to Mikhailovsky-Danilevsky, he served as a lieutenant in the Mingrelia Infantry Regiment. Recent studies, however, assert Madatov took a discharge in 1803 because of poor health, and returned to service three years later.

During the Russo-Turkish War, Madatov served in Platov's advance guard in 1809, distinguishing himself at Babadag, Girsov, Braila (Order of St. Anna, 3rd class), Kustendji (also known as Constanta, Order of St. Vladimir, 4th class), Rassevat (received a golden sword), Silistra, Kalipetri, and Kapakly (Order of St. Anna, 2nd class). Madatov transferred as a rotmistr to the Aleksandria Hussar Regiment in early 1810, and the same year fought at Shumla, Chaushkoy (Order of St. George, 4th class), Ruse, Batin (promoted to lieutenant colonel), and Giurgiu. In 1811, his regiment was moved to the Volhynia, where it was attached to the 3rd Reserve Army of Observation. During the 1812 Campaign, Madatov initially served with the 17th Brigade of the 5th Cavalry Division in Markov's corps, and later joined the advance guard of Count Lambert. He distinguished himself at Kobryn (Order of St. Anna, 2nd class), Gorodechno (promoted to colonel), Minsk, Borisov, Stakhov, Pleshenitsa, and Vilna (golden sword with diamonds).

In early 1813, Madatov served in Winzegorode's corps at Kalisch (Order of St. George, 3rd class, 6 March 1813), Glogau, Lutzen (Order of St. Vladimir, 3rd class), Bautzen, and Reichenbach. In August-September 1813, he transferred to Sacken's corps in the Army of Silesia, fighting at Leignitz, Bautzen, Bunzlau, Haynau, Hochkirch, Wurschen, and Wolnau. He was decorated for these actions with the Prussian Pour le Merite. At Leipzig, he was wounded in the left hand but continued leading the Russian cavalry charges, for which he was promoted to a major general on 9 November 1814, with seniority dating from 28 September 1813. After recuperating for a couple of weeks at Halle, Madatov joined the Russian army in Paris in March 1814. After the war, he commanded a brigade of the 2nd Hussar Division, and returned to France during the Hundred Days in 1815.

The following year, Madatov was appointed to the Independent Caucasian Corps, where he took comman of the Russian forces in the native Karabagh. He became head of the Military District of Sheki, Shirvan and Karabagh in 1817. In 1819-1821, he took part in operations against the local insurgents in Daghestan, distinguishing himself in Tabassaran (Order of St. Anna, 1st class), at Lavashi (diamond signs of the Order of St. Anna, 1st class) and Kasykumyka (Order of St. Vladimir, 2nd class). During the Russo-Persian War of 1826-1827, Madatov fought at Shamkhor and Elisavetpol, for which he received promotion to lieutenant general on 10 October 1826, and a golden sword with diamonds. In 1828, he was dispatched to the Danubian Principalities, where he served in 3rd Corps during the Russo-Turkish War of 1828-1829.

In May-August 1828, Madatov took part in the actions at Issacea, Girsov, and Kuzgun. In Pravoda on 15 August 1828, he took command of a detachment comprised of two infantry regiments, three uhlan squadrons, and a cossack regiment, and with these defended the town against superior Turkish forces. In the winter of 1829, he took command of the 3rd Hussar Division, and in the spring served at Silistra, Kulevchi, and Shumla (Order of St. Alexander of Neva).

Madatov died without warning, possibly of a stroke, near Shumla on 14 September 1829. Out of respect for Madatov, the Grand Vizier of Porte, who defended Shumla, allowed him to be buried in the Church of St. George inside the town. His remains were later transported for internment in the Alexander of Neva Monastery in St. Petersburg.

MAKAROV, Peter Stepanovich (b. 1768 — d. 19 December 1815) was born to a noble family in the Kostroma *gubernia*. He enlisted as a sub-ensign in the Life Guard Preobrazhensk Regiment on 12 January 1783, and transferred as a lieutenant to the Caucasian Musketeer Regiment on 12 January 1787. During the Russo-Turkish War of 1787-1791, he took part in the operations in the Caucasus and the Kuban Valley, distinguishing himself at Anapa and Sudjuk Kale. He transferred to the Naval Artillery Corps on 23 March 1792, and served on the galley flotilla in the Baltic Sea in 1793-1797. In 1798, he took part in the cruise to the British shores, and the following year participated in the expedituion to Holland, where he was wounded in the right side at Helder.

Returning to Russia, Makarov rose to a lieutenant colonel on 22 August 1805, and served as an adjutant to General Michelson during the Russo-Turkish War of 1806-1812. He was promoted to a colonel in the Life Guard Jager Regiment on 25 September 1807. On 8 December 1810, Makarov was decorated with the Order of St. George (4th class) for twenty-five years of service.

During the 1812 Campaign, Makarov served with the 3rd Brigade of the Guard Infantry Division in the 1st Western Army, and fought at Smolensk, Borodino (wounded in right hand), Tarutino, Maloyaroslavets, Vyazma, and Krasnyi. In 1813, he served at Lutzen and was seriously wounded in the chest at Bautzen. Promoted to a major general on 30 July 1813, Makarov fought at Pirna, Kulm (Prussian Iron Cross), Teplitz, and Leipzig. For these actions, he received the Order of St. George (3rd class) on 10 November 1813, and became chef of the Life Guard Pavlovsk Regiment on 18 December 1813. In 1814, he distinguished himself at Paris, earning the Order of St. Anna (1st class). After participating in the 1815 Campaign, Makarov fell ill and died on 19 December 1815.

MALTITS, Leontii Fedorovich became commander of the 11th Jager Regiment on 28 May 1797, and a colonel on 4 October 1797. He rose to a major general on 31 August 1798, and chef of the Friedrichsham Garrison Regiment on 5 August 1799. Promoted to a lieutenant general on 16 March 1800, Maltits served as chef of the Yaroslavl Musketeer Regiment between 13 January 1802 and 27 November 1805. During the 1805 Campaign, he led the 5th Column of the Russian army in Austria, and a division at Austerlitz on 2 December 1805.

MALUTIN, Peter Fedorovich (d. ca. 1775 — date of death unclear) was born to a noble family. He began service as a corporal in the army in 1785, and participated in the operations against the Swedes in 1788-1791. Therefter, he served in the Gatchina Troops and rose to lieutenant colonel in 1796. Later that year, Emperor Paul promoted Malutin to colonel of the Life Guard Izmailovsk Regiment and entrusted him with the inspection of the Kiev *gubernia*. Malutin became major general in 1798, and lieutenant general on 3 February 1800, commanding the Life Guard Izmailovsk Regiment between 14 June 1799 and 9 February 1808. He participated in the 1805-1807 Campaigns against Napoleon, distinguishing himself at Friedland (Order of St. George). Malutin retired because of poor health in early 1808. His date of death remains uncertain.

MANDERSTERN, Karl Yegorovich (b. 1785 — d. 1862) studied in the 2nd Cadet Corps and began service as an ensign in the Riga Infantry Corps. He served as Lieutenant General Langeron's adjutant in 1805 before transferring to the Imperial Retinue two years later. In 1808-1811, he served in the Danubian Principalities. During the 1812 Campaign, Manderstern was ober quartermaster of the 8th Corps and served in that capacity throughout the 1813-1814 Campaigns.

After the war, Manderstern became ober quartermaster of the Guard Corps in 1826, rising to the rank of major general. He participated in the bloody suppression of the Polish Uprising in 1831, and was seriously wounded in the head at Ostrolenka, for which he received the Order of St. George (3rd class). In 1839, he was appointed the Commandant of Riga, and in 1852, was named Commandant of the fortress of St. Petersburg.

MANFREDI, Osip Ignatievich (Josef Ignatius August) (b. 1778 — d. 5 July 1816) descended from Austrian noblilty. After studying the military art in Vienna, he served in the Austrian and Piedmontese armies before entering Russian service with a rank of captain on 3 September 1804. He served as an assistant to the Minister of Navy Paul Chichagov and took part in Vice Admiral Senyavin's naval campaign in the Mediterranean Sea in 1807. Manfredi garnered the Order of St. George (4th class) for his actions in the naval engagement at Mount Athons. In 1808-1810, he served in the Corps of Engineers and was promoted to colonel on 30 December 1811.

Manfredi became head of the military communications of the 1st Western Army on 5 May 1812. During the 1812 Campaign, he served in the headquarters of the 1st Western Army and commanded the 2nd Brigade of the Corps of Engineers, earning the Order of St. Anna (2nd class) with diamonds for his distinguished service at Borodino. In 1813, he served at Kalisch, Lutzen, Bautzen (received a golden sword), and Danzig, where he earned the Order of St. George (3rd class, 21 August 1814) and the rank of major general on 28 December 1813. After the war, he became head of the 9th District of the Central Office of Communications [*glavnoe upravlenie putei soobshenii*] before dying on 5 July 1816.

MANTEYFELDT, Ivan Vasilievich (Gothard Johann) (b. 21 June 1771 — d. 21 October 1813) was born to an ancient German family of counts in the Lifland *gubernia*. He enlisted as a sergeant in the Life Guard Preobrazhensk Regiment on 27 August 1783, and rose to a cornet in the Life Guard Horse Regiment on 12 January 1791. Three years later, he transferred as a premier major to the Ukraine Light Horse Regiment and served in Poland. Promoted to colonel on 6 April 1799, he participated in the 1805 Campaign in Moravia, garnering the Order of St. George (4th class, 24 May 1806) for his actions at Austerlitz in December 1805. He became chef of the St. Petersburg Dragoon Regiment on 12 January 1807. During the campaign in Poland, Manteydeldt rose to major general on 5 June 1807, and took part in the battles at Guttstadt, Heilsberg, and Friedland, where he was wounded and received the Order of St. George (3rd class) on 1 June 1808. Manteydeldt went on to serve in the Danubian Principalities in 1809-1810, where he distinguished himself at Silistra, Shumla, and Ruse.

During the 1812 Campaign, Manteyfeldt served with the 18th Brigade of the 6th cavalry Division in the Army of Danube in the Volhynia and on the Berezina. The following year, he distinguished himself at Dennewitz and Leipzig. He was mortally wounded in the latter engagement and died on 21 October 1813.

Two other Manteyfeldts served in the Russian army at the time: **MANTEYFELDT, Roman Grigorievich**, commanded the Ladoga Musketeer Regiment from 6 September 1798 to 29 February 1799. He was promoted to major general on 29 February 1799, and served as chef of the Vyatka Musketeer Regiment between February 1799 and July 1802. Colonel **MANTEYFELDT, Ernest Vasilievich**, commanded the Izumsk Hussar Regiment in 28 November 1800 and 21 February 1802.

MARKOV (Markov I), Alexander Ivanovich (b. 1781 — d. 1844) was born to a Russian noble family in the Poltava *gubernia*. He studied in the Artillery and Engineer Cadet Corps and began service in the 2nd Artillery Battalion in 1800. He participated in the 1805 Campaign, fighting at Austerlitz that December. In 1806-1807, he served in Poland and took part in the battles at Pultusk and Eylau, where he was seriously wounded in the right shoulder (golden cross). After recuperating, he fought at Heilsberg and Friedland in June 1807. Promoted to staff captain on 8 October 1808, he joined the 1st Reserve Artillery Brigade on 13 March 1811. During the 1812 Campaign, he commanded the 23rd Horse Artillery Company of the 1st Reserve Artillery Brigade in the 1st Corps, fighting at Polotsk (Order of St. Vladimir, 4th class), Orekhovo, Lupniny, Borisov, and on the Berezina.

In 1813, Markov participated in the actions at Danzig, Magdeburg, Halle, Bautzen (Order of St. George, 4th class), Dresden, and Leipzig, receiving promotion to colonel on 9 October 1813. During the invasion of France, he distinguished himself at Nogent, Provance, Morman, Bar sur Aube (promoted to major general on 11 September 1814 with seniority dating from 27 February 1814), Troyes, Arcis sur Aube, Le Fère Champenoise, and Paris, where he was decorated with the Order of St. Anna (1st class). Markov took command of the artillery of the 2nd Corps on 7 June 1814, and of the 1st Corps on 18 April 1817. He later led the 1st Artillery Division, but was relieved of command and court martialed for embezzelement and abuse of authority in 1826.

MARKOV, Yevgeny Ivanovich (b. 1769 — d. 1828) was born to a noble family in the Moscow *gubernia*. He enlisted as a private in the Permsk Infantry Regiment on 16 December 1770, and rose to an ensign on 29 November 1772. On 9 October 1779, he transferred as a lieutenant to the Semipalatinsk Field Battalion, and then as a captain to the Kursk Infantry Regiment on 12 January 1783. Promoted to a second major on 29 June 1788, he took part in the Russo-Turkish War, garnering a golden cross and the Order of St. George (4th class, 11 April 1792) at Ochakov, where he was wounded in the head. After recuperating, Markov became a premier major in the Apsheron Infantry Regiment in 1792, and served in Poland from 1792-1794, fighting at Gorodische, Dubenky, and Praga. Two years later, he took part in the Persian Expedition to the Caspian Sea, distinguishing himself at Derbent (golden sword). Markov was promoted to colonel on 15 April 1798, and given command of the Tiflis Musketeer Regiment on 27 August 1798. He rose to major general on 7 October 1798, and became chef of the Muromsk Infantry Regiment on 8 December 1798. He served under Rimsky-Korsakov in Switzerland the following year and fought at Zurich.

After a brief retirement from November 1799 through October 1800, Markov became commandant of Arensburg on 8 February 1801, and commander of the Pskov Musketeer Regiment on 9 August 1801. He led this unit during the 1805 Campaign, distinguishing himself at Dürrenstein and Austerlitz. In 1806-1807, he served with the 7th Division in Poland, fighting at Eylau (Order of St. George, 3rd class, 20 April 1807), Guttstadt, Heilsberg, and Friedland, for which he was promoted to lieutenant general on 24 December 1807.

In 1808, Markov took command of the 9th Division of the Army of Moldavia in the Danubian Principalities. He distinguished himself at Braila (wounded in the right leg), Macin, Babadag, and Bazardjik (Order of St. Alexander of Neva). While serving under Kutuzov in 1811, he was instrumental in surrounding the Turkish army at Slobodzea and Ruse, for which he was decorated with the Order of St. George (2nd class) on 27 October 1811. In 1812, Markov commanded a corps of the 3rd Reserve Army of Observation. The following year, he took command of a corps in the Army of Poland and served at Torgau and Hamburg.

After the war, he commanded the 5th Division and was relieved of command on 25 April 1816.

Other Markovs of the Russian army include: Lieutenant Colonel **MARKOV, Timofey Aleksandrovich**, who commanded the Polotsk Musketeer Regiment in 15 November 1800 – 1 June 1802; **MARKOV (Markov II), Vasily Petrovich**, who became chef of the 11th Jager Regiment on 28 January 1799, and a major general on 15 February 1799. He served as chef of the 10th Jager Regiment between 20 March 1800 and 24 August 1807; **Lieutenant Colonel Markov** (first name unclear) led the 25th Jager Regiment between 21 December 1806 and 7 January 1808. He served with 5th Division in Poland in 1806-1807, distinguishing himself at Eylau. He rose to colonel on 24 December 1807.

MARTYNOV, Andrey Dmitryevich (b. 1762 — d. 27 January 1815) was born to a Don Cossack staff officer's family. He enlisted as a Cossack in his fathers, Major General Dmitry Martynov's Cossack Regiment in January 1770, and rose to esaul on 25 May 1772. In 1773, he became a Cossack colonel and took command of a Cossack regiment, which he led throughout the Russo-Turkish of 1787-1791. He distinguished himself at Ochakov (Order of St. Vladimir, 4th class). He became a colonel of the Russian Regular Army on 7 October 1789, a brigadier on 9 July 1796, a major general on 7 February 1797, and a lieutenant general on 3 October 1798.

Martynov took a discharge on 10 November 1799, and served as a governing ataman [*nakaznoi ataman*] of the Don Cossack Host in 1807-1808. During the 1812 Campaign, he commanded the advance guard of Platov's Cossack corps, distinguishing himself at Dorogobouzh, on the Vop' River, at Smolensk, Krasnyi, on the Berezina, and Molodechna, where he was wounded in the right shoulder. He left the army and returned to the Don Host. For his service in this campaign, he was decorated with the Order of St. George (3rd class) on 6 April 1813.

MASALOV (Mosolov), Fedor Ivanovich (b. 20 February 1771 — d. 6 August 1844) was born to a Russian noble family. He enlisted as a corporal in the Life Guard Preobrazhensk Regiment in 1775. He later transferred to the Life Guard Izmailovsk Regiment and rose to captain in 1801. The following year, he took command of a squadron of the Starodoub Dragoon Regiment. In 1806-1811, he served in the Danubian Principalities, distinguishing himself at Bender, Ismail, Kunya (Order of St. Anna, 3rd class, promoted to colonel on 24 December 1807), Calipetri, Kapanly (Order of St. Vladimir, 4th class), Rassevat, Silistra, Tataritsa (Order of St. Anna, 2nd class), and Shumla.

In 1812, Masalov served with 15th Brigade of the 5th Cavalry Division in the 3rd Reserve Army of Observation. He participated in operations in Volhynia and the battle at Kobryn, Slonim, and on the Berezina River, where he was wounded in the left thigh. His unit was converted to the Starodoub Cuirassier Regiment on 29 December 1812. In May 1813, Masalov fought at Lutzen and Bautzen (Order of St. Vladimir, 3rd class), and became commander of the Novgorod Cuirassier Regiment on 27 July 1813. Promoted to major general on 27 September 1813, he took part in the battles at Leipzig, Brienne, Malmaison, Arcis sur Aube, and Paris.

After the war, he commanded the 2nd Brigade of the 3rd Cuirassier Division, transferred to the 3rd Division on 18 October 1817, and later served as an assistant to the commander of the 2nd Dragoon Division on 7 July 1820. He retired in 1834 and spent the last ten years of his life in St. Petersburg.

MASLOV, Andrey Timofeyevich (b. 1770 — d. 19 February 1820) was born to a noble family from the Pskov *gubernia*. He enlisted in the Life Guard Preobrazhensk Regiment on 24 January 1781, and rose to a sergeant in the Life Guard Semeyonovsk Regiment in 1789. During the Russo-Swedish War of 1788-1791, he distinguished himself at Rochensalmi. Maslov transferred as a captain to the Estland Jager Corps in January 1790. Two years later, he joined the Muromsk Infantry Regiment and served in Poland in 1792-1794. In 1799, he served under Rimsky-Korsakov in Switzerland, fighting at Zurich, where he was wounded in the right hand.

During the 1806-1807 Campaigns in Poland, Maslov served with the 3rd Division at

Pultusk, Janokov, Eylau (wounded in the hand, golden cross), Guttstadt, and Heilsberg, where he was seriously wounded in the right leg. He took command of the Muromsk Musketeer Regiment on 20 September 1807, and became chef of the Revel Musketeer Regiment on 12 March 1808. During the Russo-Swedish War of 1808-1809, he participated in actions at Kuopio, Uleaborg, Torneo, Skellefteå, Umeå, Sevar, and Ratan.

Rising to colonel on 8 December 1809, Maslov organized the Podolsk Musketeer Regiment and became its chef on 29 January 1811. A month later, this unit was converted to the Podolsk Infantry Regiment on 6 March 1811. In 1812, he led the 1st Brigade of the 21st Division in the Finland Corps and took part in the actions at Podolsk, Chashniki, Smolyani, Stanitsa, and Khrabrov, where he took a serious wound to the chest that disabled him for the rest of the war. After recuperaing, he commanded in succession the 21st, 7th and 10th Divisions in 1819-1821. On 15 May 1823, he became the Commandant of Smolensk. He was serving in this position when he died on 19 February 1828.

MATSNEV, Mikhail Nikolayevich (b. 1785 — d. 1842) was born to a noble family from the Orel *gubernia*. He began service as a page in the Imperial court and enlisted as a sub-lieutenant in the Life Guard Jager Battalion on 5 October 1802. During the 1805 Campaign, he distinguished himself at Austerlitz on 2 December (Order of St. Anna, 3rd class). Two years later, he served with a battalion of St. Petersburg *gubernia* militia and fought at Guttstadt, on the Passarge, at Heilsberg (Order of St. Vladimir, 4th class), and Friedland. Promoted to colonel on 26 September 1810, he served with the 3rd Brigade of the Guard Infantry Division in the 1st Western Army at Smolensk and was seriously wounded in the left shoulder at Borodino (Order of St. Anna, 2nd class, with diamonds).

Matsnev spent almost a year recuperating from his Borodino wound. He rejoined the army in the summer of 1813, becoming chef of the 11th Jager Regiment on 14 July 1813. He commanded a brigade of the 24th Division in the battle at Leipzig that October (Swedish Order of the Sword). During the 1814 Campaign, he distinguished himself at Soissons (Order of St. Vladimir, 3rd class), Craonne, Laon, and Paris. For his service, he received the rank of major general on 13 December 1814, with seniority dating from 6 March 1814 and the Prussian Pour le Merite.

After the war, Matsnev commanded the 3rd Brigade of the 7th Division. In January 1820, he became assistant to the commander of the 7th Division and later served in the same capacity in the 10th Division. On 10 July 1821, Matsnev took command of the 1st Brigade of the 9th Division. He retired on 11 February 1823.

MAYEVSKY, Sergey Ivanovich (b. 1779 — d. 1848) was born to an officer's family; his father was rotmistr in the Polish army, and after abducting his bride from the monastery, fled to Russia. Sergey Mayevsky studied in a Jesuit boarding school and began service in the *gubernia* administration in 1789. Five years later, he enlisted as an ensign in the Ukraine Corps. Under Paul I, he served under General Rosenberg in the 1799 Campaign in Italy. Later, he served as an adjutant to Essen I in 1805-1807. During the Russo-Turkish War of 1806-1812, he garnered a golden cross for his service at Bazardjik.

In 1812, Mayevsky served under prince Peter Bagration and distinguishing himself at Borodino on 7 September. He served as a courier in the main headquarters of the Russian army in

1813, becoming a colonel and senior adjutant in the General Staff. He distinguished himself at Lutzen, Bautzen, and Kulm, for which he received the Order of St. George (4th class) and was appointed chef of the 13th Jager Regiment on 1 October 1813. In 1814, he served at Craonne, Laon, and Paris, and the following year returned to France during the Hundred Days.

For his service in 1813-1814, Mayevsky was decorated with the Order of St. Anna with diamonds, the Prussian Pour le Merite, the Swedish Order of the Sword, and the Sardinian Order of St. Maurice and Lazarus.

After the war, he became a major general on 24 December 1819, and commanded the 3rd Brigade of the 3rd Grenadier Division. In 1824, he commanded the settled battalions of the 2nd and 3rd Grenadier Divisions. Under Nicholas I, Mayevsky commanded the 24th Settled Battalion and the 1st Artillery Company in Elisavetgrad, and later served in 2nd Army.

Mayevsky retired in the 1840s and spent the last years of his life writing recollections of his military service. His memoir is entitled *Moi vek ili Istoria generala Mayevskogo* [*My Century or the History of General Mayevsky*] and was published in the *Russkaya Starina* in 1873. It is especially valuable for its interesting observations on the campaigns of 1812-1813.

MAZOVSKY, Nikolay Nikolaevich major general, became chef of the Pavlovsk Grenadier Regiment on 23 October 1803. In 1805, he served with Tolstoy's corps at Hanover. In 1806-1807, his regiment was attached to the 2nd Division, and Mazovsky fought with it at Pultusk, Eylau, Guttstadt, Heilsberg, and Friedland, where he was mortally wounded on 14 June 1807.

MECKLENBURG, Karl August Christian (b. 13 July 1782 — d. 1833) was born to a prominent German family of dukes of Mecklenburg. He entered the Russian service as a captain in the Life Guard Preobrazhensk Regiment on 11 October 1798, rising to a colonel on 27 January 1798. Two years later, he became major general and chef of the Moscow Grenadier Regiment on 20 June 1800. He took part in the 1806-1807 Campaigns in Poland, serving in the 8th Division at Eylau (Order of St. George, 3rd class, 1 June 1808), Guttstadt, and Heilsberg, where he was seriously wounded in the left hand. In 1809, he was transferred to the Danubian Principalities, where he fought the Turks at Braila, Giurgiu, Tataritsa, Bazardjik (golden sword with diamonds, and a golden cross), Shumla, and Nikopol.

In 1812, Mecklenburg commanded the 1st Brigade, which belonged to the 2nd Grenadier Division, 8th Corps, 2nd Western Army. During the campaign, he also led the 2nd Grenadier Division during Prince Bagration's retreat from Volkovisk and fought at Moghilev. On 14 August 1812, as the Russian armies were launching their offensive near Smolensk, the 2nd Grenadier Division was ordered to follow the 2nd Western Army. Mecklenburg, however, had spent the previous night drinking heavily, was still drunk when his orders arrived, and did not wake until that afternoon. The result was that the division remained in the town for more than three hours, which in turn prevented General Rayevsky's corps, stacked behind, from leaving Smolensk. Napoleon's army quickly approached Smolensk that afternoon, and found a city full of enemy troops. Thus the incompetence for which Prince Mecklenburg should have been court marshaled, by sheer luck, proved advantageous for the Russians.

Mecklenburg later distinguished himself at Shevardino and Borodino, where he was wounded and received promotion to lieutenant general on 12 November 1812. In late 1812, he fought at Maloyaroslavets, Vyazma, and Krasnyi. The following year, he distinguished himself at Lutzen, Bautzen, Dresden, Kulm (Prussian Iron Cross), and Leipzig. In 1814, he participated in actions at Brienne, La Rothière, Bar sur Aube, Laon, and Paris. After the war, he left the Russian service on 18 May 1814, and returned to his principality. Another **MECKLENBURG, Friedrich Ludwig**, served as chef of the Astrakhan Grenadier Regiment between March 1799 and September 1814.

MEDINTSEV, Yakov Afanasievich took command of the Kurinsk Infantry Regiment on 12 May 1809. Promoted to a colonel on 18 September 1810, he became chef of the Ryazan Infantry Regiment on 27 May 1811, and commander of the same unit on 4 July 1815.

MEISNER, Jacob Ivanovich (b. 1756 — date of death unknown) was born to a noble family in the Lifland *gubernia*. He studied in the Artillery and Engineer Cadet Corps and began service as a shtyk junker in the 2nd Fusilier Regiment on 25 June 1773. Two years later, he transferred as an ensign to the 2nd Cannonier regiment on 13 January 1775, and later joined the Corps of Engineers with a rank of captain on 15 May 1786. He served in Poland from 1792-1794, and rose to major on 22 January 1797.

Serving in Finland in 1797-1798, Meisner earned promotion to colonel on 28 November 1799. He received the Order of St. George (4th class) for twenty-five years of military service in December 1802. In 1807, he served at Danzig and in 1808-1809, took part in the military operations in Finland. In 1812-1813, he directed the Astrakhan Engineer District and was promoted to a major general on 10 April 1813. He later served as a deputy head of the Warsaw Engineer District before retiring in 1818.

MEISTRE, Ksaverii Ksaverievich (François Xavier de) (b. 19 October 1762 — d. 13 June 1852) was born to a noble family in the Kingdom of Sardinia. He began service in the Piedmontese army and participated in several campaigns against France in 1796-1800. He entered the Russian service with a rank of captain on 17 January 1800. Four year later he retired, only to return on 16 April 1805, as a director of the Maritime Museum and of the Library of the Admiralty. Promoted to colonel on 7 September 1809, Meistre transferred to the quartermaster service in 1810. He served in the Caucasus from 1810-1811, and distinguished himself in the fighting at Akhaltsikhe, where he was wounded in the right hand.

In April 1812, Meistre transferred to the 3rd Reserve Army of Observation and later became ober-quartermaster of Kamensky's corps. During the 1812 Campaign, he fought at Kobryn, Gorodechna (earned a golden sword), Pruzhany, and Volkovisk. In early 1813, he served as the ober-quartermaster in General Bashutsky's detachment before joining Lieutenant General Wallmoden's detachment. In May 1813, he took part in the actions at Lutzen and Bautzen (wounded). Promoted to major general on 30 July 1813, Meistre became general quartermaster of the Russian troops at Danzig. On 1 October 1813, he was seriously wounded in the left shoulder while directing the construction of fortifications. He left the army to recuperate. After the war, he served in the 21st Division before retiring on 10 August 1816.

MELISSINO, Aleksey Petrovich (b. 1759 — d. 27 August 1813) was born to a prominent noble family of Greek descent. His father, General Peter Melissino, distinguished himself during the Russo-Turkish Wars under Catherine II, and directed the Artillery and Engineer Cadet Corps. Aleksey Melissino enlisted as a sergeant in the guard in 1777. Promoted to a captain in 1781, he served on the staff of General-Feldzugmeister Ivan Müller-Zako-Melsky. During the Russo-Swedish War in 1788, he trained recruits for the artillery and was promoted to major on 19 October 1788.

During the Russo-Turkish War of 1787-1791, Melissino volunteered to serve against the Turks and transferred with a rank of lieutenant colonel to the Sumsk Light Horse Regiment. He took part in actions at Akkerman, Bender, and Ismail (Order of St. George, 4th class, 5 April 1791). After the war, he rose to colonel on 16 January 1793. He later joined the Military Order Horse Grenadier Regiment (*konno-grenaderskii polk Voennago Ordena*), but was discharged from the army by Emperor Paul on 12 January 1797. He returned to service on 27 December 1800, serving in the Elisavetgrad Hussar Regiment.

On 13 January 1801, Melissino became major general and chef of the Mariupol Hussar Regiment. However, Melissino took a discharge in early 1802, but returned to the army five years later when he was ordered to organize the Lubensk Hussar Regiment. He became chef of this unit on 2 May 1807.

In 1812, he commanded cavalry in Osten-Sacken's corps in the 3rd Reserve Army of Observation and took part in the actions at Pinsk (Order of St. Anna, 1st class), Yanov, Perin, Kovel, Gorodnya, Mukhavtsy, Zadvorye, Rudnya, Gornostaye-vichy, and Volkovisk (golden sword). In 1813, Melissino served in Miloradovich's corps and fought at Warsaw, Lutzen, Nossen Bautzen, and Reichenbach. Melissino was mortally wounded on 26 August 1813, while leading a cavalry charge against the French infantry square at Dresden. He died the following day.

MENDELEYEV, Moisei (Moses) Kondratievich took command of the Podolsk Infantry Regiment on 14 April 1811, and rose to lieutenant colonel on 9 May 1812. He died on 22 March 1813.

MENSHIKOV, Alexander Sergeyevich (b. 22 September 1787 — d. 1 May 1869) was born to a prominent Russian noble family, and was the grandson of Great Prince Alexander Menshikov, whose name is inextricably entwined with the life of Peter the Great. In 1805, Menshikov served on diplomatic missions to Berlin and London. Four years later, he joined the Guard artillery and served in the Danubian Principalities, where he distinguished himself at

Turtukai (Order of St. Vladimir, 4th class) and Ruse (wounded in the leg). He was appointed flügel adjutant to Emperor Alexander in 1811. During the 1812 Campaign, Menshikov delivered communications between Emperor Alexander and Prince Bagration between June and August, and served with the Russian main headquarters throughout the 1813-1814 campaigns. He distinguished himself in the Battle of Paris, where he was wounded again.

After the Napoleonic Wars, Menshikov rose to adjutant general on 18 October 1817. However, he fell out of favor with Emperor Alexander, perhaps because he turned down command of the Black Sea Fleet, claiming (justly) that he had no knowledge or experience in naval operations. Able to read the handwriting on the all, Menshikov took a discharge in December 1824.

Determined to eeducate himself on naval affairs, Menshikov spent his retirement studying navigation and naval operations before returning to the service on 18 January 1826, and joining the Black Sea Navy. After participating in the Russo-Persian War in 1826-1827, he distinguished himself during the Russo-Turkish War of 1828-1829. He was promoted to rear admiral, captured Anapa (Order of St. George, 3rd class, with a promotion to vice admiral), and was seriously wounded in both legs in the battle at Varna.

After recuperating, Menshikov joined the State Council in March 1830, and became the Governor of Finland in 1831. Five years later, he was appointed Minister of the Navy and decorated with the Order of St. Andrew the First Called. During the Crimean War in 1854-1856, he became notorious for his incompetence and arrogance, negotiation failures with the Turks, and mishandling of the army. Anticipating removal from command, he resigned because of "poor health" in March 1855, and was appointed the Governor General of Kronshtadt on 21 December of the same year. He died almost fourteen years later on 1 May 1869.

MERLIN, Pavel Ivanovich (b. 17 November 1769, Shatsk — d. 7 January 1842, Nikolsk) was born to a noble family from the Tambov *gubernia*. He enlisted as a sergeant in the 2nd Cannonier Regiment in 1784, and rose to a shtyk junker in the the Bombardier Regiment on in 1787. Promoted to an auditor in 1787, and to a lieutenant in 1790, he served with the Bombardier Regiment during the Russo-Swedish War in 1788-1790. In 1792, he served in Poland, and two years later rose to captain in the 2nd Cannonier Regiment and adjutant in the staff of Lieutenant General von Brigman. In 1795, Merlin returned to the 2nd Bombardier Regiment and was promoted to major in January 1797. He joined Lieutenant General Bazin's Artillery Battalion in February 1797, and took a discharge on 17 November of the same year.

Merlin returned to the artillery in April 1801, and took command of a company in the 1st Horse Artillery Battalion. On 15 December 1803, he rose to lieutenant colonel. He took command of a company of the 6th Artillery Brigade on 4 September 1806. During the 1806-1807 Campaigns in Poland, he distinguished himself at Czarnow (Order of St. George, 4th class), Naselsk, Pultusk, Eylau (promoted to a colonel, golden cross), Guttstadt, Heilsberg, and Friedland, where he was wounded in the left leg and captured. Merlin was released after the Treaty of Tilsit in July 1807, and received a golden sword for courage. On 13 July 1807, he took command of a company of the 18th Artillery Brigade. In 1808-1809, he served in Finland, but did not participate in any major battles. In 1811, he led the 4th Horse Artillery Company in the 2nd Reserve Artillery Brigade.

During the 1812 Campaign, Merlin led the 2nd Reserve Artillery Brigade in the 1st Western Army, fighting at Yankovo, Kochergiski, Porechye, Smolensk, Borodino (Order of St. Vladimir, 3rd class), Tarutino, Maloyaroslavets, Vyazma, and Krasnyi, for which he was later decorated with the Order of St. George (3rd class) on 15 June 1813. For his conduct throughout the 1812 Campaign, he was promoted to major general on 7 January 1813. In early 1813, he commanded artillery in Miloradovich's corps before taking command of artillery in the Guard Corps in May 1813, which he handled well at Lutzen and Bautzen. In August 1813, he became commander of artillery in Winzegorode's corps, participating in the battles at Dennewitz and Leipzig (diamond signs of the Order of St. Anna, 1st class).

During the 1814 Campaign, Merlin commanded the artillery in Winzegorode's corps, garnering a golden sword with diamonds at Soissons. After the war, he led artillery in the 2nd Independent Corps and the 2nd Cavalry Corps. In May 1815, he took command of the 4th Corps and returned to France during the Hundred Days. Merlin became commander of artillery in the 5th Corps on 2 March 1817, and was relieved of command fives years later in March 1822. He took a discharge on 5 January 1835.

MERTENS, Aleksey, colonel, commanded the 4th Artillery Regiment between 17 August 1805 and 30 January 1806. He participated in the 1805 Campaign, distinguishing himself during the retreat from Braunau and in the battle of Austerlitz. In late 1806, he served as chef of the 4th Artillery Regiment.

MESHCHERINOV, Vasily Dmitryevich (b. 1776 — date of death unclear) was born to a noble family from the Orel *gubernia*. He enlisted as a furier in the Life Guard Izmailovsk Regiment on 14 June 1787, and transferred as a captain to the Shirvan Infantry Regiment on 12 January 1796. Rising to lieutenant colonel, he took command of the 18th Jager Regiment on 21 October 1800. Promoted to colonel on 5 May 1806, Meshcherinov became chef of the 32nd Jager Regiment on 2 May 1807, and served in Poland. The following year, he was dispatched to the Danubian Principalities, where he distinguished himself at Silistra, Shumla, and Bazardjik, for which he received a golden cross and promotion to major general on 26 June 1810.

In 1812, Meshcherinov served with the 3rd Brigade of the 18th Division in the 3rd Reserve Army of Observation, fighting on the Berezina and at Vilna. In 1813, he took part in the actions at Thorn, Koenigswartha, Katzbach, and Dresden. After serving in France in 1814, he led a brigade of the 18th Division. On 17 May 1816, he took command of the 13th Division and retired because of poor health on 11 February 1819. Meshcherinov returned to the army on 14 June 1827 and became a head of the 5th District of the Internal Guard on 14 June 1831. He finally took a discharge on 25 March 1836.

MESHCHERSKY (Meshchersky I), Stepan Vasilievich, colonel, commanded the Orel Musketeer Regimen from 30 September 1806 to 13 August 1809. During the 1806-1807 Campaigns in Poland, he served with the 9th Division of Essen I's corps. He served as chef of the Vyatka Musketeer Regiment between 13 August 1809 and 31 October 1810.

MESHCHERIAKOV, Demid Ivanovich, colonel, took command of the Kamchatka Musketeer Regiment on 27 February 1808. He served as chef of the Selengisnk Musketeer Regiment between 28 June 1808 and 4 October 1815.

MEZENTSEV, Mikhail Ivanovich (b. 1770 — d. 4 February 1848) was born to a noble family from the Smolensk *gubernia*. He enlisted as a private in the Life Guard Izmailovsk Regiment on 4 March 1785, and transferred as a captain to the Izumsk Light Horse Regiment on 12 January 1795. In December 1805, he took part in the battle of Austerlitz, and the following year joined Grand Duke Constantine's Uhlan Regiment. In 1807, he fought at Guttstadt, Heilsberg, and Friedland, garnering the Order of St. George (4th class) on 1 June 1808. On 24 December

October 1800, he served as an adjutant to General Count Tatitschev. During the 1805 Campaign, he volunteered for service and was assigned to the Novgorod Musketeer Regiment. He distinguished himself at Krems (Dürrenstein) but at Austerlitz, his regiment suffered appalling losses and Mezentsev was wounded in the head. He remained in French captivity for two years and returned to Russia in early 1808.

Mezentsev took command of the Minsk Musketeer Regiment on 15 July 1808, and was appointed chef of the Permsk Musketeer Regiment on 3 August 1808. He participated in the Russo-Swedish War of 1808-1809, and distinguished himself at Oravais (Order of St. George, 4th class, 1 June 1808), Umeå, Sevar and Ratan (Order of St. Vladimir, 3rd class). In 1812, he served in the 15th Division of the 1st Corps, fighting at Klyastitsy (promoted to a major general on 30 October with seniority since 31 July 1812), and Golovchin, where he was again seriously wounded in the head. Mezentsev rejoined the army in the summer of 1813, and took command of the 5th Division. He took part in the battle at Leipzig in October 1813, and in the actions at La Brussel, Le Fère Champenoise, and Bar sur Aube. After the war, he led the 2nd Brigade of the 5th Division before taking command of the 5th Division on 26 November 1817. He took a discharge on 14 January 1826, and lived in St. Petersburg untill his death on 14 January 1833.

1809, his regiment was converted to the Life Guard Uhlan Regiment and Mezentsev rose to colonel on 24 October 1811.

During the 1812 Campaign, Mezentsev served with 1st Brigade of the Guard Cavalry Division, 1st Reserve Cavalry Corps, 1st Western Army, and fought at Vitebsk, Smolensk, Borodino, Tarutino, and Maloyaroslavets (wounded in the left hand). In 1813, he fought at Lutzen, Bautzen, Dresden, Kulm (wounded in the leg, Prussian Iron Cross, promoted to a major general on 27 September 1813 with seniority dating from 29 August 1813), Leipzig, Magdeburg, and Hamburg. Between 18 May 1814 and 13 September 1814, he served as chef of the Byelorussia Hussar Regiment. After the war, Mezentsev took command of the 2nd Brigade of the 2nd Hussar Division on 8 February 1816, and was appointed assistant to Field Marshal Barclay de Tolly on 19 November 1816. He took command of the Bug Uhlan Division on 29 October 1823, and rose to lieutenant general on 3 September 1826. Mezentsev was relieved of command on 25 November 1827, and took a discharge from the service on 31 March 1838.

MEZENTSEV, Vladimir Petrovich (b. 2 January 1782 — d. 14 January 1833) was born to a Russian noble family. He enlisted as a sub-ensign in the Life Guard Preobrazhensk Regiment on 27 August 1782, rising to an ensign on 12 January 1796. Promoted to colonel in

MICHELSON, Ivan Ivanovich (b. 1755 — d. 17 August 1807, Bucharest), was born to a noble family from the Lifland *gubernia*. He began service as a private in the Life Guard Izmailovsk Regiment, and participated in the Seven Years War, distinguishing himself at Zornsdorf and Kunnersdorf. He transferred to the Kazan Infantry Regiment in 1758, and later served in the Novgorod Infantry, Astrakhan Grenadier, and Astrakhan Carabinier regiments, taking part in the war against the Polish Confederation of Bar in 1768. During the Russo-Turkish War of 1769-1774, he fought at Larga (rose to a premier major in the Kargopol Carabinier Regiment) and Kagul. In 1770-1772, he served in Poland and transferred as a lieutenant colonel to the St. Petersburg Carabinier Regiment.

In 1773-1774, Michelson took part in the suppression of Pugachev's peasant uprising. He defeated Pugachev's forces at Podpikovo, on the Aya River, at Kazan, and Cherny Yar. For his success, Michelson received a large estate in the Vitebsk *gubernia*, promotion to colonel, the Order of St. George (3rd class), and a golden sword with diamonds. He took command of the Military Order Cuirassier Regiment in 1775, and of the Leib Cuirassier Regiment the following year. Two years later, Michelson became a major general and garnered the Order of St. Alexander of Neva. In 1786, he rose to lieutenant general and commanded a corps during the Russo-Swedish War in 1788-1790, earning the diamond signs of the Order of St. Alexander of Neva. He became chef of the Glukhov Cuirassier Regiment in 1790, and chef of the Smolensk Dragoon Regiment on 25 February 1800.

In 1803, Michelson was appointed the Military Governor of Byelorussia, receiving the Order of St. Andrew the First Called (March 1806). During the 1805 Campaign, he commanded the Russian forces in the western provinces. In 1806, he led the Russian army against the Turks in Bessarabia and Moldavia, capturing Khotin, Bender, Akkerman, and Bucharest. However, he fell ill and died in Bucharest on 17 August 1807. His remains were transported back to Russia and buried in Nevel in the Smolensk *gubernia*.

MICHOT DE BEAURETOUR, Alexander Frantsevich (b. 1771, Nice — d. 22 June 1841, Palermo) was born to the French noble family of Michot in the Piedmont. He studied military sciene in Turin and began his long and distinguished service, initially in the Piedmontese (Sardinian) army, where he rose to major. He entered the Russian service as a captain in the Engineer Corps on 19 April 1805, and served on the Ionian Islands and in Naples from October 1805 to November 1806, distinguishing himself at Corfu and Bocco di Cattaro. Michot transferred to the Quartermaster Section of the Imperial retinue on 28 November 1806, and served under Vice Admiral Senyavin in the Mediaterranean Sea in 1807. The following year, he joined the Army of Moldavia and, in 1809-1811, commanded engineer troops in the sieges of Braila (Order of St. Vladimir, 4th class), Issacea, Tulcea, Ismail, Turtukai (Order of St. George, 4th class, 1 July 1810), Ruse, Shumla (promoted to a lieutenant colonel), Nikopol, Vatin, and Lovchea (promoted to a colonel on 27 April 1811).

In 1812, Michot was appointed to the headquarters of the 1st Western Army. In July 1812, he inspected the Drissa Camp and advised Emperor Alexander to abandon this position as soon as possible. Michot was dispatched to find locations for the fortified camps near Moscow and on the Volga River. He joined the main Russian army after the battle of Borodino, and delivered to Emperor Alexander the news of the surrender of Moscow and the battle of Tarutino. In October-November 1812, Michot took part in the battles at Vyazma, Maloyariaslavets, and Krasnyi, becoming flügel adjutant on 3 November 1812. In 1813, he fought at Lutzen, Bautzen, Dresden, Kulm (promoted to major general on 27 September 1813), and Leipzig (received promotion to adjutant general on 20 October 1813). During the invasion of France, Michot served at Brienne, Arcis sur Aube, Le Fère Champenoise, and Paris. In late 1814, he served on a diplomatic mission to the Piedmont, for which he was conferred the title of count of the Kingdom of Piedmont.

For his service in the Napoleonic Wars, Michot garnered the Austrian Order of Leopold (2nd class), the Sardinian Order of St. Maurice and Lazarus, the Prussian Order of Red Eagle (2nd class), the French Order of St. Louis, the Bavarian Order of Maximilian Order, and the Württemberg Order of Military Merit. In 1815-1823, Michot attended Emperor Alexander, receiving the title of count of the Russian Empire and the Order of St. Anna (1st class) on 24 December 1823. During this period, he also served on various diplomatic missions to Italy. Under Emperor Nicholas I, Michot rose to lieutenant general on 3 September 1826. The same year, he returned to Sardinia-Piedmont, where he lived for the next fifteen years. In 1839, King Charles Albert of Piedmont conferred on him the title of count de Beauretour. Rising to general of infantry on 25 April 1841, Michot de Beauretour died in Palermo on 22 June 1841.

Michot had two brothers: **Ludwig Michot de Beauretour** also served in the Russian engineer corps. He rose to lieutenant colonel and distinguished himself at Thorn, where a cannonball ripped off his hand. After the war, he commanded the Akhtyrsk Engineer Company before dying in 1821; **Stepan Michot de Beauretour** served as the Russian consul in Nice.

MIKHAILOVSKY-DANILEVSKY, Alexander Ivanovich (b. 26 August 1789, St. Petersburg — d. 9 September 1848, St. Petersburg) was born to a noble family in St. Petersburg. His father, Ivan Danilevsky (1751-1807), was a prominent figure in the contemporary Russian society who studied in the Kiev Academy of Theology and several European universities, receiving his doctorate in medicine. However, the older Danilevsky pursued a banking career and became the Director of the State Loan Bank. The change of the family name from Danilevsky to Mikhailovsky-Danilevsky was a result of an incident during the reign of Paul I, when Danilevsky was mistakenly accused of treason. During the interrogation, he was found innocent and released. Emperor Paul comforted him by giving him a promotion and adding "Mikhailovsky"—the emperor just moved to Mikhailovsk palace—to his surname to prevent any future confusion.

Alexander Mikhailovsky-Danilevsky studied at the Petropavlovsk College in St. Petersburg in 1797-1806, and began working as a collegial clerk at his father's State Loan Bank. He retired after his father's death in 1807, and after studying at the Goettingen University, traveled throughout Europe in 1809-1810. Returning to Russia, he briefly worked in the chancellery of the Ministry of Finance, and on 1 August 1812, became an adjutant to Field Marshal Mikhail Kutuzov, then commander of the St. Petersburg *opolchenye*. After Kuzutov was given command of the Russian army, Mikhailovsky-Danilevsky followed him to the fields of Tsarevo-Znaimische and Borodino. He distinguished himself in the latter action, receiving the Order of St. Anna (4th class). In October, he was wounded at Tarutino and left the army to recover, earning the Order of St. Vladimir (4th class).

Mikhailovsky-Danilevsky returned to the army in February 1813, and served as the adjutant to Kutuzov. After Kutuzov's death, Emperor Alexander took him into his entourage, where Mikhailovsky-Danilevsky was responsible for the foreign correspondence and the journal of the military operations. This journal described the actions of the Russian army and was personally edited by Alexander I. Participating in the campaigns of 1813-1814, Mikhailovsky-Danilevsky was decorated with Order of St. Anna (2nd class) with diamonds, the Austrian Order of St. Leopold (3rd class), the Prussian Pour le Merite and a golden sword for courage.

After the war, Mikhailovsky-Danilevsky joined the newly established General Staff and accompanied Emperor Alexander in his travels in 1815-1818. He rose to colonel in 1815, and to flügel adjutant in the following year. At this time, Mikhailovsky-Danilevsky wrote several historical articles published in the Russian periodicals (*Sin Otechestva, Russkii Vestnik* and *Otechestvennie Zapiski*). In late 1818, he married Anna Pavlovna Chemodanova, daughter of a wealthy noble family, and left Moscow to accompany his pregnant wife to his estate. He stayed with her for next five months. When he returned to the capital, he found himself out of favor with Emperor Alexander I, who gave him command of the 3rd Brigade of the 7th Division in Poltava—far from the capital and the court.

While serving in Poltava, Mikhailovsky-Danilevsky befriended the local officers who later participated in the Decembrist Rebellion of 1825. This event further tainted his career, and on 21 April 1826, was discharged from the army. He spent the next few years in St. Petersburg and in 1829, was restored in the army and became duty officer to General Ivan Diebitch during the Russo-Turkish War of 1828-1829. In 1831, Mikhailovsky-Danilevsky took part in the operations in Poland and was seriously wounded at Grochow (25 February 1830).

During this period, Mikhailovsky-Danilevsky published several works on the campaigns of 1813-1815, including his own wartime diaries *Zapiski 1814-1815 gg.* [Notes of 1814-1815] and *Zapiski o pokhode 1813 goda* [Notes on the 1813 Campaign]. Emperor Nicholas I praised these studies and ordered him to write a comprehensive history of the wars of Alexander I. This assignment resulted in a series of fundamental researches on the Napoleonic campaigns. Mikhailovsky-Danilevsky was a prolific and remarkably efficient writer with virtually unrestricted access to official diplomatic and military archives. He published *Opisanie pokhoda vo Frantsiiu v 1814 godu* [Description of the Campaign in France in 1814] in 1836, *Opisanie otechestvennoi voini v 1812 godu* [Description of the Patriotic War of 1812] in 1839, *Opisanie voini 1813 goda* [Description of the 1813 Campaign] in 1840, *Opisanie finlandskoi voini na sukhom puti i po more v 1808 i 1809 godakh* [Description of the Finnish War on land and sea in 1808 and 1809] in 1841, *Opisanie Turetskoi Voini s 1806 do 1812 goda* [Description of the War with Turkey from 1806 to 1812] in 1843, *Opisanie Pervoi Voini Imperatora Aleksandras Napoleonom v 1805 godakh* [Description of the First War of Alexander I with Napoleon in 1805] in 1844, and *Opisanie Vtoroi Voini Imperatora Aleksandra s Napoleonom v 1806 i 1807 godakh* [Description of the Second War of Alexander I with Napoleon in 1806 and 1807] in 1846.

In 1845-1849, Mikhailovsky-Danilevsky compiled a six-volume compilation with more than 200 biographies of Russian generals called

Imperator Aleksandr I i ego spodvizhniki v 1812, 1813, 1814 i 1815 godakh. Voennaia galerea zimniago dvortsa [Emperor Alexander and His Devotees in 1812, 1813, 1814 and 1815. War Gallery of the Winter Palace]. His last work was a monumental study of Suvorov's 1799 Campaign in Italy and Switzerland, but he died before finishing it. Emperor Nicholas entrusted Dmitry Miliutin, Professor of Military Statistics at the Imperial War Academy and the future Minister of War, to complete this work. The four volume *Istoriia voini 1799 goda mezhdu Rossiiei I Frantsiei v tsarstvovanie imperatora Pavla I* [History of the War of 1799 Between Russia and France During the Reign of Paul I] was published in St. Petersburg in 1852-1853. The histories of 1813-1814 Campaigns were translated into German in the 1840s, and an English edition of the 1814 Campaign appeared in 1840. Two volumes on the Russo-Turkish War of 1806-1812 were printed in English by the Nafziger Collection in 2002.

Mikhailovsky-Danilevsky's works contain narrative histories of the campaigns, without any attempt at critical analysis which, according to him, was up to the military theorists. The volumes were personally read and edited by Emperor Nicholas I, who often removed entire sections of the works. Mikhailovsky-Danilevsky also sometimes omitted individuals who had fallen from favor after the Napoleonic Wars. As a result, Mikhailovsky-Danilevsky's histories contained virtually no criticism of the Russian actions and so catered to Imperial wishes. Nevertheless, they are one of the best sources on the Russian army, and hold invaluable details unavailable elsewhere.

These works brought fame and awards to Mikhailovsky-Danilevsky. In 1834, Emperor Nicholas presented him with a snuffbox decorated with diamonds for the work on 1812 Campaign. On 6 December 1835, he was promoted to lieutenant general, and three days later, became the Chairman of the Military Censorship Committee. He later garnered the Orders of St. Vladimir (2nd class, 1836), St. George (4th class, 1836), the White Eagle (1838), the Prussian Red Eagle (1st class, 1839) and the Russian Order of St. Alexander of Neva (1843).

Mikhailovsky- Danilevsky became a member of Emperor's Council of War in 1839, and of the Imperial Academy of Science in 1843. He died on 9 September 1848, during the cholera epidemic in St. Petersburg.

MILORADOVICH, Mikhail Andreyevich (b. 12 October 1771 — d. 25 December 1825, St. Petersburg) was born to a prominent noble family of Serbian descent; son of Lieutenant general Andrey Miloradovich. He enlisted as a sub-ensign in the Life Guard Izmailovsk Regiment in 1780. Over the next seven years, he studied at the universities of Höttingen and Königsberg, as well as at Strasbourg and Metz. He began service as a ensign in the Life Guard Izmailovsk Regiment on 16 April 1787. After participating in the Russo-Swedish War in 1788-1790, he rose to a colonel on 27 September 1797. On 7 August 1798, he became major general and chef of the Apsheron Musketeer Regiment. Miloradovich took part in Field Marshal Suvorov's campaigns in Italy and Switzerland, distinguishing himself at Lecco (Order of St. Anna, 1st class), Cassano, Verderio, on the Trebbia, at Novi, and during the crossing of the Alps, for which he was decorated with the Order of St. Alexander of Neva. He became very close to Grand Duke Constantine, who gave him a golden sword inscribed "To my friend Miloradovich."

During the 1805 Campaign, Miloradovich led the 2nd Column of the Russian army during the march to Braunau. In October-November, he commanded an independent brigade, distinguishing himself at Amstetten and Dürrenstein (Krems), for which he received the Order of St. George (3rd class, 24 January 1806) and promotion to lieutenant general on 20 November 1805. At Austerlitz, he led the Russian division in the center of the Allied position and made desperate attempts to repulse the French attacks. In 1806, he took command of a corps in the Army of Moldavia, participating in the opening moves of the Russo-Turkish War of 1806-1812. He distinguished himself at Gladen, Bucharest (received a golden sword with diamonds inscribed "For Saving Bucharest") in 1806, Turbat, and Obilesti in 1807, and at Rassevat (promoted to general of infantry on 11 October 1809) and Silistra in 1809. However, Miloradovich had a conflict with Commander-in-Chief Prince Peter Bagration, who had him recalled from the army in late 1809. Between April 1810 and August 1812, he served as the Military Governor of Kiev.

In 1812, Miloradovich organized the Kaluga Reserve Corps and joined the main Russain army at Gzhatsk in August. He distinguished himself leading the Russian right flank at Borodino, garnering the diamond signs of the Order of St. Alexander of Neva. On 9 September, he took command of the Russian main rear guard and covered the Russian withdrawal from Moscow. From October through December 1812, Miloradovich commanded the Russian advance guard, fighting at Vyazma, Dorogobouzh, and Krasnyi. For his conduct during the pursuit of the French army, he was decorated with the Orders of St. George (2nd class) and of St. Vladimir (1st class) on 14 December 1812. During the 1813-1814 Campaigns, he commanded a Russian corps in major battles in Germany and France, including Kulm (Prussian Iron Cross, a golden sword with laurels and 50,000 rubles), Leipzig (Order of St. Andrew the First Called), Arcis sur Aube, Brienne, Le Fère Champenoise, and Paris. For his service in these campaigns, Miloradovich was decorated with the Prussian Orders of Black and Red Eagles, the Austrian Orders of Leopold (1st class), Maria Theresa (2nd class), the Bavarian Order of Maximilian Joseph, Baden's Order of Fidelity, and the Sardinian Order of St. Maurice and Lazarus.

After the war, Miloradovich led the Guard Corps. He became the Military Governor of St. Petersburg and a member of the State Council on 30 August 1818. During the Decembrist Uprising, he urged the insurgents to return to the barracks but was mortally shot by Lieutenant P. Kakhovsky and died on 25 December 1825. He was buried in the Alexander of Neva Monastery in St. Petersburg.

MITKOV, Fedot Konstantinovich (b. 1764 — d. 1827) was born to a noble family from the Vladimir *gubernia*. He studied in the Navy Cadet Corps and began service as a guard marine in the Baltic Fleet in 1781. Promoted to a midshipman, he served on the ship-of-the-line *"St. Nikolay"* in the Baltic Sea, participating in the Russo-Swedish War of 1788-1790. Rising to a lieutenant captain, he transferred to the ship-of-the-line *Prince Gustav* in 1799, and took part in the expedition to Holland. He returned to Russia and command of the ship-of-the-line *Yaroslav* in Vice Admiral Senyavin's squadron in the Mediterranean Sea, and fought in Naples in 1806.

The following year, Mitkov took part in the operations against the Turks, distinguishing himself in the naval battle at Mt. Athons, for which he earned the Order of St. Anna (2nd class). Made captain (1st class) in June 1808, he commanded the ship-of-the-line *Ne tron menia* in 1812-1814, and was promoted to captain commander (14 March 1814) for landing the British forces on the Dutch coast in 1814.

After the war, Mitkov transported the Russian guard units to St. Petersburg and served as ober-intendant of the Black Sea Fleet. He rose to a major general on 21 August 1823, and served in the Intendant Department of the Ministry of Navy.

MONAKHTIN, Fedor Fedorovich (b. 1775 — d. September 1812) was born to a Russian noble family. He enlisted in the guard in 1782, and after studying in the Infantry Cadet Corps, began service as a lieutenant in the Astrakhan Grenadier Regiment in 1795. He took command of the Moscow Musketeer Regiment on 10 January 1803, and became commander of the Novgorod Musketeer Regiment on 29 March 1805.

Promoted to colonel on 5 May 1806, Monakhtin served in the Army of Moldavia, where he again took command of the Moscow Musketeer Regiment on 4 February 1808. His unit was converted to the infantry regiment on 5 March 1811, and in the following year served with the 1st Brigade of the 7th Division of the 6th Corps in the 1st Western Army. During the 1812 Campaign, he distinguished himself at Smolensk. At Borodino, Monakhtin served as the chief of staff for the 6th Corps and took three wounds (two in the left leg, one in the stomach) defending the Great Redoubt. While in the army infirmary, he learned about the surrender of Moscow, and in a fury, ripped off his bandages and bled to death. He was posthumously promoted to major general on 12 November 1812 for his actions at Smolensk.

MOORE, Ustin Vasilievich (b. 1763 — d. 16 January 1835) was born to a British noble family. He began service in the British Royal Navy and entered the Russian navy as a midshipman in September 1783. During the Russo-Swedish War of 1788-1790, he led a gunboat, fighting at Gogland, Eland, Barezund (rose to a lieutenant captain, 1789), Revel, Vyborg, and Sveaborg, where he garnered the Order of St. Vladimir (4th class). Promoted to captain (1st class) on 22 February 1804, he commanded the ship-of-the-line *Maksim-Ispovednik* in the Baltic Sea. During the Russo-Swedish War of 1808-1809, he captained the ship-of-the-line *Borei*. After the declaration of war between Russia and Britain, he was discharged from the navy.

For the next four years, Moore lived in Moscow and was restored in command on 26 March 1812, when he was promoted to a captain commander with seniority dating from 20 January 1809. During the 1812 Campaign, he commanded the ship-of-the-line *Mironosets* in the Gulf of Finland and transported the Finland Corps to the Baltic provinces. In 1813-1814, he joined the British Royal Navy in its blockade of the French coast. After the war, he transported the Guard units to Russia and took command of a fifteen-vessel squadron at Kronshtadt in 1815. The following year, he commanded the ship-of-the-line *Tostislav* before serving on the ships-of-the-line *Pamiat Evstafia* in 1818, and *Prince Gustav* in 1820. Promoted to rear admiral in May 1821, he later led a brigade of the 1st Fleet Division (flotskaya divizia).

MORDVINOV, Dmitry Mikhaylovich (b. 19 June 1773 — d. 23 July 1848) was born to a Russian noble family from the Vitebsk *gubernia*; the brother of Vladimir Mordvinov. He enlisted as a sergeant in the artillery in March 1781, transferred as a sub-ensign to the Life Guard Semeyonovsk Regiment several days later, rose to ensign on 12 January 1784, and to sub-lieutenannt in 1786. In October 1802, he left the military service and was appointed actual kamerger (4th class) in the Imperial court. Over the next ten years, he served in various government institutions, including the Mining Council and the Department of Mining and Salt Affairs (*departament gornikh i solyanikh del*). He earned the Order of St. Vladimir (4th class) for effective service in 1808.

During the 1812 Campaign, Mordvinov took command of the 5th Company (*druzhina*) of the St. Petersburg *opolchenye*. He was seriously wounded and lost his leg at Polotsk (Order of St. George, 4th class) and was promoted to major general on 15 January 1813. After recuperating, he served in the Department of Mining and Salt Affairs. On 18 December 1826, he took a discharge from the military service. The same year, he received a rank of privy counsellor and was appointed to the Senate. He retired in January 1847.

MORDVINOV, Vladimir Mikhaylovich (b. 1775 — date of death unclear; removed from rosters on 6 August 1823) was born to a noble family from the Pskov *guberrnia*. He enlisted as a corporal in the Life Guard Semeyonovsk Regiment on 12 January 1784, and began service as a sergeant in 1792. Promoted to ensign in January 1794, he served with the St. Petersburg Grenadier Regiment in Poland late that year, distinguishing himself at Praga, for which he earned a golden cross and rank of sub-lieutenant. On 12 January 1795, Mordvinov transferred as a second major to the Belozersk Infantry Regiment and rose to major on 17 January 1797. Two years later, he transferred to the civil service, only to return to the army as colonel in the Leib- Grenadier Regiment on 28 March 1801. He took command of the Sevsk Musketeer Regiment on 22 February 1803.

Mordvinov participated in the 1805 Campaign and distinguished himself at Krems (Dürrenstein, earned the Order of St. Vladimir, 4th class) and Austerlitz, where he was wounded in the left leg and garnered in return a golden sword. In 1806-1807, he served with the 5th Division in Poland, fighting at Pultusk, Jankovo, Landsberg, Eylau (wounded in the right shoulder, received the Order of St. George, 4th class, 8 May 1807), Guttstadt, Heilsberg, and Torau. In the latter action, Mordvinov was seriously wounded in the right leg. After recuperating, he rejoined his division in Finland, where he fought the Swedes in 1808-1809. He was wounded again, this time in the left hand, at Ratan and took a discharge with a rank of major general on 7 June 1809. He returned to the army on 25 January 1811, and became chef of the St. Petersburg Grenadier regiment on 21 February 1811. However, a month later he was relieved of command. During the 1812 Campaign, Mordvinov became head of the Pskov *opolchenye* and served with 1st Corps at Polotsk, Chashniki, and Studenka. In January 1813, he earned a golden sword with diamonds for his actions at Elbing.

During the campaigns of 1813-1814, Mordvinov served as a duty officer in the headquarters of the Army of Reserve in the Duchy of Warsaw. After the war, he served as an assistant to the commander of the 22nd Division, and took command of the 1st Brigade in the same division on 24 February 1816. He was relieved of command because of poor health on 22 October 1818. He later led the 1st Brigade of the 16th Division on 13 June 1820, and of the 2nd Brigade of the 19th Division on 19 August of the same year. Mordvinov was transferred to the 17th Division on 21 January 1823, and died late that spring.

MORKOV, Irakly Ivanovich (b. 13 November 1753 — d. 7 April 1828) was born to a Russian noble family in the Moscow *gubernia*. He studied in the Infantry Cadet Corps and began service as a sub-lieutenant in the Life Guard Preobrazhensk Regiment on 3 October 1769. He participated in the Russo-Turkish War of 1770-1774 before fighting the Turks again in 1787-1791. Morkov distinguished himself at Ochakov (promoted to colonel and received Order of St. George, 4th class, 25 April 1789), Focsani, Rimnic, and Ismail (Order of St. George, 3rd class, 5 April 1791).

Morkov served in the Russian mission to Constantinople in 1792, and was promoted to major general for helping negotiate the Treaty of Jassy. Morkov serve din Poland in 1792-1794, fought at Gorodische (Order of St. George, 2nd class, 7 July 1792), and Dubenka (golden saber with diamonds). He was conferred the title of count of the Russian Empire on 3 October 1796, and rose to lieutenant general on 23 February 1798. Morkov became chef of the Caucasus Grenadier Regiment on 23 March 1798, and served as the inspector of the Caucasus Inspectorate before taking a discharge on 21 November 1798. During the 1812 Campaign, Morkov became head of the Moscow *opolchenye* on 14 August, and fought at Borodino, Maloyaroslavets, Vyazma, and Krasnyi. For his service, he was decorated with the Order of St. Alexander of Neva. He finally retired in 1813 and spent the rest of his life at his estate.

MUKHIN, Semen Alexandrovich (b. 1771, Kremenchug — d. 15 July 1828) was born to a petty noble family in the Poltava *gubernia*. After serving in the local administration in the Azov *gubernia*, he enlisted as a vakhmistr in the Poltava Pikinieer Regiment on 5 December 1779. He transferred as a lieutenant to the main headquarters on 23 October 1788. During the Russo-Turkish War of 1787-1791, Mukhin distinguished himself at Anapa, for which he received promotion to captain. After service in Poland in 1792-1794, Mukhin transferred as a premier major to the Mariupol Hussar Regiment, and later served in the Quartermaster Section of the Imperial Retinue. Promoted to colonel on 27 January 1799, he served on several topographic missions to map the Crimea, St. Petersburg, and Volhynia, for which he garnered the Order of St. Anna (2nd class). Mukhin rose to major general on 1 April 1805, and continued working on the maps of the Russian Empire in 1806-1811.

He became the ober quartermaster of the 2nd Corps on 25 October 1811, and in June-July 1812, briefly served as the quartermaster general of the 1st Western Army. On 30 July 1912, Emperor Alexander appointed him the head of the Department of Cartography. Mukhin became the quartermaster general of the Army of Reserve on 24 April 1813. He briefly served in the same capacity in the Army of Poland between 24 June and 5 August 1813, before returning again to the Army of Reserve. After the war, he served as the Chief of Staff of the Independent Corps of the Internal Guard in 1816-1824. Promoted to lieutenant general on 3 September 1826, he became the head of the Field Audit of the 1st Army on 25 March 1828.

MÜLLER, Anton Vasilievich (Berend Otto) (b. 19 February 1764, Mustel — d. 17 October 1848) was born to a German noble family in the Riga *gubernia*. He studied in the Navy Cadet Corps and began service as a guard marine in May 1778. After training on the British Royal Navy in 1779-1780, he rose to a midshipman in the Baltic Sea Fleet. In 1783, he took command of a gunboat in the Caspian Sea Flotilla. He returned to the Baltic Sea Fleet in 1792 and commanded the frigate *Arkhipelag* in

1795-1797. In 1798, he commanded the frigate *Narva* along the Dutch and French coasts. He rose to captain (2nd class) on 12 May 1799, and commanded the ship-of-the-line *Mstislav* during the expedition to Holland in late 1799.

After his return to Russia, Müller rose to captain commander on 13 May 1808, and commanded a squadron in the Gulf of Finland during the Russo-Swedish War of 1808-1809. Promoted to rear admiral on 19 January 1809, he became commander of the Kronstadt and director of the Navigation School of the Baltic Sea Fleet in March 1810. Two years later, he commanded a galley flotilla in the Gulf of Riga. In late 1812, he successfully landed the Russian force at Mittau and captured the town, for which he garnered the Order of St. Anna (1st class). In 1813, Müller led a squadron of newly built ships-of-the-line from Arkhangelsk to British shores and participated in the blockade of the French coastline. After the war, he transported the Russian troops to St. Petersburg and became the head of the Revel harbor. In 1817, he took part in the cruise to Spain. He became the Head of the Navy General Staff on 7 December 1821; two years later, he rose to vice admiral and charge d'affairs of the Minister of Navy on 24 December 1823. He was appointed Minister of Navy in January 1828, and received promotion to admiral on 13 January 1829. Müller took a discharge on 17 February 1839.

MÜLLER (Müller III), Ivan Ivanovich (b. 1776 – d. 1814) was born to petty noble family from the Tula *gubernia*. He studied in the Artillery and Engineer Cadet Corps and began service as a lieutenant in the Gatchina Artillery Company on 30 January 1794. Two years later, he transferred as a staff captain to the Life Guard Jager Battalion on 21 November 1796, and later rose to a colonel on 19 April 1798. In 1799, he became chef of the 8th Jager Regiment on 24 May 1799, and served with Derfelden's corps in Italy and Switzerland. He distinguished himself at Bassignana (promoted to a major general on 24 May 1799), on the Trebbia, at Novi, and during the crossing of the Alps. Returning to Russia, he became chef of the 7th Jager regiment on 20 March 1800.

He participated in the 1805 Campaign, fighting at Amstetten, Dürrenstein, and Austerlitz, where he was wounded in the left thigh and earned the Order of St. Vladimir (3rd class). He retired on 17 May 1806, only to return on 7 October 1807, continuing to serve as chef of 7th Jagers. Müller was relieved of command on 28 February 1810, and took a discharge on 11 April 1810. In 1812, he organized the Tula *opolchenye* and participated in the operations on the Berezina. In early 1813, he served at Warsaw and Modlin before taking command of the Tula *opolchenye* at the siege of Danzig on 10 April 1813. He garnered a golden sword with diamonds for repulsing a French sortie on 9 May 1813. On 17 September 813, Müller took a severe wound during the assault on the French fortifications, for which he garnered the Order of St. Anna (1st class). He retired because of wounds on 27 December 1813 and died in May 1814.

There were many Müllers serving in the Russian army during the Napoleonic Wars, including: **MÜLLER (Müller I), Karl Karlovich**, who became the commander of the Vyborg Musketeer Regiment on 23 July 1798. On 31 August 1798, he was promoted to a major general and appointed chef of the Kolyvan Musketeer Regiment. He later served as chef of the 30 Jager Regiment between 9 March 1807 and 1 October 1808. **MÜLLER (Müller II), Peter Borisovich**, who became chef of the Riga Cuirassier Regiment on 27 October 1798. Two brief appointments followed as the commander of the Riga Cuirassier Regiment in May-September 1800, and as chef of the His

Majesty's Leib Cuirassier Regiment in September — December 1800. Rising to a lieutenant general on 8 November 1800, he served as chef of the Kinburn Dragoon Regiment until 24 July 1801; **MÜLLER, Andrey Logginovich**, who took command of the Moscow Musketeer Regiment on 15 April 1802. Rising to a major general on 14 November 1802, he served as chef of the Velikii Lutsk Musketeer Regiment from 14 November 1802 to 31 October 1810.

MÜLLER–ZAKOMELSKY, Peter Ivanovich (b. 1755 — d. 21 June 1823) was born to a noble family from the Byelorussia *gubernia*; brother of Yegor Müller–Zakomelsky. He studied in the Artillery and Engineer Cadet Corps, and began service as an adjutant to Major General Ivan Müller–Zakomelsky in December 1769. Promoted to sub-lieutenant in 1772, he participated in the Russo-Turkish War in 1787-1791, garnering the Order of St. George (4th class, 25 April 1789) for his conduct at Ochakov. Made colonel in 1791, he served in Poland in 1792-1794. He became major general on 12 January 1795, and took a discharge two years later. On 19 May 1802, Müller–Zakomelsky returned to the army with the rank of lieutenant general. He became chef of the 5th Artillery Regiment on 20 June 1803, and fought at Austerlitz in 1805. Two years later, he took command of the 10th Division in Poland. On 24 December 1807, he became inspector of the Russian artillery and a member of the War College.

In 1812, after Kutuzov's departure from St. Petersburg, Müller–Zakomelsky took command of the St. Petersburg and Novgorod *opolchenye*s. In 1813-1814, he served with *opolchenye*s in the Army of Reserve in the Duchy of Warsaw and rose to general of artillery on 30 May 1814. After the war, he became the *charge d'affairs* of the Minister of War on 18 May 1819, and was officially appointed the Minister of War on 7 December 1819. Four years later, on 25 March 1823, he took an indefinite furlough because of poor health and traveled to resorts in the Caucasus, where he died on 21 June 1823.

MÜLLER–ZAKOMELSKY, Yegor Ivanovich (b. 1767 — d. 1830) was born to a noble family from the Byelorussia *gubernia*. He enlisted as a sergeant in the Life Guard Preobrazhensk Regiment in 1781 and served as an adjutant to Général-en-Chef Ivan Müller–Zakomelsky. Promoted to a colonel in the Tver Carabinier Regiment on 13 September 1793, he took a discharge from the army in 1797. Three years later, he returned to the service in the Ryazan Cuirassier Regiment on 14 November 1800. He became major general and commander of the Tver Dragoon Regiment on 27 March 1801; six months later, he became chef of this unit on 18 September 1801. On 26 September 1803, he was appointed commander of the Grand Duke Constantine's Uhlan Regiment.

Müller–Zakomelsky distinguished himself during the 1805 Campaign at Austerlitz, but was wounded and captured in action. Released the following year, he became chef of the Mariupol

Hussar Regiment on 21 November 1807, and rose to adjutant general on 13 July 1810. In early 1812, he commanded the 1st Reserve Corps; after this unit was disbanded, Müller–Zakomelsky served in the main headquarters of the 1st Western Army at Borodino, Tarutino, Maloyaroslavets and Krasnyi. He was promoted to lieutenant general on 28 June 1813, and retired on 29 December 1815.

MURAVYEV, Nikolay Nikolayevich (b. 26 September 1768, Riga — d. 1 September 1840) was born to a prominent Russian noble family. He was enlisted in the Life Guard Preobrazhensk Regiment in 1774 at the age six, and rose to a sergeant on 24 March 1776. In April 1778, he transferred as a midshipman to the Baltic Sea Fleet and began active service as a lieutenant in the Baltic Galley Flotilla on 12 May 1789. During the Russo-Swedish War, he distinguished himself at Rochensalmi and Vyborg, garnering the Order of St. Vladimir (4th class). Promoted to lieutenant captain on 26 October 1794, he served as a duty officer to Rear Admiral Senyavin in 1795-1796.

On 2 January 1797, Muravyev transferred to the army as a lieutenant colonel in the Elisavetgrad Hussar Regiment, but was discharged from the army on 28 September of the same year. In retirement, Muravyev took part in the organization of the Moscow zemstvo troops in 1806-1807, and commanded the Mozhaisk militia. In 1811, he established the Moscow Mathematical School to train column guides. During the 1812 campaign, Muravyev trained the Moscow *opolchenye*, rising to a colonel on 23 August 1812. He served as the Chief of Staff of the 3rd Opolchenye District In 1813-1814, and participated in the sieges of Modlin, Dresden, Magdeburg, and Hamburg, where he received his promotion to major general on 19 September 1815, with seniority dating from 12 May 1815.

After the war, Muravyev directed his Moscow Mathematical School, which was later converted to the School for Column Guides [*shkola kolonovazhatikh*]. He retired on 27 February 1823, and spent the rest of his life in Moscow. Muravyev had three sons:

1. His oldest son, **Aleksandr Nikolayevich Muravyev** (b. 1792 — d. 1863) studied in the University of Moscow and began service as a column guide on the Quartermaster Section of the Imperial Retinue on 1 March 1810. Promoted to sub-lieutenant on 14 September 1810, he took part in the preparations of the detailed map of the Russian western provinces. In March 1812, he was appointed an assistant to the quartermaster general of the 1st Western Army. During the 1812 Campaign, Muravyev served with the 5th Corps, fighting at Borodino (Order of St. Anna, 4th class), Tarutino, Maloyaroslavets, Vyazma (earned a golden sword), and Krasnyi.

In 1813-1814, he rose to a lieutenant on 16 March 1813, and took part in the battles of Lutzen, Bautzen, Kulm (Prussian Iron Cross), Leipzig (promoted to staff captain on 2 November 1813), Brienne, Le Fère Champenoise, and Paris. For his conduct, he was decorated with the Orders of St. Vladimir (4th class) and of St. Anna (2nd class), the Prussian Pour le Merite, the Bavarian Order of Maximilian Joseph, and the Austrian Order of Leopold. After the war, he was appointed to the Guard General Staff and promoted to captain on 20 August 1814. Made colonel on 7 March 1816, he served as ober-quartermaster in the 1st Reserve Cavalry Corps. In January 1818, Emperor Alexander had him arrested after inspecting his unit and Muravyev took a discharge on 7

October of the same year. He was active member of the Massonic lodges and other secret societies in Russia. In December 1825, Muravyev took part in the Decembrist Uprising and was arrested in January 1826. After he was court martialed, he was exiled to Siberia, where he served on various government positions for the next twenty years.

Muravyev was restored in the military service with a rank of colonel in the General Staff in May 1851. During the Crimean War, he served as the chief of staff for the 2nd Corps, becoming major general on 27 March 1855. After the war, he served as the Military Governor of Nizhegorod, rising to lieutenant general in April 1851. Muravyev left numerous letters and recollections on his service in the Russian Army and his exile to Siberia, published in a single volume *Sochinenia i pisma* [Works and Letters] in 1986. Muravyev's memoirs are particularly interesting for the insights on the Russian senior officer corps during the 1812-1814 Campaigns.

2. **Nikolay Nikolayevich Muravyev** (Muravyev-Karsky) (b. 1794 — d. 1866) began service as a column guide in the Quartermaster service and served throughout the 1812-1814 Campaigns. After the war, he served in the Caucasus and distinguished himself during the Russo-Turkish and Russo-Persian Wars in 1826-1830, earning his nickname *Karsky* [of Kars, the fortress in eastern Turkey].

3. His third son, **Mikhail Nikolayevich Muravyev** (Muravyev-Vilensky) (b. 1796 — d. 1866) studied in the University of Moscow and began service as a column guide in the quartermaster service in December 1811. Promoted to ensign in January 1812, he served in the headquarters of the 5th Corps during the 1812 Campaign. He was wounded at Borodino on 7 September 1812. After recuperating, he took part in the operations in Germany, rising to a sub-lieutenant in March 1813. Muravyev transferred to the Guard General Staff in August 1814 and served on the Caucasus Line in 1815-1820, becoming staff captain in December 1817 and captain in March 1820.

On 24 April 1820, Muravyev transferred as a lieutenant colonel to the quartermaster service and retired in November of the same year. He was involved with the secret societies in 1822-1825 and was arrested after the Decembrist Uprising, although he did not participate in it. Muravyev was soon acquited and appointed Vice Governor of Vitebsk in June 1827. The following year, he became the civil governor of Moghilev in September 1828, and received the rank of actual civic counsellor on 5 January 1830. He took part in the suppression of the Polish Uprising in 1830-1831, serving in the Army of Reserve. He later became the Civil Governor of Grodno (1831), and the Military Governor of Kursk (1835).

In December 1832, Muravyev returned to the military service, receiving the rank of major general. In 1839, he became the head of the Department of Taxes and rose to a privy counsellor on 9 August 1842. Seven years later, he again returned to the military service, changing his civil rank of privy counsellor to the military rank of lieutenant general on 21 May 1849. He joined the State Council in January 1850 and was promoted to general of infantry in August 1856. Muravyev served as the Minister of State Property in 1857-1862. He became the Governor General of the Grodno, Kovno, Vilna, and Minsk, and the Head of the Vilna Military District in May 1863. Two years later, he was conferred the title of count of the Russian Empire and became known as *Muravyev-Vilensky* (Muravyev of Vilna).

MUROMTSEV, Nikolay Seliverstovich (b. 1762 — d. 1834) was born to a noble family from the Ryazan *gubernia*. He enlisted as a sergeant in the Vologda Infantry Regiment on 26 December 1773, and rose to an ensign on 21 September 1775. After serving in Poland in 1783-1785, he took part in the Russo-Turkish War of 1787-1791, distinguishing himself at Ochakov (wounded in the left hand, received a golden cross), Kaushani, Akkerman, Bender (rose to a premier major in the Kinburn Dragoon Regiment), Killia (wounded in the left shoulder), and Macin (Order of St. Vladimir, 4th class).

In 1792-1794, Muromtsev served in Poland. He stood out at Dubenky (promoted to colonel in the Moscow Dragoon Regiment on 13 September 1792) and Praga (golden cross). He retired with a rank of major general in November

1797. In retirement, Muromtsev organized and commanded the Ryazan militia in 1806-1807. During the 1812 Campaign, he took command of the Ryazan *opolchenye* on 1 September, and the following month led the Penza and Saratov *opolchenye*s. He served at Modlin and Hamburg in 1813-1814, rising to a lieutenant general on 14 October 1814, with seniority dating from 11 September 1814. Muromtsev retired with the end of the Napoleonic Wars in 1815.

MUSIN-PUSHKIN, Ivan Alekseyevich (b. 1783 — d. 1836) was born to a prominent Russian family of counts from Yaroslavl *gubernia*. He began service as a junker in the College of Foreign Affairs in March 1799, and rose to college assessor on 29 October 1801, and to kamer-junker on 19 March 1803. In 1805-1809, he served on diplomatic missions to Baden, Prussia, and Denmark. On 14 August 1809, Musin-Pushkin was appointed to the Ministry of Justice and served in the criminal court in St. Petersburg. Made kamerger on 11 September 1811, he rose to civic counsellor on 16 January 1812. During the 1812 Campaign, he served with the 2nd Company [druzhina] of the St. Petersburg *opolchenye* at Polotsk (earned a golden sword), Chashniki, Smolyani and on the Berezina.

In 1813, Musin-Pushkin became duty officer to General Wittgenstein, fighting at Bautzen, Gorlitz (Order of St. George, 4th class, 29 June 1813, and promotion to kamerger, 4th class, on 19 July 1813), Dresden, Pirna, and Leipzig, where he was wounded and earned the Order of St. Vladimir (3rd class). In 1814, he took part in actions at Arcis sur Aube, St. Dizier, and Paris. Musin-Pushkin became duty general in the General Staff of the 2nd Army on 18 May 1814, and his civil rank was converted to the military rank of major general on 10 June 1815. In 1816, he took command of the 2nd Brigade of the 14th Division, and between March 1822 and September 1826, served as an assistant to the commander of the 3rd Division. He left the military service in February 1828, and later served as a hofmeister of the Imperial court.

MUSIN-PUSHKIN, Ivan Klavdievich (b. 1781 — d. 1822) was born to a noble family from the Kursk *gubernia*. He enlisted as a sub-ensign in the Life Guard Izmailovsk Regiment on 26 January 1785, and began service as a portupei-ensign on 13 January 1798, rising to an ensign on 19 September 1798. He participated in the 1805 Campaign, distinguishing himself at Austerlitz, where he was wounded in the right leg and received a golden sword and promotion to captain. He became adjutant to Grand Duke Constantine on 17 October 1806, and during the following year took part in the battles of Guttstadt, Heilsberg, and Friedland, where he suffered severe canister wounds to his right shoulder, stomach, and right thigh. For his conduct, Musin-Pushkin was decorated with the Order of St. Vladimir (4th class) and promoted to colonel on 28 June 1808. He took command of the 1st Battalion of the Life Guard Izmailovsk Regiment in 1810.

During the 1812 Campaign, Musin-Pushkin served with the 2nd Brigade of the Guard Infantry Division of the 5th Corps. After fighting at Ostrovno, he temporarily commanded the entire Izmailovsk Regiment at Borodino before being wounded in the chest (Order of St. Vladimir, 3rd class). After recuperating, he joined his unit in early 1813 and fought at Lutzen, Bautzen, Reichenbach, Pirna, Peterswalde, and Kulm, where he was wounded in the head and received the Prussian Iron Cross and the rank of major general on 27 September 1813. Musin-Pushkin became chef of the Vitebsk Infantry Regiment on 10 October 1813, and later took part in the battle of Leipzig and the siege of Mainz. During the invasion of France, he served at Brienne (golden sword with diamonds), La Rothière, Champaubert, and Paris, where he was wounded in the leg. After the war, he commanded the 1st Brigade in the 16th Division. Musin-Pushkin returned to France during the Hundred Days in 1815, and retired on 6 January 1816.

MUSIN-PUSHKIN, Peter Klavdievich (b. 1765 — d. 1834) was born to a noble family from the Kursk *gubernia*. He began service as a page at the Imperial court in 1778, rising to a kamer-page in 1785. During the Russo-Turkish War of 1787-1791, he joined the Sumsk Light Horse Regiment with a rank of rotmistr, and served in the Crimea and the Danubian Principalities. In December 1788, he was seriously wounded in the head at Ochakov (golden cross). After recuperating, Musin-Pushkin served in Poland in 1792-1794, rising to a lieutenant colonel.

Promoted to colonel on 24 November 1797, Musin-Pushkin took command of the Ekaterinoslavl Cuirassier Regiment on 26 April 1798, and became major general and chef of the Kazan Cuirassier Regiment on 18 February 1799. He took a discharge on 22 March 1799, but returned to the army on 10 November of the same year, when he was appointed commander of the Pavlograd Hussar Regiment. However, he was again discharged with a rank of lieutenant general on 16 March 1800, only to return to the service on 20 November of the same year. Musin-Pushkin became chef of the Chernigov Cuirassier Regiment on 1 January 1801. Three months later, he was appointed commander of the same regiment, serving in this capacity until 10 March 1803.

The following year, Musin-Pushkin became chef of the Taganrog Dragoon Regiment on 29 October 1804, and served in the Caucasus in 1807-1811. In 1812, he took command of the 24th Brigade of the 8th Cavalry Division in the 3rd Reserve Army of Observation. During the 1812 Campaign, he commanded reserve cavalry in Osten-Sacken's corps and later led a cavalry detachment at Lublin and Zamostye. In 1813-1814, Musin-Pushkin trained reserve cavalry squadrons in Moghilev and Brest-Litovsk. After the war, he continued service in the cavalry, but did not hold any high positions of responsiblity. He retired on 28 December 1833.

MYAKININ, Nikolay Diomidovich (b. 1787 — d. 30 October 1814) was born to a noble family from the Novgorod *gubernia*. He enlisted as a junker in the 1st Artillery Battalion on 25 February 1802, was quickly transferred to the Life Guard Artillery Battalion on 1 March 1802, and promoted to a portupei-junker on 24 October 1802. Made a sub-lieutenant on 12 April 1804, he distinguished himself at Austerlitz on 2 December 1805 (Order of St. Anna, 3rd class). On 26 February 1806, he was appointed adjutant to General Arakcheyev, and the next year took part in the actions at Guttstadt, Heilsberg, and Friedland, for which he was decorated with the Order of St. Vladimir (4th class) and a golden sword.

Rising to a lieutenant colonel, Myakinin served as a senior adjutant to General Arakcheyev in early 1812, and organize the reserve company of the guard artillery in July-October 1812. For his service, he received promotion to colonel on 1 December 1812, and accompanied Arakcheyev to the main Russian army in early 1813. During the 1813 Campaign, Myakinin served at Modlin, Lutzen, Bautzen (wounded in the left hand, received the Order of St. George, 4th class, 21 May 1813) and Leipzig, where he was wounded in the chest and promoted to a major general on 23 January 1814. In 1814, he commanded the Russian artillery at Craonne, garnering the Order of St. George (3rd class). After the war, Myakinin took command of the artillery of the 4th Corps on 18 May 1814, but took a furlough to recuperate from wounds. He died at St. Petersburg on 30 October 1814.

NABOKOV, Ivan Alexandrovich (b. 22 March 1787 — d. 3 May 1852, St. Petersburg) was born to a prominent noble family from the Novgorod *gubernia*; his father, Alexander Nabokov, was a general of infantry under Catherine II. Ivan Nabokov studied in the Page Corps and enlisted as a lieutenant in the Life Guard Semeyonovsk Regiment on 13 January 1806. He took part in the 1807 Campaign and fought at Heilsberg and Friedland (golden sword). Nabokov became a colonel on 13 May 1811. During the 1812 Campaign, he served with the 1st Brigade of the Guard Infantry Division of the 5th Reserve (Guard) Corps and fought at Borodino (Order of St. Anna, 2nd class), and Krasnyi. In 1813, Nabokov fought at Lutzen, Bautzen, and Kulm (wounded, promoted to major general on 27 September 1813 with seniority dating from 29 August 1813). He became chef of the Sevsk Infantry Regiment on 10 October 1813, and distinguished himself at Leipzig, for which he earned the Order of St. Vladimir (3rd class).

In 1814, Nabokov fought at Bar sur Aube (received the Order of St. Anna, 1st class), Craonne, Laon, Arcis sur Aube (wounded, golden sword with diamonds), and Paris. In 1815, he led the 3rd Brigade of the 5th Division and assumed command of the 3rd Brigade of the 1st Grenadier Division on 18 January 1816. Nabokov took command of the 3rd Infantry Division on 28 February 1822, became a lieutenant general on 3 September 1826, and later led the Combined Division of the 5th Corps (9 February 1828) and the 15th Division. He was given command of the 3rd Grenadier Division on 1 February 1830.

Nabokov took part in the suppression of the Polish Uprising in 1830-1831, fighting at Praga (received the Order of St. Vladimir, 2nd class), Ostrolenka (Order of St. George, 3rd class, 3 September 1831), and Warsaw (Order of St. Alexander of Neva). He temporarilly led the Independent Grenadier Corps on 11 September 1832, and was confirmed commander of this corps on 17 August 1833. He was promoted to general of infantry on 18 December 1835, awarded the diamond signs of Order of St. Alexander of Neva in 1836, appointed adjutant general on 13 February 1844, and chef of the Sevsk Infantry Regiment on 6 January 1847. Nabokov was relieved of his position because of poor health in December 1848, and appointed member of the Council of War and commandant of St. Petersburg fortress in March 1849. He became the Commandant of St. Petersburg on 14 May 1849. Nabokov died in St. Petersburg on 3 May 1852, and was buried near the Petropavlovsk Cathedral.

NANIY, Foma (Thomas) Petrovich (b. 1769 — d. 1853, Kiev) descended from an Italian merchant family. He began service as a cadet in the Military Order Cuirassier Regiment on 12 January 1788, and took part in the Russo-Turkish War in 1789-1791, fighting at Ismail and Macin. Naniy transferred as a sub-lieutenant to the Seversk Carabinier Regiment on 16 May 1791. He took part in the 1799 Campaign in Switzerland. In 1806-1812, he served in the Army of Danube and fought at Ruse, Ismail,

Silistra, Giurgiu, Bazardjik (Order of St. George, 4th class, 25 July 1810), and Shumla.

Naniy was appointed commander of the Starodoub Dragoon Regiment on 5 May 1809, and promoted to colonel on 24 December 1809. During the Russian Campaign of 1812, he served in the 15th Brigade, 5th Cavalry Division, 3rd Reserve Army of Observation, and fought at Kobryn, Gorodechno (wounded), Brest Litovsk, Slonim, and Borisov. In 1813, he fought at Lutzen, Bautzen, Dresden, and Leipzig. Promoted to major general on 27 September 1813, Naniy was awarded the Prussian Order of Red Eagle.

In 1814, Naniy served in the siege of Belfor as well as in the actions at Brienne, Arcis sur Aube, and Paris. He retired on 3 November 1817 and settled in Kiev.

NARYSHKIN, Lev (Levin) Alexandrovich (b. 16 February 1785 — d. 29 November 1846, Naples) was born to a prominent Russian noble family. Home-schooled by the Jesuits, he began his career at the Imperial Court and became an actual kamerger on 26 March 1799. Naryshkin enslited as a lieutenant in the Life Guard Preobrazhensk Regiment on 3 February 1803, and transferred as a staff rotmistr to the Life Guard Hussar Regiment on 25 February 1807. He took part in the 1807 Campaign and fought at Guttstadt, Heilsberg, and Friedland (wounded, awarded a golden sword). He retired in 1808 and served at the Imperial Court for the next four years. He returned to the army as a rotmistr in the Izumsk Hussar Regiment on 9 April 1812.

During the 1812 Campaign, Naryshkin's regiment was attached to the 1st Western Army and fought at Vitebsk, Ostrovno, Smolensk, and Borodino, where he was wounded in the head. He was captured by the French in late September, but liberated at Vitebsk in November in time to take part in the operations on the Berezina River. He was promoted to colonel on 1 December 1812. In 1813, he led a cavalry detachment and fought at Kalisch, Gross Beeren, Dennewitz (Order of St. George, 4th class, 21 October 1813), and Leipzig (wounded, earned the Order of St. Vladimir, 3rd class). For his actions at Leipzig, Naryshkin was promoted to major general and given command of a Cossack brigade. At the head of that outfie, he conducted operations in Holland and northern France in 1814. He remained in the Russian occupational forces under Mikhail Vorontsov in France for three years and returned to Russia in 1818.

Naryshkin left military service in April 1824, serving at the Imperial Court for the next nineteen years. He returned to the army in early 1843, served in the Imperial Retinue beginning on 3 June 1843, and rose to adjutant general on 18 December 1843. Exactly one year later, he was promoted to a lieutenant general. He died during a trip to Naples on 29 November 1846, and was buried in the Church of the Holy Spirit in St. Petersburg.

NASSAU-ZIGEN (Nassau-Siegen), Karl Heinrich Nicholas Otton (b. 16 January 1745, France — d. 1808, Tinne, near Nemirov) was born to a prominent German noble family. His father, Prince Maximilian Wilhelm Adolf of Nassau, was separated from his French wife, and Karl Nassau-Zigen was brought up in his grandmother's estate in France. He was conferred the title of prince on 14 June 1756, and served in the French Royal army during the Seven Years War. Nassau-Zigen took part in the naval expedition around the world in 1766-1769, and fought in the Anglo-Spanish War in 1782, commanding artillery near Gibraltar. For his actions, he was conferred a rank of major general in the Spanish army. Nassau-Zigen became notorious for his adventures, affairs, and duels. In 1786, he traveled to the Crimea to see Prince Gregory Potemkin. Once there, he met Empress Catherine II in early 1787. He entered the Russian service with a rank of captain in 1787, but the next year became a rear admiral in charge of a galley flotilla on the Dnieper estuary. During the Russo-Turkish War of 1787-1791, he fought the Turks at Kinburn (Order of St. George, 2nd class), Ochakov, and two minor naval combats. For these actions he was awarded a golden sword and promoted to vice admiral.

In 1789, Nassau-Zigen transferred to the Baltic Fleet. He met and defeated the Swedes at Rochensalmi (Order of St. Andrew the First Called and 3,000 rubles), but suffered a setback at the same place in July 1790. Nevertheless, he was promoted to admiral and appointed commander of the galley fleet on 27 December 1790. He traveled to Germany in 1791, and helped French èmigrès enter Russian service.

Nassau-Zigen retired on 22 May 1792, and lived at Koblentz. He briefly returned to service and was dispatched on a secret diplomatic mission to the Prussian court in 1793. However, he retired again in November 1794, and settled in Venice. He returned to Russia in 1796, and lived at his estate near Nemirov. He died there in 1808.

NAUMOV, Mikhail Fedorovich (b. 1757 — d. 29 April 1823, Smolensk) was born to a petty noble family and enlisted as a private in the Kozlov Infantry Regiment on 12 January 1772. He was promoted to ensign on 7 August 1782, and subsequently transferred as a lieutenant to the Kherson Infantry Regiment on 12 January 1786. Naumov took part in the Russo-Turkish War in 1787-1790, and distinguished himself at Ochakov in 1788 (golden cross and promotion to captain). In January 1790, the Kherson Infantry Regiment was disbanded and its two battalions were merged into the New Ingermanland Musketeer Regiment, with which Naumov continued his service. He was promoted to major in 1799, and to lieutenant colonel in 1804. Naumov participated in the 1805 Campaign, serving in Dokhturov's column, and at Austerlitz, where he was severely bruised by a cannonball (Order of St. Vladimir, 4th class).

In the summer of 1806, Naumov was appointed to the 12th Division of the Army of Dniestr and served against the Turks in 1806-1812. He took command of the New Ingermanland Musketeer Regiment on 11 September 1807, and fought at Braila (golden sword) and was promoted to colonel on 24 December 1807. He was seriously wounded in the head during the assault on Giurgiu in April 1809. Naumov requested temporary transfer from the army to recuperate and was appointed to the Vyatka Garrison Battalion on 5 December 1809. After returning to health, he was restored to the position of commander of the New Ingermanland Regiment on 3 March 1810, and served under Count Zuccato and Major General Isaev in Little Wallachia, fighting on the Island of Olmar, at Dudu, Brza-Palanka, Praiova, and Negotin in 1810. He was appointed chef of the newly formed Voronezh Musketeer Regiment on 8 February 1811, and reorganized it into a regular infantry regiment on 6 March 1811.

During the 1812 Campaign, Naumov served in the 25th Division in Finland and organized the St. Petersburg *opolchenye*. He commanded the *opolchenye* forces in Wittgenstein's corps at Polotsk, Chashniky, and Smolyani, garnering the Order of St. Vladimir (3rd class). In late November 1812, he took part in the operation on the Berezina River.

In 1813, Naumov served in the siege of Danzig, for which he received the Order of St. Anna (2nd class) and a promotion to major general on 12 October 1813. In 1814-1818, he commanded the 2nd Brigade of the 25th Division of Prince Eugene of Württemberg's Corps and returned to France during the Hundred Days in 1815. He became commander of the 8th Division (later renamed to 13th Division) on 22 March 1819, and was relieved of command on 6 August 1820. Naumov was appointed the Commandant of Smolensk on 17 May 1822.

NAZIMOV, Fedor Viktorovich (b. 20 December 1764 — d. 19 March 1827, Kiev) was born to a noble family from the Tambov *gubernia*. He enlisted as a corporal in the Life Guard Preobrazhensk Regiment on 10 February 1777, and tranferred as a captain to the Keksholm (Kexholm) Infantry Regiment on 12 February 1790. Nazimov took part in the Russo-Turkish War in 1787-1791, and the operations in Poland from 1792-1794. He became commander of the Ukraine Musketeer Regiment on 2 December 1798, a colonel on 12 August 1799, and major general on 28 May 1803. He rose to chef of the Kurin Musketeer Regiment on 16 September 1805, and was sent to the Army of Danube to fight the Turks.

In 1806-1812, Nazimov fought at Giurgiu, Braila, Ismail, Silistra, Slobodzea, and Shumla. He commanded the 2nd Brigade of the 27th Division between 8 October 1810 and November 1816. During the 1812 Campaign, Nazimov also temporarily led the 15th Division of the 3rd Reserve Army of Observation. After the war, he became the Civil Governor of Kiev on 17 November 1817, and was conferred the rank of actual state counsellor. He was relieved of his position in 1821.

NAZIMOV, Vasily Gavrilovich (b. 1759 - d. 1839) was born to a noble family from the St. Petersburg *gubernia*. He studied in the Artillery and Engineer Cadet Corps and enlisted as a shtyk-junker in the Bombardier Regiment on 9 July 1776. After service in Poland in 1779, he was promoted to lieutenant in May 1780, and returned to the Artillery and Engineer Cadet Corps six years later. Appointed major in the Neva Infantry Regiment in 1789, Nazimov retired in 1792, only to return to service as a major in the 2nd Fusilier Regiment on 19 March 1795. He retired a second time in 1797, and began service in the Senate in May 1802, before transferring as a military adviser to the Engineer Expedition.

Nazimov participated in the 1805 Campaign, serving at the Russian headquarters and was promoted to civil counsellor in 1806 before joining the naval (coastal) artillery with a rank of captain (1st class) in 1808. In 1809-1810, he commanded coastal artillery. Nazimov participated in the reorganization of the Ministry of Navy and became the head of the Artillery Office in 1810. He remained at this position for the next seventeen years, and in 1827, was promoted to major general and appointed duty general at the Naval General Staff. After rising to a lieutenant general on 11 September 1829, he transferred to the Senate, where he worked for almost ten years.

Another officer of the same last name, **NAZIMOV, Nikolay Gavrilovich,** led the 50th Jager Regiment from 10 November – 9 May 1812, and from 4 July 1815 – 11 September 1816. He became a colonel on 19 November 1811, and served as chef of the 50th Jager Regiment between 9 May 1812 and 4 July 1815.

NEBOLSIN, Peter Fedorovich (date of birth unknown — d. 1809) enlisted in the Apsheron Infantry Regiment in 1772, and transferred to the Dnieper Grenadier Regiment in 1779. He took part in the Russo-Turkish War in 1787-1790, serving in the Crimea as well as at Tulcea, Isaccea, and Ismail. Nebolsin joined the Chernigov Grenadier Corps in 1794, and was promoted to premier major.

In 1800, Nebolsin was appointed chef of the Prince Vyazemsky's Garrison Regiment. Two years later, on 17 May 1802, he took command of the Troitsk Musketeer Regiment. Nebolsin rose to major general and chef of the Troitsk Musketeer Regiment on 11 October 1804. He participated in the operations in the Kuban Valley in 1804-1805. During the Russo-Persian War in 1806-1808, he fought at Nukha, Nakhichevan, and along the Araks River. He died in late 1810 and was removed from the rosters on 1 January 1810.

NECHAEV (Nechaev II) led the Podolsk Musketeer Regiment from 30 August to 16 December 1803, and again from 9 April 1805 to 27 October 1808. He was promoted to a colonel on 24 December 1807. In 1805, he fought with the 3rd Column at Austerlitz, and in 1806-1807, served with the 8th Division in Poland, fighting at Eylau.

NESTEROV, Peter Aleksandrovich commanded the Pskov Musketeer Regiment in October 1800 — August 1801, rose to a colonel on 26 September 1803, and served as chef of the 28th Jager Regiment between 5 September 1806 and 25 January 1808.

NEVEROVSKY, Dmitry Petrovich (b. 1 November 1771, Prokhorovka, Poltava *gubernia* — d. 2 November 1813, Halle) was born to a petty noble family in the Poltava *gubernia*. He enlisted as a private in the Life Guard Semeyonovsk Regiment on 27 May 1786, and became a sergeant in early 1787. During the Russo-Turkish War of 1787-1791, he transferred as a lieutenant to the Malorosiisk (Little Russia) Grenadier Regiment on 14 October 1787, and fought at Salchea and Bender. Neverovsky went to Poland in 1792-1794, and participated in the actions at Derevitse, Gorodische (promoted to captain), Maciejowice, and Praga (golden cross and rank of second major). Promoted to colonel, he took command of the 1st Marine Regiment on 3 October 1803. The following year, on 2 April 1804, he rose to major general and chef of the 3rd Marine Regiment at Revel.

In 1805, Neverovsky served under General Tolstoy in the expedition to Hanover. He returned to Revel in early 1806, and after an Imperial inspection in May 1806, was awarded a diamond ring and the Order of St. Vladimir (3rd class). He became chef of the Pavlograd Grenadier Regiment on 21 November 1807, and was awarded the Order of St. George (4th class) for distinguished service on 8 December 1810. In late 1811, Neverovsky organized the 27th Infantry Division, which was later assigned to the 2nd Western Army. For his effective maintenance of this division, he earned the Order of St. Anna (1st class). During the 1812 Campaign, Neverovsky joined Prince Bagration on the Russian retreat and distinguished himself at Krasnyi on 14 August 1812, where he halted the French army and allowed the Russian armies to defend Smolensk. He then took part in the battles at Smolensk, Shevardino, Borodino (wounded), and Maloyaroslavets. For his actions at Borodino, he was promoted to lieutenant general on 12 November 1812.

In 1813, Neverovsky served in Osten-Sacken's corps of the Army of Silesia and fought at Katzbach (received the Prussian Order of Red Eagle). He was seriously wounded at Leipzig when a musket ball shattered his leg. He died of the gangrene in a hospital at Halle on 2 November 1813, and was buried at a local cemetery. His remains were transferred to the Borodino Battlefield on 20 July 1912. For his actions at Leipzig, Neverovsky was nominated for Orders of St. Vladimir (2nd class) and of St. George (3rd class), but he died before receiving them.

NEYDHARDT, Alexander Ivanovich (b. 5 November 1784 — d. 6 September 1845) was born to a German noble family. He enlisted as a sub-ensign in the Friedrichsham Garrison Regiment in 1798, and was promoted to ensign in December 1798. In 1807, he was appointed adjutant to General Buxhöwden and served with him in Poland (January 1807) and Finland (1808). In early 1812, Neydhardt was appointed to the Quartermaster Section of the Imperial Retinue. During the 1812 Campaign, he served under Wittgenstein and took part in the actions at Klyastitsy (wounded in the chest) and Studianka (Order of St. George, 4th class). In 1813, Neydhardt took part in the battles at Lutzen, Bautzen, Dresden, Kulm, and Leipzig (Order of St. Vladimir, 3rd class). He had to leave the army in late 1813 because of poor health, and did not participate in the 1814 Campaign. In late 1814, he took part in the delimitation of the Russo-Austrian frontiers, and in 1815, organized quarters for the Russian army in Bavaria.

In 1816-1817, Neydhardt served as the Chief of Staff of the 4th and 5th Corps and was promoted to major general on 13 January 1818. In September 1826, he temporarily served as the Chief of Staff of the Guard and Grenadier Corps. He participated in the Russo-Turkish War of 1828-1829, serving as the Chief of Staff of the Guard Corps, and distinguished himself at Varna, receiving the rank of lieutenant general.

In early 1830, Neydhardt was appointed quartermaster general for the General Staff and retained his earlier position. In 1830-1831, he took part in the suppression of the Polish Uprising, served as the Chief of Staff of the 1st Army. He was awarded the Order of St. George, (3rd class) for his actions at Warsaw. In 1832, he was dispatched on a secret diplomatic mission to Prussia. After returning to Russia, Neydhardt took command of the 1st Corps in 1834, and of the 6th Corps in 1836. Promoted to general of infantry in 1841, he briefly served as the Military Governor of Moscow and was appointed commander-in-chief of the Transcaucasian troops and commander of the Independent Caucasus Corps in October 1842. Neydhardt became a member of the Council of War in January 1845, but retired in June 1845. He died on 6 September 1845 in Moscow.

NEYDHARDT, Pavel Ivanovich (b. 22 March 1779, St. Petersburg — d. 6 September 1850, St. Petersburg) was born to a German noble family. He enlisted as a sergeant in the artillery on 17 May 1786, and transferred as a kaptenarmus to the Life Guard Preobrazhensk Regiment in April 1792. Promoted to a sergeant in December 1792, he was appointed to His Majesty's Artillery Company on 30 November 1796, and to the Quartermaster Section of the Imperial Retinue on 24 December 1796. Over the next five years, Neydhardt drafted maps of the Vyborg *gubernia* and was promoted to staff captain on 21 April 1800, to captain on 25 April 1800, and to major on 1 April 1805. During the 1805 Campaign, he was appointed to the quatermaster service and served under Ulanius and Bagration in the rearguard actions in

October 1805. At Austerlitz that December, Neydhardt fought in the 4th Column and was awarded the Order of St. Anna (2nd class).

In 1806, Neydhardt served in the 14th Division of Buhxöwden's corps, and in 1807, joined the main headquarters, fighting at Mohrungen, Jankovo, Eylau (Order of St. Vladimir, 4th class, and a golden sword), Guttstadt, on the Passarge River (golden sword), Heilsberg, and Friedland (Prussian Pour le Merite). In 1808, he served in Prince Bagration's 21st Division and took part in numerous minor actions (Bjorneborg, Hasting, Raxvalbi) leading to the capture of Abo. In March 1808, Neydhardt took part in the expedition to the Aland Islands and defended the Great Aland Island for four weeks before being captured by Swedish landing forces. Released in December 1809, he served on a topographic mission to map southern Finland, and was promoted to lieutenant colonel on 21 February 1811.

Neydhardt was appointed to the headquarters of the 1st Western Army in early 1812. During the Russian Campaign, he fought at Vitebsk and Smolensk, served as an assistant to Kutuzov and Bennigsen in August, supervised the Russian deployment at Borodino on 5-6 September, and was promoted to colonel after the battle. In October-November 1812, he served in the main Russian headquarters. In the spring of 1813, he fought at Lutzen and Bautzen before being appointed the Chief of Staff of Langeron's corps on 19 August. Neydhardt then took part in the battle at Katzbach, and was promoted to major general on 27 September 1813 with seniority dating from 2 May 1813. He distinguished himself fighting on the Parthe River during the Battle of Leipzig, and was awarded the Order of St. George (3rd class, 18 October 1813) and the Swedish Order of the Sword.

From December 1813 to February 1814, Neydhardt served with Langeron's corps at the siege of Mainz. Through February – March 1814, he fought at Soissons, Laon (Order of St. Anna, 2nd class), and Paris (Order of St. Anna, 1st class). He returned to Russia in late 1814, but served as the Chief of Staff for Langeron's corps during the Hundred Days and took part in the siege of Metz. Neydhardt became the Chief of Staff for the Grenadier Corps on 21 April 1816, and commander of the 26th Division (later 9th Division) on 27 February 1820. He was appointed the Commandant of Odessa on 3 May 1825, but was relieved of duty on 4 August 1826. A year later, he was appointed to the Senate with a rank of privy counsellor (7 July). Neydhardt was awarded the Order of St. Vladimir (2nd class) on 12 January 1840, and rose to an actual privy counsellor on 15 December 1843.

NIKITIN, Aleksey Petrovich (b. 13 May 1777 — d. 11 March 1858, St. Petersburg) was born to a petty noble family from the Tula *gubernia*. His parents died when he was an infant and Catherine II enrolled him in the Cadet Corps in 1788. Little did she know that Nikitin would eventually become one of Russia's finest artillery officers.

After graduating, he began service as a shtyk-junker in the 3rd Bombardier Battalion on 6 July 1796 and was promoted to sub-lieutenant on 1 January 1797. Nikitin transferred as a lieutenant to the Major General Basin's Field Artillery Battalion on 22 January 1797, and earned his captaincy on 31 August 1797. Nikitin served as an artillery commander for several minor fortresses in Finland in 1797-1799. He became a major on 1 February 1799, and transferred to the 1st Artillery Regiment. During military exercises, he excelled in artillery target practice was awarded the Order of St. John of

Jerusalem in 1799. When the 1st Artillery Regiment was reorganized in August 1801, Nikitin transferred to the 2nd Artillery Battalion. He was appointed to the 2nd Horse Artillery Battalion on 22 June 1803, and became a lieutenant colonel on 26 December 1804.

In the 1805 Campaign, Nikitin commanded the horse artillery in Essen I's corps, but did not participate in any actions. He was given command of the 9th Artillery Brigade on 4 September 1806, and appointed to the Army of Dnieper to fight the Turks. He fought at Khotin attached to Prince Volkonsky's 9th Division of Essen I's corps. In late 1806, Nikitin followed Essen's corps to Grodno, received promotion to colonel on 29 January 1807, and participated in the actions on the Skva River (Order of St. Anna, 2nd class). His artillery brigade was transferred to Platov's corps in April 1807, and Nikitin fought at Allenstein. He returned to Essen's corps, now commanded by General Tolstoy, in late May 1807, and fought at Olshevo-Borki. After the war, his unit was renamed to the 7th Artillery Brigade on 19 October 1809, and to the 7th Horse Artillery Company of the 3rd Reserve Brigade on 26 February 1811. In 1812, he commanded the 3rd Reserve Brigade in the 5th Corps of the 1st Western Army.

During the Russian Campaign of 1812, Nikitin fought at Disne, Beshenkovichy, Vitebsk (nominated for the second Order of St. Anna, 2nd class, but received instead an Imperial letter of gratitude), Porechye, Rudnya, Smolensk, Gedeonovo (golden sword), Gzhatsk, Gridnevo, and Kolotsk (diamond signs of the Order of St. Anna, 2nd class). At Borodino, Nikitin experienced heavy fire and lost some 90 men and 113 horses. He was severely bruised by a shell, for which he was later decorated with the Order of St. Vladimir (3rd class). During October – November, Nikitin fought at Tarutino and Maloyaroslavets (nominated for the second Order of St. Vladimir, 3rd class, but again received an Imperial letter of gratitude). He distinguished himself at Krasnyi, where he led his gunners in a daring attack to capture French artillery. For this exploit, he was promoted to a major general on 7 January 1812, and received the Order of St. Anna.

In early 1813, Nikitin distinguished himself at Kalisch (wounded, Order of St. George, 3rd class, 6 March 1813). In April, he took command of the artillery of the Russian advance guard and fought at Weissenfels, Gross-Hersen, Lutzen (Prussian Order of Red Eagle), Dresden, Bautzen, Gorlitz, Lobau, and Goldberg. For his actions, he was awarded a golden sword with diamonds. In August-October 1813, he took part in the battles at Dresden, Peterswalde (diamond signs of the Order of St. Anna, 1st class), and Leipzig (Order of St. Vladimir, 2nd class). In late October, he took command of the artillery in Osten-Sacken's Corps.

During the 1814 Campaign, Nikitin fought at Brienne, La Rothière, Soudron, Viels Maisons, Montmirail, Chateau Thierry, Meaux, Craonne, and Paris. For his actions at Brienne and La Rothière, he was nominated for a second golden sword with diamonds, but instead received a third Imperial letter of gratitude. During the Hundred Days, he led his troops from Poland to Meaux. After returning to Russia, he became commander of artillery in the Grenadier Corps on 22 January 1816. Promoted to lieutenant general on 18 January 1826, Nikitin assumed command of artillery in the Settled Grenadier Corps on 22 March 1827. On 28 September 1829, he was given command of the 2nd Reserve Cavalry Corps, which was renamed to the 1st Reserve Cavalry Corps two years later. Nikitin participated in the suppression of the Polish Uprising in 1830-1831, and was appointed chef of the Chuguev Uhlan Regiment on 25 September 1832 (Order of St. Alexander of Neva on 26 September 1832). He took command of the 1st Reserve Cavalry Corps on 14 April 1833, and was promoted to general of cavalry on 18 December 1833, which was followed by the Order of St. Vladimir (1st class) on 6 November 1835.

During the celebration of the anniversary of the Battle of Borodino in 1839, Nikitin was awarded the diamond signs of the Order of St. Alexander of Neva and appointed to take charge of the military colonies in Ukraine on 11 September 1839. He became the Inspector General of the Reserve Cavalry on 13 August 1840. For his service, he received the Order of St. Andrew the First Called on 4 October 1842, the diamond signs of the Order of the White Eagle, the diamond signs of the Order of St. Andrew the First Called (1845), a diamond ring with Emperor Nicholas' portrait (1846), and conferred the title of count of the Russian Empire on 1 October 1847. In 1850, Nicholas I renamed the Chuguev Uhlan Regiment to Nikitin's Uhlans Regiment (and so it remained until 1858). Nikitin was appointed a member of the State Council on 9 September 1856. He died on 11 March 1858, at St. Petersburg.

NILUS, Peter Bogdanovich, major general, served as chef of the Sofia Musketeer Regiment from 7 October 1807 – 31 October 1810, and as chef of the 35th Jager Regiment from 31 October 1810 – 13 September 1814.

O'GUILVI, Alexander Alexandrovich (b. 4 May 1765 — d. 6 April 1847, St. Petersburg) was born to an Irish noble family and began service in the British Royal Navy. He joined the Russian Navy in January 1783, and served on a flotilla in the Caspian Sea. He transferred to the Baltic Fleet in 1787, and took part in the Russo-Swedish War in 1788-1790, fighting at Barezund (Order of St. George, 7 December 1790) and Vyborg (received a golden sword). O'Guilvi commanded the frigate *Riga* during the expedition to Holland in 1799, and was promoted to captain (1st class) on 21 January 1803. In 1805, he participated in the transportation of the Russian troops to Hanover, and during the Russo-Swedish war in 1808-1809, commanded a coastal defense flotilla and was promoted to captain commander.

In 1812-1814, O'Guilvi commanded the ship-of-the-line *Smelyi* and participated in the British blockade of the French ports, landing the British troops in Holland in 1814. He was promoted to rear admiral on 2 March 1814. In 1815, O'Guilvi took command of the 3rd Marine Division and was promoted to vice admiral on 11 September 1824. He became commander of the 4th Brigade of the Baltic Fleet *Ekipazh* on 7 April 1827, and of the 3th Division of the Baltic Fleet on 26 March 1828. O'Guilvi was appointed inspector of the Baltic Fleet *Ekipazh* on 2 May 1830, and became a member of the Admiralty on 23 April 1836. He rose to admiral on 28 April 1841, and retired in 1843. During his career, O'Guilvi received the Order of St. Anna (1st class) with diamonds and an Imperial crown, the Order of the White Eagle, and the Order of St. Vladimir (2nd class).

OBOLENSKY, Vasily Petrovich (b. 16 January 1780 — d. 17 February 1834) was born to a Russian family of princes and enlisted in the Guard in 1785, receiving promotion to captain in August 1785. He retired in 1792 with the rank of major, but returned to service nine years later. In 1805-1807, he served in the Olonetsk Musketeer Regiment. In 1811, Obolensky was promoted to colonel (26 October) and appointed adjutant to Prince George of Holstein-Oldenburg.

During the Russian Campaign of 1812, he organized a regular Cossack regiment in Ukraine and became commander of the 3rd Ukraine Cossack Regiment on 19 June 1812. He operated in Byelorussia and made several raids into Poland from September-October 1812.

Obolensky became chef of the 3rd Ukraine Cossack Regiment on 8 March 1813, and fought at Kalisch, Lutzen, Bautzen, Reichenbach, Gorlitz, and other minor actions. He was appointed flügel adjutant on 15 September, and rose to major general on 10 October 1813. Obolensky was awarded the Order of St. Anna (1st class) for his actions at Leipzig in October 1813. In 1814, he served at Mainz and commanded the 2nd Brigade of the Ukraine Regular Cossack Division (13 September). He was appointed duty general for the headquarters of the 2nd Army on 7 November 1816, and retired because of poor health on 31 January 1822.

OBRESKOV (Obreskov III), Nikolay Vasilievich (b. 1764 — d. 1821) was born to a noble family in the Moscow *gubernia*. He began his career at the Imperial Court in 1772, becoming kamer-page in 1781 before enlisting in the Life Guard Izmailovsk Regiment on 1 March 1785. He participated in the Russo-Swedish War in 1788-1790, earning promotion to captain. Appointed colonel in the Byelorussia Jager Corps on 17 January 1794, Obreskov led the Tver Carabinier Regiment during the operations in Poland in late 1794, receiving a golden sword for Maciejowice and a golden cross for Praga. He assumed command of the Sumsk Light Horse Regiment on 12 January 1795, and participated in the Persian Campaign, capturing Baku in 1796. He was promoted to brigadier on 27 July 1796 and to major general on 10 October 1798.

Obreskov was discharged from the army on 21 February 1799. In retirement, he was first elected marshal (*predvoditel*) of the nobility of the Dmitriev *uezd* of the Moscow *gubernia*, then commanded the *uezd* militia in 1806, before becaming the marshal of the nobility of the entire Moscow *gubernia* in 1808. Obreskov was appointed the Civil Governor of the Moscow *gubernia* on 7 July 1810.

During the Russian Campaign of 1812, he organized the Moscow *opolchenye* and commanded the 4th *Opolchenye* Regiment at Borodino, Chirikov, Chernishna, and Tarutino. He returned to his position of governor in late October 1812, and was appointed to the Senate in 1816.

Two other Obreskovs served in the Russian army during the Napoleonic Wars. **OBRESKOV (Obreskov I), Alexander Vasilievich**, became chef of the Vladimir Dragoon Regiment on 14 December 1796. Promoted to lieutenant general on 21 March 1798, he rose to general of cavalry on 23 February 1800, and was confirmed chef of the Vladimir Dragoon Regiment on 11 April 1801 (served until 15 March 1802).

OBRESKOV (Obreskov II), Mikhail Alekseyevich, commanded Her Majesty's Leib Cuirassier Regiment before becoming major general and chef of the Narva Dragoon Regiment on 26 November 1797. He took command of Her Majesty's Leib Cuirassier Regiment on 27 November 1797, and became chef of the same unit on 21 December 1797 (served until 21 February 1799).

ODOYEVSKY, Ivan Sergeyevich (b. 1769 — d. 18 April 1839) was born to a prominent Russian noble family and enlisted in the Life Guard Preobrazhensk Regiment on 13 February 1776. He transferred as a sergeant to the Life Guard Semeyonovsk Regiment in 1779, becoming an ensign in 1782. In 1789, Odoyevsky transferred as a captain to the Sofia Carabinier Regiment and served as an adjutant to Prince Gregory Potemkin. During the Russo-Turkish War, he took part in the actions at Ismail (golden cross), Killya, and Macin. He was appointed commander of the Ukraine Light Horse Regiment and served in Poland from 1792-1794.

Odoyevsky was promoted to colonel on 12 January 1795, and took command of the Sofia Cuirassier Regiment on 11 April 1798. Odoyevsky became major general and chef of the Siberia Dragoon Regiment on 15 February 1799. However, he was discharged from the army on 14 March 1800, but returned to service a year later. He became chef of the Ingermanland Dragoon Regiment on 10 March 1803, and took part in the 1805 Campaign, fighting at Amstetten and Austerlitz. Odoyevsky retired on 5 May 1806, but returned to service three months later, becoming chef of the Nezhinsk Dragoon Regiment on 5 September 1806. He took another discharge on 17 April 1809. During the 1812

Campaign, Odoyevsky took part in the organization of the Moscow *opolchenye* and served as chef of the 2nd *Opolchenye* Regiment beginning on 12 August. He fought at Borodino, Maloyaroslavets, Vyazma, and Krasnyi in 1812, and served at Danzig in 1813-1814 before retiring in 1815.

OKULOV, Modest Matveyevich (b. 1768 — d. 25 July 1812, Ostrovno) enlisted as a sergeant in the Life Guard Preobrazhensk Regiment on 14 April 1784. He transferred as a captain to the army in January 1791, and became a colonel on January 1799. Okulov was discharged from the army on 28 April 1800, and after returning to service in late 1802, became commander of the Nasheburg Musketeer Regiment on 7 February 1803. He was promoted to major general and appointed chef of the Rylsk Musketeer Regiment on 28 July 1803.

During the 1812 Campaign, Okulov led the 1st Brigade of the 23rd Division, 4th Corps, and was mortally wounded at Ostrovno on July 25, dying that same day.

OLDEKOP, Karl Fedorovich (b. 1777 — d. 25 July 1831, Dubrovno) was born to a German family in the Lifland *gubernia*. He initially enlisted as a sergeant in the Regular Army in 1783, but transferred to the Life Guard Preobrazhensk Regiment on 20 August 1786. Oldekop became a vakhmistr in the Life Guard Horse Regiment in 1794, and then a captain in the Chernigov Infantry Regiment on 12 January 1795. Promoted to major in 1798, he briefly retired in 1799 before returning as a lieutenant colonel in 1800.

In 1805, Oldekop served in Essen's corps and did not participate in actions in Moravia. After rising to colonel in April 1806, he took command of the Crimea Musketeer Regiment on 19 September 1806. Serving in the Army of Dniestr, he took part in the Russo-Turkish War and fought at Khotin. Oldekop was appointed a flügel adjutant on 11 December 1806, and the following year served as a duty officer in Essen's corps. He fought at Ostrov and Ostrolenka, earning the Order of St. Vladimir (4th class) and the Prussian Pour le Merite.

In 1808, Oldekop was reduced in rank for insubordination and transferred as a duty officer to the headquarters of the Army of Moldavia. In 1809, he took part in the actions at Constanta, Rassevat, Silistra, and Tataritsa (Order of St. Vladimir, 3rd class). After Bagration's recommendation, he was restored the rank of flügel adjutant. He became chef of the Aleksapol Musketeer Regiment on 20 January 1810, and then chef of the Kolyvan Musketeer Regiment on 18 July 1810. In 1810-1811, Oldekop distinguished himself at Silistra, Shumla (Order of St. Anna, 2nd class), Ruse, and Batin (Order of St. George, 4th class, 30 April 1812).

During the Russian Campaign of 1812, Oldekop served as a duty general in the headquarters of the 3rd Reserve Army of Observation and participated in the battles at Kobryn (golden sword), Pruzhany, and Gorodechno. He was promoted to major general on 14 December 1812, with seniority dating from 12 August 1812. Between November 1812 and February 1813, Oldekop took part in the operations on the Berezina, Styr, and Vistula Rivers, and in the siege of Thorn.

In 1813, Oldekop fought at Koenigswarte, Bautzen, Dresden, Kulm (Order of St. Anna, 1st class, and the Prussian Order of Red Eagle), and Leipzig (Order of St. Vladimir, 2nd class). In 1814, Oldekop served as a duty officer in the Russian headquarters, participating in the battles at Arcis sur Aube, La Fère Champenoise, and Paris, for which he garnered the diamond signs of Order of St. Anna (1st class).

In 1815, he marched with the Russian army to France during the Hundred Days and participated in the grand review at Vertus (Hesse-Kassel Order of Military Merit). In 1816-1829, Oldekop served as a duty officer in the 1st Army, became a lieutenant general on 1 October 1821, received the Order of St. Alexander of Neva on 3 September 1826, and was finally relieved of position on 21 February 1829.

OLENIN, Yevgeny Ivanovich (b. 24 March 1774 — d. 11 November 1827) was born to a noble family from the Smolensk *gubernia*. He began service in the Life Guard Horse Regiment in 1778, and transferred as a rotmistr to the Kharkov Light Horse Regiment in January 1793. He took part in the campaign in Poland in 1794, received a golden cross for Praga, and transferred to the Smolensk Musketeer Regiment in 1797. Olenin took part in the campaigns in Italy and the Alps in 1799, and was promoted to colonel on 30 December 1800, later transferring to the Life Guard Horse Regiment on 1 January 1803.

During the 1805 Campaign, Olenin distinguished himself at Austerlitz in December. He took part there in the capture of the French eagle of the 1st Battalion of the 4th Line, but was wounded three times (Order of St. George, 4th class, 8 March 1806). He became seriously ill in late 1808 and retired with the rank of major general on 25 November 1808. Olenin returned to service on 1 August 1812, and was appointed to the Smolensk Reserve Corps. In November, he fought at Smolensk (wounded in the left leg) and Krasnyi (wounded in the head). He took a furlough to recuperate on 3 April 1813, and retired in March 1816. During his service, he was awarded the Orders of St. Vladimir (3rd class), of St. Anna (2nd class) with diamonds and of St. John of Jerusalem.

OLSUFIEV (Olsufiev III) Nikolay Dmitrevich (b. 1779 — d. 7 July 1817, Warsaw) was born to a noble family from the Moscow *gubernia*; the brother of Zakhar Olsufiev. He graduated from the Infantry Cadet Corps and enlisted in the Life Guard Izmailovsk Regiment in 1781, rising to sub-lieutenant on 27 April 1797, and to lieutenant on 19 June 1799. In early 1800, Olsufiev became an adjutant to Grand Duke Constantine and transferred to the Life Guard Horse Regiment. He was promoted to staff captain on 26 March 1801, to rotmistr on 17 October 1801, and to colonel on 29 May 1803.

During the 1805 Campaign, Olsufiev distinguished himself at Austerlitz that December, for which he earned the Order of St. Vladimir (4th class) and a golden sword. In 1807, he fought at Guttstadt, Heilsberg (Order of St. George, 4th class, 1 June 1808), and Friedland (promoted to colonel). For his actions in 1807, he was also decorated with the Order of St. Vladimir (3rd class) and the Prussian Pour le Merite. Olsufiev again served as an adjutant to Grand Duke Constantine from 1808-1811.

During the Russian Campaign of 1812, Olsufiev led a reserve squadron of the Life Guard Horse Regiment, and after fighting at Vitebsk, accompanied Grand Duke Constantine to St. Petersburg. After promotion to major general on 18 December 1812, Olsufiev took part in the battles at Lutzen, Bautzen, Dresden, Kulm (Order of St. Anna, 1st class, and the Prussian Iron Cross), and Leipzig (golden sword with diamonds). In 1814, he led the 9th Corps at Brienne, La Ferté sous Jouarre, La Rothière, Vauchamps, La Fère Champenoise, and Paris, for which he received the diamond signs of Order of St. Anna (1st class). For his actions in 1813-1814, he was also awarded the Prussian Order of Red Eagle, the Austrian Order of Leopold, and the Bavarian Order of Maximilian Joseph. He served as an adjutant to Grand Duke Constantine from 1815 - 1817, earning the Order of St. Vladimir (2nd class). Olsufiev became seriously ill on 20 June 1817, and died on 7 July 1817 in Warsaw.

Another **OLSUFIEV, Sergey Adamovich**, led the Astrakhan Dragoon Regiment before becoming major general and chef of the Ingermanland Dragoon Regiment on 1 October 1797 (he served as chef until 24 February 1798).

OLSUFIEV (Olsufiev I), Zakhar Dmitrevich (b. 1772 — d. 1 April 1835, St. Petersburg) was born to a noble family from the Moscow *gubernia*. His brother was Olsufiev (Olsufiev III) Nikolay Dmitreviche. Zakhar enlisted as an ensign in the Life Guard Izmailovsk Regiment on 15 January 1786, and participated in the Russo-Swedish War in 1789-1790. In 1795-1796, he served in the Russian naval squadron in Britain. He was promoted to colonel on 16 April 1797, and became major general and chef of the Bryansk Musketeer Regiment on 5 June 1798. However, with warning Olsufiev fell out of favor with Paul in October 1800, and retired to his estate. After Paul's assassination, Olsufiev was appointed chef of the Vyborg Musketeer Regiment on 24 November 1801.

Olsufiev participated in the 1805 Campaign against Napoleon, fighting at Austerlitz on 2 December 1805. In 1807, he served in Poland and distinguished himself at Eylau (wounded in the leg), Deppen, and Heilsberg (wounded in the hand). His actions earned him a golden sword with diamonds and a promotion to lieutenant general on 11 September 1807. Taking command of the 22nd Infantry Division in the Army of Moldavia on 11 September 1807, Olsufiev was wounded at Braila in 1809, and later led a reserve corps in Wallachia in 1810. He was again seriously wounded during the assault on Ruse and retired on 8 July 1810. He returned to service on 9 September 1811, and was given command of 17th Infantry Division in General Baggovut's 2nd Corps.

During the 1812 Campaign, Olsufiev fought at Smolensk, Valutino, and Borodino, where he defended the Utitsa Hill on the Russian left flank and received the Order of St. George (3rd class, 1 November 1812). When General Baggovut was killed in the battle of Tarutino, Olsufiev took command of the 2nd Corps. In November, he participated in the battles of Maloyaroslavets, Vyazma, Dorogobouzh, and Krasnyi. In 1813, Olsufiev fought at Lutzen, Bautzen, Katzbach, Leipzig, and Mainz.

During the 1814 Campaign, he took part in the actions at Brienne and La Rothière before his corps was decimated at Champaubert, where Olsufiev was wounded and captured. He remained in captivity in Paris until the Allied occupation of the city. Olsufiev later led the 4th Corps in late 1814, and the 17th Division in 1815-1820. He was appointed to the Senate on 22 February 1820, and retired because of poor health on 2 June 1831. Olsufiev died at St. Petersburg on 20 March 1835.

OPPERMAN, Karl Ivanovich (b. 1765, Damrstadt — d. 14 July 1831, Vyborg) was born to a German noble family in Hesse-Darmstadt. He began service in the Hessian army, rising to a captain of engineer troops before joining the Russian army with a rank of lieutenant on 23 October 1783. He participated in the Russo-Swedish War in 1789-1790, fighting at Bjorkzund (Order of St. George, 4th class, on 2 September 1789). In 1794, Opperman served in Poland and was appointed to the Engineer Expedition of the War College in 1797. He became colonel on 18 March 1797, and was transferred to the Department of Cartography. Discharged from the army with a rank of major general on 14 October 1799, Opperman returned to service on 17 December 1800, and worked in the Engineer Corps of the Department of Naval Communications. He was appointed to the Department of Cartography on 27 April 1801, and later joined the Imperial Retinue. In 1803, he supervised the repair works in the fortresses in Finland, and drafted new maps of Russia's western *gubernia*s.

In 1805, Opperman participated in the expedition to Naples and served as a quartermaster general of the Allied forces. In 1806-1807, he served in Essen's corps and fought at Ostrov and Ostrolenka. During the Russo-Swedish War, he supervised the repair work in the fortresses of Vyborg, Neischlodt, and Tavastheus, and was appointed inspector in the Engineer Department of the Ministry of War in 1809. Opperman established a new engineer school in St. Petersburg in 1810 that later became the Central Engineer School in 1819. Opperman directed construction of new fortresses at Bobruisk and Dünaburg in 1810-1811, and was promoted to lieutenant general on 11 September 1811. He became Director of the Engineer Department of the Ministry of War on 11 March 1812, and led engineer troops in the 1st Western Army. During the 1812 Campaign, Opperman took part in the battles at Borodino, Maloyaroslavets, and Krasnyi.

In early 1813, Opperman served at the sieges of Thorn (Order of St. George, 3rd class, 8 May 1813) and Modlin. He became the Chief of Staff of the Army of Poland on 15 July 1813, and participated in the battles at Dresden, Pirna, Leipzig, and in the sieges of Magdeburg and Hamburg. For his actions, Opperman was decorated with the French Legion of Honor, the Prussian Order of Red Eagle, the Swedish Order of the Sword, the Danish Order of Danebrog, the Russian Orders of St. Alexander of Neva with diamonds and St. Anna (1st class) with diamonds.

In 1815-1817, Opperman reorganized the Engineer Department and established sapper and pioneer services. He was appointed inspector general of the Corps of Engineers on 1 February 1818, and rose to general of engineer service on 24 December 1823. Opperman received the title of count of the Russian Empire on 28 July 1829. In 1830, he was ordered to repair the fortress of Sveaborg, where he died during the cholera epidemic in 1831.

ORLOV, Mikhail Fedorovich (b. 5 April 1788 — d. 31 March 1842, Moscow) was born to a prominent Russian noble family. Illegitimate son of Count Fedor Orlov, he was later declared legitimate in 1796. Orlov studied in a Jesuit boarding school in Moscow and served in the College of Foreign Affairs in 1801-1804. He enlisted as an estandart junker in the Life Guard Cavalry Regiment on 27 July 1805. During the 1805 Campaign, he distinguished himself at Austerlitz that December and was promoted to cornet on 21 January 1806. In 1807, Orlov participated in the battles at Guttstadt, Heilsberg, and Friedland (golden sword). He was promoted to lieutenant on 9 May 1808, and appointed an adjutant to Prince Volkonsky in 1810.

In the beginning of the 1812 Campaign, Orlov accompanied Minister of Police Alexander Balashov to negotiate with Napoleon at Vilna and was later promoted to staff rotmistr and appointed flügel adjutant to Alexander I on 14 July 1812. In August-September 1812, he fought at Smolensk, Shevardino, and Borodino. In October-November, Orlov served in Dorokhov's detachment and fought at Vereya (Order of St. George, 4th class, 28 November 1812), Maloyaroslavets, Vyazma, and Krasnyi (promoted to rotmistr). In 1813, he battled at Kalisch (promoted to a colonel, 6 April 1812) and served in Tilleman's detachment at Merzeburg and Leipzig. In 1814, he fought under General Orlov-Denisov at Champaubert, Troyes, Arcis sur Aube, and helped negotiate the surrender of Paris on 30 March 1814.

Promoted to a major general on 14 April 1814, Orlov was sent on a diplomatic mission to Denmark. Returning to Russia, he served as the Chief of Staff of the 7th Corps during the march of the Russian army to France in 1815. He served in the same capacity in the 4th Corps beginning 25 June 1817, before taking command of the 16th Division on 15 June 1820. He participated in various secret societies in 1821-1825 and, after the Decembrist Uprising of 24 December 1825, was detained in the Petropavlovsk Fortress. His brother Aleksey Orlov, Adjutant General to Nicholas, stood up for him and Orlov was sentenced to exile to his estate. He was allowed to return to Moscow in 1831 and died eleven years later.

Two other Orlovs served in the Russian army at this period. **Colonel ORLOV (Orlov 1, first name unclear),** led the Vladimir Dragoon Regiment between January and September 1804; Major General **ORLOV (Orlov II), Aleksey Petrovich**, commanded the Leib Cossack regiment between March 1799 and January 1803.

ORLOV-DENISOV, Vasily Vasilievich (b. 19 September 1775 — d. 5 February 1843, Kharkov) was born to a Cossack noble family; his grandfather was the first Cossack general to receive the title of count of the Russian Empire. He was named Vasily Orlov until 8 May 1801, when he was allowed to add his grandfather's family name of Denisov. Orlov-Denisov began service as a Cossack in January 1789, and was promoted to sotnik on 15 October 1789. In 1792, he joined the Krasnov's Cossack Regiment and became colonel on 14 July 1799. He transferred to the Life Guard Cossack Regiment in 1806, and participated in the 1807 Campaign in Poland, fighting at Guttstadt, Heilsberg, and Friedland (received the Order of St. George, 4th class, 1 June 1808). Promoted to major general on 24 December 1807, he took command of the Life Guard Cossack Regiment on 2 August 1808. Orlov-Denisov participated in the operations in Finland in 1808-1809 and fought at Borgo, Helsingfors and defended the coastline in southern Finland. He was appointed an adjutant general on 10 February 1811.

During the Russian Campaign, Orlov-Denisov served in the rearguard of the 1st Western Army and fought at Dubino, Vilna, Kocherzhishki, Vitebsk, Zabolotye, Borodino, Chirikov, Voronovo, Tarutino (Order of St. George, 3rd class, 4 January 1813), Maloyaroslavets, Gzhatsk, Lyakhov, Krasnyi, Vileyko, and Vilna. In 1813-1814, he led Emperor Alexander I's escort and participated in the battles at Lutzen, Bautzen, Dresden, Kulm (promoted to lieutenant general on 27 September 1813), Leipzig, and Paris. For his actions, he was decorated with the Orders of St. Alexander of Neva, the Prussian Pour le Merite, the Order of Red Eagle, the Austrian Order of Maria Theresa, the Bavarian Order of Maximilian Joseph, and the French Order of St. Louis.

After the Napoleonic Wars, Orlov-Denisov became commander of the 5th Reserve Cavalry Corps on 11 September 1825, and rose to general of cavalry on 3 September 1826. He retired in October 1827, but returned to service in April 1828. During the Russo-Turkish War of 1828-1829, Orlov-Denisov served in the headquarters of the Russian army before retiring in 1830. He was initially buried at the Preobrazhensk Monastery in Kharkov, but his remains were transferred to Novocherkassk in 1911.

O'ROURKE (O'Rourke I), Joseph Kornilovich (b. 1762 — d. 1849) was born to an Irish noble family; his father moved to Russia under Empress Elizabeth and served as a major general in the Russian army. O'Rourke enlisted as a sergeant in the Life Guard Izmailovsk Regiment in 1776, and fourteen years later, became a captain in the Pskov Dragoon Regiment. He fought in the Russo-Swedish War in 1789-1790, and participated in the 1794 Campaign in Poland. O'Rourke transferred to the Pavlograd Hussar Regiment in 1797, rising to major in 1798. In 1799, he served in General Rimsky-Korsakov's corps in Switzerland, and for his actions at Zurich, was awarded the Order of St. George (4th class) and promoted to lieutenant colonel in 1800.

During the 1805 Campaign, O'Rourke served in the Russian rearguard and fought at Schöngrabern and Austerlitz. During the 1806-1807 Campaigns in Poland, he took part in the battles at Golimyn and Eylau (awarded the Order of St. Vladimir, 3rd class). In March 1807, he was sent to Volhynia to form the Volhynia Uhlan Regiment, and was appointed chef of this unit on

19 May 1807. In 1808-1811, he served in the Danube Valley and distinguished himself at Giurgiu.

Promoted to major general on 3 August 1810, O'Rourke was dispatched to Serbia, where he defeated the Turks at Palanka and Banya, earning the Order of St. George (3rd class) on 10 December 1810. He also fought at Jasika, Varvarino, and on the Morava River. He later joined the main Russian forces and fought the Turks at Kalafat. For his actions, O'Rourke was awarded the Order of St. Anna (1st class) with diamonds and the Order of St. Vladimir (2nd class). In early 1812, he commanded Russian troops on the border of Bosnia. During the 1812 Campaign, he was recalled to Volhynia, where he commanded a cavalry detachment and fought on the Bug and Berezina Rivers, and pursued the French from Molodechno to Kovno.

In 1813, O'Rourke took part in the rearguard actions on the Oder River and in the battles at Dresden, Magdeburg, and Kulm (Prussian Iron Cross). He was promoted to lieutenant general on 10 October 1813, with seniority dating from 16 August 1813. In October 1813, he fought at Dennewitz, Leipzig, and Kassel. During the 1814 Campaign in France, O'Rourke commanded a cavalry corps in the Army of North and fought at Craonne, St. Dizier, Bar sur Aube, Laon (awarded the Order of St. Alexander of Neva), and Paris. For his actions in 1813-1814, he was awarded the Prussian Order of Red Eagle, the Swedish Order of the Sword, and Hesse-Kassel Order of Military Merit.

In August 1814, O'Rourke took command of the 2nd Uhlan Division. The next year, he accompanied Alexander I to the Congress of Vienna. In 1816-1818, he led the Lithuanian Uhlan Division and took command of the 1st Hussar Division on 4 May 1819. Relieved of duty on 25 July 1819, he retired to his estate near Minsk. During the Polish Rebellion of 1830, O'Rourke mobilized reserves in the Minsk *gubernia* and was awarded the Order of St. Alexander of Neva with diamonds. He was promoted to general of cavalry on 22 April 1841. O'Rourke died at his estate at Vselube in the Grodno *gubernia* in April 1849. During his career,

O'Rourke also received two golden swords (one with diamonds) for courage. His brother **O'ROURKE (O'Rourke I) Patrice Kornilovich**, rose to colonel and led the Volhynia Horse (later Uhlan) Regiment on 24 October 1811, but sickened and died on 10 June 1812.

OSTEN-SACKEN (Osten-Sacken I), Fabian Vilgelmovich (Fabian Gotlib von der Osten Sacken) (b. 31 October 1752, Revel — d. 19 April 1837, Kiev) was born to a family of German barons in Courland. He enlisted as a sub-ensign in the Koporsk Infantry Regiment on 29 October 1766. He participated in the Russo-Turkish War in 1769-1770, fought at Khotin, and transferred as an ensign to the Nasheburg Infantry Regiment. In 1771-1773, Sacken served in Poland. By 1785, he served as a captain in the Infantry Cadet Corps and transferred as a lieutenant colonel to the Moscow Grenadier Regiment on 24 November 1786. He joined the Rostov Musketeer Regiment on 30 July 1789, and took part in the Russo-Turkish War of 1789-1791. Promoted to colonel on 21 August 1792, Sacken received the Order of St. George (4th class, 7 December 1792) and transferred to the Chernigov Musketeer Regiment in 1793. He served against the Poles in 1794.

On 9 October 1797, Oesten-Sacken became a major general and chef of the Ekaterinoslavl Grenadier Regiment; two months later, he became chef of the Pskov Grenadier Regiment on 22 January 1798. In 1799, Oesten-Sacken served in the Russian corps in Switzerland and fought at Zurich, where he helped to cover the Russian retreat before being wounded in the head and captured by the French. Released in 1800, he became chef of the St. Petersburg Grenadier Regiment on 14 January 1801.

In 1805, Oesten-Sacken led a corps in the Grodno and Vladimir *gubernia*s. In 1806-1807, he led one of the columns in Bennigsen's army and fought at Pultusk, Jankovo, Eylau, and Launau. During the operations around Guttstadt in June 1807, his column moved very slowly and allowed Ney's corps to escape. Oesten-Sacken—whose relations with Bennigsen were deeply strained— allegedly delayed the advance to undermine the entire operation so Bennigsen would be removed from the army. Bennigsen accused Oesten-Sacken of insubordination and held him responsible for the failure of the maneuver at Guttstadt. A military court convened and found him guilty as charged. He was relieved of command on 10 June 1807.

Osten-Sacken spent the next five years in St. Petersburg before taking over as a commander of the Reserve Corps in the 3rd Reserve Army of Observation in early 1812. In October 1812, he covered the advance of Chichagov's army to the Berezina and fought at Slonim and Volkovysk. In 1813, he led a corps in the Army of Silesia and fought at Leignitz, Kaizerwalde, Bunzlau, and Katzbach. He was promoted to general of infantry on 11 September 1813, with seniority dating from 26 August 1813. He distinguished himself at Leipzig and was awarded the Order of St. George (2nd class) on 20 October 1813. In 1814, he participated in the battles at La Rothière (Order of St. Andrew the First Called), Craonne, and Paris. He was appointed Govenor General of Paris on 31 March 1813, and served until June 1814, receiving a special golden sword with the inscription "March 1814—City of Paris to General Sacken."

In 1815, Oesten-Sacken led the 3rd Corps in Poland before becoming commander-in- chief of the 1st Army and a member of the State Council on 20 June 1818. Three years later, he was honored with the title of count of the Russian Empire on 20 April 1821. He became chef of the Uglitsk Infantry Regiment on 9 February 1826; this unit was renamed "Osten-Sacken's Infantry Regiment." Oesten-Sacken was promoted to field marshal on 3 September 1826. During the Polish Uprising in 1830-1831, he governed the Kiev, Podolsk, and Volhynia *gubernia*s. He was conferred the title of prince of the Russian Empire on 20 November 1832.

During his career, Osten-Sacken also received the Orders of St. Vladimir (1st class), of St. Alexander of Neva, of St. Anna (1st class), the Prussian Orders of Red and Black Eagles, the Austrian Order of Maria Theresa, a medal "For XXXV Years of Distinguished Service" and two golden swords (one with diamonds) for courage.

Two other Osten-Sackens served in the Russian army during the Napoleonic Wars. **OSTEN-SACKEN (Osten-Sacken III), Erofei Kuzmich (Ieronim Kazimirovich)**, took command of the Pskov Dragoon Regiment on 11 April 1798. He rose to major general and chef of the same unit on 6 October 1798. The following year, he became commander of the Pskov Dragoon Regiment on 22 March 1799. Oesten-Sacken served as chef of the Elisavetgrad Hussar Regiment between 22 December 1800 and 13 January 1807, and served with the 5th Division in Poland in 1806-1807. **OSTEN-SACKEN (Osten-Sacken I), Leontii Khristoforovich,** rose to lieutenant colonel and commander of the Chernigov Musketeer Regiment on 22 January 1801. Promoted to colonel on 26 September 1803, he led the Smolensk Musketeer Regiment between 26 May 1803 and 6 January 1807. During the 1805 Campaign, the Smolensk Musketeer Regiment was attached to Major General Miloradovich's detachment at Amstteten and Austerlitz.

OSTERMAN-TOLSTOY, Alexander Ivanovich (b. 1771 — date of death unknown; removed from rosters on 18 February 1857) was born to a prominent, and one of the wealthiest, Russian noble family of Tolstoy. He began service in the Life Guard Preobrazhensk Regiment on 12 January 1774, and rose to an ensign in 1788 at the age of seventeen. During the Russo-Turkish War of 1787-1791, Tolstoy volunteered to serve in the army, earning promotion to lieutenant of the Guard, and served at Ismail (Order of St. George, 4th class, 5 April 1791) and Macin. Two years later, he transferred as a lieutenant colonel to the 2nd Battalion of the Bug Jager Corps on 12 January 1793. Promoted to colonel on 8 November 1796, he was allowed to add name and title of his childless grandfathers, Count Ostermans, to his last name. Osterman-Tolstoy became a major general and chef of the Schlüsseburg Musketeer Regiment on 12 February 1798. Two months later, he was transferred to the civil service with a rank of actual civil counsellor.

Osterman-Tolstoy returned to military service in 1801 and took command of infantry division on 8 April 1801. In 1805, he served under Count Peter Tolstoy in Pomerania and rose to lieutenant general on 27 June 1806. During the 1806 Campaign in Poland, he led the 2nd Division fighting at Czarnow (Order of St. George, 3rd class, 20 January 1807) and Pultusk. In 1807, Osterman-Tolstoy took part in the retreat from Jankovo and commanded the left flank of the Russian army at Eylau. He was seriously wounded at Guttstadt in June 1807, and left the army to recuperate. Bitterly opposed to the Tilsit peace treaty with France, he led the anti-French faction in St. Petersburg. He retired because of poor health on 4 November 1810.

During the 1812 Campaign, Osterman-Tolstoy joined the 1st Corps as a volunteer and fought at Wilkomir. On 13 July 1812, he became commander of the 4th Corps of the 1st Western Army, and distinguished himself at Ostrovno and Valutino. He was seriously bruised at Borodino, and at the council of war at Fily, urged the abandonment of Moscow. From October-November 1812, he fought at Tarutino and Krasnyi, but had to leave army because of poor health in December.

Osterman-Tolstoy returned to the army in early 1813 and was seriously wounded later that spring at Bautzen. After recuperating, he was given command of the Guard Corps on 26 August 1813. He distinguished himself at Kulm, where he was seriously wounded when a cannonball ruooed off his left hand. Osterman-Tolstoy was decorated with the Order of St. George (2nd class, 31 August 1813) and the Prussian Iron Cross before taking a furlough to recuperate. He was appointed an adjutant general on 17 March 1814, and chef of the Life Guard Pavlovsk Regiment on 28 December 1815. Osterman-Tolstoy took command of the Grenadier Corps on 21 April 1816, and rose to general of infantry on 29 August 1817. He was relieved of his position on 31 January 1826, and served as military adviser to Ibrahim Pasha of Egypt in 1831. After returning to Russia, Osterman-Tolstoy had an argument with Nicholas I and was forced to leave country in 1834. He spent the rest of his life in Switzerland, and died in Geneva in early 1857.

OZHAROVSKY, Adam Petrovich (b. 1776, Warsaw — d. December 1855, Warsaw) was born to a Polish noble family in Warsaw. He participated with the Poles during the bloody uprising in 1794, but after its defeat, entered Russian service in late 1794. He became a cornet in the Life Guard Horse Regiment on 16 June 1796, and was promoted to colonel on 27 September 1802. During the 1805 Campaign, Ozharovsky distinguished himself at Austerlitz, where he helped to capture the French eagle of the 1st Battalion of the 4th Line and earned the Order of St. George (4th class) on 8 March 1806. In June 1807, he fought at Guttstadt, Heilsberg, and Friedland (awarded the Order of St. George, 3rd class, 1 June 1808). For his actions, he earned promotion to major general and appointment as adjutant general on 3 August 1807.

During the 1812 Campaign, Ozharovsky served in the headquarters of the 1st Western Army, fought at Borodino (received a golden sword with diamonds) and led a combined corps of *opolchenye* and Cossacks at Tarutino, Maloyaroslavets, and Krasnyi. In 1813, he took part in the battles at Lutzen, Bautzen, Dresden, Kulm (Prussian Iron Cross and promotion to lieutenant general on 27 September 1813), and Leipzig. In 1814, Ozharovsky fought at Brienne, Bar sur Aube, La Fère Champenoise, and Paris, for which he was awarded the Order of St. Alexander of Neva.

After the war, he served as an adjutant general to Emperor Alexander. He was promoted to general of cavalry on 3 September 1826, and became commander of the Independent Lithuanian Corps on 1 March 1827. Ozharovsky retired in October 1827, but returned to service in 1831 to take part in operations in Poland. He was appointed a member of the State Council of the Kingdom of Poland on 24 September 1833, and served in the Polish Senate in 1841. During his career, Ozharovsky also received the Order of St. Anna (1st class), the Prussian Orders of Pour le Merite and Red Eagle, the French Order of St. Louis, the Austrian Order of Maria Theresa, the Württemberg Order of Military Merit, the Bavarian Order of Maximilian Joseph and the Sardinian Order of St. Maurice and Lazare, and a medal "For XXX Years of Distinguished Service." His brother, **Colonel Kozma Ozharovsky**, also served in the Life Guard Horse Regiment, but was killed at Friedland on 14 June 1807.

PADEYSKY, Fedor Fedorovich (b. 1759 — date of death unknown; removed from rosters on 3 April 1829) was born to a noble family from the Voronezh *gubernia*. He enlisted as a private in the Staroskol Infantry Regiment on 1 February 1769, rising to a sergeant on 11 April 1770. Three years later, he transferred as an ensign to the Tenginsk Infantry Regiment on 12 January 1773. Padeysky took part in the Russo-Turkish War in 1773-1774, and joined the Kozlov Infantry Regiment on 26 March 1788. He participated in another Russo-Turkish War in 1788-1791 (golden cross for Ochakov). From 1792-1794, he served in Poland, fighting at Gorodishe (golden sword), Maciejowice, and Praga (golden cross and promotion to premier major). He became lieutenant colonel on 7 November 1799, and took command of the Kozlov Musketeer Regiment on 16 September 1802. The same year, he received the Order of St. George (4th class) for his dedicated service on 8 December. Padeysky rose to a colonel on 12 December 1803.

Padeysky took part in the operations against the French on the Ionian Islands and in Naples in 1805-1806. In 1807, he became chef of the Kozlov Musketeer Regiment on 28 March, and distinguished himself against the Turks on the Island of Tenedos, for which he was decorated with the Order of St. George (3rd class) on 17 August 1807. Transferred to the Army of Danube in 1808, Padeysky was seriously wounded at Braila in 1809, and distinguished himself at Bazardjik (golden cross) and Shumla in 1810. A promotion to major general followed on 9 August 1810. In 1811, Padeysky served under General Kutuzov at Ruse and Viddin. During the 1812 Campaign, he commanded the 1st Brigade of the 15th Division in the 3rd Reserve Army of Observation and fought at Kobryn, Gorodechnya, Borisov, Stakhov, and Brilya. In 1813, he took part in the siege of Thorn and served as the commandant of this fortress for the next two years. Padeysky became the Commandant of Dünaburg on 20 November 1816, and of Novgorod on 19 January 1822.

PAHLEN (fon der Pahlen), Matvei Ivanovich (Karl Magnus) (b. 2 March 1779, Revel — d. 1 June 1863, Palme, Estland *gubernia*) was born to a noble family from the Estland *gubernia*. The Pahlens were an old Livonian family who had served Sweden and then Russia after Peter the Great annexed Livonia in early 1700s. Matvei Pahlen began service as a quartermaster in the Life Guard Horse Regiment in 1784, and

PAHLEN (Pahlen II, fon der Pahlen), Pavel Petrovich (Paul Karl Ernst Wilhelm Philipp) (b. 18 July 1775 — d. 21 February 1834) was born to a noble family from the Courland *gubernia*; the son of Peter Pahlen, Military Governor of Moscow. Pavel Pahlen enlisted in the guard in January 1782 at age five, and began active service as a rotmistr in the Orenburg Dragoon Regiment on 12 January 1790. He transferred as a premier major to the Moscow Carabinier Regiment in 1793, and served in Poland in 1794. Promoted to lieutenant captain in the Life Guard Semeyonovsk Regiment in August 1795, he took part in the Persian Campaign along the Caspian Sea in 1796, distinguishing himself at Derbent, Baku, and Shemakha.

Pahlen joined the His Majesty's Leib Cuirassier Regiment on 23 November 1797, and rose to colonel on 8 August 1798. He became a major general on 23 March 1800, and chef of the Izumsk Hussar regiment on 26 September 1800. However, due to his father's involvement in the assassination of Paul, Pahlen was discharged from the army on 9 August 1803. He returned to the army three years later, becoming chef of the Derpt Dragoon Regiment on 11 September 1808. He served in the Danubian Principalities in 1807-1812, fighting at Turbat, Giurgiu, Obilesti (Order of St. George, 4th class), Salchi, Tulcea, Babadag, Girsov, Constanta (Kustendji), Rassevat (Order of St. Vladimir, 3rd class), Tataritsa (Order of St. George, 3rd class), Silistra transferred as a cornet to the Riga Dragoon Regiment on 2 February 1797. Rising to lieutenant, he served with his regiment in the 5th Division in Poland in 1806-1807, fighting at Landsberg and Eylau. After transferring as a staff rotmistr to the Chevalier Guard Regiment, he served in Finland in 1808-1809, fighting at Kuopio, Brahestadt, Lappo, Idensalmi (received the Order of St. George, 4th class, 1 March 1809) and in the expedition to the Aland Islands. He rose to rotmistr in 1809 and to colonel in 1810. In 1810-1811, he fought the Turks in the Danubian Principalities, distinguishing himself at Silistra, Shumla, Ruse, Batin, and Nikopol.

During the 1812 Campaign, Pahlen initially served as duty officer to Major General Sergey Tuchkov II and later led a flying cavalry detachment. In 1813, he joined Alexander Chernishev's detachment and distinguished himself at Pirna, Luneburg (promoted to major general on 4 September 1813, with seniority dating from 2 April 1813), Gross Beeren, and Dennewitz (Order of St. George, 3rd class, 6 October 1813). He led the advance guard of the Army of North at Leipzig. In November-December 1813, Pahlen served at Hamburg. In 1814, he took part in the battles at Soissons, Craonne, Laon, Rheims, and St. Dizier. After the war, he retired on 24 July 1818, and served in the civil administration of the Estland *gubernia*.

Pahlen was conferred the rank of privy counsellor in 1828, and two years later, returned to military service with the rank of lieutenant general on 13 January 1830. Pahlen served as the Military Governor of Riga and Governor General of the Estland, Courland, and Lifland *gubernia*s. He took part in the operations against the Poles in 1830-1831, and earned promotion to general of cavalry on 22 October 1843. After becoming a member of the State Council on 29 March 1845, he took an indefinite furlough because of poor health two years later and died on 1 June 1863.

During his career, Pahlen garnered the Russian Orders of St. Alexander of Neva, of St. Vladimir (2nd class) and of St. Anna (1st class) with diamonds; he was also decorated with the Prussian Orders of Red Eagle and Pour le Merite, and the Swedish Order of the Sword.

(golden sword with diamonds), Ruse, and Shumla.

In 1812, Pahlen served with the 22nd Brigade of the 7th Cavalry Division in the Army of Danube, and fought at Vladimir-Volhynsky, Kladnev, Lubomle, Volkovysk, and on the Berezina. In 1813, he participated in the actions at Thorn, Lutzen, Bautzen, Katzbach, Lovenberg (Order of St. Anna, 1st class), and Leipzig (diamond signs of the Order of St. Anna, 1st class). In 1814, he served at Soissons, Laon, Chalons, Le Fère Champenoise (promoted to lieutenant general on 1 January 1816, with seniority dating from 25 March 1814), and Paris. After the war, he led the 2nd Horse Jager Division before taking command of the 2nd Reserve Combined Cavalry Corps on 10 March 1827, and then took over the 2nd Corps on 4 October 1829. He rose to general of cavalry on 7 July 1828. During the Polish Uprising of 1830-1831, he commanded the cavalry of the Army of Reserve.

PAHLEN (fon der Pahlen), Peter Alekseyevich (Peter Ludvig) (b. 28 July 1745 — d. 25 February 1826) was born to old Livonian family of fon der Pahlen, who had served Sweden and then Russia after Peter the Great annexed Livonia in the early 1700s. Pahlen enlisted in the Life Guard Horse Regiment in 1760, and rose to rotmistr nine years later. He distinguished himself fighting the Turks in 1769-1774, becoming a colonel and commander of the Yamburg Carabinier Regiment in 1778. Promoted to major general on 2 May 1787, he served under Prince Gregory Potemkin during the Russo-Turkish War of 1787-1791, earning the Order of St. George (4th class) at Ochakov. In 1792-1794, he served in the Baltic provinces and helped negotiate the annexation of Courland.

Promoted to lieutenant general in 1795, Pahlen became the first Governor General of the Courland *gubernia*. He later became a favorite of Emperor Paul, who made him the cavalry inspector in the St. Petersburg and Finland Inspections on 12 December 1797. Pahlen rose to general of cavalry on 11 April 1798, and was appointed the Military Governor of St. Petersburg on 8 August 1798. In March 1801, Pahlen was one of the leaders of the conspiracy against Emperor Paul and was involved in his murder. Emperor Alexander removed him from every official position and exiled him to his country estate in June 1801. Pahlen never returned to the court and died on 25 February 1826.

PAHLEN (Pahlen III, fon der Pahlen), Peter Petrovich (b. 1778 — d. 1 May 1864, St. Petersburg) was born to a noble family from the Courland *gubernia*; son of Peter Pahlen, Military Governor of St. Petersburg, brother of Pavel Pahlen. He enlisted as a vakhmistr in the Life Guard Horse Regiment on 5 November 1790, and transferred as a captain to the Orenburg

Dragoon Regiment on 12 January 1792. Rising to a premier major in this unit, Pahlen took part in the Persian Campaign in 1796, fighting at Derbent and Baku. He received promotion to colonel on 20 October 1798. Two years later, he became major general and chef of the Kargopol Dragoon Regiment on 30 September 1800. Pahlen was appointed chef of the Sumsk Hussar Regiment on 1 June 1801.

During the 1806-1807 Campaigns in Poland, Pahlen distinguished himself at Lopachin (Order of St. George, 4th class, 31 January 1807), Mohrungen, Eylau (Order of St. George, 3rd class, 20 April 1807), Launau, Guttstadt, Heilsberg, and Friedland. He took command of the 3rd Reserve Cavalry Corps in the 1st Western Army in early 1812. During the 1812 Campaign, he fought at Vitebsk, Golovchin, Porechye, and Rudnya. However, Pahlen became seriously ill and left the army in late August 1812. He was promoted to lieutenant general on 22 August 1812 with seniority dating from 27 July 1812. Returning to the army in early 1813, he participated in the actions at Bautzen, Reichenbach, Löwenberg (wounded in the head), Hollensdorf, and Leipzig, where he was wounded in the head and shoulders.

In 1814, Pahlen participated in the battles at Brienne, Mèry, Nogent, Bar sur Aube, Troyes, Arcis sur Aube, Le Fère Champenoise, and Paris, where he was decorated with the Order of St. George (2nd class) on 31 March 1814. After the war, he commanded the 3rd Reserve Cavalry Corps in 1815, and the 4th Reserve Cavalry Corps from 1816 to 1822. He took a discharge on 24 March 1823, but returned to the army four years later as the commander of the 1st Corps on 23 November 1827. Pahlen became general of cavalry and adjutant general on 18 December 1827, as well as chef of the Sumsk Hussar Regiment on 6 November 1829.

Pahlen took part in the Russo-Turkish War in 1828-1829, and fought the Polish insurgents in 1830-1831. He was relieved of command of the 1st Corps and appointed a member of the State Council on 7 February 1834. The following month, he joined the Council of War on 5 March 1834. He became Inspector General of all Russian cavalry on 10 March 1840. The same day, Pahlen was also appointed chef of the Military Order Cuirassier Regiment. On 1 May 1853, the Sumsk Huissar Regiment was renamed "Pahlen's Hussar Regiment." Pahlen was again confirmed chef of the Military Order Dragoon Regiment on 8 June 1860, and became chef of the 5th Squadron of the Life Guard Horse Regiment on 6 April 1862.

During his long career, Pahlen received the Orders of St. Andrew the First called with diamonds, St. Vladimir (1st class), St. Alexander of Neva with diamonds, the White Eagle, St. Anna (1st class) with diamonds, and St. John of Jerusalem. He was also decorated with the Prussian Orders of Black and Red Eagle, as well as the Austrian Order of Maria Theresa (3rd class).

There were several other Pahlens serving in the Russian army during the Napoleonic Wars, including **PAHLEN, Dmitry Fedorovich**, who became chef of the Lifland Dragoon Regiment on 16 September 1805. He served with the 8th Division in Poland in 1806-1807, and rose to major general on 5 June 1807. He died from the wounds received in the battle of Friedland in 1807.

PALITSYN, Ivan Ivanovich (b. 1763 – d. 10 October 1814, Lyadokhov) was born to a Russian noble family. He enlisted as a sergeant in the Schlüsselburg Infantry Regiment on 12 January 1775, and transferred to the Life Guard Preobrazhensk Regiment on 22 August 1783.

Palitsyn joined the Aleksopol Infantry Regiment with a rank of captain on 12 January 1790. He took part in the Russo-Turkish War of 1787-1791, distinguishing himself at Ismail, where he was wounded in the left leg and hand (golden cross). He rose to a colonel on 9 June 1800, and took command of the Aleksopol Musketeer Regiment on 2 May 1801. He became chef of the Phanagoria Grenadier Regiment on 5 July 1806, and chef of the Orel Musketeer Regiment on 25 September 1806.

Palitsyn took part in the Russo-Turkish War of 1806-1812, becoming a major general on 24 December 1807. In October 1810, the Orel Musketeer Regiment was converted to the 41st Jager Regiment. During the 1812 Campaign, Palitsyn commanded the 3rd Brigade of the 12th Division in the 7th Corps and fought at Saltanovka (Moghilev) and Smolensk. He was severely wounded at Borodino and left the army to recuperate. He never fully recovered from his wounds, and died at his estate in Lyakhovo on 10 October 1814.

Another **Palitsyn, Nikolay Lukich** became chef of the Pskov Grenadier Regiment on 4 November 1799, chef of the Ekaterinoslavl Grenadier Regiment on 12 April 1801, and served as chef of the Tobolsk Garrison Regiment between 10 June 1805 and 23 May 1816.

PANCHULIDZEV (Panchulidzev I), Ivan Davydovich (b. 1759 — d. 21 January 1815) was born to the Georgian noble family of Panchulidze (and brother of Semen Panchulidze). His father, David Matveyevich Panchulidzev, immigrated to Russia in 1738. The younger Panchulidzev enlisted as a kaptenarmus in the Life Guard Preobrazhensk Regiment on 12 January 1774, and transferred as a captain to the Kinburn Dragoon Regiment on 12 January 1786. He took part in the Russo-Turkish War in 1787-1791, garnering a golden cross and the rank of second major at Ochakov. He served in Poland in 1794, rising to premier major. Two years later, he participated in the Persian Campaign along the Caspian Sea, fighting at Derbent and Baku. Promoted to colonel on 22 October 1799, he took command of the Tver Dragoon Regiment on 30 January 1803, and of the Chernigov Dragoon Regiment on 20 September 1805.

During the 1805 Campaign, Panchulidzev turned in distinguished performances at Amstetten, Schöngrabern (Hollabrunn, received the Order of St. Vladimir, 4th class), and Austerlitz, where he was wounded in the left leg. He became chef of the Chernigov Dragoon Regiment on 17 March 1806, and rose to a major general on 5 June 1807. During the Russo-Turkish War of 1806-1812, he took part in the operations at Anapa (Order of St. Anna, 1st class) and Trabzon. In 1812, Panchulidzev served with the 12th Brigade of the 4th Cavalry Division in the 4th Reserve Cavalry Corps, fighting at Dashkovka (Moghilev), Nadva, Smolensk, Shevardino, Borodino, Mozhaisk, Tarutino, on the Chernyshka River, Maloyaroslavets, Vyazma, and Krasnyi, for which he was decorated with the Order of St. George (3rd classs) on 15 June 1813. In 1813, he distinguished himself at Lutzen (promoted to lieutenant general on 27 September 1813), Bautzen, Reichenbach, and Katzbach. The following year, he fought at Mainz, Rheims, Le Fère Champenoise, and Paris.

PANCHULIDZEV, (Panchulidzev II), Semen Davydovich (b. 1767 — d. 29 December 1817) was born to the Georgian noble family of Panchulidze (the brother of Ivan Panchulidze). After studying in the Infantry Cadet Corps, he enlisted as a lieutenant in the

Chernigov Infantry Regiment on 25 February 1785. He distinguished himself at Anapa during the Russo-Turkish War of 1787-1791, and served in Poland in 1794. Panchulidzev served under Rimsky-Korsakov in Switzerland in 1799. Returning to Russia, he took command of the Pavlograd Hussar Regiment on 21 January 1803.

During the 1805 Campaign, Panchulidzev distinguished himself at Lambach, Amstetten, Dürrenstein, Schöngrabern (Hollabrunn), Wischau, and Austerlitz, for which he garnered the Order of St. George (4th class) on 24 January 1806. He became chef of the Ingermanland Dragoon Regiment on 4 August 1806. In 1806-1807, he served with the 7th Division in Poland, taking part in the battles at Eylau, Guttstadt, Heilsberg, and Friedland. Promoted to major general on 24 December 1807, he led the 7th Brigade of the 2nd Cavalry Division in the 2nd Reserve Cavalry Corps in 1812.

Over the course of the 1812 Campaign, Panchulidzev participated in the battles at Ostrovno, Kakzvachino, Smolensk, Borodino (golden sword with diamonds), Tarutino, Vereya (Order of St. Anna, 1st class), Maloyaroslavets, and minor actions during the pursuit of Napoleon's army. For his conduct, he was decorated with the Order of St. George (3rd class) on 15 June 1813.

In 1813, Panchulidzev served at Bautzen, Katzbach, Dresden, and Leipzig. The following year, he took part in the battles at Brienne, La Rothière, Montmirail, Craonne, Laon, and Le Fère Champenoise. He retired because of poor health on 13 June 1815, and died in Moscow on 29 December 1817.

The third **Panchulidzev, Aleksey Davydovich** (b. 1768 — d. 1832) served as the vice-governor and governor of Saratov from 1791 to 1826.

PANKRATIEV, Nikita Petrovich (b. 1788 — d. 1836) was born to a noble family from the Kiev *gubernia*. He volunteered for service against the Turks in 1807, and took part in the actions at Trabzon and Braila in 1809. Promoted to lieutenant in 1810, he became adjutant to General Mikhail Kutuzov and participated in the battle at Ruse in July 1811. For his conduct, Pankratiev received the Order of St. Vladimir (4th class) and promotion to lieutenant in the Life Guard Jager Regiment. In 1812, Pankratiev again served as adjutant to Kutuzov at Borodino (Order of St. Anna, 2nd class) before leading Cossack troops in various partisan detachments and fighting at Nikolsk, Sharapova, Klevin, and Borovsk. In late October, Pankratiev returned to his duties of adjutant to Kutuzov and participated in the battle at Krasnyi (golden sword and diamond signs of the Order of St. Anna, 2nd class).

After Kutuzov died in April 1813, Pankratiev rose to a staff captain in the Life Guard Jager Regiment and fought at Bautzen and Dennewitz. He became a captain and flügel adjutant to Emperor Alexander on 5 October 1813, before taking part in the battle of Leipzig, where he earned promotion to colonel. In 1814, he served as a duty officer in Winzegorode's staff and participated in the actions at Soissons, Craonne, Laon, Rheims, Bar le Duc (Order of St. Vladimir, 3rd class) and Chaumont. Late in the spring of 1814, he escorted King Jerome of Westphalia to Bern and joined Emperor Alexander at Vienna. During the Hundred Days in 1815, Pankratiev commanded the 59th Jager Regiment. Promoted to major general in 1817, he took command of the 2nd Brigade of the 1st Grenadier Division. In 1822, he became commander of the 2nd Brigade of the 11th Division and, in 1827, he assumed command of the 2nd Brigade of the 20th Division in the Caucasus.

Pankratiev participated in the Russo-Persian War in 1827, receiving the Order of St. Anna (1st class), and took command of the 20th Division on 17 July 1827. He then took part in the Russo-Turkish War of 1828-1829, distinguishing himself at Bayazet, Kainly, Miliduz (earned the Order of St. George, 3rd class), Hassan Kale, and Erzerum, for which he was promoted to lieutenant general and decorated with the Order of St. Anna (1st class) with a crown. After briefly serving as the Chief of Staff of the Independent Caucasus Corps, he took part in the operations in Daghestan and briefly commanded the Russian troops in Transcaucasia in 1831, earning the Order of St. Alexander of Neva. He became a member of the State Council of the Kingdom of Poland on 16 November 1832, and the following year was appointed Military Governor of Warsaw on 30 May 1833. He presided over the court martial of the Polish officers who participated in the uprising of 1831.

PANTENIUS, Fedor Ivanovich took command of the 5th Jager Regiment on 7 March 1805. During the 1805 Campaign, he served in Buxhöwden's corps and distinguished himself at Austerlitz that December. Promoted to lieutenant colonel on 5 May 1806, he served with the 7th Division in Poland in 1806-1807, fighting at Eylau, Guttstadt, Deppen, Heilsberg, and Friedland. He rose to colonel on 24 December 1807, and became chef of the 27th Jager Regiment on 31 October 1810. After the war, he led the 27th Jager Regiment from July 1815–September 1816.

PANTZERBITER, Karl Karlovich (Karl Friedrich) (b. 1765 — d. 1819) was born to a noble family from the Lifland *gubernia*. After studying in the Infantry Cadet Corps, he began service as a sub-lieutenant in the Kiev Infantry Regiment on 1 March 1785. He took part in the Russo-Swedish War in 1788-1790, and joined the Velikii Lutsk Infantry Regiment on 26 May 1789, rising to captain on 11 July of the same year. He served in Poland in 1794, and transferred as a major to the Ryazan Musketeer Regiment on 9 April 1799. Promoted to lieutenant colonel on 18 December 1804, he served with the 14th Division in Poland in 1806-1807, distinguishing himself at Pultusk, Eylau (Order of St. Vladimir, 4th class), Heilsberg, and Friedland (wounded in the left leg). He briefly served as the Commandant of Koenigsberg in 1807, earning the Order of St. Anna (2nd class) and promotion to colonel on 24 December 1807. After taking part in the Russo-Swedish War in 1808-1809, Pantzerbiter became chef of the Aleksapol Musketeer Regiment on 31 October 1810.

During the 1812 Campaign, Pantzerbiter commanded the 2nd Brigade of the 12th Division in the 7th Corps and fought at Saltanovka (Moghilev, wounded), Smolensk, Borodino (wounded in the left hand, received the Order of St. George, 4th class, 4 January 1813), Maloyaroslavets (golden sword), and Krasnyi (decorated with the Order of St. Anna, 2nd class, with diamonds). He served at Modlin in 1813, and at Mainz and Paris in 1814. He returned to France during the Hundred Days in 1815, and was promoted to major general on 11 September of that year. After the war, Pantzerbiter served in the 12th Division until retiring in early 1816.

PAPKOV, Peter Afanasievich (b. 1722 — d. 30 May 1853) was born to a noble family from the Ekaterinoslavl *gubernia*. He enlisted as a vakhmistr in the Taganrog Dragoon Regiment on 12 January 1784, and transferred as a cadet to the Astrakhan Dragoon Regiment in 1787. In January 1790, he initially joined the Tiflis Musketeer Regiment, but later transferred as a shtyk junker to the 2nd Fusilier Regiment two months later. He served in the Caucasus in 171-1795, distinguishing himself at Anapa, for which he earned the rank of sub-lieutenant. In 1796, Papkov participated in the Persian Campaign, fighting at Derbent, Baku, and Shemakha. He rose to lieutenant on 19 June 1796, to staff captain in 1797, and finally to captain in 1798.

After a brief retirement in late 1798, Papkov joined the Life Guard Artillery Battalion in May 1799, and received the Order of St. John of Jerusalem on 15 August 1800, followed by promotion to colonel on 20 October 1800. Three years later, he took command of the artillery pontoon companies, which were later converted to the Pontoon Artillery Regiment. In 1806, he commanded the 14th Artillery Brigade in Poland, fighting at Guttstadt, Heilsberg, and Friedland, for which he received the Prussian Pour le Merite and promotion to major general in December 1807.

In 1808, Papkov left the army and became the Ober-Ceremonymeister of St. Petersburg, receiving the Order of St. George (3rd class). Beginning in 1810, he served on various civil positions in Taganrog, Rostov, and Mariupol before dying on 30 May 1853.

His brother **PAPKOV, Polikarp Afanasievich** (b. 1756 — d. 1817) studied in the Artillery and Engineer Cadet Corps and began service in the 2nd Fusilier Regiment in November 1775. He served in the Crimea from 1776-1779, and in the Caucasus from 1780-1796, serving in the garrisons of Mozdok, Kizlyar, and Perevolochensk. He served with the 1st Fusilier Regiment during the Persian campaign of 1796, fighting at Derbent (wounded in the left hand) and Baku. Transferring to the 7th Artillery Regiment in February 1797, he was promoted to a lieutenant colonel in 1798, and to colonel in 1799. In 1800, he took command of the Moscow Artillery Garrison, and the following year was appointed to the Moscow Artillery Depot. Seven years later, he rose to major general but left the military in 1810.

PARADOVSKY, Philip Osipovich commanded the Mariupol Hussar Regiment between 10 April 1806 and 20 March 1810. He served with the 9th Division in Essen I's corps in Poland in 1806-1807. During the 1812-1813 Campaign, he served as chef of the Lifland Dragoon (later Horse Jager) Regiment, and was mortally wounded at the Katzbach on 26 August 1813.

PASKEVICH, Ivan Fedorovich (b. 19 May 1782, Poltava — d. 1 February 1856, Warsaw) was born to a noble family from the Poltava *gubernia*. He began service as a kamer page at the Imperial Court in 1799, and transferred as a lieutenant to the Life Guard Preobrazhensk Regiment on 17 October 1800. He also received the rank of flügel adjutant to Emperor Paul. Under Emperor Alexander, Paskevich took an indefinite furlough, returning to the army in 1805. He served in the headquarters of the Russian army in the Danubian Principalities during the Russo-Turkish War in 1806-1812, fighting at Giurgiu (Order of St. Vladimir, 4th class) and Ismail (golden sword) in 1807. He served on diplomatic missions to Constantinople in 1808-1809.

Promoted to captain in January 1808, Paskevich distinguished himself at Braila in May 1809, where he was wounded in the head. After recuperating, he served at Macin, Constanta (Kustendji), Rassevat, Silistra, and Tataritsa (Order of St. Anna, 2nd class) in 1809. He rose to colonel and commander of the Vitebsk Musketeer Regiment on 21 June 1809. In 1810, Paskevich fought at Bazardjik (golden cross and the Order of St. Vladimir, 3rd class), Varna (Order of St. George, 4th class, 19 July 1810) and Batin, for which he was promoted to major general on 10 December 1810. The following year, he garnered the Order of St. George (3rd class, 11 February 1811) for his conduct at Lovchea and became chef of the Orel Musketeer Regiment on 29 January 1811.

In 1812, Paskevich took command of the 26th Infantry Division on 13 June and participated in Prince Bagration's retreat, distinguishing himself at the battle of Moghilev against Marshal Louis Davout. Paskevich served at Smolensk, Kolotsk, Borodino (Order of St. Anna, 1st class), Maloyaroslavets, Vyazma, and Krasnyi, garnering the Order of St. Vladimir (2nd class). In 1813, he took part in the actions at Modlin, Pirna, Dohna, Dresden, and Leipzig, for which he received promotion to lieutenant general on 20 October 1813.

In 1814, Paskevich took command of the 2nd Grenadier Division on 2 February and fought at Laon, Arcis sur Aube and Paris, for which he was decorated with the Order of St. Alexander of Neva. He returned to France during the Hundred Days in 1815. After the war, he took command of the 2nd Guard Infantry Division on 26 November 1817, and attended Grand Duke Mikhail beginning on 15 July 1819. He became commander of the 1st Guard Infantry Division on 23 May 1821, and received the rank of adjutant general on 24 December 1824.

Paskevich eventually became one of closest associates of Emperor Nicholas I, who called Paskevich "Father General." After becoming commander of the 1st Corps on 11 March 1825, Paskevich rose to general of infantry on 3 September 1826, and led troops of the Independent Caucasus Corps. He became the Commander-in-Chief of the Russian troops in the Caucasus on 9 April 1827. During the Russo-Persian War in 1827, he captured the fortress of Yerivan (Order of St. George, 2nd class, 10 November 1827), and the title of Prince of Yerivan [*kniaz Erivanskii*] in 1828. For the victory at Elisavetpol, he was awarded a golden sword with diamonds and laurels, inscribed "For the Defeat of the Persians at Elisavetpol." By the end of the war, Paskevich forced the Persians to cede the provinces of Nakhichevan and Yerivan to Russia. He became chef of the Shirvan Infantry Regiment on 29 August 1828, which was later renamed "Paskevich's Infantry Regiment" on 25 September of the same year.

During the Russo-Turkish War of 1828–29, Paskevich captured several strategic Turkish fortresses, including the fortress of Erzerum (Order of St. George, 1st class, 8 August 1829). Promoted to field marshal on 4 October 1829, he commanded the Russian army against the Polish insurgents in 1831 and captured Warsaw, where he was bruised in the left shoulder by enemy fire. For his victory, Paskevich was conferred the title of Illustrious Prince of Warsaw [*Svetleishii kniaz Warshavskii*] on 16 September 1831. He served as the Viceroy of Poland from 1832 to 1856=, and became General Inspector of all Russian infantry on 14 April 1833.

Over the next twenty years, Paskevich served as chef of several regiments that were renamed after him. He was appointed chef of the Orel Jager Regiment (renamed "Paskevich's Jager Regiment") on 22 September 1835, chef of the Aleksandria Hussar Regiment (renamed "Paskevich's Hussar Regiment") on 13 September 1845, chef of the Novorosiisk Dragoon Regiment (renamed "Paskevich's Dragoon Regiment") on 27 September 1852. The previous names of these units were restored after Paskevich's death, except for the Orel Jager Regiment, which retained Paskevich's name. Paskevich also served as chef of the 1st Prussian Infantry Regiment and the 37th Hungarian Infantry Regiment.

When the Austrian Emperor requested military assistance from Russia during the revolutions of 1848, Paskevich commanded the Russian troops that invaded Hungary in June 1849. He defeated the Hungarians in several engagements and forced them to surrender at Világos on 13 August 1849. During the Crimean War, Paskevich briefly led the Russian armies in the Danubian Principalities from April through June 1854. However, he was relieved of command after being defeated by the Turks at Silistra on 8 June 1854.

Paskevich remains one of the most decorated Russian officers in history. During his outstanding career, he garnered the Russian Orders of St. Andrew the First Called with diamonds, St. Vladimir (1st class), St. Alexander of Neva with diamonds, St. Anna (1st class) with diamonds, and the Polish Order of the White Eagle. Foreign decorations included the Prussian Orders of Red and Black Eagles with diamonds, the Austrian Orders of St. Stephan with diamonds and Maria Theresa (1st class), the Neapolitan Order of St. Ferdinand and Military Merit, the Bavarian Order of Maximilian Joseph, the Saxe-Weimar Order of the White Hawk, the Parma Order of St. Louis, the Württemberg Order of Military Merit, the Danish Order of the Elephant, the Dutch Order of Wilhelm (1st class), the Persian Order of the Lion and the Sun, and the Turkish Order of the Crescent. Paskevich also received a golden sword with diamond, a Prussian golden sword with diamonds, and a medal inscribed "For XLV Years of Distinguished Service."

Paskevich's brother, **PASKEVICH, Stepan Fedorovich** (b. 1785 — d. 21 April 1840) studied in the Page Corps and began service as a lieutenant in the Fanagoria Grenadier Regiment on 22 December 1803. He participated in the 1805 Campaign and was wounded in the right hand at Austerlitz on December 2. Promoted to staff-captain in 1806, he served in the Danubian Principalities in 1806-1812, distinguishing himself at Braila (Order of St. Anna, 4th class), Bazardjik (golden cross and the Order of St. Vladimir, 4th class, and the Order of St. Anna, 2nd class).

On 26 June 1810, Paskevich transferred as a captain to the Life Guard Jager Regiment and fought at Batin, for which he was decorated with the Order of St. George (4th class). In 1812, Paskevich transferred as a lieutenant colonel to the Orel Infantry Regiment, and with that outfit fought at Smolensk, Borodino, Tarutino, and Maloyaroslavets. In 1813, he distinguished himself at Magdeburg before retiring on 27 December of the same year. He returned to the army with the rank of colonel in February 1816. Paskevich later left the army and held various civil positions, including the Governor of Tambov (1831-1832), Kursk (1834-1835), and Vladimir (1835-1836) *gubernia*s.

PASSEK, Peter Petrovich (b. 23 March 1779 — d. 12 May 1825) was born to a noble family from the Smolensk *gubernia*. He enlisted as a sergeant in the Life Guard Preobrazhensk Regiment in 1782, and transferred as a lieutenant to the Smolensk Dragoon Regiment on 12 January 1790. He served in Poland in 1792-1794, garnering the rank of second major and a golden cross for his service at Praga. He transferred as a lieutenant colonel to the Moscow Grenadier Regiment on 7 August 1797. The following year, he rose to a colonel on 24 April, and took command of the Moscow Grenadier Regiment on 28 July 1798.

During the 1799 Campaign in Italy, Passek fought on the Adda River and was wounded in the right leg at Bassignana. Promoted to major general on 23 June 1799, he became chef of the Kiev Grenadier Regiment on the same day. Four years later, he became commander of this unit on 18 August 1803. Passek took a discharge on 27 November 1804, but returned to the army on 15 January 1807, taking command of a brigade in the 5th Division. He took part in the battles at Eylau (golden cross), Lomitten, Guttstadt, and Heilsberg, where he was wounded in the right shoulder and earned a golden sword with diamonds. Passek became chef of the Moghilev Musketeer Regiment on 7 October 1807, and took another discharge on 10 December 1807. He returned to the service on 1 August 1812, joining the Smolensk *opolchenye*.

During the 1812 Campaign, Passek fought the French at Smolensk, Borodino, Tarutino, Maloyaroslavets, Vyazma, Krasnyi, garnering the Order of St. Anna (1st class). In 1813, he briefly commanded the Smolensk *opolchenye* before joining Miloradovich's staff. He fought at Lutzen and took a severe wound in the chest at Bautzen. He retired on 28 May 1815, and died on 12 May 1825.

PATKULL, Vladimir Grigorievich (b. 21 November 1783 — date of death unclear) enlisted as a sub-ensign in the Life Guard Semeyonovsk Regiment in September 1799. Promoted to ensign in 1802, he took part in the 1805-1807 campaigns, fighting at Austerlitz, Guttstadt, Heilsberg, and Friedland (wounded in the leg, Order of St. Vladimir, 4th class). Made colonel on 19 November 1811, he served as a commanding officer of the Koporsk Infantry Regiment in 1812, fighting at Smolensk (Order of St. George, 4th class) and Borodino (wounded in the crotch, garnered the Order of St. Vladimir, 3rd class). After recuperating, he distinguished himself at Kulm (golden sword, the Prussian Iron Cross, and the Pour le Merite) and Leipzig.

In 1814, Patkull participated in the battle for Paris. He became a major general on 11 September 1816, and later led the 1st Brigade of the 1st Grenadier Division. He attended the Crown Prince of Weimar in 1824-1825, before taking command of the 2nd Guard Infantry Brigade. In 1828, he became the Commandant of Revel and rose to a lieutenant general on 22 April 1832. Promoted to general of infantry on 18 December 1848, he received the Order of St. Alexander of Neva on 12 July 1852.

PATTON, Alexander Yakovlevich (b. 1761 — d. 24 January 1815) descended from an Austrian noble family settled in Russia. He enlisted as a private in the Life Guard Preobrazhensk Regiment on 12 January 1774, and transferred as a captain to the Sofia Infantry Regiment on 12 January 1787. He later served in the 2nd Marine Regiment and the Rochensalmi Garrison Regiment until 29 January 1807, when he took command of the Neva Musketeer Regiment. Promoted to colonel on 24 December 1807, Patton served in the 21st Division during the Russo-Swedish War in 1808-1809, taking part in the actions at Tavastheus, Bjorneborg, and Abo. He became chef of the Tula Musketeer Regiment on 20 April 1809.

During the 1812 Campaign, Patton served with the 2nd Brigade of the 14th Division in the 1st Corps and took part in the actions at Polotsk, Smolnya (wounded in the right hand, promoted to major general on 8 June 1813, with seniority dating from 15 January 1813), and on the Berezina. In 1813, he participated in the combats at Pillau, Danzig, Wittenberg, Launau, and Leipzig. During the invasion of France, he commanded the 2nd Brigade of the 14th Division, fighting at Craonne and Paris. After the war, he contracted a sudden illness and died at his estate Anikshty in the Vilna *gubernia* on 24 January 1815.

PAULUCCI, Philipp (Filippo) Osipovich (b. 1779, Modena — d. 6 February 1849, Nice) was born to an Italian family of marquises in Modena. After studying in a Jesuit college, he began service in the Piedmontese army and fought the French in 1794. During Napoleon Bonaparte's victorious campaigns in 1796-1797,

Paulucci joined the Austrian army. In 1801-1806, he served in Naples, briefly joining the French army in late 1806. On 28 March 1807, he entered Russian service as a colonel in the Imperial Retinue. The same year, he was appointed an adjutant to General Ivan Michelson in the Danubian Principalities. He served in Isaev's detachment in Serbia, and successfully negotiated with the Serbian leader Karadjordje.

In 1808-1809, Paulucci participated in the Russo-Swedish War in Finland, serving as the Chief of Staff of the 6th Division. He was promoted to major general on 3 August 1808. In 1810, he was appointed the Chief of Staff of the Independent Georgian Corps and fought the Turks in southern Georgia. For his victory at Akhalkalaki, he was promoted to lieutenant general on 3 November 1810. He served as the Commander-in-Chief of the Russian troops in Georgia, and made several successful incursions in Daghestan, for which he was decorated with the Order of St. George (3rd class) on 7 May 1812.

Paulucci became adjutant general on 29 July 1812, with seniority dating from 28 February 1812. Later that year, Paulucci was appointed the Chief of Staff of the 3rd Reserve Army of Observation, and thereafter of the 1st Western Army on 3 July. However, Paulucci soon quarelled with Barclay de Tolly and was forced to resign just eight days later. He was appointed Military Governor of Riga on 29 October 1812, and two months later helped negotiate the Taurrogen Convention with the Prussian troops, and went on to capture Memel.

After the war, Paulucci served as the Governor General of the Lifland, Courland, and Estland *gubernia*s between 1812 and 1830. He directed the reconstruction in the Baltic provinces and made great efforts to restore the suburbs of Riga, which burned down in 1812. During Paulucci's time, work was begun on the landscaping of the Vermanes Park, street lighting, and the numbering of buildings. For his service, Paulucci was decorated with the Order of St. Vladimir (2nd class) and received promotion to general of infantry on 24 December 1823. He resigned from the positions on 12 January 1830, and returned to Sardinia-Piedmont, where he eventually rose to become Governor of Genoa and Inspector General of the Sardinian army.

PESTEL, Andrey Borisovich (b. 1779 — d. 12 November 1863) began service as a sergeant in the Life Guard Preobrazhensk Regiment in 1781, rising to a captain in January 1793. He transferred as a major to the 2nd Moscow Artillery Battalion in November 1798, before joining the Tenginsk Infantry Regiment on 24 November 1800. Promoted to colonel on 4 September 1806, he took command of the Tenginsk Musketeer Regiment on 15 August 1806, and served with the 4th Division in Poland in 1806-1807, receiving the Order of St. Vladimir (4th class) for his actions at Eylau. He served with his regiment in Finland in 1808-1809, where he was wounded at Idensalmi (golden sword).

Pestel became chef of the Tiflis Infantry Regiment on 24 March 1812, and took part in the operations against the Persians in Georgia and Armenia in 1812-1813 (Order of St. Anna, 2nd class). He became commander of the Tiflis Infantry Regiment on 4 July 1815, before rising to major general and commander of the 2nd Brigade of the 20th Division on 11 September 1816. In 1817-1819, he participated in the operations against the mountaineers in Daghestan. Pestel took an indefinite furlough to recuperate in May 1820, and retired in 1834.

PETROVSKY, Mikhail Andreyevich (b. 1764 — d. 21 March 1828, Moscow) was born to a noble family from the Kiev *gubernia*. After studying in the Kiev Seminary and the University of Moscow, he began service as a secretary in the administration of the Novgorod *gubernia* in 1786. Four year later, he enlisted as an ensign in the Tobolsk Infantry Regiment on 15 December 1790, and later transferred to the Pskov Dragoon Regiment. He served in Poland in 1792-1794, distinguishing himself at Maciejowice (golden sword) and Praga (golden cross).

In December 1796, Petrovsky transferred as a major to the His Majesty's Leib-Cuirassier regiment and served as an adjutant to Field

Marshal Nikolay Saltykov. Promoted to colonel on 11 August 1799, he was appointed to the Commissariat in February 1800. Petrovsky became a major general on 18 June 1804, and directed the Moscow Commissariat from 1807-1811.

During the 1812 Campaign, he served as the General-krigs-Commissar of the 1st Western Army, and established several military hospitals for the sick and wounded. In 1813, he became the Intendant General of the Army of Poland, participating in the military operations in Saxony. In 1814, he took part in the siege of Hamburg. Petrovsky retired on 12 October 1816.

PEYKER, Alexander Emmanuilovich (b. 8 December 1776, Derpt — d. 19 July 1834, Narva) was born to a noble family from the Lifland *gubernia*. After studying at a private boarding school, he enlisted as a corporal in the 5th Marine Battalion [*flotskii batalion*] in December 1790. In the summer of 1793, he prevented the escape of the prisoners in Kronstadt and was appointed as a sub-ensign to the Gatchina Troops. He rose to portupei-ensign in 1794, to sub-lieutenant in the Life Guard Semeyonovsk Regiment in late 1797, to staff captain in 1799, to captain in 1801, and finally to colonel on 19 March 1805. During his service, he was decorated with the Order of St. John of Jerusalem in 1800, and with the Order of St Anna (3rd class) in 1804.

In early 1806, Peyker transferred to the 1st Marine Regiment and became commander of this unit on 27 January 1807. On 3 February 1810, he became chef of the 2nd Marine Regiment and trained the crews of the Baltic Sea Fleet, for which he received the Order of St. Vladimir (4th class). In early 1812, he served with the 1st Brigade of the 25th Division in Finland. During the 1812 Campaign, Peyker was initially dispatched to Gatchina and later trained the St. Petersburg and Novgorod *opolchenye*s. He reinforced the 1st Corps in December 1812, and during the 1813-1814 Campaigns, took part in the sieges of Pillau and Danzig. He successfully repulsed several French sorties at Danzig, for which he was promoted to major general on 27 September 1813, and earned the Orders of St. Anna (2nd class) and St. Vladimir (3rd class), and a golden sword.

After the war, Peyker commanded a brigade comprised of the 1st and 2nd Marine Regiments, earning an allowance of 5,000 rubles in 1816, a twelve-year rent in 1818, the Order of St. Anna (1st class) in 1819, and an allowance of 40,000 rubles in 1823. He took command of the 1st Division on 23 May 1824, and rose to lieutenant general on 3 September 1826. Two years later, he was appointed the Commandant of Narva on 23 February 1828.

PHULL, Karl Ludwig August (b. 1757 — d. 25 April 1826) was born to a prominent Württemberg noble family. He began service in the Württemberg army in 1774, and transferred as a lieutenant to the Prussian army in 1779. Beginning in 1781, Phull served in the Prussian General Staff and participated in the campaigns against France. After the Prussian debacle in 1806, he entered Russian service on 8 January 1807, receiving the rank of major general.

Promoted to lieutenant general on 11 September 1809, he served at the Russian main headquarters in 1810-1811, and prepared a strategic plan of the defense of Russia in case of a French invasion, which is known as "the Drissa Plan." This plan required the 1st Western Army to retreat to a fortified camp and pin down the French forces there, while the 2nd Western Army operated against the enemy flanks and rear. Despite major flaws in this strategy, Emperor Alexander, who completely trusted Phull, ordered construction of the fortified camp at Drissa—despite the opposition of many Russian senior officers. When Napoleon invaded, triggering the start of the 1812 Campaign, Alexander realized the potential dangers of deploying his army at Drissa and allowed General Barclay de Tolly to withdraw deeper into Russia. Phull was recalled to St. Petersburg and did not participate in any military decision-making during the decisive 1813-1814 Campaigns. After the war, he was appointed the Russian envoy to Holland, where he served before retiring in May 1821.

PILLAR, Yegor Maksimovich (George Ludwig) (b. 30 March 1767 — d. 20 November 1830, Kiriya) was born to a noble family from the Estland *gubernia*. He enlisted as a sub-ensign in the Bombardier Regiment on 16 May 1780, and transferred as a sub-lieutenant to the Narva Infantry Regiment on 24 March 1785. Three years later, he joined the Vyborg Infantry Regiment on 29 March 1788. He took part in the Russo-Swedish War in 1788-1790, and Field Marshal Suvorov's campaign in Italy and Switzerland in 1799.

Taking command of the Vyborg Musketeer Regiment on 8 April 1803, Pillar fought at Austerlitz on 2 December 1805, garnering the Order of St. George (4th class, 9 April 1807). He served with the 8th Division in Poland in 1806-1807, distinguishing himself at Pultusk and Eylau. He rose to colonel and chef of the Vilna Musketeer Regiment on 2 February 1809. In 1809-1811, he served in the Danubian Principalities, fighting at Shumla, Ruse, Silistra, and Bazardjik. Pillar became chef of the 34th Jager Regiment on 31 October 1810. During the 1812 Campaign, he served with the 3rd Brigade of the 4th Division of the 2nd Corps, and fought at Vitebsk, Smolensk, Borodino (ascended to major general on 3 December 1812 with seniority dating from 7 September 1812), and Tarutino. In 1813, he took part in the actions at Lutzen, Bautzen, and Leipzig, garnering the Order of St. George (3rd class) on 10 November 1813. In 1814, he led the 17th Division and distinguished himself at Paris. After the war, Pillar led the 2nd Brigade of the 16th Division before retiring on 20 November 1817.

PIROGOV, Ippolit Ivanovich (b. 1776 — date of death unclear) was born to a noble family from the Kazan *gubernia*. After studying in the Artillery and Engineer Cadet Corps, he began service as a shtyk-junker in the 1st Bombardier Regiment on 16 August 1791. In 1792-1794, he served in Poland, fighting at Nesvizh and Grodno. During the 1806-1807 Campaigns in Poland, he distinguished himself at Pultusk (Order of St. Vladimir, 4th class), Eylau (golden cross), Guttstadt, and Heilsberg, where he was wounded in the right leg.

In 1808-1812, Pirogov served in Moscow before becoming adjutant to Major General Karl Löwenstern. He took part in the actions at Maloyaroslavets, Krasnyi, and on the Berezina. The following year, he served at Kalisch before receiving assignment to organize reserve artillery companies in the Duchy of Poland. In late 1813, he took command of the 10th Horse Artillery Company and was wounded at Dresden. After recuperating, he directed an artillery factory and was promoted to colonel on 14 May 1814.

In 1815, he returned to France during the Hundred Days, commanding the artillery of the Russian Occupation Corps. After returning to Russia, Pirogov supervised the reserve artillery parks in 1818-1822. He later led the reserve artillery in the 1st Army and served as the Intendant General of the 1st Army during the Russo-Turkish War of 1828-1829. Promoted to lieutenant general on 26 April 1829, Pirogov took part in the suppression of the Polish Uprising in 1831. He retired because of poor health on 21 September 1831.

PISAREV, Alexander Alexandrovich (27 August 1780 — d. 6 July 1848) was born to a noble family from the Moscow *gubernia*. After studying in the Infantry Cadet Corps, he began service as a sub-lieutenant in the Life Guard Semeyonovsk Regiment on 13 April 1797. He distinguished himself at Austerlitz on 2 December 1805, for which he later received the rank of captain. In 1807, Pisarev served at Heilsberg and Friedland, earning promotion to colonel on 29 August 1807. During the 1812 Campaign, he served in the 1st Brigade of the Guard Infantry Division of the 5th Reserve Corps, fighting at Borodino, Maloyaroslavets, and Krasnyi. Pisarev took command of the Kiev Grenadier Regiment on 2 February 1813, and participated in the battle at Lutzen in May. For his courage, he was later promoted to major general on 27 September 1813, with seniority dating from 2 May 1813.

Pisarev took command of a brigade in the 2nd Grenadier Division and fought at Bautzen (Order of St. George, 4th class, 21 May 1813) and Leipzig (wounded in the right leg). In 1814, he served at Arcis sur Aube and Paris, earning the Order of St. George (3rd class) on 17 May 1814. He resigned from the command because of poor health on 27 August 1815. After recuperating, he led the 10th Division before retiring on 12 January 1823.

Pisarev occupied various civil positions for the next twenty years and served in the Imperial Senate and the Council of the Kingdom of Poland, rising to a privy counsellor. On 6 April 1840, he returned to military service with the rank of lieutenant general. The same day, he was appointed the Military Governor of Warsaw. He retired on 27 July 1847 and died a year later.

PLATOV, Matvei Ivanovich (b. 19 August 1753, Pribilyanskoe — d. 15 January 1818, Epanchitskoe) was born to a Don Cossack family. He began service in the Don Cossack Chancellery in 1766, becoming an esaul in 1769. Platov distinguished himself in the campaign against the Crimean Tatars in 1771, and took command of a Cossack regiment in 1772. In 1774-1784, he served in the Kuban Valley, Chechnya, and Daghestan. During the Russo-Turkish War of 1787-1791, he fought at Ochakov (Order of St. George, 4th class, 25 April 1789), Akkerman, Bender, Kaushani (promoted to brigadier), and Ismail (Order of St. George, 3rd class, 5 April 1791). For his conduct, he was appointed ataman of the Ekaterinoslavl and Chuguev Cossacks. On 12 January 1793, Platov received promotion to major general. In 1796, he participated in the Persian Campaign along the Caspian Sea, receiving the Order of St. Vladimir (3rd class) and a golden sword for courage.

Misled by Emperor Paul's courtiers, Platov fell out of favor with the emperor on 22 May 1797, and was exiled him to Kostroma before he changed his mind and detained him in the Petropavlovsk Fortress. After verifying Platov's innocence, Paul pardoned him and awarded him the Commander Cross of the Order of St. John of Jerusalem. In 1800, Platov took part in the expedition to India, though his Cossacks got only as far as Orenburg. Platov became a lieutenant general and the campaign ataman [*pokhodnii ataman*] of the Don Cossacks on 27 September 1801. He began the reorganization of the Don Host and transferred the Cossack capital to Novocherkask.

During the 1806-1807 Campaigns in Poland, Platov commanded a Cossack corps, fighting in numerous rearguard actions and in the battles at Eylau, Guttstadt, and Friedland, garnering the Orders of St. George (2nd class, 4 December 1807), St. Alexander of Neva, and the Prussian Orders of the Black and Red Eagles. In 1808-1809, he fought the Turks in the Danube Valley, distinguishing himself at Girsov, Rassevat, Tataritsa, and Silistra, for which he received the Order of St. Vladimir (1st class) and the rank of general of cavalry on 11 October 1809.

Platov returned to the Don Host and arranged the local Cossack administration. In 1812, he commanded the Cossack Corps and supported General Bagration's 2nd Western Army. He defeated the French at Korelichi, Mir, and Romanovo, and covered Bagration's flanking movement at Moghilev. During the Russian offensive at Smolensk, Platov fought at Molevo Boloto (Inkovo). At Borodino, he led a cavalry movement against the French left flank, but failed to accomplish his assigned mission (and thus was not awarded after the battle). Ironically, the attack had a dramatic effect on Napoleon's psyche, who worried about his flank and held back the French Imperial Guard. Later that year, Platov particularly distinguished himself while leading the Cossack troops during the French retreat. For his service, Platov was conferred the title of count of the Russian Empire on 10 January 1813. He led the Cossacks throughout the 1813-1814 Campaigns in Saxony and France.

After the war, Platov accompanied Emperor Alexander to London, where he was accepted with great honors. The city presented Platov with a golden sword, and the University of Oxford conferred a honorary doctoral degree to him. Returning to Russia, Platov spent the next couple of years at Novocherkask, governing the Don Host. He died on 15 January 1818, at Epachinskoe, near Taganrog, and was initially buried in the Ascension Cathedral in Novocherkask. His remains were transferred to the Cossack Host Cathedral in Novocherkask in October 1911.

POLETAEV, Ivan Ivanovich (1759 — d. 29 October 1813, Leipzig) was born to a noble Russian family. He enlisted in the 1st Fusilier Regiment on 29 March 1770, and rose to a sub-lieutenant on 2 May 1780. During the Russo-Turkish War in 1787-1791, he served at Kinburn, Killia, Ismail (golden cross), and Macin. In 1793-1794, he fought the Poles, rising to the rank of colonel on 22 September 1797. Promoted to major general on 29 March 1798, he commanded artillery in the garrison of Rochensalmi in Finland before taking a discharge on 21 September 1799. Poletaev returned to the Moscow Artillery Depot on 12 April 1801, where he served for seven years before retiring on 15

April 1808. He volunteered for service in late 1812, and joined the Russian army in 1813, taking part in the operations in Bohemia. Poletaev was mortally wounded during the battle of Liepzig, and died on 29 October 1813.

POLIVANOV, Nikolay Petrovich (b. 12 February 1771 — d. 17 April 1839) began service as a sub-ensign in the Life Guard Preobrazhensk Regiment in 1787, and participated in the Russo-Swedish War in early 1789. The same year, he transferred to the Danubian Principalities, where he fought the Turks at Bender, Killia, and Ismail. In 1792-1794, he served in Poland, taking part in the actions at Kobryn, Krupchitse, Brest, and Praga. Promoted to lieutenant colonel in 1798, he joined the Sumsk Hussar Regiment and fought in the 1799 Campaign in Switzerland, distinguishing himself at Zurich, where he negotiated the cease fire with Andre Masséna. For these actions, Polivanov was decorated with the Prussian Pour le Merite and the Russian Order of St. Vladimir. During his return to Russia in late 1799, Polivanov negotiated with Bavarian authorities for the transit of the Russian army through the Bavarian territories. After retiring in 1802, he became an adjutant to General Rimsky-Korsakov the following year, but took another discharge on 31 January 1805. During the 1806-1807 Campaigns, Polivanov organized and led a brigade of the Pokrov *opolchenye*. He commanded the entire Pokrov *opolchenye* in 1812-1813.

POLIVANOV, Yuri Ignatievich (b. 1751 — d. 16 January 1813) was born to a noble family from the Saratov *gubernia*. He studied in the Infantry Cadet Corps and began service as a cornet in the Life Guard Horse Regiment on 27 February 1773. Promoted to sub-lieutenant on 25 March 1774, he rose to rotmistr on 12 January 1781, and transferred as a colonel to the Elisavetgrad Light Horse Regiment on 28 April 1781. During the Russo-Turkish War in 1787-1791, he distinguished himself at Ochakov (golden cross) in 1788. He joined the Chernigov Carabinier Regiment, serving at Rimnic (Order of St. George, 4th class), Ismail (golden cross and rank of brigadier), and Macin (Order of St. Vladimir, 3rd class).

Polivanov went on to serve in Poland in 1794, fighting at Brest, Kobylka (wounded), and Praga, where he was wounded and rewarded with both a golden snuffbox with diamonds on 16 November 1794, and promotion to major general on 6 December 1794. He became chef of the Ingermanland Dragoon Regiment on 14 December 1796, but took a discharge on 1 October 1797. He returned to the army three years later, serving in the Chernigov Dragoon Regiment. Polivanov led a cavalry brigade in 1805, distinguishing himself at Wischau and Austerlitz, where he was wounded in the leg. He retired again in early 1806.

During the 1812 Campaign, he served with the Kaluga *opolchenye* at Maloyaroslavets, Vyazma, Krasnyi (Order of St. Anna, 1st class, with diamonds), and Studenka on 27 November, where he was mortally wounded with a shot in the chest. He lingered for many weeks before expiring on 16 January 1813, and was buried in the local church in the village of Nikolsk in Maloyaroslavets *uezd*. Polivanov's remains were finally laid to rest at the memorial park of the 1812 Campaign in Maloyaroslavets in October 1996.

POLL, Ivan Lavrentievich (Johann Ludwig) (b. 1768, Waxholm — d. 1 May 1840, Chernyshi, Kiev *gubernia*) was born to a noble family from the Lifland *gubernia*. He enlisted as a furier in the Life Guard Preobrazhensk Regiment on 24 February 1781, and transferred as an ensign to the Keksholm (Kexholm) Infantry Regiment on 12 January 1783. Poll joined the Kiev Grenadier Regiment as a sub-lieutenant on 12 January 1786, and became a captain in the Tavrida Grenadier Regiment on 30 November 1791. He finally transferred to the Seversk Carabinier Regiment on 21 January 1794, and took part in the operations in Poland in 1794, distinguishing himself at Khelmy and Slonim (promoted to second major). Poll was bumped up again to major in December 1796, granted the Order of St. Anna (3rd class), and later promoted to lieutenant colonel on 22 October 1799, and to colonel on 27 October 1800. He joined the Novorossiisk Dragoon Regiment on 2 June 1803.

During the 1805 Campaign, Poll's regiment was sent to reinforce Kutuzov's army, but arrived after the Allies were defeated at Austerlitz on 2 December. In 1806, Poll served with the 9th Division during the opening moves of the Russo-Turkish War of 1806-1812, fighting at Khotin. The division was dispatched to reinforce the Russian army in Poland, and Poll took part in the minor action near Stanislavov on the Skhva River on 16 February 1807. He took command of the Novorossiisk Dragoon Regiment on 25 September 1807, and the following year was appointed chef of the Kargopol Dragoon Regiment on 17 November 1808.

During the 1812 Campaign, Poll served with the 7th Brigade of the 2nd Cavalry Division in the 2nd Reserve Cavalry Corps. He did not participate in any actions during the Russian retreat to Moscow, and served in the main headquarters at the battle of Borodino. During the French retreat, Poll finally engaged the French at Vyazma (promoted to major general on 30 July 1813, with seniority dating from 4 November 1812), and Krasnyi (Order of St. George (3rd class, 15 June 1813).

In the spring of 1813, Poll served under Miloradovich at Dresden, Bautzen, Reichenbach, Gorlitz, and Lobau, garnering the Order of St. Vladimir (3rd class) and the Prussian Pour le Merite. In September, he fought again at Lobau and then at the village of Nider-Putzk, for which he was decorated with the Prussian Order of Red Eagle (2nd class) and his second Order of St. Vladimir (3rd class). In October, Poll participated in the Battle of Leipzig, for which he received an Imperial letter of gratitude. After serving at Mainz in January 1814, he joined Langeron's corps, fighting at Le Fère Champenoise (Order of St. Anna, 1st class) and Neuilly (near Paris). After the war, he commanded the 2nd Brigade of the 1st Dragoon Division before becoming commander of the 2nd Brigade of the 4th Dragoon Division on 16 January 1817.

Poll retired on 10 January 1822, and spent the next eighteen years at his estate of Chernyshi in the Kiev *gubernia*, where he died on 1 May 1840.

POLTORATSKY, Constantine Markovich (b. 1782 — d. 27 March 1858) was born to a noble family from the Chernigov *gubernia*. He enlisted as a furier in the Life Guard Semeyonovsk Regiment in 1784 at the age of two, and rose to ensign in 1798. Promoted to a regimental adjutant, he took part in the battle of Austerlitz in 1805 (Order of St. Anna, 4th class, and the rank of staff captain). Two years later, aged 25, he fought at Heilsberg and Friedland, garnering the Order of St. Vladimir (4th class) and a promotion to captain. Promoted again to colonel on 1 June 1808, he served in the Army of Danube in 1810, distinguishing himself at Batin,

Silistra, Lovchea (golden sword), and in Serbia (Order of St. Vladimir, 3rd class). He became chef of the Neyshlodt Infantry Regiment on 27 May 1811. Two years later, Poltoratsky was appointed chef of the Tiflis Infantry Regiment on 22 January 1812, but just two months later became chef of the Nasheburg Infantry Regiment on 24 March.

During the 1812 Campaign, Poltoratsky served with the 1st Brigade of the 9th Division in the 3rd Reserve Army of Observation, distinguishing himself at Kobryn and Gorodechnya (Order of St. George, 4th class, 4 December 1812). In 1813, he led a brigade comprised of the Nasheburg and Apsheron Infantry Regiments at Thorn (Order of St. Anna, 2nd class), Koenigswartha (promoted to major general on 27 September 1813, with seniority dating from 19 May 1813), and Leipzig (Order of Anna, 2nd class, with diamonds, the Prussian Order of Red Eagle, and the Swedish Order of the Sword). In 1814, he participated in the combats at Brienne, La Rothière, and Champaubert, where he was wounded and captured. He was released only after the Allies captured Paris on 31 March 1814.

In 1815-1818, Poltoratsky served with the Russian Occupation Corps in France and became commander of the 3rd Brigade of the 23rd Division on 10 August 1817. Returning to Russia, he was appointed commander of the 3rd Brigade of the 14th Division until resigning on 25 March 1822. Eight years later, he transferred to civil service with the rank of privy counsellor, and became the Civil Governor of Yaroslavl on 9 February 1830. As the governor, Poltoratsky earned the Orders of St. Vladimir (2nd class) and of the White Eagle. On 20 October 1834, he returned to military service, becoming lieutenant general and Military Governor of Yaroslavl before retiring in 1842.

POLUEKTOV, Boris Vladimirovich (b. 12 July 1779 — d. 18 October 1843, Warsaw) was born to an ancient Russian noble family. He was enlisted in the Life Guard Preobrazhensk Regiment on 15 January 1791, and began active service as a sub-ensign in 1796. Promoted to portupei-ensign in 1797, he received the Order of St. John of Jerusalem in January 1798, and the rank of ensign on 1 September of the same year, at the age of nineteen. Made a sub-lieutenant in 1799, Poluektov rose to full lieutenant in 1802 and participated in the 1805 Campaign. On 2 December 1805, he fought at Austerlitz, where his brother Vsevolod, lieutenant of the Preobrazhensk Regiment, was killed. Poluektov received promotion to a staff captain in March 1806 and to captain in January 1808.

In September 1808, Poluektov served with a battalion of the Life Guard Preobrazhensk Regiment in Finland, and participated in the Russo-Swedish War. In March 1809, he took part in Prince Bagration's daring crossing of the Gulf of Bothnia to capture the Aland Islands. Latee that year, he took command of the 1st Battalion of the Preobrazhensk Regiment and received the Commander Cross of the Order of St. John of Jerusalem.

During the 1812 Campaign, Poluektov served with the 1st Brigade of the Guard Infantry Division in the 5th Reserve Corps, distinguishing himself at Borodino, for which he was decorated with the Order of St. Vladimir (3rd class). In 1813, he served at Lutzen, Bautzen (Order of St. Anna, 2nd class, with diamonds), Pirna, Berggieshubel (Order of St. George, 4th class), and Kulm (Prussian Orders of Red Eagle and the Iron Cross, as well as promotion to major general on 27 September 1813, with seniority dating from 28 August 1813). Poluektov took command of the Moscow Grenadier Regiment on 10 October 1813, and during the 1814 Campaign, participated in the battles at Brienne, Arcis sur Aube, and Paris, for which he was decorated with the Order of St. Anna (1st class). He took command of the 3rd Brigade of the 2nd Grenadier Division on 13 September 1814, and returned to France during the Hundred Days in 1815.

In April 1818, Poluektov became commander of the 2nd Brigade of the 2nd Grenadier Division and received the Order of St. Vladimir (2nd class). On 18 January 1826, Poluektov was appointed commander of the 2nd Grenadier Division and rose to lieutenant general on 3 September of the same year. During the Polish Uprising in 1831, he distinguished himself at Grochow, Ostrolenka, and Warsaw, for which he was decorated with the Order of St. George (3rd class) on 30 October 1831. Poluektov took command of the reserve divisions of the 1st, 2nd, and 3rd Corps on 7 July 1832, and became a member of the General Audit on 14 April 1833. Promoted to general of infantry on 22 October 1843, he held this rank for only a week, dying in Warsaw on 29 October.

PONCET (de Ponce), Mikhail Ivanovich (Francois Michel) (b. 1778 — d. 3 October 1829, Adrianople) was born to a French noble family in Dresden. After serving in the Saxon army, he entered the Russian service as a lieutenant in the 3rd Jager Regiment on 30 October 1806. In December 1806, he served with the 4th Division in Poland, distinguishing himself at Pultusk, where he was wounded in the left hand (Order of St. Anna, 3rd class). In 1807, he served in Barclay de Tolly's rear guard at Hof and Eylau (Order of St. Vladimir, 4th class, and a golden sword). He served in Finland in 1808 and for his good conduct was transferred as a lieutenant to the Life Guard Jager Regiment. In 1809-1810, he served in the Danubian Principalities, fighting the Turks at Ruse, Silistra, and Shumla (Order of St. George, 4th class).

Promoted to colonel on 10 January 1812, Poncet served in the headquarters of the Army of Danube during the Russian Campaign in 1812. In 1813, he served under General Mikhail Vorontsov, distinguishing himself at Rogozin, Bromberg, Kustrin, Magdeburg, Gross Beeren (Order of St. Vladimir, 3rd class, and promotion to major general on 27 September), and Uterbog, where he was wounded. In 1814, he commanded a brigade comprised of four battalions of the Tula and Navaginsk Infantry Regiments and fought at Soissons, Craonne (golden sword with diamonds), Laon, and Paris.

After the war, Poncet remained with Vorontsov's corps in France until 1818, when he took indefinite furlough due to poor health. He returned to the army only ten years later. During the Russo-Turkish War of 1828-1829, he rose to a lieutenant general on 18 December 1828, and commanded the troops on the Danube. However, Poncet became seriously ill and died in Adrianople on 3 October 1829.

POPONDOPOLO (Papadopoulos), Emmanuil Grigorievich (date of birth unknown — d. 23 June 1810, Shumla) was born to a Greek noble family. He studied in the Greek Gymnasium of the Artillery and Engineer Cadet Corps and began service as an ensign in the Russian army in 1781. During the Russo-Turkish War of 1787-1791, he served at Ochakov and Kaushani. He took command of the Ladoga Musketeer Regiment on 26 April 1799, and rose to colonel on 24 October 1799. In 1804-1806, he commanded a detachment on Corfu and the Ionian Islands, rising to a major general on 11 October 1804. In 1805, he organized the Greek Legion (*Legion Legkikh Strelkov*) and fought in Naples. Popondopolo became chef of the Kolyvan Musketeer Regiment on 25 September 1806. In 1806-1807, he organized additional Greek Legions and successfully operated against Ali Pasha of Janina. Returning to Russia in 1808, he served in the Army of Moldavia, fighting at Silistra and Ruse before being mortally wounded at Shumla on 23 June 1810.

PORTNYAGIN, Semen Andreyevich took command of the Kharkov Cuirassier Regiment on 15 December 1799. He rose to major general and chef of the Nizhegorod Dragoon Regiment on 27 October 1800. On 11 April 1801, he became chef of the Narva Dragoon Regiment, which he led throughout the Napoleonic Wars.

POSNIKOV, Fedor Nikolayevich (b. 1784 — d. 8 August 1841) was born to a noble family from the Novgorod *gubernia*. He began service as a kamer page at the Imperial Court and enlisted as a lieutenant in the Life Guard Semeyonovsk Regiment on 19 October 1798. In 1805, he was wounded in the right side at Austerlitz and received promotion to colonel on 8 May 1806. In 1807, he fought at Guttstadt, Heilsberg, and Friedland, where he took a wound to his right leg and earned the Order of St. George (4th class, 1 June 1808). He became battalion commander in the Semeyonovsk Regiment on 26 January 1808.

During the 1812 Campaign, Posnikov served with the 1st Brigade of the Guard Infantry Division in the 5th Corps and fought at Borodino (garnered the Order of St. Vladimir, 3rd class), Tarutino, Maloyaroslavets, and Krasnyi. In 1813, he took part in the actions at Lutzen, Bautzen, and Kulm (Prussian Iron Cross). He rose to a major general on 27 September 1813, and chef of the Malorossiisk Grenadier Regiment on 10 October. Posnikov participated in the Battle of Leipzig on 16-19 October. In 1814, he served with the 2nd Grenadier Division at Brienne, Le Fère Champenoise, and Paris. He retired because of poor health on 18 January 1816, but returned to the army on 1 February 1825, becoming the head of the 6th District of the Independent Corps of Internal Guard. He took a final discharge on 17 December 1834.

POTAPOV, Aleksey Nikolayevich (b. 8 November 1772, Moscow — d. 17 March 1847, St. Petersburg) was born to a noble family from the Pskov *gubernia*. He enlisted in the Life Guard Izmailovsk Regiment on 12 March 1782, and rose to an ensign on 12 January 1791. Potapov transferred as a rotmistr to the Sumsk Light Horse Regiment on 12 January 1792, and served in Poland from 1792-1794. In 1806-1807, he served with the 3rd Division in Poland, garnering the Order of St. George (4th class, 2 February 1807). He transferred to the Grand Duke Constantine's Uhlan Regiment and became adjutant to Grand Duke Constantine on 2 August 1809. Promoted to colonel on 24

POTEMKIN, Jacob Alekseyevich (b. 27 October 1781, St. Petersburg — d. 13 February 1831, Zhitomir) was born to a prominent Russian noble family. After studying in the Infantry Cadet Corps, he began service as a kamer page at the Imperial court in 1797. Two years later, he enlisted as a lieutenant in the Life Guard Horse Regiment on 30 May 1799. After brief retirement in 1800, he joined the Life Guard Jager Regiment on 21 March 1800. Potemkin rose to a staff captain on 22 March 1803, and to captain on 18 October 1804. Promoted to colonel on 12 April 1805, he participated in the 1805 Campaign, fighting at Austerlitz (Order of St. Vladimir, 4th class). Two years later, he took part in the battles at Guttstadt (Order of St. George, 4th class and the Prussian Pour le Merite), Heilsberg, and Friedland (golden sword).

Potemkin took part in the Russo-Swedish War in 1808-1809, receiving the Order of St. Vladimir (3rd class) for his actions at Kuopio. He became chef of the 2nd Jager Regiment on 5 December 1809. Poor health forced his retirement in 1810, he he returned to the army the following year, becoming chef of the 48th Jager Regiment and commander of the 3rd Brigade of the 17th Division on 29 January 1811.

During the 1812 Campaign, Potemkin served in the 2nd Corps and took part in the actions at Vitebsk (promoted to major general on 12 November 1812, with seniority dating from

October 1811, he served in the headquarters of the 5th Reserve (Guard) Corps in 1812, fighting at Ostrovno, Borodino, Tarutino, and Krasnyi.

In 1813, Potapov distinguished himself at Kulm (Prussian Iron Cross and promotion to major general on 27 September 1813, with seniority dating from 29 August 1813) and Leipzig (golden sword with diamonds). In 1814, he served at Le Fère Champenoise and Paris. After the war, he took command of the Life Guard Horse Jager Regiment on 9 May 1814. He became a duty officer in the General Staff on 11 September 1823. Potapov took part in the suppression of the Decembrist Uprising in December 1826, receiving promotions to adjutant general on 26 December 1825, and to lieutenant general on 3 September 1826. Thereafter, he participated in the Russo-Turkish War in 1828-1829, and fought the Poles in 1831. He took command of the 3rd Reserve Cavalry Corps on 14 April 1833, and earned the rank of general of cavalry on 8 October 1834. In October 1845, he was relieved of command and appointed to the State Council.

There was another Potapov serving in the Russian army during the Napolenic Wars: **Potapov, Lev Ivanovich,** took command of the Izumsk Hussar Regiment on 24 January 1804, and served with the 2nd Division in Poland in 1806-1807. Promoted to major general on 5 June 1807, he became chef of the Oliviopol Hussar Regiment on the same day. He died of illness on 25 October 1808.

25 July 1812), Smolensk, Borodino, Mozhaisk, Tarutino (Order of St. Anna, 2nd class, with diamonds), Maloyaroslavets, and Krasnyi (Order of St. Anna, 1st class). On 28 December 1812, he took command of the Life Guard Semeyonovsk Regiment, which he led throughout the 1813-1814 Campaigns. Potemkin garnered the Prussian Iron Cross, the Austrian Order of Maria Theresa, and the Russian Order of St. George (3rd class) for his actions at Kulm. After the battles of Leipzig and Paris, he rose to adjutant general on 14 April 1814. He accompanied Emperor Alexander to Britain and other European states in 1814-1815.

After briefly leading the 1st Brigade of the 1st Guard Division in 1817-1818, Potemkin took command of the 2nd Guard Division on 3 August 1819, and of the 4th Infantry Division on 23 May 1821. He rose to lieutenant general on 24 December 1824, and received the Order of St. Vladimir (2nd class, 18 October 1826) and the diamond signs of the Order of St. Anna (1st class, 1828). During the Russo-Turkish War in 1828-1829, he led the Russian advance guard at Shumla and Giurgiu, and briefly led a corps in Wallachia (golden sword with diamonds and the Order of St. Alexander of Neva with diamonds). He was appointed temporary governor general of the Podlosk and Volhynia *gubernia*s on 10 December 1830.

POTOZKY, Stanislav Stanislavovich (b. 1787 — d. 16 July 1831, St. Petersburg) was born to a Polish noble family. He enlisted as a cornet in the Life Guard Horse Regiment in 1793, and began active service as a lieutenant in the Her Majesty's Leib-Cuirassier Regiment on 26 May 1803. He transferred to the Life Guard Horse Regiment in 1804, and served as an adjutant to Grand Duke Constantine in 1805. Two years later, Potozky served at Guttstadt, Heilsberg, and Friedland. In 1809-1810, he joined the Army of Moldavia in the Danubian Principalities and rose to a flügel adjutant on 14 December 1810.

Promoted to colonel in the Life Guard Preobrazhensk Regiment on 27 September 1811, Potozky served with the 1st Brigade of the Guard Infantry Division of the 5th Corps at Borodino in 1812. The following year, he took part in the actions at Kalisch, Lutzen, Bautzen, and Leipzig, garnering the rank of major general on 27 September 1813, and the Order of St. George (4th class) on 20 October 1813. Potozky attended Emperor Alexander I during the Invasion of France in 1814, taking part in the battles at Brienne, Arcis sur Aube, and Paris. After the war, he became adjutant general on 13 July 1817, and retired on 18 September 1822. Six years later, he transferred to civil service with the rank of privy counsellor (the equivalent of lieutenant general), and served as the Ober-Ceremonymeister of the Imperial court.

POTULOV, Pavel Vasilievich (b. 1758 — date of death unclear) was born to a noble family from the Tambov *gubernia*. He enlisted as a private in the Life Guard Semeyonovsk Regiment on 12 January 1775, and transferred as a lieutenant to the Smolensk Dragoon Regiment in 14 March 1778. After serving in Poland from 1783-1785, Potulov took part in the Russo-Turkish War of 1787-1791, distinguishing himself at Ochakov, where he was wounded in the head and earned a golden cross and promotion to second major. He left the army to recuperate and returned in October 1790. In 1792-1794, he again served in Poland and distinguished himself at Mir in 1792, earning the Order of St. George (2nd class) on 9 July 1792.

Potulov served as an adjutant with premier major's rank to Lieutenant General V. Zubov. In 1794, he barely escaped the Polish insurgents in

Warsaw and fought at Slonim, Brest, Belostock (golden sword), and Praga, where he garnered a golden cross and rank of lieutenant colonel. In 1796, Potulov served under V. Zubov during the Persian Campaign along the Caspian Sea, taking part in the actions at Derbent, Baku, and Shemakha, for which he was decorated with the Order of St. Vladimir (4th class). He rose to a colonel and commander of the Smolensk Dragoon Regiment on 31 August 1798.

In 1799-1802, Potulov served in Georgia, where he took command of the Ekaterinoslavl Cuirassier Regiment on 4 June 1803. He was promoted to major general on 2 December 1803. During the 1805 Campaign, he fought at Wischau (wounded in the right leg) and Austerlitz (wounded in the right leg, received the Order of St. Vladimir, 3rd class). Potulov became chef of the Ekaterinoslavl Cuirassier Regiment on 30 January 1806, and in the 1806 Campaign in Poland, served with the 6th Division. He was appointed head of the cavalry supplies depot in Moscow on 6 February 1807.

During the 1812 Campaign, he took command of the 8th *Opolchenye* Infantry Regiment of the 2nd Moscow *Opolchenye* Division on 19 August 1812, and fought at Borodino, Mozhaisk, Tarutino, Maloyaroslavets, and Vyazma, where he was wounded in the hand and earned the Order of St. Anna (1st class). Potulov headed the cavalry supplies depot in Warsaw in 1813-1814, and briefly served in the siege of Danzig before retiring on 17 September 1814.

There was another Potulov prominent in the Russian army during the Napoleonic Wars: **POTULOV, Alexander Alexandrovich**, took command of the Odessa Infantry Regiment on 10 November 1811, and became chef of the same unit on 9 May 1812. During the 1812 Campaign, he served in the 2nd Western Army and distinguished himself at Smolensk, where he was mortally wounded on 17 August 1812.

POVALO-SHVEIKOVSKY, Yakov (Jacob) Ivanovich (b. 20 October 1750 — d. 9 October 1807) was born to a noble family from the Smolensk *gubernia*. He enlisted as a corporal in the Life Guard Semeyonovsk Regiment in April 1768, rising to furier in 1769, and then to sergeant in 1770. On 12 January 1771, Povalo-Shveikovsky transferred as a lieutenant to the Novgorod Infantry Regiment. He became a captain on 18 May 1772, and major on 21 July 1773. He participated in the Russo-Turkish War in 1771-1774, serving in Generals Essen's and Weisman's corps. He transferred as a captain to the Life Guard Preobrazhensk Regiment on 10 July 1778. Six years later, he became a colonel in the Ukraine Light Horse Regiment in May 1784. During the next Russo-Turkish War in 1787-1791, he led this regiment at Ochakov and received promotion to brigadier on 2 May 1789. On 5 April 1791, he became a major general and chef of the Smolensk Musketeer Regiment. In 1792-1794, he served in Poland.

Povalo-Shveikovsky rose to a lieutenant general on 17 February 1798, and commanded a corps during Alexander Suvorov's campaigns in Italy and Switzerland in 1799. He distinguished himself at Palazollo, Lecco, on the Adda River, at Milan, Valence, Alessandria, on the Tidone and Trebbia rivers, at Novi, and during the crossing of the Alps (Diamond Cross of the Order of St. John of Jerusalem). For his conduct, Povalo-Shveikovsky received the Order of St. Alexander of Neva on 26 May 1799, the Order of St. John of Jerusalem on 4 October 1799, and promotion to general of infantry on 8 October 1799. He was appointed the Military Governor of Kiev on 25 April 1800, and was discharged from service on 22 September of the same year. He received the civil rank of actual privy counselor and served in the Senate before dying on 9 October 1807.

There was also another Povalo-Shveikovsky in the Russian army at the time: **Povalo-Shveikovsky II, Peter Zakharovich**, who served as chef of the Rostov Musketeer Regiment between 4 and 6 November 1799, and as chef of the Murom Musketeer Regiment from 6 September 1799 to 5 October 1800.

POZZO DI BORGO, Charles-André (b. 8 March 1764, Alata, Corsica — d. 27 February 1842 Paris) was born to a petty noble family on Corsica. After studying law in Pisa, he actively participated in the Corsican politics during the French Revolution. He politically allied with Napoleon Bonaparte early in his life, and was one of the two Corsican delegates to the National Assembly, where he facilitated the incorporation of Corsica into France. Pozzo sat with the Girondists until the events of August 1792. When he returned to Corsica, he found himself alienated from the Bonapartes, who were in the process of joining the Jacobins. While in Corsica, Pozzo became the *procureur-général-syndic* (chief of the civil government) and refused to obey the summons to the bar of the Convention. Pozzo and famous Corsican leader Pascuale Paoli found themselves allied with the British, who established a protectorate over Corsica from 1794 to 1796.

When the French restored their authority over the island in 1796, Pozzo accompanied Sir Gilbert Elliot, the former British viceroy in Corsica, to Vienna, where Pozzo entered Russian service on 10 October 1805. During the 1805 Campaign, he served as the Russian commissioner with the Anglo-Neapolitan forces in Italy, and in 1806, served in similar capacity with the Prussians. In 1807, Pozzo was sent on a diplomatic mission to Constantinople. When Alexander I and Napoleon concluded the Treaty of Tilsit, Pozzo's diplomatic career in Russia ended and he moved to Vienna. Napoleon demanded his extradition, but Clemence Metternich allowed him to leave for England. Pozzo di Borgo remained in England until 1812, when he was recalled to Russia.

Pozzo negotiated with Sweden in early 1813, ensuring its alliance against the French. He then served with the Army of North at Gross Beeren, Dennewitz, and Leipzig, receiving promotion to major general on 15 September 1813, with seniority dating from 13 July 1813.

In 1814, when the Allies entered Paris, Pozzo served as commissary general to the French provisional government and rose to adjutant general on 14 April 1814. During the First Restoration, he became the Russian ambassador to France and sought to arrange a marriage between the Duc de Berry and the Grand Duchess Anna (Alexander's sister). Pozzo was present at the Congress of Vienna, and during the Hundred Days, traveled with Louis XVIII to Belgium. After the Second Restoration, Pozzo remained as the Russian ambassador to Paris for the next fifteen years. He received promotion to lieutenant general in the Russian army on 17 March 1817, and was made a count and peer of France in 1818. On 3 September 1826, he was conferred the title of count of the Russian Empire, and on 3 May 1829, received the rank of general of infantry. Pozzo was made the Russian ambassador to Britain on 17 January 1835. However, as his health declined, he retired on 9 January 1840, and died in Paris on 27 February 1842.

PRENDEL, Victor Antonovich (b. 1766 — d. 10 November 1852, Kiev) was born to an Austrian noble family from Tyrol. After traveling extensively throughout Europe in 1781-1791, he joined the Austrian army in 1792, and took part in the campaigns against France in 1794-1797. He served under Alexander Suvorov during the campaigns in Italy and Switzerland in 1799, and entered Russian service on 30 October 1804, becoming a staff captain in the Chernigov Dragoon Regiment. During the 1805 Campaign, he served as an assistant to Mikhail Kutuzov and distinguished himself at Austerlitz, receiving the Order of St. Vladimir (4th class) and the rank of captain.

After briefly serving against the Turks in 1806, Prendel served with Essen's corps in Poland in 1807. He became an adjutant to General Löwis in 1808, and to General Sergey Golitsyn in 1809, taking part in the campaign against Austria in Galicia. In January 1810, he was dispatched to Vienna, where he conducted intelligence operations. Promoted to major in the Kharkov Dragoon Regiment in May 1810, he traveled through France, Italy, Holland, and Germany to gather military intelligence on the French military. After returning to Russia, Prendel fought at Smolensk on 15-17 August, and led a partisan detachment from September through December 1812, earning the rank of lieutenant colonel. In 1813, he commanded a Cossack detachment and successfully operated against the French lines of communication. After capturing the French dispatches, Prendel often copied them and sent the originals to the addressee marked with a special Cossack seal.

Prendel took part in the actions at Kalisch (promoted to colonel), Dresden, Lutzen (Order of St. Vladimir, 3rd class), Bautzen, Gross Beeren, Dennewitz, and Leipzig, for which he was decorated with the Order of St. Anna (2nd class) with diamonds. He later received the Swedish Order of the Sword for crossing the Elbe River. Between November 1813 and 1816, Prendel served as the commandant of Leipzig. In 1816-1818, he supervised the roads and hospitals in Saxony. Returning to Russia, he served in the headquarters of the 1st Army and received the rank of major general in 1831. He retired four years later.

PRIOUDA, Peter Karlovich (date of birth unclear — d. 28 March 1807) took command of the 6th Jager Regiment on 8 April 1799, and participated in the 1799 Campaign in Italy and Switzerland, rising to colonel on 4 August 1799. Returning to Russia, he became commander of the 5th Jager Regiment on 20 March 1800, and, later, chef of the 8th Jager Regiment on 21 July of the same year. He took command of the 24th Jager Regiment on 5 July 1806, and served with the 5th Division in Poland. He died of wounds received at Eylau on 28 March 1807.

PROTASOV, Aleksey Andrianovich (b. 1780, Zhelchino, Ryazan *gubernia* — d. 30 December 1833, Moscow) was born to a noble family from the Ryazan *gubernia*. He enlisted in the Life Guard Horse Regiment in 1795, rising to cornet on 26 March 1801, and to staff rotmistr in 1805. During the 1805 Campaign, he distinguished himself at Austerlitz on 2 December. In 1807, Protasov participated in the battles at Heilsberg and Friedland, where he was wounded in the left hand and earned the Order of St. Vladimir (4th class).

Promoted to colonel on 10 December 1808, Protasov took command of the Combined Cuirassier Regiment, comprised of reserve squadrons of the Chevalier Guard Regiment, Life Guard Horse Regiment, His Majesty Leib Cuirassier Regiment, and Her Majesty's Leib Cuirassier Regiment. Serving in the 1st Corps, he fought at Skolitsy, Svolnya, Volyntsy, both battles of Polotsk (Order of St. George, 4th class, 16 September 1812), Chasniki, and on the Berezina. After his unit was disbanded in early

1813, Protasov served with the Life Guard Horse Regiment in Saxony, distinguishing himself at Dresden and Kulm, for which he earned the Prussian Iron Cross and promotion to major general on 27 September 1813. He took command of the Malorossiisk Cuirassier Regiment on 10 October 1813, and was wounded in the right side at Leipzig. In 1814, he took part in the battles at Arcis sur Aube and Paris. Returning to Russia, he briefly served in the Independent Corps of the Internal Guard before retiring because of poor health on 19 March 1817.

PROZOROVSKY, Alexander Alexandrovich (b. 1732 – d. 9 August 1809) was born to an ancient noble family tracing its origin from Rurik, the founder of the Russian state. In 1742, he was enlisted in the Guard Regiment at age ten; two years later, he received the rank of corporal. He reached the rank of sergeant by 1753, and in 1756 made captain. Prozorovsky participated in the Seven Year's War and was wounded at the battle of Grossjägerndorf. Promoted to second major in 1758, he participated in the battles of Kunersdorf, Zordforf, and Kustrin. In 1760, he was conferred the rank of lieutenant colonel and took part in the capture of Berlin.

Prozorovsky became a colonel iIn 1761, and five years later, rose to major general. He served in Poland in 1767-68 and in 1769 led the Russian troops against the Turks on the Dniestr River. Prozorovsky distinguished himself in several battles against the Turks and was awarded the Order of St. George (3rd class). In 1771-1773, Prozorovsky took part in the operations against the Turks in the Crimea, where he captured Perekop and suppressed the local Tatar uprising. In 1773, he was promoted to lieutenant general, and the next year, transferred to the Danube Valley, where he garnered a golden sword with diamonds. In 1777, Prozorovsky took a furlough because of poor health and returned to the army in 1779, when he was appointed to the Ukraine Division of Count Peter Rumyantsev-Zadunaisky. In 1781, Prozorovsky became the Governor of Orel and Kursk; nine years later, he became the Military Governor of Moscow.

Prozorovsky was relieved of authority in 1795, though a year later, Emperor Paul I gave him command of the 1st Smolensk Division. Without warning he fell out of the emperor's favor in January 1797, and for next three years Prozorovsky lived at his estates. He was recalled only in late 1805, when he took command of the militia in the 6th Military District. In 1807, Prozorovsky was promoted to field marshal and appointed the Commander-in-Chief of the Army of Moldavia. He spent the next two years fighting the Turkish troops in the Danube Valley, but failed to achieve any success of note. When his irrational assault on Braila resulted in some 5,000 killed and wounded, he unjustly accused his officers and soldiers of cowardice. Prozorovsky died near Macin on 9 August 1809

PRZHEBISHEVSKY, Ignatii Yakovlevich (b. 1755 — date of death unclear) was born to a Polish noble family in Volhynia. He began service in the Polish army, but after the Second Partition of Poland, entered the Russian service with the rank of colonel on 17 May 1793. He rose to major general in the Astrakhan Grenadier Regiment on 26 May 1795, and became chef of the Kursk Musketeer Regiment on 26 September 1797. He served in Rimsky-Korsakov's corps in Switzerland in 1799, becoming a lieutenant general on 15 June 1799, and distinguishing himself at Zurich in September of the same year. Six years later, Przhebishevsky led a division in Langeron's 2nd Column at Austerlitz, leading the Allied attack on Sokolnitz. His troops were soon routed and Przhebishevsky was captured. After he returned to Russia in 1806, he was court martialed for surrendering to the French, but the General Audit acquited him of the charges. Thereafter, however, Przhebishevsky was put on trial by the State Council, which found him guilty of not following the battle disposition. He was reduced in rank and discharged from the army in December 1810.

PYSHNITSKY, Dmitry Ilyich (b. 6 November 1764 — d. 17 October 1844) was born to a noble family from the Smolensk *gubernia*. He enlisted as a sergeant in the Apsheron Infantry Regiment on 18 February 1776, and served in Poland in 1779-1781. He rose to an ensign in May 1784, and to lieutenant in January 1786. He participated in the Russo-Turkish War of 1787-1791, and served again in Poland in 1792-1794, rising to a premier major. In 1799, he served with the Apsheron Musketeers in Italy and Switzerland. Returning to Russia, Pyshnitsky took command of the Nizov Musketeer Regiment on 31 January 1800, and became a colonel on 20 October of the same year. Five years later, he became chef of the Kremenchug Musketeer Regiment on 10 October 1806.

During the Russo-Swedish War of 1808-1809, Pyshnitsky served with the 17th Division in Finland. In 1812, he served in the 1st Brigade of the 4th Division of the 2nd Corps and took part in the actions at Smolensk (wounded), Borodino (promoted to major general on 3 December 1812, with seniority dating from 7 September 1812), Tarutino, and Vyazma, garnering the Order of St. George (3rd class, 15 June 1813). In February 1813, he served at Kalisch before taking command of the 4th Division and fighting at Lutzen (wounded in the right hand), Bautzen (bruised), Reichenbach (wounded in the leg), Pirna, Dresden, Kulm, Teplitz, and Leipzig. In 1814, Pyshnitsky distinguished himself at Paris, for which he received promotion to a lieutenant general on 7 May 1815, with seniority dating from 30 March 1814. He was relieved of command of the 4th Division on 21 April 1816, and retired on 1 January 1834.

RADOZHITSKY, Ilya Timofeyevich (b. 1788 — d. 21 April 1861) studied in the Imperial Military Orphanage and began service as a sub-lieutenant in the Kherson Artillery Garrison on 13 June 1806. Two years later, he transferred to the 2nd Artillery Brigade on 1 October 1808, and rose to lieutenant on 19 January 1810. In September 1811, his unit was renamed as the 11th Artillery Brigade. During the 1812 Campaign, Radozhitsky served in the 3rd Light Company of the 11th Artillery Brigade, 6th Corps, 1st Western Army, fighting at Ostrovno (Order of St. Anna, 4th class), Smolensk, Borodino (bruised in the head), and Vyazma. In 1813, he served at Lutzen, Bautzen, and Leipzig, garnering two Orders of St. Vladimir (4th class). In 1814, he distinguished himself at Paris, and was promoted to staff captain.

After the war, Radozhitsky completed a topographic mission to the Grodno *gubernia* and was appointed to the General Staff in July 1815. He rose to captain on 11 September 1817, and to lieutenant colonel on 27 September 1819, before retiring on 8 January 1820. He subsequently returned to the army in February 1823, and served in the 22nd Artillery Brigade before taking command of the 4th Battery Company of the 21st Artillery Brigade in 1824. He also headed the Caucasian Mobile Reserve Artillery Park.

Radozhitsky took part in the Russo-Turkish War of 1828-1829, fighting the Turks in the Transcaucasia. He was appointed to command the 3rd Light Company of the 20th Artillery Brigade on 21 September 1830, but was unable to join the unit because of illness and was instead transferred to the Artillery Department. On 4 August 1831, he became an assistant to the director of the weapon factory in Tula and received a promotion to colonel on 24 December 1835. For his long and dedicated service, Radozhitsky received the Order of St. George (4th class) in January 1836. He took a discharge on 14 December 1838. Ten months later, Radozhitsky again returned to the artillery, serving in Georgia. He retired with a rank of major general in 1850.

Radozhitsky was a brilliant intellectual and left a diverse literary legacy. His study *Istoricheskoe izvestie o pokhode rossiiskikh voisk v 1796 g. v Daghestan i Persiu pod komandoi grafa V.A. Zubova* [Historical Bulletin on the Expedition of the Russian Forces under Count V.A. Zubov to Daghestan and Persia in 1796] appeared in the *Otechestvennie zapiski* in 1827. Radozhitsky's memoirs, *Pokhodnie zapiski artillerisra s 1812 po 1816 god* [Artillerist's Recollections on the Campaigns in 1812-1816], were published in Moscow in 1835, and contain detailed and interesting accounts of his exploits during the Napoleonic Wars. In 1857, the *Voennii Zhurnal* printed his *Pokhodnie zapiski artillerista v Azii s 1829 po 1831 g.* [Artillerist's Recollections on the Campaigns in Asia in 1829-1831]. In addition to his historical writtings, Radozhitsky studied botany. He is the author of the monumental fifteen-volume study *Vsermirnaia flora* [World Flora].

RADT, Semen Lukich (b.1766 — d. 1822) descended from a Swiss noble family. After serving in the Swiss and Dutch armies, he entered the Russian army as a captain in Général-en-Chef Saltykov's staff on 21 March 1788. During the Russo-Turkish War of 1787-1791, he fought at Khotin and Hadjibey (Odessa). He transferred to the Kekshlom Infantry Regiment in April 1790, and was assigned to the galley flotilla in the Baltic Sea. He took part in the operations against the Swedes in 1790, distinguishing himself in the naval engagements at Bjorkzund, Vyborg and Rochensalmi (Order of St. Vladimir, 4th class). Promoted to lieutenant captain, Radt sailed to Britain in 1792-1793. After returning to Russia, he was promoted to lieutenant colonel in 1794 and transferred to the Kursk Musketeer Regiment. Made a colonel on 20 April 1797, Radt served as an adjutant to Grand Duke Alexander.

He became a major general and chef of the Little Russia (Malorossiiskii) Grenadier Regiment on 19 April 1798. Two years later, he was apromoted to lieutenant general and appointed infantry inspector in the Ukraine Inspection.

After brief retirement in late 1800, Radt served in the War College and took a discharge because of poor health in 1802. During the 1807 Campaign in Poland, he organized and commanded militia in the Estland *gubernia*. After returning to the army in 1811, Radt headed the St. Petersburg recruiting depot and was assigned to the headquarters of the 3rd Reserve Army of Observation on 27 May 1815. After the battle of Borodino, Radt transferred to the main Russian headquarters and fought at Maloyaroslavets, Krasnyi, and on the Berezina. The following year, he served at Zamostye and remained in the Duchy of Warsaw in 1814.

After the war, Radt took command of the 24th Division on 29 September 1814, but was releived of command on 23 September 1816. He retired because of poor health three years later.

RAKHMANOV, Pavel Alexanderovich (b. 1769 — d. 1845) was born to a noble family from the Moscow *gubernia*. He enlisted as a kaptenarmus in the Life Guard Preobrazhensk Regiment on 28 April 1788, and fought the Swedes in 1788-1790, rising to an ensign on 13 January 1790. He served with the Moscow Musketeer Regiment in Poland from 1792-1794, garnering a golden cross for Praga; he transferred as a lieutenant to the Bombardier Company of the Life Guard Preobrazhensk Regiment. He served under Rimsky-Korsakov in Switzerland in 1799, distinguishing himself at Zurich.

After returning to Russia, Rakhmanov retired in April 1800. In 1807, he organized militia in the Volokolamsk and Klin uezds. In 1812, he led the *opolchenye* of these uezds at Mozhaisk, Krymsk, Maloyaroslavets, Vyazma, and Krasnyi, garnering in return a golden sword with diamonds. In 1813, he served at Modlin and Danzig, where he earned the Order of St. Anna (1st class). He retired in May 1814.

RAKHMANOV, Vasily Sergeyevich (b. 1764 — d. 22 November 1816) was born to a noble family from the Kursk *gubernia*. He studied in the Infantry Cadet Corps and began service as a lieutenant in the Tula Infantry Regiment on 17 February 1785. He took part in the Russo-Swedish War of 1788-1790, and served in Poland in 1794, where he received the Order of St. George (4th class, 7 December 1795) for his actions at Maciejowice. In 1799, he participated in the expedition to Holland, where his distinguished service at Bergen earned him a promotion to colonel on 16 June 1799. Returning to Russia, he took command of the Kolyvan Musketeer Regiment on 23 June 1803. The same year, he became major general and chef of the Nizov Musketeer Regiment on 9 September.

During the 1806-1807 Campaigns in Poland, Rakhmanov served with the 6th Division at Pultusk, Guttstadt (golden sword with diamonds) and Friedland. He took part in the Russo-Swedish War in 1808-1809, distinguishing himself at Kuopio and Idensalmi. From 1810-1811, Rakhmanov served as the Commandant of Uleaborg in Finland. During the 1812 Campaign, he served with the Finland Corps at Riga, Polotsk, Chashniki, and Elbing (Order of St. George, 3rd class, 12 August 1813). In 1813, Rakhmanov took part in the siege of Danzig. After the war, he led the 1st Brigade of the 6th Division. He became a lieutenant general and commander of the 24th Division on 23 September 1816, but died two months later on 22 November 1816.

RAKOV, Semen Ilyich, colonel, took command of the Ekaterinoslavl Grenadier Regiment on 12 November 1808. He served in the Danubian Principalities from 1808-1812, serving as chef of the Apsheron Musketeer Regiment (31 October 1810) and of the Okhotsk Musketeer (later Infantry) Regiment (2 December 1810). During the Russo-Turkish War in 1809-1811, he distinguished himself in battles at Rassevat, Silistra, Shumla, and Ruse.

RALL, Fedor Fedorovich (b. 1786 — d. 19 June 1837) began service as a page at the Imperial Court before joining the Leib-Grenadier Regiment in 1803. He fought at Austerlitz in 1805 and transferred as a lieutenant to the Life Guard Jager Regiment in 1806. Rall was engaged at Guttstadt, Heilsberg, and Friedland in 1807, garnering in return a golden sword for courage. In 1812, he served at Smolensk, Borodino, Tarutino, and Maloyaroslavets, and in 1813 was decorated with the Order of St. George (4th class) for his actions at Kulm. He took part in the invasion of France in 1814.

After the war, Rall took command of the 1st Carabinier Regiment but retired because of poor health in 1818. Eight years later, he returned to the army with a rank of colonel and command of the Field Marshal Duke Wellington's Infantry Regiment. He participated in the Russo-Turkish War in 1828-1829, rising to a major general and commander of the 3rd Brigade of the 10th Division. For his conduct in the battle at Pravoda, Rall garnered a golden sword with diamonds. During the Polish Uprising of 1830-1831, he led the 3rd Brigade of the 9th Division and later commanded the 2nd Brigade of the 7th Division in 1833. He retiring in 1835, and died on 19 June 1837.

RAYEVSKY, Nikolay Nikolayevich (b. 25 September 1771 — d. 28 September 1829) was born to a prominent Russian family. His father, Colonel Nikolay Semeyonovich Rayevsky, died at Jassy before Rayevsky was born; his mother, Catherine Samoilova, was the niece of Prince Gregory Potemkin. Nikolay the younger was enlisted in the Life Guard Preobrazhensk Regiment at the age of three in 1774, becoming a sergeant on 11 May 1777, an ensign on 12 January 1786, a sub-lieutenant on 12 January 1788, and a lieutenant in 1789. During the Russo-Turkish War of 1787-1791, he transferred as a premier major to the Nizhegorod Dragoon Regiment on 11 April 1789, and served in Moldavia and Wallachia, fighting at Akkerman and Bender. Rayevsky was promoted to lieutenant colonel on 12 September 1790, and at age nineteen, took command of the Great Hetman Bulava (*Bulavy Velikogo Getman*) Cossack Regiment.

Promoted to colonel on 11 February 1792, Rayevsky served in Poland in the same year, distinguishing himself at Gorodische (Order of St. George, 4th class) and Daragosta (golden sword). In 1793, he took part in the operations around Moghilev, for which he earned the Order of St. Vladimir (4th class). In 1794, he led the Nizhegorod Dragoon Regiment in the Caucasus and took part in the Persian Campaign in 1796, fighting at Derbent.

Rayevsky was discharged from the army during Emperor Paul's purges in May 1797. He was restored in the army with a rank of major general after Paul's assassination on 27 March 1801, but he took another discharge on 31 December of the same year due to his poor health and family problems. Rayevsky returned to the service in 1805, when he was appointed to the Imperial Retinue and served under Prince Peter Bagration during the Russian retreat from Braunau to Austerlitz. In April 1807, he took command of a jager brigade in Bagration's advance guard in Poland. He distinguished himself at Guttstadt (Order of St. Vladimir, 3rd class), Quetz, Deppen, Heislberg (wounded in the leg), and Friedland (Order of St. Anna, 1st class).

Rayevsky participated in the Russo-Swedish War in 1808, leading a detachment in Bagration's 21st Division. In the spring of 1808, he took part in the actions at Kumo, Bjorneborg, Normark, Christianstadt, and Vaasa, earning the Order of St. Vladimir (2nd class), promotion to lieutenant general on 26 April 1808, and command of the 21st Division two days later. Rayevsky fought at Gamle-Kalerby, Lappo, Kuortaine, Brahestadt, and Uleaborg. In 1809, he led the 11th Division in the Danubian Principalities, distinguishing himself at Silistra (golden sword with diamonds) and Shumla. On 12 April 1811, he took command of the 26th Division. The following year, 1812, he led the 7th Corps of the 2nd Western Army. On 22-23 July of that year, Rayevsky led an attack with his two sons, Alexander (16 years old) and Nikolay (10 years old) at the battle at Saltanovka (near Moghilev), where he engaged the French under Marshal Davout. Although he suffered a tactical defeat, Rayevsky inflicted nearly twice as many casualties as he suffered. His subsequent defense of Smolensk on 15-16 August 1812, allowed the Russian armies time to regroup and retreat to Borodino.

On 7 September 1812, Rayevsky played a prominent role in the battle of Borodino, where he defended an artillery battery in center of the Russian position known as the Great Redoubt (or Rayevsky's Redoubt). Although the French eventually captured it, his extraordinary defense of the key position earned him the Order of Alexander of Neva. At the council of war at Fily, Rayevsky urged that Moscow be abandoned. In October- November 1812, he participated in the battles of Tarutino, Maloyaroslavets (Order of St. George, 3rd class, 27 February 1813), and Krasnyi. When he became seriously ill, he took a furlough in December 1812, but returned to the army in late April 1813.

During the campaigns of 1813-1814, Rayevsky commanded the Grenadier Corps, fighting at Koenigswartha, Bautzen, Drezden, Kulm (Order of St. Vladimir, 1st class), and Dohna. He was seriously wounded in the neck at Leipzig, but remained on the battlefield. His actions earned him a promotion to general of cavalry on 20 October 1813, and the Austrian Order of Maria Theresa (3rd class). After the battle, he left the army to recuperate from the wound and returned in early 1814, when he replaced General Wittgenstein on 20 February 1814.

In 1814, Rayevsky fought at Arcis sur Aube, Vitry, Le Fère Champenoise, and Paris, for which he was awarded the Order of St. George (2nd class) on 31 March 1814. In 1815, he led his corps to France during the Hundred Days and attended a military parade at Vertus. After the war, he led the 3rd Corps (25 January 1816), and then the 4th Corps, before retiring on 7 December 1824.

Rayevsky was both surprised and angered when he learned in December 1825, that his two sons, Alexander and Nikolay, brother V. Davydov, and two sons-in-law, Mikhail Orlov and Sergey Volkonsky, took part in the Decembrist Uprising. They were all arrested and exiled to Siberia. Despite his family's involvement in the uprising, Rayevsky was appointed a member of the State Council on 7 February 1826, and over the next four years tried in vain to secure amnesty for the members of his family. Before he could do so, he became seriously ill and died on 28 September 1829. Rayevsky was buried in the village of Boltyshka in the Kiev *gubernia*.

REHBINDER, Maxim Vasilievich (b. 1730 — d. 22 February 1804) descended from a Westphalian noble family. After enlisting in the army in 1759, he served with the Azov Musketeer Regiment in the Russo-Turkish War in 1769-1774. During the next Russo-Turkish War in 1787-1791, Rehbinder distinguished himself in the campaign in the Kuban Valley and commanded the Schlüsselburg Musketeer Regiment until July 1797. He became major general and chef of the Azov Musketeer Regiment on 29 July 1797. In 1799, he led one of the divisions in Suvorov's army in Italy and Switzerland, fighting on the Adde and Trebbia Rivers, at Novi, and in the Alps. He retired after the campaign and died on 22 February 1804.

Several other Rehbinders also served in the Russian army: **Colonel Rehbinder** (first name unclear) led the Rostov Musketeer Regiment from 23 December 1807 to 11 September 1808, and the Count Arakcheyev's Musketeer Regiment from 11 September 1808 to 4 September 1809; **REHBINDER, Alexander Ottovich**, led the Tiflis Musketeer Regiment from 15 April 1805 to 19 February 1806; **REHBINDER, Otto Ivanovich**, took led the Kiev Cuirassier Regiment on 18 October 1801. He rose to major general and chef of the Zhitomir Dragoon Regiment on 16 September 1805. He took part in the Russo-Turkish War in 1806-1809, distinguishing himself at Obilesti on 19 June 1807. He died of illness in 1809 (removed from rosters on 9 December 1809); **REHBINDER, Roman Ivanovich**, commanded the Kazan Cuirassier Regiment between March and September 1798.

REHREN (Rehren I, Reren), Ivan Bogdanovich (Johann Friedrich) (b. 18 December 1775, Leppist — 19 October 1813, Leipzig) was born to a noble family in the Lifland *gubernia*. He studied in the Artillery and Engineer Cadet Corps and began service as a sub-lieutenant in the 1st Marine Battalion on 15 December 1792. Six years later, he led a grenadier battalion before becoming the commander of the Schlüsselburg Musketeer regiment on 17 March 1803. Promoted to colonel on 5 May 1806, he served with the 8th Division in Poland in 1806-1807, distinguishing himself at Eylau, where he was seriously wounded in the chest and left side (Order of St. George, 4th class, on 8 May 1807). In 1808-1811, he served in the Danubian Principalities, fighting at Frasin and Giurgiu.

In 1812, Rehren served with the 2nd Brigade of the 8th Division in the Army of Danube, and took part in the actions at Brest, Volkovisk, and Rudnya. In 1813, he fought at Lutzen, Bautzen, Reichenbach, Katzbah (promoted to major general on 27 September 1813), and was mortally wounded at Leipzig on 19 October 1813.

REMI, Gabriel Pavlovich (b. 1790 — date of death unclear) was born to a Dutch noble family. After serving in the Dutch army, he entered the Russian service as a lieutenant in the Engineer Corps on 20 March 1787. During the Russo-Turkish War of 1787-1791, he served at Ochakov, Bender (promoted to quartermaster), Tulcea, Issacea, Ismail (golden cross), and Braila. Promoted to captain on 9 February 1791, he served in the Black Sea Fleet from 1792 to 1796. Rising to a major in January 1797, he transferred to artillery and received the rank of lieutenant colonel on 8 October 1797. On 14 November

1798, he became colonel in Prince Mishetsky's Artillery Battalion. Two years later, Remi returned to the Engineer Corps and was promoted to major general on 14 June 1804. He served in the Engineer Expedition (Section) of the War College, receiving the Order of St. George (4th class) for twenty five years of service in 1809. He served in Kiev during the 1812-1814 Campaigns.

RENNI, Robert (Roman) Yegorovich (b. 23 April 1778 — d. 7 November 1832) was born to a Scottish family living in Riga. He was enlisted as a clerk in Major General Lunin's staff at age two. Promoted to ensign in October 1782 at the age of four, he transferred as a lieutenant to the Selenginsk Infantry Regiment in 1783. In 1785, he took a two-year furlough to travel to Scotland, but became seriously ill. When he did not return to the army on time, he was discharged for absence in 1787. After returning to Russia, Renni studied in the boarding school in Riga and returned to the service, joining the Yeletsk Infantry regiment in May 1794. The same year he served in Poland and was promoted to captain. In 1795-1796, he served on a mission to map Lithuania. In April 1796, he was appointed to the Quartermaster Section of the Imperial Retinue, and later served as ober-quartermaster in the Moscow Inspection.

Promoted to major in 1799, Renni participated in the expedition to Holland, fighting at Helder, Bergen, and Castricum, for which he garnered the Order of St. Anna (4th class). Returning to Russia, he rose to lieutenant colonel in March 1805, and served with Tolstoy's corps in nothern Germany in the fall of that year. In 1806-1807, Renni attended General Tolstoy in Poland, distinguishing himself at Eylau (wounded, Order of St. Vladimir, 4th class) and Heilsberg. After Tilsit, he took part in delimitation of the Russian state borders in Poland and was promoted to colonel on 6 January 1809. In 1810-1811, he served as a military agent at the Russian embassy in Berlin and was decorated with the Order of St. Anna (2nd class). Renni became quartermaster general for the 3rd Reserve Army of Observation in 1812 and fought at Kobryn (Order of St. Vladimir, 3rd class) and Gorodechnya, for which he was promoted to major general on 14 December 1812.

In 1813-1814, Renni served as the Chief of Staff of Winzegorode's corps, fighting at Kalisch (Order of St. George, 3rd class, 6 March 1813), Lutzen, Bautzen, Dennewitz (Swedish order of the sword), Leipzig (diamond signs of the Order of St. Anna, 1st class), Soissons (Order of St. Vladimir, 2nd class), Laon, St. Dizier (golden sword with diamonds), and Paris. For his service, he was also decorated with the Prussian Pour le Merite and Hesse-Kassel Order of Military Merit. He was appointed Chief of Staff of the 4th Corps in 1814, and returned to France during the Hundred Days in 1815. He retired because of poor health on 13 January 1816, and spent the next sixteen years at his estate in the St. Petersburg *gubernia*.

RENTEL, Vladimir Evdokimovich (date of birth unclear — d. 1829) was born to a German noble family. After studying in the Navy Cadet Corps, he began service as a guard marine in the Baltic Sea Fleet in 1788. During the Russo-Swedish War in 1788-1790, he served on the ship-of-the-line *Deris* at Gogland and on the ship-of-the-line *Boreslav* at Eland, Revel, and Vyborg. He continued serving in the Baltic Sea Fleet from 1792-1795, rising to lieutenant in May 1793.

In 1796-1802, Rentel took part in several cruises to Britain and commanded the transport vessel *Minerva* in 1803. The following year, he transfererd to the ship-of-the-line *Retvizan* and took part in the operations in the Ionian Islands and Naples in 1805-1806. In 1807, he fought the Turks at the Dardanelles and Mt. Athons, garnering the Orders of St. Anna (3rd class) and of St. George (4th class). He was in Senyavin's squadrons in Lisbon in 1808, and was promoted to lieutenant captain on 23 January 1808.

In 1809, Rentel returned to Russia and commanded gunboats on the Aya River near Riga, and in 1812 was decorated with the order of St. Vladimir (4th class) for his actions against the French. In 1813, he served at the siege of Danzig (Order of St. Anna, 2nd class). After the war, he commanded the 2nd Gallery *Ekipazh* and rose to captain (2nd class) in 1816. He served in the Gulf of Finland in 1816-1820, becoming captain (1st class) in September 1821. He led the ship-of-the-line *St. Andrew* in 1822, and commanded the 6th and later, the 16th, Fleet *Ekipazhs*. Rentel became rear admiral on 18 December 1827, and commanded the 3rd Brigade of the 1st Baltic Fleet Division until his death in 1829.

REPNIN-VOLKONSKY, Nikolay Grigorievich (b. 1778 — d. 18 January 1845) was born to the prominent Russian family of Princes Volkonsky and the grandson of Field Marshal Repnin. Born Volkonsky. He assumed the title of Prince Repnin-Volkonsky after the death of Field Marshal N. Repnin on 24 July 1801. Repnin-Volkonsky studied in the Infantry Cadet Corps and began service as an ensign in the Life Guard Izmailovsk Regiment on 20 October 1792. He transferred to the Leib-Hussar (Life Guard Hussar) Regiment on 25 April 1799. He took part in the 1799 Campaign in Holland, becoming to flügel adjutant to Emperor Paul I on 10 October 1799, and colonel on 9 October 1800. Two years later, he joined the Chevalier Guard Regiment on 29 September 1802. In 1805, he led a squadron at Austerlitz, where he was severely wounded in the chest and captured. He was released several weeks later and decorated with the Order of St. George (4th class) on 11 February 1806 for his courage at Austerlitz.

Unable to remain in the field, Repnin-Volkonsky retired because of his wound on 23 September 1806, receiving the rank of major general. After more than a two-year absence, he returned to the army on 23 November 1808, and because of his retirement, his seniority was dated from 13 January 1809. In 1809, he served as a Russian envoy to Westphalia. In February 1810, he was appointed the Russian *charge d'affairs* to Madrid, but Napoleon delayed him in Paris to prevent Russian involvement in Spanish affairs. Throughout this period, Repnin-Volkonsky gathered intelligence on the French military preparations. He was recalled on 23 April 1811.

In 1812, he led the reserve cavalry squadrons in the 1st Corps, fighting at Klyastitsy, Svolnya, Polotsk, and Chashniki, garnering the Order of St. George (3rd class) on 16 September 1812. In early 1813, he commanded a flying detachment, capturing Berlin and pursuing the French to the Elba River, for which he received promotion to adjutant general on 30 March 1813. He then fought at Dresden, Kulm (Prussian Iron Cross), and Leipzig.

Repnin-Volkonsky became the Governor General of Saxony on 20 October 1813, and commanded the Russian troops in Saxony. Promoted to lieutenant general on 17 March 1814, he left Saxony on 20 November 1814, and took part in the Congress of Vienna in 1815. For his service in the Napoleonic wars, he was decorated with the Prussian Pour le Merite, the Orders of the Black and Red Eagles, the Austrian

Order of Leopold (2nd class), and the French Order of St. Louis. He was appointed Military Governor of Malorossiia (Little Russia) in October 1816, and rose to general of cavalry on 7 July 1828. Repnin-Volkonsky attempted to implement a number of administrative, social, and economic reforms in the region, and often spent his personal finances to fund these projects. However, he faced stiff opposition from the local nobles, as well as from the conservative Minister of Finances Kankrin. Unjustly accused of embezzelement, Repnin-Volkonsky was removed from the position on 18 December 1834. Two years later, while still under investigation, he was discharged from military service. Disappointed by the unfair nature of the system to which he had devoted his life, Repnin-Volkonsky left Russia with his family to live in Europe for three years. He returned to Malorossia in 1842, and died on 18 January 1845, at his estate of Yagotin in the Poltava *gubernia*.

REPNINSKY (Repninsky II in 1812), Sergey Yakovlevich (b. 8 August 1775 — d. 6 April 1818) was born to a Russian noble family from the Kiev *gubernia*. He enlisted in the Life Guard Preobrazhensk Regiment on 12 January 1782, and transferred as a lieutenant to the Life Guard Semeyonovsk Regiment in 1792. After retiring as a captain in 1797, Repninsky returned to the army as a colonel and commander of the Vladimir Musketeer Regiment on 20 April 1799. He became major general and chef of the Smolensk Musketeer Regiment on 18 October 1800. Made a member of the War College on 19 April 1801, Repninsky took command of the Riga Musketeer Regiment on 17 January 1802, and became chef of the Novgorod Musketeer Regiment on 24 November 1802.

During the 1805 Campaign, Repninsky commanded the 4th Column on the march to Braunau. In November-December 1805, he distinguished himself at the head of a brigade at Dürrenstein (Krems) and again at Austerlitz, where he was wounded five times (three times in the right leg, once in the waist, and once in the head) but remained with his regiment. In 1806-1811, he participated in the Russo-Turkish War, fighting at Kuchbey, Babyli, Ismail, Galati, Braila (wounded in the head), Issacea, Tulcea, Girsov, Constanta (Kustendji), Rassevat (Imperial letter of gratitude), Tataritsa (another Imperial letter of gratitude), Silistra, Bazardjik (Order of St. Anna, 1st class), Shumla (Order of St. George, 5 December 1810), Batin, Giurgiu, and Viddin (Order of St. Vladimir, 3rd class). His unit (Novgorod Musketeers) was converted to the 43rd Jager Regiment on 31 October 1810.

In 1812, Repninsky served with the 3rd Brigade of the 16th Division in Major General Liders' detachment in Serbia and joined the 3rd Western Army in late 1812. In 1813, he took part in minor operations in Saxony, and in 1814, distinguished himself at Craonne and Laon. His wounds and active service took a toll, and after the war he retired to his estate in the village of Uvarovskoe in the Kaluga *gubernia*. He died there on 6 April 1818, and was buried at the Novodevichii Monastery in Moscow.

REPNINSKY (Repninsky I in 1812), Stepan Yakovlevich (b. 7 January 1774 — d. 3 July 1851, Kiev) was born to a Russian noble family from the Kiev *gubernia*. He enlisted in the Life Guard Semeyonovsk Regiment in 1776, rising to a sergeant on 12 January 1782. In May 1788, he was appointed flügel adjutant to Général-en-Chef Bruce. The following year, he became senior adjutant in Bruce's staff on 24 August 1789. He transferred as a premier major to the St. Petersburg Dragoon Regiment on 23 April 1792, and served in Poland in 1794, distinguishing himself at Vilna and Pogulyanka. Promoted to lieutenant colonel on 4 October 1797, he was discharged from the army on 23 September 1798. He returned to the army after Emperor Paul's murder in March 1801 and served in the Akhtyrsk Hussar Regiment. Repninsky took command of this unit on 30 July 1805, and distinguished himself at Austerlitz that December.

In 1806-1807, Repninsky served with the 10th Division in Poland, fighting at Pultusk and in numerous rear guard actions, including Jablonovo (Order of St. Vladimir, 4th class) and Sirotskoe (wounded, Order of St. George, 4th class, 13 December 1807). He was promoted to major general on 24 December 1807, and appointed chef of the Tiraspol Dragoon Regiment on 9 May 1808.

In 1809-1811, Repninsky served in the Danubian Principalities, taking part in the actions at Giurgiu, Turno, Bazardjik (Order of St. Anna, 1st class and a golden cross), Shumla, Ruse, and Viddin (Order of St. george, 3rd class, 28 February 1812). In early 1812, he served with the 22nd Brigade of the 7th Cavalry Division in the Army of Danube.

During the 1812 Campaign, Repninsky led a cavalry detachment in Volhynia and the Duchy of Warsaw, fighting at Ustilug and Rubezhev. In early 1813, he commanded troops at Novy-Zamostye and later served in Silesia and Saxony. In 1814, he commanded the Russian troops in the siege of Hamburg and became commander of the 2nd Brigade of the 2nd Horse Jager Division on 13 September 1814. In 1815, he led his brigade to France during the Hundred Days and was decorated with the Prussian Order of Red Eagle (2nd class).

Repninsky took command of the 2nd Dragoon Division on 8 October 1823, and rose to lieutenant general on 24 December 1824. He was relieved of command on 1 October 1830, and later presided over the military court investigating special cases of embezzelement and abuse of authority in the Kiev, Podolsk, and Volhynia *gubernia*s. For his service, he was promoted to general of cavalry on 29 March 1849. He died in Kiev on 3 July 1851, and was buried in the Kiev-Vydubitsk Monastery.

REPNINSKY, Nikolay Yakovlevich (b. 1790 — d. 13 March 1841) began service as a junker in the Life Guard Jager Regiment in October 1806, and served with this regiment at Guttstadt, on the Passarge, Heilsberg, and Friedland in 1807. Promoted to an ensign on 4 November 1807, he served in Finland from 1808-1809. In 1812, he fought at Smolensk, Borodino (wounded three times, Order of St. Vladimir, 4th class).

In 1813-1814, Repninsky took part in the battles at Lutzen, Bautzen, Pirna, Teplitz, Kulm, Leipzig, and Paris. Promoted to colonel on 7 November 1816, he served as a battalion commander in the Life Guard Lithuanian Regiment before taking command of the Penza Infantry regiment on 28 March 1819. After brief retirement in 1820, Repninsky took command of the Kamchatka Infantry Regiment in January 1822. He rose to a major general on 7 July 1827, and led the reserves of the 6th Corps during the Russo-Turkish War of 1828-1829. He retired on 28 February 1830.

RESLEYN, Fedor (Friedrich) Ivanovich (b. 1760 — d. 23 December 1838, Kazan) was born to a German noble family. He began service in the artillery in 1770s and took part in the Russo-Turkish War of 1787-1791, distinguishing himself at Ochakov (golden cross). Promoted to colonel in the 2nd Artillery Battalion on 15

August 1800, he took command of a company in the Leib Guard Artillery Battalion in 1804, and fought at Austerlitz on 2 December 1805.

After returning to Russia, Resleyn's keen administrative talents were put to outstanding use when he became the director of the Kazan gunpowder factory on 8 May 1806. He was also promoted to major general on 8 February 1809. He remained at the Kazan facility for the next twenty-five years, receiving the Order of St. Anna (2nd class). Resleyn retired in September 1830, and died on 23 December 1838.

REZVYI, Dmitry Petrovich (b. 1762 — d. 31 January 1823) was born to a middle class family in St. Petersburg. He enlisted as a furrier (fourrier) in the Guard in September 1781, rising to the rank of sergeant in the Life Guard Artillery Regiment in January 1786. On 23 May 1786, he transferred as an ensign to the staff of Général-en-Chef Ivan Müller-Zakomelsky, becoming a captain in June 1788. During the Russo-Turkish War of 1787-1791, Rezvyi fought at Ochakov (golden cross, 1788), Akkerman and Bender in 1789, and Macin in 1791. He took part in the operations in Poland in 1794, serving at Kruchitse, Brest, Kobylka, and Praga, where he earned the Order of St. George (4th class, 12 January 1795) and a golden cross.

On 8 August 1796, he was promoted to major in the 2nd Cannonier Regiment, and on 4 January 1797, transferred as a lieutenant colonel to the Schlüsselburg Infantry Regiment.

Promoted to colonel on 24 August 1798, Rezvyi served under Rimsky-Korsakov in Switzerland in 1799. Promoted to major general on 26 October 1799, Rezvyi was decorated by Emperor Paul I with the Order of St. John of Jerusalem on 16 December 1800. Between 18 March 1800 and 8 September 1801, Rezvyi served as chef of the 2nd Artillery Regiment. He became chef of the 3rd Artillery Battalion on 8 September 1801, and of the 4th Artillery Battalion on 5 October 1801. From 30 June 1803 to October 1806, he served again as chef of the 2nd Artillery Regiment. He actively participated in the artillery reforms of Aleksey Arakcheyev, earning the Order of St. Anna (2nd class) with diamonds. In June 1805, Emperor Alexander conferred him with noble status.

Rezvyi participated in the 1806-1807 Campaigns in Poland, fighting at Jankovo, Wolfsdorf, Eylau (wounded, right hand, Order of St. Anna), Guttstadt, Heilsberg, and Friedland (golden sword with diamonds). He led artillery in the Army of Moldavia in 1808-1811, where he served at Ruse, Rassevat, Tataritsa (wounded, Order of St. George, 3rd class), Braila, and Silistra. Rezvyi commanded the artillery in the main Russian army in early 1813, fighting at Lutzen, Bautzen, Dresden, and Leipzig.

Rezvyi served at Hamburg in 1814. However, his quarrel with powerful General Arakcheyev ruined his career. In early 1812, Rezvyi had made fun of Arakcheyev, which the thin-skinned officer never forgot. Arakcheyev refused Rezvyi the command of the Russian artillery in late 1812, and two years later, did not approve Rezvyi's promotion to lieutenant general— even though Rezvyi had served capably as a major general for more than fifteen years. Adding insult to injury, Arakcheyev forced Rezvyi out of the army on 29 December 1815. Rezvyi spent the next eight years in St. Petersburg, where he died on 31 January 1823.

REYCHEL, Abram Abramovich (b. 1767 — date of death unclear, ca. 1822) descended form a Saxon noble family. He entered the Russian civil service in February 1788, and in

October of that year became an adjutant with ensign's rank to Général-en-Chef Krechetnikov. He transferred to the Novotulsk Infantry Regiment on 20 June 1789, and joined the Astrakhan Grenadier Regiment on 14 July 1790. During the Russo-Turkish War in 1787-1791, he distinguished himself at Ismail (golden cross). After service in Poland in 1794, Reychel transferred to the Ladoga Musketeer Regiment on 18 December 1796. He took command of the Apsheron Musketeer Regiment on 11 November 1806, and rose to colonel on 24 December 1807.

Reychel fought in the Russo-Turkish War of 1806-1812 at Bucharest, Obilesti, Rassevat, Ruse (Order of St. George, 4th class), and Silistra. During the 1812 Campaign, he led the 2nd Brigade, 9th Division, 2rd Reserve Army of Observation, and fought at Kobryn. After the battle, he escorted Saxon prisoners to Zhitomir and later took part in the actions at Brest and on the Berezina. In 1813, he served at Thorn and Leipzig (wounded). He was discharged with the rank of major general on 24 January 1814.

REYTER (Reiter), Yemelyan Ivanovich (b. 1764 — date of death unknown, ca. 1837) was born to a noble family from the Lifland *gubernia*. He enlisted as a corporal in the Life Guard Preobrazhensk Regiment in January 1778, and transferred as a sub-ensign to the Pskov Infantry Regiment on 12 January 1780. He rose to sub-lieutenant in August 1785, and to lieutenant on 12 January 1786. After studying in the Infantry Cadet Corps, he graduated with a rank of captain on 13 August 1791.

Over the next seven years, Reyter enjoyed rapid promotions, becoming a major on 11 December 1796, a lieutenant colonel on 14 February 1798, a colonel on 31 August 1798, and a major general on 11 October 1799. He was discharged from the army on 19 March 1800, but returned to serve in the Commissariat on 7 November 1801. In 1801-1812, he directed the Commission of the Giorgievsk Supply Depot in the Caucasus and supplied the Russian troops on the Caucasian Line.

After the Napoelonic wars, Reychel served in the Committee of the Supply Depot and in the Supply Department of the Ministry of War.

REYTERN, Khristofor Romanovich (b. 10 October 1782 — d. September 1833) was born to a German noble family from the Lifland *gubernia*. He began service as a clerk to General Benckendorf on 30 May 1792, and transferred as an ensign to the Nasheburg Infantry Regiment in March 1793. He was discharged from the army on 30 January 1796, but returned to the service on 3 June 1797, serving in the Starodoub Cuirassier Regiment. Promoted to lieutenant on 30 June 1798, Reytern served in Rimsky-Korsakov's corps in Switzerland in 1799. He served in Moravia in 1805, and fought on the Passarge as well as at Guttstadt, Heilsberg, and Friedland in 1807. Reytern transferred to the Life Guard Hussar Regiment in late 1807, and again as a lieutenant colonel to the Alexander (*Aleksandriisky*) Hussar Regiment in 1811.

During the 1812 Campaign, Reytern served with Alexander Hussars in the 3rd Reserve Army of Observation and fought at Kobryn, Pruzhani, Borisov, on the Berezina, and at Vilna. In 1813, he distinguished himself at Lutzen (promoted to colonel), Bunzlau, Katzbach, and Leipzig (Order of St. Anna, 2nd class, the diamond signs to this order, and the Order of St. Vladimir, 4th class). The following year, he served at St. Dizier, Brienne, La Rothière, and Craonne, where he earned a golden sword.

After the war, he took command of the Alexander Hussar Regiment on 13 June 1815, and rose to major general on 24 December 1819. He commanded the 1st Brigade of the 1st Hussar Division before taking command of the Bug Uhlan Division on 29 November 1829.

During the Russo-Turkish War of 1828-1829, Reytern served at Braila (Order of St. Anna, 1st class), Giurgiu, Turno, Varna, Kozludji, Kulevchi, Shumla (Order of St. Vladimir, 2nd class), Slivno, and Adrianople. Promoted to lieutenant general on 1 January 1830, he participated in the suppression of the Polish Uprising in 1830-1831. In 1832, he took command of the 2nd Uhlan Division, but resigned because of poor health in July 1833.

RIBAS (Ribas y Boyons), Joseph (b. 17 June 1749, Naples — d. 14 December 1800) was born to a Spanish noble family. His father,

Michel de Ribas, served in Naples for nineteen years. The younger Ribas (the image above was painted later in life, but is almost certainly Ribas) began service in the Neapolitan army as a sub-lieutenant in the Regimento Samnio d'Infanteria in 1765. He entered Russian service as a captain in the Infantry Cadet Corps on 17 March 1774, and volunteered for service against the Turks. Serving in Mikhail Kamensky's corps, Ribas fought at Kozlitse, Yeni-Bazaar, and Bulanika. Returning to Russia, he worked as a censor in the Infantry Cadet Corps and rose to a lieutenant colonel in May 1776. Three years later, he transferred as a colonel to the Regular Army and took command of the Mariupol Light Horse Regiment. He took part in the campaign in the Crimea in 1783-1784.

During the Russo-Turkish War of 1787-1791, Ribas led land troops and flotillas at Ochakov (Order of St. Vladimir, 3rd class), Hadjibey (Orders of St. George, 3rd class, and of St. Vladimir, 2nd class), Akkerman, Bender, Tulcea, Issacea, and Ismail (golden sword with diamonds and a large estate). After becoming a rear admiral in 1791, Ribas commanded a cavalry detachment at Macin, for which he was decorated with the Orders of St. George (2nd class) and St. Alexander of Neva. In 1792-1793, he was placed in command of a flotilla in Kherson and earned a promotion to vice admiral. He was instrumental in establishing a harbor and developing the city infrastucture in Hadjibey (Odessa) in 1794-1796.

However, under Emperor Paul I, Ribas was removed from command in January 1797 but, after a brief period of disfavor, was appointed general-kriegs-commissar on 13 January 1798. Ribas rose to admiral on 19 May 1799, and headed the Forest Department. He was relieved of this position for embezzelement on 13 March 1800, but appointed to the Admiralty on 27 November 1800. However, he became seriously ill and died on 14 December 1800.

RICHELIEU, Armand-Emmanuel du Plessis (b. 25 September 1766, Paris — d. 17 May 1822, Paris) was born to a prominent French noble family, the son of Louis-Antoine-Armand du Plessis, duc de Fronsac, and direct descendant of Cardinal Louis-François-Armand de Vignerot du Plessis, duc de Richelieu. Armand Richelieu took over his grandfather's duties at court as first gentleman of the bedchamber in 1785. During the French Revolution, he left France and briefly served in the Russian army in 1790, standing out at Ismail, for which he earned a golden sword. He returned to France in early 1791 to arrange the funeral of his father. In August of the same year, he returned to Russia, where Empress Catherine II conferred him the honorary rank of colonel of the Russian army. In 1792, he delivered the Russian financial aid to Prince de Condé and served as the Russian agent in the Austrian army in the Rhineland from 1793-1794.

Richelieu returned to Russia and was appointed a lieutenant colonel in the Military Order Cuirassier Regiment in March 1795, and colonel in June of the same year. In 1797, he became a major general and commander of the His Majesty's Leib Cuirassier Regiment on 28 September 1797. Two months later, Emperor Paul appointed him chef of the same regiment on 12 December 1797. In 1802, Richelieu returned to France and met First Consul Napoleon Bonaparte. After returning to Russia, Emperor Alexander I appointed Richelieu Governor of Odessa (1803) and the Governor General of Novorosiisk (1805). Richelieu transformed the Black Sea village of Odessa into a modern city, constructing port facilities and encouraging agriculture and commerce.

During the Russo-Turkish War of 1806-1812, Richelieu commanded the 13th Division and did not participate in any major battles, though he did occupy Palanka, Akkerman, and Killia in 1806. Richelieu returned to France in 1814, but when Napoleon escaped from Elba in 1815, he again joined the Russian army. After Waterloo, Richelieu succeeded Charles Talleyrand as the Prime Minister with control of foreign affairs in September 1815. His friendship with Emperor Alexander helped him to mitigate the Allied demands on France, and at the Congress of Aix-la-Chapelle in 1818, he obtained the withdrawal of the Allied forces from France and the inclusion of France into the Quadruple Alliance.

Richelieu resigned in 1818, but became Prime Minister again in 1820. He retired from politics in 1821 and died on 17 May 1822 in Paris.

RICHTER, Boris Khristoforovich (Burhard Adam) (b. 23 November 1782 — d. 15 October 1832, Dresden) was born to a German noble family in the Lifland *guberniia*. He began service in the Tavrida Grenadier Regiment on 17 December 1797, rising to ensign the following year. In 1799, he took part in the expedition to Holland. Returning to Russia, he transferred to the Life Guard Horse Regiment in 1803, and in 1805 distinguished himself at Austerlitz, earning the Order of St. Anna (3rd class). Two years later, he fought at Heilsberg and Friedland, rising to staff rotmistr on 27 November 1807. Promoted to colonel on 30 March 1810, Richter took command of a battalion in the Life Guard Jager Regiment.

In 1812, Richter served with the 3rd Brigade of the Guard Infantry Division in the 5th Corps, fighting at Smolensk, Borodino (Order of St. George, 4th class, 3 December 1812), and Tarutino. In 1813, he served at Lutzen, Bautzen, Kulm (Prussian Iron Cross, promoted to major general on 27 September 1813, with seniority dating from 29 August 1813), and Teplitz, where he was wounded in the right hand and chest. In 1814, Richter led temporarily the Life Guard Finland Regiment. After the war, he took command of the 3rd Brigade of the 3rd Grenadier Division and was confirmed as commander of the Life Guard Finland Regiment on 23 January 1816. Five years later, he became commander of the Guard Settled Infantry Brigade [*gvardeiskaia posellennaia peshaia brigada*] of the Independent Lithuanian Corps on 15 February 1821.

Promoted to lieutenant general on 3 September 1826, Richter rose to adjutant general on 24 May 1829. In 1830, he led the Combined Guard and Grenadier Divisions of the Reserve Corps in Warsaw. On 28 November, he was arrested by the Polish insurgents and remained in captivity until the Russian army captured Warsaw in late 1831. Thereafter, he took command of the 3rd Guard Infantry Division on 18 October 1831.

Another **RICHTER, Yegor Khristo-forovich**, took command of the Revel Musketeer regiment on 24 August 1807, and rose to lieutenant colonel on 24 December 1807. He became commander of the Muromsk Musketeer Regiment on 12 March 1808, and was promoted to a colonel on 19 November 1811. During the campaign of 1812- 1813, he led the Life Guard Pavlovsk Grenadier Regiment between 22 January 1812 and 15 September 1813.

RIDIGER (Rüdiger), Fedor Vasilievich (b. 1783, Mitau — d. 23 June 1856, St. Petersburg) was born to a German noble family in the Courland *gubernia*. He enlisted as a sub-ensign in the Life Guard Semeyonovsk Regiment on 12 April 1799, begining a long and distinguished career that would span more than half a century of service. After reaching ensign on 7 November 1800, Ridiger transferred as a lieutenant to the Sumsk Hussar regiment in 1802, and served as an adjutant to Major General Pahlen. Promoted to staff captain on 11 March 1805, he served in General Knorring's troops in Prussia during the 1805 Campaign. Ridiger took part in minor actions against the French in May-June 1806, and garnered a golden saber on 1 June 1806. Ridiger transferred to the Grodno Hussar Regiment on 29 August 1806, and served with the 14th Division and in Bagration's rearguard in Poland in 1806-1807. Ridiger distinguished himself at Deppen, Heilsberg, and Friedland, earning in return the Order of St. Anna (2nd class).

After becoming a major on 4 November 1807, Ridiger again served under Prince Bagration in Finland from 1808-1809, fighting at Tavastheus, Nakili, Lapfert, Vaasa (Order of St. Vladimir, 4th class), Gamle Kalerby (Order of St. George, 4th class, 27 February 1809), Lappo, Kolmar, Kartane (wounded in the left leg, promoted to lieutenant colonel on 31 December 1808), Viganda, and Uleaborg. In 1810, Ridiger commanded the coastal defenses between Revel and Pernov (Piarnu). In 1812, he served in the 1st Corps and distinguished himself at Druya (Drouia), where he captured French General St. Germaine and was promoted to colonel on 26 August 1812. Ridiger served at Klyastitsy (Order of St. Vladimir, 3rd class), Svolnya (Order of St. Anna, 2nd class), two battles at Polotsk (diamond signs of the Order of St. Anna, 2nd class, for the first battle, and the Order of St. George, 3rd class, for the second battle), Chashniki (promoted to major general on 8 June 1813 with seniority dating from 31 October 1812), Borisov, on the Berezina, at Vilna, Koenigsberg, and Elbing. Ridiger rose to chef of the Grodno Hussar Regiment on 12 November 1812.

In early 1813, Ridiger served in the blockades of Danzig, Spandau, Magdeburg, and Halle. He fought at Lutzen (Prussian Order of Red Eagle, 2nd class), Bautzen (Prussian Order of Red Eagle, 1st class), Reichenbach (Order of St. Anna, 1st class), Dresden, Peterswalde, Kulm, and Leipzig (diamond signs of the Order of St. Anna, 1st class). In 1814, he served at Strasburg, Brienne, Nogent, Bar sur Aube, Troyes (order of St. Vladimir, 2nd class), Malmaison, Arcis sur Aube, Le Fère Champenoise, and Paris. Ridiger took command of the 2nd Brigade of the 1st Hussar Division on 29 December 1814, of the 1st Hussar Division on 9 December 1816, of the 2nd Dragoon Division on 4 June 1819, and of the 3rd Division on 8 October 1823. Ridiger rose to lieutenant general on 18 January 1826.

During the Russo-Turkish War of 1828-1829, Ridiger led the Russian advance guard, distinguishing himself at Constanta (Kustendji), Mangalia, Varna, Bazardjik, Shumla, Eski-

Istambul and Shumla, where he garnered a golden sword with diamonds on 3 November 1828. In the winter of 1829, he led the 7th Corps in Bulgaria and fought at Arnau-Lare, Kulevchi (Order of St. Alexander of Neva), Shumla, Slivno and Adrianople, garnering the Order of St. Vladimir (1st class).

After the war, Ridiger took command of the 4th Reserve Cavalry Corps on 4 October 1829, and led the Russian troops in Moldavia. He rose to adjutant general on 9 May 1831. During the Polish Uprising in 1831, Ridiger successfully operated in Volhynia in the spring of 1831, and was promoted to adjutant general on 9 May 1831. He later defeated Polish General Dwernicki at Boromel and drove the Polish forces to the Galician frontier. Fos his conduct, Ridiger received an allowance of 50,000 rubles and the rank of general of cavalry on 18 October 1831. He was appointed commander of the 3rd Corps on 14 November of the same year. Ridiger became chef of the Klyastitsy Hussar Regiment on 26 May 1845. In 1846, he suppressed the Polish uprising in Krakov, for which he received the Austrian Order of Leopold (1st class) and the title of count of the Russian Empire on 15 October 1847.

In 1848-1849, Ridiger commanded the Russian troops dispatched to assist the Austrians against the Hungarian Uprising and was decorated with the Order of St. Andrew the First Called and the Dutch Order of Wilhelm (2nd class). Due to his poor health, Ridiger resigned as head of the 3rd Corps on 6 September 1850, and later served in the State Council, receiving the Austrian Order of St. Stephan. During the Crimean War, he took command of the Guard and Grenadier Corps on 3 March 1855, garnering the diamond signs of the Order of St. Andrew the First Called. Ridiger retired because of illness late the same year, and he died in St. Petersburg on 23 June 1856.

RIDINGER, Alexander Karlovich (b. 28 October 1782 — d. 7 October 1825) was born to a prominent German noble family in the Estland *gubernia*; son of Karl Ridinger, Governor of Vyborg. He studied in the Infantry Cadet Corps and began service as a page at the Imperial Court in December 1796, rising to kamer-page on 20 October 1798. On 17 October 1801, he transferred as a lieutenant to the Life Guard Jager Regiment and distinguished himself at Austerlitz in 1805. In 1806-1807, he fought at Eylau, on the Passarge, and at Friedland, garnering a golden sword for the latter.

Promoted to colonel on 4 November 1807, Ridinger rose to become the Commandant of Wilmanstrand and chef of the Wilmanstrand Garrison Battalion on 23 April 1809. Two years later, he was appointed chef of the 44th Jager Regiment on 12 October 1811. During the 1812 Campaign, he served in the 3rd Brigade of the 21st Division in the Finland Corps, fighting in the Baltic provinces. In 1813, he distinguished himself at Pillau and Leipzig, for which he was promoted to major general on 23 January 1814, with seniority dating from 18 October 1813. In 1814, he served at Soissons (Order of St. George, 3rd class, 3 October 1814), Craonne, Laon, and Paris. After the war, Ridinger commanded a brigade of the 21st Division.

RIMSKY-KORSAKOV, Alexander Mikhailovich (b. 24 August 1753 — d. 25 May 1840, St. Petersburg) was born to a Russian noble family. He enlisted as a corporal in the Life Guard Preobrazhensk Regiment in 1768, rising to a sub-ensign in 1769, to a sergeant in 1770, to an ensign in 1774 and to a lieutenant in 1775. Promoted to lieutenant colonel in 1778, he transferred to the Chernigov Infantry Regiment and served in Poland from 1778-1779. During the Russo-Turkish War of 1787-1791, he was assigned to the Austrian Corps, fighting at Khotin and Gangur in 1788. The following year, he led a detachment at Byrlad, Maximeni, on the Siret River, and at Galati. He had the honor of delivering the news of the Russian victories to Catherine II, who decorated him with the Order of St. George (4th class) and promoted him to brigadier.

Rimsky-Korsakov transferred to the Life Guard Semeyonovsk Regiment on 25 July 1789, and served on the galley flotilla against the Swedes at Friedrichsham, Neischlodt, and Julaksioki (Order of St. Vladimir, 3rd class). He became a major general in 1793, and briefly visited Britain in 1794. He joined the Austrian army in the Netherlands and took part in various actions against the French in late 1794. Rimsky-Korsakov returned to Russia in 1795 and, during the following year, participated in the Persian Expedition along the Caspian Sea, distinguishing himself at Derbent (Order of St. Anna, 1st class) and Gandja (Order of St. Alexander of Neva). Under Emperor Paul, Rimsky Korsakov became the infantry inspector for the St. Petersburg Inspection and received promotion to a lieutenant general on 15 January 1798. He became chef of the Rostov Musketeer Regiment on 28 September 1798.

In 1799, Rimsky-Korsakov commanded a corps against the French in Switzerland and was decisively defeated at Zurich in September 1799. He was removed from command and discharged from the army in November of the same year. He returned to the service in March 1801, receiving rank of general of infantry on 27 March 1801, with seniority dating from 5 December 1799.

In 1802, Rimsky-Korsakov became the Governor of Byelorussia. One year later, he was appointed infantry inspector in Moscow. In 1805-1806, he commanded the Russian reserves in the western provinces and became the Military Governor of Lithuania on 1 October 1806. Rimsky-Korsakov organized local militias during the campaigns in Poland in 1806-1807, for which he was decorated with the Order of St. Vladimir (1st class). Following a bitter disagreement with General Aleksey Arakcheyev, Rimsky-Korsakov took a discharge on 15 July 1809. In 1812, he was again appointed the Military Governor of Lithuania, serving at this position for the next eighteen years. He became a member of the State Council in 1830, and died in St. Petersburg on 25 May 1840.

RITTER, George Ivanovich (b. 1731 — date of death unclear) was born to a German noble family. After service in the Württemberg army, he entered Russian service as a sub-lieutenant in the 1st Moscow Regiment in 1766. After a brief retirement in 1767-1769, Ritter returned to the army as a sub-lieutenant in the St. Petersburg Legion. He participated in the Russo-Turkish War in 1770-1774, rising to a lieutenant in January 1771, and then served in Poland from 1775-1776. He became captain in the Revel Infantry Regiment in January 1777, and transferred as a major to the Polotsk garrison on 12 November 1780.

Ritter again served in Poland in 1794, rising to lieutenant colonel on 21 December 1797. A year later he made colonel on 27 June and later that year became Commandant of Polotsk and chef of the Polotsk Garrison Battalion on 14 December 1798. Promoted to a major general on 19 June 1799, he retired with a rank of lieutenant general on 16 March 1800. Ritter returned to the army nine months later on 18 December, and became chef of the Perma Musketeer Regiment on 23 December. He was appointed

Commandant of Arensburg in August 1801, and of Pernov on 16 October 1804.

RODIONOV (Rodionov II in 1812), Mark Ivanovich (b. 1770 — d. 1826) was born to a prominent Cossack noble family in Cherskassk. He began service as a clerk in January 1782, and rose to sotnik in April 1782. During the Russo-Turkish War of 1787-1791, he distinguished himself at Ochakov (golden cross and rank of esaul), Kaushani, Bender (wounded in the head), and Ismail, where he received a golden cross and promotion to captain. Rodionov commanded a Cossack regiment in Poland in 1794, garnering a golden cross and rank of premier major for Praga. After becoming a colonel on 29 March 1799, he served in the Don Cossack Host from 1801-1811.

During the 1812 Campaign, Rodionov served with the 1st Corps at Drissa, Zhiltsy, Goropatki (promoted to major general on 12 November 1812, with seniority dating from 20 September 1812), Polotsk (wounded in the head), Smolyani, and on the Berezina (Order of St. George, 3rd class, 12 August 1813). In February 1813, he distinguished himself at Tempelberg, near Danzig and was later decorated with the Order of St. George (4th class) on 23 July 1813. Rodionov also served at Berlin, Dresden, Wittenberg, Bautzen, and Magdeburg. In 1814, he took part in the operations in Hanover. After the war, he returned to the Don Cossack Host.

ROMODANOVSKY-LADYZHENSKY, Alexander Nikolaevich was born to a prominent Russian family, son of Senator Nikolay Ivanovich Romodanovsky-Ladyzhensky and Baroness Maria Isaevna Shafirova. He was enlisted in the Guard in 1770, but later served as a kamer page at the court. In August 1783, he transferred as a lieutenant to the Horse Guards and rose to rotmistr in 1789. In January 1795, he transferred to the regular army as a colonel and the following year joined the Orenburg Dragoon Regiment, which he led until December 1797. Promoted to major general on 20 December 1797, Romodanovsky-Ladyzhensky served as chef of the Malorosiisk Cuirassier Regiment until 6 November 1798, when he became chef of the Kharkov Cuirassier Regiment. The following year, he again became chef of the Malorossiisk Cuirassier Regiment on 3 February 1799 (served until 29 May 1806) and rose to lieutenant general on 25 November 1799.

ROOP, Evstafii (Gustav) Antonovich (b. 1788 — d. 25 April 1840, Gatchina) was born to a noble family from Estland *gubernia*. He began service in the Kazan Dragoon Regiment on 13 January 1803, and rose to ensign in 1804. He served with the 5th Division in Poland in 1806-1807, and was seriously wounded in the right shoulder and face at Eylau. After a transfer to the Life Guard Dragoon Regiment on 24 December 1809, Roop was promoted to lieutenant in 1810. He was elevated to staff captain on 2 February 1813, and distinguished himself at Kulm, for which he was decorated with the Order of St. Vladimir (4th class) and the Prussian Iron Cross.

In the Battle of Leipzig, Roop was wounded in the left leg and chest, but managed to remain with the regiment for the rest of the campaign. In 1814, he served as a liason officer between Quartermaster General Diebitch and Field Marshal Blücher, and fought at La Rothière, Arcis sur Aube, and Le Fère Champenoise, (golden sword for courage and the Order of St. Anna, 2nd class). After the war, Roop trained the cavalry squadrons, becoming a captain on 6 April 1816, a colonel on 26 May 1819, and a major general on 6 April 1828. He became the Director of Gatchina on 22 January 1832.

His brother **ROOP, Bogdan (Emmanuel) Antonovich** (b. 1795 — d. 1865), also served in the Life Guard Dragoon Regiment, distinguishing himself at Dresden, Kulm (Order of St. Anna, 4th class), Leipzig, La Rothière, Le Fère Champenoise (Order of St. Vladimir, 4th class), Sezanne, Rheims, and Paris.

ROSEN (Rosen III in 1812), Alexander Vladimirovich (b. 29 October 1779 — d. 1 September 1832) was born to a noble family from the Estland *gubernia*. He was enlisted as a sergeant in the Life Guard Preobrazhensk Regiment on 12 January 1787, transferred as a vakhmistr to the Life Guard Horse Regiment on 12 January 1794, and rose to captain in the Azov Infantry Regiment in January 1795. Promoted to major on 3 October 1796, he joined the Riga Musketeer Regiment in May 1797. In 1799, he served as an adjutant to Field Marshal Alexander Suvorov during the campaigns in Italy and Switzerland, distinguishing himself at Brescia, on the Adda River (Order of St. Anna, 2nd class), at Tortona, Marengo, Turin (Order of St. John of Jerusalem and the Sardinian Order of St. Maurice and Lazarus), Alessandria, Seravalle, Novi (Order of St. Anna, 2nd class, with diamonds), and in the crossing of the Alps (Austrian Order of Maria Theresa).

Rosen was elevated to a lieutenant colonel on 22 January 1800, and served in the Riga Musketeer Regiment before transfering to the Life Guard Preobrazhensk Regiment on 25 December 1801. He was promoted to colonel on 29 September 1802. In 1805, he served with the Pavlograd Hussar Regiment at Ems, Amstetten, Hollabrunn, Wischau, and Austerlitz (Order of St. George, 4th class, 24 January 1806). He took command of the Pavlograd Hussar Regiment on 21 December 1806, and serving in the 2nd Division, fought at Golymin, Eylau, Guttstadt, Heilsberg, and Friedland, garnering the Order of St. Vladimir (3rd class). He became chef of the His Majesty's Leib Cuirassier Regiment on 23 August 1810.

In 1812, Rosen served with the 1st Cuirassier Brigade of the 1st Cuirassier Division in the 1st Western Army, fighting at Borodino (promoted to major general on 3 Decemebr 1812), Tarutino, Maloyaroslavets, Vyazma, and Krasnyi (Order of St. Anna, 1st class).

During the campaigns in Germany and France in 1813-1814, Rosen served at Lutzen, Bautzen, Leipzig, Brienne, Le Fère Champenoise, and Paris. After the war, he led the 1st Brigade of the 3rd Dragoon Division before taking command of the 3rd Dragoon Division on 13 January 1819. He was removed because of poor health on 11 April 1822, and died in St. Petersburg on 1 September 1832.

ROSEN, Andrey Fedorovich (b. 1773 — date of death unclear; removed from rosters on 22 May 1829) was born to a noble family from the Lifland *gubernia*. He enlisted as a corporal in the Life Guard Horse Regiment in 1787, rising to a vakhmistr in 1790, and to a lieutenant in the Chevalier Guard Corps in 1792. He transferred to the Kinburn Dragoon Regiment in 1796, and served in Switzerland in 1799. Returning to Russia, he joined the Starodoub Cuirassier Regiment in 1802. The following year, he transferred to the Pereyaslavl Dragoon Regiment.

After retirement in 1804-1805, Rosen took part in the Russo-Turkish War of 1806-1812, fighting at Killia, Karmankun, and Ismail in 1806-1807. He joined the Smolensk Dragoon Regiment in late 1807, and became an adjutant to Field Marshal Prozorovsky in 1809. In 1809-

1810, he served in the Alexandria Hussar Regiment and participated in the actions at Rassevat, Tataritsa, Silistra, Shumla, Batin, Ruse, Giurgiu, and Nikopol, garnering the Orders of St. Vladimir (4th class), St. Anna (2nd class), and a golden saber. During the 1812 Campaign, Rosen served with the 3rd Reserve Army of Observation at Kobryn, Gorodechna, Borisov, and on the Berezina.

In 1813, Rosen fought at Kalisch, Lutzen (rose to a colonel on 2 May 1813), Bautzen, Gross Beeren, Dennewitz (Order of St. George, 4th class), and Leipzig, where he was wounded in the left leg. In 1814, he led a detachment through Holland and fought at Soissons, Craonne, Laon, Rheims, St. Dizier, and in other minor actions, for which he was decorated with the Order of St. Vladimir (3rd class). After the war, he took command of the Grodno Hussar Regiment from 1815-1819. Rosen was appointed commandant of Baku in Azerbaidjan in 1825, and repulsed the Persian offensive in 1826. He died in early 1829.

ROSEN (Rosen IV), Fedor Fedorovich (Friedrich Otto) (b. 9 July 1767, Revel — d. 17 July 1851, Revel) was born to a noble family of barons from the Lifland *gubernia*. He enlisted as a private in the Life Guard Preobrazhensk Regiment on 12 January 1777, and soon transferred to the Life Guard Izmailovsk Regiment, where he became a sergeant in 1779. However, he remained at home until age eighteen and began actual service in 1785. Rosen transferred as a captain to the 4th Battalion of the Estland Jager Corps in January 1789. He took part in the Russo-Swedish War in 1789-1790, serving on the galley flotilla at Bjorkzund, Vybog, and Rochensalmi. Rosen served in Poland in 1792-1794, transferring to the St. Petersburg Grenadier Regiment on 27 March 1795. He rose to a major on 3 January 1799 and received the Order of St. Anna (3rd class) at the military review in Revel in June 1804. On 29 March 1804, he was appointed platz-major in Revel and rose to lieutenant colonel on 18 December of the same year.

Rosen took command of the St. Petersburg Grenadier Regiment on 1 April 1805, and served in Tolstoy's corps in Hanover in late 1805. During the 1806-1807 Campaigns in Poland, Rosen served in the 2nd Division at Pultusk, Jankovo, and Eylau, where he seriously wounded in the left hand. For his conduct, he was promoted to colonel on 24 December 1807. In 1808, he served in the Baltic coastal defense against the British and Swedish navies, and in 1809-1810, remained with his regiment at Kobryn. He became chef of the newly formed Lithuanian Musketeer (later Infantry) Regiment on 29 January 1811. In 1812, he led the 2nd Brigade of the 21st Division in the Finland Corps and served at Mitau, Polotsk, Ushach, Chashniki, Smolyani, on the Berezina, and at Labiau (Order of St. Vladimir, 3rd class).

In 1813, Rosen took part in the actions at Danzig and commanded a brigade of the 21st Division at Gross Beeren, Dennewitz, and Leipzig, for which he was promoted to major general on 23 January 1814, with seniority dating from 18 October 1813. In 1814, he fought at Soissons, Rheims (served as commandant of the town), Craonne, Laon (Order of St. Anna, 1st class), and Paris.

After the war, Rosen briefly served as an assistant to the 21st Division and took command of the 3rd Brigade of the 14th Division on 6 January 1816. He resigned from this position because of poor health on 1 October 1821. He served as the Commandant of Sebastopol from 24 May 1832 to 21 September 1842, and was promoted to lieutenant general during this posting (14 April 1833). Rosen received the Order of St. Vladimir (2nd class) on 14 April 1834, and was relieved of command because of poor health on 21 February 1842. He rose to general of infantry on 29 March 1845, and lived in Revel until his death on 17 July 1851.

ROSEN (Rosen III in 1812), Gregory Vladimirovich (b. 11 October 1782 — d. 18 August 1841) was born to a noble family from the Estland *gubernia*; the brother of Alexander Rosen. He was enlisted by his family as a sub-ensign in the Life Guard Preobrazhensk Regiment on 17 March 1789, rising to portupei-ensign on 1 January 1796, ensign on 1 February 1797, lieutenant on 20 September 1798, staff captain on 15 May 1799, and captain on 2 June 1803. During the 1805 Campaign, Rosen distinguished himself at Austerlitz, receiving in return a golden sword and later, the rank of colonel on 10 April 1806. In 1807, he became chef of the 1st Jager Regiment (27 January 1807), and served as a duty officer to Platov in the actions at Guttstadt, Launau, Bergfried (Order of St. George, 4th class), Heilsberg, and Welau, garnering the Order of St. Vladimir (3rd class) and the Prussian Pour le Merite.

Rosen participated in the Russo-Swedish War of 1808-1809 and distinguished himself at Helsinger (major general on 9 April 1809) and in the expedition to the Aland Islands. Rosen transferred to the guard on 26 September 1810, when he took command of the Guard Brigade comprised of the Life Guard Preobrazhensk and Semeyonovsk Regiments. During the 1812 Campaign, he took part in the rearguard actions at Mikhailovka, Semleva, Belomirskoe, Vyazma, and Kolotsk before fighting at Borodino (Order of St. Anna, 1st class), Mozhaisk, and Krasnyi (Order of St. George, 3rd class, 15 June 1813). He took command of the Life Guard Preobrazhensk Regiment on 28 December 1812.

In 1813, Rosen fought at Lutzen (took command of the 1st Guard Division on 11 May 1813), Bautzen (Prussian Order of Red Eagle, 1st class), Dresden, Pirna, Teplitz, Kulm (Prussian Iron Cross, promoted to lieutenant general on 11 September 1813, with seniority dating from 29 August 1813), and Leipzig. He took part in the invasion of France in 1814, receiving the Order of St. Vladimir (2nd class, 15 May 1814) and a silver medal for the capture of Paris. After the war, Rosen led the 20th Division and later the 1st Guard Infantry Division, rising to adjutant general on 4 March 1818. On 23 May 1821, he took command of the 15th Division, receiving the diamond signs of the Order of St. Anna (1st class) on the military review in 1823. He took command of the Combined Division of the 5th Corps on 13 May 1826.

On 3 September 1826, Rosen became a general of infantry and commander of the 1st Corps. The following year, he assumed command of the Independent Lithuanian Corps on 8 November 1827, and received the order of St. Alexander of Neva. He distinguished himself during the Polish Campaign of 1830-1831. For his service, he was decorated with the Order of St. George (2nd class) on 25 September 1831, and on the same day, was appointed Commander of the Independent Caucasian Corps and the Civil Governor of Transcaucasia. He launched several expeditions to subdue Chechnya and Shamkhal in 1832-1833, and received the Persian Order of the Lion and the Sun. In 1834-1837, Rosen fought Imam Shamil in Daghesstan and Chechnya, but failed to subdue the Chechens. On 12 December 1837, he resigned from his position and later served in the Senate.

ROSEN (Rosen I in 1812), Ivan Karlovich (b. 1753 — d. 14 July 1817, Kiev) was born to a noble family from the Lifland *gubernia*. He began service in the College of Foreign Affairs in November 1767, and enlisted as an ensign in the Tenginsk Infantry Regiment in 1769, rising to a sub-lieutenant on 20 January 1770, lieutenant on 5 December 1770, and captain on 5 December 1771. Rosen took part in the Russo-Turkish War of 1769-1774, fighting at Khotin, Larga, Kagul, Giurgiu (wounded in the leg), Bucharest, Turno, and Ruse. After fighting in Poland in 1777-1779, he served on the staff of Prince Gregory Potemkin in 1781-1786, rising to second major on 22 May 1780, premier major on 9 July 1783, and lieutenant colonel on 12 January 1786.

During the Russo-Turkish War of 1787-1791, Rosen served at Kinburn and Ochakov before becoming an ober-quartermaster in General Krechetnikov's detachment. Rosen returned to Poland in 1792 and distinguished himself at Opsau, Prevozh, and Kamenets-Podolsk. He was promoted to colonel on 19 October 1794, and received the Order of St,. George (4th class) for twenty-five years of service. Rosen became major general and chef of the New Ingermanland Regiment on 19 October 1797. Made lieutenant general on 30 September 1799, he led the advance guard of Gudovich's corps in 1799, and the 6th Column of the Army of Podolsk in 1805. He was diverted to the Danubian Principalities in the opening of the 1805 Campaign, but was later ordered to reinforce General Kutuzov in Moravia.

Rosen was dispatched to Georgia in 1806, where he took command of the 20th Division and fought the Turks in southern Georgia and Armenia in 1807-1809. In 1810, he helped to defeat and capture King Solomon II of Imereti, and later served as the Military Governor of Tbilisi. However, after King Solomon escaped from the Tbilisi Prison, Rosen was removed from command. He later led a corps in the Army of Poland in 1813 and served at Glogau. In 1814, Rosen again took command of the 20th Division, but was relieved on 28 August 1816.

ROSEN (Rosen VI), Otto Fedorovich (b. 1782 — d.) began service as a private in the Revel Garrison Regiment on 17 March 1797, quickly becoming a portupei-ensign on 17 July 1797, ensign on 4 April 1798, sub-lieutenant on 1 June 1798, and lieutenant on 10 December 1798. He transferred to the Tobolsk Infantry Regiment on 22 January 1802, and rose to staff captain on 4 August 1803, and to a captain on 6 December 1806. During the 1806-1807 Campaigns in Poland, Rosen fought at Pultusk, Landsberg, Eylau (golden cross), and minor rearguard actions. Promoted to major on 19 November 1808, Rosen joined the Elisavetgrad Hussar Regiment on 26 March 1811.

During the 1812 Campaign, Rosen fought at Kochergamki, Ostrovno, Vitebsk (wounded in the left leg, received the Imperial letter of gratitude), Porechye, Smolensk, and Borodino (Order of St. Anna, 2nd class). He later served in Lieutenant General Dorokhov's detachment, participating in various skirmishes and raids, for which he garnered the Orders of St. George (4th class) and St. Vladimir (4th class). Rosen distinguished himself at Vereya (golden sword), Maloyaroslavets (Imperial letter of gratitude), Vyazma, Dorogobouzh, and Krasnyi (Imperial letter of gratitude). In 1813, he became a lieutenant colonel on 11 February 1813, and after the battle of Dennewitz, received promotion to colonel on 6 September 1813. At Leipzig, he was wounded in the head and decorated with the Order of St. Anna (2nd class).

In December 1813, Rosen briefly served at Hamburg before marching to France, where he took part in the actions at Soissons, Craonne, Laon (Order of St. Vladimir, 3rd class), Rheims, and St. Dizier (Prussian Pour le Merite). He took command of the Elisavetgrad Hussar Regiment on 15 September 1814, and returned to France during the Hundred Days in 1815. He led the Elisavetgrad Hussars between 1815-1820, and receivrf four Imperial letters of gratitude (1816, 1817, 1819 and 1820) for excellent maintenance of the unit. Rosen was promoted to major general on 31 March 1820, and late the same year, served as an assistant to the commander of the 1st Horse Jager Division.

Rosen took command of the 2nd Brigade of the 1st Dragoon Division (2 September 1821), of the 2nd Brigade of the 1st Hussar Division (14 April 1822) of the 2nd Brigade of the 2nd Uhlan Division on 2 August 1825, of the 1st Brigade of the 2nd Uhlan Division on 12 September 1825, and of the 2nd Uhlan Division (11 February 1826). He fought in the Russo-Persian War in 1826-1827, at Echmiadzin, Nakhichevan, Abbas-Abad, Djevan Bulak (Order of St. Anna, 1st class), Yerivan, and Sardar-Abad (Order of St. George, 3rd class). In 1828, he was dispatched with a mission to the Shah of Persia, who decorated him with the Persian Order of the Lion and the Sun. Rosen was elevated to lieutenant general in 1829, but was murdered by his former adjutant in late 1831.

His brother, **ROSEN, Peter Fedorovich** (ca. 1778 - 1831), became the Deputy Head of the Supreme Military Police [*vischaia voennaia politsia*] in the Ministry of War in March 1812. During the 1812-1813 Campaign, he served as the Director of the Supreme Military Police in the main Russian army, earning the Order of St. Anna (2nd class). He distingusihed himself in the Battle of Leipzig, for which he was later decorated with the diamond signs of the Order of St. Anna (2nd class, 13 July 1814). On 28 April 1813, his civil rank was converted to colonel, and on 2 November of the same year, became the Head of the Police in Saxony, receiving the Order of St. Vladimir on 11 January 1814. After earning the Prussian Order of Red Eagle (2nd class) in 1814, Rosen became the Head of the Military Police in the 1st Army on 22 March 1815. He later supervised the Russian hospitals in Germany until 13 September 1816.

ROSEN, Roman Fedorovich (b. 11 November 1782 — d. 4 October 1848) was born to a noble family from the Lifland *gubernia*. He enlisted in the Revel Garrison Regiment on 17 March 1797, rising to a portupei-ensign on 17 July 1797, ensign on 11 February 1798, sub-lieutenant on 4 April 1798, and lieutenant on 11 December 1798. He joined the Tobolsk Infantry Regiment on 22 January 1802, becoming a staff captain on 31 July 1802, and captain on the 17 October 1806.

Rosen took part in the campaigns in Poland in 1806-1807, fighting at Pultusk, Landsberg, and Eylau (wounded in the right side, Prussian Pour le Merite). He was promoted to a major on 19 November 1808. At Borodino four years later, Rosen distinguished himself in action and received a promotion to lieutenant colonel on 28 October 1812, and the Order of St. George (4th class).

In 1813, Rosen took part in the actions at Lutzen, Pirna, Dresden, and Leipzig, garnering the Order of St. Vladimir (4th class). The following year, he fought at Nogent, Bar sur Aube, Troyes (Order of St. Vladimir, 3rd class), Le Fère Champenoise, and Paris, where he earned the Order of St. Anna with diamonds. Rosen took command of the Tambov Infantry Regiment on 28 May 1814, and on 11 September of the same year, became chef of this unit. The following year, he again became commander of the Tambov Infantry Regiment on 4 July 1815. He rose to a major general on 24 October 1819, and took command of the 3rd Brigade of the 27th Division. He was appointed commander of the 14th Division on 8 April 1829, and received promotion to a lieutenant general on 4 October of the same year.

Rosen participated in operations across southern Georgia during the Russo-Turkish War of 1828-1829. He served in the Independent Caucasus Corps between 1831 and 1834, taking command of the 2nd Division on 25 May 1835, and of the 2nd Grenadier Division on 11 January 1837. During his service in the Caucasus, Rosen earned the Order of St. Vladimir (2nd class), and the Order of the White Eagle. In October 1840, he became a member of the Audit General and rose to a general of infantry on 29 March 1845. He died in. St. Petersburg on 4 October 1848.

ROSENBERG, Andrey Grigorievich (b. 1739 — d. 6 September 1813, Chernov) was born to a German noble family from the Courland *gubernia*. He began service in 1753 and took part in the Seven Years War in 1756-1763. In 1768-1769, he took part in the operations against the Turks in the Mediterannean and Black Sea, receiving promotion to a lieutenant captain. Rosenberg served in the Crimea in 1770, and became a captain in the Life Guard Preobrazhensk Regiment on 25 December 1770. He transferred as a colonel to the regular army on 16 January 1772, and served in Poland in 1778-1779. He was promoted to brigadier on 5 December 1780. Two years later, Rosenberg became major general and chef of the Tavrida Jager Regiment on 9 July 1782. In 1788, he was appointed the Military Governor of Smolensk.

Rosenberg received the rank of lieutenant general on 16 February 1790. On 14 December 1796, he was elevated to chef of the Vitebsk Musketeer Regiment and in 1798 served as the inspector for the Smolensk division. In 1799, Rosenberg led a corps in Field Marshal Alexander Suvorov's army in Italy and Switzerland, fighting at Brescia, on the Adda River, and Milan. On 12 May 1799, Rosenberg approached the Po River at Bassignana, where he encountered the entire French army. Grand Duke Constantine urged him to attack the French positions across the river, but Rosenberg refused. When he argued that the French were in superior numbers, Constantine called him a coward. An infuriated Rosenberg recklessly attacked across the river and suffered heavy casualties, losing up to 1,500 men, including a general, 58 officers, and a pair of guns. After receiving a severe reprimand from Suvorov, Rosenberg led one of the Russian corps on the march to Turin.

In June-August 1799, Rosenberg took part in the battles on the Tidone, Trebbia, and Nure Rivers (promotion to general of cavalry), and at Novi. From September-November of the same year, Rosenberg took part in the crossing of the Alps, fighting at St. Gothard, the Devil's Bridge, Altdorf, Muothatal Valley, and Panixer Pass. After Suvorov left the army in March 1800, Rosenberg led the troops to Russia. He became chef of the Vladimir Musketeer Regiment on 20 June 1800, and served as the Military Governor of Kamenets-Podolsk and the Infantry Inspector of the Dnieper Inspection.

In October 1803, he became the Military Governor of Kherson and the Infantry Inspector in the Crimea. Two years later, Rosenberg took a discharge because of poor health on 25 March 1805. He died at his estate of Chernov, near Kamenets-Podolsk on 6 September 1813.

ROSSI, Ignatius Petrovich (b. 28 January 1765 — d. 22 November 1814) descended from an Italian noble family settled in Russia. His grandfather was invited by Peter the Great to build palaces in Russia. He studied in the Artillery and Engineer Cadet Corps in 1772-1780, and began service as a sub-lieutenant in the Narva Infantry Regiment on 15 May 1780. He rose to lieutenant on 1 May 1783, and transferred as a captain to the Sofia Infantry Regiment on 12 January 1786. During the Russo-Swedish War in 1789-1790, he served on the galley flotilla of Prince Nassau-Zigen, distinguishing himself at Rochensalmi (promoted to a second major). On 2 January 1793, he was promoted to lieutenant colonel, and seven years later, Rossi rose to colonel on 22 April 1800. He transferred to the Pskov Musketeer Regiment on 18 April 1802, and became chef of the Volhynia Musketeer Regiment on 25 July 1805. He was dispatched to reinforce Kutuzov, but joined him only after the battle of Austerlitz had been fought and lost.

In 1806, Rossi's unit was attched to the 6th Division and he fought at Pultusk. In January 1807, he served in Essen I's corps and joined the main Russian army in June of the same year, fighting at Heilsberg and Friedland. He was promoted to major general for his service in this campaign on 24 December 1807. In 1812, he commanded a brigade of the 4th Division in the 2nd Corps and fought at Smolensk on 16-17 August. At Borodino, he was seriously wounded in the head, and despite subsequent treatment, suffered from severe headaches for the rest of his life. For his conduct at Borodino, Rossi received the Order of St. Vladimir (3rd class).

After recuperating, he returned to the army in July 1813, serving in the Army of Poland. He then took command of the 13th Division and distinguished himself at the battle of Leipzig, for which he was decorated with the Order of St. Anna (1st class). In 1814, he served at Magdeburg (Prussian Order of Red Eagle, 2nd class) and Hamburg (golden sword with diamonds).

After the war, Rossi was still suffering from severe headaches and took a furlough to recover. He did not, and died on 22 November 1814, at his estate in the Courland *gubernia*.

ROTH, Loggin Osipovich (b. 1780 — d. 13 February 1851) descended from a French noble family. After fleeing the French Revolution, he served in Prince de Conde's émigré corps before entering Russian service on 10 September 1797, rising to a sub-lieutenant in 1799. He took part in the operations in Switzerland in 1799, and was wounded at Constance. After briefly leaving the Russian service, he returned to Russia in 1802 and rose to lieutenant in the Vyborg Musketeer Regiment. In 1805, he served in Buxhöwden's corps and fought at Austerlitz on 2 December 1805. Promoted to a staff captain on 4 April 1806, he served with the 8th Division in Poland in 1806-1807, distinguishing himself at Eylau (golden cross and the Prussian Pour le Merite), on the Passarge River (Order of St. Vladimir, 4th class), and at Heilsberg.

Roth received the rank of captain on 11 September 1808, and was dispatched to the Danubian Principalities. Over the next two years, he fought at Braila (wounded in the head and right shoulder, received a golden sword), Ruse (wounded in the left leg), Lovchea (Order of St. George, 4th class, 20 June 1812). He was conferred the rank of captain in the Life Guard Finland Battalion on 30 March 1809. In 1811, Roth received a promotion to colonel on 30 July, took command of the 45th Jager regiment on 5 September, and became chef of the 26th Jager Regiment on 15 November.

During the 1812 campaign, Roth served with the 3rd Brigade of the 14th Division in the 1st Corps, fighting at Klyastitsy, Smela (Order of St. George, 3rd class, 13 November 1812), and two battles of Polotsk (wounded in the right hand in the second battle), for which he was promoted to major general on 15 January 1813, with seniority dating from 18 October 1812.

In 1813, Roth served at Lutzen, Bautzen (Order of St. Anna, 1st class, and the Prussian Order of Red Eagle, 1st class), Peterswalde, Dresden, and Teplitz, where he was wounded in the lower jaw and garnered the Order of St. Vladimir (2nd class) and the Austrian Order of Maria Theresa (3rd class). In 1814, he served at Arcis sur Aube, Le Fère Champenoise, and Panten (near Paris), where he was wounded in the left thigh and received promotion to lieutenant general on 8 May 1814, with seniority dating from 30 March 1814.

After the war, he commanded the 3rd Grenadier Division (8 May 1814), the 15th Infantry Division (11 September 1818), the 4th Corps (16 March 1820), the 3rd Corps (8 October 1823), again the 4th Corps (28 September 1826), and the 6th Corps (29 May 1827). During the Russo-Turkish War of 1828-1829, he led the 5th Corps and rose to the rank of general of infantry on 10 July 1828. He distinguished himself at Adrianople, for which he was later decorated with the Order of St. George (2nd class) on 3 October 1829. Roth became assistant to the commander-in-chief of the 1st Army in February 1833, and received rank of adjutant general on 24 November 1835.

RTISCHEV (Rtyschev), Nikolay Fedorovich (b. 1754 — d. 20 January 1835) was born to an ancient Russian family. After studying in the Infantry Cadet Corps, he began service as a lieutenant in the regular army on 27 July 1773, and became adjutant to General Field Marshal Zakhar Chernyshev on 11 October of the same year. He rose to second major in the 2nd Grenadier Regiment on 11 October 1779, and continued to serve as an adjutant to Chernyshev until 15 September 1784, when Rtischev was promoted to a colonel in the Navaginsk Infantry Regiment. Five years later, he became brigadier in the newly formed St. Petersburg Grenadier Regiment on 2 May 1789. During the Russo-Swedish War in 1789-1790, he served on the galley flotilla in several naval engagements, garnering a golden sword for his courage.

Promoted to major general on 12 January 1793, Rtischev served under General Igelstrom in Poland. He was appointed chef of the Narva Musketeer Regiment on 14 December 1796. Two years later, he became lieutenant general, commandant of Astrakhan and chef of the Astrakhan Garrison Regiment on 5 April 1798. However, he retired on on 3 October of the same year only to return to the army on 15 April 1806. He organized and later took command of the 16th Division (9 October 1806), garnering the Order of St. Anna (1st class). Rtischev took part in the operations in the Danubian Principalities in 1807-1809, distinguishing himself at Braila. He took command of the 25th Division on 27 May 1809, and participated in the campaign against Austria in Galicia late that year. He received the Order of St. George (4th class) for dedicated service on 8 December 1810.

Rtischev was appointed commander of the 19th Division on 20 January 1811, and on 19 July of the same year, became Commander-in-Chief of the Russian troops on the Caucasian Line. The following year, he was appointed Commander-in-Chief of the troops in Georgia and the Governor of Transcaucasia. He took vigorous measures against the North Caucasian mountaineers and suppressed the uprisings in Daghestan, Kakheti, Kartli, and mountain region of Georgia. In 1812-1813, he successfully repulsed several Persian armies in Armenia and southern Georgia, forcing Persia to sign the peace treaty at Gulistan on 24 October 1813. Under this agreement, Persia acknowledged Russia's annexation of Transcaucasia and the Khanates of Karabagh, Gandja, Sheka, Shirvan, Derbent, Baku, etc.

For his military and diplomatic successes, Rtischev was decorated with the Order of St. Alexander of Neva (12 December 1812), the Persian Order of the Lion and the Sun and received promotion to general of infantry in 1813. He resigned from his position on 21 April 1816, and was replaced by General Aleksey Yermolov. The following year, he was appointed to the Senate in June 1817, and served as the senator for fifteen years.

RUDZEVICH, Alexander Yakovlevich (b. 1775 — d. 4 April 1829) was born to a petty noble family of Tatar descent from the Crimea. He enlisted as a sergeant in the Life Guard Preobrazhensk Regiment on 17 April 1786, and studied in the Greek Cadet Corps before starting service as a captain in the Russian main headquarters on 7 April 1792. He took part in the campaign in Poland in 1794, fighting at Pesochna, Sluzhev, Warsaw, Maciejowice, Kobylka and receiving a golden cross for Praga. In 1795-1798, Rudzevich served on various topographical missions to map Vyborg and Kazan provinces. In January 1799, he was appointed to General Lassi's troops at Kovno, receiving the rank of lieutenant colonel on 20 November of the same year. In March 1800, he was recalled to St. Petersburg, and the following year, completed the topographic maps of the Gulf of Finland coastline.

Rudzevich transferred to the Troitsk Musketeer Regiment on 2 May 1801, and served in the Kuban Valley and Caucasus for the next ten years. He rose to a colonel on 18 December 1804, and took command of the Troitsk Musketeer Regiment on 29 March 1805. In 1804-1805, he took part in the actions in the Kuban Valley, distinguishing himself at Arba (Orders of St. Anna, 3rd class), Ergioki, Kizburun (Order of St. Vladimir, 4th class), and in Chechnya (Order of St. Anna, 2nd class, with diamonds). On 28 January 1806, he became chef of the Tiflis Musketeer Regiment, but retired because of illness on 2 May 1807. He returned to the army two years later, becoming chef of the 22nd Jager Regiment on 15 December 1809.

In 1810-1811, Rudzevich again fought in the Kuban Valley, distinguishing himself at Kumatyr Aul, Sudjuk Kale (Order of St. George, 3rd class, 18 July 1811) and Anapa. Promoted to major general on 20 February 1811, Rudzevich served with the 3rd Brigade of the 13th Division in the Crimea in 1812. He joined the Army of Danube in late 1812 and participated in the battle on the Berezina and the pursuit of the French, for which he was decorated with the Order of St. Anna (1st class). In 1813, he led a jager brigade of the 10th and 22nd Jager Regiments at Thorn and was decorated with the diamond signs of the Order of St. Anna (1st class). In May, he took part in the actions at Koenigswartha and Bautzen, briefly commanding the Russian rearguard.

Rudzevich transferred to Langeron's corps in the summer of 1813, and took command of the advance guard.. On 18 August, he was appointed the Chief of Staff of this corps, but since Rudzevich led the advance guard, Colonel Heydhardt carried his staff duties. During August – September 1813, Rudzevich fought the French near Zibeneichen on the Bober River, Goldberg, Katzbach, Hochkirch, and after a brief furlough, at Wolkau. For his conduct in these actions, he was decorated with the Prussian Order of Red Eagle (2nd class) and received promotion to lieutenant general on 27 September 1813. From October-December, he secured the crossing at Düben and fought at Klein Widderitzsch, Gross Widderitzsch, and Leipzig, where he earned the Order of St. Alexander of Neva and the Swedish Order of the Sword.

In 1814, Rudzevich briefly commanded the 10th Corps at Kassel until 3 February, when he took command of the 22nd Division. He defended Soissons in early March 1814, and later commanded the 8th Corps at Paris, for which he was decorated with the Order of St. George (2nd class, 31 March 1814) and the Prussian Order of Red Eagle (1st class).

After the war, Rudzewich commanded the 13th Division, and between 7 November 1814 and 13 January 1816, served as the Military Governor of Kherson and commander of the 6th Corps. He became the Chief of Staff of the 2nd Army on 21 April 1816. Three years later, Rudzevich was appointed commander of the 7th Corps on 6 March 1819 and later of the 3rd Corps on 20 November 1826. He rose to general of infantry on 3 September 1826. During the

Russo-Turkish of 1828-1829, he led the 3rd Corps at Ismail, Issacea, Babadag, Constanta (Kustendji), Macin, Bazardjik, and Shumla, garnering the diamond signs of the Order of St. Alexander of Neva.

In 1829, Rudzevich deployed his troops in Wallachia, but soon thereafter learned his son had been killed at Varna. The news devastated Rudzevich. He died on 4 April 1829, and was buried at his estate of Karasubazaar in the Crimea.

RUSANOV, Vasily Akimovich (b. 1779 — date of death unclear) began service as a page at the Imperial Court and transferred as a lieutenant to the Life Guard Hussar Regiment on 19 October 1798. He rose to a staff rotmistr on 1 October 1799, rotmistr on 21 December 1801, and to colonel on 12 December 1803. He joined the Aleksandria Hussar Regiment on 25 January 1805, and served with the 6th Division in Poland in 1806-1807. He was wounded in the left shoulder and chest at Eylau (Order of St. George, 4th class).

Rusanov commanded the Aleksadria Hussar Regiment between 10 December 1807 and 17 February 1809. He fell ill and after recuperating, retired with a rank of major general on 17 February 1809, only to return to the army on 16 July of the same year. Rusanov later headed the 8th District of the Independent Corps of Internal Guard in 1810-1811. In 1812-1814, Rusanov organized six infantry and two jager regiments in Voronezh, Ryazan and Tambov. He retired on 12 October 1827.

RYKOV, Vasily Dmitryevich (b. 1759 — d. 6 August 1827, Kiev) was born to a noble family from the Saratov *gubernia*. He enlisted as a furier (fourrier) in the Life Guard Preobrazhensk Regiment in 1776, rising to a sergeant in 1779, and to an ensign in 1782. He participated in the Russo-Swedish War in 1788-1790, and after transfering as a captain to the Orenburg Dragoon Regiment, served in Poland in 1792-1794. Promoted to major in 1797, he took command of the Orenburg Dragoon Regiment on 22 November 1798. Two years later, he became a lieutenant colonel on 6 June 1800, and received the Order of St. John of Jerusalem for dedicated service. He transferred to the Lifland Dragoon Regiment on 10 September 1805, and took command of this regiment on 26 February 1806.

Rykov served with the 8th Division in Poland in 1806-1807, fighting at Landsberg, Eylau (wounded in the left leg, golden cross and a golden sword), Guttstadt, Heilsberg, and Friedland, for which he was decorated with the Order of St. Vladimir (4th class). He became a colonel on 24 December 1807. From 1808-1811, he served in the Danubian Principalities and distinguished himself at Silistra, Braila, Bazardjik (Order of St. Vladimir, 3rd class), Shumla (Order of St. George, 4th class, 23 April 1811), Batin, Nikopol, Ruse, and Slobodzea. In May 1812, he became the commandant of the main headquarters of the Army of Danube, and later led the Lifland Dragoons at Pavlovichi, Lokachi, Lubomle, Brest-Litovsk, Brilya, and Stakhov.

In 1813, Rusanov fought at Thorn, Koenigswartha, Bautzen (Order of St. Anna, 2nd class), Dresden (Order of St. Anna, 2nd class, with diamonds), Kulm (Prussian Iron Cross), and Leipzig, for which he was promoted to major general on 19 December 1813. The following year, he served at Brienne, La Rothière, Bar sur Aube, Arcis sur Aube, and Paris, receiving in return the Prussian Pour le Merite.

After the war, Rusanov led the 3rd Brigade of the 1st Uhlan Division (13 December 1815), before taking command of the 2nd Brigade of the Ukraine Cossack Division on 3 November 1816, of the 2nd Brigade of the Bug Uhlan Division on 28 November 1817, and of the Bug Uhlan Division on 18 May 1818. He was decorated with the Order of St. Anna (1st class) in 1820. Rykov was relieved of command on 29 October 1823, and spent the rest of his life in Kiev, where he died on 6 August 1827.

RYLEYEV, Alexander Nikolayevich (b.1778 — d. 9 June 1840) was born to a noble family from the Kaluga *gubernia*. He enlisted as a sergeant in the Life Guard Preobrazhensk Regiment on 4 June 1794, and transferred as a vakhmistr to the Chevalier Guard Corps in late 1795. He joined the Leib-Hussar (Life Guard Hussar) Regiment on 5 January 1797, becoming a lieutenant on 21 December 1801, staff rotmistr on 12 April 1803, and rotmistr on 27 January 1805. He took part in the 1805 Campaign, receiving the Order of St. Anna (3rd class) at Austerlitz. Ryleyev took a discharge with a rank of colonel on 4 August 1806. Two years later, he returned to the army as a lieutenant colonel in the Pavlograd Hussar Regiment on 11 March 1807. He rose to a colonel on 11 September 1811, and organized reserve cavalry squadrons in Ukraine in early 1812.

During the 1812 Campaign, Ryleyev served in the 3rd Reserve Army of Observation at Kobryn, Gorodechnya, Slonim, Stakhov, and on the Berezina. In 1813, he took part in the actions at Thorn, Magdeburg, Gross Beeren, Dennewitz (promoted to major general on 27 September 1813), and Leipzig, for which he was decorated with the Order of St. Anna (2nd class) and the Prussian Order of Red Eagle (2nd class).

In 1814, Ryleyev served at Sedan, Craonne, and Laon (wounded in the right hand, received a golden sword with diamonds). After the war, he served in the 3rd Hussar and 3rd Dragoon Divisions. He took command of the 1st Brigade of the 1st Dragoon Division on 24 December 1816. Ryleyev resigned from this position because of poor health on 6 August 1818, and later served on the military court in St. Petersburg, receiving the Order of St. George (4th class) for twenty-five years of service. He finally retired on 15 October 1829, and lived in Saratov, where he died on 9 June 1840.

RYLEYEV (Ryleyev I), Mikhail Nikolayevich (b. 1771 — d. 1831) was born to a noble family from the Kostroma *gubernia*. He enlisted as a vakhmistr in the Life Guard Horse Regiment on 13 January 1785, transferred as a captain to the Moscow Grenadier Regiment on 12 January 1794, and later switched to the Siberia Grenadier Regiment on 12 February 1796. He rose to major on 14 November 1799, and served as a battalion commander of the Siberia Grenadier Regiment on the Ionian Islands and Naples in 1804-1806. His unit transferred to the Danubian Principalities in 1806, and Ryleyev took part in the actions at Turbat, Giurgiu, and Obilesti (Order of St. Vladimir, 4th class). He took command of the Siberia Grenadier Regiment on 12 February 1807, and after being wounded, briefly served in the Akhtyarsk Garrison Battalion between 16 May 1808 and 11 January 1809.

Ryleyev joined the Butyrsk Infantry Regiment in January 1809, and took command of the Smolensk Musketeer Regiment on 13 January 1810. He distinguished himself at Bazardjik (golden cross and a golden sword), Shumla (Order of St. Anna, 2nd class), Ruse, and Nikopol. Promoted to colonel on 11 September 1811, he became chef of the Koporsk Infantry Regiment on 10 June 1812, but still remained with 12th Division, leading the 1st Brigade comprised of the Smolensk and Narva Infantry Regiment. During the 1812 Campaign, his brigade was attached to the 7th Corps of the 2nd Western Army. With that army Ryleyev distinguished himself in the battle at Saltanovka (Moghilev), where he took a severe wound to his left leg. For his courage, Ryleyev was promoted to major general on 28 December 1812, with seniority dating from 23 July 1812.

After recuperating, Ryleyev returned to the Army in late 1813, serving as the Commandant of Dresden in 1814. In 1815, he led the 25th Division in the 2nd Corps during the Hundred Days. After the war, he took command the 2nd Brigade of the 13th Division on 4 July 1818, and received the Order of St. George (4th class) for twenty-five years of dedicated service in 1819. In 1820-1822, Ryleyev commanded Third Settled Battalions of the 7th, 8th and 9th Division and, beginning on 27 October 1823, Ryleyev led the Third Settled Battalions of the 16th, 18th, and 19th Divisions. On 21 May 1824, he took command of a detachment in the Corps of Military Settlements in the Moghilev *gubernia*. Promoted to lieutenant general on 31 March 1826, Ryleyev received the Order of St. Anna (1st class) on 3 September 1826 and became the Commandant of Novgorod on 3 April 1829.

RYNKEVICH, Yefim Yefimovich (b. 1772, Yamburg — d. 1834) was born to a noble family from the Lifland *gubernia*. He began service in the Life Guard Izmailovsk Regiment and transferred as a captain to the Pskov Musketeer Regiment on 12 January 1790. He took part in the Russo-Swedish War in the spring of 1790. He joined the Kozlov Musketeer Regiment on 14 July 1791, and fought in Poland in 1792. Rynkevich returned to Poland two years later, fighting at Shikochin, Pesochna, Warsaw, Maciejowice, and Praga (golden cross).

Promoted to second major on 10 October 1794, Rynkevich transferred to the Poltava Musketeer Regiment on 1 September 1798, and he assumed command of this regiment on 23 January 1799, becoming a lieutenant colonel on 26 September 1799. He earned the Order of St. Anna (2nd class) on 11 February 1800, and was promoted to colonel on 23 December 1800. However, he retired on 5 January 1802, and returned to military service only four years later, when he took part in the organization of the militias in the western provinces of Russia from 1806-1807.

In 1812, Rynkevich joined the Ryazan *opolchenye* and led the 8th Opolchenye Infantry Regiment. In 1813, he served at Dresden, Magdeburg and Hamburg, earning a golden sword for courage. He retired again on 25 April 1815, and served as the Vice Governor of Simbirsk in 1815-1817, and as a Vice Governor of Moscow in 1817-1821.

RZHEVSKY, Pavel Alekseyevich (b. 1784 — d. 11 February 1852, Moscow) was born to a noble family from the Ryazan *gubernia*. He began service in the College of Foreign Affairs in 1798, and transferred to the military service as a lieutenant in the Life Guard Semeyonovsk Regiment on 24 January 1802. In 1803, he became adjutant to Major General Leontii Depreradovich and fought at Austerlitz in 1805, earning the Order of St. Anna (3rd class). Promoted to staff captain in April 1806, Rzhevsky served at Guttstadt, Heilsberg, and Friedland, where he was wounded in the hand and chest at the latter battle. For his courage, Rzhevsky received the Order of St. Vladimir (4th class, 1 June 1808), and was promoted to captain on 29 August 1808. The same year, he transferred as a rotmistr to the Life Guard

Hussar Regiment on 19 November. He took a discharge with a rank of colonel on 18 January 1809.

During the 1812 Campaign, Rzhevsky returned to the cavalry with the rank of major on 1 August and attended General Nikolay Tuchkov. He fought at Borodino, Tarutino, Chernyshka, Maloyaroslavets (wounded in the right hand, promoted to lieutenant colonel, 27 October 1812), Chernov, Krasnyi, and Yakovlevichi, for which he was decorated with the Order of St. Anna (2nd class) on 12 January 1813. During the 1813 campaign, Rzhevsky served under Wittgenstein at Dresden (Order of St. Anna, 2nd class, with diamonds, and the Prussian Pour le Merite), Hodendorf, Kulm, Wachau, Liebertwolkwitz, Holzhausen, and Leipzig (promoted to colonel). In 1814, he took part in the actions at Nogent, Bar sur Aube, Troyes, Le Fère Champenoise, and Paris, garnering a golden sword and the Order of St. Vladimir (3rd class).

After the war, Rzhevsky retired because of poor health on 23 October 1817. He later served in the commission directing constructions in Moscow in 1827-1840, rising to civic counsellor on 3 January 1835. He died in Moscow on 11 February 1852.

Another **Rzhevsky, Gregory Pavlovich** (b. 1763 — d. 23 May 1830) began service in the the Life Guard Semeyonovsk Regiment in 1773, and participated in the Russo-Swedish War in 1790. Promoted to lieutenant colonel, he commanded the 4th Battalion of the Lifland Jager Corps in Poland in 1794, fighting at Krupchitse and Brest-Litovsk (golden sword). Rzhevsky retired in May 1796, and died in St. Petersburg on 23 May 1830.

S

SABANEYEV, Ivan Vasilievich, (date of birth unclear 1770/1772 — d. 6 September 1829, Dresden) was born to a noble family in the Yarosvlavl *gubernia*. He enlisted as a corporal in the Life Guard Preobrazhensk Regiment on 18 January 1787. After graduating from the University of Moscow, he became a captain in the Malorosiisky (Little Russia) Grenadier Regiment on 12 January 1791. During the Russo-Turkish War in 1787-1791, he volunteered for the Army of Moldavia and took command of the 1st Battalion of the Bug Jager Corps, distinguishing himself at Macin in July 1791. Sabaneyev served in Poland in 1792-1794, and in the Caucasus in 1796. After the Bug Jager Corps was disbanded on 10 December 1796, he continued service with the 13th (later 12th) Jager Regiment. In 1799, he served in General Rosenberg's Corps in Italy, fighting at Novi, Gavi, Tortona (promotion to major), St. Gothard, the Devil's Bridge, and Altdorf. Aleksandr Suvorov recommended Sabancycv be promoted to lieutenant colonel and awarded the Order of St. Anna (2nd class) with diamonds. Sabaneyev was seriously wounded in the left hand in the action in the Muottethal Valley and was captured by the French at Glarus, where Suvorov left his wounded troops before crossing the Panixer Pass. Sabaneyev remained a prisoner of war in France until early 1801, when after the rapprochement between Napoleon and Paul, the Russian prisoners were released. He became commander of the 12th Jager Regiment on 14 March 1802, and took part in the 1803 Campaign in the Kuban Valley against the North Caucasian mountaineers, for which he received the Order of St. Vladimir (4th class).

Sabaneyev retired because of poor health on 18 January 1805, recovered, and returned to the army with the rank of colonel on 17 January 1807. During the 1807 Campaign in Poland, he served with the 3rd Jager Regiment in the advance guard of General Peter Bagration, and fought at Guttstadt, Deppen, Heilsberg, and Friedland, where he was seriously wounded in the face. His gallant conduct earned him the Order of St. Vladimir (3rd class) and a golden sword. After recuperating, Sabaneyev took command of the 3rd Jager Regiment on 16 February 1808, and participated in the Russo-Swedish War. In 1808, he fought under Barclay de Tolly and Kamensky II at Jorois, Kuopio, and Alavo, where he was wounded in the right leg. Sabaneyev returned to his regiment in early 1809 and participated in the crossing of the frozen Gulf of Bothnia. He fought at Sävar and Ratan, for which he received the Order of St. George (3rd class) on 6 December 1809 as well as promotion to major general on 8 December 1809.

Sabaneyev rose to command the 7th Jager Regiment in the Army of Moldavia on 28 February 1810. Later that year he fought at Silistra and Razgrad, for which he was awarded the Order of St. Anna (1st class) and a pension of 1,000 rubles for 12 years. Sabaneyev went on to distinguish himself at the battles of Shumla (Order of St. Anna, 1st class, with diamonds and a golden sword with diamonds), Batin (Order of St. Vladimir, 2nd class), and Turnovo. In 1811, he served under General Mikhail Kutuzov and participated in the destruction of the Turkish army at Ruse in late 1811, and was promoted to lieutenant general on 10 January 1812. He was appointed the second plenipotentiary to the Bucharest congress, where the Russo-Turkish peace treaty was negotiated. In May 1812, Sabaneyev became the Chief of Staff of the Army of Danube and led the reserve corps.

During the 1812 Campaign, Sabaneyev took part in the actions at Lokachy, Losna, and on the Beresina. In 1813, he served as the Chief of Staff of the 3rd Western Army and took part in the actions at Thorn (Order of Alexander of Neva), Koenigswartha, Bautzen, Dresden, Kulm, and Leipzig; his actions in the latter two battles garnered the Orders of St. Alexander of Neva and of St. Vladimir (1st class). Sabaneyev also participated in the 1814 Campaign, fighting at Brienne, Arcis sur Aube, Le Fère Champenoise, and Paris (received allowance of 30,000 rubles).

After Napoleon's return in 1815, Sabaneyev was dispatched with the 27th Infantry Division to France and served at Metz. After briefly serving with the Russian occupation corps in France, he led the 8th Corps (later re-designated the 6th Corps of the 2nd Army). He was stationed with his corps in southern Ukraine from 1816-1823. He rose to general of infantry on 24 December 1823, and led the 2nd Army the following year. However, four years later, Sabaneyev had to retire because of poor health. While traveling in Europe to recuperate, he died at Dresden on 6 September 1829.

SABLIN, Jacob Ivanovich (b. 1785 — date of death unclear) was born to a Russian noble family. After graduating from the 2nd Cadet Corps, he began service as a sub-lieutenant in the Life Guard Artillery Battalion in 1804. He participated in the 1805 Campaign and received the Order of St. Anna (3rd class) for Austerlitz. In 1807, he distinguished himself at Heilsberg (golden sword) and Friedland. He rose to lieutenant colonel on 16 December 1811, and led of the 12th Artillery Brigade and the 22nd Light Artillery Company. During the 1812 Campaign, Sablin served with the 2nd Western Army and fought at Saltanovka, Smolensk, Borodino (bruised, Order of St. Vladimir, 4th class), and Krasnyi (Order of St. Anna, 2nd class). He was promoted to colonel on 26 April 1813.

Another Sablin, **Alexander Yakovlevich Sablin II** (b. 1787 — date of death unclear) graduated from the 2nd Cadet Corps and began service as a sub-lieutenant in the 3rd Artillery Regiment in 1804. He was captured by the French at Austerlitz in 1805. He returned to Russia in 1806 and fought at Heilsberg in 1807, where he was wounded in the leg and received the Order of St. Anna (3rd class).

Sablin was elevated to lieutenant on 6 November 1808, and served in Finland in 1808-1809. He transferred to the 4th Reserve Artillery Brigade in April 1811. In 1812, he fought at Novy Borisov, and the following year, at Bautzen and Leipzig (Order of St. Anna, 2nd class). In 1814, Sablin became a staff captain on 3 February, and distinguished himself at Soissons, for which he garnered a golden sword.

SABLUKOV Nikolay Aleksandrovich (date of birth unclear, 12 January/12 May 1776, St. Petersburg — date of death unclear, 2/3 July 1848, St. Petersburg) was born to a noble family in St. Petersburg. He was home schooled and enlisted at an early age in the Life Guard Preobrazhensk Regiment. His active service began in the Life Guard Horse Regiment in 1790. Sablukov rose to cornet in January 1792. In 1795-1796, he traveled in Europe and studied at various universities. After he returned to Russia, Sablukov was promoted to colonel and squadron commander in the Life Guard Horse Regiment on 12 June 1799. He retired with a rank of major general in April 1801, and traveled to Britain, where he lived for the next five years.

In 1806, Sablukov returned to service as the head of the commissariat of the Ministry of Navy. The following year, he directed the Accounting Section of the Admiralty. However, he again left service in 1809 and spent another three years in Britain.

During the 1812 Campaign, Sablukov returned to the military service on 20 August 1812, and served as an adjutant to General Fedor Korf. He distinguished himself at Krasnyi, for which he received the Order of St. Vladimir (3rd class) and a golden sword. He left the service for the third time and final time on 10 April 1813, and settled in St. Petersburg.

SAINT PRIEST (St. Priest) Emmanuel (b. 10 May 1776, Istanbul — d. 29 March 1814, Laon) was born to a prominent French noble family. His father, Francois Saint Priest, was the French ambassador to Portugal, Spain, and the Ottoman Empire, as well as Minister of War under King Louis XVI. He fled to Russia after the French Revolution of 1789.

Emmanuel St. Priest studied at the University of Heidelberg and joined Prince Conde's corps in 1792. The next year, his father helped him enter Russian service and join the Artillery and Engineer Cadet Corps on 14 February 1793. Two years later, St. Priest transferred as a lieutenant to the Life Guard Semeyonovsk Regiment on 26 December 1795. In 1799, he took a discharge with a rank of captain on 25 August, and served in Prince Conde's Corps as an aide-de-camp of the Duke of Angouleme. Though Napoleon declared amnesty for most émigrés, St. Priest was excluded from the list and returned to Russia. Emperor Alexander welcomed him back with the rank of colonel in the Life Guard Semeyonovsk Regiment on 12 April 1801.

In 1805, St. Priest took command of a company of the Life Guard Jager Battalion on 4 March, and led the unit with some distinction at Austerlitz on 2 December 1805, for which he was awarded the Order of St. George (4th class).

He became commander of the Life Guard Jager Regiment on 24 June 1806. During the 1807 Campaign, St. Priest distinguished himself again at Guttstadt, where he was seriously wounded (Order of St. Vladimir, 3rd class). He stayed with the Duke of Angouleme at Mittau to recuperate, and was appointed chef of the 6th Jager Regiment on 1 December 1809. He rejoined the Army of Moldavia and fought at Bazardjik, Shumla, Batin, Sistov, and Lovech. For his conduct in these battles, St. Priest was promoted to major general on 26 June 1810, and to general adjutant on 26 September 1810. He also received the Orders of St. Anna (1st class), St. George (3rd class), and St. Vladimir (2nd class). In 1811, he participated in drafting of the new military regulations, *Uchrezhdenie dlia upravlenia bolshoi deistvuiushei armii* [Establishment for the Administration of the Large Active Army].

In 1812, St. Priest was appointed the Chief of Staff of the 2nd Western Army of Peter Bagration. He took part in all actions of this army during its retreat to Smolensk and was wounded at Borodino on 7 September 1812. He was promoted to lieutenant general on 2 November 1812, and served in Adjutant General Kutuzov's cavalry detachment and General Wittgenstein's corps. After the Russians liberated Vilna, Emperor Alexander instructed St. Priest to take care of the French prisoners of war there.

In 1813, St. Priest led the advance guard of Miloradovich's Corps. He fought at Glogau, Lutzen, Bautzen, and Reichenbach. In August 1813, he took command of the 8th Corps and participated in the actions at Hochkirch, Lobau, Wartenburg, and Leipzig. In early 1814, St. Priest served at Koblenz and Mainz, and during the invasion of France, advanced from St. Dizier to Rheims, which he occupied (Order of St. George, 2nd class). However, St. Priest was caught by surprise and defeated by Napoleon on 13-14 March 1814. He was seriously wounded when a cannonball struck him in the chest. He was transported to Laon, where he lingered for two weeks before dying on 29 March 1814.

SANDERS, Fedor Ivanovich (b. 1755 — d. 1836) was born to a noble family in the Lifland *gubernia*. He enlisted in the Kiev Infantry

Regiment on 4 August 1765. In 1769, he became a sergeant and took part in the Russo-Turkish War in 1770-1774, rising to an ensign in January 1771, and to lieutenant in December 1771. In 1778, he transferred to the Aleksopol Infantry Regiment, where he served for the next nine years before joining the Lifland Jager Regiment in 1787. During the Russo-Turkish War of 1787-1791, Sanders distinguished himself at Ochakov (golden cross), Hadjibey (Odessa), and Ismail, for which, on Aleksandr Suvorov's firm recommendation, he received the rank of premier major and a golden cross.

During the Polish Campaign of 1794, Sanders took part in the capture of Praga, which earned him a promotion to lieutenant colonel and a golden cross. After the campaign, he joined the 8th Jager Battalion, but retired in 1797.

Sanders returned to the army in 1806 and served in the 11th Jager Regiment in the Army of Moldavia. He took part in General Michelson's operations against the Turks in 1806, including the capture of Bender and the combat at Ismail, for which he was awarded a golden sword. In March 1807, Sanders joined General Meyendorff in besieging Ismail and stood out on several occasions, including a combat on 29 March for which he was awarded the Order of St. Anna (2nd class). On 20 April, he repulsed a Turkish sortie to the Island Cetal. Although wounded in the right leg, he personally led a counter charge, capturing two guns and two stands of colors. For this feat, he was decorated with the Order of St. Vladimir (3rd class). Two months later, Sanders distinguished himself again, this time in an action on 8 June, during which he was wounded in the left hand and left leg. For his actions, Sanders was not only made colonel and commander of the 11th Jager Regiment on 12 August 1807, but also garnered the Order of St. Anna (2nd class).

In 1809, Sanders again fought at Ismail and was wounded in the face below the left eye, on 7 September. Nevertheless, he remained with his men and directed construction of an artillery battery. Sanders took command of the 29th Jager Regiment on 28 February 1810, and distinguished himself in a series of actions at Turtukay, Razgrad, and Ruse. He rose to a major general on 28 June 1810. During the assault on Ruse in late 1810, he led the Russian right flank and was wounded again. After taking part in siege of Giurgiu and Turnu, he commanded the fifth square in the battle at Ruse a year later in 1811, for which he earned the Order of St. Anna (1st class). Later that same year, he participated in the actions at Vidin and Lom-Palanka.

In May 1812, Sanders became inspector in the Army of Danube and late that year fought at Brest and on the Berezina. During the 1813 Campaign, he led the 1st Brigade of the 12th Infantry Division and distinguished himself at Bautzen and Dresden. For his actions at Leipzig in October 1813, he was awarded a golden sword and temporarily appointed military governor of the city. In 1814, Sanders fought at Bremen, Soissons, Craonne, Laon, and Paris.

After the war, Sanders took an extended furlough to recuperate and returned to service in 1816, when he became the Military Governor of Ismail on 4 April 1816. He rose to lieutenant general on 16 April 1830, and retired four years later on 21 May 1834. Sanders died on 13 January 1836 in St. Petersburg.

SANTI, Alexander Frantsevich (b. 1757 — d. 1831) was born to a Piedmontese noble family. His father, Francis Santi, settled in Russia under Peter the Great. Alexander enlisted as a private in the Life Guard Preobrazhensk Regiment in 1762, and began service as a cadet in the same unit in 1771. He rose to sub-ensign in 1774, and transferred as a sub-lieutenant to the

St. Petersburg Legion in January 1775 and later as a lieutenant to the Kargopol Carabinier Regiment in 1778. Santi took part in operations in Poland in 1781-1783, and was wounded at Minsk-Mazovetsky. He participated in the Russo-Turkish War in 1787-1791, distinguishing himself at Ochakov (golden cross and rank of premier major), Focsani, Rimnic (Order of St. Vladimir, 4th class), Killia, Ismail (wounded in the right thigh, golden cross, and rank of lieutenant colonel), Babadag, and Macin. For his actions in the last battle, he received promotion to colonel and appointment as commander of the Rostov Carabinier Regiment on 29 July 1791. In 1792-1794, Santi served against the Poles, fighting at Dubenka (wounded in the left hand), Brest, and Bely-Podlyaska, for which he was promoted to brigadier. He became a major general on 16 April 1797.

In 1799, Santi took part in the expedition to Holland, where he was wounded and captured at Alkmar. He was released in 1800 and returned to Russia, where he took a discharge from the army. Santi returned to military service (although he was not officially accepted) seven years later, when he took part in the formation of the Moscow *opolchenye* in 1807. In 1812, he took command of the 5th *Opolchenye* Infantry Regiment of the 2nd Moscow *Opolchenye* Division. Following the battle at Borodino, Santi led his unit in various minor rear guard actions against the French, and fought at the battles at Tarutino and Vyazma. Santi became seriously ill in late 1812 and left army to recuperate in Kaluga. He did not serve again, and died in 1831.

SAVOINI, Eremei (Geronimo) Yakovlevich (12 May 1776, Florence — 19 April 1836, St. Petersburg) was born to an Italian noble family from Florence. He entered the Russian service as a sergeant in the Mariupol Light Horse Regiment on 24 August 1784, and transferred as a sub-ensign to the Nikolaev Coastal [*primosrskii*] Grenadier Regiment. He participated in the Russo-Turkish War in 1788-1791, fighting at Bender, Ismail (golden cross and promotion to sub-lieutenant), and Macin. Savoini became commander of the Ladoga Infantry Regiment on 16 May 1808, and took part in the Russo-Turkish War in 1808-1812. He was appointed chef of this regiment on 11 March 1811.

During the Russian Campaign of 1812, Savoini served with the 1st Brigade of the 26th Division of the 7th Corps in the 2nd Western Army. He participated in Prince Bagration's retreat from Volkovysk and fought at Saltanovka, Smolensk, Borodino (wounded in the left leg and hand), Zhernovka, and Krasnyi. For his conduct at Borodino, he was promoted to major general on 15 December 1812, with seniority dating from 7 September 1812.

In 1813, Savoini served at Modlin, Dresden, and Leipzig, and in 1814, took part in the siege of Hamburg, for which he received the Order of St. George (3rd class) on 9 February 1814. After the war, Savoini led the 1st Brigade of the 26th Division in 1815, and took over the 4th Division on 9 December 1816. Between 1817-1825, he commanded in succession the 28th, 27th, and 24th Divisions. He became lieutenant general on 2 June 1825, commander of the 4th Corps on 4 October 1829, and general of infantry on 18 December 1833.

SAXE-COBURG-SAALFELD, Leopold Georg (b. 16 December 1790, Coburg — d. 10 December 1865, Laeken) was born to a prominent ducal family of Saxe-Coburg-Saalfeld, the son of the Duke Francis Frederick of Saxe-Coburg-Saalfeld. Leopold entered the Russian service as a lieutenant colonel in the Life

Guard Izmailovsk Regiment on 9 April 1799, and transferred as a colonel to the Life Guard Horse Regiment on 13 February 1801. He rose to a major general on 28 May 1803, and in 1805, served in the Imperial Retinue at Austerlitz. Two years later, Prince Leopold served in Poland, distinguishing himself at Guttstadt, Heilsberg, and Friedland. In 1808, he attended Alexander at Erfurt. In 1809-1812, he returned to his principality and lived in Coburg. On 8 July 1813, Prince Leopold returned to the Russian army and served with the Life Guard Cuirassier Regiment at Kulm (Order of St. George, 4th class) and Leipzig (golden sword). In 1814, he took part in the battles at Brienne, Laon, Le Fère Champenoise, and Paris.

After the war, he took command of the 1st Uhlan Division on 13 June 1815, and rose to lieutenant general. He left the Russian service in 1819 and settled in Britain, where he married Charlotte Augusta, Princess of Great Britain, Ireland, and Hanover. In 1830, Prince Leopold declined the Greek crown.

After Belgium achieved its independence from the Netherlands in October 1830, the Belgian National Congress offered Leopold to become king of the newly-formed country. He accepted the proposal on 26 June 1831, and was crowned King Leopold I of Belgium on 21 July of the same year. He successfully contained the Dutch attempts to conquer his kingdom in 1831-1839. His second marriage was to Princess Louise-Marie Thérèse Charlotte Isabelle d'Orléans, daughter of King Louis Philippe of France in 1832.

SAXE-COBURG, Ferdinand Ernst August (b. 13 January 1784 — d. 10 February 1844) was born to a prominent family of Saxe-Coburg-Saafeld, the son of the Grand Duke Francis. He entered Russian service as a captain in the Life Guard Izmailovsk Regiment in 1790, and rose to colonel on 1 December 1796. Five years later, he transferred as a major general to the Life Guard Horse Regiment on 31 March 1801. In 1805, he served in the Imperial Retinue at Austerlitz. In 1806, Prince Ferdinand briefly served in the Prussian army, but after its collapse at Jena-Auerstadt, returned to the Russian army. He took part in the 1807 Campaign in Poland, fighting at Heilsberg and Friedland, for which he garnered a golden sword with diamonds.

After Tilsit, Ferdinand Saxe-Coburg ascended the throne of Duchy of Saxe-Coburg and avoided military involvement for the next five years. He joined the Allies on 30 July 1813, and took part in the battles at Kulm (Order of St. George, 4th class) and Leipzig (diamond signs of the Order of St. Alexander of Neva). He was officially restored in the Russian service with the rank of lieutenant general on 28 December 1813. In 1814, he served in the Imperial Retinue and participated in the actions at Brienne, La Rothière, Arcis sur Aube, St. Dizier, Le Fère Champenoise, and Paris. After the war, he returned to his principality, but remained in the Russian military service, rising to general of cavalry on 18 December 1832.

SAXE-WEIMAR EISENACH, Karl (Charles) August (b. 3 September 1757, Weimar — d. 14 June 1828, Graditz) was born to a prominent princely family of Saxe-Weimar. He entered Russian service as a lieutenant general and chef of the Kiev Grenadier Regiment on 18 August 1803. In 1805, he took part in the campaign against France, distinguishing himself at Austerlitz. The following year, Prince Karl left the Russian army for Prussia, but was captured after the destruction of the Prussian armies at Jena-Auerstadt on 14 October 1806. Released in 1807, he joined the Austrian army two years later and fought at Aspern and Wagram. He lived in Saxe-Weimar from 1810-1812, and joined the Russian army in early 1813. Serving in the 1st Cuirassier Division, he fought at Lutzen, Bautzen, Reichenbach, Dresden, Pirna, Kulm (golden sword), and Leipzig. For his actions in these battles, he was officially accepted into the Russian service with a rank of general of cavalry on 28 December 1813. In 1814, he took part in the battles at Brienne, Laon, Le Fère Champenoise, and Paris for which he received the Order of St. Vladimir (1st class). After the war, he returned to Saxe-Weimar.

SAZONOV, Aleksey Gavrilovich (b. 1791 — date of death unclear) was born to a petty noble family in the Ryazan *gubernia*. He studied in the 2nd Cadet Corps and began service as a sub-lieutenant in the 12th Battery Company of the 12th Artillery Brigade on 30 October 1806. In 1807-1811, he served in the Danubian Principalities, fighting the Turks at Ismail, Braila, Bazardjik (golden cross), Varna, Silistra, Shumla, and Nikopol. In 1812, he served with the 2nd Western Army at Saltanovka (wounded in the leg, golden sword), Smolensk, Borodino (Order of St. Vladimir, 4th class), Maloyaroslavets (wounded in the back), Vyazma (promoted to lieutenant, 29 July 1813), and Krasnyi.

SAZONOV, Fedor Vasilievich (b. 10 August 1789, Voronezh — date of death unclear) was born to a noble family from the Ryazan *gubernia*. He graduated from the Infantry Cadet Corps and began service as a page at the Imperial Court. He became a lieutenant in the Life Guard Jager Battalion on 6 October 1802. During the 1805 Campaign, he took part in the battle at Austerlitz and was wounded in the right leg. In 1807, he distinguished himself at Lomitten, where he was again wounded, this time in the left leg (Order of St. Vladimir, 4th class). Sazonov became colonel on 10 January 1810, and volunteered for service against the Turks in the Danubian Principalities. He assumed command of the 11th Jager Regiment on 8 April 1810, and became chef of the 40th Jager Regiment on 11 June 1811.

During the 1812 Campaign, Sazonov served with the 3rd Brigade of the 24th Division of the 6th Corps in the 1st Western Army. He took part in the actions at Vitebsk, Smolensk, Solovyeovo, Mikhalevka, Belomirovka, the Kolotsk Monastery, and Borodino, where he was wounded twice. After recuperating, he returned to the army in late 1813 and served at Modlin, for which he received the diamond signs of the Order of St. Anna. Sazonov was promoted to major general on 18 March 1814, and retired because of poor health on 20 February 1816. Sazonov participated in the grand celebration on the Borodino battlefield in August 1839.

SAZONOV, Ivan Terentievich (b. 1755 — d. 21 March 1823, Tambov) was born to a noble family in the Tambov *gubernia*. He enlisted as a private in the Orel Infantry Regiment on 24 October 1770, and rose to ensign in January 1772. He served in the Kuban Valley in 1775, and transferred as lieutenant to the Life Guard Grenadier Regiment in 1779. During the Russo-Swedish War in 1788-1790, he led a battalion of the Life Guard Grenadier Regiment and rose to a lieutenant colonel in 1790. He was discharged from the army in 1796, but returned to service in April 1801. Sazonov became a major general and chef of the Neva Musketeer Regiment on 1 March 1803. During the Russo-Swedish War in 1808-1809, he took part in the action at Lemo and commanded one of Prince Bagration's columns during the crossing of the

Gulf of Bothnia in April 1809. Sazonov took command of the 14th Division on 1 October 1810.

During the 1812 Campaign, Sazonov, whose division was attached to Wittgenstein's corps, fought at Klyastitsy, Pogorische, Polotsk (Order of St. Vladimir, 2nd class), Glubokoe, and Chashniki (golden sword with diamonds). However, he became seriously ill in late October and left army to recuperate. He was promoted to lieutenant general on 30 October 1812, with seniority dating from 17 August 1812. Sazonov was removed from command of the 14th Division on 13 January 1813. He did not hold any positions in the army after the war.

SCHPERBERG, Ivan Yakovlevich (b. 1770 — d. 1856) was born to a German noble family in the Lifland *gubernia*. He was enlisted as a kaptenarmus in the Izumsk Light Horse Regiment on 24 December 1790. In 1792-1794, he served in Lithuania and Poland and was promoted to cornet on 15 April 1795. In 1796, Schperberg participated in the Persian Campaign along the Caspian Sea. He transferred to the Pavlograd Hussar Regiment on 15 June 1797, served under Rimsky-Korsakov in Switzerland in 1799, and was wounded at Zurich. He transferred as a lieutenant to the Life Guard Horse Regiment on 21 November 1802. In 1805, Schperberg distinguished himself at Austerlitz, and in 1807, fought at Heilsberg (Order of St. George, 4th class, 13 December 1807) and Friedland (promotion to rotmistr). After Tilsit, Schperberg was appointed adjutant to Grand Duke Constantine and rose to colonel on 24 October 1811.

During the Russian Campaign, Schperberg served as a duty officer in Ataman Platov's Cossack corps and participated in Prince Bagration's retreat to Smolensk, fighting at Mir, Romanovo, Saltanovka, Molevo Boloto, Solovyevo, and Dorogobouzh. He distinguished himself at Borodino, where he was seriously wounded in the head but remained with his regiment. Schperberg was again seriously wounded at Mozhaisk on 8 September, and left the army to recuperate. He returned to service in June 1813 and fought at Dresden, Pirna, Leipzig, and Frankfurt. In 1814, he participated in the actions at Montmirail, Chateau Thierry, Etoges, and Paris (major general, 28 May 1814).

After the war, Schperberg attended Grand Duke Constantine and filled a series of posts: assistant to the commander of the 3rd Hussar Division on 25 September 1820; commander of the 2nd Brigade of the Lithuanian Uhlan Division on 11 April 1821; commander of the 2nd Brigade of the 4th Dragoon Division on 21 January 1822.

Schperberg retired because of poor health on 15 March 1823. During his career, he received the Prussian Orders of Red Eagle (2nd class) and Pour le Merite, Swedish Order of the Sword, and the Bavarian Order of Maximilian Joseph.

SCHWANEBACH, Christian Fedorovich (b. 1763 — d. 1820) was born to an Austrian noble family. His father entered Russian service in 1740. Schwanebach studied in the Artillery and Engineer Cadet Corps and began service as an ensign in the corps of engineers. On 1 October 1800, he rose to major general and chef of the 1st Pioneer Regiment, and served at this position until 13 September 1814. Over the next nine years, Schwanebach served in the Engineer Expedition that supervised the Russian engineer forces. He also tutored Grand Duke Nicholas Pavlovich, garnering the Orders of St. George (4th class) and St. Anna (1st class).

In March 1812, Schwanebach was appointed the deputy director of the Engineer

Department, where he served for the next three years. In November 1812, he also became inspector of the Engineer Corps.

SCHROEDER, Peter Petrovich (b. 28 April 1770 — d. 24 January 1824) was born to a German noble family in the Lifland *gubernia*. He was enlisted as a sergeant in the Bombardier Regiment on 23 March 1780, and began service as a sub-ensign in the Life Guard Semeyonovsk Regiment on 16 April 1785. He transferred as a lieutenant to the 4th Battalion of the Siberia Jager Corps on 2 May 1787. Schroeder served in Poland in 1792-1794, and was appointed premier major to the Simbirsk Dragoon Regiment on 1 November 1795. He rose to colonel on 12 October 1800, and transferred to the Velikii Lutsk Musketeer Regiment. In the 1805 Campaign, he served in Pomerania. He was appointed commander of the Velikii Lutsk Musketeer Regiment on 9 March 1806, and chef of the Tobolsk Musketeer Regiment on 5 September 1806.

Schroeder participated in the campaigns in Poland in 1806-1807 and fought at Eylau (wounded in the right shoulder, golden cross) and Danzig (golden sword). In 1810, he supervised construction of the Dünaburg fortress. During the Russian Campaign of 1812, his regiment was attached to the 1st Western Army and Schroeder fought at Vitebsk, Smolensk (promoted to major general on 12 November 1812, with seniority dating from 16 August 1812) and Borodino (wounded in both legs, Order of St. Vladimir, 3rd class).

After recuperating, Schroeder led the 4th Division on 18 January 1813, and fought at Kalisch, where he was wounded in the left hand. On 9 April 1813, he became the Commandant of Memel. After the war, he led the 2nd Brigade of the 4th Division before resigning on 30 May 1816. Schroeder was appointed to the Ministry of War in 1820, and retired because of poor health in 1822.

SCHREITERFELDT (Schreiterfeldt II in 1812) Karl Ivanovich (b. 8 May 1761 — d. 18 January 1825) was born to a German family in the Lifland *gubernia*; his full name was Carl Fabian Wilhelm Shreiter von Schreiterfeldt. He studied in the Artillery and Engineer Cadet Corps and served on various missions in the Crimea in 1784-1786, and in St. Petersburg and Vyborg from 1786-1788. During the Russo-Swedish War of 1789-1790, he served on the galley fleet and fought at Rochensalmi (golden sword, promoted to captain). In 1792-1796, he worked on fortifications of Revel and Dünamud fortresses. In 1798-1799, he served against the French in the Adriatic Sea and was promoted to colonel on 27 November 1799. From 1800-1801, he served on the Russian naval squadron in the Mediterranean Sea and in the Crimea. Schreiterfeldt was awarded the Order of St. George (4th class) for excellent service on 8 December 1802.

During the Russo-Turkish War of 1806-1812, Schreiterfeldt participated in the sieges of Anapa, Sukhumi, and Sudjuk Kale. He became lieutenant general and head of the Riga Engineer District on 8 February 1811. During the 1812 Campaign, he organized the defense of Riga. In 1813-1814, he served at Danzig, Stattin, and Lübeck. After the war, he headed the Lifland Engineer District, and was later discharged because of poor health with the rank of lieutenant general on 27 January 1824.

SELYAVIN, Nikolay Ivanovich (b. 1774 — d. 18 October 1833, St. Petersburg) was born to a noble family from the Moscow *gubernia*. He began service as a sergeant in the Ekaterinoslavl Grenadier Regiment in 1790, and transferred as a

SENYAVIN, Dmitry Nikolaevich (b. 1763 — d. 1831) was born to a noble family from the Kaluga *gubernia*. He studied in the Naval Cadet Corps and began service in the Baltic Fleet in 1778, becoming a midshipman in 1780. He took part in a cruise to Portugal in 1780-1781 and transferred to the Black Sea Fleet, where he commanded a packetboat in 1786. He participated in the Russo-Turkish War of 1788-1791, becoming adjutant general in 1788 and taking command of the ship-of-the-line *Navarkhia* in the battle of Cape Kaliakria.

In 1790s, Senyavin served under Admiral Fedor Ushakov and took command of the ship-of-the-line *St. Peter* in 1796. In 1798-1799, he took part in Ushakov's expedition in the Mediterranean Sea. Returning to Russia, Senyavin became the Commandant of Kherson port and later rose to rear admiral and the Commandant of Revel. In August 1805, he became a vice admiral and led the Russian naval squadron in the Adriatic Sea. Senyavin fought the French at Cattaro (Kotor) and Ragusa in 1806.

During the Russo-Turkish War of 1806-1812, Senyavin defeated the Turkish fleet at the Dardanelles, Tenedos, and Mt. Athos. However, the Treaty of Tilsit undermined his successes and forced him to seek neutral ports at Trieste and Lisbon, where he was blockaded by the British Royal Navy in 1808. Senyavin was forced to transfer his ships to the British and returned to Russia in 1809. However, he was disgraced at the Russian court for losing his ships, and thus fell out of favor. Senyavin served as the Commandant of the Revel port in 1810 before retiring three years later. Emperor Nicholas recalled him to active duty in 1826-1829, when Senyavin commanded the Baltic Fleet.

SESLAVIN (Seslavin II), Alexander Nikitich (b. 1780, Esemovo, Tver *gubernia* — d. 7 May 1858, Tver *gubernia*) was born to a noble family from the Tver *gubernia*. He studied in the Artillery and Enginner Cadet Corps and began service as a sub-lieutenant in the Life Guard Artillery Battalion on 1 March 1798. During the 1805 Campaign, he served in Count Tolstoy's sub-lieutenant to the Azov Musketeer Regiment in March 1797. In 1799, he served as a company commander in this unit during Field Marshal Suvorov's campaigns in Italy and Switzerland. As the Russian army retreated across the Panixer pass, Suvorov ordered Selyavin to remain with the Russian wounded left behind at Glarus. He was captured by the French and released in late 1800. Returning to Russia, he was promoted to captain in the Quartermaster Section of the Imperial Retinue. During the 1805 Campaign in Moravia and the Russo-Swedish War of 1808-1809, he served as an adjutant to General Paul Sukhtelen and received his colonelcy on 27 September 1811.

In 1812, Selyavin joined the quartemaster service of the 1st Western Army, but took part only in its initial retreat to the Drissa Camp. He was subsequently recalled to St. Petersburg and returned to the army in late 1812. In 1813-1814, he served as a duty officer in the General Staff of the Russian army and rose to major general on 16 October 1813. For his actions in 1813-1814, he garnered the Prussian Orders of Red Eagle and Pour le Merite, the Bavarian Order of Maximilian Joseph, and the Austrian Order of Leopold (2nd class).

After the war, he continued his work in the quartemaster service for the next sixteen years. He rose to lieutenant general on 3 September 1826.

corps in Pomerania. Two years later, he took part in the campaign in Poland, distinguishing himself at Heilsberg, where he was wounded in the chest and earned the Order of St. Vladimir (4th class).

Seslavin took a discharge and retired to his estate to recuperate. He returned to the military service in 1810, when he volunteered for service against the Turks in the Danubian Principalities. He distinguished himself in the battles at Razgrad, Silistra (Order of St. Anna, 2nd class), Shumla (promoted to staff captain, 15 August 1810), and Ruse, where he was seriously wounded in the right shoulder. For his actions, he earned promotion to captain on 22 May 1811. Seslavin became adjutant to General Mikhail Barclay de Tolly on 24 December 1811.

During the 1812 Campaign, Seslavin took part in the actions at Ostrovno, Smolensk (golden sword), Gridnevo (wounded in the leg) and Borodino (wounded, Order of St. George, 4th class, 17 November 1812). In October-November 1812, Seslavin commanded a partisan detachment and distinguished himself by bold raids on the French communication and supply lines. He was first to obtain intelligence on Napoleon's retreat from Moscow, which facilitated quick redeployment of the Russian army to Maloyaroslavets. Seslavin distinguished himself at Vyazma, Lyakhov, Borisov, Oshmyani, and Vilna, where he was wounded in the left hand. For his conduct, he was promoted from a captain of the Life Guard Horse Artillery Company to a colonel on 12 November 1812;

Seslavin took command of the Sumsk Hussar Regiment on the same day and rose to flügel adjutant on 1 December 1812.

In 1813, Seslavin took part in numerous rear guard actions as well as in the battles at Dresden and Leipzig, receiving promotion to major general on 27 September 1813 and the Order of St. Anna (1st class). In 1814, he participated in the combats at Brienne, La Rothière, Arcis sur Aube, and Le Fère Champenoise. His actions in 1814 earned him the Austrian Order of Maria Theresa and the Prussian Red Eagle. After the war, he served in the 1st Hussar Division and took a discharge because of poor health on 29 August 1820.

Two other Seslavins of note served in the Russian army during the Napoleonic wars. **Fedor Nikitich Seslavin** (b. 1787) graduated from the 2nd Cadet Corps and began service in the 9th Artillery Regiment in 1805. After briefly serving in the Siberia, he transferred to the 1st Reserve Artillery Brigade on 13 April 1811, and rose to a staff captain on 11 December 1811. In 1812, he served with the 1st Corps at Klyastitsy (golden sword), two battles of Polotsk (earned the Order of St. Vladimir, 4th class), and on the Berezina. In 1813-1814, he fought at Bautzen, Gross Beeren (Prussian Pour le Merite and promotion to captain), Wittenberg (transferred to the 21st Artillery Brigade on 14 September 1813), Leipzig, Soissons, and Paris (Imperial letter of gratitude).

Sergey Nikitich Seslavin (Seslavin IV) (b. 1789) also graduated from the 2nd Cadet Corps and began service as a sub-lieutenant in the Engineer Corps on 31 December 1809. He transferred to the 27th Battery Company of the 1st Reserve Artillery Brigade on 3 May 1812. During the 1812 Campaign, he served with the 1st Corps at Klyastitsy and fought at both battles of Polotsk, as well as on the Berezina. In 1813-1814, he remained in the Duchy of Warsaw and became a lieutenant on 12 October 1813.

SHABELSKY, Ivan Petrovich (b. 1796 — d. 30 May 1874) was born to a noble family from the Ekaterinoslavl *gubernia*. He began service in the Engineer Corps in 1811, and was assigned to the 1st Corps of Wittgenstein in 1812. During the 1812 Campaign, he served at Klyastitsy,

Svolnya, and Polotsk, where he skillfully constructed two pontoon bridges under the enemy fire, for which he received the rank of lieutenant and the Order of St. Vladimir (4th class). In late 1812, he fought at Koenigsberg, Braunsberg, and Elbing, earning promotion to captain. The following year, he became adjutant to General d'Auvray (Dovre) and served at Lutzen, Bautzen (Prussian Pour le Merite), Dresden, and Leipzig. For his actions in the last two battles, he received two Orders of St. Anna (3rd and 2nd classes) and was transferred with the same rank to the Life Guard Semeyonovsk Regiment.

In 1814, Shabelsky fought at Bar sur Aube, Le Fère Champenoise, Troyes, Arcis sur Aube, and Paris. For his service in 1814, he was promoted to colonel, but Shabelsky took the unusual step of declining the rank, claiming he was too young for it. Instead, Emperor Alexander I decorated him with the Order of St. Anna (2nd class) and a golden sword.

Shabelsky ultimately became a colonel in 1817, and transferred to the Derpt Horse Jager Regiment. In 1821, he took command of the Nizhegorod Dragoon Regiment and later reached the rank of major general. He participated in the Russo-Persian War in the Caucasus in 1826-1827, where he fought on the Araks River and at Sardar-Abad and Yerevan, earning the Orders of St. George (4th class), St. Vladimir (3rd class), and a golden sword with diamonds.

After the war, he led a brigade of the 2nd Uhlan Division. In 1830-1831, he served against the Polish insurgents and rose to commander of the 6th Light Cavalry division in 1833. He was promoted to lieutenant general in 1835, and later commanded in succession the 4th and 2nd Cavalry Divisions in 1836-1845, and the 3rd Reserve Cavalry Corps in 1845. He took part in the campaign against the Hungarian insurgents in 1849 and rose to general of cavalry in 1850. During the Crimean War, he commanded the Russian troops around Odessa. In 1855, he also took command of the 1st Reserve Corps. After the war, he was awarded a golden crown of the Prussian Pour le Merite in 1863. He died on 30 May 1874.

SHAKHOVSKY (Shakovskoi), Ivan Leontievich (b. 3 April 1777 — d. 1 April 1860, St. Petersburg) was born to a Russian family of princes. He was enlisted as a sergeant in the Life Guard Izmailovsk Regiment on 12 January 1786, and transferred as a captain to the Kherson Grenadier Regiment on 12 January 1794. He served in Poland in 1794, and distinguishing himself at Brest-Litovsk, Kobylka and Praga (Order of St. George, 4th class, 12 January 1795). Shakhovsky was promoted to colonel on 14 December 1799, transferred to the Life Guard Jager Battalion in 1802, rose to major general on 20 November 1804, and became chef of the 20th Jager Regiment on 7 January 1804.

During the 1812 Campaign, he led the 3rd Brigade of the 3rd Division of the 3rd Corps and fought at Vitebsk, Smolensk, Borodino (golden sword with diamonds), Tarutino, Maloyaroslavets, and Krasnyi. For his actions in 1812, he garnered the Orders of St. Anna (1st class) and St. Vladimir (2nd class).

In 1813, Shakhovsky served at Kalisch (Order of St. George, 3rd class, 6 March 1813), Lutzen, Bautzen, Kulm, and Leipzig (promoted to lieutenant general on 1 August 1814, with seniority dating from 16 October 1813). In 1814, he participated in actions at Bar sur Aube, Le Fère Champenoise, and Paris, for which he earned the Order of St. Alexander of Neva. In 1815-1816, Shakhovsky led the 4th Division. He became commander of the 2nd Grenadier Division on 26 November 1817, commander of the Grenadier Corps on 20 September 1823, and rose to general of infantry on 3 September 1826. He participated in the suppression of the Polish Uprising in 1831, fighting at Belolenke, Grochow, Ostrolenka, and Warsaw, for which he garnered the Order of St. George (2nd class) on 30 October 1831. He also earned the Order of St. Vladimir (1st class) for pursuing the Polish forces to the Prussian borders. Shakhovsky became chef of the Ekaterinoslavl Grenadier Regiment on 18 October 1831, and was relieved of command of the Grenadier Corps on 23 June 1832. He was appointed head of the General Audit on 13 January 1836, and became a member of the State Council on 13 July 1839. For his exemplary service, Shakhovsky was decorated with the Order of St. Andrew the First Called in 1843, and became an adjutant general in 1850. During the Crimean War, Shakhovsky commanded the St. Petersburg *opolchenye* from March-July 1855.

SHAKHOVSKY (Shakovskoi), Nikolay Leontievich (b. 1757 — d. 12 February 1837) was born to a Russian family of princes. He enlisted as a private in the 1st Fusilier Regiment in 1769, and rose to sergeant on 3 October 1770. He transferred to the 2nd Moscow Regiment in 1773, where he became regimental adjutant in 1776. He participated in the Russo-Turkish War in 1774-1777, fighting at Silistra and in the Crimea. In 1782, Shakhovsky became general staff quartermaster under Field Marshal General Chernyshev, and was promoted to second major in 1774. He soon transferred to the Moscow Carabineer Regiment and then to the Little Russia (Malorossiisky) Grenadier Regiment in 1786. Two years later, he briefly served in Poland before joining the Russian army in the Danubian Principalities.

Shakhovsky became a premier major in the Uglitsk Infantry Regiment on 25 July 1788, and fought on the Solchea River in 1789. In 1790, he joined the Astrakhan Grenadier Regiment and distinguished himself at Ismail, where he took two serious wounds (left palm cut off, injury in the head) and earned the Order of St. George (4th class) on 5 April 1791, and promotion to lieutenant colonel in the Kherson Grenadier Regiment.

After recuperating, Shakhovsky served in Poland in 1794, fighting at Krupchitse (Order of St. Vladimir, 4th class) and Praga (Order of St. Vladimir, 3rd class). After the campaign, he transferred to the Commissariat in 1798, and took a discharge with the rank of major general in 1799. He returned to the army in 1805, when he was appointed proviantmaster general. In 1806-1807, he served in this capacity for the Russian army in Poland and earned the Prussian Pour le Merite. He retired in late 1807, and three years later, entered the civil service with the rank of privy counselor.

Another **Shakhovsky, Peter Ivanovich**, served as the Governor General of the Pskov *gubernia* in 1812, and provided supplies to Wittgenstein's corps during the Russian Campaign.

SHATILOV, Ivan Yakovlevich (b. 1771 — date of death unclear) was born to a noble family in the Tver *gubernia*. He enlisted in the Life Guard Izmailovsk Regiment in 1782, and transferred as a lieutenant to the Moscow Grenadier Regiment in 1793. He served in Poland in 1794 and joined the Pavlovsk Grenadier Regiment. In 1799, Shatilov took part in the expedition to Holland. Back in Russia, he returned to the Moscow Grenadier Regiment in 1805. Two years later, he served with the 8th Division in Poland, fighting at Eylau, Guttstadt, Heilsberg, and Friedland, where he was wounded and received a golden sword. He took command of the Moscow Grenadier Regiment on 3 December 1807, and became lieutenant colonel on 24 December 1807. In 1808-1811, Shatilov served in the Danubian Principalities, where he distinguished himself at Lovchea and Bazardjik for which he earned the Order of St. George (4th class) and rank of colonel on 25 April 1811.

In 1812, Shatilov fought at Smolensk and Borodino, where he was wounded and garnered the Order of St. Anna (2nd class). After recuperating, Shatilov became chef of the Borodino Infantry Regiment on 2 June 1813, and commander of the Borodino Infantry Regiment on 4 July 1816. He rose to major general and commander of the 1st Brigade of the 17th Division on 11 September 1816. Shatilov retired because of poor health on 6 December 1824.

SHELE, Gustav Khristianovich (date of birth unclear, ca. 1759/1760 — d. 18 February 1820, Aland Islands) was born to a Swedish noble family. He enlisted as a cadet in the Bombardier Company of the Life Guard Preobrazhensk Regiment in 1774. Over the next nine years, he was promoted to bombardier, furier and kaptenarmus before retiring with the rank of lieutenant on 12 January 1783. He returned to the army seven months later, joining the Pskov Infantry Regiment. Shele participated in the Russo-Swedish War in 1788-1790 and fought at Brakela, Friedrixham, and on the Kumen River.

At the end of the war, Shele transferred as a captain to the Neva Infantry Regiment in January 1789, and distinguished himself during the Russo-Turkish War in 1789-1791, for which he received the Order of St. George (4th class). He rose to major in December 1799 and to lieutenant colonel in May 1806. In 1807, he led a battalion of the Neva Musketeer Regiment.

During the Russo-Swedish War in 1808-1809, Shele distinguished himself at Abo, Lemo, Helsing, and the Aland Islands. He became commander of the Neva Musketeer Regiment on 7 June 1809, and was garrisoned on the Aland Islands. He was promoted to colonel on 11 September 1811.

During the 1812 Campaign, Shele served in the 2nd Brigade of the 21st Division of the Finland Corps and fought at Dalenkirchen, Eckau, Garozen, Chashniki, and Smolyani (Order of St. Anna, 2nd class). In 1813, he was attached to Major General Sievers' detachment, and took part in the actions at Pillau and Danzig. Shele's unit was sent to the Army of North and he fought at Teltov, Gross Beeren, and Leipzig (Order of St. Vladimir, 3rd class). In 1814, Shele distinguished himself at Soissons, Craonne, Laon, and Paris. He was promoted to major general on 13 December 1814, with seniority dating from 6 March 1814.

After the war, Shele served in the 28th Division (29 March 1815), briefly led reserve battalions of the 2nd Corps, and finally became commander of the 3rd Brigade of the 28th Division on 20 March 1816. He was appointed the Commandant of the Aland Islands on 27 April 1816.

SHENSHIN, Vasily Nikanorovich (b. 28 April 1784 — d. 28 May 1831) was born to a noble family from the Orel *gubernia*. He was enlisted at age two in the Life Guard Izmailovsk Regiment on 8 June 1786, and rose to a sergeant on 4 October 1790, at the age of six; Shenshin became an ensign on 11 October 1798, lieutenant on 21 September 1802, and staff captain on 14 February 1805. He participated in the 1805 Campaign and fought at Austerlitz, for which he received the Order of St. Anna (4th class). In 1807, he took part in the battles at Guttstadt, Heilsberg, and Friedland (wounded in the left leg, received promotion to captain on 4 November 1807, and the Order of St. Vladimir, 4th class).

In 1809, Shenshin transferred as a colonel to the Arkhangelogorod Musketeer Regiment (26 April) in the Danubian Principalities and was appointed chef of this unit on 29 June 1811. He received the Order of St. Anna (2nd class) for actions at Giurgiu in 1811, where he was wounded in the left arm. During the 1812 Campaign, he served in the 1st Brigade of the 8th Division in the Army of Danube and participated in the operations at Gornostaevichy, Volkovysk, and on the Berezina. In 1813, Shenshin served at Thorn, Bautzen, Dresden, Pirna (promoted to major general on 27 September 1813), and Leipzig (wounded in the stomach, Orders of St. George, 3rd class, and of St. Vladimir, 18 October 1813). In 1814, Shenshin distinguished himself at Montmirail, where he was wounded in the right hand, receiving in return the Order of St. Anna (2nd class) and the Prussian Red Eagle (2nd class).

After the war, Shenshin became commander of the 2nd Brigade of the 8th Division on 18 May 1814, commander of the 1st Brigade of the 23rd Division on 2 March 1818, commander of the Life Guard Finland Regiment on 10 June 1821, commander of the 1st Brigade of the 2nd Guard Infantry Division on 19 February 1823, and commander of the 1st Brigade of the 1st Guard Infantry Division on 26 March 1825. During the Decembrist Uprising, Shenshin was one of the first to pledge allegiance to Emperor Nicholas I and was appointed adjutant general on 27 December 1825, and promoted to lieutenant general on 3 September 1826.

Shenshin participated in the Russo-Turkish War in 1828-1829 and distinguished himself at Varna. Shenshin took command of the 1st Guard Infantry Division on 5 October 1829. In 1831, he took part in the suppression of the Polish uprising, but died during the cholera epidemic on 28 May 1831.

SHEPELEV, Dmitry Dmitrievich (b. 1771 — d. 1841) was born to a noble Russian family. He was enlisted as sergeant in the Life Guard Preobrazhensk Regiment in 1782, promoted to ensign in 1792, and transferred as a second major to the Mariupol Light Horse (*legkokonnii*) Regiment in 1793. He served in Poland in 1794, and distinguished himself at Khelm (Order of St. George, 4th class, 7 December 1795) and Praga (wounded in the right hand, golden cross). In 1796, he participated in the Persian Campaign along the Caspian Sea. Shepelev served under Rimsky-Korsakov in Switzerland in 1799, and rose to colonel on 19 July of that year. Returning to Russia, he became chef of the Vladimir Dragoon Regiment on 10 November 1800, commander of the Georgian Hussar Regiment on 3 February 1801, and chef of this unit on 4 March 1801. He became flügel adjutant on 25 April 1801, and after his regiment (Georgian Hussars) was disbanded, was confirmed as flügel adjutant on 5 May 1802.

During the 1805 Campaign, Shepelev served in Buxhöwden's corps and fought at Austerlitz that December. He became chef of the Grodno Hussar Regiment on 5 July 1806, and participated in the Polish campaign the following year at Guttstadt, on the Passarge River (Order of St. George, 3rd class, 3 September 1807), Heilsberg, and Friedland. Promoted to major general on 5 June 1807, he served under Prince Bagration during the Russo-Swedish War in

1808-1809, and took part in the expedition to the Aland Islands. He retired in 1810, but returned to the army in July 1812.

During the 1812 Campaign, Shepelev commanded the Guard Cavalry Brigade comprised of the Life Guard Horse Regiment and Chevalier Guard Regiment. He led this unit at Maloyaroslavets and Krasnyi. In 1813, he led the advance guard of Wittgenstein's corps, captured Koenigsberg (earned promotion to lieutenant general on 13 January 1813) and served at Hamburg and in Holstein. He became commander of the 2nd Hussar Division in 1815, but retired because of poor health on 14 April 1816. Shepelev returned to service on 7 July 1826 but was discharged on 1 February 1830.

SHEPELEV, Vasily Fedorovich (b. 1768 — d. 11 February 1813) was born to a noble family in the Kaluga *gubernia*. He was enlisted in the Life Guard Preobrazhensk Regiment on 12 May 1780, and transferred as a cornet to the Life Guard Horse Regiment on 12 January 1786. He served in Poland in 1792-1794, and was promoted to colonel on 20 May 1797. Shepelev became major general and chef of St. Petersburg Dragoon Regiment on 31 September 1798. He served under Rimsky-Korsakov in Switzerland in 1799 and fought at Zurich.

After returning to Russia, he was promoted to lieutenant general and appointed cavalry inspector of the Smolensk Inspection on 26 September 1800. He was discharged on 8 November 1800, but returned to service the following year and was appointed chef of the Vladimir Dragoon Regiment and cavalry inspector of the Caucasus Inspection on 3 February 1801.

Shepelev became chef of the Taganrog Dragoon Regiment on 11 April 1801, and was relieved of his inspector position on 21 April 1801. Less than a year later, he became cavalry inspector of the Caucasus Inspection on 15 March 1802, and then chef of the St. Petersburg Dragoon Regiment on 25 November 1803. He participated in the 1805 Campaign and fought at Austerlitz. In 1806, Shepelev served in the 8th Division and retired on 13 January 1807. He returned to service in 1812, and was elected head of the Kaluga *opolchenye*. In 1812-1813, he operated around Bryansk, Mstislavl and Moghilev. During his career, Shepelev was also decorated with the Orders of St. Anna (1st class), St. Vladimir (3rd class), St. John of Jerusalem, and a golden sword.

SHERBATOV (Sherbatov I in 1812), Aleksey Grigorievich (b. 5 March 1776 — d. 30 December 1848, Moscow) descended from a prominent Russian family of princes. He enlisted in the Life Guard Semeyonovsk Regiment on 21 April 1782, and began service as a sub-ensign on 12 January 1792. Under Paul I, Sherbatov enjoyed rapid promotions, earning the Order of St. John of Jerusalem in 1798, and a colonelcy on 16 April 1799. Sherbatov became major general and chef of the Tenginsk Musketeer Regiment on 9 November 1800. He retired on 5 October 1804, but returned to service on 16 September 1805, when he was appointed chef of the Kostroma Musketeer Regiment. However, because of retirement, his seniority was changed to 21 October 1801.

Sherbatov participated in the 1806-1807 Campaigns in Poland, serving in the 4th Division. He distinguished himself at Golymin (Order of St. George, 4th class, 10 February 1807), Pultusk, Hof, and Eylau. In the spring of 1807, he defended Danzig against the French and refused to accept the French offers to surrender. Although he finally capitulated, Sherbatov preferred to remain in French captivity rather than accept the French stipulation of not serving against France for a year. Napoleon detained Sherbatov in Dresden and released him after the treaty at Tilsit was signed. Sherbatov was dispatched to the Danubian Principalities, where he took part in operations against the Turks and was seriously wounded in the chest at Shumla in 1810.

During the Russian Campaign of 1812, Sherbatov commanded the 18th Division of the 3rd Reserve Army of Observation and fought at Brest-Litovsk, Kobryn (Order of St. Anna, 1st class), Gorodechnya, Borisov, and Studenka and Podubie (Order of St. George, 3rd class, 4 December 1812). For his actions in 1812, he was promoted to lieutenant general on 4 June 1813, with seniority dating from 28 November 1812. In 1813, Sherbatov served at Thorn (Order of St. Vladimir, 2nd class), Koenigswartha (diamond signs of the Order of St. Anna), and Bautzen, where he was seriously wounded.

After recuperating, he commanded the 6th Corps in the Army of Silesia and fought at Katzbach, Löwenberg (Order of St. Alexander of Neva), and Leipzig (golden sword with diamonds). In 1814, he distinguished himself at Brienne (Order of St. George, 2nd class, 29 January 1814), Soissons and Paris. In 1815-1816, he led the 18th Division, became commander of the 6th Corps on 21 April 1816, was appointed adjutant general on 11 September 1816, and just over seven years later, rose to general of infantry on 24 December 1823.

Sherbatov was appointed commander of the 4th Corps on 7 December 1824, commander of the 2nd Corps on 28 September 1826, chef of the Kostroma Infantry Regiment on 18 October 1831, head of the General Audit on 23 June 1832, and chef of the Kostroma Jager Regiment on 14 April 1833. He participated in the suppression of the Polish uprising in 1831, and received the Order of St. Vladimir (1st class) and a golden sword with diamonds and laurels for the capture of Warsaw. Sherbatov retired because of poor health on 25 December 1835, but returned to service on 6 May 1839, and was confirmed chef of the Kostroma Jager Regiment.

Sherbatov became the Military Governor of Moscow on 26 April 1844, and was relieved of command because of poor health on 18 May 1848. He died on 30 December 1848 in Moscow.

During his career, Sherbatov received the Orders of St. Andrew the First Called, St. Vladimir (1st class), St. Alexander of Neva with diamonds, St. Anna (1st class) with diamonds, St. John of Jerusalem, two medals "For Military Merit" and "For XXX Years of Distinguished Service), the Prussian Order of Red Eagle (1st class), and the Sardinian Order of St. Maurice and Lazarus.

SHERBATOV, Alexander Fedorovich (b. 24 July 1773 — d. 12 May 1817) was born to a prominent Russian family of princes. He was enlisted as a sergeant in the Life Guard Preobrazhensk Regiment in 1776 and began service as a lieutenant on 15 May 1788. He transferred to the commissariat as ober-proviantmeister with the rank of premier major in 1790, and became kriegs-commissar with the rank of lieutenant colonel on 21 February 1792. In 1796, he transferred as a lieutenant colonel to the Voronezh Infantry Regiment and took part in the Persian Campaign along the Caspian Sea. He was promoted to colonel on 6 February 1797, and transferred to the Life Guard Horse Regiment in 1798. In 1799, he served as an adjutant to Grand Duke Constantine and participated in the campaigns in Italy and Switzerland, where he distinguished himself on the Adde River. He was promoted to major general and appointed adjutant general on 18 May 1799.

Returning to Russia, Sherbatov was discharged from service for authority abuses on 6 April 1800. He was restored in rank on 8 April 1801, and appointed to the Life Guard Hussar Regiment. However, he retired on 27 September 1802. During the 1812 Campaign, he organized and commanded two cavalry regiments in the Tula *opolchenye*. He participated in the actions at Krasnyi, Chashniki, and on the Berezina. For his actions, Sherbatov was awarded a golden sword with diamonds and the Order of St. George (4th class). In 1813, he fought at Kalisch, Lutzen, Bautzen, Teplitz (Order of St. Anna, 1st class), and in 1814, led the advance guard in Ataman Platov's detachment. After the war, Sherbatov served as director of horse stud farms.

SHERBATOV (Sherbatov II in 1812), Nikolay Grigorievich (date of birth unclear; 7 or 31 July 1777 — d. 7 January 1849, Moscow) was born to a prominent Russian family of princes; the brother of Aleksey Sherbatov. He was enlisted as a sub-ensign in the Life Guard Semeyonovsk Regiment on 27 January 1785, and began service as an ensign on 13 January 1791. After serving ten years in the Guard, Sherbatov transferred as a lieutenant colonel to the quartermaster service on 24 March 1801. He participated in the 1806-1807 Campaigns in Poland and fought at Ostrolenka, Heilsberg, and Friedland, receiving a golden sword for courage and the Order of St. Vladimir (4th class).

After Tilsit, Sherbatov was appointed to the Life Guard Hussar Regiment and promoted to colonel on 27 February 1808. He retired in 1810 but returned to service in early 1812, taking command of the 2nd Ukraine Cossack Regiment attached to the Ukraine Cossack Brigade. During the Russian Campaign of 1812, he joined the 3rd Reserve Army of Observation and fought at Kovel and Lubomle. In 1813, he became chef of the 2nd Ukraine Cossack Regiment on 8 March 1813, and served at Glogau, Katzbach (promoted to major general on 27 September), Löwenberg (Order of St. George, 3rd class, 10 November 1813), and Dresden.

In 1814, he served at Metz and Paris. After the war, he was put in command of the 1st Brigade of the Ukraine Cossack (later Uhlan) Division. He retired because of poor health on 31 December 1819, and spent the next thirty years in Moscow. During his career, Sherbatov was also awarded the Orders of St. Anna (2nd class) with diamonds, St. Vladimir (3rd class), Prussian Orders Pour le Merite and Red Eagle (3rd class), and the Swedish Order of the Sword.

SHEVICH, Ivan Georgievich (b. 1754 — d. 16 October 1813) was born to a Serbian noble family. His grandfather served as a lieutenant general in the Austrian army and entered Russian service in 1752. Shevich enlisted as a vakhmistr in the Moscow Legion on 12 May 1770, transfererd to the Illyrian Hussar Regiment, and rose to ensign on 12 May 1772. He participated in the suppression of Pugachev's peasant uprising in 1773-1774, then went on to serve in the Kuban Valley in 1776-1777. Shevich took part in the Russo-Turkish War in 1788-1790, and fought at Ochakov, Kaushani, and Bender. He served in Poland in 1794, became a colonel on 30 June 1798, and rose to command the Glukhov Cuirassier Regiment on 12 October 1799. However, he took a discharge with the rank of major general on 6 March 1800.

Shevich returned to service on 6 January 1807, and his seniority was changed to 12 October 1801. He was appointed to the Army of Moldavia and led the detachment in Little Wallachia. He soon became commander of the Life Guard Hussar Regiment on 10 December 1808. During the 1812 Campaign, Shevich commanded the Guard Cavalry Brigade and fought at Borodino (Order of St. Anna, 1st class), Spas Kupla, and Krasnyi (Order of St. George, 3rd class, 9 March 1813). In 1813, Shevich fought at Lutzen, Bautzen, and Kulm (promoted to lieutenant general on 11 September 1813) before taking a mortal wound at Leipzig on 16 October 1813.

SHISHKIN, Nikolay Andreyevich (b. 1767 — date of death unclear) was born to a noble family in the Ryazan *gubernia*. He enlisted as a vakhmistr in the Life Guard Horse Regiment on 5 May 1784, and rose to cornet on 3 October 1786. He participated in the Russo-Swedish War in 1788-1790, and fought at Memel, Pardakoski, and Kernikoski (wounded, promoted to lieutenant). Shishkin transferred as a second major to the Voronezh Hussar Regiment on 12 January 1791, and took part in Russo-Turkish War, fighting at Babadag and Macin. He served in Poland in 1792-1794, and fought at Vladimir-Volhynsk, Dubenka, Gorodische, Maciejowice (golden sword), Radojitze (Order of St. George, 4th class, 7 December 1795), and Praga (golden cross). Shishkin transferred as a major to the Pavlograd Hussar Regiment on 15 July 1797.

In 1799, Shishkin served under Rimsky-Korsakov in Switzerland and fought at Constance (promoted to lieutenant colonel) and Zurich. Returning to Russia, he was promoted to colonel and transferred to the Seversk Dragoon Regiment in November 1800. However, he was soon discharged from the army for improper reporting.

Shishkin returned to service in July 1801. He participated in the 1805 Campaign and fought at Amstetten, Wischau, and Austerlitz (wounded in the neck and shoulder). He took command of the Seversk Dragoon Regiment on 11 November 1806, and served in Poland at the battles of Plotsk, Ostrolenka, Eylau (wounded, golden cross) and Guttstadt (wounded in the left thigh). He left the army to recuperate and retired because of his wounds with the rank of major general on 7 October 1807.

Shishkin returned to service again during the Russian Campaign of 1812, when he joined the Ryazan *opolchenye* on 7 August and took part in minor actions against the French at the head of two *opolchenye* cavalry regiments. In 1813, he served at Kalisch and Glogau (golden sword with diamonds) and remained in the Duchy of Warsaw for the remaining of war. He retired on 18 January 1815.

SHISHKOV, Alexander Semenovich (b. 20 March 1754 —. 21 April 1841) was born to a noble family in the Moscow *gubernia*. He studied in the Naval Cadet Corps and receiving the rank of guard marine in 1769. He took part in expeditions to Naples in 1773-1776 and in

1778-1779. He participated in the Russo-Swedish War in 1788-1790, and fought at Gogland, Eland (promoted to captain 2nd class) and Vyborg (golden sword). Shishkov was appointed to the Black Sea Fleet in 1796, becoming a captain (1st class) on 24 November 1796. The following year, he was appointed squadron-major (*eskadr-maior*) to Paul I on 20 January 1797, and captain-commander and adjutant general on 21 July 1797. In 1798, Shishkov served on a diplomatic mission to Prussia and was promoted to rear admiral on 4 November 1798, and vice admiral on 20 May 1799. He served as the Official Historian of the Russian Navy and published several works on the Russian naval history. In 1803, he became a member of the Admiralty, and in 1805 was appointed to the Naval Science Committee.

Shishkov became a secretary to Alexander in 1810, and was appointed State Secretary on 21 April 1812, replacing Mikhail Speransky. During the 1812 Campaign, he accompanied Alexander to the Drissa Camp and later urged the Emperor to leave the army. In 1813, he witnessed the battles of Lutzen, Bautzen, Dresden, Kulm, and Leipzig. He attended Alexander throughout the 1814 Campaign in France.

After the war, Shishkov became a member of the State Council and rose to admiral on 18 December 1823. He became the Minister of Education (*narodnogo prosveshenia*) on 27 May 1824 and was dismissed on 7 May 1828.

SHKAPSKY, Mikhail Andreyevich (b. 1754 — d. 22 July 1815) was born to an ober-officer's family in the Moscow *gubernia*. He enlisted as a private in the Moscow Legion on 12 September 1769, and transferred as a sub-ensign to the Siberia Dragoon Regiment on 2 April 1770. He participated in the suppression of Pugachev's peasant uprising in 1772-1774. Shkapsky transferred to the Kabarda Infantry Regiment in 1776, and participated in campaigns in the Kuban Valley. For his actions, he was promoted to ensign on 2 May 1778.

Six years later, he transferred as a captain to the Vladimir Infantry Regiment and fought the Caucasian mountaineers, receiving the Order of St. Vladimir (4th class) for his actions at Anapa. He was soon transferred to the Nizhegorod Infantry Regiment and fought in Poland in 1792-1794.

In 1799, Shkapsky served under Rimsky-Korsakov in Switzerland and distinguished himself at Schaffhausen, where he was wounded in the right leg and hand and earned promotion to lieutenant colonel. He received the Order of St. George (4th class) for excellent service on 8 December 1803. Shkapsky participated in the 1805 Campaign and distinguished himself at Austerlitz, receiving the rank of colonel on 5 May 1806. He then served in Poland in 1806-1807, fighting at Eylau, Heilsberg, and Friedland (wounded in the left leg). After recuperating, he was appointed chef of the Staroskol Musketeer Regiment and served in the Danubian Principalities from 1809-1811. He distinguished himself at Ruse and rose to major general on 30 July 1811.

During the Russian Campaign of 1812, Shkapsky served in the Army of Danube and participated in the operations in Volhynia. In 1813-1814, he served at Lublin (Order of St. George, 3rd class, 11 April 1813), Breslau, Katzbach, Leipzig, and Mainz. In 1815, he led the 2nd Brigade of the 22nd Division and marched to France during the Hundred Days. However, he became seriously ill and died on 22 July 1815. For his actions in 1813-1814, Shkapsky was also awarded the Order of St. Anna (1st class) and the Swedish Order of the Sword.

SHOSTAKOV (Shestakov), Gerasim Alekseyevich (b. 1756 — d. 1837) was born to a noble family in the Chernigov *gubernia* He enlisted as a private in the Akhtyrsk Hussar Regiment on 6 May 1775. Shostakov participated in the Russo-Turkish War in 1787-1791, and distinguished himself at Ochakov (golden cross) and Killia. He served in Poland in 1792-1794, and retired with a rank of lieutenant colonel on 15 October 1800. Shostakov returned to the Akhtyrsk Hussars in July 1801, and then transferred as a lieutenant colonel to the Elizavetgrad Hussar Regiment. In 1806-1807, his regiment was attached to the 5th Division and took part in the operations in Poland, where he fought at Eylau. Shostakov was promoted to colonel on 24 December 1808, and took command of the Elizavetgrad Hussar Regiment on 20 March 1810.

During the Russian Campaign of 1812, he served in the 8th Brigade of the 2nd Cavalry Division of the 2nd Corps and fought at Ostrovno, Vitebsk, Smolensk, Borodino, Vyazma, Dorogobouzh, and Krasnyi. In 1813, he distinguished himself at Torgau and Leipzig. During the 1814 Campaign in France, Shostakov received the Order of St. George (3rd class, 26 March 1814) for his actions at St. Dizier. After the war, he became chef of the Elizavetgrad Hussar Regiment on 18 May 1814, and led the 2nd Brigade of the 2nd Hussar Division (September 1814). Shostakov retired on 1 April 1818.

SHUBERT, Fedor Fedorovich (b. 23 February 1789 — d. 15 November 1865) was born to a German noble family in St. Petersburg. He began service in the Quartermaster Service of the Imperial Retinue and served on a diplomatic mission to China in 1805. Returning to Russia, Shubert rose to a sub-lieutenant in the quartersmaster service and took part in the campaigns in Poland in 1806-1807, fighting at Eylau (wounded, Order of St. Vladimir, 4th class). After recuperating, he joined the Russian army in Finland and fought at Forsbü, Revelholm, and the capture of the Aland Islands. In the summer of 1809, he took part in the Russo-Swedish negotiations leading to the Peace Treaty of Fridrixham on 17 September 1809. Shubert served under the Russian Foreign Minister Nikolay Rumyantsev and served on several diplomatic missions to Napoleon between late 1809 and early 1810.

In the spring of 1810, Shubert joined the Army of Danube and fought at Silistra, Shumla, Ruse, and Batin, where he was wounded and earned promotion to captain and a golden sword. During the 1812 Campaign, he served as ober-quartermaster of the 2nd Cavalry Corps in the 1st Western Army and took part in the actions at Ostrovno, Smolensk, Borodino, Spas Kuplya, Tarutino, Maloyaroslavets, Vyazma, and Krasnyi. For the 1812 Campaign, Shubert garnered the Order of St. Anna (2nd class) with diamonds and a promotion to lieutenant colonel. In 1813, he served with the 2nd Cavalry Corps at Glogau, Lutzen, Bautzen, Reichenbach, Löwenberg, Goldberg, Katzbach, Zobten, and Leipzig, where he earned the rank of colonel and the Prussian Orders of Red Eagle and the Pour le Merite.

In 1814, Shubert served in the Army of Silesia and distinguished himself at Le Fère Champenoise and Paris. In March-December 1814, he served as a liaison officer between the Russian and Prussian headquarters. In July 1815, he became ober-quartermaster of the Russian occupation corps in France, where he remained for the next three years. He returned to Russia and became director of the III Section of the Military Topographic Depot in 1819, director of the Toporgraphic Corps in 1822, and director of the Military Topographic Depot in 1832. In 1829-1837, he headed the Hydrographic Bureau of the Naval General Staff, rising to major general in 1820, to lieutenant general in 1831, and general of infantry in 1845. He served as general quartermaster of the General Staff in 1834-1843, before becoming a member of the War Council in 1843 and head of the Military Academic Committee in 1846. Shubert was instrumental in completing numerous topographic maps and surveys of various Russian provinces.

SHUKHANOV, Danil Vasilievich (b. 1745 — d. 1813) was born to a Moldavian noble family. He enlisted in the Bakhmutsk Hussar Regiment in 1755, and participated in the Russo-Turkish Wars in 1770s and 1780s, earning the Order of St. George (4th class) for his actions at Kinburn in 1787, and a golden cross for Ismail in 1791. In 1792-1794, Shukhanov served in Poland. He rose to colonel on 1 July 1799. During the Russo-Turkish War of 1806-1812, he served with the Oliviopol Hussar Regiment and distinguished himself at Shumla, Bazardjik (golden cross), and Ruse. In 1812, he took part in the operations of the Army of Danube in Volhynia and on Berezina. In 1813, he distinguished himself at Michelsdorf (Order of St. Vladimir, 3rd class) and Dresden, where he earned promotion to major general on 27 September 1813. However, he passed away in late 1813 (cause unclear), and was removed from rosters on 25 December 1814.

SHULGIN, Alexander Sergeyevich (date of birth unclear, ca. 1775 — d. 11 May 1841, Moscow) was born to a Russian noble family. He studied in the Artillery and Engineer Cadet Corps and became cornet in the Sumsk Light Horse Regiment on 4 February 1795. He served under Rimsky-Korsakov in Switzerland in 1799, and fought at Zurich. Returning to Russia, he retired with the rank of lieutenant colonel in 1802, but returned to service in early 1805. During the 1805 Campaign, he served with the Grand Duke Constantine's Uhlan Regiment and distinguished himself at Austerlitz (Order of St. Vladimir, 4th class). In 1807, Shulgin took part in the battles at Guttstadt, Heilsberg, and Friedland (Order of St. George, 4th class, 1 June 1808). After the treaty was signed at Tilsit, he became adjutant to Grand Duke Constantine. His regiment was renamed to the Life Guard Uhlan Regiment on 24 December 1809, and Shulgin became colonel on 24 October 1811.

Shulgin served as an assistant to general policemeister in the 1st Western Army during the 1812 Campaign, and was awarded the Order of St. Anna (2nd class) for his conduct at Borodino. In 1813-1814, he served as an adjutant to Grand Duke Constantine and distinguished himself at Le Fère Champenoise, for which he received promotion to major general on 22 May 1814, with seniority dating from 25 March 1814. For his service in 1813-1814, he also received the Prussian Red Eagle, Pour le Merite, and the Bavarian Order of Maximilian Joseph.

After the war, he became the Chief of Police (ober-policemeister) of Moscow on 26 March 1816, and ober-policemeister of St. Petersburg on 14 August 1825. He took indefinite furlough because of poor health on 11 February 1826, and retired from service on 11 January 1834.

SHULMAN (Shulman I), Fedor Maksimovich (b. 1773 — date of death unclear) was born to a noble family from the Lifland *gubernia*. He studied in the Artillery and Engineer Cadet Corps and began service as a shtyk junker in the 2nd Cannonier Regiment in 1791. In 1792-1794, he served in the Courland *gubernia*. He took part in minor actions in the 1805-1807 Campaigns, and served during the Russo-Swedish War at Sveaborg, for which he received the Order of St. George (4th class). Shulman became lieutenant colonel and commander of the 6th Artillery Brigade and the 6th Battery Artillery Company on 21 February 1811.

In 1812, he served in the 1st Corps and fought at Chashniki and on the Ushach River, earning the Order of St. Vladimir (4th class). In 1813, he rose to colonel on 8 June and participated in the siege of Danzig, garnering the Orders of St. Anna (2nd class), St. Vladimir (3rd class), Prussian Pour le Merite, and a golden sword.

His brother, **Levin Maksimovich Shulman,** also graduated from the Artillery and Engineer Cadet Corps and began service in Herbel's Battalion. He distinguished himself against the French at Eylau (wounded) in 1807, and against the Turks at Ruse (Order of St. Vladimir, 4th class) in 1811. He rose to lieutenant colonel on 21 February 1811, and later commanded the 10th Battery Company of the 19th Artillery Brigade.

SHUSHERIN, Zakhar Sergeyevich (b. 1785 — date of death unclear) was born to a noble family in the Tula *gubernia*. He studied in the Artillery and Engineer Corps and began service as a sub-lieutenant in the Life Guard Artillery Battalion in 1799. In 1806-1807, he served in Poland, fighting at Suchochin, Eylau, Heilsberg (Order of St. Anna, 3rd class) and Friedland. Promoted to lieutenant colonel, Shusherin took command of the 8th Horse Artillery Company of the 3rd Reserve Artillery Brigade on 21 February 1811. During the 1812 Campaign, he fought at Borodino (Order of St. Anna, 2nd class), Tarutino, and Krasnyi (Order of St. Vladimir, 4th class). In 1813, he served at Kalisch, Lutzen, Bischofswerde (golden sword), Liwerbach (diamond signs of the Order of St. Anna, 2nd class), Bautzen (Order of St. George, 4th class, and the Prussian Pour le Merite), and Leipzig. In 1814, he took part in the actions at Soissons and Paris.

SHUVALOV, Pavel Andreyevich (b. 1 June 1776 — d. 13 December 1823) was born to a noble family and enlisted as a cornet in the Life Guard Horse Regiment on 23 February 1786. He became a sub-lieutenant on 14 January 1793. Shuvalov served in Poland in 1794 and distinguished himself at Praga, for which he garnered the Order of St. George (4th class) on 12 January 1795. Promoted to colonel on 29 August 1798, Shuvalov was discharged from army on 16 April 1799. However, he volunteered for the 1799 Campaign in Italy and Switzerland, where he distinguished himself at St. Gothard. He was officially restored in the army with the rank of major general on 27 September 1801.

Shuvalov became chef of the Glukhovsk Cuirassier Regiment on 23 June 1803, chef of the Serpukhov Dragoon Regiment on 5 September 1806, and again chef of the Glukhovsk Cuirassier Regiment on 17 October 1806. During the

1806-1807 Campaigns in Poland, he served with the 9th Division in General Essen I's corps. During the Russo-Swedish War of 1808-1809, Shuvalov led a corps and captured Torneo in the spring of 1809, for which he was promoted to lieutenant general on 1 April 1809, and adjutant general on 19 July 1808. He completed several diplomatic missions to Vienna between December 1809 and May 1811.

During the 1812 Campaign, Shuvalov commanded the 4th Corps in the 1st Western Army, but was replaced by General Alexander Osterman Tolstoy on 13 July 1812, because of poor health. After recuperating, he attended Emperor Alexander I during the campaigns in Germany and France in 1813-1814, and distinguished himself at Kulm (Prussian Iron Cross), Leipzig (Order of St. Alexander of Neva), Brienne, Arcis sur Aube, Le Fère Champenoise, and Paris. Shuvalov took part in the negotiations for the surrender of Paris in March 1814, and as the Russian representative, accompanied Napoleon to Elba.

After the war, Shuvalov continued diplomatic service until his death on 13 December 1823. During his service, Shuvalov also received the Russian Orders of St. Alexander of Neva, St. Vladimir (2nd class), St. Anna (1st class), St. John of Jerusalem, Prussian Red Eagle (1st class), French Order of St. Louis, Austrian Order of Leopold, Württemberg Order of Military Merit, Bavarian Order of Maximilian Joseph, and the Sardinian Order of St. Maurice and Lazarus.

SIBIRSKY, Alexander Vasilievich (b. 19 November 1779 — d. 1836) was born to a princely family of the Turkish descent. He was enlisted in the Life Guard Preobrazhensk Regiment upon his birth and rose to captain at age eleven. Four years later, he became a major in the Black Sea Grenadier Corps. He took command of the Apsheron Musketeer Regiment on 11 February 1805, and of the Narva Musketeer Regiment on 20 September 1805. During the 1805 Campaign, Sibirsky distinguished himself at Krems (Dürrenstein) and Austerlitz, where he was wounded three times in the left leg and captured by the French.

He remained in captivity for two years. After returning to Russia, Sibirsky served in Finland in 1808-1809, where he became chef of the Moghilev Musketeer Regiment on 3 August 1808, and distinguished himself at Oravais and Torneo, for which he received promotion to major general on 26 April 1809.

During the 1812 Campaign, Sibirsky served in the 2nd Brigade of the 5th Division in Wittgenstein's corps and fought at Sventsyani, Jakubovo, Klyastitsy, and Polotsk (Order of St. George, 3rd class, 16 September 1812). He was wounded in the right leg during an assault on Polotsk on 19 September 1812, and left the army to recuperate. He returned in late 1812 and served at Lutzen, Bautzen, and Reichnebach, where he took a serious wound to the right hand and was transported to Warsaw.

After the war, he remained in the Duchy of Warsaw commanding the 1st Brigade of the 5th Division and the 1st Brigade of the 16th Division (August 1816 – January 1817). Sibirsky took command of the 18th Division on 29 January 1818, and rose to lieutenant general on 24 December 1824. He was discharged because of poor health on 13 January 1827.

SIEVERS (Syvers), Egor Karlovich (George Alexander), (b. 28 August 1779, Wenden — d. 30 June 1827) was born to a noble family from the Lifland *gubernia*. He graduated from the Page Corps with the rank of kamer-page and transferred as a lieutenant to the Life Guard Izmailovsk Regiment on 9 February 1798.

He rose to staff captain on 22 October 1799, and to captain on 28 November 1800. Despite a promising career, he took a discharge to pursue academic studies. For the next five years, he attended various universities in Germany before returning to the service as a colonel in the 1st Pioneer Regiment on 1 May 1806. Sievers served in this regiment for the next six years.

During the 1812 Campaign, he supervised the communication and supply services in Wittgenstein's corps, and fought at Klyastitsy, Svolnya, and Polotsk. For his effective service, he received the Orders of St. Anna (2nd class) with the diamond signs, and St. Vladimir (3rd class), as well as promotion to major general on 15 January 1813, with seniority dating from 19 October 1812.

In 1813, Sievers was appointed chief engineer of the main Russian army, as well as chef of the newly established Sapper Regiment on 1 March 1813. He took part in the battles at Bautzen, Lutzen, and Dresden, and commanded the siege works at Erfurt. In January 1814, he was entrusted with selecting the crossing site over the Rhine for the invasion of France. He fought at Brienne, fortified Langres and Nogent, and secured the Allied supply lines. For his actions, he was awarded the Orders of St. Anna (1st class) and St. Vladimir (2nd class). While in Paris, Sievers became acquainted with French engineering and Emperor Alexander instructed him to establish contacts between the European and Russian engineer schools. In 1816, Sievers joined the staff of the Engineer Corps and was transferred as chief engineer to the 1st Army.

In 1817, Sievers was appointed chairman of the commission working to draft engineer manuals for the military colonies. In 1819, he became chief of the engineer section of Military-Academic [*Voenno-uchebnii*] Committee of the General Staff, and the next year he became Head of the General Engineer Institute. For his excellent service in this institute, Sievers received the diamond signs of the Order of St. Anna (1st class). In 1821, he became a member of the council on the military colonies and sat on two other committees (transportation and communications). For his service, he also earned a golden snuffbox with a jewel-encrusted portrait of Emperor Alexander. He was promoted to lieutenant general on 10 April 1825.

SIEVERS (Syvers) Ivan Khristianovich (George Joachim Johann) (b. 1775 — d. 22 January 1843, Sebastopol) was born to a noble family from the Lifland *gubernia*. He studied in the Artillery and Engineer Cadet Corps and began service as a sub-lieutenant in the Gatchina Artillery Troops on 10 March 1793. Three years later, he transferred as a captain to the Life Guard Artillery Battalion on 21 November 1796, and received his colonelcy on 1 January 1798. The following year, he became a major general and chef of the 9th Artillery Battalion on 16 January 1799. The same year, he served under General Rimsky-Korsakov in Switzerland, fighting at Zurich and Schaffhausen. Returning to Russia, he led the Life Guard Artillery Battalion and became a member of the Artillery Section of the War College in 1801.

On 26 December 1803, Sievers was appointed chef of the 6th Artillery Regiment. Three years later, he served in the Army of Moldavia and took part in the opening moves of the Russo-Turkish War. In 1807-1812, he served at Ismail, Obilesti (Order of St. Anna, 1st class), Braila (seriously wounded in the chest and right shoulder), Shumla, Batin, Ruse, and Slobodzea. In early 1812, he took command of the artillery of the 3rd Reserve Army of Observation and fought at Brest, Kobryn, Gorodechna, Borisov and Studenka.

In 1813-1814, Sievers served at Modlin, Breslavl, and Glogau (golden sword with diamonds). After the war, he was appointed to command the artillery of the 2nd Army on 22 November 1814, and became artillery commander of the Southern District in the Crimea on 17 June 1816. Two years later, he received the Order of St. George (4th class) for twenty-five years of excellent service. Sievers became a lieutenant general on 3 September 1826, and took a discharge because of poor health on 4 June 1831.

SIEVERS, Karl Karlovich (Karl Gustav) (b. 19 November 1772 — d. 30 March 1856) was born to a noble family from the Lifland *gubernia*.

SIEVERS, Karl Karlovich (Karl Gustav)

He graduated from the Artillery and Engineer Cadet Corps and enlisted as a shtyk junker in the 2nd Artillery Battalion on 17 December 1789. He transferred to the Rostov Carabinier Regiment on 15 February 1792, and served in Poland later that year. Sievers rose to lieutenant colonel in 1798, and to colonel on 19 March 1799. However, in the spring of the same year, he was dismissed from the service during Emperor Paul's military purges. Sievers returned to the army in December 1800 and served in Voinov's Cuirassier Regiment. He took command of the Starodoub Dragoon Regiment on 29 January 1802. On 28 May 1803, he became a major general and chef of Novorossiisk Dragoon Regiment.

Sievers served in Lieutenant General Essen's corps during the 1805 Campaign. In early 1806, he marched with the corps to the Danubian Principalities, where he participated in the capture of Khotin. In 1807, as Essen's corps was recalled to Poland, Sievers fought the French at Troschin, Stanislavov, Drengev, Ostrolenka, and on the Omulev, Ruzhan, and Narew rivers. For his actions, he was awarded the Order of St. Anna (1st class) in January 1808. The following year, he participated in the campaign against Austria and led the advance guard at Pnev, on the Son River, and distinguished himself by occupying Krakow in June 1809. On 16 February 1810, Sievers took command of a brigade of the 4th Cavalry Division, but kept his position of chef of Novorossiisk Dragoon Regiment. On 15 May 1812, he assumed command of the 4th Cavalry Division in the 2nd Western Army of General Peter Bagration.

During the 1812 Campaign, Sievers constructed bridges at Nikolaev for the 2nd Western Army and covered its movement to Bobruisk in July. He distinguished himself during the forced march to Moghilev, when his troops covered more than 80 miles in 36 hours—an astonishing military feat. On 23 July, he fought Marshal Davout's forces at Saltanovka (Moghilev). He followed Bagration to Smolensk, where he engaged the French on 16 August and covered the Russian retreat to Dorogobouzh, where he commanded the observation corps. Sievers took command of the rear guard of the 2nd Western Army and waged a fighting retreat through Luzhky, Gzhatsk, Popov, Kolotsk, and Elnya. On 7 September 1812, he fought at Borodino, where he led a desperate counterattack of the cuirassier and dragoon regiments. After the battle, he again participated in rear guard actions at Mozhaisk, Tatarka, Krasnaya Pakhra, and Chirikov. For his actions at Borodino, Sievers received the Order of St. George (3rd class) on 1 November 1812.

On 15 December 1812, Sievers was appointed to command cavalry in Wittgenstein's corps, and fifteen days later, crossed the Nieman River and occupied Koenigsberg. On 8 February 1813, he captured the fortress of Pillau and its entire French garrison. He became the Commandant of Koenigsberg on 20 February, and on 14 April, Military Governor of Eastern Prussia and Koenigsberg. On 1 November 1813, Sievers was promoted to lieutenant general and on 13 September 1814, transferred from the artillery service to cavalry. He remained military governor of Koenigsberg for the next two years, earning the Prussian Order of the Red Eagle (1st Class) for his service.

In March 1829, Sievers was appointed to the military tribunal, where he served until 1830. In 1833, he was appointed to the Senate, and on 13 January 1837, transferred to civil service with the civil rank of privy court counsellor. In January 1840, he received the Order of the White Eagle for his service. In 1841-1848, Sievers served in various departments in the Senate and became general of cavalry on 22 October 1843. He retired on 21 June 1853, and spent the rest of his life at his estate, where he died on 30 March 1856.

His brother, **Yakov Karlovich Sievers** (b. 1774 — d. 1810) graduated from the Artillery and Engineer Cadet Corps in 1789, and began service as a shtyk junker in the 2nd Bombardier Regiment. In 1803, he transferred to the 5th Artillery Regiment and fought the French in Moravia in 1805, for which he received the Order of St. Vladimir (3rd class) and a promotion to colonel. In 1807, he distinguished himself at Eylau, earning the Order of St. George (4th class) and the Prussian Pour le Merite. He became major general on 16 June 1807.

SINELNIKOV, Alexander Nikitich (b. 1790 — date of death unclear) was born into a middle class family, the son of a court singer. He studied in the 2nd Cadet Corps and began service as a sub-lieutenant in the 5th Artillery Regiment in 1806. He took part in the Russo-Turkish War in 1806-1811, fighting at Galati, Giurgiu (Order of St. Anna, 3rd class), Silistra, and Braila. Sinelnikov transferred to the 7th Artillery Brigade on 13 October 1809, and rose to lieutenant on 19 December 1810. During the 1812 Campaign, he served at Smolensk (promoted to staff captain), Borodino (golden sword), Tarutino, Maloyaroslavets, and Krasnyi. The following year, he fought at Bautzen (Order of St. Vladimir, 4th class), Pirna, Kulm (Order of St. Anna, 2nd class, and a rank of captain), and Leizpig. He ended the war at Paris, for which he received the colonelcy on 6 October 1814.

SIPYAGIN, Nikolay Martemianovich (b. 1785 — d. 22 October 1828) was born to a noble family from the Kostroma *gubernia*; the son of Vice Admiral Martemian Sipyagin. He began service in the College of Foreign Affairs in 1799, and enlisted as a junker in the Life Guard Semeyonovsk Regiment on 14 February 1800. An ensign in 1804, he participated in the 1805 Campaign in Moravia, where he was wounded at Austerlitz and received the Order of St. Vladimir (4th class). Two years later, Sipyagin took part in the battles at Guttstadt, Heilsberg, and Friedland for which he garnered a golden sword. He rose to a regimental adjutant on 1 October 1808, and to flügel adjutant on 26 July 1811.

During the 1812 Campaign, Sipyagin served first as adjutant to Grand Duke Constaine and later to Prince Bagration and distinguished himself at Shevardino, Borodino, and Krasnyi (earned promotion to colonel, 7 January 1813). In 1813, he served at Glogau, Bautzen, Reichenbach, Gorlitz (Order of St. George, 4th class, 23 July 1813), Kulm (Prussian Iron Cross and the rank of major general on 27 September 1813), and Leipzig (Order of St. Anna, 1st class). In 1814, he led a mobile detachment and distinguished himself at Arcis sur Aube and Paris, for which he received promotion to adjutant general on 14 April 1814, and the Order of St. George (3rd class) on 15 May 1814.

After the war, Sipyagin served as the Chief of Staff of the Guard Corps, establishing the new library and printing press. However, he had sharp conflict with Aleksey Arakcheyev that led to his transfer to command the 6th Division on 22 March 1819. Sipyagin rose to lieutenant general and commander of the Combined Division of the 5th Corps on 3 September 1826. The following year, he was appointed the Commandant of Tiflis (Tbilisi) in Georgia on 9 April 1827. While serving in the Caucasus, he took part in the Russo-Turkish War in 1828, but became seriously ill and died 22 October 1828, in Tiflis.

SISOEV (Sysoev), Vasily Alekseyevich (b. 1772 — date of death unclear; removed from rosters on 19 September 1839) was born to a Cossack staff officer's family. He began service as a private Cossack on 12 June 1786, and participated in the Russo-Swedish War in 1788-1790. He served in Poland in 1792-1794, where he received a golden cross for Praga and rose to esaul in 1794. In 1805, Sisoev commanded a Cossack regiment in Bagration's detachment and distinguished himself at Schöngrabern. In 1807, he served in the 8th Division, fighting at Eylau (golden cross), Guttstadt, Heilsberg, and Friedland. For his actions, Sisoev was decorated with the Order of St. George (4th class) on 17 August 1807.

Sisoev served in the Danubian Principalities from 1808-1811 and earned the Order of St. George (3rd class) on 27 October 1811, and a golden cross for his actions at Bazardjik. In 1812, he led a Cossack regiment in General Ilovaisky V's Cossack detachment in the 2nd Western Army. He fought well at Mir, Romanovo, Saltanovka (Moghilev), Borodino, Tarutino, Maloyaroslavets, Polotsk Monastery, and Markovo, for which he was promoted to major general on 18 December 1812. Sisoev did not participate in the campaigns in Europe, serving instead in the Caucasus, where he fought the Chechens. In 1826-1827, he served in the Black Sea Cossack Host and distinguished himself fighting the Turks in the Danube Valley from 1828-1829, earning promotion to lieutenant general on 18 December 1828. In 1830-1831, he participated in the suppression of the Polish uprising.

SKALON, Anton Antonovich (b. 17 September 1767, Biisk — d. 17 August 1812, Smolenks; Scalon in French) was born to a French noble family that settled in Russia under Peter the Great. His father was a lieutenant general in the army under Catherine the Great.

Skalon was enlisted as a private in the Life Guard Preobrazhensk Regiment in 1775, and transferred to the Life Guard Semeyonovsk Regiment in 1782. He rose to lieutenant on 24 January 1783, and later served in the Siberia Dragoon Regiment. Promotions followed quickly as Skalon became colonel on 22 March 1799, commander of the Siberia Dragoon Regiment on 20 May 1798, major general on 27 October 1800, chef of the Siberia Dragoon Regiment on 23 April 1800, and chef of the Irkutsk Dragoon Regiment on 11 April 1802. He took a discharge on 9 December 1802, and returned to service four years later, when he was restored as chef of the Irkutsk Dragoon Regiment on 8 May 1806.

During the campaign against Austria in 1809, Skalon organized six regiments in Siberia and marched them to Volhynia, for which he received the Order of St. Vladimir (3rd class). During the 1812 Campaign, he led the 10th Brigade of the 3rd Cavalry Division of the 3rd Reserve Cavalry Corps. He stood out during the defense of Smolensk on 17 August 1812, when he led the charge of his cavalry brigade, but was mortally wounded. He was buried after the battle by the French troops near the Royal Bastion at Smolensk.

SOKOLOVSKY, Osip (Joseph) Karlovich (b. 1763 — date of death unclear) was born to a Byelorussian noble family in the Moghilev *gubernia*. He began his career in the Polish army, but soon entered the Russian service as a sublieutenant in the Arkhangelogorod Infantry Regiment on 1 January 1787. He served against the Turks in 1787-1791, and distinguished himself at Khotin, where he was wounded. In 1792-1794. He fought the Poles and rose to the rank of captain. After serving under Rimsky-Korsakov in Switzerland in 1799, he took command of the Yaroslavl Musketeer Regiment on 13 May 1804. In 1805, Sokolovsky served in Maltitz's division and fought at Krems and Austerlitz. He received his colonelcy on 5 May 1806, and served with the 10th Division of Essen I's corps in Poland in 1806-1807.

In 1810, Sokolovsky transferred with his unit to the Danubian Principalities, where he participated in the actions at Derekoy and Shumla. He became chef of the Jaroslavl Infantry Regiment on 21 June 1811. In 1812 Campaign, he served with the 2nd Brigade of the 10th Division in the Army of Danube and fought at Volkovisk and Rudnya. In 1813, Sokolovsky participated in combats at Czenstow, Bunzlau, Katzbach (promoted to major general on 27 September), and Leipzig. The following year, he commanded the Russian troops blockading the fortress of Lindau.

After the war, he took over the 2nd Brigade of the 15th Division and later became the Commandant of Kazan on 13 November 1821. He took a discharge on 16 July 1831. During his career, Sokolovsky received the Orders of St. Anna (1st class), St. Vladimir (4th class), St. George (4th class), as well as the Baden Orders of Military Merit of Charles Frederick, and of the Lion of Zaehringen.

SOKOVNIN, Boris Sergeyevich (b. 1780 — d. 1849) was born to a noble family in the Orel *gubernia*. He enlisted as a vakhmistr in the Life Guard Horse Regiment on 4 August 1791, and rose to cornet on 13 October 1799. In 1805, he distinguished himself at Austerlitz, and in 1807, took part in the battles at Heilsberg and Friedland. For these actions, he received promotion to colonel on 19 November 1807. Four years later, he took command of the Novgorod Cuirassier Regiment on 24 October 1811.

During the 1812 Campaign, he served in the 8th Corps of the 2nd Western Army and participated in Prince Bagration's retreat to Smolensk. Sokovnin distinguisheed himself at Borodino, where he was seriously wounded in the head and leg and captured by the French. He remained in captivity until 7 November 1812, when he was finally rescued by Russian troops. He was promoted to major general on 14 February 1813, for his actions at Borodino, and awarded the Order of St. George on 1 March 1813. Sokovnin spent the rest of war recuperating from his wounds.

He became the Commandant of Kazan and chef of the Kazan Garrison Regiment on 16 January 1816. The next year, he transferred to the civil service as the Civil Governor of Orel on 23 October 1817. On 25 February 1821, he returned to the military service with the rank of major general and retired on 25 March 1836.

STAHL (Stahl II in 1812), Egor Fedorovich (George Johann) (b. 9 November 1777 — d. 23 April 1862, Revel) was born to a noble family from the Estland *gubernia*. He enlisted as a vakhmistr in the Life Guard Horse Regiment on 13 January 1785. After service in the Baltic Navy in 1792-1794, he transferred as a captain to the Astrakhan Grenadier Regiment on 13 January 1796. Stahl briefly retired in 1802, but returned to the army with a rank of lieutenant colonel the following year. During the 1805 Campaign, he took part in the actions at Amstetten, Schöngrabern (Order of St. Vladimir, 4th class), Raussnitz, and Austerlitz, In 1806-1807, he distinguished himself at Golymin, Jankovo, Eylau, Guttstadt, and Heilberg. After joining the Pavlograd Hussar Regiment on 24 December 180, he was promoted to colonel on 25 August 1811.

In ealy 1812, Stahl was temporarily transferred to the Luvensk Hussar Regiment in the 3rd Reserve Army of Observation. He took part in the battles at Kobryn, Gorodechno, Vyzva (Order of St. George, 4th class, 4 December 1812), Brest-Litovsk, Slonim, and on the Berezina. In 1813, he served at Magdeburg, Wittenberg, Gross Beeren, Dennewitz (promoted to a major general on 27 September 1813), and Leipzig. In 1814, he took part in operations in the Netherlands. After the war, Stahl served in the 4th Dragoon Division and retired because of poor health on 29 February 1816.

STAHL (Stahl I in 1812), Karl Gustavovich (b. 10 September 1777, Rappele — d. 28 February 1853, Moscow) was born to a noble family from the Lifland *gubernia*. He enlisted as a corporal in the Life Guard Preobrazhensk Regiment in 1785, and as a captain transferred to the Pereyaslavl Horse Jager Regiment in 1796. After serving in Switzerland in 1799, he served well in Poland in 1806-1807, fighting at Pultusk (Order of St. George, 4th class, 20 January 1807), Jankovo, Hoff, Eylau, Guttstadt, and Friedland. Stahl became colonel and adjutant to Grand Duke Constantine on 24 October 1811. During the 1812 Campaign, he served with the 5th Reserve (Guard) Corps in the 1st Western Army. In 1813, he took part in the battles at Bautzen, Dresden, Kulm (Prussian Iron Cross), and Leipzig, for which he received promotion to major general on 19 February 1814, with seniority dating from 16 October 1813.

During the invasion of France, Stahl assumed command of the Astrakhan Cuirassier Regiment on 20 January 1814, and fought at Troyes, Bar sur Aube, Labrussel, Arcis sur Aube, Le Fre Champenoise, and Paris. After the war, he served as intendant general for the 2nd Army before retiring on 12 January 1820. He returned to the army seven years later and was appointed Commandant of Moscow in 1830. Stahl became a lieutenant general on 6 August 1833, senator on 8 May 1838, and general of cavalry on 22 October 1843.

During his long career, Stahl earned the Orders of St. Alexander of Neva with diamonds,

St. Anna (1st class) with diamonds and crown, St. Vladimir (1st class) of the White Eagle, two Prussian Pour le Merite, the Austrian Order of Leopold, the Bavarian Order of Maximilian Joseph, and a medal "For XXXV Years of Distinguished Service."

STAVITSKY, Maxim Fedorovich (b. 1778 — d. 2 November 1841, St. Petersburg) was born to a noble family from the Poltava *gubernia*. He studied in the Artillery and Engineer Cadet Corps and began service as a shtyk-junker in the Artillery Battalion of the Baltic Galley Fleet (*artilleriiskii grebonogo flota batalion*) on 18 May 1791. The following year, he transferred to the Bombardier Regiment. Stavitsky served in Poland in 1794, where he was captured. He was released after the Russian army took Warsaw and was promoted to sub-lieutenant in November 1794. After returning to Russia, he became adjutant in 1796, lieutenant in the field artillery battalion in June 1797, captain the the same year, and a major in the 1st Artillery Regiment on 19 March 1800. In 1801, he was appointed to the Quartermaster Section of the Imperial Retinue and accomplished several missions to France, Turkey, and the Far East from 1802-1804.

During the 1805 Campaign, Stavitsky served as a brigade major under General Bennigsen and became a flügel adjutant on 10 October 1806. From December 1806 – January 1807, he served in the Russian headquarters in Poland and fought at Czarnow, Pultusk (Order of St. George, 4th class), and Jankovo. After the fight of Eylau, he delivered the news of the battle to Emperor Alexander, for which he received the Order of St. Anna (2nd class) and quick promotions to lieutenant colonel on 6 February 1807, and to colonel nine days later. In June 1807, he fought at Wolfsdorf, Ankendorf (golden sword), Heilsberg, and Friedland, where he was seriously wounded in the left shoulder and garnered the Order of St. Vladimir (3rd class). In 1808, he trained a newly organized battalion in St. Petersburg, and during the 1809 Campaign in Galicia, served as brigade major under Prince Sergey Golitsyn and negotiated the Russian acquisition of the Tarnopol region.

Stavitsky took command of a brigade of the 27th Division on 6 December 1811. During the 1812 Campaign, he served with the 2nd Western Army at Smolensk, Shevardino (wounded in the right hand), and Borodino, where he took another serious wound to the left leg. For his actions in the last two battles, he was promoted to major general on 3 December 1812, with seniority dating from 5 September 1812. After recuperating, Stavitsky returned to the army in August 1813, in time to participate in the battles at Bunzlau (two battles, received the Order of St. Anna, 1st class, and the Prussian Red Eagle, 2nd class), Katzbach, Leipzig (wounded in the right hand), and Mainz. During the invasion of France, he distinguished himself at Brienne and La Rothière, where he suffered another severe wound when a musket ball shattered both of his jaws. For his courage, Stavitsky was decorated with the Order of St. Vladimir (2nd class).

Unable to continue in the service, Stavitsky took a discharge on 30 September 1815, and received a twelve-year rent for an estate in the Courland *gubernia*. He soon transferred to civil service and rose to an actual counsellor and senator on 18 September 1826. However, a month later, he returned to military service as a lieutenant general on 23 September 1826, with seniority dating from 3 September 1826. During the last years of his career, Stavitsky garnered the Orders of St. Anna (1st class) with crown, the White Eagle, St. John of Jerusalem, and a medal "For XL Years of Distinguished Service."

STAVRAKOV, Semen Khristoforovich (b. 1763/1764, Omelnik, Poltava *gubernia* — d. 16 March 1819) was born to a Greek noble family from the Poltava *gubernia*. He enlisted as a corporal in the Kozlov Infantry Regiment on 2 November 1783, and transferred as a sergeant to the Tavrida Grenadier Regiment on 21 May 1789. Stavrakov took part in the Russo-Turkish War in 1789-1791, fighting at Killia, Babadag, and Macin. In 1794, he served in Poland as a registrar in General Alexander Suvorov's field chancellery. He distinguished himself at Krupchitse, Kobylka, and Praga, for which he received a golden cross and promotion to ensign on 18 September 1794. He served as Suvorov's secretary for the next two years, becoming a sub-lieutenant in the Fanagoria Grenadier Regiment on 2 May 1795, lieutenant in the Azov Infantry Regiment on 8 November 1796, and lieutant captain in Suvorov's staff on 12 November 1796.

After Suvorov's staff was disbanded, Stavrakov took a discharge with the rank of staff captain on 29 January 1797. Two years later, on 22 February 1799, Suvorov recalled him to participate in the campaigns in Italy. Stavrakov took part in the battles at Palazollo, Bergamo, Cassano (Order of St. Anna, 3rd class), Marengo, Tidone, Trebbia (Order of St. John of Jerusalem), Alessandria, Seravalle, Novi (Order of St. Anna, 2nd class, with diamonds), and in all actions involved during the crossing of the Alps. For the 1799 Campaign, he received the Order of St. Anna (2nd class) on 17 June 1799, and became adjutant to Suvorov on 25 June 1799. In December of that year, he was elevated to major and garnered the Austrian Order of Maria Theresa (3rd class) and the Sardinian Order of St. Maurice and Lazarus.

After Suvorov's death, Stavrakov was appointed to the quartemaster services on 30 July 1801. During the 1805 Campaign, he served as a brigade major in the headquarters of the Russian army and distinguished himself at Austerlitz, where he was wounded in the right leg. He was promoted to lieutenant colonel on 11 February 1806. Two years later, he took part in the battles at Eylau (golden cross), Guttstadt, Heilsberg (Order of St. George, 4th class, 1 June 1808), and Friedland (wounded in the right hand, received a golden sword). Stavrakov then participated in the Russo-Swedish War in 1808-1809, serving as a brigade major in the Russian headquarters. He distinguishing himself at Kuortain and Oravais, for which he rose to a colonel on 30 October 1808. For his service in 1809, he received two diamonds rings. In early 1811, he transferred to the Danubian Principalities, where he continued service in the headquarters and received a golden sword for the battle of Ruse.

In March 1812, Stavrakov became the Commandant of the Headquarters of the 1st Western Army, and during the 1812 Campaign, he fought at Ostrovno, Smolensk, Borodino, Tarutino, Maloyaroslavets, Vyazma, Krasnyi, and on the Berezina. He was promoted to major general on 3 December 1812. In 1813, Stavrakov took part in the battles at Lutzen, Bautzen, Dresden, Kulm (Prussian Iron Cross), and Leipzig. The following year, he served at Brienne, La Rothière, Bar su Aube, Arcis sur Aube, and Paris, earning the Order of St. Anna (1st class) and the Prussian Red Eagle (2nd class) for his service in 1813-1814, and the Order of St. George (4th class) for twenty-five years of exemplary service.

After the war, he became wagonmeister general of the General Staff on 23 January 1816, and a week later, was appointed inspector of military hospitals on 3 February 1816.

STEINGELL, Faddey Fedorovich (Fabian Gothard) (b. 14 October 1762 — d. 19

March 1831, Helsingfors) was born to a noble family in the Estland *gubernia*. His father, Jacob Friedrich von Steingell, served as a lieutenant in the Russian army. Faddey Steingell began service as a column guide in the main headquarters on 19 October 1776, was appointed an adjutant in the Vologodsk Infantry Regiment on 10 October 1777, and enrolled as an ensign in the Infantry Cadet Corps on 7 December 1782. After graduating from the Cadet Corps, he rose to the rank of lieutenant in November 1786, and reached captain in February 1788.

During the Russo-Swedish War in 1788-1790, Steingell fought in minor actions in the summer of 1788 before transferring to the quartemaster service with the rank of premier major. He became a lieutenant colonel on 1 December 1789. In 1790, he distinguished himself at Pardakoski and was awarded the Order of St. Vladimir (4th class). In 1791-1792, he served under General Alexander Suvorov in Finland. He transferred to the Velikii Lutsk Infantry Regiment in 1796, and was appointed colonel in the Quartermaster Section of the Imperial Retinue on 16 October 1797. In 1798, he successfully completed a topographic mission in Vyborg *gubernia*, for which he received the Order of St. Anna (2nd class) and a promotion to major general on 13 March 1799, with seniority dating from 31 August 1798. He was also appointed chef of the Old Ingermanland Musketeer Regiment on 13 March 1799, but was discharged from the army on 12 August 1799.

In 1800, Steingell was appointed the Director of the Cartography Depot of the Quartemaster Section of the Imperial Retinue, and served on topographic missions to Arkhangelsk and Finland in 1801. In late 1802, he was awarded an annual allowance of 3,000 rubles and the Order of St. George (4th class) for twenty-five years of excellent service. Two years later, he received the Order of St. Anna for excellent service.

During the 1805 Campaign, Steingell was appointed the quartermaster general in General Bennigsen's corps, but he did not participate in any battles. Returning to Russia, he accomplished several topographic missions in the St. Petersburg, Novgorod, and Olonetsk *gubernia*s between March and August 1806. Once again, he found himself the quartemaster general in Bennigsen's corps in September 1806. During the 1806-1807 Campaigns in Poland, Steingell took part in the battles at Zargze, Pultusk (Order of St. Vladimir, 3rd class, and the Prussian Red Eagle, 1st class), Eylau (Order of St. George, 3rd class, and annual allowance of 3,000 rubles, 20 April 1807), Heilsberg, and Friedland (bruised by a cannonball, received the Order of St. Vladimir, 2nd class). He was elevated to lieutenant general on 11 September 1807.

After the Russo-Swedish War of 1808-1809, Steingell led the Russian troops and flotilla on the Aland Islands in 1809-1810. He became the Governor General of Finland and the Commander-in-Chief of the Russian troops in Finland on 19 February 1810. For his service, he received the diamond signs of the Order of St. Anna (1st class) on 23 February 1811, and the title of count of the Russian Empire on 18 September 1812.

During the 1812 Campaign, Steingell landed his corps near Revel and fought the French at Eckau, Bausk, Polotsk (golden sword), Kubluchi (Order of Alexander of Neva), Chasniki, Smolyani, and on the Berezina. He left the army because of poor health in February 1813, and returned to Finland to recuperate.

After the war, Steingell resumed the duties of the Governor General of Finland and commanded the Finland Corps. In 1816, he was awarded a large estate in Lifland *gubernia* for his excellent service in Finland. He became a general of infantry on 13 January 1819. Steingell retired because of poor health on 11 September 1823, and settled at Helsingfors.

Over the next eight years, he conducted various scientific researches and was elected a member of the St. Petersburg Academy of Sciences, St. Petersburg Pharmaceutical Society, Finland Mineralogical Society, and other scientific institutions. He died on 19 March 1831 at Helsingfors.

STROGANOV, Pavel Aleksandrovich (b. 18 June 1774, Paris – d. 22 June 1817, Copenhagen) was born to a prominent Russian noble family, the son of Count Alexander Sergeyevich Stroganov, ober kamerger and actual privy counsellor under Catherine the Great and Paul I. His parents lived in Paris until 1778, when they returned to Russia. He was baptized by Emperor Paul, brought up with Grand Duke Alexander, and tutored by Gilbert Romme, who later played an important role in the French Revolution. Stroganov enlisted as a cornet in the Life Guard Horse Regiment in 1779, and in 1781-1790, traveled extensively in Russia and France. In 1787, he studied in Geneva, and two years later arrived in Paris, where he lived under the alias of Paul Otcher.

Stroganov witnessed the events of the French Revolution in 1789. After his tutor, Gilbert Romme founded the Society *Amis de la roi*, Stroganov took part in the policial debates and met many political figures of the Revolution. In 1790, Stroganov joined the Jacobin Club, but was quickly recalled to Russia, where he was put under home arrest at an estate near Moscow.

He began actual military service as a lieutenant in the Life Guard Preobrazhensk Regiment in 1791. Stroganov enjoyed rapid promotions under Paul I, becoming a kamer-junker in 1792, and kamerger in 1798. When Alexander took the throne, Stroganov became the Emperor's close confidant and urged him to grant a constitution.

From 1801-1803, Stroganov was one of the figures behind the Unofficial Committee of advisors that Alexander assembled to prepare a program of reforms, and he became a privy counsellor and senator in 1802. During the 1805 Campaign, Stroganov accompanied Emperor Alexander at Austerlitz, and after the battle, was dispatched with a diplomatic mission to Britain. Returning to the continent, he volunteered for service in the army and took command of a Cossack Regiment in Ataman Platov's advance guard. In June 1807, he distinguished himself in the actions at Guttstadt, Quetz, Deppen, Heilberg, and Friedland. For his conduct throughout the campaign, he received the Order of St. George (3rd class) on 3 September 1807.

After the treaty was signed at Tilsit, Stroganov became a major general on 2 January 1808, with seniority dating from 13 November 1805, and was transferred to the Life Guard Izmailovsk Regiment on 8 February 1808. During the Russo-Swedish War, he initially led reserves at Wilmanstrand in 1808, and served under Prince Peter Bagration during the expedition to the Aland Islands in the spring of 1809. On 9 June of that year, Stroganov took command of the Life Grenadier Regiment and of the brigade of the 1st Grenadier Division. In July, he followed Prince Bagration to the Danubian Principalities. From September to December he fought the Turks at Macin, Constanta, Rassevat (golden sword), Silistra (Order of St. Anna, 1st class), and Tataritsa (Order of St. Vladimir, 2nd class). In 1810, he participated in the battles at Silistra (diamond signs of the Order of St. Anna, 1st class), Shumla, Djuma, and other minor actions. In early 1811, he temporarily left the army because of his father's death.

In 1812, Stroganov commanded the 1st Grenadier Division in the 3rd Corps and fought at Lubino and Borodino, where he took led the 3rd Corps after the death of General Tuchkov. His actions earned him a promotion to lieutenant general on 12 November 1812.

Between October and November 1812, Stroganov led his corps in the battles at Tarutino, Maloyaroslavets, and Krasnyi. He took a furlough in late 1812 because of poor health and returned to the army in time to fight at Leipzig, for which he garnered the Order of St. Alexander of Neva. From December 1813 to February 1814, he served at Hamburg. During the invasion of France, Stroganov served under Winzegorode and distinguished himself at Craonne (where his only son, Alexander, was killed), Laon, and Paris, for which he was decorated with the Order of St. George (2nd class) on 5 May 1814. He became commander of the 2nd Guard Division on 15 September 1814. The death of his son at Craonne was a crushing blow to Stroganov, who contracted pulmonary tuberculosis while accompanying his son's remains back to Russia.

He lingered into 1816, and traveled to Copenhagen to recuperate, but died there on 22 June 1817. His remains were transported to St. Petersburg and buried beside those of his son at the Alexander Nevsky Monastery. He left his mark on the world in a way he could never have imaginaed: Stroganov's favorite dish, a combination of beef, mushrooms, and sour cream, is popularly known as "Beef Stroganoff."

STTADEN Yevstafiy Yevstafevich (Reinhold Gustav), (b. 23 September 1774 — d. 17 February 1845, Tula) was born to a German noble family in the Courland *gubernia*. He began service in the Bombardier Regiment on 5 June 1784, and was promoted to lieutenant on 30 December 1796. Sttaden participated in the 1805 Campaign and distinguished himself at Austerlitz (Order of St. Vladimir, 4th class). He was promoted to colonel on 15 June 1811. During the 1812 Campaign, he commanded the 14th Artillery Brigade of the 1st Corps and fought at Jakubovo (golden sword and the Order of St. George, 4th class, 5 August 1812), Golovchin, Smolyani, and on the Berezina. Sttaden was promoted to major general on 7 June 1813, with seniority dating from 28 November 1812.

In 1813, Sttaden fought at Wittenberg, Lutzen (received Ordet of St. George, 3rd class, 10 November 1813) and Bautzen. After 28 May 1813, he supervised supply and ammunition trains and depots in Germany. After the war, he became commander of the artillery of the 1st Corps. He was appointed head of the Tula weapon factory on 18 April 1817, and inspector of all weapon factories on 19 April 1824. Another promotion, this time to lieutenant general, arrived on 13 January 1826. He became the Military Governor of Tula on 4 June 1831, though retired soon thereafter. He returned to service on 26 February 1838, and continued working as inspector of weapon factories, reaching the rank of general of artillery on 28 April 1841.

SUKHAREV, Alexander Dmitryevich (b. 1771 — d. 12 May 1853) was born to a Russian noble family. He enlisted as a corporal in the Life Guard Preobrazhensk Regiment on 1 July 1775, and transferred to the Life Guard Izmailovsk Regiment in 1776. Sukharev served on the galley fleet during the Russo-Swedish War of 1789-1790, becoming ensign on 9 September

1789 and receiving a medal for courage in the naval engagements in 1789. He rose to captain in 1798, but transferred to civil service with the rank of college counsellor on 19 September 1798 (promoted to court counsellor on 24 May 1800). Sukharev returned to the military as a major general on 17 July 1801, and served in the War College.

During the 1812 Campaign, Sukharev commanded the 16th Company (*druzhina*) of the St. Petersburg *Opolchenye* but did not participate in any combat. In 1813, Sukharev fought at Dresden and Hamburg, for which he received the Order of St. George (4th class) on 18 October 1813. In early 1814, he became the head of the Audit in the Army of Poland, and the following year, directed the military hospitals in Frankfort. Sukharev retired on 16 January 1816, but returned to the army on 21 April 1826, before transferring to civil service as a privy counsellor in 1832. He eventually rose to actual privy counsellor.

SUKHOZANET, Ivan Onufrievich (b. 15 July 1788, Vesekh — d. 20 February 1861) was born to a noble family of Polish descent in the Vitebsk *gubernia*. He studied in the Artillery and Engineer Cadet Corps and began service as a sub-lieutenant in the Engineer Corps on 22 August 1803. The next year, he transferred to the 1st Artillery Regiment. During the 1806-1807 Campaigns in Poland, he distinguished himself at Pultusk, Eylau (wounded in the left side, golden cross), Wolfsdorf, Guttstadt, Heilsberg, and Friedland, where he barely survived after being trampled by the charging French cavalry. For his actions, Sukhozanet was transferred to the Life Guard Artillery Battalion and served as an adjutant to General Leo Yashvil (Iashvili). He became lieutenant colonel in late 1811.

During the 1812 Campaign, Sukhozanet served in Wittgenstein's 1st Corps and participated in the battles at Wilkomir, Klyastitsy, Polotsk (Order of St. George, 4th class, 16 September 1812), Chashniki (promotion to colonel), and on the Berezina. In 1813, he led the 1st Artillery Brigade, distinguishing himself at Bautzen (promoted to major general on 7 June 1813), Dresden, Kulm, and Leipzig, where he ably directed the Russian artillery fire against the charging French cavalry. In 1814, he fought at Brienne, Le Fère Champenoise, and Paris. After the war, he commanded the artillery in the 1st Army and became chief of the artillery of the Guard Corps on 12 January 1820.

During the Decembrist Uprising in December 1825, Sukhozanet commanded the artillery battery and opened canister fire against the insurgents, a move that earned him a promotion to lieutenant general on 3 September 1826. In 1828-1829, he fought the Turks in the Danube Valey and received the Order of St. George (3rd class) for his actions at Braila. He also served as chief of staff of the Guard Corps at Shumla. Sukhozanet was serving in Poland in

1830-1831 when he lost a leg at the battle of Grochow (Order of St. Vladimir, 1st class).

After the war, he became intendant of the artillery and engineer schools on 26 December 1831, and member of the Council of War on 9 July 1833. He rose to general of artillery on 4 May 1834. Between 16 September 1833 and 11 June 1836, he directed the Page Corps and served as chef of the Noble Regiment. From 1832-1854, he served as director of the Imperial Military Academy.

Sukhozanet had two brothers: **Peter Onufrievich**, who graduated from the 2nd Cadet Corps in 1805 and served with his brother in the 1st Corps in 1812; and **Nikolay Onufrievich** (1794-1871), who graduated from the Page Corps and served with his brother throughout the 1812-1814 campaigns. Nikolay eventually fought in the Crimean War and became Russia's Minister of War in 1856-1861.

SUKHTELEN, Pavel Petrovich (b. 3 September 1788, St. Petersburg — d. 1 April 1833, Orenburg) was born to a Dutch noble family; the son of Peter Kornilovich Sukhtelen. He began service as a column guide in the quartermaster service on 7 February 1802, and rose to sub-lieutenant on 23 September of that year. He transferred as a cornet in the Chevalier Guard Regiment on 5 October 1804. In 1805, Sukhtelen distinguished himself at Austerlitz, where he was captured after being wounded in the right leg and head. After the battle, he was introduced to Napoleon, who praised his courage. Sukhtelen was released in February 1806 and received the rank of lieutenant and a golden sword for his actions at Austerlitz. Two years later, he fought at Eylau (golden cross), Heilsberg, and Friedland.

In 1808, Sukhtelen volunteered to fight the Swedes and served in the Grodno Hussar Regiment in Finland in 1808-1809. He distinguished himself during the capture of the fortress of Svartholm, for which he was appointed flügel adjutant. Returning to Russia, he transferred as a lieutenant colonel to the Byelorussia Hussar Regiment in 1809, and served against the Turks in the Danubian Principalities in 1810-1811. In late 1811, he was dispatched on a diplomatic mission to London and returned to Russia in October 1812, just in in time to fight the French on the Berezina. In early 1813, Sukhtelen served in Chernishev's detachment in Saxony and served at Spandau (promoted to colonel, 4 March 1813) and Zeghauzen, where he was seriously wounded in the left hand. He briefly served as the Chief of Staff in Wallmoden's detachment before becoming a duty officer in Wittgenstein's corps. From August-October 1813, he participated in the battles at Dresden, Pirna, Kulm (Prussian Iron Cross and the Order of St. George, 4th class, 11 October 1813), and Leipzig (order of St. Vladimir, 3rd class).

Sukhtelen took command of the Volhynia Uhlan Regiment in early 1814 and distinguished himself at Soissons, for which he was promoted to major general on 13 December 1814, with seniority dating from 14 February 1814. After the war, he commanded the 1st Brigade of the 2nd Hussar Division (1816-1818) and then the 1st Brigade of the Lithuanian Uhlan Division (12 August 1819). He moved on to serve as an assistant to the commander of the Guard Light Cavalry Division (5 December 1819), and took command of the 1st Brigade of the 1st Hussar Division (8 October 1823). He became quartermaster general of the General Staff on 1 June 1826. Sukhtelen participated in the Russo-Persian War in 1827-1828, serving as a duty officer in the headquarters of the Caucasian Corps, and distinguishing himself at Yerivan

(Order of St. George, 3rd class, 10 November 1827). He rose to adjutant general on 6 April 1828, and transferred to the Danubian Principalities to fight the Turks in 1828-1829. After the war, he became the Military Governor of Orenburg and commander of the Independent Orenburg Corps on 3 May 1830.

SUKHTELEN, Peter Kornilovich (Johann Peter) (b. 13 August 1751, Netherlands — d. 18 January 1836, Stockholm) was born to a Dutch noble family. He began service in the Dutch engineer troops and fought against Britain in 1773-1779. In 1783, he transferred as a lieutenant colonel to the Russian engineer service. He took part in the Russo-Swedish War in 1788-1790, commanding engineer troops in the Russian army and distinguishing himself at Vyborg and Fridriexham, for which he received promotion to major general on 26 April 1789 as well as a golden sword and the Order of St. George (4th class) on 28 August 1789. In 1794, he was on a diplomatioc mission to Warsaw and was wounded and captured by Polish insurgents. He was liberated after the Russian troops captured Warsaw in late 1794.

After the campaign, Sukhtelen served as inspector of fortifications in the Vilna *gubernia*. He became a lieutenant general on 31 December 1797, and was appointed chief engineer of the Finland Inspection. He rose to general of engineer service on 10 July 1799, and served as inspector of engineer troops in the Estland and Lifland Inspections. In 1802, he was appointed the head of all Russian quartermaster services. In the 1805 Campaign, he accompanied Alexander at Austerlitz. During the Russo-Swedish War of 1808-1809, he served as the Chief of Staff of the Russian army and distinguished himself at Svartholm and Sveaborg, for which he was decorated with a golden sword with diamonds. He played an important role in the Russo-Swedish negotiations during and after the war, and served as an ambassador to Sweden from 1809-1811.

In 1812, Sukhtelen negotiated a treaty with Britain and in return was conferred the title of baron on 18 September 1812. In 1813, he served in the headquarters of the Army of the North and fought at Gross Beeren, Dennewitz, and Leipzig. In 1814, he served at Hamburg and negotiated a treaty between Denmark and Russia. The following year, he served as an observer in the Swedish army during the invasion of Norway. He returned to Stockholm as the Russian ambassador to Sweden. From 1822-1836, Sukhtelen served as a member of the State Council, a member of the Imperial Military Academy, and as inspector of the Engineer Corps. He received the title of count of the Russian Empire on 3 February 1822.

During his illustrious career, Sukhtelen received the Orders of St. Andrew the First Called with diamonds, St. Vladimir (1st class), St. Alexander of Neva, St. Anna (1st class), St. John of Jerusalem, as well as the Swedish Orders of the Sword and of the Seraphim.

SULIMA, Akim Semenovich (b. 1737 — d. 1818) was born to a noble family of the Prussian descent. He studied in the Kiev Academy and Cadet Corps, from which he graduated with a golden medal and rank of sergeant in 1759. He remained at the Cadet Corps, training the cadets while rising to lieutenant in 1761 and to captain in 1763. Sulima transferred as a premier major to the Azov Infantry Regiment on 10 May 1764, but returned to the Cadet Corps two years later. In 1764-1766, Sulima translated several French military treatises for the Russian cadets and completed a new statute of the Corps that incorporated the ideas of the Enlightenment. For his contributions, Sulima was elevated to lieutenant colonel of the regular army and second major of the Cadet Corps on 12 February 1767, soon followed by another promotion to colonel of the regular army on 18 June 1770. In 1773, he served as an assistant to the Count Zakhar Chernyshev, Governor General of Byelorussia, and for his effective service, was promoted to a brigadier on 20 October 1775.

Sulima took a discharge with the rank of major general on 9 October 1778, and spent the next eighteen years in his estate in Little Russia. In 1796, Emperor Paul I recalled him for an appointment as a judge of the Supreme Court (*Generalnii sud*) of Little Russia (Malorossia). On 13 May 1797, he was conferred civil rank of actual court counsellor. In 1802, after the Supreme Court was abolished, Sulima retired and received the Order of St. Vladimir and an annual allowance of 1,200 rubles. In 1805, he was appointed column guide in the Quartermaster Section of the Imperial Retinue and took part in the battle of Austerlitz on 2 December 1805.

After the war, Sulima returned to his estate where he lived until his death in 1818.

SULIMA, Joseph Ivanovich began service as a cadet in the Kherson Corps in 1792 and rose to guard marine in January 1794. He served on the Black Sea Fleet in 1794-1798, becoming a midshipman in 1796. He was posted to the brigantine *Prokpor* in the Black Sea from 1797-1798, on the *Elen* in the Azov Sea in 1800, and on the *Galata* in the Black Sea in 1801-1802. Sulima became a lieutenant on 22 March 1804, and commanded a schooner in the expedition to Corfu and Venice in 1805-1807. In 1808-1809, he served on various frigates (*Pospeshnii*, *Krepkii*, and *Derzski*) in Trieste and Venice before returning to Russia in 1810. He was promoted to lieutenant captain on 17 January 1811.

In 1812, Sulima served on the *Lesnoe* in Sebastopol, and the following year joined the Russian troops at Thorn. He was involved in constructing the pontoon bridges across the Bobr, Oder, and Saale Rivers, for which he received the Order of St. Anna (2nd class) and the Prussian Pour le Merite. In 1814, he attended General Langeron at Soissons, Laon, and Paris. After the war, Sulima commanded a corvette in the Black Sea in 1816-1819, and was decorated with the Order of St. George (4th class) for the eighteen naval campaigns in which he had served. In 1820, he commanded the brig *Ganimed*, and after serving in Sebastopol in 1821-1822, captained the frigate *Pospeshnii* in the Black Sea. He rose to captain 2nd class on 11 September 1824, and captain 1st class on 18 December 1827.

On 3 September 1831, Sulima ascended to the rank of rear admiral and took command of the 3rd Brigade of the 2nd Naval (*flotskoi*) Division. In 1834-1835, he was the Military Governor of Sveaborg, and in 1836-1842, served in the same capacity in Arkhangelsk. He rose to vice admiral in December 1837 and received the Orders of St. Stanslaus (1st class, 1838), St. Anna (1st class, 1840), and St. Vladimir (2nd class, 1846). Sulima became a member of the Admiralty Council in May 1842, and took his discharge on 18 February 1852.

SULIMA, Nikolay Semenovich (b. 1777 — d. 2 November 1840, St. Petersburg) was born to an ancient noble family of Prussian descent. He briefly studied in the Infantry Cadet Corps in 1791, and enlisted in the Life Guard Preobrazhensk Regiment in 1792. The following year, he transferred as a sergeant to the jager company in the Life Guard Semeyonovsk Regiment. In early 1797, he became an ensign in the Nasheburg Infantry Regiment, but later transferred with the same rank to the Life Guard Izmailovsk Regiment, where he received promotion to sub-lieutenant on 8 May 1797. Over the next five years, Sulima enjoyed a series of quick promotions: lieutenant and regimental adjutant in 1799, staff captain in 1800, captain in early 1803, and colonel on 23 December 1803. He transferred to the Moscow Musketeer Regiment in 1804, and the next year became its commander on 21 January 1805.

During the 1805 Campaign, Sulima served in Dokhturov's column, distinguishing himself at Krems (Dürrenstein) and earning in return the Order of St. Vladimir (4th class). At Austerlitz, after two horses were shot under him, Sulima led his regiment's bayonet charge, but took a serious sabre cut to the head and was captured. He was exchanged for a French officer two weeks later and was discharged in November 1806. He returned to the military service on the eve of Napoleon's 1812 invasion of Russia, and took command of the Tavrida Grenadier Regiment on and 30 September 1811.

During the 1812 Campaign, Sulima served with the 3rd Brigade of the 1st Grenadier Division in the 3rd Corps and fought at Vitebsk, Smolensk, and Borodino (for which he was later promoted to major general on 3 December 1812). In October 1812, Sulima assumed command of the 3rd brigade of the 1st Grenadier Division and fought at Tarutino (bruised by cannoball in the right leg), Maloyaroslavets, Vyazma, and Krasnyi (Order of St. George, 3rd class, 15 June 1813). In 1813, he served at Lutzen (golden sword), Koenigswartha, Bautzen (Prussian Red Eagle, 2nd class), Reichenbach, Gorlitz, Dresden, Kulm, and Leipzig (Order of St. Anna, 1st class). During the 1814 Campaign, he participated in the actions at Brienne, La Rothière, Arcis sur Aube, and Paris.

After the war, Sulima took command of the 2nd Brigade of the 1st Grenadier Division and later of the 1st Brigade of the 13th Division on 13 June 1815. He took a discharge because of poor health on 12 February 1816, but returned to the army on 27 May 1817, when he assumed command of the 3rd Brigade of the 14th Division. In 1822, he transferred to the 17th Division, which was soon transformed into the 5th Division. Two years later, he led the Combined Brigade of the 14th Division and was decorated for excellent service with the Order of St. Vladimir (2nd class) on 3 September 1826. He took command of the 11th Division on 28 September 1826, of the 16th Division on 13 January 1827, and rose to a liuetenant general on 29 May 1827.

During the Russo-Turkish War of 1828-1829, Sulima fought at Silistra (golden sword with diamonds) and Shumla in 1828. He took command of the 5th Division on 25 January 1829, and participated in the operations at Silistra, Kulevchi, Slivno, and Adrianople. In 1830-1831, he fought the Polish insurgents at Mariampol, Keidan, Shadova, Levoshniki, Vilna, and Warsaw, for which he garnered the Order of St. Alexander of Neva. After the war, he assumed command of the 4th Division on 14 April 1833, and became the Governor General of Eastern Siberia on 18 December 1833. The following year, he was appointed the Governor General of Western Siberia and commander of the Siberian Corps on 10 October 1834. For his service in Siberia, Sulima received the diamond signs of the Order of St. Alexander of Neva on 18 December 1835. He was relieved of command because of poor health on 9 February 1836, and appointed a member of the Council of War. The following year, he became a member of the State Control Council on 25 January 1837. He spent his remaining years in St. Petersburg, where he died on 2 November 1840.

SUTGOV (Suthof), Nikolay Ivanovich (b. 20 December 1765, Vyborg — d. 13 October 1836) was born to a Finnish merchant family. After civil service in Vyborg from 1784-1785, he enlisted as a lieutenant in the 4th Battalion of the Finland Jager Corps on 29 November 1786. He took part in the Russo-Swedish War in 1788-1790, and rose to platz-major in the Life Grenadier Regiment. Sutgov received his colonelcy and command of the Voronezh Musketeer Regiment on 5 May 1806. Two years later, he became chef of this unit on 18 January 1808. He participated in the Russo-Turkish war in 1808-1811, fighting at Girsov, Rassevat,

Silistra, Tataritsa, Braila, Shumla, and Ruse. His regiment was transformed into the 37th Jager Regiment on 31 October 1810.

During the 1812 Campaign, Sutgov served in the 3rd Brigade, 8th Division, Army of Danube, and fought at Volkovysk and Pruzhany. In 1813, he served at Glogau, Bautzen (wounded in the chest), and Leipzig (wounded to both legs). After recuperating, Sutgov took part in the 1814 Campaign in France and was wounded and captured on 14 February 1814. He was released on 30 March 1814, and promoted to major general on 13 June 1815, with seniority dating from 14 February 1814. During the Hundred Days in 1815, he served in the siege of Metz.

After the war, he led a brigade of the 13th Division and became the Commandant of Helsingfors on 26 October 1826. Sutgov retired on 16 January 1834.

SUVOROV, Aleksandr Vasilievich (b. 24 November 1730, Moscow — d. 18 May 1800), who would rise to become one of the most famous and influential generals in Russian history, was born to a Russian noble family of Swedish descent. He enlisted in the Life Guard Semeyonovsk Regiment on 3 November 1842 at age twelve and spent the next five years studying at home. He began active service on 12 January 1748, rising to sub-ensign in January 1750, and to sergeant on 19 June 1751. Suvorov became a lieutenant on 6 May 1754, and joined the New Ingermanland Infantry Regiment two weeks later. In January 1756, Suvorov became oberquartermaster in Novgorod, and on 9 November of the same year, was appointed general-audit-lieutenant in the War College, receiving the rank of premier major on 15 December 1756.

Suvorov participated in the Seven Years War from 1757-1763, taking part in several major battles of the war. He became colonel and commander of the Astrakhan Infantry Regiment on 6 September 1762, and on 17 April 1763, took command of the Suzdal Infantry Regiment. Suvorov led the Russian troops in Poland from 1769-1772. In his first campaigns against the Turks in 1773-1774, he laid the foundation of his military reputation, achieving decisive victories at Turtukai, Kosludji, and other places. In 1775, he took part in the suppression of the rebellion of Emelyan Pugachev. From 1777-1783, Suvorov served in the Kuban Valley and the Caucasus, becoming a lieutenant-general in 1780, and general of infantry in 1783. In 1785, he took command of the St. Petersburg Division and rose to général-en-chef on 9 November 1786. On 17 January 1787, he assumed command of the Kremenchug Division.

From 1787 to 1791, Suvorov was again fighting the Turks and won many victories, including those scored at Kinburn, Ochakov, and Focsani. For his triumphant victory on the Rimnic River, Empress Catherine II made him a count with the name "Rimniksky" in addition to his own name, and the Emperor Joseph II of Austria made him a count of the Holy Roman Empire. In 1790, Suvorov became notorious when the storming of the fortress of Ismail in Bessarabia led to the massacre of the Turkish garrison and residents. In 1794, he led the Russian army in Poland, crushing the Polish forces in a series of engagements. His assault on Praga was again followed by a bloody massacre of the residents.

Under Emperor Paul, Suvorov opposed the introduction of the Prussian military regulations and uniform into the Russian army. In response, Paul I put him under house arrest at his estate of Konchaiskoe, near Moscow. In February 1799, Suvorov was summoned by Paul to take command of the Russian army against the French Revolutionary armies in Italy. Suvorov opened this campaign with a series of decisive victories at Cassano, Trebbia, and Novi, which virtually expelled the French from the Italian peninsula. However, the Austrians became concerned by the expansion of the Russian influence in the region and saw that Suvorov was recalled to Switzerland. Meanwhile, General Rimsky-Korsakov, in charge of a Russian corps in Switzerland, was defeated by General Andre Masséna at Zurich, which left Suvorov virtually surrounded in the Alps. Undeterred by his perilous situation, Suvorov launched his legendary crossing of the Alps during October-November of 1799, fighting his way through the mountains.

After returning to Russia, Suvorov fell out of favor when it was discovered he had a general serving as his duty officer—a privilege reserved to members of the Imperial family. Emperor Paul refused to give him an audience. Exhausted and seriously ill, Suvorov died on 18 May 1800, at St Petersburg. He was buried in the Church of the Annunciation in the Alexander of Neva Monastery, with a simple inscription on his grave "Here lies Suvorov."

Suvorov left an indelible imprint on the Russian army and was one of the most important Russian military figures in all of Russian history. He enjoyed legendary status during his own lifetime, and was idolized by his troops. He established the spirit of self-sacrifice, resolution, and indifference to losses in the Russian army. His character of leadership responded to the character of the Russian soldier, and many subsequent leaders emulated him. He was a man of great simplicity in manners and living; and while on a campaign often lived as a private soldier, sleeping on straw and contenting himself with the humblest food.

SUVOROV, Arkadii Aleksandrovich (b. 15 August 1784 — d. 25 April 1811) was the son of the famous Field Marshal Aleksander Suvorov. He enjoyed a brilliant career at the court due to his father's successes. Paul I made him adjutant general and Alexander appointed him lieutenant general. Suvorov participated in 1809 Campaign against Austria and led the 9th Division against Turks in the Danubian Principalities in 1810-1811. However, he drowned on 25 April 1811, in the Rimnic River while trying to save his coachman.

SVECHIN, Nikanor Mikhaylovich (b. 14 July 1772, Dubrovka, Tver *gubernia* — d. 25 February 1849, St. Petersburg) was born to a noble family from the Tver *gubernia*. He was enlisted as a sergeant in the Life Guard Preobrazhensk Regiment at an early age and studied at the Tver Boarding School. He began his service in February 1791, and enjoyed rapid promotions to to sub-ensign in 1796, portupei-ensign in September 1798, ensign on 25 December 1798, sub-lieutenant in October 1799, and to lieutenant in August 1803. In 1805, Svechin accompanied his regiment to Moravia, but as he crossed a creek near Olmutz, his horse fell in the river and Svechin was badly bruised. His injuries left him unable to participate at Austerlitz that December.

In 1806-1807, he served under General Rimsky-Korsakov, who was forming a new reserve army around Vilna and Grodno, and Svechin received the rank of staff captain. He returned to his regiment in late 1807; two years later he was promoted to captain in April 1809. He was appointed to the 2nd Battalion of the Life Guard Preobrazhensk Regiment, deployed at Vaasa in Finland. Returning to Russia, he rose to colonel on 8 February 1810, and took command of the 2nd Battalion of the Life Guard Preobrazhensk Regiment in July of the same year.

During the 1812 Campaign, Svechin served with the 1st Brigade of the Guard Infantry Division, 5th reserve (Guard) Corps, 1st Western Army. He took part in the battles at Borodino (Order of St. Anna, 2nd class) and Spas Kuplya, as well as in the pursuit of the French in late 1812. In May 1813, he served at Lutzen and Bautzen (Order of St. Vladimir, 3rd class). On 28 August, Svechin distinguished himself at Berggieshubel, where he led a bayonet charge through the French lines and cleared the road to Teplitz for retreating Russian army. For his actions, Svechin received the Order of St. George (4th class, 22 December 1813). The following day, 29 August, he fought at Kulm and received a promotion to major general on 27 September 1813, as well as the Prussian Iron Cross. On 10 October 1813, he became chef of the New Ingermanland Infantry Regiment. Svechin took part in the battle at Leipzig on 16-18 October (Prussian Order of the Red Eagle, 2nd class). From 22 December 1813 to 28 January 1814, he served in the blockade of Wessel.

Over the course of the invasion of France, Svechin fought at Craonne, Laon (Order of St. Anna, 1st class), Rheims, and Paris. In late 1814, he led the 2nd Brigade of the 12th Division of the 5th Corps, and the following year, led his brigade back to France after Napoleon's escape from Elba. However, Svechin became seriously ill while passing through Germany and left the army to recuperate. He was relieved of command because of poor health on 29 September 1815, but two months later took command of the 2nd Brigade of the 11th Division on 7 December 1815. He became commander of the 2nd Division on 10 May 1822, and of the 19th Division on 13 February 1823. He rose to lieutenant general on 3 September 1826. During the Russo-Turkish War in 1828-1829, Svechin served at Babadag, Constanta, Mangalia, Bazardjik, Shumla, and Varna.

Svechin took a discharge because of poor health on 25 February 1829, and settled in St. Petersburg, where he died on 25 February 1849.

TALYZIN, Alexander Ivanovich (b. 1777 — d. 12 September 1847) was born to a noble family from the Moscow *gubernia*. He enlisted as a sergeant in the Life Guard Izmailovsk Regiment on 12 January 1793. Talyzin became a colonel on 15 March 1801, and distinguished himself at Austerlitz in 1805, where he was wounded and awarded the Order of St. George (4th class) on 8 March 1806. He retired because of poor health with a rank of major general on 13 November 1806, but returned to service two years later. In 1809-1811, he served as assistant to the governor of Moscow.

During the Russian Campaign of 1812, Talyzin organized the Moscow *Opolchenye* and became chef of the 2nd *Opolchenye* Jager Regiment. He took part in the battles at Borodino, Tarutino, Maloyaroslavets (Order of St. Anna, 1st class), Vyazma, and Krasnyi (golden sword with diamonds). In the 1813 Campaign, he fought at Lutzen, Bautzen (commanded 2nd Brigade of the 7th Division), Katzbach, and Leignitz. In 1814, Talyzin distinguished himself at La Ferte sous Jouane. He led the 2nd Brigade of the 7th Division in 1815, and took command of the 3rd Brigade of the 17th Division on 25 September 1816, before becoming assistant to the commander of the 17th Division on 23 February 1817. He retired in November 1817 and settled in Moscow.

TALYZIN (Talyzin III), Fedor Ivanovich (b. 1773 — d. 15 February 1844) was born to a noble family in the Moscow *gubernia*. He enlisted as a private in the Life Guard Preobrazhensk Regiment in 1775, and transferred to the Life Guard Izmailovsk Regiment the following year. His actual service began as a sergeant in 1789, and he was promoted to ensign on 12 January 1790. Talyzin became a colonel on 29 September 1798, and major general and chef of the Selengin Musketeer Regiment on 15 November 1799.

He was discharged from the army on 8 September 1800, but returned to service the next year as chef of the Butyrsk Musketeer Regiment (17 November 1801 – 29 January 1802). He was appointed chef of the Sebastopol Musketeer Regiment on 11 February 1804, and served in the Caucasus, where he distinguished himself fighting the Persians and mountaineers at Anakur, Godoret, Mleta, Gamashichur, and Lori. Talyzin was seriously wounded (two muskets shots to the right leg and a saber cut to the head) during combat in the Abaran Valley.

Talyzin retired because of his wounds on 30 November 1804, and spent the next eight years at his estate. He returned to the army during the 1812 Campaign and was appointed chef of the 3rd *Opolchenye* Jager Regiment on 26 August 1812. He led the 3rd *Opolchenye* Division at Borodino and was given command of the 2nd Brigade of the 7th Infantry Division on 12 September 1812. He took part in the actions at Chirikov, Tarutino, and Maloyaroslavets (Order of St. Anna, 1st class). In 1813, he fought at Kalisch, Lutzen, Bautzen (golden sword with diamonds), and Reichenbach. In August 1813, he rose to lead the 7th Division and fought at Katzbach, Dresden, Leipzig, and Mainz. During the crossing of the Rhine River on 1 January 1814, he captured French fortifications with six guns, for which he earned the Order of St. George (3rd class) and the Prussian Red Eagle. He went on to fight at Ligny, St. Dizier, Brienne, La Rothière, Montmirail (Order of St. Vladimir, 2nd class), Chateau Thierry, Mery sur Seine, Craonne, Laon, Soissons, and Paris.

Talyzin led a brigade of the 18th Division in 1815 before becoming commander of the 16th Division on 21 April 1816, the 4th Division on 26 November 1817, and the 11th Division on 11 June 1824. He was promoted to lieutenant general on 8 April 1820. Talyzin's career collapsed when he was relieved of his position for embezzlement on 28 September 1826, and court martialed on 30 December 1828. He returned to the army in September 1839 in time to celebrate the Borodino anniversary, and was granted an army retirement with pension.

TALYZIN (Talyzin I), Stepan Alexandrovich (b. 1765 — d. 1 May 1815) was born to a prominent Russian noble family from the Moscow *gubernia*, but turned in a checkered military career. He enlisted as a sergeant in the Life Guard Izmailovsk Regiment on 21 April 1775, and after studying in Germany, began his active service as ensign in January 1784. During the Russo-Swedish War in 1788-1789, he served on a galley flotilla and rose to captain-lieutenant in January 1789. He transferred that same year as a lieutenant colonel to the 2nd Battalion of the Byelorussia Jager Corps and took part in the operations against the Turks on the Salche River, at Bender, Ismail (Order of St. George, 4th class), Babadag, and Macin. In 1792-1794, Talyzin served in Poland and fought at Dubenka, Pesochna (golden sword) and Praga (wounded). He became colonel and commander of the Orlovsk Infantry Regiment on 2 January 1795.

Talyzin rose to major general and chef of the Orlovsk Regiment on 12 October 1797. He was discharged for ineffective service on 25 February 1798, but restored on 9 April and appointed Military Governor of Astrakhan and chef of the Astrakhan Garrison Regiment on 3 October 1798. He was dismissed a second time for inefficient command on 20 January 1799. He returned to service only after Emperor Alexander I took the throne. Appointed chef of the Pavlovsk Grenadier Regiment on 22 April 1801, Talyzin retired because of poor health on 14 May 1802. During the 1807 Campaign in Poland, he led militia in the Moscow *gubernia*, but retired again in late January 1808.

During the Russian Campaign of 1812, Talyzin organized *opolchenye* in various districts of the Moscow *gubernia*, returned to the regular army on 20 August, and commanded *opolchenye* detachments at Tarutino, Maloyaroslavets, Vyazma, and Krasnyi. On 28 January 1813, he was appointed assistant to the commander of the 8th Division and fought at Kalisch, Lutzen, Bautzen, Katzbac, Leipzig, and Wachau (wounded in the right thigh, golden sword with diamonds). In 1814, Talyzin fought at Brienne and La Rothière, where he was severely wounded in the chest and right hand. He retired in late 1814 and died because of complications from his wounds in May 1815.

Another **TALYZIN (Talyzin II) Peter Alexandrovich**, lieutenant general, led the Life Guard Preobrazhensk Regiment between 15 May 1799 and 23 May 1801.

TARASOV, Nikita Maksimovich was appointed commander of the Belevsk Musketeer Regiment on 27 June 1805, and promoted to colonel on 5 May 1806. Appointed chef of the Saratov Musketeer Regiment on 27 August 1808, he became chef of the Vologda Musketeer Regiment on 11 September 1808. Tarasov died in early 1811 and was excluded from rosters on 6 March 1811.

TARNOVSKY, Peter Ivanovich was promoted to lieutenant colonel on 19 November 1811 and commanded the Pavlovsk Grenadier Regiment between 29 August 1810 and 22 January 1812.

TATISHEV, Alexander Ivanovich (b. 1762 — d. 29 June 1833) was born to a prominent Russian noble family. Enlisted in the army at an early age, he became a cornet in the Prince Potemkin's Cuirassier Regiment in 1776. Tatishev distinguished himself at Ochakov during the Russo-Turkish War of 1787-1791, and later served in Poland in 1792. The following year, he transferred as a lieutenant colonel to the Poltava Light Horse Regiment. In 1794, Tatishev served at the Imperial Court, where he rose to colonel but transferred to civil service with the rank of actual state counselor in 1798.

After Emperor Paul I's death, Tatishev returned to the army with the rank of major general in the Commissariat and took a discharge in 1803. Three years later, he was elected head of the Moscow militia. In March 1808, he became general kriegs-commissar in the Russian army, serving in this capacity throughout the Napoleonic Wars. After the war, Tatishev became the Minister of War on 26 March 1823, and was elevated to general of infantry. He was conferred the title of count of the Russian Empire in 1826, and then retired because of illness in 1827.

TATISHEV, Nikolay Alekseyevich (b. 1739 — d. 1823) was born to a prominent Russian noble family. He enlisted in the Life Guard Preobrazhensk Regiment at the age of four in 1743, and began active service as a lieutenant in 1759. He transferred to the Nizhegorod Carabinier Regiment, rising to a rotmistr in 1763. Tatishev served in Poland in 1768, distinguishing himself during the assault on Warsaw. He served at Kagul (rank of premier major and the Order of St. George, 4th class), Bucharest (promoted to colonel), Turno, Cernavoda, Ruse, and Turtukai during the Russo-Turkish War of 1769-1774. In early 1777, he rose to colonel and commander of the Prince Potemkin's Novo Troitsk Cuirassier Regiment. He became a brigadier in 1782, and the following year, temporarily led the Life Guard Preobrazhensk Regiment.

During the Russo-Swedish War in 1789-1790, Tatishev commanded a detachment of the Guard battalions in Finland, receiving the Order of St. Anna (1st class). Emperor Paul discharged him with the rank of lieutenant general, but Tatishev returned to the army with the rank of general of infantry after the Emperor was assassinated in March 1801. He commanded the Life Guard Preobrazhensk Regiment between 26 May 1801 and 4 June 1803. On 27 September 1801, he was conferred the title of count of the Russian Empire. In 1806, he was appointed head of the 1st Zemstvo District militia.

TAUBE, Maksim Maksmovich (b. 1783 — d. 6 August 1749) was born to a noble family in the Lifland *gubernia*; the brother of Roman Taube. He graduated from the Artillery and Engineer Cadet Corps and began service as a sub-lieutenant in the 5th Artillery Regiment on 25 December 1798. Taube participated in the Russo-Turkish War in 1806-1810 and fought at Bucharest, Giurgiu (Order of St. Anna, 3rd class), Zimnik, Silistra (golden sword, 1810) and Ruse (Imperial letter of gratitude, 1811). He was promoted to captain on 25 January 1811, and was appointed to the 13th Artillery Brigade before becoming commander of the 56th Light Company of the 1st Reserve Artillery Brigade on 26 March 1812. Taube was promoted to lieutenant colonel on 8 September 1812.

In 1813, Taube served in the Duchy of Warsaw and Silesia and participated in the actions at Dresden and Leipzig (Order of St. George, 4th class). In 1814, he fought at Craonne, Laon (Order of St. Anna, 2nd class, with diamonds), and Paris, for which he earned the rank of colonel and the Order of St. Anna (2nd class) with diamonds. After the war, Taube commanded 26th Artillery Brigade (1 November 1814) and later served in Vorontsov's corps in France. In 1819, he took command of the Tambov Infantry Regiment, and in 1822, rose to major general and led the 1st Brigade of the 15th Division and then the 3rd Brigade of the 3rd Division.

In 1825-1831, Taube served in the Caucasus, fighting in Chechnya and Daghestan. In 1835, he became the Civil Governor of Caucasus and a lieutenant general in 1836. Appointed to the Senate in 1839, he died on 6 August 1849.

TAUBE, Roman Maksimovich (b. 1782 — date of death unclear) was born to a noble family in the Lifland *gubernia*; the brother of Maksim Taube. He studied in the Artillery and Engineer Cadet Corps and was appointed as sub-lieutenant to the Pioneer Regiment in 1797. He transferred to the Life Guard Artillery Battalion in 1799. He participated in the 1805 Campaign and fought at Austerlitz. In 1807, he took part in the battles at Guttstadt, Heilsberg, and Friedland (wounded in the hand). For his actions in 1807, he was awarded the Order of St. Vladimir (4th class) and a golden sword for courage.

In 1808-1809, Taube served in Finland, earning the Order of St. George (4th class) for his actions in 1808. He was wounded in a combat on 16 April 1809, and promoted to captain on 16 August of the same year. During the Russian Campaign of 1812, Taube led the 2nd Battery Company of the Life Guard Artillery Brigade and fought at Borodino, where he was mortally wounded after a cannonball tore off his leg.

TELEPNEV, Ivan Ivanovich was appointed commander of the Mariupol Hussar Regiment on 5 February 1799. He became major general and chef of Aleksandria Hussar Regiment on 14 October 1799 and commanded the Glukhov Cuirassier Regiment between 1 November 1801 and 29 March 1804.

TEPLOV, Nikolay Afanasievich, major, was appointed commander of the Shirvan Infantry Regiment on 1 June 1812. He served with the 24th Division at Smolensk, Borodino and Krasnyi in 1812, and at Leipzig in 1813. He was killed on 30 January 1814, during the invasion of France.

TESLEV, Alexander Petrovich (b. 26 November 1778, Vyborg — d. 15 November 1847) was born to a Lutheran noble family at Vyborg. He began service as a corporal of the Neva Infantry Regiment on 4 March 1793. Promoted to ensign on 28 November 1797, he was appointed to the Quartermaster Section of the Imperial Retinue on 28 July 1798. In 1798-1805, Teslev served in Finland to map the southern provinces. Thereafter, he was attached to the embassy to China to map the Far Eastern provinces between Omsk and the Amur River. Teslev returned to St. Petersburg in 1807 and was appointed to Bennigsen's army in Poland, fighting at Guttstadt, Heilsberg, and Friedland.

During the Russo-Swedish War of 1808-1809, Teslev served in the battles of Kuopio, Sigaioki, Lappo, Alavo, Kuortaine, and Idensalmi, and later served as an adjutant to Lieutenant General Steingell (golden sword). In 1810, he completed mapping the Aland Islands, and the next year, was dispatched to map Siberia and Mongolia. In late 1811, he was appointed ober-quartermaster of the Finland Corps. During the Russian Campaign, Teslev's corps marched to Riga, defended the Baltic provinces, and fought at Eckau, Polotsk (promoted to a colonel on 23 February 1813), Chashniki, Smolyani (Order of St. Vladimir, 3rd class), and Borisov.

During the 1813 Campaign in Saxony, Teslev served at Wittenberg, Lutzen, Bautzen, Pirna, Kulm, Dresden, and Leipzig (Order of St. George, 4th class, 3 February 1814). For his actions at Dresden, he was promoted to major general on 4 March 1814, with seniority dating from 22 August 1813. In 1814, he fought at Bar sur Aube, Labrusselle, Arcis sur Aube, Le Fère Champenoise, and Paris, where he garnered a golden sword with diamonds.

After the war, he served as chief of staff for the 1st Infantry Corps (1815) and commanded, in succession the 21st, 23rd, and 2nd Divisions over the course of 1819-1831. Teslev became a lieutenant general on 3 September 1826. He was relieved of his position on 1 April 1831, and appointed assistant to the governor of Finland on 8 March 1832. Receiving the Order of St. Alexander of Neva in 1839, he became general of infantry on 13 July 1841.

TETERIN, Dmitry Kuzmich (b. 1791 — date of death unclear) was born to officer's family, but orphaned at an early age. He studied in the Military Orphanage and was appointed sub-lieutenant in the 4th Artillery Brigade on 6 May 1809. He became brigade adjutant in the 3rd Artillery Brigade on 28 February 1811. During the Russian Campaign, he fought at Smolensk, Borodino (St. Anna sword), and Vitebsk. In 1813, he served at Kalisch, Lutzen, and Bautzen, receiving the Order of St. Anna (2nd class) and St. Vladimir (4th class).

TETTENBORN, Friedrich Karl Freiherr von (b. 2 March 1778, Tubingen — d. 21 December 1845, Vienna) was born to a noble family in Baden. He studied in the universities of Göttingen and Jena and served in the Austrian cavalry against the French on the Rhine River and in Holland in 1795-1800. During the 1805 Campaign, he served in Archduke Ferdinand's cavalry and escaped the surrender at Ulm. He was awarded the Order of Maria Theresa on 9 June 1806. Tettenborn served at the Austrian embassy in St. Petersburg in 1808, and took part in the 1809 Campaign against the French, distinguishing himself at Wagram.

During the Russian Campaign of 1812, he entered Russian service on 12 September 1812, and served under Winzegorode. Tettenborn fought on the Berezina River and at Lepel and Kovno. For his actions, he was awarded the Order of St. George (4th class) and promoted to colonel on 18 December 1812. In 1813, he led a cavalry detachment and fought at Koenigsberg and Berlin. Tettenborn occupied Hamburg on 19 March 1813, and defended it for a couple of weeks against the French before abandoning it on 30 May 1813. For his actions at Hamburg, he was promoted to major general on 28 March 1813, and awarded the Order of St. George (3rd class) on 12 August 1813.

In August-October 1813, Tettenborn took part in minor actions in Mecklenburg, Göhrde, and Bremen. In 1814, he fought in Holstein,

Kolon, St. Dizier, Arcis sur Aube, and Paris (golden sabre with diamonds). In 1815, Tettenborn commanded the 3rd Uhlan Division and marched to France during the Hundred Days. He left the Russian army on 11 April 1818, and returned to Baden, later serving as the ambassador to Vienna. He wrote a memoir *Geschichte der Kriegszuge des Generals Tettenborn... 1813 und 1814*, published at Stuttgart in 1814.

TEYL VAN SERASKERKEN, Fedor Vasilievich (Dideric Jacob) (b. 1771, Netherlands — date of death unknown; excluded from rosters on 9 July 1826) was born to a Dutch noble family and began service in the Dutch army. He entered Russian service with the rank of captain on 5 December 1803, and served in the Quatermaster Section of the Imperial Retinue. In 1805, he served with the Russian squadron in the Mediterranean Sea and fought at Corfu (promoted to major). He served as a quartermaster in Bennigsen's army in 1807, fighting at Guttstadt, Heilsberg, and Friedland.

During the Russo-Swedish War, Teyl served in the Russian headquarters and was promoted to lieutenant colonel in 1808, and to colonel on 26 April 1809. In 1810-1811, he served on diplomatic and intelligence missions to Vienna. During the Russian Campaign of 1812, Teyl served as quartermaster general of the 3rd Reserve Observational Army and took part in the actions at Kobryn, Gorodechnya, etc. He was promoted to major general on 7 June 1813. Teyl participated in the 1813-1814 Campaign serving in the Russian headquarters and was awarded the Prussian Red Eagle and the Austrian Order of Leopold. In 1815-1826, he served on diplomatic missions to Naples, the Vatican and the United States.

TIMOFEYEV, Paul Petrovich (b. 1780 — date of death unclear) graduated from the Artillery and Engineer Cadet Corps in 1794 and began service as a sub-lieutenant in the 13th Artillery Battalion in 1794. He participated in the 1806-1807 Campaigns in Poland, fighting at Pultusk, Jankovo, Guttstadt, and Friedland (Order of St. Vladimir, 4th class). Timofeyev served in Finland during the Russo-Swedish War of 1808-1809 and was awarded a golden sword for courage in 1808. He was promoted to lieutenant colonel on 21 February 1811, and appointed commander of the 4th Light Company of the 11th Artillery Brigade on 10 October 1811. During the Russian campaign, he fought at Smolensk, Borodino, Ostrovno and Chernishnya.

TISHENINOV, Nikolay Vasilievich (b. 1786 — date of death unclear) was born to a petty noble family. He graduated from the 2nd Cadet Corps and began service as a sub-lieutenant in the 11th Artillery Battalion in 1803. He participated in the campaign in Poland in 1807 and fought at Landsberg, Eylau, on the Passarge River (Order of St. Anna, 3rd class), and Heilsberg (golden sword). In 1808, he transferred to the Danubian Principalities, and from 1809-1811 took part in the actions at Braila, Macin, Silistra (wounded in the right leg), Shumla, Giurgiu, Ruse (received Imperial gratitude), and Slobodzea. Tisheninov was appointed to the 12th Light Company of the 7th Artillery Brigade on 31 December 1811, and was promoted to staff captain on 10 January 1812. During the Russian Campaign, Tisheninov fought at Smolensk, Borodino (Order of St. Vladimir, 4th class), Tarutino, Maloyaroslavets, and Krasnyi (Order of St. Vladimir, 3rd class).

TITOV, Nikolay Maksimovich (b. 1789 — date of death unclear) was born to a noble family in the Nizhegorod *gubernia*. He graduated from the 1st Cadet Corps and began service as a sub-lieutenant in the 5th Artillery Brigade in 1807. He was promoted to lieutenant on 21 February 1811, and transferred to the 3rd Horse Artillery Company of the 1st Reserve Artillery Brigade on 13 March 1811. During the Russian Campaign, he served under Wittgenstein and fought at Klyastitsy, Polotsk, Borisov, Wilkomir, Belyi, Yuriev, and Chashniki. In 1813, he served at Danzig, Lutzen, and Bautzen.

Other Titovs serving in the Russian army included: **TITOV, Adam Ageyevich**, colonel, was appointed commander of the Tarnopol Infantry Regiment on 10 November 1811, chef of the Tarnopol Infantry Regiment on 9 May 1812, and commander of the Tarnopol Infantry Regiment on 4 July 1815.

TITOV (Titov II), Vasily Petrovich was appointed commander of the Malorossiiskii (Little Russia) Grenadier Regiment on 24 August 1798. He rose to major general and chef of the Muromsk Musketeer Regiment on 29 November 1798. He served as chef of the 5th and 4th Jager Regiments (March 1799-July 1800), and as chef of the Muromsk Musketeer Regiment on 20 March 1802 (until 18 January 1810).

TITOV (Titov I), Nikolay Fedorovich was appointed commander of the Caucasus Grenadier Regiment on 27 August 1798. He became major general and chef of the Kherson Grenadier Regiment on 18 November 1798, and served until 29 January 1811.

TOKMACHEV, Peter Lukianovich (b. 1785 — date of death unclear) was born to a noble family in the Kostroma *gubernia*. He graduated from the 2nd Cadet Corps and was appointed as sub-lieutenant to the 4th Artillery Regiment in 1805. He served at Austerlitz in 1805. During the campaign in Poland in 1807, Tokmachev fought at Eylau, Heilsberg (Order of St. Anna, 3rd class), and Friedland (wounded in the chest). In 1808-1809, he served in Finland. He was promoted to staff captain on 21 February 1811, and appointed to the 10th Light Company of the 5th Artillery Brigade on 6 March 1811. During the 1812 Campaign, Tokmachev took part in rear guard actions in July and fought at Riga. In 1813, he took part in the actions at Langfurt and Wollinberg.

TOLBUKHIN, Pavel Petrovich, colonel, commanded the 7th Jager Regiment between 20 May 1804 and 23 November 1808. He took part in the 1805 Campaign, fighting at Austerlitz, and served with the 8th Division in Poland in 1806-1807, fighting at Eylau. Tolbukhin later served as chef of the 6th Jager Regiment between 23 November 1808 and 31 October 1809.

TOLBUZIN (Tolbuzin I), Mikhail Ivanovich, colonel, served as chef of the Glukhov Cuirassier Regiment between 28 July 1808 and 28 October 1812. He served with the 2nd Cuirassier Division of the 2nd Western Army in 1812, fighting at Smolensk. He was mortally wounded at Borodino and died on 31 October 1812. His brother, **TOLBUZIN (Tolbuzin II) Sergey Ivanovich**, colonel, served as chef of the Courland Dragoon Regiment from 2 February 1809 to 22 May 1812.

TOLL, Karl Fedorovich (Karl Wilhelm) (b. 19 April 1777, Estland — d. 5 May 1842, St. Petersburg) descended from a Dutch noble family that settled in Sweden in the 15th Century. One of his ancestors served as the Swedish ambassador to Tsar Ivan the Terrible and settled in Estland. In 1782-1796, Toll studied in the

Cadet Corps, where he became close to General Mikhail Kutuzov, then Director of the Cadet Corps. He was appointed as lieutenant to the main headquarters on 10 December 1796, and was dispatched on a mission to strengthen defenses in the Crimea in 1797. Toll served under Field Marshal Alexander Suvorov in Italy and Switzerland in 1799 and took part in the actions at Serravalle, Novi (golden sword), St. Gothard, Devil's Bridge, Altdorf, and in the Muothatal Valley. He was promoted to captain on 14 November 1799, and to major on 12 May 1800.

During the 1805 Campaign, Toll served at the Russian headquarters and attended Alexander I after the December battle of Austerlitz, for which he was awarded the Order of St. Vladimir (4th class). In 1806, Toll was appointed to the quartermaster service of the Army of Dniestr and took part in the actions against the Turks at Giurgiu and Ismail, receiving the rank of lieutenant colonel and the Order of St. Anna (2nd class). In early 1809, he participated in the failed assault on the fortress of Braila, and after briefly leading a battalion of the 20th Jager Regiment, returned to the main quatermaster service under Prince M. Volkonsky on 13 July 1810. He was promoted to colonel on 27 September 1811.

During the 1812 Campaign, Toll served as the Quartermaster General in the 1st Western Army. He participated in the actions at Ostrovno, Vitebsk, and supported the offensive at the council of war at Smolensk. On 15-19 August, Toll fought at Smolensk and Lubino, receiving the Order of St. Vladimir (3rd class). However, Barclay de Tolly and Bagration criticised him for poor perfomance at Dorogbouzh and Tsarevo-Znaimische, and ordered him to leave the army. After Mikhail Kutuzov became the Russian commander- in-chief, he recalled his old protégé and made him Quatermaster General of all the Russian armies. During the rest of the 1812 Campaign, Toll gradually gained considerable influence over Kutuzov's decisions. He took part in the Battle of Borodino (Order of St. George, 4th class), supported the decision to abandon Moscow at the council of war at Fily, and fought in the actions on the Nare and Chernishna Rivers, at Tarutino (Order of St. Anna, 1st class), Maloyaroslavets, Vyazma, and Krasnyi. For his service, he was promoted to major general and awarded the Order of St. George (4th class) on 3 December 1812.

After Kutuzov's death in April 1813, Toll was appointed the quartermaster general in the main Allied headquarters and attended Emperor Alexander at Lutzen and Bautzen, receiving the Prussian Order of Red Eagle. In June 1813, Toll transferred as the quartemaster general to Field Marshal Schwarzenberg's army and fought at Dresden, Kulm (Order of St. Vladimir, 2nd class, and the Austrian Order of Leopold), and Leipzig (promoted to lieutenant general, 19 October 1813). He urged the invasion of France at the council of war in Frankfurt in December 1813.

During the 1814 Campaign, Toll fought at Brienne (Austrian Order of Maria Theresa), La Ferte sur Aube, Fontet, Bar sur Aube, Troyes, Arcis sur Aube, Le Fère Champenoise, and Paris. For his actions, he was awarded a 12-year allowance of 4,257 rubles and conferred the title of baron of the Austrian Empire. In 1815, Toll participated in the Congress of Vienna and delivered Emperor Alexander's letters to the Allied commanders-in-chief in the Netherlands in June 1815.

Toll met Blücher and Wellington before the battle of Waterloo before returning to the Russian army to attend Emperor Alexander during the Russian army's march to France. Toll took part in the organization of the grand military parade at Vertus and was appointed quatermaster general of the newly established General Staff on 24 December 1815.

Toll served at this position for the next eight years, distinguishing himself at the maneuvers at Peterhof in 1817. He was awarded a 12-year allowance of 5,066 rubles in 1820 and appointed adjutant general (4 May 1823) and the Chief of Staff of the 1st Army on 18 April 1824. He garnered the Order of St. Alexander of Neva in 1824 and the diamond signs of this order in 1826. Toll rose to general of infantry on 3 September 1826.

During the Russo-Turkish War of 1828-1829, Toll served as the Chief of Staff of the 2nd Army (21 February 1829) and participated in the actions at Silistra, Kulevci, Shumla, and Adrianople. For his service, he was conferred the title of count of the Russian Empire (21 June 1829), presented with a gift of 300,000 rubles and the Orders of St. Vladimir (1st class) and of St. George (2nd class, 11 October 1829). He was appointed chef of the 20th Jager Regiment on 4 October 1829, and became a member of the State Council on 25 January 1830, and the Chief of Staff of the 1st Army on 13 December 1830.

Toll participated in the suppression of the Polish Uprising in 1831, fighting at Kalushino, Minsk, Milosna, Vav, Grochow (Order of the White Eagle), and Ostrolenka. He briefly commanded the Russian army after Diebitch's death and took part in the battles at Bolimov, Shimanov, and Warsaw, where he was bruised by enemy fire. Toll resigned from his positions on 17 September 1831, and settled in St. Petersburg. He was appointed chef of the Nizhegorod Infantry Regiment on 14 April 1833, and headed the Department of Communications and Public Buildings on 13 October 1833. For his service, he was awarded the diamond signs of Order of St. Andrew the First Called on 19 April 1835, and large estates in the Kingdom of Poland in 1837. He died on 5 May 1842 in St. Petersburg.

TOLSTOY (the American), Fedor Ivanovich (b. 17 February 1782 — d. 5 November 1846, Moscow) was born to a prominent Russian noble family. He enlisted at an early age in the Life Guard Preobrazhensk Regiment and began active service as ensign in 1798. In 1803, he volunteered for a naval expedition around the world commanded by Lieutenant Kruzenshtern. His insubordination and lack of discipline, however, convinced Kruzenshtern to abandon Tolstoy on the Aleutian Islands, where he spent a couple of years.

After a brief trip to America, Tolstoy returned to Russia in 1805 and was appointed to the Neischlodt Garrison Battalion. Tolstoy participated in the Russo-Swedish War, serving as adjutant to Prince Mikhail Dolgorukov and transferred to the Life Guard Preobrazhensk Regiment on 12 November 1808.

Notorious for his gambling and duels, Tolstoy retired on 24 October 1811, but returned to service during the 1812 Campaign. He served in the Moscow *opolchenye* at Borodino, where he was seriously wounded in the leg and promoted to colonel. He retired from the army and settled at Moscow, where his house became a popular literary salon.

TOLSTOY, Nikolay Ivanovich (b. 6 November 1758 — d. 27 February 1818, Moscow) was born to a noble family from the Tula *gubernia*. He enlisted as corporal in the Life Guard Preobrazhensk Regiment on 17 January 1774, and was promoted to ensign on 12 January 1781. He participated in the Russo-Swedish War in 1788-1790 and fought at Rochensalmi, Vyborg (Order of St. Vladimir, 4th class) and Swenkzund, where he was wounded in the right hand and captured. Tolstoy returned to Russia in late 1790, and after being promoted to colonel in January 1792, retired from army. He returned to service in late 1801 and was appointed to the Commissariat Expedition of the War College on 21 October 1801.

Tolstoy became major general on 23 April 1804, and served as head of the military hospital in Moscow. During the Russian Campaign of 1812, he supervised evacuation of the wounded at Borodino (Order of St. Vladimir, 3rd class) and directed the military hospital in Moscow.

TOLSTOY, Peter Alexandrovich (b. 1769 — d. 10 October 1844, Moscow) was born to a prominent Russian noble family and enlisted as a corporal in the Life Guard Preobrazhensk Regiment on 12 January 1775. His active service began as a sub-lieutenant on 1 June 1785. That same year, he became a flügel adjutant in the headquarters of Général-en-Chef Field Marshal Prince Saltykov. He was promoted to lieutenant colonel in the regular army on 25 July 1788, and appointed adjutant general to Prince Saltykov on 15 November 1788. Tolstoy participated in the Russo-Swedish War in 1789-1790, joined the Ingermanland Carabineer Regiment on 8 April 1792, and transferred to the Pskov Dragoon Regiment on 25 April 1793.

Tolstoy served in Poland in 1792-1795, fighting at Brest (promoted to colonel, 9 July 1794), Maciejowice, Warsaw, and Praga (wounded in the left hand, awarded the Order of St. George, 3rd class, 12 January 1795). He was promoted to major general and appointed chef of the Nizhegorod Dragoon Regiment on 20 November 1797. He was appointed adjutant general to Emperor Paul on 10 December 1797, and awarded the Order of St. Anna (1st class) in early 1798. In 1799, Tolstoy served as a liaison officer between Archduke Johann [John] and Field Marshal Suvorov during operations in Italy and Switzerland. He was promoted to lieutenant general and appointed to the Imperial Retinue on 4 November 1799.

Tolstoy was appointed to the War College on 18 December 1799, and to the Senate on 29 February 1800. He became the Military Governor of Vyborg and head of the Finland Inspection on 6 November 1802. In 1803-1805, he served as the Military Governor of St. Petersburg, became commander of the Life Guard Preobrazhensk Regiment on 4 June 1803, and infantry inspector of the St. Petersburg Inspection on 25 May 1803. After a military parade in late 1803, Tolstoy was nominated for the Order of St. Alexander of Neva, but he declined it and accepted a snuffbox with Alexander's anagram.

In 1805, Tolstoy led an expeditionary corps in Hanover. In 1806, he served as a liaison officer between the King of Prussia and General Levin Bennigsen. After the Prussian disaster at Jena, Tolstoy was appointed a duty general in Bennigsen's headquarters and temporarily commanded the 6th Division and Tuchkov's corps, fighting at Ostrolenka and along the Narew River. In October 1807-October 1808, he served as the Russian ambassador to Paris and was recalled because of his criticism of Napoleon and opposition to the Treaties of Tilsit and Erfurt. Returning to Russia, he served as an inspector of the recruitment depots.

In 1812, Tolstoy commanded *opolchenye*s of the 3rd District, which included the Kazan, Nizhegorodsk, Penza, Kostroma, Simbirsk, and Vyatsk *gubernias*. Tolstoy joined the main army in early 1813 and fought at Dresden, Magdeburg, and Hamburg (Prussian Orders of Red and Black Eagles, the French Legion of Honor, October 1814). He was promoted to general of infantry on 14 October 1814, with seniority dating from 1 July 1814.

After the war, Tolstoy commanded the 4th Corps (25 January 1816) and 5th Corps in Moscow before becoming a member of the State Council on 11 September 1823. Appointed chef of the Moscow Infantry Regiment on 29 May 1827, Tolstoy also served as the commander-in-chief of troops in St. Petersburg and Kronstadt on 4 May 1828.

From 1828-1830, Tolstoy served in the main headquarters and supervised military settlements. For his service, he was awarded the

Order of St. Vladimir (1st class) on 4 October 1830. During the Polish Uprising of 1831, he was given command of the Army of Reserve on 21 April 1831, and operated with it in Lithuania (golden sword with diamonds and inscription "For Vanquishing the Polish Rebels"). In 1831-1836, he was involved with military settlements and briefly served as the Commandant of Moscow in 1836.

TORMASOV, Alexander Petrovich (b. 22 August 1752 — d. 25 November 1819) was born to ancient Russian noble family. His grandfather served in St. Petersburg Admiralty under Peter the Great. Tormasov began his career as a page at the Imperial Court in February 1762, and enlisted as a lieutenant in the Vyatka Infantry regiment on 13 March 1772. He was promoted to captain in May and served as adjutant to Count Bruce, who was appointed commander of the Finland Division in 1774. Tormasov became lieutenant colonel and commander of the Finland Jager Battalion in 1777. He served in the Crimea in 1782-1783, and led the Aleksandria Light Horse Regiment in 1784. From 1788-1791, he participated in the Russo-Turkish War, commanding a cavalry brigade that remained in reserve at Ochakov. After a promotion to brigadier on 5 April 1789, and then to major general on 1 April 1791, he distinguished himself at Babadag and Macin (Order of St. George, 3rd class, 29 March 1792).

From 1792-1794, Tormasov served against the Polish insurgents, fighting at Vishnepol, Mobar, Warsaw, Maciejowice, and Praga. For his actions, he was awarded the Polish Orders of the White Eagle and St. Stanslaus, the Russian Order of St. Vladimir (2nd class), and a golden sword with diamonds. He was appointed chef of the Military Order Cuirassier Regiment on 14 December 1796, and promoted to lieutenant general on 18 February 1798. However, Tormasov had an argument with Emperor Paul in 1799 and was discharged from the army on 23 July 1799. He returned to service on 28 November 1800, and was restored as chef of the Life Guard Horse Regiment on 18 December 1800. Two days later, he was appointed commander of the Life Guard Horse Regiment. Tormasov was promoted to general of cavalry on 27 September 1801, and enjoyed a quick succession of promotions, including to cavalry inspector of the Dniestr Inspection on 23 July 1801, and cavalry inspector of the Lifland Inspection on 20 February 1802.

After briefly retiring in late 1802, Tormasov became the Military Governor of Kiev on 7 February 1803. In 1804, he was awarded an estate in the Courland *gubernia*, and in 1805 began organizing the Army of the Dniestr against the Turks. He took a prolonged furlough because of poor health in 1806 and was awarded the Order of St. Alexander of Neva. After recuperating, Tormasov was appointed the Military Governor of Riga on 28 March 1807, but retired again for health reasons on 23 December 1807. After the death of his wife, Tormasov returned to the army on 21 June 1808, and was appointed commander-in-chief of the troops in Georgia and the Caucasus on 15 September 1808.

Tormasov secured the Russian administration in the Transcaucasia, defeating several Persians raids into Georgia and launching a successful offensive against the Turks in Western Georgia. He simultaneously forced the remaining independent Georgian principalities, including the Kingdom of Imereti, into Russian submission. After capturing the fortresses of Poti and Akhaltsikhe he negotiated with the Persians at the fortress of Askoran in early 1810. Tormasov crushed Persian Prince Abbas Mirza at Migri and Akhalkalaki in September 1810 (diamond signs of Order of St. Alexander of Neva). From October to December, Tormasov suppressed an uprising in Daghestan, then engaged King Solomon of Imereti at Akhaltsikhe and prevented a Turkish invasion of southern Georgia (Order of St. Vladimir, 1st class, early 1811). Thereafter, Tormasov was appointed commander-in-chief of the 3rd Reserve Army of Observation in Volhynia on 27 March 1812.

During the Russian Campaign of 1812, Tormasov engaged the Austrian and French troops at Brest, Kobryn (received 50,000 rubles and Order of St. George, 2nd class, 9 August 1812), and Gorodechnya. He took command of the 2nd Western Army after Prince Peter Bagration's death in late September 1812, but arrived at the Tarutino Camp after the two Russian armies were merged. Tormasov assumed command of the main Russian forces, excluding the advance guard. In November 1812, he fought at Maloyaroslavets and Krasnyi, and pursued the French to Vilna. In early 1813, he briefly led the Russian army after Kutuzov's death and took part in the battle of Lutzen. However, poor health again drove him from the army. He received an appointment as a member of the State Council and returned to St. Petersburg.

Tormasov became the Military Governor of Moscow on 11 September 1814, and was conferred the title of count of the Russian Empire on 11 September 1816. He died on 25 November 1819, and was buried in the Don Monastery in Moscow.

TORNOV, Fedor Grigorievich (b. 1777 — date of death unclear) was born to a Lutheran noble family in the Riga *gubernia*. He studied in the Artillery and Engineer Cadet Corps and was appointed as shtyk-junker in the 1st Fusillier Regiment in 1791. He participated in the campaign in Switzerland in 1799, in Poland in 1807, and in Galicia in 1809. Tornov was promoted to lieutenant colonel on 21 February 1811, and became commander of the 3rd Artillery Brigade on six days later. During the 1812 Campaign, he fought at Smolensk, Borodino (wounded, golden sword), and Vitebsk. In 1813, he served at Kalisch, was promoted to colonel on 25 March 1813, and fought again at Lutzen.

TREFURT, Fedor Fedorovich was appointed commander of the Tobolsk Musketeer Regiment on 2 August 1808, and promoted to colonel on 25 May 1813. During the 1812 Campaign, he served with the 2nd Brigade of the 4th Division fighting at Borodino, Mozhaisk, Tarutino and Vyazma. In 1813, Trefurt led his unit at Kalisch, Lutzen, Bautzen, Reichenbach, Pirna, Dresden, Kulm, Teplitz, and Leipzig. During the invasion of France, he took part in the Battle for Paris on 30 March 1814, and became commander of the Tobolsk Infantry Regiment on 11 September 1814.

TREIDEN, Leontii Ivanovich was appointed commander of the Taganrog Dragoon Regiment on 19 March 1799. He became colonel on 23 March 1800, and commander of Vladimir Dragoon Regiment on 20 August 1800. Treiden commanded the Taganrog Dragoon Regiment between 11 April 1801 and 5 September 1806. He was appointed chef of Tiraspol Dragoon Regiment on 5 September 1806, and rose to major general on 24 December 1807. Treiden died on 25 January 1808.

TRESKIN, Mikhail Lvovich (b. 1765 — d. 1839) was born to a noble family from the Tambov *gubernia*. He began service as a kapternamus in the Life Guard Preobrazhensk Regiment on 26 March 1783, and transferred as a sergeant to the Life Guard Izmailovsk Regiment on 25 October 1784. The following year, Treskin transferred to the 6th Orenburg Field Battalion with the rank of lieutenant. He participated in the Russo-Turkish War of 1789-1791 and fought on the Kuban River and at Anapa (promoted to second major). He was appointed major of the Butyrsk Musketeer Regiment on 12 January 1797.

Treskin served under Alexander Suvorov in Italy in 1799 and distinguished himself at Novi, where he was wounded in the right leg. For his actions, he was promoted to lieutenant colonel on 21 October 1800, and appointed commander of the Butyrsk Musketeer Regiment on 13 December 1804. During the 1805 Campaign, Treskin served under Dokhturov and was wounded and captured at Austerlitz. He was released in February 1806 and promoted to colonel on 5 May for his actions at Austerlitz. In late 1806, Treskin was sent to the Danubian Principalities, where he remained for three years. He took part in actions at the Island of Chetal, Ismail (golden sword), and Braila (wounded in the left hand). Treskin was appointed chef of the Azov Musketeer Regiment on 14 September 1809, and sent on garrison duty to Finland.

During the Russian Campaign of 1812, Treskin was attached to the 3rd Brigade of the 6th Division of the Finland Corps. He operated near Riga and fought the French on the Ushach River, at Chashniky, Borisov, and on the Berezina. In early 1813, he served in the siege of Danzig, was promoted to major general on 27 September 1813, and awarded the Order of St. George (3rd class) on 9 January 1814. He retired on 31 March 1816.

TRETYAKOV, Nikolay Ivanovich (b. 1770 — date of death unknown, ca. 1829) was born to a noble family in the St. Petersburg *gubernia*. He studied at the Artillery and Engineer Cadet Corps and enlisted as a shtyk-junker in the 1st Fusilier Regiment on 21 September 1787. He took part in the Russo-Turkish War in 1787-1788, and was seriously wounded in the right shoulder at Ochakov in 1788. After recuperating, he transferred as lieutenant to the Bombardier Regiment on 26 February 1790, and served on the galley flotilla of Prince Nassau-Zigen. The same year, Tretyakov was seriously wounded and captured by the Swedes in the battle at Swenkzund, but returned to Russia in October.

In 1794, Tretyakov served in Poland and was promoted to captain-lieutenant for his actions at Praga. He transferred to the Life Guard Artillery Battalion on 28 April 1798, and promoted to captain on 19 September 1800. That same year, he transferred from the Guard to the field artillery with a rank of colonel (16 October) and led an artillery company in 1805. He distinguished himself at Dürrenstein (golden sword) and Austerlitz (wounded in the hand). In 1806, he took command of the 18th Artillery Brigade (4 September) and fought at Pultusk, where he was wounded in the left leg and was awarded the Order of St. Vladimir (4th class).

In 1807, Tretyakov took part in the battles at Guttstadt, Heilsberg, and Friedland, where he was seriously wounded in the head. After recuperating, he took part in the invasion of Finland in 1808 and served at Sveaborg, Tavastheus, Kuopio, and Idensalmi. In 1809, he served in Prince Bagration's corps during the crossing of the Gulf of Bothnia to the Aland Islands. Tretyakov was appointed head of the Lifland Artillery District on 18 March 1812, and during the Russian Campaign of 1812, fought at Riga, Olae, and along the Dvina River. In 1813, he took part in the siege of Elbing and was promoted to major general on 11 September 1813.

After the war, Tretyakov was awarded the Order of St. George (4th class, 8 December 1816) for distinguished service and appointed head of gunpowder factory at Shostkinsk on 3 January 1817. He retired because of poor health in 1829 and died shortly thereafter.

TROSHINSKY, Ivan Yefimovich (b. 1783 — d. 1832) was born to a Russian noble family in the Poltava *gubernia*. He initially served in the College on Foreign Affairs and enlisted as a lieutenant in the Life Guard Hussar Regiment

TROTSKY, Peter Ivanovich (b. 1790 — date of death unclear) was born to a noble family in the Voronezh *gubernia*. He graduated from the 2nd Cadet Corps and began service as a sub-lieutenant of the 21st Artillery Brigade on 6 March 1810. He transferred to the 11th Light Company of the 6th Artillery Brigade on 21 February 1811. During the Russian Campaign, he fought on the Uschatch River and at Chashniki. In 1813, he served at Danzig.

on 27 March 1807. During the 1805 Campaign, he joined Mikhail Kutuzov's army at Olmutz and fought at Austerlitz on 2 December. In 1807, he participated in the actions at Guttstadt, Heilsberg, and Friedland, where he was seriously wounded in the left leg and awarded the Order of St. George (4th class, 1 June 1808). He was promoted to colonel on 23 August 1809.

During the Russian Campaign of 1812, Troshinsky served in the 1st Western Army and took part in the retreat to Smolensk. He was seriously wounded in the chest at Borodino and spent rest of campaign recuperating. In 1813, Troshinsky took part in the battles at Bautzen, Dresden, Kulm (Iron Cross), and Leipzig. For his actions, he was promoted to major general on 27 September 1813, and appointed chef of the Lubensk Hussar Regiment on 20 January 1814. He served in the siege of Hamburg later that year. Returning to Russia, he assumed command of the 2nd Brigade of the 2nd Uhlan Division.

Troshinsky became assistant to the commander of the 2nd Uhlan Division on 30 May 1816, assistant to the commander of the Ukraine Uhlan Division on 31 July 1818, and commander of the 3rd Uhland Division on 10 December 1823. He was promoted to lieutenant general on 3 September 1826, and became commander of the 4th Hussar Division on 15 April 1827. Troshinsky retired because of poor health on 30 January 1828.

TROUSSON, Christian Ivanovich (b. 26 March 1742, Koblentz — d. 20 March 1813, St. Petersburg) descended from a French noble family. He joined the Russian army in December 1782 and served as a captain in the Engineer Corps. He participated in the Russo-Turkish War of 1787-1791 and was severely wounded in both legs at Ochakov in 1788. After recuperating, he took part in the actions at Bender and Killia. In 1796, he fought in the Persian Campaign at Derbent and Baku (promoted to colonel, 18 October 1796).

In 1797-1798, Trousson worked on various construction projects on the Dnieper and Dvina Rivers and was promoted to major general on 25 January 1798. He was appointed to the Department of Naval Communications with the rank of actual civil counsellor in 1799. However, he returned to the engineer service in 1800, took part in the construction of the Tula armory, and was promoted to lieutenant general on 27 June 1806. Trousson was appointed head of engineer troops of the 1st Western Army on 31 March 1812, and took part in the retreat to Smolensk and Borodino. However, he became seriously ill in late 1812 and had to leave the army.

TRUBETSKOY, Vasily Sergeyevich (b. 4 April 1776 — d. 22 February 1841, St. Petersburg) was born to a prominent Russian family in St. Petersburg. He enlisted as a private in the Life Guard Preobrazhensk Regiment in 1781 and transferred to the Life Guard Horse Regiment three years later. He began his actual service as a cornet on 16 January 1793. and was promoted to sub-lieutenant on 12 January 1796, to kamer-junker on 15 February 1796, and transferred to the Imperial Court with the rank of actual kamerger in 1798. Two years later, he became a privy counsellor and member of the Kamer College. Under Emperor Alexander I, however, he was reduced in rank and became a kamerger.

In 1805, Trubetskoy was appointed lieutenant of the Mariupol Hussar Regiment and adjutant to Prince Peter Bagration. He participated in Bagration's rear-guard actions from October to November 1805, and distinguished himself at Austerlitz (golden sword). For these actions, he was appointed flügel adjutant to Alexander I on 13 June 1806, and promoted to colonel, taking command of the Life Guard Cavalry Regiment on 25 September 1806. During the 1806-1807 Campaigns, he fought at Pultusk (Order of St. Vladimir, 4th class), Wolfsdorf (Order of St. Vladimir, 3rd class), Eylau (promoted to major general and appointed adjutant general to Alexander I, 27 February 1807), Guttstadt (Order of St. George, 4th class), Heilsberg (Order of St. George, 3rd class), and Friedland. Trubetskoy accompanied Alexander at Tilsit and participated in the negotiations with Napoleon.

In 1809, Trubetskoy was dispatched with instructions to Prince Prozorovsky in Wallachia and served under Prince Peter Bagration from September to December 1809. Trubetskoy distinguished himself again at Constanta (Kustendji, Order of St. Anna, 1st class), Rassevat (golden sword with diamonds), and Tataritsa (Order of St. Vladimir, 2nd class). His criticisms of Count Nikolay Kamensky's actions in 1810, however, temporarily forced him out of the army.

During the Russian Campaign of 1812, he served as adjutant general to Alexander I and delivered the Imperial manifesto to St. Petersburg. He commanded cavalry in General Winzegorode's Corps and participated in minor actions with the French. In 1813-1814, he attended Alexander and took part in every major battle, including Lutzen, Bautzen (promoted to lieutenant general on 27 September 1813), Leipzig (golden sword with diamonds), and Paris.

From 1814-1822, Trubetskoy served on diplomatic missions and accompanied Alexander to the Congresses at Vienna, Aachen, and Verona. In 1826, he was awarded the Order of St. Alexander of Neva, promoted to general of cavalry on 3 September 1826, and appointed to the Senate on 18 December 1826. During the Russo-Turkish War of 1828-1829, he served in the headquarters and took part in the actions at Shumla and Varna (diamond signs of Order of St. Alexander of Neva). He became a member of the State Council on 18 December 1835.

During his long career, Trubetskoy was also awarded the Prussian Pour le Merite, Iron Cross, Orders of Red and Black Eagles with diamonds, Austrian Order of Leopold, Bavarian Order of Maximilian Joseph, Sardinian Order of St.

Maurice and Lazarus, and the French Order of St. Louis.

TSEBRIKOV, Gregory Ivanovich (b. 1789 — date of death unclear) graduated from the 2nd Cadet Corps in 1806 and began service as a sub-lieutenant in the St. Petersburg Artillery Garrison in 1806. He participated in the campaign against Austria in 1809, and was promoted to lieutenant on 19 January 1810. Tsebrikov transferred to the 10th Horse Company of the 3rd Reserve Artillery Brigade in February 1811.

During the Russian Campaign of 1812, he fought at Borodino, Tarutino (Order of St. Anna, 3rd class), and Krasnyi (golden sword). In 1813-1814, he took part in the battles at Dresden (Order of St. Vladimir, 4th class), Leipzig (Order of St. Anna, 2nd class), Magdeburg, Arcis sur Aube, and Paris.

TSITSIANOV, Pavel Dmitryevich (b. 19 September 1754 — d. 20 February 1806, Baku) was born to a prominent Georgian noble family. He was enlisted by his family as a corporal in the Life Guard Preobrazhensk Regiment in 1761. Promoted to ensign in 1772, he rose to a lieutenant captain in 1777, and assumed command of a jager company of the Life Guard Preobrazhensk Regiment. In 1778, Tsitsianov transferred as a lieutenant colonel to the Tobolsk Infantry Regiment. He became a colonel in 1785, and took command of the St. Petersburg Grenadier Regiment in 1786. During the Russo-Turkish War of 1787-1791, he fought at Khotin, on the Salchea River, at Ismail, and Bender. Made brigadier on 16 February 1790, Tsitsianov became a major general in 1793 and served in Poland in 1794, distinguishing himself at Grodno and Vilna, for which he garnered the Orders of St. Vladimir (3rd class) and of St. George (3rd class). He garnered a golden sword with diamonds for capturing some 5,000 Poles at Lubany in the Minsk *gubernia* in August 1794.

In 1795-1797, Tsitsianov participated in the Persian expedition along the Caspian Sea, serving as the Commandant of Baku in 1796-1797. He became chef of the Suzdal Musketeer Regiment on 14 December 1796, and chef of the Tobolsk Musketeer Regiment on 29 December 1796. Tsitsianov took a discharge because of poor health on 20 September 1797. Emperor Alexander appointed him to the Chancellery of the State Council on 19 May 1801, and promoted him to lieutenant general in late 1801. The following year, he made Tsitsianov the Commander-in-Chief of the Russian troops in Georgia and the Military Governor of the Astrakhan *gubernia*. Tsitsianov launched a series of administrative and social reforms in Georgia and succeeded in forcing the Caucasian mountaineers to pledge allegiance to the Russian emperor. He brought into submission the tribes in Daghestan and constructed the fortress of Aleksandrovsk on the Alazani River. For his actions, he was decorated with the Order of St. Alexander of Neva.

Simultaneously, Tsitsianov suppressed anti-Russian fractions within the Georgian nobility and forced Prince Gregory Dadiani of Mingrelia to accept Russian sovereignty. To secure the Georgian frontiers, he captured the major fortress of Gandja in January 1804, for which he was promoted to general of infantry. Returning to Georgia, he forced King Solomon of Imereti to pledge an oath to Emperor Alexander. In the summer of 1804, he advanced against the Persian forces in Armenia and fought at Gumri, Echmiadzin, on the Zang River (Order of St. Vladimir, 1st class), and Yerevan. His aggressive actions forced the Khans of Sheka, Shagakha, and Shurag to pledge allegiance to the

Russian Emperor in early 1805. Thus, within two years, Tsitsianov pacified most of Georgia and conquered neighboring principalities, greatly extending the Russian sphere of influence.

In July 1805, Tsitsianov repulsed the Persian invasion on the Araks River and launched a counteroffensive in the fall of 1805. He occupied Shirvan, compelling the local khan to accept Russian rule in January 1806. In February he reached Baku, intending to impose Russian authority on the local khan. On 20 February 1806, the Khan of Baku agreed to personally meet Tsitsianov and sign the pledge. An overconfident Tsitsianov rode to the meeting accompanied only by his adjutant. Shortly after his arrival, he and his adjutant were hacked to death by the Khan's guards. Their bodies were thrown into a ditch near the city walls. After the Russians captured Baku a few months later, Tsitsianov's body was recovered and buried in the local Armenian Church. Five years later, his remais were transferred to the Zion Cathedral in Tbilisi (Georgia).

TSVILENEV, Alexander Ivanovich (b. 1769 — d. 12 June 1824) was born to a petty noble family from Smolensk *gubernia*. He enlisted as a furier (fourrier) in the Life Guard Semeyonovsk Regiment on 1 April 1784, rising to a kaptenarmus on 12 January 1785, and to sergeant in 1786. He participated in the Russo-Swedish War from 1788-1790 and served on the galley flotilla in 1789. He transferred as a captain to the Belozersk Infantry Regiment on 12 January 1790, and to the Moscow Grenadier Regiment on 23 January 1793. Tsvilenev served in Poland fighting at Sventsyani, Oshmyani, and Vilna (promoted to major). He was appointed to the Pavlovsk Grenadier Regiment on 17 December 1796, became commander of this regiment on 28 May 1799, and was promoted to lieutenant colonel on 30 July 1799.

Tsvilenev took part in the expedition to Holland and fought at Heldern and Bergen. For his actions, he was awarded the Order of St. John of Jerusalem and was promoted to colonel on 24 October 1800. In 1805, he was serving with Tolstoy's Corps in northern Germany. The following year he was appointed chef of the New Ingermanland Musketeer Regiment on 4 April and attached to the Army of the Dniester. He took part in the opening moves of the Russo-Turkish War and fought at Braila and Silistra in 1806-1807, garnering a golden sword for his actions. In 1809, Tsvilenev was garrisoned at Jassy and did not take part in any actions. In early 1810, he was assigned to Major General Isaev's detachment on the Serbian border and fought at Dudu (Order of St. George, 4th class, 14 May 1810), Praiova, Negotin, Kladovo, and Bregov. He was promoted to major general on 7 October 1810, with seniority dating from 6 October. Tsvilenev's regiment was attached to the newly established army under Prince Bagration in the Podolsk *gubernia* in early 1811, and a year later Tsivilenev assumed command of the 2nd Brigade of the 1st Grenadier Division of the 3rd Corps in the 1st Western Army.

Tsvilenev served well during the Russian Campaign of 1812, fighting at Lubino, Borodino (Order of St. Anna, 1st class), Tarutino, Maloyaroslavets (remained in reserve), and Krasnyi (Order of St. George, 3rd class, 15 June 1813). In 1813, he took part in battles at Lutzen (replaced Konovnitsyn as commander of the 1st Grenadier Division, golden sword with diamonds), Bautzen (in reserve), and Dresden (in reserve). He was seriously wounded in the right hand leading the 1st Grenadier Division at Kulm and received the Order of St. Vladimir, (2nd class) and the Prussian Order of Red Eagle. He left the army to recuperate and did not participate in the balance of the 1813-1814 Campaigns.

After the occupation of Paris, Tsvilenev led the 11th Division of the 4th Corps in late 1814, and marched back to France in 1815. After participating in the grand parade at Vertus, he was promoted to lieutenant general on 11 September 1815. He commanded the 11th Division for the next five years, was relieved of command on 6 August 1820, but restored on 8 October 1823. He resigned because of poor health on 25 April 1824, and died on 12 June at Starodub.

TSVILENEV, Ivan Petrovich (b. 1784 — date of death unclear) was born to a noble family in the Kaluga *guberniia*. He graduated from the 2nd Cadet Corps and began service as a sub-lieutenant in the 2nd Horse Artillery Battalion in 1804. He took part in the 1807 Campaign, earned promotion to lieutenant on 29 January 1807, and subsequently fought at Eylau, Heilsberg, and Friedland. He transferred to the 2nd Horse Company of the 1st Reserve Artillery Brigade on 13 March 1811. During the 1812 Campaign, he served at Smolensk, Borodino, Mozhaisk, Borisov, Oshmyani, and Vilno. He was promoted to captain on 14 December 1812.

Another **Tsvilenev, Prokhor Grigorievich**, directed the Tula weapon factory during the Napoleonic Wars.

TSYBULSKY, Ivan Denisovich (b. 1771 — d. 1837) was born to a noble family in the Smolensk *guberniia*. He enlisted in the Guard on 18 October 1789 and transferred to the Baltic fleet on 26 May 1792. After briefly leaving the service in October 1796, he joined the Pavlovsk Grenadier Regiment with the rank of captain in November and was soon transferred to the Life Guard Semeyonovsk Regiment. He became a colonel on 3 January 1799, and rose to major general and chef of the Ufa Musketeer Regiment on 31 May 1800. He served under Prince Sergey Golitsyn in the 1809 Campaign against Austria.

Tsybulsky led the 1st Brigade of the 24th Division, 6th Corps, 2nd Western Army, during the Russian Campaign of 1812. He took part in Prince Bagration's retreat to Smolensk and distinguished himself defending the Great Redoubt at Borodino, where he was twice wounded. After recuperating, he returned to the army and took part in the battle at Maloyaroslavets.

In November 1812-1814, he used a brigade of the 27th Division to secure order in the Smolensk *guberniia*, and became commander of a brigade of the 24th Division in late 1814. He was relieved of command on 23 September 1816, and retired on 26 January 1834.

TUCHKOV (Tuchkov IV), Alexander Alekseyevich (b. 18 March 1777, Kiev — d. 7 September 1812, Borodino) was born to a prominent Russian noble family; his ancestors immigrated from Prussia in the 13th century and Tuchkov's father, Aleksey, served as the Senator and lieutenant general of engineer troops under Empress Catherine II. Alexander Tuchkov was enlisted as a shtyk-junker in the Bombardier Regiment in 1788, served as a flügel adjutant and adjutant general to his father in 1789-1791, and was appointed captain of the 2nd Artillery Battalion on 8 July 1794. In 1795-1797, he served in succession in the Merten's Artillery Battalion, 6th Artillery Regiment, 12th Artillery Regiment, and 1st Artillery Battalion (promoted to major in 1797). Tuchkov rose to lieutenant colonel in 1798, colonel on 6 May 1799, and was appointed commander of the 6th Artillery Regiment on 27 November 1800.

Tuchkov retired in 1801 and traveled throughout Europe. He returned to military service in 1804 and was appointed to the Murom Musketeer Regiment. In 1806, he transferred to the Tavrida Grenadier Regiment and fought the French at Golymin (Order of St. Vladimir, 4th class). Tuchkov became chef of the Revel Musketeer regiment on 15 December 1806. In early 1807, he was attached to the 6th Division and did not take part in the battle of Eylau. In June 1807, he served in Prince Bagration's advance guard at Guttstadt (Order of St. George, 4th class, 8 January 1808) and distinguished himself at Deppen, Heilsberg, and Friedland (Order of St. Vladimir, 3rd class). In 1808, he was attached to Barclay de Tolly's corps and operated in Savolax region in north Finland, fighting at Kuopio and Idensalmi. Tuchkov was promoted to major general on 24 December 1808, and led the advance guard of Prince Shuvalov's corps operating at Tornea in March 1809.

In May 1809, Tuchkov led a daring march across the thawing ice on the Gulf of Bothnia to capture Skelleftea, a move that earned him the Order of St. Anna (2nd class) with diamond signs. In June 1809, he became a duty general to Barclay de Tolly and remained in Finland until April 1810. During the Russian Campaign of 1812, he commanded the 1st Brigade of the 3rd Division, 3rd Corps, 1st Western Army, and with it fought at Vitebsk, Smolensk, and Lubino. At Borodino, Tuchkov commanded a brigade under his brother Nikolay Tuchkov's corps at Utitsa. During the fighting, he personally led the counterattack of the Revel Musketeer Regiment, but was killed when several cannonballs ripped him apart. His body was never found and his remains were presumably buried in a common grave. His wife, Margarita Tuchkov, built a church on the site of Tuchkov's death in 1820.

TUCHKOV (Tuchkov I), Nikolay Alekseyevich (b. 27 April 1765, Kiev — d. 11 November 1812, Jaroslavl) was enrolled as a conductor in the Engineer Corps on 27 March 1773, and began active service as a sergeant in the artillery in 1778. He was appointed flügel adjutant to general-feldzugmeister in September 1778, then transferred as a sub-lieutenant to the Canonier Regiment in 1783 and became adjutant general to General-Feldzugmeister Müller-Zakomelsky in 1785. Tuchkov was promoted to captain of the Bombardier Regiment in 1787, and participated in the Russo-Swedish War in 1788-1790. He transferred as a major to Muromsk Infantry Regiment in 1791, and served in Poland in 1792-1794, fighting at Nesvizh, Zelva, Brest-Litovsk, and Warsaw. At Maciejowice, he led a battalion of the Velikolutsk Musketeer Regiment and captured the local castle and a gun. For his actions, he was sent with the good news to Catherine the Great, who awarded Tuchkov with the Order of St. George (4th class). He was promoted to colonel and transferred to the Belozersk Infantry Regiment on 15 October 1794.

Tuchkov became major general and chef of the Sevsk Musketeer Regiment on 15 October 1797. Between 11 November 1798 and 9 April 1801, this regiment was named after its chef as the Tuchkov I's Musketeer Regiment. In 1799, he served in General Rimsky-Korsakov's corps and distinguished himself at Zurich. His actions in this capacity earned him a promotion to lieutenant general on 24 September 1799, and he was appointed infantry inspector in the Lifland Inspection on 2 October 1800. Tuchkov served in the Inspection for the next four years before joining Bennigsen's corps during the 1805 Campaign. His troops reached Silesia by December 1805, but had to return to Russia after the disastrous battle of Austerlitz. In 1806, he was given command of the 5th Division in Buxhöwden's corps. Tuchkov remained in reserve during the battles of Pultusk and Golymin. He took part in the council of war at Novogrod and led the Russian right wing during the offensive in early January 1807.

Tuchkov assumed command of the corps on 26 January 1807, and covered the right flank at Eylau (Order of St. Vladimir, 3rd class, and the Prussian Red Eagle). In April, Tuchkov was given command of Essen's corps and fought with it on the Narew River. After the Treaty of Tilsit, Tuchkov participated in the invasion of Finland and operated in the north. He occupied Kuopio in early March and advanced to Vaasa. Unable to halt the Swedish offensive in April 1808, he was recalled to the headquarters at Abo, where he arrived in time to command troops against a Swedish landing force. Tuchkov led the Russian troops in Savolax region and fought at Idensalmi in October 1808. He took a prolonged furlough because of poor health in November 1808 and was awarded the Order of St. Alexander of Neva. Tuchkov was appointed the Military Governor of Kamenets-Podolsk on 20 January 1811, and took command of the 3rd Corps in the 1st Western Army in early 1812.

During the 1812 Campaign, Tuchkov fought at Ostrovno, Vitebsk, and Smolensk. He and his brother, Pavel Tuchkov III, distinguished themselves in the battle at Valutina Gora (Lubino). At Borodino, Tuchkov's corps was deployed on the extreme left flank, where it repulsed Prince Poniatowski's attacks at Utitsa. Tuchkov was severely wounded in the chest while leading a bayonet attack of the Pavlovsk Grenadier Regiment. He was transported to Jaroslavl, where he died on 11 November 1812. He was buried at Tolgsk Monastery,

TUCHKOV (Tuchkov III), Pavel Alekseyevich (b. 1776, Vyborg — d. 5 February 1858, St. Petersburg) enlisted as a sergeant in the Bombardier Regiment on 29 December 1785, and served as an adjutant to his father in 1787. He became a shtyk-junker in 1788, and captain of the 2nd Bombardier Regiment on 4 August 1791. He was promoted to major in early 1797, and served in von Mertens' (later Baturin's) Artillery Battalion. At a military parade in 1798, he was promoted to lieutenant colonel and appointed to the Life Guard Artillery Battalion, earning the Order of St. Anna. He became a colonel and received the Order of St. John of Jerusalem in 1799. Tuchkov was promoted to major general and appointed chef of the 1st Artillery Colonel on 20 October 1800. Three years later, he became chef of the 9th Artillery Regiment on 30 June, but retired on 18 November. He returned to service on 23 March 1807, and was appointed chef of the Wilmandstrand Musketeer Regiment.

Tuchkov led the 1st Brigade of the 17th Division in 1807, but did not take part in operations in Poland. In 1808, he participated in Russo-Swedish War and commanded a detachment of 17th Division. He fought in the actions at Kuskoski, Helsingfors, Tavastheus, Sveaborg, Gangud (Hango), and defended the coastline of southern Finland. For his actions, he was awarded the Order of St. Anna (1st class). Tuchkov defended the islands of Sando and Kimiton in the summer of 1808, led a corps at Uleaborg in late 1808, and participated in Prince Bagration's advance across the frozen Gulf of Bothnia to the Aland Islands in March 1809. In 1810, Tuchkov commanded a brigade of the 17th Division, attached to the 1st Western Army, and helped in the construction of the fortress of Dünaburg. In early 1812, his brigade was attached to the 2nd Corps in the 1st Western Army.

During the Russian Campaign of 1812, Tuchkov fought at Orzhishki, Koltyniani, and commanded the Russian rear guard during the retreat of the 1st Western Army to Smolensk. After the Battle of Smolensk, Tuchkov was dispatched ahead of his brother Nikolay Tuchkov I's corps to defend the road junction at Lubino (Valutina Gora). He anticipated the French troops there and resolutely defended his positions against the superior enemy. In the evening, he led a counterattack with the Ekaterinoslavl Grenadier Regiment, but was captured after receiving a bayonet wound to the abdomen and several saber cuts to the head. He was well-treated by Marshal Alexander Berthier, who kept him at his quarters and loaned him 6,000 franks. Napoleon interviewed Tuchkov on 25 August 1812, and offered to deliver a peace proposal to Emperor Alexander, which Tuchkov declined. That fall, Tuchkov was transported to Metz. He remained in captivity for the next two years. After receiving an allowance of 2,000 franks from the French government, he was transferred to Brittany in January 1814. Tuchkov was finally released in April 1814, and after a six-month leave, returned to the Russian army.

Tuchkov served under General Rayevsky during the Russian advance to France in 1815 and took command of the 8th Division on 16 December 1815. He retired on 21 February 1819, and was awarded the Order of St. George (4th class) for twenty-five years of service. Tuchkov was appointed to the Senate in 1828 and chaired various charity societies. He was awarded the Order of St. Anna (1st class) and Order of St. Vladimir (2nd class) in 1831, Order of the White Eagle in 1834, Order of St. Alexander of Neva in 1838, the diamond signs of the Order of St. Alexander of Neva in 1842, and the Order of St. Vladimir (1st class) in 1845. He became privy counsellor in 1840 and died on 5 February 1858, in St. Petersburg.

TUCHKOV (Tuchkov II), Sergey Alekseyevich (b. 12 October 1767 — d. 15 February 1839, Moscow) enlisted in the 2nd Fusilier Regiment on 26 February 1773. He began active service as a sergeant on 15 July 1783, and was promoted to sub-lieutenant on 14 March 1785. During the Russo-Swedish War in 1788-1790, Tuchkov served on galley fleet and participated in several naval battles. In the Battle of Rochensalmi, he was wounded and later awarded a golden sword. In 1794, he commanded a horse artillery battalion in Poland and distinguished himself at Vilna (Order of St. Vladimir, 4th class) and Praga (golden cross, promoted to premier major). In 1796, Tuchkov participated in the Persian Campaign, fighting at Derbent and on the Iori River. His actions again earned the attention of his superiors, and he was promoted to lieutenant colonel on 22 December 1797, and commander of the Fanagoria Grenadier Regiment on 19 July 1798.

Tuchkov was elevated again, this time to major general, and appointed chef of the Caucasus Grenadier Regiment on 22 November 1798. He remained in the Transcaucasia for the next six years, fighting the Chechens, Circassians, Turks, and Persians. He retired on 30 November 1804, but returned to service two years later, becoming chef of the Kamchatka Musketeer Regiment on 5 September 1806. In 1808, he was sent to the Army of Moldavia and took part in operations in the Danube Valley. However, he was accused of abandoning the siege of Silistra in 1810 and was under investigation for the next four years.

Tuchkov served as a duty officer in the headquarters of the Army of Danube in 1811 and commanded the 2nd Reserve Corps at Mozyr in 1812. He took part in the operation on the

Berezina River in November 1812, and later served in the sieges of Modlin and Magdeburg in 1813. He became the Military Governor of Babadag in 1826, rose to lieutenant general on 26 April 1829, and assumed the role of Commandant of Ismail on 8 January 1830. He founded the small town of Tuchkov near Ismail and retired in 1836.

TUMANSKY, Gregory Vasilievich, commanded the Malorossiiskii (Little Russia) Grenadier Regiment between 6 January 1798 and 18 December 1799. Promoted to major general on 18 December 1799, he led the Astrakhan Grenadier Regiment until 28 March 1807, serving with the 9th Division in Poland in 1806-1807.

TURCHANINOV, Andrey Petrovich (b. 1779 — d. 1830) was born to a wealthy noble family from the Moghilev *gubernia*; his father was a secretary to Catherine II. Turchaninov began service as a sub-ensign in the Life Guard Preobrazhensk Regiment on 7 June 1795, transferred to the Life Guard Jager Battalion, and rose to ensign on 17 June 1799. In 1805, his regiment joined Kutuzov's army at Olmutz and Turchaninov fought at Austerlitz, where he was wounded in the right leg. His battalion was transformed into the Life Guard Jager Regiment on 22 May 1806. During the Polish Campaign in 1807, he fought at Guttstadt, Heilsberg, and Friedland. In 1808-1809, Turchaninov served in Finland and was appointed commander of the 3rd Jager Regiment on 20 March 1810.

During the Russian Campaign of 1812, Turchaninov served with the 6th Division in Finland and fought at Riga, Eckau, Polotsk, Chashniky (wounded), and Smolyani. In 1813, he took part in the siege of Danzig and was promoted to major general on 27 September 1813, with seniority dating from 1 September 1813. After the war, Turchaninov served in the 23rd Division in 1815, and commanded the 3rd Brigade of the 23rd Division and then the 2nd Brigade of the 20th Division from 1816-1826. He became commander of the 22nd Division on 18 December 1826, and was promoted to lieutenant general on 18 December 1828. Turchaninov was appointed the Commandant of Sebastopol on 15 September 1829. After a mutiny in 1830, he was court martialed for failing to suppress it, reduced in ranks, and stripped of his decorations.

TURCHANINOV, Pavel Petrovich (b. 1776 — d. 6 March 1839) was born to a noble family in the Moghilev *gubernia*; the brother of Andrey Turchaninov. He was enlisted as a sergeant in the Life Guard Preobrazhensk Regiment on 29 August 1789, and rose to ensign on 29 October 1794. During the Russo-Swedish War of 1788-1790, he served on the galley fleet of Prince Nassau Zigen and was awarded a golden medal. He joined the Old Ingermanland Infantry Regiment with the rank of captain on 14 March 1796, and served as an adjutant to General Alexander Suvorov. Turchaninov was promoted to second major on 9 July 1796, and to major on 10 December 1796. In 1797-1798, he served on a special mission to contain the cholera epidemic in the Ukraine. In 1799, he took part in the expedition to Holland and was seriously wounded at Alkmar.

Turchaninov was promoted to lieutenant colonel on 28 January 1800. He retired on 28 June of that year, but returned to service the following May to become commander of the Arkhangelogorod Musketeer Regiment on 2 October 1801. He was put in charge of the Ekaterinoslavl Grenadier Regiment on 16

January 1805 and served in General Essen I's corps. He was promoted to colonel on 5 May 1806, and was attached to the 7th Division of Buxhöwden's corps. He participated in the 1806-1807 Campaigns in Poland and distinguished himself at Golymin (golden sword), Mohrungen, Eylau (Order of St. George, 4th class, 8 May 1807, and the Prussian Pour le Merite), Liebstadt (Order of St. Vladimir, 4th class), Heilsberg (wounded in the right thigh), and Friedland, where he commanded the 7th Division and earned the Order of St. Anna (2nd class).

Turchaninov was appointed chef of the Olonetsk Musketeer Regiment on 19 February 1808, and led the 1st Brigade of the 22nd Division of the Army of Moldavia. In 1809-1811, he participated in the actions at Giurgiu, Kladovo, the Island of Oltmar, Brza-Palanka, Praiova (received diamond signs of Order of St. Anna, 2nd class), Bregov (Order of St. Vladimir, 3rd class), Gurgusovtsy (promoted to major general on 5 January 1811), and Lovcha. Turchaninov distinguished himself during the entrapment of the Turkish army at Ruse in 1811, and was awarded a golden sword with diamonds and appointed a duty general to General Mikhail Kutuzov. He took command of the 2nd Brigade of the 22nd Division in June 1812, and served in the reserve corps of Lieutenant General Sabaneyev.

During the Russian Campaign of 1812, Turchaninov was attached to Lieutenant General Sacken's Corps in October and he took part in the combats at Pruzhani, Gornostaevichi, and Volkovisk. In early 1813, he served under Lieutenant General Saint Priest at Glogau and fought at Waldheim, Nossen, Dresden, Weissig, Bischofswerde, Bautzen, Reichenbach, Lauban, Lewenberg, Goldberg, and Klein Rosen. In June 1813, he took command of the 22nd Division attached to the 10th Corps of the Army of Silesia. He fought at Katzbach and Lobau (awarded the Order of St. Anna, 1st class, with diamonds), on the Bobr River and at Leipzig (Orders of St. Vladimir, 2nd class, Swedish Order of the Sword, and the Prussian Order of Red Eagle). From December 1813 to February 1814, he participated in the blockade of Kassel.

During the 1814 Campaign, Turchaninov fought at Soisson, Laon, and Paris. In 1815, he commanded the 1st Brigade of the 22nd Division before becoming assistant to the commander of the 22nd Division on 24 December 1816, commander of the 1st Brigade of the 14th Division on 7 December 1818, and commander of the 13th Division on 24 September 1824. Turchaninov resigned from his position to arrange his family affairs on 22 July 1826, and was appointed the Commandant of Abo on 9 October 1829. He became the Military Governor of Podolsk on 6 January 1835, Military Governor of Kaments and the Civil Governor of the Podolsk *gubernia* on 24 February 1835, and the Commandant of Kiev on 29 October 1835.

TVOROGOV, Stepan Trofimovich (b. 1769 — date of unknown; removed from rosters on 29 April 1816) was born to a noble family in the St. Petersburg *gubernia*. He studied in the Artillery and Engineer Cadet Corps and enlisted as a sergeant in the 1st Cannonier Regiment on 20 December 1780. He was discharged from service with the rank of shtyk-junker on 23 Jaanuary 1783, but returned to the service the following year and served as a sub-lieutenant in the Permsk Infantry Regiment (30 June 1784). He tranferred to the artillery in 1786 and was promoted to lieutenant on 12 June 1788. Serving in the Black Sea Fleet, he participated in the Russo-Turkish War in 1789-1791 and fought in the naval battle at Ochakov (Order of St. George, 4th class, 11 August 1788). In

1789-1791, he served at Hajibey (Odessa), Akkerman, Ismail (promoted to captain), and Macin.

Tvorogov transferred to the Caspian Sea Flotilla in 1796 and commanded the schooner *St. Olga* during the Persian Campaign. He joined the 1st Siege Artillery Battalion on 27 February 1797, and served in the 11th Artillery Battalion (June 1799). He became adjutant to General Aleksey Arakcheyev on 4 June 1803, and participated in the 1805 Campaign, where he distinguished himself at Austerlitz (golden sword). Returning to Russia, Tvorogov was appointed commander of the St. Petersburg Reserve Artillery Brigade on 4 September 1806. He became a flügel-adjutant to Alexander on 2 January 1808, and during the Russo-Swedish War in 1808-1809, served at the fortress of Sveaborg (Order of St. Anna, 2nd class). He was appointed duty general in the Ministry of Navy on 18 June 1811, and conferred the rank of captain (1st class) of the naval artillery. Late that year, he was promoted to zeichmeister with a major general's rank on 24 December.

During the Russian Campaign of 1812, Tvorogov took part in the organization of the St. Petersburg *Opolchenye* and led an *opolchenye* artillery company. He joined the main army in late 1812 and fought at Stakhov, Smorgon, Oschmyani, Vilna, and Kovno. In 1813, he served at Danzig and was awarded a golden sword. He was appointed adjutant to the Minister of War on 7 September 1814.

TYRTOV, Ivan Alexandrovich (b. 1791 — date of death unclear) graduated from the 2nd Cadet Corps and began service as a sub-lieutenant in the 18th Artillery Brigade on 27 November 1807. He served in the Danubian Principalities in 1810-1811, and fought at Bazardjik (golden medal and Imperial letter of gratitude), Batin, Silistra, and Ruse. He was promoted to lieutenant on 21 February 1811. In 1812, he took part in the actions at Kobryn, Gorodechnya (Order of St. Order, 3rd class), Stakhovo, and Brilev (Order of St. Vladimir, 4th class). In 1813, he served at Thorn, Katzbach, and participated in some minor actions in 1814.

UDOM (Udom I), Ivan Fedorovich (b. 9 November 1768 — 30 July 1821) was born to a noble family in the Lifland *gubernia*. He enlisted in the Life Guard Preobrazhensk Regiment on 18 March 1782, and took part in the Russo-Swedish War in 1788. He transferred as a captain to the Uglitsk Infantry Regiment on 12 January 1789, and as a major to the Life Grenadier Regiment in November 1789. He participated in the Russo-Turkish War in 1789-1791, fighting at Salche, Braila, Tulcea, Babadag, and Macin, and then served in Poland from 1792-1794. He became a flügel adjutant on 17 April 1801, and was promoted to colonel on 26 August 1805. Udom distinguished himself at Austerlitz in 1805 and in 1807, fought at Eylau, Guttstadt (received the Order of St. George, 4th class), Heilsberg, and Friedland. He was appointed chef of the Keksholm (Kexholm) Musketeer Regiment on 24 December 1810, and commander of the Life Guard Lithuanian Regiment on 1 December 1811.

During the 1812 Campaign, Udom served in the Guard Division of the 5th Guard Corps and fought at Vitebsk and Smolensk. He stood out at Borodino (wounded in the hand) and received a promotion to major general on 3 December 1812, with seniority dating from 7 September. In October-November, he fought at Tarutino, Maloyaroslavets, and Krasnyi. In 1813-1814, he participated in the battles at Lutzen, Bautzen, Dresden, Kulm, Leipzig, Brienne, and Paris.

After the war, he commanded the 1st Brigade of the 2nd Guard Division and was appointed to the Imperial Retinue on 25 April 1819. He became commander of the Life Guard Semeyonovsk Regiment on 5 February 1821, but died a few months later on 30 July.

UDOM (Udom II), Yevstafiy Yevstafievich (b. 1760 — d. 1836) was born to a petty noble family in the Lifland *gubernia*. He enlisted as a sergeant in the Nasheburg Infantry Regiment on 13 July 1771, and served in Poland for the next eight years. Promoted first to ensign on 10 June 1776, then to sub-lieutenant in 1778, Udom transferred as a lieutenant to the Uglitsk Infantry Regiment in 1779, and became a captain in 1783. He took part in the Russo-Turkish War in 1787-1791, fighting at Gangur, Ismail, Bender, and Macin. Transferred to the Siberia Grenadier Regiment in late 1791, he took part in the operations in Poland in 1792-1794, fighting at Dubenka (Order of St. George, 4th class) and Warsaw. He became a second major on 10 September 1796, lieutenant colonel in 1799, and colonel on 26 September 1803.

In 1804-1806, Udom served on the naval squadron in the Black and Mediterranean Seas. He took part in the operations at Corfu and Naples. Returning to Russia, he was appointed chef of the Galicia Musketeer Regiment on 25 September 1806, and took part in the 1809 Campaign against Austria. After his regiment was converted into the 38th Jager Regiment, Udom became its chef on 31 October 1810. In 1810-1811, he served in the Danubian Principalities, leading a brigade in St. Priest's detachment and distinguishing himself at Lovchea. He was promoted to major general on 12 March 1811. Udom accompanied General Arkadii Suvorov (the son of Field Marshal Alexander Suvorov) to the Danubian Principalities and barely survived when their carriage was swept away by the flooding Rimnic River; Suvorov, who was not as fortunate drowned. In the summer of 1811, Udom participated in the operations around Ruse and was deployed at Slobodzea. After the victory at Ruse, he was honored with the Order of St. Anna.

During the 1812 Campaign, Udom served with the 3rd Brigade, 9th Division, 3rd Reserve Army of Observation, and fought at Kobryn, Divino, and Tukhenichi, where he was severely wounded in the left leg and lost some of his toes. After recuperating, he returned to the army in early 1813 and led a brigade of the 10th and 38th Jager Regiments. He took part in minor actions (Löwenberg, Goldberg) in Silesia in August 1813 and distinguished himself at Katzbach (Order of St. Vladimir, 3rd class, and Prussian Order of Red Eagle), and Leipzig (golden sword with diamonds and Swedish Order of the Sword). In December 1813, he served at Cassel, and in 1814 fought at Brienne (Order of St. Vladimir, 2nd class), Champaubert, Soissons, Laon, and Paris.

Returning to Russia, Udom was dispatched with the 9th Division back to France during the Hundred Days and served in the blockade of Metz. He took part in the grand parade at Vertus and was awarded the French Legion of Honor. He took command of the 9th Division on 6 January 1816, and remained with the occupational forces in France for two years. He was promoted to lieutenant general on 24 December 1824 and relieved of command on 19 September 1826. Udom became Commandant of Riga on 1 August 1827, was relieved of command on 10 November 1828, and discharged with a pension on 3 November 1833.

ULAN (Ulan IV) David Aleksandrovich rose to command the Tatar Lithuanian Horse Regiment on 19 June 1801, and became commander of the Tatar Horse Regiment on 17 November 1803. Promoted to colonel on 24 December 1808, he led the Narva Dragoon Regiment from 18 February 1813 to 22 October 1814.

ULANIUS, Karl Karlovich (b. 1762 – d. 1808) served as an adjutant in the 1st Battalion of the Bug Jager Corps in 1785, and participated in the Russo-Turkish War in 1787-1791. He served in Poland from 1792-1794, rising to second major in the Bug Jager Corps. He commanded the Old Ingermanland Musketeer Regiment between 14 February 1800 and 2 July 1804, and served as chef of the 6th Jager Regiment in 2 July 1804 – 23 November 1808. He became major general on 13 November 1804. In 1805-1807, Ulanius served under Prince Bagration in Moravia and Poland, and in 1808, commanded the advance guard of General Miloradovich's corps in the Danubian Principalities, where he died in November 1808.

ULANOV, Gabriel Petrovich (b. 1753 — date of death unknown; excluded from rosters on 30 January 1819) was born to a petty noble family. He enlisted as a corporal in the New Ladoga (*Novoladozhski kanal*) Battalion on 23 November 1772, and transferred to the Bombardier Regiment two years later. He became a sub-lieutenant on 22 May 1784, and took part in the Russo-Turkish War in 1787-1791. Ulanov was wounded at Ochakov, and also fought at Akkerman, Bender, and Killia. He briefly served as Commandant of Tiraspol in 1797 and rose to colonel on 4 December 1798. He participated in the 1799 Campaign in Italy and Switzerland, and was wounded at Mantua.

After returning to Russia, Ulanov was made a major general and chef of the 3rd Siege Artillery

Battalion on 19 September 1802, and commander of the 2nd Artillery Regiment on 30 June 1803. In 1805, he served in General Tolstoy's corps in northern Germany. Ulanov was given the command of the Riga Citadel Artillery Garrison on 9 March 1806, and made commander of the Okhtensk gunpowder factory on 29 January 1807. He became the head of the Riga supply depot on 21 June 1808, and was put in charge of the Riga Artillery Garrison on 16 March 1810. He became the Commandant of Dünaburg on 19 October 1810. During the 1812 Campaign, he defended Dünaburg from 12-27 July, and then joined the 1st Western Army. He became head of the artillery garrisons of the St. Petersburg District on 22 August 1814.

ULRICHSEN Karl Grigorievich took command of the Dnieper Musketeer Regiment on 11 February 1808. He earned promotion to lieutenant colonel on 26 June 1810 and became commander of the Estland Infantry Regiment on 20 November 1811 before rising to colonel on 30 October 1812.

UMANETS, Andrey Semenovich (b. 1761 — d. 1828, Stary Bikhov) was born to a noble family in the Chernigov *gubernia*. He graduated from the Infantry Cadet Corps and enlisted as a lieutenant in the Staroskol Infantry Regiment in 1782. After a transfer to the Glukhov Carabineer Regiment on 12 August 1787, he took part in the Russo-Turkish War in 1788-1791, fighting at Khotin (became a rotmistr in 1789), Salche, Ismail, Babadag, and Macin. In 1792-1794, he served in Poland and participated in the actions at Brest, Kobylka, and Praga, for which he received a cross. He was promoted to second major in 1795, to lieutenant colonel in 1798, and to colonel in 1800. His carabineer unit was converted to a cuirassier regiment in August 1798.

Umanets was appointed chef of the Kinburn Dragoon Regiment on 23 February 1808, and participated in the Russo-Turkish War. In 1809, he fought at Rassevat and Silistra. In 1810, he took part in the capture of Silistra (Order of St. Vladimir, 4th class), and in the actions at Ruse and Nikopol. The next year, 1811, he participated in the battle at Ruse but his regiment was routed by the Turks. Despite Imperial reprimands, Umanets was awarded a golden sword for courage. In late 1811, he took part in the entrapment of the Ottoman army on the Danube River and was promoted to major general. During the 1812 Campaign, he served in the 3rd Reserve Army of Observation and fought at Pavlovichi, Lubomle, and Stakhov, for which he earned the Order of St. Vladimir (3rd class).

In 1813, Umanets took part in the actions at Koenigswarta, Bautzen (Order of St. Anna, 2nd class, with diamonds), and Leignitz. He was later attached to Korff's corps of the Army of Silesia and fought at the Katzbach (golden sword with diamonds) and Leipzig. In 1814, he fought at Brienne (Order of St. Anna, 1st class), Montmirail, Chateau Thierry, Craonne, and Le Fère Champenoise (Order of St. Anna, 1st class, with diamonds and Prussian Order of Red Eagle).

After the war, Umanets served as an assistant to the commander of the 3rd Dragoon Division and became the head of the Field Audit of the 1st Army on 28 March 1817. He was promoted to lieutenant general on 24 December 1824, and retired four years later because of poor health.

URAKOV, Aleksey Vasilievich, colonel, commanded the Ufa Musketeer Regiment from 13 March 1801 - 24 January 1803, and the Rylsk Musketeer Regiment between 16 October 1804 and 1 July 1806. He served as chef of the Revel Musketeer Regiment from July to December 1806, and as chef of the Tiflis Musketeer Regiment from 9 July 1807 to 30 October 1808.

URAKOV, Ivan Afanasievich commanded the Uglitsk Musketeer Regiment from March 1800 to December 1802, and May 1806 to October 1808. Promoted to colonel on 5 May 1806, he served as chef of the Tiflis Musketeer Regiment from 30 October 1808 to 22 November 1811.

URUSOV (Urusov II), Alexander Petrovich (b. 1768 — d. 29 October 1835) was born to a prominent Russian family of princes. He enlisted in the Life Guard Preobrazhensk Regiment on 14 January 1779, transferred as a captain to the Navaginsk Infantry Regiment on 12 January 1790, and participated in the final stage of the Russo-Swedish War. He was promoted to colonel on 27 February 1790. Urusov was appointed commander of the Ladoga Musketeer Regiment on 8 August 1804, and was promoted to major general and appointed chef of the Kaluga Musketeer Regiment on 16 September 1805. However, Urusov was relieved of command in November 1806 for failing to adequately maintain his unit.

He returned to military service in 1812 and was appointed brigade commander in the 4th Corps on 9 September. He took part in actions at Voronovo, Vyazma, and Vilna. In 1813, he commanded the 8th Division and fought at Nossen, Dresden, Bautzen, Goldberg, and Leipzig. In 1814, Urusov's command was routed at Etoges, where he was wounded three times and captured. He was soon released and retired on 25 December 1814.

URUSOV, Nikolay Yurievich (b. 1767 — d. 16 August 1821) was born to a Russian noble family. He enlisted in the Life Guard Preobrazhensk Regiment on 18 August 1778, and was promoted to ensign on 12 January 1789. He took part in the Russo-Swedish War in 1789-1790. He was promoted to colonel in February 1798, and the following year he rose to major general, commandant of Astrakhan, and commander of the local garrison on 21 January. He retired in March 1800-July 1801 and was appointed chef of the Vyatka Musketeer Regiment on 5 July 1802. He led a brigade in Dokhturov's Division in 1805 and fought at Austerlitz. In 1806, Urusov was attached to the 10th Division of Essen I's corps and fought in Poland. He retired because of poor health in January 1808, but returned to service three years later.

Urusov became the head of the 7th District of the Internal Garrisons on 5 July 1811, and during the 1812 Campaign, oversaw the formation of reserve battalions in the Yaroslavl, Kostroma, and Vladimir *gubernia*s. He led a detachment during the French retreat in late 1812 and was given command of a brigade in the 3rd Corps of the Army of Reserve in early 1813. After the war, he commanded a corps of the Internal Guard in the 9th District until he retired on 30 January 1819.

USHAKOV, Ivan Mikhaylovich (b. 1778 — date of death unknown; removed from rosters on 28 March 1840) was born to a noble family from the Kursk *gubernia*. He enlisted in the Life Guard Preobrazhensk Regiment on 26 September 1784, and rose to sub-lieutenant on 25 December 1796. He took part in the 1806-1807 Campaigns in Poland, fighting at Pultusk, Landsberg, Eylau (wounded), and Heilsberg. He served as adjutant to Generals Prozorovsky and Kutuzov in 1808-1809, and became commander of the Chernigov Musketeer Regiment on 30 March 1810.

During the 1812 Campaign, Ushakov's regiment was attached to the 1st Western Army and fought at Ostrovno and Vitebsk (promoted to colonel). He was severely wounded at Borodino when a musket ball shattered his jaw and a cannonball took off his left leg. Somehow he survived, and was awarded the Order of George (4th class) on 4 January 1813. He retired with the rank of major general on 18 March 1814.

Three years later, Ushakov returned to service and was appointed to the court of Grand Duke Nicholas on 16 August 1817. He took part in the suppression of the Decembrist Uprising in December 1825 and was appointed adjutant general to Emperor Nicholas I on 26 December 1825. He rose to lieutenant general on 3 September 1826. His later years are a mystery.

USHAKOV (Ushakov III), Pavel Nikolayevich (b. 13 November 1779, Potikino, Jaroslavl *gubernia* — 13 May 1853, St. Petersburg) was born to a prominent Russian noble family. His father served in the War College. Educated at a private boarding school in Moscow, Pavel Ushakov was enlisted as a sub-ensign in the Life Guard Preobrazhensk Regiment soon after birth in 1779. He later transferred to the Life Guard Izmailovsk Regiment, rising to ensign on 14 February 1799. He took part in the 1805 Campaign and was wounded at Austerlitz that December. In 1807, he took part in the combat at Heilsberg and was wounded in the right hand at Friedland. He was promoted to colonel on 23 August 1809.

During the 1812 Campaign, Ushakov served in the 2nd Brigade of the Guard Infantry Division of the 5th Reserve (Guard) Corps and took part in the retreat to Vitebsk. After the battle of Ostrovno, he led the Rylsk Infantry Regiment and fought at Lubino, Zabolotye, Borodino (Order of St. George, 4th class, 4 January 1813), Maloyaroslavets, Vyazma, and Krasnyi. In 1813, he served as a battalion commander in the Life Guard Izmailovsk Regiment and fought at Lutzen and Bautzen. For his conduct, he was promoted to major general on 27 September and became chef of the Poltava Infantry Regiment on 10 October. Ushakov took part in the battle of Leipzig that October and served in the siege of Hamburg in 1814.

Ushakov returned with the Russian army to France during the Hundred Days and took part in the blockade of Soissons in 1815. He briefly commanded a brigade of the 26th Division in late 1815 until he retired on 11 September 1816. He returned to the army on 16 August 1817, and led the 2nd Brigade of the 9th Division. Ushakov became commander of the 2nd Brigade of the 4th Division on 20 April 1821, commander of the 7th Division on 5 November 1824, and a lieutenant general on 3 September 1826. He participated in the Russo-Turkish War in 1828-1829 at the head of the 2nd Guard Infantry Divison (10 October 1828) and distinguished himself at Varna (Order of St. George, 3rd class).

Ushakov took command of the 1st Guard Infantry Division on 18 June 1831, and took part in the suppression of the Polish uprising, fighting at Warsaw. He was promoted to adjutant general on 18 December 1831, and led the infantry of the Independent Guard Corps on 3 August 1837. He became general of infantry on 28 April 1841, and commander of the 4th Corps on 6 November 1842. However, he was court martialed for ineffective service and embezzlement of state funds on 21 February 1853, and was sentenced to six months in jail, where he died on 13 May 1853.

Many other Ushakovs served in the Russian army during the Napoleonic Wars, including: **USHAKOV, Aleksey Aleksandrovich,** colonel, commanded the Sumsk Hussar Regiment between 11 February 1804 and 25 January 1808. He served with the 3rd Division in Poland in 1806-1807; **USHAKOV (Ushakov I), Fedor Aleksandrovich**, major general, served as chef of the Senate Regiment from April 1800-April 1801, as chef of the Lithuanian Musketeer Regiment from 10 April 1801 - 31 October 1810, and as chef of the 33rd Jager Regiment between 31 October and 8 December 1810; **USHAKOV, Fedor Ivanovich**, commanded the Caucasus Grenadier Regiment from 25 September 1807 - 15 February 1811. He took command of the Georgian Grenadier Regiment on 15 February 1811, was promoted to lieutenant colonel on 11 September 1811, and led the Vitebsk Musketeer Regiment from 12 June 1812 - 13 June 1816; **USHAKOV (Ushakov III), Ivan Fedorovich**, was given command of the Kherson Grenadier Regiment on 4 July 1800. He became major general and chef of the Vologda Musketeer Regiment on 28 May 1803; **USHAKOV (Ushakov II) Nikolay Aleksandrovich**, took command of the Lithuanian Musketeer Regiment on 26 April 1801. He rose to major general and chef of the Kurinsk Musketeer Regiment on 12 January 1803. Between 16 September 1805 and 1 October 1810, he served as chef of the Odessa Musketeer Regiment.

USHAKOV, Sergey Nikolayevich (b. 1776, Potikino, Yaroslavl *gubernia* — d. 7 March 1814, Craonne) enlisted as a vakhmistr in the Life Guard Horse Regiment on 18 March 1790, and was promoted to a cornet on 19 February 1799. He transferred to the Chevalier Guard Regiment in 1800, and was promoted to colonel on 7 June 1804. He participated in the 1805 Campaign and distinguished himself at Austerlitz at the head of a squadron of the Chevalier Guard Regiment. In 1807, he fought at Guttstadt, Heilsberg, and Friedland. He became chef of the Courland Dragoon Regiment on 22 May 1812, and served in the 3rd Cavalry Corps of the 1st Western Army. He took part in the battles at Smolensk, Borodino (Order of St. George, 4th class), Spas-Kuplia, Vyazma, Dorogobouzh, and Krasnyi (Order of St. George, 3rd class). He was promoted to major general on 18 December 1812. In 1813, he fought at Katzbach and Leipzig, but he was mortally wounded leading a charge at Craonne in 1814.

UVAROV Fedor Petrovich (b. 23 April 1773, Khruslavka, Tula *Gubernia* — 2 December 1824, St. Petersburg) was born to a petty noble family in the Tula *gubernia*. He was enlisted as a sergeant in the artillery in 1776 at the age of three, transferred as a kaptenarmus to the Life Guard Preobrazhensk Regiment in November 1780, and rose to vakhmistr in the Life Guard Horse Regiment in late 1786. His active service began as a captain of the Sofia Infantry Regiment on 12 January 1788, and served in the Olonetsk Horse Jager Squadron from 1789-1790. He became a second major in the Smolensk Dragoon Regiment in September 1790. Uvarov served in Poland in 1792-1794, fighting at Stolbtsy, Mir, Natsybov, Warsaw (promoted to premier major), Sali, and Vilna, and was promoted to lieutenant colonel on 25 May 1795. Under Paul I, he rapidly achieved promotions. Uvarov transferred to the His Majesty's Life Guard Cuirassier Regiment on 20 March 1797, became colonel on 23 April 1798, briefly served in the Zorn's Cuirassier Regiment, transferred to the Life Guard Horse Regiment on 14 September 1798, was promoted to major general, and appointed adjutant general on 30 September 1798.

Uvarov transferred to the Chevalier Guard Corps on 22 January 1799, and after reorganization of the corps, became chef of the Chevalier Guard Regiment on 21 August 1799. He was promoted to lieutenant general on 17 November 1800. Although he took part in the conspiracy against Paul, he did not play an active role in his assassination. Uvarov distinguished himself leading the Russian cavalry at Austerlitz in 1805 (Order of St. Alexander of Neva and Order of St. George, 3rd class). In 1807, he fought at Guttstadt (Order of St. Vladimir, 2nd class), Heilsberg, and Friedland (golden sword with diamonds). After the Treaty at Tilsit, he commanded the Chevalier Guard Regiment in St. Petersburg and was given command of the advance guard of the Army of Moldavia in April 1810. Uvarov took part in the actions at Silistra, Shumla, Ruse, and Batin (Order of St. George, 2nd class).

In late 1811, Uvarov was recalled to St. Petersburg and appointed commander of the 1st Reserve Cavalry Corps of the 1st Western Army in April 1812. He participated in the retreat to Smolensk and fought at Kolotsk Monastery. During the Battle of Borodino, he and Platov led their failed cavalry attack on the French left flank, whic is often referred to as "Uvarov's Diversion" or "Platov's Raid." However, both Uvarov and Cossack commander Ataman Platov failed to accomplish the assigned mission at Borodino, and (significantly) were not awarded after the battle. Ironically, the attack had a dramatic effect on Napoleon's psyche, causing him to worry about his flank enough to hold back the French Imperial Guard. After the battle, Uvarov and his command covered the retreat to Moscow, and at the council of war at Fily, urged to fight another battle. In October, Uvarov's corps remained in reserve and was not engaged at Maloyaroslavets or Krasnyi, but was involved in the fighting at Vyazma and Krasnyi.

In 1813-1814, Uvarov attended Emperor Alexander I at Lutzen, Bautzen, Dresden, Kulm, Leipzig, Brienne, Arcis sur Aube, Le Fère Champenoise, and Paris. His solid performance at Leipzig earned him a promotion to general of cavalry on 20 October 1813, and the Order of St. Vladimir (1st class) for his conduct in France.

After returning to Russia, Uvarov was involved with the committee assisting the invalides of the Napoleonic Wars and accompanied Emperor Alexander to the Congresses in Vienna, Aachen, and Lambach between 1815 and 1820. He led the Guard Corps beginning 13 November 1821, and became a member of the State Council on 11 September 1823. Uvarov was awarded the Order of St. Andrew the First Called on 24 December 1823. He became seriously ill in the summer of 1824 and died on 2 December 1824, in St. Petersburg.

V

VADBOLSKY, Ivan Mikhaylovich (b. 1781 — d. 1861) was born to a Russian family of princes. He enlisted as a sergeant in the Life Guard Preobrazhensk Regiment on 30 April 1790, and transferred to the Chevalier Guard Corps on 2 December 1796. The following year, he joined the Life Guard Horse Regiment. In 1805, he distinguished himself at Austerlitz (golden sword), and in 1807 fought at Guttstadt, Heilsberg, and Friedland (wounded in the neck, Order of St. George, 4th class, 1 June 1808, and the Prussian Pour le Merite). Vadbolsky was promoted to colonel on 24 August 1807. He rose to command the Lithuanian Uhlan Regiment on 1 January 1809, and participated in the campaign against Austria. He assumed command of the Mariupol Hussar Regiment on 1 February 1812.

During the 1812 Campaign, Vadbolsky served with the 11th Brigade, 3rd Cavalry Division, 1st Western Army, and fought at Oshmyani, Kozyani, Beshenkovichi, Vitebsk (Order of St. Vladimir, 3rd class), Smolensk (Order of St. Anna, 2nd class), Borodino (wounded in the head, second Order of St. Vladimir, 3rd class), Mozhaisk, and Znamenskoe. Vadbolsky took command of a partisan detachment on 30 September 1812, and harrassed the French lines of communications, taking part in the capture of Vereya on 10 October 1812, and was awarded his second Order of the St. Anna (2nd class). During the French Retreat, he fought at Maloyaroslavets, Vyazma, Dorogobouzh, Krasnyi and minor rearguard actions. In 1813, he was promoted to major general on 1 June 1813 and distinguished himself at Liegnitz, Bunzlau, Katzbach (received the Order of St. Anna, 1st class) and, in 1814, he fought at St. Dizier and Brienne. At La Rothière, Vadbolsky received a sabre cut to his side and was awarded the Order of St. George (3rd class) on 1 February 1814.

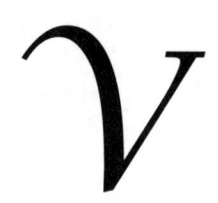

Vadbolsky became commander of the 1st Brigade of the 2nd Hussar Division on 10 September 1814, and of the 3rd Hussar Division in December 1816. He was relieved of command on 7 October 1823, and three years later, was appointed to the Independent Caucasian Corps. He served under General Ivan Paskevich during the operations against the Turks in 1826-1828, and distinguished himself at Abbas-Abad (promoted to lieutenant general on 14 October 1827). Between August 1827 and February 1828, he led the Karabakh Detachment on the Russian flank and captured the fortress of Ardebil on 14 February 1828. In August 1828, he took part in the assaults on Kars (Order of St. Vladimir, 2nd class), Akhalkalaki, Akhaltsikhe, and Atskuri. He took a furlough in late 1828 to recuperate and was relieved of command on 15 May 1829. Vadbolsky was discharged on 1 January 1834.

VADKOVSKY, Yakov (Jacob) Yegorovich (b. 1774 — d. 2 April 1820) was born to a noble family and began service in the Life Guard Preobrazhensk Regiment on 12 January 1790. He transferred as a kapenarmus to the Life Guard Semeyonovsk Regiment on 26 May 1790. In 1793, he became an ensign, and by 1800 reached the rank of colonel. He took command of the Petrov Musketeer Regiment on 5 October 1805, and became chef of the Libau Musketeer Regiment on 5 September 1806. In 1806-1807,

Vadkovsky remained in reserves in Russia and did not participate in military operations in Poland. During the Russo-Swedish War, he distinguished himself at Abo and received the Order of St. George (3rd class) on 26 June 1808. He was promoted to major general on 28 June 1808.

Vadkovsky retired because of poor health on 6 January 1812, but returned to the army on 20 August of that year. At Borodino, Vadkovsky led a brigade of the 17th Division and received the Order of St. Vladimir (3rd class). Later that year he fought at Maloyaroslavets and Krasnyi.

Vadkovsky left the army because of poor health in 1813 and was discharged from the military service on 4 July 1814. He was awarded the Order of St. Anna (1st class) with diamonds for his excellent overall service in 1812-1813.

VASILCHIKOV (Vasilchikov II in 1812), Dmitry Vasilievich (b. 1778 — date of death unclear; removed from rosters on 17 December 1859) was born to a noble family in the Pskov *gubernia*; the brother of Illarion and Nikolay Vasilchikov. He was enlisted in the Life Guard Preobrazhensk Regiment in 1785, and began service as a vakhmistr in the Life Guard Horse Regiment in 1794, rising to cornet in 1796. Emperor Paul appointed him actual kamerger in July 1799. Two years later, Vasilchikov returned to military service with the rank of rotmistr in the Chevalier Guard Regiment, and rose to colonel in 1802. During the 1807 Campaign in Poland, he distinguished himself at Guttstadt, Heilsberg, and Friedland. He transferred to the Akhtyrsk Hussar Regiment in 1809, took part in operations in Galicia, and assume command of the Akhtyrsk Hussar Regiment on 9 April 1811.

During the Russian Campaign of 1812, Vasilchikov served with the 14th Brigade, 4th Cavalry Division, 2nd Western Army, and fought at Mir, Saltanovka, Smolensk, Borodino, and Vyazma. For his service, Vasilchikov received the Order of St. George (4th class, 4 January 1813) and a promotion to major general on 7 January 1813. In 1813-1814, Vasilchikov fought at Bautzen, Katzbach, Leipzig (Order of St. George, 3rd class, 19 October 1813), La Rothière, Craonne, and Paris. In 1814-1815, he led a brigade in the 2nd Hussar Division. After the war, he took command of the 1st Uhlan Division on 9 January 1817. Poor health forced him to retire on 28 December 1822. Eight years later, he began service at the court with a rank of privy counsellor and was appointed ober-jagermeister of the Imperial Court.

Vasilchikov rose to actual privy counsellor on 2 May 1838, and supervised the construction of the Isakievsk Cathedral in St. Petersburg. He became a member of the State Council on 13 July 1846. He transferred to the military service with enlistment in the Akhtyrsk Hussar Regiment in 1858, and was promoted to general of cavalry on 11 June 1858. During his career, Vasilchikov received the Russian Orders of St. Andrew the First Called with diamonds, St. Vladimir (1st class), St. Alexander of Neva with diamonds, the White Eagle, a medal "For XLV Years of Distinguished Service," the Prussian Orders of the Red Eagle (1st class) and the Pour le Merite, and the Württemberg Order of Fridriech and Hesse-Darmstadt Order of Ludwig.

VASILCHIKOV (Vasilchikov I in 1812), Illarion Vasilievich (date of birth unclear, ca. 1775/1776 — d. 5 March 1847) was born to a noble family in the Pskov *gubernia*; brother of Dmitry and Nikolay Vasilchikov. He began service as vakhmistr in the Life Guard Horse Regiment in 1792, and rose to cornet in 1793. Emperor Paul I appointed him kamerger in

1799. Vasilchikov was promoted to major general and appointed adjutant general on 4 August 1801. Two years later, he became chef of the Akhtyrsk Hussar Regiment on 5 July 1803. During the campaigns in Poland, his regiment was attached to the 10th Division in 1806, and in 1807, distinguished himself at Guttstadt.

Vasilchikov led a brigade in the 4th Cavalry Corps in the 2nd Western Army during the 1812 Campaign. He fought at Mir, Romanovo, Saltanovka, and Smolensk (Order of St. George, 3rd class, 12 February 1813). At Borodino, he commanded the 12th Division and was wounded defending the the Great Redoubt. He was promoted for his conduct to lieutenant general on 12 November 1812, with seniority dating from 5 August 1812. In October-November 1812, Vasilchikov took command of the 4th Cavalry Corps and fought at Tarutino, Maloyaroslavets, Vyazma, Krasnyi, and on the Berezina. In 1813, he took part in the battles at Bautzen, Koenigswartha (wounded), Katzbach (golden sabre with diamonds), Dresden, and Leipzig (Russian Order of St. Alexander of Neva and the Prusian Red Eagle, 1st class). In 1814, he commanded cavalry of the Army of Silesia and fought at Brienne, La Rothière and Chateau Thierry, and received the Order of St. George (2nd class, 29 January 1814) for his service.

After the war, Vasilchikov became chef of the Life Guard Horse Jager Regiment on 15 April 1814, commander of the Guard Light Cavalry Division in 1815, and commander of the 1st Reserve Cavalry Corps on 29 July 1818. He was instrumental in suppressing the Decembrist Uprising in December 1825, for which he was awarded the Order of St. Andrew the First Called on 3 September 1826. He attended Emperor Nicholas I during the Russo-Turkish War in 1828-1829. Vasilchikov took command of the troops in St. Petersburg and its surroundings on 6 July 1831, and was conferred title of count of the Russian Empire on 18 December 1831. Vasilchikov became the head of the Department of Laws in the State Council on 13 January 1833, inspector general of cavalry on 14 April 1833, and chef of the Akhtyrsk Hussar Regiment on 30 January 1835. In 1838, he presided over the State Council and the Cabinet and received title of prince of the Russian empire on 13 January 1839. In January 1843, the Akhtyrsk Hussar Regiment was renamed Vasilchikov's Hussar Regiment, and the following year, Vasilchikov became chef of the Military Order Cuirassier Regiment on 10 May 1844.

During his career, Vasilchikov also received the Prussian Orders of Red and Black Eagles, the Austrian Order of Maria Theresa, and a medal "For XL Years of Distinguished Service."

VASILCHIKOV, Nikolay Vasilievich (b. 1781 — d. 1849) was born to a noble family from the Pskov *gubernia*; the brother of Dmitry and Illarion Vasilchikov. He began service in the Guard in 1784 and rose to cornet in 1796 and colonel in 1802. He became commander of the Pskov Dragoon Regiment on 10 October 1806. During the 1806-1807 Campaigns in Poland,

Vasilchikov distinguished himself at Eylau (Order of St. George, 4th class, on 8 May 1807). For his conduct in the spring of 1807, he also earned another Order of St. George (4th class) on 11 September 1807. He transferred to the Lifland Dragoon Regiment on 31 July 1810, and served against the Turks in the Danubian Principalities. He became chef of the Vyatka Infantry Regiment on 14 July 1812, and served with the 1st Brigade of the 22nd Division in the Army of Danube.

In late 1812, Vasilchikov took part in operations around Volkovysk (Order of St. George, 3rd class, 1 April 1813) and on the Berezina River. In 1813, he distinguished himself at Lutzen, for which he garnered promotion to major general on 27 September 1813, with seniority dating from 11 May 1813. For his service, he also received the Prussian Pour le Merite and the Red Eagle (2nd class), as well as the Swedish Order of the Sword (4th class).

After the war, Vasilchikov led several cavalry and infantry brigades before retiring on 30 January 1824. He served as governor of Orel in 1837-1841.

VASILIEV, Vasily Kuzmich (b. 1786 — date of death unclear) was born to a Russian noble family. He graduated from the 2nd Cadet Corps in 1806 and began service as a sub-lieutenant in the 3rd Artillery Regiment. In 1807, he fought at Eylau and Heilsberg. Two years later, he served under Prince Sergey Golitsyn in Galicia and was promoted to lieutenant on 19 January 1810. Vasiliev transferred to the 14th Battery Company of the 14th Artillery Brigade on 12 March 1811. During the 1812 Campaign, Vasiliev served in Wittgenstein's corps and fought at Klyastitsy, two battles of Polotsk, and Chashniki. In 1813, he took part in the battles at Pillau and Lutzen and received the Orders of St. Anna (3rd class) and of St. Vladimir (4th class).

VELIKOPOLSKY, Anton Petrovich (b. 1770 — d. 3 February 1830, St. Petersburg) was born to a noble family from the Pskov *gubernia*. He enlisted as a kaptenarmus in the Life Guard Izmailovsk Regiment on 18 February 1777, and rose to sergeant in 1778. He transferred as a rotmistr to the Kazan Cuirassier Regiment on 12 January 1789. Velikopolsky participated in the Russo-Swedish War in 1789-1790, fighting on the Kumen River, and later briefly served under Prince Gregory Potemkin in Moldavia in 1790-1791. In 1792, he joined the Military Order Cuirassier Regiment but returned to the Kazan Cuirassiers. In 1793-1794, Velikopolsky served as a duty officer to General Mikhail Kutuzov in Istanbul. After returning to Russia, he became a second major and attended King Stanislas of Poland in 1795-1796. He was promoted to lieutenant colonel on 13 February 1798, and colonel on 8 April 1799.

In 1800, Velikopolsky was dispatched to the Baltic provinces to prepare the coastline defenses against possible British landing. He became major general on 30 May 1803, and chef of the Seversk Dragoon Regiment on 22 June 1803. However, Velikopolsky retired on 24 June 1803, and returned to service as chef of the Siberia Dragoon Regiment on 30 September 1803. He was discharged from the army for incompetence on 11 July 1806.

During the 1812 Campaign, Velikopolsky was elected head of the 15th Company (*druzhina*) of the St. Petersburg *opolchenye*, and later led the 5th Brigade of this *opolchenye*. He took part in the actions at Gorodnya, Sirotin, Strunya, Polotsk (Order of St. Vladimir, 3rd class), Chashniki, Smolyani (bruised by a cannonball in the right side), and Studyanka. Suffering from the wound, Velikopolsky left the army and became the Commandant of Urburg, where he established a large hospital for 2,400 men. He returned to his *opolchenye* troops in Koenigsberg in early 1813 and commanded the St. Petersburg and Novgorod *opolchenyes* at Danzig. In July 1813, Velikopolsky took command of the 2nd *Opolchenye* Brigade, but was recalled to the main army and served as a duty officer to Barclay de Tolly. Velikopolsky took part in the actions at Peterswalde and Leipzig, where he was wounded in the right leg. He was officially restored in the military service on 12 December 1813, and appointed to the Army of Reserve in the Duchy of Warsaw. Velikopolsky served in the military court in St. Petersburg in 1828.

VELYAMINOV, Ivan Alexandrovich (date of birth unclear, ca. 1771-1772 — d. 8 December 1837, St. Petersburg) was born to a noble family in the Tula *gubernia*. He began service as a page at the Imperial Court and enlisted as a lieutenant in the Life Guard Semeyonovsk Regiment in January 1797. He quickly rose through the ranks, becoming staff-captain in 1798, captain in 1799, and colonel in 1800. He received the Order of St. John of Jerusalem for exemplary service in 1800. During the 1805 Campaign, Velyaminov commanded a battalion of the Life Guard Semeyonosvk Regiment and distinguished himself at the Battle of Austerlitz, for which he received the Order of St. George (4th class). In 1807, he fought at Guttstadt, Deppen, Heilsberg, and Friedland, where he was wounded in the chest. For his actions in 1807, he received the Order of St. Vladimir (3rd class), the Prussian Pour le Merite, and a golden sword for courage. Velyaminov became major general and chef of the Keksholm (Kexholm) Musketeer Regiment on 24 December 1807.

Velyaminov served under Prince Peter Bagration during the Russo-Swedish War, and distinguished himself at Helsinge in 1808 and during the march to the Aland Islands in the spring of 1809. After returning to Russia, he was discharged for poorly maintaining his unit on 8 December 1810, but was restored in rank on 2 October 1811. Velyaminov assumed command of the 33rd Division on 27 March 1812. During the 1812 Campaign, he fought at Shavli, Janisek, Eckau, Riga, Nizoten, and numerous minor actions. Velyaminov received the Order of St. Anna (1st class) for his service in these battles. In 1813, he served in the siege of Danzig, where he was seriously wounded in the chest on 24 March 1813. After recuperating, he became the chief of staff of the Russian forces besieging Danzig. After the capture of this city, Velyaminov led the 1st Infantry Corps of the Army of Reserve. He took command of the 25th Division on 10 September 1814, and became lieutenant general the following day.

In 1815, Velyaminov marched to France during the Hundred Days, but was ordered back after the Battle of Waterloo. On 13 January 1818, he was appointed commander of the 20th Division in the Independent Georgian Corps. For his service, he received the Order of St. Vladimir (2nd class) on 3 November 1819, and a rent for twelve years in 1821. Velyaminov rose to command the Independent Siberia Corps and become Governor General of Western Siberia on 7 July 1827. The same year, he was awarded 35,000 rubles for an exemplary service. He rose to general of infantry on 7 July 1828. Velyaminov was relieved of command and appointed to the Council of War of the Ministry of War on 10 October 1834.

VELYAMINOV, Nikolay Stepanovich (b. 1781 — date of death unclear) was born to a noble family in the Ryazan *gubernia*. He graduated from the Artillery and Engineer Cadet Corps and began service as a sub-lieutenant in the Major General Mamontov's Artillery Battalion in 1797. He served in the Danubian Principalities in 1806-1812, distinguishing himself at Giurgiu and Ismail in 1807. He transferred to the Life Guard Artillery Brigade in 1810, and rose to captain on 1 May 1811. In 1813, he led the 3rd Artillery Brigade and fought at Thorn, Koenigswartha, and Bautzen. During his service, Velyaminov received the Orders of St. George (4th class), of St. Anna (3rd and 2nd classes), and of St. Vladimir (4th and 3rd class), the Prussian Pour le Merite, and a golden sword for courage.

VENANSON, Osip (Joseph) Petrovich (b. 1777 — date of death unknown) was born to a Sardinian noble family. He began service in the Piedmontese army, but after Napoleon's victorious campaigns in Italy, entered Russian service in 1798 and served under Field Marshal Alexander Suvorov in Italy in 1799. Returning to Russia, Venanson was appointed to the quartermaster section of the Imperial Retinue on 1 November 1802. He took part in the 1805 Campaign and fought at Austerlitz on 2 December 1805. From 1807-1812, he served in the headquarters of the Army of Moldavia and the Army of Danube, earning colonelcy on 20 February 1812.

During the Russian Campaign of 1812, Venanson served in the staff of General Osten-Sacken's corps and took part in operations in Volhynia. In 1813-1814, he participated in the battles at Bautzen, Katzbach, Leipzig, Brienne, and La Rothière. For his service, Venanson was promoted to major general on 9 November 1814. After the war, he served in the 8th Division but left Russian service on 14 May 1816, and returned to Piedmont.

During his career in the Russian army, Venanson also received the Orders of St. Anna (2nd class) with diamonds, St. Vladimir (3rd class), St. John of Jerusalem, the Prussian Pour le Merite, and the Sardinian Order of St. Maurice and Lazarus.

VERBOVSKY, Platon Vasilievich (b. 1779 — date of death unclear) was born to a noble family in the Ekaterinoslavl *gubernia*. He graduated from the Artillery and Engineer Cadet Corps and began service as a shtyk junker in the Bombardier Regiment in 1796. He took part in the 1805-1807 Campaigns in Moravia and Poland. In 1810-1811, Verbovsky served in the Black Sea Fleet and took part in expedition against the Circassians, for which he received the Order of St. Vladimir (4th class) in 1811. He became lieutenant colonel on 21 February 1811, and commander of the 19th Light Artillery Company of the 10th Artillery Brigade on 26 February 1811. In 1813-1814, Verbovsky fought at Katzbach (Order of St. George, 4th class), Leipzig (golden sword), Brienne, La Rothière (Order of St. Anna, 2nd class), Craonne, and Paris.

VESELITSKY, Gavriil (Gabriel) Petrovich (b. 21 July 1774 — d. 12 October 1829) was born to a noble family from Dalmatia that settled in Russia in early 18th century. He graduated with a rank of shtyk-junker from the Artillery and Engineer Cadet Corps in 1790, and was assigned to the galley fleet of Prince Nassau-Zigen in the Baltic Sea. He took part in operations against the Swedes and distinguished himself at Friedrichsham and Bjorko Zund (promoted to sub-lieutenant). In August 1791, Veselitsky transferred to the 2nd Artillery Fusilier Regiment. The following year, he served against the Polish confederates. Veselitsky was promoted to lieutenant of the 10th Artillery Battalion in January 1797, to staff captain in 1798 and to captain in 1800. Three years later, he took command of a company in the 6th Artillery Regiment.

In 1805, Veselitsky became a major and in 1806, his company was attached to the 11th Artillery Brigade, 11th Division, Army of Moldavia. In 1806-1812, Veselitsky served against the Turks in the Danubian Principalities. He fought at Gloden, on the Jalomits River, and Bucharest in 1806; Turbat (Order of St. Vladimir, 4th class) and Obilesti in 1807; Giurgiu, Rassevat (Order of St. George, 4th class), and Silistra in 1809; Turtukai (golden sword), Ruse, Batin (promoted to lieutenant colonel), and Turno in 1810. Veselitsky took command of the 7th Reserve Artillery Brigade in Langeron's Corps on 7 April 1811, and participated in battle at Ruse, for which he earned the Order of St. Anna (2nd class) and a promotion to colonel on 10 January 1812.

During the 1812 Campaign, Veselitsky became commander of the artillery in the 3rd Western Army and fought at Brest-Litovsk, Borisov, and on the Berezina. In 1813, he directed artillery during the siege of Thorn, for which he garnered the Order of St. George (3rd class, 8 May 1813) and the Prussian Red Eagle (2nd class). Veselitsky fought at Koenigswartha, Bautzen (promoted to major general on 7 June 1813), Löwenberg, Goldberg, Katzbach (Order of St. Anna, 1st class, for last three battles), and Leipzig (diamonds signs of the Order of St. Anna, 1st class, and the Swedish Order of the Sword, 2nd class). In 1814, he distinguished himself at Soissons and Paris (golden sword). For his service in 1813-1814, he was also awarded the Order of St. Vladimir (3rd class) and a rent for twelve years. In 1815, Veselitsky led the artillery of the 6th Corps and marched to France during the Hundred Days.

After the war, Veselitsky became chief of staff of the Intependent Orenburg Corps on 1 February 1817, and presided over the Orenburg Border Comission. He was promoted to lieutenant general on 3 September 1826, and was awarded the Order of St. Vladimir (2nd class) for distinguished service in January 1829.

VESELITSKY, Peter Petrovich (b. 1775 — d. 7 September 1812, Borodino) was born to a noble family from Dalmatia that settled in Russia in early 18th century. He was the younger brother of Gavriil Veselitsky. Peter Veselitsky graduated from the Artillery and Engineer Cadet Corps and began service as a shtyk junker in the 2nd Fusilier Regiment in 1794. He participated in the 1807 Campaign, distinguishing himself at Eylay (golden sword) and Friedland (Order of St. Vladimir, 4th class). He became colonel on 21 February 1811, and took command of the 24th Battery Company of the 24th Artillery Brigade. In 1812, he fought at Smolensk and was mortally wounded at Borodino.

VISTITSKY (Vistitsky II in 1812), Mikhail Stepanovich (b. 1768 — d. 1832) was born to a noble family from the Smolensk *gubernia*. He enlisted as a corporal in the Life Guard Izmailovsk Regiment on 12 January 1776, and transferred as a rotmistr to the Kiev Carabinier Regiment on 12 January 1786. He took part in the Russo-Turkish War in 1788-1791 and distinguished himself at Macin, for which he was appointed ober-quartermaster with the rank of premier major. He rose to colonel on 17 January 1799, and served as the quartermaster general in Alexander Rimsky-Korsakov's corps in Switzerland in 1799. Returning to Russia, Vistitsky became a major general on 21 October 1800.

During the 1812 Campaign, Vistitsky served as the quartermaster general of the 2nd Western Army and participated in the actions at Saltanovka, Smolensk, Shevardino, Borodino (Order of St. Anna, 1st class, with diamonds) and Tarutino (wounded). In October-December 1812, he served as quartermaster general of the main Russian army. In 1813, he served in the same capacity in the Army of Reserve in the Duchy of Warsaw. He retired because of poor health in November 1816.

VLASOV, Maxim Grigorevich (b. 24 August 1767, Razdorskoe — d. 3 July 1848, Ust-Medveditskoe) was born to a Cossak ober-officer's family. He studied in the Kiev-Pechora Monastery and began service as a private in the Grekov's Cossak Regiment on 12 March 1791. In 1792-1794, he served in Poland and rose to sotnik on 21 July 1792 and esaul in 1794. In 1805, he directed Ataman Platov's chancellery before transferring to the Ataman Cossack Regiment. Vlasov took part in the 1807 Campaign in Poland and fought at Guttstadt and Heilsberg. For his service, he earned promotion to sergeant as well as the Order of St. Vladimir (4th class) and the Prussian Pour le Merite. He was appointed to the Army of Danube in 1809 and took part in operations against the Turks. He was promoted to lieutenant colonel in 1810, and took command of the Vlasov's Cossack Regiment on 4 January 1812.

During the 1812 Campaign, Vlasov participated in the actions at Bolshie Soleshniky, Olshani (golden sword), Kamen, Molevo Boloto, Smolensk, Borodino, and Kovno (Order of St. George, 4th class, 7 April 1813). He became colonel on 4 March 1813, and during the 1813 Campaign, served in General Alexander Chernishev's detachment. He distinguished himself at Berlin, Luneburg, Beltzig (Order of St. George, 3rd class), Kassel (promoted to major general on 15 January 1815, with seniority dating from 18 September 1813), and Hanau. In 1814, Vlasov participated in minor actions in Holland as well as in the battles at Soissons, Laon, and Rheims.

After the war, Vlasov commanded Cossack regiments in Georgia and suppressed uprisings in Western Georgia and Shirvan. He led the Black Sea Cossack Host between 18 December 1820 and August 1826. Vlasov's fortunes took a turn for the worse when he was accused of brutally destroying two Circassian villages in 1826. He was under investigation for several years until finally acquitted of the charges in March 1830.

Vlasov became the head of the Don Cossack Host on 2 June 1830. In 1831, he participated in suppression of the Polish uprising and distinguished himself at Wawer, where he was wounded ten times. For his outstanding courage in this battle, Vlasov was promoted to lieutenant general on 27 March 1831, with seniority dating from 11 March 1831. He became ataman of the Don Cossak Host on 16 January 1836, and general of cavalry on 22 October 1843.

Vlasov died during the cholera epidemic at Ust-Medveditskoe on 3 July 1848.

VLASTOV, Egor Ivanovich (date of birth unclear, ca. 1769/1770 — d. 10 February 1837) was born to a Greek family in Constantinople (Istanbul). He was brought to Russia and studied in the Cadet Corps of Fellow Co-Believers, which he graduated with the rank of sub-lieutenant in the Estland Jager Corps on 29 March 1790. During the Russo-Swedish War in 1790, he served on the galley fleet of Prince Nassau-Zigen. In 1792-1794, he served in Poland, fighting at Pashuchi, Zelva (promoted to captain), Brest-Litovsk, Borun, and Vilna. In

1795, he transferred to the St. Petersburg Grenadier Regiment. In 1799, Vlastov became a major and battalion commander of the St. Petersburg Grenadier Regiment. He received the Order of St. Anna (3rd class) for good maintenance of his battalion in 1804. During the 1805 Campaign, Vlastov served in Count Tolstoy's corps in Pomerania and was promoted to lieutenant colonel. He took command of the 24th Jager Regiment on 8 August 1806.

During the 1806-1807 Campaigns in Poland, Vlastov fought at Pultusk, Zurkviten, Eylau (Order of St. Vladimir, 4th class), Glotau, Quez, and Heilsberg, where he was seriously wounded in the chest. For his actions in the last two battles, Vlastov was awarded the Order of St. Anna (2nd class). After recuperating, he became a colonel and chef of the 24th Jager Regiment on 24 December 1807. In 1808-1809, he served with the 5th Division against the Swedes in Finland and took part in the actions at Lenowerde, Lintulaks, Saarijärvi, Karstula (Order of St. George, 3rd class, 11 September 1808), Perho, Torneo, Hernefors (Order of St. Anna, 2nd class), and Umeå. Vlastov also earned the Order of St. Vladimir (3rd class) for his service in 1808.

During the 1812 Campaign, he served with the 3rd Brigade, 5th Division, Wittgenstein's corps, and fought at Jakubovo, Klyastitsy, and Golovchitsa (promotion to major general, 30 October 1812), both battles of Polotsk (golden sword for the first battle, and a lifetime rent for the second battle), Belyi (Order of St. Anna, 1st class), and on the Berezina.

In 1813, Vlastov participated in the battles at Dresden (diamond signs of the Order of St. Anna, 1st class), Dohna, Peterswalde, Leipzig, and Liebertwolkwitz (Order of St. Vladimir, 2nd class, for the last two battles). In 1814, he served at Strasbourg, Bar sur Aube, Troyes, Arcis sur Aube, Le Fère Champenoise, and Paris. For his actions at the French capital, he was promoted to lieutenant general on 13 June 1815, with seniority dating from 30 March 1814.

After the war, Vlastov led the 3rd Brigade of the 5th Division. Quick succession of commands followed: the 14th Division (29 March 1815), 6th Division (June 1815), and 5th Division (1819). He took a prolonged furlough because of poor health in April 1822, and died at his estate at Knyazhevo in the Vladimir *gubernia* on 10 February 1837.

His son, **Constantine Egorovich Vlastov**, served in the 24th Jager Regiment in 1809 and received the Order of St. Anna (3rd class) for his actions against the Swedes. In 1814, he served with the 5th Division and earned the Order of St. Vladimir (4th class) for courage at Paris.

VLODEK, Mikhail Fedorovich (b. 1780 — d. 1849) was born to a noble family from the Vilna *gubernia*. He began service as a lieutenant in the Life Guard Horse Regiment and led a squadron at Austerlitz in 1805. He rose to a flügel adjutant on 21 June 1808, and to a colonel on 10

December 1808. In 1810-1811, he served in the Army of Danube against the Turks and received the Order of St. George (4th class) on 1 December 1810. From 1812-1814, he served in the Imperial Retinue and attended Emperor Alexander throughout the campaigns in Russia, Germany, and France. He became a major general on 27 September 1813.

After the war, Vlodek commanded the 1st Brigade of the 2nd Uhlan Division (2 May 1818) and the Lithuanian Uhlan Division (4 May 1819). He was promoted to lieutenant general on 3 September 1826, and appointed adjutant general on 18 October 1831. He became a member of the General Audit on 23 June 1832, and served in the State Council of the Kingdom of Poland after 22 August 1833. Ten years later, he rose to general of cavalry on 22 October 1843.

During his career, Vlodek received the Orders of St. Alexander of Neva, St. Anna (1st class) with crown, St. Vladimir (2nd class), the White Eagle, Austrian Order of Leopold, Prussian Order of the Red Eagle, Württemberg Order of Charles, French Order of St. Louis, and the Bavarian Order of Maximilian Joseph.

VNUKOV, Vasily Mikhailovich (b. 1791 — date of death unclear) was born to a noble family from the Kostroma *gubernia*. He graduated from the 2nd Cadet Corps in 1807, and began service as a sub-lieutenant in the 10th Artillery Brigade on 2 January 1808. The following year, he served in Prince Sergey Golitsyn's corps against the Austrians in Galicia. He transferred to the 7th Artillery Brigade on 12 March 1811. During the 1812 Campaign, Vnukov served at Smolensk, Borodino, and Tarutino. In 1813, he fought at Bautzen, Gros Beeren, Dennewitz (Prussian Pour le Merite), and Leipzig for which he received the Order of St. Anna (3rd class). In 1814, he distinguished himself at Soissons and Laon.

VOINOV, Alexander Lvovich (b. 1770 — date of death unclear; removed from rosters on 29 October 1832) was born to a Russian noble family. He began service in the Life Guard Preobrazhensk Regiment in 1780 and rose to cornet in 1785. He transferred as a lieutenant colonel to the Izumsk Light Horse Regiment in 1793 and distinguished himself at Vilna and Kovno (Order of St. George, 4th class, 9 July 1794) against the Polish confederates in 1794. He became colonel on 4 December 1797, and commander of the Ingermanland Dragoon Regiment on 29 March 1798. Voinov rose to major general and chef of the Starodoub Cuirassier Regiment on 26 April 1799.

During the 1799 Campaign, Voinov served in Switzerland. After returning to Russia, his regiment was reorganized to the Starodoub Dragoon Regiment on 1 August 1801. During the Russo-Turkish War in 1806-1812, Voinov distinguished himself at Ismail, Shumla, Bazardjik (golden cross), and Ruse for which he earned the Order of St. George (3rd class) on 4 October 1811. He was promoted to lieutenant general on 26 June 1810, and took command of the 12th Division on 1 October 1810. During the 1812 Campaign, Voinov led the 3rd Corps of the Army of Danube and took part in the operations at Pruzhani and on the Berezina. In 1813, he served at Thorn.

After the war, Voinov took command of the 3rd Reserve Cavalry Corps in 1822 and of the 1st Infantry Corps on 28 February 1822. He was promoted to general of cavalry on 24 December 1824. Exactly one year later, he took command of the Guard Corps. During the Decembrist Uprising, Voinov swiftly moved his troops to suppress the insurgents and was rewarded with an appointment as adjutant general on 27

December 1825, and commander of the 7th Corps on 20 November 1826. He commanded the Russian cavalry during the Russo-Turkish War in 1828-1829, and retired because of poor health in 1830.

VOLKHOVSKY, Peter Mikhailovich (b. 1789 — date of death unclear) was born to a noble family in the Nizhegorod *gubernia*. He graduated from the 2nd Cadet Corps in 1805, and began service as a sub-lieutenant in the 5th Artillery Regiment. During the 1805 Campaign, he distinguished himself at Amstetten and Austerlitz, where he was seriously wounded in the left leg and captured.

After returning to Russia in 1806, Volkhovsky rose to lieutenant on 6 November 1808, and transferred to the 8th Reserve Artillery Brigade on 26 February 1811. He fought at Ust-Lug and Rubishov during the 1812 Campaign, and was promoted to staff captain on 20 April 1813. He took part in the actions at Czentochow, Sttednitz., Bunzlau, Bautzen, and Leipzig, and the following year, 1814, served at Brienne, Laon, Soissons, and Paris.

VOLKONSKY, Andrey Aleksandrovich (b. 1788 — date of death unclear) was born to a prominent Russian family in the Vladimir *gubernia*. He graduated from the 2nd Cadet Corps and began service as a sub-lieutenant in the 18th Artillery Brigade on 30 October 1806. Volkonsky served in the Danubian Principalities in 1810-1811 and distinguished himself at Bazardjik (golden cross), Shumla, and Batin. He was elevated to lieutenant on 19 January 1810. In 1812, he served with the 3rd Western Army and fought at Kobryn and Gorodechnya (Order of St. Anna, 3rd class). The following year, Volkonsky participated in the actions at Thorn, Bautzen (Order of St. Vladimir, 4th class), and Katzbach. During the 1814 Campaign, he distinguished himsef at Brienne, La Rothière (promotion to staff captain), Montmirail (Order of St. Anna, 2nd class), and Paris.

VOLKONSKY (Volkonsky I in 1812), Dmitry Mikhaylovich (b. 1770 — d. 19 May 1835, Moscow) was born to the Tula branch of a prominent Russian family of princes. He was enlisted as a sergeant in the Life Guard Preobrazhensk Regiment on 11 January 1775, at the age of five, and began his active service as a lieutenant in the Life Guard Izmailosvk Regiment on 11 February 1788. Volkonsky participated in the Russo-Swedish War in 1788-1789, and fought at Rochensalmi and Vyborg (Order of St. George, 4th class, 7 December 1789, and a golden sword for courage). Volkonsky served in Prince Repnin's corps against the Turks and distinguished himself at Babadag and Macin. In 1794, he transferred to the Apsheron Infantry Regiment and served in Poland. He became a colonel in the Moscow Garrison Regiment on 12 May 1797, and the following year rose to major general and commander of the Moscow Garrison Regiment on 23 April 1798. Eight months later, Volkonsky was appointed commandant of Malta on 27 December 1798, and participated in Field Marshal Alexander Suvorov's campaign in Italy.

Returning to Russia, Volkonsky enjoyed quick succession of promotions, serving as chef of the St. Petersburg Grenadier Regiment from 5 April to 15 May 1800, chef of the Shirvan Musketeer Regiment, and infantry inspector in the Siberia Inspection from 25 August to 27 October 1800. After brief service in the Life Guard Preobrazhensk Regiment between 22 and 26 October 1800, Volkonsky served as chef of the 4th Jager Regiment from 30 December 1800 to 1 January 1801, before serving as the Military Governor of Vyborg and infantry inspector of the Finland Inspection from 1 January to 23 July 1801. He became infantry inspector in the Ukraine Inspection on 22 March 1803, and took command of the Russian troops in Georgia on 16 September 1803. Two years later, Volkonsky was appointed duty officer to the headquarters of General Mikhail Kutuzov's army and was wounded at Austerlutz on 2 December 1805.

In 1806, Volkonsky assumed command of the 6th Division and distinguished himself at Guttstadt, Heilsberg, and Friedland (wounded in the right leg, decorated with a golden sword with diamonds and the Order of St. Anna, 1st class). After Tilsit, Volkonsky retired because of his wounds. He returned to the military service during the 1812 Campaign, when he took command of a corps in the 3rd Western Army. In the spring of 1813, he took part in the actions at Glogau, Lutzen, and Bautzen. In the summer of 1813, he led the Tula *opolchenye* at Danzig, garnering the Orders of St. George (3rd class, 24 November 1813), St. Vladimir (2nd class), and Prussian Red Eagle (1st class).

After the war, Volkonsky was appointed to the Senate in 1816. During his career, Volkonsky was also decorated with the Order of St. John of Jerusalem, Austrian Order of Maria Theresa, and the Sardinian Order of St. Maurice and Lazarus.

VOLKONSKY (Volkonsky III in 1812), Nikita Grigorievich (b. 1781, Moscow — d. 1844, Assis, Italy) was born to the Chernigov branch of a prominent Russian family of princes; the brother of Sergey Volkonsky. He enlisted as an ensign in the Life Guard Izmailovsk Regiment on 20 October 1792, and began service as a lieutenant on 12 January 1796. Volkonsky took a discharge with the rank of camptain on 28 November 1800, and served at the Imperial Court, rising to a kamer-junker on 27 September 1801. Six years later, he transferred as a lieutenant colonel to the military service and became adjutant to General Ivan Michelson. He took part in the Russo-Turkish War in 1807-1812 and was decorated with a golden sword for courage. Volkonsky was promoted to colonel and flügel adjutant of Emperor Alexander on 27 September 1807.

During the 1812 Campaign, Volkonsky served with the St. Petersburg *opolchenye* and fought at Polotsk on 18-19 October, where he took a serious wound to his right side. He retired because of wounds on 1 November 1812, but returned to the army within two months on 31 December 1812. In 1813, he served in Alexander's entourage and fought at Lutzen, Bautrzen, Dresden (promoted to major general on 27 September 1813), and Leipzig (golden sword with diamonds). In 1814, he distinguished himself at Brienne, La Rothière, Bar sur Aube, Arcis sur Aube, Le Fère Champenoise, and Paris. In 1815, he attended Emperor Alexander during the Congress of Vienna. Twelve years later, he transferred to the Imperial Court as jagermeister with the rank of privy counsellor on 18 December 1827. He spent last few years of his life in Italy, where he converted to Catholicism.

VOLKONSKY (Volkonsky II in 1812), Peter Mikhaylovich (b. 7 May 1776, St. Petersburg — 7 September 1852, Peterhof) was born to a prominent Russian family of princes. He was enlisted as a sergeant in the Life Guard Preobrazhensk Regiment within a year of birth. He was transferred to the Life Guard Horse Regiment, where he rose to vice-vakhmistr and vakhmistr in 1783. In 1792, Volkonsky joined the Life Guard Semeyonosvk Regiment, where he began his service as an ensign on 12 January 1793. The following year, he became a sub-lieutenant. After Paul's accession to the throne in November 1796, Volkonsky was appointed among the first regimental adjutants and promoted to lieutenant on 22 November 1796. A quick series of promotions soon followed, as he became a staff-captain on 3 May 1794, and adjutant to Grand Duke Alexander on 18 November 1797. Volkonsky earned the Order of St Anna (3rd class) on 26 May 1798, the Order of St. John of Jerusalem in 1800, and promotions to captain on 5 May 1799, and colonel on 7 June 1800. The following year, Emperor Alexander I made him a major general, adjutant general and deputy head of the Imperial Campaign Chancellery (*voenno-pokhodnaia kantselaria*) on 27 September 1801. For his dutiful service, Volkonsky received the Order of St. Anna (2nd class) with diamonds in 1803.

In 1805, Volkonsky became a duty general and quartermaster general of the Allied armies and distinguished himself at Austerlitz, where he personally led several countercharges (Order of St. George, 3rd class, on 9 February 1806). In 1806-1807, he served in the Imperial Campaign Chancellery and attended Emperor Alexander during his review of the Russian army in April 1807, where Volkonsky received the Prussian Order of the Red Eagle (1st class).

Volkonsky took part in the meeting of two emperors at Tilsit and spent the next two years studying the French military system. He returned to Russia in the spring of 1810 and was appointed head of the quartermaster service on 4 June. He was instrumental in reorganizing the quartermaster service along the French lines, including the establishment of the new Cartography Department and adoption of the *Uchrezhdenie dlia upravlenia bolshoi deistvuiushei armii* [Establishment for the Administration of the Large Active Army]. For his effective service, he was decorated with the Order of St. Vladimir (2nd class).

During the 1812 Campaign, he persuaded Emperor Alexander to abandon Phull's plan and withdraw from the Drissa Camp. In July-August 1812, he accompanied Alexander to Moscow and St. Petersburg. He joined the main Russian army on 27 September 1812, where he remained for over month until ordered to raise *opolchenye* in Novgorod. In November, Volkonsky took part in the battle on the Berezina and became the Chief of Staff of the Russian army on 9 January 1813.

During the 1813 Campaign, Volkonsky took part in the battles at Lutzen (promoted to lieutenant general on 5 May 1813 with seniority dating from 2 May 1813), Bautzen, Dresden (decorated with the Austrian Order of Leopold, 1st class, prior to the battle on 18 August), Kulm and Leipzig (Order of St. Alexander of Neva and the Austrian Order of the Maria Theresa). In late 1813, he participated in the meeting of the Allied powers at Frankfurt. In 1814, he fought at Brienne and Arcis sur Aube and urged the Allied commanders to advance on Paris. Volkonsky distinguished himself at Le Ferè Champenoise, where he swiftly moved General Rayevsky's corps to reinforce the Allied forces, and at Paris. For his service, he received the Order of St. Vladimir (1st class), the French Order of St. Louis, the Swedish Order of the Sword, the Bavarian Order of Maximilian Joseph and the Württemberg Order of the Military Merit. In April-December 1814, he accompanied Alexander I to London, St. Petersburg and Vienna and laid foundation to the Guard General Staff. During the Hundred Days, Volkonsky again served as the Chief of Staff of the Russian army and organized the grand military review at Vertus in September 1815.

After returning to Russia, Volkonsky was instrumental in the establishment of the General Staff on 24 December 1815, and was promoted to general of infantry on 24 December 1817. He directed the General Staff for seven years, and his effective service earned him the diamond signs of the Order of St. Alexander of Neva. He became a member of the State Council in 1821 and accompanied Emperor Alexander to the Congresses at Aix-la-Chapelle, Troppau, Laibach, and Verona in 1819-1822. In 1824, Volkonsky was appointed ambassador to the France, where King Charles X awarded him the Order of the Holy Spirit. Volkonsky returned to Russia in 1825 in time to attend Emperor Alexander on his deathbed. Under Nicholas I, Volkonsky became the Minister of the Imperial Court (*ministr imperatorskogo dvora*) on 3

September 1826. For his excellent service at this position, he received permission to wear the uniform of the Life Guard Semeyonovsk Regiment in 1826, as well as large estates in the Tambov *gubernia* in 1827, the diamond signs of the Order of St. Andrew the First Called in 1828, Emperor Nicholas' portrait encrusted with diamonds in 1830, another permission to wear the uniform of the Guard General Staff in 1832, the title of his higness prince (*svetleishii kniaz*) in 1834, and another two Imperial portraits with diamonds in 1837.

Volkonsky was appointed the Inspector General of the Reserve in 1837, chef of the Belozersk Infantry Regiment on 21 August 1839, and promoted to general field marshal on 18 December 1850. In January 1843, the Belozersk Infantry Regiment was renamed to the Adjutant General Prince Volkonsky's Infantry Regiment. Prince Volkonsky died in St. Petersburg on 7 September 1852.

Volkonsky was one of the most decorated officers in the history of the Russian Empire. In addition to aforementioned awards, he also received the Russian Orders of St. Andrew the First Called, St. Stanislaus (1st class), and a medal "For LV Years of Distinguished Service." He also received 31 foreign awards, including the Polish Order of the White Eagle, Prussian Black Eagle with diamonds, Austrian Order of St. Stephan (1st class), French Order of St. Louis (1st class), Swedish Order of the Seraphim, British Order of Bath (1st class), Dutch Order of the Elephant, Baden Orders of Fidelity (1st class), Lion of Zaehringen (1st class), Military Merit of Charles Frederick (1st class), Anhaldt Order of Albrecht the Bear, Saxe-Weimar Orders of Vigilance and the White Falcon, Hessian Order of the Lion of Gold, Hesse-Darmstadt Order of Ludwig, Dutch Order of the Lion (1st class), Hanoverian Order of the Guelphs (1st class), Sardinian Order of the Annunziata, and the Neapolitan Orders of St. Ferdinand and Military Merit.

VOLKONSKY (Volkonsky IV in 1812), Sergey Grigorievich (b. 19 December 1788 — d. 10 December 1865, Voronki) was born to the Chernigov branch of this prominent Russian noble family; the son of General Gregory Volkonsky, Governor General of Orenburg. He enlisted as a sergeant in the Kheron Grenadier Regiment on 12 June 1796, transferred as a rotmistr to the Ekaterinoslavl Cuirassier Regiment in 1797, and began his service as a lieutenant in the Chevalier Guard Regiment on 10 January 1806. During the 1806-1807 Campaigns in Poland, Volkonsky served as an adjutant to General Osterman-Tolstoy and fought at Pultusk (Order of St. Vladimir, 4th class), Jankovo, Hof, Eylau (wounded, golden cross), Guttstadt, Heilsberg, and Friedland. In early 1810, he was appointed to the headquarters of the Army of Moldavia and took part in the actions at Bazardjik and Silistra, for which he was promoted to staff-rotmistr and appointed flügel aadjutant on 18 September 1810.

In 1812, Volkonsky transferred to the Imperial Retinue, and during the 1812 Campagn, served with Wittgenstein's corps at Orekhovo (promoted to colonel) and on the Berezina (Order of St. Vladimir, 3rd class). In 1813, he served at Kalisch (Order of St. George, 4th class), Gross Beeren, Dennewitz (promoted to major general on 27 September 1813), and Leipzig (Order of St. Anna, 1st class). In 1814, he distinguished himself at Laon and received the Prussian Order of the Red Eagle (2nd class).

After the war, Volkonsky took command of a brigade of the 2nd Uhlan Division in 1816, and of a brigade of the 19th Division in 1821.

Inspired by the ideas fostered by the Enlightenment, Volkonsky joined the Union of Welfare in 1819 and the Southern Society in 1821 with a goal of transforming the Russian monarchy. He became one of the most active members of the Decembrist Uprising and was arrested on 17 January 1826. He was initially sentenced to death, but was pardoned and sentenced instead to twenty years of hard labor and stripped of nobility and titles on 22 July 1826. The following month, his sentence was reduced to fifteen years of hard labor, and in 1832, it was reduced again to ten years.

Volkonsky was not allowed to enter European Russia until 1856, when he received amnesty (his nobility was reinstated on 7 September 1856) and settled on his estate in Chernigov *gubernia*, where he died on 10 December 1865. Volkonsky's wife was Maria Rayevsky, the daughter of General Nikolay Rayevsky, who followed Volkonsky into exile.

Volkonsky left very interesting and insightful memoirs entitled *Zapiski Sergeya Grigorievicha Volkonskogo (Dekabrista)*, which were published in St. Petersburg in 1901.

VOLKOV, Mikhail Mikhaylovich (b. 1776 — d. 12 December 1820, Belgorod) was born to an ancient Russian noble family. He was enlisted at the age of five as a sergeant in the Life Guard Preobrazhensk Regiment on 15 March 1781, and began service as a rotmistr in the Poltava Light Horse Regiment on 12 January 1794. He transferred to the Ekaterinoslavl Cuirassier Regiment, and in 1796, joined the Rostov Dragoon Regiment. He was promoted to major in September 1798, but was discharged in May 1799. Volkov returned to the army in November 1800 and was restored in his rank in the Ekaterinoslavl Cuirassier Regiment, and promoted to lieutenant colonel soon thereafter.

Volkov served with the 6th Division during the 1806-1807 Campaigns in Poland, fighting at Pultusk, Eylau, Heilsberg, and Friedland, for which he earned the Order of St. Vladimir (4th class). He rose to colonel on 24 December 1807. In 1809, he served in Prince Sergey Golitsyn's corps in Galicia and took command of the Ekaterinoslavl Cuirassier Regiment on 9 November 1811.

During the 1812 Campaign, Volkov served in the 2nd Cuirassier Division in the 8th Corps. He took part in Prince Bagration's retreat to Smolensk and fought at Shevardino and Borodino, where he was wounded in the left leg and chest. For his courage, he received the Order of St. George (4th class) on 4 January 1813. After recuperating, Volkov participated in the battles at Tarutino, Maloyaroslavets, and Krasnyi, for which he was decorated with the Order of St. Anna (2nd class). In 1813, Volkov served at Lutzen, Bautzen, and Leipzig (Order of St. Vladimir, 3rd class). For his actions, he was promoted to major general on 27 September 1813. He took part in the pursuit of the French army to the Rhine, but was unable to continue campaign because of poor health. He left the army in early 1814 and returned to his estate in Belgorod in the Kursk *gubernia*, where he died on 12 December 1820.

VOLZHINSKY, Peter Lvovich (b. 1789 — date of death unclear) was born to a noble family, son of college counsellor. He graduated from the Grodno Cadet Corps in 1805 and began service as a sub-lieutenant in the 3rd Artillery Regiment. He participated in the 1807 Campaign in Poland, distinguishing himself at Eylau and Heilsberg. In 1812, he served under Wittgenstein at Polotsk, Chashniki, and on the Berezina. In 1813-1814, he took part in the actions at Danzig, Spandau, Magdeburg, Soissons, and Paris. For his actions, he received the Orders of St. Anna (3rd class), St. Vladimir (4th class), the Prussian Pour le Merite, and a golden sword for courage.

VOLZHINSKY, Nikolay Lvovich (b. 1790 — date of death unclear) was born to a noble family from the Smolensk *gubernia*. He graduated from the Grodno Cadet Corps in 1806 and began service as a sub-lieutenant in the 2nd Artillery Brigade. He participated in the 1807 Campaign in Poland, distinguishing himself at Guttstadt (Order of St. Anna, 3rd class), Heilsberg, and Friedland. He rose to lieutenant on 19 November 1810, and transferred to the 24th Artillery Brigade on 23 March 1811.

During the 1812 Campaign, Volzhinsky fought at Smolensk, Borodino (golden sword), Tarutino, Maloyaroslavets, Krasnyi, and Vitebsk. In 1813, he took part in the actions at Gross Beeren, Dennewitz, Leipzig, and Hamburg, while the following year, he he was promoted to staff captain on 13 January 1814 and participated in the battles at Craonne and Paris.

VORONTSOV, Mikhail Semenovich (b. 29 May 1782 — d. 18 November 1856, Odessa) was born to a prominent Russian family of princes. He was the son of Général-en-chef Semen Vorontsov, Russian Ambassador to London. Mikhail Vorontsov was enlisted as a corporal in the Life Guard Preobrazhensk Regiment in 1786 ate the age of four, and became actual kamerger on 19 September 1797. He began service as a sub-lieutenant in this unit in 1801. Two years later, Vorontsov was appointed to the Russian troops in the Caucasus and took part in operations against the Persians. He distinguished himself at Yerivan for which he received the Order of St. George (4th class) on 9 August 1804. During the 1805 Campaign, he served with General Tolstoy's corps in Pomerania. In 1806-1807, he served in Poland and distinguished himself at Pultusk (promotion to colonel, 22 January 1807) and Friedland. In 1807, Vorontsov took command of the 1st Battalion of the Life Guard Preobrazhensk Regiment. Two years later, he was appointed chef of the Narva Musketeer Regiment, Army of Moldavia, on 11 October 1809. He participated in the actions at Bazardjik (promoted to major general on 26 June 1810, golden cross), Shumla, Ruse, and Viddin (Order of St. George, 3rd class, 22 March 1812). In early 1812, he took command of the 2nd Grenadier Division of the 2nd Western Army.

Vorontsov participated in Bagration's retreat during the 1812 Campaign, and fought at Saltanovka, Smolensk, and Borodino, where he lost two-thirds of his division defending the fleches and took a serious bayonet wound. After recuperating, he assumed command of the advance guard of the 3rd Western Army and fought at Bromberg, Rogazen, and Poznan in early 1813. For his action, Vorontsov was promoted to lieutenant general on 20 February 1813. Later that year, he served in the Army of the North and participated in the battles at Gross Beeren, Dennewitz, Leipzig, and Kassel. In 1814, Vorontsov distinguished himself at Craonne (Order of St. George, 2nd class, 7 March 1814), Laon, and Paris.

After the war, he led the 12th Division in late 1814 and assumed command of the Russian Occupation Corps in France. He rose to adjutant general on 11 September 1815, and led the 3rd Corps on 2 March 1820. Three years later, he was appointed Governor General of Novorossiisk and Viceroy (*namestnik*) of Bessarabia on 19 May 1823.

Vorontsov received a promotion to general of infantry on 10 April 1825, and became a member of the State Council in 1826. In

1828-1829, he participated in the Russo-Turkish War and distinguished himself at Varna, for which he earned a golden sword inscribed "For the Capture of Varna." On 8 January 1845, he became Viceroy and Commander-in-Chief of the Russian troops in the Caucasus.

Over the next ten years, Vorontsov undertook many administrative and social reforms in the Transcaucasian provinces, and launched massive offensives against the Chechens, who were led by Imam Shamil. Vorontsov was conferred the title of his highness prince (*svetleishii kniaz*) on 14 April 1852, and received the rank of general field marshal on 5 September 1856.

During his long career, Vorontsov earned numerous foreign awards, including the French Order of St. Louis (1st class), British Order of Bath (1st class), Austrian Orders of St. Stephan and of Maria Theresa, Swedish Orders of the Seraphim and of the Sword, Prussian Orders of the Black and Red Eagles, Hanoverian Order of the Guelph, Hesse-Kassel Order of Military Merit, Sardinian Order of St. Maurice and Lazarus, and others.

VOYEIKOV, Aleksey Ivanovich (d. 1776 — d. 7 September 1812, Borodino) was born to a Russian noble family. Graduating from the Artillery and Engineer Cadet Corps, he began service as a shtyk-junker in the 1st Pontoon Company in 1789. He served in southern Russia in 1789-1794 and fought under Alexander Suvorov in Italy in 1799. During the 1805 Campaign, he distinguished himself at Austerlitz. In 1806-1807, he fought at Pultusk (Order of St. Anna, 3rd class), Eylau (Order of St. Vladimir, 4th class), Heilsberg, and Friedland. Voyeikov took command of the 4th Artillery Brigade on 24 March 1811, and rose to colonel on 25 June 1811. During the 1812 Campaign, he fought at Smolensk and was mortally wounded at Borodino on 7 September.

VOYEIKOV, Aleksey Vasilievich (b. 20 December 1778 — d. 5 July 1825) was born to an ancient noble family from the Orel *gubernia*. He enlisted as a sergeant in the Life Guard Preobrazhensk Regiment in 1793. He studied at the University of Moscow Boarding School and graduated second in his class on 30 May 1796. The following year, he transferred as a sub-ensign to the Yaroslavl Musketeer Regiment on 2 February 1797. He served under General Alexander Rimsky-Korsakov in Switzerland in 1799 and fought at Zurich.

After returning to Russia, he became a lieutenant on 31 January 1800, staff captain in the Crimea Musketeer Regiment in 1803, and captain in 8 March 1805. In early 1806, his regiment was attached to the 9th Division, Army of Moldavia. He took part in the opening moves of the Russo-Turkish War, fought at Khotin, marched with the 9th Division to Poland, and participated in the battle of Ostrolenka, for which he received the Order of St. Vladimir (4th class).

In May 1807, Voyeikov became adjutant to General Peter Tolstoy, the new commander of the 9th Division, and fought at Olshova Borka on 11 June 1807. After Tilsit, Voyeikov was promoted to major in the Life Guard Grenadier Regiment. During the Russo-Swedish War, he served as a brigade-major to Lieutenant Generals Mikhail Barclay de Tolly and Tuchkov I. Voyeikov took part in the battle at Idensalmi (golden sword for courage) and the crossing of Kvarken in 1809. He negotiated an armistice with the Swedes and was promoted to lieutenant colonel. In May 1809, he became an adjutant to Barclay de Tolly, and after the war was transferred as a lieutenant colonel to the Life Guard Preobrazhensk Regiment on 3 October

1809. Further promotions followed as Voyeikov became colonel on 13 January 1810, and flügel adjutant to Emperor Alexander I on 11 October that same year. After Barclay de Tolly became the Minister of War, Voyeikov became involved in the military reorganizations in 1811 and received the Order of St. Anna (2nd class) for his service. He led the 3rd Brigade of the 27th Division, 2nd Western Army, on 31 March 1812.

During the 1812 Campaign, Voyeikov participated in the actions at Krasnyi, Smolensk, Shevardino, Borodino, Chirikov, Spas Kuplya, Maloyaroslavets, and Krasnyi. Voyeikov was promoted to major general on 3 December 1812. He left the army in late December to marry his fiance and returned in April 1813, when he assumed command of the Jager Brigade of the 27th Division. He fought at Haynau and Kaiserswalde, where he was seriously wounded in the right hand. For his courage, he garnered a golden sword with diamonds and the Prussian Order of the Red Eagle (2nd class).

Voyeikov spent the rest of campaign recuperating from his wound and was furloughed on 1 May 1814. He was discharged on 29 June 1815. He never fully recovered and died on 5 July 1825, at the village of Rasskazovo in the Tambov *gubernia* from complications relating to his injury. He was buried at the Treguliaevo Predtechevo Monastery.

VSEVOLOZHSKY, Aleksey Matveyevich (b. 1763 — d. 26 January 1813, Kaluga) was born to a noble family from the Vladimir *gubernia*. He began service as a private in the Kargopol Carabinier Regiment in 1778 and rose to vakhmistr in 1780 and cornet in 1784. After fighting the Turks in 1787-1791, he served in Poland in 1792-1794. During the 1805 Campaign, he distinguished himself at Austerlitz and was promoted to colonel. He took part in the 1807 Campaign in Poland and earned a promotion to major general for his actions at Eylau on 24 December 1807. Vsevolozhsky became chef of the Elisavetgrad Hussar Regiment on 25 January 1808. During the 1812 Campaign, he served with the 8th Brigade of the 2nd Cavalry Division in the 1st Western Army and fought at Vitebsk, Smolensk, Valutino, and Borodino. Vsevolozhsky fell seriously ill in late 1812 and traveled to Kaluga to recuperate. He died there at the local hospital on 26 January 1813.

VTOROV, Osip Maksimovich (b. 1772 — date of death unclear) was born to a noble family in the Kursk *gubernia*. He began service as a sub-ensign in the Belozersk Infantry Regiment and rose to ensign in 1789. He participated in the Russo-Swedish War in 1788-1790 and in the operations in Poland in 1794. In 1805, Vtorov served in the Olonetsk Infantry Regiment and distinguished himself at Austerlitz, for which he received a promotion to lieutenant colonel. In 1807, he assumed comand of the Olonetsk Musketeer Regiment on 10 December 1807. From 1806-1812, he served in the Danubian Principalities, where he participated in numerous battles against the Turks and became colonel on 25 April 1811. He was appointed chef of the Ukraine Infantry Regiment on 31 March 1812.

During the 1812 Campaign, Vtorov served with the 1st Brigade, 8th Division, Army of Danube, and took part in operations in Volhynia, including a combat at Volkovysk, where he was wounded. In 1813-1814, Vtorov distinguished himself at Dresden, Leipzig, Magdeburg (wounded), and Hamburg. He was promoted to major general on 11 September 1814, but took a discharge due to poor health on 13 June 1815.

VUICH, Nikolay Vasilievich (b. 1765 — d. 8 April 1836, Nezhin) was born to a Serbian family that settled in Russia in mid-18th century. He enlisted as a company quartermaster (*rotnii kvartemistr*) in the Akhtyrsk Hussar Regiment on 23 December 1777, and became an adjutant with sub-ensign's rank in the 3rd Battalion of the Byelorussia Jager Corps on 19 April 1787. Vuich participated in the Russo-Turkish War in 1787-1791, fighting at Byrlad (promoted to lieutenant), Maksimeni, Galati (wounded in the right leg), and Ismail (promoted to captain, golden cross). In 1792-1794, he served in Poland and took part in the actions at Lubar, Divin, Kobryn, Krupchitsa, Tiraspol, Warsaw, and Praga. For his actions, Vuich was promoted to second major in late 1794. In 1797, he joined the 12th Jager

Regiment, and in November 1799, became a lieutenant colonel. On 22 September 1800, he took command of the 11th Jager Regiment but was removed from command on 8 April 1803, only to be appointed again commander of this unit on 9 September 1803. Vuich received his colonelcy on 30 September 1803. Three years later, he became chef of the newly established 25th Jager Regiment on 4 July 1806.

During the 1806-1807 Campaigns in Poland, Vuich served in the Russian advance and rear guards and fought at Mohrungen, Wolfsdorf, Landsberg, Eylau (Order of St. Vladimir, 3rd class), Launau, Guttstadt, Deppen (Order of St. Anna, 2nd class), Elditten, Heilsberg, and Friedland. For his role in the last two battles, he received the Order of St. George (3rd class) on 1 June 1808. That same year he served under Prince Peter Bagration in Finland, where he distinguished himself at Ulfsby and captured Great Aland Island, where he was later garrisoned. In May 1808, he was captured by the superior Swedish landing forces after a desperate defense of the island. Vuich remained in the Swedish captivity until August 1809. He returned to Russia, where he was acquitted of any wrongdoing in losing the island.. He became chef of the 19th Jager Regiment on 24 March 1812.

During the 1812 Campaign, Vuich led a brigade of the 24th Division, 6th Corps, 1st Western Army. He participated in the battles at Vitebsk, Smolensk, Mikhalevka, Borodino (promoted to major general on 2 December 1812, with seniority dating from 7 September 1812), Vereya (diamond signs of the Order of St. Anna, 2nd class), Maloyaroslavets (golden sword with diamonds), and Krasnyi. In 1813, he assumed command of the 24th Division and participated in the battles at Gross Beeren, Dennewitz, Leipzig (Order of St. Anna, 1st class), and Rotenburg. In 1814, he served at Craonne, Laon (diamond signs of the Order of St. Anna, 1st class), and Paris. In 1815, Vuich took command of the 3rd Brigade of the 24th Division, and during the Hundred Days, marched to France, where he took part in the siege of Verdun and the grand military parade at Vertus. Returning to Russia, he took command of the 24th Division on 9 December 1816, and of the 18th Division on 23 November 1827. Vuich rose to lieutenant general on 24 December 1824, and was relieved of command because of poor health on 9 February 1828.

VYAZEMSKY, Vasily Vasilievich (b. 1775 — d. 17 December 1812, Minsk) was born to a prominent Russian family of princes. He enlisted in the Guard in 1786 and studied in the University of Moscow Boarding School and the Mountain Engineer Corps before beginning service in the Life Guard Preobrazhensk Regiment in 1790. Two years later, he became a duty officer to General Alexander Suvorov and served in Poland in 1792-1794, garnering a golden cross for his actions at Praga. He transferred to regular infantry with a rank of premier major in 1795, and was promoted to colonel on 12 October 1799. In 1800, Vyazemsky became commander of the 11th Jager Regiment on 25 July and chef of the 13th Jager Regiment on 8 August. Three years later, he rose to major general on 5 December 1803.

In 1805-1806, Vyazemsky participated in the expeditions to Naples and Illyria. In 1809-1812, he served in the Danubian Principalities, where he distinguished himself at Braila, Ruse, and Turtukai, for which he received the Order of St. Anna (1st class). In 1812, he led the 3rd Brigade, 15th Division, 3rd Reserve Army of Observation, at Kobryn, Gorodechnya, and Borisov, where he was seriously wounded on 21 November 1812. He died at a military hospital in Minsk on 17 December 1812.

WALLMODEN-GIMBORN, Ludwig George Thedel Graf von (b. 6 February 1769, Hanover — d. 20 March 1862, Vienna) began service as a lieutenant in the Hanoverian Leibgarde-Regiment and transferred into the Prussian army in 1790. He fought during the Revolutionary Wars against France, served as Rittmeister in the 6th Husarenregiment Wolffradt, and was awarded the Prussian Order Pour le Merite in 1794 for his actions at Kaiserslautern, when he was wounded in the chest. He entered Austrian service as a Rittmeister (2 Classe) in the Vécsey Hussar Regiment in October 1795. He was promoted to Rittmeister (1 Classe) on 1 January 1797, then transferred to the Karaczay Chevaulegers Regiment and became major in the General Staff on 16 April 1797. Wallmoden was appointed to the 2nd Dragoon Regiment on 7 June 1798, and promoted to oberst-lieutenant in the 1st Uhlan Regiment on 3 August 1798. He became commander of the 1st Uhlan Regiment on 16 August 1801 and rose to major general on 1 April 1807.

During the 1809 Campaign, Wallmoden served on diplomatic mission to London to negotiate subsidies, but returned in time to fight at Wagram, serving as a brigade commander in Feldmarschall-Lieutenant Graf Klenau's 6th Army Corps. After the battle, he served in the rearguard and distinguished himself at Hollabrunn. For his actions, he was awarded the Austrian Order of Maria Theresa on 13 July 1809. He was promoted to feldmarschall-lieutenant on 21 August 1809. After briefly remaining in British service, he entered Russian service on 30 March 1813, and commanded light cavalry detachments under Generals Dörenberg, Tettenborn, and Chernishev in Northern Germany. He participated in the battle at Dennewitz (Order of St. George, 3rd class, 2 October 1813) and Gohrde. In late 1813, he successfully operated around Hamburg and Mecklenburg. He left Russian service on 29 June 1815, and returned to Austrian army.

In August 1816, Wallmoden led Austrian troops in Naples and became colonel-proprietor of the 6th Cuirassier Regiment on 30 August 1819. In 1820, Wallmoden commanded a division in the General Frimont's corps and suppressed a disturbance in Naples. He remained there until March 1827, when he was transferred to Milan and led the 1st Corps between August 1830 and March 1848. He became a privy councilor on 20 January 1831, and was promoted to general of cavalry on 18 September 1838. Wallmoden remained in Milan until 1 March 1848, when he was appointed deputy to Feldmarschall Graf Radetzky. He retired on 19 October 1848, and was awarded the Grand Cross of the Order of Leopold. Wallmoden spent the rest of his life in Vienna, where he died on 20 March 1862.

During his long career, he was also awarded the Russian Orders of St. Alexander of Neva, St Vladimir (2nd class), St. Anna (1st class) with diamonds, Prussian Red Eagle (1st class) and the Pour le Merite with a crown, British Order of the Bath, Hanoverian Order of Guelphs, Swedish Order of the Sword, and the Sicilian Order of St. George.

WINZEGORODE (Wintzingerode), Ferdinand Fedorovich (b. 26 February 1770, Allendorf, Hesse-Kassel — d. 30 June 1818, Wisbaden) was born to a prominent Hessian family. He studied at the Kassel Cadet Corps from 1778 to 1785 and began service in the Hessian Guard. However, he soon took a discharge and spent the next three years serving in the armies of various lesser German states. Winzegorode served in the Austrian army in Netherlands in 1790, and on the Rhine in 1792-1793 and again in 1795-1796. He entered Russian service with a rank of major in the Military Order Cuirassier Regiment on 19 June 1797. He became lieutenant colonel in the Life Guard Izmailovsk Regiment and adjutant to Grand Duke Constantine in early 1798, and was promoted to colonel on 5 June 1798.

On 14 February 1799, Winzegorode was allowed to leave the Russian service to take command of the Archduke Ferdinand's Dragoon Regiment and participate in operations against the French. Winzegorode returned to Russia on 24 November 1801, and was appointed to the Quartemaster Section of the Imperial Retinue. He rose to major general and adjutant general on 24 April 1802. Between 28 May and 23 September 1803, he served as chef of the Odessa Hussar Regiment.

In early 1805, Winzegorode served on diplomatic mission to the Prussian Court and took part in the drafting of the Allied operational plan against France. During the 1805 Campaign, he served at the Russian headquarters and distinguished himself at Krems (Dürrenstein), for which he received the Order of St. George (3rd class, 20 May 1806). At Hollabrun (Schöngrabern), he and Prince Peter Bagration tricked Marshal Joachim Murat into a one-day armistice that helped General Mikhail Kutuzov rescue his army. Winzegorode fought at Austerlitz, but was held responsible for the defeattafter the battle was held responsible for defeat. He left the Russian service on 15 January 1807, and from 1807 to 1811 served in the Austrian army. In 1809, he distinguished himself at Aspern-Essling, where he was severly wounded. He was promoted to feldmarshal lieutenant on 5 June 1809, for his actions in the latter battle. He returned to the Russian army on 23 May 1812.

During the 1812 Campaign, Winzegorode led a partisan detachment in the Smolensk *gubernia* and covered the St. Petersburg route. For his actions, he received a promotion to lieutenant general on 18 September 1812, and the Order of St. Alexander of Neva on 21 October 1812. On 22 October, as the French withdrew from Moscow, Winzegorode entered the town with his adjutant to negotiate with the French and prevent them from destroying the Kremlin. The French detained him and Napoleon wanted to court martial him for treason, claiming Hessian Winzegorode was his subject (Hesse became part of the Confederation of the Rhine). However, as he was transported from Moscow, Winzegorode was rescued by the Cossacks near Radoshkevichi, between Minsk and Vilna. He assumed command of corps at Grodno and distinguished himself pursuing the retreating French forces. In 1813, he took part in the actions at Kalisch (Order of St. George, 2nd class, 14 February 1813), Lutzen (Order of St. Vladimir, 2nd class, 3 May 1813), Gros Beeren, Dennewitz, and Leipzig for which he was promoted to general of cavalry on 20 October 1813.

In 1814, Winzegorode led a corps and fought at Soissons (Order of St. Vladimir, 1st class), Craonne, Laon, and St. Dizier. Later that year, he led the 2nd Independent Corps. After returning to Russia, he took command of the 2nd

Cavalry Corps, with which he marched back to France during the Hundred Days in 1815.

After the war, Winzegorode took command of 2nd Corps (21 April 1816) and later of the Independent Lithuanian Corps on 7 July 1817. In May 1818, he traveled to Germany to recuperate from wounds but died at Wisbaden on 30 June 1818.

WITTE, Ivan Osipovich (b. 1781, Paris — d. 3 July 1840) was born to a prominent noble family from the Kamenets-Podolsk *gubernia*; his father was the Commandant of Kamenets-Podolsk under Empress Catherine II. Witte enlisted as a cornet in the Life Guard Horse Regiment on 28 September 1792, and transferred as a staff rotmistr to the Chevalier Guard Regiment on 13 January 1800. He was elevated to colonel in 1801, and distinguished himself at Austerlitz in 1805, where he was seriously wounded in the right leg by a cannonball. After recuperating, he took a discharge in 1807 and traveled to France, where he volunteered in the French army and took part in the 1809 Campaign against Austria. In 1810-1812, Witte served as a Russian spymaster in the Duchy of Warsaw and provided the Russian command with intelligence on the French forces and their movements.

In 1812, Witte organized and led a brigade of four regular Cossack regiments in the Ukraine. On 8 March 1813, he became chef of the 1st Ukraine Cossack Regiment and fought at Kalisch (Order of St. George, 3rd class, 6 March 1813), Lutzen, Bautzen, and Leipzig. In 1814, he took part in the actions at Laon, Craonne, and Paris.

After the war, he commanded a military settlement in the Ukraine and rose to lieutenant general on 18 May 1818. He took command of the 1st Reserve Cavalry Corps on 29 October 1823. During the Russo-Turkish War of 1828-1829, he became general of cavalry on 3 May 1829. Witte took part in the suppression of the Polish Uprising in 1831, for which he received an appointment as chef of the Ukraine Uhlan Regiment on 11 September 1831, and the Order of St. George (2nd class) on 30 October. The following year, he became inspector of all Russian reserve cavalry on 22 April 1832.

During his long career, Witte also received the Orders of St. Andrew the First Called with diamonds, St. Vladimir (1st class), St. Alexander of Neva with diamonds, the White Eagle, St. Anna (1st class), St. John of Jerusalem, Prussian Order of the Red Eagle and the Pour le Merite, the Swedish Order of the Sword, as well as medals inscribed "For Military Merit" and "For XXX Years of Distinguished Service."

WITTGENSTEIN, Peter Khristiano-vich (Ludwig Adolf) (b. 5 January 1769, Pereyaslavl — d. 11 June 1843, Lvov) was born to a prominent Prussian family, the son of a Prussian lieutenant general in the Russian service. He enlisted as a sergeant in the Life Guard Semeyonovsk Regiment on 1 April 1781, and transferred as vakhmistr to the Life Guard

Horse Regiment on 1 April 1789. He rose to cornet on 12 January 1790, sub-lieutenant on 12 January 1792, and transferred as premier major to the Ukraine Light Horse Regiment on 2 May 1793. Wittgenstein served in Poland in 1794, distinguishing himself at Ostrolenka (Order of St. George, 4th class, 12 January 1795) and Praga (golden cross). In 1796, he took part in the Persian Campaign along the Caspian Sea, and after the capture of Derbent, delivered the city keys to St. Petersburg. The same year, Wittgenstein transferred to the Elisavetgrad Hussar Regiment, then to the Rostov Dragoon Regiment on 2 May, and to General Lindener's Hussar Regiment on 21 August. He rose to colonel on 9 February 1798, and became commander of the Akhtyrsk Hussar Regiment on 5 May 1799. A month later, Wittgenstein was elevated to major general and chef of the Mariupol Hussar Regiment on 1 July 1799. He was discharged on 13 January 1801, but returned to service on 1 May 1801. Wittgenstein was appointed commander of the Elisavetgrad Hussar Regiment on 14 October 1801, and chef of the Mariupol Hussar Regiment on 13 January 1802.

Wittgenstein participated in the 1805 Campaign against Napoleon, fighting at Amstetten (Order of St. George, 3rd class, 24 January 1806), Wischau, and Austerlitz (Order of St. Anna, 1st class). In 1806, he transferred to the Army of Moldavia and took part in the opening moves of the Russo-Turkish War of 1806-1812. Later that year, he led the advance guard of General Essen's corps, covering the Russian border from the Bug River to Grodno. He fought the French at Ostrolenka and in several rear guard actions. For his service, he was decorated with the Order of St. Vladimir (3rd class) and a golden sword for courage. Wittgenstein became chef of the Life Guard Hussar Regiment on 10 November 1807, and lieutenant general on 24 December. In 1808-1811, he commanded a corps in the southern Finland.

In 1812, Wittgenstein commanded the 1st Independent Corps, which covered the routes to St. Petersburg. He engaged the French at Wilkomir, Klyastitsy (wounded in the head, received 12,000 rubles and the Order of St. George, 2nd class, 10 November 1812), Kokhanovichi, Polotsk (two battles), Chashniki, Smolyani, and on the Berezina. After successful battles at Polotsk, he became increasingly popular in Russian society and was called "the Savior of St. Petersburg." For the capture of Polotsk, he was promoted to general of cavalry on 3 November 1812, with seniority dating from 18 October 1812. Wittgenstein committed several mistakes during the operation on the Berezina River that ultimately allowed Napoleon to rescue save much of his army, though Admiral Paul Chichagov was largely blamed for the fiasco. Wittgenstein occupied Berlin from February to April 1813 and fought at Mockern, for which he received the diamond signs of the Order of St. Alexander of Neva and the Prussian Orders of the Black and Red Eagles.

Wittgenstein assumed command of the Russian army on 25 April 1813, after the death of Mikhail Kutuzov. However, he mishandled the army at Lutzen (Order of St. Andrew the First Called) and Bautzen. After these defeats, Wittgenstein resigned and was replaced by General Mikhail Barclay de Tolly. In August-October 1813, he took part in the battles at Berggieshubel, Dresden, Pirna, Hellendorf, and Leipzig, for which he was decorated with a golden sword with laurels and diamonds. At the head of the 6th Corps in 1814, Wittgenstein was seriously wounded in the right thigh at Bar sur Aube. He took a furlough and traveled to Ramstadt to recuperate.

After the war, he took command of the 2nd Army on 15 May 1818, and became a member of the State Council on 7 September 1818. He was appointed chef of the Wittgenstein (earlier Mariupol) Hussar Regiment on 9 February 1826, and received promotion to general field marshal on 3 September 1826.

Wittgenstein became the Commander-in-Chief of the Russian army during the Russo-Turkish War in 1828-182, and captured Macin and Braila. However, he was virtually ignored by his General Staff, which operated independently from him. Despite Wittgenstein's requests for a discharge, Emperor Nicholas I kept him in command and even awarded him the diamond signs of the Order of St. Andrew the First Called on 21 June 1828.

Wittgenstein was finally relieved of command because of poor health on 21 February 1829. He settled at his estate of Kamenka in the Podolsk *gubernia*, where he spent the next decade. On 13 May 1834, the King of Prussia conferred upon him the title of prince for his role in the 1813 Campaign, and two years later Emperor Nicholas gave him the title of His Highness Prince (*svetleishii prince*). While traveling in Europe to recover his health, Wittgenstein died at Lvov on 11 June 1843. He is buried there.

WOLFE, Ivan Pavlovich (Peter Johann Paul Wilhelm) (b. 7 June 1783, Munster — 11 April 1828, Derpt) was born to a noble family from the Estland *gubernia*. He enlisted as a sub-ensign in the Tobolsk Musketeer Regiment on 1 October 1798, and began service as ensign on 18 December 1798. Wolfe participated in the expedition to Holland in 1799 and took part in the battles at Texel and Helder, for which he received the Order of St. Anna (3rd class) and a promotion to lieutenant. He participated in the 1806-1807 Campaigns in Poland, where he fought at Pultusk. At Eylau, he was seriously wounded in the left hand and right leg and received a golden cross and rank of staff captain. After recuperating, he joined his unit in Finland, where he served for the next two years.

During the 1812 Campaign, Wolfe served with the 2nd Brigade, 4th Division, 2nd Corps, 1st Western Army, and fought at Smolensk (promotion to lieutenant colonel), Gedeonovo (Order of St. Vladimir, 4th class), and Borodino, where he assumed command of the Tobolsk Infantry Regiment and repulsed several French cavalry charges. For his actions, he garnered the Order of St. George (4th class, 4 January 1813). In October-November 1812, he distinguished himself at Tarutino (Imperial letter of gratitude), Maloyaroslavets (golden sword), Vyazma (Imperial letter of gratitude), and Krasnyi (Order of St. Anna, 2nd class). In 1813, Wolfe served at Lutzen (received promotion to colonel), Batuzen, Dresden, Kulm (Prussian Iron Cross), and Leipzig, where he took two serious wounds to the head and right shoulder.

After recuperating, Wolfe returned to his unit during the campaign in France in 1814 and served at Brienne, La Rothière, Bar sur Aube, Troyes, and Paris for which he was promoted to major general on 17 January 1815, with seniority dating from 30 March 1814.

After the war, he led the 1st Brigade, 4th Division, and the 1st Brigade, 22nd Division, in 1815-1824. He took a discharge because of poor health on 18 February 1824, but returned to the army two years later and assumed command of the 1st Brigade, 1st Division, on 31 March 1826. The following year, Wolfe became commander of the Combined Division of the 5th Corps on 9 April 1827, and assumed command of the 18th Division on 9 February 1828.

WOLZOGEN, Ludwig Adolf Friedrich (b. 15 February 1774, Meininhen — d. 16 June 1845, Berlin) was born to a Saxon noble family. He served in the Württemberg and Prussian armies in 1792-1806, rising to a lieutenant colonel of the Württemberg army. He entered Russian service as a major in the quartermaster service on 5 October 1807. His deep knowledge of military theory earned Wolzogen the confidence of Emperor Alexander I, who made him his flügel adjutant on 23 January 1811, and a lieutenant colonel on 27 September 1811. During 1811-1812, Wolzogen made several missions to the Russian western provinces to evaluate Russian military deployment on the eve of Napoleon's invasion. He submitted his own plan of operations against Napoleon and opposed to the idea of defending the Drissa Camp. He earned his colonelcy on 24 June 1812.

During the 1812 Campaign, Wolzogen served in the Quartermaster Section of the Imperial Retinue, and as the quartemaster on the staff of the 1st Western Army. After Emperor Alexander's departure from the army, Wolzogen became a duty officer to General Barclay de Tolly and, in October–November 1812, to General Levin Bennigsen. He took part in the actions at Vitebsk, Smolensk, Borodino (bruised, Order of St. Anna, 2nd class, with diamonds) and Tarutino (golden sword). In 1813, he served in the headquarters of the Russian army and took part in the battles at Bautzen, Gros Beeren,

Dresden, and Leipzig, for which he was promoted to a major general on 20 October 1813. In 1814, Wolzogen distinguished himself at La Rothière, for which he garnered the Order of St. Anna (1st class).

After the war, he left the Russian service for the Prussian army, where he eventually rose to general of infantry in 1836. Wolzogen penned interesting memoirs on his participation in the Napoleonic Wars, which are entitled *Memoiren des Königlich Preussischen Generals der Infanterie Ludwig Freiherrn von Wolzogen*, published in Leipzig in 1851.

WÜRTTEMBERG, Alexander Friedrich von (b. 5 May 1771, Mempelgard — d. 4 July 1833, Gotha) was born to a ruling family of the Kingdom of Württemberg. His sister was Empress Consort Maria Feodorovna, the wife of Emperor Paul I of Russia. He began service as a colonel in the Württemberg army on 21 April 1791, and transferred as a colonel to the Austrian army in 1793, with which he took part in campaigns against France in 1796-1799, fighting at Rastadt, Wurtzburg, Offenbach, Stockach, and Zurich. Prince Alexander Württemberg became major general in 1796 and feldmarshal lieutenant in the Austrian army in July 1798. On Suvorov's recommendation, he entered Russian service as a lieutenant general and chef of the Riga Cuirassier Regiment on 19 May 1800. His unit was reorganized as the Riga Dragoon Regiment on 1 August 1800, and Württemberg was promoted to general of cavalry on 26 August 1800. He was appointed Military Governor of Byelorussia on 15 April 1811.

During the 1812 Campaign, Württemberg served in the headquarters of the 1st Western Army and fought at Vitebsk, Smolensk, Borodino, Tarutino (Order of St. George, 3rd class, 4 January 1813), Maloyaroslavets, Vyazma, and Krasnyi. In 1813, he led the Russian troops besieging Danzig, for which he received a golden sword inscribed "For the Capture of Danzig," and the Order of St. George (2nd class, 31 August 1813). After the war, he returned to his duties of Military Governor of Byelorussia and was confirmed as chef of the Riga Dragoon Regiment on 17 February 1818. He became the head of the Communications Departments on 14 August 1822, and began construction of several channels to improve navigation on the major rivers in the western Russia.

Württemberg was appointed chef of the Ekaterinoslavl Cuirassier Regiment on 13 January 1826, member of the State Council on 17 December 1826, and again chef of the Riga Dragoon Regiment on 7 July 1827. He took a discharge on 15 September 1832, and left Russia on 24 November of the same year.

During his long career, Alexander of Württemberg also garnered the Russian Orders of St. Andrew the First Called with diamonds, St. Anna (1st class), St. Alexander of Neva, St. Vladimir (1st class), St. John of Jerusalem, Prussian Orders of the Black and Red Eagles, Württemberg Orders of the Crown and the Military Merit, and the Bavarian Order of Maximilian Joseph.

WÜRTTEMBERG, Eugene (Friedrich Karl Paul Ludwig) von (b. 8 January 1788, Els — d. 16 September 1857, Karlsruhe) was born to a ruling family of the Kingdom of Württemberg. He entered Russian service as a colonel in the Life Guard Horse Regiment on 25 November 1797, and became chef of the Pskov Dragoon Regiment on 23 March 1799. He enjoyed close relations with Emperor Paul I. After Paul was assassinated, he left the Russian army, but Emperor Alexander made him chef of the Tavrida Grenadier Regiment on 18 April 1801.

Eugene of Württemberg lived in Europe for the next six years and returned to the Russian army in 1806. He participated in the campaigns in Poland, distinguishing himself at Pultusk (Order of St. George, 4th class, 10 March 1807), Eylau, Wolfsdorf, and Friedland.

After Tilsit, Württemberg took command of a brigade of the 3rd Division, and in 1810-1811, led the 9th Division. He took command of the 4th Division in the 1st Western Army on 8 June 1811, and, during the 1812 Campaign participated in the actions at Smolensk, Gedeonovo, Borodino (Order of St. George, 3rd class and promotion to lieutenant general, 1 November 1812), Tarutino, Vyazma, and Krasnyi. In 1813, he commanded the 2nd Corps at Kalisch, Lutzen, Dresden, Pirna, Kulm, and Leipzig (Order of St. George, 2nd class, 20 October 1813). In 1814, he distinguished himself at Bar sur Aube and Paris for which he was promoted to general of infantry on 29 March 1814.

After the war, he commanded the 1st Corps in 1816-1821. During the Decembrist Uprising in December 1825, he supported Emperor Nicholas I and defended the Winter Palace. In return, Nicholas renamed the Tavrida Grenadier Regiment to Eugene von Württemberg's Grenadier Regiment on 6 January 1826.

During the Russo-Turkish War in 1828, von Württemberg commanded the 7th Corps but had a disagreement with General Diebitch that led to his resignation. He left the Russian service the same year and returned to Württemberg.

During his career, he received the Russian Orders of St. Andrew the First Called with diamonds, St. Alexander of Neva with diamonds, St. Vladimir (1st class), St. Anna (1st class), St. John of Jerusalem, Prussian Orders of the Black and Red Eagles, Württemberg Orders of the Golden Eagle and of the Military Merit, Bavarian Order of Maximilian Joseph, Austrian Order of Maria Theresa, Saxe-Weimar Order of the White Hawk, Hannoverian Order of Guelphs, and the French Order of St. Louis.

Another offspring of Württemberg family, Prince **Paul Karl Friedrich August von Württemberg** (b. 30 October 1785 — d. 1852, Paris) entered the Russian army with a rank of major general on 28 December 1813, and commanded the Anhalt-Turring Brigade during the 1814 Campaign in France. In 1814-1816, he served in the 14th Division and thereafter returned to Württemberg.

YAFIMOVICH, Ivan Lvovich (b. 1781 — d. 8 July 1831, Warsaw) was born to a noble family in the Smolensk *gubernia*. He graduated from the Infantry Cadet Corps on 13 August 1800, and was appointed lieutenant of the Moscow Grenadier Regiment on 11 October 1800. During the 1805 Campaign, Yafimovich was wounded at Austerlitz on 2 December 1805. In 1806-1807, his regiment was attached to the 8th Division and Yafimovich fought at Eylau (golden cross) and Heilsberg (wounded in the left hand, golden sword). He transferred as a staff captain to the Life Guard Jager Regiment on 14 March 1808, and served as an adjutant to Prince Karl von Mecklenburg in the Danube Valley in 1809-1810. Yafimovich distinguished himself at Bazardjik (Order of St. Vladimir, 4th class, and promotion to captain) but took a severe wound to the head and right hand at Ruse.

During the 1812 Campaign, Yafimovich served in the 3rd Brigade of the Guard Infantry Division and fought at Ostrovno and Borodino, where he was seriously wounded again, this time in the right leg. His courage earned him the Order of St. Anna (2nd class). After a short convalescence, he took part in the battle of Krasnyi, after which he was promoted to colonel on 1 February 1813. During the 1813-1814 Campaigns, he participated in the battles of Lutzen, Bautzen, Kulm (Prussian Iron Cross), Leipzig, and Paris. In 1815, he marched with the Russian army to France during the Hundred Days and attended the grand military parade at Vertus. He was promoted to major general on 8 January 1816, with seniority dating from 27 September 1815.

After the war, Yafimovich served as an assistant to the commander of the 3rd Grenadier Division (3 February 1816), led the 1st Brigade of the 14th Division (9 January 1817), and the 1st Brigade of the 11th Division (11 February 1817). After briefly serving as an assistant to the commander of the 7th Division, he assumed command of the reserve battalions of the 7th and 15th Divisions in 1819. He became commander of the 1st Brigade of the 4th Division on 28 September 1826, and participated in the Russo-Turkish War of 1828-1829, serving at Braila and Varna. Yafimovich took command of the 1st Brigade of the 6th Division on 16 October 1829, and was severely wounded at Silistra. In 1830, he marched to suppress the Polish uprising. His luck finally ran out, and and Yafimovich was mortally wounded in the battle of Warsaw.

YASHVIL, Vladimir Mikhailovich, *see* **Iashvili Vladimir Mikhailovich**

YASHVIL, Leo Mikhailovich, *see* **Iashvili Leo Mikhailovich**

YAZIKOV, Peter Grigorevich (b. 1756 — date of death unknown; removed from rosters on 30 March 1826) was born to a noble family in the Vladimir *gubernia*. He was enlisted at the age of twelve as a corporal in the Tobolsk Musketeer Regiment on 23 October 1768, and rose to ensign on 20 June 1769. Yazikov served in Poland in 1771-1773, and participated in the suppression of Emelyan Pugachev's peasant rebellion in 1774. He transferred as a major to the Russian main headquarters in April 1776, and became lieutenant colonel of the Pskov Infantry Regiment on 21 September 1778. Yazikov took part in the Russo-Swedish War in 1788-1790, rising to colonel on 2 May 1789, and receiving the Order of St. George (4th class) on 19 September 1790. In 1792-1794, he served in Poland, where he distinguished himself at Praga (golden cross) and Warsaw (golden sword). Yazikov was promoted to brigadier and appointed the deputy commandant of Warsaw on 12 January 1795. However, Yazikov was discharged from army during Paul's purges in June 1797 and returned to service in 1801.

Yazikov became a major general and served in the capacity of duty general in the War College on 31 July 1801. Two years later, he became the

Commandant of Voronezh and chef of the Voronezh Garrison Battaion on 30 April 1803. Yazikov remained at Voronezh for next seven years and was relieved of command on 3 October 1810. Yazikov became chef of the Saratov Infantry Regiment and brigade commander of the 13th Division on 29 January 1811.

During the 1812 Campaign, he marched from the Crimea to Volhynia and participated in several minor actions late in the war, including Pavlovichi, Ustilug, Lukov, and Golovnya. In early 1813, he served in the siege of Modlin and was seriously wounded when a cannoball struck him in the right thigh. Yazikov recovered and became commander of the 2nd Brigade of the 13th Division on 7 October 1814. He rose to become Chief of Staff of the 8th Corps on 9 January 1817, and was soon transferred in the same capacity to the 6th Corps. Yazikov was appointed commander of the 1st District of the Independent Corps of the Internal Guard on 15 March 1819.

YERMOLOV, Aleksey Petrovich, see Ermolov Aleksey Petrovich

YURKOVSKY, Anastasiy Antonovich (b. 1755 — d. 1831) was born to a Hungarian noble family and began service as a vakhmistr in the Hungarian Hussar Regiment on 12 June 1772. He participated in the Russo-Turkish War in 1772-1774 and was promoted to ensign on 12 January 1774. During the Russo-Turkish War of 1788-1791, he distinguished himself at Ochakov (twice wounded in the head), Ismail, and Braila (twice wounded in the head). For his courage, Yurkovsky was awarded the Order of St. George (4th class) on 9 July 1791. Promoted to colonel on 12 November 1798, he took command of the Aleksandria Hussar Regiment on 27 July 1800.

Yurkovsky became major general and chef of the Elisavetgrad Hussar Regiment on 13 January 1807. During the Polish Campaigns of 1806-1807, he served in the 5th Division and distinguished himself at Bartenstein (Order of St. George, 3rd class, 20 April 1807) Eylau, Guttstadt, and Heilsberg (wounded in the right hand). He retired on 25 January 1808, and returned to service on 2 December 1812, to command a Cossack detachment during the French retreat in 1812. In 1813-1814, Yurkovsky participated in the battles at Leignitz, Bunzlau, Katzbach, Reichenbach, Torgau, Lutzen, Leipzig, St. Dizier, Brienne, Montmirail, and Meaux.

After the war, Yurkovsky served as the Commandant of the Sebastopol fortress from 1816-1826.

YURLOV, Ivan Ivanovich (b. 1769 — date of death unknown) was born to Russian noble family from the Nizhegorod *gubernia*. He studied in the Infantry Cadet Corps and was assigned as a lieutenant in the Moscow Carabinier Regiment on 14 March 1787. He participated in the campaign in Poland in 1794-1794, receiving the rank of second major for his actions at Maciejowice and a golden cross for Praga. He became a major on 27 February 1797, and served under General Rimsky-Korsakov in Switzerland, where Yurlov was wounded at Zurich. He was promoted to lieutenant colonel in 1800 and transferred to the Kazan Dragoon Regiment on 8 July 1801. During the Polish Campaign of 1806-1807, his regiment was attached to the 5th Division and Yurlov fought at Pultusk (Order of St. Vladimir, 4th class), Eylau (wounded, golden cross, promoted to colonel on 6 May 1807), Guttstadt, Heilsberg, and Friedland (wounded in the head). Beginning in May 1808, Yurlov served as commanding officer of the Kazan Dragoon Regiment, and went on to earn the Order of St. George (4th class) for 25 years of distuinguished service. Yurlov rose to become full commander of his regiment on 23 August 1810.

During the Russian Campaign of 1812, Yurlov served in General Winzegorode's detachment and took part in minor actions against the French. In 1813, he fought at Kalisch, Lutzen, Bautzen (golden sword), Danzig (promoted to major general, 27 September 1813; Order of St. Vladimir, 3rd class, 13 January 1814). He became commander of the 1st Brigade of the 2nd Dragoon Division on 13 January 1814, and almost three years later retired because of poor health on 23 November 1816. He became the Governor of the Vladimir *gubernia* in March 1817, received the rank of actual civic counsellor, and served in the Commissariat of the Ministry of War in 1818-1828.

YUSHKOV, Alexander Ivanovich (b. 1781 — date of death unknown) was enlisted as a sub-ensign in the Life Guard Preobrazhensk Regiment on 3 February 1792, at the age of eleven, rising to ensign on 2 January 1799. He participated in the 1805-1807 Campaigns, fighting at Austerlitz and Friedland. He was promoted to colonel and appointed battalion commander of the Life Guard Preobrazhensk Regiment on 24 February 1810.

During the 1812 Campaign, Yushkov served in the 1st Brigade of the Guard Infantry Division of the 5th Reserve (Guard) Corps and distinguished himself at Borodino (Order of St. Anna, 2nd class). In 1813, he took part in the battles at Lutzen, Bautzen, Pirna, and Kulm (Prussian Iron Cross). He was promoted to major general on 27 September with seniority dating from 28 August 1813, and became chef of the Yakutsk Infantry Regiment on 10 October 1813. He served as the brigade commander of the 9th Division at Leipzig. In 1814, Yushkov participated in the battles at Brienne, La Rothière, Champaubert, Soissons, Laon, and Paris.

After the war, Yushkov led the 2nd Brigade of the 27th Division, served as an assistant to the commander of the 9th Division (2 April 1816), commanded the 2nd Brigade of the 15th Division (6 March 1819), the 3rd Brigade of the 15th Division (20 June 1821), and the 5th Division (5 November 1824). During the Russo-Turkish War of 1828, Yushkov fought at Silistra, Kulevchi, and on the Kamcha River (wounded in the thigh). He was relieved of command of the 5th Division on 25 January 1829, and commanded the 7th Division from 26 April – 16 October 1829. Yushkov retired in January 1836.

During his career, Yshkov also received the Prussian Order of Red Eagle (2nd class), Baden's Order of the Lion, and a medal for 25 years of distinguished service.

YUZEFOVICH. Dmitry Mikhailovich (b. 1777 — d. 7 October 1821, Romny) was born to a Polish noble family in the Poltava *gubernia*. He enlisted in the Life Guard Preobrazhensk Regiment in 1789, was promoted to captain on 12 January 1795, and appointed adjutant to Général-en-Chef Branitsky. He transferred as a rotmistr to the Ekaterinoslavl Cuirassier Regiment in January 1797 and rose to major in October 1798. He transferred to the Rostov Dragoon Regiment in January 1799, but after this regiment was disbanded, returned to the Kharkov Dragoon Regiment in March 1800. He became lieutenant colonel on 8 January 1801. Yuzefovich temporarily commanded the Kharkov Dragoon Regiment from 22 July 1803 –

January 1804, and later served as a squadron commander in the same regiment.

During the 1805 Campaign, Yuzefovich participated in the retreat from Branau but did not take part in any rearguard actions. At Austerlitz, he served under Uvarov on the north flank and received a golden sword for courage. He took command of the Kharkov Dragoon Regiment on 5 July 1806. During the Polish Campaigns of 1806-1807, Yuzefovich was attached to the 10th Division of Essen I's Corps and distinguished himself at Shumovo (Order of St. George, 4th class, 21 September 1807), Ostrovo, Ostrolenka, and in the rearguard actions on the Bobr River in June 1807. For his conduct, he was promoted to colonel on 24 December 1807, and became chef of the Kharkov Dragoon Regiment on 23 August 1810. Yuzefovich participated in the 1809 Campaign against Austria, but did not participate in any combat.

During the Russian Campaign, Yuzefovich served in the 4th Cavalry Corps of the 2nd Western Army and participated in Bagration's retreat to Smolensk, leading a cavalry detachment comprised of Kharkov Dragoons and Cossacks. In August, he served under General Neverovsky at Krasnyi, where he led a cavalry charge but was routed by Murat's horsemen. At Smolensk on 16-17 August, Yuzefovich led a detachment of the Kharkov Dragoons along with the Bykhalov Cossack Regiment, and counterattacked several times during the battle. After Smolensk, he transferred to the main rear guard and took part in the rearguard actions between Smolensk and Borodino. He distinguished himself at Shevardino and Borodino, served in the rearguard under Platov and Miloradovich in September and fought at Tarutino, Maloyaroslavets, Vyazma (Order of St. Vladimir, 3rd class), and Krasnyi. He transferred to the advance guard of General Vasilchikov and captured Belostock in December 1812. For his perfomance at Borodino, he was promoted to major general on 7 January 1813.

In early 1813, Yuzefovich's regiment was attached to Miloradovich's troops and took part in the capture of Warsaw. He participated in the sieges of Modlin, Kalisch, and Glogau in February-April 1813. In May, Yuzefovich arrived late to take part in battle of Lutzen, but covered the Allied retreat and fought at Nossen. He distinguished himself at Bischofswerda (11 May), Zeiten (15 May), Bautzen (22 May), and Gorlitz. For his courage in these actions, he was awarded the Order of St. Anna, a golden sword with diamonds and the Prussian Order of Red Eagle. In August, he served in St. Priest's Corps in the Army of Silesia and took part in the actions on the Katzbach and Bobr Rivers, the battles of Katzbach and Puzkau (Order of St. George, 3rd class). In October, Yuzefovich commanded a cavalry detacment in the Army of Silesia and fought at Leipzig on 16-19 October (Order of St. Anna, 1st class). After the battle he took part in the pursuit, leading the advance guard of St. Priest's Corps. He captured Düsseldorf (Prussian Order of Red Eagle, 1st class). In December 1813, Yuzefovich was appointed the Commandant of Koblenz and occupied Cologne.

On 19 January 1814, Yuzefovich led troops in the blockade of Metz, but was recalled on 24 March to suppress a local uprising. After returning to Metz, he accepted the French surrender of this fortress on 11 April, and was appointed Commandant of Nancy and commander of the Russian troops in Lotharingia. In September 1814, he returned to Russia and took command of the 2nd Brigade of the 4th Dragoon Division. Yuzefovich rose to command the 1st Dragoon Division on 9 December 1816, the 1st Horse Jager Division on 13 January 1819, and the 2nd Uhlan Division on 5 February 1820. He became seriously ill in the fall of 1821, was relieved of command on 11 September, and died on 7 October at Romny in the Poltava *gubernia*.

Z

ZAGRYAZHSKY, Peter Petrovich (b. 1778 — d. 10 February 1849) enlisted as a vakhmistr in the Pavlograd Light Horse Regiment in 1796 and rose to ensign in 1797. In 1799, he transferred to the Life Guard Hussar Regiment and was promoted to colonel on 7 October 1800 at age of twenty-two. He participated in the 1805-1807 Campaigns against the French and distinguished himself at Guttstadt, Heilsberg, and Friedland, where he was wounded fourteen times and captured clinging to life. After he recovered and returne to Russia, he was awarded the Order of St. George (4th class) on 1 June 1808. The next year, Zagryazhsky was appointed chef of the Nezhinsk Dragoon Regiment on 5 May 1809.

During the 1812 Campaign, Zagryazhsky served with the 4th Brigade of the 1st Cavalry Division of the 1st Reserve Cavalry Corps in the 1st Western Army. He fought at Ostrovno, Borodino, Maloyaroslavets, Orsha, Vilna, and Kovno. For his actions, he was promoted to major general on 1 August 1813, with seniority dating from 17 November 1812. Through 1813-1814, Zagryazhsky fought at Spandau, Leipzig, and Paris, and took command of a brigade of the 1st Horse Jager Division in late 1816. He was appointed commander of the 1st Hussar Division on 25 July 1819 and later assumed command of the 1st Dragoon Division on 4 November 1819. Zagryazhsky became lieutenant general on 18 January 1826, and commander of the 1st Horse Jager Division on 13 November 1828. During the Russo-Turkish War, he took command of the reserve cavalry on 25 February 1829.

After the conclusion of the war, Zagryazhsky was relieved of command on 1 October 1830, and retired with a full pension on 28 December 1833.

ZAITSEV, Aleksey Dmitryevich (b. 1770 — date of death unclear) enlisted at an early age in the Azov Infantry Regiment. He participated in the campaigns against the Northern Caucasian mountaineers in 1787-1789 and against the Poles in 1792-1794, where he distinguished himself at Zelva, Brest-Litovsk, Tiraspol, and Praga (golden cross, promoted to ensign). In 1795, Zaitsev transferred as a sub-lieutenant to the Polotsk Infantry Regiment, although he soon returned to the Azov Regiment, where he became a lieutenant on 20 August 1798. During Suvorov's campaigns in Italy in 1799, Zaitsev served with Lieutenant General Rehbinder's Corps, earning the rank of captain. He participated in Suvorov's Swiss campaign in late 1799 and garnered the Orders of St. Anna (3rd class) and of St. John of Jerusalem. Emperor Paul also appointed him Commandant of the fortress of Vyborg.

Over the next eight years, Zaitsev repaired and reorganized the fortress and received two diamond rings and a golden snuffbox for his service. Through 1808-1809, Zaitsev defended the fortress against the Swedes and was awarded the Order of St. Anna (2nd class). In 1809, he was promoted to colonel and appointed chef of the Rochensalmi Garrison Regiment. Three years later, he took command of the Voronezh Garrison Battalion and later led the 2nd Brigade of the 6th District of the Internal Guard Corps. In 1828, he became major general and served in the 10th and 5th Districts of the Internal Guard Corps. Zaitsev retired in 1831 with a full pension.

ZAKHAROV, Rostislav Ivanovich (b. 1784 — d. 7 September 1812, Borodino) was born to a Russian noble family. He studied in the Artillery and Engineer Cadet Corps and began his service as a sub-lieutenant in the Life Guard Artillery Battalion in 1800. He distinguished himself at Austerlitz in 1805, and in 1807, fought at Heilsberg and Friedland, where he was wounded in the right hand. In 1809-1810, Zakharov served in the Danubian Principalities, earning promotion to captain on 14 February 1810. In 1811, he led the 1st Light Horse Artillery Battery in the Guard Horse Artillery.

During the 1812 Campaign, Zakharov was mortally wounded at Borodino on 7 September 1812.

ZAKHARZHEVSKY, Jacob Vasilievich (b. 3 November 1780 — d. 13 March 1865) was born to a noble family in the Poltava *gubernia*. He graduated from the Shklov Cadet Corps and began service as a sub-lieutenant in the 1st Siege Artillery Battalion on 30 June 1799. The following year, he transferred to the 1st Artillery Regiment. He participated in the 1806-1807 Campaigns in Poland and distinguished himself at Eylau on 8 February 1807. During the Russo-Swedish War, he served in General Rayevsky's corps in Finland. In 1812, Zakharzhevsky became staff captain in the 6th Horse Artillery Company of the 2nd Reserve Artillery Brigade and fought at Smolensk, Lubino, and Borodino, where he was wounded in the right foot and later received the Order of St. Vladimir (4th class). After recuperating, he participated in the battles at Vyazma, Krasnyi, and on the Berezeina.

In the spring of 1813, Zakharzhevsky served at Lutzen, Bautzen, and Reichebach. For his actions, he was promoted to colonel on 29 July 1813. He particularly distinguished himself at Leipzig in October 1813, where his horse artillery company suppressed the French artillery fire. At the height of the action, however, Zakharzhevsky was seriously wounded when a cannonball tore off his right foot. For his valor, he was awarded the Order of St. George (4th class) and the Prussian Pour le Merite as well as the 3,000 rubles allowance.

Zakharzhevsky remained at Altenburg in 1814, recuperating from the wound. He returned to service only in 1815, when he commanded some reserve horse artillery companies. He was promoted to major general on 27 January 1815. After returning to Russia, he served as an administrator for the Imperial mansions at Tsarskoe Selo, Gatchina, and Peterhof. He supervised the Imperial palaces for almost fifty years and was generously awarded by the Emperors Alexander I, Nicholas II, and Alexander II. Zakharzhevsky was promoted to lieutenant general on 18 December 1828, and to general of artillery on 22 October 1843. He was awarded the Orders of the White Eagle, St. Alexander of Neva with diamonds, St. Vladimir (1st class) and St. Andrew the First Called. Zakharzhevsky also received a medal for sixty years of distinguished service. He died on 13 March 1865, and was buried at the Catherine Cathedral at Tsarskoe Selo.

ZAKREVSKY, Arsenii Andreyevich (b. 24 September 1786, Bernikovo, Tver *gubernia* — d. 23 January 1865, Florence) was born to a petty noble family in the Tver *gubernia*. He graduated from the Shklov Cadet Corps and began service as an ensign in the Arkhangelogorod Musketeer Regiment on 1 December 1802. He served as battalion and then regimental adjutant to Count Nikolay Kamensky, who commanded the Arkhangelogorod Musketeer Regiment. Zakrevsky participated in the 1805 Campaign and fought at Austerlitz, where he earned the Order of St. Anna (3rd class). In 1807, he fought at Jankowo, Koenigsberg, Eylau (golden cross), and Danzig. During the Russo-Swedish War of 1808-1809, he fought at Alavo, Kuortain, and Oravais. In 1810, he followed Kamensky to the Army of Danube and participated in the actions at Ruse (wounded in the hand and foot) and Batin (Order of St. George, 4th class, 4 October 1811).

In 1811, Zakrevsky was recalled to St. Petersburg to report on Kamensky's death and was appointed an adjutant to Barclay de Tolly, serving as the Director of the Special Chancellery (Military Intelligence) of the Ministry of War. In addition, Emperor Alexander conferred upon him the rank of lieutenant colonel of the Life Guard Preobrazhensk Regiment. On 25 February 1812, Zakrevsky rose to colonel. During the 1812 Campaign, he participated in the battles at Smolensk, Lubino, and Borodino (Order of St. Vladimir, 3rd class). He was promoted to flügel adjutant to Alexander on 15 December 1812. In 1813, he distinguished himself at Lutzen, Bautzen, Kulm, and Leipzig. For his conduct in these battles, he was promoted to major general on 27 September and to adjutant general on 20 October 1813. In 1814, Zakrevsky served at the main Russian headquarters and fought at Brienne, Le Fère Champenoise, and Paris.

After the war, Zakrevsky served as a duty officer at the main headquarters and became lieutenant general on 11 September 1821. He took command of the Independent Finland Corps and became the Governor of Finland on 11 September 1823. After the Decembrist Uprising, Zakrevsky was appointed a member of the military court sentencing the conspirators, but he did not actually participate in the proceedings. Zakrevsky was promoted to general of infantry on 3 May 1829, and was conferred the title of count of the Russian Empire on 14 August 1830.

Zakrevsky served as the Minister of Internal Affairs in 1828-1831. He retired in 1831 and spent the next seventeen years traveling in Europe. He returned to service in 1848, when he became Military Governor of Moscow on 18 May. He remained at this position for the next eleven years, concentrating enormous power in his hands. Zakrevsky became a member of the State Council on 15 November 1848. In 1852, he celebrated the 40th anniverssary of the liberation of Moscow from the French with a grand festivity attended by thousands of veterans of the Napoleonic Wars. Zakrevsky retired because of poor health on 28 April 1859, and traveled to Italy to recuperate. He died at Florence on 23 January 1865.

During his career, Zakrevsky received the Orders of St. Andrew the First Called with diamonds, St. Anna (1st class) with diamonds, of St. Vladimir (1st class), St. Alexander of Neva with diamonds, White Eagle, Prussian Orders Pour le Merite and the Red Eagle (2nd class), Austrian Order of Leopold (2nd class), Württemberg Order of Military Merit, Bavarian Order of Maximilian Joseph (3rd class), French Order of St. Louis, Dutch Order of the Lion, Persian Order of the Lion and the Sun, and a medal inscribed "For XXXV Years of Distinguished Service."

ZAKREVSKY, Dmitry Andreyevich (b. 1769 — d. 1835) enlisted in the Caucasian Musketeer Regiment in 1773 and rose to ensign on 27 November 1787. He transferred to the Jager Corps in 1788 and became an adjutant to Lieutenant General Potemkin. During the Russo-Turkish War of 1787-1791, Zakrevsky distinguished himself at Ochakov, Akkerman, and Bender. Zakrevsky was promoted to second major on 11 October 1788, and to premier major on 26 December 1789. In 1790-1791, he served as an adjutant to Prince Gregory Potemkin and received his colonelcy on 23 February 1792. After a transfer to the Revel Musketeer Regiment, Zakrevsky took part in the campaign against the Polish insurgents in 1793-1794, receiving the Order of St. Vladimir (4th class) for his actions at Vilna. On 16 October 1797, Zakrevsky was elevated to major general and the Commandant of Revel. However, two days later, he retired from the military service with the lower rank of colonel. Emperor Alexander restored his rank of major general on 25 July 1801.

ZAPOLSKY, Andrey Vasilievich (b. 1768 — d. 19 March 1813) enlisted in the Life Guard Preobrazhensk Regiment on 27 March 1791, becoming ensign on 12 January 1794. Five years later he rose to colonel on 27 December 1799. He was appointed chef of Ekaterinoslavl Grenadier Regiment on 5 September 1804. Zapolsky participated in the campaigns against Napoleon in 1805-1807 and received the Order of St. George (3rd class, 20 April 1807) for Eylau. In December 1811, he took command of a brigade of the 1st Grenadier Division, and in March 1812, was appointed commander of the 35th Division. In late 1812, he assumed command of the 2nd Reserve Corps and took part in minor actions against the French. In 1813, he briefly led a brigade of 1st Corps of the Army of Reserve before falling ill and dying on 19 March 1813.

ZASS (Zass II), Alexander Pavlovich (Christopher Alexander), (b. 1 July 1785, Pernov — d. 30 August 1843, St. Petersburg) descended from a noble family from the Lifland *gubernia*. On 21 November 1793, he enlisted as a sergeant in the Life Guard Semeyonovsk Regiment. Three years later, after becoming ensign on 25 November 1796, he quickly rose to flügel adjutant the following month. In 1805, he served as an adjutant to Buxhöwden and fought at Austerlitz on 2 December 1805. On 26 July 1806, he was promoted to captain and participated in the first Polish Campaign. Zass fought at Worlfsdorf, Guttstadt, Heilsberg, and Friedland, all which worked to his advantage with a promotion to colonel on 24 December 1807. In 1809-1811, Zass served in the Army of Danube against the Turks. On 17 November 1810, he commanded the 27th Jager Regiment and captured Girsov, earning the Order of St. George (4th class). In 1811, he distinguished himself at Vidin and was appointed chef of the Belostock Infantry Regiment on 15 November 1811.

In 1812, Zass led the 1st Brigade of the 10th Division of the 3rd Corps of the Army of Danube. He took part in the actions at Kovel, Lutsk, and Lubomle. During the 1813 Campaign, he distinguished himself at Katzbach, for which he was promoted to major general and received command of the 2nd Brigade of the 10th Infantry Division. In October 1813, he distinguished himself at Leipzig and took command of the 10th Division. The following year, Zass led the 27th Division and fought at Brienne, La Rothière, Montmirail, Chateau Thierry, Craonne, Laon, and Paris. For his actions, he was decorated with the Order of St. George (3rd class). In 1815, he took command of the 3rd Brigade of the 15th Division, and during the Hundred Days, participated in the blockades of Faltzburg and Metz. In June 1821, he became commander of the 2nd Brigade of the 8th Infantry Division and two years later, received command of the 8th Division (8 October 1823).

During the Russo-Turkish War of 1828-1829, Zass distinguished himself at Shumla and Silistra, garnering the Orders of St. Vladimir (2nd class) and St. Anna (1st class), as well as the rank of lieutenant general (4 June 1828). In 1829, he took command of the 7th Division (16 October) and the following year, participated in the operations against the Polish insurgents. His role in the capture of Warsaw earned a golden sword for courage. On 14 April 1833, Zass became commander of the 6th Division and led it until September 1839, when he was appointed the General Auditor of the Russian army. He died on 30 August 1843, in St. Petersburg.

ZASS (Zass I), Andrey Andreyevich (Gideon Henrich), (b. 1776 — d. 28 January 1830, Warsaw) was born to a noble family in the Lifland *gubernia*; the son of Lieutenant General Andrey Pavlovich Zass. He enlisted as a vakhmistr in the prestigious Chevalier Guard Regiment on 12 January 1787. In March 1792, he transferred to the Kiev Horse Jager Regiment and took part in the campaign in Poland, where he fought at Slonim (golden cross for Praga). Zass was elevated to second major in late 1794. Three years later, he transferred to the Military

Order Cuirassier Regiment with a rank of premier major on 18 February 1797.

After retirement in 1804-1806, Zass returned to military service in early 1807, joining the Pskov Dragoon Regiment on the campaign in Poland. He fought at Guttstadt, Heilsberg, and Friedland, receiving the Order of St. Vladimir (4th class). He was promoted to colonel on 27 April 1810, and given command of the Pskov Dragoon Regiment on 31 July 1810.

In 1812, Zass served in the 6th Brigade, 2nd Cavalry Division, 2nd Reserve Cavalry Corps, 1st Western Army. He fought at Borodino (Order of. St. George, 4th class) and was wounded in the left hand at Mozhaisk on 9 September. After recuperating, he joined the army in late 1812 and participated in the 1813 Campaign, fighting at Kalisch, Lutzen, Bautzen, and Dresden before being wounded in the right thigh at Kulm. For his conduct, he received the Prussian Iron Cross and was promoted to major general on 27 September 1813, with seniority dating from 29 August 1813. After fighting at Leipzig in October 1813, Zass took part in the invasion of France. On 2 October 1814, he received command of the 2nd Brigade of the 2nd Cuirassier Division.

After Napoleon's return in 1815, Zass was dispatched to join the Allied forces in France, and reached Paris after the battle of Waterloo. In February 1820, Zass was promoted to command the 1st Horse Jager Division. Six years later, he rose to lieutenant general (3 September) and received command of the 2nd Cuirassier Division.

Zass took command of the 2nd Dragoon Division on 31 December 1827, and participated in the Russo-Turkish War of 1828-1829. He distinguished himself at Kulevchi on 20 June 1829, and was awarded a golden sword for courage. The next year, he was dispatched to suppress the Polish Uprising, but died during the cholera epidemic in Warsaw.

ZASS, Andrey Pavlovich (Andreas Burchard Friedriech) (b. 1753, Riga — d. 5 January 1816, Riga) was born to a noble family in the Lifland *gubernia*. He enlisted as a sub-ensign in the Life Guard Preobrazhensk Regiment on 26 May 1768, becoming an ensign on 12 January 1773. Six years later, he transferred as a lieutenant colonel to the Leib Cuirassier (Life Guard Cuirassier) Regiment on 12 January 1779. After participating in the Russo-Turkish War in 1787-1789, he organized and took command of the Pereyaslavl Horse Jager Regiment (1790-1793). In 1793-1794, Zass led the Kiev Horse Jager Regiment against the Polish insurgents. He was promoted to major general on 8 February 1797, and served as chef of the Staroskol Musketeer Regiment between 15 December 1796 and 7 April 1797, when he was discharged from the service. Zass was restored in the army on 7 April 1801, and became commander of the Ekaterinoslavl Cuirassier Regiment on 16 November 1802. The next year, on 4 June 1803,

Zass became chef of the Pereyaslavl Dragoon Regiment (held this position until 8 April 1814).

In late 1805, Zass was sent to the Army of Danube and took part in the opening moves of the Russo-Turkish War in 1806. On 27 June 1806, he was promoted to lieutenant general. In 1807-1808, he led a cavalry detachment against the Turks. In 1809, he became commander of the 25th Division on 1 January and of the 16th Division four months later in May. During Prince Bagration's offensive in August-October 1809, Zass invested and captured the fortress of Ismail, and led a corps in Greater Wallachia.

In May-June 1810, Zass captured the fortress of Tutrukan (Order of St. George, 3rd class, 25 June 1810) before investing Ruse. In August, he commanded the right wing of the Russian army in Little Wallachia and Serbia. He captured the fortress of Kladovo and defeated Ismail Bey at Kalafat in 1811, earning in return Orders of St. Alexander of Neva, St. Anna (1st Class), and St. Vladimir (1st Class), as well as a golden sword for courage. Age and poor health, however, caught up with Zass and prevented him from continuing on campaign in late 1811.

Zass took a prolonged furlough to recuperate and returned to the army on 18 November 1812. He led a cavalry detachment in the 3rd Western Army and fought on the Bug and Nieman Rivers. In 1813, he fought at Thorn and Bautzen, for which he garnered second golden sword for courage. Zass took another furlough because of deteriorating health in June 1813, and retired on 8 April 1814. After the war, Zass lived in Riga, where he died on 5 January 1816.

ZASYADKO (Zasyadko II), Alexander Dmitryevich (b. 1779 — d. 8 June 1837) was born to a noble family in the Poltava *gubernia*. He graduated from the Artillery and Engineer Cadet Corps and began service as a sub-lieutenant in the 10th Artillery Battalion on 11 March 1797. Two years later, he participated in the campaign in Italy, where he fought at Mantua. In 1804-1806, Zasyadko took part in the expeditions to Corfu and Naples, where he distinguished himself at Castel Nuovo and was awarded the Order of St. George (4th class). In 1807, Zasyadko served in the Danube Valley and distinguished himself at Ismail, Turtukai (Orders of St. Anna, 2nd class, and of St. Vladimir, 4th class), Razgrad (golden sword) and was wounded in the left knee at Ruse (diamond signs of the Order of St. Anna). He took command of the 29th Light Company of the 15th Artillery Brigade on 5 August 1809.

In the summer of 1810, Zasyadko commanded the Russian artillery during the sieges of Giurgiu and Ruse, and took part in the destruction of the Turkish army near Ruse in 1811. In 1812, Zasyadko led the 15th Artillery Brigade and fought at Gorodechnya and Borisov. The next year, he fought at Thorn, for which he was promoted to colonel and earned the Prussian Pour le Merite. He also took part in the actions at Bautzen, Goldberg, Heinesdorf, Katzbach (Order of St. Vladimir, 3rd class), and Leipzig (Order of St. George, 3rd class). In 1814, Zasyadko served in the siege of Mainz and was in charge of ammunition supplies.

After the war, Zasyadko devoted his time to various artillery experiements and was successful in testing rockets. He was promoted to major general and appointed duty general in the 2nd Army in 1819. The next year, he became the head of the St. Petersburg laboratory and the Okhtensk gunpowder factory. He spent the rest of his life working on methods to improve gunpowder, rockets, and artillery equipment. He was promoted to lieutenant general in 1829, and retired because of poor health two years later. Zasyadko settled in Kharkov, where he died on 8 June 1837.

His brother, **ZASYADKO (Zasyadko I), Dmitry Dmitryevich** (b. 1781 — date of death unclear) became colonel in 1811 and took command of the 5th Battery Company of the 15th Artillery Brigade on 2 February 1812. Serving with the 3rd Reserve Army of Observation, he fought at Kobryn and Gorodechnya (Order of St. Anna, 2nd class) in 1812. The following year, he served at Thorn (Order of St. George, 4th class), Koenigsberg, Bautzen, Goldberg, Heinesdorf, and Leipzig, for which he garnered the Prussian Order of Red Eagle (3rd class). Zasyadko received his colonelcy in December 1813. In 1814, he fought at Mainz, Brienne, La Rothière (golden sword) and Champaubert, where he was seriously wounded in the head and captured by the French. He remained in captivity until 31 March 1814.

ZAVYASKIN, Mikhail Vasilievich (b. 1790 — date of death unclear) was born to a noble family from the Tambov *gubernia*. He studied in the 1st Cadet Corps and began service as a sub-lieutenant in the 10th Artillery Regiment on 27 November 1807. He served against the Austrians in Galicia in 1809. Two years later, Zavyaskin transferred to the 7th Artillery Brigade on 12 March 1811. During the 1812 Campaign, he fought at Smolensk, Borodino, Tarutino, and Maloyaroslavets, where he was wounded in the right leg. In 1813, he participated in minor actions in Silesia and served at Berlin and Wittenberg, for which he garnered the Order of St. Vladimir (4th class) and the Prussian Pour le Merite. Zasyadkin distinguished himself at in 184 at the battles of Soissons, Laon, and Paris.

ZBIEWSKY, Timofei Ivanovich (b. 1767 — d. 2 March 1828, Bender) was born to a Polish noble family. His family became Russian residents after the Second Partition of Poland. Zbiewsky began his career as a private in the 2nd Battalion of the Ekaterinoslavl Jager Corps on 13 April 1783. In 1788-1790, he participated in the Russo-Turkish War and fought at Ochakov, Akkerman. and Bender, as well as in a series of naval engagements. He distinguished himself during the assault on Ismail, for which he received a golden cross and promotion to lieutenant on 22 December 1790. In 1791, he fought at Braila and Babadag. Two years later, Zbiewsky transferred to the newly established Life Guard Grenadier Battalion. In 1796, he joined the Tavrida Grenadier Regiment, but was dismissed for leaving his regiment without the Imperial permission. However, an investigation acquitted him and he was appointed to the Vladimir Musketeer Regiment. Zbiewsky was promoted to captain in 1797, to major in 1798, and to lieutenant colonel two years later. Four years later, he became commander of the Vladimir Musketeer Regiment on 6 April 1804.

In 1805, Zbiewsky took part in the campaign against Napoleon and distinguished himself at Austerlitz, fighting in Dokhturov's column (Order of St. George, 4th class, 10 February 1806, promotion to colonel on 5 May 1806). In 1806-1807, Zbiewsky fought at Golymin (Order of St. Vladimir, 4th class), Eylau (Order of St. Anna, 2nd class), and Guttstadt, where he was wounded and decorated with a golden sword for courage. After recuperating, he was appointed chef of the Mingrelia Musketeer Regiment on 14 September 1809, and took part in the operations against the Turks at Braila, Silistra (Order of St. Anna, 2nd class), Shumla, Vidin (Order of St. George, 3rd class, 4 September 1811), and Kalafat. For his actions, he earned the rank of major general on 19 August 1810.

In 1812, Zbiewsky served in the 2nd Brigade, 16th Division, 4th Corps, Army of Danube, and temporarily led this brigade from 31 March 1812. He took part in the actions along the Narew River and around Volkovysk and Tsekhanovets. In the spring of 1813, he remained in the Duchy of Warsaw and joined the Army of Poland later that year. In 1814, he served in the siege of Hamburg and was confirmed as commander of the 2nd Brigade, 16th Division, on 13 September 1814. In 1817, Zbiewsky was appointed the Commandant of Bender (20 February), where he remained for the rest of his life.

ZHELTUKHIN (Zheltukhin II), Peter Fedorovich (b. 1777, Kazan — date of death unknown; excluded from rosters on 6 November 1829) was born to a noble family in the Kazan *gubernia*. He began service in the Life Guard Izmailovsk Regiment in 1796 and rose to ensign in the following year. During the 1805 Campaign, he served as a captain and fought at Austerlitz, receiving a golden sword for courage. Promoted to colonel in 1806, he was wounded at Friedland on 14 June 1807, and earned the Order of St. George (4th Class) and the Prussian Pour le Merite. During the Russo-Swedish War of 1808-1809, he served as a commanding officer in the Life Guard Grenadier Regiment, and later led the 1st Brigade, 1st Grenadier Division. In 1812, he served in the Life Guard Grenadier Regiment, which was attached to the 1st Brigade, 1st Grenadier Division, 3rd Corps, 1st Western Army. Zheltukhin distinguished himself at Borodino, Maloyaroslavets, and Krasnyi, earning the Order of St. George (3rd class, 15 June 1813). He was promoted to major general on 3 December 1812, with seniority dating from 7 September 1812.

During the 1813 Campaign, Zheltukhin fought at Bautzen and Leipzig, receiving the Prussian Pour le Merite and the Order of Red Eagle (2nd class). In 1814, he took part in the capture of Paris. After the war, he was given command of the Life Guard Grenadier Regiment on 18 July 1817, and later became commander of the 1st Brigade of the 2nd Grenadier Division on 30 April 1819. In 1819-1823, he served as the Chief of Staff of the Guard Corps and was appointed to the Imperial Retinue in April 1823.

After Emperor Alexander's death, he retired in January 1825 with a full pension. However, he returned to service two years later (24 January 1827), becoming lieutenant general and the Military Governor of Kiev on 9 February 1827. During the Russo-Turkish War of 1829, Zheltukhin was instrumental in supplying the Russian troops in the Danubian Principalities. He represented the Divans of Moldavia and Wallachia during the Russo-Turkish negotiations before falling ill and dying on 23 December 1829, during a fever epidemic.

In addition to above-mentioned awards, Zheltukhin also received the Orders of St. Anna (1st class) with diamonds and St. Vladimir (2nd class) along with two golden swords for courage.

ZHELTUKHIN (Zheltukhin I), Sergey Fedorovich (b. 1776, Kazan — d. 14 June 1833, Kazan) was born to a noble family in the Kazan *gubernia*; and the brother of Peter Zheltukhin. He enlisted as a sergeant in the Life Guard Izmailovsk Regiment on 28 November 1784, and was promoted to ensign in 1797. The next year, he became flügel adjutant to Emperor Alexander I and received a promotion to sublieutenant. He became colonel on 13 April 1804, and participated in the campaigns against the

French in 1805-1807. He fought at Austerlitz on 2 December 1805, receiving the Order of St. Vladimir (4th Class), and was wounded at Friedland on 14 June 1807, for which he earned the Order of St. Vladimir (3rd Cass) and the Prussian Pour le Merite.

In 1808, Zheltukhin took command of the Siberia Grenadier Regiment (4 October) and served in the Army of Moldavia. The following year, he became chef of the Penza Musketeer Regiment on 14 July 1809. He took part in the actions at Giurgiu, Lovech and Kladovo, and captured the Island of Olmar on the Serbian border. For his actions, Zheltukhin was promoted to major general on 10 October, while his unit was converted to the 45th Jager Regiment later that month. Zheltukhin served in the Divan of the Moldavia and Wallachia in 1810. During the battle at Ruse in 1811, he led the central square of the Russian army.

In 1812, Zheltukhin served with the 3rd Brigade of the 22nd Division of the 1st Corps of the Army of Danube. He took part in the operations against the French in late October and fought at Borisov and on the Berezina. In 1813, he led the 10th Infantry Corps. Zheltukhin was wounded in the left at Leipzig and decorated with the Order of St. Anna (1st Class). In late 1813, he joined General Stroganov's corps besieging Hamburg and transferred to Baron Winzegorode's troops thereafter. During the 1814 Campaign, Zheltukhin distinguished himself at Laon and Paris, earning the Order of St. Vladimir (2nd Class), the Prussian Order of Red Eagle, and the Swedish Order of the Sword. From 1815 - 1819, Zheltukhin headed up the 3rd Brigade of the 22nd Division and became commander of the 13th Division on 14 February 1819. He was promoted to lieutenant general on 24 December 1824. Three years later, he took command of the 18th Division on 13 January 1827. Over the next two years, he also led the 12th Division and the Combined Division of the 4th Corps. He was put in charge of the reserves of the 2nd Army in May 1829, but was relieved of command that December. He died three years later at Kazan.

ZHEMCHUZHNIKOV, Apollon Stepanovich (b. 2 January 1765, St. Petersburg — d. 5 August 1840) was born to a noble family in St. Petersburg. He was the son of Vice Admiral Stepan Zhemchuzhnikov of the Russian Navy. Apollon Zhemchuzhnikov graduated from the Infantry Cadet Corps in 1785 and joined the Revel Musketeer Regiment as a lieutenant. He took part in the campaigns in Poland in 1792-1794, and after distinguishing himself at Vilna, was promoted to second major by Alexander Suvorov. On 21 March 1801, he became a colonel and the next year was transferred to the Tavrida Grenadier Regiment. After the 1805 Campaign, Zhemchuzhnikov fought at Pultusk and Eylau in December 1806 – January 1807. On 28 April 1807, he took command of the Tavrida Grenadier Regiment (until September 1811) and fought at Landsberg (wounded in the hand and chest), Heilsberg, and Friedland. In 1811, he trained the recruits and commanded a company in Tver in 1812, missing all the military operations of that year.

Zhemchuzhnikov joined the main army in the spring of 1813 and fought at Spandau, Lutzen, Bautzen, Leipzig, Magdeburg, and Hamburg (Orders of St. Anna, 1st Class, St. George, 3rd Class, and the Prussian Order of Red Eagle). He was promoted to major general on 27 September 1813, with seniority dating from 2 May 1813. In 1814, he took part in the siege of Hamburg. During the Hundred Days, he marched with the Russian army back to the

Rhine River. He was soon appointed to command the 1st Brigade of the 8th Division and rose to command the 29th Division on 13 January 1819. Zhemchuzhnikov was promoted to lieutenant general on 3 September 1826, and retired because of poor health on 2 February 1838.

ZHEREBTSOV, Alexander Alexandrovich (b. 1781 — d. 1832) was born to a prominent noble family, the son of ober-hofmeister Alexander Zherebtsov (1754-1807) of Catherine the Great. He was enlisted at age of four as a sergeant in the Life Guard Semeyonovsk Regiment on 2 May 1785, but transferred to the Life Guard Preobrazhensk Regiment in 1794, becoming ensign in 1795 at age of fourteen. Three years later, he became kamer-junker to Emperor Paul I and rose to an actual kamerger on 15 April 1798. In 1802, he became kamerger to Emperor Alexander I.

In 1806-1807, Zherebtsov participated in the organization of St. Petersburg *zemtsvo* troops and was appointed to the Ministry of Internal Affairs on 21 October 1809. The following year, he transferred to the Ministry of Police on 28 March 1810. During the Russian Campaign, Zherebtsov was instrumental in organizing the St. Petersburg *opolchenye* and led the 4th Company (*druzhina*). He fought at Polotsk (Order of St. Vladimir, 4th class) and Chashniky. Later, he led the 2nd Brigade of the St. Petersburg *opolchenye* and took part in the actions at Smolyani, Batur, Stary Borisov, and on the Berezina, earning the Order of St. George (4th class, 10 November 1813).

In 1813, Zherebtsov participated in the capture of Koenigsberg and the siege of Danzig, commanding throughout the campaign the Novgorod *opolchenye*. He distinguished himself in repulsing the sortie of the French garrison at Danzig in April 1813, and was awarded a golden sword for courage. On 31 May 1815, his civil rank of actual kamerger was changed to the military rank of major general with seniority dating from 13 June 1813 (later, the seniority was changed to 31 August 1812).

After the war, Zherebtsov served as an assistant to the commander of the 5th Division before taking command of the 3rd Brigade of the 5th Division on 9 December 1816. Relieved of command on 2 October 1820, he retired in 1828 and died in 1832. He was buried at the Predtechev monastery in Vyazma.

ZHERVE, Alexander Karlovich (b. 6 November 1779 — d. 1858, Paris) was born a Prussian noble family at Vyborg, the son of Karl Eremevich Zherve, Commandant of Vybog. Alexander graduated from the 2nd Cadet Corps and began service as a sub-lieutenant in the 1st Siege Artillery Battalion on 25 December 1798. He continued his studies at the Cadet Corps until 1806, when Grand Duke Constantine chose him for the service in the Life Guard Finland Regiment. Zherve participated in the 1807 Campaign and fought at Guttstadt, Heilsberg, and Friedland, earning a golden sword for courage. In 1812, he was already a colonel leading the 3rd Battalion of the Life Guard Finland Regiment. At its head he distinguished himself at Borodino, where he led his regiment in a bayonet attack. Zherve was wounded in the right foot and garnered the Order of St. Anna (2nd class) with diamonds.

After recuperating, Zherve returned to the army in late 1812 and fought at Lutzen, Bautzen, Dippoldiswalde, and Kulm in 1813. He particularly distinguished himself at Leipzig (Order of St. George, 4th class, and Prussian Pour le Merite). In 1814, he participated in the invasion of France. Two years later, Zherve became major general and commander of the

2nd Jager Regiment. In 1817, he became assistant to the commander of the 21st Division and led the 3rd Brigade of this division for the next ten years.

Zherve took command of the 1st Division in 1827 and participated in the suppression of the Polish Uprising four years later. He fought at Grochow and Minsk and was awarded the Order of St. Anna (1st class) and the Polish Medal Virtuti militari. In November of 1831, he became commander of the 14th Division. Zherve rose to lieutenant general on 18 December 1833, and was appointed the Commandant of Tobolsk. He retired with a pension on 12 January 1840, and settled in Paris, where he died in 1858.

ZHERVE, Karl (Hannibal) Eremevich (b. 1755 — d. 1818, Vyborg) descended from a Prussian noble family and immigrated to Russia in the mid-18th century. He began service in the Russian army in 1772, and joined as an ensign the Life Guard Izmailovsk Regiment on 11 August 1775. He was enrolled in the Infantry Cadet Corps, and after graduation was assigned as a premier major to the Keksholm (Kexholm) Infantry Regiment. He soon transferred to the marine battalion and served on the ship-of-the-line *Twelve Apostles*. He participated in the naval actions against the Swedes in 1790-1791. In 1793, Zherve transferred to the Velikii Lutsk Infantry Regiment. He was promoted to colonel in 1798 and to major general in 1799.

Appointed chef of the Yeletsk Musketeer Regiment on 27 October 1799, Zherve became chef of the Chernigov Musketeer Regiment three days later. In November 1800, he transferred to the Life Guard Semeyonovsk Regiment, and in January 1801, became Commandant of Keksholm. On 16 February 1802, he was appointed chef of the Vyborg Garrison Regiment, where he served for the next seven years.

During the Russo-Swedish War, Zherve served in the Reserve Corps in Karelia and provided the army with supplies and ammunition. In 1809, he became the Commandant of Vyborg. Three years later during the invasion of Russia by Napoleon, Zherve supervised the evacuation of the Imperial treasury, paintings, and private correspondence from St. Petersburg to Vyborg, where he protected it for eight months. After the war, Zherve remained Commandant of Vyborg before falling ill and dying in 1818.

ZHEVAKHOV (Javakhishvili), Ivan Semenovich (b. 1762 — d. 5 August 1837) descended from a prominent Georgian noble family. His grandfather, Siush (Semen) Javakhishvili, immigrated to Russia with the Georgian King Vakhtang VI in 1724. Zhevakhov enlisted as a cadet in the Ukraine Hussar Regiment in 1775, and became an ensign in 1786. He fought the Circassians in the North Caucasus in 1777 and the Turks in the Crimea from 1789 to 1791, taking a wound at Ochakov. From 1792 to 1794, Zhevakhov served in the operations to crush the Polish insurgents. Zhevakhov was promoted to colonel on 24 November 1800. He distinguished himself during the 1807 Campaign in Poland (Order of St. George, 4th class, on 21 September 1807). The next year, Zhevakhov took command of the Akhtyrsk Hussar Regiment on 1 June. In 1811, he rose to become chef of the Serpukhov Dragoon Regiment on 12 February.

During the Russian Campaign, Zhevakhov's regiment was attached to the 26th Cavalry Brigade, Lambert's Cavalry Corps, 3rd Reserve Army of Observation. He fought at Janov, Pinsk, and Kobryn, garnering the Order of St. Vladimir (3rd class). In late 1812, he led a cavalry detachment in General Osten-Sacken's corps and fought with it at Slonim, Volkovysk, Gornostaevichi, and Isabelin. His unit, the Serpukhov Dragoons, was converted into an uhlan regiment on 8 January 1813. During the Saxon Campaign, Zhevakhov took part in the sieges of Modlin and Czeistohow before fighting at Dresden. He was promoted to major general on 20 April 1813.

Zhevakhov retired because of poor health after the war on 12 February 1817, and spent the rest of his life at Odessa on the Black Sea coast.

ZHEVAKHOV (Javakhishvili), Spiridon Eristovich (Estatovich) (b. 1768 — d. 6 August 1815, Weimarn) was born to a prominent Georgian noble family. He enlisted as a sergeant in the Life Guard Preobrazhensk Regiment in 1779, and after eleven years transferred as a rotmistr (captain) to the Aleksandria Light Horse (later Hussar) Regiment in 1790. He participated in the Russo-Turkish War in 1790-1791, and fought the Poles in 1792-1794. In 1796, he took part in the Persian Campaign along the Caspian Sea, and in 1799 served with the Pavlograd Hussar Regiment in Italy and Switzerland.

Zhevakhov participated in the 1805 Campaign against Napoleon, serving under Prince Peter Bagration at Krems, Schöngrabern, and Austerlitz. The following year, he distinguished himself at Guttstadt and Heilsberg and was promoted to colonel on 24 December 1807. Three years later, he was appointed commander of the Pavlograd Hussar Regiment on 15 December 1810.

During the 1812 Russian Campaign, Zhevakhov served in the 14th Brigade, 4th Cavalry Division, 3rd Reserve Army of Observation. He fought at Gorodechnya (golden sword for courage), Vizhye, Slonim, and on the Berezina. In 1813, he served in General Alexander Chernyshev's cavalry detachment and distinguished himself at Leipzig. He was promoted to major general on 27 September 1813, and took part in the 1814 Campaign (Order of St. George, 3rd class, for his actions on 10 March 1814).

After the war, Zhevakhov commanded the 3rd Hussar Division, but died suddenly on 6 August 1815.

ZHEVAKHOV (Javakhishvili), Philip Semenovich (b. 1752 — date of death unknown) descended from a prominent Georgian noble family. He began his service in the Sumsk Hussar Regiment in 1766 and rose to ensign in 1771. Zhevakhov participated in the Russo-Turkish Wars in 1771-1791, serving in the Kharkov Hussar, Izumsk Hussar, Akhtyrsk Hussar, and the Life Guard Hussar Regiments. He was elevated to colonel in 1790.

Zhevakhov retired in 1801 with a rank of major general and settled in the Poltava *gubernia*. In 1812, he was elected head of the Poltava *opolchenye* and briefly served in the siege of Zamostye before retiring in 1814.

ZHIRKEVICH, Ivan Stepanovich (b. 1785 — date of death unclear) was born to a noble family in the Smolensk *gubernia*. He studied in the 1st Cadet Corps and began service as a sub-lieutenant in the Life Guard Artillery Battalion in 1805. He participated in the battle of Austerlitz on 2 December 1805, for which he earned the Order of St. Anna (3rd class). Two years later, he fought at Guttstadt, Heilsberg, and Friedland, garnering a golden sword for valor.

Zhirkevich served as an adjutant to General Arakcheyev from 1807-1808. In 1809, he joined Prince Golitsyn's corps in Galicia and was promoted to lieutenant on 16 August 1809, and the Order of St. Anna (2nd class). In 1812, Zhirkevich served with the Life Guard Artillery Brigade and distinguished himself at Smolensk and Borodino (Order of St. Vladimir, 4th class). The following year, he became staff captain on 25 September 1813, and fought at Lutzen, Bautzen (Imperial letters of gratitude), Dresden, and Leipzig.

Zhirkevich penned his memoirs *Zapiski of I. Zhikevicha* [Recollections of I. Zhirkevich], which were published in the *Russkaya Starina* in 1874. They provide interesting details on the Russian army during the Napoleonic Wars.

ZVARYKIN, Fedor Vasilievich (b. 21 April 1765, Kostroma — d. 25 September, 1826, Kislovodsk) was born to a noble family in the Kostroma *gubernia*. He graduated from the Cadet Corps in 1785, and began service as a lieutenant in the St. Petersburg Grenadier Regiment on 1 March 1785. He took part in the Russo-Turkish War in 1787-1791, and participated in the capture of Khotin and in the battles at Salcha, Killia, and Macin.

Zvarykin transferred as a captain to the Tavrida Jager Corps in 1792, and fought the Polish insurgents from 1792-1794. For his actions, Zvarykin was promoted to second major and transferred to the Smolensk Dragoon Regiment. In 1797, he became a major and joined the Old Ingermanland Musketeer Regiment. Rising to lieutenant colonel on 19 December 1799, he took command of the Ukraine Musketeer Regiment on 8 April 1803. Three years later, he advanced to colonel on 5 May 1806, and briefly served in the siege of Khotin. He marched with Essen's corps to Poland and participated in operations against the French. In 1808, Zvarykin became chef of the Shirvan Musketeer Regiment on 8 February 1808, and the following year took part in the campaign against Austria in Galicia.

During the 1812 Campaign, Zvarykin served in the 1st Brigade, 24th Division, 6th Corps, 1st Western Army. He was wounded in the left arm at Smolensk, for which he received Order of St. Vladimir (4th class). Zvarykin stayed in the army but was unable to participate in its subsequent battles. In 1813, he served under General Winzegorode and distinguished himself at Leipzig, for which he was promoted to major general on 23 January 1814, with seniority dating from 18 October 1813. Zvarykin participated in the actions at Rotenburg later that year, and crossed the Rhine River near Düsseldorf. During the invasion of France, he fought at Soissons and was wounded leading a bayonet attack at Craonne (Order of St. Anna for valor).

In 1815, Zvarykin led the 2nd Brigade, 24th Division, and participated in the grand military parade at Vertus. After returning to Russia, he became the Commandant of Vitebsk on 18 October 1817. Four years later, he transferred to Astrakhan on 12 May 1821, where he served as the commandant for the next five years. He fell ill and died on 25 September 1826 at Kislovodsk.

ZUCCATO (Tsukato), Yegor Gavrilovich (date of birth unclear — d. 1810) descended from an ancient Venetian family. He served in Württemberg army before entering Russian service in 1788 as a second major. During the Russo-Turkish War of 1787-1791, he distinguished himself at Ochakov, earning the Order of St. George (4th class). In 1791, Zuccato advanced to lieutenant colonel and joined the 1st Marine Regiment. In October 1794, he was appointed to the Horse Grenadier Regiment of the Military Order (*Konno-grenadersky Voennogo Ordena Polk*) and fought at Praga, garnering the Order of St. Vladimir (4th class). He retired in March 1797, but returned to service in 1799 and was assigned to General Rosenberg's corps.

Zuccato participated in the Italian and Swiss Campaigns of 1799, distinguishing himself on the Tidone and Trebbia rivers, and at Novi. Skipping the rank of colonel, he was promoted to major general in October 1799. Returning to Russia, Zuccato was discharged in March 1800, but restored in rank in November of the same year. He served in the War College until late 1808. Zuccato transferred to the Army of Moldavia in 1809 and was awarded the Order of St. George (3rd class) for his actions in the battle of Rassevat. In the summer of 1810, he led the Russian troops in Serbia and captured several

Turkish fortresses along the Danube River (Order of St. Anna, 1st class, July 1810). Zuccato took sick and died of an undisclosed illness in August 1810.

ZYKOV, Peter Yakovlevich (b. 1791 — date of death unclear) was born to a Russian noble family. He graduated from the 2nd Cadet Corps in 1807 and began service as a sub-lieutenant in the 8th Artillery Brigade on 1 January 1808. Over the next three years, he served in the Danubian Principalities and distinguished himself at Ismail and Ruse in 1809. He became a brigade adjutant on 14 May 1811.

During the 1812 Campaign, Zykov served in the 3rd Western Army and fought at Brest-Litovsk and Volkovysk. In 1813, he participated in the combats at Glogau, Bautzen (Order of St. Vladimir, 4th class), and Leipzi. The following year, Zykov distinguished himself at Brienne, Arcis sur Aube (Order of St. Anna, 3rd class), and Paris.

Bibliography

The book is based on a wide variety of sources. I was able to obtain a number of *formuliars*, records of service from the Rossiiskii Gosudarstvennii Voenno-Istoricheskii Arkhiv (Russian State Military Historical Archive, RGVIA). I also consulted the collection of archival materials from the RGVIA stored at Florida State University's Special Collections. With more than one thousand files, it contains detailed descriptions of most of the campaigns and orders of battle for Russian forces throughout the Napoleonic Wars.[1]

Despite its importance to the course of European history, the Russian officer corps remains largely unexplored. It is particularly true for the Western historiography, where only a few Russian commanders are well known to the public. Russian historians dedicated most of their work to various issues related to the crucial 1812 Campaign, thus failing to examine other issues of this important epoch. The late 19th century witnessed increasing numbers of publications on the Napoleonic Wars, but most contained only general information on Russian generals and field marshals. One of the first publications, S. Ushakov's *Deiania Rossiiskikh Polkovodtsev i Generalov oznamenovavshikh sebia v dostopamiatnuiu voinu s Frantsiei v 1812, 1813, 1814 i 1815 godakh* [*Deeds of the Russian Commanders and Generals Distinguished During the Memorable War against France in 1812, 1813, 1814 and 1815*] was published in St. Petersburg in 1822. It contains biographies of twelve prominent Russian commanders. Eighteen years later, prominent Russian historian Bantysh-Kamensky completed his two-volume *Biographii rossiiskikh generalissimusov i general-feldmarshalov*, which offers well-researched and detailed biographies on Russian field marshals and generalissimos. This study was followed by N. Polevoi's *Russkie polkovodtsy* that contained brief biographies of major Russian commanders from the times of Peter the Great to Emperor Nicholas I.

At the same time Alexander Mikhailovsky-Danilevsky, one of Russia's greatest historians, wrote his monumental six-volume work on more than one hundred and fifty participants of the 1812 Campaign.[2] This work still remains one of the best sources for biographical details of the Russian generals. Mikhailovsky-Danilevsky participated in the Napoleonic Wars and served as official historian of the Russian Empire, so he had virtually unrestricted access to the official diplomatic and military archives. He was also a prolific and remarkably efficient writer. He published *Opisanie pokhoda vo Frantsiiu v 1814 godu* [*Description of the Campaign in France in 1814*] in 1836, *Opisanie otechestvennoi voini v 1812 godu* [*Description of the Patriotic War of 1812*] in 1839, *Opisanie voini 1813 goda* [*Description of the 1813 Campaign*] in 1840, *Opisanie finlandskoi voini na sukhom puti i po more v 1808 i 1809 godakh* [*Description of the Finnish War on land and sea in 1808 and 1809*] in 1841, *Opisanie Turetskoi Voini s 1806 do 1812 goda* [*Description of the War with Turkey from 1806 to 1812*] in 1843, *Opisanie Pervoi Voini Imperatora Aleksandra s Napoleonom v 1805 godakh* [*Description of the First War of Alexander I with Napoleon in 1805*] in 1844, and *Opisanie Vtoroi Voini Imperatora Aleksandra s Napoleonom v 1806 i 1807 godakh* [*Description of the Second War of Alexander I with Napoleon in 1806 and 1807*] in 1846.

One of the trademarks of Mikhailovsky-Danilevsky's work is the level of detail he was able to extract from both official materials and the participants themselves. He contacted and interviewed large numbers of veterans and gathered personal correspondence from descendents of the senior officers. After all these years, many of his works are still widely considered one of the best available on its topic. On the negative side, these studies contain narrative histories of the campaigns without any attempt at critical analysis. Emperor Nicholas I personally read and edited them, often removing entire sections of the manuscripts critical of Russian actions. As a result, Mikhailovsky-Danilevsky's histories contain virtually no criticism of Russian army and its commanders.

The period between 1870 and 1912 witnessed an increase in publications on military topics. Most were regimental histories celebrating various anniversaries and contain interesting factual data on their participation in the Napoleonic Wars, as well as some biographical details on officers. At the same time, the Russian Imperial Historical Society published 25 volumes of the *Russkii biograficheskii slovar* [*Russian Biographical Dictionary*] in 1896-1918. Another monumental encyclopedia, Brokgauz-Efron's *Entrsiklopedicheskii slovar* was published in 41 volumes and contained several hundreds of entries on Russia's prominent statesmen and commanders during the Revolutionary and Napoleonic eras.[3]

Despite an outpouring of new studies, only a few were dedicated to the development of the Russian officer corps. In 1887, N. Glinoetsky published his brief study of Russian military ranks. In 1912, A. Andronikov, V. Fedorov and A. Nikiforov wrote separate chapters on the military service for the massive 13-volume collection *Stoletie Voennogo Ministerstva, 1802-1902*.[4] Another book, *The War Gallery of 1812*, was published in 1912 to commemorate the centennial anniversary of the campaign. It offers more than 320 portraits and detailed biographies of the participants. However, this publication concentrates only on senior officers whose portraits were presented in the War Gallery of the Hermitage, and contains no analysis of the Russian officer corps during the Napoleonic Wars.[5] From 1958 and 1973, prominent Russian historian Liubomir Beskrovny published two important works on the Russian army of the 18th-19th centuries.[6] Beskrovny's works are based on extensive research in the Russian archives and, despite some factual errors and Soviet propaganda elements, remains one of the best sources on the subject. Another important study, P. Zaionchkovsky's *Samoderzhavie i russkaia armiia na rubezhe XIX i XX veka* was published in 1971, but it covers the Russian officer corps of the late 19th century.[7] In 1972, Yu. Prudnikov attempted to study the Russian officer corps of the late 18th century, but he focused only on a limited number of regiments of the Russian army.[8] In 1987, a new book eneitled *Geroi 1812 goda,* was dedicated to the officers of 1812, but its tone is more hagiographic than academic. Incredibly, many prominent Russian commanders, including Prince Peter Bagration, are not included in the book.[9]

A new generation of historians emerged with the collapse of the USSR. Sergey Volkov's *Russkii ofitserskii korpus*[10] provides an engaging general history of the Russian officer corps from its foundation to the October Revolution of 1917. The author analyzed various aspects of the corps, including education, social status, advancement and training of the officers. However, Volkov specializes in late 19th century Russian military history and his volume heavily focuses on this period. Recently, several biographical dictionaries were published in Russia, including Shikman's *Deyateli Otechestvennoi istorii*, Solovyev's *General-Feldmarshali Rossii*, Buganov's *Polkovodtsy XVIII veka*, and Yashenko's *Polkovodtsy, voenachalniki i voennyi deyateli Rossii v Voennoi entsiklopedii I. D. Sytina*.[11] In 1996, several prominent Russian historians united their efforts to create a dictionary of the Russian generals of the Napoleonic Wars.[12] With more than 550 biographies, it is one of the largest biographical dictionaries on the Napoleonic Wars. Sadly, almost every biography was published with factual errors. Furthermore, as demonstrated by Alexander Podmazo, some contributors may have distorted facts and falsified archival documents. Therefore, this volume should be used with only the greatest caution.[13]

In 1997, Alexander Podmazo published *Shefy i komandiri reguliarnikh polkov russkoi armii*, an excellent study of the Russian regimental commanders.[14] Based on extensive work in the archives, this book contains a wealth of information on every Russian regiment and its leaders during the Napoleonic Wars. Finally, in 2002, Dmitry Tselorungo completed his seminal study of the Russian officers during the 1812 Campaign entitle *Ofitsery Russkoi Armii—uchastniki Borodinskogo Srazhenia*.[15] Tselorungo's study is based on thousands of records of service and offers a systematic analysis of the Russian officer corps during the 1812 Campaign. With its numerous statistical tables and details on the Russian officers, his study remains unmatched. One can only hope similar works will appear in the near future.

Notes

1. This collection contains ninety-two reels of microfilm with thousands of documents arranged by Napoleonic campaigns. The materials are organized in fond (f.), inventories (*opis*), files (*delo*) and pages (*listi*).

2. Alexander Mikhailovsky-Danilevsky, *Imperator Aleksandr i ego spodvizhniki v 1812, 1813, 1814, 1815 godakh*, [*Emperor Alexander and His Devotees in 1812, 1813, 1814, 1815 Campaigns*]. 6 vols. St. Petersburg, 1845-1850.

3. *Russkii biograficheskii slovar* [*Russian Biographical Dictionary*]. Ed. Polovtsov, A. A.; Modzalevskii, B. L.; Kurdiumov, M. G. 25 volumes. + 5 recent volumes, St. Petersburg: Izd. imp. Rus. ist. obshchestva, 1896-1918. Publication of the Russian Biographical Dictionary was interrupted by the October Revolution in 1917. Although drafts for the seven remaining volumes were completed, they were not published until 1997. *Entsiklopedicheskii slovar* [*Encyclopedical Dictionary*]. 41 vols. St. Petersburg: Izd. F. A. Brokgauz & Efron, 1890-1907. Brokgauz-Efron's encyclopedia was recently reprinted in St. Petersburg in 1990-1993.

4. N. Glinoetsky, *Istoricheskii ocherk razvitia ofitserskikh chinov i sistemi chinoproizvodstva v russkoi armii*, in *Voennii sbornik,* 4 (1887); A. Andronikov, V. Fedorov, *Prokhozhdenie sluzhbi po voennomu vedomstvu* in *Stoletie Voennogo Ministerstva*, 1802-1802 [Centennial Anniversary of the Ministry of War, 1802-1902] (St. Petersburg, 1912), IV, Part 3, Book 1, Section III; A. Nikoforov, *Chinoproizvodstvo po voennomu vedomstvu*, in Ibid., IV, Part 3, Book 1.

5. *Voennaya galerea 1812 goda* [*Military Gallery of 1812*]. St. Petersburg, 1912.

6. Liubomir Beskrovny, *Russkaia armia i flot v XVIII veke* [*Russian Army and Fleet in XVIII Century*]. Moscow, 1958.

7. See also Zaionchkovsky's articles, "*Russkii oficertskii korpus na rubezhe stoletii, 1881-1903 [Russian Officer Corps on Between the Two Centuries, 1881-1903].*" in *Voenno-istoricheskii zhurnal*, No. 8 (1971), No. 3 (1973).

8. Yu. Prudnikov, "*Komplektovanie ofitserskogo korpusa russkoi armii v 1794-1804 gg [Organization of the Officer Corps of the Russian Army in 1794-1804].*" in *Vestnik MGU*, No. 2 (1972).

9. *Geroi 1812 goda*, [*Heroes of 1812 Campaign*]. Moscow, 1987.

10. S. Volkov, *Russkii ofitserskii korpus* [*Russian Officer Corps*]. Moscow, 1993.

11. A. P. Shikman, *Deyateli Otechestvennoi istorii: biograficheskii slovar-spravochnik,* 2 vols. Moscow, 1997; B.I. Solovyev, *General-Feldmarshali Rossii* [*General Field Marshals of Russia*]. Rostov na Donu: Phoenix, 2000; V.I,. Buganov, *Polkovodtsy, XVIII vek* [*Military Commanders, XVIII Century*]. Moscow, 1992; *Polkovodtsy, voenachalniki i voennyi deyateli Rossii v Voennoi entsiklopedii* I.D. Sytina [*Russian Military Commanders, Leaders and Statesmen from I.D. Sytin's Military Encyclopedia*], ed. V. Yashenko, 3 vols. St. Petersburg, 1995-1997.

12. *Slovar russkikh generalov, uchastnikov boevikh deistvii protiv armii Napoleona Bonaparta v 1812-1815 gg.* [*Dictionary of the Russian Generals – Participants of the Military Operations against the Forces of Napoleon Bonaparte in 1812-1815*], ed. V. Bezotosny, A. Gorshman, L. Ivchenko and et. al. in *Rossiiskii Arkhiv*, vol. VII, Moscow, 1996.

13. Alexander Podmazo, "Ostorozhno – Falshivka! Kak Polkovnika I.S. Kutuzova proizveli v general maiori spustia dva stoletia posle smerti [Warning – A Forgery! How Colonel I.S. Kutuzov was Promoted to Major General Two Centuries After His Death]." in *Otechestvennie arkhivi*, Moscow, No. 2 (2003).

14. Alexander Podmazo, *Shefy i komandiri reguliarnikh polkov russkoi armii, 1796-1815* [*Chefs and Commanders of the Regular Regiments of the Russian Army, 1796-18*15], Moscow, 1997. I would like to thank the author for his permission to work on the English edition of this work. Parts of the works were published on-line on the Napoleon Series web-site (www.napoleon-series.org).

15. Dmitry Tselorungo, *Ofitsery Russkoi Armii – uchastniki Borodinskogo Srazhenia* [Officers of the Russian Army – Participants of the Battle of Borodino]. Moscow, 2002.

Archival Sources

Rossiiskii Gosudarstvennii Voenno-Istoricheskii Arkhiv (RGVIA) [Russian State Military Historical Archive]
   fond 846, opis 16, Napoleonic Wars: delos 3106 – 4255 – This massive collection of over thousand files contains valuable information on the Russian involvement in the Napoleonic Wars.

Primary Sources

A. V. Suvorov: Pisma [A.V. *Suvorov: Letters*]. V. Lopatin ed. Moscow, 1987.

A. V. Suvorov: Dokumenti [*A.V.Suvorov: Documents*]. Moscow, 1952.

Afanas'ev A. *1812-814: Sekretnaya perepiska General P.I. Bagrationa, lichnie pis'ma general N.N. Raevskogo, zapiski Generala Vorontsova, dnevniki ofitserov Russkoi armii – iz sobrania Gosudarstvennogo Istoricheskogo Muzea* [*1812-1814: Secret Correspondence of General P.I. Bagration, Private letters of General N.N. Rayevsky, Notes of General Vorontsov, Diaries of the Officers of the Russian Army - from the collection of the State Historical Museum*]. Moscow: Terra, 1992.

Aglamov, S. *Otechestvennaya voina 1812 goda: Istoricheskie materiali Leib-Gvardii Semyenovskogo polka* [*The Patriotic War of 1812: Historical Materials of the Semyenovsky Lifeguard Regiment*]. Poltava, 1912.

Akti sobrannie Kavkazskoi arkheograficheskoi komissiei [*Acts Compiled by the Caucasian Archeographical Commission*]. Tiflis, 1869.

Aleksey Petrovich Yermolov 1777-1861: Biographicheskii ocherk [*Aleksey Petrovich Yermolov, 1777-1861: Biographical Treatise*]. St. Petersburg, 1912.

Al'tshuller R and Tartarovsky A. *Listovki Otechestvennoi voini 1812 goda* [*Leaflets of the Patriotic War of 1812*]. Moscow, 1912.

Al'tshuller R. *Borodino: Dokumenti, pis'ma, vospominaniya* [*Borodino: Documents, Letters, Recollections*]. Moscow, 1962.

Andreev, N. *Iz vospominanii,* [*From the Memoirs of N. I. Andreev*], in *Russkii arkhiv*, No. 10 (1879).

Anekdoti Kniazia Italiiskogo Grafa Suvorova Rimnikskago, [*Stories About Suvorov, Count of Rimnic, Prince of Italy*]. St. Petersburg, 1827.

Anekdoti ili dostopiamiatnie skazania o ego svetlosti general-feldmarshale kniaze Mikhaile Larionoviche Golenisheve-Kutuzove Smolenskom [*Stories or Interesting Traditions on His Excellency General Field Marshal Prince Mikhail Larionovich Golenischev-Kutuzov of Smolenk*]. St. Petersburg, 1814.

Atlas Shveitsraskoi kampanii A. V. Suvorova: iz fondov Rossiiskogo gosudarstvennogo voenno-istoricheskogo arkhiva [*Atlas of Suvorov's Swiss Campaign: From the Materials of the Russian State Military Historical Archive*]. Zurich, 2000.

Austerlitz: Vospominania suvorovskogo soldata [*Austerlitz: Recollections of Suvorov's Soldier*]. Moscow, 1901.

Austerlitz raconté par les Témoins de la Bataille des Trois Empereurs. Geneva, 1969.

Bagration v Dunaiskikh kniazhestvakh: Sbornik Dokumentov [*Bagration in the Danubian Principalities: Compilation of Documents*]. Chisineu, 1949.

Barclay de Tolly, Mikhail. *Izobrazhenie voennikh deistvii 1812 g* [*Survey of Military Operations During 1812 Campaign*]. St. Petersburg, 1912.

———, *Opravdanie v deistviyakh ego vo vremia Otechestvennoi voini s frantsuzami v 1812 godu* [*Justification by Commander-in-Chief Barclay de Tolly of His Actions during the Patriotic War with the French in 1812*]. in *Zhurnal Imperatorskogo Russkogo voenno-istoricheskogo obshestva*. St. Petersburg, 1911.

Bennigsen, Levin. *Memoirs on 1807 Campaign*, in *Russkaya starina* No. 100 (July-October 1899), No. 101 (January, 1901).

———. *Zapiski o kampanii 1812 g.* [Memoirs on 1812 Campaign], in *Russkaya starina*, Nos. 138-139 (1909).

———. *Mémoires du général Bennigsen, Avec une introduction, des annexes et des notes de E. Cazalas*. Paris: Charles-Lavauzelle, 1907.

Bernhardi, Theodor von. *Denkwurdigkeiten aus dem Leben des Kaiserl russ. Generals von der Infantrie Carl Friedrich Grafen von Toll*. Leipzig: O. Wignad, 1856-1858.

Beskrovny, Liubomir. *M. I. Kutuzov: Sbornik Dokumentov, pod redaktsiei polkovnika L. G. Beskrovnogo* [*M. I. Kutuzov: Compilation of Documents*]. 5 vols. Moscow: Voenizdat, 1951-1954.

Besedi i chastnaya perepiska mezhdu imperatorom Aleksandrom i knyazem A. Chartorizhskim [*Conversations and Private Correspondence of the Emperor Alexander with the Prince A. Czartoriski*]. Moscow, 1912.

Brett-James A. *1812: Eyewitness Accounts of Napoleon's Defeat in Russia*. New York: Harper, 1966.

Boitsov, M. *K chesti Rossii: iz chastnoi perepiski 1812 goda perepiski* [*To Russia's Honor: From the Private Correspondence*]. Moscow: Sovremennik, 1988.

Bumagi, otnosiashiesia do Otechestvennoi voini 1812 g., sobrannie i izdannie P.I. Shukinim, [*Materials on The Patriotic War of 1812, compiled and published by P.I. Shukin*]. Moscow, 1904.

Butenev, Apolonarius. *Diplomat Pri Armii Kniazya Bagrationa: Vospominania A.P. Buteneva o 1812 godu* [*Diplomat At the Army of Prince Bagration: Recollections of A.P. Butenev on 1812 Campaign*]. Moscow, 1911.

Buturlin, Dmitri. *Istoriya nashestviya Imperatora Napoleona na Rossiyu v 1812 godu.* [*The Emperor Napoleon's Invasion of Russia in 1812*], 2 vols. St. Petersburg: Voenn. Tip. Glavnogo Shtaba, 1837-1838.

Davidov, Denis. *In the Service of the Tsar Against Napoleon: the Memoirs of Denis Davidov, 1806-1814*, translation by Greg Troubetskoy, London: Greenhill, 1999.

———, *Sochineniya* [*Compilation of Writtings*]. St. Petersburg, 1848 (reprint Moscow, 1962).

———, *Voyenniye zapiski* [*Military Notes*]. Moscow, 1982.

Dokumenti shtaba M.I. Kutuzova, 1805-1806 [*Documents of M.I. Kutuzov's Headquarters, 1805-1806*]. ed. by Karvyalis V. A., Solovyeov A.E. Vilna, 1951.

Donskie kazaki v 1812 godu, sbornik dokumentov ob uchastii donskogo kazachestva v Otechestvennoi voine 1812 goda [*Don Cossacks in 1812: a Compilation of the Documents on the Role of Don Cossacks in the Patriotic War of 1812*]. Rostov na Donu, 1954.

Dubrovin, Nikolay. *Pisma glavneishikh deiatelei v tsarstvovanie imperatora Aleksandra I s 1807-1829 god* [*Letters of Prominent Statesmen during the Reign of Emperor Alexander I in 1807-1829*]. St. Petersburg, 1883.

———, *Otechestvennaya voina v pismakh sovremenikov,* [*The Patriotic War in Correspondence of the Contemporaries*]. St. Petersburg, 1882.

———, *Pis'ma glavneishikh deyatelei v tsarstsvivanii Aleksandra I* [*Letters of Major Statesmen during the Reign of Alexander I*]. St. Petersburg, 1883.

Durova, Nadejda. *The Cavalry Maiden: Journals of a Female Russian Officer in the Napoleonic Wars*. Ann Arbor: Ardis, 1988.

Engelhart, L. *Zapiski* [*Notes*]. Moscow, 1868.

Ermolov, Aleksey, *Zapiski A. P. Ermolova* [*Memoirs of A. P. Ermolov*], Moscow, extended 2-volume edition (1865); one volume edition, Moscow, 1991.

Eugene, Duke of Württemberg. *Memoiren des Herzogs Eugen von Wurttemberg*. Frankfurt, 1862.

Feldmarshal Kutuzov: Sbornik dokumentov i materialov [*Field Marshal Kutuzov: Compilation of Documents and Materials*]. Moscow, 1947.

General Bagration: Sbornik dokumentov i materialov [*General Bagration: Compilation of Documents and Materials*], ed. S. N. Golubov. Moscow, 1945.

Generalisimus Suvorov: Sbornik Dokumentov i Materialov [*Generalissimo Suvorov: Compilation of Documents and Materials*]. Moscow, 1947.

Glinka, Feydor. *Pis'ma russkogo ofitsera* [*Letters of Russian Officer*]. Moscow, 1985.

———, *Vospominaniya o 1812 gode (ocherki Borodinskogo srazheniya)* [*Recollections of 1812 Campaign (Narrative of the Battle of Borodino)*]. Moscow 1839.

Golitsyn, Nikolay. *Ofitserskiye zapiski ili vospominaniya o pokhodakh 1812, 1813, 1814 godov* [*Officer's Notes or Recollections of the 1812, 1813 and 1814 Campaigns*]. Moscow, 1838.

———, *Otrivki iz oficerskikh zapisok Kniazya N.V. Golitsyna o pokhodakh 1812, 1813, i 1814 godov* [*Excerpts From the Memoirs of the Prince N. V. Golitsyn on the 1812, 1813 and 1814 Campaigns*], in *Russkii Invalid*, No. 208 (1838).

Grabbe, Paul, *Iz Pamiatnikh Zapisok grafa Pavla Khristoforovicha Grabbe* [*From Memorable Recollections of Count Paul Khristoforovich Grabbe*]. Moscow, 1873.

Journal Voennykh Deistvii Imperatorskoi Rossiiskoi Armii [*Journal of Military Operations of the Russian Imperial Army*]. St. Petersburg, 1807.

Kallash V. *Dvenadtsatii god v vospominanyakh i perepiske sovremennikov* [*1812 Campaign in Memoirs and Correspondence of Contemporaries*]. Moscow, 1912.

Kharkevich V. *1812 god v dnevnikakh, zapiskakh i vospominaniyakh sovremennikov,* [*1812 Campaign in Diaries, Notes and Memoirs of Contemporaries*]. Vilno, 1900.

———, *Perepiska imperatora Aleksandra i Barklaia de Tolli v Otechestvennuiu voinu* [*Correspondence of the Emperor Alexander with Barclay de Tolly from the Commencement of War to the Departure of the Tsar from the Army*]. in *Voennii sbornik*, Nos. 11-12 (1903), No.1 (1904), No.3 (1906).

———, *Voina 1812 goda. Ot Nemana do Smolenska* [*The War of 1812. From the Nieman to Smolensk*]. Vilna, 1901.

Langeron, Alexander Andrault. *Journal inedit de la campagne de 1805*, Paris: La Vouivre, 1998.

———, *Zapiski* [*Notes*], in *Voennii sbornik*, No. 11 (1900)

———, *Zapiski Grafa Langerona. Voina s Turtsiei v 1806-1812 gg.* [*Count Langeron's Recollections. War against Turkey in 1806-1812*]. in *Russkaia starina*, Nos. 130-132 (1907), Nos. 133-136 (1908).

Löwernstein, Waldemar Hermann. *Memoires du general-major russe baron de Löwernstein (1776-1858)*. Paris: Fontemoing, 1903.

———, *Zapiski* [*Notes*], in *Russkaya Starina*, No. 11 (1900).

———, *Denkwürdigkeiten eines Livländers: Aus den Jahren 1790-1815*. Leipzig, 1858.

Muraviyev, A. *Avtographiobicheskie zapiski* [*Autobiographical Notes*], in *Dekabristi: Novie Materially*. Moscow, 1955.

———, *Sochinenia i pisma* [*Writings and Letters*]. Irkutsk, 1986.

Otechestvennaia voina 1812 g.: Materiali Voenno-Uchebnogo arkhiva Glavnogo Shtaba [*Patriotic War of 1812: Materials of Military - Academic Archive of the General Staff*], 22 vols. St. Petersburg, 1900-1914.

Platov, Matvei. *Is Perepiski M. I. Platova* [*From Platov's Correspondence*], in *Voennii sbornik*, 1906

Radozhitsky, Ilya. *Poxodnie zapiski artilerista s 1812 po 1816* [*Campaign Recollections of the Artilleryman, 1812-1816*]. Moscow, 1835.

Rayevsky G. *Arkhiv Rayevskogo* [*Rayevsky's Archive*]. St. Petersburg, 1908.

Razskazi starogo, *voina o Suvorove* [*Old Soldier's Stories about Suvorov*]. Moscow, 1847.

Rossia i Shvetsia: dokumenti i materiali 1809-1818 [*Russia and Sweden: Documents and Materials 1809-1818*]. Moscow, 1985.

Shukin, P. I. *Bumagi otnosiashiesia do Otechestvennoi voini 1812 goda* [*Materials Related to the Patriotic War of 1812*]. Moscow: Mamontov's Typography, 1900.

Sukhtelen, Paul. *Narrative of the Conquest of Finland by the Russians in the Years 1808-9: From an Unpublished Work by a Russian Officer of Rank*, ed. by Gen. Monteith, London, 1854.

Vigel, Filip, *Zapiski [Recollections]*. 2 vols. Moscow, 1928.

Vneshnaya politika Rossii XIX i nachala XX veka: dokumenti Rossiiskogo Ministerstva Inostrannikh del [*Foreign Policy of Russia in XIX and beginning of XX century: Documents of the Ministry of Foreign Affairs of Russia*]. 5 vols. Moscow, 1961.

Volkonsky, Sergey. *Zapiski Sergia Grigorievicha Volkonskogo (Dekabrista)* [*Recollections of Sergey Grigorievich Volkonsky (the Decembrist)*]. St. Petersburg, 1901.

Voyensky, K. *Otechestvennaya voina 1812 goda v zapiskakh sovremennikov* [*Patriotic War of 1812 in Recollections of Contemporaries*]. St. Petersburg, 1911.

Wilson, Robert, *Narrative of events during the Invasion of Russia by Napoleon Bonaparte and the Retreat of the French army, 1812*. London, 1860.

———, *Brief Remarks on the Character and Composition of the Russian army, and a Sketch of the Campaigns in Poland in the Years 1806 and 1807*. London, 1810.

———, *General Wilson's Journal, 1812-1814*, edited by Antony Brett-James. London: Kimber, [1964].

Wolzogen und Neuhaus, Ludwig. *Memoiren des Königlich Preussischen Generals der Infanterie Ludwig Freiherrn von Wolzogen*. Leipzig, 1851.

Zapiski Grafa E. F. Komarovskogo [*Recollections of Count E. F. Komarovsky*]. St. Petersburg, 1914.

Zapiski donskogo atamana Denisova [*Recollections of the Don Cossack Ataman Denisov*]. St. Petersburg, 2000.

Zhikharev, Stepan. *Zapiski Stepana Petrovicha Zhikhareva* [*Recollections of Stepan Petrovich Zhikharev*]. Moscow, 1890.

Zhirkevich, Ivan. *Zapiski [Recollections]*. in *Russkaya starina*, No. 8 (1874).

Secondary Sources

Andolenko, C.R. *Aigles de Napoleon contre drapeaux du Tsar*. Paris, 1969.

Angeli, Moritz Edler von, "Ulm und Austerlitz. Studie auf Grund archivalischer Quellen Ìber den Feldzug 1805 in Deutschland," in *Mittheilungen des Kaiserlichen und Koniglichen Kriegsarchivs*. Vienna, 1877.

Antelava, Irakli. *Gruzini v Otechestvenoi voine 1812 goda* [*Georgians in the Patriotic War of 1812*]. Tbilisi: Merani, 1983.

Bantysh-Kamensky, *Biographii rossiiskikh generalissimusov i general-feldmarshalov* [*Biographies of Russian Generalissimos and General Field Marshals*]. Moscow, 1991.

Beskrovny, Liubomir. *Russkoe voennoe isskustvo XIX v.* [*Russian Military Art in XIX century*]. Moscow, 1974.

———. *Borodinskoye srazheniye* [*The Battle of Borodino*]. Moscow: Moskovskii rabochii, 1971.

———. *Russkaya armiya i flot v XVIII veke* [Russian Army and Navy in XIX century]. Moscow, 1958.

———. *Russkaya armiya i flot v XIX veke* [Russian Army and Navy in XIX century]. Moscow: Nauka, 1973.

———, *Otechestvennaia voina 1812 goda* [*The Patriotic War of 1812*]. Moscow: Moskovskii rabochii, 1968.

———, *Tysiacha vosem'sot dvenadtsatyi god: k stopiatidesiatiletiiu Otechestvennoi voiny* [*The year of 1812 - to the 150th Anniversary of the Patriotic War (compilation of articles)*]. Moscow, 1962.

Bezotosnyi V. *Donskoi generalitet i ataman Platov v 1812 godu: maloizvestnue i neizvestnye fakty na fone znamenitykh sobytii*, [*Don Cossack Generals and Ataman Platov in 1812: Less Known And Unknown Facts of Celebrated Events*]. Moscow, 1999.

Biograficheskii entsiklopedicheskii slovar [Biographical Encyclopedia.] ed. Landa, N. M. Moscow: Bol'shaia Rossiiskaia entsiklopediia, 2000.

Bogdanovich, M. *Pokhodi Suvorova v Italii i Shveitsarii* [*Suvorov's Campaigns in Italy and Switzerland*]. St. Petersburg, 1846.

———, *Istoria tsarsvovania imperatora Aleksandra I i Rossii v ego vremia* [History of Reign of Emperor Alexander I and Russia During His Times]. St. Petersburg, 1869-1871.

———, *Istoria Otechestvennoi voini 1812 goda po dostovernum istochnikam* [History of the Patriotic War of 1812 Based on Original Sources]. St. Petersburg: tip. Torgovogo doma S. Strugovshikova, 1859.

Boguslavsky, L.A. *Istoria Apsheronskogo polka. 1700-1892* [*History of the Apsheron Regiment, 1700-1892*]. St. Petersburg, 1892.

Bolshaia Sovetskaya Entsiklopedia [Large Soviet Encyclopedia], Moskva: Sovetskaia entsiklopedia, Izd.1, 1926-1947; Izd.2, 1950-57; Izd.3, 1970-78.

Buturlin, Dmitri. *Relation historique et critique de la campagne de 1799 des Austro-Russes en Italie*. St. Petersburg, 1812.

Chandler, David. *The Campaigns of Napoleon*. New York: Macmillan, 1966.

Djevegelov A., Makhnevich N. and etc. *Otechestvennaia voina i Russkoye obshestvo* [*The Patriotic War and Russian Society*]. 7 vols. Moscow, 1911-1912.

Duffy, Christopher. *Russia's Military Way to the West: Origins and Nature of Russian Military Power, 1700-1800*. London, 1981.

———. *Austerlitz, 1805*. London, 1977.

———. *Borodino*. London, 1972.

Entsiklopedicheskii slovar [*Encyclopedical Dictionary*]. 41 vols. St. Petersburg: Izd. F. A. Brokgauz & Efron, 1890-1907.

Entsiklopedicheskii slovar Russkogo Bibliograficheskogo Instituta Granat [*Encyclopedical Dictionary of the Russian Bibliographical Institute Granat*]. 58 vols. Moscow: R. B. I Granat, 1910-1948.

Fabry, Gabriel Joseph. *Campaign de Russie*. 5 vols. Paris, 1900.

Gachot, Edourd. *La Campagne d'Helvétie, 1799*. Paris, 1914.

———, *Les Campagnes de 1799: Souvarow en Italie*. Paris, 1903.

Höpfner, Friedrich Eduard Alexander von. *Der Krieg von 1806 und 1807 [i.e. achtzehnhundertsechs und achtzehnhundertsieben]: ein Beitrag zur Geschichte der Preussischen Armee nach den Quellen des Kriegs-Archivs bearbeitet*. vol. 3 Berlin 1850.

Inostrantsev, *Otechestvennaya voina 1812 goda, Operatsii 2-oi Zapadnoi armii kniazya Bagrationa ot nachala voini do Smolenska* [Patriotic War of 1812. Operations of the 2nd Western Army of the Prince Bagration from the Commencement of War to Smolensk]. St. Petersburg, 1914.

Istoria Leib-Gvardii Egerskogo polka za 100 let. 1796-1896 [*A Hundred Year History of the Life Guard Jager Regiment, 1796-1896*]. St. Petersburg, 1896.

Istoria rodov russkogo Dvoriantsva [History of the Russian Noble Families], 2 vols. Moscow, 1991.

Josselson, Michael. *The Commander: Life of Barclay de Tolly*. Oxford, 1980.

Kafengauz, Boris. *Geroi Otechestvennoi voiny 1812 goda* [Heroes of the Patriotic War of 1812]. Moscow, 1966.

Karnovich, E. *Velikii Knyaz Konstantin Pavlovich* [Grand Duke Constantine Pavlovich]. St. Petersburg, 1899.

Kavtaradze A.G. *General A. P. Ermolov*. Toula, 1977.

Kersnovsky, A. *Istoria russkoi armii* [*History of the Russian Army*]. 4 vols. Moscow: Golos, 1992.

Kharkevich V. *Voina 1812 goda. Ot Nemana do Smolenska* [*The Campaign of 1812. From the Nieman to Smolensk*]. Vilna, 1901.

Khataevich, N. *Partizan A. N. Seslavin*. Moscow, 1973.

Kochetkov, A. *Barclay de Tolly*. Moscow: Moskovskii rabochii, 1970.

Kraivanova, I. *General A. I. Osterman-Tolstoi*. Moscow, 1972.

Lettow-Vorbeck, Oscar von. *Der krieg von 1806 und 1807*. Berlin, 1896.

Levchenko, V. Geroi *1812 goda [Heroes of 1812]*. Moscow, 1987.

Longworth, Philip. *The Art of Victory: The Life and Achievements of Generalissimo Suvorov, 1729-1800*. London, 1965.

Luppol, A. *Geroi Otechestvennoi voiny 1812 goda: putevoditel po nekropolu Donskogo monastyria [Heroes of the Patriotic War of 1812: A Guide to Necropolis of the Don Monastery]*. Moscow, 1988.

Maksutov, V. *Istoria 25-go pekhotnogo Smolenskogo polka za 200 let ego sushestvovania, 1700-1900 [History of the 25th Infantry Smolensk Regiment During 200 Years of its Existence, 1700-1900]*. St. Petersburg, 1901.

Manzej K. *Istoria Leib-Gvardii Gusarskogo Ego Velitshestva polka, 1775-1857 [History of the His Majesty's Life Guard Hussar Regiment, 1775-1857]*. 4 vols. Petersburg , 1859.

Mikhailovsky-Danilevsky, Alexander; Miliutin, Dmitri. *Istoriia voini Rossii s Frantsiei v 1799 godu [History of the War between Russia and France in 1799]*. 4 vols. St. Petersburg, 1852. (reprint in 3 vols. St. Petersburg 1857)

——. *Opisanie pervoi voini Imperatora Aleksandra s Napoleonom v 1805 godu [Description of the First Campaign of Emperor Alexander against Napoleon in 1805]*, in *Polnoe Sobranie Sochinenii*. St. Petersburg, 1849.

——. *Opisanie vtoroi voini Imperatora Aleksandra s Napoleonom v 1806-1807 godakh [Description of the Second War of the Emperor Alexander against Napoleon in 1806-1807]*. St. Petersburg. 1846.

——. *Opisanie Finliandskoi Voini v 1808 i 1809 godakh [Description of the War in Finland in 1808-1909]*. St. Petersburg, 1841.

——. *Russo-Turkish War of 1806-1812*, translation by Alexander Mikaberidze, West Chester: Nafziger Collection, 2002.

——. *Opisanie otechestvennoi voiny 1812 g. [Description of the Patriotic War of 1812]*, 4 vols. St. Petersburg, 1839.

——. *Imperator Aleksandr I i ego spodvizhniki v 1812, 1813, 1814, 1815 godakh: Voennaia galereia Zimnego Dvortsa [Emperor Alexander I and His Devotees in 1812, 1813, 1814 and 1815: War Gallery of the Winter Palace]*. 6 vols. St. Petersburg, 1845-1850.

Modern Encyclopedia of Russian and Soviet History. Joseph L. Wieczynski, ed. 63 vols. Gulf Breeze, FL: Academic International Press, 1976-1996

Nersisyan, M. *Otechestvennaia voina 1812 i narodi Kavkaza [The Patriotic War of 1812 and the People of Caucasus]*. Yerevan, 1965.

Nikolay Mikhailovich, Grand Duke, *Russkie portrety XXVIII i XIX stoletii [Russian Potraits of XVIII and XIX Centuries]*. 6 vols. St. Petersburg, 1906-1913,

Panchulidzev, S. A. *Sbornik biografii Kavalergardov [Collection of Biographies of Chevalierguards]*. vol. 3 (1801-1826). St. Petersburg, 1906.

Pavlova, L. *Dekabristy – uchastniki voin 1805-1814 [Decembrists—Participants of 1805-1814 Campaigns]*. Moscow, 1979.

Pestrikov, N. S. *Istoriia Leib-gvardii moskovskago polka [History of the Life Guard Moscow Regiment]*. 2 vols. St. Petersburg, 1903-1904.

Petre, Lorain. *Napoleon's Campaign in Poland*. London, 1976.

Petrov, A. *Voina Rossii s Turtsiei, 1806-1812 [History of the War Between Russia and Turkey, 1806-1812]*. 3 vols. St. Petersburg, 1885-1887,

——. *Vlianie Turetskikh voin s polovini proshlogo stoletia na razvitie Russkago voennago iskusstva [Influence of the Russo-Turkish Wars of the Last Century on the Development of the Russian Military Art]*. St. Petersburg, 1894.

Pisarev, A.A. *Biografii shtab i ober-ofitserov grenaderskogo Grafa Arakcheyeva polka, polozhivshikh zhisn svoiu, sashishaia Gosudaria i otechestvo v srazheniakh 1812-1814 [Biographies of Staff and Ober-Officers of Count Arakcheyev's Grenadier Regiment, Who Sacrificed Their Lives for the Emperor and Motherland in the Battle of 1812-1814]*. St. Petersburg, 1816.

Plotho, Carl von. *Tagebuch während des Krieges zwischen Russland und Preussen einerseits, und Frankreich andrerseits, in den Jahren 1806 und 1807.* Berlin, 1811.

Pochko, Nonna Andreyevna. *General N. N. Raevskii.* Moscow, 1971.

Podmazo, Alexander. *Shefi i komandiri reguliarnikh polkov Russkoi armii v 1796-1815* [*Chefs and Commanders of Regular Regiments of the Russian Army in 1796-1815*]. Moscow, 1997.

Polevoi, N. *Russkie polkovodtsy ili Zhizn i podvigi rossiiskikh polkovodtsev ot vremen imperatora Petra velikogo do tsarstvovania imperatora Nikolaia I* [*Russian Commanders or Life and Exploits of Russian Commanders from the Time of Emperor Peter the Great to the Reign of Emperor Nicholas I*]. St. Petersburg, 1845.

Polikarpov, N. *K istorii Otechestvennoi Voini 1812 g.: Po pervositochnikam* [*On the History of The Patriotic War of 1812: Primary Sources*]. Moscow, 1911.

Polkovodets Kutuzov: Sbornik Statei [*Commander Kutuzov: Compilation of Articles*]. Moscow, 1965.

Potto V.A. *Istoria Akhtyrskogo polka* [*History of the Akhtyrsk Regiment*]. 2 vols. St. Petersburg, 1902.

Romanov D. *Polkovodets D. S. Dokhturov* [*Commander D.S. Dokhturov*]. Tula, 1979.

Russkii biograficheskii slovar [*Russian Biographical Dictionary*]. ed. Polovtsov, A. A.; Modzalevskii, B. L.; Kurdiumov, M. G. 25 volumes. + 5 recent volumes, St. Petersburg: Izd. imp. Rus. ist. obshchestva, 1896-1918.

Rüstow, Friedrich Wilhelm. *Der Krieg von 1805 in Deutschland und Italien.* Frauenfeld, 1853.

Shilder, Nikolay. *Imperator Aleksandr Pervii: Ego zhizn i tsarstvovanie* [*Emperor Alexander the First: His Life and Reign*]. St. Petersburg, 1897-1905.

———, *Imperator Pavel I* [*Emperor Paul I*]. Moscow, 1997.

Shilov, D.N. *Gosudartsvennie deiateli Rossiiskoi Imperii: glavy vysshikh i tsentralnikh uchrezhdenii 1802-1917.* St. Petersburg, 2002.

Shirokorad, A. *Russko-Turetskie voini 1676-1918 gg.* [*Russo-Turkish Wars in 1676-1918*]. Moscow, 2000.

Shishov, Alexander, *Generalissimus Suvorov* [*Generalissimo Suvorov*]. Moscow: Olma Press, 2003.

———, *Neizvestnii Kutuzov: novoe prochtenie biographii* [*Unknown Kutuzov: New Interpretation of Biography*]. Moscow, 2001.

Smirnoi, N. *Zhizn i podvigi M.I. Platova* [Life and Exploits of M.I. Platov]. Moscow, 1821

Smith, Digby. *The Greenhill Napoleonic Wars Data Book.* London, 1998.

Sudravski, V.K. *Istoria Leib-Gvardii Grenaderskogo polka.* St. Petersburg, 1906.

Sweden Armen, Generalstaben, *Krigshistoriska avdelningen. Shveidskaia voina 1808-1809 g.g. sostavlena voenno-istoricheskim otdelom Shvedskogo Generalnogo Shtaba* [*The Swedish Campaign of 1808-1809, Compiled by the Military History Section of the Swedish General Staff*]. translation by Russian General Staff. 2 vols. St. Petersburg, 1906.

Tarle, Eugene. *Nashestvie Napoleona na Rossiyu 1812* [*Napoleon's Invasion of Russia, 1812*]. Moscow: Voenizdat, 1992.

Tartarovsky A.G. *Nerazgadannyi Barklai: legendy i byl' 1812 goda* [*Unknown Barclay: Legends and Tales of 1812*]. Moscow, 1996.

———, *1812 god i russkaia memuaristika* [*1812 Campaign and Russian Historiography*]. Moscow: Nauka, 1980.

Troitsky, Nikolay. *1812: Velikii god Rossii* [*1812: The Glorious Year of Russia*]. Moscow: Nauka, 1988.

Volodin, P. M. *Partisan Aleksandr Figner* [*Partisan Alexander Figner*]. Moscow, 1971.

Voronov P. N. *Istoria Leib-Gvardii Pavlovskogo polka. 1790-1890* [*History of the Life Guard Pavlovsk Regiment, 1790-1890*]. St. Petersburg, 1890.

Voennaia entsiklopediia. [Military Encyclopedia]. O. Novitskii, ed. 18 vols. St. Petersburg: Izd-vo I. D. Sytina, 1911-1915.

Zakharov, G. *Russko-Shvedskaya Voina 1808-1809 gg.* [*Russo-Swedish War of 1808-1809*]. Moscow, 1940.

Zhilin, Pavel, *Mikhail Illarionovich Kutuzov: Zhizn i polkovodcheskaya deyatelnost* [*Mikhail Illarionovich Kutuzov: Life and Military Career*]. Moscow, 1978.

―――, *Gibel' Napoleonovskoi armii v Rossii* [*Destruction of Napoleon's Army in Russia*]. Moscow: Nauka, 1974.

―――, *Otechestvennaya voina 1812 goda* [*The Patriotic War of 1812*]. Moscow: Voenizdat, 1988.

Zhizn i podvigi general-leitenanta Dmitria Petrovicha Neverovskogo 1771-1813 [*Life and Exploits of Lieutenant General Dmitry Petrovich Neverovsky, 1771-1813*]. Moscow, 1912.

Znosko-Borovski, N. *Istoria Leib-Gvardii Izmailovskogo polka* [*History of the Life Guard Izmailovsk Regiment*]. St. Petersburg, 1882.

Articles

Chkhartichvili, K. "General Ivan Gurieli." *Tsiskari,* No.5 (1973): 155-158.

Colin, "Campagne de 1805." *Revue Historique*. Nos. 70, 71, 72 (1906), Nos. 75, 77 (1907).

Degterev L. "Maloizvestnye Geroi Borodina [*Unknown Heroes of Borodino*]." *Voprosi Istorii*, No.11 (1984): 182-186

Dubrovin, Nikolay. "Russkaya zhizn v nachale XIX veka [Russian Life in Early XIX Century." *Russkaya starina*, No. 12 (1898)

―――, "Materiali dlia istorii tsarstvovania Aleksandra I [Materials for the History of Reign of Alexander I]." *Voennii sbornik,* No. 11 (1864).

Povstianoi, V. "Geroi Otechestvennoi voini 1812 goda (Jacob Kulnev) [Heroes of the Patriotic War of 1812 (Jacob kulnev)]." *Voenno-istoricheskii zhurnal*, No. 7 (1963): 127-128.

Shvedov, S. "Komplektovanie, chislenost' i poteri russkoi armii v 1812 g [Organization, Strength and Losses of the Russian army in 1812]." *Istoria SSSR*, N4 (1987)

Smirnov, D.P. "Neverovsky: K 200-letiu so dnia rozhdenia [Neverovsky: 200th Anniversary of His Birth]." *Voenno-istoricheskii zhurnal*, No. 12 (1971): 120-122. ü

Periodicals

Russkii Invalid ili Voennie Vedomosti, St. Petersburg, 1910-1912

Russkii Arkhiv, St. Petersburg, 1864-1911

Russkaya Starina, St. Petersburg, 1871-1912